W9-CBC-218

ROMANOV'S

Russian-English
English-Russian

DICTIONARY

ROMANOV'S
RUSSIAN-ENGLISH ENGLISH-RUSSIAN Dictionary

Two Volumes in One

Part I by E. Wedel, Ph. D.

Part II by A. Romanov

LANGENSCHEIDT

HODDER AND STOUGHTON

Published in the British Commonwealth
by Hodder & Stoughton Limited,
Saint Paul's House, Warwick Lane,
London E C 4

First Edition 1964

Printers: Druckhaus Langenscheidt, Berlin-Schöneberg
Printed in Germany — Bn. IV. Ah. (B,w. IV. Aw. LKG/HS)

Preface

This Russian-English dictionary has been compiled with the same care and diligence as all other publications of Langenscheidt Publishers, which have been appreciated as standard works for many decades.

The dictionary is meant to be used in all walks of life and at school. In its two parts it contains more than 35,000 vocabulary entries with many translations and idioms as well as their phonetic transcriptions. Americanisms have received special consideration, and in the Russian-English part cases of particular American usage are even cited in the first place, being followed by their respective British semantic (or orthographic) equivalents.

English pronunciation follows that laid down by Daniel Jones in his *An English Pronouncing Dictionary* (1953). In the Russian-English part pronunciation is only given after those Russian words and parts of words which deviate from the basic rules of pronunciation. Generally speaking, Russian words can be pronounced properly if the place of the accent is known. Therefore every Russian word has been given its stress. Shift of stress, as far as it takes place within the inflection, is also indicated. A detailed account of Russian pronunciation with the help of the symbols of I. P. A.'s phonetic transcription can be found on pages 21—27.

References to full-length inflection tables in the supplement to the dictionary, as given after nouns, adjectives and verbs, enable the user to employ the words in question in all their modifications.

In addition to the vocabulary this dictionary contains lists of geographical names (American and British), abbreviations, numerals, measures and weights and a survey of the most important differences between British and American spelling and pronunciation.

Publishers and editors hope of this book that it may contribute to the mutual understanding between nations and thus help to deepen their cultural relations.

Предисловие

Настоящий словарь русского и английского языков составлен с такой же тщательностью и аккуратностью, как и все издания Лангеншейдта, зарекомендовавшие себя образцовыми трудами на протяжении многих десятков лет.

Словарь предназначается преимущественно для работников разных профессий и учащихся. Он содержит в обеих частях более 35000 заглавных слов в алфавитном порядке, с указанием произношения, переводом и устойчивыми оборотами речи, причём учитываются в должной мере особенности американского варианта английского языка.

Английское произношение даётся по словарю Daniel Jones, An English Pronouncing Dictionary (1953).

К словнику прилагаются: списки географических названий (американских и английских), сокращений, имён числительных, мер длины и веса, грамматические таблицы, а также перечень важнейших различий между языком британцев и американцев в отношении правописания и произношения.

Издательство и сотрудники надеются изданием настоящего словаря способствовать взаимопониманию и укреплению культурных связей между народами.

Contents

Оглавление

page стр.

Careful reading and observation of the following preliminary notes will both facilitate the use and help to open up the full value of the dictionary.

Preliminary Notes

1. Arrangement. Material in this dictionary has been arranged in alphabetical order. In the Russian-English part, proper names (Christian, geographical, etc.) as well as abbreviations appear in their individual alphabetical order within the vocabulary itself. In the case of a number of prefixed words, especially verbs, not explicitly listed because of the limited size of the dictionary, it may prove useful to drop the prefix, which is often but a sign of the perfective aspect (see below), and look up the primary (imperfective) form thus obtained.

Compounds not found in their alphabetical places should be reduced to their second component in order to find out their main meaning, e. g.:
термоя́дерный → я́дерный = nuclear.

To save space with the aim of including a maximum of material, compounds, derivatives, and occasionally just similar words, have, wherever possible, been arranged in groups, the vertical stroke (|) in the first entry word of such a group separating the part common to all following items of the group, and the tilde (~) in the run-on words replacing the part preceding the vertical stroke in the first entry and consequently not repeated in the other articles of the group. The tilde may also stand for the whole first entry, which then has no separation mark since it is entirely repeated in the run-on items of the group.

Besides the bold-faced tilde just mentioned, the same mark in standard type (~) is employed within a great number of entries to give phrases and idioms of which the entry word or any component of its inflection system forms part.

A tilde with circlet (~̊) indicates a change in the initial letter (capital to small and vice versa) of a run-on word.

Examples: **Аме́рик|а ...; ~̊а́нский = америка́нский**
англи́|йский ...; ˈ~̊я = ˈАнглия (for stress see below, 3).

Within brackets: square [ ], round ( ), acute-angled ⟨ ⟩, instead of the tilde a hyphen (-) with the same function (mark of repetition) has been used, e. g.:

то́лстый [14; толст, -а́, -о] = [14; толст, толста́, то́лсто]
брать [беру́, -рёшь; брал, -а́, -о] = [беру́, берёшь; брал, брала́, бра́ло]
весели́ть ...; (-ся) = весели́ться
cf. **убира́ть ...,** ⟨убра́ть⟩ ...; **-ся = убира́ться,** ⟨убра́ться⟩
проси́ть ..., ⟨по-⟩ = ⟨попроси́ть⟩.

Of the two main aspects of a Russian verb the imperfective form appears first, in boldface type, followed, in acute-angled brackets ⟨ ⟩ and in standard type, by its perfective counterpart. Verbs occurring only as perfective aspects (or whose imperfective or iterative aspect is hardly ever used) bear the mark *pf.*; those used only in the imperfective aspect have no special designation at all; verbs whose perfective aspect coincides with the imperfective are marked thus: *(im)pf.*

If in a certain meaning (or meanings) only one member of an aspect pair may be used, the cases concerned are preceded by the abbreviations *impf.* or *pf.* respectively and thus separated from the meanings to which both aspects apply, these latter being always given in the first place. Similarly in a noun the abbreviation *pl.* (or *sg.*) after one or more translation items designates the word(s) following it as referring only to the plural (or singular) form of the entry otherwise used in both numbers. Number differences between a Russian entry and its English counterpart(s) are indicated by adding the abbreviation *pl.* or *sg.* behind the latter, whereas a noun used only in the plural bears the mark *pl.* right after the entry itself, i. e. where usually the gender is given (see below).

In the English equivalents of Russian verbs the particle 'to' of the infinitive has been omitted for reasons of space economy.

Also, a number of quite similar international words, particularly nouns terminating in **-áция, -и́ция** or **-и́зм, -и́ст** = -ation, -ition, -ism, -ist, or likewise obvious cases such as **тайфу́н** 'typhoon' have not been included in the dictionary, especially since there are no stress or inflectional peculiarities about the Russian nouns in question nor is there, on the whole, any difficulty in deducing their semantic values.

Moreover, English adjectives used as nouns (and nouns used as adjectives) alike have, in connection with successive pertinent entries, been given but once, whereas the Russian words naturally appear in their different forms, i. e. parts of speech; e. g.:

америк|áнец *m* ..., **~áнка** *f* ..., **~áнский** ... = American (i. e. man, woman, *adj.*)
квадрáт *m* ..., **~ный** ... square = square (*su.*) & square (*adj.*)
cf. **лими́т** *m* ..., **~и́ровать** ... *(im)pf.* = limit (*su.*) & limit (*vb.*).

Otherwise the adjectival use of an English noun (and occasionally other parts of speech) corresponding to a Russian adjective has as a rule been noted by adding dots (...) to the noun, etc. form concerned, irrespective of the mode of its orthographic combination with another noun, i. e. whether they are spelled in one word, hyphenated or written separately.

2. Pronunciation. As a rule pronunciation in individual Russian entry words has been given only in cases and places that differ from the standard pronunciation of Russian vowel and consonant letters (for this cf. pp. 21—27), e. g.:

г = g, but in лёгкий = (-x-)
ч = tʃ, but in что = (ʃ-)
не = ɲɛ, but in (the loan word) пенснé = (-ˈnɛ)

To transcribe Russian sounds and (Cyrillic) letters, the alphabet of the International Phonetic Association (I.P.A.) has been used.

3. Stress. The accent mark (ʹ) is placed above the stressed vowel of a Russian entry (or any other) word having more than one syllable and printed in full, as well as of run-on words, provided their accentuated vowel is not covered by the tilde or hyphen (= marks of repetition), e. g.:

дока́з|ывать, 〈~áть〉 = 〈доказáть〉. Since ё is always stressed the two dots over it represent implicitly the accent mark.

Wherever the accent mark precedes the tilde ('~) the last syllable but one of the part for which the tilde stands is stressed.

Examples: **уведом|ля́ть** ..., 〈'~ить〉 = 〈увéдомить〉.
выполн|я́ть ..., 〈'~ить〉 = 〈вы́полнить〉.

An accent mark over the tilde (~́) implies that the last (or sole) syllable of the part replaced by the tilde is to be stressed.

Examples: **наход|и́ть** ...; **~́ка** = **нахо́дка**
прода|ва́ть ..., 〈~́ть〉 = 〈продáть〉
по́езд ...; **~́ка** = **поéздка**
труб|á ...; **~́ка** = **тру́бка.**

In special cases of phonetic transcription, however, the accent mark precedes the stressed syllable, cf. **антéнна** [-ˈtɛn-], this usage being in accordance with I.P.A. rules.

Two accents in a word denote two equally possible modes of stressing it, thus:

и́нáче = **инáче** *or* **и́наче**
загр|ужáть ..., 〈~узи́ть〉 [... -у́зи́шь] = [... загру́зишь *or* загрузи́шь]
нали|вáть ..., 〈~́ть〉 [... нáли́л ...] = [... нáлил *or* нали́л ...].

Quite a number of predicative (or short) adjectives show a shift, or shifts, of stress as compared with their attributive forms. Such divergences are recorded as follows:

хоро́ший [17; хорóш, -á] = [17; хорóш, хорошá, хорошó (*pl.* хороши́)]
плохо́й [16; плох, -á, -о] = [16; плох, плохá, плóхо (*pl.* плóхи)]
до́брый [14; добр, -á, -о, дóбры́] = [14; добр, добрá, дóбро (*pl.* дóбры *or* добры́)].

The same system of stress designation applies, by the way, to accent shifts in the preterite forms of a number of verbs, e. g.:

да|вáть ..., 〈~ть〉 [... дал, -á, -о; ...(дан, -á)] = [... дал, далá, дáло (*pl.* дáли); ... (дан, данá, данó, даны́)].

Insertion of "epenthetic" o, e between the two last stem consonants in masculine short forms has been noted in all adjectives concerned.

Examples: **лёгкий** [16; лёгок, легкá; *a.* лёгки] = [16; лёгок, легкá, легкó (*pl.* легки́ *or* лёгки)]
бéдный [14; -ден, -днá, -о; бéдны́] = [14; бéден, беднá, бéдно (*pl.* бéдны *or* бедны́)]
больно́й [14; бóлен, больнá] = [14; бóлен, больнá, больнó (*pl.* больны́)]
по́лный [14; пóлон, полнá, пóлнó] = [14; пóлон, полнá, пóлно *or* полнó (*pl.* пóлны *or* полны́)].

If the stress in all short forms conforms to that of the attributive adjective the latter is merely provided with the abbreviation *sh.* (for *short form*) that indicates at the same time the possibility of forming such predicative forms, e. g.:

бога́тый [14 *sh.*] = [14; бога́т, бога́та, бога́то, бога́ты]
паху́чий [17 *sh.*] = [17; паху́ч, паху́ча, паху́че, паху́чи]
сво́йственный [14 *sh.*] = [14; сво́йствен, сво́йственна, сво́йственно, сво́йственны].

4. Inflected forms. All Russian inflected parts of speech appearing in the dictionary are listed in their respective basic forms, i. e. nominative singular (nouns, adjectives, numerals, certain pronouns) or infinitive (verbs). The gender of Russian nouns is indicated by means of one of three abbreviations in italics (*m*, *f*, *n* — cf. list, pp. 487—488) behind the entry word.* Each inflected entry is followed, in square brackets [ ], by a figure, which serves as reference to a definite paradigm within the system of conjugation and declension as tabulated at the end of the book, pp. 483—491. Any variants of these paradigms are stated after the reference figure of each entry word in question.

Examples: **ло́жка** *f* [5; *g/pl.*: -жек], like **ло́жа** *f* [5], is declined according to paradigm 5, except that the former example inserts in the genitive plural "epenthetic" e between the two last stem consonants: ло́жек; cf. **ло́дка** *f* [5; *g/pl.*: -док] = [*g/pl.*: ло́док]. **кусо́к** *m* [1; -ска́] = "epenthetic" o is omitted in the oblique cases of the singular and in all cases of the plural; cf. **коне́ц** *m* [1; -нца́] = [конца́, концу́, etc.].

го́род *m* [1; *pl.*: -да́, *etc. e.*] = the example stresses its stem in the singular, but the endings in the plural, the nominative plural being in -á (instead of in -ы́): города́, городо́в, etc.

край *m* [3; в -аю́; *pl.*: -ая́, *etc. e.*] = declined after paradigm 3, but the ending of the prepositional singular, with prepositions в, на, is in -ю́ (stressed); as for the plural, see го́род, above. Cf. also **печь** *f* [8; в -чи́; *from g/pl e.*], where, in addition to the stressed ending of the prepositional singular (after в, на), the accent shifts onto the ending in the genitive plural and all following cases of that number.

кури́ть [13; курю́, ку́ришь] = conjugated after paradigm 13, except that stress shifts onto the stem syllable in the 2nd and all following persons (singular and plural).

As the prefixed forms of a verb follow the same inflection model and (with the exception of perfective aspects having the stressed prefix вы́-) mode of accentuation as the corresponding unprefixed verb, differences in stress, etc. have in cases of such aspect pairs been marked but once, viz. with the imperfective form.

---

* For users of part II: Any Russian noun ending in a **consonant** *or* **-й** is of masculine gender;
those ending in **-а** *or* **-я** are of feminine gender;
those ending in **-о** *or* **-е** are of neuter gender.
In case of deviation from this rule, as well as in nouns terminating in **-ь**, the gender is indicated.

5. Government. Government, except for the accusative, is indicated with the help of Latin and Russian abbreviations (cf. list, pp. 33—35). Emphasis has been laid on differences between the two languages, including the use of prepositions. Whenever a special case of government applies only to one of several meanings of a word, this has been duly recorded in connection with the meaning concerned. To ensure a clear differentiation of person and thing in government, the English and Russian notes to that effect show the necessary correspondence in sequence.

6. Semantic distinction. If a word has different meanings and, at the same time, different forms of inflection or aspect, such significations have been differentiated by means of figures (e. g. бить, коса́, коси́ть); otherwise a semicolon separates different meanings, a comma mere synonyms. Italicized additions serve to specify individual shades of meaning, e. g. **поднима́ть** ... take up (*arms*); hoist (*flag*); set (*sail*); give (*alarm*); make (*noise*); scare (*game*); **приёмный** ... reception (*day*; *room* ...); ... office (*hours*); entrance (*examination*); foster (*father* ...). For further definitions with the help of illustrative symbols and abbreviations cf. list below, pp. 33—35.

In a number of Russian verbs the perfective aspect indicated (particularly with the prefixes ⟨за-⟩ and ⟨по-⟩) has, strictly speaking, the connotations "to begin to do s. th." (the former) and "to do s. th. a (little) while" (the latter); but since these forms are very often rendered into English by means of the equivalent verb without any such additions they have occasionally been given as simple aspect counterparts without further indication as to their aforesaid semantic subtlety.

7. Orthography. In both the Russian and English parts newest spelling standards have been applied, and in the latter differences between American and British usage noted wherever possible and feasible.

A hyphen at the end of a line and at the beginning of the next one denotes a hyphenated word.

In parts of words or additions given in brackets a hyphen is placed within the respective bracket.

Полноценное пользование словарём возможно лишь при точном соблюдении нижеследующих указаний!

Предварительные замечания

1. Порядок. Все заглавные слова, включая и неправильные производные формы отдельных частей речи, расположены в алфавитном порядке, напр.: *bore, born, borne* от *bear*; *men* от *man*; в русско-английской части: лучше, лучший от хороший.

Американские и английские географические названия, а также сокращения даны в особых списках на стр. 493—505.

Тильда (~ ~) служит в гнёздах слов знаком повторения. Жирная тильда (~) заменяет или всё заглавное слово или же его составную часть, стоящую перед вертикальной чертой (|). Светлая тильда (~) заменяет: а) непосредственно предыдущее заглавное слово, которое уже само может быть образовано посредством жирной тильды; б) в указании произношения произношение всего предыдущего заглавного слова. Чёрточка (-) в указании произношения даётся вместо повторения неизменяемой части заглавного слова.

При изменении начальной буквы (прописной на строчную или наоборот) вместо простой тильды ставится соответствующая тильда с кружком ~ (~).

Примеры: abandon [əˈbændən], ~ment [-mənt = əˈbændənmənt] certi|ficate, ~fication, ~fy, ~tude.

2. Произношение. Произношение сложных английских слов как правило не указывается, если каждая из их составных частей приводится в алфавитном порядке как самостоятельное заглавное слово с указанием произношения.

3. Дополнения **курсивом** служат только для уточнения отдельных английских значений.

Дальнейшие пояснения даны в виде **условных знаков и сокращений** (см. стр. 33—35).

4. Точка с запятой отделяет различные оттенки значений; синонимы даны через запятую.

5. Прибавление (**~ally**) к английскому имени прилагательному означает, что его наречие образуется посредством добавления ~ally к заглавному слову, напр.: dramatic (~ally = dramatically).

6. Переносный знак в конце строчки и в начале последующей означает, что данное английское слово пишется через чёрточку, напр.: air-conditioned = air--conditioned.

The Russian Alphabet

Printed	Written	Russian name	Transcribed	Printed	Written	Russian name	Transcribed
А а	*А* *а*	а	a	П п	*П* *п*	пэ	pɛ
Б б	*Б* *б*	бэ	bɛ	Р р	*Р* *р*	эр	ɛr
В в	*В* *в*	вэ	vɛ	С с	*С* *с*	эс	ɛs
Г г	*Г* *г*	гэ	gɛ	Т т	*Т* *т*	тэ	tɛ
Д д	*Д* *д*, *д*	дэ	dɛ	У у	*У* *у*	у	u
Е е	*Е* *е*	е	jɛ	Ф ф	*Ф* *ф*	эф	ɛf
Ё ё	*Ё* *ё*	ё	jɔ	Х х	*Х* *х*	ха	xa
Ж ж	*Ж* *ж*	жэ	ʒɛ	Ц ц	*Ц* *ц*	цэ	tsɛ
З з	*З* *з*, *з*	зэ	zɛ	Ч ч	*Ч* *ч*	че	tʆe
И и	*И* *и*	и	i	Ш ш	*Ш* *ш*	ша	ʃa
Й й	*Й* *й*	и[1])		Щ щ	*Щ* *щ*	ща	ʆtʆa
К к	*К* *к*	ка	ka	Ъ ъ	- *ъ*	[2])	
Л л	*Л* *л*	эль	ɛl̡	Ы ы	- *ы*	ы[3])	ɨ
М м	*М* *м*	эм	ɛm	Ь ь	- *ь*	[4])	
Н н	*Н* *н*	эн	ɛn	Э э	*Э* *э*	э[5])	ɛ
О о	*О* *о*	о	ɔ	Ю ю	*Ю* *ю*	ю	ju
				Я я	*Я* *я*	я	ja

[1]) и кра́ткое short i [2]) твёрдый знак hard sign, jer [3]) *or* еры́
[4]) мя́гкий знак soft sign, jeŗ [5]) э оборо́тное reversed e
Until 1918 in addition the following letters were used in Russia:
i, v = и, ѣ = е, ѳ = ф.

Explanation of Russian Pronunciation with the Help of Phonetic Symbols

Объяснение русского произношения при помощи фонетических знаков

I. Vowels

1. All vowels in stressed position are half-long in Russian.
2. In unstressed position Russian vowels are very short, except in the first pretonic syllable, where this shortness of articulation is less marked. Some vowel letters (notably о, е, я), when read in unstressed position, not only differ in length (quantity), but also change their timbre, i. e. acoustic quality.

Russian letter	Explanation of its pronunciation		Transcription symbol
a	stressed	= **a** in 'father': ма́ма (ˈmamə) 'mamma, mother'	a
	unstressed	1. = **a** in the above examples, but shorter – in first pretonic syllable: каза́к (kaˈzak) 'Cossack'	a
		2. = **a** in '**a**go, **a**bout' – in post-tonic or second, etc. pretonic syllable(s): ата́ка (aˈtakə) 'attack' абрико́с (əbŗiˈkɔs) 'apricot'	ə
		3. = **i** in 's**i**t' – after ч, щ in first pretonic syllable: часы́ (tʃ̡ɪˈsɨ) 'watch, clock' щади́ть (ʃ̡[t]ʃ̡ɪˈḑiţ) 'spare'	ɪ
e	Preceding consonant (except ж, ш, ц) is soft, i. e. palatalized.		
	stressed	1. = **ye** in '**ye**t' – in initial position, i. e. at the beginning of a word, or after a vowel, ъ, ь (if not ё) before a hard consonant: ем (jɛm) '[I] eat' бытие́ (bɨţiˈjɛ) 'being' съел (sjɛɫ) 'ate [up]' премье́р (pŗɪˈm̡jɛr) 'premier'	jɛ
		2. = **e** in 'set' – after consonants, soft or hard (ж, ш, ц), before a hard consonant, as well as in final position, i. e. at the end of a word, after consonants: нет (ņɛt) 'no' шест (ʃɛst) 'pole' цел (tsɛɫ) 'whole, sound' в стране́ (fstraˈņɛ) 'in the country' на лице́ (nəliˈtsɛ) 'on the face'	ɛ
		3. = **ya** in '**Y**ale' (but without the i-component) – in initial position or after a vowel, ъ, ь, both before a soft consonant: ель (jeļ) 'fir' бие́ние (b̡iˈjeņɪe) 'palpitation, throb' съесть (sjeşţ) 'to eat [up]'	je

Russian letter	Explanation of its pronunciation	Transcription symbol
	4. = **a** in 'pale' – after consonants, soft or hard (ж, ш, ц), before a soft consonant: петь (p̡eţ) 'to sing' сесть (şeşţ) 'to sit down' шесть (ʃeşţ) 'six' цель (tseļ) 'aim'	e
	unstressed 1. = **i** in 'sit', but preceded by (j) – in initial position, i. e. also after a vowel: ещё (jɪˈʃ[t]ʃɔ) 'still, yet' знáет (ˈznajɪt) '[he, she, it] knows'	jɪ
	2. = **i** in 'sit' – after soft consonants: рекá (r̡ɪˈka) 'river'	ɪ
	3. = **ы** (cf.) after ж, ш, ц: женá (ʒɨˈna) 'wife' пшенó (pʃɨˈnɔ) 'millet' ценá (tsɨˈna) 'price'	ɨ
ё	Preceding consonant (except ж, ш, ц) is soft.	
	only stressed 1. = **ya** in 'yacht' or **yo** in 'beyond' – in initial position, i. e. also after a vowel, ъ, ь, before a hard consonant, or in final position: ёлка (ˈjɔłkə) 'Christmas tree' даёт (daˈjɔt) '[he, she, it] gives' подъём (padˈjɔm) 'rise' бельё (b̡ɪˈļjɔ) 'linen'	jɔ
	2. = **o** in 'cost' – after both soft and hard consonants before hard consonants: лёд (ļɔt) 'ice' шёлк (ʃɔłk) 'silk'	ɔ
и	Preceding consonant (except ж, ш, ц) is soft.	
	stressed = **ee** in 'seen': и́ва (ˈivə) 'willow' юри́ст (juˈr̡ist) 'lawyer'	i
	Note: In the instr/sg. of он/онó and the oblique forms of они́ initial и- may be pronounced (ji-): их (ix *or* jix) 'of them'.	i/ji
	unstressed 1. = **ee** in 'seen', but shorter – in first pretonic syllable: мину́та (m̡iˈnutə) 'minute'	i
	2. = **i** in 'sit' – in post-tonic or second, etc. pretonic syllable(s): хóдит (ˈxɔḑɪt) '[he, she, it] goes' приписáть (p̡r̡ɪp̡iˈsaţ) 'to ascribe'	ɪ
	stressed & unstressed = **ы** (cf.) after ж, ш, ц: жить (ʒɨţ) 'to live' ши́рма (ˈʃɨrmə) 'screen' цили́ндр (tsɨˈļindr) 'cylinder'	ɨ
о	stressed = **o** in 'cost': том (tɔm) 'volume'	ɔ

Russian letter	Explanation of its pronunciation		Transcription symbol
	unstressed	1. = **a** in 'father', but shorter – in first pretonic syllable: водá (va'da) 'water' Москвá (ma'skva) 'Moscow'	a
		2. = **a** in '**a**go', '**a**bout' – in post-tonic or second, etc. pretonic syllable(s): гóрод ('gɔrət) 'town, city' огорóд (əga'rɔt) 'kitchen garden'	ə
		Note: In foreign words unstressed o is pronounced (ɔ) in final position, cf.: рáдио ('raḑiɔ) 'radio', какáо (ka'kaɔ) 'cocoa' as against Russian (native) мáсло ('masłə) 'butter'.	ɔ
у	stressed & unstressed	= **oo** in '**boo**m': бýду ('budu) '[I] will (*Brt.* shall) be'	u
ы	stressed & unstressed	a retracted variety of **i**, as in 'h**i**ll'; no English equivalent: вы (vɨ) 'you' рóзы ('rɔzɨ) 'roses'	ɨ
э	stressed & unstressed	1. = **e** in 's**e**t' – before a hard consonant: э́то ('ɛtə) 'this' эпóха (ɛ'pɔxə) 'epoch'	ɛ
		2. resembles the English sound **a** in 'pale' (but without the i-component) or **é** in French 'été' – before a soft consonant: э́ти ('eţı) 'these' элемéнт (eļı'm̧ɛnt) 'element'	e
ю	Preceding consonant is soft.		
	stressed & unstressed	1. like **yu** in '**yu**le', but shorter – in initial position, i. e. also after a vowel, and after ь: юг (juk) 'south' знáю ('znaju) '[I] know' вьюга ('v̧jugə) 'snowstorm'	ju
		2. = **u** in 'r**u**le' – after consonants: рю́мка ('ŗumkə) 'wineglass' люблю́ (ļu'bļu) '[I] like, love'	u
я	Preceding consonant is soft.		
	stressed	1. = **ya** in '**ya**rd', but shorter – in initial position, i. e. also after a vowel and ъ, as well as after ь: я́ма ('jamə) 'pit' мая́к (ma'jak) 'lighthouse' изъя́н (iz'jan) 'defect' статья́ (sta'ţja) 'article' рья́ный ('ŗjanɨj) 'zealous'	ja
		2. = **a** in 'f**a**ther' – after a consonant and before a hard consonant: мя́со ('m̧asə) 'meat; flesh'	a
		3. = **a** in 'b**a**d' – in interpalatal position, i. e. between soft consonants: пять (p̧æţ) 'five'	æ

Russian letter	Explanation of its pronunciation	Tran-scription symbol
	unstressed 1. = **i** in 'sit', but preceded by (j) – in initial position, i. e. also after a vowel and ъ: язы́к (jɪ'zɨk) 'tongue; language' та́ять ('tajɪţ) 'to thaw' изъяви́ть (ɪzjɪ'v̡iţ) 'to express, show'	jɪ
	2. = **i** in 'sit' – after soft consonants: мясни́к (m̡ɪş'ņik) 'butcher' Ряза́нь (r̡ɪ'zaņ) 'Ryazan [town]'	ɪ
	3. = **a** in 'ago' (preceded by j after vowels) – in final position: ня́ня ('ņaņə) '(wet) nurse' а́рмия ('arm̡ɪjə) 'army'	(j)ə
	II. Semivowel	
й	1. = **y** in 'yet' – in initial position, i. e. also after a vowel, in loan words: (Нью-)Йо́рк (jɔrk) '(New) York' майо́р (ma'jɔr) 'major'	
	2. in the formation of diphthongs as their second element:	j
ай	= (ɪ) of (aɪ) in 'time': май (maj) 'May'	aj
ой	= [stressed] **oi** in 'noise': бой (bɔj) 'fight', большо́й (baļ'ʃɔj) 'big'	ɔj
	= [first pretonic] **i** in 'time': война́ (vaj'na) 'war'	aj
	= [post-tonic] **a** in 'ago' + **y** in 'yet': но́вой ('nɔvəj) 'of/to the new'	əj
уй	= **u** in 'rule' + (j): бу́йвол ('bujvəł) 'buffalo'	uj
ый	= ы (cf.) + (j): вы́йти ('vɨjţɪ) 'to go out', кра́сный ('krasnɨj) 'red'	ɨj
ий	= и (cf.) + (j): кий (ķij) 'cue', си́ний ('şiņɪj) 'blue'	ij ɪj
ей	(j +) **a** in 'pale' ей (jej) 'to her', пей (p̡ej) 'drink!', нейтро́н (ņej'trɔn) 'neutron'	(j)ej
юй	= ю (cf.) + (j): плюй (p̡ļuj) 'spit!'	(j)uj
яй	= [stressed] (j +) **a** in bad + (j): я́йца ('jæjtsə) 'eggs'	(j)æj
	= [unstressed] **yi** in **Yi**ddish: яйцо́ (jɪ'tsɔ) 'egg'	jɪ

III. Consonants

1. As most Russian consonants may be palatalized (or 'softened') there is, beside the series of normal ('hard') consonants, a nearly complete set of 'soft' parallel sounds. According to traditional Russian spelling, in writing or printing this 'softness' is marked by a combination of such palatalized consonants with the vowels е, ё, и, ю, я or, either in final position or before a consonant, the so-called 'soft sign' (ь). In phonetic transcription palatalized

consonants are indicated by means of a small hook, or comma, attached to them. As a rule a hard consonant before a soft one remains hard; only з, с may be softened before palatalized з, с, д, т, н.

2. Always hard are ж, ш, ц.
3. Always soft are ч, щ.
4. The voiced consonants б, в, г, д, ж, з are pronounced voicelessly (i. e. = п, ф, к, т, ш, с) in final position.
5. The voiced consonants б, в, г, д, ж, з, when followed by (one of) their voiceless counterparts п, ф, к, т, ш, с, are pronounced voicelessly (regressive assimilation) and vice versa: voiceless before voiced is voiced (except that there is no assimilation before в).
6. The articulation of doubled consonants, particularly those following a stressed syllable, is marked by their lengthening.

Russian letter		Explanation of its pronunciation	Transcription symbol
б	hard	= **b** in '**b**ad': бок (bɔk) 'side'	b
	soft	as in 'Al**b**ion': бе́лка ('b̦ɛłkə) 'squirrel'	b̦
в	hard	= **v** in '**v**ery': во́дка ('vɔtkə) 'vodka'	v
	soft	as in '**v**iew': ве́ра ('v̦ɛrə) 'faith, belief'	v̦
г	hard	= **g** in '**g**un': гора́ (ga'ra) 'mountain'	g
	soft	as in 'ar**g**ue': гимн (g̦imn) 'anthem'	g̦
		Note: 1. = (v) in endings -ого, -его: больно́го (bal̦'nɔvə) 'of the sick, ill' рабо́чего (ra'bɔtʃɪvə) 'of the worker'	v
		2. = (x) in бог (bɔx) 'God' and in the combinations -гк-, -гч-: мя́гкий ('m̦axk̦ɪj) 'soft' мя́гче ('m̦axtʃ̦ɪ) 'softer'	x
д	hard	= **d** in '**d**oor': да́ма ('damə) 'lady'	d
	soft	as in '**d**ew': дя́дя ('d̦æd̦ə) 'uncle'	d̦
	-здн-	– in this combination д is mute: по́здно ('pɔznə) 'late'	
ж	hard	= **s** in 'mea**s**ure', **but hard**: жа́жда ('ʒaʒdə) 'thirst'	ʒ
	-жж-	may also be soft: во́жжи ('vɔʒ̦ʒ̦ɪ) 'reins'	ʒ̦ʒ̦
	-жч-	= щ: мужчи́на (mu'ʃ̦[t]ʃ̦inə) 'man'	ʃ̦[t]ʃ̦
з	hard	= **z** in '**z**oo': зал (zał) 'hall'	z
	soft	as in 'pre**s**ume': зе́ркало ('z̦ɛrkələ) 'mirror'	z̦
	-зж-	= hard or soft doubled ж: по́зже ('pɔʒʒɛ *or* 'pɔʒ̦ʒ̦ɛ) 'later'	ʒʒ/ʒ̦ʒ̦
	-зч-	= щ: изво́зчик (iz'vɔʃ̦[t]ʃ̦ɪk) 'coachman'	ʃ̦[t]ʃ̦
к	hard	= **c** in '**c**ome': как (kak) 'how, as'	k
	soft	like **k** in '**k**ey': кирпи́ч (k̦ir'p̦itʃ̦) 'brick'	k̦
л	hard	= **ll** in General American 'ca**ll**': ла́мпа ('łampə) 'lamp'	ł
	soft	= **ll** in English 'mi**ll**ion': ли́лия ('l̦il̦ɪjə) 'lily'	l̦
м	hard	= **m** in '**m**an': мак (mak) 'poppy'	m
	soft	as in '**m**ute': мир (m̦ir) 'world; peace'	m̦

Russian letter	Explanation of its pronunciation	Transcription symbol
н	hard = **n** in '**n**oise': нос (nɔs) 'nose'	n
	soft = **n** in '**n**ew': нет (ɳɛt) 'no'	ɳ
п	hard = **p** in '**p**art': пол (pɔł) 'floor'	p
	soft as in 'scor**p**ion': пить (p̡iţ) 'to drink'	p̡
р	hard = trilled **r**: рот (rɔt) 'mouth'	r
	soft as in 'O**r**ient': ряд (ɽat) 'row'	ɽ
с	hard = **s** in '**s**ad': сад (sat) 'garden'	s
	soft as in 'a**ss**ume': сюда́ (ʂu'da) 'hither, here'	ʂ
	-сч- = щ: сча́стье ('ʆ[t]ʆæʂţjɪ) 'happiness; luck'	ʆ[t]ʆ
т	hard = **t** in '**t**ent': там (tam) 'there'	t
	soft as in '**t**une': тюльпа́н (ţuɭ'pan) 'tulip'	ţ
	-стн-, -стл- – in these combinations -т- is mute: ле́стница ('ɭeʂɳɪtsə) 'staircase' счастли́вый (ʆ[t]ʆɪs'ɭivɨj) 'happy; lucky'	
ф	hard = **f** in '**f**ar': фа́брика ('fabɽɪkə) 'factory'	f
	soft as in '**f**ew': фильм (fiɭm) 'film'	f̡
х	hard = **ch** in Scotch 'lo**ch**': холм (xɔłm) 'hill'	x
	soft like **ch** in German 'i**ch**'; no English equivalent: хи́мия ('x̧iɱɪjə) 'chemistry'	x̧
ц	hard = **ts** in '**ts**ar': царь (tsaɽ) 'tsar, czar'	ts
ч	soft = **ch** in '**ch**eek': час (tʆas) 'hour'	tʆ
ш	hard = **sh**: шум (ʃum) 'noise'	ʃ
щ	soft = **sh** + **ch** in '**ch**eek', cf. fre**sh** **ch**eeks, or = doubled (ʆʆ) as in '**s**ure': щека́ (ʆ[t]ʆɪ'ka) 'cheek', щи (ʆ[t]ʆi) 'cabbage soup'	ʆ[t]ʆ

IV. 'Surds'

Russian letter	Explanation of its pronunciation	Transcription symbol
ъ	The *jer* or 'hard sign' separates a hard (final) consonant of a prefix and the initial vowel, preceded by (j), of the following root, thus marking both the hardness of the preceding consonant and the distinct utterance of (j) before the vowel: предъяви́ть (pɽɪdjɪ'ʋiţ) 'to show, produce' съезд (sjɛst) 'congress'. *Note*: Until 1918 the 'hard sign' was also used at the end of a word terminating in a hard consonant: братъ (brat) 'brother'.	

Russian letter	Explanation of its pronunciation	Transcription symbol
ь	The *jeŗ* or 'soft sign' serves to represent the palatal or soft quality of a (preceding) consonant in final position or before another consonant, cf.:	‚
	брат (brat) 'brother' and брать (braţ) 'to take' по́лка ('pɔłkə) 'shelf' and по́лька ('pɔḷkə) 'polka, Pole (= Polish woman)'.	
	It is also used before vowels to indicate the softness of a preceding consonant as well as the pronunciation of (j) with the respective vowel, e. g.:	
	семья́ (şım̧'ja) 'family' – *cf.* се́мя ('şem̧ə) 'seed',	j
	and in foreign words, such as батальо́н (bəta'ḷjɔn) 'battalion'.	j

Объяснение английского произношения при помощи фонетических знаков

Explanation of English Pronunciation with the Help of Phonetic Symbols

А. Гласные и дифтонги

В английском языке существуют краткие и долгие гласные, независимо от ударения.

[ɑ:] — долгий, глубокий и открытый звук «а», как в слове «мама».

[ʌ] — краткий, неясный звук, похожий на русский неударный звук «о», который слышится в слове «Москва», или «а» в слове «варить».
Английский звук [ʌ] встречается главным образом в ударном слоге.

[æ] — звонкий, не слишком краткий звук, средний между «а» и «э», более открытый, чем «э». При произнесении рот широко открыт.

[εə] — дифтонг, напоминающий не слишком долгий открытый звук, близкий к русскому «э» (в слове «этот»), за которым следует неясный гласный [ə] (примерно эа).

[ai] — этот дифтонг похож на русское «ай»; его первый элемент близок к русскому «а» в слове «два». Второй элемент — очень краткий звук [i].

[au] — этот дифтонг похож на русское «ау» (в слове «пауза»). Его первый элемент тот же, что и в [ai]; однако этот звук переходит постепенно в очень краткий звук [u].

[ei] — дифтонг, напоминающий русское «эй». Он состоит из звука [e] и очень краткого звука [i].

[e] — краткий звук, напоминающий «э» в слове «эти», но короче.

[ə] — нейтральный, неясный, безударный гласный звук, напоминающий русский беглый гласный в словах: «комната», «водяной» (в первом слоге).

[i:] — долгий гласный звук, похожий на русское протяжное «и» в словах: «ива», «вижу».

[i] — короткий открытый гласный, напоминающий средний звук между «и» и «ы», похожий на «и» в слове «шить».

[iə] — дифтонг, состоящий из полуоткрытого, полудолгого звука [i] и неясного звука [ə].

[ou] — дифтонг, напоминающий русское «оу». Первый его элемент — полуоткрытый звук «о» — переходит в слабое «у», причём губы слегка округляются, а язык остается неподвижным.

[ɔ:] — открытый, долгий гласный, похожий на протяжное русское «о» в слове «бор».
При произнесении этого гласного губы округлены (но не выпячены), положение рта почти как при русском «а», однако язык отодвинут назад.

[ɔ] — краткий открытый звук, похожий на русское «о».
При произнесении этого звука надо открыть рот как при «а» и, отодвигая язык назад, не выпячивая губ, произнести «о».

[o] — закрытый, краткий (близкий к «у») звук «о» в безударных слогах.

[ə:] — В русском языке нет звука, похожего на [ə:]. При его произнесении надо рот приоткрыть только слегка, губы растянуть, а язык оставить в нейтральном положении.
В закрытом слоге этот гласный орфографически представлен сочетаниями -er, -ir и -ur.

[ɔi] — дифтонг, состоящий из звука [ɔ] и очень краткого [i].

[u:] — долгий гласный, напоминающий протяжно произнесенное русское «у» под ударением, напр.: сук, губка.

При произнесении этого звука губы вперёд не выдвигаются.

[uə] — дифтонг, состоящий из звука [u] и неясного гласного [ə].

[u] — краткий звук, похожий на русский неударный звук «у» в словах: «тупой», «сума». При произнесении этого звука губы не выдвигаются.

Б. Согласные

Согласные: [b] — б, [f] — ф, [g] — г, [k] — к, [m] — м, [p] — п, [s] — с, [v] — в, [z] — з почти не отличаются от соответствующих русских.

Английские звонкие согласные, в противоположность русским, сохраняют на конце слова свою звонкость и произносятся чётко и энергично.

[r] — произносится только перед гласными, в конце слова только, если следующее слово начинается с гласного. При произнесении этого звука кончик языка поднят к нёбу и только слегка прикасается к нему выше альвеол. Английское [r] произносится, в отличие от соответствующего русского звука «р», без раскатистой вибрации языка.

[ʒ] — звук, похожий на смягченное русское «ж».

[ʃ] — звук, похожий на смягченное русское «ш».

[θ] — аналогичного звука в русском языке нет. Для получения этого согласного пропускается струя воздуха между кончиком языка и краем верхних зубов; этот звук приближается к русскому «с» в слове «сын», если его произнести с чуть высунутым языком.

[ð] — отличается от [θ] только присутствием голоса. Следует избегать звука, похожего на русское «з».

[s] — соответствует русскому «с».

[z] — соответствует русскому «з».

[ŋ] — носовой заднеязычный согласный. В русском языке аналогичного звука нет. (Чтобы научиться произносить этот звук, надо с открытым ртом задней частью спинки языка попробовать произнести «м» так, чтобы воздух проходил не через рот, а через нос.)

[ŋk] — согласный звук, отличающийся от [ŋ] только присутствием [k].

[w] — согласный, похожий на очень краткое русское «у». При произнесении этого звука воздух проходит между губами, которые сначала слегка вытягиваются вперёд, а затем быстро занимают положение, нужное для следующего гласного звука.

[h] — простой, безголосный выдох.

[j] — звук, похожий на русский «й».

[f] — соответствует русскому согласному «ф».

[v] — соответствует русскому согласному «в».

Ударение в английских словах обозначается знаком (ˈ) и ставится перед ударным слогом, напр.: onion (ˈʌnjən).

В английском языке, кроме слов с ударением на одном слоге, бывают слова с одинаково сильным ударением на двух слогах, напр.: unsound (ˈʌnˈsaund), а также (длинные слова) с главным и побочным ударением, напр.: conglomeration (kɔnˈglɔməˈˈreiʃn).

Две точки (:) обозначают **долготу звука,** напр.: ask (ɑ:sk), astir (əsˈtə:).

Английский алфавит

a (ei), **b** (bi:), **c** (si:), **d** (di:), **e** (i:), **f** (ef), **g** (dʒi:), **h** (eitʃ), **i** (ai), **j** (dʒei), **k** (kei), **l** (el), **m** (em), **n** (en), **o** (ou), **p** (pi:), **q** (kju:), **r** (ɑ:, *Am.* ɑ:r), **s** (es), **t** (ti:), **u** (ju:), **v** (vi:), **w** (ˈdʌblju:), **x** (eks), **y** (wai), **z** (zed, *Am.* zi:).

Американская орфография

отличается от британской главным образом следующим:

1. Вместо **...our** пишется **...or**, напр.: hon*or* = honour, lab*or* = labour.
2. Окончанию **...re** соответствует **...er**, напр.: cent*er* = centre, theat*er* = theatre, meag*er* = meagre; исключения представляют og*re* и слова, оканчивающиеся на ...cre, напр.: massa*cre*, na*cre*.
3. Вместо **...ce** пишется **...se**, напр.: defen*se* = defence, licen*se* = licence.
4. Во всех словах, производных от глаголов, оканчивающихся на **...l** и **...p**, согласная на конце не удваивается, напр.: travel — trave*l*ed — trave*l*er — trave*l*ing, worship — worshi*p*ed — worshi*p*er — worshi*p*ing. Также и в некоторых других словах вместо двойной пишется одна согласная, напр.: wa*g*on = waggon, woo*l*en = woollen.
5. В некоторых случаях немое **e** опускается, напр.: abrid*gm*ent = abridgement, acknowled*gm*ent = acknowledgement, jud*gm*ent = judgement, ax = ax*e*, good-by = good-by*e*.
6. В некоторых словах написанию приставки **en...** предпочитается **in...**, напр.: *in*close = enclose, *in*snare = ensnare.
7. Написания **æ** и **œ** часто заменяются простым **e**, напр.: an*e*mia = anæmia, diarrh*ea* = diarrhœa.
8. Немой конечный слог в словах французского происхождения часто опускается, напр.: catalog = catalog*ue*, program = program*me*, prolog = prolog*ue*.
9. Особые случаи: st*a*nch = staunch, m*o*ld = mould, m*o*lt = moult, gr*a*y = grey, pl*ow* = plough, ski*ll*ful = skilful, t*i*re = tyre.

Американское произношение

отличается от английского главным образом следующим:

1. ɑ: произносится как протяжное æ: в словах ask (æ:sk = ɑ:sk), castle (kæ:sl = kɑ:sl), grass (græ:s = grɑ:s), past (pæ:st = pɑ:st) и т. д.; так же в словах branch (bræ:ntʃ = brɑ:ntʃ), can't (kæ:nt = kɑ:nt), dance (dæ:ns = dɑ:ns) и т. д.
2. ɔ произносится как ɑ в таких словах: common ('kamən = 'kɔmən), not (nat = nɔt), on (an = ɔn), rock (rak = rɔk), bond (band = bɔnd) и во многих других.
3. ju: произносится как u:, напр.: due (du: = dju:), duke (du:k = dju:k), new (nu: = nju:).
4. r произносится между предшествующим гласным и последующим согласным звонко, коротко, причём кончик языка оттягивается назад и касается твёрдого нёба несколько выше альвеол, напр.: clerk (klə:rk = klɑ:k), hard (hɑ:rd = hɑ:d); так же и в конце слова, напр.: far (fɑ:r = fɑ:), her (hə:r = hə:).
5. Глухие p, t, k в начале безударного слога (следующего за ударным слогом) произносятся звонко, т. е. как b, d, g, напр.: property, water, second.
6. Разница между слогами с сильным и слабым ударением выражена гораздо меньше; в более длинных словах слышится ясно второстепенное ударение, напр.: dictionary (''dikʃə'nɛri = 'dikʃənri), ceremony (''serə'mouni ='seriməni), inventory (''inven'touri = 'invəntri), secretary (''sekrə'tɛri = 'sekrətri).
7. Перед, а часто также и после носовых согласных (m, n, ŋ) гласные и дифтонги произносятся с носовым оттенком, напр.: stand, time, small.

Symbols and Abbreviations

Условные знаки и сокращения

1. Symbols — Знаки

□ после английского имени прилагательного или причастия указывает на возможность правильного образования от них наречий путем прибавления суффикса *...ly* или изменения *...le* на *...ly* или *...y* на *...ily*, напр.: rich □ = *richly*; acceptable □ = *acceptably*; happy □ = *happily*.

□ after an English adjective or participle means that from it an adverb may be formed regularly by adding *...ly*, or by changing *...le* into *...ly* or *...y* into *...ily*; as: rich □ = *richly*; acceptable □ = *acceptably*; happy □ = *happily*.

F *familiar* = *colloquial language* разговóрный язы́к.

P *popular* просторéчие.

⚒ *rare, little used* рéдко, малоупотреби́тельно.

† *obsolete* устарéвшее слóво, выражéние.

📖 *scientific term* наýчный тéрмин.

⚘ *botany* ботáника.

⊕ *handicraft, engineering* тéхника.

⚒ *mining* гóрное дéло.

⚔ *military term* воéнное дéло.

⚓ *nautical term* судохóдство.

☤ *commercial term* торгóвля.

🚂 *railroad, railway* железнодорóжное дéло.

✈ *aviation* авиáция.

📯 *postal affairs* пóчта.

♪ *musical term* мýзыка.

△ *architecture* архитектýра.

⚡ *electrical engineering* электротéхника.

⚖ *jurisprudence* юриспрудéнция.

∡ *mathematics* математика.

⚘ *farming* сéльское хозя́йство.

⚗ *chemistry* хи́мия.

⚕ *medicine* медици́на.

& *and* и.

= *equal to* равнó.

2. Abbreviations — Сокращения

a. *also* тáкже.

abbr. *abbreviation* сокращéние.

acc. *accusative* (*case*) вини́тельный падéж.

adj. *adjective* и́мя прилагáтельное.

adv. *adverb* нарéчие.

Am. *Americanism* американи́зм.

anat. *anatomy* анатóмия

art. *article* арти́кль, член.

ast. *astronomy* астронóмия.

attr. *attributively* атрибути́вное употреблéние (т. е. в кáчестве определéния).

biol. *biology* биолóгия.

Brt. *British* (*English*) *usage* британское (англи́йское) словоупотреблéние.

b. s. *bad sense* в дурнóм смы́сле.

cap. *capitalized* с большóй бýквы.

cf. *compare* сравни́.

ch. *chess* ша́хматы.

cj. *conjunction* сою́з.

co. *comic(ally)* шутли́во.

coll. *collective (noun)* собира́тельное и́мя (существи́тельное).

com. *commonly* обыкнове́нно.

comp. *comparative (degree)* сравни́тельная сте́пень.

compd(s). *compound(s)* сло́жное сло́во (сло́жные слова́).

cond. *conditional* усло́вное наклоне́ние.

contp. *contemptuously* пренебрежи́тельно.

cook. *cookery* кулина́рия.

dat. *dative (case)* да́тельный паде́ж.

dem. *demonstrative pronoun* указа́тельное местоиме́ние.

dim. *diminutive* уменьши́тельная фо́рма.

e. *endings stressed (throughout)* ударе́ние (сплошь) на оконча́ниях.

eccl. *ecclesiastical term* церко́вное выраже́ние.

econ. *economy* эконо́мика.

educ. *education* шко́ла, шко́льное де́ло, педаго́гика.

e. g. *for example* наприме́р.

esp. *especially* осо́бенно.

etc. *et cetera (and so on)* и т. д. (и так да́лее).

f *feminine (gender)* же́нский род.

fenc. *fencing* фехтова́ние.

fig. *figuratively* в перено́сном значе́нии.

form. *formerly* пре́жде.

f/pl. *feminine plural* мно́жественное число́ же́нского ро́да.

fr. *French* францу́зское сло́во, выраже́ние.

ft. *future (tense)* бу́дущее вре́мя.

gen. *genitive (case)* роди́тельный паде́ж.

geogr. *geography* геогра́фия.

geol. *geology* геоло́гия.

geom. *geometry* геоме́трия.

ger. *gerund* геру́ндий.

g/pl. *genitive plural* роди́тельный паде́ж мно́жественного числа́.

g. pr. *(pt.) present (past) gerund* дееприча́стие настоя́щего (проше́дшего) вре́мени.

gr. *grammar* грамма́тика.

hist. *history* исто́рия.

hunt. *hunting* охо́та.

imp. *imperative* повели́тельное наклоне́ние.

impers. *impersonal (form), -ly* безли́чная фо́рма, безли́чно.

impf. *imperfective (aspect)* несоверше́нный вид.

(im)pf. *imperfective and perfective (aspect)* несоверше́нный и соверше́нный вид.

ind(ecl). *indeclinable word* несклоня́емое сло́во.

inf. *infinitive* инфинити́в, неопределённая фо́рма глаго́ла.

instr. *instrumental (case)* твори́тельный паде́ж.

int. *interjection* междоме́тие.

interr. *interrogative(ly)* вопроси́тельная фо́рма, вопроси́тельно.

iro. *ironically* ирони́чески.

irr. *irregular* непра́вильный.

iter. *iterative, frequentative (aspect)* многокра́тный вид.

ling. *linguistics* лингви́стика, языкозна́ние.

lit. *literary* кни́жное выраже́ние.

m *masculine (gender)* мужско́й род.

metall. *metallurgy* металлу́ргия.

min. *mineralogy* минерало́гия.

mot. *motoring* автомобили́зм.

m/pl. *masculine plural* мно́жественное число́ мужско́го ро́да.

mst *mostly* бо́льшей ча́стью.

n *neuter (gender)* сре́дний род.

no. *number* но́мер.

nom. *nominative (case)* имени́тельный паде́ж.

n/pl. *neuter plural* мно́жественное число́ сре́днего ро́да.

npr. *proper name* (or *noun*) и́мя со́бственное.

o. a. one another друг дру́га, друг дру́гу.

obj. *objective* (*case*) объéктный падéж.

obl. *oblique* (*cases*) кóсвенные падежи́.

oft. *often* чáсто.

once *semelfactive* (*aspect*) однокрáтный вид.

op. *opposite* противоположно.

opt. *optics* óптика.

o. s. oneself себя́, себé, -ся.

p. *participle* причáстие.

p. person лицó.

P. *person* человéк.

paint. *painting* жи́вопись.

parl. *parliamentary term* парлáментское выражéние.

part. 1. *particle* части́ца; 2. *particular*(*ly*) осóбенно.

part. g. *partitive genitive* роди́тельный раздели́тельный.

pers. *pers. person*(*al form*) лицó (ли́чная фóрма).

pf. *perfective* (*aspect*) совершéнный вид.

pharm. *pharmacy* фармацéвтика.

phon. *phonetics* фонéтика.

phot. *photography* фотогрáфия.

phys. *physics* фи́зика.

pl. *plural* мнóжественное числó.

poet. *poetic* поэти́ческое слóво, выражéние.

pol. *politics* поли́тика.

poss. *possessive* (*form*) притяжáтельная фóрма.

p. pr. a. (*p.*) *present participle active* (*passive*) действи́тельное (страдáтельное) причáстие настоя́щего врéмени.

p. pt. a. (*p.*) *past participle active* (*passive*) действи́тельное (страдáтельное) причáстие прошéдшего врéмени.

pr. *present* (*tense*) настоя́щее врéмя.

pred(*ic.*) *predicative* предикати́вное употреблéние (т. е. в кáчестве именнóй чáсти сказýемого).

pref. *prefix* пристáвка.

pr(*e*)*s.* *present* (*tense*) настоя́щее врéмя.

pron. *pronoun* местоимéние.

prov. *proverb*(*ial saying*) пословица, поговóрка.

prp. *preposition* предлóг.

prpos. *prepositional* (*case*) предлóжный падéж.

psych. *psychology* психолóгия.

pt. *preterite, past* (*tense*) прошéдшее врéмя.

rad. *radio* рáдио.

refl. *reflexive* (*form*) возврáтная фóрма.

rel. *relative* (form) относи́тельная фóрма.

rhet. *rhetoric* ретóрика.

s. *see* смотри́.

s. b. somebody ктó- (когó-, комý-) -нибудь.

s. b.'s somebody's чéй-нибудь.

sg. *singular* еди́нственное числó.

sh. *short* (*predicative*) *form* крáткая фóрма.

sl. *slang* жаргóн.

Sov. *Soviet term* выражéние совéтского периода.

st. *stem stressed* (*throughout*) ударéние (сплошь) на оснóве.

s. th. something чтó-либо.

su. *substantive* и́мя существи́тельное.

sup. *superlative* превосхóдная стéпень.

surv. *surveying* топогрáфия.

tel. *telegraphy* телегрáф.

teleph. *telephony* телефóн.

text. *textiles* ткáни.

th. *thing* вещь, предмéт.

thea. *theater* теáтр.

typ. *typography* типогрáфское дéло.

univ. *university* университéт.

usu. *usually* обы́чно.

v/aux. *auxiliary verb* вспомогáтельный глагóл.

vb. *verb* глагóл.

vet. *veterinary* ветеринáрия.

v/i. *verb intransitive* непереходный глагóл.

voc. *vocative* (*case*) звáтельный падéж.

v/refl. *verb reflexive* возврáтный глагóл.

v/t. *verb transitive* перехóдный глагóл.

zo. *zoology* зоолóгия.

Russian Abbreviations — Русские сокращения

И имени́тельный паде́ж nominative (case).

Р роди́тельный паде́ж genitive (case).

Д да́тельный паде́ж dative (case).

В вини́тельный паде́ж accusative (case).

Т твори́тельный паде́ж instrumental (case).

П предло́жный паде́ж prepositional *or* locative (case).

и т. д. (и так да́лее) *etc.* (*et cetera*)*e*

и т. п. (и тому́ подо́бное) *and th. like.*

лат. лати́нский язы́к Latin.

тж. та́кже *also.*

PART ONE

RUSSIAN-ENGLISH VOCABULARY

A

а 1. *cj.* but, and; а то or else; а что? why so?; **2.** *int.* ah!; **3.** *part.* F eh?

аб|ажу́р *m* [1] lamp shade; **~ба́т** *m* [1] abbot; **~ба́тство** *n* [9] abbey; **~за́ц** *m* [1] paragraph; **~онеме́нт** *m* [1] subscription; **~оне́нт** *m* [1] subscriber; **~орда́ж** ⚓ *m* [1] grappling, boarding; **~о́рт** *m* [1] abortion; **~рико́с** *m* [1] apricot; **~солю́тный** [14; -тен, -тна] absolute; **~стра́ктный** [14; -тен, -тна] abstract; **~су́рд** *m* [1] absurdity; **~су́рдный** [14; -ден, -дна] absurd; **~сце́сс** *m* [1] abscess.

аван|га́рд *m* [1] advance guard; vanguard; **~по́ст** *m* [1] outpost; **~с** *m* [1] advance(d money); **~сом** (*payment*) in advance; **~тю́ра** *f* [5] adventure; **~тюри́ст** *m* [1] adventurer; **~тюри́стка** *f* [5; *g/pl.*: -ток] adventuress.

авар|и́йный [14] emergency...; **~ия** *f* [7] accident; wreck.

а́вгуст *m* [1] August.

авиа|ба́за *f* [5] air base; **~бо́мба** *f* [5] air bomb; **~констру́ктор** *m* [1] aircraft designer; **~ли́ния** *f* [7] airline; **~ма́тка** *f* [5; *g/pl*: -ток], **~но́сец** *m* [1; -сца] aircraft carrier; **~по́чта** *f* [5] air mail; **~тра́сса** *f* [5] air route; **~цио́нный** [14] air(craft)...; **~ция** *f* [7] aviation; aircraft *pl.*; **~шко́ла** *f* [5] flying school.

аво́сь F perhaps, maybe; на ~ at random.

австр|али́ец *m* [1; -и́йца], **~али́йка** *f* [5; *g/pl.*: -и́ек], **~али́йский** [16] Australian; **~а́лия** *f* [7] Australia; **~и́ец** *m* [1; -и́йца], **~и́йка** *f* [5; *g/pl.*: -и́ек], **~и́йский** [16] Austrian; **'~ия** *f* [7] Austria.

автобиогр|афи́ческий [16], **~афи́чный** [14; -чен, -чна] autobiographic(al); **~а́фия** *f* [7] autobiography.

авто́бус *m* [1] (motor) bus.

авто|го́нки *f/pl.* [5; *gen.*: -нок] (car) race; **~граф** *m* [1] autograph; **~жи́р** *m* [1] autogiro; **~заво́д** *m* [1] car factory, automobile plant; **~кра́тия** *f* [7] autocracy; **~магистра́ль** *f* [8] highway; **~ма́т** *m* [1] automaton; slot machine; submachine gun; **~мати́ческий** [16], **~мати́чный** [14; -чен, -чна] automatic; **~ма́тчик** *m* [1] submachine gunner; **~маши́на** *f* [5] *s.* ~моби́ль; **~мобили́ст** *m* [1] motorist; **~моби́ль** *m* [4] (motor-) car; го́ночный ~моби́ль *m* racing car, racer; **~но́мия** *f* [7] autonomy.

а́втор *m* [1] author; **~изова́ть** [7] (*im*)*pf.* authorize; **~ите́т** *m* [1] authority; **~ский** [16] author's; ~ское пра́во *n* copyright; **~ство** *n* [9] authorship.

авто|ру́чка *f* [5; *g/pl.*: -чек] fountain pen; **~стра́да** *f* [5] (motor, super)highway.

ага́ (a'ha) aha!; (oh,) I see!

Ага́фья *f* [6; *g/pl.*: -фий] Agatha.

аге́нт *m* [1] agent; **~ство** *n* [9], **~у́ра** *f* [5] agency.

агит|ацио́нный [14] agitation..., propaganda...; **~и́ровать** [7], ⟨с-⟩ agitate; **~ка** F *f* [5; *g/pl.*: -ток] (agitation) leaflet; **~про́п** (агитацио́нно-пропаганди́стский отде́л) *m* [1] *pol.* agitation and propaganda department; **~пу́нкт** *m* [1] (*local*) agitation center (*Brt.* -tre).

агра́рный [14] agrarian.

агресс|и́вный [14; -вен, -вна] agressive; **~ия** *f* [7] aggression.

агрикульту́ра *f* [5] agriculture.

агро|но́м *m* [1] agriculturist; **~номи́ческий** [16] agronomi(cal); **~но́мия** *f* [7] agronomy.

ад *m* [1; в -у́] hell.

Ада́м *m* [1] Adam.

ада́птер (-tɛr) ⚡ *m* [1] pickup.

адвока́т *m* [1] lawyer; attorney (at law), *Brt.* barrister; solicitor; **~у́ра** *f* [5] ⚖ bar.

адми|нистрати́вный [14] administrative; **~нистра́ция** *f* [7] administration; **~ра́л** *m* [1] admiral; **~ралте́йство** *n* [9] admiralty.

а́дрес *m* [1; *pl.*: -а́, *etc. e.*] address (не по Д at wrong); **~а́т** *m* [1], **~а́тка** *f* [5; *g/pl.*: -ток] addressee; consignee; **~ный** [14]: ~ный стол *m* register-office; **~ова́ть** [7] (*im*)*pf.* address, direct.

адриати́ческий [16] Adriatic...

а́дский [16] hellish, infernal.

адъюта́нт *m* [1] aide-de-camp.

аз *m* [1 *e.*]: ~ы́ *pl.* elementaries; F с ~о́в from scratch.

аза́рт *m* [1] passion, vehemence; hazard; войти́ в ~ get excited; **~ный** [14; -тен, -тна] hot-tempered, hazardous; venturesome.

а́збу|ка *f* [5] alphabet; **~чный** [14] alphabetic(al); ~чная и́стина *f* truism.

азербайджа́н|ец *m* [1, -нца] Azerbaijanian; **~ский** [16] Azerbaijan.

ази|а́т *m* [1], **~а́тка** *f* [5; *g/pl.*: -ток], **~а́тский** [16] Asian; Asiatic; **'~я** *f* [7] Asia; Ма́лая '~я Asia Minor.

азо́вский [16] Asov...

азо́т *m* [1] nitrogen; **~ный** [14] nitric.
а́ист *m* [1] stork; **~овый** [14] stork...
ай ah!, oh!
айва́ *f* [5] quince.
акаде́м|ик *m* [1] academician; graduate; **~и́ческий** [16] academic; **~ия** *f* [7] academy; ♀ия нау́к Academy of Sciences; ♀ия худо́жеств Academy of Arts.
ака́ция *f* [7] acacia.
акваре́ль *f* [8] water colo(u)r.
акклиматизи́ровать [7] (*im*)*pf.* acclimatize.
аккомпан|еме́нт ♪ *m* [1] accompaniment; **~и́ровать** ♀ [7] accompany.
акко́рд ♪ *m* [1] chord; **~ный** [14]: ~ная рабо́та *f* piecework.
аккредит|и́в *m* [1] letter of credit; **~ова́ть** [7] (*im*)*pf.* accredit.
аккура́тный [14; -тен, -тна] accurate, punctual; tidy, neat.
акт *m* [1] act(ion); *thea.* act; document; *parl.* bill; **~ёр** *m* [1] actor.
акти́в *m* [1] asset(s); body of active functionaries; **~ный** [14; -вен, -вна] active.
актри́са *f* [5] actress.
актуа́льный [14; -лен, -льна] topical.
аку́ла *f* [5] shark.
аку́ст|ика *f* [5] acoustics; **~и́ческий** [16] acoustic(al).
акуше́р|ка *f* [5; *g/pl.*: -рок] midwife; **~ство** *n* [9] midwifery.
акце́нт *m* [1] accent; stress.
акцептова́ть † [7] (*im*)*pf.* accept.
акци|оне́р *m* [1] stockholder, *Brt.* shareholder; **~оне́рный** [14] joint-stock (*company*); **'~я** *f* [7] share; *pl. a.* stock.
алба́н|ец *m* [1; -нца], **~ка** *f* [5; *g/pl.*: -нок], **~ский** [16] Albanian.
а́лгебра *f* [5] algebra.
алеба́стр *m* [1] alabaster.
Алексе́й *m* [3] Alexis.
але́ть [8] blush, grow crimson; glow.
Алжи́р *m* [1] Algeria; Algiers.
алиме́нты *m/pl.* [1] alimony.
алкого́л|ик *m* [1] alcoholic; **~ь** *m* [4] alcohol.
аллегори́ческий [16] allegorical.
алле́я *f* [6; *g/pl.*: -е́й] avenue, alley.
алма́з *m* [1], **~ный** [14] diamond.
алта́рь *m* [4 *e.*] altar.
алфави́т *m* [1] alphabet; **~ный** [14] alphabetical.
а́лчн|ость *f* [8] greed(iness); **~ый** [14; -чен, -чна] greedy (of, for к [Д]).
а́лый [14 *sh.*] crimson.
альбо́м *m* [1] album; sketchbook.
альмана́х *m* [1] almanac.
альпини́|зм *m* [1] mountain climbing, Alpinism; **~ст** *m* [1], **~стка** *f* [5; *g/pl.*: -ток] climber, Alpinist.
'Альпы *f/pl.* [5] Alps.
альт *m* [1 *e.*] alto.
а́льф|а *f* [5]: от ~ы до оме́ги from beginning to end.
алюми́ний *m* [3] aluminium.
Аля́ска *f* [5] Alaska.
амба́р *m* [1] barn; granary.
амбразу́ра *f* [5] embrasure.
амбулато́р|ия *f* [7] ambulance station, dispensary; **~ный** [14]: ~ный больно́й *m* outpatient.
Аме́рик|а *f* [5] America; ♀а́нец *m* [1; -нца], ♀а́нка *f* [5; *g/pl.*: -нок], ♀а́нский [16] American.
ами́нь amen.
амнист|и́ровать [7] (*im*)*pf.*, **¿ия** *f* [7] amnesty.
амортиз|а́ция *f* [7] amortization; **~и́ровать** [7] (*im*)*pf.* amortize, pay off.
а́мпула *f* [5] ampoule.
ампут|а́ция *f* [7] amputation; **~и́ровать** [7] (*im*)*pf.* amputate.
амуни́ция *f* [7] ammunition.
амфи́бия *f* [7] amphibian.
амфитеа́тр *m* [1] amphitheater (*Brt.* -tre); *thea.* circle.
ана́лиз *m* [1] analysis; **~и́ровать** [7] (*im*)*pf.*, ⟨про-⟩ analyze (*Brt.* -se).
ана|логи́чный [14; -чен, -чна] analogous, similar; **~ло́гия** *f* [7] analogy; **~на́с** *m* [1] pineapple; **¿рхия** *f* [7] anarchy.
анатом|и́ровать [7] (*im*)*pf.* anatomize; **~и́ческий** [16] anatomical; **¿ия** *f* [7] anatomy.
анга́р *m* [1] hangar.
а́нгел *m* [1] angel.
анги́на *f* [5] quinsy, tonsillitis.
англи́|йский [16] English; **~ча́нин** *m* [1; *pl.*: -ча́не, -ча́н] Englishman; **~ча́нка** *f* [5; *g/pl.*: -нок] Englishwoman; **'♀я** *f* [7] England.
Андре́й *m* [3] Andrew.
'Анды *f/pl.* [5] Andes.
анекдо́т *m* [1] anecdote.
ане|ми́я *f* [7] anemia; **~стези́я** (-nεstε-) *f* [7] anesthesia.
ани́с *m* [1] anise.
Анкара́ *f* [5] Ankara.
анке́та *f* [5] questionnaire; form.
аннекс|и́ровать [7] (*im*)*pf.* annex; **¿ия** *f* [7] annexation.
аннули́ровать [7] (*im*)*pf.* annul.
ано́д *m* [1] anode; **~ный** [14] anodic.
анома́лия *f* [7] anomaly.
анони́мный [14; -мен, -мна] anonymous.
анса́мбль *m* [4] ensemble.
антагони́зм *m* [1] antagonism.
Антаркт|и́да *f* [5] Antarctica; **¿ика** *f* [5], ♀и́ческий [16] Antarctic.
анте́нна (-'tεn-) *f* [5] aerial; *zo.* antenna.
антиква́р *m* [1] antiquary; dealer in antiquarian goods; **~ный** [14] antiquarian.
антило́па *f* [5] antelope.
анти|пати́чный [14; -чен, -чна] antipathetic; **~па́тия** *f* [7] antipathy; **~санита́рный** [14] insani-

tary; **~се́птика** *f* [5] antisepsis; antiseptic; **~те́за** *f* [5] antithesis.
анти́чн|ость *f* [8] antiquity; **~ый** [14] antique.
антоло́гия *f* [7] anthology.
Анто́н *m* [1] Anthony; **~и́на** *f* [5] Antonia.
антра́кт *m* [1] intermission, *Brt.* interval; interlude.
антропо́л|ог *m* [1] anthropologist; **~о́гия** *f* [7] anthropology.
анчо́ус *m* [1] anchovy.
апат|и́чный [14; -чен, -чна] apathetic; **~ия** *f* [7] apathy.
апелл|и́ровать [7] (*im*)*pf.* appeal (to к Д); **~яцио́нный** [14] (*court*) of appeal; ~яцио́нная жа́лоба *f* = **~я́ция** ⚖ *f* [7] appeal.
апельси́н *m* [1] orange.
аплоди́|ровать [7], ⟨за-⟩ applaud; **~сме́нты** *m/pl.* [1] applause.
апоге́й *m* [3] apogee.
аполити́чн|ость *f* [8] indifference toward(s) politics; **~ый** [14; -чен, -чна] indifferent to politics.
апологи́ческий [16] apologetic.
апопле́ксия *f* [7] apoplexy.
апо́стол *m* [1] apostle.
апофео́з *m* [1] apotheosis.
аппара́т *m* [1] apparatus; camera.
аппе́нд|икс *m* [1] *anat.* appendix; **~ици́т** *m* [1] appendicitis.
аппети́т *m* [1] appetite; прия́тного ~а! bon appétit!; **~ный** [14; -и́тен, -и́тна] appetizing.
апре́ль *m* [4] April.
апте́ка *f* [5] drugstore, *Brt.* chemist's shop; **~рь** *m* [4] druggist, *Brt.* (pharmaceutical) chemist.
ара́|б *m* [1], **~бка** *f* [5; *g/pl.*: -бок] Arab; **~бский** [16] (*a.* **~ви́йский** [16]) Arabian, Arabic; Arab (*Ligue, etc.*); **~п** † *m* [1] Moor, Negro.
арби́тр *m* [1] arbiter; umpire; **~а́ж** ⚖ *m* [1] arbitration.
арбу́з *m* [1] watermelon.
Аргенти́н|а *f* [5] Argentina; **♀ец** *m* [1; -нца], **♀ка** *f* [5; *g/pl.*: -нок], **♀ский** [16] Argentine.
арго́ *n* [*indecl.*] argot.
аргуме́нт *m* [1] argument; **~и́ровать** [7] (*im*)*pf.* argue.
аре́на *f* [5] arena; sphere.
аре́нд|а *f* [5] lease, rent; сдава́ть (брать) в ~у lease (rent); **~а́тор** *m* [1] lessee; tenant; **~ова́ть** [7] (*im*)*pf.* rent.
аре́ст *m* [1] arrest; **~а́нт** *m* [1], **~а́нтка** *f* [5; *g/pl.*: -ток] prisoner; **~о́вывать** [1], ⟨~ова́ть⟩ [7] arrest.
аристокра́тия *f* [7] aristocracy.
арифме́т|ика *f* [5] arithmetic; **~и́ческий** [16] arithmetic(al).
а́рия *f* [7] aria; air.
а́рка *f* [5; *g/pl.*: -рок] arc; arch.
арка́да *f* [5] arcade.
'**Аркти|ка** *f* [5] Arctic (Zone); **♀ческий** (-'ţi-) [16] arctic.
армату́ра *f* [5] fittings, armature.
Арме́ния *f* [7] Armenia.
а́рмия *f* [7] army.
армя́н|и́н *m* [1; *pl.*: -мя́не, -мя́н], **~ка** *f* [5; *g/pl.*: -нок], **~ский** [16] Armenian.
арома́т *m* [1] aroma, perfume, fragrance; **~и́ческий** [16], **~ный** [14; -тен, -тна] aromatic, fragrant.
арсена́л *m* [1] arsenal.
арте́ль *f* [8] workmen's cooperative association.
арте́рия *f* [7] artery.
артилле́р|ия *f* [7] artillery; **~и́ст** *m* [1] artilleryman; **~и́йский** [16] artillery...
арти́ст *m* [1] artist(e); actor; **~ка** *f* [5; *g/pl.*: -ток] artist(e); actress.
артишо́к *m* [1] artichoke.
а́рфа *f* [5] harp.
архео́лог *m* [1] archeologist; **~и́ческий** [16] archeologic(al); **~ия** *f* [7] archeology.
архи́в *m* [1] archives *pl.*
архиепи́скоп *m* [1] archbishop.
архипела́г *m* [1] archipelago.
архите́кт|ор *m* [1] architect; **~у́ра** *f* [5] architecture; **~у́рный** [14] architectonic.
арши́н *m* [1; *g/pl.*: арши́н] arshine (†, = *0.711 m.* = *2 ft. 4 in.*).
арьерга́рд *m* [1] rear guard.
асбе́ст *m* [1] asbestos.
асе́птика (-'sɛ-) *f* [5] asepsis.
аспира́нт *m* [1] candidate (*for university teacher's/researcher's career*).
ассамбле́я *f* [6; *g/pl.*: -ле́й]: Генера́льная ♀ Организа́ции Объединённых На́ций United Nations, General Assembly.
ассигнова́|ть [7] (*im*)*pf.* assign, allocate, allot; **~ние** *n* [12] assignment, allocation, allotment.
ассимил|и́ровать [7] (*im*)*pf.* assimilate (**-ся** o. s.); **~я́ция** *f* [7] assimilation.
ассисте́нт *m* [1], **~ка** *f* [5; *g/pl.*: -ток] assistant.
ассортиме́нт *m* [1] assortment.
ассоци|а́ция *f* [7] association; **~и́ровать** [7] (*im*)*pf.* associate.
АССР (Автоно́мная Сове́тская Социалисти́ческая Респу́блика *f*) Autonomous Soviet Socialist Republic.
а́стра *f* [5] aster.
астроно́м *m* [1] astronomer; **~и́ческий** [16] astronomic(al); **~ия** *f* [7] astronomy.
асфа́льт *m* [1] asphalt.
ата́к|а *f* [5] attack, charge; **~ова́ть** [7] (*im*)*pf.* attack, charge.
атама́н *m* [1] hetman.
ателье́ (-tɛ-) *n* [*indecl.*] studio, atelier.
атланти́ческий [16] Atlantic...
а́тлас[1] *m* [1] atlas.
атла́с[2] *m* [1] satin.
атле́т *m* [1] athlete; **~ика** *f* [5] athletics; **~и́ческий** [16] athletic.
атмосфе́р|а *f* [5] atmosphere; **~ный** [16] atmospheric.
а́том *m* [1] atom; **~ный** [14] atomic.

аттеста́т *m* [1] certificate.
ауди|е́нция *f* [7] audience; **~то́рия** *f* [7] lecture hall; audience.
аукцио́н *m* [1] auction (by с P).
Афана́сий *m* [3] Athanasius.
Афганиста́н *m* [1] Afghanistan.
афе́р|а *f* [5] speculation, fraud, shady deal; **~и́ст** *m* [1], **~и́стка** *f* [5; *g/pl.*: -ток] speculator, swindler.
Афи́ны *f/pl.* [5] Athens.
афи́ша *f* [5] playbill, poster.
афори́зм *m* [1] aphorism.
ˈ**Африка** *f* [5] Africa.
африка́н|ец *m* [1; -нца], **~ка** *f* [5; *g/pl.*: -нок], **~ский** [16] African.
ах ah!; **~ать** [1], *once* ⟨~нуть⟩ [20] groan, lament; be amazed.
ацетиле́н *m* [1] acetylene.
аэро|дина́мика *f* [5] aerodynamics; **~дро́м** *m* [1] airdrome (*Brt.* aero-); **~навига́ция** *f* [7] aerial navigation; **~пла́н** *m* [1] airplane (*Brt.* aero-); **~по́рт** *m* [1] airport; **~по́чта** *f* [5] air mail; **~сни́мок** *m* [1; -мка] aerial view; **~ста́т** *m* [1] balloon; **~(фото)съёмка** *f* [5; *g/pl.*: -мок] aerial photography.

Б

б *s.* бы; б. *abbr.*: бы́вший.
ба́б|а *f* [5] (country)woman; peasant's wife; *fig.* milksop; сне́жная ~а snowman; **~а-яга́** *f* [5] old witch, hag; **~ий** [18] womanish, effeminate; ~ье ле́то *n* Indian summer; ~ьи ска́зки *f/pl.* old wives' tales; **~ка** *f* [5; *g/pl.*: -бок] grandmother; повива́льная ~ка midwife; *pl.* knucklebones; **~очка** *f* [5; *g/pl.*: -чек] butterfly; **~ушка** *f* [5; *g/pl.*: -шек] grandmother; granny; вот тебе́ ~ушка и ˈЮрьев день! a pretty business this!
бага́ж *m* [1*e.*] baggage, *Brt.* luggage; ручно́й ~ small baggage; сдать в ~ check one's baggage, *Brt.* register one's luggage; **~ный** [14]: ~ный ваго́н *m* baggage car, *Brt.* luggage van.
багров|е́ть [8], ⟨по-⟩ become purple, redden; **~ый** [14 *sh.*] purple.
бадья́ *f* [6] bucket, pail, tub.
ба́за *f* [5] base, basis, foundation.
база́р *m* [1] market, bazaar; F revel, row; **~ный** [14] market...; *fig.* vulgar, cheap.
ба́зис *m* [1] basis.
байда́рка *f* [5; *g/pl.*: -рок] canoe.
ба́йка *f* [5] baize.
Байка́л *m* [1] (Lake) Baikal.
бак *m* [1] ⚓ forecastle; container, receptacle; tank; boiler.
бакал|е́йный [14]: ~е́йный магази́н *m*, ~е́йная ла́вка *f* grocery, grocer's store (*Brt.* shop); ~е́йные това́ры *m/pl.* = ~е́я; **~е́йщик** *m* [1] grocer; **~е́я** *f* [6] groceries *pl.*
ба́к|ен *m* [1] beacon; **~енба́рды** *f/pl.* [5], **~и** *m/pl.* [1; *gen.*: бак] whiskers.
баклажа́н *m* [1] eggplant.
баклу́ш|а *f* [5]: бить ~и F idle, dawdle, fool (away).
бактерио́лог *m* [1] bacteriologist; **~и́ческий** [16] bacteriological; **~ия** *f* [7] bacteriology.
бакте́рия *f* [7] bacterium.
бал *m* [1; на -у́; *pl. e.*] ball (at на П).
балага́н *m* [1] booth, show.
балагу́р F *m* [1] joker; **~ить** F [13] joke, crack jokes.
балала́йка *f* [5; *g/pl.*: балала́ек] balalaika.
баламу́тить F [15], ⟨вз-⟩ trouble, stir up.
бала́нс *m* [1] balance (*a.* ✝); торго́вый ~ balance of trade; **~и́ровать** [7] balance; **~овый** [14] balance...
балбе́с *m* [1] simpleton, booby.
балда́ *m/f* [5] blockhead, dolt.
балдахи́н *m* [1] canopy.
бале|ри́на *f* [5] (female) ballet dancer; **~т** *m* [1] ballet.
ба́лка *f* [5; *g/pl.*: -лок] beam; hollow.
балка́нский [16] Balkan...
балко́н *m* [1] balcony.
балл *m* [1] grade, mark; point.
балла́да *f* [5] ballad.
балла́ст *m* [1] ballast.
баллисти́ческий [16] ballistic.
балло́н *m* [1] balloon.
баллоти́р|овать [7] ballot; **~о́вка** *f* [5; *g/pl.*: -вок] vote, poll.
бало́в|анный F [14 *sh.*] spoilt; **~а́ть** [7] (*a.* **-ся**) be naughty; trifle; ⟨из-⟩ spoil, coddle; ˈ**~ень** *m* [4; -вня] darling, pet; **~ни́к** *m* [1 *e.*] urchin, brat; **~ни́ца** *f* [5] tomboy; **~ство́** *n* [9] naughtiness, spoiling, trifling.
балти́йский [16] Baltic...
бальза́м *m* [1] balm; **~и́ровать** [7], ⟨на-⟩ embalm.
балюстра́да *f* [5] balustrade.
бамбу́к *m* [1] bamboo.
бана́ль|ность *f* [8] banality; commonplace; **~ный** [14; -лен, льна] banal, trite.
бана́н *m* [1] banana.
ба́нда *f* [5] gang.
банда́ж *m* [1*e.*] bandage; truss.
бандеро́ль *f* [8] (postal) wrapper.
банди́т *m* [1] bandit, gangster.
банк *m* [1] bank; **~а** *f* [5; *g/pl.*: -нок] jar; can, *Brt.* tin.
банке́т *m* [1] banquet.
банки́р *m* [1] banker.
банкно́т *m* [1], **~а** *f* [5] bank note.

банкро́т *m* [1] bankrupt; **~иться** [15], ⟨о-⟩ go bankrupt; **~ство** *n* [9] bankruptcy.
бант *m* [1] bow.
ба́нщ|ик *m* [1], **~ица** *f* [5] attendant (at baths).
ба́ня *f* [6] bath(s).
бар *m* [1] saloon, (snack) bar.
бараба́н *m* [1] drum; **~ить** [13], ⟨про-⟩ (beat the) drum; **~ный** [14]: ~ный бой *m* beat of the drum; ~ная перепо́нка *f* eardrum; **~щик** *m* [1] drummer.
бара́к *m* [1] barracks, hut.
бара́н *m* [1] wether; ⚔ ram; **~ий** [18] wether...; согну́ть в ~ий рог bully, intimidate; **~ина** *f* [5] mutton; **~ка** *f* [5; *g/pl.*: -нок] (*kind of*) round cracknel.
барахло́ *n* [9] junk, *Brt.* lumber.
бара́хтаться F [1] flounce, flounder.
бара́шек *m* [1; -шка] lamb(skin).
барбари́с *m* [1] barberry.
барелье́ф *m* [1] bas-relief.
Ба́ренцово [19]: ~ мо́ре *n* Barents Sea.
ба́ржа *f* [5] barge.
ба́рий *m* [3] barium.
ба́рин *m* [1; *pl.*: ба́ре *or* ба́ры, бар] nobleman; landlord; master; sir.
барито́н *m* [1] baritone.
ба́рка ⚓ *f* [5; *g/pl.*: -рок] bark, barque; **´с** ⚓ *m* [1] launch.
баро́метр *m* [1] barometer.
баррика́да *f* [5] barricade.
барс *m* [1] panther.
ба́р|ский [16] lordly; manorial; жить на ~скую но́гу live in grand style; **~ство** *n* [9] the noble class; gentility; idleness; haughtiness.
барсу́к *m* [1*e.*] badger.
ба́рхат *m* [1] velvet; **~ный** [14] velvet(y).
ба́рщина *f* [5] statute labo(u)r, corvée.
ба́рын|я *f* [6] lady; mistress; madam, ma'am.
бары́ш *m* [1*e.*] profit, gain(s); **~ник** *m* [1] forestaller; horsedealer; **~ничать** [1] buy up, practise usury; **~ничество** *n* [9] forestallment.
ба́рышня *f* [6; *g/pl.*: -шень] young lady; miss.
барье́р *m* [1] barrier.
бас ♪ *m* [1; *pl. e.*] bass.
баск *m* [1] Basque.
баскетбо́л *m* [1] basketball.
басно|пи́сец *m* [1; -сца] fabulist; **~сло́вный** [14; -вен, -вна] fabulous, incredible.
ба́сня *f* [6; *g/pl.*: -сен] fable.
басо́н *m* [1] galloon, lace.
бассе́йн *m* [1] basin; region; ~ для пла́вания swimming-pool.
ба́ста that will do; no more of this!
баста́рд *m* [1] bastard; hybrid.
бастио́н *m* [1] bastion.
бастова́ть [7], ⟨за-⟩ (be ⟨go⟩ on) strike.
батальо́н *m* [1] battalion; **~ный** [14] battalion...; ~ный (команди́р) battalion commander.
батаре́|йка *f* [5; *g/pl.*: -ре́ек] flashlight (*Brt.* torch, pocket lamp); **~я** ⚡, ⚔ *f* [6; *g/pl.*: -е́й] battery.
бати́ст *m* [1] cambric; **~овый** [14] of cambric.
батра́к *m* [1 *e.*] day labo(u)rer, farm hand.
ба́тюшк|а *m* [5; *g/pl.*: -шек] father, papa; priest; (F *address*) dear friend, old boy; как вас по ~е? what's your father's name?; ~и (мой)!, ~и све́ты! good gracious!, o(h) dear!
бахва́л P *m* [1] braggart; **~иться** [13] boast, brag; **~ьство** *n* [9] brag(ging), vaunt.
бахрома́ *f* [5] fringe.
бахчево́дство *n* [9] melon-growing.
баци́лла *f* [5] bacillus.
ба́шенка *f* [5; *g/pl.*: -нок] turret.
башка́ P *f* [5] head, noddle.
башлы́к *m* [1 *e.*] (*kind of*) hood.
башма́к *m* [1 *e.*] shoe; clog; drag; быть под ~о́м be henpecked.
ба́шня *f* [6; *g/pl.*: -шен] tower; ⚔ turret, cupola.
баю́кать [1], ⟨у-⟩ lull.
бая́н *m* [1] (*kind of*) accordion.
бде́ние *n* [12] wake(fulness); care.
бди́тель|ность *f* [8] vigilance; **~ный** [14; -лен, -льна] vigilant, watchful.
бег *m* [1; на бегу́] run(ning); *pl.* [бега́, *etc. e.*] race(s); escape; барье́рный ~ hurdle race; эстафе́тный ~ relay race; на ~у́ while running; *s.* бего́м.
бе́ганье *n* [12] running (*a. for. s. th., on business*); ~ на конька́х skating.
бе́гать [1], ⟨по-⟩ run (around); F shun (*a.* р. от Р); *fig.* run after (*a* р. за Т); ~ вза́пуски F race, vie in a run.
бегемо́т *m* [1] hippopotamus.
бегле́ц *m* [1 *e.*] runaway.
бе́гл|ость *f* [8] fluency, agility; cursoriness; **~ый** [14] fluent, agile; cursory; fugitive.
бег|ово́й [14] race...; **~о́м** in full career; **~отня́** F *f* [6] running about, bustle; **´ство** *n* [9] flight (put to обрати́ть в В), escape, stampede.
бегу́н *m* [1 *e.*] runner; trotter.
бед|а́ *f* [5; *pl.*: бе́ды] misfortune, disaster, mischief; что за ~а́? what does it matter?; не ~а́ it doesn't matter; ~а́ не велика́ there's no harm in that; в то́м-то и ~а́ that's the trouble; на ~у́ F unluckily; ~а́ как F awfully; **´ненький** [16] poor, pitiable; **~не́ть** [8], ⟨о-⟩ grow (become) poor; **´ность** *f* [8] poverty; **~нота́** *f* [5] the poor *coll.*; **´ный** [14; -ден, -дна́, -дно] poor (in Т); **~ня́га** F [5], **~ня́жка** *m/f* [5; *g/pl.*: -жек] poor fellow, wretch; **~ня́к** *m* [1 *e.*] poor man, pauper; small farmer.

бедро́ *n* [9; *pl.*: бёдра, -дер, -драм] thigh; hip; loin.

бе́дств|енный [14 *sh.*] disastrous, miserable; ~енное положе́ние *n* distress, emergency; **~ие** *n* [12] distress, disaster; **~овать** [7] suffer want, live in misery.

бежа́ть [4; бегу́, бежи́шь, бегу́т; беги́!; бегу́щий], ⟨по-⟩ (be) run (-ning, *etc.*); flee; avoid, shun (*a.* p. от P); ~ сломя́ го́лову F run for one's life *or* head over heels.

бе́жевый [14] beige.

бе́жен|ец *m* [1; -нца], **~ка** *f* [5; *g/pl.*: -нок] refugee.

без, ~о (P) **1.** without, ...less; out of (*work*); **2.** less (*with quantities*); **3.** to (*with time*): ~о всего́ without anything; ~ вас ... *a.* ... while you were out.

безала́берный F [14; -рен, -рна] slovenly, disorderly.

безалкого́льный [14] nonalcoholic.

безапелляцио́нный [14; -о́нен, -о́нна] unappealable; peremptory.

безбе́дный [14; -ден, -дна] well off.

безбиле́тный [14]: ~ пассажи́р *m* [1] stowaway.

безбо́ж|ие *n* [12], **~ность** *f* [8] atheism, ungodliness; **~ник** *m* [1], **~ница** *f* [5] atheist; **~ный** [14; -жен, -жна] atheistic, godless, impious; unscrupulous; F awful.

безболе́зненный [14 *sh.*] painless.

безборо́дый [14] beardless.

безбоя́зненный [14 *sh.*] fearless.

безбра́ч|ие *n* [12] celibacy; **~ный** [14; -чен, -чна] unmarried.

безбре́жный [14; -жен, -жна] shoreless, boundless.

безве́рие *n* [12] unbelief.

безве́стный [14; -тен, -тна] unknown.

безве́тр|енный [14 *sh.*] **~ие** *n* [12] calm.

безви́нный [14; -и́нен, -и́нна] guiltless, innocent.

безвку́с|ие *n* [12], **~ица** *f* [5] tastelessness, bad taste; **~ный** [14; -сен, -сна] tasteless, insipid.

безвла́стие *n* [12] anarchy.

безво́дный [14; -ден, дна] arid.

безвозвра́тный [14; -тен, -тна] irretrievable.

безвозду́шный [14] void of air.

безвозме́здный [-mezn-) [14] gratuitous; without compensation.

безволо́сый [14] hairless, bald.

безво́льный [14; -лен, -льна] lacking willpower, weak-willed.

безвре́дный [14; -ден, -дна] harmless.

безвре́менный [14] premature.

безвы́ездный [14] (-jiznyj) permanent.

безвы́ходный [14; -ден, -дна] **1.** continual; **2.** desperate, hopeless.

безголо́вый [14] headless; stupid; forgetful.

безгра́мотн|ость *f* [8] illiteracy, ignorance; **~ый** [14; -тен, -тна] illiterate; faulty.

безграни́чный [14; -чен, -чна] boundless, unlimited.

безда́рный [14; -рен, -рна] untalented, dull; bungling.

безде́йств|ие *n* [12] inactivity; **~овать** [7] be inactive, idle.

безде́л|ица *f* [5], **~ка** *f* [5; *g/pl.*: -лок], **~у́шка** *f* [5; *g/pl.*: -шек] trifle; (k)nick-(k)nack.

безде́ль|е *n* [12] idleness; **~ник** *m* [1], **~ница** *f* [5] idler; good-for-nothing; **~ничать** [1] idle, lounge.

безде́нежье *n* [10] want of money.

безде́тный [14; -тен, -тна] childless.

безде́ятельный [14; -лен, -льна] inactive.

бе́здна *f* [5] abyss; *fig.* F lots (of).

бездо́мный [14; -мен, -мна] homeless.

бездо́нный [14; -до́нен, -до́нна] bottomless; *fig.* unfathomable.

бездоро́ж|ье *n* [12] impassability; **~ный** [14; -жен, -жна] impassable.

бездохо́дный [14; -ден, -дна] unprofitable.

безду́шный [14; -шен, -шна] soulless; heartless.

безжа́лостный (biʒʒ-sn-) [14; -тен, -тна] ruthless.

безжи́зненный (biʒʒ-) [14 *sh.*] lifeless; *fig.* dull.

беззабо́тный [14; -тен, -тна] careless; carefree.

беззаве́тный [14; -тен, -тна] unselfish; unreserved.

беззако́н|ие *n* [12] lawlessness; anarchy; **~ность** *f* [8] illegality; **~ный** [14; -о́нен, -о́нна] illegal; lawless.

беззасте́нчивый [14 *sh.*] shameless; impudent; unscrupulous.

беззащи́тный [14; -тен, -тна] defenseless; unprotected.

беззвёздный (-zn-) [14; -ден, -дна] starless.

беззву́чный [14; -чен, -чна] soundless; silent; mute.

безземе́льный [14] landless.

беззло́бный [14; -бен, -бна] good-natured.

беззу́бый [14] toothless.

безли́чный [14; -чен, -чна] impersonal.

безлю́дный [14; -ден, -дна] deserted, uninhabited.

безме́рный [14; -рен, -рна] immeasurable; immense.

безмо́зглый F [14] brainless, stupid.

безмо́лв|ие *n* [12] silence; **~ный** [14; -вен, -вна] silent.

безмяте́жный [14; -жен, -жна] quiet, calm; undisturbed.

безнадёжный [14; -жен, -жна] hopeless.

безнадзо́рный [14; -рен, -рна] uncared for.

безнака́занный [14 *sh.*] unpunished, with impunity.
безнали́чный [14]: ~ расчёт *m* † cashless settlement.
безнра́вственный [14*sh.*] immoral.
безоби́дный [14; -ден, -дна] inoffensive; harmless.
безо́блачный [14; -чен, -чна] cloudless; serene.
безобра́з|ие *n* [12] ugliness; deformity; mess; disgrace; ~ие! scandalous!, shocking!; **~ничать** [1] behave in an improper *or* mischievous manner; **~ный** [14; -зен, -зна] ugly; deformed; shameful, disgusting, abominable; indecent, mischievous.
безогово́рочный [14; -чен, -чна] unconditional.
безопа́с|ность *f* [8] safety; security; Сове́т ≈ности Security Council; **~ный** [14; -сен, -сна] safe, secure (from от P); ~ная бри́тва *f* safety razor.
безору́жный [14; -жен, -жна] unarmed; defenseless.
безостано́вочный [14; -чен, -чна] continuous; nonstop...
безотве́тный [14; -тен, -тна] without response; humble; dumb.
безотве́тственный [14 *sh.*] irresponsible.
безотлага́тельный [14; -лен, -льна] undelayable, urgent.
безотра́дный [14; -ден, -дна] desolate, wretched.
безотчётный [14; -тен, -тна] unaccountable; unconscious, involuntary.
безоши́бочный [14; -чен, -чна] faultless.
безрабо́т|ица *f* [5] unemployment; **~ный** [14] unemployed.
безразли́ч|ие *n* [12] (к Д) indifference (to, toward); **~ный** [14; -чен, -чна] indifferent; э́то мне ~но it is all the same to me.
безрассу́дный [14; -ден, -дна] thoughtless, reckless, rash.
безрезульта́тный [14; -тен, -тна] futile, vain.
безро́потный [14; -тен, -тна] humble, meek, submissive.
безрука́вка *f* [5; *g/pl.:* -вок] sleeveless jacket, waistcoat.
безуда́рный [14; -рен, -рна] unstressed.
безу́держный [14; -жен, -жна] unrestrained; impetuous.
безукори́зненный [14 *sh.*] irreproachable, unobjectionable.
безу́м|ец *m* [1; -мца] madman, lunatic; madcap; **~ие** *n* [12] madness, folly; **~ный** [14; -мен, -мна] mad, insane; nonsensical, absurd; rash.
безумо́лчный [14; -чен, -чна] incessant, uninterrupted.
безу́мство *n* [9] folly.
безупре́чный [14; -чен, -чна] blameless, irreproachable.
безусло́в|но certainly, surely; **~ный** [14; -вен, -вна] absolute, unconditional.
безуспе́шный [14; -шен, -шна] unsuccessful.
безуста́нный [14; -а́нен, -а́нна] incessant; indefatigable.
безуте́шный [14; -шен, -шна] disconsolate, inconsolable.
безуча́стный [14; -тен, -тна] indifferent.
безымя́нный [14] anonymous; ~ па́лец *m* ring finger.
безыску́сственный [14 *sh.*] unaffected, unsophisticated.
безысхо́дный [14; -ден, -дна] hopeless, desperate.
бейсбо́л *m* [14] baseball.
бека́с *m* [1] snipe.
белёсый [14] whitish.
беле́ть [8], ⟨по-⟩ grow *or* turn white; *impf.* (*a.* **-ся**) appear *or* show white.
белизна́ *f* [5] whiteness.
бели́ла *n/pl.* [9] ceruse.
бели́ть [13; белю́, бе́лишь; белённый] **1.** ⟨вы́-⟩ bleach; **2.** ⟨на-⟩ paint (white); **3.** ⟨по-⟩ whitewash.
бе́лка *f* [5; *g/pl.:* -лок] squirrel.
беллетри́стика *f* [5] fiction.
бело|боро́дый [14] white-bearded; **~бры́сый** F [14] flaxen-haired.
белова́тый [14 *sh.*] whitish.
бело|ви́к *m* [1 *e.*], **~во́й** [14]: ~вой экземпля́р *m* fair copy; **~воло́сый** [14] white-haired; **~гварде́ец** *m* [1; -е́йца] White Guard (*member of troops fighting against the Red Guards and the Red Army in the Civil War 1918-1920*); **~голо́вый** [14] white-headed.
бело́к *m* [1; -лка́] albumen; white [(*of egg or eye*).]
бело|кали́льный [14] white hot; **~кро́вие** *n* [12] leukemia; **~ку́рый** [14 *sh.*] blond, fair; **~ру́с** *m* [1], **~ру́ска** *f* [5; *g/pl.*: -сок] Byelorussian, White Russian; **≈ру́ссия** *f* [7] Byelorussia, White Russia; **~ру́сский** [16] Byelorussian; **~сне́жный** [14; -жен, -жна] snow-white; **~шве́йка** *f* [5; *g/pl.*: -шве́ек] seamstress.
белу́га *f* [5] sturgeon.
бе́л|ый [14; бел, -á, -о] white; light, fair; secular; ~ый свет *m* (wide) world; ~ые стихи́ *m/pl.* blank verse; средь ~а дня F in broad day-light.
бель|ги́ец *m* [1; -ги́йца], **~ги́йка** *f* [5; *g/pl.*: -ги́ек], **~ги́йский** [16] Belgian; **≈гия** *f* [7] Belgium.
бельё *n* [12] linen; ни́жнее ~ underwear.
бельм|о́ ꝑ *n* [9; *pl.:* бе́льма, бельм] wall-eye; *pl.* goggle-eyes; вы́пучить ~а F stare; он у меня́ как ~о́ на глазу́ he is an eyesore to me.
бельэта́ж *m* [1] *thea.* dress circle; second (*Brt.* first) floor.

бемо́ль ♪ *m* [4] flat.
бенефи́с *m* [1] benefit(-night).
бензи́н *m* [1] benzine; gasoline, *Brt.* petrol.
бензо|ба́к *m* [1] gasoline *or* petrol tank; **~коло́нка** (*a.* ~запра́вочная коло́нка) *f* [5; *g/pl.:* -нок] filling station; **~л** *m* [1] benzol.
бенуа́р *m* [1] *thea.* parterre box.
бе́рег *m* [1; на -гу́; *pl.*: -ра́, *etc. e.*] bank, shore, coast; land; вы́йти (вы́ступить) из ~о́в overflow the banks; приста́ть к ~у land; **~ово́й** [14] coast(al), shore... ~ово́е судохо́дство *n* coasting.
бережли́вый [14 *sh.*] economical.
бе́режный [14; -жен, -жна] cautious, careful.
берёза *f* [5] birch.
берёзовый [14] birch(en).
бере́йтор *m* [1] horse-breaker.
бере́мен|ная [14] pregnant; **~ность** *f* [8] pregnancy.
бере́т *m* [1] cap, beret.
бере́чь [26 г/ж: берегу́, бережёшь] **1.** ⟨по-⟩ guard, watch (over); **2.** ⟨по-, с-⟩ spare, save, take care of; **3.** ⟨с-⟩ [сбережённый] keep; preserve; **-ся** take care (of o. s.); береги́сь! take care!, look out!, attention!
Бе́рингов [19]: ~ проли́в *m* Bering Strait; ~о мо́ре *n* Bering Sea.
берло́га *f* [5] bear's lair; den.
берцо́|вый [14]: ~вая кость *f* shin-bone.
бес *m* [1] demon.
бесе́д|а *f* [5] conversation, talk; conference, discussion; **~ка** *f* [5; *g/pl.*: -док] arbo(u)r, summer-house; **~овать** [7] converse.
бесёнок *m* [2; -нка; *pl.*: бесеня́та] imp.
беси́ть F [15], ⟨вз-⟩ [взбешённый] enrage, madden; **-ся** (fly into a) rage; romp.
бесконе́ч|ность *f* [8] infinity; до ~ности endlessly; **~ный** [14; -чен, -чна] endless, infinite; unlimited, boundless; eternal; ~но ма́лый ⚹ infinitesimal.
бескоры́ст|ие *n* [12] unselfishness; **~ный** [14; -тен, -тна] disinterested.
бескро́в|ие *n* [12] an(a)emia; **~ный** [14; -вен, -вна] an(a)emic; bloodless.
бесново́|тый [14] possessed, demoniac; **~ться** [7] rage, rave.
бесо́вщина *f* [5] devilry.
беспа́мят|ность *f* [8] forgetfulness; **~ный** [14; -тен, -тна] forgetful; unconscious; **~ство** *n* [9] unconsciousness, swoon.
беспарти́йный [14] (*pol.*) independent; non-party (man).
бесперебо́йный [14; -бо́ен, -бо́йна] uninterrupted, smooth.
беспереме́нный [14] invariable; unalterable.
беспереса́дочный [14] through...
беспе́ч|ность *f* [8] carelessness; **~ный** [14; -чен, -чна] careless.
беспла́т|ный [14; -тен, -тна] free (of charge), gratuitous; ~но gratis.
беспло́д|ие *n* [12] sterility; **~ный** [14; -ден, -дна] sterile; fruitless, vain.
бесповоро́тный [14; -тен, -тна] unalterable, irrevocable.
бесподо́бный [14; -бен, -бна] incomparable, matchless.
беспозвоно́чный [14] invertebrate.
беспок|о́ить [13], ⟨(п)о-⟩ upset, worry; disturb, bother, trouble; **-ся** worry, be anxious (about о П); **~о́йный** [14; -ко́ен, -ко́йна] restless; uneasy; **~о́йство** *n* [9] unrest; trouble; anxiety; прости́те за ~о́йство sorry to (have) trouble(d) you.
бесполе́зный [14; -зен, -зна] useless.
беспо́мощный [14; -щен, -щна] helpless.
беспоро́чный [14; -чен, -чна] blameless, irreproachable.
беспоря́до|к *m* [1; -дка] disorder, mess; *pl.* disorders; **~чный** [14; -чен, -чна] disorderly, incoherent.
беспоса́дочный [14]: ~ перелёт nonstop flight.
беспо́шлинный [14] duty-free.
беспоща́дный [14; -ден, -дна] pitiless, ruthless, relentless.
беспреде́льный [14; -лен, -льна] boundless, infinite, unlimited.
беспрекосло́вный [14; -вен, -вна] absolute, unquestioning, implicit.
беспрепя́тственный [14 *sh.*] unhampered, unhindered.
беспреры́вный [14; -вен, -вна] uninterrupted, continuous.
беспреста́нный [14; -а́нен, -а́нна] incessant, continual.
беспри́быльный [14; -лен, -льна] unprofitable.
беспризо́рн|ик *m* [1] waif, stray; **~ый** [14; -рен, -рна] homeless, uncared-for.
беспримéрный [14; -рен, -рна] unprecedented, unparalleled.
беспринци́пный [14; -пен, -пна] unprincipled, unscrupulous.
беспристра́ст|ие *n* [12] impartiality; **~ный** (-sn-) [14; -тен, -тна] impartial, unprejudiced, unbias(s)ed.
беспричи́нный [14; -и́нен, -и́нна] groundless; unfounded.
бесприю́тный [14; -тен, -тна] homeless.
беспробу́дный [14; -ден, -дна] deep (*about sleep*); unrestrained.
беспро́волочный [14] wireless.
беспросве́тный [14; -тен, -тна] pitch-dark; *fig.* hopeless.
беспроце́нтный [14] without charge for interest.
беспу́тный [14; -тен, -тна] dissolute.

бессвя́зный [14; -зен, -зна] incoherent, rambling.
бессерде́чный [14; -чен, -чна] heartless, unfeeling, callous.
бесси́|лие *n* [12] debility; impotence; **~льный** [14; -лен, -льна] weak, powerless, impotent.
бессла́вный [14; -вен, -вна] infamous, disgraceful, inglorious.
бессле́дный [14; -ден, -дна] without leaving a trace, entire.
бесслове́сный [14; -сен, -сна] speechless, dumb; taciturn.
бессме́рт|ие *n* [12] immortality; **~ный** [14; -тен, -тна] immortal.
бессмы́сл|енный [14 *sh.*] senseless; dull; **~ица** *f* [5] nonsense.
бессо́вестный [14; -тен, -тна] unscrupulous.
бессодержа́тельный [14; -лен, -льна] empty, insipid, dull.
бессозна́тельный [14; -лен, -льна] unconscious.
бессо́нн|ица *f* [5] insomnia; **~ый** [14] sleepless.
бесспо́рный [14; -рен, -рна] indisputable; doubtless, certain.
бессро́чный [14; -чен, -чна] termless, not limited in time.
бесстра́ст|ие *n* [12] dispassionateness, calmness; **~ный** [14; -тен, -тна] dispassionate, composed.
бесстра́ш|ие *n* [12] fearlessness; **~ный** [14; -шен, -шна] fearless, intrepid.
бессты́д|ный [14; -ден, -дна] shameless, impudent; indecent; **~ство** *n* [9] impudence, insolence.
бессчётный [14] innumerable.
бесталанный [14; -а́нен, -а́нна] **1.** untalented; **2.** ill-fated.
бе́стия *f* [7] brute, beast; artful dodger.
бестолко́в|щина *f* [5] nonsense; mess; confusion; **~ый** [14 *sh.*] absurd, confused.
бестре́петный [14; -тен, -тна] intrepid, undaunted.
бесхи́тростный [14; -тен, -тна] artless, naïve, ingenuous, unsophisticated.
бесхозя́йствен|ность *f* [8] mismanagement; **~ный** [14] thriftless.
бесцве́тный [14; -тен, -тна] colo(u)rless.
бесце́льный [14; -лен, -льна] aimless.
бесце́н|ный [14; -е́нен, -е́нна] invaluable, priceless; **~ок:** за ~ок F for a song *or* a trifling sum.
бесцеремо́нный [14; -о́нен, -о́нна] unceremonious, bold, inconsiderate.
бесчелове́ч|ие *n* [12], **~ность** *f* [8] inhumanity; **~ный** [14; -чен, -чна] inhuman, cruel.
бесче́ст|ный [14; -тен, -тна] dishonest; dishono(u)rable; **~ье** *n* [10] dishono(u)r, disgrace.
бесчи́нство *n* [9] excess, outrage; **~вать** [7] behave outrageously.
бесчи́сленный [14 *sh.*] innumerable, countless.
бесчу́вств|енный (bi'ʃtʃustv-) [14 *sh.*] insensible, callous, hard-hearted; **~ие** *n* [12] insensibility; unconsciousness, swoon.
бесшаба́шный F [14; -шен, -шна] reckless, careless; wanton.
бесшу́мный [14; -мен, -мна] noiseless, quiet.
бето́н *m* [1] concrete; **~и́ровать** [7], ⟨за-⟩ concrete; **~ный** [14] concrete...
бечёвка *f* [5; *g/pl.*: -вок] string.
бе́шен|ство *n* [9] **1.** ⚕ hydrophobia; **2.** fury, rage; **~ый** [14] **1.** rabid; **2.** furious, frantic, wild; **3.** enormous.
библе́йский [16] Biblical; Bible...
библиографи́ческий [16] bibliographic(al).
библиоте́|ка *f* [5] library; **~карь** *m* [4] librarian; **~чный** [14] library...
би́блия *f* [7] Bible.
бив(у)а́к *m* [1] bivouac; стоя́ть ~ом *or* на ~ах bivouac.
би́вень *m* [4; -вня] tusk.
бидо́н *m* [1] can.
бие́ние *n* [12] beat, throb.
бизо́н *m* [1] bison.
биле́т *m* [1] ticket; card; note, bill; обра́тный ~ round-trip ticket, *Brt.* return-ticket.
биллио́н *m* [1] billion, *Brt.* milliard.
билья́рд *m* [1] billiards.
бино́кль *m* [4] binocular(s); glass; театра́льный ~ opera glasses; полево́й ~ field glass.
бинт *m* [1 *e.*] bandage; **~ова́ть** [7], ⟨за-⟩ bandage, dress.
био́граф *m* [1] biographer; **~и́ческий** [16] biographic(al); **~ия** *f* [7] biography.
био́лог *m* [1] biologist; **~и́ческий** [16] biological; **~ия** *f* [7] biology.
биохи́мия *f* [7] biochemistry.
бипла́н *m* [1] biplane.
би́ржа *f* [5] (stock) exchange; ~ труда́ labor registry office, *Brt.* labour exchange.
бирже|ви́к *m* [1 *e.*], stockbroker; **~во́й** [14]: ~во́й ма́клер = ~ви́к.
Би́рм|а *f* [5] Burma; **~а́нец** *m* [1; -нца], **~а́нка** *f* [5; *g/pl.*: -нок], **~а́нский** [16] Burmese.
бирюза́ *f* [5] turquoise.
бис encore!
би́сер *m* [1] *coll.* (glass) beads *pl.*
бискви́т *m* [1] sponge cake.
би́тва *f* [5] battle.
бит|ко́м *s.* наби́тый; **~о́к** *m* [1; -тка́] (mince)meat ball.
бить [бью, бьёшь; бей!; би́тый] **1.** ⟨по-⟩ beat; churn (*butter*); **2.** ⟨про-⟩ [про́би́л, -би́ла, про́би́ло] strike (*clock*); **3.** ⟨раз-⟩ [разобью́, -бьёшь] break, smash; **4.** ⟨у-⟩ shoot, kill; trump (*card*); **5.** *no pf.* spout; ~ в глаза́ strike the eye; ~ в наба́т,

~ тревóгу sound the alarm (bell) (отбóй the retreat); ~ ключóм 1. bubble; 2. boil over; 3. sparkle; 4. abound in vitality; прóбил егó час his hour has struck; би́тый час *m* one solid hour; **-ся** fight; beat (*heart*); drudge, toil; -ся головóй о(б) стéну dash against the rock; -ся об заклáд bet; он бьётся как ры́ба об лёд he exerts himself in vain.
бифштéкс *m* [1] (beef)steak.
бич *m* [1 *e.*] whip; *fig.* scourge; **~евáть** [7] lash, scourge.
благови́дный [14; -ден, дна] attractive; *fig.* seemly.
благово|лéние *n* [12] benevolence, goodwill; **~ли́ть** [13] wish (a. p. к Д) well, be kind (to a. p.); deign.
благовóн|ие *n* [12] fragrance; **~ный** [14] fragrant.
благовоспи́танный [14 *sh.*] well-bred.
благогo|вéйный [14; -вéен, -вéйна] devout, reverent, respectful; **~вéние** *n* [12] awe (of), reverence, respect (for) (пéред Т); **~вéть** [8] (пéред Т) worship, venerate.
благодар|и́ть [13], ⟨по-, от-⟩ (В/за В) thank (a p. for s. th.); **∠ность** *f* [8] gratitude; thanks; не стóит ∠ности you are welcome, *Brt.* don't mention it; **∠ный** [14; -рен, -рна] grateful, thankful (to a p. for s. th. Д/за В); **~я́** (Д) thanks *or* owing to.
благодáт|ный [14]; -тен, -тна] blessed; **~ь** *f* [8] blessing.
благодéтель *m* [4] benefactor; **~ница** *f* [5] benefactress; **~ный** [14; -лен, -льна] beneficent; beneficial.
благодея́ние *n* [12] benefit.
благоду́ш|ие *n* [12] good nature, kindness; **~ный** [14; -шен, -шна] kindhearted, benign.
благожелáтель|ность *f* [8] benevolence; **~ный** [14; -лен, -льна] benevolent.
благозву́ч|ие *n* [12], **~ность** *f* [8] euphony, sonority; **~ный** [14; -чен, -чна] sonorous, harmonious.
благонадёжный [14; -жен, -жна] reliable, trustworthy.
благонамéренный [14 *sh.*] well-meaning, well-meant.
благонрáвный [14; -вен, -вна] well-mannered, modest.
благообрáзный [14; -зен, -зна] attractive, comely, sightly.
благополу́ч|ие *n* [12] well-being, prosperity, happiness; **~ный** [14; -чен, -чна] happy; safe.
благоприя́т|ный [14; -тен, -тна] favo(u)rable, propitious; **~ствовать** [7] (Д) favo(u)r, promote.
благоразу́м|ие *n* [12] prudence, discretion; **~ный** [14; -мен, -мна] prudent, judicious.
благорóд|ный [14; -ден, -дна] noble; high-minded, distinguished; lofty; precious; **~ство** *n* [9] nobility.
благосклóнный [14; -óнен, -óнна] favo(u)rable, well-disposed (to [-ward(s)] ∠ р. к Д).
благосло|вéние *n* [12] benediction, blessing; **~вля́ть** [28], ⟨~ви́ть⟩ [14 *e.*; -влю́, -ви́шь] bless.
благосостоя́ние *n* [12] prosperity.
благотвори́тельный [14] beneficent, charitable.
благотвóрный [14; -рен, -рна] wholesome, salutary.
благоустрóенный [14 *sh.*] well-furnished, comfortable.
благоухá|ние *n* [12] fragrance, odo(u)r; **~ть** [1] scent, exhale fragrance.
благочести́вый [14 *sh.*] pious.
блажéн|ный [14 *sh.*] blissful; **~ство** *n* [9] bliss; **~ствовать** [7] enjoy felicity.
блаж|и́ть P [16 *e.*; -жу́, -жи́шь] be capricious, cranky; **~нóй** P [14] capricious; preposterous; **~ь** F *f* [8] caprice, whim, freak, fancy; folly.
бланк *m* [1] form; letterhead.
блат P *m* [1] profitable connections; по ∠у on the quiet, illicitly, through good connections; **~нóй** P [14] trickster, rogue; ~нóй язы́к *m* thieves' slang, cant.
бледнéть [8], ⟨по-⟩ turn pale.
бледно|вáтый [14 *sh.*] palish; **~ли́цый** [14 *sh.*] with a pale face.
блéд|ность *f* [8] pallor; **~ный** [14; -ден, -днá, -о] pale.
блёк|лый [14] faded, withered; **~нуть** [21], ⟨по-⟩ fade, wither.
блеск *m* [1] luster, shine, brilliance, glitter, splendo(u)r.
блест|éть [11; *a.* блéщешь], *once* ⟨блесну́ть⟩ [20] shine, glitter; flash; не всё то зóлото, что ~и́т all is not gold that glitters; **~ки** ('bʲɔski) *f/pl.* [5; *gen.*: -ток] spangle; **~я́щий** [17 *sh.*] brilliant.
блеф *m* [1] bluff.
блéять [27], ⟨за-⟩ bleat.
ближ|áйший [17] (*s.* бли́зкий) the nearest, next; **∠е** nearer; **∠ний** [15] near(-by); *su.* fellow creature.
близ (Р) near, close; **∠иться** [15; 3*rd p. only*], ⟨при-⟩ approach (a p. к Д); **∠кий** [16; -зок, -зкá, -о; *comp.*: бли́же], (к Д) near, close; ∠кие *pl.* folk(s), one's family, relatives; ∠ко от (Р) close to, not far from; **~лежáщий** [17] nearby, neighbo(u)ring.
близнéц *m* [1 *e.*] twin.
близору́кий [16 *sh.*] short-sighted.
бли́зость *f* [8] nearness, proximity; intimacy.
блин *m* [1 *e.*] pancake.
блистáтельный [14; -лен, -льна] brilliant, splendid, magnificent.
блистáть [1] shine, beam.

блок *m* [1] **1.** bloc, coalition; **2.** pulley.
блок|áда *f* [5] blockade; **~úровать** [7] (*im*)*pf.* blockade, block up.
блокнóт *m* [1] notebook.
блондúн *m* [1] blond; **~ка** *f* [5; *g/pl.*: -нок] blonde.
блохá *f* [5; *nom/pl. st.*: блóхи] flea.
блуд *m* [1] licentiousness; **~úть** P **1.** [15] roam, wander; **2.** [15 *e.*; -жý, -дúшь] debauch; **~лúвый** [14 F *sh.*], **∠ный** [14] wanton; ∠ный сын *m* prodigal son.
блуждá|ть [1], ⟨про-⟩ roam, wander; ~ющий огонёк *m* will-o'-the-wisp; ~ющая пóчка *f* floating kidney.
блýз|а *f* [5] blouse, smock; **~ка** *f* [5; *g/pl.*: -зок] (ladies') blouse.
блюдечко *n* [9; *g/pl.*: -чек] saucer.
блюдо *n* [9] dish; course.
блюдце *n* [11; *g/pl.*: -дец] saucer.
блюстú [25], ⟨со-⟩ observe, preserve, maintain; watch; **~тель** *m* [4], **~тельница** *f* [5] keeper, guardian.
бля́ха *f* [5] metal plate, badge.
боá [*indecl.*] **1.** *m zo.* boa; **2.** *n* boa (*wrap*).
боб *m* [1 *e.*] bean; haricot; остáться на ~áх have one's trouble for nothing.
бобёр *m* [1; -брá] beaver (*fur*).
бобúна *f* [5] bobbin, spool, reel.
бобóв|ый [14]: ~ые растéния *n/pl.* legumes.
бобр *m* [1 *e.*], **~óвый** [14] beaver.
бóбслей *m* [3] bobsleigh.
бобы́ль *m* [4 *e.*] landless peasant; *fig.* solitary man, (old) bachelor.
бог (bɔx) *m* [1; *voc.*: бóже; *from g/pl. e.*] God; god, idol; ~ весть, ~ (егó) знáет F God knows; бóже (мой)! oh God!, good gracious!; дай ~ God grant; I (let's) hope (so); ей ∠у! by a God!; рáди ∠а for God's (goodness') sake; сохранú (не дай, избáви, упасú) ~ (бóже) God forbid!
богат|éть [8] ⟨раз-⟩ grow (become) rich; **∠ство** *n* [9] wealth; **∠ый** [14 *sh.*; *comp.*: богáче] rich (in T), wealthy.
богаты́рь *m* [4 *e.*] hero; athlete.
богáч *m* [1 *e.*] rich man.
Богéм|ия *f* [7] Bohemia; **2ский** [16] Bohemian.
богúня *f* [6] goddess.
богомáтерь *f* [8] the Blessed Virgin.
бого|мóлец *m* [1; -льца], **~мóлка** *f* [5; *g/pl.*: -лок] devotee; pilgrim; **~мóлье** *n* [10] prayer; pilgrimage.
богоотстýпник *m* [1] atheist.
богорóдица *f* [5] the Blessed Virgin, Our Lady.
богослóв *m* [1] theologian; **~ие** *n* [12] theology, divinity; **~ский** [16] theological.
богослужéние *n* [12] divine service.
боготворúть [13] adore, deify.
богохýль|ник *m* [1] blasphemer; **~ничать** [1] blaspheme; **~ный** [14] blasphemous; **~ство** *n* [9] blasphemy; **~ствовать** [7] = богохýльничать.
бодáть [1], ⟨за-⟩, *once* ⟨боднýть⟩ [20] (*a.* **~ся**) butt, gore (*a. o.a.*).
бóдр|ость *f* [8] vivacity, sprightliness; **~ствовать** [20] be awake; **~ый** [14; бодр, -á, -о] awake; sprightly, vivacious, brisk; vigorous.
боевúк *m* [1 *e.*] hit, draw.
боевóй [14] battle..., fighting, war-..., military; live (*shell, etc.*); pugnacious, militant; ~ пáрень *m* dashing fellow; ~ порЯдок *m* battle array.
бое|припáсы *m/pl.* [1] ammunition; **~спосóбный** [14; -бен, -бна] effective.
боéц *m* [1; бойцá] soldier, fighter.
бóже *s.* бог; **~ский** [16] godlike, divine; **∠ственный** [14 *sh.*] divine; **~ствó** *n* [9] deity, divinity.
бóжий [18] God's, divine.
божúться [16 *e.*; -жýсь, -жúшься], ⟨по-⟩ swear.
бой *m* [3; бóя, в боЮ; *pl.*: бои́, боёв, *etc. e.*] battle, combat, fight; брать (взять) бóем *or* с бóю take by assault (storm); рукопáшный ~ close fight; ~ часóв the striking of a clock; **∠кий** [16; бóек, бойкá, бóйко; *comp.*: бóйч(é)е] brisk, lively, busy; smart, quick, sharp; voluble, glib; **∠кость** *f* [8] liveliness, smartness.
бойкотúровать [7] (*im*)*pf.* boycott.
бойнúца *f* [5] loophole, embrasure.
бóйня *f* [6; *g/pl.*: бóен] slaughterhouse; *fig.* massacre, slaughter.
бок *m* [1; на бокý; *pl.*: бокá, *etc. e.*] side; нá ~, ∠ом sideways; ~ ó ~ side by side; пóд ∠ом F close by; барáний ~ leg of mutton.
бокáл *m* [1] wineglass.
боковóй [14] lateral.
бокс *m* [1] boxing; **~ёр** *m* [1] boxer; **~úровать** [7] box.
болвáн *m* [1] dolt, blockhead.
болгáр|ин *m* [4; *pl.*: -ры, -р] Bulgarian; **2ия** *f* [7] Bulgaria; **~ка** *f* [5; *g/pl.*: -рок], **~ский** [16] Bulgarian.
бóлее (*s.* бóльше) more (than P); ~ высóкий higher; ~ úли мéнее more or less; не ~ at (the) most.
болéзненный [14 *sh.*] sickly, ailing, morbid; painful.
болéзнь *f* [8] sickness (on the score of по Д), illness; disease; (*mental*) disorder; sick (*leave* ... по Д).
болéльщик *m* [1] *sport*: fan.
болéть 1. [8] be sick, ill (with T); be anxious (for, about за В о П), apprehensive; **2.** [9; *3rd p. only*] hurt, ache; у меня́ болúт головá (зуб, гóрло) I have a headache (a toothache, a sore throat).
болóт|истый [14 *sh.*] boggy

swampy; **~ный** [14] bog..., swamp-...; **~о** *n* [9] bog, swamp.
болт *m* [1 *e.*] bolt.
болта́ть [1] **1.** ⟨вз-⟩ shake up; **2.** (**-ся**) dangle; **3.** F ⟨по-⟩ [20] chat (-ter); **~ся** F loaf *or* lounge about.
болтли́вый [14 *sh.*] talkative.
болтовня́ F *f* [6] idle talk, gossip.
болту́н *m* [1; -на́], **~ья** *f* [6] babbler, chatterbox.
боль *f* [8] pain, ache.
больни́|ца *f* [5] hospital; **~чный** [14] hospital...; ~чная ка́сса *f* sick-fund; ~чный листо́к *m* medical certificate.
бо́льн|о painful(ly); P very; мне ~о it hurts me; глаза́м ~о my eyes smart; **~о́й** [14; бо́лен, больна́] sick, ill (*a. su.*), sore; patient, invalid; *fig.* delicate, burning; tender.
бо́льше bigger; more; ~ всего́ most of all; above all; ~ не ... no more *or* longer; как мо́жно ~ as much as possible; **~ви́зм** *m* [1] Bolshevism; **~ви́к** *m* [1 *e.*], **~ви́чка** *f* [5; *g/pl.*: -чек] Bolshevik; **~ви́стский** (-'ʏis-sķij) [16] Bolshevist(ic).
бо́льш|ий [17] bigger, greater; **~инство́** *n* [9] majority; most; **~о́й** [16] big, large, great; grownup.
бо́мб|а *f* [5] bomb; **~ардирова́ть** [7] bomb, shell; bombard (*a. fig.*); **~ардиро́вка** *f* [5; *g/pl.:* -вок] bombardment, bombing; **~ардиро́вщик** *m* [1] bomber; **~ёжка** F *f* [5; *g/pl.:* -жек] = ~ардиро́вка; **~и́ть** [14 *e.*; -блю́, -би́шь; (раз-) бомблённый], ⟨раз-⟩ bomb.
бомбо|во́з *m* [1] = бомбардиро́вщик; **~убе́жище** *n* [11] air-raid shelter.
бонбонье́рка *f* [5; *g/pl.:* -рок] bonbonnière, box for candies.
бо́нда́рь *m* [4 & 4 *e.*; *pl. a.* -ря́, *etc. e.*] cooper.
бор *m* [1] **1.** [в бору́] pine wood *or* forest; **2.** ⚗ boron.
бордо́ *n* [*indecl.*] claret.
бордю́р *m* [1] border, trimming.
боре́ц *m* [1; -рца́] fighter; wrestler; *fig.* champion, partisan.
бор|зо́й [14] swift, fleet (*dog*); ~за́я (соба́ка) *f* borzoi, greyhound.
бо́рзый [14; борз, -а́, -о] brisk, swift.
Бори́с *m* [1] Boris (*masc. name*).
бормота́ть [3], ⟨про-⟩ murmur, mutter.
бо́ров *m* [1; *from g/pl. e.*] boar.
борода́ *f* [5; *ac/sg.:* бо́роду; *pl.:* бо́роды, боро́д, -да́м] beard.
борода́вка *f* [5; *g/pl.:* -вок] wart.
борода́|тый [14 *sh.*] bearded; **~ч** *m* [1 *e.*] bearded man.
боро́дка *f* [5; *g/pl.:* -док] small beard; bit (*key*).
борозд|а́ *f* [5; *pl.:* бо́розды, боро́зд -да́м] furrow; **~и́ть** [15 *e.*; -зжу́ -зди́шь], ⟨вз-⟩ furrow.
боро|на́ *f* [5; *ac/sg.:* бо́рону; *pl.:* бо́роны, боро́н, -на́м] harrow; **~ни́ть** [13], **~нова́ть** [7], ⟨вз-⟩ harrow.
боро́ться [17; боря́сь] fight, struggle (for за B); wrestle.
борт *m* [1; на -ту́; *nom/pl.:* -та́] **1.** braid, lace; border; **2.** board; на ~у́ су́дна on board a ship; бро́сить за́ ~ throw overboard; челове́к за ~ом! man overboard!; **~ово́й** [14] board...
борщ *m* [1 *e.*] borsch(t), red-beet soup.
Бо́ря *m* [6] *dim. of* Бори́с.
босико́м barefoot.
босо́й [14; бос, -а́, -о] barefooted; на бо́су но́гу = босико́м.
босоно́гий [16] = босо́й.
Босфо́р *m* [1] Bosporus.
턴бося́к *m* [1 *e.*] tramp, vagabond.
бота́ни|к *m* [1] botanist; **~ка** *f* [5] botany; **~ческий** [16] botanic(al).
боти́нок *m* [1; *g/pl.:* -нок] shoe, *Brt.* (lace-)boot.
ботфо́рты *m/pl.* [1] jackboots.
бо́ты *m/pl.* [1; *g/pl. a.* бот] overshoes.
бо́цман *m* [1] boatswain.
боча́р *m* [1 *e.*] cooper.
бо́чка *f* [5; *g/pl.:* -чек] cask, tun.
бочко́м sideway(s), sidewise.
бочо́но|к *m* [1; -нка] (small) barrel; **~чный** [14]: ~чное пи́во *n* draught beer.
боязли́вый [14 *sh.*] timid, fearful.
боя́знь *f* [8] fear, dread.
боя́р|ин *m* [4; *pl.:* -ре, -р], **~ыня** *f* [6] boyar(d) (*member of old nobility in Russia*).
боя́рышник *m* [1] hawthorn.
боя́ться [бою́сь, бои́шься; бо́йся, бо́йтесь!], ⟨по-⟩ be afraid (of P), fear; бою́сь сказа́ть I don't know exactly, I'm not quite sure.
бра́вый [14] brave, courageous.
бразды́ *f/pl.* [5] *fig.* reins.
брази́|лец [1; -льца] Brazilian; **♀лия** *f* [7] Brazil; **~льский** [16], **~лья́нка** *f* [5; *g/pl.:* -нок] Brazilian.
брак *m* [1] **1.** marriage; matrimony; **2.** (*no pl.*) defective articles, spoilage.
бракова́ть [7], ⟨за-⟩ scrap, reject.
бракосочета́ние *n* [12] wedding.
брани́ть [13], ⟨по-, вы́-⟩ scold, rebuke, abuse; **-ся** quarrel, wrangle; swear, curse.
бра́нный [14] **1.** abusive; **2.** battle-..., military.
бранчли́вый [14 *sh.*] quarrelsome.
брань *f* [8] **1.** abuse, quarrel([l]ing); invective; **2.** battle, fight.
брасле́т *m* [1] bracelet.
брат *m* [1; *pl.:* бра́тья, -тьев, -тьям] brother; (*address:*) old boy!; ваш ~ F of your kind; наш ~ F (such as) we.
брата́|ние *n* [12] fraternization; **~ться** [1], ⟨по-⟩ fraternize.
бра́тец *m* [1; -тца] dear brother; (*address:*) old fellow!, dear friend!

бра́тия *f* [7] fraternity; friary; ни́щая ~ beggary.
брато|уби́йство *n* [9], **~уби́йца** *m/f* [5] fratricide.
бра́т|ский [16; *adv.*: (по-)бра́тски] brotherly, fraternal; **~ство** *n* [9] brotherhood, fraternity, fellowship.
брать [беру́, -рёшь; брал, -á, -о; ˈ...бранный], ⟨взять⟩ [возьму́, -мёшь; взял, -á, -о; взя́тый (взят, -á, -о)] take; ~ напрока́т hire; ~ приме́р (с Р) take (a p.) for a model; ~ верх над (Т) be victorious over, conquer; ~ на пору́ки be (-come) bail (for В); ~ сло́во take (have) the floor; ~ (с Р) сло́во make (s. o.) promise; ~ (свои́ слова́) обра́тно withdraw (one's words); ~ себя́ в ру́ки *fig.* collect o.s., pull o.s. together; ~ на себя́ assume; ~ за пра́вило make it a rule; его́ взяла́ охо́та писа́ть he took a fancy to writing; он взял да сказа́л F he said it without further consideration; возьми́те напра́во! turn (to the) right!; *s. a.* взима́ть; **-ся** [бра́лся, -ла́сь, -ло́сь], ⟨взя́ться⟩ [взя́лся, -ла́сь, взяло́сь, взяли́сь] (за В) undertake; set about; take hold of seize; ~ за́ руки join hands; ~ за кни́гу (рабо́ту) set about *or* start reading a book (working); отку́да э́то берётся? where does that come from?; отку́да у него́ де́ньги беру́тся? wherever does he get his money from?; отку́да ни возьми́сь all of a sudden.
бра́чный [14] matrimonial, conjugal.
брев|е́нчатый [14] log...; **~но́** *n* [9; *pl.*: брёвна, -вен, -внам] log; beam.
бред *m* [1] delirium; **ˊить** [15], ⟨за-⟩ rave, talk deliriously (about Т); **ˊни** *f/pl.* [6; *gen.*: -ней] nonsense, fantasies; raving.
бре́зг|ать [1] (Т) disdain; **~ли́вость** *f* [8] squeamishness, disgust; **~ли́вый** [14 *sh.*] squeamish, fastidious (in к Д).
брезе́нт *m* [1] tarpaulin.
бре́зжить [16], **-ся** glimmer; dawn.
бре́мя *n* [13; *no pl.*] burden, load.
бренча́ть [4*e.*; -чу́, -чи́шь], ⟨за-, про-⟩ clink, jingle; strum.
брести́ [25], ⟨по-⟩ drag, lag; grope.
брешь *f* [8] breach; gap.
брига́|да *f* [5] brigade (*a.* ⚔), team, group of workers; уда́рная ~да shock brigade; **~ди́р** *m* [1] brigadier; foreman.
бри́джи *pl.* [*gen.*: -жей] breeches.
бриллиа́нт *m* [1], **~овый** [14] brilliant.
брита́н|ец *m* [1; -нца] Briton, Britisher; **ˇния** *f* [7] Britain; **~ский** [16] British; ˇская Импе́рия *f* British Empire; ˇские острова́ *m/pl.* British Isles.
бри́т|ва *f* [5] razor; **~венный** [14]: ~венный прибо́р *m* shaving things.
брить [бре́ю, бре́ешь; бре́й(те)!; бре́я; брил; бри́тый], ⟨вы́-, по-⟩ shave; **-ся** *v/i.* get shaved, (have a) shave; **~ё** *n* [10] shaving.
бров|ь *f* [8; *from g/pl. e.*] eyebrow; хму́рить **ˊи** frown; он и **ˊью** не повёл F he did not turn a hair; попа́сть не в ~ь, а в глаз F hit the nail on the head.
брод *m* [1] ford.
броди́ть [15] **1.** ⟨по-⟩ wander, roam; **2.** (*impers.*) ferment.
бродя́|га *m* [5] tramp, vagabond; **~жничать** F [1] stroll, tramp; **~жничество** *n* [9] vagrancy; **~чий** [17] vagrant.
броже́ние *n* [12] fermentation; *fig.* agitation, unrest.
бром *m* [1] bromine.
броне|ви́к *m* [1 *e.*] armo(u)red car; **~во́й** [14] armo(u)red; **~но́сец** *m* [1; -сца] battleship; **~по́езд** *m* [1] armo(u)red train; **~та́нковый** [14]: ~та́нковые ча́сти *f/pl.* armo(u)red troops.
бро́нз|а *f* [5] bronze; **~овый** [14] bronzy, bronze...
брони|рова́ть[1] [7], ⟨за-⟩ armo(u)r; **ˊровать**[2] [7], ⟨за-⟩ reserve secure.
бро́нх|и *m/pl.* [1] bronchi *pl.* (*sg.* ~ bronchus); **~и́т** *m* [1] bronchitis.
броня́[1] *f* [6; *g/pl.*: -не́й] armo(u)r.
бро́ня[2] *f* [6; *g/pl.*: -ней] reservation.
броса́ть [1], ⟨бро́сить⟩ [15] throw, (*a.* ⚓) cast, fling (*a.* out) (s. th. at В *or* Т/в В); leave, abandon, desert; give up, quit, leave off; (*impers.*) break into, be seized with (в В); lay down (*one's arms*); F waste, squander; брось(те) ...! F (oh) stop ...!; **-ся** dash, rush, plunge, dart (off -ся бежа́ть); fall (up)on (на В); go to (в В); -ся в глаза́ strike the eye.
бро́со|вый [14] catchpenny; under (*price*); ~вый э́кспорт *m* dump.
бросо́к *m* [1; -ска́] hurl, throw.
бро́шка *f* [5; *g/pl.*: -шек] brooch.
брошю́|ра *f* [5] brochure, pamphlet; **~рова́ть** [7], ⟨с-⟩ stitch.
брус *m* [1; *pl.*: бру́сья, бру́сьев, бру́сьям] (square) beam; bar; *pl.* (*a.* паралле́льные **ˊья**) (*gymnastics*) parallel bars; **~ко́вый** [14] bar...
брусни́ка *f* [5] red bilberry, -ries *pl.*
брусо́к *m* [1; -ска́] **1.** bar; **2.** (*a.* точи́льный ~) whetstone.
бру́тто [*indecl.*] gross (weight).
бры́з|гать [1 *or* 3] *once* ⟨~нуть⟩ [20] splash, spatter, sprinkle; gush; **~ги** *f/pl.* [5] splash, spray.
брык|а́ть [1], *once* ⟨~ну́ть⟩ [20] (*a.* **-ся**) kick.
брюз|га́ F *m/f* [5] grumbler, griper, grouch; **~гли́вый** [14 *sh.*] morose, sullen, peevish, grouchy; **~жа́ть**

[4*e.*; -жу́, -жи́шь], ⟨за-⟩ grumble, growl, grouch.
брю́ква *f* [5] turnip.
брю́ки *f/pl.* [5] trousers, pants.
брюне́т *m* [1] brunet; **~ка** *f* [5; *g/pl.:* -ток] brunette.
Брюссе́ль *m* [4] Brussels; **2ский** [16]: 2ская капу́ста *f* Brussels sprouts.
брю́хо P *n* [9] belly, paunch.
брюш|и́на *f* [5] peritoneum; **~но́й** [14] abdominal; ~но́й тиф *m* typhoid fever.
бря́кать [1], *once* ⟨бря́кнуть⟩ [20] **1.** *v/i.* clink; **2.** *v/t.* plump.
бряца́ть [1] clank, jingle; rattle.
БССР (Белору́сская Сове́тская Социалисти́ческая Респу́блика *f*) Byelorussian Soviet Socialist Republic.
бу́бен *m* [1; -бна; *g/pl.:* бу́бен] (*mst pl.*) tambourine; **~е́ц** *m* [1; -нца́], **~чик** *m* [1] jingle, small bell.
бу́блик *m* [1] (round) cracknel.
бу́бн|ы *f/pl.* [5; *g/pl.:* бубён, -бна́м] (*cards*) diamonds.
бугор *m* [1; -гра́] hillock.
Будапе́шт *m* [1] Budapest.
бу́дет (*s.* быть) (*impers.*) (it's) enough!, that'll do!
буди́льник *m* [1] alarm clock.
буди́ть [15] **1.** ⟨раз-⟩ (a)wake, waken; **2.** ⟨про-⟩ [пробуждённый] *fig.* (a)rouse.
бу́дка *f* [5; *g/pl.:* -док] booth, box.
бу́дни *m/pl.* [1; *gen.:* -дней] weekdays; everyday life, monotony; **~чный** [14] everyday; humdrum.
будора́жить [16], ⟨вз-⟩ excite.
бу́дто as if, as though (*a.* ~ бы, ~ б); that; allegedly.
бу́дущ|ее *n* [17] future; **~ий** [17] future (*a. gr.*); **~ность** *f* [8] futurity, future.
бу́ер *m* [1; *pl.:* -pá, *etc. e.*] iceboat.
буза́ P *f* [5] row, shindy.
бузина́ *f* [5] elder.
буй *m* [3] buoy.
бу́йвол *m* [1] buffalo.
бу́йный [14; бу́ен, буйна́, -о] impetuous, violent, vehement; unbridled; exuberant.
бу́йство *n* [9] mischief, rage, outrage, violence; **~вать** [7] behave outrageously, rage.
бук *m* [1] beech.
бу́к|ва *f* [5] letter; прописна́я (строчна́я) ~ва capital (small) letter (with с P); **~ва́льный** [14] literal, verbal; **~ва́рь** *m* [4*e.*] ABC book, primer; **~вое́д** *m* [1] pedant.
букини́ст *m* [1] second-hand bookseller
бу́ковый [14] beechen, beech...
букс *m* [1] box(wood).
букси́р *m* [1] tug(boat); tow; взять на ~ take in tow; **~ный** [14] tug...; **~овать** [7] tow, tug.
була́вка *f* [5; *g/pl.:* -вок] pin; англи́йская ~ safety pin.
була́ный [14] dun (*horse*).
була́т *m* [1] Damascus steel; **~ный** [14] steel...; damask...
бу́лка *f* [5; *g/pl.:* -лок] small loaf; roll.
бу́лоч|ка *f* [5; *g/pl.:* -чек] roll; bun; **~ная** *f* [14] bakery; **~ник** *m* [1] baker.
булы́жник *m* [1] cobblestone.
бульва́р *m* [1] boulevard, avenue; **~ный** [14] boulevard...; ~ный рома́н *m* dime novel, *Brt.* penny dreadful; ~ная пре́сса *f* gutter press.
бу́лькать [1] gurgle.
бульо́н *m* [1] broth, bouillon.
бума́|га *f* [5] paper; document; **~жка** *f* [5; *g/pl.:* -жек] slip of paper; P note (*money*); **~жник** *m* [1] wallet; **~жный** [14] **1.** paper...; **2.** cotton...; **~зея** *f* [6] fustian.
бунт *m* [1] **1.** revolt, mutiny, insurrection, uprising; **2.** bale, pack; **~а́рь** *m* [4*e.*] = ~овщи́к.
бунтов|а́ть [7] rebel, revolt; ⟨вз-⟩ instigate; **~ско́й** [14] rebellious, mutinous; **~щи́к** *m* [1 *e.*] mutineer, rebel.
бура́ *f* [5] borax.
бура́в *m* [1 *e.*] drill, auger; **~ить** [14], ⟨про-⟩ bore, drill.
бура́н *m* [1] snowstorm, blizzard.
бурда́ F *f* [5] wash, wish-wash.
бурдю́к *m* [1 *e.*] wineskin.
буреве́стник *m* [1] (stormy) petrel.
буре́ние *n* [12] drilling, boring.
буржуа́ *m* [*indecl.*] bourgeois; **~зи́я** *f* [7] bourgeoisie; **~зный** [14] bourgeois...
буржу́й *contp.* P *m* [3], **~ка** *f* [5; *g/pl.:* -жу́ек] *s.* буржуа́.
бури́ть [13], ⟨про-⟩ bore.
бу́рка *f* [5; *g/pl.:* -рок] felt, cloak.
бурла́к *m* [1 *e.*] (barge) hauler.
бурли́ть [13] rage; seethe.
бурми́стр *m* [1] steward; mayor.
бу́рный [14; -рен, -рна] stormy, storm...; violent, boisterous.
буру́н *m* [1 *e.*] surf.
бурча́|нье *n* [12] grumbling; rumbling; **~ть** [4 *e.*; -чу́, -чи́шь] mumble; grumble; rumble.
бу́ры *m/pl.* [1] Boers.
бу́рый [14] brown, fulvous; ~ у́голь *m* brown coal, lignite.
бурья́н *m* [1] wild grass (*steppe*).
бу́ря *f* [6] storm, tempest.
бу́сы *f/pl.* [5] *coll.* (glass)beads.
бутафо́рия *f* [7] *thea.* properties *pl.*
бутербро́д (-tɛr-) *m* [1] sandwich.
буто́н *m* [1] bud.
бу́тсы *f/pl.* [5] football boots.
буты́л|ка *f* [5; *g/pl.:* -лок] bottle; **~очка** *f* [5; *g/pl.:* -чек] small bottle; **~ь** *f* [8] large bottle; carboy.
буф *m* [1] (*mst pl.*) puff; рука́в (взду́тый) **~ом** puffed sleeve.
бу́фер *m* [1; *pl.:* -pá, *etc. e.*] buffer.
буфе́т *m* [1] sideboard; bar, lunch-

room, refreshment room; **~чик** *m* [1] barkeeper; **~чица** *f* [5] barmaid.
буффо́н *m* [1] buffoon.
бух bounce!, plump!
Бухара́ *f* [5] Bokhara.
Бухаре́ст *m* [1] Bucharest.
буха́нка *f* [5; *g/pl.:* -нок] loaf.
бу́хать [1], *once* ⟨бу́хнуть⟩ plump.
бухга́лтер (buˈha-) *m* [1] bookkeeper; **~ия** *f* [7] bookkeeping; **~ский** [16] bookkeeper('s)..., bookkeeping... [бу́хать.
бу́хнуть [21] **1.** ⟨раз-⟩ swell; **2.** *s.*
бу́хта *f* [5] **1.** bay; **2.** coil.
бушева́ть [7; бушу́ю, -у́ешь] roar, rage, storm.
бушла́т *m* [1] (sailor's) jacket.
бушпри́т *m* [1] bowsprit.
буя́н *m* [1] brawler, rowdy, ruffian; **~ить** [13] brawl, riot, kick up a row.
бы, *short* б, *is used to render subjunctive and conditional patterns:* a) *with the preterite, e.g.* я сказа́л ~, е́сли ~ (я) знал I would say it if I knew it; (*similarly*: *should, could, may, might*); b) *with the infinitive, e.g.:* всё ~ ему́ знать he would like to know everything; не вам ~ говори́ть you had better be quiet.
быва́лый [14] experienced; former; common; *cf.* быва́ть.
быва́|ть [1] **1.** occur, happen; как ни в чём не **~ло** as if nothing had happened; он, **~ло**, гуля́л he would (*or* used to) go for a walk; бо́ли как не **~ло** F the pain had (*or* has) entirely disappeared; **2.** ⟨по-⟩ (у P) be (at), visit, stay (with).
бы́вший [17] former, late, ex-...
бык *m* [1 *e.*] **1.** bull; **2.** abutment.
были́на *f* [5] Russian epic.
были́нка *f* [5; *g/pl.:* -нок] blade of grass.
бы́ло (*s.* быть) (*after verbs*) already: я уже́ заплати́л ~ де́ньги ... I had already paid the money, (but) ...; almost nearly, was (were) just going to ...; я чуть ~ не сказа́л I was on the point of saying, I nearly said.
был|о́й [14] bygone, former; **~о́е** *n* past; **~ь** *f* [8] true story *or* ocurrence; past.
быстро|но́гий [16] swift(-footed); **~та́** *f* [5] quickness, swiftness, rapidity; **~хо́дный** [14; -ден, -дна] fast.
бы́стрый [14; быстр, -á, -o] quick, fast, swift.
быт *m* [1; в быту́] way of life, manners *pl.*; **~ие́** *n* [12] existence, being; *Bibl.* Genesis; **~ность** *f* [8] stay; в мою **~ность** в (П) during my stay in, while staying in; **~ово́й** [14] of manners, popular, genre; common, everyday.
быть (*3rd p. sg. pr.:* есть, *cf.*; *3rd p. pl.:* † суть; *ft.:* бу́ду, -дешь; будь[те]!; бу́дучи; был, -á, -o; не́ был, -o, -и) be; (*cf.* бу́дет, быва́ть, бы́ло); ~ (Д) ... will (inevitably) be *or* happen; мне бы́ло (бу́дет) ... (го́да *or* лет) I was (I'll be) ... (years old); как (же) ~? what is to be done?; так и ~! I don't care; будь что бу́дет come what may; будь по-ва́шему have it your own way!; бу́дьте до́бры (любе́зны), ... be so kind as ..., would you please ...
бюва́р *m* [1] writing case.
бюдже́т *m* [1], **~ный** [14] budget.
бюллете́нь *m* [4] bulletin; ballot, *Brt.* voting paper; medical certificate.
бюро́ *n* [*indecl.*] office, bureau; спра́вочное ~ inquiry office; information; ~ путеше́ствий travel bureau, *Brt.* tourist(s') office.
бюрокра́т *m* [1] bureaucrat; **~и́зм** *m* [1] red tape; **~и́ческий** [16] bureaucratic; **~ия** *f* [7] bureaucracy.
бюст *m* [1] bust; **~га́льтер** (-ˈhaltɛr) *m* [1] bra(ssière).
бязь *f* [8] cheap cotton goods.

В

в, во **1.** (В): (*direction*) to, into; for; в окно́ out of (in through) the window; (*time*) in, at, on, within; в сре́ду on Wednesday; в два часа́ at two o'clock; (*measure, price, etc.*) at, of; в день a *or* per day; длино́й в четы́ре ме́тра four meters long; чай в два рубля́ килогра́мм tea at 2 roubles a kilo(gram); в де́сять раз бо́льше ten times as much; (*promotion*) to the rank of; идти́ в солда́ты become a soldier; **2.** (П): (*position*) in, at, on; (*time*) in; в конце́ (нача́ле) го́да at the end (beginning) of the year; (*distance*) в пяти́ киломе́трах от (Р) five kilometers from.
в. *abbr.*: век.
Вавило́н *m* [1] Babylon.
ваго́н 🚂 *m* [1] car(riage, *Brt.*); **~-рестора́н** *m* dining car; **~е́тка** *f* [5; *g/pl.:* -ток] lorry, trolley, truck; **~овожа́тый** *m* [14] streetcar (*Brt.* tram) driver.
ва́жн|ичать [1] put on (*or* give o.s.) airs; **~ость** *f* [8] importance; conceit; **~ый** [14; ва́жен, -жна́, -o, ва́жны́] important, significant; haughty; F не**~о** rather bad; э́то не**~о** that doesn't matter *or* is of no importance.
ва́за *f* [5] vase, bowl.
вака́н|сия *f* [7] vacancy; **~тный** [14; -тен, -тна] vacant.

вáкса *f* [5] (shoe) polish, blacking.
вакци́на *f* [5] vaccine.
вал *m* [1; на -ý; *pl. e.*] **1.** rampart; bank; wall; **2.** billow; **3.** ⊕ shaft, axle.
валéжник *m* [1] brushwood.
вáленок *m* [1; -нка] felt boot.
валерья́н|ка F *f* [5], **~овый** [14]: ~овые кáпли *f/pl.* valerian.
валéт *m* [1] (*cards*) knave.
вáлик *m* [1] **1.** ⊕ roller **2.** bolster.
вал|и́ть [13; валю́, вáлишь; вáленный], ⟨по-, с-⟩ **1.** overturn, tumble (down; *v/i.* **-ся**), fell; heap (up), dump; **2.** [3*rd p. only*: -и́т] flock, throng; снег ~и́т it is snowing heavily.
валовóй [14] gross, total.
валу́н *m* [1 *e.*] boulder.
вáльдшнеп *m* [1] woodcock.
вальс *m* [1] waltz; **~и́ровать** [7], ⟨про-⟩ waltz.
вальцевáть [7] ⊕ roll.
валю́т|а *f* [5] (foreign) currency; золотáя ~а gold standard; **~ный** [14] currency..., exchange...; ~ный курс *m* rate of exchange.
валя́ть [28], ⟨по-⟩ roll; knead; full; P валя́й! go!; ~ дуракá idle; play the fool; **-ся** wallow, loll; lie about (in disorder).
вани́ль *f* [8] vanilla.
вáнн|а *f* [5] tub; bath; сóлнечная ~а sun bath; приня́ть ~у take a bath; **~ая** *f* [14] bath(room).
Вáнька *m* [5] **1.** *s.* Вáня; **2.** ♀-встáнька *m* [5] tumbler (*toy*).
Вáня *m* [6] *dim. of* Ивáн John.
вáрвар *m* [1] barbarian; **~ский** [16] barbarous; **~ство** *n* [9] barbarity.
Варвáра *f* [5] Barbara, Babette.
вáрежка *f* [5; *g/pl.*: -жек] mitten.
вар|éние *n* [12] = вáрка; **~éник** *m* [1] (*mst pl.*) boiled pieces of paste enclosing curd *or* fruit; **~ёный** [14] cooked, boiled; **~éнье** *n* [10] jam, preserves *pl.*
Вáренька *f* [5] *dim. of* Варвáра.
вариáнт *m* [1] variant, version.
вари́ть [13; варю́, вáришь; вáренный], ⟨с-⟩ **1.** cook, boil (*v/i.* **-ся**); brew; **2.** digest.
вáрка *f* [5] cooking, boiling.
Варшáва *f* [5] Warsaw.
варьетé *n* (-ˈtɛ) [*indecl.*] vaudeville, *Brt.* variety (*show & theater, -tre*).
варьи́ровать [7] vary.
Вáр|я *f* [6] *dim. of* ~вáра.
варя́г *m* [1] Varangian.
василёк *m* [1; -лькá] cornflower.
Васи́лий *m* [3] Basil.
вассáл *m* [1] vassal.
Вáся [6] *dim. of* Васи́лий.
вáт|а *f* [5] absorbent cotton, *Brt.* cotton wool; wadding; на ~е wadded.
ватáга *f* [5] gang, band, troop.
ватер|ли́ния (-tɛr-) *f* [7] water line; **~пáс** *m* [1] level.
вáтный [14] cotton(-wool)...; wadded.
ватру́шка *f* [5; *g/pl.*: -шек] curd *or* jam patty.
вáфля *f* [6; *g/pl.*: -фель] waffle, wafer.
вáхт|а ⚓ *f* [5] watch; стоя́ть на ~е keep watch; **~енный** [14] sailor on duty; **~ер** (*a.* **~ёр**) *m* [1] guard, watchman.
ваш *m*, **~а** *f*, **~е** *n*, **~и** *pl.* [25] your; yours; по-~ему in your opinion (*or* language); (пусть бу́дет) по-~ему (have it) your own way, (just) as you like; как по-~ему? what do you think?; *cf.* наш.
Вашингтóн *m* [1] Washington.
вая́|ние *n* [12] sculpture; **~тель** *m* [4] sculptor; **~ть** [28], ⟨из-⟩ form, cut, model.
вбе|гáть [1], ⟨~жáть⟩ [4; -гу́, -жи́шь, -гу́т] run *or* rush in.
вби|вáть [1], ⟨~ть⟩ [вобью́, вобьёшь; вбéй(те)!; вбил; вби́тый] drive (*or* hammer) in; ~ть себé в гóлову take it into one's head; **~рáть** [1], ⟨вобрáть⟩ [вберу́, -рёшь] absorb, imbibe.
вблизи́ nearby; close (to P).
вброд: переходи́ть ~ ford.
вв. *or* **в. в.** *abbr.*: векá.
ввáл|ивать [1] ⟨~и́ть⟩ [13; ввалю́, ввáлишь; ввáленный] throw (in[to]), dump; **-ся** fall *or* tumble in; flock in.
введéние *n* [12] introduction.
ввезти́ *s.* ввози́ть.
вверг|áть [1] ⟨~нуть⟩ [21] fling *or* cast (into в В); plunge (*v/i.* **-ся**); ~áть в отчáяние drive to despair.
ввер|я́ть [14], ⟨~ить⟩ entrust, commit, give in charge.
ввёртывать [1], ⟨ввертéть⟩ [11; вверчу́, ввéртишь], *once* ⟨ввернуть⟩ [20; ввёрнутый] screw in; *fig.* put in (*a word, etc.*).
вверх up(ward[s]); ~ по лéстнице upstairs; ~ дном (*or* ногáми) upside down; ~ тормáшками F headlong; ру́ки ~! hands up!; **~у́** above; overhead.
ввести́ *s.* вводи́ть.
ввиду́ in view (of P), considering; ~ тогó, что as, since, seeing that.
ввин|чивать [1], ⟨~ти́ть⟩ [15 *e.*; -нчу́, -нти́шь] screw in.
ввод|и́ть [15], ⟨ввести́⟩ [25] introduce; bring *or* usher (in); ~и́ть в курс дéла acquaint with an affair; ~и́ть в строй (*or* дéйствие, эксплуатáцию) ⊕ put into operation; **~ный** [14] introductory; ~ное слóво *or* предложéние *n gr.* parenthesis.
ввоз *m* [1] import(s); importation; **~и́ть** [15], ⟨ввезти́⟩ [24] import; **~ный** [14] import...
ввóлю (P) F plenty of; to one's heart's content.
ввя́з|ываться [1], ⟨~áться⟩ [3] meddle, interfere (with в В); get involved (in).
вглубь inward(s), deep (into).

вгля́д|ываться [1], ⟨~е́ться⟩ [11] (в В) peer (into), look narrowly (at).
вгоня́ть [28], ⟨вогна́ть⟩ [вгоню́, вго́нишь; вогна́л, -а́, -о; во́гнанный (во́гнан, -ана)] drive in(to).
вдава́ться [5], ⟨вда́ться⟩ [вда́мся, вда́шься, *etc. s.* дать] jut out; press in; indulge (in в В), plunge *or* go (into).
вда́в|ливать [1], ⟨~и́ть⟩ [14] press in.
вдал|еке́, ~и́ far off, far (from от Р); **~ь** into the distance.
вдви|га́ть [1], ⟨~нуть⟩ [20] put *or* push in.
вдво́|е twice (as..., *comp.*: ~е бо́льше twice as much *or* many); *vb.* + ~е *a.* double; **~ём** both *or* two (of us, *etc.*, *or* together); **~йне́** twice (as much, *etc.*), doubly.
вде|ва́ть [1], ⟨~ть⟩ [вде́ну, вде́нешь; вде́тый] (в В) thread.
вде́л|ывать, ⟨~ать⟩ [1] set (in).
вдоба́вок in addition (to); into the bargain, to boot.
вдов|а́ *f* [5; *pl. st.*] widow; **~е́ц** *m* [1; -вца́] widower.
вдо́воль (Р) F quite enough; plenty of.
вдо́вый [14 *sh.*] widowed.
вдого́нку after, in pursuit of.
вдоль (Р, по Д) along; lengthwise; ~ и поперёк throughout, far and wide.
вдохнов|е́ние *n* [12] inspiration; **~е́нный** [14; -ве́нен, -ве́нна] inspired; **~ля́ть** [28], ⟨~и́ть⟩ [14 *e.*; -влю́, -ви́шь] inspire; **-ся** get inspired (with *or* by Т).
вдре́безги into smithereens.
вдруг suddenly, all of a sudden.
вду|ва́ть [1], ⟨~ть⟩ [18] blow in.
вду́м|чивый [14 *sh.*] thoughtful; **~ываться,** ⟨~аться⟩ [1] (в В) ponder (over), reflect ([up]on), dive (into).
вдыха́ть [1], ⟨вдохну́ть⟩ [20] inhale; *fig.* inspire (with).
вегета|риа́нец *m* [1; -нца] vegetarian; **~ти́вный** [14] vegetative.
ве́д|ать [1] **1.** † know; **2.** (Т) be in charge of, manage; **~е́ние** *n* [12] running, directing; ~е́ние книг bookkeeping; **~ение** *n* [12] knowledge, lore; authority, charge, competence; **~омо** known; без моего́ ~ома without my knowledge; **~омость** *f* [8; *from g/pl. e.*] list, roll; bulletin; **~омство** *n* [9] department, administration.
ведро́ *n* [9; *pl.*: вёдра, -дер, -драм] bucket, pail; ~ для му́сора garbage can, *Brt.* dust-bin.
вёдро † *n* [9] serene weather.
веду́щий [17] leading; basic.
ведь indeed, sure(ly); why, well; then; you know!; ~ уже́ по́здно it is late, isn't it?
ве́дьма *f* [5] witch, hag.
ве́ер *m* [1; *pl.*: -ра́, *etc. e.*] fan.
ве́жлив|ость *f* [8] politeness; **~ый** [14 *sh.*] polite.
везде́ everywhere.
везти́ [24], ⟨по-, с-⟩ *v/t.* drive (be driving, *etc.*), transport; pull; ему́ (не) везёт F he is (un)lucky.
век *m* [1; на веку́; *pl.*: века́, *etc. e.*] **1.** century; age; **2.** life(time); сре́дние ~а́ *pl.* Middle Ages; на моём ~у́ in my life(time); ~ с тобо́й мы не вида́лись we haven't met for ages.
ве́ко *n* [9; *nom/pl.*: -ки] eyelid.
веково́й [14] secular.
ве́ксель *m* [4; *pl.*: -ля́, *etc. e.*] bill of exchange, promissory note.
веле́ть [9; ве́ленный] (*im*)*pf.*; *pt. pf. only* order, tell (p. s. th. Д/В).
велика́н *m* [1] giant.
вели́к|ий [16; вели́к, -а́] great; (too) large *or* big; от ма́ла до ~а everybody, young and old; ~ая пя́тница *f* Good Friday; Пётр ♀ий Peter the Great.
Велико|брита́ния *f* [7] Great Britain; **♀ду́шие** *n* [12] magnanimity; **♀ду́шный** [14; -шен, -шна] magnanimous, generous; **♀ле́пие** *n* [12] splendo(u)r, magnificence; **♀ле́пный** [14; -пен, -пна] magnificent, splendid; **♀ру́с** *m* [1], **♀ру́сский** [16] (Great) Russian.
велича́|вый [14 *sh.*] sublime, majestic, lofty; **~ть** [1] praise, glorify; style.
вели́ч|ественный [14 *sh.*] majestic, grand, stately; **~ество** *n* [9] Majesty; **~ие** *n* [12] grandeur; **~ина́** *f* [5; *pl. st.*: -чи́ны] size; quantity; celebrity; ~ино́й в *or* с (В) ... big *or* high.
вело|го́нки *f/pl.* [5; *gen.*: -нок] cycle race; **~дро́м** *m* [1] cycling ground.
велосипе́д *m* [1] bicycle; е́здить на ~е cycle; **~и́ст** *m* [1] cyclist; **~ный** [14] (bi)cycle..., cycling...
вельмо́жа *m* [5] magnate.
ве́на *f* [5] **1.** *anat.* vein; **2.** ♀ Vienna.
венге́р|ец *m* [1; -рца] **~ка** *f*, [5; *g/pl.*: -рок], **~ский** [16] Hungarian.
Ве́нгрия *f* [7] Hungary.
венери́ческий [16] venereal.
Венесуэ́ла *f* [5] Venezuela.
вене́ц *m* [1; -нца́] wreath, garland; crown; halo; идти́ под ~ † marry.
венеци|а́нский [16] Venetian; **'♀я** (-ˈnɛ-) *f* [7] Venice.
ве́нзель *m* [4; *pl.*: -ля́] monogram.
ве́ник *m* [1] broom, besom.
вено́к *m* [1; -нка́] wreath, garland.
вентил|и́ровать [7], ⟨про-⟩ ventilate, air; **~я́тор** *m* [1] ventilator, fan.
венча́|льный [14] wedding...; **~ние** *n* [12] wedding (ceremony); **~ть** [1] **1.** ⟨у-⟩ wreathe, crown; **2.** ⟨об-, по-⟩ marry; **-ся** get married (in church).
ве́ра *f* [5] **1.** faith, belief, trust (in в В); religion; **2.** ♀ Vera.

ве́рба *f* [5] willow.
верблю́|д *m* [1] camel; **~жий** [18]: ~жья шерсть *f* camel's hair.
ве́рбн|ый [14]: ~ое воскресе́нье *n* Palm Sunday.
вербов|а́ть [7], ⟨за-, на-⟩ enlist, recruit; engage, hire; **∠ка** *f* [5] enlistment; hire; **∠щик** *m* [1] enlister; hirer.
верёв|ка *f* [5; *g/pl.*: -вок] rope; **~очка** *f* [5; *g/pl.*: -чек] string, cord; **~очный** [14] rope...
верени́ца *f* [5] file, chain, line.
ве́реск *m* [1] heather.
веретено́ *n* [9; *pl. st.*: -тёна] spindle.
верещáть [16 *e.*; -щу́, -щи́шь] chirp.
верзи́ла F *m* [5] big (stupid) fellow, spindlelegs.
ве́рить [13], ⟨по-⟩ believe (in в В); believe, trust (*acc.* Д); ~ на́ слово take on trust; **-ся** (*impers.*) (мне) не ве́рится one (I) can hardly believe (it).
вермише́ль *f* [8] *coll.* vermicelli.
ве́рно *adv.* **1.** & **2.** *s.* ве́рный 1. & 2.; **3.** probably; **~сть** *f* [8] **1.** faith (-fulness), fidelity, loyalty; **2.** correctness, accuracy.
верну́ть(ся) [20] *pf.*, *s.* возвраща́ть(ся).
ве́рн|ый [14; -рен, -рна́, -о] **1.** faithful, true; loyal; **2.** right, correct; accurate, exact; **3.** safe, sure, reliable; **4.** inevitable, certain; ~ée (сказа́ть) or rather.
ве́ро|вание *n* [12] faith, belief; **~вать** [7] believe (in в В).
вероисповéдание *n* [12] creed.
вероло́м|ный [14; -мен, -мна] perfidious, treacherous; **~ство** *n* [9] perfidy, treachery.
вероотсту́пник *m* [1] apostate.
веротерпи́мость *f* [8] toleration.
вероя́т|ие *n* [12] likelihood; **~ность** *f* [8] probability; по всей ~ности in all probability; **~ный** [14; -тен, -тна] probable, likely.
ве́рсия *f* [7] version.
верста́ *f* [5; *pl. st.*: вёрсты] verst (= *3500 ft.*); **~к** *m* [1 *e.*] workbench; **~ть** [1], ⟨с-⟩ [свёрстанный] *typ.* make up.
ве́рт|ел *m* [1; *pl.*: -ла́] spit; **~е́ть** [11; верчу́, ве́ртишь], ⟨по-⟩ turn; twist; (**-ся**) **1.** turn, revolve; **2.** fidget; **3.** loaf; **4.** make subterfuges; -ся на языке́ be on the tip of one's tongue; **~ика́льный** [14; -лен, -льна] vertical; **~ля́вый** [14 *sh.*] fidgety, restless; **~олёт** *m* [1] helicopter; **~у́н** *m* [1 *e.*] fidget; **~у́шка** [5; *g/pl.*: -шек] light-minded woman.
ве́рующий [17] pious; believer.
верфь *f* [8] dockyard.
верх *m* [1; на -у́; *pl. e.*] **1.** top, upper part; **2.** right side (*fabric, clothes*); *fig.* **1.** summit, apex, pink; **2.** upper hand; **~и́** *pl.* **1.** heads, leaders; ... в ~а́х summit ...; **2.** ♪ high notes; **3.** surface; superficial knowledge; **∠ний** [15] upper.
верхо́в|ный [14] supreme, high; ~ная власть *f* supreme power; ~ный суд *m* supreme court; **~о́й** [14] riding...; rider, horseman; ~а́я езда́ *f* riding; **~ье** *n* [10; *g/pl.*: -ьев] upper (course).
верхо́м *adv.* astride; on horseback; е́здить ~ ride, go on horseback.
верху́шка *f* [5; *g/pl.*: -шек] top, crest; the highest ranks.
верши́на *f* [5] peak, summit.
верши́ть [16 *e.*; -шу́, -ши́шь; -шённый], ⟨за-, с-⟩ **1.** (re)solve, decide; **2.** direct (Т); **3.** accomplish.
вершо́к *m* [1; -шка́] vershok (†, = *4.45 cm.* = *1.75 in.*).
вес *m* [1] weight; на ~ by weight; уде́льный ~ *phys.* specific gravity; по́льзоваться больши́м ∠ом enjoy great credit; ∠ом в (В) weighing...
вес|ели́ть [13], ⟨раз-⟩ amuse, divert (**-ся** o. s., enjoy o. s.); **~ёлость** *f* [8] gaiety, mirth; **~ёлый** [14; ве́сел, -а́, -о] gay, merry, cheerful; как ∠ело! it's such fun!; ему́ ∠ело he enjoys himself, is of good cheer; **~е́лье** *n* [10] merriment, merrymaking, fun; **~ельча́к** *m* [1 *e.*] merry fellow.
весе́нний [15] spring...
ве́с|ить [15] *v/i.* weigh; **~кий** [16; ве́сок, -ска] weighty.
весло́ *n* [9; *pl.*: вёсла, -сел] oar.
весн|а́ *f* [5; *pl.*: вёсны, вёсен] spring (in [the] Т); **~у́шка** *f* [5; *g/pl.*: -шек] freckle.
весов|о́й [14] **1.** weight...; balance-...; **2.** sold by weight; **~щи́к** *m* [1 *e.*] weigher.
вести́ [25], ⟨по-⟩ **1.** (be) lead(ing, *etc.*), conduct, guide; **2.** carry on; **3.** keep; **4.** drive; ~ (своё) нача́ло spring (from от Р); ~ себя́ behave (o.s.); **~сь** be conducted *or* carried on; так уж у нас ведётся that's a custom among us.
вестибю́ль *m* [4] entrance hall.
Вест-'Индия *f* [7] West Indies.
ве́ст|ник *m* [1] messenger; bulletin; **~ово́й** ⚔ *m* [14] orderly; **~ь** *f* [8; *from g/pl. e.*] **1.** news, message; **2.** gossip, rumo(u)r.
весы́ *m/pl.* [1] scales, balance.
весь *m*, вся *f*, всё *n*, *pl.*: все [31] **1.** *adj.* all, the whole; full, life (*size*; at в В); **2.** *su. n* all over; everything, *pl. a.* everybody; лу́чше всего́ (всех) best of all, the best; при всём том *or* со всем тем for all that; во всём ми́ре all over the world; по всей стране́ throughout the country; всего́ хоро́шего! good luck!; во всю F *s.* си́ла; **3.** всё *adv.* always, all the time; only, just; всё

(ещё) не not yet; всё бо́льше (и бо́льше) more and more; всё же nevertheless, yet.
весьма́ very, extremely; ~ вероя́тно most probably.
ветв|и́стый [14 *sh.*] branchy; **~ь** *f* [8; *from g/pl. e.*] branch.
ве́тер *m* [1; -тра] wind; встре́чный ~ contrary *or* head wind; попу́тный ~ fair wind; броса́ть де́ньги (слова́) на ~ waste money (words); держа́ть нос по ве́тру be a timeserver.
ветерина́р *m* [1], **~ный** [14]: ~ный врач *m* veterinarian.
ветеро́|к [1; -рка́], **~чек** [1; -чка] *m* light wind, breeze, breath.
ве́тка *f* [5; *g/pl.*: -ток] branch(let), twig; 🚂 branch line.
ве́то *n* [*indecl.*] veto; наложи́ть ~ veto; **~шь** *f* [8] rags, tatters *pl.*
ве́тр|еный [14 *sh.*] windy (*a. fig.* = flippant); **~яно́й** [14] wind...; ~яна́я ме́льница *f* windmill; **~яный** [14]: ~яная о́спа *f* chicken pox.
ве́тх|ий [16; ветх, -á, -о; *comp.*: ве́тше] old, dilapidated; worn-out, shabby; decrepit; **~ость** *f* [8] decay, dilapidation; приходи́ть в ~ость fall into decay.
ветчина́ *f* [5] ham.
ветша́ть [1], ⟨об-⟩ decay, dilapidate, weaken.
ве́ха *f* [5] landmark; ⚓ spar buoy.
ве́чер *m* [1; *pl.*: -pá, *etc. e.*] **1.** evening; **2.** evening party; soiree; ~ом in the evening; сего́дня ~ом tonight; вчера́ ~ом last night; по́д ~ toward(s) the evening; **~е́ть** [8; *impers.*] decline (*of the day*); **~и́нка** *f* [5; *g/pl.*: -нок] = ве́чер 2.; **~ко́м** F = ~ом; **∠ний** [15] evening..., night...; **∠ня** *f* [6; *g/pl.*: -рен] vespers *pl.*, evensong; **~я** *f* [6]: та́йная ~я *or* ~я госпо́дня the Lord's Supper.
ве́чн|ость *f* [8] eternity; (це́лую) ~ость F for ages; **~ый** [14; -чен, -чна] eternal, everlasting; perpetual.
ве́ша|лка *f* [5; *g/pl.*: -лок] hanger, tab; peg, rack; cloakroom; **~ть** [1], **1.** ⟨пове́сить⟩ [15] hang (up); **-ся** hang o. s.; **2.** ⟨взве́сить⟩ [15] weigh.
вещево́й [14]: ~ мешо́к *m* knapsack.
вещ|е́ственный [14] corporeal, real, material, substantial; **~ество́** *n* [9] matter, substance; **~и́ца** *f* [8] knickknack; piece; **~ь** *f* [8; *from g/pl. e.*] thing; object; work, piece, play; *pl.* belongings; baggage, *Brt.* luggage.
ве́я|лка *f* [5; *g/pl.*: -лок] winnowing machine; **~ние** *n* [12] waft; 🌾 winnowing; *fig.* trend; influence; **~ть** [27] **1.** *v/i.* breathe; spread; **2.** ⟨про-⟩ *v/t.* winnow.
вжи|ва́ться [1], ⟨**∠ться**⟩ [-ву́сь, *etc. s.* жить] accustom o.s. (to в B).
взад back(ward[s]); ~ и вперёд back and forth, to and fro; up and down.
взаи́мн|ость *f* [8] reciprocity; **~ый** [14; -мен, -мна] mutual, reciprocal; спаси́бо, ~о F thanks, the same to you.
взаимо|де́йствие *n* [12] interaction; coöperation; **~де́йствовать** [7] interact; cooperate; **~отноше́ние** *n* [12] mutual (*or* inter-, cor)relation; **~по́мощь** *f* [8] mutual aid; **~понима́ние** *n* [12] mutual understanding.
взаймы́ on credit *or* loan; брать ~ borrow (from у, от P); дава́ть ~ lend.
вза|ме́н (P) instead of, in exchange for; **~перти́** locked up, under lock and key; **~пра́вду** P = впра́вду.
взба́л|мошный F [14; -шен, -шна] extravagant; **~тывать,** ⟨взболта́ть⟩ [1] shake *or* stir up.
взбе|га́ть [1], ⟨**~жа́ть**⟩ [4; взбегу́, -жи́шь, -гу́т] run up.
взбива́ть [1], ⟨взбить⟩ [взобью́, -бьёшь; взбил, -а; взби́тый] fluff; whip, froth.
взбира́ться [1], ⟨взобра́ться⟩ [взберу́сь, -рёшься; взобра́лся, -ла́сь, -ло́сь] climb (s. th. на B).
взболта́ть *s.* взба́лтывать.
взбудора́живать [1] = будора́жить.
взбух|а́ть [1], ⟨**∠нуть**⟩ [21] swell.
взва́ливать [1], ⟨взвали́ть⟩ [13; взвалю́, -а́лишь; -а́ленный] load, charge (with на B).
взвести́ *s.* взводи́ть.
взве́|шивать [1], ⟨**~сить**⟩ [15] weigh; **-ся** weigh o. s.
взви|ва́ть [1], ⟨**~ть**⟩ [взовью́, -вьёшь, *etc. s.* вить] whirl up; **-ся** soar up, rise.
взви́зг|ивать [1], ⟨**~нуть**⟩ [20] squeak, scream.
взви́н|чивать [1], ⟨**~ти́ть**⟩ [15 *e.*; -нчу́, -нти́шь; -и́нченный] excite; raise (*prices*).
взвить *s.* взвива́ть.
взвод *m* [1] platoon.
взводи́ть [15], ⟨взвести́⟩ [25] lead up; lift; impute (s. th. to a p. B/на B); ~ куро́к cock (*firearm*).
взволно́|ванный [14 *sh.*] excited; uneasy; **~ва́ть(ся)** *s.* волнова́ть.
взгля|д *m* [1] look; glance; gaze; stare; *fig.* view, opinion; на ~д in appearance, by sight; на мой ~д in my opinion; на пе́рвый ~д at first sight; с пе́рвого **∠**да on the face of it; at once; **∠дывать** [1], *once* ⟨**~ну́ть**⟩ [19] (на B) (have a) look, glance (at).
взгромо|жда́ть [1], ⟨**~зди́ть**⟩ [15 *e.*; -зжу́, -зди́шь; -можде́нный] load, pile up; **-ся** clamber, perch (on на B).
вздёр|гивать [1], ⟨**~нуть**⟩ [20] jerk up; ~нутый нос *m* pug nose.

вздор *m* [1] nonsense; **∠ный** [14; -рен, -рна] foolish, absurd; F quarrelsome.
вздорожá|ние *n* [12] rise of price(s); **~ть** *s.* дорожáть.
вздох *m* [1] sigh; испустúть послéдний ~ give up the ghost; **~нýть** *s.* вздыхáть.
вздрáгивать [1], *once* ⟨вздрóгнуть⟩ [20] start, wince; shudder.
вздремнýть F [20] *pf.* nap.
взду|вáть [1], ⟨~ть⟩ [18] **1.** whirl up; **2.** *v/i.* **-ся** inflate; **3.** F thrash; **∠тие** *n* [12] swelling.
вздýма|ть [1] *pf.* conceive the idea, take it into one's head; **-ся:** емý ~лось = он ~л; как ~ется at one's will.
взды|мáть [1] raise, whirl up; **~хáть** [1], *once* ⟨вздохнýть⟩ [20] sigh; ~хáть (по, о П) long (for); *pf.* F draw breath, breathe again.
взи|мáть [1] levy, raise (from с Р); **~рáть** [1] (на В) look (at); не взирáя на without regard to, notwithstanding.
взлáмывать [1], ⟨взломáть⟩ [1] break *or* force open.
взлез|áть [1], ⟨~ть⟩ [24 *st.*] (на В) climb up.
взлёт *m* [1] ascent, rise.
взлет|áть [1], ⟨~éть⟩ [11] fly up, soar.
взлом *m* [1] breaking in; **~áть** *s.* взлáмывать; **∠щик** *m* [1] burglar.
взмах *m* [1] stroke; sweep; **∠ивать** [1], *once* ⟨~нýть⟩ [20] swing.
взмет|áть [3], *once* ⟨~нýть⟩ [20] whirl *or* throw up; flap.
взмóрье *n* [10] seashore, seaside.
взнос *m* [1] payment; fee.
взнýзд|ывать [1], ⟨~áть⟩ bridle.
взобрáться *s.* взбирáться.
взойтú *s.* восходúть & всходúть.
взор *m* [1] look; gaze; eyes *pl.*
взорвáть *s.* взрывáть.
взрóслый [14] grown-up, adult.
взрыв *m* [1] explosion; detonation; *fig.* outburst; **~áтель** *m* [4] fuse; **~áть** [1], ⟨взорвáть⟩ [-вý, -вёшь; взóрванный] blow up; *fig.* enrage; **-ся** explode; **~нóй** [14], **∠чатый** [14] explosive (*su.*: ∠чатое вещество).
взрыхлять [28] *s.* рыхлúть.
взъе|зжáть [1] ⟨∠хать⟩ [взъéду, -дешь; взъезжáй(те)!] ride *or* drive up; **~рóшивать** [1], ⟨~рóшить⟩ [16 *st.*] dishevel, tousle; **-ся** bristle up.
взывáть [1], ⟨воззвáть⟩ [-зовý, -зовёшь; -звáл, -á, -о] cry, call; invoke; appeal (to к Д).
взыск|áние *n* [12] **1.** levy, collecting; **2.** punishment, reprimand: **~áтельный** [14; -лен, -льна] exacting, exigent; **∠ивать** [1], ⟨~áть⟩ [3] (с Р) **1.** levy, exact; collect; recover (from); **2.** call to account; impose a penalty (on); не взыщú(те)! no offence!
взят|ие *n* [12] seizure, capture; **~ка** *f* [5; *g/pl.*: -ток] **1.** bribe; дать ~ку bribe, P grease; **2.** trick (*cards*); **~очник** *m* [1] bribe taker, corrupt official; **~очничество** *n* [9] bribery; **~ь** *s.* брать.
вибр|áция *f* [7] vibration; **~úровать** [7] vibrate.
вид *m* [1] **1.** look(s), appearance, air; **2.** sight, view; **3.** kind, sort; species; **4.** *gr.* aspect; в ∠е (Р) in the form of, as, by way of; при ∠е at the sight of; на ~ý (у Р) in sight; visible (to); с (*or* по) ∠у by sight; judging from one's appearance; ни под какúм ∠ом on no account; у негó хорóший ~ he looks well; дéлать *or* покáзывать ~ pretend; (не) терять *or* выпускáть из ∠у lose sight of (keep in view); стáвить на ~ reproach (a p. with Д/В); ∠ы *pl.* prospects (for на В).
видáть F [1], ⟨у-; по-⟩ егó давнó не ~ I *or* we haven't seen him for a long time; **-ся** (*iter.*) meet, see (o. a.; a p. с Т).
видéние *n* [12] vision.
вúдеть [11 *st.*], ⟨у-⟩ see; catch sight of; ~ во сне dream (of В); вúдишь (-ите) ли? you see?; **-ся** = видáться (*but a. once*).
вúдим|о apparently, evidently; ~о-не~о F lots of, immense quantity; **~ость** *f* [8] **1.** visibility; **2.** appearance; **~ый 1.** [14 *sh.*] visible; **2.** [14] apparent.
видн|éться [8] appear, be seen; **∠о** it can be seen; it appears; apparently; (мне) ничегó не ∠о I don't *or* can't see anything; **∠ый 1.** [14; -ден, -днá, -о] visible; **2.** [14] outstanding, eminent, prominent; F stately, portly.
видоизмен|éние *n* [12] variation; variety; **~ять** [1], ⟨~úть⟩ [13] alter, change.
видоискáтель *m* [4] (view) finder.
вúза *f* [5] visa.
визант|úец *m* [1; -úйца], **~úйка** *f* [5; *g/pl.*: úек], **~úйский** [16] Byzantine; **~úя** *f* [7] Byzantium.
виз|г *m* [1] scream, shriek; yelp; **~глúвый** [14 *sh.*] shrill, squeaky; **~жáть** [4 *e.*; -жý, -жúшь], ⟨за-⟩ shriek; yelp.
визúровать [7] (*im*)*pf.* visa.
визúт *m* [1] visit, call; **~ный** [14]: ~ная кáрточка *f* calling card.
вúка *f* [5] vetch.
вúл|ка *f* [5; *g/pl.*: -лок] **1.** fork; **2.** (штéпсельная) ~ка ⚡ plug; **~ы** *f/pl.* [5] pitchfork.
вилять [28], ⟨за-⟩, *once* ⟨вильнýть⟩ [20] wag (one's tail хвостóм); *fig.* prevaricate, shuffle.
вин|á *f* [5] **1.** guilt; fault; **2.** reason; вменять в ~ý impute (to Д); свáливать ~ý lay the blame (on на В); это не по моéй ~é it's not my fault.

винегре́т *m* [1] vinaigrette (salad).
вини́т|ельный [14] *gr.* accusative (*case*); **~ь** [13] blame (for за В), accuse (of в П).
ви́н|ный [14] wine...; ~ный ка́мень *m* tartar; ~ная я́года *f* (dried) fig; **~о́** *n* [9; *pl. st.*] wine; F vodka.
винова́т|ый [14 *sh.*] guilty (of в П); ~! sorry!, excuse me!; (I beg your) pardon!; вы в э́том (не) ~ы it's (not) your fault; я ~ пе́ред ва́ми I must apologize to you, (*a.* круго́м ~) it's all my fault.
вино́в|ник *m* [1] **1.** culprit; **2.** originator, author; **~ный** [14; -вен, -вна] guilty (of в П).
виногра́д *m* [1] **1.** vine; **2.** *coll.* grapes *pl.*; сбор ~а vintage; **~арство** *n* [9] winegrowing; **~арь** *m* [4] winegrower; **~ник** *m* [1] vineyard; **~ный** [14] (of) grape(s).
вино|де́лие *n* [12] winemaking; **~ку́ренный** [14]: ~ку́ренный заво́д *m* distillery; **~торго́вец** [1; -вца] wine merchant.
винт *m* [1 *e.*] screw; **ʼик** *m* [1] small screw; у него́ ʼика не хвата́ет F he has a screw loose; **~о́вка** *f* [5; *g/pl.*: -вок] rifle; **~ово́й** [14] screw...; spiral; ~ова́я ле́стница *f* spiral (winding) stairs.
винье́тка *f* [5; *g/pl.*: -ток] vignette.
виолонче́ль *f* [8] (violon)cello.
вира́ж *m* **1.** [1 *e.*] bend, curve; **2.** [1] *phot.* toning solution.
виртуо́з *m* [1] virtuoso.
ви́селица *f* [5] gallows, gibbet.
висе́ть [11] hang.
ви́ски *n* [*indecl.*] whisk(e)y.
виско́за *f* [5] viscose.
Ви́сла *f* [5] Vistula.
ви́смут *m* [1] bismuth.
ви́снуть F [21], ‹по-› *v/i.* hang, be suspended.
висо́к *m* [1; -ска́] *anat.* temple.
високо́сный [14]: ~ год *m* leap year.
вися́чий [17] hanging; suspension-...; ~ замо́к *m* padlock.
витами́н *m* [1] vitamin.
вит|а́ть [1] **1.** stay, linger; **2.** soar; **~ева́тый** [14] affected, bombastic.
вито́к *m* [1; -тка́] coil.
витри́на *f* [5] shopwindow; show-case.
вить [вью, вьёшь; ве́й(те)!; вил, -а́, -о; ви́тый (вит, -а́, -о)], ‹с-› [совью́, совьёшь] wind, twist; build (*nests*); **-ся 1.** wind; spin, whirl; **2.** twine, creep; curl; **3.** hover.
ви́тязь *m* [4] hero.
вихо́р *m* [1; -хра́] forelock.
вихрь *m* [4] whirlwind.
ви́це-... (*in compds.*) vice-...
вишн|ёвый [14] cherry...; **ʼя** *f* [6; *g/pl.:* -шен] cherry.
вишь P look, there's; you see.
вка́пывать [1], ‹вкопа́ть› dig in; drive in; *fig* как вко́панный stock-still, transfixed.
вка́т|ывать [1], ‹~и́ть› [15] roll in, wheel in.
вклад *m* [1] deposit; *fig.* contribution (to в В); **ʼка** [5; *g/pl.:* -док] insert; **ʼчик** *m* [1] depositor; **ʼывать** [1], ‹вложи́ть› [16] put in, insert, enclose; invest; deposit.
вкле́|ивать [1], ‹~ить› [13] glue *or* paste in; **~йка** *f* [5; *g/pl.:* -е́ек] gluing in; sheet, *etc.*, glued in.
вкли́ни|вать(ся) [1], ‹ʼʼть(ся)› [13; *a. st.*] (be) wedge(d) in.
включ|а́ть [1], ‹~и́ть› [16 *e.*; -чу́, -чи́шь; -чённый] include; insert; ⚡ switch *or* turn on; **-ся** join (s. th. в В); ~а́я including; **~е́ние** *n* [12] inclusion; insertion; ⚡ switching on; **~и́тельно** included.
вкол|а́чивать [1], ‹~оти́ть› [15] drive *or* hammer in.
вконе́ц F completely, altogether.
вкопа́ть *s.* вка́пывать.
вкорен|я́ться [28], ‹~и́ться› [13] take root; ~и́вшийся established, (deep-)rooted.
вкось askew, aslant, obliquely; вкривь и ~ pell-mell; amiss.
ВКП(б) = Всесою́зная Коммунисти́ческая па́ртия (большевико́в) C.P.S.U.(B.) = Communist Party of the Soviet Union (Bolsheviks); (*since 1952*: КПСС, *cf.*).
вкра́|дчивый [14 *sh.*] insinuating, ingratiating; **~дываться** [1], ‹~сться› [25] creep *or* steal in; *fig.* insinuate o.s.
вкра́тце briefly, in a few words.
вкруту́ю: яйцо́ ~ hard-boiled egg.
вкус *m* [1] **1.** taste; flavo(u)r; **2.** style; прия́тный на ~ savo(u)ry; прия́тно на ~ = ʼно; быть *or* прийти́сь по ʼу be to one's taste, relish (*or* like) s. th.; име́ть ~ (P) taste (of); **ʼный** [14; -сен, -сна́, -о] tasty; (э́то) ʼно it tastes well *or* nice.
вку|ша́ть [1], ‹~си́ть› [15; вкушённый] **1.** taste; **2.** enjoy, experience.
вла́га *f* [5] moisture.
владе́|лец *m* [1; -льца] owner, proprietor, possessor; **~ние** *n* [12] possession (of Т); **~тель** *m* [4] **1.** owner; **2.** ruler; **~ть** [8], ‹за-, о-› (Т) own, possess; rule, govern; master, manage; ~ть собо́й control o.s.
Влади́мир *m* [1] Vladimir.
влады́|ка *m* [5] **1.** lord, sovereign; **2.** archbishop; **~чество** *n* [9] rule, sway.
вла́жн|ость *f* [8] humidity; **~ый** [14; -жен, -жна́, -о] humid, damp.
вла́мываться [1], ‹вломи́ться› [14] break in.
вла́ст|вовать [7] rule, dominate; **~ели́н** *m* [1] sovereign; **~и́тель** *m* [4] master, ruler; **~ный** [14; -тен, -тна] imperious, commanding; в э́том я не ~ен I have no power

over it; **~ь** *f* [8; *from g/pl. e.*] authority, power; rule, regime; control; *pl.* authorities.

влачи́ть [16 *e.*; -чу́, -чи́шь] drag; eke out.

вле́во (to the) left.

влез|а́ть [1], ⟨~ть⟩ [24 *st.*] climb *or* get in(to); climb up.

влет|а́ть [1], ⟨~е́ть⟩ [11] fly in; rush in.

влеч|е́ние *n* [12] inclination; **~ь** [26], ⟨по-, у-⟩ drag, pull; *fig.* attract, draw; ~ь за собо́й involve, entail.

вли|ва́ть [1], ⟨~ть⟩ [волью́, -льёшь; влей(те)!; влил, -а́, -о; вли́тый (-та́, -о)] pour in; **-ся** flow *or* fall in; **~я́ние** *n* [12] influence; **~я́тельный** [14; -лен, -льна] influential; **~я́ть** [28], ⟨по-⟩ (have) influence.

ВЛКСМ (Всесою́зный Ле́нинский Коммунисти́ческий Сою́з Молодёжи) Leninist Young Communist League of the Soviet Union.

вложи́ть *s.* вкла́дывать.

вломи́ться *s.* вла́мываться.

влюб|лённость *f* [8] amorousness; **~ля́ться** [28], ⟨~и́ться⟩ [14] fall in love (with в В); ~лённый enamo(u)red; lover; **~́чивый** [14 *sh.*] amorous.

вмен|я́емый ⚖ [14 *sh.*] responsible, accountable; **~я́ть** [28], ⟨~и́ть⟩ [13] consider (as в В), impute; ~я́ть (себе́) в обя́занность pledge s. o. (o. s.) (to *inf.*).

вме́сте together, along with; ~ с тем at the same time.

вмести́|мость *f* [8] capacity; **~тельный** [14; -лен, -льна] capacious, spacious; **~ть** *s.* вмеща́ть.

вме́сто (P) instead, in place (of); as.

вмеш|а́тельство *n* [9] interference, intervention; ⚕ operation; **~́ивать** [1], ⟨~а́ть⟩ [1] (В/в В) mingle (with); involve (in); **-ся** interfere, intervene, meddle (with в В).

вме|ща́ть [1], ⟨~сти́ть⟩ [15 *e.*; -ещу́, -ести́шь; -ещённый] **1.** put, place; **2.** hold, contain, accomodate; **-ся** find room; hold.

вмиг in an instant, in no time.

внаём *or* **внаймы́:** отда́ть (сдать) ~ rent, *Brt.* let; взять ~ rent, hire.

внача́ле at first, at the beginning.

вне (P) out of, outside; beyond; быть ~ себя́ be beside o. s.

внебра́чный [14] illegitimate.

внедр|е́ние *n* [12] introduction; **~я́ть** [28], ⟨~и́ть⟩ [13] inculcate; introduce; **-ся** take root.

внеза́пный [14; -пен, -пна] sudden, unexpected.

внекла́ссный [14] out-of-class.

внеочередно́й [14] extra(ordinary).

внес|е́ние *n* [12] entry; **~ти́** *s.* вноси́ть.

внешко́льный [14] nonschool.

вне́шн|ий [15] outward, external; foreign; **~ость** *f* [8] appearance; exterior.

вниз down(ward[s]); **~у́ 1.** (P) beneath, below; **2.** down(stairs).

вник|а́ть [1], ⟨~́нуть⟩ [19] (в В) penetrate (into), fathom.

внима́|ние *n* [12] attention; care; приня́ть во ~ние take into consideration; принима́я во ~ние in view of, with regard to; оста́вить без ~ния disregard; **~тельность** *f* [8] attentiveness; **~тельный** [14; -лен, -льна] attentive; **~ть** [1], ⟨внять⟩ [*inf. & pt. only*; внял, -а́, -о] (Д) hear *or* listen (to); follow, watch; comply with.

вничью́: сыгра́ть ~ draw (*game*).

вновь 1. again; **2.** newly.

вноси́ть [15], ⟨внести́⟩ [24 -с-: -су́, -сёшь; внёс, внесла́] carry *or* bring in; enter, include; pay (in); contribute; make (*correction*).

внук *m* [1] grandson; *cf.* внуча́та.

вну́тренн|ий [15] inner, inside, internal, interior; inland...; home...; **~ость** *f* [8] interior; (*esp. pl.*) internal organs, entrails.

внутр|и́ (P) in(side); within; **~ь** (P) in(to), inward(s), inside.

внуч|а́та *m/f pl.* [2] grandchildren; **~́ка** *f* [5; *g/pl.*: -чек] granddaughter.

внуш|а́ть [1], ⟨~и́ть⟩ [16 *e.*; -шу́, -ши́шь; -шённый] (Д/В) suggest; inspire (a p. with); inculcate (upon); **~е́ние** *n* [12] suggestion; infusion; reprimand; **~и́тельный** [14; -лен, -льна] imposing, impressive; **~и́ть** *s.* ~а́ть.

вня́т|ный [14; -тен, -тна] distinct; intelligible; **~ь** *s.* внима́ть.

вобра́ть *s.* вбира́ть.

вовл|ека́ть [1], ⟨~е́чь⟩ [26] drag in; *fig.* involve.

во́время in *or* on time, timely.

во́все quite; ~ не(т) not at all.

вовсю́ F with all one's might.

во-вторы́х second(ly).

вогна́ть *s.* вгоня́ть.

во́гнутый [14 *sh.*] concave.

вод|а́ *f* [5; *ac/sg.*: во́ду; *pl.*: во́ды, вод, во́дам] water; на ~е́ и на су́ше by sea and by land; в му́тной ~е́ ры́бу лови́ть fish in troubled waters; вы́йти сухи́м из ~ы́ come off clear; толо́чь ~́у (в сту́пе) beat the air.

водвор|я́ть [28], ⟨~и́ть⟩ [13] settle; install; (re)establish.

водеви́ль *m* [4] musical comedy.

води́тель *m* [4] driver.

вод|и́ть [15], ⟨по-⟩ **1.** lead, conduct, guide; **2.** drive; **3.** move (T); **4.** breed; ~и́ть дру́жбу be on friendly terms; **-ся** be (found), live; be customary *or* the custom; (у P, за T) have; (с T) associate (with); э́то за ним ∠ится F that's in his way, to be sure!

во́дка *f* [5; *g/pl.:* -док] vodka (*kind of whisky*); дать на во́дку tip.

водо|боя́знь *f* [8] hydrophobia; **~во́з** *m* [1] water carter; **~воро́т** *m* [1] whirlpool, eddy; **~ём** *m* [1] reservoir; **~измеще́ние** ⚓ *n* [12] displacement, tonnage; **~ка́чка** *f* [5; *g/pl.:* -чек] waterworks.

водо|ла́з *m* [1] diver; **~лече́ние** *n* [12] hydropathy, water cure; **~напо́рный** [14]: ~напо́рная ба́шня *f* water tower; **~непроница́емый** [14 *sh.*] watertight; **~но́с** *m* [1] water carrier; **~па́д** *m* [1] waterfall; **~по́й** *m* [3] watering place; watering (*of animals*); **~прово́д** *m* [1] water pipe; **~разде́л** *m* [1] divide, *Brt.* watershed; **~ро́д** *m* [1] hydrogen; **~ро́дный** [14]: ~ро́дная бо́мба *f* hydrogen bomb; **′~росль** *f* [8] alga, seaweed; **~снабже́ние** *n* [12] water supply; **~сто́к** *m* [1] drain(age), drainpipe; **~сто́чный** [14]: ~сто́чная труба́ *f* gutter; **~храни́лище** *n* [11] reservoir.

водру|жа́ть [1], ⟨~зи́ть⟩ [15 *e.*; -ужу́, -узи́шь; -ужённый] set up; hoist.

вод|яни́стый [14 *sh.*] watery; **~я́нка** *f* [5] dropsy; **~яно́й** [14] water...

воева́ть [14], wage *or* carry on war, be at war.

воеди́но together.

военача́льник *m* [1] commander.

военизи|а́ция *f* [7] militarization; **~и́ровать** [7] (*im*)*pf.* militarize.

военно|-возду́шный [14]: ~-возду́шные си́лы *f/pl.* air force; **~-морско́й** [14]: ~-морско́й флот *m* navy; **~пле́нный** [14] prisoner of war; **~-полево́й** [14]: ~-полево́й суд *m* court-martial; **~слу́жащий** [17] military man, soldier.

вое́нн|ый [14] **1.** military, war...; **2.** military man, soldier; ~ый врач *m* medical officer; ~ый кора́бль *m* man-of-war, warship; ~ое положе́ние *n* martial law (under на П); поступи́ть на ~ую слу́жбу enlist, join; ~ые де́йствия *n/pl.* hostilities.

вож|а́к [1 *e.*] guide; leader; **~а́тый** [14] leader, guide; streetcar (*Brt.* tram) driver; **~дь** *m* [4 *e.*] chief(-tain); leader; **∠жи** *f/pl.* [8; *from g/pl. e.*] reins.

воз *m* [1; на -у́; *pl. e.*] cart(load).

возбу|ди́мый [14 *sh.*] excitable; **~ди́тель** *m* [4] exciter; **~жда́ть** [1], ⟨~ди́ть⟩ [15 *e.*; -ужу́, -уди́шь] excite, stir up; arouse; incite; raise; bring, present; **~жда́ющий** [17] stimulating; ~жда́ющее сре́дство *n* stimulant; **~жде́ние** *n* [12] excitement; **~ждённый** [14] excited.

возвели́ч|ивать [1], ⟨~ить⟩ [16] exalt, praise, glorify.

возвести́ *s.* возводи́ть.

возве|ща́ть [1], ⟨~сти́ть⟩ [15 *e.*; -ещу́, -ести́шь; -ещённый] (В/Д *or* о П/Д) announce.

возв|оди́ть [15], ⟨~ести́⟩ [25] (в *or* на В) lead up; raise, elevate; erect; make.

возвра́|т *m* [1] **1.** = ~ще́ние 1. & 2.; **2.** ⚕ relapse; **~ти́ть(ся)** *s.* ~ща́ть (-ся); **~тный** [14] back...; relapsing; *gr.* reflexive; **~ща́ть** [1], ⟨~ти́ть⟩ [15 *e.*; -ащу́, -ати́шь; -ащённый] return; give back; restore, reimburse; recover; **-ся** return, come back (from из *or* с Р); revert (to к Д); **~ще́ние** *n* [12] **1.** return; **2.** restitution.

возв|ыша́ть [1], ⟨~ы́сить⟩ [15] raise, elevate; **-ся** rise; tower (over над Т); **~ыше́ние** *n* [12] rise; elevation; **~ы́шенность** *f* [8] **1.** sublimity, loftiness; **2.** hill (range); **~ы́шенный** [14] elevated, lofty.

возгл|авля́ть [28], ⟨~а́вить⟩ [14] (be at the) head.

во́згла|с *m* [1] exclamation, (out-)cry; **~ша́ть** [1], ⟨~си́ть⟩ [15 *e.*; -ашу́, -аси́шь; -ашённый] proclaim.

возд|ава́ть [5], ⟨~а́ть⟩ [-да́м, -да́шь, *etc. s.* дава́ть] reward; show, do; ~а́ть до́лжное do justice (to Д).

воздвиг|а́ть [1], ⟨∠нуть⟩ [21] erect, construct, raise.

возде́йств|ие *n* [12] influence, impact; **~овать** [7] (*im*)*pf.* (на В) influence; act upon, affect.

возде́л|ывать, ⟨~ать⟩ [1] till.

воздержа́ние *n* [12] abstinence; abstention.

возде́рж|анный [14 *sh.*] *s.* ~ный; **~иваться** [1], ⟨~а́ться⟩ [4] abstain (from от Р); при двух ~а́вшихся *pol.* with two abstentions; **~ный** [14; -жен, -жна] abstemious, temperate.

во́здух *m* [1] air; на (откры́том *or* све́жем) ~е in the open air, outdoors; **~опла́вание** *n* [12] aeronautics.

возду́ш|ный **1.** [14] air...; ~ная трево́га *f* air-raid warning; ~ные за́мки *m/pl.* castles in the air; **2.** [14; -шен, -шна] airy.

воззва́|ние *n* [12] appeal; proclamation; **~ть** *s.* взыва́ть.

вози́ть [15] drive, transport; **-ся** (с Т) busy o.s. (with), mess (around with); dawdle; fidget; romp, frolic.

возл|ага́ть [1], ⟨~ожи́ть⟩ [16] (на В) lay (on); entrust (with); ~ага́ть наде́жды на (В) rest one's hopes upon.

во́зле (Р) by, near, beside.

возложи́ть *s.* возлага́ть.

возлю́блен|ный [14] beloved; *m* lover; ~ная *f* mistress, sweetheart.

возме́здие *n* [12] requital.

возме|ща́ть [1], ⟨~сти́ть⟩ [15 *e.*; -ещу́, -ести́шь; -ещённый] com-

pensate, recompense; **~ще́ние** *n* [12] compensation, indemnification.
возмо́жн|о it is possible; possibly; о́чень ~о very likely; **~ость** *f* [8] possibility; chance; по (ме́ре) ~ости as ... (far) as possible; **~ый** [14; -жен, -жна] possible; сде́лать всё ~ое do one's utmost.
возмужа́лый [14] mature, virile.
возму|ти́тельный [14; -лен, -льна] revolting, shoking; **~ща́ть**, ⟨~ти́ть⟩ [15 *e.*; -щу́, -ути́шь] revolt; **-ся** be shocked *or* indignant (at T); **~ще́ние** *n* [12] indignation; revolt; **~щённый** [14] indignant.
вознагра|жда́ть [1], ⟨~ди́ть⟩ [15 *e.*; -ажу́, -ади́шь; -аждённый] reward, recompense, indemnify; **~жде́ние** *n* [12] reward, recompense.
возначе́ри|ваться [1], ⟨~ться⟩ [13] intend, decide.
вознес|е́ние *n* [12] ascension; **~ти́(сь)** *s.* возноси́ть(ся).
возник|а́ть [1], ⟨~нуть⟩ [21] arise, originate, emerge; **~нове́ние** *n* [12] rise, origin.
возн|оси́ть [15], ⟨~ести́⟩ [24 -с-: -су́, -сёшь; -нёс, -несла́; -несённый] raise, elevate; exalt; **-ся**, ⟨-сь⟩ **1.** rise; **2.** become haughty.
возня́ *f* [6] **1.** fuss, bustle, romp; **2.** trouble, bother.
возобнов|ле́ние *n* [12] renewal; resumption; **~ля́ть** [28], ⟨~и́ть⟩ [14 *e.*; -влю́, -ви́шь; -влённый] renew; resume.
возра|жать [1], ⟨~зи́ть⟩ [15 *e.*; -ажу́, -ази́шь] **1.** object (to про́тив Р); **2.** return, retort (to на В); (я) не ~жа́ю I don't mind; **~же́ние** *n* [12] objection; rejoinder.
во́зраст *m* [1] age (at в П); **~а́ние** *n* [12] growth, increase; **~а́ть** [1], ⟨~и́⟩ [24 -ст-: -расту́; -ро́с, -ла́; -ро́сший] grow up; increase, rise.
возро|жда́ть [1], ⟨~ди́ть⟩ [15 *e.*; -ожу́, -оди́шь; -ождённый] revive, regenerate (*v/i.*: **-ся**); **~жде́ние** *n* [12] rebirth, revival; эпо́ха ~жде́ния Renaissance.
во́зчик *m* [1] wag(g)oner, carter.
во́ин *m* [1] warrior, soldier; **~ский** [16] military; ~ская обя́занность († пови́нность) *f* conscription; **~ственный** [14] martial, bellicose.
вои́стину truly, really.
вой *m* [3] howl(ing), wail(ing).
во́йло|к *m* [1] **~чный** [14] felt.
войн|а́ *f* [5; *pl. st.*] war (at на П); warfare; идти́ на ~у́ take the field; поджига́тель ~ы́ warmonger; втора́я мирова́я ~а́ World War II.
во́йск|о *n* [9; *pl. e.*] host; army; *pl.* troops, (*land, etc.*) forces.
войти́ *s.* входи́ть.
вокза́л *m* [1] railroad (*Brt.* railway) station, depot.
вокру́г (Р) (a)round; верте́ться ~ да о́коло F beat about the bush.

вол *m* [1 *e.*] ox.
Во́лга *f* [5] Volga.
волды́рь *m* [4 *e.*] blister, swelling.
волейбо́л *m* [1] volleyball.
во́лей-нево́лей willy-nilly.
во́лжский [16] (on the) Volga...
волк *m* [1; *from g/pl. e.*] wolf; смотре́ть ~ом F scowl.
волн|а́ *f* [5; *pl. st., from dat. a. e.*] wave; ⚡ дли́нные, сре́дние, коро́ткие ~ы long, medium, short waves; **~е́ние** *n* [12] agitation, excitement, unrest; *pl.* troubles, riots; **~и́стый** [14 *sh.*] wavy, undulating; **~ова́ть** [7], ⟨вз-⟩ (**-ся** be) agitate(d), excite(d); worry; **~у́ющий** [17] exciting, thrilling.
воло́вий [18] ox...
Воло́дя *m* [6] *dim. of* Влади́мир.
волоки́т|а F [5] **1.** *f* red tape; a lot of fuss and trouble; **2.** *m* lady-killer, ladies' man; **~ство** *n* [9] flirtation.
волокн|и́стый [14 *sh.*] fibrous; **~о́** *n* [9; *pl.*: -о́кна, -о́кон, *etc. st.*] fiber, *Brt.* fibre.
волонтёр *m* [1] volunteer.
во́лос *m* [1; *g/pl.*: -ло́с; *from dat. e.*] (*a. pl.*) hair; **~а́тый** [14 *sh.*] hairy; **~о́к** *m* [1; -ска́] (small) hair; ⚡ filament; быть на ~о́к (*or* на ~ке́) от сме́рти F be on the verge (within a hair's breadth *or* ace) of death; висе́ть (*or* держа́ться) на ~ке́ hang by *or* on a thread.
во́лость *f* [8; *from g/pl. e.*] district.
волосяно́й [14] hair...
волочи́ть [16], ⟨по-⟩ drag, pull, draw; **-ся** drag o.s., crawl along; F (за Т) run after, court.
волхв *m* [1 *e.*] magician, wizard.
во́лчий [18] wolfish; wolf('s)...
волчо́к *m* [1; -чка́] top (*toy*).
волчо́нок *m* [2] wolf cub.
волше́б|ник *m* [1] magician; **~ница** *f* [5] sorceress; **~ный** [14] magic, fairy...; [-бен, -бна] *fig.* enchanting; **~ство́** *n* [9] magic, witchery.
волы́нка *f* [5 *g/pl.*; -нок] bagpipe.
вольно|ду́мец *m* [1; -мца] freethinker; **~слу́шатель** *m* [4] auditor, irregular student.
во́льн|ость *f* [8] liberty; freedom; **~ый** [14; -лен, -льна́, -о] free, easy, unrestricted; ⚔ ~о! at ease!
вольт *m* [1] volt.
вольфра́м *m* [1] wolframite.
во́л|я *f* [6] **1.** will; си́ла ~и will power; **2.** liberty, freedom; ~я ва́ша (just) as you like; по до́брой ~е of one's own will; отпусти́ть на ~ю set free; дать ~ю give free rein.
вон 1. F there; ~ там over there; **2.** ~! get out!; пошёл ~! out *or* away (with you)!; вы́гнать ~ turn out; ~ (оно́) что! F you don't say!; oh, that's it!
вонз|а́ть [1], ⟨~и́ть⟩ [15 *e.*; -нжу́,

-зи́шь; -зённый] thrust, plunge, transfix.
вон|ь *f* [8] stench, stink; **~ю́чий** [17 *sh.*] stinking; **~ю́чка** *f* [5; *g/pl.*: -чек] skunk; **~я́ть** [28] stink (of T).
вообра|жа́емый [14 *sh.*] imaginary, supposed; **~жа́ть** [1], ⟨~зи́ть⟩ [15 *e.*; -ажу́, -ази́шь; -ажённый] (*a.* ~жа́ть себе́) imagine, fancy; ~жа́ть себя́ imagine o. s. (s. b. T); ~жа́ть о себе́ be conceited; **~же́ние** *n* [12] imagination; fancy; **~зи́мый** [14 *sh.*] imaginable.
вообще́ generally, in general; at all.
воодушев|ле́ние *n* [12] enthusiasm; **~ля́ть** [28], ⟨~и́ть⟩ [14 *e.*; -влю́, -ви́шь; -влённый] (**-ся** feel) inspire(d by T).
вооруж|а́ть [1], ⟨~и́ть⟩ [16 *e.*; -жу́, -жи́шь; -жённый] **1.** arm, equip (with T); **2.** stir up (against про́тив P); **~е́ние** *n* [12] armament, equipment.
воо́чию with one's own eyes.
во-пе́рвых first(ly).
вопи́|ть [14 *e.*; -плю́, -пи́шь], ⟨за-⟩ cry out, bawl; lament, wail; **~ю́щий** [17] crying, flagrant.
вопло|ща́ть [1], ⟨~ти́ть⟩ [15 *e.*; -ощу́, -оти́шь; -ощённый] embody, personify; ~щённый *a.* incarnate; **~ще́ние** *n* [12] embodiment, incarnation.
вопль *m* [4] outcry, clamo(u)r; wail.
вопреки́ (Д) contrary to; in spite of.
вопро́с *m* [1] question; под ~ом questionable, doubtful; ~ не в э́том that's not the question; спо́рный ~ point at issue; что за ~! of course!; **~и́тельный** [14] interrogative; ~и́тельный знак *m* question mark.
вор *m* [1; *from g/pl. e.*] thief.
ворва́ться *s.* врыва́ться.
ворко|ва́ть [7], ⟨за-⟩ coo; **~тня́** F *f* [6] grumble.
вороб|е́й *m* [3 *e.*; -бья́] sparrow; ста́рый (*or* стре́ляный) ~е́й F cunning fellow; **~ьи́ный** [14] sparrow('s)...
ворова́ть [7], ⟨F c-⟩ steal; **~ка** *f* [5; *g/pl.*: -вок] (female) thief; **~ско́й** [16] thievish; thieves'...; **~ство́** *n* [9] theft, larceny.
ворожи́ть [16 *e.*; -жу́, -жи́шь], ⟨по-⟩ tell fortunes.
во́рон *m* [1] raven; **~а** *f* [5] crow; воро́н счита́ть F stand gaping about.
воро́нка *f* [5; *g/pl.*: -нок] **1.** funnel; **2.** crater.
вороно́й [14] black; *su.* *m* black horse.
во́рот *m* [1] **1.** collar; **2.** windlass; **~а** *n/pl.* [9] gate; **~и́ть** [15] **1.** (*pf.*) F *cf.* возвраща́ть; **2.** (*impf.*) P move, roll; turn off, round; **3.** *s.* воро́чать **2.**; **~ни́к** *m* [1 *e.*] collar; **~ничо́к** *m* [1; -чка] (small) collar.
во́рох *m* [1; *pl.*: -ха́, *etc. e.*] pile, heap.
воро́|чать [1] **1.** *s.* ~ти́ть **2.**; **2.** F manage, boss (T); **-ся** toss; turn; stir; **~ши́ть** [16 *e.*; -шу́, -ши́шь; -шённый] turn (over).
ворч|а́ние *n* [12] grumbling, growl; **~а́ть** [4 *e.*; -чу́, -чи́шь], ⟨за-, п(р)о-⟩ grumble, growl; **~ли́вый** [14 *sh.*] grumbling, surly; **~у́н** F *m* [1 *e.*], **~у́нья** *f* [6] grumbler.
восвоя́си F home.
восемна́дца|тый [14] eighteenth; **~ть** [35] eighteen; *s.* пять, пя́тый.
во́семь [35; восьми́, *instr.* восемью́] eight; *cf.* пять & пя́тый; **~десят** [35; восьми́десяти] eighty; **~со́т** [36; восьмисо́т] eight hundred; **~ю** eight times.
воск *m* [1] wax.
воскл|ица́ние *n* [12] exclamation. **~ица́тельный** [14] exclamatory; ~ица́тельный знак *m* exclamation mark *or* point; **~ица́ть** [1], ⟨~и́кнуть⟩ [20] exclaim.
восково́й [14] wax(en)...
воскр|еса́ть [1], ⟨~е́снуть⟩ [21] rise (from из P); recover; Христо́с ~е́с(е)! Christ has arisen! (*Easter greeting*); (*reply*:) вои́стину ~е́с(е)! (He has) truly arisen!; **~есе́ние** *n* [12] Resurrection; **~есе́нье** *n* [10] Sunday (on: в В, *pl.* по Д); **~еша́ть** [1], ⟨~еси́ть⟩ [15 *e.*; -ешу́, -еси́шь; -ешённый] resuscitate, revive.
воспал|е́ние *n* [12] inflammation; ~е́ние лёгких (по́чек) pneumonia (nephritis); **~ённый** [14 *sh.*] inflamed; **~и́тельный** [14] inflammatory; **~я́ть** [28], ⟨~и́ть⟩ [13] inflame (*v/i.* **-ся**).
воспе|ва́ть [1], ⟨~ть⟩ [-пою́, -поёшь; -пе́тый] sing of, praise.
воспит|а́ние *n* [12] education, upbringing; **~анник** *m* [1], **~анница** *f* [5] foster child; pupil; **~анный** [14 *sh.*] well-bred; пло́хо ~анный ill-bred; **~а́тель** *m* [4] educator; (private) tutor; **~а́тельный** [14] educational, pedagogic(al); **~ывать** [1], ⟨~а́ть⟩ bring up; educate.
воспламен|я́ть [28], ⟨~и́ть⟩ [13] inflame (*v/i.* **-ся**).
восполн|я́ть [28], ⟨~ить⟩ [13] fill (up); make up (for).
воспо́льзоваться *s.* по́льзоваться.
воспомина́ние *n* [12] remembrance, recollection, reminiscence; *pl. a.* memoirs.
воспре|ща́ть [1], ⟨~ти́ть⟩ [15 *e.*; -ещу́, -ети́шь; -ещённый] prohibit, forbid; вход ~щён! no entrance!; кури́ть ~ща́ется! no smoking!; **~ще́ние** *n* [12] interdiction, prohibition.
воспри|и́мчивый [14 *sh.*] sensitive; susceptible (to к Д); **~нима́ть** [1], ⟨~ня́ть⟩ [-приму́, -и́мешь; -и́нял, -а́, -о; -и́нятый] take (up); conceive; **~я́тие** *n* [12] perception.

воспроизв|еде́ние *n* [12] reproduction; **~оди́ть** [15], ⟨~ести́⟩ [25] reproduce.
воспря́нуть [20] *pf.* rise, jump up; ~ ду́хом cheer up.
воссоедин|е́ние *n* [12] reun(ification)ion; **~я́ть** [28], ⟨~и́ть⟩ [13] reunite.
восста|ва́ть [5], ⟨**~**ть⟩ [-ста́ну, -ста́нешь] (a)rise; revolt.
восстан|а́вливать [1], ⟨~ови́ть⟩ [14] **1.** reconstruct, restore; **2.** stir up, dispose **~ие** *n* [12] insurrection, revolt; **~ови́ть** *s.* ~а́вливать; **~овле́ние** *n* [12] reconstruction, restoration.
восто́к *m* [1] east; ♀ the East, Orient; Бли́жний (Да́льний) ♀ the Near (Far) East; на ~ (to[ward] the) east, eastward(s); на ~е in the east; с ~а from the east; к ~у от (Р) (to the) east of.
восто́р|г *m* [1] delight, rapture; я в ~ге I am delighted (with от Р); приводи́ть (приходи́ть) в ~г = **~га́ть(ся)** [1] *impf.* (be) delight(ed) (with Т); **~женный** [14 *sh.*] enthusiastic, exalted.
восто́чный [14] east(ern, -erly); oriental.
востре́бова|ние *n* [12]: до ~ния poste restante; **~ть** [7] *pf.* call for.
восхвал|е́ние *n* [12] praise, eulogy; **~я́ть** [28], ⟨~и́ть⟩ [13; -алю́, -а́лишь] praise, extol.
восхи|ти́тельный [14; -лен,-льна] delightful; **~ща́ть** [1], ⟨~ти́ть⟩ [15 *e.*; -ищу́, -ити́шь; -ищённый] delight, transport; **-ся** (Т) be delighted (with), admire; **~ще́ние** *n* [12] admiration, delight; приводи́ть (приходи́ть) в ~ще́ние *s.* ~ща́ть(ся).
восхо́|д *m* [1], **~жде́ние** *n* [12] rise; ascent; ~д со́лнца sunrise; **~ди́ть** [15], ⟨взойти́⟩ [взойду́, -дёшь; взошёл, -шла́; взоше́дший] rise, ascend.
восше́ствие *n* [12] ascent; ~ на престо́л accession to the throne.
восьм|ёрка *f* [5; *g/pl.*: -рок] eight (*cf.* дво́йка); **~еро** [37] eight (*cf.* дво́е).
восьми|деся́тый [14] eightieth; *cf.* пя́т(идеся́т)ый; **~ле́тний** [14] of eight, aged 8; **~со́тый** [14] eight hundredth; **~часово́й** [14] eight-hour...
восьм|о́й [14] eighth; *cf.* пя́тый; **~у́шка** *f* [5] eighth of lb.; octavo.
вот here (is); there; now; well; that's ...; ~ и всё F that's all; ~ (оно́) как *or* что! you don't say!, is that so?; ~ те(бе) ра́з *or* на́! there you are!; a pretty business this!; ~ како́й ... such a ...; ~ челове́к! what a man!; ~-~! yes, indeed; ~-~ every *or* (at) any moment.
воткну́ть *s.* втыка́ть.
во́тум *m* [1] vote.
во́тчина *f* [5] patrimony (*estate*).
воцар|я́ться [28], ⟨~и́ться⟩ [13] **1.** accede to the throne; **2.** set in; be restored.
вошь *f* [8; вши; во́шью] louse.
вощи́ть [16 *e.*], ⟨на-⟩ wax.
вою́ющий [17] belligerent.
впа|да́ть [1], ⟨~сть⟩ [25; впал, -а] (в В) fall (flow, run) in(to); **~де́ние** *n* [12] flowing into; mouth, confluence; **~дина** *f* [5] cavity, socket; **~лый** [14] hollow, sunken; **~сть** *s.* ~да́ть.
впервы́е for the first time.
вперего́нки́ F *s.* наперего́нки́.
вперёд forward, ahead (of Р), on (-ward); in future; in advance, beforehand; *s. a.* зад.
впереди́ in front, ahead (of Р) before.
вперемё́жку F alternately.
впер|я́ть [28], ⟨~и́ть⟩ [13] fix (one's eyes on взор в В).
впечатл|е́ние *n* [12] impression; **~и́тельный** [14; -лен, льна] sensitive.
впи|ва́ть [1], ⟨~ть⟩ [вопью́, -пьёшь; впил, -а́, -о] suck in, imbibe; **-ся** (в В) cling to; seize; stick; fix.
впи́с|ывать [1], ⟨~а́ть⟩ [3] enter, insert.
впи́т|ывать [1], ⟨~а́ть⟩ soak up *or* in; absorb, imbibe; **~ь** *s.* впива́ть.
впи́х|ивать [1], *once* ⟨~ну́ть⟩ [20] push *or* squeeze in(to) (в В).
вплавь by swimming.
впле|та́ть [1], ⟨~сти́⟩ [25 -т-: вплету́, -тёшь] interlace, braid.
вплот|ну́ю (к Д) (quite) close(ly) by, (right) up to; *fig.* F seriously; **~ь** (к Д) (right) up to; even (till).
вполго́лоса in a low voice.
вполз|а́ть [1], ⟨~ти́⟩ [24] creep *or* crawl in(to), up.
вполне́ quite, fully, entirely.
впопа́д F to the point, relevantly.
впопыха́х *s.* второпя́х.
впо́ру: быть ~ fit.
впосле́дствии afterward(s), later.
впотьма́х in the dark.
впра́вду F really, indeed.
вправ|ля́ть [28], ⟨~ить⟩ [14] set.
впра́ве: быть ~ have the right.
впра́во (to the) right.
впредь henceforth, in future.
впро́голодь starv(el)ing.
впрок **1.** for future use; **2.** to a p.'s benefit; э́то ему́ ~ не пойдёт he won't profit by it.
впро́чем by the way; however.
впры́г|ивать [1], *once* ⟨~нуть⟩ [20] jump in(to) *or* on; (в, на В).
впры́с|кивание *n* [12] injection; **~кивать** [1], *once* ⟨~нуть⟩ [20] inject.
впря|га́ть [1], ⟨~чь⟩ [26 г/ж; *cf.* напря́чь] harness, put to (в В).
впус|к *m* [1] admission; **~ка́ть** [1], ⟨~ти́ть⟩ [15] let in, admit.
впусту́ю F in vain, to no purpose.
впу́т|ывать [1], ⟨~ать⟩ entangle,

involve (in в В); **-ся** become entangled.
впя́тер|о five times (*cf.* вдвóе); **~óм** five (together).
враг *m* [1 *e.*] enemy; † devil.
враж|дá *f* [5] enmity; **~дéбность** *f* [8] animosity; **~дéбный** [14; -бен, -бна] hostile; **~довáть** [7] be at enmity (with с T); **∠еский** [16], **∠ий** [18] (the) enemy('s)...
вразбрóд F separately, scatteringly.
вразрéз: идтú ~ be contrary (to с T).
вразум|и́тельный [14; -лен, -льна] intelligible, clear; **~ля́ть** [1], ⟨~и́ть⟩ [13] bring to reason; instruct, make wise.
врá|ль F *m* [4 *e.*] liar; tattler; **~ньё** *n* [12] lies, fibs *pl.*, idle talk.
врас|плóх unawares, by surprise; **~сыпну́ю:** брóситься ~сыпну́ю disperse.
враст|áть [1], ⟨~ú⟩ [24 -ст-: -сту́; врос, -лá] grow in(to); settle *or* subside.
вратáрь *m* [4 *e.*] goalkeeper.
врать F [вру, врёшь; врал, -á, -о], ⟨со-⟩ [сóвранный], lie; make a mistake; be inaccurate; tell (tales).
врач *m* [1 *e.*] doctor, physician; **~éбный** [14] medical.
вращ|áть [1] (В *or* T) turn, revolve, rotate (*v/i.* **-ся**; -ся в П associate with); ~áющийся revolving, rotatory; **~éние** *n* [12] rotation.
вред *m* [1 *e.*] harm, damage; detriment; **~и́тель** *m* [4] ✓ pest; saboteur; **~и́тельство** *n* [9] sabotage; **~и́ть** [15 *e.*; -ежу́, -еди́шь], ⟨по-⟩ (do) harm, (cause) damage (to Д); **∠ный** [14; -ден, -днá, -о] harmful, injurious (to Д *or* для Р).
врез|áть [1], ⟨∠ать⟩ [3] (в В) cut in(to); lay *or* put in(to); **-ся** run in(to); project into; impress (on).
врéмен|ный [14] temporary, transient, provisional; **~щи́к** *m* [1 *e.*] favo(u)rite, minion.
врéм|я *n* [13] time; *gr.* tense; weather; ~я гóда season; во ~я (Р) during; в настоя́щее ~я at (the) present (moment); от ~ени до ~ени, по ~енáм, ~енáми from time to time, (every) now and then, sometimes; в скóром ~ени soon; в то (же) ~я at that (the same) time; в то ~я как whereas; за послéднее ~я lately, recently; на ~я for a (certain) time, temporarily; in (*the long*) run; со ~енем in the course of time; тем ~енем meanwhile; скóлько ~ени? how long?; what's the time?; хорошó провести́ ~я have a good time; **~яисчислéние** *n* [12] chronology; **~я(пре)провождéние** *n* [12] pastime.
врóвень even, abreast (with с T).
врóде like; such as; kind of.
врождённый [14 *sh.*] innate.
вроз(н)ь separately, apart.
врун F *m* [1 *e.*], **∠ья** F *f* [6] lier.
вруч|áть [1], ⟨~и́ть⟩ [16] hand over; entrust.
вры|вáть [1], ⟨~ть⟩ [22] dig in; **-ся,** ⟨ворвáться⟩ [-ву́сь, -вёшься; -вáлся, -лáсь] rush in(to); enter (by force).
вряд: ~ ли hardly, scarcely.
всáдни|к *m* [1] horseman; **~ца** *f* [5] horsewoman.
всá|живать [1], ⟨~ди́ть⟩ [15] thrust *or* drive in(to), hit; **~сывать** [1], ⟨всосáть⟩ [-су́, -сёшь] suck in *or* up, imbibe.
всё, все *s.* весь.
все|вéдущий [17] omniscient; **~возмóжный** [14] of all kinds *or* sorts.
всегдá always; **~шний** [15] constant, habitual.
всегó (-ˈvɔ) altogether, in all; sum total; ~ (тóлько, лишь, -нáвсего) only, merely; прéжде ~ above all.
всел|éнная *f* [14] universe, world; **~я́ть** [28], ⟨~и́ть⟩ [13] settle, move in(to) (*v/i.* **-ся**); *fig.* inspire.
все|мéрный every (*or* all) ... possible; ~мéрно in every possible way; **~ми́рный** [14] world..., universal; **~могу́щий** [17 *sh.*] = ~си́льный; **~нарóдный** [14; -ден, -дна] national, nation-wide; *adv.:* ~нарóдно in public; **∠нощная** *f* [14] vespers *pl.*; **~óбщий** [17] universal, general; **~объéмлющий** [17 *sh.*] universal; **~росси́йский** [16] All-Russian.
всерьёз F in earnest, seriously.
все|си́льный [14; -лен, -льна] omnipotent, almighty; **~сою́зный** [14] All-Union, ... of the U.S.S.R.; **~сторóнний** [15] all-round.
всё-таки nevertheless, (but) still.
всеуслы́шание: во ~ in public.
всецéло entirely, wholly.
вскá|кивать [1], ⟨вскочи́ть⟩ [16] jump *or* leap (up/on на В); start (from с Р); F rise *or* swell; **~пывать,** ⟨вскопáть⟩ [1] dig up.
вскарáбк|иваться, ⟨~аться⟩ [1] (на В) climb (up).
вскáрмливать [1], ⟨вскорми́ть⟩ [14] raise, rear *or* bring up.
вскачь at full gallop.
вскип|áть [1], ⟨~éть⟩ [10 *e.*; -плю́, -пи́шь] boil (up); *fig.* fly into a passion.
всклó(кó)|чивать [1], ⟨~чить⟩ [16] tousle; ~ченные *or* ~чившиеся вóлосы *m/pl.* dishevel(l)ed hair.
всколы́х|ивать [1], ⟨~áть⟩ [3 *st.* & 1], *once* ⟨~нуть⟩ [20] stir up, rouse.
вскользь in passing, cursorily.
вскопáть *s.* вскáпывать.
вскóре soon, before long.
вскорми́ть *s.* вскáрмливать.
вскочи́ть *s.* вскáкивать.
вскри́|кивать [1], ⟨~чáть⟩ [4 *e.*

-чу́, -чи́шь], *once* ⟨~кнуть⟩ [20] cry out, scream.

вскружи́ть [16; -жу́, -у́жи́шь] *pf.*; ~ (Д) го́лову turn a p.'s head.

вскры|ва́ть [1], ⟨~ть⟩ [22] **1.** open; reveal; **2.** dissect; **-ся 1.** open; be disclosed; **2.** break (up); **ʼтие** *n* [12] **1.** opening; disclosure; **2.** dissection, autopsy; **3.** breaking up.

всласть F to one's heart's content.

вслед (за T; Д) (right) after, behind, following; **ʼствие** (P) in consequence of, owing to; ʼствие э́того consequently.

вслепу́ю F blindly, at random.

вслух aloud.

вслу́ш|иваться [1], ⟨~аться⟩ (в B) listen attentively (to).

всма́триваться [1], ⟨всмотре́ться⟩ [9; -отрю́сь, -о́тришься] (в B) peer, look narrowly (at).

всмя́тку: яйцо́ ~ soft-boiled egg.

всо́|вывать [1], ⟨всу́нуть⟩ [20] put, slip (into в B); **~са́ть** *s.* вса́сывать.

вспа́|хивать [1], ⟨~ха́ть⟩ [3] plow (*Brt.* plough) *or* turn up; **~шка** *f* [5] tillage.

всплес|к [1] splash; **ʼкивать** [1], ⟨~ну́ть⟩ [20] splash; ~ну́ть рука́ми throw up one's arms.

всплы|ва́ть [1], ⟨~ть⟩ [23] rise to the surface, emerge.

всполоши́ть F [16 *e.*; -шу́, -ши́шь; -шённый] *pf.* startle (*v/i.* **-ся**).

вспом|ина́ть [1], ⟨ʼнить⟩ [13] (B *or* о П) remember, recall; (Д + **-ся** = И + *vb.*); **~ога́тельный** [14] auxiliary; **~яну́ть** P [19] = ʼнить.

вспорхну́ть [20] *pf.* fly up.

вспры́г|ивать [1], *once* ⟨~нуть⟩ [20] jump *or* spring (up/on на B).

вспры́с|кивать [1], ⟨~нуть⟩ [20] sprinkle; wet; inject.

вспу́г|ивать [1], *once* ⟨~ну́ть⟩ [20] start, frighten away.

вспух|а́ть [1], ⟨ʼнуть⟩ [21] swell.

вспыл|и́ть F [13] *pf.* get angry; **ʼьчивость** *f* [8] irascibility; **ʼьчивый** [14 *sh.*] quick-tempered.

вспы́|хивать [1], ⟨~хнуть⟩ [20] **1.** flare up, flash; blush; **2.** burst into a rage; break out; **~шка** *f* [5; *g/pl.*: -шек] flare, flash, outburst, outbreak.

вста|ва́ть [5], ⟨~ть⟩ [вста́ну, -нешь] stand up; get up, rise (from с P); arise; **ʼвка** *f* [5; *g/pl.*: -вок] setting in, insertion, inset; **~вля́ть** [28], ⟨ʼвить⟩ [14] set *or* put in, insert; **~вно́й** [14] (to be) put in; ~вны́е зу́бы *m/pl.* false teeth.

встрепену́ться [20] *pf.* start, shudder, shake up.

встрёпк|а P *f* [5] reprimand; зада́ть ~у (Д) P bowl out, blow up (a p).

встре́|тить(ся) *s.* ~ча́ть(ся); **~ча** *f* [5] meeting, encounter; reception; тёплая ~ча warm welcome; **~ча́ть** [1], ⟨~тить⟩ [15 *st.*] **1.** meet (*v/t.*, with B), encounter; come across; **2.** meet, receive, welcome; ~ча́ть Но́вый год celebrate the New Year; **-ся 1.** meet (*v/i.*, o. a., with с T); **2.** (*impers.*) occur, happen; there are (were); **~чный** [14] counter..., (coming from the) opposite (direction), (s. b. *or* s. th.) on one's way; пе́рвый ~чный the first comer.

встря́|ска *f* [5; *g/pl.*: -сок] **1.** F shock; **2.** P = встрёпка; **~хивать** [1], *once* ⟨~хну́ть⟩ [20] shake (up); stir (up); (**-ся** *v/i.*, o. s.).

вступ|а́ть [1], ⟨~и́ть⟩ [14] (в B) enter, join; set one's foot, step (into); begin, enter *or* come into, assume; ~и́ть в брак contract marriage; ~и́ть на трон accede to the throne; **-ся** (за B) intercede (for), protect; take a p.'s side; **~и́тельный** [14] introductory; opening; entrance...; **~ле́ние** *n* [12] entry, entrance; accession; beginning; introduction.

всу́|нуть *s.* всо́вывать; **~чивать** F [1], ⟨~чи́ть⟩ [16] foist (s.th. on B/Д).

всхлип *m* [1], **ʼывание** *n* [12] sob(bing); **ʼывать** [1], *once* ⟨ʼнуть⟩ [20 *st.*] sob.

всход|и́ть [15], ⟨взойти́⟩ [взойду́, -дёшь; взошёл, -шла́; взоше́дший; *g. pt.*: взойдя́] **1.** go *or* climb ([up]on на B), ascend, rise; come up, sprout; **2.** = входи́ть; **ʼы** *m/pl.* [1] standing *or* young crops.

всхрапну́ть F [20] *pf.* nap.

всып|а́ть [1], ⟨ʼать⟩ [2 *st.*] pour *or* put (into в B); P thrash (a p. Д).

всю́ду everywhere, all over.

вся́|кий [16] **1.** any, every; any-, everybody (*or* -one); **2.** = **~ческий** [16] all kinds *or* sorts of, sundry; every possible; ~чески in every way; ~чески стара́ться take great pains; **~чина** F *f* [5]: ~кая ~чина whatnot(s), hodgepodge.

вта́|йне in secret; **~лкивать** [1], ⟨втолкну́ть⟩ [20] push *or* shove in(to); **~птывать** [1], ⟨втопта́ть⟩ [3] tramp(le) in(to); **~скивать** [1], ⟨~щи́ть⟩ [16] pull *or* drag in, up.

вте|ка́ть [1], ⟨~чь⟩ [26] flow in(to).

втере́ть *s.* втира́ть.

вти|ра́ть [1], ⟨втере́ть⟩ [12; вотру́, -рёшь; втёр] rub in; worm; ~ра́ть очки́ (Д) throw dust in (p.'s) eyes; **-ся** F worm into; **ʼскивать** [1], ⟨ʼснуть⟩ [20] press *or* squeeze in.

втихомо́лку F on the quiet.

втолкну́ть *s.* вта́лкивать.

втоптать *s.* вта́птывать.

втор|га́ться [1], ⟨ʼгнуться⟩ [21] (в B) intrude, invade, penetrate; meddle (with); **~же́ние** *n* [12] invasion, incursion; **ʼить** [13] ♪ sing (*or* play) the second part; echo, repeat; **~и́чный** [14] second, repeated; secondary; ~и́чно once more,

for the second time; **ꙇник** *m* [1] Tuesday (on: во В, *pl.*: по Д); **~óй** [14] second; upper; из ~ы́х рук second hand; *cf.* пéрвый & пя́тый; **~оку́рсник** *m* [1] sophomore.
второпя́х in a hurry, being in a great haste, hastily.
второстепéнный [14; -éнен, -éнна] secondary, minor.
в-трéтьих third(ly).
втри́дорога F very dearly.
втрó|е three times (as ..., *comp.*; *cf.* вдвóе); *vb.* + ~е *a.* treble; **~ём** three (of us, *etc.*, *or* together); **~ййнé** three times (as much, *etc.*), trebly.
втуз *m* [1] (вы́сшее техни́ческое учéбное заведéние *n*) technical college, institute of technology.
вту́лка *f* [5; *g/pl.*: -лок] plug.
втунé in vain; without attention.
втыкáть [1], ⟨воткну́ть⟩ [20] put *or* stick in(to).
втя́|гивать [1], ⟨~ну́ть⟩ [19] draw *or* pull in(to), on; envolve, engage; **-ся** (в В) fall in; enter; (become) engage(d) in; get used (to).
вуáль *f* [8] veil.
вуз *m* [1] (вы́сшее учéбное заведéние *n*) university, college; **ꙇовец** *m* [1; -вца] college student.
вулкáн *m* [1] volcano; **~и́ческий** [16] volcanic.
вульгáрный [14; -рен, -рна] vulgar.
вход *m* [1] entrance; плáта за ~ entrance *or* admission fee.
входи́ть [15], ⟨войти́⟩ [войду́, -дёшь; вошёл, -шлá; вошéдший; *g. pt.*: войдя́] (в В) enter, go, come *or* get in(to); go in(to), have room *or* hold; run into (*debts, etc.*); penetrate into; be included in; ~ во вкус (Р) take a fancy to; ~ в довéрие (ми́лость) к (Д) gain a p.'s confidence (favo[u]r); ~ в положéние (Р) appreciate a p.'s position; ~ в привы́чку *or* быт (послóвицу) become a habit (proverbial); ~ в (состáв [Р]) form part (of), belong (to).
входнóй [14] entrance..., admission...
вцеп|ля́ться [28], ⟨~и́ться⟩ [14] (в В) grasp, catch hold of.
ВЦСПС (Всесою́зный Центрáльный Совéт Профессионáльных Сою́зов) the All-Union Central Council of Trade Unions.
вчерá yesterday; **~шний** [15] yesterday's, (of) yesterday.
вчернé in the rough; in a draft.
вчéтверо four times (as ..., *comp.*; *cf.* вдвóе); **ꙇм** four (of us, *etc.*).
вчи́т|ываться [1], ⟨~áться⟩ (в В) become absorbed in *or* familiar with s.th. by reading.
вшéстеро six times (*cf.* вдвóе).
вши|вáть [1], ⟨~ть⟩ [вошью́, -шьёшь; *cf.* шить] sew in(to); **ꙇвый** [14] lousy; **~ть** *s.* ~вáть.

въе|дáться [1], ⟨ꙇсться⟩ [*cf.* есть[1]] eat (in[to]).
въе|зд *m* [1] entrance, entry; ascent; разрешéние на ~зд entry permit; **~зжáть** [1], ⟨ꙇхать⟩ [въéду, -дешь; въезжáй(те)!] enter, ride *or* drive in(to), up/on (в, на В); move in(to); **ꙇсться** *s.* ~дáться.
вы [21] you (*polite form a.* 2); ~ с ним you and he; у вас (был) ... you have (had) ...
вы́б|áлтывать F [1], ⟨ꙇолтать⟩ blab *or* let out; **~егáть** [1], ⟨ꙇежать⟩ [4; вы́бегу, -ежишь] run out; **~ивáть** [1], ⟨ꙇить⟩ [вы́бью, -бьешь, *etc.*, *cf.* бить] **1.** beat *or* knock out; break; smash; drive out; hollow out; **2.** stamp, coin; **-ся** break out *or* forth; -ся из сил be(come) exhausted, fatigued; -ся из колей come off the beaten track; **~ирáть** [1], ⟨ꙇрать⟩ [вы́беру, -решь; -бранный] choose, pick out; elect; take out; find; **-ся** get out; move (out); **ꙇить** *s.* ~ивáть.
вы́бор *m* [1] choice, selection; на ~ (*or* по ~у) at a p.'s discretion; random (*test*); *pl.* election(s); всеóбщие ~ы *pl.* general election; дополни́тельные ~ы by-election; **~ка** *f* [5; *g/pl.*: -рок] selection; *pl.* excerpts; **~ный** [14] electoral; *su.* delegate.
вы́бр|áсывать [1], ⟨~осить⟩ [15] throw (out *or* away); thrust (out); discard *or* dismiss; exclude, omit; strand; ~áсывать (зря) дéньги waste money; **-ся** throw o. s. out; **~ать** *s.* выбирáть; **~ить** [-ею, -еешь; -итый] *pf.* shave clean; (*v/i.* **-ся**); **~осить** *s.* ~áсывать.
вы́б|ывáть [1] ⟨ꙇыть⟩ [-уду, -удешь] leave, withdraw, drop out.
выв|áливать [1], ⟨ꙇалить⟩ [13] discharge, throw out; P stream; **-ся** fall out; stream out; **~áривать** [1], ⟨ꙇарить⟩ [13] extract; boil down; **~éдывать**, ⟨ꙇедать⟩ [1] find out, (try to) elicit; **ꙇезти** *s.* ~ози́ть; **~ёртывать** [1], ⟨ꙇернуть⟩ [20] unscrew; tear out; dislocate; turn (inside out); *v/i.* **-ся**; slip out, extricate o. s.
вы́вес|ить *s.* вывéшивать; **~ка** *f* [5; *g/pl.*: -сок] sign(board); **~ти** *s.* выводи́ть.
выв|éтривать [1], ⟨ꙇетрить⟩ [13] (remove by) air(ing); **-ся** weather; **~éшивать** [1], ⟨ꙇесить⟩ [15] hang out *or* put up; **~и́нчивать** [1], ⟨ꙇинтить⟩ [15] unscrew.
вы́вих *m* [1] dislocation; **~нуть** [20] *pf.* dislocate, sprain (one's ... себé В).
вы́вод *m* [1] **1.** withdrawal; **2.** breeding, cultivation; **3.** derivation, conclusion; сдéлать ~ draw a conclusion; **~и́ть** [15], ⟨вы́вести⟩ [25] **1.** take, lead *or* move (out, to);

2. derive, conclude; 3. hatch; cultivate; 4. construct; 5. remove, extirpate; 6. write *or* draw carefully; 7. depict; ~ить (В) из себя́ make s. b. lose his temper; **-ся**, ‹-сь› disappear; **~ок** *m* [1; -дка] brood.

вы́воз *m* [1] export(s); **~и́ть** [15], ‹вы́везти› [24] remove, get *or* take *or* bring out; export; **~но́й** [14] export...

выв|ора́чивать F [1], ‹~оротить› [15] = вывёртывать, вы́вернуть.

выг|а́дывать, ‹~адать› [1] gain *or* save (s. th. from В/на П).

вы́гиб *m* [1] bend, curve; **~а́ть** [1], ‹вы́гнуть› [20] arch, curve.

вы́гля|деть [11 *st.*] *impf.* look (s. th. Т, like как); как она́ ~дит? what does she look like?; он ~дит моло́же свои́х лет he doesn't look his age; **~дывать** [1], *once* ‹~нуть› [20 *st.*] look *or* peep out (of в В, из Р).

вы́гнать *s.* выгоня́ть.

вы́гнуть *s.* выгиба́ть.

выгов|а́ривать [1], ‹'~орить› [13] 1. pronounce; utter; 2. F stipulate; 3. *impf.* F (Д) rebuke; **'~ор** *m* [1] 1. pronunciation; 2. reproof, reprimand.

вы́год|а *f* [5] profit; advantage; **~ный** [14; -ден, -дна] profitable; advantageous (to Д, для Р).

вы́гон *m* [1] pasture; **~я́ть** [28], ‹вы́гнать› [вы́гоню, -нишь] turn *or* drive out; expel *or* fire.

выгор|а́живать [1], ‹'~одить› [15] enclose; P exculpate, free from blame; **~а́ть** [1], ‹'~еть› [9] 1. burn down; 2. fade; 3. F click, come off.

выгр|ужа́ть [1], ‹~узить› [15] unload; discharge; disembark; (*v/i.* -ся); **~узка** [5; *g/pl.*: -зок] unloading; disembarkation.

выдава́ть [5], ‹вы́дать› [-дам, -дашь, *etc. cf.* дать] 1. give (out), pay (out); distribute; 2. draw *or* issue; 3. betray; 4. extradite; ~ (себя́) за (В) [make] pass (o.s. off) for; ~ (за́муж) за (В) give (*a girl*) in marriage to; **-ся** 1. stand out; 2. F happen *or* turn out.

выд|а́вливать [1], ‹~авить› [14] press *or* squeeze out; **~а́лбливать** [1], ‹~олбить› [14] hollow out.

вы́да|ть *s.* ~ва́ть; **~ча** *f* [5] 1. distribution; delivery; payment; 2. issue; grant; 3. betrayal; 4. extradition; день ~чи зарпла́ты payday; **~ю́щийся** [17; -щегося, *etc.*] outstanding, distinguished.

выдви|га́ть [1], ‹'~нуть› [20] 1. pull out; 2. put forward, propose, promote; **-ся** 1. step forth, move forward; 2. project; 3. advance; 4. *impf. s.* ~жно́й; **~же́нец** *m* [1; -нца] promoted worker; **~жно́й** [14] pull-out..., sliding.

выд|еле́ние *n* [12] separation, detachment; discharge, secretion; **~елка** *f* [5; *g/pl.*: -лок] manufacture; workmanship; **~е́лывать,** ‹~елать› [1] work, make; elaborate; curry (*leather*); **~еля́ть** [28], ‹~елить› [13] 1. separate, detach; 2. mark (out); emphasize; 3. ⚖ allot; satisfy (*coheirs*); 4. ⚕ secrete; 5. ⚗ evolve; **-ся** *v/i.* 1,4; stand out, come forth; rise above, excel; **~ёргивать,** ‹~ернуть› [20] pull out.

выде́рж|ивать [1], ‹'~ать› [4] stand, bear, endure; pass (*exam.*); observe (*size, etc.*); '~ать хара́ктер be firm; '~анный self-restrained; consistent; mature; **'~ка** *f* [5; *g/pl.*: -жек] 1. self-control; 2. extract, quotation 3. *phot.* exposure; на '~ку at random.

выд|ира́ть F [1], ‹~рать› [-деру, -ерешь] tear out; pull; *pf.* thrash; **~олбить** *s.* ~а́лбливать; **~охнуть** *s.* ~ыха́ть; **~ра** *f* [5] otter; **~рать** *s.* ~ира́ть; **~умка** *f* [5; *g/pl.*: -мок] invention; **~у́мывать,** ‹~умать› [1] invent, contrive, devise.

выд|ыха́ть [1], ‹~охнуть› [20] breathe out; **-ся** become stale; *fig.* exhaust o.s.

вы́езд *m* [1] departure; drive, ride; exit; gateway; visit.

выезжа́ть[1] [1], ‹вы́ехать› [вы́еду, -едешь; -езжа́й(те)!] *v/i.* (из, с Р) 1. leave, depart; 2. drive *or* ride out, on(to); 3. (re)move (from); 4. (begin to) visit (*social affairs, etc.*); ~[2] *a.* **вые́зживать** [1], ‹вы́ездить› [15] *v/t.* break in (*a horse*).

вы́емка *f* [5; *g/pl.*: -мок] excavation; hollow.

вы́ехать *s.* выезжа́ть.

вы́ж|ать *s.* ~има́ть; **~дать** *s.* ~ида́ть; **~ива́ть** [1], ‹~ить› [-иву, -ивешь; -итый] survive; go through; stay; F oust; ~ить из ума́ be in one's dotage; **~ига́ть** [1], ‹~ечь› [26 г/ж: -жгу, -жжешь, -жгут; -жег, жгла; -жженный] burn out, down *or* in; brand; **~ида́ть** [1], ‹~дать› [-жду, -ждешь; -жди (-те)!] (Р *or* В) wait for *or* till (after); **~има́ть** [1], ‹~ать› [-жму, -жмешь; -жатый] squeeze, press *or* wring out; *sport* lift; **~ить** *s.* ~ива́ть.

вы́звать *s.* вызыва́ть.

выздор|а́вливать [1], ‹'~оветь› [10] recover; **~а́вливающий** [17] convalescent; **~овле́ние** *n* [12] recovery.

вы́з|ов *m* [1] call; summons; invitation; challenge; **~у́бривать** [1] = зубри́ть; **~ыва́ть** [1], ‹~вать› [-ову, -овешь] 1. call (to; for *thea.*; up *tel.*; [up]on *pupil*); send for; 2. summon (to к Д; before a court в суд); 3. challenge (to на В); 4. rouse, cause; evoke; **-ся** undertake *or* offer; **~ыва́ющий** [17] defiant, provoking.

выи́гр|ывать, ⟨'~ать⟩ [1] win (from у P), gain, benefit; **'~ыш** *m* [1] win(ning[s]), gain(s); prize; profit; быть в '~ыше have won (profited); **'~ышный** [14] advantageous, profitable; lottery...
вы́йти *s.* выходи́ть.
вык|а́зывать F [1], ⟨~азать⟩ [3] show, prove; display; **~а́лывать** [1], ⟨~олоть⟩ [17] put out; cut out; **~а́пывать,** ⟨~опать⟩ [1] dig out *or* up; **~ара́бкиваться,** ⟨~арабкаться⟩ [1] scramble *or* get out; **~а́рмливать** [1], ⟨~ормить⟩ [14] bring up, rear, breed; **~а́тывать** [1] **1.** ⟨~атать⟩ [1] mangle; roll; **2.** ⟨~атить⟩ [15] push *or* move out; ~атить глаза́ P stare.
выки́|дывать [1], *once* ⟨'~инуть⟩ [20] **1.** throw out *or* away, discard; omit; strand; stretch (out); **2.** hoist (up); **3.** miscarry; **4.** F play (*trick*); **'~идыш** *m* [1] miscarriage, abortion.
вы́кл|адка *f* [5; *g/pl.*: -док] laying out, spreading; exposition; border, trimming; computation, calculation; ⚔ outfit; **~а́дывать** [1], ⟨вы́ложить⟩ [16] **1.** take *or* lay out, spread; set forth; **2.** border; **3.** brick *or* mason; **4.** compute.
выкликáть [1] call up(on *or*, F, out).
выключ|а́тель *m* [4] ⚡ switch; **~а́ть** [1], ⟨'~ить⟩ [16] **1.** switch *or* turn off; stop; **2.** exclude; **~е́ние** *n* [12] switching off, stopping.
вык|о́вывать [1], ⟨~овать⟩ [7] forge; *fig.* mo(u)ld; **~ола́чивать** [1], ⟨~олотить⟩ [15] beat *or* knock out; dust; P exact (*debts, etc.*); **~олоть** *s.* ~а́лывать; **~опать** *s.* ~а́пывать; **~ормить** *s.* ~а́рмливать; **~орчёвывать** [1], ⟨~орчевать⟩ [7] root up *or* out.
выкр|а́ивать [1], ⟨~оить⟩ [13] cut out; F hunt (up), spare; **~а́шивать** [1], ⟨~асить⟩ [15] paint, dye; **~и́кивать** [1], *once* ⟨~икнуть⟩ [20] cry *or* call (out); **~оить** *s.* ~аивать; **~ойка** *f* [5; *g/pl.*: -оек] pattern.
выкр|ута́сы F *m/pl.* [1] flourishes, scrolls; dodges, subterfuges; **~у́чивать** [1], ⟨~утить⟩ [15] twist; wring (out); F unscrew; **-ся** F slip out.
вы́куп *m* [1] redemption; ransom; **~а́ть**[1] [1], ⟨~ить⟩ [14] redeem; ransom; **~ать**[2] *s.* купа́ть.
выку́р|ивать [1], ⟨'~ить⟩ [13] **1.** smoke (out); **2.** distill.
выл|а́вливать [1], ⟨~овить⟩ [14] fish out *or* up; **~азка** *f* [5; *g/pl.*: -зок] **1.** ⚔ sally; **2.** excursion, outing; **~а́мывать,** ⟨~омать⟩ [1] break out.
выл|еза́ть [1], ⟨~езть⟩ [24] climb *or* get out; fall out (*hair*); **~епля́ть** [28], ⟨~епить⟩ [14] model.
вы́лет *m* [1] ✈ start, taking off; flight; **~а́ть** [1], ⟨~еть⟩ [11] fly out; ✈ start, take off (for в B); rush out *or* up; fall out; slip (a p.'s memory ~еть из головы́).
выл|е́чивать [1], ⟨~ечить⟩ [16] cure, heal (*v/i.* **-ся**); **~ива́ть** [1] ⟨~ить⟩ [-лью, -льешь; *cf.* лить] pour (out); **~итый** [14] poured out; ⊕ cast; F just like (s. b. И).
вы́л|овить *s.* ~а́вливать; **~ожить** *s.* выкла́дывать; **~омать** *s.* ~а́мывать; **~упля́ть** [28], ⟨~упить⟩ [14] shell; **-ся** hatch.
вым|а́зывать [1], ⟨~азать⟩ [3] smear; soil (**-ся** o.s.) (with T); **~а́ливать** [1], ⟨~олить⟩ [13] get *or* obtain by entreaties; **~а́нивать** [1], ⟨~анить⟩ [13] lure (out of из P); coax *or* cheat (a p. out of s. th. у P/B); **~а́ривать** [1], ⟨~орить⟩ [13] extirpate; ~а́ривать го́лодом starve (out); **~а́рывать,** ⟨~арать⟩ [1] **1.** soil; **2.** delete, cross out; **~а́чивать** [1], ⟨~очить⟩ [16] drench, soak *or* wet; **~а́щивать** [1], ⟨~остить⟩ [15] pave; **~е́нивать** [1], ⟨~енять⟩ [28] exchange (for на B); **~ереть** *s.* ~ира́ть; **~ета́ть** [1], ⟨~ести⟩ [25 -т- *st.*: -ету, -етешь] sweep (out); **~еща́ть** [1], ⟨~естить⟩ [15] avenge o.s. (on Д); vent (on p. на П); **~ира́ть** [1], ⟨~ереть⟩ [12] die out, become extinct.
вымога́т|ельство *n* [9] blackmail, extortion; **~ь** [1] extort (s.th. from B *or* P/у P).
вым|ока́ть [1], ⟨~окнуть⟩ [21] wet through, get wet; **~олвить** [14] *pf.* utter, say; **~олить** *s.* ~а́ливать; **~орить** *s.* ~а́ривать; **~остить** *s.* ~а́щивать; **~очить** *s.* ~а́чивать.
вы́мпел *m* [1] pennant, pennon.
вым|ыва́ть [1], ⟨~ыть⟩ [22] wash (out, up); ~ыть го́лову (Д) F bawl out, blow up; **~ысел** *m* [1; -сла] invention; falsehood; **~ыть** *s.* ~ыва́ть; **~ышля́ть** [28], ⟨~ыслить⟩ [15] invent; **~ышленный** *a.* fictitious.
вы́мя *n* [13] udder.
вын|а́шивать [1], ⟨~осить⟩ [15] **1.** wear out; **2.** evolve, bring forth; **3.** train; **4.** nurse; **~ести** *s.* ~оси́ть.
вын|има́ть [1], ⟨~уть⟩ [20] take *or* draw out, produce.
вын|оси́ть[1] [15], ⟨~ести⟩ [24 -с-: -су, -сешь; -с, -сла] **1.** carry *or* take out (away), remove; transfer; **2.** endure, bear; **3.** acquire; **4.** submit; express (*gratitude*); pass (*a.* ⚖); **~осить**[2] *s.* ~а́шивать; **~оска** *f* [5; *g/pl.*: -сок] marginal note, footnote; **~о́сливость** *f* [8] endurance; **~о́сливый** [14 *sh.*] enduring, sturdy, hardy, tough.
вын|ужда́ть [1], ⟨~удить⟩ [15] force, compel; extort (s. th. from B/у *or* от P); **~ужденный** [14 *sh.*] forced; of necessity.

вы́нырнуть [20] *pf.* emerge.
вы́па|д *m* [1], **~де́ние** *n* [12] falling out; *fenc.* lunge; *fig.* thrust, attack; **~да́ть** [1], ⟨**~сть**⟩ [25] **1.** fall *or* drop (out); slip out; **2.** fall (to Д, *a.* на до́лю to a p.'s share *or* lot), devolve on; **3.** lunge.
вып|а́ливать [1], ⟨**~́алить**⟩ [13] blurt out; F shoot (with из P); **~а́лывать** [1], ⟨**~́олоть**⟩ [17] weed (out); **~а́ривать** [1], ⟨**~́арить**⟩ [13] steam; evaporate.
вып|eка́ть [1], ⟨**~́ечь**⟩ [26] bake; **~ива́ть** [1], ⟨**~́ить**⟩ [-пью, -пьешь; *cf.* пить] drink (up); F booze; **~́ить** (ли́шнее) F overdrink o.s.; **~́ить** ча́шку ча́ю have a cup of tea; **~́ивка** F *f* [5; *g/pl.*: -вок] booze; **~́ивший** [17] drunk; tipsy.
вы́п|иска *f* [5; *g/pl.*: -сок] **1.** writing out, copying; **2.** extract; ⚕ statement (of account из счёта); **3.** order, subscription; **4.** discharge; notice of departure; **~и́сывать** [1], ⟨**~́исать**⟩ [3] **1.** write out (*or* down); copy; **2.** *s.* выводи́ть 6.; **3.** order, subscribe; **4.** discharge, dismiss; **-ся** register one's departure; -ся из больни́цы leave hospital.
вы́пла|вка *f* [5] smelting; **~кать** [3] *pf.* weep (one's eyes глаза́) out; F obtain by weeping; **~та** *f* [5] payment; **~́чивать** [1], ⟨**~тить**⟩ [15] pay (out *or* off).
выпл|ёвывать [1], *once* ⟨**~́юнуть**⟩ [20] spit out; **~ёскивать** [1] ⟨**~́ескать**⟩ [3], *once* ⟨**~́еснуть**⟩ [20] dash *or* splash (out).
выпл|ыва́ть [1], ⟨**~́ыть**⟩ [23] emerge, come out, appear.
выпол|а́скивать [1], ⟨**'~оскать**⟩ [3] rinse; gargle; **~за́ть** [1], ⟨**'~зти**⟩ [24] creep or crawl out; **~не́ние** *n* [12] fulfil(l)ment, execution, realization; **~ня́ть** [1], ⟨**'~нить**⟩ [13] carry out, fulfil(l); make (up); **'~оть** *s.* выпа́лывать.
вы́пр|авка *f* [5; *g/pl.*: -вок] **1.** correction; **2.** carriage (*of a soldier*); **~авля́ть** [28], ⟨**~авить**⟩ [14] set right *or* straight; correct; **~а́шивать** [1], ⟨**~осить**⟩ [15] (try to) obtain by request; **~ова́живать** F [1], ⟨**~оводить**⟩ [15] see out; **2.** turn out; **~ы́гивать** [1], ⟨**~ыгнуть**⟩ [20] jump out *or* off; **~яга́ть** [1], ⟨**~ячь**⟩ [26 г/ж: -ягу, -яжешь; -яг] unharness; **~ямля́ть** [28], ⟨**~ямить**⟩ [14] straighten; **-ся** erect o.s.
вы́пуклый [14] convex; prominent; *fig.* expressive, distinct.
вы́пуск *m* [1] letting out; omission; ⊕ output; ⚕ issue; publication; instal(l)ment; (age) class of graduates; **~а́ть** [1], ⟨вы́пустить⟩ [15] let out (*or* go); ⚖ release; ⊕ produce; issue; publish; omit, leave out; graduate; ~а́ть в прода́жу put on sale; **~ни́к** *m* [1 *e.*] graduate; **~но́й** [14] graduate ..., graduation ..., final, leaving; ⊕ discharge-...; outlet ...
вып|у́тывать, ⟨**~́утать**⟩ [1] disentangle *or* extricate (o. s. **-ся**); **~у́чивать** [1], ⟨**~́учить**⟩ [16] **1.** bulge; **2.** P *s.* тара́щить.
вып|ы́тывать, ⟨**~́ытать**⟩ [1] find out, (try to) elicit.
выпя́|ливать P [1], ⟨**'~лить**⟩ [13] *s.* тара́щить; **~чивать** F [1], ⟨**'~тить**⟩ [15] protrude.
выраб|а́тывать, ⟨**'~отать**⟩ [1] manufacture, produce; elaborate, work out; develop; earn, make; **'~отка** *f* [5; *g/pl.*: -ток] manufacture, production; output, performance; elaboration.
выр|а́внивать [1], ⟨**~́овнять**⟩ [28] level, ⊕ plane; smooth (*a. fig.*); **-ся** straighten; ⚔ dress; develop, grow up.
выра|жа́ть [1], ⟨**'~зить**⟩ [15] express, show; ~жа́ть слова́ми put into words; **~же́ние** *n* [12] expression; **~зи́тельный** [14; -лен, -льна] expressive; F significant.
выр|аста́ть [1], ⟨**~́асти**⟩ [24 -ст-: -асту; *cf.* расти́] **1.** grow (up); increase; develop into; **2.** emerge, appear; **~а́щивать** [1], ⟨**~́астить**⟩ [15] grow; breed; bring up; *fig.* train; **~́вать 1.** *s.* **~**ыва́ть[1]; **2.** *s.* рвать 3.
вырез|а́ть [1], ⟨**'~ать**⟩ [15] **1.** cut out, clip; **2.** carve; engrave; **3.** slaughter; **'~ка** *f* [5; *g/pl.*: -зок] cutting (out), clipping; carving; engraving; tenderloin; **~но́й** [14] carved.
вы́ро|док *m* [1; -дка] degenerate; monster; **~жда́ться** [1], ⟨**~диться**⟩ [15] degenerate; **~жде́ние** *n* [12] degeneration.
вы́ро|нить [13] *pf.* drop; **~сший** [17] grown.
выр|уба́ть [1], ⟨**~́убить**⟩ [14] **1.** cut down *or* fell; **2.** cut out *or* carve; **~уча́ть** [1], ⟨**~́учить**⟩ [16] **1.** help, rescue, relieve; redeem; **2.** ⚕ gain; **~́учка** *f* [5] rescue, relief, help (to на В); ⚕ proceeds.
выр|ыва́ть[1] [1], ⟨**~́вать**⟩ [-ву, -вешь] **1.** pull out; tear out; **2.** snatch away; extort (s.th. from a p. В/у Р); **-ся** break away, rush (out); escape; **~ыва́ть**[2], ⟨**~́ыть**⟩, [22] dig out, up.
вы́с|адка *f* [5; *g/pl.*: -док] disembarkation, landing; **~а́живать** [1], ⟨**~адить**⟩ [15] **1.** land, disembark; **2.** help out; make *or* let a p. get out; **3.** (trans)plant; **-ся** = 1. *v/i.*; *a.* get out, off.
выс|а́сывать [1], ⟨**~́осать**⟩ [-осу, -осешь] suck out; **~ве́рливать** [1], ⟨**~́верлить**⟩ [13] bore, drill; **~вобожда́ть** [1], ⟨**~́вободить**⟩ [15] free.

выс|ева́ть [1], ⟨∠еять⟩ [27] sow; **~ека́ть** [1], ⟨∠ечь⟩ [26] **1.** hew, carve; strike (*fire*); **2.** *s.* сечь²; **~еле́ние** *n* [12] expulsion, eviction; transfer; **~еля́ть** [28], ⟨∠елить⟩ [13] expel, evict; transfer, move; **∠еять** *s.* ~е́ивать; **~и́живать** [1], ⟨∠идеть⟩ [11] sit (out), stay; hatch.

выск|а́бливать [1], ⟨∠облить⟩ [13] scrub clean; erase; **~а́зывать** [1], ⟨∠азать⟩ [3] express, tell, give; **-ся** express o.s.; express one's opinion, thoughts, *etc.* (about о П); declare o.s. (for за В; against про́тив Р); **~а́кивать** [1], ⟨∠очить⟩ [16] jump, leap *or* rush out; **~а́льзывать, ~ользáть** [1], ⟨∠ользнуть⟩ [20] slip out; **∠облить** *s.* ~а́бливать; **∠очить** *s.* ~а́кивать; **∠очка** *m/f* [5; *g/pl.:* -чек] upstart; F forward pupil; **~реба́ть** [1], ⟨∠рести⟩ [25 -б-; *cf.* скрести́] scrub clean; scratch out.

вы́сл|ать *s.* высыла́ть; **~е́живать** [1], ⟨~едить⟩ [15] track down; **~у́живать** [1], ⟨~ужить⟩ [16] F serve; obtain by *or* for service; **-ся** advance, rise; insinuate o.s.; **~у́шивать,** ⟨~ушать⟩ [1] listen (to), hear; ⚕ auscultate.

высм|е́ивать [1], ⟨∠еять⟩ [27] deride, ridicule.

выс|о́вывать [1], ⟨∠унуть⟩ [20 *st.*] put out; **-ся** lean out.

высо́кий [16; высо́к, -а́, -со́ко́; *comp.*: вы́ше] high; tall (*a.* ~ ро́стом); *fig.* lofty.

высоко|благоро́дие *n* [12] (Right) Hono[u]r(able); **~ка́чественный** [14] (of) high quality; **~квалифици́рованный** [14] highly skilled; **~ме́рие** *n* [12] haughtiness; **~ме́рный** [14; -рен, -рна] haughty, arrogant; **~па́рный** [14; -рен, -рна] bombastic, high-flown; **~превосходи́тельство** *n* [9] Excellency; **~уважа́емый** [14] dear (*polite address*).

вы́сосать *s.* выса́сывать.

высо|та́ *f* [5; *pl.:* -о́ты, *etc. st.*] height; (✈, *astr.*, *geogr.*) altitude; hill; level; *fig.* climax; ~то́й в (В) ... *or* ... в ~ту́ ... high.

вы́сох|нуть *s.* высыха́ть; **~ший** [17] dried up, withered.

выс|очáйший [17] highest; supreme, imperial; **~о́чество** *n* [9] Highness; **∠паться** *s.* высыпа́ться.

вы́спренний [15] bombastic.

вы́став|ить *s.* ~ля́ть; **~ка** *f* [5; *g/pl.:* -вок] exhibition, show; **~ля́ть** [28], ⟨~ить⟩ [14] **1.** put (take) out, put forward (*a. fig.*); **2.** exhibit, display, expose; (re)present (o.s. себя́); **3.** mark, provide (*with date, no.*); ⚔ post; P turn out; ~ля́ть напока́з show off; **-ся** come out, emerge; **~очный** [14] (of the) exhibition, show...

выстр|а́ивать(ся) [1] *s.* стро́ить(-ся); **∠ел** *m* [1] shot; (*noise*) report; на (расстоя́ние, -ии) ∠ел(а) within gunshot; **∠елить** *s.* стреля́ть.

высту́к|ивать, ⟨'~ать⟩ F [1] strike, [tap; ⚕ percuss.]

вы́ступ *m* [1] projection; **~а́ть** [1], ⟨~ить⟩ [14] **1.** step forth, forward; come *or* stand out; appear; **2.** set out, march off; **3.** speak (sing, play) in public; ~а́ть с ре́чью (в пре́ниях) deliver a speech (take the floor); ~а́ть в похо́д ⚔ take the field; **~ле́ние** *n* [12] **1.** appearance; **2.** departure; *pol.* speech, declaration; *thea.* performance, turn.

вы́сунуть(ся) *s.* высо́вывать(ся).

высу́ш|ивать [1], ⟨'~ить⟩ [16] dry (up); drain, *fig.* exhaust.

вы́сш|ий [17] highest, supreme; higher (*a. educ.*), superior; ~ая ме́ра наказа́ния supreme penalty, capital punishment.

выс|ыла́ть [1], ⟨∠лать⟩ [вы́шлю, -лешь] send forward; send out, away; banish; **∠ылка** *f* [15] dispatch; exile; **~ыпа́ть** [1], ⟨∠ыпать⟩ [2] pour out *or* in, on; *v/i.* swarm forth, out; **~ыпа́ться** [1], ⟨вы́спаться⟩ [-сплюсь, -спишься] sleep one's fill (*or* enough), have a good night's rest; **~ыха́ть** [1], ⟨∠охнуть⟩ [21] dry up, wither; **~ь** *f* [8] height.

выт|а́лкивать, F ⟨∠олкать⟩ [1], *once* ⟨∠олкнуть⟩ [20 *st.*] push out; **~а́пливать** [1], ⟨∠опить⟩ [14] **1.** heat; **2.** melt (down); **~а́скивать** [1], ⟨∠ащить⟩ [16] take *or* pull out; F pilfer.

выт|ека́ть [1], ⟨∠ечь⟩ [26] flow out; *fig.* follow, result; **∠ереть** *s.* ~ира́ть; **∠ерпеть** [14] *pf.* endure, bear; F не ∠ерпел couldn't help; **~есня́ть** [28], ⟨∠еснить⟩ [13] force, push out; oust, expel; **∠ечь** *s.* ~ека́ть.

выт|ира́ть [1], ⟨∠ереть⟩ [12] dry, wipe (o. s. **-ся**); wear out.

вы́точенный [14] well-turned.

вы́тр|ебовать [7] *pf.* ask for, demand, order, summon; obtain on demand; **~яса́ть** [1], ⟨∠ясти⟩ [24 -с-] shake out.

выть [22], ⟨вз-⟩ howl.

выт|я́гивать [1], ⟨∠януть⟩ [20 *st.*] draw, pull *or* stretch (out); drain; F elicit; endure, bear; **-ся** stretch, extend (o.s.); ⚔ come to attention; F grow (up); **∠яжка** *f* [5] drawing, stretching (out); ⚗ extract; на ∠яжку ⚔ at attention.

выу́|живать [1], ⟨'~дить⟩ [15] fish out (*a. fig.*).

выу́ч|ивать [1], ⟨'~ить⟩ [16] learn, memorize; (В + *inf. or* Д) teach (a p. to ... *or* s.th.); **-ся** learn (s.th. from Д/у Р).

вых|а́живать F [1], ⟨∠одить⟩ [15] **1.** rear, bring up; nurse, restore to

health; **2.** go (all) over, through; **~ва́тывать** [1], ⟨**~**ватить⟩ [15] snatch away, from, out; snap up, off.
вы́хлоп *m* [1] exhaust; **~но́й** [14] exhaust...; **~отать** [1] *pf.* obtain.
вы́ход *m* [1] **1.** exit; way out (*a. fig.*); outlet; **2.** departure; withdrawal, retirement; **3.** appearence, publication; *thea.* entrance (*on the stage*), performance; **4.** yield, output; ~ за́муж marriage (*of women*); ~ в отста́вку retirement, resignation; **~ец** *m* [1; -дца] immigrant, native of; come *or* originate from.
выходи́ть[1] [15], ⟨вы́йти⟩ [вы́йду, -дешь; вы́шел, -шла; вы́шедший; вы́йдя] **1.** go *or* come out, leave; get out, off; withdraw, retire; **2.** appear, be published *or* issued; **3.** come off; turn out, result; happen, arise, originate; **4.** spend, use up, run out of; ✝ become due; F вы́шло! it's clicked!; вы́йти в офице́ры rise to the rank of an officer; ~ в отста́вку (на пе́нсию) retire, resign; ~ за преде́лы (P) transgress the bounds of; ~ (за́муж) за (B) marry (*v/t.*; *of women*); ~ из себя́ be beside o.s.; ~ из терпе́ния lose one's temper (patience); окно́ выхо́дит на у́лицу the window faces the street; ~ из стро́я fall out, be out of action; из него́ вы́шел ... he has become ...; из э́того ничего́ не вы́йдет nothing will come of it.
вы́ход|ить[2] *s.* выха́живать; **~ка** [5; *g/pl.:* -док] trick, prank; excess; **~но́й** [14] exit...; outlet...; holiday-...; festive; **~но́й** день *m* holiday, day off; (have one's быть T).
вы́холенный [14] well-groomed.
выцве|та́ть [1], ⟨'**~**сти⟩ [25 -т-: -ету] fade, wither.
выч|ёркивать [1], ⟨**~**еркнуть⟩ [20] strike out, obliterate; **~ёрпывать**, ⟨**~**ерпать⟩ [1], *once* ⟨**~**ерпнуть⟩ [20 *st.*] scoop; dredge (out); **~есть** *s.* **~**ита́ть; **~ет** *m* [1] deduction.
вычисл|е́ние *n* [12] calculation; **~я́ть** [1], ⟨'**~**ить⟩ [13] calculate, compute.
вы́чи|стить *s.* **~**ща́ть; **~та́емое** *n* [14] subtrahend; **~та́ние** *n* [12] subtraction; **~та́ть** [1], ⟨вы́честь⟩ [25 -т-: -чту; -чел, -чла; *g. pt.*: вы́чтя] deduct; ⅍ subtract; **~ща́ть** [1], ⟨**~**стить⟩ [15] clean, scrub, brush, polish.
вы́чурный [14; -рен, -рна] ornate, flowery; fanciful.
вы́швырнуть [20 *st.*] *pf.* turn out.
вы́ше higher; above; beyond; он ~ меня́ he is taller than I (am); э́то ~ моего́ понима́ния that's beyond my reach.
вы́ше... above..., afore...
выш|иба́ть F [1], ⟨**~**ибить⟩ [-бу, -бешь; -б, -бла; -бленный] knock *or* throw out; **~ива́ние** *n* [12] embroidery; **~ива́ть** [1], ⟨**~**ить⟩ [-шью, -шьешь] embroider; **~ивка** *f* [5; *g/pl.:* -вок] embroidery.
вышина́ *f* [5] height; *cf.* высота́.
вы́шка *f* [5; *g/pl.:* -шек] tower.
выяв|ля́ть [28], ⟨'**~**ить⟩ [14] discover, uncover, reveal.
выясн|е́ние *n* [12] clarification; **~я́ть** [28], ⟨'**~**ить⟩ [13] clear up, find out, ascertain; **-ся** turn out; come to light.
вью|га *f* [5] snowstorm; **~к** *m* [1] pack, bale, load; **~н** *m* [1 *e.*] loach (*fish*); **~чить** [16], ⟨на-⟩ load; **~чный** [14] pack...; **~щийся** [17] curly; **~**щееся расте́ние *n* creeper.
вя́жущий [17] astringent.
вяз *m* [1] elm.
вяза́н|ка *f* [5; *g/pl.:* -нок] fag(g)ot; '**~ый** [14] knitted; **~ье** *n* [10] (*a.* **~ие** *n* [12]) knitting; crochet.
вяз|а́ть [3], ⟨с-⟩ **1.** tie, bind (together); **2.** knit; (крючко́м) crochet; **-ся** *impf.* match, agree, be in keeping; F make sense; work (well), get on; **~кий** [16; -зок, -зка́, -о] viscous, sticky; swampy, marshy; **~нуть** [21], ⟨за-, у-⟩ sink in, stick.
вя́лить [13], ⟨про-⟩ dry, sun.
вя́|лый [14 *sh.*] withered, faded; flabby; *fig.* sluggish; dull (*a.* ✝); **~нуть** [20], ⟨за-, у-⟩ wither, fade; droop, flag.

Г

г *abbr.*: грамм.
г. *abbr.:* **1.** год; **2.** го́род; **3.** господи́н.
га 1. ha(h)!; **2.** *abbr.*: гекта́р.
Гаа́га *f* [5] The Hague.
Гава́нна *f* [5] **1.** Havana; **2.** ♀ Havana cigar.
га́вань *f* [8] harbo(u)r.
Гаври|и́л *m* [1], P **~ла** [5] Gabriel.
га́га *f* [5] *zo.* eider.
гад *m* [1] reptile (*a. fig.*).
гада́|лка *f* [5; *g/pl.:* -лок] fortuneteller; **~ние** *n* [12] fortunetelling; guessing, conjecture; **~ть** [1] **1.** ⟨по-⟩ tell fortunes; (by cards на ка́ртах); **2.** *impf.* guess, conjecture.
га́д|ина F *f* [5] = гад; **~ить** [15] **1.** ⟨на-, за-⟩ F soil; (Д) P harm; **2.** ⟨из-⟩ P spoil, botch; **~кий** [16; -док, -дка́, -о] nasty, ugly, disgusting, repulsive; **~ли́вый** [14 *sh.*] squeamish; **~ость** F *f*[8] vermin; villainy, ugly thing (act, word); **~ю́ка** *f* [5] *zo.* viper (*a.*, P, *fig.*), adder.
газ *m* [1] **1.** gas; свети́льный ~

coal gas; дать ~ *mot.* step on the gas; на по́лном ~е (~у́) at full speed (throttle); *pl.* ⚕ flatulences; **2.** gauze.
газе́ль *f* [8] gazelle.
газе́т|а *f* [14] newspaper; **~ный** [14] news...; ~ный киоск *m* newsstand, *Brt.* news stall; **~чик** *m* [1] newsman, newsboy.
газиро́ван|ный [14]: ~ная вода́ *f* soda water.
га́з|овый [14] **1.** gas...; ~овый счётчик *m* = ~оме́р; ~овая педа́ль *f mot.* accelerator (pedal); **2.** gauze...; **~оме́р** *m* [1] gas meter; **~о́метр** *m* [1] gasometer.
газо́н *m* [1] lawn.
газо|обра́зный [14; -зен, -зна] gaseous; **~прово́д** *m* [1] gas pipe line.
га́йка *f* [5; *g/pl.:* га́ек] ⊕ nut.
галантер|е́йный [14]: ~е́йный магази́н *m* notions store, *Brt.* haberdashery; ~е́йные това́ры *m/pl.* = **~е́я** *f* [6] notions *pl.*, dry goods *pl.*, *Brt.* fancy goods *pl.*
галд|ёж P *m* [1 *e.*] row, hubbub; **~е́ть** P [11], ⟨за-⟩ clamo(u)r, din.
гал|ере́я *f* [6] gallery; **~ёрка** F *f* [5] *thea.* gallery.
галифе́ *pl. indecl.* ⚔ breeches.
га́лка *f* [5; *g/pl.:* -лок] jackdaw.
гало́п *m* [1] gallop; ~ом at a gallop; **~и́ровать** [7] gallop.
гало́ши *f/pl.* [5] galoshes, rubbers.
га́лстук *m* [1] (neck)tie.
галу́н *m* [1 *e.*] galloon, braid.
гальван|изи́ровать [7] *(im)pf.* galvanize; **~и́ческий** [16] galvanic.
га́лька *f* [5; *g/pl.:* -лек] pebble.
гам F *m* [1] din, row, rumpus.
гама́к *m* [1 *e.*] hammock.
гама́ши *f/pl.* [5] gaiters.
га́мма *f* [5] ♪ scale; range.
ган|гре́на ⚕ *f* [5] gangrene; **~дика́п** *m* [1] handikap; **~те́ли** (-ˈtɛ-) *f/pl.* [8] dumbbells.
гара́ж *m* [1 *e.*] garage.
гарант|и́ровать [7] *(im)pf.*, **~́ия** *f* [7] guarantee, warrant.
гардеро́б *m* [1] wardrobe; (*a.* **~ная** *f* [14]) check-, cloakroom; **~щик** *m* [1], **~щица** *f* [5] cloakroom attendant.
гарди́на *f* [5] curtain.
гармо́|ника *f* [5] (*kind of*) accordion; губна́я ~ника mouth organ, harmonica; **~ни́ровать** [20] harmonize, be in harmony (with с T); **~ни́ст** *m* [1] accordionist; harmonist; **~ни́ческий** [16] harmonic; *a.* = **~ни́чный** [14; -чен, -чна] harmonious; **~ния** *f* [7] harmony; F *a.* = **~нь** F *f* [8], **~шка** *f* [5; *g/pl.:* -шек] = ~ника.
гарни|зо́н *m* [1] garrison; **~́р** *m* [1], **~́ровать** [7] *(im)pf., cook.* garnish; **~ту́р** *m* [1] set.
гарпу́н *m* [1 *e.*], **~ить** [13] harpoon.
гарцева́ть [7] prance.
гарь *f* [8] (s. th.) burnt, char.
гаси́ть [15], ⟨по-, за-⟩ extinguish, put *or* blow out; slake.
га́снуть [21], ⟨по-, у-⟩ go out, die away; *fig.* fade, wither.
гастрол|ёр *m* [1] guest actor *or* artist, star; **~и́ровать** [7] tour, give performance(s) on a tour; **~́ь** *f* [8] starring (performance).
гастроно́м *m* [1] **1.** gastronome(r); gourmet; **2.** *a.* = ~и́ческий магази́н *m* delicatessen, (dainty) food store *or* shop; **~и́ческий** [16] gastronomic(al); *cf.* ~ **2.**; **~ия** *f* [7] gastronomy; dainties, delicacies *pl.*
гауптва́хта *f* [5] guardhouse.
гвалт F *m* [1] rumpus, din.
гвард|е́ец *m* [1; -е́йца] guardsman; **~́ия** *f* [7] Guards *pl.*
гвозд|ик *dim. of* ~ь, *cf.* ; **~и́ка** *f* [5] carnation, pink; (*spice*) clove; **~ь** *m* [4 *e.*; *pl.:* гво́зди, -де́й] nail; *fig.* main feature, hit.
гг. *or* **г.г.** *abbr.:* **1.** го́ды; **2.** господа́.
где where; F *s.* куда́ F; ~-~ = ко́е-где́, *cf.*; *cf.* ни; ~ F = **~́-либо, ~́-нибудь, ~́-то** any-, somewhere; ~́-то здесь hereabout(s).
ГДР *cf.* герма́нский.
гей! F heigh!
гекта́р *m* [1] hectare.
гектоли́тр *m* [1] hectoliter.
ге́ли|й *m* [3] helium; **~копте́р** (-ˈtɛ) *m* [1] *s.* вертолёт; **~отерапи́я** *f* [7] heliotherapy.
генеало́гия *f* [7] genealogy.
генера́|л *m* [1] general; ~л-майо́р *m* major general; **~льный** [14] general; ~льная репети́ция *f* dress rehearsal; **~тор** *m* [1] generator.
ген|иа́льный [14; -лен, -льна] of genius; ingenious; **~́ий** *m* [3] genius.
гео́|граф *m* [1] geographer; **~графи́ческий** [16] geographic(al); **~гра́фия** *f* [7] geography; **~лог** *m* [1] geologist; **~ло́гия** *f* [7] geology; **~ме́трия** *f* [7] geometry.
Гео́рг|ий *m* [3] George; **2и́н(а** *f* [5]) *m* [1] dahlia.
гера́нь *f* [8] geranium.
Гера́сим *m* [1] Gerasim (*m. name*).
герб *m* [1 *e.*] (coat of) arms; emblem; **~́овый** [14] stamp(ed).
Герма́н|ия *f* [7] Germany; Федерати́вная Респу́блика ~ии (ФРГ) Federal Republic of Germany; **2ский** [16] German; ~ская Демократи́ческая Респу́блика (ГДР) German Democratic Republic (*Eastern Zone of Germany*).
гермети́ческий [16] hermetic.
геро|и́зм *m* [1] heroism; **~и́ня** *f* [6] heroine; **~и́ческий** [16] heroic; **~́й** *m* [3] hero; **~́йский** [16] heroic.
ге́тры *f/pl.* [5] gaiters.
г-жа *abbr.:* госпожа́.
гиаци́нт *m* [1] hyacinth.
ги́бель *f* [7] ruin, destruction; loss;

⚓ wreck; death; P immense number, lots of; **~ный** [14; -лен, -льна] disastrous, fatal.
ги́бк|ий [16; -бок, -бка́, -о] supple, pliant, flexible (*a. fig.*); **~ость** *f* [8] flexibility.
ги́б|лый P [14] ruinous; **~нуть** [21], ⟨по-⟩ perish.
Гибралта́р *m* [1] Gibraltar.
гига́нт *m* [1] giant; **~ский** [16] gigantic, huge.
гигие́н|а *f* [5] hygiene; **~и́ческий** [16], **~и́чный** [14; -чен, -чна] hygienic.
гид *m* [1] guide.
гидравли́ческий [16] hydraulic.
гидро|пла́н, ~самолёт *m* [1] seaplane, hydroplane; **~(электро)ста́нция** *f* [7] hydroelectric power station.
гие́на *f* [5] hyena.
гик *m* [1], **∠анье** *n* [10] whoop(ing).
ги́льза *f* [5] (*cartridge*) case; shell.
Гимала́и *m/pl.* [3] The Himalayas.
гимн *m* [1] hymn; anthem.
гимна|зи́ст *m* [1] pupil *of* **∠зия** *f* [7] high school, *Brt.* grammar school; **∠ст** *m* [1] gymnast; **~стёрка** *f* [5; *g/pl.*: -рок] ⚔ blouse, *Brt.* tunic; **∠стика** *f* [5] gymnastics; **~сти́ческий** [16] gymnastic.
гипе́рбол|а *f* [5] hyperbole; ⅍ hyperbola; **~и́ческий** [16] hyperbolic, exaggerated.
гипно́|з *m* [1] hypnosis; **~тизи́ровать** [7], ⟨за-⟩ hypnotize.
гипо́теза *f* [5] hypothesis.
гиппопота́м *m* [1] hippopotamus.
гипс *m* [1] *min.* gypsum; ⊕ plaster of Paris; **∠овый** [14] gypsum..., plaster...
гирля́нда *f* [5] garland.
ги́ря *f* [6] weight.
гита́ра *f* [5] guitar.
глав|а́ [5; *pl. st.*] **1.** *f* head; top, summit; cupola; chapter (*in books*); (быть, стоя́ть) во ~е́ (be) at the head; lead (by с Т); **2.** *m/f* head, chief; **~а́рь** *m* [4 *e.*] (ring) leader, chieftain.
главе́нство *n* [9] priority, hegemony; **~вать** [7] (pre)dominate.
главнокома́ндующий *m* [17]: ~ commander in chief; Верхо́вный ~ Commander in Chief; Supreme Commander.
гла́вн|ый [14] chief, main, principal, central; head...; ... in chief; ~ая кни́га *f* ⚕ ledger; ~ое (де́ло) *n* the main thing; above all; ~ый го́род *m* capital; ~ым о́бразом mainly, chiefly.
глаго́л *m* [1] *gr.* verb; † word, speech; **~ьный** [14] verb(al).
глад|и́льный [14] ironing; **∠ить** [15] **1.** ⟨вы́-⟩ iron, press; **2.** ⟨по-⟩ stroke, caress; F ∠ить по голо́вке treat with indulgence *or* favo(u)r; **∠кий** [16; -док, -дка́, -о] smooth (*a. fig.*); lank (*hair*); plain (*fabric*); P well-fed; **∠кость, ~ь** *f* [8] smoothness.
глаз *m* [1; в -у́; *pl.*: -а́, глаз, -а́м] eye; look; (eye)sight; F heed, care; в ~а́ (Д) to s.b.'s face; (*strike*) the eye; в мои́х ~а́х in my view *or* opinion; за ~а́ in s.b.'s absence, behind one's back; plentifully; на ~ approximately, by eye; на ~а́х (*poss. or* у P) in s.b.'s presence, sight; с ∠у на ~ privately, tête-à-tête; просты́м (невооружённым) ∠ом with the naked eye; темно́, хоть ~ вы́коли F it is pitch-dark; **~а́стый** F [14 *sh.*] goggle-eyed; sharp-sighted; **~е́ть** P [8] stare *or* gape (around); **~но́й** [14] eye..., optic; ~но́й врач *m* oculist; **~о́к** *m* [1; -зка́] **1.** [*pl. st.*: -зки, -зок] *dim. of* ~; аню́тины ∠ки *pl.* pansy; **2.** [*pl. e.*: -зки́, -зко́в] ⚘ bud; *zo.* ocellus, eye; peephole.
глазоме́р *m* [1]: на ~ estimate(d) by the eye; (*sure, etc.*) eye.
глазу́нья *f* [6] fried eggs *pl.*
глазур|ова́ть [7] (*im*)*pf.* glaze; **∠ь** *f* [8] glaze.
гла|си́ть [15 *e*; *3. p. only*] say, read, run; **∠сность** *f* [8] public(ity); **∠сный** [14] public; (*a. su.*) vowel; *su.* council(l)or; **~ша́тай** *m* [3] town crier; *fig.* herald.
гле́тчер *m* [1] glacier.
гли́н|а *f* [5] loam; clay; **~истый** [14 *sh.*] loamy; **~озём** *m* [1] *min.* alumina; **~яный** [14] earthen; loamy.
глист *m* [1 *e.*], **~а́** *f* [5] (intestinal) worm; (ле́нточный) ~ tapeworm.
глицери́н *m* [1] glycerine.
гло́бус *m* [1] globe.
глода́ть [3], ⟨об-⟩ gnaw (at, round).
глот|а́ть [1], ⟨про~и́ть⟩ [15], *once* ⟨~ну́ть⟩ [20] swallow; F devour; **∠ка** *f* [5; *g/pl.*: -ток] throat; во всю ∠ку *s.* го́лос; **~о́к** *m* [1; -тка́] draught, gulp (at Т).
гло́хнуть [21] **1.** ⟨о-⟩ grow deaf; **2.** ⟨за-⟩ fade, die away, out; go out; grow desolate.
глуб|ина́ *f* [5] depth; remoteness (*past*); *fig.* profundity; *thea.* background; Т/в (В) ..., *or* ... в В ... deep; **~о́кий** [16; -бо́к, -бока́, -бо́ко́] deep; low; remote; *fig.* profound; complete; great (*age*); ~о́кой зимо́й (но́чью) in the dead of winter (late at night).
глубоко|мы́сленный [14 *sh.*] thoughtful, sagacious; **~мы́слие** *n* [12] thoughtfulness; **~уважа́емый** [14] dear (*polite address*).
глубь *f* [8] *s.* глубина́.
глум|и́ться [14 *e.*; -млю́сь, -ми́шься] sneer, mock, scoff (at над Т); **~ле́ние** *n* [12] mockery.
глуп|е́ть [8], ⟨по-⟩ become stupid; **~е́ц** *m* [1; -пца́] fool, blockhead; **~и́ть** F [14 *e.*; -плю́, -пи́шь] fool; **∠ость** *f* [8] stupidity; foolery; non-

sense; ∠ый [14; глуп, -á, -о] foolish, silly, stupid.
глух|áрь *m* [4 *e.*] capercailie, wood grouse; **~óй** [14; глух, -á, -о; *comp.*: глýше] deaf (*a. fig.*; к Д to; *cf.* слепóй); dull, vague; desolate, wild; out-of-the-way; ⚠ tight, solid, blind; late, the dead of; *gr.* voiceless; **~онемóй** [14] deaf-mute; **~отá** *f* [5] deafness.
глуш|íтель ⊕ *m* [4] muffler; **~íть** [16 *e.*; -шý, -ши́шь; -шённый] **1.** ⟨о-⟩ deafen, stun; **2.** ⟨за-⟩ deafen; deaden; muffle; smother, suppress (*a.*⚘); ⊕ switch off, throttle; ⚡ jam; **~ь** *f* [8] thicket; wilderness; solitude, lonely spot, nook.
глы́ба *f* [5] lump, clod; block.
гля|дéть [11; гля́дя], ⟨по-⟩, *once* ⟨∠нуть⟩ [20] look, glance (at на В); F look after, take care of (за Т); peep (out of, from из Р); F ~ди́ very likely; look out!; тогó и ~ди́ ... may + *inf.* (unexpectedly); кудá глазá ~дя́т at random; after one's nose.
гля́н|ец *m* [1; -нца] polish; luster; **~цев(и́т)ый** [14 (*sh.*)] glossy, lustrous; glazed *paper*; **~уть** *s.* глядéть.
г-н *abbr.*: господи́н.
гнать [гоню́, гóнишь; гони́мый; гнал, -á -о; '...гнанный], ⟨по-⟩ **1.** *v/t.* (be) drive (-ving, *etc.*); F send; float; **2.** distil; **3.** pursue, chase; (*a.* **-ся** за Т; *fig.* strive for); **4.** *v/i.* speed along.
гнев *m* [1] anger; **∠аться** [1], ⟨раз-, про-⟩ be(come) angry (with на В); **∠ный** [14; -вен, -внá, -о] angry.
гнедóй [14] sorrel, chestnut (*horse*).
гнезд|и́ться [15] nest; **~ó** *n* [9; *pl.*: гнёзда, *etc. st.*] nest, aerie.
гнёт *m* [1] press(ure); oppression.
гни|éние *n* [12] putrefaction; **~лóй** [14; гнил, -á, -о] rotten, putrid; wet; **~ль** *f* [8] rottenness; **~ть** [гнию́, -ёшь; гнил, -á, -о], ⟨с-⟩ rot, putrefy.
гно|éние *n* [12] suppuration; **~и́ть (-ся)** [13] fester; **~й** *m* [3] pus; **∠йный** [14] purulent.
гнуса́вить [14] snuffle, twang.
гнýсн|ость *f* [8] meanness; **~ый** [14; -сен, -снá, -о] vile, mean, base.
гнуть [20], ⟨со-⟩ bend, curve; bow; F drive (at к Д); *fig.* bully.
гнушáться [1], ⟨по-⟩ (Р *or* Т) scorn, despise, disdain.
говé|нье *n* [12] fast; **~ть** [1] fast.
гóвор *m* [1] talk, hum, murmur; rumo(u)r; accent; dialect, patois; **~и́ть** [13], ⟨по-; сказáть⟩ [3] speak *or* talk (about, of о П, про В; to *or* with р. с Т); say, tell; ~я́т, ~и́тся they say, it is said; ~и́ть по-рýсски speak Russian; инáче ~я́ in other words; не ~я́ ужé о (П) let alone; по прáвде (сóвести) ~я́ to tell the truth; что вы ~и́те! you don't say!; что (как) ни ~и́ whatever you (one) may say; что и ~и́ть, и не ~и́(те)! yes, of course, sure!; **~ли́вый** [14 *sh.*] talkative.
говя́|дина *f* [5], **~жий** [18] beef.
гóгот *m* [1], **~áть** [3], ⟨за-⟩ cackle; P roar (with laughter).
год *m* [1; *pl.*: -ды & -дá, *from g/pl. e.* & лет, *etc.* 9 *e.*] year (в ~ a *or* per year); в э́том (прóшлом) ~ý this (last) year; из ∠а в ∠ year in year out; ∠ от ~у year by year; крýглый ~ all the year round; (с) ~áми for (after a number of) years; *cf.* пят(и-десят)ый.
годи́т|ься [15 *e.*; гожýсь, годи́шься], ⟨при-⟩ be of use (for для Р, к Д, на В), do; fit; *pf.* come in handy; э́то (никудá) не ~ся that's no good (for anything), that won't do, it's (very) bad.
годи́чный [14] annual.
гóдный [14; -ден, -днá, -о, гóдны́] fit, suitable, useful, good, ⚔ able(-bodied) (to, *a.* + *inf.*, for для Р, к Д, на В); ни на чтó не ~ good-for-nothing.
годов|óй [14] annual; one year (old); **~щи́на** *f* [5] anniversary.
гол *m* [1] goal; заби́ть ~ score.
гол|ени́ще *n* [11] bootleg; **∠ень** *f* [8] shank.
голлáнд|ец *m* [1; -дца] Dutchman; **Ωия** *f* [7] Holland; **~ка** *f* [5; *g/pl.*: -док] Dutchwoman; **~ский** [16] Dutch.
голов|á [5; *pl.*: гóловы, голóв, -вáм] **1.** *f* [*ac/sg.*: '~у] head; **2.** *m* head, chief; ~á сáхару sugar loaf; как снег нá ~у all of a sudden; с ~ы́ до ног from head to foot; в ~áх at the head; на свою́ '~у F to one's own harm; повéсить '~у become discouraged *or* despondent; ~á идёт кругóм (у Р s.b.'s) thoughts are in a whirl; **∠ка** *f* [5; *g/pl.*: -вок] small head; head (*pin, nail, etc.*); bulb, clove (*onion, garlic*); **~нóй** [14] head...; ⚔ advance...; ~нáя боль *f* headache.
голово|кружéние *n* [12] giddiness; **~кружи́тельный** [14] dizzy, giddy; **~лóмка** *f* [5; *g/pl.*: -мок] puzzle; **~мóйка** *f* [5; *g/pl.*: -мóек] F blowup; **~рéз** F *m* [1] daredevil; cutthroat, thug; **~тя́п** F *m* [1] booby, bungler.
гóлод *m* [1] **1.** hunger; **2.** *s.* ~óвка; **~áть** [1] starve; **∠ный** [14; гóлоден, -днá, -о, гóлодны́] hungry; starv(el)ing; **~óвка** *f* [5; *g/pl.*: -вок] starvation; famine; hunger strike.
гололéдица *f* [5] ice-crusted ground.
гóлос *m* [1; *pl.*: -cá, *etc. e.*] voice; vote; прáво ~а suffrage; во весь ~ at the top of one's voice; в оди́н ~ unanimously; ~á зá и прóтив the yeas (ayes) & noes; **~и́ть** P [15 *e.*; -ошý, -оси́шь] bawl; **~лóвный**

[14; -вен, -вна] unfounded; empty; **~ова́ние** *n* [12] voting, poll(ing); закры́тое ~ова́ние secret vote; **~ова́ть** [7], ⟨про-⟩ vote; **~ово́й** [14] vocal (cords свя́зки *f/pl*).

голуб|е́ц *m* [1; -бца́] stuffed cabbage; **~о́й** [14] (sky) blue; **∠(уш)ка** *f* [5; *g/pl.*: -бок (-шек)], **∠чик** *m* [1] (F *address*) (my) dear; **'~ь** *m* [4] pigeon; **~я́тня** *f* [6; *g/pl.*: -тен] dovecote.

го́л|ый [14; гол, -á, -o] naked, nude; bare (*a. fig.*); poor, miserable; **~ь** *f* [8] poverty; waste (land).

гомеопа́тия *f* [7] homeopathy.

гомин(ь)да́н *m* [1] Kuomintang.

го́мон F *m* [1] din, hubbub.

гондо́ла *f* [5] gondola (*a.* ✈).

гон|е́ние *n* [12] persecution; **~е́ц** *m* [1; -нца́] courier; **∠ка** *f* [5; *g/pl.*: -нок] rush; chase; F haste; ⚗ distil(l)ment; *pl.* race(s), ⚓ regatta; F blowup; ∠ка вооруже́ний arms race.

Гонко́нг *m* [1] Hong Kong.

го́нор *m* [1] airs *pl.*; **~а́р** *m* [1] fee.

го́ночный [14] race..., racing.

гонт *m* [1] *coll.* shingles.

гонча́р *m* [1 *e.*] potter; **~ный** [14] potter's; ~ные изде́лия *n/pl.* pottery.

го́нчая *f* [17] (*a.* ~ соба́ка) hound.

гоня́ть(ся) [1] drive, *etc.*, *s.* гнать.

гор|а́ *f* [5; *ac/sg.*: го́ру; *pl.*: го́ры, гор, гора́м] mountain; heap, pile; (*a. pl.*) (toboggan) slide; в ∠у *or* на́ ~у uphill; *fig.* up(ward); по́д ~у *or* с ~ы́ downhill; под ~о́й at the foot of a hill (*or* mountain); не за ~а́ми not far off; пир ~о́й F sumptuous feast; стоя́ть ~о́й (за В) defend s.th. *or* s.b. with might & main; у меня́ ~а́ с плеч свали́лась F a load's been (*or* was) taken off my mind.

гора́здо *used with the comp.* much, far; P quite.

горб *m* [1 *e.*; на -у́] hump, hunch; **~а́тый** [14 *sh.*] humpbacked; curved; aquiline (*nose*); **∠ить** [14], ⟨с-⟩ stoop, bend, curve (*v/i.* **-ся**); **~у́н** *m* [1 *e.*] hunchback; **~у́шка** *f* [5; *g/pl.*: -шек] top crust, heel (*bread*).

горд|ели́вый [14 *sh.*] haughty, proud; **~е́ц** *m* [1 *e.*] proud man; **~и́ться** [15 *e.*; горжу́сь, горди́шься], ⟨воз-⟩ be(come) proud (of T); **∠ость** *f* [8] pride; **∠ый** [14; горд, -á, -o] proud (of T).

го́р|е *n* [10] grief, distress; trouble; misfortune, disaster; с ~я out of grief; ~е мне! woe is me!; ему́ и ~я ма́ло F he doesn't care a bit; с ~ем попола́м F hardly, with difficulty; **~ева́ть** [6], ⟨по-⟩ grieve; regret (s. th. о П).

горе́л|ка *f* [5; *g/pl.*: -лок] burner; **~ый** [14] burnt.

горемы́ка F *m/f* [5] poor wretch.

го́рест|ный [14; -тен, -тна] sad, sorrowful; **~ь** *f* [8] *cf.* го́ре.

гор|е́ть [9], ⟨с-⟩ burn (*a. fig.*), be on fire; glow, gleam; не ~и́т F there's no hurry; де́ло ~и́т (в рука́х у Р) F the matter is top urgent (makes good progress).

го́рец *m* [1; -рца] mountaineer.

го́речь *f* [8] bitter taste (*or* smell); *fig.* bitterness; grief, affliction.

горизо́нт *m* [1] horizon; **~а́льный** [14; -лен, -льна] horizontal, level.

гори́стый [14 *sh.*] mountainous; hilly.

го́рка *f* [5; *g/pl.*: -рок] *dim. of* гора́, *s.*; hill; whatnot, small cupboard.

горла́нить P [13], ⟨за-, про-⟩ bawl.

го́рл|о *n* [9] throat; gullet; (*vessel*) neck (*a.* **~ышко** *n* [9; *g/pl.*: -шек]); по ~о F up to the eyes; я сыт по ~о F I've had my fill (*fig.* I'm fed up with [T]); во всё ~о *s.* го́лос.

горн *m* [1] **1.** ⊕ (*a.* **~и́ло** *n* [9]) furnace, forge; crucible (*a. fig.*); **2.** ♪ horn, bugle; **~и́ст** *m* [1] bugler.

го́рничная *f* [14] parlo(u)rmaid.

горно|заво́дский [16], **~промы́шленный** [14] mining, metallurgical; **~рабо́чий** *m* [17] miner.

горноста́й *m* [3] ermine.

го́рн|ый [14] mountain(ous), hilly; *min.* rock...; ⊕ mining; ~ый про́мысел *m*, ~ое де́ло *n* mining; ~ое со́лнце *n* sun lamp; **~я́к** *m* [1 *e.*] miner.

го́род *m* [1; *pl.*: -да́, *etc. e.*] town; city (*large town*; F *down town*); за́ ~(ом) *go* (*live*) out of town; **~и́ть** P [15], ⟨на-⟩ (вздор, *etc.*) talk nonsense; **~о́к** *m* [1; -дка́] small town; quarter; **~ско́й** [14] town..., city..., municipal; *s. a.* горсове́т.

горожа́н|ин *m* [1; *pl.*: -жа́не, -жа́н] townsman; *pl.* townspeople; **~ка** *f* [5; *g/pl.*: -нок] townswoman.

горо́|х *m* [1] pea (*plant*); *coll.* peas (*seeds*) *pl.*; **~ховый** [14] pea(s)...; pea green; чу́чело ~ховое *n*, шут ~ховый *m* F *fig.* scarecrow; boor, merry-andrew; **~шек** *m* [1; -шка] *coll.* (small) peas *pl.*; **~шин(к)а** *f* [5 (*g/pl.*: -нок)] pea; dot.

горсове́т (городско́й сове́т) *m* [1] city *or* town soviet (council).

го́рст|очка *f* [5; *g/pl.*: -чек] *dim.* of **~ь** *f* [8; *from g/pl. e.*] hollow (*hand*); handful (*a. fig.*).

горта́н|ный [14] guttural; **~ь** *f* [8] larynx.

горчи́ца *f* [5] mustard.

горшо́к *m* [1; -шка́] pot.

го́рьк|ий [16; -рек, -рька́, -o; *comp.*: го́рче] bitter (*a. fig.*); *f su.* vodka, bitters *pl.*; ~ий пья́ница *m* dipsomaniac.

горю́ч|ее *n* [17] (engine) fuel; gasoline, *Brt.* petrol; **~ий** [17 *sh.*] combustible; P bitter (*tears*).

горя́ч|ий [17; горя́ч, -á] hot (*a. fig.*); fiery, hot-tempered; ardent, passionate; violent; warm (*scent*); cordial; hard, busy; **~и́ть** [16 *e.*;

-чу́, -чи́шь], ⟨раз-⟩ heat (*a. fig.*); **-ся** get *or* be excited; **~ка** *f* [5] fever (*a. fig.*); **~ность** *f* [8] vehemence, hot temper.

гос = госуда́рственный state... (*of the U.S.S.R.*); **2ба́нк** *m* [1] State Bank; **2изда́т** (2уда́рственное изда́тельство) *m* [1] State Publishing House; **2пла́н** (2уда́рственный пла́новый комите́т) *m* [1] State Planning Committee.

го́спиталь *m* [4] ⚔ hospital.

господ|и́н *m* [1; *pl.*: -пода́, -по́д, -да́м] gentleman; master (*a. fig.*); Mr. (*with name or title*); (ladies &) gentlemen (*a. address*); *pl.* (*servants*:) master & mistress; уважа́емые ~а́ dear Sirs (*in letters, a.* ✝); я сам себе́ ~и́н I am my own master; **∠ский** [16] seignorial, (land)lord's, master's; manor (house); **∠ство** *n* [9] rule; supremacy; **∠ствовать** [7] rule, reign; (pre)dominate, prevail (over над T); command (*region*); **∠ь** *m* [го́спода, -ду; *voc.*: -ди] Lord, God (*a. as int., cf.* бог).

госпожа́ *f* [5] lady; mistress; Mrs. *or* Miss (*with name*).

гостеприи́м|ный [14; -мен, -мна] hospitable; **~ство** *n* [9] hospitality.

гост|и́ная *f* [14] drawing room; **~и́нец** *m* [1; -нца] present, gift; **~и́ница** *f* [5] hotel; inn; **~и́ть** [15 *e.*; гощу́, гости́шь] be on a visit, stay with (у P); **~ь** *m* [4; *from g/pl. e.*] guest; visitor (*f* **∠ья** [6]); идти́ (е́хать) в ∠и go to see (s.b. к Д); быть в ~я́х (у P) = и́ть.

госуда́рственный [14] state...; national; ⚖ public; high (*treason*); ~ переворо́т *m* coup d'état; ~ стро́й *m* political system, regime; *s. a.* ГПУ.

госуда́р|ство *n* [9] state; **~ь** *m* [4] sovereign; Czar; ми́лостивый ~ь (dear) Sir (*a. pl., in letters, a.* ✝).

готова́льня *f* [6; *g/pl.*: -лен] (case of) drawing utensils *pl.*

гото́в|ить [14] **1.** ⟨при-⟩ prepare (o.s. *or* get ready for **-ся** к Д); **2.** ⟨под-⟩ prepare, train; **3.** ⟨за-⟩ store up; lay in (*stock*); **~ность** *f* [8] readiness; willingness; **~ый** [14 *sh.*] ready (for к Д *or inf.*), on the point of; finished; willing; ready-made (*clothes*); будь ~! — всегда́ ~! be ready! — always ready! (*slogan of pioneers, cf.* пионе́р).

ГПУ (Госуда́рственное полити́ческое управле́ние) G.P.U. = Political State Administration (*predecessor, 1922—35, of* НКВД, [*cf.*).

гр. *abbr.*: граждани́н.

граб *m* [1] hornbeam.

граб|ёж *m* [1 *e.*] robbery; **~и́тель** *m* [4] robber; **∠ить** [14], ⟨о-⟩ rob, plunder.

гра́бли *f/pl.* [6; *gen.*: -бель & -блей] rake.

грав|ёр *m* [1] engraver; **∠ий** *m* [3] gravel; **~ирова́ть** [7], ⟨вы́-⟩ engrave; **~иро́вка** *f* [5; *g/pl.*: -вок] engraving, etching, print (*a.* **~ю́ра** *f* [5]).

град *m* [1] hail (*a. fig.* = shower); ~ идёт it is hailing; **∠ом** thick & fast, profusely.

гра́дус *m* [1] degree (of в B); под ~ом F tipsy; **~ник** *m* [1] thermometer.

гражд|ани́н *m* [1; *pl.*: гра́ждане, -ан], **~а́нка** *f* [5; *g/pl.*: -нок] citizen (*U.S.S.R. a.* = [wo]man, & *in address, mst. without name*); **~а́нский** [16] civil (*a. war*); civic (*a. right*); **~а́нство** *n* [9] citizenship; citizens *pl.*; дать (получи́ть) пра́во ~а́нства (be) accept(ed) (in public); приня́ть ... ~а́нство become a ... citizen.

грамза́пись *f* [8] recording.

грамм *m* [1] gram(me).

грамма́т|ика *f* [5] grammar; **~и́ческий** [16] grammatical.

граммофо́н *m* [1] gramophone.

гра́мот|а *f* [5] reading & writing; document; patent; diploma; † letter; вери́тельная ~а credentials; э́то для меня́ кита́йская ~а F it's Greek to me; **~ность** *f* [8] literacy; **~ный** [14; -тен, -тна] literate; trained, expert.

грана́т *m* [1] pomegranate; *min.* garnet; **~а** *f* [5] shell; grenade.

грандио́зный [14; -зен, -зна] mighty; grand.

гранёный [14] facet(t)ed; cut.

грани́т *m* [1] granite.

грани́|ца *f* [5] border, frontier; boundary; *fig.* limit, verge; за ~цу (~цей) *go* (*be*) abroad; из-за ~цы from abroad; **~чить** [16] border *or* verge ([up]on с T).

гра́н|ка *f* [5; *g/pl.*: -нок] *typ.* galley (proof); **~ь** *f* [8] *s.* грани́ца; ⚘ plane; facet; edge; *fig.* verge.

граф *m* [1] earl (*Brt.*); count.

граф|а́ *f* [5] column; **∠ик** *m* [1] diagram, graph; **∠ика** *f* [5] graphic arts.

графи́н *m* [1] decanter, carafe.

графи́ня *f* [6] countess.

графи́|т *m* [1] graphite; **~ть** [14 *e.*; -флю́, -фи́шь; -флённый], ⟨раз-⟩ line *or* rule (*paper*), draw columns; **~ческий** [16] graphic(al).

граци|о́зный [14; -зен, -зна] graceful; **'~я** *f* [7] grace(fulness).

грач *m* [1 *e.*] rook.

греб|ёнка *f* [5; *g/pl.*: -нок] comb; стри́чь(ся) под ~ёнку (have one's hair) crop(ped); **∠ень** *m* [4; -бня] comb; crest; **~е́ц** *m* [1; -бца́] oarsman; **~ешо́к** *m* [1; -шка́] *s.* ∠ень; **∠ля** *f* [6] rowing; **~но́й** [14] row(ing)...

грёз|а *f* [5] (day)dream; **~ить** ('grʒe-) [15] *impf.* dream (of о П); ⚘

rave; **-ся,** ⟨по-, при-⟩: мне гре́зится (И) I dream (of *or v/t.*).
грек *m* [1] Greek.
гре́лка *f* [5; *g/pl.*: -лок] hot-water bottle; электри́ческая ~ heating pad.
грем|е́ть [10 *e.*; гремлю́, -ми́шь], ⟨про-, за-⟩ thunder, peal (*a. voice, bell, etc.*); rattle, clank, tinkle (*sword, chains, keys*); clatter (*dishes*); *fig.* ring; be famous (for, as); **~у́чий** [17] rattling; ⚗ oxy-hydrogen; fulminating; ~у́чая змея́ *f* rattlesnake; **~у́шка** *f* [5; *g/pl.*: -шек] rattle (*toy*).
гренки́ *m/pl.* [1 *e.*] toast (*sg.*: -нóк).
Гренла́ндия *f* [7] Greenland.
грести́ [24 -б-: гребу́; грёб, гребла́], ⟨по-⟩ row; scull; rake; scoop.
греть [8; ...гре́тый], ⟨со-, на-, разо-, обо-, подо-⟩ warm (o.s. **-ся**) (up); heat; -ся на со́лнце sun.
грех *m* [1 *e.*] sin; fault; F = грешно́; с ~о́м попола́м F so-so; *cf.* го́ре; есть тако́й ~ F well, I own it; как на ~ F unfortunately.
Гре́|ция *f* [7] Greece; **2цкий** [16]: 2цкий оре́х *m* walnut; **2ча́нка** *f* [5; *g/pl.*: -нок], **2ческий** [16] Greek.
греч|и́ха, ~ка *f* [5] buckwheat; **~невый** [14] buckwheat...
греш|и́ть [16 *e.*; -шу́, -ши́шь], ⟨со-⟩ sin (*a.* against про́тив Р); **~ник** *m* [1], **~ница** *f* [5] sinner; **~но́** (it's a) shame (on Д); **~ный** [14; -шен, -шна́, -о] sinful; F *sh.*: sorry.
гриб *m* [1 *e.*] mushroom; **~о́к** [1; -бка́] *dim. of* ~; fungus.
гри́ва *f* [5] mane.
гри́венник F *m* [1] ten-kopeck coin.
Григо́рий *m* [3] Gregory.
грим *m* [1] *thea.* make-up.
грима́с|а *f* [5] grimace; **~ничать** [1] make faces *or* grimaces.
гримирова́ть [7], ⟨за-, на-⟩ make up (*v/i.* **-ся**).
грипп *m* [1] influenza.
гри́фель *m* [4] slate pencil.
Гри́ш(к)а *m* [5] *dim. of* Григо́рий.
гр-ка *abbr.*: гражда́нка.
гроб *m* [1; в -у́; *pl.*: -ы́ & -а́, *etc. e.*] coffin; † grave; **~ни́ца** *f* [5] tomb; **~ово́й** [14] coffin...; tomb...; deadly; **~овщи́к** *m* [1 *e.*] coffin maker.
гроза́ *f* [5; *pl. st.*] (thunder)storm (*a fig.*); disaster; danger, menace; terror.
грозд|ь *m* [4; *pl.*: -ди, -де́й, *etc. e.*, & -дья, -дьев] bunch (*grapes*); cluster.
грози́ть [15 *e.*; грожу́, -зи́шь], ⟨по-⟩ threaten (a p. with Д/Т) (*a.* **-ся**).
гро́з|ный [14; -зен, -зна́, -о] menacing; formidable; P severe, cruel; Ива́н 2ный Ivan the Terrible; **~ово́й** [14] storm(y).
гром *m* [1; *from g/pl.*: *e.*] thunder (*a. fig.*); ~ греми́т it thunders; как ~ом поражённый *fig.* thunderstruck.
грома́д|а *f* [5] giant, colossus; mass, heap; **~ный** [14; -ден, -дна] huge, tremendous.
громи́|ть [14 *e.*; -млю́, -ми́шь; -млённый], ⟨раз-⟩ smash, crush; rout.
гро́мк|ий [16; -мок, -мка́, -о; *comp.*: гро́мче] loud; noisy; *fig.* famous, great, noted; notorious; (*words, etc.*) pompous; **~оговори́тель** *m* [4] loud-speaker.
громо|во́й [14] thunder..., thunderous; **~гла́сный** [14; -сен, -сна] roaring; *mst. adv.* in public; **~зди́ть** (**-ся**) [15 *e.*; -зжу́, -зди́шь] *cf.* взгромозжда́ть(ся); **~здкий** [16; -док, -дка] bulky, cumbersome; **~отво́д** *m* [1] lightning rod *or* conductor.
громыха́ть F [1] rattle.
грот *m* [1] grotto.
гро́х|нуть F [20] *pf.* crash, tumble (*v/i.* **-ся**); **~от** *m* [1] rumble; **~ота́ть** [3], ⟨за-⟩ rumble; P roar.
грош *m* [1 *e.*] half-kopeck; piece; ни ~а́ not a stiver *or* farthing; ~ цена́ *or* ~а́ ло́маного не сто́ит not worth a pin; ни в ~ не ста́вить not care a straw (for В); **~о́вый** [14] worth 1 ~; *fig.* (dirt-)cheap, paltry.
груб|е́ть [8], ⟨за-, о-⟩ harden, become callous; **~и́ть** [14 *e.*; -блю́, -би́шь], ⟨на-⟩ say rude things; **~ия́н** F *m* [1] rude fellow; **~ость** *f* [8] rudeness; **~ый** [14; груб, -а́, -о] coarse; rough; rude; gross (*error, etc.*).
гру́да *f* [5] pile, heap, mass.
груд|и́нка *f* [5; *g/pl.*: -нок] brisket; bacon; **~но́й** [14]: ~на́я кле́тка *f* thorax, chest; **~ь** *f* [8; в, на -ди́; *from g/pl. e.*] breast; bosom; стоя́ть ~ью (за В) defend bravely.
груз *m* [1] load, freight; ⚓ cargo.
грузи́н *m* [1; *g/pl.*: грузи́н], **~ка** *f* [5; *g/pl.*: -нок] Georgian; **~ский** [16] Georgian.
грузи́ть [15 & 15 *e.*; -ужу́, -у́зи́шь], ⟨на-, за-, по-⟩ load, embark.
Гру́зия *f* [7] Georgia (*Caucasus*).
гру́з|ный [14; -зен, -зна́, -о] massive, heavy; **~ови́к** *m* [1 *e.*] truck, *Brt.* lorry; **~ово́й** [14] freight..., goods..., ⚓ cargo...; ~ово́й автомоби́ль *m* = ~ови́к; **~оподъёмность** *f* [8] carrying capacity, ⚓ tonnage; **~чик** *m* [1] loader, ⚓ stevedore.
грунт *m* [1] soil; ground (*a. paint.*); **~ово́й** [14] ground...; unpaved.
гру́пп|а *f* [5] group; **~ирова́ть** (**-ся**) [7], ⟨с-⟩ (form a) group.
груст|и́ть [15 *e.*; -ущу́, -сти́шь], F ⟨взгрустну́ть⟩ [20] grieve; long (for) (по П); **~ный** [14; -тен, -тна́,

-o] sad, sorrowful; dreary; F deplorable; мне ∠но I feel sad; ~ь *f* [8] sadness, grief, melancholy.
гру́ша *f* [5] pear (*a. tree*).
гры́жа *f* [5] hernia, rupture.
грыз|ня́ F *f* [6] squabble; ~**ть** [24; *pt. st.*], ⟨раз-⟩ gnaw (*a. fig.*), nibble; bite; crack (*nuts*); **-ся** bite o. a.; F squabble; ~**у́н** *m* [1 *e.*] *zo.* rodent.
гряд|а́ *f* [5; *nom/pl. st.*] ridge, range (*a. fig.* = line); ⚒ bed (*a.* ∠**ка** *f* [5; *g/pl.*: -док]).
гряду́щий [17] future, coming; на сон ~ for a nightcap.
гряз|ево́й [14] mud...; ~**езащи́тный** [14]: ~езащи́тное крыло́ *n* fender, mudguard; ~**елече́бница** *f* [5] mud bath; ∠**и** *f/pl.* [8] (curative) mud; ~**ни́ть** [13], ⟨за-⟩ soil (*a. fig.*); **-ся** get dirty; ∠**нуть** [20], ⟨по-⟩ sink (*mud, etc., & fig.*); ∠**ный** [14; -зен, -зна́, -о, гря́зны́] dirty (*a. fig.*); muddy; slop... (*pail*); ~**ь** *f* [8; в -зи́] dirt; mud (*street, etc.*); в ~и́ dirty; не уда́рить лицо́м в ~ь save one's face.
гря́нуть [19 *st.*] *pf.* crash, thunder, (re)sound, ring, roar; break out, burst, start.
губ|а́ *f* [5; *nom/pl. st.*] lip; bay; gulf; ∠а не ду́ра (у P p.'s) taste isn't bad.
губерн|а́тор *m* [1] governor; ∠**ия** *f* [7] government, province.
губи́т|ельный [14; -лен, -льна] pernicious; ~**ь** [14], ⟨по-, F с-⟩ destroy, ruin; waste (*time*).
гу́б|ка *f* [5; *g/pl.*: -бок] **1.** *dim. of* ~а́; **2.** sponge; ~**но́й** [14] labial; ~на́я пома́да *f* lipstick.
гуверн|а́нтка *f* [5; *g/pl.*: -ток] governess; ~**ёр** *m* [1] tutor.
гуд|е́ть [11], ⟨за-⟩ buzz; honk, hoot, whistle; ~**о́к** *m* [1; -дка́] honk, hoot, signal; horn; siren, whistle.
гул *m* [1] boom, rumble; hum; ∠**кий** [16; -лок, -лка́, -о] booming, loud; resonant.
гуля́|нье *n* [10] walk(ing); revel(ry), open-air merrymaking, (popular) festival; ~**ть** [28], ⟨по-⟩ [20] go for a walk (*a.* идти́ ~ть), stroll; *fig.* sweep (*wind, etc.*); make merry.
ГУМ (госуда́рственный универма́г) *m* [1] state department store.
гума́нн|ость *f* [8] humanity, humaneness; ~**ый** [14; -а́нен, -а́нна] humane.
гумно́ *n* [9; *pl. st., gen.*: -мен & -мён] ⚒ floor.
гур|т *m* [1 *e.*] drove (*cattle*); ~то́м F wholesale; ~**ьба́** F *f* [5] crowd (in T).
гу́сеница *f* [5] caterpillar (*a.* ⊕).
гуси́ный [14] goose (*a.* flesh ко́жа *f*).
густ|е́ть [8], ⟨за-⟩ thicken; ~**о́й** [14; густ, -а́, -о] thick, dense; deep, rich (*colo[u]r, sound*); ~**ота́** *f* [5] thickness; density; depth.
гус|ь *m* [4; *from g/pl. e.*] goose; *fig.* хоро́ш ~ь F a fine fellow indeed!; как с ∠я вода́ F like water off a duck's back, thick-skinned; ~**ько́м** in single file.
гу́ща *f* [5] grounds *pl.*; sediment; thicket; *fig.* center (*Brt.* -tre), middle.
ГЭС *abbr.*: гидро(электро)ста́нция.

Д

д. *abbr.*: **1.** дере́вня; **2.** дом.
да 1. *part.* yes; oh (yes), indeed (*a. interr.*); (oh) but, now, well; *imp.* do(n't) ...!; *tags:* aren't, don't, *etc.*; may, let; **2.** *cj.* (*a.* ~ и) and; but; ~ и то́лько continually; ~ что́ вы! you don't say!
дабы́ † (in order) that *or* to.
да|ва́ть [5], ⟨~ть⟩ [дам, дашь, даст, дади́м, дади́те, даду́т ('...-) дал, -а́, -о; ('...)да́нный (дан, -а́)] give; let; bestow; take (*oath*), pledge; make (*way*); ~ва́й(те)! come on!; *with vb.* (*a.* ∠й[те]) let us (me); ни ∠ть ни взять exactly like; ~ва́ть ход де́лу set s.th. going *or* further it; **-ся** let o.s. (*be caught. cheated* в В); (turn out to) be (*e.g. hard*, for Д); (can) master (s.th. И); *pt.* F take to.
дави́ть [14] **1.** ⟨на-⟩ press; squeeze (⟨вы́-⟩ out); **2.** ⟨за-, раз-⟩ crush; run over, knock down; **3.** ⟨по-⟩ oppress; suppress; **4.** ⟨при-, с-⟩ press (down *or* together), jam, compress; throng, crowd; **5.** ⟨у-⟩ strangle; **-ся** choke; F hang o.s.
да́в|ка F *f* [5] throng, jam; ~**ле́ние** *n* [12] pressure (*a. fig.*).
да́вн|(и́шн)ий [15] old; ~**о́** long ago; for a long time, long since; ~**опроше́дший** [17] long past; ~опроше́дшее вре́мя *n gr.* past *or* pluperfect; ~**ость** *f* [8] remoteness; ⚖ limitation; ~**ы́м-~о́** F (a) very long (time) ago.
да́же (*a.* ~ и) even; ~ не not even.
да́л|ее *s.* да́льше; и так ~ее and so on (*or* forth); ~**ёкий** [16; -лёк, -лека́, -леко́ & -лёко; *comp.*: да́лее, да́льше], far, distant (from от P); long (*way*); *fig.* wide (of); strange (to); F smart, clever; ~**еко́**, ~**ёко** far (off, away); a long way (to до P); (Д) ~еко́ до (P) F can't match with; ~еко́ не F by no means; ~еко́ за (B) long after; (*age*) well over; ~**ь** *f* [8; в -ли́] distance; open (space); ~**ьне́йший** [17] further;

в ~ьнейшем later *or* further on; **~ьний** [15] distant (*a. relative*); remote; *s. a.* ~ёкий; **~ьневосточный** [14] Far Eastern.

дально|бойный ⚔ [14] long range; **~видный** [14; -ден, -дна] clear-sighted; **~зоркий** [16; -рок, -рка] far-, long-sighted; **'~сть** *f* [8] remoteness; ⚔, ⊕ (long) range.

дальше farther; further(more); then, next; (читайте) ~! go on (reading); не ~ как *or* чем this very; only.

дам|а *f* [5] lady; partner (*dance*); queen (*card*); **~ский** [16] ladies', women's; **~ба** *f* [5] dam, dike; **~ка** *f* [5; *g/pl.:* -мок] king (*draughts*).

Дани|ил [1], P **~ла** *m* [5] Daniel.

Дания *f* [7] Denmark.

дан|ный [14] given, present, this; ~ная *f* & quantity; ~ные *pl.* data, facts; statistics.

дантист *m* [1] dentist.

дань *f* [8] tribute (*a. fig.*).

дар *m* [1; *pl. e.*] gift (*a. fig.*); **~ить** [13], ⟨по-⟩ give (a p. s.th. Д/В), present (a p. with В/Т); **~моед** F *m* [1] sponger; **~ование** *n* [12] gift, talent; **~овитый** [14 *sh.*] gifted, talented; **~овой** [14] gratis, free.

даром *adv.* gratis, for nothing; in vain; ~ что (al)though; это ему ~ не пройдёт F he will smart for it.

Дарья *f* [6] Darya (*first name*).

дат|а *f* [5] date; **~ельный** [14] *gr.* dative (*case*); **~ировать** [7] (*im*)*pf.* (задним числом ante)date.

дат|ский [16] Danish; **~чанин** *m* [1; *pl.:* -чане, -чан], **~чанка** *f* [5; *g/pl.:* -нок] Dane.

дать(ся) *s.* давать(ся).

дач|а *f* [5] giving; cottage, summer residence, villa; на ~е out of town, in the country; **~ник** *m* [1] summer resident; **~ный** [14] suburban; country...; garden (city посёлок).

Даш([ень]к)а *f* [5] *dim. of* Дарья.

два *m, n,* две *f* [34] two; *cf.* пять & пятый; в ~ счёта F in a jiffy.

двадцат|илетний [15] twenty-years-old, of 20; **~ый** [14] twentieth; *cf.* пят(идесят)ый; **'~ь** [35; -ти] twenty; *cf.* пять.

дважды twice; ~ два & two by two; как ~ два (четыре) as sure(ly) as two & two makes four.

двенадцат|и... (*in compds.*) twelve-...; dodec(a)...; duodecimal, -denary; **~ый** [14] twelfth; *cf.* пятый; **~ь** [35] twelve; *cf.* пять.

двер|ной [14] door...; **~ца** *f* [5; *g/pl.:* -рец] *dim. of* **~ь** *f* [8; в -ри; *from g/pl. e.*; *instr. a.* -рьми] door (*a. pl.* ~и).

двести [36] two hundred.

дви|гатель *m* [4] engine, motor; **~гать** [1 & 3], ⟨~нуть⟩ [20] (В & Т) move, push, drive (on); stir; **-ся** move, advance; set out, start; **~жение** *n* [12] movement (*a. pol.*); stir; *phys.* motion; traffic; *fig.* emotion; *pl.* (light) gymnastics; приводить (приходить) в ~жение set going (start [moving]); **~жимый** [14 *sh.*] movable; **~нуть** *s.* ~гать.

двое [37] two (*in a group, together*); нас было ~ we (there) were two (of us); **~брачие** *n* [12], **~жёнство** *n* [9] bigamy; **~точие** *n* [12] colon.

двоиться [13], ⟨раз-⟩ bifurcate.

двой|ка *f* [5; *g/pl.:* двоек] two (*a. boat*; *team*; P *bus, etc., no. 2*; *cards, a.* deuce); pair; F (*mark*) = плохо, *cf.*; **~ник** *m* [1 *e.*] double(ganger); **~ной** [14] double (*a. fig.*); **~ня** *f* [6; *g/pl.:* двоен] twins *pl.*; **~ственный** [14 *sh.*] double, twofold, -faced; dual (*a. gr.* number число).

двор *m* [1 *e.*] (court)yard; farm(-stead); court; на ~е outside, outdoors; **~ец** *m* [1; -рца] palace; **~ник** *m* [1] janitor, (yard &) street cleaner; F *mot.* windshield (*Brt.* windscreen) wiper; **~ня** *f* [6] *coll.*, † servants, domestics *pl.*; **~няга** F *f* [5], **~няжка** F *f* [5; *g/pl.:* -жек] mongrel; watchdog; **~овый** [14] yard-..., house...; servant...; **~цовый** [14] court...; palace...; **~янин** *m* [1; *pl.:* -яне, -ян] nobleman; **~янка** *f* [5; *g/pl.:* -нок] noblewoman; **~янский** [16] noble; **~янство** *n* [9] nobility.

двоюродн|ый [14]: ~ый брат *m*, ~ая сестра *f* cousin.

двояк|ий [16 *sh.*] double, twofold; **~о** in two ways.

дву|бортный [14] double-breasted; **~главый** [14] double-headed; **~гласный** [14] diphthong(al); **~жильный** P [14] sturdy, tough; **~колка** *f* [5; *g/pl.:* -лок] cart; **~кратный** [14] double; done twice; **~личие** *n* [12] duplicity; **~личный** [14; -чен, -чна] double-faced; **~рушник** *m* [1] double-dealer; **~рушничество** *n* [9] double-dealing; **~смысленный** [14 *sh.*] ambiguous; **~стволка** *f* [5; *g/pl.:* -лок] double-barrel(l)ed gun; **~ствольный** [14]: ~ствольное ружьё *n* = ~стволка; **~створчатый** [14]: ~створчатая дверь *f* folding doors; **~сторонний** [15] bilateral; two-way (*traffic*); reversible (*fabric*).

двух... (*cf. a.* дву...): **~дневный** [14] two days'; **~колейный** 🚂 [14] double-track; **~колёсный** [14] two-wheel(ed); **~летний** [15] two-years-old; two years'; **~местный** [14] two-seat(ed); **~месячный** [14] two months' *or* two-months-old; **~моторный** [14] twin-engine(d); **~недельный** [14] two weeks', *Brt. a.* a fortnight's; **~сотый** [14] two hundredth; **~этажный** [14] two-storied (*Brt.* -reyed).

двуязы́чный [14; -чен, -чна] bilingual.
дебат|и́ровать [7] debate; **ׅ**~**ы** *m/pl.* [1] debate.
дебе́лый F [14 *sh.*] plump, fat.
де́бет ✝ *m* [1] debit; занести́ в ~ = ~**ова́ть** [7] (*im*)*pf.* debit (*sum* against *or* to a p. В/Д).
дебито́р *m* [1] debtor.
дебо́ш *m* [1] riot, row.
де́бри *f/pl.* [8] thicket; wilderness.
дебю́т *m* [1] debut; opening.
де́ва *f* [5]: (ста́рая) ~ (old) maid.
девальва́ция *f* [7] devaluation.
дева́ть [1], ⟨деть⟩ [де́ну, -нешь] put; place; leave, mislay; куда́ ~ *a.* what to do with, how to spend; **-ся** go, get; *vb.* + И = put, leave + *obj.*; be (*pr.*); куда́ мне ~ся? where shall I go *or* stay? куда́ он де́лся? what has become of him?
де́верь *m* [4; *pl.*: -рья́, -ре́й, -рья́м] (*wife's*) brother-in-law.
деви́з *m* [1] motto.
дев|и́ца *f* [5] maid, girl; ~**и́чий** [18] maiden, girl's; ~ичий монасты́рь *m* nunnery; ~**ка** *f* [5; *g/pl.*: -вок] wench; P maid; P whore; ~**очка** *f* [5; *g/pl.*: -чек] (little) girl; ~**ственный** [14 *sh.*] maiden; virgin...; primeval; ~**ушка** *f* [5; *g/pl.*: -шек] (grown-up) girl; † parlo(u)rmaid; ~**чо́нка** F *f* [5; *g/pl.*: -нок] slut; girl.
девя|но́сто [35] ninety; ~**но́стый** [14] ninetieth; *cf.* пя́т(идеся́т)ый; ~**тисо́тый** [14] ninehundredth; ~**тка** *f* [5; *g/pl.*: -ток] nine (*cf.* дво́йка); ~**тна́дцатый** [14] nineteenth; *cf.* пять & пя́тый; ~**тна́дцать** [35] nineteen; *cf.* пять; ~**тый** [14] ninth; *cf.* пя́тый; '~**ть** [35] nine; *cf.* пять; ~**тьсо́т** [36] nine hundred; '~**тью** nine times.
дегенера́т *m* [1] degenerate.
дёготь *m* [4; -гтя] tar.
де́д|(ушка *m* [5; *g/pl.*: -шек]) *m* [1] grandfather; old man; *pl.* ~ы *a.* forefathers; ♀ Моро́з *m* Jack Frost; Santa Claus, Father Christmas.
дееприча́стие *n* [12] *gr.* gerund.
дежу́р|ить [13] be on duty; sit up, watch; ~**ный** [14] (p.) on duty; ~**ство** *n* [9] duty; (night) watch.
дезерти́р *m* [1] deserter; ~**овать** [7] (*im*)*pf.* desert; ~**ство** *n* [9] desertion.
дезинф|е́кция *f* [7] disinfection; ~**ици́ровать** [7] (*im*)*pf.* disinfect.
дезорганиз|ова́ть [7] (*im*)*pf.*, *impf.* *a.* ~**о́вывать** [1] disorganize.
де́йств|енный [14 *sh.*] efficient; ~**ие** *n* [12] action; activity; ⚔, ⊕, ⅍ operation; *thea.* act; effect; efficacy; influence, impact; ме́сто ~ия scene; свобо́да ~ий free play; ~**и́тельно** really; indeed; ~**и́тельность** *f* [8] reality; validity; ~**и́тельный** [14; -лен, -льна] real, actual; valid; ⚔, *gr.* active (*service*; *voice*); ~**овать** [7], ⟨по-⟩ act, work (*a.* upon на В); operate, function; apply; have effect (on на В); get (*on one's nerves*); ~**ующий** [17] active; acting; ⚔ field...; ~ующее лицо́ *n* character, personage.
дека́брь *m* [4 *e.*] December.
дека́н *m* [1] dean.
декла|ми́ровать [7], ⟨про-⟩ declaim; ~**ра́ция** *f* [7] declaration.
декольт|е́ (dɛ-; -ˈtɛ) *n* [*indecl.*] décolleté; ~**иро́ванный** [14 *sh.*] low-necked.
декора́|тор *m* [1] decorator; ~**ция** *f* [7] decoration; *thea.* scenery.
декре́т *m* [1] decree, edict; ~**и́ровать** [7] (*im*)*pf.* decree.
де́ла|нный [14 *sh.*] affected, forced; ~**ть** [1], ⟨с-⟩ make, do; ~ть не́чего F it can't be helped; **-ся** (Т) become, grow, turn; happen (with, to с Т), be going on; что с ним сде́лалось? what has become of him?
делега́|т *m* [1] delegate; ~**ция** *f* [7] delegation.
дел|ёж F *m* [1 *e.*] distribution, sharing; ~**е́ние** *n* [12] division (*a.* ⅍); partition; point (*scale*).
деле́ц *m* [1; -льца́] (sharp) businessman, moneymaker.
делика́тн|ость *f* [8] tact(fulness), delicacy; ~**ый** [14; -тен, -тна] delicate.
дели́|мое *n* [14] ⅍ dividend; ~**тель** *m* [4] ⅍ divisor; ~**ть** [13; делю́, де́лишь] **1.** ⟨раз-, по-⟩ (на В) divide (in[to]), *a.* ⅍ (by); **2.** ⟨по-⟩ share (*a.* **-ся** [Т/с Т s.th. with s.b.], exchange; confide [s.th. to], tell; ⅍ be divisible).
дели́шки F *n/pl.* [9; *gen*: -шек] [business.]
де́л|о *n* [9; *pl. e.*] affair, matter, concern; work, business (on по Д), line; art *or* science; deed, act(ion); ⚖ case, (*a. fig.*) cause; file; ⚔ action, battle; говори́ть ~о F talk sense; де́лать ~о *fig.* do serious work; то и ~о continually, incessantly; в чём ~о? what's the matter?; в том то и ~о F that's just the point; что вам за ~о? *or* э́то не ва́ше ~о that's no business of yours; на ~е in practice; на (*or* в) са́мом ~е in reality, in fact; really, indeed; по ~а́м on business; как ~а́? F how are you?; ~о идёт *cf.* идти́.
делов|и́тый [14 *sh.*], ~**о́й** [14] businesslike; expert; ~о́й *a.* business...; work(ing).
делопроизводи́тель *m* [4] secretary.
де́льный [14] competent; sensible.
демаго́г *m* [1] demagogue; ~**и́ческий** [16] demagogic(al).
демаркацио́нный [14] (of) demarcation.
демилитаризова́ть [7] (*im*)*pf.* demilitarize.
демобилизова́ть [7] (*im*)*pf.* demobilize.

демокра́т *m* [1] democrat; **~и́ческий** [16] democratic; **~ия** [7] democracy.
демонстр|а́ция *f* [7] demonstration; **~и́ровать** [7] (*im*)*pf*., *a*. ⟨про-⟩ demonstrate; show, project (*film*).
демонта́ж *m* [1] dismantling.
де́нежный [14] money..., monetary, pecuniary; currency...; F rich.
день *m* [4; дня] day; в ~ a *or* per day; в э́тот ~ (on) that day; ∠ за́ ~ day after day; изо дня́ в ∠ day by day; ∠ ото дня́ from day to day; весь ~ all day (long); на (э́тих) днях the other day; one of these days; три часа́ дня 3 p.m., 3 o'clock in the afternoon; *cf*. днём.
де́ньги *f*/*pl*. [*gen*.: де́нег; *from. dat. e*.] money.
департа́мент *m* [1] department.
депе́ша *f* [5] dispatch, wire(less).
депози́т ⚕ *m* [1] deposit.
депута́т *m* [1] deputy, delegate; member of the Supreme Soviet.
дёр|гать [1], *once* ⟨~нуть⟩ [20] pull, tug (*a*. за В at), jerk, twist; F press a p. hard, importune.
дерев|ене́ть [8], ⟨за-, о-⟩ stiffen; grow numb; **~е́нский** [16] village-..., country..., rural, rustic; ~е́нский жи́тель *m* villager; **∠ня** *f* [6; *g*/*pl*.: -ве́нь, *etc*. *e*.] village; country(side); **'~о** *n* [9; *pl*.: -е́вья, -е́вьев] tree; *sg*. wood; кра́сное '~о mahogany; чёрное '~о ebony; резьба́ по ~у wood engraving; **~я́нный** [14] wooden (*a*. *fig*.).
держа́ва *f* [5] power; *hist*. orb.
держа́ть [4] hold; keep; support; have (*a*. ⚕ in stock; *a*. *exam*.); read (*proofs*); ~ сто́рону side with; ~ себя́ (кого́-либо) в рука́х (have) control (over) o.s. (a p.); ~ себя́ conduct o.s., behave = **-ся 1.**; **2.** ⟨у~ся⟩ (за В; Р) hold (on[to]); *fig*. stick (to); keep; hold out, stand.
дерз|а́ть [1], ⟨~ну́ть⟩ [20] dare, venture; **∠кий** [16; -зок, -зка́, -о; *comp*.: -зче] impudent, insolent; bold, daring, audacious; (*a*. = † **~нове́нный** [14; -е́нен, -е́нна] & **∠остный** [14; -тен, -тна]); **∠ость** *f* [8] impudence, cheek.
дёрн *m* [1] turf; **~уть** *s*. дёргать.
дес|а́нт *m* [1] landing; troops *pl*. landed (авиа... airborne...); **~е́рт** *m* [1] dessert; **~на́** *f* [5; *pl*.: дёсны, -сен, *etc*. *st*.] gum; **∠пот** *m* [1] despot.
десяти|дне́вный [14] ten days'; **~кра́тный** [14] tenfold; **~ле́тие** *n* [12] decade; tenth anniversary; **~ле́тка** *f* [5; *g*/*pl*.: -ток] ten-grades (*or* -forms) standard school (*leading to maturity*) (*U.S.S.R.*); **~ле́тний** [15] ten years'; ten-years-old.
десят|и́на *f* [5] †, = *approx*. $2^3/_4$ *acres*; tithe; **~и́чный** [14] decimal; **∠ка** *f* [5; *g*/*pl*.: -ток] ten (*cf*. дво́йка); **∠ник** *m* [1] foreman; **∠ок** *m* [1; -тка] ten; *pl*. dozens of, many; *s*. идти́; не ро́бкого ∠ка F not a craven; **∠ый** [14] tenth (*a*., *f*, part; 3,2 — *read:* три це́лых и две ∠ых = 3.2); *cf*. пя́т(идеся́т)ый; из пя́того в ∠ое discursively, in a rambling manner; **'~ь** [35 *e*.] ten; *cf*. пять & пя́тый; **'~ью** ten times.
дета́ль *f* [8] detail; ⊕ part; **~но** in detail; **~ный** [14; -лен, -льна] detailed, minute.
дет|вора́ *f* [5] *coll*. F = ∠и; **~ёныш** *m* [1] young one; cub, *etc*.; **∠и** *n*/*pl*. [-е́й, -ям, -ьми́, -ях] children, kids; дво́е, (тро́е, че́тверо, *etc*.) ~е́й two (three, four) children; *sg*.: дитя́ (*a*. ребёнок), *cf*.; **∠ский** [16] child(ren)'s, infant(ile); childlike; childish; ∠ский дом *m* (orphan) boarding school; ∠ский сад *m* kindergarten; ∠ская *f* nursery (room); **∠ство** *n* [9] childhood.
де́ть(ся) *s*. дева́ть(ся).
дефе́ктный [14] defective.
дефици́тный [14; -тен, -тна] unprofitable; scarce.
деш|еве́ть [8], ⟨по-⟩ cheapen, become cheaper; **~еви́зна**, F **~ёвка** *f* [5] cheapness, low price(s); **~ёвый** [14; дёшев, дешева́, дёшево; *comp*.: деше́вле] cheap (*a*. *fig*.); low (*price*).
де́ятель *m* [4] man; representative; госуда́рственный ~ statesman; нау́чный ~ scientist; обще́ственный ~ public man; полити́ческий ~ politician; **~ность** *f* [8] activity, -ties *pl*.; work; **~ный** [14; -лен, -льна] active.
джу́нгли *f*/*pl*. [*gen*.: -лей] jungle.
диа́|гноз *m* [1] diagnosis; **~гона́ль** *f* [8] diagonal; **~ле́кт** *m* [1] dialect; **~ле́ктный** [14] dialectic(al); **~ле́ктика** *f* [5] dialectic(s); **~лекти́ческий** [16] dialectic(al); **~ло́г** *m* [1] dialogue; **~ма́т** *m* [1] dialectical materialism; **~метр** *m* [1] diameter; **~пазо́н** *m* [1] ♪ diapason (*a*. *fig*.); ⊕ range; **~позити́в** *m* [1] (lantern) slide; **~фра́гма** *f* [5] diaphragm.
дива́н *m* [1] divan, sofa.
диверс|а́нт *m* [1] saboteur; **∠ия** *f* [7] sabotage; ⚔ diversion.
диви́зия ⚔ *f* [7] division.
див|и́ться [14 *e*.], ⟨по-⟩ wonder (at Д *or* на В); **∠ный** [14; -вен -вна] wonderful; delightful; **∠о** *n* [9] wonder, miracle, marvel (*a*. it is a ...); на ∠о excellently; что за ∠о! (most) wonderful!; no wonder.
дие́т|а (-'ɛta) *f* [5] diet; **~и́ческий** [16] dietetic(al).
дизентери́я *f* [7] dysentery.
дик|а́рь *m* [4 *e*.] savage (*a*. *fig*.); F shy person; **∠ий** [16; дик, -а́, -о] wild, savage (*a*. *fig*.); odd, bizarre; shy, unsociable; drab; ⚘ proud

(*flesh*); dog (*rose*); ~ость *f* [8] wildness, savagery, -geness; absurdity.

дикт|áнт *m* [1] *s.* ~óвка; **~áтор** *m* [1] dictator; **~áторский** [16] dictatorial; **~атýра** *f* [5] dictatorship; **~овáть** [7], ⟨про-⟩ dictate; **~óвка** *f* [5; *g/pl.:* -вок] dictation; **~óр** *m* [1] (radio) announcer.

дилетáнт *m* [1] dilettante; **~ский** [16] dilettant(e)ish.

динáм|ика *f* [5] dynamics; **~и́т** *m* [1] dynamite; **~и́ческий** [16] dynamic; **~о(-маши́на** *f* [5]) *n* [*indecl.*] dynamo.

динáстия *f* [7] dynasty.

диплóм *m* [1] diploma; F thesis to degree.

дипломáт *m* [1] diplomat; **~и́ческий** [16] diplomatic; **~ия** *f* [7] diplomacy.

дирек|ти́ва *f* [5] directive; **~тор** *m* [1; *pl.:* -pá, *etc. e.*] manager, director; (*school*) principal, *Brt.* headmaster; **~ция** *f* [7] management, directorate.

дириж|áбль *m* [4] airship; **~ёр** *m* [1] ♪ conductor; **~и́ровать** [7] (T) ♪ conduct.

дисгармóния *f* [7] discord.

диск *m* [1] disk; **~óнт** *m* [1], **~онти́ровать** [7] (*im*)*pf.* discount; **~ýссия** *f* [7] discussion.

дисп|ансéр (-ˈsɛr) *m* [1] dispensary; **~éтчер** *m* [1] dispatcher; 🚂 traffic superintendent; **~ут** *m* [1] dispute, disputation.

дис|сертáция *f* [7] dissertation, thesis; **~сонáнс** *m* [1] dissonance, discord; **~тáнция** *f* [7] distance; 🚂 section; **~тилли́ровать** [7; -óванный] (*im*)*pf.* distil(l); **~ципли́на** *f* [5] discipline.

дитя́ *n* [-я́ти ✎; *pl.* дéти, *cf.*] child.

диф|ирáмб *m* [1] dithyramb; **~тери́т** *m* [1], **~тери́я** *f* [7] diphtheria; **~фамáция** *f* [7] defamation.

дифференц|иáл *m* [1], **~иáльный** [14] ⚗, ⊕ differential; **~и́ровать** [7] (*im*)*pf.* differentiate.

дич|áть [1], ⟨о-⟩ run wild; *fig.* grow (**~и́ться** F [16 *e.*; -чýсь, чи́шься] be) shy, unsociable; shun (a p. P); **~ь** *f* [8] game, wild fowl; F wilderness; F nonsense, bosh.

длин|á *f* [5] length; в ~ý (at) full length, lengthwise; ~óй в (В) ... *or* в ~ý ... long; **~но...** (*in compds.*) long...; **~ный** [14; -и́нен, -иннá, -и́нно] long; too long; F tall.

длит|ельный [14; -лен, -льна] long; protracted, lengthy; **~ься** [13], ⟨про-⟩ last.

для (P) for, to; because of; ~ тогó, чтóбы (in order) to, that ... may; ~ чегó? wherefore?; я́щик ~ пи́сем mail (*Brt.* letter) box.

Дми́трий *m* [3] Demetrius (*name*).

днев|áльный [14] ⚔ orderly; p. on duty; **~áть** [6] spend the day; have a day of rest; **~ни́к** *m* [1 *e.*] journal, diary (*vb.:* вести́ keep); **~нóй** [14] day('s), daily; day(light свет *m*).

днём by day, during the day.

Днепр *m* [1 *e.*] Dnieper; **~óвский** [16] Dnieper...

дн|о *n* [9; *pl.:* дóнья, -ньев] bottom; золотóе ~о *fig.* gold mine; вы́пить до ~а drain, empty; идти́ ко ~у *v/i.* (пусти́ть на ~о *v/t.*) sink.

до (P) *place:* to, as far as, up (*or* down) to; *time:* till, until, to; before; *degree:* to, up (*or* even) to; *age:* under; *quantity:* up to; about; ~ тогó so (much); (Д) не ~ F not be interested in *or* disposed for, *or* have no time, *etc.*, for, to.

добáв|ить *s.* ~ля́ть; **~лéние** *n* [12] addition; supplement; **~ля́ть** [28], ⟨~ить⟩ [14] add; **~очный** [14] additional, extra; supplementary.

добе|гáть [1], ⟨~жáть⟩ [-егý, -ежи́шь, -егýт] run up to (до P).

доб|ивáть [1], ⟨~и́ть⟩ [-бью, -бьёшь; -бéй(те)!; -би́тый] beat completely *or* utterly, smash; kill, finish; **-ся** (P) (try to) get, obtain *or* reach; strive for; find out (about); он ~и́лся своегó he gained his end(s); **~ирáться** [1], ⟨~рáться⟩ [-берýсь, -рёшься] get to, reach.

дóблест|ный [14; -тен, -тна] valiant, brave; **~ь** *f* [8] valo(u)r.

добрó[1] *n* [9] good; F property; ~м F kindly, amicably; ~[2] F well; ~ бы if only; ~ пожáловать! welcome!; please; **~вóлец** *m* [1; -льца] volunteer; **~вóльный** [14; -лен, -льна] voluntary; **~дéтель** *f* [8] virtue; **~дéтельный** [14; -лен, -льна] virtuous; **~дýшие** *n* [12] good nature; **~дýшный** [14; -шен, -шна] good-natured; **~желáтельный** [14; -лен, -льна] benevolent; **~желáтельство** *n* [9] benevolence; **~кáчественный** [14 *sh.*] (of) good (quality); ⚕ benign; **~сердéчный** [14; -чен, -чна] good-hearted; **~сóвестный** [14; -тен, -тна] conscientious; **~сосéдский** [16] good neighbo(u)rly; **~м** *s.* ~[1].

добр|отá *f* [5] kindness; **~óтный** [14; -тен, -тна] (very) good, solid; **~ый** [14; добр, -á, -о, дóбры́] kind; good; F solid; ~ое ýтро *n* (~ый день *m*, вéчер *m*)! good morning (afternoon, evening)!; в ~ый час!, всегó ~ого! good luck!; чегó ~ого after all; бýдь(те) ~(ы) will you be so kind.

добы|вáть [1], ⟨~ть⟩ [-бýду, -дешь; дóбы́л, -á, дóбы́ло; дóбы́тый (дóбы́т, добы́та, дóбы́то)] get, obtain, procure; ⚒ extract, mine; *hunt.* bag; **~ча** *f* [5] procurement; ⚒ extraction, mining; booty, spoil; (*animals'*) prey (*a. fig.*); *hunt.* bag.

довезти́ *s.* довози́ть.

дове́р|енность *f* [8] (на В) ⚖ letter of attorney; † = ~ие; **~енный** [14] deputed; proxy, agent; **~ие** *n* [12] confidence, trust (in к Д); **~ить** *s.* ~я́ть; **~чивый** [14 *sh.*] trusting, trustful; confidential; **~ша́ть** [1], ⟨~ши́ть⟩ [16 *e.*; -шу́, -ши́шь] finish; complete; **~ше́ние** *n* [12] completion; в ~ше́ние *or* к ~ше́нию (Р) to complete *or* crown (s.th.); **~я́ть** [28], ⟨~ить⟩ [13] trust (a p. Д); confide *or* entrust (s.th. to В/Д); entrust (a p. with Д/В); **-ся** (Д) *a.* trust, rely (on).

дов|ести́ *s.* ~оди́ть; **~од** *m* [1] argument; **~оди́ть** [15], ⟨~ести́⟩ [25] (до Р) see (a p. to); lead ([up] to); bring (to); drive (to), make.

довое́нный [14] prewar.

дов|ози́ть [15], ⟨~езти́⟩ [24] (до Р) take *or* bring ([right up] to).

дово́ль|но enough, sufficient; rather, pretty, fairly; **~ный** [14; -лен, -льна] content(ed), satisfied (with Т); **~ствие** ⚔ *n* [12] ration, allowance; **~ство** *n* [9] contentment, satisfaction; F prosperity; **~ствоваться** [7] content o.s. (with Т).

довы́боры *m/pl.* [1] by-election.

догад|а́ться *s.* ~ываться; **~ка** *f* [5; *g/pl.*: -док] guess, conjecture; **~ливый** [14 *sh.*] quick-witted; **~ываться,** ⟨~а́ться⟩ [1] (о П) guess, surmise.

до́гма *f* [5], **~т** *m* [1] dogma.

догна́ть *s.* догоня́ть.

догов|а́ривать [1], ⟨~ори́ть⟩ [13] finish (speaking), speak; **-ся** (о П) agree (upon), arrange; ~а́ривающиеся сто́роны *f/pl.* contracting parties; **~о́р** *m* [1] contract; *pol.* treaty; **~ори́ть(ся)** *s.* ~а́ривать(ся); **~о́рный** [14] contract(ual).

дог|оня́ть [28], ⟨~на́ть⟩ [-гоню́, -го́нишь, *cf.* гнать] catch up (with), overtake; drive *or* bring to; *impf.* *a.* pursue, try to catch up, be (on the point of) overtaking; **~ора́ть** [1], ⟨~оре́ть⟩ [9] burn down; *fig.* fade, die out.

дод|е́лывать, ⟨~е́лать⟩ [1] finish, complete; **~у́мываться,** ⟨~у́маться⟩ [1] (до Р) find, reach *or* hit upon (s. th., by thinking).

доезжа́|ть [1], ⟨дое́хать⟩ [-е́ду, -е́дешь] (до Р) reach; не ~я short of.

дожд|а́ться *s.* дожида́ться; **~еви́к** F *m* [1 *e.*] raincoat; **~ево́й** [14] rain(y); ~ево́й зо́нтик *m* umbrella; ~ево́й червь *m* earthworm; **~ли́вый** [14 *sh.*] rainy; **~ь** *m* [4 *e.*] rain (in под Т, на П); ~ь идёт it is raining.

дож|ива́ть [1], ⟨~и́ть⟩ [-живу́, -вёшь; до́жил, -а́, -о; до́житый (до́жит, -а́, -о)] *impf.* live one's last years, *etc.*; (до Р) *pf.* live (till *or* up to); (live to) see; come to; **~ида́ться** [1], ⟨~да́ться⟩ [-ду́сь, -дёшься; *cf.* ждать] (Р) wait (for, till); *pf.* *a.* [see.]

до́за *f* [5] dose.

дозво|ля́ть [28], ⟨~лить⟩ [13] permit, allow; ~ленный *a.* licit; **~ни́ться** F [13] *pf.* reach (a p. by phone до Р), ring till the door *or* phone is answered.

дозна́ние ⚖ *n* [12] inquest.

дозо́р ⚔ *m* [1], **~ный** ⚔ [14] patrol.

дои́ск|иваться F [1], ⟨~а́ться⟩ [3] (Р) (try to) find (out).

дои́ть(ся) [13], ⟨по-⟩ (give) milk.

дойти́ *s.* доходи́ть.

док *m* [1] ⚓ dock.

доказ|а́тельство *n* [9] proof, evidence; **~ывать** [1], ⟨~а́ть⟩ [3] prove; argue.

док|а́нчивать [1], ⟨~о́нчить⟩ [16] finish, end.

докла́д *m* [1] report; lecture (on о П); **~на́я** [14] (*a.* запи́ска *f*) memorandum, report; **~чик** *m* [1] lecturer; reporter; **~ывать** [1], ⟨доложи́ть⟩ [16] report (s.th. В *or* on о П); announce (a p. о П).

доко́нчить *s.* дока́нчивать.

до́ктор *m* [1; *pl.* -ра́, *etc. e.*] doctor.

доктри́на *f* [5] doctrine.

докуме́нт *m* [1] document.

докуча́ть F [1] = надоеда́ть.

долби́ть [14 *e.*; -блю́, -би́шь; -блённый] **1.** ⟨вы́-, про-⟩ hollow (out); peck (*bird*); chisel; *impf.* F strike; **2.** P ⟨в-⟩ inculcate; cram.

долг *m* [1; *pl. e.*] debt; *sg.* duty; (last) hono(u)rs *pl.*; в ~ = взаймы́; в ~у́ indebted (*a. fig.*, to у Р, пе́ред Т); **~ий** [16; до́лог, долга́, -о] long; **~о** long, (for) a long time *or* while.

долго|ве́чный [14; -чен, -чна] perennial (*a.* ♀), durable; **~во́й** [14]: ~во́е обяза́тельство *n* promissory note; **~вре́менный** [14] (very) long; **~вя́зый** F [14 *sh.*] lanky; **~игра́ющий** [17]: ~игра́ющая пласти́нка *f* long-playing record; **~ле́тие** *n* [12] longevity; **~ле́тний** [15] longstanding; of several years; **~сро́чный** [14] long-term; **~та́** *f* [5; *pl.*: -го́ты, *etc. st.*] length; *geogr.* longitude; **~терпели́вый** [14 *sh.*] long-suffering.

до́л|ее = ~ьше, *cf.*; **~ета́ть** [1], ⟨~ете́ть⟩ [11] (до Р) fly ([up] to), reach; *a.* = доноси́ться.

до́лж|ен *m*, ~на́ *f*, ~но́ *n* (*cf.* ~но́²), ~ны́ *pl.* **1.** must [*pt.*: ~ен был, ~на́ была́, *etc.* had to]; **2.** (Д) owe (a p.); **~ни́к** *m* [1 *e.*] debtor; **~но¹** one (it) must *or* ought to (be ...); proper(ly); **~но́²** P = ~но́ быть probably, apparently; **~ностно́й** [14] official; **~ность** *f* [8] post; office; **~ный** [14] due (*a. su.* ~ное *n*), proper; ~ным о́бразом duly.

доли|ва́ть [1], ⟨~ть⟩ [-лью́, -льёшь; *cf.* лить] fill (up), add.

доли́на *f* [5] valley.

до́ллар *m* [1] dollar.
доложи́ть *s.* докла́дывать.
доло́й F off, down; ~ ... (В)! down *or* off with ...!; с глаз ~! out of my sight!
долото́ *n* [9; *pl. st.*: -ло́та] chisel.
до́льше (*comp. of* до́лгий) longer.
до́ля *f* [6; *from g/pl. e.*] lot, fate; grain (*of truth*), spark (*of wit, etc.*); в восьму́ю (четвёртую) до́лю листа́ octavo (quarto), in 8vo (4to).
дом *m* [1; *pl.*: -а́, *etc. e.*] house; home; family; household; вы́йти и́з ~у leave (one's home), go out; на́ ~ = ~о́й; на ~у́ = **∠а** at home; как ∠а at one's ease; (у Р) не все ∠а (be) a bit off (one's head), nutty; **~а́шний** [15] home..., house(hold)-...; private; domestic; *pl. su.* folks; ~а́шний стол *m* plain fare; **∠енный** [14]: ∠енная печь *f* = ∠на; **∠ик** *m* [1] *dim. of* дом.
домин|ио́н *m* [1] (*Brt.*) dominion; **~и́ровать** [7] (pre)dominate; **~о́** *n* [*indecl.*] domino(es).
домкра́т *m* [1] (lifting) jack. [nace.]
до́мна *f* [5; *g/pl.*: -мен] blast fur-
дом|ови́тый [14 *sh.*] thrifty, careful; notable (*housewife*); **~овладе́лец** *m* [1; -льца] house owner; **~о́вый** [14] house... [solicit.]
домога́ться [1] (Р) strive for,
домо́|й home; **~ро́щенный** [14] homebred; **~се́д** *m* [1] stay-at-home; **~управле́ние** *n* [12] house management; **~ча́дцы** *m/pl.* [1] folks; inmate.
домрабо́тница *f* [5] housemaid.
до́мысел *m* [1; -сла] conjecture.
Дон *m* [1; на -ну́] Don; **~ба́сс** (= Доне́цкий бассе́йн) ⚒ *m* [1] Donets Basin.
доне|се́ние *n* [12] report; **~сти́**(**сь**) *s.* доноси́ть(ся); **∠цкий** [14] *s.* Донба́сс.
до́н|изу to bottom; **~има́ть** F [1], ⟨~я́ть⟩ [дойму́, -мёшь; *cf.* заня́ть] press, exhaust (with Т).
доно́с ⚖ *m* [1] denunciation, information (against на В); **~и́ть** [15], ⟨донести́⟩ [24; -су́, -сёшь] carry *or* bring ([up] to); report (s.th., about, on о П); denounce, inform (against на В); ~и́ть *pf.* wear out; *a.* **-ся** (до Р) waft (to), reach, (re-)sound; **~чик** *m* [1] informer.
донско́й [16] (*adj. of* Дон) Don...
доны́не to this day, till now.
доня́ть *s.* донима́ть.
допи|ва́ть [1], ⟨∠ть⟩ [-пью́, -пьёшь; *cf.* пить] drink up.
допла́|та *f* [5] additional payment, extra (*or* sur)charge; **~чивать** [1], ⟨~ти́ть⟩ [15] pay in addition.
допо́длинный F [14] true, real.
дополн|е́ние *n* [12] addition; supplement; *gr.* object; **~и́тельный** [14] additional, supplementary; extra; *adv. a.* in addition; more; **~я́ть** [28], ⟨∠ить⟩ [13] add, supply, complete, fill up; enlarge (*edition*).
допото́пный [14] antediluvian.
допр|а́шивать [1], ⟨~оси́ть⟩ [15] ⚖ interrogate, examine; *impf.* question; **~о́с** *m* [1] ⚖ interrogation, examination; F questioning; **~оси́ть** *s.* ~а́шивать.
до́пу|ск *m* [1] access, admittance; **~ска́ть** [1], ⟨~сти́ть⟩ [15] admit (*a.* of), concede; allow; tolerate; suppose; make (*mistake*); **~сти́мый** [14 *sh.*] admissible, permissible; **~ще́ние** *n* [12] admission.
допы́т|ываться [1], ⟨~а́ться⟩ F (try to) find out.
дореволюцио́нный [14] pre-revolutionary, before the revolution.
доро́г|а *f* [5] road, way (*a. fig.*); passage; trip, journey; больша́я ~а highroad; желе́зная ~а railroad, *Brt.* railway; ~ой *or* в (по) ~е on the way; туда́ ему́ и ~а F that serves him right; *cf. a.* путь.
дорого|ви́зна *f* [5] dearness, high price(s); **∠й** [16; до́рог, -а́, -о; *comp.*: доро́же] dear (*a. fig.*), expensive.
доро́дный [14; -ден, -дна] stout, burly.
дорож|а́ть [1], ⟨вз-, по-⟩ become dearer, rise in price; **~и́ть** [16 *e.*; -жу́, -жи́шь] (Т) esteem (highly), (set a high) value (on).
доро́ж|ка *f* [5; *g/pl.*: -жек] path; бегова́я ~ка race track (*Brt.* -way); лётная ~ка ✈ runway; **~ный** [14] road...; travel(l)ing.
доса́|да *f* [5] vexation; annoyance, fret; F кака́я ~да! how annoying!, what a pity!; **~ди́ть** *s.* ~жда́ть; **~дливый** [14 *sh.*] fretful, peevish; **~дный** [14; -ден, -дна] annoying, vexatious; deplorable; (мне) ~дно it is annoying (annoys me); **~довать** [7] feel *or* be annoyed, vexed (at, with на В); **~жда́ть** [1], ⟨~ди́ть⟩ [15 *e.*; -ажу́, -ади́шь] vex, annoy (a p. with Д/Т).
доск|а́ *f* [5; *ac/sg.*: до́ску; *pl.*: до́ски, досо́к, доска́м] board, plank; (*a.* кла́ссная ~а́) blackboard; plate; гри́фельная ~а́ slate; от ~и́ до ~и́ (*read*) from cover to cover; на одну́ ∠у on a level.
доскона́льный [14; -лен, -льна] thorough.
досло́вный [14] literal, verbal.
досм|а́тривать [1], ⟨~отре́ть⟩ [9; -отрю́, -о́тришь] see up to *or* to the end (до Р); watch, look after (за Т); не ~отре́ть overlook; **~о́тр** *m* [1] supervision; (customs) examination; **~отре́ть** *s.* ~а́тривать.
доспе́хи *m/pl.* [1] armo(u)r; outfit.
досро́чный [14] preschedule.
дост|ава́ть [5], ⟨~а́ть⟩ [-ста́ну, -ста́нешь] take (out, *etc.*); get; procure; ([до] Р) touch; reach (to); F (Р) suffice, have enough; **-ся** (Д)

fall to a p.'s share; (turn out to) be, cost (*fig.*); F catch it; **~áвить** *s.* ~авля́ть; **~áвка** *f* [5; *g/pl.*: -вок] delivery; conveyance; с ~áвкой (нá дом) carriage paid; free to the door; **~авля́ть** [28], ⟨~áвить⟩ [14] deliver, hand; bring; *fig.* procure, cause, give; **~áток** *m* [1; -тка] prosperity, (good) fortune; F sufficiency; **~áточно** considerably; (P) (be) enough, sufficient; suffice; **~áточный** [14; -чен, -чна] sufficient.

дости|гáть [1], ⟨∠гнуть⟩, ⟨∠чь⟩ [21 -г-: -сти́гну, -гнешь] (P) reach, arrive at, attain (*a. fig.*); (*prices*) amount *or* run up (to); **~жéние** *n* [12] attainment; achievement; **~жи́мый** [14 *sh.*] attainable.

достовéрный [14; -рен, -рна] authentic, reliable; positive.

достó|инство *n* [9] dignity; merit, advantage; (*money, etc.*) worth, value; **~йный** [14; -óин, -óйна] worthy (*a.* of P); well-deserved; **~пáмятный** [14; -тен, -тна] memorable, notable; **~примечáтельность** *f* [8] (*mst. pl.*) sight(s); **~примечáтельный** [14; -лен, -льна] remarkable, noteworthy; **~я́ние** *n* [12] property (*a. fig.*), fortune.

дóступ *m* [1] access; **∠ный** [14; -пен, -пна] accessible (*a. fig.*); approachable, affable; comprehensible; susceptible; moderate (*price*).

досу́г *m* [1] leisure; на ~е at leisure, during one's leisure hours.

дóс|уха (quite) dry; **∠ы́та** one's fill.

дот ⚔ *m* [1] pillbox.

дотлá completely, utterly; to the ground.

дотр|áгиваться [1], ⟨~óнуться⟩ [20] (до P) touch.

дóх|лый [14] dead; **~ля́тина** *f* [5] carrion; **~нуть** [21], ⟨из-, по-⟩ die; P croak, kick off; **~ну́ть** *s.* дышáть.

дохóд *m* [1] income, revenue; proceeds *pl.* **~и́ть** [15], ⟨дойти́⟩ [дойду́, -дёшь; *cf.* идти́] (до P) go *or* come (to), arrive (at), reach: *hist.* come down to; (*price*) rise, run up to; **~ный** [14; -ден, -дна] profitable.

доцéнт *m* [1] lecturer, instructor.

дóчиста (quite) clean; F completely.

дочи́т|ывать, ⟨~áть⟩, [1] finish (*book, etc.*) *or* read up to (до P).

дóч|ка *f* [5; *g/pl.*: -чек] F = **~ь** *f* [дóчери, *etc.* = 8; *pl.*: дóчери, -рéй, *etc. e.*; *instr.*: -рьми́] daughter.

дошкóльный *m* [1] preschool.

дощ|áтый [14] of boards, plank...; **~éчка** *f* [5; *g/pl.*: -чек] *dim. of* доскá.

доя́рка *f* [5; *g/pl.*: -рок] milkmaid.

драгоцéнн|ость *f* [8] jewel, gem (*a. fig.*); precious thing *or* possession; **~ый** [14; -цéнен, -цéнна] precious (*a. stone*), costly, valuable.

дразни́ть [13; -ню́, дрáзнишь] **1.** ⟨по-⟩ tease, banter; nickname; **2.** ⟨раз-⟩ excite.

дрáка *f* [5] scuffle, fight.

дракóн *m* [1] dragon.

дрáма *f* [5] drama; **~ти́ческий** [16] dramatic; **~ту́рг** *m* [1] playwright, dramatist.

драп|ировáть [7], ⟨за-⟩ drape; **∠овый** [14] (of thick) cloth (драп).

дра|ть [деру́, -рёшь; драл, -á, -о; '... дранный], ⟨со-⟩ (*cf.* сдирáть) pull (off); tweak (p.'s *ear* В/за В; F *cf.* выдирáть & раздирáть; **-ся,** ⟨по-⟩ scuffle, fight, struggle; **~чли́вый** [14 *sh.*] pugnacious.

дребе|дéнь F *f* [8] trash; **'~зг** F *m* [1] clash; *cf.* вдрéбезги; **~зжáть** [4; -зжи́т], ⟨за-⟩ rattle.

древ|еси́на *f* [5] wood substance *or* material(s); **~éсный** [14] tree...; wood(y); ~éсный спирт *m* methyl alcohol; ~éсный у́голь *m* charcoal; **∠ко** *n* [9; *pl.*: -ки, -ков] flagpole.

дрéвн|ий [15; -вен, -вня] ancient (*a. su.*), antique; (very) old; **~ость** *f* [8] antiquity (*a. pl.* = -ties).

дрейф ⚓, ✈ *m* [1], **~овáть** [7] drift.

дрем|áть [2], ⟨за-⟩ doze (off), slumber; **~óта** *f* [5] drowsiness; slumber, doze; **~у́чий** [17] dense; ~у́чий лес *m* primeval forest.

дрессировáть [7], ⟨вы́-⟩ train.

дроб|и́ть [14 *e.*; -блю́, -би́шь; -блённый], ⟨раз-⟩ break to pieces, crush; dismember, divide *or* split up; *impf.* F drum; **∠ный** [14; -бен, -бна] fractional; rolling; drumming; **~ь** *f* [8] *coll.* (small) shot; (*drum*) roll; ⅍ [*from g/pl. e.*] fraction; decimal.

дров|á *n/pl.* [9] (fire)wood; **∠ни** *m/pl.* [4; *a. from g/pl. e.*] peasant's sled(ge); **~осéк** *m* [1] lumberman, *Brt.* woodcutter.

дрó|ги *f/pl.* [5] dray; **~гнуть 1.** [21], ⟨про-⟩ shiver *or* shake (*with cold*), chill; **2.** [20 *st.*] *pf.* start; waver, falter; shrink, flinch; **~жáть** [4 *e.*; -жу́, -жи́шь], ⟨за-⟩ tremble, shake, shiver (with от P); flicker, glimmer; dread (s.th. пéред T); be anxious (about за B); guard, save (над T); **~жжи** *f/pl.* [8; *from gen. e.*] yeast, barm; **~жки** *f/pl.* [5; *gen.*: -жек] droshky; **~жь** *f* [8] trembling, shiver; vibration; ripples *pl.*

дро|зд *m* [1 *e.*] thrush; **~к** *m* [1] ⚘ broom; **∠тик** *m* [1] dart, javelin; **~фá** *f* [5; *pl. st.*] *zo.* bustard.

друг[1] *m* [1; *pl.*: друзья́, -зéй, -зья́м] friend; (*address a.*) dear; **~**[2]**:** ~ ∠а each (one an)other; ~ за ∠ом one after another; ~ с ∠ом with each other; **~óй** [14] (an)other, different; else, next, second; (н)и тóт (н)и ~óй both (neither); на ~óй день the next day.

дру́ж|ба *f* [5] friendship; **~елю́бный** [14; -бен, -бна] amicable, friendly; **~еский** [16], **~ественный** [14 *sh.*] friendly; **~и́на** *f* [5] bodyguard, retinue; militia; troop, (*fire*) brigade; **~и́ть** [16; -жу́, -у́жи́шь] be friends, be on friendly terms (with с T); **~и́ще** *m* F [11] old chap *or* boy; **~ка** [5; *g/pl.*: -жек] **1.** *f* F = друг[2]; **2.** *m* best man; **~ный** [14; -жен, -жна́, -о, дру́жны́] friendly, on friendly terms; harmonious, concurrent, unanimous; ♀, ⚔ vigorous; *adv. a.* hand in hand, together; at once.

дря́|блый [14; дрябл, -á, -о] limp, flabby; **~зги** F *f/pl.* [5] squabbles; **~нно́й** P [14] wretched, mean, trashy; **~нь** F *f* [8] rubbish, trash (*a. fig.*); P rotten, lousy (thing, p.); **~хлый** [14; дряхл, -á, -о] decrepit; F dilapidated.

дуб *m* [1; *pl. e.*] oak; **~и́льный** [14] tan...; **~и́льня** *f* [6; *g/pl.*: -лен] tannery; **~и́на** *f* [5] club, cudgel; P boor, dolt; **~и́ть** [14 *e.*; -блю́, -би́шь], ⟨вы́-⟩ tan; **~лёр** *m* [1] *thea.* understudy, double; **~ова́тый** F [14 *sh.*] dull; **~о́вый** [14] oak(en); *fig.* dull; **~ра́ва** *f* [5] (oak) wood, forest.

дуг|á *f* [5; *pl. st.*] arc (*a.* ⚡); (shaft) bow (*harness*); ~о́й arched; **~ово́й** [14]: ~ова́я ла́мпа *f* arc light.

ду́дк|а *f* [5; *g/pl.*: -док] pipe; F ~и! fudge!, rats!; пляса́ть под ~у *or* по ~е dance to s.b.'s tune *or* piping.

ду́ло *n* [9] muzzle; barrel (*gun*).

ду́ма *f* [5] **1.** thought; meditation; **2.** (*Russia, prior to 1917*) duma = council; elective legislative assembly; **~ть** [1], ⟨по-⟩ think (about, of о П); reflect, meditate (on над T, о П); (+ *inf.*) intend, be going to; care (for о П); F suspect (на B); как ты ~ешь? what do you think?; мно́го ~ть о себе́ be conceited; не до́лго ~я without hesitation; **-ся** seem, appear; ([one, you] must, can) think.

Дуна́й *m* [3] Danube.

дун|ове́ние *n* [12] waft, breath; **∠уть** *s.* дуть.

Ду́ня *f* [6] *dim. of* Евдоки́я.

дупло́ *n* [9; *pl. st.*: ду́пла, -пел, -плам] hollow (*tree*); cavity (*tooth*).

ду́р|а *f* [5] silly woman; **~а́к** *m* [1 *e.*] fool, simpleton; ~а́к ~ако́м arrant fool; **~а́цкий** [16] foolish, silly; fool's; **~а́чество** F *n* [9] tomfoolery; **~а́чить** F [16], ⟨о-⟩ fool, hoax; **-ся** fool, play tricks; **~е́ть** F [8], ⟨о-⟩ grow stupid; become stupefied; **~и́ть** F [13] *s.* ~а́читься; be naughty *or* obstinate.

дурма́н *m* [1] jimson weed, thorn apple; *fig.* narcotic; **~ить** [13], ⟨о-⟩ stupefy.

дурн|е́ть [8], ⟨по-⟩ grow plain *or* ugly; **~о́й** [14; ду́рен, -рна́, -о] bad; plain, ugly; P stupid; мне ∠о I feel (am) sick *or* unwell; **~ота́** F *f* [5] giddiness, sickness.

дурь F *f* [8] folly, caprice; trash.

ду́т|ый [14] blown (*glass*); *fig.* inflated; false; **~ь** [18], ⟨по-⟩, *once* ⟨ду́нуть⟩ [20] blow; ду́ет there is a draught (draft); **-ся**, ⟨на-⟩ swell; F sulk, be angry with (на B); P give o.s. airs.

дух *m* [1] spirit; mind; courage; ghost; F breath; P scent; (не) в ∠е in a good (bad) temper *or* in high (low) spirits, ([+ *inf.*] in no mood to); в моём ∠е to my taste; на ~у́ at the confession; P ∠ом in a jiffy *or* trice; at one draught; во весь ~ *or* что́ есть ∠у at full speed, with all one's might; **~и́** *m/pl.* [1 *e.*] perfume.

духов|е́нство *n* [9] *coll.* clergy; **∠ка** *f* [5; *g/pl.*: -вок] oven; **~ни́к** *m* [1 *e.*] (father) confessor; **∠ный** [14] spiritual; mental; ecclesiastical, clerical, religious, sacred; ∠ная *f* (*form.*) testament, will; ∠ный оте́ц *m* = ~ни́к; ∠ное лицо́ *n* clergyman; **~о́й** [14] ♪ wind (*instrument*); ~о́й орке́стр *m* brassband.

духота́ *f* [5] sultriness, sultry air.

душ *m* [1] shower (bath); douche.

душ|á *f* [5; *ac/sg.*: ду́шу; *pl. st.*] soul; mind, disposition; temper (-ament); feeling, emotion; person; *hist.* serf; F *address*: dear, darling; ~а́ в ∠у in perfect harmony; в глубине́ ~и́ in one's heart of hearts; от (всей) ~и́ from (with all) one's heart; по ~а́м heart-to-heart; ~а́ в пя́тки ушла́ have one's heart in one's mouth.

душ|евнобольно́й [14] mentally sick *or* deranged (person); **~е́вный** [14] mental, psychic(al); sincere, hearty; **∠енька** F *f* [5] darling; **~ераздира́ющий** [17] heart-rending.

душ|и́стый [14 *sh.*] fragrant; sweet (*peas*); **~и́ть** [16] **1.** ⟨за-⟩ strangle, choke (*a. fig.*); **2.** ⟨на-⟩ perfume (o.s. **-ся**); **∠ный** [14; -шен, -шна́, -о] stuffy; sultry.

дуэ́|ль *f* [8] duel; **~т** *m* [1] duet.

ды́б|ом (*stand*) on end (*hair*); **~ы:** (встать, *etc.*) на ~ы rear (*a.* up, *fig.*), prance.

дым *m* [1] smoke; **~и́ть** [14 *e.*; -млю́, -ми́шь], ⟨на-⟩ *or* **~и́ться** smoke; steam; **∠ка** *f* [5] haze; gauze; **∠ный** [14] smoky; **~ово́й** [14] smoke...; **~о́к** *m* [1; -мка́] small stream *or* puff of smoke; **~охо́д** *m* [1] flue.

ды́ня *f* [6] muskmelon.

дыр|á *f* [5; *pl. st.*], **∠ка** *f* [5; *g/pl.*: -рок] hole; **~я́вый** [14 *sh.*] having a hole *or* full of holes; (*clothes, shoes*)

tattered; F bad (*memory*); ~я́вая голова́ F forgetful person.
дыха́|ние *n* [12] breath(ing); **~тельный** [14] respiratory; ~тельное го́рло *n* windpipe.
дыша́ть [4], ⟨по-⟩, F (*a. once*) ⟨дохну́ть⟩ [20] breathe (s. th. T); *a.* devote o.s. to, indulge in; foam with; ~ све́жим во́здухом take the air; е́ле ~ *or* ~ на ла́дан F have one foot in the grave.
ды́шло *n* [9] (*wagon, cart*) pole.
дья́вол *m* [1] devil; **~ьский** [16] devilish.
дья|к, ~чо́к *m* [1; -чка́] clerk & chanter, sexton; **∠кон** *m* [1] deacon.
дю́жий P [17; дюж, -а́, -е] sturdy.
дю́жин|а *f* [5] dozen; ~ами, по ~ам by the dozen; **~ный** [14] common (-place), mediocre.
дю|йм *m* [1] inch; **∠на** *f* [5] dune.
дюралюми́ний *m* [3] duralumin.
дя́д|ька *m* [5; *g/pl.*: -дек] F & *contp.* = ~я; † tutor, instructor; **~я** *m* [6; *g/pl.*: -дей] uncle (*a. in* F *address*); F (strong) fellow, guy.
дя́тел *m* [1; -тла] woodpecker.

Е

'Ева *f* [5] Eve (*name*).
Ева́нгелие *n* [12] Gospel (♀ *fig.*).
Евге́ни|й *m* [3] Eugene; **~я** *f* [7] Eugenia.
Евдоки́я *f* [7] Eudoxia.
евре́й *m* [3] Jew; **~ка** *f* [5; *g/pl.*: -ре́ек] Jewess; **~ский** [16] Jewish.
Евро́п|а *f* [5] Europe *n*; **♀е́ец** *m* [1; -пе́йца], **♀е́йка** *f* [5; *g/pl.*: -пе́ек], **♀е́йский** [16] European.
е́герь *m* [4; *pl.*: *a.* -ря́, *etc. e.*] hunter; ⚔ chasseur.
Еги́п|ет *m* [1; -пта] Egypt; **♀етский** [16] Egyptian; **♀тя́нин** *m* [1; *pl.*: -я́не, -я́н], **♀тя́нка** *f* [5; *g/pl.*: -нок] Egyptian.
его́ (ji'vɔ) his; its; *cf.* он.
Его́р P *m* [1] George.
еда́ *f* [5] food; meal.
едва́ (*a.* ~ ли) hardly, scarcely; *s. a.* е́ле; no sooner; ~ не almost, nearly; ~ ли не perhaps.
един|е́ние *n* [12] unity, union; **~и́ца** *f* [5] ⅍ one; digit; unit; F (*mark*) very bad; *pl.* (a) few; **~и́чный** [14; -чен, -чна] single, isolated.
едино... (*cf. a.* одно...): **~бо́рство** *n* [9] (single) combat, duel; **~вла́стие** *n* [12] autocracy; **~вре́менный** [14] single; † simultaneous; **~гла́сие** *n* [12] unanimity; **~гла́сный** [14; -сен, -сна] unanimous; ~гла́сно unanimously; **~ду́шие** *n* [12] unanimity; **~ду́шный** [14; -шен, -шна] unanimous; **~ли́чный** [14] individual (*a.* peasant ~ли́чник *m*), personal; **~мы́слящий** [17] like-minded; **~мы́шленник** *m* [1] like-minded p., associate, confederate; **~обра́зный** [14; -зен, -зна] uniform; **~ро́г** *m* [1] unicorn.
еди́нствен|ный [14 *sh.*] only, single, sole; ~ный в своём ро́де unique; ~ное число́ *n gr.* singular.
еди́н|ство *n* [9] unity; unanimity; **~ый** [14 *sh.*] one, single; only (one), sole; one whole; united; (one and the) same; все до ~ого all to a man.
е́дкий [16; е́док, едка́, -о] caustic.
едо́к *m* [1 *e.*] (F good) eater.
её her; its; *cf.* она́.
ёж *m* [1 *e.*] hedgehog.
ежеви́ка *f* [5] blackberry, -ries *pl.*
еже|го́дный [14] annual; **~дне́вный** [14] daily; everyday; **~ме́сячный** [14] monthly; **~мину́тный** [14] (occuring) every minute; continual; **~неде́льный** [14] weekly; **~ча́сный** [14] hourly.
ёжиться [16], ⟨съ-⟩ shrink; be shy.
ежо́в|ый [14]: держа́ть в ~ых рукави́цах rule with a rod of iron.
езд|а́ *f* [5] ride, drive; **∠ить** [15], go (by T), ride, drive; come, visit; travel; **~о́к** *m* [1 *e.*] rider, horseman.
ей: ~(-~) P, ~-бо́гу F really, indeed.
Екатери́на *f* [5] Catherine.
е́ле (*a.* ~-~) hardly, scarcely, barely; slightly; with (great) difficulty.
еле́й *m* [3] (holy) oil; *fig.* unction; **~ный** [14] unctuous.
Еле́на *f* [5] Helen.
Елизаве́та *f* [5] Elizabeth.
ёлка *f* [5; *g/pl.*: ёлок] fir; (рожде́ственская, новогóдняя) ~ Christmas (*Sov.*: New Year's) tree *or* (children's) party (на В to, for; на П at).
ел|о́вый [14] fir(ry); **~ь** *f* [8] fir; **∠ьник** *m* [1] fir wood (*or* greens *pl.*).
ёмк|ий [16; ёмок, ёмка] capacious; **~ость** *f* [8] capacity; ме́ра ~ости cubic measure.
Енисе́й *m* [3] Yenisei (*Siber. river*).
ено́т *m* [1] raccoon.
епи́скоп *m* [1] bishop.
ерала́ш F *m* [1] mess, muddle, jumble.
е́ре|сь *f* [8] heresy; **~ти́к** *m* [1 *e.*] heretic.
ёрзать F [1] fidget; slip.
еро́шить [16] = взъеро́шивать, *s.*
ерунда́ F *f* [5] nonsense; trifle(s).
е́сли if, in case; once (*a.* ~ уж[е́]); а *or* и ~ if ever; whereas; ~ и *or*

да́)же even though; ах *or* о, ~ (ы) ... oh, could *or* would ...; ~ бы не but for; ~ то́лько provided.
естеств|енный [14 *sh.*] natural; **~о́** [9] nature; **~ове́д** *m* [1] naturalist, scientist; **~ове́дение, ~озна́ние** *n* [12] natural science; **~оиспыта́тель** *m* [4] *s.* ~ове́д.
есть[1] [ем, ешь, ест, еди́м, еди́те, едя́т; ешь(те)!; ел; ...е́денный] **1.** ‹ съ-, по-› eat (*pf. a.* up), have; **2.** ‹разъ-› eat away (*rust*); ⚗ corrode; bite; **3.** F ‹по-, разъ-› bite, gnaw, sting; P torment.
есть[2] *cf.* быть; am, is, are; there is (are); у меня́ ~ ... I have ...; так и ~ indeed!; ~ тако́е де́ло! F O.K.; ~! ⚔ yes, sir!
ефре́йтор ⚔ *m* [1] private first class, *Brt.* lance-corporal.
е́ха|ть [е́ду, е́дешь; поезжа́й!], ‹по-› (be) go(ing, *etc.*) (by T), ride, drive (in, on T *or* в, на П); come; run; (в, на В) leave (for), go (to); (за T) go for, fetch; по~ли! *s.* идти́.
ехи́д|ный [14; -ден, -дна] spiteful, malignant; **~ство** *n* [9] spite, malice.
ещё (не) (not) yet; (всё) ~ still (*a. with comp.*); another, more (& more ~ и ~); ~ раз once more; else; already; as early (late, *etc.*) as; possibly, probably; more or less, somewhat; ~ бы! (to be) sure!, I should think so!, of course!; it would be worse still if ...

Ж

ж *s.* же.
жа́б|а *f* [5] toad; грудна́я ~а angina pectoris; **~ра** *f* [5] gill.
жа́воронок *m* [1; -нка] (sky)lark.
жадн|ичать F [1], ‹по-› be greedy *or* avaricious; **~ость** *f* [8] greed (-iness), avarice; **~ый** [14; -ден, -дна́, -o] greedy (of на В, до Р, к Д), avaricious.
жа́жда *f* [5] thirst (*a. fig.* for P, *or inf.*); **~ть** [-ду, -дешь] thirst, crave (for P, *or inf.*).
жаке́т *m* [1], F **~ка** *f* [5; *g/pl.*: -ток] jacket.
жале́ть [8], ‹по-› **1.** pity; (о П) regret; **2.** (P *or* B) spare; grudge.
жа́лить [13], ‹у-› sting, bite.
жа́лк|ий [16; -лок, -лка́, -o; *comp.*: жа́льче] pitiable; miserable, wretched; **~o** *s.* жаль.
жа́ло *n* [9] sting (*a. fig.*).
жа́лоб|а *f* [5] complaint; ⚖ action; **~ный** [14; -бен, -бна] mournful, plaintive; (of) complaint(s).
жа́лова|нье *n* [10] pay, salary; reward; **~ть** [7], ‹по-› (T) reward, award; give; appoint (в И *pl.*); F like; come (to see a p. к Д); **-ся** (на В) complain (of); F inform (against); ⚖ sue, go to law.
жа́лост|ливый F [14 *sh.*] compassionate; sorrowful; **~ный** F [14; -тен, -тна] mournful; compassionate; **~ь** *f* [8] pity, compassion.
жаль it is a pity (как ~ what a pity); unfortunately; (Д ~ В): мне ~ его́ I am sorry for (*or* pity) him; *a.* regret; grudge.
жар *m* [1; в -у́] heat; fever; *fig.* ardo(u)r; **~а́** *f* [5] heat, hot weather; **~еный** [14] fried; roast(ed); *s. a.* ~ко́е; **~ить** [13], ‹за-, из-, P с-› roast; fry; F (*sun*) burn; **~кий** [16; -рок, -рка́, -o; *comp.*: жа́рче] hot; *fig.* ardent, vehement, intense; мне ~ко I am hot; **~ко́е** *n* [16] roast meat.
жа́т|ва *f* [5] harvest; crop; **~венный** [14] reaping.
жать[1] [жму́, жмёшь; ...жа́тый], ‹с-›, *cf.*, & ‹по-› press, squeeze (*a.* out); shake (hands with ру́ку Д); pinch (*shoes, etc.*); F *fig.* oppress; **-ся** shrink (with от Р); crowd; snuggle; F vacillate; **~**[2] [жну, жнёшь; ... жа́тый], ‹с-› [сожну́], ‹по-› reap, harvest.
жва́ч|ка *f* [5] rumination; cud; P chewing gum (*or* tobacco); **~ный** [14]: ~ные (живо́тные) *n/pl.* ruminants.
жгут *m* [1 *e.*] strap.
жгу́чий [17 *sh.*] burning; poignant.
ж. д. *abbr.*: желе́зная доро́га; *cf.* R. R., Ry.
ждать [жду, ждёшь; ждал, -á, -o], ‹подо-› wait (for P); expect, await; вре́мя не ждёт time presses; ~ не дожда́ться wait impatiently (for P).
же 1. *conj.* but, and; whereas, as to; **2.** = ведь, *cf.*; *a.* do + *vb.*; the (this) very, same (*a.* place, time, *etc.*); just; too; *interr.* ever, on earth; for goodness' sake.
жева́|ть [7 *e.*; жую, жуёшь] chew; **~тельный** [14] masticatory; chewing.
жезл *m* [1 *e.*] staff, rod, wand.
жела́|ние *n* [12] wish, desire; по (согла́сно) ~нию at, by (as) request(ed); **~нный** [14; -а́нен, -а́нна] desired, long wished for; welcome; beloved; **~тельный** [14; -лен, -льна] desirable; desired; мне ~тельно I am anxious to; **~ть** [1], ‹по-› wish (a p. s.th. Д/Р), desire; love; **~ющие** *pl.* [17] p.s wishing to ...
желе́ *n* [*indecl.*] jelly (*a. fish, meat*).
железа́ *f* [5; *pl.*: же́лезы, желёз, железа́м] gland.

желез|нодоро́жник *m* [1] railroad (*Brt.* railway-) man; **~нодоро́жный** [14] railroad..., *Brt.* railway...; **∠ный** [14] iron...; rail...; **∠о** *n* [9] iron; кро́вельное ∠о sheet iron; куй ∠о, пока́ горячо́ strike while the iron is hot; **~обето́н** *m* [1] reinforced concrete.
жёлоб *m* [1; *pl.*: -ба́, *etc. e.*] gutter.
желт|е́ть [8], ⟨по-⟩ grow *or* turn yellow; *impf.* (*a.* **-ся**) appear *or* show yellow; **~изна́** *f* [5] yellow (-ness); **~ова́тый** [14 *sh.*] yellowish; **~о́к** *m* [1; -тка́] yolk; **~у́ха** *f* [5] jaundice.
жёлтый [14; жёлт, -а́, -о] yellow.
желу́до|к *m* [1; -дка] stomach; **~чный** [14] gastric, stomachic(al).
жёлудь *m* [4; *from g/pl. e.*] acorn.
жёлч|ный [14] gall...; [жёлчен, -чна, -о] bilious (*a. fig.*); **~ь** *f* [8] bile, gall (*a. fig.*); grief.
жема́н|иться F [13] mince; be prim; **~ница** F *f* [5] prude; **~ный** [14; -а́нен, -а́нна] affected, mincing, prim; **~ство** *n* [9] primness, prudery.
же́мч|уг *m* [1; *pl.*: -га́, *etc. e.*] *coll.* pearls *pl.*; **~у́жина** *f* [5] pearl; **~у́жный** [14] pearl(y).
жен|а́ *f* [5; *pl. st.*: жёны] wife; † woman; **~а́тый** [14 *sh.*] married (*man*; to a p. на П); **~и́ть** [13; женю́, же́нишь] (*im*)*pf.* marry (*a man* to на П); **-ся** marry (*v/t.* на П; *of men*); **~и́тьба** *f* [5] marriage (to на П); **~и́х** [1 *e.*] fiancé; bridegroom; suiter; F marriageable young man; **~олю́б** *m* [1] lady-killer, ladies' man; **~оненави́стник** *m* [1] woman hater **~оподо́бный** [14; -бен, -бна] womanlike; **∠ский** [16] female, woman('s) *or* women's; girls'; *gr.* feminine; **∠ственный** [14 *sh.*] womanly; womanish, effeminate; **∠щина** *f* [5] woman.
жердь *f* [8; *from g/pl. e.*] pole.
жереб|ёнок *m* [2] foal, colt; **~е́ц** *m* [1; -бца́] stallion.
жерло́ *n* [9; *pl. st.*] crater; aperture, mouth; muzzle (*gun, etc.*).
жёрнов *m* [1; *pl. e.*: -ва́] millstone.
же́ртв|а *f* [5] sacrifice; (*p.*:) victim; **~овать** [7], ⟨по-⟩ (Т) sacrifice (*v/t.*; o.s. собо́й); (В) give; **~оприноше́ние** *n* [12] offering.
жест *m* [1] gesture; **~икули́ровать** [7] gesticulate.
жёсткий [16; -ток, -тка́, -о; *comp.*: -тче] hard; rough, rude, coarse, harsh (*a. fig.*); tough; stiff, rigid, severe, rigorous; ~ ваго́н (ordinary) passenger car, *Brt.* second-class carriage.
жесто́к|ий [16; жесто́к, -а́, -о] cruel; terrible, dreadful, fierce, grim; rigorous, violent; **~осе́рдие** *n* [12] hard-heartedness; **~ость** *f* [8] cruelty; severity.

жест|ь *f* [8] tin (plate); **~я́нка** [5; *g/pl.*: -нок] can, *Brt.* tin; **~яно́** [14] tin...; **~я́нщик** *m* [1] tinsmith
жето́н *m* [1] counter; medal; toke
жечь, ⟨с-⟩ [26 г/ж: (со)жгу, -жжёшь, -жгу́т; (с)жёг, (со)жгла, сожжённый] burn (*a. fig.*); tor ment.
живи́т|ельный [14; -лен, -льна vivifying; crisp (*air*); **~ь** [14 *e.*; жив лю́, -ви́шь], ⟨о-⟩ vivify, animate.
жив|о́й [14; жив, -а́, -о] living alive (*pred.*); lively, vivid, vivaciou quick, nimble; real, true; в ~ы́ alive; ~ и здоро́в safe & sound ни ~ ни мёртв more dead tha alive; заде́ть за ~о́е sting to th quick; **~опи́сец** *m* [1; -сца] painte **~опи́сный** [14; -сен, -сна] pictur esque; **∠опись** *f* [8] painting **∠ость** *f* [8] vivacity; vividness.
живо́т *m* [1 *e.*] P belly; stomach † life; **~во́рный** [14; -рен, -рна vivifying; **~новодство** *n* [9] cattl breeding; **~ное** *n* [14] animal; ~ный [14] animal; *fig.* brutal.
жив|отрепе́щущий [17] livin (*fish*); *fig.* burning; **~у́чий** [17 *sh.* hardy, tough; enduring; **~ьём** alive.
жи́дк|ий [16; -док, -дка́, -о; *comp.* жи́же] liquid, fluid; watery, weak thin; sparse, scanty; **~ость** *f* [8 liquid; scantiness.
жи́ж|а, **~ица** F *f* [5] slush; broth.
жи́зне|нность *f* [8] viability; vital ity; vividness; **~нный 1.** [14 *sh.* (of) life('s), worldly; vivid; living **2.** [14] vital; **~описа́ние** *n* [12] bi ography; **~ра́достный** [14; -тен -тна] cheerful, merry; **~спосо́бны** [14; -бен, -бна] viable.
жизн|ь *f* [8] life; practice; в ~ь (∠и не ... never (in one's life); при ∠и in a p.'s lifetime; alive; не на ~ь, на смерть of life & death.
жи́л|а *f* [5] F sinew, tendon; vei (*a.* ⚒); **~е́т** *m* [1], **~е́тка** *f* [5; *g/pl.* -ток] vest, *Brt.* waistcoat; **~е́ц** *n* [1; -льца́] lodger, roomer; inmate † = жи́тель; **~истый** [14 *sh.* sinewy, stringy (*a. meat*), wiry **~и́ще** *n* [11] dwelling, lodging(s) **~и́щный** [14] housing; **~ка** *f* [5 *g/pl.*: -лок] *dim. of* ~а; veinlet; vei (*leaf, wing, marble, & fig.*); **~о́й** [14 dwelling; inhabited; living, *cf.* ~ **пло́щадь** *f* [8] living space; **~ьё** [10] habitation; F dwelling.
жир *m* [1; в -у́; *pl. e.*] fat; grease ры́бий ~ cod-liver oil; **~е́ть** [8] ⟨о-, раз-⟩ grow fat; **∠ный** [14 -рен, -рна́, -о] fat; (of) grease greasy; ♀ fleshy; *fig.* rich; *typ.* bol -(-faced); **∠о** ✝ *n* [*indecl.*] endorse ment; **~ово́й** [14] fat(ty).
жит|е́йский [16] worldly, (of life('s); everyday; **∠ель** *m* [4] **∠ельница** *f* [5] inhabitant, resident

ˆельство *n* [9] residence; вид на ˆельство residence (*or* stay) permit; **~ие́** *n* [12] life (*a. of a saint*).
жи́тница *f* [5] granary.
жить [живу́, -вёшь; жил, -а́, -о; не́ жил(и)] live (T, на B [up]on; T *a.* for); reside, lodge; exist, be; как живёте? how are you (getting on)?; жи́л(и)-бы́л(и) ... once upon a time there was (were) ... (*in fairy tales*); **ˆся:** ему́ хорошо́ живётся he is well off; **~ё(-бытьё)** F *n* [10] life, living; residence, stay; (Д) be well off.
жму́рить [13], ⟨за-⟩ screw up *or* contract (one's eyes **-ся**; blink).
жн|е́йка *f* [5; *g/pl.:* -е́ек], **~ея́** *f* [6] reaping machine, harvester; **~ец** *m* [1 *e.*] reaper; **~ивьё** *n* [10; *pl.*: жни́вья, -вьев] stubble(s); **~и́ца** *f* [5] reaper.
жо́л..., жо́р... *s.* жёл..., жёр...
жрать P [жру, жрёшь; жрал, -а́, -о], ⟨со-⟩ eat; devour, gorge, gobble.
жре́бий *m* [3] lot (*a. fig.* = destiny); броса́ть (тяну́ть) ~ cast (draw) lots; ~ бро́шен the die is cast.
жрец *m* [1 *e.*] (*pagan*) priest (*a. fig.*).
жужжа́|ние *n* [12], **~ть** [4 *e.*; жужжу́, -и́шь] buzz, hum.
жу|к *m* [1 *e.*] beetle; ма́йский ~к cockchafer; P = **ˆлик** F *m* [1] swindler, cheat(er), trickster; filcher, pilferer; **ˆльничать** F [1], ⟨с-⟩ cheat, trick.
жу́пел *m* [1] bugaboo, bugbear.
жура́вль *m* [4 *e.*] (*zo., well*) crane.
жури́ть F [13], ⟨по-⟩ scold, rebuke.
журна́л *m* [1] magazine, periodical, journal; diary; ⚓ log(book); **~и́ст** *m* [1] news(paper)man, journalist; **~и́стика** *f* [5] journalism.
журча́|ние *n* [12], **~ть** [-чи́т] purl, murmur.
жу́т|кий [14; -ток, -тка́, -о] weird, uncanny, dismal, sinister; мне ~ко I am terrified; **~кость**, F **~ь** *f* [8] dismay, dread(ful P *pred.*).
жюри́ *n* [*indecl.*] jury (*prizes*).

З

за 1. (В): (*direction*) behind; over, across, beyond; out of; (*distance*) at; (*time*) after; over, past; before (*a.* ~ ... до Р); (with)in, for, during; (*object*[*ive*], *favo*[*u*]*r*, *reason*, *value*, *substitute*) for; ~ то, что because; ~ что? what for?, why?; **2.** (Т): (*position*) behind; across, beyond; at, over; after (*time & place*); because of; with; ~ мной ... *a.* I owe ...; ко́мната ~ мной I take (reserve) the room.
заба́в|а *f* [5] amusement, entertainment; **~ля́ть** [28], ⟨(по)~ить⟩ [13] amuse (**-ся** o.s., be amused at Т); **~ник** F *m* [1] joker, wag; **~ный** [14; -вен, -вна] amusing, funny.
забасто́в|ка *f* [5; *g/pl.*: -вок] strike, walkout; **~очный** [14] strike ...; **~щик** *m* [1] striker.
забве́ние *n* [12] oblivion.
забе|га́ть [1], ⟨~жа́ть⟩ [4; забегу́, -ежи́шь, -егу́т; -еги́!] run in(to), get; run off, away; F drop in (on к Д); ~га́ть вперёд forestall.
заб|ива́ть [1], ⟨~и́ть⟩ [-бью́, -бьёшь; *cf.* бить] drive in; nail up; stop up, choke (up); block (up); F outdo, beat; (*fountain*) spout forth; sound (*alarm*); F stuff (*head*); take (*into one's head*); **-ся** F hide, get; *pf.* begin to beat.
заб|ира́ть [1], ⟨~ра́ть⟩ [-беру́, -рёшь; *cf.* брать] take (*a.*, F, away); capture, (*a. fig.*) seize; arrest; put (into); turn, steer; (Т) close, partition (off); **-ся** climb *or* creep (in, up); steal in, penetrate; hide; get (far off).
заби́|тый [14] browbeaten, cowed, (in)timid(ated); **~ть** *s.* ~ва́ть; **~я́ка** F *m/f* [5] bully, squabbler.
заблаго|вре́менно in (due) time, beforehand; **~вре́менный** [14] preliminary; timely; **~рассу́диться** [15; *impers.*, *with* Д] think fit.
забл|уди́ться [15] *pf.* lose one's way, go astray; **~у́дший** [17] lost; stray; **~ужда́ться** [1] be mistaken, err; **~ужде́ние** *n* [12] error, mistake; ввести́ в ~ужде́ние mislead.
забол|ева́ть [1], ⟨~е́ть⟩ [8] fall sick *or* ill (of Т), be taken ill with; ache; *su.*: **~ева́ние** *n* [12] *a.* = боле́знь.
забо́р *m* [1] fence; **~ный** [14] fence...; *fig.* vulgar, trashy.
забо́т|а *f* [5] care (about, of о П), concern, anxiety, worry, trouble; без ~ careless; carefree; **~иться** [15], ⟨по-⟩ (о П) care (for), take care of, look after; worry, be anxious (about); **~ливый** [14 *sh.*] careful, provident; attentive; anxious, solicitous.
забр|а́сывать [1] **1.** ⟨~оса́ть⟩ (Т) fill up; heap (*a. fig.* = overwhelm); pelt (*stones*); bespatter (*dirt*); **2.** ⟨~о́сить⟩ [15] throw, fling, (*a. fig.*) cast; neglect, give up; **~а́ть** *s.* забира́ть; **~еда́ть** [1], ⟨~ести́⟩ [25] wander *or* get ([in]to, far); **~оса́ть**, **~о́сить** *s.* ~а́сывать; **~о́шенный** [14] deserted; unkempt.
забры́згать [1] *pf.* splash, sprinkle.
заб|ыва́ть [1], ⟨~ы́ть⟩ [-бу́ду, -дешь] forget (*o.s.* **-ся**; *a.* nap, doze); **~ы́вчивый** [14 *sh.*] forgetful; **~ытьё** *n* [12; в -тьи́] unconscious-

ness, swoon; drowsiness; slumber; reverie; frenzy.

зава́л *m* [1] heap, drift; obstruction, abatis; **\~ивать** [1], ⟨\~и́ть⟩ [13; -алю́, -а́лишь] fill *or* heap (up); cover; block, obstruct, close; F overburden (*with work, etc.*); **-ся** fall; sink; collapse.

зава́р|ивать [1], ⟨\~и́ть⟩ [13; -арю́, -а́ришь] boil (*a.* down), make (*tea*); scald; P *fig.* concoct.

зав|еде́ние *n* [12] establishment, institution; (закры́тое) учёбное \~еде́ние (boarding) school; **\~е́довать** [7] (T) be in charge *or* the head (chief) of, manage; **\~е́домый** [14] notorious, indubitable; \~е́домо knowingly; admittedly, certainly; **\~е́дующий** [17] (T) chief, head; director; **\~езти́** *s.* \~ози́ть.

зав|ере́ние *n* [12] assurance; **\~е́рить** *s.* \~еря́ть; **\~ерну́ть** *s.* \~ёртывать; **\~ерте́ть** [11; -ерчу́ -е́ртишь] *pf.* start turning (*v/i.* **-ся**); **\~ёртывать** [1], ⟨\~ерну́ть⟩ [20] wrap (up); turn (*a.* up; off, screw up); F drop in; **\~ерша́ть** [1], ⟨\~ерши́ть⟩ [16 *e.*; -шу́, -ши́шь; -шён-ный] finish, complete, accomplish; crown; **\~ерше́ние** *n* [12] conclusion, end; completion; **\~еря́ть** [28], ⟨\~е́рить⟩ [13] assure (a p. of В/в П); attest, authenticate.

заве́|са *f* [5] curtain; screen (*a.* ⚔); *fig.* veil; **\~сить** *s.* \~шивать; **\~сти́** *s.* заводи́ть.

заве́т *m* [1] legacy; precept, maxim; vow; *Bibl.* (Ве́тхий Old, Но́вый New) \~ Testament; **\~ный** [14] sacred; dear, precious; fond; cherished; intimate; † forbidden.

заве́|шивать [1], ⟨\~сить⟩ [15] cover, hang with, curtain.

завеща́|ние *n* [12] testament, will; **\~ть** [1] (*im*)*pf.* bequeath; instruct, leave as precept.

завзя́тый F [14] inveterate; enthusiastic; true, genuine.

зав|ива́ть [1], ⟨\~и́ть⟩ [-вью́, -вьёшь; *cf.* вить] wave, curl; wind round; **\~и́вка** *f* [5; *g/pl.:* -вок] waving; холо́дная (шестиме́сячная) \~и́вка water (permanent) wave.

зави́д|ный [14; -ден, -дна] enviable, desirable; envious (of Д/И); **\~овать** [7], ⟨по-⟩ envy (a p. a th. Д/в П), be envious (of).

зави́н|чивать [1], ⟨\~ти́ть⟩ [15 *e.*; -инчу́, -инти́шь] screw up.

зави́с|еть [11] depend (on от Р); **\~имость** *f* [8] dependence; в \~имости от (Р) depending on; **\~имый** [14 *sh.*] dependent.

зави́ст|ливый [14 *sh.*] envious, jealous; **'\~ь** *f* [8] envy (of, at к Д).

зави|то́й [14] curly; **\~то́к** *m* [1; -тка́] curl, ringlet; flourish; **\~ть** *s.* \~ва́ть.

завко́м *m* [1] (заводско́й комите́т) works council.

завлад|ева́ть [1], ⟨\~е́ть⟩ [8] (T) take possession *or* hold of, seize.

завл|ека́тельный [14; -лен, -льна] enticing, tempting; **\~ека́ть** [1], **\~е́чь** [26] (al)lure, entice, tempt; involve; carry away.

заво́д[1] *m* [1] works, factory, plant (at/to на П/В); stud (*a.* ко́нский \~); \~[2] winding mechanism; *typ.* edition; **\~и́ть** [15], ⟨завести́⟩ [25] take, bring, lead; put; establish, set up, found (*business, etc.*); form, contract (*habit, friendship, etc.*); get, procure, acquire (*things*); start (*a. motor*), begin (*talk, dispute, etc.*; *a.* to keep [*animals*]); wind up (*watch, etc.*); **-ся,** ⟨завести́сь⟩ appear; nest; get, have; **\~но́й** [14] ⊕ starting; mechanical (*toy*); **\~ский, \~ско́й** [16] works..., factory...; stud...

заво|ева́ние *n* [12] conquest; *fig.* (*mst pl.*) achievement(s); **\~ева́тель** *m* [4] conqueror; **\~ёвывать** [1], ⟨\~ева́ть⟩ [6] conquer; win, gain.

зав|ози́ть [15], ⟨\~езти́⟩ [24] take, bring, drive; leave, F deliver.

завол|а́кивать [1], ⟨\~о́чь⟩ [26] cover, overcast; get cloudy.

завор|а́чивать [1], ⟨\~оти́ть⟩ [15] turn (in, up, down, about); direct.

завсегда́тай *m* [3] habitué.

за́втра tomorrow; **\~к** *m* [1] breakfast (at за Т; for на В, к Д); (второ́й \~к) lunch; **\~кать** [1], ⟨по-⟩ (have, take) breakfast (lunch); **\~шний** [15] tomorrow's; \~шний день *m* tomorrow; *fig.* (near) future.

завыва́ть [1], ⟨завы́ть⟩ [22] howl.

зав|яза́ть[1] [3], ⟨\~я́знуть⟩ [21] sink in, stick; F *fig.* get stuck *or* involved in; **\~яза́ть**[2] *s.* \~я́зывать; **\~я́зка** *f* [5; *g/pl.:* -зок] string, tie; beginning, starting point; entanglement, plot; **\~я́зывать** [1], ⟨\~яза́ть⟩ [3] tie (up), bind, fasten; *fig.* begin, start; entangle, knit (*plot*); **'\~язь** ⚘ *f* [8] ovary; **\~я́нуть** *s.* вя́нуть.

заг|ада́ть *s.* \~а́дывать; **\~а́дить** *s.* \~а́живать; **\~а́дка** *f* [5; *g/pl.:* -док] riddle, enigma; **\~а́дочный** [14; -чен, -чна] enigmatic(al); mysterious; **\~а́дывать** [1], ⟨\~ада́ть⟩ [1] propose (*a riddle*); try to find out (*by a guess, fortunetelling, etc.*); F fix upon; plan; **\~а́живать** F [1], ⟨\~а́дить⟩ [15] soil, befoul.

зага́р *m* [1] sunburn, tan. [trouble.]

загво́здка F *f* [5; *g/pl.:* -док] hitch,

заги́б *m* [1] bend; dog-ear (*page*); *pol.* deviation; **\~а́ть** [1], ⟨загну́ть⟩ [20] bend, fold (over), turn (up).

загла́в|ие *n* [12] title (*book, etc.*); **\~ный** [14] title...; \~ная бу́ква *f* capital letter.

загла́|живать [1], ⟨\~дить⟩ [15] smooth; press, iron; *fig.* make up (*or* amends) for, expiate.

загл|óхнуть *s.* глóхнуть 2.; **~óхший** [17] deserted, desolate; **~ушáть** [1], 〈~ушúть〉 [16] *s.* глушúть 2.

загля́|дывать [1], 〈~нýть〉 [19] glance; peep; look (through, up); have a look (at); F drop in *or* call (on к Д); **~дываться** [1], 〈~дéться〉 [11] (на В) gaze, gape *or* stare (at), feast one's eyes *or* gloat ([up]on).

заг|нáть *s.* ~онять; **~нýть** *s.* ~ибáть; **~овáривать** [1], 〈~оворúть〉 [13] **1.** *v/i.* begin, start (*or* try) to talk *or* speak; **2.** *v/t.* tire with one's talk; exorcise; **3. -ся** F drivel, talk nonsense; be(come) confused; talk (too) long, much; **~óвор** *m* [1] conspiracy, plot; exorcism; составля́ть ~óвор conspire, plot; **~оворúть** *s.* ~овáривать; **~овóрщик** *m* [1] conspirator.

заголóвок *m* [1; -вка] heading, title.

загóн *m* [1] enclosure; быть в ~е F suffer neglect; **~я́ть** [28], 〈загнáть〉 [-гоню́, -гóнишь; *cf.* гнать] drive (in, off); exhaust, fatigue.

загор|áживать [1], 〈~одúть〉 [15 & 15 *e.*; -рожý, -рóдишь] enclose, shut in; block (up), bar (*way*); **-ся** fence, protect; **~áть** [1], 〈~éть〉 [9] become sunburnt; **-ся** catch *or* take fire; light up, kindle, flash; blush, blaze up; *fig.* (get) inflame(d); break out; **~éлый** [14] sunburnt; **~одúть** *s.* ~áживать; **~óдка** F *f* [5; *g/pl.*: -док] fence, enclosure; partition; **′~одный** [14] country (*house, etc.*); out-of-town.

загот|áвливать [1] & **~овля́ть** [28], 〈~óвить〉 [14] prepare; store up; lay in (*stock*); **~óвка** *f* [5; *g/pl.*: -вок], **~овлéние** *n* [12] storage, laying in (*stocks, supplies*).

загра|дúтельный [14] ⚔ curtain (*fire*), barrage (*a. balloon*); **~ждáть** [1], 〈~дúть〉 [15 *e.*; -ажý, -адúшь; -аждённый] block (up), bar; **~ждéние** *n* [12] block(ing), obstruction; прóволочное ~ждéние wire entanglement.

загранú|чный [14] foreign; ... abroad.

загре|бáть [1], 〈~стú〉 *s.* грестú.

загрóбн|ый [14] sepulchral (*voice*); ~ый мир *m* the other world; ~ая жизнь *f* the beyond.

загромо|ждáть [1], 〈~здúть〉 [15 *e.*; -зжý, -здúшь; -мождённый] block (up), (en)cumber, crowd; overload; **~ждéние** *n* [12] blocking; overloading.

загрубéлый [14] callous, coarse.

загр|ужáть [1], 〈~узúть〉 [15 & 15 *e.*; -ужý, -ýзúшь] (T) load; ⊕ charge; F busy, assign work to; be occupied (*or* taken) by work (*time*); **~ýзка** *f* [5] load(ing, *etc.*), charge; **~ызáть** [1], 〈~ы́зть〉 [24; *pt. st.*; загры́зенный] bite (*fig.* worry) to death, kill.

загрязн|éние *n* [12] soiling; pollution; infection; **~я́ть** [28], 〈~úть〉 [13] (**-ся** become) soil(ed), pollute(d) (*water, etc.*), infect(ed) (*air*).

загс *m* [1] (*abbr.*: отдéл зáписей áктов граждáнского состоя́ния) registrar's (registry) office.

зад *m* [1; на -ý; *pl. e.*] back, rear *or* hinder part; posterior(s), rump; *pl.* F things already (well-)known *or* learned; **~óм** напере́д back to front.

зад|áбривать [1], 〈~óбрить〉 [13] (В) insinuate o.s. (with), gain upon.

зад|авáть [5], 〈~áть〉 [-дáм, -дáшь, *etc.*, *cf.* дать; зáдал, -á, -о; зáданный (зáдан, -á, -о)] set, assign (*task*); give (*a.* ♪ *keynote*), F dress (down); ask (*question*); **-ся** [*pt.*: -дáлся, -лáсь] цéлью (мы́слью) take it into one's head, set one's mind on doing s.th.; F happen to be.

задáв|ливать [1], 〈~úть〉 [14] crush; run over, knock down; *fig.* suppress; P strangle, kill.

задáние *n* [12] assignment, task; (com)mission (*a.* ⚔); домáшнее ~ homework.

задáток *m* [1; -тка] earnest money; deposit; *pl.* rudiments.

задá|ть *s.* ~вáть; **~ча** *f* [5] problem (*a.* ♘); task; object(ive), aim, end; **~чник** *m* [1] book of problems.

задв|игáть [1], 〈~úнуть〉 [20] push (into, *etc.*); shut (*drawer*); draw (*curtain*); slide (*bolt*); **~úжка** [5; *g/pl.*: -жек] bolt; **~ижнóй** [14] sliding (*door*); sash (*window*).

задвóрки *f/pl.* [*gen.*: -рок] backyards.

зад|евáть [1], 〈~éть〉 [-éну, -éнешь; -éтый] be caught (by за В), brush against, touch (*a. fig.*, [up]on); excite; hurt, wound; ⚕ affect; **~éлывать,** 〈~éлать〉 [1] stop up, choke (up); wall up.

задёр|гать [1] *pf.* overdrive; F harrass; **~гивать** [1], 〈~нуть〉 [20] draw (*curtain*); cover.

задержáние *n* [12] arrest.

задéрж|ивать [1], 〈~áть〉 [4] detain, hold back *or* up, stop; delay, check; arrest; slow down; **-ся** stay; be delayed; linger; stop; be late; **~ка** *f* [5; *g/pl.*: -жек] delay; (*a.* ⊕) trouble, break.

задёрнуть *s.* задёргивать.

задéть *s.* задевáть.

зад|ирáть F [1], 〈~рáть〉 [-дерý, -рёшь; *cf.* драть] lift *or* pull (up); stretch; *impf.* provoke, vex, pick a quarrel (with); ~(и)рáть нос be haughty, turn up one's nose.

зáдний [15] back, hind(er); reverse [(*gear*).

задóлго (до Р) long before.

зад|олжáть F [1] *pf.* run into debt; owe (money); **~óлженность** *f* [8] debts *pl.*, indebtedness.

зáдом backward(s); *cf.* зад.

задóр *m* [1] fervo(u)r; quick temper;

provocative tone *or* behavio(u)r; **~ный** [14; -рен, -рна] fervent; provoking, teasing; frolicsome.
задра́ть *s.* задира́ть.
зад|ува́ть [1], ‹~у́ть› [18] blow out; F begin to blow; *impf.* blow (in).
заду́|мать *s.* ~мывать; **~мчивый** [14 *sh.*] thoughtful, pensive; **~мывать** [1], ‹~мать› conceive; resolve, decide; plan, intend; **-ся** think (about, of о П); reflect, meditate (on над Т); begin to think, (be) engross(ed, lost) in thought(s); hesitate; **~ть** *s.* ~ва́ть.
задуше́вный [14] heart-felt, warm-hearted, affectionate; intimate, in(ner)most.
зад|ыха́ться [1], ‹~охну́ться› [21] gasp, pant; choke (*a. fig.*, with от Р).
зае́з|дить F [15] *pf.* fatigue, exhaust; **~жа́ть** [1], ‹зае́хать› [-е́ду, -е́дешь; -езжа́й!] call on (*on the way*), drive, go *or* come (to [see, *etc.*] к Д *or* into в В); pick up, fetch (за Т); get; **~жий** [17] visitant.
заём *m* [1; за́йма] loan.
за|е́хать *s.* ~езжа́ть; **~жа́ть** *s.* ~жима́ть; **~же́чь** *s.* ~жига́ть.
заж|ива́ть [1], ‹~и́ть› [-иву́, -вёшь; за́жил, -а́, -о] **1.** heal (up); close, skin (over); **2.** *pf.* begin to live.
за́живо alive.
зажига́|лка *f* [5; *g/pl.*: -лок] (cigarette) lighter; **~ние** *n* [12] lighting; ignition; **~тельный** [14] incendiary (*bomb, & fig.*); **~ть** [1], ‹заже́чь› [26 г/ж: -жгу́, -жжёшь; *cf.* жечь] light, kindle (*a. fig.*); (*match a.*) strike; turn on (*light*); **-ся** light (up), kindle.
зажи́м *m* [1] ⊕ clamp; *fig.* suppression; **~а́ть** [1], ‹зажа́ть› [-жму́, -жмёшь; -жа́тый] press, squeeze; clutch; *fig.* F (sup)press; stop (*mouth*), hold (*nose*), close (*ears*).
зажи́|точный [14; -чен, -чна] prosperous; **~точность** *f* [8] prosperity; **~ть** *s.* ~ва́ть.
заздра́вный [14] (to s.b.'s) health.
зазева́ться F [1] gape (at на В); be (-come) heedless, absent(-minded).
зазем|ле́ние *n* [12], **~ля́ть** [28], ‹~ли́ть› [13] ⚡ ground, *Brt.* earth.
зазна|ва́ться F [5], ‹~ться› [1] be (-come) presumptuous, put on airs.
заз|о́рный †, P [14; -рен, -рна] shameful, scandalous; **~ре́ние** *n* [12]: без ~ре́ния (со́вести) without remorse *or* shame.
зазу́бр|ивать [1] *s.* зубри́ть; **~ина** *f* [5] notch.
заи́грывать F [1], (с Т) flirt, coquet (with), make advances (to); ingratiate o.s. (with).
заи́к|а *m/f* [5] stutterer; **~а́ние** *n* [12] stutter; stammer; **~а́ться** [1], *once* ‹~ну́ться› [20] stutter; stammer; F (give a) hint (at о П), suggest, mention; stir; *pf.* stop short.
заи́мствова|ние *n* [12] borrowing, taking; loan word (*a.* ~нное сло́во); **~ть** [7] (*im*)*pf.*, *a.* ‹по-› borrow, take (over).
заи́ндевелый [14] frosty.
заинтересо́в|ывать(ся) [1], ‹~а́ть (-ся)› [7] (be[come]) interest(ed in T), rouse a p.'s interest (in в П); я ~ан(а) I am interested (in в П).
заи́скивать [1] ingratiate o.s. (with у Р).
зайти́ *s.* заходи́ть.
за́йчик *m* [1] *dim. of* заяц; F speck(le).
закабал|я́ть [28], ‹~и́ть› [13] enslave.
закавка́зский [16] Transcaucasian.
закады́чный F [14] bosom (*friend*).
зака́з *m* [1] order; дать ~ (на В/Д) ✝ place an order (for ... with); **~а́ть** *s.* ~ывать; на ~ = **~но́й** [14] made to order; ~но́й лес (p)reserve; ~но́е (письмо́) *n* registered (letter); **~чик** *m* [1] customer; **~ывать** [1], ‹~а́ть› [3] order (o.s. себе́); † forbid.
зака́л *m* [1], **~ка** *f* [5] ⊕ tempering; *fig.* hardening; endurance, hardiness; breed, kind; **~я́ть** [28], ‹~и́ть› [13] ⊕ temper; *fig.* harden; ~ённый tempered (*metal*); *fig.* hardened, tried, experienced.
зак|а́лывать [1], ‹~оло́ть› [17] kill, slaughter; stab; pin (up); у меня́ ~оло́ло в боку́ I have a stitch in the side; **~а́нчивать** [1], ‹~о́нчить› [16] finish, conclude; **~а́пывать** [1], ‹~опа́ть› [1] bury; fill up.
зака́т *m* [1] sunset; *fig.* decline; end; **~ывать** [1] **1.** ‹~а́ть› [1] roll up; **2.** ‹~и́ть› [15] roll (into, under, *etc.* в, под В); turn up (*eyes*); **-ся** roll; set (*sun, etc.*); *fig.* end; F burst (out laughing *or* into tears).
заква́|ска *f* [5] ferment; leaven; *fig.* F breed; **~шивать** [1], ‹~сить› [15] sour.
заки́|дывать [1] **1.** ‹~да́ть› [1] F fill up, cover; *fig.* ply, assail, pelt (with T); **2.** ‹~нуть› [20] throw (in [-to], on, over, behind, *etc.* в, на, за ... В; *a.* out [*net*], back [*head*]); fling, (*a. fig.*) cast.
зак|ипа́ть [1], ‹~ипе́ть› [10; -пи́т] begin to boil; *cf.* кипе́ть; **~иса́ть** [1], ‹~ки́снуть› [21] turn sour.
закла́д *m* [1] † = зало́г; *s. a.* би́ться; **~ка** *f* [5; *g/pl.*: -док] laying; walling (up); harnessing, putting to; bookmark; **~но́й** [14] pawn...; ~на́я mortgage (bond); **~чик** *m* [1] pawner; pawnbroker; **~ывать** [1], ‹заложи́ть› [16] put (*a.* in, *etc.*), lay (*a.* out [*garden*], the foundation [stone] of, found), place; F mislay; heap, pile (with T); wall up; pawn, pledge; harness, put (*horse[s]*) to, get ready (*carriage*); mark, put in (*bookmark*); *impers.* F obstruct (*hearing, nose*), press (*breast*).

акл|ёвывать [1], ⟨~евáть⟩ [6 *e.*; -клюю́, -юёшь] peck to death *or* wound (badly) (by pecking); F wreck, ruin; **~éивать** [1], ⟨~éить⟩ [13] glue *or* paste up (over); **~ёпка** *f* [5; *g/pl.*: -пок], **~ёпывать,** ⟨~е-пáть⟩ [1] rivet.

аклинá|ние *n* [12] conjuration, incantation; exorcism; **~тель** *m* [4] conjurer, exorcist; (*snake*) charmer; **~ть** [1] conjure, adjure.

аключ|áть [1], ⟨~и́ть⟩ [16 *e.*; -чу́, -чи́шь; -чённый] enclose, put; confine, imprison; conclude (= finish, with Т; = infer, from из Р, по Д — что; *v/t.*: *treaty*, [= make] *peace, etc.*); *impf.* (*a.* в себé) contain; **~áться** [1] consist (in в П); end (with Т); **~éние** *n* [12[confinement, imprisonment (*a.* тюрéмное); conclusion; **~ённый** [14] prisoner; **~и́тельный** [14] final, concluding.

аклЯ́тый [14] implacable; sworn.

акóв|ывать [1], ⟨~áть⟩ [7 *e.*; -кую́, куёшь] put in (irons), chain; *fig.* freeze; prick (*horse*).

акол|áчивать F [1], ⟨~оти́ть⟩ [15] drive in; nail up; board up; *fig.* beat to death; thrash; **~дóвывать** [1], ⟨~довáть⟩ [7] enchant; bewitch, charm; ~дóванный круг *m* vicious circle; **~оти́ть** *s.* ~áчивать; **~óть** *s.* закáлывать.

акóн *m* [1] law; rule; ~ бóжий (God's) Law; religion (*form. school subject*); объяви́ть вне ~а outlaw; по (вопреки́) ~у according (contrary) to law; охраня́емый ~ом ⚕/⚖ registered; **~ность** *f* [8] legality; law; **~ный** [14; -óнен, -óнна] legal, lawful, legitimate.

аконо|вéд *m* [1] jurist, jurisprudent; **~дáтель** *m* [4] legislator; **~дáтельный** [14] legislative; **~дá-тельство** *n* [9] legislation; **~мéр-ность** *f* [8] regularity; **~мéрный** [14; -рен, -рна] regular; **~положé-ние** *n* [12] regulation(s); **~проéкт** *m* [1] bill, draft.

акó|нчить *s.* закáнчивать; **~пáть** *s.* закáпывать; **~птéлый** [14] smoky; **~ренéлый** [14] deep-rooted, inveterate,in grained; **~рю́чка** F *f* [5; *g/pl.*: -чек] flourish; trick, ruse; hitch; **~снéлый** [14] = ~ре-нéлый; **~у́лок** *m* [1; -лка] alleyway, (*Brt.*) (narrow) lane; nook; **~ченé-лый** [14] (be)numb(ed), stiff.

акрá|дываться [1], ⟨~сться⟩ [25; *pt. st.*] creep in; **~шивать** [1], ⟨~сить⟩ [15] paint over.

акреп|лéние *n* [12] fastening; strengthening; securing; (за Т) assignment (*a.* ⚖); ⚔ fortification; **~ля́ть** [28], ⟨~и́ть⟩ [14 *e*; -плю́, -пи́шь; -плённый] fasten, (*a. phot.*) fix; strengthen, consolidate, fortify (*a.* ⚔); secure; assign (to за Т, *a.* ⚖); ⚒ strut.

закрепо|щáть [1], ⟨~сти́ть⟩ [15 *e.*; -ощу́, -ости́шь; -ощённый] enslave; **~щéние** *n* [12] enslavement.

закрóйщи|к *m* [1], **~ца** *f* [5] cutter.

закругл|éние *n* [12] rounding (off); curve; **~я́ть** [28], ⟨~и́ть⟩ [13] round (off).

закру́|чивать [1], ⟨~ти́ть⟩ [15] turn (round, off, up); twist.

закр|ывáть [1], ⟨~ы́ть⟩ [22] shut, close; lock (up); cover, hide; turn off (*tap*); ~ывáть глазá (на В) shut one's eyes (to); **~ы́тие** *n* [12] closing, close; **~ы́ть** *s.* ~ывáть; **~ы́тый** [14] closed; secret; boarding (*school*); high-necked (*dress*); в ~ы́-том помещéнии indoor(s).

закули́сный [14] (lying *or* passing) behind the scenes; secret.

закуп|áть [1], ⟨~и́ть⟩ [14] buy (*a.* in), purchase; **⌐ка** *f* [5; *g/pl.*: -пок] purchase.

заку́пор|ивать [1], ⟨~ить⟩ [13] cork (up), (*cask*) bung (up); **~ка** *f* [5; *g/pl.*: -рок] corking; ⚕ embolism; constipation.

заку́пщик [1] purchasing agent, buyer.

заку́р|ивать [1], ⟨~и́ть⟩ [13; -урю́, -у́ришь] light (*cigar, etc.*), begin to smoke; F (blacken with) smoke; ~и́(те)! have a cigar(ette)!

заку́с|ка *f* [5; *g/pl.*: -сок] snack, lunch; hors d'oeuvres; на ~ку *a.* for the last bit; **~óчная** *f* [14] lunchroom, snackbar; **~ывать** [1], ⟨~и́ть⟩ [15] bite (*a. one's lip*[*s*]); take *or* have a snack, lunch; eat (s.th. [with, after a drink] Т); ~и́ть язы́к stop short, hold one's tongue.

заку́т|ывать, ⟨~ать⟩ [1] wrap up.

зáл *m* [1], † **~а** *f* [5] hall; room.

зал|егáние *n* [12] *geol.* deposit(ion); **~егáть** [1], ⟨~éчь⟩ [26; -ля́гу, -ля́жешь] lie (down); hide; *fig.* root; ⚕ be obstructed (with phlegm).

заледенéлый [14] icy; numb.

зал|ежáлый [14] stale, spoiled (by long storage); ~ежáлый товáр *m* drug; **~ёживаться** [1], ⟨~ежáть-ся⟩ [4 *e.*; -жу́сь, -жи́шься] lie (too) long (*a. goods, & spoil thus*), stale; **⌐ежь** *f* [8] *geol.* deposit; 🌾 fallow.

зал|езáть [1], ⟨~éзть⟩ [24 *st.*] climb up, in(to), *etc.*; hide; steal *or* get in(to); **~епля́ть** [28], ⟨~епи́ть⟩ [14] stop, close; glue *or* paste up; stick over; **~етáть** [1], ⟨~етéть⟩ [11] fly in(to), up, far off, beyond; come, get; **~ётный** [14] stray(ing); migratory (*bird*); F visitant.

залéч|ивать [1], ⟨~и́ть⟩ [16] heal; F cure to death; **~ь** *s.* ~егáть.

зал|и́в *m* [1] gulf, bay; **~ивáть** [1], ⟨~и́ть⟩ [-лью́, -льёшь; зáли́л, -á, -о; зали́тый] (Т) flood, overflow; pour (all) over, cover; fill; extinguish; **-ся** break into *or* shed (*tears* слезáми), burst out (laughing смé-хом); trill, warble, roll, quaver;

~ивной [14] floodable, flooded; jellied; resonant; **~и́ть** *s.* ~ива́ть.
зал|о́г *m* [1] pledge (*a. fig.*); pawn; security; *gr.* voice; дать в ~о́г pawn, pledge; **~ожи́ть** *s.* закла́дывать; **~о́жник** *m* [1], **~о́жница** *f* [5] hostage.
залп *m* [1] volley; ~ом F (*drink*) at one draught; (*smoke, etc.*) at a stretch; (*read*) at one sitting; blurt out.
зама́|зка *f* [5] putty; **~зывать** [1], ⟨~зать⟩ [3] smear, soil; paint over; putty; F *fig.* veil, hush up; **~лчивать** F [1], ⟨замолча́ть⟩ [4 *e.*; -чу́, -чи́шь] conceal, keep secret; **~нивать** [1], ⟨~ани́ть⟩ [13; -маню́, -ма́нишь] lure, decoy, entice; **~нчивый** [14 *sh.*] alluring, tempting; **~хиваться** [1], *once* ⟨~хну́ться⟩ [20] lift one's arm (*etc.* against Т/на В), threaten (with); **~шка** F *f* [5; *g/pl.*: -шек] habit, manner.
замедл|е́ние *n* [12] delay; **~я́ть** [28], ⟨~ить⟩ [13] slow down, reduce; delay, retard (*a.* с Т); не ~я́ть с (Т) (do, *etc.*) soon.
заме́|на *f* [5] substitution (of/for Т/Р), replacement (by Т); ⚖ commutation; substitute; **~ни́мый** [14 *sh.*] replaceable, exchangeable; **~ни́тель** *m* [4] substitute; **~ня́ть** [28], ⟨~ни́ть⟩ [13; -меню́, -ме́нишь; -менённый] replace (by Т), substitute (p., th. for Т/В); ⚖ commute (for, into); (И/В) (be) follow(ed).
замере́ть *s.* замира́ть.
замерза́|ние *n* [12] freezing; то́чка ~ния freezing point; **~ть** [1], ⟨замёрзнуть⟩ [21] freeze, congeal; be frozen (to death, *a.* F = feel very cold).
за́мертво (as if) dead, unconscious.
замести́ *s.* замета́ть.
замести́|тель *m* [4] deputy, assistant, vice-...; **~ть** *s.* замеща́ть.
заме|та́ть [1], ⟨~сти́⟩ [25 -т-: -мету́] sweep (up); drift, cover; block up (*roads*); wipe out (*tracks*).
заме́|тить *s.* ~ча́ть; **~тка** *f* [5; *g/pl.*: -ток] mark; note; paragraph, (brief) article, item; **~тный** [14; -тен, -тна] noticeable, perceptible; marked, remarkable; ~тно *a.* one (it) can (be) see(n), notice(d); **~ча́ние** *n* [12] remark, observation; *pl.* criticism; reproof, rebuke; досто́йный ~ча́ния worthy of notice; **~ча́тельный** [14; -лен, -льна] remarkable, outstanding; wonderful; noted (for Т); **~ча́ть** [1], ⟨~тить⟩ [15] notice; mark; observe, remark; reprove.
замеша́тельств|о *n* [9] confusion, embarrassment; в ~е confused, disconcerted, embarrassed.
зам|е́шивать, ⟨~еша́ть⟩ [1] involve, entangle; ~е́шан(а) в (П) *a.* mixed up with; (-**ся** be) mingle(d) in, with (в В *or* П, ме́жду Т); supervene; **~е́шкаться** F [1] *pf.* be delayed, tarry; **~еща́ть** [1], ⟨~ести́ть⟩ [15 *e.*; -ещу́, -ести́шь; -ещённый] replace; substitute; act for, deputize; fill (*vacancy*); **~еще́ние** *n* [12] substitution (*a.* ⚗, ♟); replacement; deputizing; filling.
зам|ина́ть F [1], ⟨~я́ть⟩ [-мну́, -мнёшь; -мя́тый] crumple; smother, hush up; -**ся** falter, halt, stick, be(come) confused, stop short, flag; **~и́нка** *f* [5; *g/pl.*: -нок] halt, hitch; **~ира́ть** [1], ⟨~ере́ть⟩ [12; за́мер, -рла́, -о] be(come) *or* stand stockstill, transfixed (with от Р); stop; fade, die away; у меня́ се́р‑дце ~ерло my heart stood still.
за́мкнутый [14 *sh.*] closed; secluded; reserved; *cf.* замыка́ть.
за́м|ок¹ *m* [1; -мка] castle; **~о́к²** *m* [1; -мка́] lock; америка́нский ~о́к springlock; на ~ке́ *or* под ~ко́м under lock & key.
замо́л|вить [14] *pf.*: ~вить сло‑в(е́чк)о F put in a word (for a p. за В, о П); **~ка́ть** [1], ⟨~кнуть⟩ [21] become silent, stop (speaking, *etc.*), cease, break off; die away *or* off; **~ча́ть** [4 *e.*; -чу́, -чи́шь] *pf.* **1.** *v/i.* *s.* ~ка́ть; **2.** *v/t.* *s.* зама́лчивать.
замор|а́живать [1], ⟨~о́зить⟩ [15] freeze, congeal; **'~озки** *m/pl.* [1] (light morning *or* night) frost; **~ский** [16] (from) oversea; foreign.
за́муж *s.* выдава́ть & выходи́ть; **~ем** married (to за Т, *of women*); **~ество** *n* [9] marriage (*of women*); **~ний** [15]: ~няя (же́нщина) married (woman).
замуро́в|ывать [1], ⟨~а́ть⟩ [7] immure; wall up.
заму́ч|ивать [1], ⟨~ить⟩ [16] torment to death; fatigue, exhaust.
за́мш|а *f* [5], **~евый** [14] chamois, suede.
замыка́|ние *n* [12]: коро́ткое ~ние ⚡ short circuit; **~ть** [1], ⟨замкну́ть⟩ [20] (en)close; † lock (up); -**ся** isolate o.s. (in в В *or* Т); -**ся** в себе́ become unsociable.
за́м|ысел *m* [1; -сла] intention, plan, design; conception; **~ы́слить** *s.* ~ышля́ть; **~ыслова́тый** [14 *sh.*] intricate, ingenious; fanciful; **~ышля́ть** [28], ⟨~ы́слить⟩ [15] plan, intend; resolve; conceive.
замя́ть(ся) *s.* замина́ть(ся).
за́нав|ес *m* [1] curtain (*a. thea.*); желе́зный ~ес *pol. a.* iron curtain; **~е́сить** *s.* ~е́шивать; **~е́ска** *f* [5; *g/pl.*: -сок] (*window*) curtain; **~е́шивать** [1], ⟨~е́сить⟩ [15] curtain.
зан|а́шивать [1], ⟨~оси́ть⟩ [15] soil; wear out; **~емо́чь** [26 г/ж: -могу́, -мо́жешь; *cf.* мочь¹] *pf.* fall sick, *Brt.* ill; **~ести́** *s.* ~оси́ть 1.
занима́|ние *n* [12] borrowing; **~тельный** [14; -лен, -льна] interesting, entertaining, amusing; engaging, captivating; **~ть** [1], ⟨з…

ня́ть› [займу́, -мёшь; за́нял, -а́, -о; заня́вший; за́нятый (за́нят, -а́, -о)] **1.** borrow (from у P); **2.** (T) occupy, (*a. time*) take; employ, busy; reserve, secure (*place*); interest, engross, absorb; entertain; ~ть дух у (P) F take one's breath away; **-ся** [заня́лся́, -ла́сь] **1.** *v/t.* (& T) occupy *or* busy o.s. (with); (*a. sport*) engage in; attend (to); learn, study; set about, begin to (read, *etc.*); **2.** *v/i.* blaze *or* flare up; break, dawn; *s. a.* заря́.

за́ново anew, afresh.

зано́|за *f* [5] splinter; **~зи́ть** [15 *e.*; -ожу́, -ози́шь] *pf.* run a splinter (into B).

зано́с *m* [1] drift; **~и́ть** [15] **1.** ‹занести́› [24 -с-: -су́, -сёшь] bring; carry; note down, enter, register; (*a. impers.*) (be) cast, get; drift, cover, block up; lift, raise (*arm, etc.*), set (*foot*); **2.** *pf.*, *s.* зана́шивать; **~чивый** [14 *sh.*] arrogant, presumptuous.

заня́т|ие *n* [12] occupation, work, business; exercise (of T); *pl.* F lessons, school, lecture(s) (to на B, at на П); ⚔ capture; **~ный** [14; тен, -тна] F = занима́тельный; **~ь** (**-ся**) *s.* занима́ть(ся); **~о́й** [14] busy; **'~ый** [14; за́нят, -а́, -о] occupied, busy, engaged.

заодно́ conjointly; together; at one; F at the same time, besides, too.

заостр|я́ть [28], ‹~и́ть› [13] point, sharpen (*a. fig.*); **-ся** taper.

зао́чн|ик [1] student of a correspondence school, college, *etc.*; **~ый** [14] in a p.'s absence; behind one's back; ~ое обуче́ние *n* instruction by correspondence; ~ое реше́ние *n* ⚖ judg(e)ment by default.

за́пад *m* [1] west; ♀ the West, Occident; *cf.* восто́к; **~а́ть** [1], ‹запа́сть› [25; -па́л, -а] fall in, sink; impress (*a.* on на *or* в B); **~ник** *m* [1] *hist.* Westerner; **~ный** [14] west(ern, -erly); occidental.

западня́ *f* [6; *g/pl.*: -не́й] trap.

запа́|здывать, ‹запозда́ть [1] be late (for на B), be tardy (with с T); **~ивать** [1], ‹~я́ть› [28] solder (up); **~ко́вывать** [1], ‹~кова́ть› [7] pack (up); wrap up.

запа́л *m* [1] ⚔, ⚒ fuse; touchhole; (*horse*) heaves; F fit, passion; **~ьный** [14] touch...; ~ьный шнур *m* match; ~ьная свеча́ *f* ⚡ spark(ing) plug; **~ьчивый** [14 *sh.*] quick-tempered, irascible; provoking.

запа́с *m* [1] stock (*a. fig.*, *of words, etc.* = store, fund), supply, (*a.* ⚔) reserve; в ~е in stock, on hand; про ~ in store *or* reserve; **~а́ть** [1], ‹~ти́› [24 -с-: -су́, -сёшь]; **-ся**, ‹~ти́сь› provide o.s. (with T); **~ли́вый** [14 *sh.*] provident; **~но́й**, **~ный** [14] spare (*a.* ⊕); reserve... (*a.* ⚔; *su.* reservist), emergency..., side... (*a.* 🚗); **~ть** *s.* запада́ть.

за́п|ах *m* [1] smell, odo(u)r, scent; **~а́хивать** [1] **1.** ‹~аха́ть› [3] plow (*Brt.* plough) *or* turn up, in; **2.** ‹~ахну́ть› [20] lap (over), wrap (o.s. **-ся**) up (in в B, T); F slam; **~а́шка** *f* [5] tillage; **~ая́ть** *s.* ~а́ивать.

запе|ва́ла *m/f* [5] precentor, (*a. fig.*) leader; **~ва́ть** [1] lead (*chorus*); **~ка́нка** *f* [5; *g/pl.*: -нок] baked pudding; spiced brandy; **~ка́ть** [1], ‹~́чь› [26] bake (in); **-ся** clot, coagulate (*blood*); crack (*lips*); **~ре́ть** *s.* запира́ть; **~́ть** *pf.* [-пою́, -поёшь; -пе́тый] start singing, strike up.

запеча́т|ать *s.* ~ывать; **~лева́ть** [1], ‹~ле́ть› [8] embody, render; impress (on в П), retain; mark, seal; **~ывать**, ‹~ать› [1] seal (up); close, glue up.

запе́чь *s.* запека́ть.

запи|ва́ть [1], ‹~́ть› [-пью́, -пьёшь; *cf.* пить] wash down (with T), drink *or* take after, thereupon; F take to drink.

зап|ина́ться [1], ‹~ну́ться› [20] stumble (over, against за *or* о B), falter; pause, hesitate; **~и́нка** *f* [5]: без ~и́нки fluently, smoothly.

запира́|тельство *n* [9] disavowal, denial; **~ть** [1], ‹запере́ть› [12; за́пер, -ла́, -о; за́пертый (за́перт, -а́, -о)] lock (up; *a.* ~ть на ключ, замо́к); ⚔, ⚓ blockade; **-ся** *impf.* F (в П) deny, disavow.

запис|а́ть *s.* ~́ывать; **~́ка** *f* [5; *g/pl.*: -сок] note, slip; (brief) letter; memorandum, report; *pl.* notes, memoirs, reminiscences; transactions, proceedings; **~но́й** [14] note...; F inveterate; **~́ывать** [1], ‹~а́ть› [3] write down, note (down); record (*a. on tape, etc.*); enter, enrol(l), register; ⚖ transfer (to Д, на B, за T), deed; **-ся** enrol(l), register, matriculate; subscribe (to; for в, на B), book; make an appointment (with a doctor к врачу́); **'~ь** *f* [8] entry; enrol(l)ment; registration; record (-ing); subscription; ⚖ deed.

запи́ть *s.* запива́ть.

запи́х|ивать F [1], ‹~а́ть› [1], *once* ‹~ну́ть› [20] push in; cram, stuff.

запла́ка|нный [14 *sh.*] tearful, in tears, tear-stained; **~ть** [3] *pf.* begin to cry.

запла́та [5] patch.

запле́сневелый [14] mo(u)ldy.

запле|та́ть [1], ‹~сти́› [25 -т-: -плету́, -тёшь] braid, plait; **-ся** F: но́ги ~та́ются totter, stagger; язы́к ~та́ется slur, mumble.

заплы|ва́ть [1], ‹~́ть› [23] swim (far), get (*by swimming*); (T) be covered *or* closed (*a. by swelling, with fat*); swell, bloat, puff up.

запну́ться *s.* запина́ться.
запове́д|ник *m* [1] reserve; nursery; **~ный** [14] forbidden, reserved; secret; dear; intimate, inmost; **~овать** [7], ⟨~ать⟩ [1] command; **~ь** ('za-) *f* [8] *Bibl.* commandment.
запод|а́зривать († -о́зр-) [1], ⟨~о́зрить⟩ [13] suspect (of в П).
запозда́|лый [14] (be)late(d), tardy; out-of-date; **~ть** *s.* запа́здывать.
запо́|й *m* [3] hard drinking; пить ~ем booze, tipple, be a hard drinker.
заполз|а́ть [1], ⟨~ти́⟩ [24] creep (in).
заполн|я́ть [28], ⟨~ить⟩ [13] fill (up); (*form*) fill out (*Brt.* in).
запом|ина́ть [1], ⟨~нить⟩ [13] remember, keep in mind; memorize; **-ся** (Д) remember, stick to one's memory.
за́понка *f* [5; *g/pl.*: -нок] cuff link; collar button (*Brt.* stud).
запо́р *m* [1] bar, bolt; lock; ⚕ constipation; на ~е bolted.
запор|а́шивать [1], ⟨~оши́ть⟩ [16 *e.*; *3rd p. only*] powder *or* cover (with *snow* Т).
запоте́лый F [14] moist, sweaty.
заправ|и́ла *m* F [5] boss, chief; **~ля́ть** [28], ⟨~ить⟩ [14] put, tuck (in); (Т) dress, season (*meals* with); get ready; tank, refuel (*car, plane*); **~ка** *f* [5; *g/pl.*: -вок] refuel(l)ing; seasoning, condiment; **~очный** [14]: ~очная коло́нка *f* filling (gas) station; **~ский** F [16] true, real.
запр|а́шивать [1], ⟨~оси́ть⟩ [15] ask, inquire (with/about у Р/о П); (*a.* Р) request; charge, ask (*excessive price*; с Р).
запре́|т *m* [1] = ~ще́ние; **~ти́тельный** [14] prohibitive; **~ти́ть** *s.* ~ща́ть; **~тный** [14] forbidden; ~тная зо́на *f* prohibited area; **~ща́ть** [1], ⟨~ти́ть⟩ [15 *e.*; -ещу́, -ети́шь; -ещённый] forbid, prohibit, interdict; **~ще́ние** *n* [12] prohibition, interdiction.
заприхо́довать [7] *pf.* enter, book.
запроки́|дывать [1], ⟨~нуть⟩ [20] F throw back; P overturn.
запро́с *m* [1] inquiry (about о П, *esp.* ⚖ на В); *pl.* demands, requirements, claims, interests; F overcharge; ⚖ цена́ без ~а fixed price; **~и́ть** *s.* запра́шивать; **'~то** plainly, unceremoniously.
запру́|да *f* [5] dam(ming); **~живать** [1], ⟨~ди́ть⟩ **1.** [15 & 15 *e.*; -ужу́, -у́ди́шь] dam up; **2.** [15 *e.*; -ужу́, -уди́шь] F jam, crowd.
запр|яга́ть [1], ⟨~я́чь⟩ [26 г/ж: -ягу́, -яжёшь; *cf.* напря́чь harness; put (*horse[s]*) to (в В); yoke (*oxen*); get ready (*carriage*); **~я́жка** *f* [5; *g/pl.*: -жек] harness(ing); team; **~я́тывать** F [1], ⟨~я́тать⟩ [3] hide, conceal; put (away); P confine; **~я́чь** *s.* запряга́ть.
запу́г|ивать, ⟨~а́ть⟩ [1] intimidate; ~анный (in)timid(ated).
за́пус|к *m* [1] start; **~ка́ть** [1], ⟨~ти́ть⟩ [15] **1.** neglect; disregard; let grow (*beard*); leave untilled (*land*); **2.** ⊕ start, set going; fly (*kite*); F (*a.* Т / в В) fling, hurl (s. th. at); put, slip, thrust, drive (into); **~те́лый** [14] desolate; **~ти́ть** *s.* ~ка́ть.
запу́|тывать, ⟨~тать⟩ [1] (**-ся** become, get) tangle(d, *etc.*); *fig.* confuse, perplex; complicate; F entangle, involve (in в В); ~танный *a.* intricate; **~щенный** [14] deserted, desolate; neglected, uncared-for, unkempt.
запыха́ться F [1] pant.
запя́стье *n* [10] wrist; † bracelet.
запята́я *f* [14] comma; F hitch, fix.
зараб|а́тывать, ⟨~о́тать⟩ [1] earn; **-ся** F overwork o.s.; **'~отный** [14]: '~отная пла́та *f* wages *pl.*; salary; pay; **'~оток** *m* [1; -тка] earnings *pl.*; job; на '~отки in search of a job; ... to hire o.s. out.
зара|жа́ть [1], ⟨~зи́ть⟩ [15 *e.*; -ражу́, -рази́шь; ражённый] infect (*a. fig.*); **-ся** become infected (with Т), catch; **~же́ние** *n* [12] infection; ~же́ние кро́ви blood poisoning.
зара́з F at once; at the same time.
зара́|за *f* [5] infection; contagion; pest; **~зи́тельный** [14; -лен, -льна] infectious; **~зи́ть** *s.* ~жа́ть; **~зный** [14; -зен, -зна] infectious, contagious; infected.
зара́нее beforehand, in advance.
зара|ста́ть [1], ⟨~сти́⟩ [24; -сту́, -стёшь; *cf.* расти́] be overgrown.
за́рево *n* [9] blaze, glow, gleam.
заре́з *m* [1] slaughter; P ruin; до ~у F (*need s.th.*) very badly.
заре|ка́ться [1], ⟨~чься⟩ [26] forswear, abjure; **~комендова́ть** [7] *pf.* recommend; ~комендова́ть себя́ (Т) show o. s., prove.
заржа́вленный [14] rusty.
зарисо́вка *f* [5; *g/pl.*: -вок] drawing, sketch.
зарни́ца *f* [5] sheet (heat) lightning.
зар|оди́ть(ся) *s.* ~ожда́ть(ся); **~о́дыш** *m* [1] embryo, germ (*a. fig.*); в ~о́дыше in the bud; **~ожда́ть** [1], ⟨~оди́ть⟩ [15 *e.*; -ожу́, -оди́шь; -ождённый] *fig.* engender; † bear; (**-ся**) arise; (be) conceive(d); **~ожде́ние** *n* [12] origin, rise; conception.
заро́к *m* [1] vow, pledge, promise.
зарони́ть [13; -роню́, -ро́нишь] *pf.* rouse; infuse; F drop, cast; **-ся** impress (on в В).
за́росль *f* [8] underbrush; thicket.
зар|пла́та *f* [5] F *s.* ~аботный.
заруб|а́ть [1], ⟨~и́ть⟩ [14] kill, cut down; notch, cut in; ~и́(те) на носу́ (на лбу, в па́мяти)! mark it well!
зарубе́жный [14] foreign.

р|уби́ть *s.* ~уба́ть; ~у́бка *f* [5; */pl.:* -бок] incision, notch; ~убце-а́ться [7] *pf.* cicatrize.
руч|а́ться [1], ⟨~и́ться⟩ [16 *e.*; учу́сь, -учи́шься] (T) secure.
р|ыва́ть [1], ⟨~ы́ть⟩ [22] bury.
р|я́ *f* [6; *pl.:* зо́ри, зорь, заря́м & о́рям] (у́тренняя) ~я́ (*a. fig.*) dawn ⚔ [*acc.* зо́рю] reveille); вече́рняя я́ evening glow; (⚔ tattoo, retreat); а ~е́ at dawn, daybreak (*a.* с ~ёй); *ig.* at the earliest stage *or* beginning; от ~и́ до ~и́ from morning to ight, all day (night); ~я́ занима́ет-я it dawns.
ря́|д *m* [1] charge (⚔, ⚡); shot; hell, cartridge; *fig.* store; ~ди́ть *s.* жа́ть; ~дка *f* [5] ⚔ loading; ⚡ harge, -ging; *sport:* gymnastics ., bodily exercise; ~дный [14] harge..., loading; ~дный я́щик *m* mmunition wag(g)on; ~жа́ть [1], ~ди́ть⟩ [15 & 15 *e.*; -яжу́, -я́ди́шь; я́женный & -яжённый] ⚔, *phot.* oad; ⚡ charge; *fig.* inspire, imbue; *f.* F (set in &) reiterate *or* go on & on.
са́|да *f* [5] ambush; попа́сть в ~ду e ambushed; ~живать [1], ⟨~-и́ть⟩ [15] plant; F confine; compel (*do s.th.*); -ся F, ⟨засе́сть⟩ [25; ся́ду, -дешь; -се́л] sit down; ettle, retire, stay; hide, lie in amush; (за B) set *or* begin to, bury s. in (*work*).
са́л|ивать [1] 1. ⟨~ить⟩ [13] rease, smear; 2. ⟨засоли́ть⟩ [13; олю́, -о́ли́шь; -о́ленный] salt; orn (*meat*).
с|а́ривать [1] & засоря́ть [28], ~ори́ть⟩ [13] litter, soil; stop (up), bstruct (*a. fig.*); ⚕ constipate; e(come) weedy; ~ори́ть глаз(а́) ave (get) s.th. in(to) one's eye(s).
с|а́сывать [1], ⟨~оса́ть⟩ [-су́, сёшь; -о́санный] suck in; engulf, wallow up.
са́харенный [14] candied, sugared.
свет|ло by daylight; ~и́ть(ся) 13; -све́тится] *pf.* light (up).
свиде́тельствовать [7] *pf.* tesfy; attest, authenticate.
се́|в *m* [1] sowing; ~ва́ть [1], ять⟩ [27] sow.
седа́|ние *n* [12] session (⚖, *parl.*); eeting; (*prp.:* in, at на П); ~тель [4] assessor; ~ть [1] 1. be in ession; sit; meet; 2. ⟨засе́сть⟩ ся́ду, -дешь; -се́л] stick.
се|ка́ть [1], ⟨~чь⟩ [26] 1. [-се́к, ла́; -сечённый] notch, mark; stop *ime with stop watch*); 2. [-се́к, се́кла; -се́ченный] flog to death.
сел|е́ние *n* [12] colonization; я́ть [28], ⟨~и́ть⟩ [13] people, opulate; occupy, inhabit.
се́|сть *s.* заса́живаться & ~да́ть ; ~чь *s.* ~ка́ть; ~ять *s.* ~ва́ть.
си́|живать [1], ⟨~де́ть⟩ [11] женный [му́хами]) flyblow(n);

-ся sit, stay *or* live (too) long; sit up late.
заскору́злый [14] hardened.
засло́н|ка *f* [5; *g/pl.:* -нок] (stove, *etc.*) door, screen, trap; ~я́ть [28], ⟨~и́ть⟩ [13] protect, screen; shut off, take away (*light*); repress, oust.
заслу́|га *f* [8] merit, desert; он получи́л по ~гам (it) served him right; ~женный [14] merited, (well-)deserved, just; meritorious, worthy; hono(u)red (*a. in Sov. titles*); ~живать [1], ⟨~жи́ть⟩ [16] merit, deserve (*impf. a.* P); F earn.
заслу́ш|ивать, ⟨~ать⟩ [1] hear; -ся listen (to T, P) with delight.
засм|а́триваться [1], ⟨~отре́ться⟩ [9; -отрю́сь, -о́тришься] (на B) feast one's eyes *or* gloat ([up]on), look (at) with delight.
засну́ть *s.* засыпа́ть 2.
зас|о́в *m* [1] bar, bolt; ~о́вывать [1], ⟨~у́нуть⟩ [20] put, slip, tuck; F mislay; ~оли́ть *s.* ~а́ливать 2.
засор|е́ние *n* [12] obstruction; ⚕ constipation; ~и́ть, ~я́ть *s.* заса́ривать.
засоса́ть *s.* заса́сывать.
засо́х|ший [17] dry, dried up; ⚘ dead; ~нуть *s.* засыха́ть.
за́спанный F [14] sleepy.
заста́|ва *f* [5] *hist.* (toll)gate, turnpike; ⚔ frontier post; outpost; ~ва́ть [5], ⟨~ть⟩ [-а́ну, -а́нешь] find, meet with; surprise; take ...; ~вля́ть [28], ⟨~вить⟩ [14] 1. compel, force, make; ~вить ждать keep waiting; ~вить замолча́ть silence; 2. (T) block (up); fill; ~ре́лый [14] inveterate, chronic; ~ть *s.* ~ва́ть.
заст|ёгивать [1], ⟨~егну́ть⟩ [20; -ёгнутый] button (one's coat, *etc.*, *a.* -ся, up); buckle, clasp, hook (up); ~ёжка *f* [5; *g/pl.:* -жек] clasp.
застекл|я́ть [28], ⟨~и́ть⟩ [13] glaze.
засте́н|ок *m* [1; -нка] torture chamber; ~чивый [14 *sh.*] shy, timid.
засти|га́ть [1], ⟨~гнуть⟩, ⟨~чь⟩ [21 -г-: -и́гну, -и́гнешь; -и́г, -и́гла; -и́гнутый] surprise, catch; take...
заст|ила́ть [1], ⟨~ла́ть⟩ [-телю́, -те́лешь; за́стланный] cover; cloud.
засто́|й *m* [3] standstill, deadlock; stagnation; ~йный [14] stagnant; chronic; ✝ unsalable; ~льный [14] table...; drinking; ~я́ться [-ою́сь, -ои́шься] *pf.* stand *or* stay too long; be(come) stagnant, stale.
застр|а́ивать [1], ⟨~о́ить⟩ [13] build on; build up, encumber; ~axо́вывать [1], ⟨~axова́ть⟩ [7] insure; *fig.* safeguard; ~ева́ть [1], ⟨~я́ть⟩ [-я́ну, -я́нешь] stick; F come to a standstill; be delayed; be lost; ~е́ливать [1], ⟨~ели́ть⟩ [13; -елю́, -е́лишь; -е́ленный]

shoot, kill; **~е́льщик** *m* [1] ⚔ skirmisher; *fig.* instigator; initiator; **~о́ить** *s.* ~а́ивать; **~о́йка** *f* [5; *g/pl.*: -о́ек] building (on); **~я́ть** *s.* ~ева́ть.

за́ступ *m* [1] spade.

заступ|а́ть [1], ⟨~и́ть⟩ [14] take (*s. b.'s place*), relieve; F start (*work* на В); **-ся** (за В) take s.b.'s side; protect; intercede for; **~ник** *m* [1] protector, patron; advocate; **~ница** *f* [5] protectress, patroness; **~ничество** *n* [9] intercession.

засты|ва́ть [1], ⟨~ть⟩ [-ы́ну, -ы́нешь] cool down, congeal; stiffen, be(come) *or* stand stockstill; (*a. blood*) freeze (F to death), chill.

засу́нуть *s.* засо́вывать.

за́суха *f* [5] drought.

засу́ч|ивать [1], ⟨~и́ть⟩ [16] turn *or* tuck up.

засу́ш|ивать [1], ⟨~и́ть⟩ [16] dry (up); F make arid; **~ливый** [14 *sh.*] droughty.

засчи́т|ывать, ⟨~а́ть⟩ [1] reckon, (ac)count; credit.

зас|ыпа́ть [1] **1.** ⟨~ы́пать⟩ [2] (T) fill up; cover, drift; *fig.* heap, ply, overwhelm; F pour, strew; **2.** ⟨~ну́ть⟩ [20] fall asleep; **~ыха́ть** [1], ⟨~о́хнуть⟩ [21] dry up; wither.

зата́|ивать [1], ⟨~и́ть⟩ [13] conceal, hide; hold (*breath*); bear (*grudge*); ~ённый *a.* secret.

зат|а́пливать [1] *&* **~опля́ть** [28], ⟨~опи́ть⟩ [14] **1.** light (make) a fire; **2.** flood; sink; **~а́птывать** [1], ⟨~опта́ть⟩ [3] trample, tread (down); **~а́скивать** [1] **1.** F, ⟨~аска́ть⟩ [1] wear out; ~а́сканный worn, shabby; hackneyed; **2.** ⟨~ащи́ть⟩ [16] drag, pull (in, *etc.*); mislay.

затв|ердева́ть [1], ⟨~ерде́ть⟩ [8] harden; **~е́рживать** [1], ⟨~ерди́ть⟩ [15 *e.*; -ржу́, -рди́шь; -ржённый] memorize, learn (by heart).

затво́р *m* [1] bolt, bar; (*a.* ⚔) lock; gate; *phot.* shutter; **~я́ть** [28], ⟨~и́ть⟩ [13; -орю́, -о́ришь; -о́ренный] shut, close; **-ся** shut o.s. up.

зат|ева́ть F [1], ⟨~е́ять⟩ [27] start, undertake; conceive; resolve; **~е́йливый** [14 *sh.*] fanciful; ingenious, intricate; **~ека́ть** [1], ⟨~е́чь⟩ [26] flow (in, *etc.*); swell; be(come) numb, asleep (*limbs*), bloodshot (*eyes*).

зате́м then; for that purpose, that is why; ~ чтобы in order to (*or* that); ~ что † because.

затемн|е́ние *n* [12] ⚔ blackout; obscuration; **~я́ть** [28], ⟨~и́ть⟩ [13] darken, overshadow, (*a. fig.*) obscure; ⚔ black out.

затер|е́ть *s.* затира́ть; **~я́ть** F [28] *pf.* lose; **-ся** get *or* be lost; disappear; lie in the midst of.

зате́|чь *s.* затека́ть; **~я** *f* [6] plan, undertaking; invention, freak; diversion; trick; **~ять** *s.* ~ва́ть.

зат|ира́ть [1], ⟨~ере́ть⟩ [12] wi *or* blot out; jam, block (up); F we out; efface, stunt; **~иха́ть** [⟨~и́хнуть⟩ [21] become silent quiet, stop (speaking, *etc.*); d away *or* off; calm down, abat **~и́шье** *n* [10] lull, calm; shelte quiet spot, nook.

заткну́ть *s.* затыка́ть.

затм|ева́ть [1], ⟨~и́ть⟩ [14 *e.*; *1st. p. sg.*; -ми́шь], **~е́ние** *n* [1 eclipse.

зато́ but (then, at the same time instead, in return, on the oth hand; therefore.

затова́ривание † *n* [12] glut.

затоп|и́ть, ~ля́ть *s.* зата́пливат **~та́ть** *s.* зата́птывать.

зато́р *m* [1] jam, block, obstructio

заточ|а́ть [1], ⟨~и́ть⟩ [16 *e.*; -ч -чи́шь; -чённый] confine, impri on; exile; **-е́ние** *n* [12] confin ment, imprisonment; exile.

затра́|вливать [1], ⟨~ви́ть⟩ [1 bait (*a. fig.* F), course, chase dow **~гивать** [1], ⟨затро́нуть⟩ [2 touch (*a. fig.*, [up]on); affect; hu

затра́|та *f* [5] expense, expenditu **~чивать** [1], ⟨~тить⟩ [15] spen

затро́нуть *s.* затра́гивать.

затрудн|е́ние *n* [12] difficul trouble; embarrassment; в ~е́н *a.* at a loss; **~и́тельный** [14; -ле -льна] difficult, hard, straitene ~и́тельное положе́ние *n* predic ment; **~я́ть** [28], ⟨~и́ть⟩ [13] en barrass, (cause) trouble; rend (more) difficult, inconvenien aggravate, complicate; **-ся** *a.* be a loss (for в П, Т).

зату|ма́нивать(ся) [1], ⟨~мани (-ся)⟩ [13] fog; dim; **~ха́ть** F [⟨~хнуть⟩ [21] die out; (*a. rad* fade; **~шёвывать** [1], ⟨~шева́т [6] shade; *fig.* F smooth over; - efface; **~ши́ть** F [16] *s.* туши́ть.

за́тхлый [14] musty, fusty.

зат|ыкать [1], ⟨~кну́ть⟩ [20] st (up), (про́бкой) cork (up); F tuc slip; **~ы́лок** *m* [1; -лка] back of t head; nape (of the neck).

заты́чка *f* F [5; *g/pl.*: -чек] bun plug.

затя́|гивать [1], ⟨~ну́ть⟩ [tighten, draw tight; gird, lace, e close, press; draw in, *etc.*; involv cover; *impers.*: sink; close, sk (over); protract, delay; begin (sing); **~жка** *f* [5; *g/pl.*: -же drawing tight; protraction; inha tion (*smoking*); **~жно́й** [14] lo lengthy, protracted.

зау|ны́вный [14; -вен, -вна] sa mournful, melancholy; **~ря́дн** [14; -ден, -дна] common(plac ordinary, mediocre; **~се́ница** *f* [agnail.

зау́треня *f* [6] matins *pl.* [rize

зау́ч|ивать [1], ⟨~и́ть⟩ [16] memo

ахва́т *m* [1] seizure, capture; ısurpation; **~ывать** [1], ⟨**~и́ть**⟩ [15] grasp, grip(e); take (along [with one, *a.* с собой]); seize, capture; ısurp; absorb, captivate; F catch, snatch, take (away [*breath*], up, *etc.*); **~нический** [16] aggressive; **~чик** *n* [1] invader, aggressor; **~ывать** *s.* ~и́ть.
ахворать F [1] *pf.* fall sick, ill.
ахл|ёбываться [1], ⟨**~ебну́ться**⟩ [20] choke, stifle (with T, от P); *fig.* be beside o.s.; ⚔, ⊕ break down, stop; **~ёстывать** [1], ⟨**~естну́ть**⟩ [20; -хлёстнутый] lash (round, on [-to], together); swamp (*boat*, *etc.*); *fig.* seize; **~о́пывать(ся)** [1], ⟨**~о́пнуть(ся)**⟩ [20] slam, bang.
ахо́д *m* [1] (со́лнца sun)set; call (*at a port*); ✈ approach; **~и́ть** [5], ⟨зайти́⟩ [зайду́, -дёшь; *g. pt.*: зайдя́; *cf.* идти́] go *or* come in *or* to (see, *etc.*), call *or* drop in (on, at к Д, в В); pick up, fetch (за Т); ⚓ call *or* touch at, enter; get, advance; pass, draw out; (*a.* ✈) approach; ⚔ outflank; turn, disappear, go behind (за В); *ast.* set; речь зашла́ о (П) (we, *etc.*) began (came) to (*or* had a) talk (about).
ахолу́ст|ный [14] out-of-the-way, provincial, country...; rustic, boorish; **~ье** *n* [10] solitude, lonely *or* dreary spot (suburb).
ахуда́лый [14] down & out; mean.
ацеп|ля́ть [28], ⟨**~и́ть**⟩ [14] (*a.* за B) catch, hook on, grapple; fasten; F & **-ся** *s.* задева́ть.
ачаро́в|ывать [1], ⟨**~а́ть**⟩ [7] charm.
ачасту́ю F often, frequently.
ача́|тие *n* [12] conception; **~ток** *m* [1; -тка] germ; *pl.* rudiments; **~точный** [14] rudimentary; **~ть** [-чну́, -чнёшь; зача́л, -á, -о; зача́тый (зача́т, -á, -о)] conceive.
ачём why, wherefore, for what (*or* what for); ~-то for some purpose (reason) (or other).
ач|ёркивать [1], ⟨**~еркну́ть**⟩ [20; -чёркнутый] strike out, obliterate; **~е́рпывать** [1], ⟨**~ерпну́ть**⟩ [20; -чёрпнутый] scoop, dip; **~ерстве́лый** [14] stale; *fig.* unfeeling; **~е́сть** *s.* ~и́тывать¹; **~ёсывать** [1], ⟨**~еса́ть**⟩ [3] comb (back); **~ёт** *m* [1] examination, test; F *educ.* credit.
ач|и́нщик *m* [1] instigator; **~исля́ть** [28], ⟨**~и́слить**⟩ [13] enrol(l), enlist, engage; ✝ enter; **~и́тывать¹** [1], ⟨**~е́сть**⟩ [25 -т-: -чту́, -чтёшь; *cf.* проче́сть] reckon, charge, account; *educ.* credit; **~и́тывать²**, ⟨**~ита́ть**⟩ [1] read (to, aloud); F thumb, wear out, tear; not return (*borrowed book*); **-ся** be(come) absorbed (in T); read (too) long.
ачумлённый [14 *sh.*] infected with pestilence.
аш|ива́ть [1], ⟨**~и́ть**⟩ [-шью́, -шьёшь; *cf.* шить] sew up; **~нуро́вывать** [1], ⟨**~нурова́ть**⟩ [7] lace (up); **~то́панный** [14] darned.
защёлк|ивать [1], ⟨**~нуть**⟩ [20] snap, catch.
защем|ля́ть [28], ⟨**~и́ть**⟩ [14 *e.*; -емлю́, -еми́шь; -емлённый] squeeze (in), pinch, jam; *impers. fig.* oppress with grief.
защи́|та *f* [5] defense (*Brt.* -nce), protection, cover; maintenance; **~ти́ть** *s.* ~ща́ть; **~тник** *m* [1] defender; protector; ⚖ advocate (*a. fig.*), counsel([l]or) for the defense; *sport*: back; **~тный** [14] protective; safety...; khaki ...; crash (*helmet*); **~ща́ть** [1], ⟨**~ти́ть**⟩ [15 *e.*; -ищу́, -ити́шь; -ищённый] (от P) defend (from, against); protect (from); vindicate, advocate, (*a. thesis*) maintain, support; *impf.* ⚖ defend, plead (for).
заяв|и́ть *s.* ~ля́ть; **~ка** *f* [5; *g/pl.*: -вок] application (for на B); claim; request; **~ле́ние** *n* [12] declaration, statement; petition, application (for о П); **~ля́ть** [28], ⟨**~и́ть**⟩ [14] (*a.* о П) declare, announce, state; claim, present; enter, lodge; notify, inform; show, manifest.
зая́длый F [14] = завзя́тый.
зая́|ц *m* [1; за́йца] hare; F speck(le); P stowaway; **~чий** [18] hare('s)...; F cowardly; ~чья губа́ *f* harelip.
зва́|ние *n* [12] rank; title; class; standing; **~ный** [14] invited; **~ный** обе́д (ве́чер) *m* dinner (evening) party; **~тельный** [14] *gr.* vocative (*case*); **~ть** [зову́, зовёшь; звал, -á, -о; (ˈ...)зва́нный (зван, -á, -о)] **1.** ⟨по-⟩ call; invite (to [*a.* ~ть в го́сти] к Д, на B); **2.** ⟨на-⟩ (T) F (be) call(ed); как вас зову́т? what is your (first) name?; меня́ зову́т Петро́м *or* Пётр my name is Peter.
звезда́ [5; *pl.* звёзды, *etc. st.*] star (*a. fig.*); морска́я ~ *zo.* starfish.
звёзд|ный [14] star..., stellar; starry (*sky*); starlit (*night*); **~очка** *f* [5; *g/pl.*: -чек] starlet; *print.* asterisk.
звен|е́ть [9], ⟨за-, про-⟩ ring, jingle, clink; у меня́ ~и́т в уша́х my ears ring.
звено́ *n* [9; *pl.*: зве́нья, -ьев] link; *fig.* part, branch; ✈ flight; squad.
звери́н|ец *m* [1; -нца] menagerie; **~ый** [14] animal; feral; *s.* зве́рский.
зверо|бо́й *m* [3] (*seal, walrus, etc.*) hunter; **~ло́в** *m* [1] trapper; hunter.
звéр|ский [16] *s.* звери́ный; *fig.* brutal, atrocious; F beastly, awful, dog(-*tired*); **~ство** *n* [9] brutality; *pl.* atrocities; **~ь** *m* [4; *from g/pl. e.*] (wild) animal, beast; *fig.* brute.
звон *m* [1] ring, jingle, peal, chime; **~а́рь** *m* [4 *e.*] bell ringer, sexton; **~и́ть** [13], ⟨по-⟩ ring (*v/t.* в B), chime, peal; (Д) telephone, call up; **~кий** [16; зво́нок, -нка́, -о; *comp.*:

звóнче] sonorous, clear; resonant; *gr.* voiced; hard (*cash*); **~óк** *m* [1; -нкá] bell; ring; the bell rings.
звук *m* [1] sound; tone (*a.* ♪); tune; **~овóй** [14] sound...; talking (*picture*); **~онепроницáемый** [14] soundproof; **~оподражáние** *n* [12] onomatopoeia; **~оподражáтельный** [14] onomatopoe(t)ic.
звуч|áние *n* [12] sounding; **~áть** [4 *e.*; *3rd p. only*], ⟨про-⟩ (re)sound; ring; clang; **∠ный** [14; -чен, -чнá, -о] sonorous, clear; resonant.
звя́к|ать [1], ⟨~нуть⟩ [20] clink.
зги: (ни) згú не видáть *or* не ви́дно it is pitch-dark.
здáние *n* [12] building.
зде|сь here; local (*on letter*); ~сь! present!; **∠шний** [15] local; я не ∠шний I am a stranger here.
здорóв|аться [1], ⟨по-⟩ (с T) greet *or* salute (o. a.), welcome; wish good morning, *etc.*; ~аться зá руку shake hands; ~о[1] P hi!, hello!; ′~о[2] P awfully; well done, dandy; **~ый** [14 *sh.*] healthy (*a. su.*), sound (*a. fig.*); wholesome, salubrious; P strong; in good health; бýдь(те) ~(ы)! good-by(e)!, good luck!; your health!; **~ье** *n* [10] health; кáк вáше ~ье? how are you?; за вáше ~ье! your health!, here's to you!; на ~ье! good luck (health)!; éшь(те) на ~ье! help yourself (-ves), please!
здрáв|ие *n* [12] † = здорóвье; ~ия желáю (-лáем) ⚔ good morning (*etc.*), sir!; **~ица** *f* [5] toast; **~ница** *f* [5] sanatorium; sanitarium; **~омы́слящий** [17] sane, sensible; **~оохранéние** *n* [12] public health service; **~ствовать** [7] be in good health; ~ствуй(те)! hello!, hi!, good morning! (*etc.*); how do you do?; да ~ствует ...! long live ...!; **~ый** [14 *sh.*] † = здорóвый; *fig.* sound, sane, sensible; ~ый смысл *m* common sense; в ~ом умé in one's senses; ~ и невреди́м safe & sound.
зев *m* [1] throat, gullet, *anat.* pharynx; † jaws *pl.*; **~áка** F *m/f* [5] gaper; **~áть** [1], *once* ⟨~нýть⟩ [20] yawn; F gape (at на B); ~áть по сторонáм stand gaping around; F dawdle; не ~áй! look out!; **~óк** *m* [1; -вкá] yawn; **~óта** *f* [5] yawning.
зелен|éть [8], ⟨за-, по-⟩ grow, turn *or* be green; *impf.* (*a.* **-ся**) appear *or* show green; **~нóй** [14] greengrocer's; **~овáтый** [14 *sh.*] greenish; **~щи́к** *m* [1 *e.*] greengrocer.
зелёный [14; зéлен, -á, -о] green (*a. fig.*), verdant; ~ теáтр open-air stage; ~ юнéц F greenhorn.
зéл|ень *f* [8] verdure; green; potherbs, greens *pl.*; **~ье** *n* [10] herb; poison.
земéльный [14] land...; landed.
землевладé|лец *m* [1; -льца] landowner; **~ние** *n* [12] (крýпное grea landed property, (real) estate.
земледéл|ец *m* [1; -льца] farme **~ие** *n* [12] agriculture, farmin **~ьческий** [16] agricultural.
земле|кóп *m* [1] digger; *Brt.* navv **~мéр** *m* [1] (land) surveyor; **~тр сéние** *n* [12] earthquake; **~чер пáлка** [5; *g/pl.*: -лок] dredge.
земли́стый [14 *sh.*] earthy; ashy.
земл|я́ *f* [6; *ac/sg.*: зéмлю; *pl* зéмли, земéль, зéмлям] earth (*planet* ♁я́); land; ground, soil; country; на ∠ю to the ground; **~я́** *m* [1 *e.*] (fellow) countryman; **~я ни́ка** *f* [5] (wild) strawberry, -ri *pl.*; **~я́нка** *f* [5; *g/pl.*: -нок] (*a.* ⚔ dugout; (mud) hut; **~янóй** [1 earth(en), mud...; land...; ashy; ~ янóй орéх *m* peanut; ~янáя грýш *f* (Jerusalem) artichoke.
земновóдный [14] amphibian.
земнóй [14] (of the) earth, te restrial; earthly; *fig.* earthy.
зéм|ский [16] *hist.* State...; count ...; ⚔ Territorial (*Army*); ~ски собóр *m* diet; ~ский начáльник sheriff, bailiff; **~ство** *n* [9] zemstv county council (*1864—1917*).
зени́т *m* [1] zenith (*a. fig.* = climax **~ный** ⚔ [14] anti-aircraft...
зени́ц|а *f* [5] † pupil, eye; берéч как ~у óка cherish like the apple one's eye.
зéркал|о *n* [9; *pl. e.*] looking glas (*a. fig.*) mirror; **∠ьный** [14] *fi* (dead-)smooth; plate (*glass*).
зерн|и́стый [14 *sh.*] grainy, gran ular; **~ó** *n* [9; *pl.*: зёрна, зёрен, зёр нам] grain (*a. coll.*), corn, (*a. fig* seed; **~овóй** [14] grain...; *su.* р cereals. [-зен, -зна] zigzag.
зигзáг *m* [1], **~ообрáзный** [14;
зим|á *f* [5; *ac/sg.*: зи́му; *pl. st.*] win ter (in [the] T; for the на B); **∠ни** [15] winter..., wintry; **~овáть** [7 ⟨за-, пере-⟩ winter; hibernate; **~ óвка** *f* [5; *g/pl.*: -вок], **~óвье** *n* [1(wintering; hibernation; winter hu
зия́|ние *n* [12] gaping; *ling.* hiatus **~ть** [28] gape.
злак *m* [1] herb; grass; *pl.* ⚘ gra mineous plants; хлéбные ~и *pl.*
злато... † *poet.* gold(en). [cereals.
злить [13], ⟨обо-, разо-⟩ vex, ange *or* make angry, irritate; **~ся** b (-come) *or* feel angry (with на B) *fig.* rage.
зло *n* [9; *pl. gen.* зол *only*] evil.
злóб|а *f* [5] spite; rage; ~а дн topic of the day; **~ный** [14; -бен -бна] spiteful, malicious; **~однéвный** [14; -вен, -вна] topical, burn ing; **~ствовать** [7] *s.* зли́ться.
злов|éщий [17 *sh.*] ominous, ill-bod ing; **~óние** *n* [12] stench; **~óнны** [14; -óнен, óнна] stinking, fetid **~рéдный** [14; -ден, -дна] mali cious, malign(ant).

злоде́|й *m* [3] malefactor, evildoer; criminal; villain; **~йский** [16] vile, villainous, outrageous; malicious; **~йство** *n* [9], **~я́ние** *n* [12] misdeed, outrage, villainy, crime.
злой [14; зол, зла, зло] wicked, (*a. su. n*) evil; malicious, spiteful; angry (with на В); fierce; severe; bad; mordant; ⚕ malignant.
зло|ка́чественный [14 *sh.*] malignant; **~ключе́ние** *n* [12] misfortune; **~наме́ренный** [14 *sh.*] malevolent; **~нра́вный** [14; -вен, -вна] ill-natured; **~па́мятный** [14; -тен, -тна] vindictive; **~полу́чный** [14; -чен, -чна] unfortunate, ill-fated; **~ра́дный** [14; -ден, -дна] mischievous.
злосло́ви|е *n* [12], **~ть** [14] slander.
зло́ст|ный [14; -тен, -тна] malicious, spiteful; malevolent; **~ь** *f* [8] spite; rage.
зло|сча́стный [14; -тен, -тна] *s.* ~полу́чный.
злоумы́шленн|ик *m* [1] plotter; malefactor; **~ый** [14] malevolent.
злоупотреб|ле́ние *n* [12], **~ля́ть** [28], ⟨~и́ть⟩ [14 *e.*; -блю́, -би́шь] (Т) abuse; (make) excessive use.
зме|и́ный [14] snake('s), serpent('s), -tine; **~и́ться** [13] meander, wind (o.s.); **~й** *m* [3] dragon; (*a.* бума́жный ~й) kite; †, P = **~я́** *f* [6; *pl. st.*: зме́и, змей] snake, serpent (*a. fig.*).
знак *m* [1] sign, mark, token; symbol; omen; badge; signal; ~и *pl.* препина́ния punctuation marks; в ~ (P) in (*or* as a) token (sign) of.
знако́м|ить [14], ⟨по-⟩ introduce (a p. to В/с Т); *a.* ⟨о-⟩) acquaint (with с Т); **-ся** (с Т) *p.*: meet, make the acquaintance of, (*a. th.*) become acquainted with; *th.*: familiarize o.s. with, go into; **~ство** *n* [9] acquaintance (-ces *pl.*); **~ый** [14 *sh.*] familiar, acquainted (with с Т); known; *su.* acquaintance; бу́дьте ~ы = ~ьтесь, ..., meet ...
знамена́тель *m* [4] denominator; **~ный** [14; -лен, -льна] memorable, remarkable; significant, suggestive; *gr.* notional.
знаме́н|ие *n* [12] †, *s.* знак; **~и́тость** *f* [8] fame, renown; *p.*: celebrity; **~и́тый** [14 *sh.*] famous, renowned, celebrated (by, for Т).
знам|ено́сец *m* [1; -сца] standard bearer; **~я** *n* [13; *pl.*: -мёна, -мён] banner, flag; ⚔ standard; colo(u)rs.
зна́ни|е *n* [12] (*a. pl.* ~я) knowledge; со ~ем де́ла with skill *or* competence.
зна́т|ный [14; -тен, -тна́, -о] noble; distinguished, notable, eminent; **~о́к** *m* [1 *e.*] expert; connoisseur.
знать[1] **1.** [1] know; дать ~ (Д) let know; дать себя́ (о себе́) ~ make o.s. felt (send news); то и зна́й = то и де́ло; кто́ его́ зна́ет goodness knows; **-ся** F associate with (с Т); (get to) know; **2.** P apparently, probably; ~² *f* [8] nobility, notables.
знач|е́ние *n* [12] meaning, sense; significance, importance (*vb.*: име́ть be of); **~и́тельный** [14; -лен, -льна] considerable; large; important; significant, suggestive; **~ить** [16] mean, signify; matter; ~ит consequently, so; well (then); **-ся** be registered; *impers.* (it) say(s); **~о́к** *m* [1; -чка́] badge; sign.
зноби́т|ь: меня́ ~ I feel chilly.
зной *m* [3] heat, sultriness; **~ный** [14; зно́ен, зно́йна] sultry, hot.
зоб *m* [1] crop, craw; ⚕ goiter, -tre.
зов *m* [1] call; F invitation.
зо́дчество *n* [9] architecture.
зол|а́ *f* [5] ashes *pl.*; **~о́вка** *f* [5; *g/pl.*: -вок] sister-in-law (*husband's sister*).
золоти́|стый [14 *sh.*] golden; **~ть** [15 *e.*; -очу́, -оти́шь], ⟨по-, вы́-⟩ gild.
зо́лот|о *n* [9] gold; на вес ~а worth its weight in gold; **~оиска́тель** *m* [4] gold digger; **~о́й** [14] gold(en) (*a. fig.*); dear; ~ы́х дел ма́стер *m* † jewel(l)er.
золоту́|ха F *f* [5] scrofula; **~шный** F [14; -шен, -шна] scrofulous.
золочёный [14] gilt, gilded.
зо́н|а *f* [5] zone; **~а́льный** [14] zonal.
зонд *m* [1], **~и́ровать** [7] sound.
зонт, ~ик *m* [1] umbrella; sunshade.
зоо́|лог *m* [1] zoölogist; **~логи́ческий** [16] zoölogical; **~ло́гия** *f* [7] zoölogy; **~па́рк, ~са́д** *m* [1] zoo (-logical garden).
зо́ркий [16; зо́рок, -рка́, -о; *comp.*: зо́рче] sharp-sighted (*a. fig.*); observant, watchful, vigilant.
зрачо́к *m* [1; -чка́] *anat.* pupil.
зре́л|ище *n* [11] sight; spectacle; show; **~ость** *f* [8] ripeness, maturity; **~ый** [14; зрел, -а́, -о] ripe, mature; deliberate.
зре́ни|е *n* [12] (eye)sight; по́ле ~я range of vision, eyeshot; *fig.* horizon; то́чка ~я point of view, standpoint, angle (*prp.*: с то́чки ~я = под угло́м ~я from ...).
зреть 1. [8], ⟨со-, вы́-⟩ ripen, mature; **2.** † [9], ⟨у-⟩ see; look.
зри́тель *m* [4] spectator, onlooker, looker-on; **~ный** [14] visual, optic; ~ный зал *m* hall, auditorium; ~ная труба́ spyglass.
зря F in vain, to no purpose, (all) for nothing; it's no good (use) ...ing.
зря́чий [17] seeing (*one that can see*).
зуб *m* [1; *from g/pl. e.*; ⊕ зу́бья, зу́бьев] tooth; ⊕ *a.* cog, dent; до ~о́в to the teeth; не по ~а́м too tough (*a. fig.*); сквозь ~ы through clenched teeth; (*mutter*) indistinctly; име́ть *or* точи́ть ~ (на В) have a grudge against; **~а́стый** [14 *sh.*]

large-, sharp-toothed; *fig.* sharp--tongued; **~éц** *m* [1; -бцá] ⊕ = зуб; ⚔ battlement; **~úло** *n* [9] chisel; **~нóй** [14] tooth...; dental; ~нóй врач *m* dentist; ~нáя боль *f* toothache; **~очúстка** *f* [5; *g/pl.*: -ток] toothpick.

зубр *m* [1] bison; *fig.* fossil.

зубр|ёжка F *f* [5] cramming; **~úть 1.** [13], ⟨за-⟩ notch; зазýбренный jagged; **2.** F [13; зубрю́, зýбрúшь], ⟨вы́-, за-⟩ [зазýбренный] cram, learn by rote.

зубчáтый [14] ⊕ cog(wheel)..., gear...; indented.

зуд *m* [1], **~éть** F [9] itch (*a. fig.*).

зы́б|кий [16; зы́бок, -бкá, -о; *comp.:* зы́бче] loose; shaky; unsteady, unstable; swelling, rippled; vague; **~ýчий** [17 *sh.*] = ~кий; **~ь** *f* [8] ripples *pl.*; swell; † wave.

зы́чный [14; -чен, -чна; *comp.:* -чнée] ringing.

зя́б|кий [16; -бок, -бкá, -о] chilly; **~левый** [14] winter...; **~лик** *m* [1] chaffinch; **~нуть** [21], ⟨(пр)о-⟩ feel chilly; freeze; **~ь** *f* [8] winter tillage.

зять *m* [4; *pl. e.*: зятья́, -ьёв] son- *or* brother-in-law (*daughter's or sister's husband*).

И

и 1. *cj.* and; and then, and so; but; (even) though, much as; (that's) just (what ... is, *etc.*), (this) very *or* same; **2.** *part.* oh; too, (n)either; even; и ... и ... both ... and ...

úбо because, since, as.

úва *f* [5] willow.

Ивáн *m* [1] Ivan; John.

úволга *f* [5] oriole.

игл|á *f* [5; *pl. st.*] needle (*a.* ⊕, ⚕, *min.*, ⚘); thorn, prickle; quill, spine, bristle; **~úстый** [14 *sh.*] prickly, thorny; spiny; crystalline.

Игнá|тий *m* [3], F **~т** [1] Ignatius.

игнорúровать [7] (*im*)*pf.* ignore.

úго *n* [8] *fig.* yoke.

игóл|ка *f* [5; *g/pl.:* -лок] *s.* иглá; как на ~ках on tenterhooks; с ~(оч)ки brand-new, spick-and--span; **~ьный** [14] needle('s)...

игóрный [14] gambling; card...

игрá *f* [5; *pl. st.*] play; game (of в В); effervescense; sparkle; ~ слов play on words, pun; ~ не стóит свеч it isn't worth while *or* doesn't pay; **~лище** *n* [11] sport, plaything; **~льный** [14] playing (*card*); **~ть** [1], ⟨по-, сыгрáть⟩ play (*sport, cards, chess, etc.*, в В; ♪ на П); gamble; (*storm, etc.*) rage; (*a. wine, etc.*) sparkle; *thea. a.* act.

игрú|вый [14 *sh.*] playful, sportive; equivocal, immodest; **~стый** [14 *sh.*] sparkling.

игрóк *m* [1 *e*] player, gambler.

игрýшка *f* [5; *g/pl.*: -шек] toy, plaything.

игýмен *m* [1] abbot, superior.

идеáл *m* [1] ideal; **~úзм** *m* [1] idealism; **~úст** *m* [1] idealist; **~истúческий** [16] idealistic; **~ьный** [14; -лен, -льна] ideal.

идéйный [14; -éен, -éйна] ideologic(al); ideal; high-principled.

идеóлог *m* [1] ideologist; **~úческий** [16] ideologic(al); **∠ия** [7] ideology.

идéя *f* [6] idea.

идúлл|ия *f* [7] idyl(l); **~úческий** [16] idyllic.

идиомáт|ика *f* [5] stock of idioms; idiomology; **~úческий** [16] idiomatic(al).

идиóт *m* [1] idiot; **~úзм** *m* [1] idiocy; **~ский** [16] idiotic.

úдол *m* [1] idol; *contp.* blockhead.

идтú [идý, идёшь; шёл, шла; шéдший; идя́, F úдучи; ...дённый], ⟨пойтú⟩ [пойдý, -дёшь; пошёл, -шлá] (be) go(ing, *etc.*; *a. fig.*), walk; come; run, pass, drive, sail, fly, *etc.*; (за Т) follow, *a.* go for, fetch; leave; move (*a. chess*, Т), flow, drift, blow; (в, на В) enter (*school*), join (*army, etc.*), become; proceed, be in progress, take place; be on (*thea., film*); lead (*road*; *a. card* с Р); (на В) attack; spread (*rumo*[*u*]*r*); (be) receive(d); † sell; ⊕ work; (в, на, под В) be used, spent (for); (в В) be sent to; ([к] Д) suit; (за В) marry; ~ в счёт count; ~ на вёслах row; ~ по отцý take after one's father; идёт! all right!, done!; пошёл (пошлú)! (let's) go!; дéло (речь) идёт о (П) the question *or* matter is (whether), it is a question *or* matter (of); ... is at stake; емý идёт *or* пошёл шестóй год (деся́ток) he is over *or* past five (fifty).

иезуúт *m* [1] Jesuit (*a. fig.*).

иерóглиф *m* [1] hieroglyph(ic).

Иерусалúм *m* [1] Jerusalem.

иждивéн|ец *m* [1; -нца] dependent; **~ие** *n* [12]: на ~ии (Р) (*live*) at s.b's. expense, depend on.

из, ~о (Р) from, outof; of; for, through; with; in; by; что ж ~ э́того? what does that matter?

избá *f* [5; *pl. st.*] (peasant's) house, hut, cottage; room (*therein*); ~-читáльня *f* [5/6] village reading room.

избав|úтель *m* [4] rescuer, saver, deliverer; **∠ить** *s.* ~ля́ть; **~лéние** *n* [12] deliverance, rescue; **~ля́ть** [28], ⟨∠ить⟩ [14] (от Р from) deliver,

free; save; relieve; redeem; **-ся** (от P) escape, get rid of.
избало́ванный [14] spoilt.
избе|га́ть [1], ⟨**~жа́ть**⟩ [4; -егу́, -ежи́шь, -егу́т], ⟨**~гнуть**⟩ [21] (P) avoid, shun; escape, evade; **~жа́ние** *n* [12]: во ~жа́ние (P) (in order) to avoid.
изб|ива́ть [1], ⟨**~и́ть**⟩ [изобью́, -бьёшь; *cf.* бить] beat, thrash; † slaughter, extirpate; F damage; **~ие́ние** *n* [12] beating; extermination, massacre.
избира́тель *m* [4] voter, elector; *pl. a.* electorate; constituency; **~ный** [14] electoral; election...; ~ный уча́сток *m* polling place; ~ное пра́во *n* franchise; ~ное собра́ние *n* caucus, *Brt.* electoral assembly.
изб|ира́ть [1], ⟨**~ра́ть**⟩ [-беру́, -рёшь; *cf.* брать] choose; elect (В/ в И *pl. or* /Т); **~ранный** *a.* select(ed).
изби́|тый [14] *fig.* beaten (*path, etc.*); hackneyed, trite; **~ть** *s.* ~ва́ть.
избра́|ние *n* [12] election; **~нник** *m* [1] the elect; **~ть** *s.* избира́ть.
избы́т|ок *m* [1; -тка] superfluity, surplus; abundance, plenty; в ~ке, с ~ком in plenty, plentiful(ly); **~очный** [14; -чен, -чна] superfluous, surplus...
изваяние *n* [12] statue; *s.* вая́ть.
изве́д|ывать, ⟨**~ать**⟩ [1] learn, (come to) know, see; experience.
и́звер|г *m* [1] monster; **~га́ть** [1], ⟨**~гнуть**⟩ [21] cast out (*a. fig.*); vomit; erupt; **~же́ние** *n* [12] ejection, eruption.
изверну́ться *s.* изворачиваться.
извести́ *s.* изводи́ть.
изве́ст|ие *n* [12] news *sg.*; information; *pl. a.* bulletin; после́дние ~ия *rad.* news(cast); **~и́ть** *s.* извеща́ть.
извёстк|а *f* [5], **~о́вый** [14] lime.
изве́стн|ость *f* [8] notoriety; reputation, fame; по́льзоваться (мирово́й) ~остью be (world-)renowned *or* famous *or* well known; ста́вить (В) в ~ость bring to a p.'s notice (s. th. о П); **~ый** [14; -тен, -тна] known (for Т; as как, P за В), familiar; well-known, renowned, famous; notorious; certain; ~ое (P ~о) де́ло of course; (мне) ~о it is known (I know); (ему́) э́то хорошо́ ~о it is a well-known fact (he is well aware of this).
извест|ня́к *m* [1 *e.*] limestone; [**'~ь** *f* [8] lime.]
изве|ща́ть [1], ⟨**~сти́ть**⟩ [15 *e.*; -ещу́, -ести́шь; -ещённый] inform (of о П); notify; ✝ *a.* advise; **~ще́ние** *n* [12] notification, information, notice; ⚖ summons, writ.
изви|ва́ться [1] wind, twist, wriggle, meander; **~лина** *f* [5] bend, curve; turn; **~листый** [14 *sh.*] winding, tortuous.
извин|е́ние *n* [12] pardon; apology, excuse; **~и́тельный** [14; -лен, -льна] pardonable; [*no sh.*] apologetic; **~я́ть** [28], ⟨**~и́ть**⟩ [13] excuse, pardon; forgive (a p. a th. Д/В); ~и́(те)! excuse me!, (I'm) sorry!; нет, (уж) ~и́(те)! oh no!, on no account!; **-ся** apologize (to/for пе́ред Т/в П); beg to be excused (on account of Т); ~я́юсь! P = ~и́(те)!
извл|ека́ть [1], ⟨**~е́чь**⟩ [26] take *or* draw out; extract (*a.* ℞); derive (*a. profit*); **~ече́ние** *n* [12] extract(ion).
извне́ from outside *or* without.
изводи́ть F [15], ⟨**извести́**⟩ [25] use up; exhaust, ruin.
изво́зчик *m* [1] cabman, cab driver; [cab.]
изво́л|ить [13] please, deign; † want (*or just polite form of respect*); ~ь(те) + *inf.* (would you) please + *vb.*; *a. order, admonition:* (if you) please; *discontent*: how can one ...; F ~ь(те) all right, O. K.; please; *cf.* уго́дно.
извор|а́чиваться [1], ⟨**изверну́ться**⟩ [20] F dodge; shift; (try to) wriggle out; **~о́тливый** [14 *sh.*] nimble (*a. fig.*), elusive; shifty.
извра|ща́ть [1], ⟨**~ти́ть**⟩ [15 *e.*; -ащу́, -ати́шь; -ащённый] distort; pervert.
изги́б *m* [1] bend, curve, turn; *fig.* shade; **~а́ть** [1], ⟨**изогну́ть**⟩ [20] bend, curve, crook (*v/i.* **-ся**).
изгла́|живать [1], ⟨**~дить**⟩ [15] (**-ся** be[come]) efface(d), erase(d); smooth out.
изгна́|ние *n* [12] expulsion, banishment; exile; **~нник** *m* [1] exile; **~ть** *s.* изгоня́ть.
изголо́вье *n* [10] head (*bed*); bolster.
изг|оня́ть [28], ⟨**~на́ть**⟩ [-гоню́, -го́нишь; -гна́л, -ла́, -о; и́згнанный] drive out; oust; expel; exile, banish.
и́згородь *f* [8] fence; hedge(row).
изгот|а́вливать [1], **~овля́ть** [28], ⟨**~о́вить**⟩ [14] make, produce, manufacture; F prepare (*food*); **~овле́ние** *n* [12] production, manufacture; making.
изда|ва́ть [5], ⟨**~ть**⟩ [-да́м, -да́шь, *etc., cf.* дать; и́зданный (и́здан, -а́, -о)] publish; edit; (*order*) issue; (*law*) enact; (*sound*) utter, emit.
и́зда|вна at all times; from of old; long since; **~лека́, ~лёка, ~ли** from afar; afar off.
изда́|ние *n* [12] publication; edition; issue; **~тель** *m* [4] publisher; editor (*of material*); **~тельство** *n* [9] publishing house, publishers *pl.*; **~ть** *s.* издава́ть.
издева́т|ельство *n* [9] derision (of над Т), scorn, scoff; **~ься** [1] jeer, sneer, mock (at над Т); bully.
изде́лие *n* [12] make; product(ion), article; (needle)work; *pl. a.* goods.

издéрж|ивать [1], ⟨~áть⟩ [4] spend; use up; **-ся** F spend much (*or* run short of) money; **~ки** *f/pl.* [5; *gen.*: -жек] expenses; ⚖ costs.
издыхá|ть [1] *s.* дóхнуть; **~ние** *n* [12] (last) breath *or* gasp.
изж|ивáть [1], ⟨~и́ть⟩ [-живý, -вёшь; -жи́тый, F -тóй (изжи́т, -á, -о)] eliminate, extirpate; complete, end (*life, etc.*); endure; ~и́ть себя́ be(come) outdated, have had one's day; **~óга** *f* [5] heartburn.
из-за (Р) from behind; from; because of; over; for (the sake of); ~ чегó? what for?; ~ э́того therefore.
излагáть [1],⟨изложи́ть⟩ [16] state, set forth, expound, expose.
излеч|éние *n* [12] cure, (medical) treatment; recovery; **~ивать** [1], ⟨~и́ть⟩ [16] cure; **~и́мый** [14 *sh.*] curable.
изл|ивáть [1], ⟨~и́ть⟩ [изолью́, -льёшь; *cf.* лить] shed; ~и́ть дýшу, мы́сли unbosom o.s.; *anger*: vent ... on (на В).
изли́ш|ек *m* [1; -шка] surplus, (*a.* **~ество** *n* [9]) excess, & = избы́ток; **~ний** [15; -шен, -шня, -не] superfluous, excessive; needless.
изл|ия́ние *n* [12] outpouring, effusion; **~и́ть** [28] = ~ивáть.
изловчи́ться F [16 *e.*; -чýсь, -чи́шься] *pf.* contrive.
излож|éние *n* [12] exposition, statement; **~и́ть** *s.* излагáть.
излóманный [14] broken; angular; spoilt, deformed, unnatural.
излуч|áть [1], ⟨~и́ть⟩ [16 *e.*; -чý, -чи́шь; -чённый] radiate.
излýчина *f* [5] *s.* изги́б.
излю́бленный [14] favo(u)rite.
измéн|а *f* [5] (Д to) treason; unfaithfulness; **~éние** *n* [12] change, alteration, modification; впредь до ~éния until further notice; **~и́ть** *s.* ~я́ть; **~ник** *m* [1] traitor; **~чивый** [14 *sh.*] changeable, variable; fickle; **~я́ть** [28], ⟨~и́ть⟩ [13; -ню́, -éнишь] **1.** *v/t.* change (*v/i.* **-ся**), alter; modify; vary; **2.** *v/i.* (Д) betray; be(come) unfaithful (to); break, violate (*oath, etc.*); fail (*memory, etc.*), desert.
измер|éние *n* [12] measurement; & dimension; **~и́мый** [14 *sh.*] measurable; **~и́тель** *m* [4] meter, measure, measuring instrument; **~я́ть** [28], ⟨~ить⟩ [13] measure; fathom (*a. fig.*).
измождённый [14 *sh.*] exhausted.
измóр: взять ~ом ⚔ starve (out).
и́зморозь *f* [8] rime; mist.
и́зморось *f* [8] drizzle.
измýчи|вать [1], ⟨~ть⟩ [16] (**-ся** be[come]) fatigue(d), exhaust(ed), wear (worn) out; *refl. a.* pine.
измышл|éние *n* [12] invention; **~я́ть** [28], ⟨измы́слить⟩ [13; -ы́шленный] invent; contrive, devise.
изнáнка *f* [5] back, inside; (*fabric*) wrong side; *fig.* seamy side.
изнáшивать [1], ⟨износи́ть⟩ [15] wear out (by use); *v/i.* **-ся.**
изнéженный [14] coddled; effeminate.
изнем|огáть [1], ⟨~óчь⟩ [26 г/ж: -огý, -óжешь, -óгут] be(come) exhausted *or* enervated; collapse; **~ожéние** *n* [12] exhaustion, weariness.
изнóс *m* [1] wear and tear; **~и́ть** *s.* изнáшивать.
изнур|éние *n* [12] exhaustion, fatigue; **~и́тельный** [14; -лен, -льна] wearisome, wasting; **~я́ть** [28], ⟨~и́ть⟩ [13] (**-ся** be[come]) fatigue(d), exhaust(ed), waste(d).
изнутри́ from within; within.
изны|вáть [1], ⟨~ть⟩ [22] pine (for по Д); *impf. a.* (от Р) die of, be wearied *or* bored to death.
изоби́л|ие *n* [12] abundance, plenty (of Р, *a.* в П); **~овать** [7] abound (in Т); **~ьный** [14; -лен, -льна] rich, abundant (in Т).
изоблич|áть [1], ⟨~и́ть⟩ [16 *e.*; -чý, -чи́шь; -чённый] convict (of в П); unmask; *impf.* reveal, show.
изобра|жáть [1], ⟨~зи́ть⟩ [15 *e.*; -ажý, -ази́шь; -ажённый] represent (*a. impf.* + собóю), depict, describe; express; ~жáть из себя́ (В) F act, set up for; **~жéние** *n* [12] representation; description; image, picture; **~зи́тельный** [14; -лен, -льна] graphic, descriptive; (*no sh.*) fine (*arts*).
изобре|сти́ *s.* ~тáть; **~тáтель** *m* [4] inventor; **~тáтельный** [14; -лен, -льна] inventive, resourceful; **~тáть** [1], ⟨~сти́⟩ [25 -т-: -бретý, -тёшь] invent; **~тéние** *n* [12] invention.
изогнýть *s.* изгибáть.
изóдранный [14] F = изóрванный.
изол|и́ровать [7] (*im*)*pf.* isolate; ⚡ *a.* insulate; **~я́тор** *m* [1] ⚡ insulator; ⚕ isolation ward; cell *or* jail (for close solitary confinement); **~я́ция** *f* [7] isolation; ⚡ insulation.
изóрванный [14] torn, tattered.
изощр|ённый [14] refined, subtle; **~я́ть** [28], ⟨~и́ть⟩ [13] (**-ся** become) refine(d), sharpen(ed); *refl. impf. a.* exert o.s., excel (in в П *or* Т).
из-под (Р) from under; from; from the vicinity of; буты́лка ~ молокá milk bottle.
изразéц *m* [1; -зцá] (Dutch) tile.
Изрáиль *m* [4] Israel.
и́зредка occasionally; here & there.
изрéз|ывать [1], ⟨~ать⟩ [3] cut up.
изре|кáть [1], ⟨~чь⟩ pronounce; **~чéние** *n* [12] aphorism, maxim.
изруб|áть [1], ⟨~и́ть⟩ [14] chop, mince; cut (up, down); saber (-bre).
изря́дный [14; -ден, -дна] (fairly) good *or* big, fair (*amount*).
изувéр *m* [1] fanatic; monster.
изувéч|ивать [1], ⟨~ить⟩ [16] mutilate.

изум|и́тельный [14; -лен, -льна] amazing, wonderful; **~и́ть(ся)** *s.* ~ля́ть(ся); **~ле́ние** *n* [12] amazement; **~ля́ть** [28], ‹~и́ть› [14 *e*; -млю́, -ми́шь; -млённый] (**-ся** Д be) amaze(d), astonish(ed), surprise(d at, wonder).
изумру́д *m* [1] emerald.
изу́стный [14] oral.
изуч|а́ть [1], ‹~и́ть› [16] study, learn; familiarize o. s. with, master; scrutinize; **~е́ние** *n* [12] study.
изъе́з|дить [15] *pf.* travel (all) over, through; **~женный** [14] beaten; bumpy (*road*).
изъяв|и́тельный [14] *gr.* indicative; **~ля́ть** [28], ‹~и́ть› [14] express, show; (*consent*) give.
изъя́н *m* [1] defect; stain; loss.
изыма́ть [1], ‹изъя́ть› [изыму́, изы́мешь] withdraw; seize.
изыска́ние *n* [12] investigation, research; survey; ⚒ prospect.
изы́сканный [14 *sh.*] refined, elegant; choice, exquisite; far-fetched.
изы́ск|ивать [1], ‹~а́ть› [3] find.
изю́м *m* [1] *coll.* raisins *pl.*
изя́щн|ый [14; -щен, -щна] graceful, elegant, (*a.*, †, *arts*) fine; ~ое *n su.* the beautiful; ~ая литерату́ра *f* belles-lettres *pl.*
Иису́с *m* [1; *voc.*: -у́се] Jesus.
ик|а́ть [1], ‹~ну́ть› [20] hiccup.
ико́|на *f* [5] icon; **~та** *f* [5] hiccup.
икра́ *f* [5] (hard) roe, spawn; caviar; *mst. pl.* [*st.*] calf (*leg*).
ил *m* [1] silt.
и́ли or; or else; ~ ... ~ either ... or.
иллю́|зия *f* [7] illusion; **~мина́ция** *f* [7] illumination; **~минова́ть** [7] (*im*)*pf.* illuminate; **~стра́ция** *f* [7] illustration; **~стри́ровать** [7] (*im*)*pf.* illustrate.
Ил|ья́ *m* [6], F *dim.* **~ю́ша** [5] Elias.
им. *abbr.*: и́мени, *s.* и́мя.
имби́рь *m* [4 *e.*] ginger.
име́ние *n* [12] estate.
имени́|ны *f*/*pl.* [5] name day; **~тельный** [14] *gr.* nominative; **~тый** [14 *sh.*] eminent, notable.
и́менно just, very (*adj.*), exactly, in particular; (*a.* а ~, и ~) namely, to wit, that is to say; (*a.* вот ~) F indeed.
именова́ть [7], ‹на-› call, name.
име́ть [8] have, possess; ~ де́ло с (Т) have to do with; ~ ме́сто take place; ~ в виду́ have in view, mean, intend; remember, bear in mind; **-ся** be at, in *or* on hand; (у Р) have; there is, are, *etc.*
иммигра́нт *m* [1] immigrant.
иммуните́т *m* [1] immunity.
императ|ор *m* [1] emperor; **~ри́ца** *f* [5] empress.
империали́|зм *m* [1] imperialism; **~ст** *m* [1] imperialist; **~сти́ческий** [16] imperialist(ic).
импе́рия *f* [7] empire.

и́мпорт *m* [1], **~и́ровать** [7] (*im*)*pf.* import.
импровизи́ровать [7] (*im*)*pf.* & ‹сымпровизи́ровать› improvise.
и́мпульс *m* [1] impulse.
иму́щ|ество *n* [9] property; belongings *pl.*; (не)дви́жимое ~ество ⚖ (im)movables *pl.*; **~ий** [17] well-to-do.
и́мя *n* [13] (*esp.* first, Christian) name (*a. fig.* & *gr.*; *parts of speech*: = *Lat.* nomen); и́мени: шко́ла им. Че́хова Chekhov school; и́менем, во ~; от и́мени (*all 3*) in the name of (P); на ~ addressed to, for; по и́мени named; in name (only); (*know*) by name.
и́на́че differently; otherwise, (or) else; не ~, как just; та́к и́ли ~ one way or another, anyhow.
инвали́д *m* [1] invalid; ~ труда́ (войны́) disabled worker (veteran, *Brt.* ex-serviceman).
инвент|ариза́ция *f* [7] inventory, stock-taking; **~а́рь** *m* [4 *e.*] inventory; (живо́й live)stock; implements, fittings *pl.*
инд|е́ец *m* [1; -е́йца] (*Am.* Red) Indian; **~е́йка** *f* [5; *g*/*pl.*: -е́ек] turkey; **~е́йский** [16] (Red) Indian; ~е́йский пету́х *m* = ~ю́к; **~иа́нка** *f* [5; *g*/*pl.*: -нок] *fem. of* ~е́ец & ~и́ец.
индиви́д, ~уум *m* [1] individual; **~уа́льный** [14; -лен, -льна] individual.
инди́|ец *m* [1; -и́йца] (East) Indian, Hindu; **~йский** [16] Indian (*a.* Ocean: ♀йский океа́н *m*), Hindu.
И́ндия *f* [7] India.
Индо|кита́й *m* [3] Indo-China; **~не́зия** *f* [7] Indonesia; **~ста́н** *m* [1] Hindustan.
инду́с *m* [1], **~ка** *f* [5; *g*/*pl.*: -сок], **~ский** [16] Hindu.
индустриализ|а́ция *f* [7] industrialization (*Brt.* -sa-); **~(и́р)ова́ть** [7] (*im*)*pf.* industrialize (*Brt.* -se).
инд|устриа́льный [14] industrial; **~у́стрия** *f* [7] industry.
индю́к *m* [1 *e.*] turkey cock.
и́ней *m* [3] (white *or* hoar)frost.
ине́р|тный [14; -тен, -тна] inert; **~ция** *f* [7] inertia; по ~ции mechanically.
инжене́р *m* [1] engineer; ~-строи́тель *m* [1/4] civil engineer; **~ный** [14] (*a.* ⚔ & ~ное де́ло *n*) engineering.
инициа́|лы *m*/*pl.* [1] initials; **~ти́ва** *f* [5] initiative; **~тор** *m* [1] initiator.
иногда́ sometimes, now and then.
иногоро́дний [15] nonresident, foreign.
инозе́м|ец *m* [1; -мца] foreigner; **~ный** [14] foreign.
ино́|й [14] (an)other, different; some, many a; ~й раз sometimes; не кто ~й (не что ~е), как ... nobody (nothing) else but ...

иносказа́тельный [14; -лен, -льна] allegorical.
иностра́н|ец *m* [1; -нца], **~ка** *f* [5; *g/pl.*: -нок] foreigner; **~ный** [14] foreign; *s. a.* министе́рство.
инста́нция *f* [7] ⚖ instance; *pl.* (official) channels; hierarchy.
инсти́нкт *m* [1] instinct; **~и́вный** [14; -вен, -вна] instinctive.
институ́т *m* [1] institute; (*a.* ⚖) institution; *form.* (girls') boarding school (**~ка** *f* [5; *g/pl.*: -ток] pupil *thereof*).
инструме́нт *m* [1] instrument.
инсцени́р|овать [7] (*im*)*pf.* stage, screen; *fig.* feign; **~о́вка** *f* [5; *g/pl.*: -вок] staging, *etc.*; direction; dramatization.
интегра́л *m* [1] integral; **~ьный** [14; *fig.* -лен, -льна] integral.
интеллектуа́льный [14; -лен, -льна] intellectual.
интеллиге́н|т *m* [1] intellectual; **~тность** *f* [8] intelligence; **~тный** [14; -тен, -тна] intelligent; intellectual; **~ция** *f* [7] intelligentsia, intellectuals *pl.*
интенда́нт *m* [1] ⚔ commissary; **~ство** *n* [9] commissariat.
интенси́вный (-tɛn-) [14; -вен, -вна] intense, (*a. econ.*) intensive.
интерва́л *m* [1] interval.
интерве́нция *f* [7] intervention.
интервью́ (-tɛr-) *n* [*indecl.*], **~и́ровать** (-tɛr-) [7] (*im*)*pf.* interview.
интере́с *m* [1] interest (in к Д; be of/to име́ть ~ для P; in the/of в ~ах P); F use; **~ный** [14; -сен, -сна] interesting; F handsome, attractive; **~ова́ть** [7], ⟨за-⟩ (**-ся** be[come]) interest(ed, take an interest in T).
интерна́т *m* [1] boarding school; hostel.
Интернациона́л *m* [1] International(e); **ℒьный** [14; -лен, -льна] international.
интерни́рова|ние (-tɛr-) *n* [12] internment; **~ть** (-tɛr-) [7] (*im*)*pf.* intern.
инти́мн|ость *f* [8] intimacy; **~ый** [14; -мен, -мна] intimate.
интри́г|а *f* [5] intrigue; **~а́н** *m* [1] intriguer; **~а́нка** *f* [5; *g/pl.*: -нок] intrigante; **~ова́ть** [7], ⟨за-⟩ intrigue.
интуити́вный [14; -вен, -вна] intuitive.
Интури́ст *m* [1] (Sov.) State bureau of foreign tourism.
инфе́кция *f* [7] infection.
инфля́ция *f* [7] inflation.
информ|а́ция *f* [7] information; **ℒбюро́** *n* [*indecl.*] (Communist) Information Bureau, Cominform; **~и́ровать** [7] (*im*)*pf.* & ⟨про-⟩ inform.
и. о. = исполня́ющий обя́занности.
ипподро́м *m* [1] race track (course).
и пр(оч). *abbr.*: и про́чее, *s.* про́чий.
Ира́|к *m* [1] Iraq; **~н** *m* [1] Iran.
ири́дий *m* [3] iridium.
и́рис *m* [1] iris (⚘, *anat.*).
ирла́нд|ец *m* [1; -дца] Irishman; **~ка** *f* [5; *g/pl.*: -док] Irishwoman; **~ский** [16] Irish (*a.* Sea: ℒское мо́ре); **ℒия** *f* [7] Ireland; Eire.
ирон|изи́ровать [7] mock, sneer (at над T); **~и́ческий** [16] ironic(al), derisive; **ℒия** *f* [7] irony.
иск ⚖ *m* [1] suit, action.
иска|жа́ть [1], ⟨**~зи́ть**⟩ [15 *e.*; -ажу́, -ази́шь; -ажённый] distort, disfigure; **~же́ние** *n* [12] distortion.
иска́ть [3], ⟨по-⟩ (B) look for; (*mst.* P) seek; ⚖ sue (a p. for с P/B).
исключ|а́ть [1], ⟨**~и́ть**⟩ [16 *e.*; -чу́, -чи́шь; -чённый] exclude, leave out; expel; **~а́я** (P) except(ing); **~ено́** impossible; **~е́ние** *n* [12] exclusion; expulsion; exception (with the за T; as an в ви́де P); **~и́тельный** [14; -лен, -льна] exceptional; exclusive; extraordinary; F excellent; *adv. a.* solely, only; **~и́ть** *s.* **~а́ть**.
иско́мый [14] sought, looked for;
иск|они́ † = и́здавна; **~о́нный** [14] (ab)original, native; arch...
ископа́ем|ый [14] (*a. fig.* & *su.* *n*) fossil; mined; *pl. su.* minerals; поле́зные **~ые** treasures of the soil.
искорен|я́ть [28], ⟨**~и́ть**⟩ [13] extirpate.
и́скоса askance, asquint.
и́скра *f* [5] spark(le); spangle.
и́скренн|ий [15; -ренен, -ренна, -е & -о, -и & -ы] sincere, frank, candid; **~о** пре́данный Вам Sincerely (*or* Respectfully) yours; **~ость** *f* [8] sincerity, frankness.
искрив|ля́ть [28], ⟨**~и́ть**⟩ [14 *e.*; -влю́, -ви́шь; -влённый] (**-ся** become) bend (-t), crook(ed); distort(ed), disfigure(d).
искр|и́стый [14 *sh.*] sparkling; **ℒиться** [13] sparkle, scintillate.
искуп|а́ть [1], ⟨**~и́ть**⟩ [14] (B) atone for, expiate; **~ле́ние** *n* [12] atonement, expiation.
иску́с *m* [1] trial (*fig.*); **~и́тель** *m* [4] tempter; **~и́ть** *s.* искуша́ть.
иску́с|ный [14; -сен, -сна] skil(l)ful, skilled; **~ственный** [14 *sh.*] artificial; false (*tooth, etc.*), imitation (*pearls, etc.*); **~ство** *n* [9] art; skill.
иску|ша́ть [1], † ⟨**~си́ть**⟩ [15 *e.*; -ушу́, -уси́шь] tempt; **~ше́ние** *n* [12] temptation; **~шённый** [14] tried; versed, (*a.* **~ённый** о́пытом) experienced.
исла́м *m* [1] Islam.
Исла́ндия *f* [7] Iceland.
испа́н|ец *m* [1; -нца], **~ка** *f* [5; *g/pl.*: -нок] Spaniard; **ℒия** *f* [7] Spain; **~ский** [16] Spanish.
испар|е́ние *n* [12] evaporation; *pl. a.* vapo(u)r(s); **~я́ть** [28], ⟨**~и́ть**⟩ [13] evaporate (*v/i.* **-ся**, *a. fig.*).
испе|пеля́ть [28], ⟨**~пели́ть**⟩ [13] burn to ashes; **~стря́ть** F [28],

⟨~стри́ть⟩ [13], **~щря́ть** [28], ⟨~щри́ть⟩ [13] mottle, speckle, variegate; stud; interlard.

испи́с|ывать [1], ⟨~а́ть⟩ [3] write (*sheet, etc.*), write upon (*on both sides, etc.*), fill (up, *book*); ~сан full of notes, *etc.*; F use up; **-ся** F write o.s. out; be(come) used up (by writing).

испито́й F [14] emaciated.

испове́д|ание *n* [12] confession; creed; **~ать** [1] † = ~овать; **~ник** *m* [1] confessor; **~овать** [7] (*im*)*pf.* confess (*v/i.* **-ся,** to a p. пе́ред T; s.th. в П); profess (*religion*); F interrogate; **~ь** ('is-) *f* [8] confession (*eccl.* [*prp.*: на В/П to/at] & *fig.*).

и́спод|воль F gradually; **~ло́бья** frowningly; **~тишка́** F on the quiet.

испоко́н: ~ ве́ку (веко́в) = и́здавна.

исполи́н *m* [1] giant; **~ский** [16] gigantic.

исполко́м *m* [1] (исполни́тельный комите́т) executive committee.

исполн|е́ние *n* [12] execution; fulfil(l)ment, performance; приводи́ть в ~е́ние = ~я́ть; **~и́мый** [14 *sh.*] realizable; practicable; **~и́тель** *m* [4] executor; *thea.*, ♪ performer; ⚖ (court) bailiff; **~и́тельный** [14] executive; [-лен, -льна] industrious; **~я́ть** [28], ⟨~́ить⟩ [13] carry out, execute; fulfil(l), do (*duty*); hold, fill (*office, etc.*); keep (*promise*); *thea.*, ♪ perform; **-ся** come true; (*age*) be: ему́ ~́илось пять лет he is five; (*period*) pass (since [с тех пор] как).

испо́льзова|ние *n* [12] use, utilization; **~ть** [7] (*im*)*pf.* use, utilize.

испо́р|тить *s.* по́ртить; **~ченный** [14 *sh.*] spoilt, broken; depraved.

исправ|до́м F *m* [1] (~и́тельный дом) reformatory, reform school; **~и́тельный** [14] correctional; *s.* ~дом; **~ле́ние** *n* [12] correction; improvement; reform; **~ля́ть** [28], ⟨~́ить⟩ [14] correct; improve; reform; repair; *impf.* hold (*office*); **-ся** reform.

испра́вн|ость *f* [8] intactness; accuracy; в ~ости = **~ый** [14; -вен, -вна] intact, in good order; accurate, correct; diligent, industrious.

испражн|е́ние *n* [12] ⚕ evacuation; *pl.* f(a)eces; **~я́ться** [28], ⟨~и́ться⟩ [13] ⚕ evacuate.

испу́г *m* [1] fright; **~а́ть** *s.* пуга́ть.

испус|ка́ть [1], ⟨~ти́ть⟩ [15] utter; emit; exhale; give up (*ghost*).

испыт|а́ние *n* [12] test, (*a. fig.*) trial; examination (at на П); **~́анный** [14] tried; **~а́тельный** [14] test...; **~у́ющий** [17] searching; **~́ывать,** ⟨~а́ть⟩ [1] try (*a. fig.*), test; experience, undergo, feel.

иссле́дова|ние *n* [12] investigation, research; exploration; examination; ⚗ analysis; treatise, paper, essay (on по Д); **~тель** *m* [4] research worker, researcher; explorer; **~тельский** [16] research... (*a.* нау́чно-~тельский); **~ть** [7] (*im*)*pf.* investigate; explore; examine (*a.* ⚕); ⚗ analyze; ⚓ sound.

иссо́хнуть *s.* иссыха́ть.

и́сстари = и́здавна, *cf.*

исступл|е́ние *n* [12] ecstasy, frenzy; rage; **~ённый** [14] frantic.

исс|уша́ть [1], ⟨~уши́ть⟩ [16] *v/t.*, **~ыха́ть** [1], ⟨~о́хнуть⟩ [21] *v/i.* & **~яка́ть** [1], ⟨~я́кнуть⟩ [21] *v/i.* dry (*v/i.* up); *fig. a.* exhaust, wear out (*v/i.* o.s. *or* become ...).

ист|ека́ть [1], ⟨~е́чь⟩ [26] flow out; *impf.* spring; elapse (*time*), expire, become due (*date*); dissolve (in *tears* T); ~ека́ть кро́вью bleed to death; **~е́кший** [17] past, last.

исте́р|ика *f* [5] hysterics *pl.*; **~и́ческий** [16], **~и́чный** [14; -чен, -чна] hysterical; **~и́я** *f* [7] hysteria.

исте́ц *m* [1; -тца́] plaintiff.

истече́ни|е *n* [12] expiration (*date*), lapse (*time*); ⚕ discharge; ~е кро́ви bleeding; по ~и (P) at the end of.

исте́чь *s.* истека́ть.

и́стин|а *f* [5] truth; **~ный** [14; -инен, -инна] true, genuine; right (*way, fig.*); plain (*truth*).

истл|ева́ть [1], ⟨~е́ть⟩ [8] mo(u)lder, rot, decay; die away.

и́стовый [14] true; grave; zealous.

исто́к *m* [1] source (*a. fig.*).

истолк|ова́ние *n* [12] interpretation; **~о́вывать** [1], ⟨~ова́ть⟩ [7] interpret, expound, (*a.* себе́) explain (to o.s.).

исто́м|а *f* [5] languor; **~ля́ть** [28], ⟨~и́ть⟩ [14 *e.*; -млю́, -ми́шь; -млённый] (**-ся** be[come]) tire(d), fatigue(d), weary (-ied).

истоп|ни́к *m* [1 *e.*] stoker; **~та́ть** F [3] *pf.* trample; wear out.

исторг|а́ть *m* [1], ⟨~́нуть⟩ [21] wrest; draw; deliver, save.

исто́р|ик *m* [1] historian; **~и́ческий** [16] historical; **~ия** *f* [7] history; story; F affair, thing; ве́чная ~ия! always the same!

источ|а́ть [1], ⟨~и́ть⟩ [16 *e.*; -чу́, -чи́шь] draw; shed; exhale, emit; **~́ник** *m* [1] spring; (*a. fig.*) source.

истощ|а́ть [1], ⟨~и́ть⟩ [16 *e.*; -щу́, -щи́шь; -щённый] (**-ся** be[come]) exhaust(ed), use(d) up.

истра́чивать [1] *s.* тра́тить.

истреб|и́тель *m* [4] destroyer (*a.* ⚓); ✈ pursuit plane, fighter; **~и́тельный** [14] destructive; fighter...; **~и́ть** *s.* ~ля́ть; **~ле́ние** *n* [12] destruction; extermination; **~ля́ть** [28], ⟨~и́ть⟩ [14 *e.*; -блю́, -би́шь; -блённый] destroy, annihilate; exterminate.

истука́н *m* [1] idol; dolt; statue.

и́стый [14] true, genuine; zealous.

истяза́|ние *n* [12], **~ть** [1] torment.
исхо́д *m* [1] end, outcome, result; way out, outlet, vent; † exit; *Bibl.* Exodus; быть на ~е come to an end; run short of; **~и́ть** [15] (из P) come, emanate; originate, proceed; start from; † depart; *pf.* F go all over; *s. a.* истека́ть; **~ный** [14] initial, of departure.
исхуда́лый [14] emaciated, thin.
исцара́пать [1] *pf.* scratch (all over).
исцел|е́ние *n* [12] healing; recovery; **~я́ть** [28], ⟨~и́ть⟩ [13] heal, cure; **-ся** recover.
исчез|а́ть [1], ⟨**∠**нуть⟩ [21] disappear, vanish; **~нове́ние** *n* [12] disappearance; **∠нуть** *s.* ~а́ть.
исче́рп|ывать, ⟨~ать⟩ [1] exhaust, use up; settle (*dispute, etc.*); ~ывающий exhaustive.
исчисл|е́ние *n* [12] calculation; 𝔄 calculus; **~я́ть** [28], ⟨∠ить⟩ [13] calculate.
ита́к thus, so; well, then, now.
Ита́лия *f* [7] Italy.
италья́н|ец *m* [1; -нца], **~ка** *f* [5; *g/pl.*: -нок]; **~ский** [16] Italian; ~ская забасто́вка *f* sit-down strike.
и т. д. *abbr.*: и так да́лее.
ито́г *m* [1] sum, total; result; в ~е in the end; подвести́ ~ sum up; **~о́** (-'vɔ) altogether; in all, total.
и т. п. *abbr.*: и тому́ подо́бное.
итти́ *s.* идти́.
их (*a.* jix) their (*a.*, P, ∠ний [15]); *cf.* они́.
ишь P (just) look, listen; there; oh; now.
ище́йка *f* [5; *g/pl.*: -е́ек] bloodhound, sleuthhound.
ию́|ль *m* [4] July; **~нь** *m* [4] June.

Й

йод *m* [1] iodine.
йо́т|а *f* [5]: ни на ~у not a jot.

К

к, ко (Д) to, toward(s); *time a.* by; for.
к. *abbr.*: копе́йка, -ки, -е́ек.
-ка F (*after vb.*) just; will you.
каба́к *m* [1 *e.*] tavern, pub; mess.
кабала́ *f* [5] serfdom, bondage.
каба́н *m* [1 *e.*] (*a.* wild) boar.
ка́бель *m* [4] cable.
каби́н|а *f* [5] cabin, booth; ✈ cockpit; **~е́т** *m* [1] study; office; ⚕ (consulting) room; *pol.* cabinet.
каблу́к *m* [1 *e.*] heel; быть под ~о́м *fig.* be henpecked.
каб|ота́ж *m* [1] coasting; **~ы́** P if.
кавале́р *m* [1] cavalier; knight; **~и́йский** [16] cavalry...; **~и́ст** *m* cavalryman; **~и́я** *f* [7] cavalry, horse.
ка́верз|а F *f* [5] intrigue; trick; **~ный** [14] trick(s)y.
Кавка́з *m* [1] Caucasus (*prp.*: на В/П to/in); ♀**ец** *m* [1; -зца] Caucasian; ♀**ский** [16] Caucasian.
кавы́чк|и *f/pl.* [5; *gen.*: -чек] quotation marks; в ~ах *iron.* so-called.
кади́|ло *n* [9] cencer; **~ть** [15 *e.*; кажу́, кади́шь] cence.
ка́дка *f* [5; *g/pl.*: -док] tub, vat.
ка́дмий *m* [3] cadmium.
кадр *m* [1] (*mst. pl.*) cadre, key group, van(guard); skilled workers; (*film*) shot; close-up; **∠овый** [14] ⚔ regular, active; commanding; skilled.
кады́к F *m* [1 *e.*] Adam's apple.
каждодне́вный [14] dayly.
ка́ждый [14] every, each; either (*of two*); *su.* everybody, everyone.
ка́ж|ется, ~ущийся *s.* каза́ться.
каза́к *m* [1 *e.*; *pl. a.* 1] Cossack.
каза́рма ⚔ *f* [5] barracks *pl.*
каза́|ться [3], ⟨по-⟩ (T) seem, appear, look; мне ка́жется (~лось), что ... it seems (seemed) to me that; он, ка́жется, прав he seems to be right; *a.* apparently; ка́жущийся seeming; ~лось бы one would think.
каза́х *m* [1], **~ский** [16] Kazak(h); ♀ская ССР Kazak Soviet Socialist Republic; ♀**ста́н** *m* [1] Kazakstan.
каза́|цкий [16], **~чий** [18] Cossack('s)...
каз|ённый [14] state..., government...; official, public; formal, perfunctory; commonplace; на ~ённый счёт *m* gratis; **~на́** *f* [5] treasury, exchequer; **~наче́й** *m* [3] treasurer; ⚔ paymaster.
казн|и́ть [13] (*im*)*pf.* execute, put to death; *impf. fig.* scourge; **~ь** *f* [8] execution; (*a. fig.*) punishment.
Каи́р *m* [1] Cairo.
кайма́ *f* [5; *g/pl.*: каём] border.
как how; as; (as) like; what; but; since; F when, if; (+*su.*, *adv.*) very (much), awfully; (+ *pf. vb.*) suddenly; я ви́дел, как он шёл ... I saw him going ...; ~ бу́дто, ~ бы as if, as it were; ~ бы мне (*inf.*) how am I to ...; ~ ни however; ~ же! sure!; ~ (же) так? you don't say!;

~ ..., так и ... both ... and ...; ~ когда́, *etc.* that depends; ~ не (+ *inf.*) of course ...; ~ мо́жно (нельзя́) скоре́е (лу́чше) as soon as (in the best way) possible.
акао *n* [*indecl.*] cocoa.
а́к-нибу́дь somehow (or other); anyhow; sometime.
ако́в [-ва́, -о́] how; what; what sort of; (such) as; ~! just look (at him)!; ~о́? what do you say?; **~о́й** [14] which.
ако́й [16] what, which; such as; F any; that; ещё ~! and what ... (*su.*)!; како́е там! not at all!; **~-либо, ~-нибудь** any, some; F no more than, (only) about; **~-то** some, a.
а́к-то 1. *adv.* somehow; somewhat; F (*a.* ~ раз) once, one day; **2.** *part.* such as.
аламбу́р *m* [1] pun.
аланча́ *f* [5; *g/pl.*: -че́й] watchtower; F maypole.
ала́ч *m* [1 *e.*] small (*padlock-shaped*) white loaf; тёртый ~ *fig.* F cunning fellow.
але́ка *m/f* [5] cripple.
алenда́рь *m* [4 *e.*] calendar.
алёный [14] red-hot; roasted.
але́чить [16], ‹ис-› cripple, maim.
а́лий *m* [3] potassium.
али́на *f* [5] snowball tree.
али́тка *f* [5; *g/pl.*: -ток] gate, wicket.
али́ть [13] **1.** ‹на-, рас-› heat, incandesce; roast; **2.** ‹за-› ⊕ temper.
ало́рия *f* [7] calorie.
ало́ши *s.* гало́ши.
а́льк|а *f* [5; *g/pl.*: -лек] tracing; tracing paper; *fig.* loan translation; **~и́ровать** [7], ‹с-› trace.
алькул|и́ровать [7], ‹с-› ✝ calculate; **~я́ция** *f* [7] calculation.
альсо́ны *f/pl.* [5] drawers, underpants.
а́льций *m* [3] calcium.
а́мбала *f* [5] flounder.
амен|е́ть [8], ‹о-› turn (in)to stone, petrify; **~и́стый** [14 *sh.*] stony; **~ноуго́льный** [14] coal (mining)...; **'~ный** [14] stone...; *fig.* stony; rock (*salt*); '~ный у́голь *m* (pit) coal (*hard & soft*); **~оло́мня** *f* [6; *g/pl.*: -мен] quarry; **~отёс** *m* [1] stonemason; **'~щик** *m* [1] bricklayer, (*a. hist.*) mason; **'~ь** *m* [4; -мня; *from g/pl. e.* (*a.*, ⚒, -ме́нья, -ме́ньев)] stone; rock; ⚕ *a.* calculus, gravel; *fig.* weight; ка́мнем like a stone; '~ь преткнове́ния stumbling block.
а́мер|а *f* [5] (*prison*) cell; ⚕ ward; 🚂 (cloak)room, office; *parl.* (†), ⚖, ⊕, ⚔ chamber; *phot.* camera; bladder (*ball*); tube (*wheel*); **~ный** [14] ♪, ⊕ chamber...
ами́н *m* [1] fireplace.
амка́ *f* [5] damask (*fabric*).
амо́рка *f* [5; *g/pl.*: -рок] closet, small room.
кампа́ния *f* [7] ⚔, *pol.* campaign.
камфара́ *f* [5] camphor.
Камча́т|ка *f* [5] Kamchatka; **♀(н)ый** [14] damask...
камы́ш *m* [1 *e.*], **~о́вый** [14] reed.
кана́ва *f* [5] ditch; gutter; drain.
Кана́д|а *f* [5] Canada; **♀ец** *m* [1; -дца], **♀ка** *f* [5; *g/pl.*: -док]; **♀ский** [16] Canadian.
кана́л *m* [1] canal; (*a. fig.*) channel; pipe; **~иза́ция** *f* [7] canalization; (*town*) severage.
канаре́йка *f* [5; *g/pl.*: -е́ек] canary.
кана́т *m* [1], **~ный** [14] rope, cable.
канва́ *f* [5] canvas; *fig.* basis; outline.
кандалы́ *m/pl.* [1 *e.*] fetters, shackles.
кандида́т *m* [1] candidate; *a. lowest Sov. univ. degree, approx.* = master.
кани́кулы *f/pl.* [5] vacation, *Brt. a.* holidays (during на П, в В).
каните́ль F *f* [8] fuss; trouble; humdrum, monotony.
канон|а́да *f* [5] cannonade; **~е́рка** *f* [5; *g/pl.*: -рок] gunboat.
кану́н *m* [1] eve.
ка́нуть [20] *pf.* sink, fall; как в во́ду ~ disappear without leaving a trace; ~ в ве́чность pass into oblivion.
канцеля́р|ия *f* [7] (secretary's) office, secretariat; **~ский** [16] office...; writing; clerk's; **~щина** *f* [5] red tape.
ка́п|ать [1 & 2], *once* ‹~нуть› [20] drip, drop, trickle; leak; **~елька** *f* [5; *g/pl.*: -лек] droplet; *sg.* F bit, grain.
капита́л *m* [1] ✝ capital; stock; **~и́зм** *m* [1] capitalism; **~и́ст** *m* [1] capitalist; **~исти́ческий** [16] capitalist(ic); **~овложе́ние** *n* [12] investment; **~ьный** [14] capital; dear, expensive; main; thorough.
капита́н *m* [1] ⚔, ⚓ captain.
капитул|и́ровать [7] (*im*)*pf.* capitulate; **~я́ция** *f* [7] capitulation.
капка́н *m* [1] trap (*a. fig.*).
ка́пл|я *f* [6; *g/pl.*: -пель] drop; *sg.* F bit, grain; ~ями by drops; как две ~и воды́ (as like) as two peas.
капо́т *m* [1] dressing gown; overcoat; ⊕ hood, *Brt.* bonnet.
капри́з *m* [1] whim, caprice; **~ничать** F [1] be capricious; **~ный** [14; -зен, -зна] capricious, whimsical.
ка́псюль ⚔ *m* [4] percussion cap.
капу́ста *f* [5] cabbage; ки́слая ~ sauerkraut.
капу́т P *m* [*indecl.*] ruin, end.
капюшо́н *m* [1] hood.
ка́ра *f* [5] punishment.
караби́н *m* [1] carbine.
кара́бкаться [1], ‹вс-› climb.
карава́й *m* [3] (big) loaf.
карава́н *m* [1] caravan.
кара́емый [14 *sh.*] ⚖ punishable.
кара́кул|ь *m* [4], **~евый** [14] astrakhan; **~я** *f* [6] scrawl.

каран|даш *m* [1 *e.*] pencil; **~тин** *m* [1] quarantine.
карапуз F *m* [1] tot; hop-o'-my--thumb.
карась *m* [4 *e.*] crucian (*fish*).
кара|тельный [14] punitive; **~ть** [1], ‹по-› punish.
караул *m* [1] sentry, guard; взять (сделать) на ~! present arms!; стоять на ~е stand sentinel; F ~! help!, murder!; **~ить** [13], ‹по-› guard, watch (F *a.* for); **~ьный** [14] sentry... (*a. su.*); ~ьная *f* (*su.*) = **~ьня** *f* [6; *g/pl.*: -лен] guardroom.
карболовый [14] carbolic (*acid*).
карбункул *m* [1] carbuncle.
карбюратор *m* [1] carburet(t)or.
карел *m* [1] Karelian; **2ия** *f* [7] Karelia; **~ка** *f* [5; *g/pl.*: -лок] Karelian.
карета *f* [5] carriage, coach.
карий [15] (dark) brown; bay.
карикатур|а *f* [5] caricature, cartoon; **~ный** [14] caricature...; [-рен, -рна] comic(al), funny.
каркас *m* [1] frame(work), skeleton.
карк|ать [1], *once* ‹~нуть› [20] croak (*a.*, F, *fig.*), caw.
карлик *m* [1] dwarf, pygmy; **~овый** [14] dwarf...; dwarfish.
карман *m* [1] pocket; это мне не по ~у F I can't afford that; это бьёт по ~у that makes a hole in my (*etc.*) purse; держи ~ (шире) that's a vain hope; он за словом в ~ не лезет he has a ready tongue; **~ный** [14] pocket...; note(*book*); ~ный вор *m* pickpocket; *cf.* фонарик.
карнавал *m* [1] carnival.
карниз *m* [1] cornice.
Карпаты *f/pl.* [5] Carpathian Mts.
карт|а *f* [5] map; ⚓ chart; (playing) card; menu; ставить (всё) на ~у stake (have all one's eggs in one basket); **~авить** [14] jar (*or* mispronounce) *Russ.* r &/*or* l (*esp. as uvular* r *or* u, v); **~ёжник** *m* [1] gambler (*at cards*); **~ель** (-ˈtel) *f* [8] cartel; **~ечь** *f* [8] case shot.
картин|а *f* [5] picture (in на П); movie, image; painting; scene (*a. thea.*); **~ка** *f* [5; *g/pl.*: -нок] (small) picture, illustration; **~ный** [14] picture...; picturesque, vivid.
картон *m* [1] cardboard, pasteboard; † = **~ка** *f* [5; *g/pl.*: -нок] (cardboard) box; hatbox.
картотека *f* [5] card index.
картофель *m* [4] *coll.* potatoes *pl.*
карточ|ка *f* [5; *g/pl.*: -чек] card; F ticket; photo; menu; **~ный** [14] card(s)...; ~ная система *f* rationing system; ~ный домик *m* house of cards.
картошка P *f* [5; *g/pl.*: -шек] potato(es).
картуз *m* [1 *e.*] cap; † pack(age).
карусель *f* [8] merry-go-round.
карцер *m* [1] dungeon; lockup.

карьер *m* [1] full gallop (at T); места в ~ on the spot; **~а** *f* [5] career; fortune; **~ист** *m* [1] careerist
каса|тельная ⩘ *f* [14] tangent; **~тельно** ([† до] P) concerning; **~ться** [1], ‹коснуться› [20] ([до] † P) touch (*a. fig.*); concern; F be about, deal *or* be concerned with; дело ~ется *a.* = дело идёт о, ; идти; что ~ется ..., то as for (to).
каска *f* [5; *g/pl.*: -сок] helmet.
каспийский [16] Caspian.
касса *f* [5] pay desk *or* office; (билетная ~) 🚂 ticket window, *Br.* booking office; *thea.* box office; bank; fund; cash; cash register; money box *or* chest, safe.
кассац|ионный [14] *s.* апелляционный; **~ия** ⚖ *f* [7] reversal.
кассета *f* [5] *phot.* plate holder.
кассир *m* [1], **~ша** F *f* [5] cashier.
каста *f* [5] caste (*a. fig.*).
касторовый [14] castor (*oil*; *hat*).
кастрировать [7] (*im*)*pf.* castrate.
кастрюля *f* [6] saucepan; pot.
каталог *m* [1] catalogue.
катанье *n* [10] driving, riding, skating, *etc.* (*cf.* катать[ся]).
катастроф|а *f* [5] catastrophe; **~ический** [16] catastrophic.
катать [1] roll (*a.* ⊕); mangle; ‹по-› (take for a) drive, ride, row, *etc.*; **-ся** (go for a) drive, ride (*a.* верхом, *etc.*), row (на лодке), skate (на коньках); sled(ge) (на санях), *etc.*; roll.
катег|орический [16] categorical; **~ория** *f* [7] category.
катер ⚓ *m* [1; *pl.*: -ра, *etc. e.*] cutter; торпедный ~ torpedo boat.
катить [15], ‹по-› roll, drive, wheel (*v/i* **-ся**; sweep; move, flow; *cf. a.* кататься).
катод *m* [1] cathode; **~ный** [14] cathodic.
каток *m* [1; -тка] (skating) rink; mangle; ⊕ roll.
катол|ик *m* [1], **~ичка** *f* [5; *g/pl.*: -чек], **~ический** [16] (Roman) Catholic.
катор|га *f* [5] hard labo(u)r in (*Siberian*) exile; place of such penal servitude; *fig.* drudgery, misery; **~жанин** *m* [1; *pl.*: -ане, -ан] **~жник** *m* [1] (exiled) convict; **~жный** [14] hard, penal; *s.* ~га; *su.* = ~жник. [⚡ coil.
катушка *f* [5; *g/pl.*: -шек] spool;
Катюша [5], **Катя** *f* [6] (*dim. of* Екатерина) Kitty, Kate.
каучук *m* [1] caoutchouc, rubber.
кафе (-ˈfɛ) *n* [*indecl.*] café.
кафедра *f* [5] platform, pulpit; lecturing desk; chair, cathedra.
кафель *m* [4] (Dutch) tile.
кача|лка *f* [5; *g/pl.*: -лок] rocking chair; **~ние** *n* [12] rocking; swing(-ing); pumping; **~ть** [1] **1.** ‹по-›, *once* ‹качнуть› [20] rock; swing

hake (*a.* one's head голово́й), toss; ⚓ roll, pitch; (**-ся** *v/i.*; stagger, urch); **2.** ⟨на-⟩ pump.
ачéли *f/pl.* [8] swing.
áчеств|енный [14] qualitative; **~о** [9] quality; в ~е (P) as, in one's capacity as in the capacity of.
áч|ка ⚓ *f* [5] rolling (бортова́я *or* бокова́я ~ка); pitching (килева́я ~ка); **~ну́ть(ся)** *s.* ~а́ть(ся).
áш|а *f* [5] mush, *Brt.* porridge; gruel; pap; F slush; *fig.* mess, jumble; **~ева́р** ⚔ *m* [1] cook.
áш|ель *m* [4; -шля], **~ля́ть** [28], *once* ⟨~лянуть⟩ [20] cough.
ашнé (-ˈnɛ) *n* [*indecl.*] neckscarf.
аштáн *m* [1], **~овый** [14] chestnut.
аю́та ⚓ *f* [5] cabin, stateroom.
áяться [27], ⟨по-⟩ (в П) repent.
в. *abbr.:* **1.** квадра́тный; **2.** квартира.
вадрáт *m* [1], **~ный** [14] square.
вáк|ать [1], *once* ⟨~нуть⟩ [20] croak.
валифи|ка́ция *f* [7] qualification(s); **~ци́рованный** [14] qualified, competent; skilled, trained.
вартáл *m* [1] quarter (= district; months); block, F building (*betw. cross streets*); **~ьный** [14] quarter(ly); district... (*a.*, *su.*, *form.*: district inspector).
вартúр|а *f* [5] apartment, *Brt.* flat; ~а в две ко́мнаты two-room apt./flat; lodgings *pl.*; ⚔ quarter(s); billet; ~а и стол board and lodging; **~áнт** *m* [1], **~áнтка** *f* [5; *g/pl.:* -ток] lodger, roomer, subtenant; **~ный** [14] housing, house-...; ~ная пла́та = **квартпла́та** *f* [5] rent.
вас *m* [1; -а & -у; *pl. e.*] quass (*Russ. drink*); **∠ить** [15], ⟨за-⟩ sour.
васц|óвый [14] aluminous; **~ы́** *m/pl.* [1] alum.
вáшеный [14] sour, leavened.
вéрху up, upward(s).
вит|áнция *f* [7] receipt; check, ticket; **∠(ы)** F quits, even, square.
вóта *f* [5] quota, share.
вт(ч) *abbr.* = kw. (K.W.H.)
ег|ельбáн *m* [1] bowling alley; **∠ля** *f* [6; *g/pl.*: -лей] pin (*pl.*: ninepins), *Brt.* skittle(s).
едр *m* [1] cedar; сиби́рский ~ cembra pine.
екс *m* [1] cake.
ёльн *m* [1] Cologne.
ельт *m* [1] Celt; **∠ский** [16] Celtic.
éлья *f* [6] *eccl.* cell.
ем = T *of* кто, *cf.*
енгуру́ *m* [*indecl.*] kangaroo.
éп|и *n* [*indecl.*], **~ка** *f* [5; *g/pl.*: -пок] cap.
ерáм|ика *f* [5] ceramics; **~ико́вый** [14], **~и́ческий** [16] ceramic.
еросúн *m* [1], **~овый** [14] kerosene.
éта *f* [5] Siberian salmon.
ефúр *m* [1] kefir.

киби́тка *f* [5; *g/pl.*: -ток] tilt cart (*or* sledge).
кив|а́ть [1], *once* ⟨~ну́ть⟩ [20] nod; beckon; point (to на В); **∠ер** *m* [1; *pl.*: -рá, *etc. e.*] shako; **~óк** *m* [1; -вкá] nod.
кидá|ть(ся) [1], *once* ⟨ки́нуть(ся)⟩ [20] *s.* броса́ть(ся); меня́ ~ет в жар и хо́лод I'm hot and cold all over (have a shivering fit).
Ки́ев *m* [1] Kiev; **♀ля́нин** *m* [1; *pl.*: -я́не, -я́н], **♀ля́нка** *f* [5; *g/pl.*: -нок] Kiever; **♀ский** [16] Kiev...
кий *m* [3; кия́; *pl.:* кии́, киёв] cue.
кило́ *n* [*indecl.*] = ~гра́мм; **~вáтт -(~чáс)** *m* [1; *g/pl.*: -вáтт] kilowatt(-hour); **~грáмм** *m* [1] kilogram (-me); **~мéтр** *m* [1] kilometer (*Brt.* -tre).
киль *m* [4] keel; **~вáтер** (-tɛr) *m* [1] wake; **∠ка** *f* [5; *g/pl.*: -лек] sprat.
КИМ *m* [1] *abbr.*: Communist Youth International (*1919—1943*).
кинематóгр|аф *m* [1] cinema(tograph), movie theater; **~áфия** *f* [7] cinematography.
кинжáл *m* [1] dagger.
кинó *n* [*indecl.*] movie, motion picture, *Brt.* the pictures, cinema (to/at в В/П); *coll.* screen, film; **~актёр** *s.* ~арти́ст; **~актри́са** *s.* ~арти́стка; **~арти́ст** *m* [1] screen (*or* film) actor; **~арти́стка** *f* [5; *g/pl.*: -ток] screen (*or* film) actress; **~ателье́** (-tɛ-) *n* [*indecl.*] (film) studio; **ʹ~варь** *f* [8] cinnabar; **~журнáл** *m* [1] newsreel; **~звездá** F *f* [5; *pl.*: -звёзды] filmstar; **~карти́на** *f* [5] film; **~лéнта** *f* [5] reel, film (copy); **~оперáтор** *m* [1] cameraman; **~плёнка** *f* [5; *g/pl.*: -нок] film (strip); **~режиссёр** *m* [1] film director; **~сеáнс** *m* [1] show, performance; **~сценáрий** *m* [3] scenario; **~съёмка** *f* [5; *g/pl.*: -мок] shooting (of a film), filming; **~теáтр** *m* [1] movie theater, cinema; **~хрóника** *f* [5] newsreel.
ки́нуть(ся) *s.* кида́ть(ся).
киóск *m* [1] kiosk, stand, stall.
киóт *m* [1] *eccl.* image case, shrine.
ки́па *f* [5] pile, stack; bale, pack.
кипари́с *m* [1] cypress.
кипé|ние *n* [12] boiling; то́чка ~ния boiling point; **~ть** [10 *e.*; -плю́, -пи́шь], ⟨за-, вс-⟩ boil; seethe; surge (up), rage, overflow, teem with; be in full swing (*work*, *war*).
Ки́пр *m* [1] Cyprus.
кипу́чий [17 *sh.*] seething; lively, vigorous, exuberant, vehement; busy.
кипят|и́ть [15 *e.*; -ячу́, -яти́шь], ⟨вс-⟩ boil (up; *v/i.* **-ся**); F be(come) excited; **~óк** *m* [1; -ткá] boiling *or* boiled (hot) water.
кирги́з *m* [1], **~ский** [16] Kirghiz.
Кири́лл *m* [1] Cyril; **♀ица** *f* [5] Cyrillic alphabet.

кирка́ *f* [5; *g/pl.*: -ро́к] pick(ax[e]), mattock.
кирпи́ч *m* [1 *e.*], **~ный** [14] brick.
кисе́ль *m* [4 *e.*] (*kind of*) jelly.
кисе́т *m* [1] tobacco pouch.
кисея́ *f* [6] muslin.
кисл|ова́тый [14 *sh.*] sourish; **~оро́д** *m* [1] oxygen; **~ота́** *f* [5; *pl. st.*: -о́ты] acid; **∠ый** [14; -сел, -сла́, -о] sour, (*a.* ⚗) acid...
ки́снуть [21], ⟨с-, про-⟩ turn sour; F *fig.* get rusty.
ки́ст|очка *f* [5; *g/pl.*: -чек] (*paint, shaving*) brush; tassel; *dim. of* **~ь** *f* [8; *from g/pl. e.*] brush; tassel; cluster, bunch; hand.
кит *m* [1 *e.*] whale.
кита́|ец *m* [1; -та́йца], Chinese; **♀й** *m* [3] China; **~йский** [16] Chinese; ♀йская Наро́дная Респу́блика (КНР) Chinese People's Republic; **~янка** *f* [5; *g/pl.*: -нок] Chinese.
ки́тель *m* [4; *pl.* -ля́, *etc. e.*] jacket.
китобо́й *m* [3], **~ный** [14] whaler.
кич|и́ться [16 *e.*; -чу́сь, -чи́шься] put on airs; boast (of T); **~ли́вый** [14 *sh.*] haughty, conceited.
кише́ть [киши́т] teem, swarm (with T; *a.* кишмя́ ~).
киш|е́чник *m* [1] bowels, intestines *pl.*; **~е́чный** [14] intestinal, enteric; digestive (*tract*); **~ка́** *f* [5; *g/pl.*: -шо́к] intestine (small то́нкая, large то́лстая), gut; *pl.* F bowels; hose.
кла́виш *m* [1], **~а** *f* [5] ♪, ⊕ key.
клад *m* [1] treasure (*a. fig.*); **∠бище** *n* [11] cemetery; **∠ка** *f* [5] laying, (*brick-, stone*)work; **~ова́я** *f* [14] pantry, larder; stock- *or* storeroom; **~овщи́к** *m* [1 *e.*] stockman, storekeeper; **~ь** *f* [8] freight, load.
кла́ня|ться [28], ⟨поклони́ться⟩ [13; -оню́сь, -о́нишься] (Д) bow (to); greet; **~йтесь** ему́ от меня́ give him my regards; F cringe (to пе́ред T); present (a p. s. th. Д/T).
кла́пан *m* [1] ⊕ valve; ♪ key, stop.
класс *m* [1] class; *shool*: grade, *Brt.* form; classroom; **∠ик** *m* [1] classic; **~ифици́ровать** [7] (*im*)*pf.* class(ify); **~и́ческий** [16] classic(al); **∠ный** [14] class(*room, etc.*); **∠овый** [14] class (*struggle, etc.*).
класть [кладу́, -дёшь; клал] **1.** ⟨положи́ть⟩ [16] (в, на, *etc.*, B) put, lay (down, on, *etc.*), deposit; apply, spend; take (*as a basis* в B); F fix; rate; make; leave (*mark*); **2.** ⟨сложи́ть⟩ [16] lay (down); erect.
клева́ть [6 *e.*; клюю́, клюёшь], *once* ⟨клю́нуть⟩ [20] peck, pick; bite (*fish*); ~ но́сом F nod.
кле́вер *m* [1] clover, trefoil.
клевет|а́ *f* [5], **~а́ть** [3; -вещу́, -ве́щешь], ⟨о-⟩ *v/t.*, ⟨на-⟩ (на B) slander; **~ни́к** *m* [1 *e.*] slanderer; **~ни́ческий** [16] slanderous.
клевре́т *m* [1] accomplice.
клеён|ка *f* [5], **~чатый** [14] oilcloth.

кле́|ить [13], ⟨с-⟩ glue, paste; **-с**[я] stick; F work, get on *or* along; **~й** [3; на клею́] glue, paste; ры́бий ~ isinglass; **~йкий** [16; клёек, клёйка] sticky, adhesive.
клейм|и́ть [14 *e.*; -млю́, -ми́шь] ⟨за-⟩ brand; *fig. a.* stigmatize; **~о́** [9; *pl. st.*] brand; *fig.* stigma, stai[n]; фабри́чное ~о́ trademark.
клён *m* [1] maple.
клепа́ть [1], ⟨за-⟩ rivet; hammer
клёпка *f* [5; *g/pl.*: -пок] riveting; stave.
кле́т|ка *f* [5; *g/pl.*: -ток] cage; square, check; *biol.* (*a.* ~очка) cell; в ~(оч)ку (~[оч]ками) check(er)ed, *Brt.* chequered; **~ча́тка** *f* [5] cellulose; cellular tissue; **~чатый** [1...] checkered (*Brt.* chequered); cellula[r]
кле|шня́ *f* [6; *g/pl.*: -не́й] claw (*of the crayfish*); **∠щи́** *f/pl.* [5; *gen.* -ще́й, *etc. e.*] pincers.
клие́нт *m* [1] client.
кли́зма *f* [5] enema.
клик *m* [1] cry, shout; shriek; **∠а** [5] clique; **∠ать** [3], *once* ⟨∠нуть⟩ [20] shriek; P call.
кли́мат *m* [1] climate; **~и́чески[й]** [16] climatic.
клин *m* [3; *pl.*: кли́нья, -ьев] wedge; gusset; **∠ом** pointed (*beard*); св[ет] не ∠ом сошёлся the world is large; there is always a way out.
кли́ника *f* [5] clinic.
клино́к *m* [1; -нка́] blade.
клич *m* [1] call; cry; **∠ка** *f* [5; *g/pl.*: -чек] (*dog's, etc.*) name; nickname.
клише́ *n* [*indecl.*] cliché (*a. fig.*).
клок *m* [1 *e.*; *pl.*: -о́чья, -ьев *or* клоки́, -ко́в] tuft; shred, rag, tatter, piece, frazzle.
клокота́ть [3] seethe, bubble.
клон|и́ть [13; -оню́, -о́нишь], ⟨на-, с-⟩ bend, bow; *fig.* incline; driv[e] (*or* aim) at (к Д); † cast down; мен[я] **∠ит** ко сну I am (feel) sleepy; (-с[я] *v/i.*; *a.* decline; approach).
клоп *m* [1 *e.*] bedbug, *Brt.* bug.
кло́ун *m* [1] clown.
клочо́к *m* [1; -чка́] wisp; scrap.
клуб¹ *m* [1; *pl. a. e.*] cloud, pu[ff] (*smoke, etc.*); s. *a.* ~о́к; **~²** [1] clu[b] (-house); **∠ень** *m* [4; -бня] tube[r], bulb; **~и́ть** [14 *e.*; *3rd p. only*] pu[ff] (up), whirl, coil (*v/i.* **-ся**).
клубни́ка *f* [5] strawberry, -ries *p[l.]*
клубо́к *m* [1; -бка́] clew; tangle.
клу́мба *f* [5] (flower) bed.
клык *m* [1 *e.*] tusk; canine, fang.
клюв *m* [1] beak, bill.
клюка́ *f* [5] crutch(ed stick), staff.
клю́ква *f* [5] cranberry, -ries *pl.*
клю́нуть *s.* клева́ть.
ключ *m* [1 *e.*] key (*a. fig.*, clue; *a.* ⊕ [га́ечный ~] = wrench; англи́йский ~ monkey wrench); ♪ cle[f]; spring, source; ⩓ keystone; **~и́ца** [*f*] [5] clavicle, collarbone; **∠ница** *f* [5] housekeeper.

клюшка *f* [5; *g/pl.*: -шек] club.
клякса *f* [5] blot.
клянчить F [16] beg for.
кляп *m* [1] gag.
кля|сть [-яну́, -нёшь; -ял, -á, -о] = проклина́ть, *cf.*; **-ся**, ⟨покля́сться⟩ swear (s. th. в П; by Т); **∠тва** *f* [5] oath; дать ∠тву (*or* ∠твенное обеща́ние) take an oath, swear; **~твопреступле́ние** *n* [12] perjury.
кляуза *f* [5] intrigue, denunciation; † captious suit; pettifoggery.
кля́ча *f* [5] jade.
кни́г|а *f* [5] book (*a.* ⚕); *teleph.* directory; register; **~опеча́тание** *n* [12] (book) printing, typography; **~опрода́вец** *m* [1; -вца] bookseller; **~охрани́лище** *n* [11] archives, storerooms *pl.*; library.
кни́ж|ка *f* [5; *g/pl.*: -жек] book (-let); notebook; passport; **~ный** [14] book...; bookish; **~о́нка** *f* [5; *g/pl.*: -нок] trashy book.
кни́зу down, downward(s).
кно́пка *f* [5; *g/pl.*: -пок] thumbtack, *Brt.* drawing pin; ⚡ (push) button; patent (*or* snap) fastener.
кнут *m* [1 *e.*] whip, knout, scourge.
кня|ги́ня *f* [6] princess (*prince's consort*; *daughter*: **~жна́** *f* [5; *g/pl.*: -жо́н]); **~зь** *m* [4; *pl.*: -зья́, -зе́й] prince; вели́кий ~зь grand duke.
коа|лицио́нный [14] coalition ...; **~ли́ция** *f* [7] coalition.
ко́бальтовый [14] cobaltic.
кобура́ *f* [5] holster; saddlebag.
кобы́ла *f* [5] mare; *sport:* horse.
ко́ваный [14] wrought (*iron*).
кова́р|ный [14; -рен, -рна] artful, guileful, insidious; **~ство** *n* [9] craft, guile, wile.
кова́ть [7 *e.*; кую́, куёшь] **1.** ⟨вы́-⟩ forge; **2.** ⟨под-⟩ shoe (*horse*).
ковёр *m* [1; -вра́] carpet, rug.
кове́ркать [1], ⟨ис-⟩ distort, deform; mutilate; murder (*fig.*).
ко́в|ка *f* [5] forging; shoeing; **~кий** [16; -вок, -вка́, -о] malleable.
коври́жка *f* [5; *g/pl.*: -жек] gingerbread.
ковче́г *m* [1] ark; Но́ев ~ Noah's Ark.
ковш *m* [1 *e.*] scoop; bucket; haven.
ковы́ль *m* [4 *e.*] feather grass.
ковыля́ть [28] toddle; stump, limp.
ковыря́ть [28], ⟨по-⟩ pick, poke.
когда́ when; F if; ever; sometimes; *cf.* ни; **~-либо, ~-нибудь** (at) some time (or other), one day; *interr.* ever; **~-то** once, one day, sometime.
ко́|готь *m* [4; -гтя; *from g/pl. e.*] claw; **~д** *m* [1] code.
ко́е|-где́ here & there, in some places; **~-ка́к** anyhow, somehow; with (great) difficulty; **~-како́й** [16] some; any; **~-когда́** off & on; **~-кто́** [23] some(body); **~-куда́** here & there, (in)to some place(s), somewhere; **~-что́** [23] something, some things.
ко́ж|а *f* [5] skin; leather; из ~и (во́н) лезть F do one's utmost; **~аный** [14] leather...; **~е́венный** [14] leather...; ~е́венный заво́д *m* tannery; **~е́вник** *m* [1] tanner; **~ица** *f* [5] peel; rind (*a.* **~ура́** *f* [5]); cuticle.
коз|á *f* [5; *pl. st.*] (she-)goat; **~ёл** *m* [1; -зла́] (he-)goat; **∠ий** [18] goat...; **~лёнок** *m* [2] kid; **∠лы** *f/pl.* [5; *gen.*: -зел] (coach) box; trestle.
ко́зни *f/pl.* [8] intrigues, plots.
козу́ля *f* [6] roe (deer).
коз|ырёк *m* [1; -рька́] peak (*cap*); **∠ырь** *m* [4; *from g/pl. e.*] trump; **~ыря́ть** F [28], *once* ⟨~ырну́ть⟩ [20] trump; boast; ⚔ salute.
ко́йка *f* [5; *g/pl.*: ко́ек] cot; bed.
коке́т|ка *f* [5; *g/pl.*: -ток] coquette; **~ливый** [14 *sh.*] coquettish; **~ничать** [1] coquet, flirt; **~ство** *n* [9] coquetry.
коклю́ш *m* [1] whooping cough.
ко́кон *m* [1] cocoon.
кок|о́с *m* [1] coco; **~о́совый** [14] coco(nut)...; **~с** *m* [1] coke.
кол *m* **1.** [1 *e.*; *pl.*: ко́лья, -ьев] stake, pale; **2.** [*pl.* 1 *e.*] P *s.* едини́ца; ни ~á ни двора́ neither house nor home.
колбаса́ *f* [5; *pl. st.*: -а́сы] sausage.
колд|ова́ть [7] conjure; **~овство́** *n* [9] magic, sorcery; **~у́н** *m* [1 *e.*] sorcerer, magician, wizard; **~у́нья** *f* [6] sorceress, enchantress.
колеб|а́ние *n* [12] oscillation; vibration; *fig.* vacillation, hesitation; (*a.* ⚕) fluctuation; **~а́ть** [2 *st.*: -е́блю, *etc.*; -е́бли(те)!; -е́бля], ⟨по-⟩, *once* ⟨~ну́ть⟩ [20] shake (*a. fig.*); **-ся** shake; (*a.* ⚕) fluctuate; waver, vacillate, hesitate; oscillate, vibrate.
коле́н|о *n* [*sg.*: 9; *pl.*: 4] knee; стать на ~и kneel; [*pl.*: -нья, -ньев] ⚘ joint, knot; [*pl. a.* 9] bend; ⊕ crank; [*pl.* 9] degree, branch (*pedigree*); P ♪ pas(sage); trick; **~чатый** [14] *biol.* geniculate; ⊕ crank(*shaft*).
колес|и́ть F [15 *e.*; -ешу́, -еси́шь] travel (much); take a roundabout way; **~ни́ца** *f* [5] chariot; **~о́** *n* [9; *pl. st.*: -лёса] wheel; кружи́ться как бе́лка в ~е́ fuss, bustle about; вставля́ть па́лки в колёса (Д) put a spoke in a p.'s wheel; но́ги ~о́м bowlegged.
колея́ *f* [6; *g/pl.*: -ле́й] rut, (*a.* 🚂) track (*both a. fig.*).
коли́бри *m/f* [*indecl.*] hummingbird.
ко́лики *f/pl.* [5] colic, gripes.
коли́честв|енный [14] quantitative; *gr.* cardinal (*number*); **~о** *n* [9] quantity; number; amount; по ~у quantitatively.
ко́лка *f* [5] splitting, chopping.
ко́лк|ий [16; ко́лок, колка́, -о]

prickly; biting, pungent; ~ость *f* [8] sarcasm, gibe.
коллéг|а *m* /*f* [5] colleague; **~ия** *f* [7] board, staff; college.
коллекти́в *m* [1] collective, group, body; **~иза́ция** *f* [7] collectivization; **~ный** [14] collective.
коллéк|тор *m* [1] ⚡ collector; **~ционéр** *m* [1] (*curiosity*) collector; **~ция** *f* [7] collection.
колóд|а *f* [5] block; trough; pack, deck (*cards*); **~ец** [1; -дца] well; shaft, pit; **~ка** *f* [5; *g*/*pl.*: -док] last; (foot) stock(s); ⊕ (*brake*) shoe; **~ник** *m* [1] convict (*in stocks*).
кóлок|ол *m* [1; *pl.*: -лá, *etc. e.*] bell; **~óльня** *f* [6; *g*/*pl.*: -лен] bell tower, belfry; **~óльчик** *m* [1] (little) bell; ⚘ bellflower.
колони|áльный [14] colonial; **~зáция** *f* [7] colonization; **~з(и́р)овáть** [7] (*im*)*pf.* colonize; **'~я** [7] colony.
колóн|ка *f* [5; *g*/*pl.*: -нок] *typ.* column; (*gas*) station; water heater, *Brt.* geyser; *a. dim. of* **~на** *f* [5] column (⚠ *a.* pillar; *typ.* †).
кóлос *m* [1; *pl.*: -лóсья, -ьев], **~и́ться** [15 *e.*; *3rd p. only*] ear; **~ни́к** *m* [1 *e.*] grate.
колоти́ть [15] knock (at, on в В, по Д).
колóть [17] **1.** ⟨рас-⟩ split, cleave; break (*sugar*); crack (*nuts*); **2.** ⟨на-⟩ chop (*firewood*); кóлотый lump (*sugar*); **3.** ⟨у-⟩, *once* ⟨кольну́ть⟩ [20] prick, sting; *fig.* F taunt; **4.** ⟨за-⟩ stab; kill, slaughter (*animals*); *impers.* have a stitch; ~ глазá (Д) be a thorn in one's side.
колпáк *m* [1 *e.*] cap; shade; bell glass.
колхóз *m* [1] collective farm, kolkhoz; **~ный** [14] kolkhoz...; **~ник** *m* [1], **~ница** *f* [5] collective farmer.
колчáн *m* [1] quiver.
колчедáн *m* [1] pyrites.
колыбéль *f* [8] cradle; **~ный** [14]: ~ная (пéсня) *f* lullaby.
колых|áть [3 *st.*: -ы́шу, *etc.*, *or* 1], ⟨вс-⟩, *once* ⟨~ну́ть⟩ [20] sway, swing; stir; heave; flicker; **-ся** *v*/*i*.
кóлышек *m* [1; -шка] peg.
кольну́ть *s.* колóть 3. *&* *impers.*
коль|цевóй [14] ring...; circular; **~цó** *n* [9; *pl. st.*, *gen.*: колéц] ring; circle; **~чу́га** *f* [5] mail.
колю́ч|ий [17 *sh.*] thorny, prickly; barbed (*wire*); *fig. s.* кóлкий; **~ка** *f* [5; *g*/*pl.*: -чек] thorn, prickle; barb.
Кóля *m* [6] (*dim. of* Николáй) Nick.
коля́ска *f* [5; *g*/*pl.*: -сок] carriage, victoria; baby carriage, *Brt.* perambulator.
ком *m* [1; *pl*: кóмья, -ьев] lump, clod; снéжный ~ snowball.
комáнд|а *f* [5] command; detachment; ⚓ crew; *sport:* team; (*fire*) company (*or* department), *Brt.* brigade; F gang.
командúр *m* [1] commander; **~овáть** [7] (*im*)*pf.*, *a.* ⟨от-⟩ send (on a mission); detach; **~óвка** *f* [5; *g*/*pl.*: -вок] mission; sending.
комáнд|ный [14] command(ing); team...; **~овáние** *n* [12] command; **~овáть** [7] ([над] T) command (*a.* = [give] order, ⟨с-⟩); F domineer; **~ующий** [17] (T) commander.
комáр *m* [1 *e.*] mosquito, gnat.
комбáйн ⚒ *m* [1] combine.
комбин|áт *m* [1] combine of complementary industrial plants (*Sov.*); **~áция** *f* [7] combination; **~и́ровать** [7], ⟨с-⟩ combine.
комéдия *f* [7] comedy; F farce.
комендá|нт *m* [1] commandant; superintendent; **~ту́ра** *f* [5] commandant's office.
комéта *f* [5] comet.
ком|и́зм *m* [1] comicality; **~ик** *m* [1] comedian, comic (actor).
Коминтéрн *m* [1] (Third) Communist International (*1919—1943*).
комиссáр *m* [1] commissar (*Sov.*); commissioner; **~иáт** *m* [1] commissariat.
коми|сснóнный [14] commission (*a.* ✝; *pl. su.* = *sum*); **~ссия** *f* [7] commission (*a.* ✝), committee; **~тéт** *m* [1] committee
коми́ч|еский [16], **~ный** [14; -чен, -чна] comic(al), funny.
кóмкать [1], ⟨ис-, с-⟩ crumple.
коммент|áрий *m* [3] comment(ary); **~áтор** *m* [1] commentator; **~и́ровать** [7] (*im*)*pf.* comment (on).
коммер|сáнт *m* [1] (wholesale) merchant; **~ческий** [16] commercial.
коммýн|а *f* [5] commune; **~áльный** [14] municipal; **~и́зм** *m* [1] communism; **~икáция** *f* [7] communication (*pl.* ⚔); **~и́ст** *m* [1], **~и́стка** *f* [5; *g*/*pl.*: -ток], **~исти́ческий** [14] communist (*a. cap.*, *cf.* КПСС).
коммутáтор *m* [1] commutator; *teleph.* switchboard; operator(s' room).
кóмнат|а *f* [5] room; **~ный** [14] room...; ⚘ indoor.
комó|д *m* [1] bureau, *Brt.* chest of drawers; **~к** *m* [1; -мкá] lump, clod
компáн|ия *f* [7] company (*a.* ✝) водúть ~ию с (T) associate with **~ьóн** *m* [1] ✝ partner; F companion
компáртия *f* [7] Communist Party
кóмпас *m* [1] compass.
компенс|áция *f* [7] compensation **~и́ровать** [7] (*im*)*pf.* compensate.
компетéн|тный [14; -тен, -тна] competent; **~ция** *f* [7] competence line.
кóмплек|с *m* [1], **~сный** [14] complex; **~т** *m* [1] (complete) set; **~тный** [14], **~товáть** [7], ⟨у-⟩ complete.
комплимéнт *m* [1] compliment.

компо|зи́тор *m* [1] composer; **~стúровать** [7], ⟨про-⟩ punch; **∠т** *m* [1] sauce, *Brt.* stewed fruit.
компрéсс *m* [1] compress.
компром|етúровать [7], ⟨с-⟩, **~и́сс** *m* [1] compromise (*v/i. a.* идтú на ~и́сс).
комсомо́л *m* [1] Komsomol, *cf.* ВЛКСМ; **~ец** *m* [1; -льца], **~ка** *f* [5; *g/pl.*: -лок], **~ьский** [16] Young Communist.
комфо́рт *m* [1] comfort, convenience; **~а́бельный** [14; -лен, -льна] comfortable, convenient.
конвéйер *m* [1] (belt) conveyor; assembly line.
конвéнция *f* [7] convention.
конвéрт *m* [1] envelope.
конв|óир *m* [1], **~оúровать** [7], **~óй** *m* [3], **~óйный** [14] convoy.
конгрéсс *m* [1] congress.
конденс|áтор (-dɛ-) *m* [1] condenser; **~úровать** [7] (*im*)*pf.* condense; evaporate (*milk*).
кондúтер *m* [1] confectioner; **~ская** *f* [16] confectioner's shop; ~ские издéлия *pl.* confectionery.
Кондрáт|ий *m* [3], ~ P [1] Conrad.
кондýктор *m* [1; *pl. a.* -á, *etc. e.*] conductor (🚂 *Brt.* guard).
коневóдство *n* [9] horse breeding.
конёк *m* [1; -нька́] skate; F hobby.
кон|éц *m* [1; -нцá] end; close; point; ⚓ rope; F distance; part; case; без ~цá endless(ly); в ~éц (до ~цá) completely; в ~цé (P) at the end of; в ~цé ~цóв at long last; в одúн ~éц one way; в óба ~цá there & back; на худóй ~éц at (the) worst; под ~éц in the end; трéтий с ~цá last but two.
конéчно (-ʃnə) of course, certainly.
конéчности *f/pl.* [8] extremities.
конéчн|ый [14; -чен, -чна] *philos.*, & finite; final, terminal; ultimate.
конкрéтный [14; -тен, -тна] concrete.
конкур|éнт *m* [1] competitor; **~éнция** ✝ *f* [7] competition; **~úровать** [7] compete; **'~с** *m* [1] competition; ✝ bankruptcy.
кóнн|ица *f* [5] cavalry; **~ый** [14] horse...; (of) cavalry.
конопáтить [15], ⟨за-⟩ calk.
конопля́ *f* [6] hemp; **~ный** [14] hempen.
коносамéнт *m* [1] bill of lading.
консерв|атúвный [14; -вен, -вна] conservative; **~атóрия** *f* [7] conservatory, *Brt.* school of music, conservatoire; **~úровать** [7] (*im*)*pf.*, *a.* ⟨за-⟩ conserve, preserve; can, *Brt.* tin; **∠ный** [14]: ∠ная фáбрика *f* cannery; **∠ы** *m/pl.* [1] canned (*Brt.* tinned) goods; safety goggles.
кóнский [16] horse(*hair, etc.*).
конспéкт *m* [1] summary, abstract; sketch; **~úвный** [14; -вен, -вна] concise, sketchy; **~úровать** [7], ⟨за-⟩ outline, epitomize.
конспир|атúвный [14; -вен, -вна] secret; **~áция** *f* [7] conspiracy.
конст|атúровать [7] (*im*)*pf.* state; find; **~итýция** *f* [7] constitution.
констр|уúровать [7] (*im*)*pf.*, *a.* ⟨с-⟩ design; **~ýктор** *m* [1] designer; **~ýкция** *f* [7] design; construction.
кóнсул *m* [1] consul; **~ьский** [16] consular; **~ьство** *n* [9] consulate; **~ьтáция** *f* [7] consultation; advice; advisory board; **~ьтúровать** [7], ⟨про-⟩ advise; **-ся** consult (with с T).
контáкт *m* [1] contact.
контингéнт *m* [1] contingent, quota.
континéнт *m* [1] continent.
контóр|а *f* [5] office; **~ский** [16] office...; ~ский слýжащий *m*, **~щик** *m* [1] clerk.
контрабáнд|а *f* [5] contraband; занимáться ~ой smuggle; **~úст** *m* [1] smuggler.
контр|агéнт *m* [1] contractor; **~-адмирáл** *m* [1] rear admiral.
контрáкт *m* [1] contract.
контрáст *m* [1], **~úровать** [7] contrast.
контратáка *f* [5] counterattack.
контрибýция ⚔ *f* [7] contribution.
контрол|ёр *m* [1] (ticket) inspector (🚂 *a.* ticket collector); **~úровать** [7], ⟨про-⟩ control, check; **∠ь** *m* [4] control, checkup; **∠ьный** [14] control ..., check...; ∠ьная рабóта *f* test (paper).
контр|развéдка *f* [5] counterespionage, secret service; **~революция** *f* [7] counterrevolution.
контýз|ить [15] *pf.* bruise, contuse; **~ия** *f* [7] contusion, bruise.
кóнтур *m* [1] contour, outline.
конурá *f* [5] kennel.
кóнус *m* [1] cone; **~ообрáзный** [14; -зен, -зна] conic(al).
конферéнция *f* [7] conference (at на П).
конфéта *f* [5] candy, *Brt.* sweet(s).
конфи|денциáльный [14; -лен, -льна] confidential; **~сковáть** [7] (*im*)*pf.* confiscate.
конфлúкт *m* [1] conflict.
конфýз|ить [15], ⟨с-⟩ (**-ся** be [-come]) embarrass(ed), confuse(d); **~ливый** F [14 *sh.*] bashful, shy.
конц|ентрациóнный [14] *s.* ~лáгерь; **~ентрúровать** [7], ⟨с-⟩ concentrate (**-ся** *v/i.*); **~éрт** *m* [1] concert (at на П); ♪ concerto; **~лáгерь** *m* [4] concentration camp.
конч|áть [1], ⟨∠ить⟩ [16] finish, end (**-ся** *v/i.*); graduate from; P stop; ∠ено! F enough!; **∠чик** *m* [1] tip; end; **~úна** *f* [5] decease.
конь *m* [4 *e.*; *nom/pl. st.*] horse; *poet.* steed; *chess*: knight; **~кú** *m/pl.* [1] (рóликовые roller) skates; **~кобé-**

жец *m* [1; -жца] skater; **~кобéжный** [14] skating.
коньяк *m* [1 *e.*; *part. g.*: -ý] cognac.
кóн|юх *m* [1] groom, (h)ostler; **~юшня** *f* [6; *g/pl.*: -шен] stable.
коопер|ати́в *m* [1] coöperative (store); **~áция** *f* [7] coöperation.
координи́ровать [7] (*im*)*pf.* coördinate.
копáть [1], ⟨вы-⟩ dig (up); **-ся** dig, root; rummage (about); dawdle.
копéйка *f* [5; *g/pl.*: -éек] kopeck.
кóпи *f/pl.* [8] mine, pit.
копи́лка *f* [5; *g/pl.*: -лок] money box.
копир|овáльный [14]: **~овáльная** бумáга *f* carbon paper; **~овать** [7], ⟨с-⟩ copy; **~óвщик** *m* [1] copyist.
копи́ть [14], ⟨на-⟩ save; store up.
кóп|ия *f* [7] copy (*vb.* снять **~ию** с P); **~нá** *f* [5; *pl.*: кóпны, -пён, -пнáм] stack.
кóпоть *f* [8] soot, lampblack.
копоши́ться [16 *e.*; -шýсь, -ши́шься], ⟨за-⟩ swarm; F stir; mess around.
копти́ть [15 *e.*; -пчý, -пти́шь; -пчённый], ⟨за-⟩ smoke; soot.
копы́то *n* [9] hoof.
копьё *n* [10; *pl. st.*] spear.
корá *f* [5] bark; crust.
кораб|лекрушéние *n* [12] shipwreck; **~лестроéние** *n* [12] shipbuilding; **~ль** *m* [4 *e.*] ship; nave (*church*).
корáлл *m* [1] coral; **~овый** [14] coral..., coralline.
Кордильéры *f/pl.* [5] Cordilleras.
корé|ец *m* [1; -ейца], **~йский** [16] Korean.
корен|áстый [14 *sh.*] thickset, stocky; **~и́ться** [13] root; **~нóй** [14] native, aboriginal; fundamental, radical; molar (*tooth*); **'~ь** *m* [4; -рня; *from g/pl. e.*] root; в кóрне totally; пусти́ть кóрни take root; вы́рвать с кóрнем pull up by the roots; **~нья** *n/pl.* [*gen.*: -ьев] roots.
корешóк *m* [1; -шкá] rootlet; stalk (*mushroom*); back (*book*); stub, *Brt.* counterfoil.
Корé|я *f* [6] Korea; **♀янка** *f* [5; *g/pl.*: -нок] Korean.
корзи́н(к)а *f* [5 (*g/pl.*: -нок)] basket.
коридóр *m* [1] corridor, passage.
кори́нка *f* [5; *g/pl.*: -нок] currant.
корифéй *m* [3] *fig.* luminary, coryphеus, leader.
кори́ца *f* [5] cinnamon.
кори́чневый [14] brown.
кóрка *f* [5; *g/pl.*: -рок] crust; rind, peel.
корм *m* [1; *pl.*: -мá, *etc. e.*] fodder; seed; **~á** *f* [5] stern.
корм|и́лец *m* [1; -льца] breadwinner; **~и́лица** *f* [5] wet nurse; **~и́ть** [14], ⟨на-, по-⟩ feed; **~и́ть** грýдью nurse; F board; ⟨про-⟩ *fig.* maintain, support; **-ся** live on (T); **~лéние** *n* [12] feeding; nursing; **~овóй** [14] feed(ing), fodder...; ⚓ stern...
корнеплóды *m/pl.* [1] edible roots.
кóроб *m* [1; *pl.*: -бá, *etc. e.*] basket; **~éйник** *m* [1] hawker; **~ить** [14], ⟨по-⟩ warp; *fig.* offend, sicken; **~ка** *f* [5; *g/pl.*: -бок] box, case.
корóв|а *f* [5] cow; дóйная **~а** milch cow; **~ий** [18] cow...; **~ка** *f* [5; *g/pl.*: -вок]: бóжья **~ка** ladybird; **~ник** *m* [1] cowshed.
королéв|а *f* [5] queen; **~ский** [16] royal, regal; **~ство** *n* [9] kingdom.
корол|ёк *m* [1; -лькá] wren: **~ь** *m* [4 *e.*] king.
коромы́сло *n* [9; *g/pl.*: -сел] yoke (*a. scale*) beam; dragonfly.
корóн|а *f* [5] crown; **~áция** coronation; **~ка** *f* [5; *g/pl.*: -нок] (*tooth*) crown; **~овáние** *n* [12] coronation; **~овáть** [7] (*im*)*pf.* crown.
корóста *f* [5] scab, scabies.
корот|áть F [1], ⟨с-⟩ while away, beguile; **~кий** [16; кóрóток, -ткá, кóроткó, кóрóтки́; *comp.*; корóче] short, brief; *fig.* intimate, в **~ких** словáх in a few words; корóче (говоря́) in a word, in short (brief); **'~ко** и я́сно (quite) plainly; дóлго ли, **~ко** ли sooner or later.
кóрпус *m* [1] body; [*pl.*: -cá, *etc. e.*] frame, case; building; (*a.* ⚔) corps.
коррект|и́в *m* [1] correction; **~и́ровать** [7], ⟨про-⟩ correct; *typ.* proofread; **~ный** [14; -тен, -тна] correct, proper; **~ор** *m* [1] proofreader; **~ýра** *f* [5] proof(reading); держáть **~ýру** *s.* **~и́ровать** (*typ.*).
корреспонд|éнт *m* [1] correspondent; **~éнция** *f* [7] correspondence.
корсéт *m* [1] corset, *Brt. a.* stays *pl.*
кóртик *m* [1] cutlass, hanger.
кóрточк|и *f/pl.* [5; *gen.*: -чек]: сесть (сидéть) на **~и** (**~ах**) squat.
корчевá|ние *n* [12] rooting out; **~ть** [7], ⟨вы́-, рас-⟩ root out.
кóрчить [16], ⟨с-⟩ *impers.* (& **-ся**) writhe (with pain от бóли); convulse; (*no pf.*) F make (*faces*); (*a.* **~** из себя́) play, pose, put on airs, set up for.
кóршун *m* [1] vulture.
коры́ст|ный [14; -тен, -тна] selfish, self-interested; *a.* = **~олюби́вый** [14 *sh.*] greedy (of gain), mercenary; **~олю́бие** *n* [12] self-interest, greed; **~ь** *f* [8] gain, profit; use; greed.
коры́то *n* [9] trough.
корь *f* [8] measles.
коря́вый [14 *sh.*] knotty, gnarled, rugged, rough; crooked; clumsy.
косá *f* [5; *ac/sg.*: кóсу; *pl. st.*] **1.** plait, braid; **2.** [*ac/sg. a.* косý] scythe; spit (of land); **~рь** *m* [4 *e.*] mower.
кóсвенный [14] oblique, indirect (*a. gr.*); ⚖ circumstantial (*evidence*).
коси́|лка *f* [5; *g/pl.*: -лок] mowing machine; **~ть**, ⟨с-⟩ **1.** [15; кошý

ко́сишь] mow; **2.** *a.* ⟨по-⟩ [15 *e.*; -кошу́, коси́шь] squint; twist (*mouth*), be(come) (a)wry; **-ся**, ⟨по-⟩ *v/i.*; *a.* look askance (at на В); **~чка** *f* [5; *g/pl.*: -чек] *dim.* of коса́ 1.

косма́тый [14 *sh.*] shaggy.

косм|е́тика *f* [5] cosmetics *pl.*; **~ети́ческий** [16] cosmetic; **~и́ческий** [16] cosmic; **~она́вт** *m* [1] astronaut.

косн|е́ть [8], ⟨за-⟩ persist, sink, fossilize (*fig.*); **∠ость** *f* [8] sluggishness, indolence; stagnation; **~у́ться** *s.* каса́ться; **∠ый** [14; -сен, -сна] sluggish, dull; stagnant, fossil.

косо|гла́зый [14 *sh.*] squint-eyed; **~го́р** *m* [1] slope; **∠й** [14; кос, -а́, -о] slanting, oblique; squint -(-eyed); F wry; **~ла́пый** [14 *sh.*] bandy-legged; F *s.* неуклю́жий.

костене́ть [8], ⟨о-⟩ ossify; stiffen, grow numb; be(come) transfixed.

костёр *m* [1; -тра́] (camp)fire, bonfire; pile, stake; meeting.

кост|и́стый [14 *sh.*] bony; **~ля́вый** [14 *sh.*] scrawny, raw-boned; **∠очка** *f* [5; *g/pl.*: -чек] bone; ⚘ stone; stay.

косты́ль *m* [4 *e.*] crutch; ⊕ spike.

кост|ь *f* [8; в -ти́; *from g/pl. e.*] bone; die; F бе́лая **~ь** blue blood; игра́ть в **∠и** (play at) dice.

костю́м *m* [1] suit; costume; **~и́рованный** [14]: **~иро́ванный** бал *m* fancy(-dress) ball.

костя́|к *m* [1 *e.*] skeleton; framework; **~но́й** [14] bone...

косу́ля *f* [6] roe (deer).

косы́нка *f* [5; *g/pl.*: -нок] kerchief.

косьба́ *f* [5] mowing.

кося́к *m* [1 *e.*] lintel; slant; felloe; herd; flock; shoal.

кот *m* [1 *e.*] tomcat; *s. a.* ко́тик; купи́ть **~а́** в мешке́ buy a pig in a poke; **~** напла́кал F very little.

кот|ёл *m* [1; -тла́] boiler, caldron; kitchen; **~ело́к** *m* [1; -лка́] kettle, pot; ⚔ mess kit; derby, *Brt.* bowler.

котёнок *m* [2] kitten.

ко́тик *m* [1] *dim. of* кот; fur seal; seal(skin; *adj.*: **~овый** [14]).

котле́та *f* [5] rissole (*without paste*); cutlet, chop.

котлови́на *f* [5] hollow, basin.

котомка *f* [5; *g/pl.*: -мок] knapsack; bag.

кото́р|ый [14] which; who; that; what; many a; P some; one; **~ый** раз how many times; **~ый** час? what time is it?; в **~ом** часу́? (at) what time?; **~ый** ему́ год? how old is he?

ко́фе *m* [*indecl.*] coffee; **∠йник** *m* [1] coffee pot; **∠йница** *f* [5] coffee mill; coffee box; **∠йный** [14] coffee...; **∠йная** *f* = **∠йня** *f* [6; *g/pl.*: -е́ен] coffee house, café.

ко́фт|а *f* [5] (woman's) jacket; blouse; (вя́заная **~а**) jersey, cardigan; **~очка** *f* [5; *g/pl.*: -чек] blouse.

коча́н *m* [1 *e.*] head (of cabbage).

кочев|а́ть [7] wander, roam; F move; travel; **∠ник** *m* [1] nomad; **~о́й** [14] nomadic.

кочега́р *m* [1] fireman, stoker.

кочене́ть [8], ⟨за-, о-⟩ grow numb, stiffen.

кочерга́ *f* [5; *g/pl.*: -рёг] poker.

ко́чка *f* [5; *g/pl.*: -чек] mound, hillock.

коша́чий [18] cat('s); feline.

кошелёк *m* [1; -лька́] purse.

ко́шка *f* [5; *g/pl.*: -шек] cat.

кошма́р *m* [1] nightmare; **~ный** [14; -рен, -рна] dreadful, horrible; F awful.

кощу́нств|енный [14 *sh.*] blasphemous; **~о** *n* [9] blasphemy; **~овать** [7] blaspheme (*v/t.* над Т).

коэффицие́нт *m* [1] coefficient.

КПСС (Коммунисти́ческая па́ртия Сове́тского Сою́за) Communist Party of the Soviet Union.

кра́деный [14] stolen (goods *n su.*).

краеуго́льный [14] *fig.* corner (*stone*); fundamental.

кра́жа *f* [5] theft; **~** со взло́мом burglary.

край *m* [3; с кра́ю; в -аю́; *pl.*: -ая́, -аёв, *etc. e.*] edge; (b)rim; brink (*a. fig.* =) edge; end; fringe, border, outskirt; region, land, country; **∠ний** [15] outermost, (*a. fig.*) utmost, extreme(ly, utterly, most, very, badly **∠не**); в **∠нем** слу́чае as a last resort; in case of emergency; **∠ность** *f* [8] extreme; extremity; до **∠ности** = **∠не**, *s.*; впада́ть в (доходи́ть до) **∠йности** go *or* run to extremes.

крамо́ла † *f* [5] sedition, revolt.

кран *m* [1] tap; ⊕ crane.

кра́пать [1 *or* 2 *st.*] drop, drip.

крапи́в|а *f* [5] nettle; **~ник** *m* [1] wren; **~ный** [14] nettle (*a.*, ⚕, *rash*).

кра́пинка *f* [5; *g/pl.*: -нок] speckle, spot.

крас|а́ *f* [5] † *s.* **~ота́**; **~а́вец** *m* [1; -вца] handsome man; **~а́вица** *f* [5] beauty, beautiful woman; **~и́вый** [14 *sh.*] beautiful; handsome; *a. iron.* fine.

крас|и́льный [14] dye...; **~и́льня** *f* [6; *g/pl.*: -лен] dye shop; **~и́льщик** *m* [1] dyer; **~и́тель** *m* [4] dye(stuff); **∠ить** [15], ⟨(п)о-, вы́-, рас-⟩ paint, colo(u)r, dye; F ⟨на-⟩ paint, make up; rouge; **∠ка** *f* [5; *g/pl.*: -сок] colo(u)r, paint, dye.

красне́ть [8], ⟨по-⟩ redden, grow *or* turn red; blush; *impf.* be ashamed; (*a.* **-ся**) appear, show red.

красно|арме́ец *m* [1; -ме́йца] Red Army man; **~ба́й** *m* [3] glib talker; **~ва́тый** [14 *sh.*] reddish; **~знамённый** [14] decorated with the Order of the Red Banner; **~ко́жий** [17] redskin(ned); **~речи́вый** [14 *sh.*] eloquent; **~ре́чие** *n* [12] eloquence;

~та́ *f* [5] redness; ruddiness; **~фло́тец** *m* [1; -тца] Red Navy man; **~щёкий** [16 *sh.*] ruddy.
красну́ха *f* [5] German measles.
кра́с|ный [14; -сен, -сна́, -о] red (*a. fig.*); † *s.* ~и́вый; ⚘ coniferous; ~ный зверь *m* deer; ~ная строка́ *f typ.* paragraph, new line; ~ная цена́ *f* ✝ F outside price; ~ное словцо́ *n* F witticism; проходи́ть ~ной ни́тью stand out.
красова́ться [7] shine, show (off).
красота́ *f* [5; *pl. st.*: -со́ты] beauty.
красть [25 *pt. st.*; кра́денный], ⟨у-⟩ steal (**-ся** *v/i.*, *impf.*; *a.* prowl slink).
кра́тк|ий [16; -ток, -тка́, -о; *comp.*: кра́тче] short, brief, concise; и́ ~ое *or* и́ с ~ой *the letter* й; *cf. a.* коро́ткий; **~овре́менный** [14; -енен, -енна] short; passing; **~осро́чный** [14; -чен, -чна] short; short-dated; short-term; **~ость** *f* [8] brevity.
кра́тный [14; -тен, -тна] divisible; *n su.* multiple; ...~ ...fold.
крах *m* [1] failure, crash, ruin.
крахма́л *m* [1], **~ить** [13], ⟨на-⟩ starch; **~ьный** [14] starch(ed).
кра́шеный [14] painted; dyed.
креди́т *m* [1] credit; в ~ on credit; **~ный** [14], **~ова́ть** [7] (*im*)*pf.* credit; **~о́р** *m* [1] creditor; **~оспосо́бный** [14; -бен, -бна] solvent.
кре́йс|ер *m* [1] cruiser; **~ерство** *n* [9] cruise; **~и́ровать** [7] cruise; ply.
крем *m* [1] cream.
креме́нь *m* [4; -мня́] flint.
кремл|ёвский [16], **♀ь** *m* [4 *e.*] Kremlin.
кре́мн|ий [3] silicon; **~и́стый** [14 *sh.*] gravelly, stony; siliceous.
крен ⚓, ✈ *m* [1] list, careen.
крендель *m* [4] cracknel.
крен|и́ть [13], ⟨на-⟩ list (**-ся** *v/i.*).
креп *m* [1] crepe, crape.
креп|и́ть [14 *e.*; -плю́, -пи́шь] fix, secure; reinforce; ⚓ belay; furl; *fig.* strengthen; **-ся** take courage; F persevere; **∠кий** [16; -пок, -пка́, -о; *comp.*: кре́пче] strong; firm, solid, sound; robust; hard; affectionate; **∠ко** *a.* fast; deep(ly); **∠нуть** [21], ⟨о-⟩ grow strong(er).
крепост|ни́чество *n* [9] serfdom; **~но́й** [14] (of, in) bond(age); *su.* serf; ~но́е пра́во *s.* ~ни́чество; (of a) fortress; **'~ь** *f* [8; *from g/pl. e.*] fortress; strength; firmness; ⚖ deed.
кре́сло *n* [9; *g/pl.*: -сел] armchair; *pl. thea.* † stall.
крест *m* [1 *e.*] cross (*a. fig.*); ~-на́~ crosswise; **~и́ны** *f/pl.* [5] baptism, christening; **~и́ть** [15; -щённый] (*im*)*pf.*, ⟨о-⟩ baptize, christen; godfather, godmother, sponsor; ⟨пере-⟩ cross (o.s. **-ся**); **∠ник** *m* [1] godson; **∠ница** *f* [5] goddaughter; **∠ный** [14] **1.** (of the) cross; **2.** ('kŗɔs-) ~ный (оте́ц) *m* godfather; ~ная (мать) *f* godmother
крестья́н|ин *m* [1; *pl.*: -я́не, -я́н] peasant, farmer; **~ка** *f* [5; *g/pl.* -нок] countrywoman, country girl, farmer's wife; **~ский** [16] farm(-er['s]), peasant...; country...; **~ство** *n* [9] peasantry.
креще́ние *n* [12] baptism (⚔ боево́е ~ baptism of fire), christening; ♀ Epiphany.
крив|а́я ⚲ *f* [14] curve; **~изна́** [5] crookedness, curvature; **~и́ть** [14 *e.*; -влю́, -ви́шь; -влённый] ⟨по-, с-⟩ (**-ся** be[come]) crook(ed), twist(ed); ~и́ть душо́й (со́вестью) palter; **~ля́ние** *n* [12] grimacing, twisting; **~ля́ться** [28] (make) grimace(s); mince; **~о́й** [14; крив, -а́, -о] crooked (*a. fig.*), wry; curve(d); F one-eyed; **~оно́гий** [16 *sh.*] bandy-legged; **~ото́лки** *m/pl.* [1] rumo(u)rs, gossip; **~оши́п** ⊕ *m* [1] crank.
кри́зис *m* [1] crisis.
крик *m* [1] cry, shout; bawl, outcry; (*fashion*) cri; **~ли́вый** [14 *sh.*] shrill, clamorous; (*a. dress, etc.*) loud; **∠нуть** *s.* крича́ть; **~у́н** F *m* [1 *e.*], **~у́нья** F *f* [6] bawler, clamo(u)rer, tattler.
кри|мина́льный [14] criminal; **~ста́лл** *m* [1] crystal; **~ста́льный** [14; -лен, -льна] crystalline.
крите́рий *m* [3] criterion.
кри́ти|к *m* [1] critic; **~ка** *f* [5] criticism; critique, review; **~кова́ть** [7] criticize; **∠ческий** [16], **∠чный** [14; -чен, -чна] critical.
крича́ть [4 *e.*; -чу́, -чи́шь], ⟨за-⟩, *once* ⟨кри́кнуть⟩ [20] cry (out), shout (at на В); scream.
кров *m* [1] shelter; home; † roof.
крова́|вый [14 *sh.*] bloody, sanguinary; **~ть** *f* [8] bed; bedstead.
кро́вельщик *m* [1] tiler; slater.
кровено́сный [14] blood (*vessel*).
кро́вля *f* [6; *g/pl.*: -вель] roof(ing).
кро́вный [14] (*adv.* by) blood; full-blooded, pure-, thoroughbred; vital; arch...
крово|жа́дный [14; -ден, -дна] bloodthirsty; **~излия́ние** ⚕ *n* [12] extravasation, hemorrhage; **~обраще́ние** *n* [12] circulation of the blood; **~пи́йца** *m/f* [5] bloodsucker; **~подтёк** *m* [1] bruise; **~проли́тие** *n* [12] bloodshed; **~проли́тный** [14; -тен, -тна] *s.* крова́вый; **~пуска́ние** *n* [12] bloodletting; **~смеше́ние** *n* [12] incest; **~тече́ние** *n* [12] bleeding; *s.* ~излия́ние; **~точи́ть** [16 *e.*; -чи́т] bleed.
кров|ь *f* [8; в -ви́; *from g/pl. e.*] blood (*a. fig.*); **~яно́й** [14] blood...
кро|и́ть [13; кро́енный], ⟨вы́-, с-⟩ cut (out); **∠йка** *f* [5] cutting (out).
крокоди́л *m* [1] crocodile.
кро́лик *m* [1] rabbit.
кро́ме (P) except, besides (*a.* ~ того́), apart (*or* aside) from; but.

кромса́ть [1], ⟨ис-⟩ hack, mangle.
кро́на *f* [5] crown.
кропи́ть [14 *e.*; -плю́, -пи́шь; -плённый], ⟨о-⟩ sprinkle.
кропотли́вый [14 *sh.*] laborious, toilsome; painstaking, assiduous.
кроссво́рд *m* [1] crossword puzzle.
крот *m* [1 *e.*] *zo.* mole.
кро́ткий [16; -ток, -тка́, -о; *comp.*: кро́тче] gentle, meek.
кро|ха́ *f* [5; *ac/sg.*: кро́ху; *from dat/pl. e.*] crumb; bit; **ﾉхотный** F [14; -тен, -тна], **ﾉшечный** F [14] tiny; **~ши́ть** [16], ⟨на-, по-, ис-⟩ crumb(le); P crush; **ﾉшка** *f* [5; *g/pl.*: -шек] crumb; bit; F baby, little one.
круг 1. *m* [1; в, на -у́; *pl. e.*] circle (*a. fig.*); sphere, range; orbit; F average; slice; **~лова́тый** [14 *sh.*] roundish; **~лоли́цый** [14 *sh.*] chubby-faced; **ﾉлый** [14; кругл, -а́, -о] round; F perfect, complete; **~ово́й** [14] circular; mutual (*responsibility*); **~оворо́т** *m* [1] circulation; succession; **~озо́р** *m* [1] horizon, scope; **~о́м** round; around, round about; ~о́м! ⚔ about face (*Brt.* turn)!; F entirely; **~ооборо́т** *m* [1] circulation; **~ообра́зный** [14; -зен, -зна] circular; **~осве́тный** [14] round the world; ⚓ circum...
кру́ж|ево *n* [9; *pl. e.*; *g/pl.*: кру́жев] lace **~и́ть** [16 & 16 *e.*; кружу́, кру́жи́шь], ⟨за-, вс-⟩ turn (round), whirl; circle; rotate, revolve, spin; stray about; (**-ся** *v/i.*); голова́ ~ится (у Р) feel giddy, **~ка** *f* [5; *g/pl.*: -жек] mug; box.
кру́жный F [14] roundabout.
кружо́к *m* [1; -жка́] (small) circle, disk; *fig.* circle; slice.
круп *m* [1] (⚕ & *horse*) croup.
круп|а́ *f* [5] grits, groats *pl.*; sleet; **~и́нка** *f* [5; *g/pl.*: -нок] grain (*a. fig.* = **~и́ца** *f* [5]).
кру́пный [14; -пен, -пна́, -о] coarse(-grained), gross; big, large(-scale), great; outstanding; † wholesale; (*film*) close(*up*); F ~ разгово́р *m* high words.
крутизна́ *f* [5] steep(ness).
крути́ть [15], ⟨за-, с-⟩ twist; twirl; roll (up); turn; whirl; P *impf.* trick.
круто́|й [14; крут, -а́, -о; *comp.*: кру́че] steep, sharp, abrupt, sudden; hard (*a.*-boiled); harsh; **'~сть** *f* [8] steepness; harshness.
кру́ча *f* [5] *s.* крутизна́.
кручи́на P *f* [5] grief, affliction.
круше́ние *n* [12] 🚂 accident; ⚓ wreck; ruin, breakdown.
крыжо́вник *m* [1] gooseberry, -ries *pl.*
крыл|а́тый [14 *sh.*] winged (*a. fig.*); **~о́** *n* [9; *pl.*: кры́лья, -льев] wing (*a.* ✈, ⚠, ⚔, *pol.*); sail (*windmill*); splashboard; **~ьцо́** *n* [9; *pl.*: кры́льца, -ле́ц, -льца́м] steps *pl.*, (outside) staircase, porch.
Крым *m* [1; в -у́] Crimea; **'2ский** [16] Crimean.
кры́с|а *f* [5] rat; **~ий** [18] rat('s).
крыть [22], ⟨по-⟩ cover; coat; trump; **-ся** *impf.* lie *or* consist in (в П); be at the bottom of.
кры́ш|а *f* [5] roof; **~ка** *f* [5; *g/pl.*: -шек] lid, cover; P (Д р.'s) end, ruin.
крюк *m* [1 *e.*; *pl. a.* крю́чья, -ьев] hook; F detour.
крюч|кова́тый [14 *sh.*] hooked; **~котво́рство** *n* [9] pettifoggery; **~о́к** *m* [1; -чка́] hook; crochet needle; flourish; F hitch.
кряж *m* [1] range; chain of hills.
кря́к|ать [1], *once* ⟨~нуть⟩ [20] quack.
кряхте́ть [11] groan, moan.
кста́ти to the point (*or* purpose); opportune(ly), in the nick of time; apropos; besides, too, as well; incidentally, by the way.
кто [23] who; ~ ..., ~ ... some ..., others ...; ~ бы ни whoever; ~ бы то ни́ был who(so)ever it may be; ~ F = **ﾉ-либо, ﾉ-нибудь, ﾉ-то** [23] any-, somebody (*or* -one).
куб *m* [1] Ⓐ cube; boiler.
ку́барем F head over heels.
ку́би|к *m* [1] (small) cube; block (*toy*); **ﾉческий** [16] cubic(al).
ку́бок *m* [1; -бка] goblet; *prize*: cup.
кубоме́тр *m* [1] cubic meter (-tre).
куве́рт † *m* [1] cover; envelope.
кувши́н *m* [1] jug; pitcher.
кувырк|а́ться [1], *once* ⟨~ну́ться⟩ [20] somersault, tumble; **~о́м** *s.* ку́барем.
куда́ where (... to); what ... for; F (*a.* ~ как[о́й], *etc.*) very, awfully, how; at all; by far, much; (*a.* + Д [& *inf.*]) how can ...; (*a.* ~ тут, там) (that's) impossible!, certainly not!, what an idea!, (*esp.* ~ тебе́!) rats!; ~ ..., ~ ... to some places ..., to others ...; ~ вы (*i. e.* идёте)? where are you going?; хоть ~ P tiptop, smart; *cf.* ни; ~ F = **~-либо, ~-нибудь, ~-то** any-, somewhere.
куда́хтать [3] cackle, cluck.
куде́сник *m* [1] wizard.
ку́др|и *f/pl.* [-е́й, *etc. e.*] curls; **~я́вый** [14 *sh.*] curly(-headed); tufty; ornate.
Кузба́сс ⚒ *m* [1] Kuznetsk Basin.
кузн|е́ц *m* [1 *e.*] (black)smith; **~е́чик** *m* [1] *zo.* grasshopper; **ﾉица** *f* [5] smithy.
ку́зов *m* [1; *pl.*: -ва́, *etc. e.*] body; box.
кукаре́кать [1] crow.
ку́киш P *m* [1] fig, fico.
ку́к|ла *f* [5; *g/pl.*: -кол] doll; **~олка** *f* [5; *g/pl.*: -лок] **1.** *dim. of* ~ла; **2.** *zo.* chrysalis; **~ольный** [14] doll('s); dollish; ~ольный теа́тр *m* puppet show.

кукуру́за *f* [5] corn, *Brt.* maize.
куку́шка *f* [5; *g/pl.*: -шек] cuckoo.
кула́|к *m* [1 *e.*] fist; ⊕ cam; kulak; **~цкий** [16] kulak...; **~чество** *n* [9] kulaks *pl.*; **~чный** [14] boxing (*match*); club (*law*); ⊕ cam...
кулёк *m* [1; -лька́] (paper) bag.
кули́к *m* [1 *e.*] curlew; snipe.
кули́са *f* [5] wing, side scene; за ~ми behind the scenes.
кули́ч *m* [1 *e.*] Easter cake.
кулуа́ры *m/pl.* [1] lobbies.
куль *m* [4 *e.*] sack, bag.
культ *m* [1] cult; **~иви́ровать** [7] cultivate; **~рабо́та** *f* [5] cultural & educational work (*Sov.*); **~у́ра** *f* [5] culture; **~у́рный** [14 *sh.*] cultural; cultured, civilized; polite, well-bred.
кум *m* [1; *pl.*: -мовья́, -овьёв] godfather; **~а́** *f* [5] godmother; gossip.
кума́ч *m* [1 *e.*] red bunting.
куми́р *m* [1] idol.
кумовство́ *n* [9] sponsorship, friendship; *fig.* nepotism.
кумы́с *m* [1] k(o)umiss.
куни́ца *f* [5] marten.
купа́|льный [14] bathing (~льный костю́м *m* bathing suit, *Brt.* bathing costume); **~льня** *f* [6; *g/pl.*: -лен] (swimming) bath, bathhouse; **~льщик** *m* [1] bather; **~ть(ся)** [1], ⟨вы́-, F ис-⟩ (take a) bath; bathe.
купе́ (-ˈpɛ) [*ind.*] 🚃 *n* compartment.
купе́|ц *m* [1; -пца́] merchant; **~ческий** [16] merchant('s); **~чество** *n* [9] merchants *pl.*
купи́ть *s.* покупа́ть.
купле́т *m* [1] couplet, stanza; song.
ку́пля *f* [6] purchase.
ку́пол *m* [1; *pl.*: -ла́] cupola, dome.
купоро́с *m* [1] vitriol.
ку́пчая *f* [14] purchase deed.
курга́н *m* [1] burial mound, barrow.
ку́р|ево P *n* [9] tobacco, smoke; *a.* = **~е́ние** *n* [12] smoking; **~и́льщик** *m* [1] smoker.
кури́|ный [14] chicken...; hen's; F short (*memory*); night... (*blindness*).
кури́|тельный [14] smoking; **~ть** [13; курю́, ку́ришь], ⟨по-, вы́-⟩ smoke (**-ся** *v/i.*); distil(l).
ку́рица *f* [5; *pl.*: ку́ры, *etc. st.*] hen; chicken, fowl.
курно́сый F [14 *sh.*] snub-nosed.
куро́к *m* [1; -рка́] cock (*gun*).
куропа́тка *f* [5; *g/pl.*: -ток] partridge.
куро́рт *m* [1] health resort.
курс *m* [1] course (⚓, ✈; ♪; *educ.*; держа́ть ~ на [В] head for; *univ. a* year); ⚕ rate of exchange; *fig.* line, policy; держа́ть (быть) в ~е (P keep (be) (well) posted on; **~а́нт** *m* [1] student; ⚔ cadet; **~и́в** *m* [1] *typ* italics; **~и́ровать** [7] ply.
ку́ртка *f* [5; *g/pl.*: -ток] jacket.
курча́вый [14 *sh.*] curly(-headed).
курь|ёз *m* [1] fun(ny thing); curiosity; **~е́р** *m* [1] messenger; courier; **~е́рский** [16]: ~е́рский по́езд *m* express (train).
куря́тник *m* [1] hen house.
куря́щий *m* [18] smoker.
кус|а́ть [1], ⟨укуси́ть⟩ [15] bite (**-ся** *v/i.*, *impf.*), sting; **~ково́й** [14] lump (*sugar*); **~о́к** *m* [1; -ска́] piece, bit, morsel; scrap; lump (*sugar*); cake (*soap*); slice; ~ка́ми by the piece; на ~ки́ to pieces; ~о́к хле́ба F living; **~о́чек** *m* [1; -чка] *dim. of* ~о́к
куст *m* [1 *e.*] bush, shrub; **~а́рник** *m* [1] bush(es), shrub(s); *pl. a.* underwood.
куста́р|ный [14] handicraft...; home(-made); *fig.* homespun; **~ь** *m* [4 *e.*] (handi)craftsman.
ку́тать(ся) [1], ⟨за-⟩ muffle, wrap
кут|ёж *m* [1 *e.*], **~и́ть** [15] carouse
кух|а́рка *f* [5; *g/pl.*: -рок] cook; **~ня** *f* [6; *g/pl.*: ку́хонь] kitchen; cuisine, cookery; **~онный** [14] kitchen...
ку́цый [14 *sh.*] dock-tailed; short.
ку́ч|а *f* [5] heap, pile; a lot of; ~ами in heaps *or* in crowds; класть в ~у pile up; **~ер** *m* [1; *pl.*: -pá, *etc. e.*] coachman; **~ка** *f* [5; *g/pl.*: -чек] *dim. of* ~а; group.
куш *m* [1] stake; F lot, sum.
куша́к *m* [1 *e.*] belt, girdle.
ку́ша|нье *n* [10] dish; meal; food; **~ть** [1], ⟨по-⟩ eat (up ⟨с-⟩); drink
куше́тка *f* [5; *g/pl.*: -ток] lounge

Л

лабири́нт *m* [1] labyrinth.
лаборато́рия *f* [7] laboratory.
ла́ва *f* [5] lava.
лави́на *f* [5] avalanche.
лави́ровать [7] tack (⚓ & *fig.*).
ла́в|ка *f* [5; *g/pl.*: -вок] bench; (small) store, *Brt.* shop; **~очник** *m* [1] store-, shopkeeper; **~р** *m* [1] laurel; **~ро́вый** [14] (of) laurel(s).
ла́гер|ь 1. [4; *pl.*: -ря́, *etc. e.*] camp (*a.*, *pl.*: -ри, *etc. st.*, *fig.*); располага́ться (стоя́ть) ~ем camp (out); **~ный** [14] camp...
лад *m* [1; в -у́; *pl. e.*] F harmony, concord; order; way; tune; (не) в ~у (~а́х) *s.* (не) ~ить; идти́ на ~ work (well), get on *or* along; **~ан** *m* [1] incense; **~ить** F [15], ⟨по-, с-⟩ get along *or* on (well), *pf. a.* make it up; manage; fix; tune; не ~ить *a.* be at odds *or* variance; out of keeping; **-ся** F *impf. s.* идти́ на ~ & ~ить

ˆно F well, all right, O. K.; ˆный F [14; -ден, -днá, -о] harmonious; fine, good(-looking).
áдожск|ий [16]: ˆое óзеро n Lake Ladoga.
адó|нь f [8], ˜ша P f [5] palm; как на ˜ни (lie) spread before the eyes; бить в ˜ши clap (one's hands).
адья́ f [6] boat; chess: rook.
азарéт ⚔ m [1] hospital.
аз|éйка f [5; g/pl.: -éек] loophole; ˆить [15] climb (v/t. на В); creep.
азý|рный [14; -рен, -рна], ˜рь f [8] azure; ˜тчик m [1] scout, spy.
ай m [3] bark(ing), yelp; ˆка f [5; g/pl.: лáек] 1. Eskimo dog; 2. kid (leather); ˆковый [14] kid...
ак m [1] varnish, laquer; ˆовый [14] varnish(ed), laquer(ed); patent leather...; ˜áть [1], ⟨вы́-⟩ lap.
акéй m [3] footman, lackey; flunk(e)y; ˜ский [16] lackey('s); fig. servile.
акировáть [7], ⟨от-⟩ laquer; varnish.
áком|иться [14], ⟨по-⟩ (T) enjoy, relish (a. fig.), eat with delight; be fond of dainties; ˜ка F m/f [5] lover of dainties; быть ˜кой a. have a sweet tooth; ˜ство n [9] dainty, delicacy; pl. sweetmeats, Brt. sweets; ˜ый [14 sh.] dainty; † (a. ˜ый до P) fond of (dainties); ˜ый кусó(че)к m tidbit, Brt. titbit.
аконúч|еский [16], ˜ный [14; -чен, -чна] laconic(al).
Ла-Мáнш m [1] English Channel.
áмп|а f [5] lamp; rad. tube, Brt. valve; ˜áд(к)а f [5 (g/pl.: -док)] (icon) lamp; ˜овый [14] lamp...; ˜очка f [5; g/pl.: -чек] bulb.
андшáфт m [1] landscape.
áндыш m [1] lily of the valley.
ань f [8] fallow deer; hind, doe.
áп|а f [5] paw; fig. clutch; ˜оть m [4; -птя; from g/pl. e.] bast shoe.
апшá f [5] noodles pl.; noodle soup.
арёк m [1; -рькá] stand, Brt. stall.
арéц [1; -рцá] box, chest, casket.
áск|а f 1. [5] caress; F affection; 2. [5; g/pl.: -сок] weasel; ˜áтельный [14] endearing, pet; † flattering; s. a. ˜овый; ˜áть [1], ⟨при-⟩ caress; pet, fondle; impf. cherish; flatter (o.s. with себя́ T); -ся endear o.s. (to к Д); fawn (dog); † (T) cherish; ˜овый [14 sh.] affectionate, tender; caressing.
áсточка f [5; g/pl.: -чек] swallow.
атáть P [1], ⟨за-⟩ patch, mend.
атвúйский [16] Latvian.
атúнский [16] Latin.
áтка P f [5; g/pl.: -ток] patch.
атýк m [1] lettuce.
атýнь f [8] brass.
áты f/pl. [5] armo(u)r.

латы́нь f [13] Latin.
латы́ш m [1 e.], ˜ка f [5; g/pl.: -шек] Lett; ˜ский [16] Lettish.
лауреáт m [1] prize winner.
лафéт m [1] gun carriage.
лачýга f [5] hovel, hut.
лáять [27], ⟨за-⟩ bark.
лгать [лгу, лжёшь, лгут; лгал, -á, -о] 1. ⟨со-⟩ lie; tell a p. (Д, пéред T) a lie; 2. ⟨на-⟩ (на В) defame.
лгун m [1 e.], ˆья f [6] liar.
лебёдка f [5; g/pl.: -док] windlass.
лебе|дúный [14] swan...; ′˜дь m [4; from g/pl. e.] (poet. a. f) swan; ˜зúть F [15 e.; -бежý, -безúшь] fawn (upon пéред T).
лев m [1; льва] lion; ♌ Leo.
лев|шá m/f [5; g/pl.: -шéй] left-handed person; ˆый [14] left (a. fig.), left-hand; wrong (side; on с P).
легáльный [14; -лен, -льна] legal.
легéнд|а f [5] legend; ˜áрный [14; -рен, -рна] legendary.
легиóн m [1] legion.
лёгкий (-xk-) [16; лёгок, легкá; a. лёгки] light (a. fig.); easy; slight; F lucky; (Д) легкó + inf. it is very well for ... + inf.; лёгок на помúне F talk of the devil!
легко|вéрный (-xk-) [14; -рен, -рна] credulous; ˜вéсный [14; -сен, -сна] light; fig. shallow; ˜вóй [14]: ˜вóй автомобúль m (a. ˜вáя [авто]машúна f) auto(mobile), car.
лёгкое (-xk-) n [16] lung.
легкомы́сл|енный (-xk-) [14 sh.] light-minded, frivolous; thoughtless; ˜ие n [12] levity; frivolity; flippancy.
лёгкость (-xk-) f [8] lightness; easiness; ease.
лёд m [1; льда; на льдý] ice.
лед|енéть [8], ⟨за-, о-⟩ freeze, ice; grow numb (with cold); chill; ˜енéц m [1; -нцá] (sugar) candy; ˜енúть [13], ⟨о(б)-⟩ freeze, ice; chill; ˆник[1] m [1] ice cellar; refrigerator, icebox; ˜нúк[2] m [1 e.] glacier; ˜никóвый [14] glacial; ice...; ˜окóл m [1] icebreaker; ˜охóд m [1] ice drift; ˜янóй [14] ice...; icy (a. fig.); chilly.
лежáлый [14] stale, old, spoiled.
лежá|ть [4 e.; лёжа] lie; be (situated); rest, be incumbent; form (the basis в П); ˜чий [17] lying; (a. ⚘) prostrate; turndown (collar).
лéзвие n [12] edge.
лезть [24 st.: лéзу; лезь!; лез, -ла], ⟨по-⟩ (be) climb(ing, etc.; v/t. на В); creep; penetrate; F reach into; (к Д [с T]) importune, press; fall out (hair); (на В) fit (v/t.); P meddle.
лейбори́ст m [1] Labo(u)rite.
лéй|ка f [5; g/pl.: лéек] watering pot, can; ˜тенáнт m [1] (second) lieutenant.

лека́р|ственный [14] medicinal, curative; **~ство** *n* [9] medicine, remedy (against, for от, про́тив Р); **'~ь** † & P *m* [4; *from g/pl. e.*] doctor.
ле́ксика *f* [5] vocabulary.
ле́к|тор *m* [1] lecturer; **~ция** *f* [7] lecture (at на П; *vb.*: слу́шать [чита́ть] attend [give, deliver]).
леле́ять [27] cherish, fondle.
ле́ме́х *m* [1 & 1 *e*; *pl.*: -ха́, *etc. e.*] plowshare (*Brt.* plough-share).
лён *m* [1; льна] flax.
лени́в|ец *m* [1; -вца] *s.* лентя́й; **~ица** *f* [5] *s.* лентя́йка; **~ый** [14 *sh.*] lazy, idle; sluggish.
Ленингра́д *m* [1] Leningrad; **♀ец** *m* [1; -дца] Leningrader.
ле́нин|ец *m* [1; -нца], **~ский** [16] Leninist.
лени́ться [13; леню́сь, ле́нишься], be lazy.
ле́нта *f* [5] ribbon; band; ⊕ tape.
лентя́й F *m* [3], **~ка** *f* [5; *g/pl.*: -я́ек] lazybones; **~ничать** F [1] idle.
лень *f* [8] laziness, idleness; listlessness; F (мне) ~ I hate, don't want, won't.
лепе|сто́к *m* [1; -тка́] petal; **'~т** *m* [1], **~та́ть** [4], ‹про-› babble, prattle.
лепёшка *f* [5; *g/pl.*: -шек] scone; lozenge.
леп|и́ть [14], ‹вы́-, с-› sculpture, model, mo(u)ld; F ‹на-› stick (to на В); **∠ка** model(l)ing, mo(u)lding; F sculpture; **~но́й** [14] plastic.
ле́пта *f* [5] mite.
лес *m* [1; из лесу & из ле́са; в лесу́; *pl.*: леса́, *etc. e.*] wood, forest; lumber, *Brt.* timber; *pl.* scaffold(ing); **∠ом** through a (the) wood; как в **~у́** F *fig.* at sea; **∠а́** *f* [5; *pl.*: лёсы, *etc. st.*] (fishing) line; **~и́стый** [14 *sh.*] woody, wooded; **∠ка** *f* [5; *g/pl.*: -сок] *s.* **∠а́**; **~ни́к** *m* [1 *e.*] ranger; **~ни́чество** *n* [9] forest district; **~ни́чий** *m* [17] forester; **~но́й** [14] forest...; wood(y); lumber...; *Brt.* timber...
лесо|во́дство *n* [9] forestry; **~насажде́ние** *n* [12] afforestation; (af)forested tract; wood; **~пи́лка** F *f* [5; *g/pl.*: -лок], **~пи́льный** [14]: ~пи́льный заво́д *m* = **~пи́льня** *f* [6; *g/pl.*: -лен] sawmill; **~ру́б** *m* [1] lumberman, woodcutter.
ле́стница *f* [5] (-ʂɲ-) (flight of) stairs *pl.*, staircase; ladder; *fig.* scale.
ле́ст|ный [14; -тен, -тна] flattering; **~ь** *f* [8] flattery.
лёт *m* [1] flight; на лету́ in the air, on the wing; F *fig.* in haste; instantly, quickly.
лета́, лет *s.* ле́то; *cf. a.* год.
лета́тельный [14] flying.
лета́ть [1] fly.
лете́ть [11], ‹по-› (be) fly(ing).
ле́тний [15] summer...
лётный [14] flying; run...
ле́т|о *n* [9; *pl. e.*] summer (in [the] ~ for the на В); *pl.* years, age (at в В); ско́лько вам ~? how old are you (*cf.* быть); в ~а́х elderly, advanced in years; **~опи́сец** *m* [1; -сца] chronicler; **~о́пись** *f* [8] chronicle; **~осчисле́ние** *n* [12] chronology, era.
лету́ч|ий [17 *sh.*] flying; fleeting; offhand, short; ⚗ volatile; ~ая мышь *f zo.* bat; ~ий листо́к = **~ка** F *f* [5; *g/pl.*: -чек] leaflet.
лётчи|к *m* [1], **~ца** *f* [5] aviator, flier, pilot, air(wo)man.
лече́бн|ица *f* [5] clinic, hospital; **~ый** [14] medic(in)al.
леч|е́ние ⚕ *n* [12] treatment; **~и́ть** [16] treat; **-ся** undergo treatment, be treated; treat (one's ... от Р).
лечь *s.* ложи́ться; *cf. a.* лежа́ть.
ле́ший *m* [17] satyr; P Old Nick.
лещ *m* [1 *e.*] *zo.* bream.
лж|е... false; pseudo...; **~ец** *m* [1 *e.*] liar; **~и́вость** *f* [8] mendacity; **~и́вый** [14 *sh.*] false, lying; mendacious.
ли, (*short, after vowels, a.*) ль **1.** (*interr. part.*:) зна́ет ~ он ...? (= он зна́ет ...?) does he know ...?; **2.** (*cj.*) whether, if; ... ~, ... ~ whether ... or ...
либера́л *m* [1], **~ьный** [14; -лен, -льна] liberal.
ли́бо or; ~ ..., ~ ... either ... or ...
Лива́н *m* [1] Lebanon.
ли́вень *m* [4; -вня] downpour.
ливре́я *f* [6; *g/pl.*: -ре́й] livery.
ли́га *f* [5] league.
ли́дер *m* [1] (*pol., sport*) leader.
Ли́з(очк)а *f* [5] Liz(zy), Lise.
лиз|а́ть [3], *once* ‹~ну́ть› lick.
лик *m* [1] face; countenance; image.
ликвиди́ровать [7] (*im*)*pf.* liquidate.
ликова́ть [7], ‹воз-› exult.
ли́лия *f* [7] lily.
лило́вый [14] lilac(-colo[u]red).
лими́т *m* [1], **~и́ровать** [7] (*im*)*pf.* limit.
лимо́н *m* [1] lemon; **~а́д** *m* [1] lemonade.
ли́мфа *f* [5] lymph.
лингви́стика *f* [5] *s.* языкозна́ние.
лине́й|ка *f* [5; *g/pl.*: -е́ек] line; ruler; slide rule; † carriage; **~ный** [14] linear; ⚔ (of the) line; ~ battle...
ли́н|за *f* [5] lens; **~ия** *f* [7] line (*a. fig.*; in по Д); **~ко́р** *m* [1] battleship; **~ова́ть** [7], ‹на-› rule.
Линч: зако́н (*or* суд) **∠а** lynch law; **♀ева́ть** [7] (*im*)*pf.* lynch.
линь *m* [4 *e.*] *zo.* tench; ⚓ line.
ли́н|ька *f* [5] mo(u)lt(ing); **~ю́чий** F [17 *sh.*] fading, faded; mo(u)lting

~ялый F [14] faded; mo(u)lted; **~ять** [28], ⟨вы́-, по-⟩ fade; mo(u)lt.
и́па *f* [5] linden, lime tree.
и́п|кий [16; -пок, -пка́, -о] sticky; sticking (*plaster*); **~нуть** [21], ⟨при-⟩ stick.
и́р|а *f* [5] lyre; **~ик** *m* [1] lyric poet; **~ика** *f* [5] lyric poetry; **~и́ческий** [16], **~и́чный** [14; -чен, -чна] lyric(al).
ис|(и́ц)а́ *f* [5; *pl. st.*] fox (silver... серебри́стая, черно-бу́рая); **'~ий** [18] fox...; foxy.
ист *m* **1.** [1 *e.*] sheet; certificate; ⚖ deed; *typ.* leaf (= 16 pp.); **2.** [1 *e.*; *pl. st* : ли́стья, -ьев] ⚘ leaf; *a.* = ~ва́; **~а́ть** F [1] leaf, thumb (through); **~ва́** *f* [5] foliage, leaves *pl.*; **'~венница** *f* [5] larch; **'~венный** [14] foliose, leafy; deciduous; **'~ик** *m* [1] *dim. of* ~; **~о́вка** *f* [5; *g/pl.*: -вок] *pol.* leaflet; **~о́к** *m* [1; -тка́] *dim. of* ~; slip; (news)paper; **~ово́й** [14] leaf(y); sheet...; folio...
Литва́ *f* [5] Lithuania.
итей|ная *f* [14], **~ный** [14]: ~ный заво́д *m* foundry; **~щик** *m* [1] founder.
и́тер|а *f* [5] letter, type; **~а́тор** *m* [1] man of letters; writer; **~ату́ра** *f* [5] literature; **~ату́рный** [14; -рен, -рна] literary.
итов|ец *m* [1; -вца], **~ка** *f* [5; *g/pl.*: -вок], **~ский** [16] Lithuanian.
итой [14] cast.
итр *m* [1] liter (*Brt.* -tre; = *ap*-*prox.* 1qt.).
ить [лью, льёшь; лил, -а́, -о; лей(-те)! ли́тый (лит, -а́, -о)] pour; shed; ⊕ cast; дождь льёт как из ведра́ it's raining cats and dogs; **-ся** flow, pour; spread; sound; **~ё** *n* [10] founding, cast(ing).
ифт *m* [1] elevator, *Brt.* lift; **~ёр** *m* [1] elevator boy, *Brt.* lift man.
и́фчик *m* [1] waist, bodice; bra(ssière).
их|о́имец † *m* [1; -мца] usurer; bribe taker; **~о́й** [14; лих, -а́, -о] bold, daring; dashing; nimble; smart; **~ора́дка** *f* [5] fever; **~ора́дочный** [14; -чен, -чна] feverish; **'~ость** *f* [8] bravery; smartness.
ицев|а́ть [7], ⟨пере-⟩ face; turn; **~о́й** [14] face...; front...; right (*side*).
ицеме́р *m* [1] hypocrite; **~ие** *n* [12] hypocricy; **~ный** [14; -рен, -рна] hypocritical; **~ить** [13] dissemble.
ице́нзия *f* [7] license (for на В).
иц|о́ *n* [9; *pl. st.*] face; countenance (*change v/t.* в П); front; person, individual(ity); в ~о́ by sight; to s. b.'s face; от ~а́ (Р) in the name of; ~о́м к ~у́ face to face; быть (Д) к ~у́ suit *or* become a p.; нет ~а́ (на П) be bewildered; *s. a.* де́йствующий.
ичи́н|а *f* [5] mask, guise; **~ка** *f* [5; *g/pl.*: -нок] larva; maggot.

ли́чн|ый [14] personal; **~ость** *f* [8] personality; identity (*card*).
лиша́й *m* [3 *e.*] ⚘ lichen (*a.* ~ник); ⚕ herpes.
лиш|а́ть [1], ⟨~и́ть⟩ [16 *e.*; -шу́, -ши́шь; -шённый] deprive, bereave, strip (of Р); ~а́ть (себя́) жи́зни commit murder (upon В) (suicide); ~ённый *a.* devoid of, lack(-ing); **-ся** (Р) lose; ~и́ться чувств faint; **~е́ние** *n* [12] (de)privation; loss; *pl.* privations, hardships; ~е́ние прав disfranchisement; ~е́ние свобо́ды imprisonment; **~и́ть(ся)** *s.* ~а́ть(ся).
ли́шн|ий [15] superfluous, odd, excessive, over..., sur...; spare; extra; needless, unnecessary; outsider; ~ее *n* undue (things, *etc.*), (*a.* a glass) too much; ... с ~им over ...; ~ий раз *m* once again; (Д) не ~е *inf.* (р.) had better.
лишь (*a.* + то́лько) only; merely, just; as soon as, no sooner ... than, hardly; ~ бы if only.
лоб *m* [1; лба; во, на лбу́] forehead.
ло́бзик *m* [1] fret saw.
ло́б|ный *anat.*, **~ово́й** [14] ⚔ frontal.
лови́ть [14], ⟨пойма́ть⟩ [1] catch; (en)trap; grasp, seize; ~ на сло́ве take at one's word.
ло́вк|ий [16; ло́вок, ловка́, -о] dexterous, adroit, deft; **~ость** *f* [8] adroitness, dexterity.
ло́в|ля *f* [6] catching; fishing; **~у́шка** *f* [5; *g/pl.*: -шек] trap; snare.
логари́фм *m* [1] logarithm.
ло́ги|ка *f* [5] logic; **'~ческий** [16], **'~чный** [14; -чен, -чна] logical.
ло́гов|ище *n* [11], **~о** *n* [9] lair, den.
ло́д|ка *f* [5; *g/pl.*: -док] boat; **~очник** *m* [1] boatman.
лоды́жка *f* [5; *g/pl.*: -жек] ankle.
ло́дырь F *m* [4] idler, loafer.
ло́жа *f* [5] *thea.* box; lodge; stock.
ложби́на *f* [5] hollow.
ло́же *n* [11] couch, bed; stock.
ложи́ться [16 *e.*; -жу́сь, -жи́шься], ⟨лечь⟩ [26 г/ж: ля́гу, ля́жешь, ля́гут; ля́г(те)!; лёг, легла́] lie down; ~ в (В) go to (*bed*, *a.* ~ [спать]); fall.
ло́жка *f* [5; *g/pl.*: -жек] spoon.
ло́ж|ный [14; -жен, -жна] false; ~ный путь *m* wrong tack; **~ь** *f* [8; лжи; ло́жью] lie, falsehood.
лоза́ *f* [5; *pl. st.*] vine; switch ⚘.
ло́зунг *m* [1] slogan, watchword.
локализова́ть [7] (*im*)*pf.* localize.
локо|моти́в *m* [1] locomotive, engine; **'~н** *m* [1] curl, lock; **'~ть** *m* [4; -ктя; *from g/pl. e.*] elbow.
лом *m* [1; *from g/pl. e.*] crowbar, pry; scrap (metal); **'~аный** [14] broken; **~а́ть** [1], ⟨с-⟩ break (*a.* up); pull (down), tear; ~а́ть го́лову rack one's brains (over над Т); **-ся** break; P clown, jest; mince, be prim.

ломба́рд *m* [1] pawnshop.
лом|и́ть [14] F = ~а́ть; *impers.* ache, feel a pain in; **-ся** bend, burst; F force (*v/t.* в В), break (into); **ˊка** *f* [5] breaking (up); **ˊкий** [16; ло́мок, ломка́, -о] brittle, fragile; **~ово́й** [14] breaking; scrap...; cart(er)...; **~о́та** *f* [5] acute pains *pl.*; **~о́ть** *m* [4; -мтя́] slice; **ˊтик** *m* [1] *dim. of* ~о́ть.
ло́но *n* [9] lap; bosom (in на П).
ло́па|сть *f* [8; *from g/pl. e.*] blade; vane, fan; **ˊта** *f* [8] shovel, spade; **ˊтка** *f* [5; *g/pl.*: -ток] **1.** *dim. of* ˊта; **2.** shoulder blade.
ло́п|аться [1], ‹~нуть› [20] burst; crack, break; tear; F be exhausted.
лопу́х *m* [1 *e.*] burdock.
лоск *m* [1] luster, gloss, polish.
лоску́т *m* [1 *e.*; *pl. a.*: -ку́тья, -ьев] rag, shred, scrap, frazzle.
лос|ни́ться [13] be glossy *or* sleek, shine; **ˊо́сь** *m* [4] salmon.
лось *m* [4; *from g/pl. e.*] elk.
лот *m* [1] plummet, lead.
лотере́я *f* [6] lottery.
лото́к *m* [1; -тка́] hawker's stand, tray.
лоха́н|ка *f* [5], **~ь** *f* [8] tub.
лохм|а́тый [14 *sh.*] shaggy, dishevel(l)ed; **~о́тья** *n/pl.* [*gen.*: -ьев] rags.
ло́цман ⚓ *m* [1] pilot.
лошад|и́ный [14] horse...; ~и́ная си́ла *f* horsepower; **ʹ~ь** *f* [8; *from g/pl. e., instr.*: -дьми́ & -дя́ми] horse.
лоша́к *m* [1 *e.*] hinny.
лощи́|на *f* [5] hollow, valley; **~ть** [16 *e.*; -щу́, -щи́шь; -щённый] ‹на-, вы́-› gloss, polish.
лоя́льн|ость *f* [8] loyalty; **~ый** [14; -лен, -льна] loyal.
лу|бо́к *m* [1; -бка́] ⚕ splint; cheap popular print (*or* literature).; **~г** *m* [1; на -у́; *pl.* -а́, *etc. e.*] meadow.
луди́ть [15] tin.
лу́ж|а *f* [5] puddle, pool; сесть в ~у F be in a pretty pickle (*or* fix).
лужа́йка *f* [5; *g/pl.*: -а́ек] (small) glade.
лук *m* [1] **1.** onion(s); **2.** bow.
лука́в|ить [14], ‹с-› dissemble, dodge; **~ство** *n* [9] cunning, slyness, ruse; **~ый** [14 *sh.*] crafty, wily.
лу́ковица *f* [5] bulb; onion.
лун|а́ *f* [5] moon; **~а́тик** *m* [1] sleepwalker; **ˊный** [14] moon(lit); *astr.* lunar.
лу́па *f* [5] magnifier, magnifying glass.
лупи́ть [14], ‹об-› peel (*v/i.* **-ся**).
луч *m* [1 *e.*] ray, beam; **~ево́й** [14] radial; **~еза́рный** [14; -рен, -рна] radiant; **~еиспуска́ние** *n* [12] radiation; **~и́на** *f* [5] (burning) chip, spill; **~и́стый** [14 *sh.*] radiant.
лу́чш|е *adv., comp. of* хорошо́; **~ий** [17] better; best (at ... в ~ем слу́чае).
лущи́ть [16 *e.*; -щу́, -щи́шь], ‹вы́-› shell, husk.
лы́ж|а *f* [5] ski (*vb.*: ходи́ть, *etc* на ~ах); **~ник** *m* [1], **~ница** *f* [5] skier; **~ный** [14] ski...
лы́ко *n* [9; *nom/pl.*: лы́ки] bast.
лы́с|ый [14] bald; **~ина** *f* [5] bald head; blaze.
ль *s.* ли.
льви́|ный [14] lion's; ~ный зев *m* snapdragon; **~ца** *f* [5] lioness.
льго́т|а *f* [5] privilege; **~ный** [14; -тен, -тна] privileged; reduced; favo(u)rable.
льди́на *f* [5] ice floe.
льну́ть [20], ‹при-› cling, nestle.
льняно́й [14] flax(en); linen...
льст|е́ц *m* [1 *e.*] flatterer; **~и́вый** [14 *sh.*] flattering; **~ить** [15], ‹по-› (Д) flatter (o.s. with себя́ T).
любе́зн|ичать F [1] (с T) court, flirt, spoon; **~ость** *f* [8] amiability, kindness; favo(u)r; *pl.* compliments; **~ый** [14; -зен, -зна] amiable, kind, dear; *su.* sweetheart; F lovely.
люби́м|ец *m* [1; -мца], **~ица** *f* [5] favo(u)rite, pet; **~ый** [14] beloved, darling; favo(u)rite, pet.
люби́тель *m* [4], **~ница** *f* [5] lover, fan; amateur; **~ский** [16] amateur(-ish).
люби́ть [14] love; like, be (‹по-› grow) fond of; *pf.* fall in love with.
любов|а́ться [7], ‹по-› (T *or* на В) admire, (be) delight(ed) (in); **ˊник** *m* [1] lover; **ˊница** *f* [5] mistress; **ˊный** [14] love...; loving, affectionate; **ˊная** связь *f* amour; **ˊь** *f* **1.** [8; -бви́; -бо́вью] love (of, for к Д); **2.** ♀ [8] *fem. name* (*cf.* Amanda).
любо|зна́тельный [14; -лен, -льна] inquisitive, curious; inquiring; **ˊй** [14] any(one *su.*); **~пы́тный** [14; -тен, -тна] curious, inquisitive; interesting; мне ~пы́тно ... I wonder ...; **~пы́тство** *n* [9] curiosity; interest.
лю́бящий [17] loving, affectionate.
люд *m* [1] *coll.* F, **ˊи** *pl.* [-е́й, -ям, -ьми́, -ях] people; † servants; вы́йти в ˊи arrive, make one's way in life (*or* fortune); на ˊях in public; **ˊный** [14; -ден, -дна] populous, crowded; **~oе́д** *m* [1] cannibal; ogre; **~ско́й** [16] man...; man's; human(e); servants' (room *su. f*).
люк *m* [1] hatch(way).
лю́лька *f* [5; *g/pl.*: -лек] cradle.
лю́стра *f* [5] chandelier, luster.
лю́тик *m* [1] buttercup.
лю́тый [14; лют, -а́, -о; *comp.*: -те́е] fierce, cruel, grim.
люце́рна *f* [5] alfalfa, *Brt.* lucerne.
ляг|а́ть(ся) [1], ‹~ну́ть› [20] kick.
лягу́шка *f* [5; *g/pl.*: -шек] frog.
ля́жка *f* [5; *g/pl.*: -жек] thigh, haunch.
лязг *m* [1], **ˊать** [1] clank, clang; chatter.
ля́мк|а *f* [5; *g/pl.*: -мок] strap; тяну́ть ~у F drudge, toil.

М

мавзоле́й *m* [3] mausoleum.
магази́н *m* [1] store, *Brt.* shop.
магистра́ль *f* [8] main (✈ air) line 🚂 (✈ *a.* route) *or* waterway; thoroughfare; trunk (line); main.
маг|и́ческий [16] magic(al); **~нети́ческий** [16] magnetic(al).
ма́гний *m* [3] magnesium.
магни́т *m* [1] magnet.
магомета́н|ин *m* [1; *pl.*: -а́не, -а́н], **~ка** *f* [5; *g/pl.*: -нок] Mohammedan.
мадья́р *m* [1], **~ский** [16] Magyar.
маёвка *f* [5; *g/pl.*: -вок] May Day meeting, outing *or* picnic.
ма́з|анка *f* [5; *g/pl.*: -нок] mud hut; **~ать** [3] **1.** ⟨по-, на-⟩ smear; rub (in); anoint; spread, butter; whitewash; **2.** ⟨c-⟩ oil, lubricate; **3.** F ⟨за-⟩ soil; *impf.* daub; **~ня́** F *f* [6] daub(ing); **~о́к** *m* [1; -зка́] touch, stroke; ⚕ swab; **~ь** *f* [8] ointment; grease.
май *m* [3] May; **2ка** *f* [5; *g/pl.*: ма́ек] sleeveless sports shirt; **~о́р** *m* [1] major; **2ский** [16] May(-Day)...
мак *m* [1] poppy.
мак|а́ть [1], *once* ⟨~ну́ть⟩ [20] dip.
маке́т *m* [1] model; dummy.
ма́клер *m* [1] broker.
макну́ть *s.* мака́ть.
макре́ль *f* [8] mackerel.
максима́льный [14; -лен, -льна] maximum.
маку́шка *f* [5; *g/pl.*: -шек] top; crown.
мала́|ец *m* [1; -ла́йца], **~йка** *f* [5; *g/pl.*: ла́ек], **~йский** [16] Malay(an).
малева́ть F [6], ⟨на-⟩ paint, daub.
мале́йший [17] least, slightest.
ма́ленький [16] little, small; short; trifling, petty.
мали́н|а *f* [5] raspberry, -ries *pl.*; **~овка** *f* [5; *g/pl.*: -вок] robin (redbreast); **~овый** [14] raspberry-...; crimson; soft, sonorous.
ма́ло little (*a.* ~ что); few (*a.* ~ кто); a little; not enough; less; ~ где in few places; ~ когда́ seldom; F ~ ли что much, many things, anything; (*a.* ~ что) yes, but ...; that doesn't matter, even though; ~ того́ besides, and what is more; ~ того́, что not only (that).
мало|ва́жный [14; -жен, -жна] insignificant, trifling; **~ва́то** F little, not (quite) enough; **~вероя́тный** [14; -тен, -тна] unlikely; **~во́дный** [14; -ден, -дна] shallow; **~говоря́щий** [17] insignificant; **~гра́мотный** [14; -тен, -тна] uneducated, ignorant; faulty; **~ду́шный** [14; -шен, -шна] pusillanimous; **~зна́чащий** [17 *sh.*], **~значи́тельный** [14; -лен, -льна] *s.* ~ва́жный; **~иму́щий** [17 *sh.*] poor; **~кро́вие** *n* [12] an(a)emia; **~кро́вный** [14; -вен, -вна] an(a)emic; **~ле́тний** [15] minor, underage; little (one); **~лю́дный** [14; -ден, -дна] poorly populated (*or* attended); **~-ма́льски** F a little bit; somewhat; **~общи́тельный** [14; -лен, -льна] unsociable; **~о́пытный** [14; -тен, -тна] inexperienced; **~-пома́лу** F gradually, little by little; **~ро́слый** [14 *sh.*] undersized; **~содержа́тельный** [14; -лен, -льна] vapid.
ма́л|ость *f* [8] smallness; F trifle; a bit; **~оце́нный** [14; -е́нен, -е́нна] inferior; **~очи́сленный** [14 *sh.*] small (in number), few; **~ый** [14; мал, -а́; *comp.*: ме́ньше] small, little; short; *cf.* ~енький; *su.* fellow, guy; lad; без ~ого almost, just shtor of; ~ и стар young & old; с ~ых лет from (one's) childhood; **~ы́ш** F *m* [1 *e.*] kid(dy).
ма́льч|ик *m* [1] boy; lad; **~и́шеский** [16] boyish; mischievous; **~и́шка** F *m* [5; *g/pl.*: -шек] urchin; greenhorn; **~уга́н** F *m* [1] *s.* малы́ш; *a.* = ~и́шка.
малю́тка *m/f* [5; *g/pl.*: -ток] baby, infant; *fig.* pygmy..., miniature...
маля́р *m* [1 *e.*] (house) painter.
маляри́я *f* [7] malaria.
ма́м|а *f* [5] ma(mma), mum, mother; **~а́ша** F *f* [5], F **~енька** *f* [5; *g/pl.*: -нек] mammy, mummy.
мандари́н *m* [1] mandarin.
манда́т *m* [1] mandate.
ман|ёвр *m* [1], **~еври́ровать** [7] maneuver, manoeuvre; 🚂 shunt, switch; **~еке́н** *m* [1] mannequin.
мане́р|а *f* [5] manner; **~ка** *f* [5; *g/pl.*: -рок] canteen, *Brt.* water bottle; **~ный** [14; -рен, -рна] affected.
манже́т(к)а *f* [5 (*g/pl.*: -ток)] cuff.
манипули́ровать [7] manipulate.
мани́ть [13; маню́, ма́нишь], ⟨по-⟩ (T) beckon; (al)lure, entice, tempt.
ман|и́шка *f* [5; *g/pl.*: -шек] dick(e)y; **2ия** *f* [7] (вели́чия megalo)mania; **~ки́ровать** [7] (*im*)*pf.* (T) neglect.
ма́нная [14]: ~ крупа́ *f* semolina.
мануфакту́ра *f* [5] textiles *pl.*
мара́ть F [1], ⟨за-⟩ soil, stain; ⟨на-⟩ scribble, daub; ⟨вы́-⟩ delete.
ма́рганец *m* [1; -нца] manganese.
маргари́тка *f* [5; *g/pl.*: -ток] daisy.
маринова́ть [7], ⟨за-⟩ pickle.
ма́рк|а *f* [5; *g/pl.*: -рок] stamp; mark; counter; make; brand, trademark; **~и́за** *f* [5] awning; **~си́стский** [16] Marxist, Marxian.
ма́рля *f* [6] gauze.
мармела́д *m* [1] fruit candy (*or* drops).
март *m* [1], **2овский** [16] March.

мар|ты́шка *f* [5; *g/pl.*: -шек] marmoset; '**♀фа** Martha.
марш *m* [1], **~ирова́ть** [7] march; **~ру́т** *m* [1] route.
ма́ск|а *f* [5; *g/pl.*: -сок] mask; **~ара́д** *m* [1] (*a.* бал-~ара́д) masked ball, masquerade; **~ирова́ть** [7], ⟨за-⟩, **~иро́вка** *f* [5; *g/pl.*: -вок] mask; disguise, camouflage.
ма́сл|еница *f* [5] (last week of) carnival; F feast; **~ёнка** *f* [5; *g/pl.*: -нок] butter dish; lubricator; **~е́ный** [14] *s.* ~яный; **~и́на** *f* [5] olive; **~ичный** [14] olive....; oil ...; **~о** *n* [9; *pl.*: -сла́, -сел, -сла́м] (*a.* коро́вье, сли́вочное ~о) butter; (*a.* расти́тельное ~о) oil; как по ~у *fig.* (*go*) on wheels; **~обо́йка** *f* [5; *g/pl.*: -о́ек] churn; oil mill; **~яный** [14] oil(y); butter(y); greasy, unctuous.
ма́сс|а *f* [5] mass; bulk; multitude; **~а́ж** *m* [1], **~и́ровать** [7] (*pt.a.pf.*) massage; **~и́в** *m* [1] massif; **~и́вный** [14; -вен, -вна] massive; **~овый** [14] mass...
ма́стер *m* [1; *pl.*: -ра́, *etc. e.*] master; foreman; craftsman; expert; ~ на все ру́ки jack-of-all-trades; **~и́ть** F [13], ⟨с-⟩ work; make; **~ска́я** *f* [16] workshop; atelier, studio; **~ско́й** [16] masterly (*adv.* ~ски́); **~ство́** *n* [9] mastery, skill; trade, handicraft.
масти́тый [14 *sh.*] venerable.
масть *f* [8; *from g/pl. e.*] colo(u)r; suit.
масшта́б *m* [1] scale (on в П); *fig.* scope; caliber (*Brt.* -bre); repute; standard.
мат *m* [1] mat; (check)mate.
Матве́й *m* [6] Matthew.
математи́|к *m* [1] mathematician; **~ка** *f* [5] mathematics; **~ческий** [16] mathematical.
материа́л *m* [1] material; **~и́зм** *m* [1] materialism; **~и́ст** *m* [1] materialist; **~исти́ческий** [16] materialistic; **~ьный** [14; -лен, -льна] material; economic; financial.
матери́к *m* [1 *e.*] continent.
матери́|нский [16] mother('s), motherly, maternal; **~ство** *n* [9] maternity; **'~я** *f* [7] matter; fabric, material; stuff.
ма́тка *f* [5; *g/pl.*: -ток] *zo.* female; queen (*bee*); *anat.* uterus.
ма́товый [14] dull, dim, mat.
матра́|с, **~ц** *m* [1] mattress.
ма́трица *f* [5] *typ.* matrix; stencil.
матро́с *m* [1] sailor.
матч *m* [1] match (*sport*).
мать *f* [ма́тери, *etc.* = 8; *pl.*: ма́тери, -ре́й, *etc. e.*] mother.
мах *m* [1] stroke, flap; с (одного́) ~у at one stroke *or* stretch; at once; дать ~у miss one's mark, make a blunder; **~а́ть** [3, F 1], *once* ⟨~ну́ть⟩ [20] (T) wave; wag; strike, flap; *pf.* F jump, go; ~ну́ть руко́й на (B) give up; **~ови́к** *m* [1 *e.*], **~ово́** [14]: ~ово́е колесо́ *n* flywheel.
махо́рка *f* [5] (poor) tobacco.
ма́чеха *f* [5] stepmother.
ма́чта *f* [5] mast.
Ма́ш([ень]к)а [5] *dim. of* Мари́я.
маши́н|а *f* [5] machine; engine; car, bike, *etc.*; **~а́льный** [14; -лен, -льна] mechanical, perfunctory; **~и́ст** *m* [1] machinist; 🚂 engineer, *Brt.* engine driver; **~и́стка** *f* [5; *g/pl.*: -ток] (girl) typist; **~ка** *f* [5; *g/pl.*: -нок] (small) machine; typewriter; clipper (под ~ку cropped); **~ный** [14] machine..., engine...; *cf.* МТС; **~опись** *f* [8] typewriting; **~острое́ние** *n* [7] mechanical engineering.
мая́к *m* [1 *e.*] lighthouse.
ма́я|тник *m* [1] pendulum; **~тьс**я P [27] drudge; **~чить** F [16] loom.
МВД *abbr.*: Министе́рство вну́тренних дел (*s.* министе́рство).
мгл|а *f* [5] darkness; mist, haze; **~и́стый** [14 *sh.*] hazy, misty.
мгнове́н|ие *n* [12] moment; instant, twinkling; **~ный** [14; -е́нен, -е́нна] momentary, instantaneous.
ме́б|ель *f* [8] furniture; **~лирова́ть** [7] (*im*)*pf.*, ⟨об-⟩ furnish (with T); **~лиро́вка** *f* [5] furnishing(s).
мёд *m* [1; *part. g.*: мёду; в меду́; *pl. e.*] honey; mead.
меда́ль *f* [8] medal; **~о́н** *m* [1] locket.
медве́|дица *f* [5] she-bear; *ast.* ♀дица Bear; **~дь** *m* [4] bear (F *fig.*); **~жий** [18] bear('s, -skin); bad (*service*); **~жо́нок** *m* [2] bear cub.
ме́ди|к *m* [1] medical man (F student); **~каме́нты** *m/pl.* [1] medicaments, medical supplies; **~ци́на** *f* [5] medicine; **~ци́нский** [16] medical; medicinal.
ме́дл|енный [14 *sh.*] slow; **~и́тельный** [14; -лен, -льна] sluggish, slow, indolent; **~ить** [14], ⟨про-⟩ delay, linger, be slow *or* tardy; hesitate.
ме́дный [14] copper(y); brazen.
медо́вый [14] honey(ed).
мед|осмо́тр *m* [1] medical examination; **~пу́нкт** *m* [1] first-aid post; **~сестра́** *f* [5; *pl. st.*: -сёстры, -сестёр, -сёстрам] nurse.
медь *f* [8] copper; жёлтая ~ brass.
меж *s.* ~ду; **~а́** *f* [5; *pl.*: ме́жи, меж, межа́м] border; balk; **~доме́тие** *n* [12] *gr.* interjection; **~доусо́бный** [14] internal, civil (*war, etc.*).
ме́жду (T; *a.* P *pl.* †) between; among(st); ~ тем meanwhile, (in the) meantime; ~ тем как whereas, while; **~горо́дный** [14] *teleph.* long-distance..., *Brt.* trunk... (*e. g.* exchange, *su. f*)); interurban; **~наро́дный** [14] international; **~ца́рствие** *n* [12] interregnum.
межплане́тный [14] interplanetary.

Ме́ксик|а *f* [5] Mexico; **2а́нец** *m* [1; -нца], **2а́нка** *f* [5; *g/pl.*: -нок], **2а́нский** [16] Mexican.
мел *m* [1; в -у́] chalk; whitewash.
меланхо́л|ик *m* [1] melancholiac; **~и́ческий** [16], **~и́чный** [14; -чен, -чна] melancholy, melancholic; **~ия** *f* [7] melancholy.
меле́ть [8], ⟨об-⟩ (grow) shallow.
ме́лк|ий [16; -лок, -лка́, -о; *comp.*: ме́льче] small, little; petty; fine, shallow; flat (*plate*); ~ий дождь *m* drizzle; **~ово́дный** [14; -ден, -дна] shallow; **~ость** *f* [8], F **~ота́** *f* [8] shallowness; ~ота́ *a.* = ме́лочь *coll.*
мелоди́|ческий [16] melodic; melodious; **~чный** [14; -чен, -чна] melodious; **'~я** *f* [7] melody.
ме́лоч|ность *f* [8] pettiness, paltriness; **~ный** & **~но́й** [14; -чен, -чна] petty, paltry; **~ь** *f* [8; *from g/pl. e.*] trifle; trinket; *coll.* small fry; (small) change; *pl.* details, particulars.
мел|ь *f* [8] shoal, sandbank; на ~и́ aground; F in a fix.
мельк|а́ть [1], ⟨~ну́ть⟩ [20] flash; gleam; flit; fly (past); loom; turn up; **¿ом** in passing.
ме́льни|к *m* [1] miller; **~ца** *f* [5] mill.
мельч|а́ть [1], ⟨из-⟩ become (**~и́ть** [16 *e.*; -чу́, чи́шь] make) small(er) *or* shallow(er).
мелюзга́ F *f* [5] *s.* ме́лочь *coll.*
мемуа́ры *m/pl.* [1] memoirs.
ме́на *f* [5] exchange; barter.
ме́нее less; ~ всего́ least of all; тем не ~ nevertheless.
менов́ой [14] exchange...; *cf.* ме́на.
ме́ньш|е less; smaller; *s. a.* ме́нее; **~еви́к** *m* [1 *e.*] Menshevik; **~ий** [17] smaller, lesser; smallest, least; F (= † **~о́й**) youngest; **~инство́** *n* [9] minority.
меню́ *n* [*indecl.*] menu, bill of fare.
меня́ть [28], ⟨по-, об-⟩ exchange, barter (for на В); change (*cf.* пере~); **-ся** *v/i.* (s. th. with Т/сТ).
ме́р|а *f* [5] measure; degree; way; по ~е (Р) *or* того́ как according as, to (*a.* в ~у Р); as far as; while the ..., the ... (+ *comp.*); по кра́йней (ме́ньшей) ~е at least.
мере́щиться F [16], ⟨по-⟩ (Д) seem (*to hear, etc.*); appear; loom.
мерз|а́вец F *m* [1; -вца] rascal; **¿кий** [16; -зок, -зка́, -о] vile, odious.
мёрз|лый [14] frozen; **~нуть** [21], ⟨за-⟩ freeze; be cold, numb.
ме́рзость *f* [8] meanness; nasty thing.
мери́ло *n* [9] standard; criterion.
ме́рин *m* [1] gelding.
ме́р|ить [13], ⟨с-⟩ measure; ⟨при-, по-⟩ F try on; **~иться,** ⟨по-⟩ cope, try conclusions with (с Т); **~ка** *f* [5; *g/pl.*: -рок] measure(s) (to по Д).
ме́ркнуть [21], ⟨по-⟩ fade, darken.
мерлу́шка *f* [5; *g/pl.*: -шек] astrakhan.
ме́р|ный [14; -рен, -рна] measured; **~оприя́тие** *n* [12] measure, action.
ме́ртв|енный [14 *sh.*] deadly (pale); **~е́ть** [8], ⟨о-⟩ deaden; grow *or* turn numb (pale, desolate); **~е́ц** *m* [1 *e.*] corpse; **~е́цкая** F *f* [14] mortuary.
мёртв|ый [14; мёртв, мертва́, мёртво; *fig.:* мертво́, мертвы́] dead; ~ый час *m* after-dinner rest; ~ая то́чка *f* ⊕ dead center; *fig.* deadlock (at на П).
мерца́|ние *n* [12], **~ть** [1] twinkle.
меси́ть [15], ⟨за-, с-⟩ knead.
мести́ [25 -т-: мету́, метёшь; мётший], ⟨под-⟩ sweep.
ме́стн|ость *f* [8] region, district, locality, place; **~ый** [14] local; ~ый жи́тель *m* native.
ме́ст|о *n* [9; *pl. e.*] place, spot; seat; F job, post; passage; package; *pl. a.* = ~ность; о́бщее (*or* изби́тое) ~о commonplace; (заде́ть за) больно́е ~о tender spot (touch on the raw); (не) к ~у in (out of) place; не на ~е in the wrong place; ~а́ми in (some) places, here & there; **~ожи́тельство** *n* [9] residence; **~оиме́ние** *n* [12] *gr.* pronoun; **~онахожде́ние, ~оположе́ние** *n* [12] location, position; **~опребыва́ние** *n* [12] whereabouts; residence; **~орожде́ние** *n* [12] deposit, field.
месть *f* [8] revenge.
ме́ся|ц *m* [1] month; moon; в ~ц a month, per month; **~чный** [14] month's; monthly; moon...
мета́лл *m* [1] metal; **~и́ст** *m* [1] metalworker; **~и́ческий** [16] metal(lic); **~у́ргия** *f* [7] metallurgy.
мет|а́тельный [14] missile; **~а́ть** [3], *once* ⟨~ну́ть⟩ [20] throw; bring forth; keep (*bank*); baste; ~а́ть икру́ spawn; **-ся** toss, jerk; rush about.
мете́л|ица *f* [5], **~ь** [8] snowstorm.
метеоро́лог *m* [1] meteorologist; **~и́ческий** [16] meteorological; **¿ия** *f* [7] meteorology.
ме́т|ить [15], ⟨по-⟩ mark; (в, на В) aim, drive at, mean; **~ка** [5; *g/pl.*: -ток] mark(ing); **~кий** [16; -ток, -тка́, -о] well-aimed; good (*shot*); keen, accurate, steady; pointed; neat; ready(-witted).
мет|ла́ *f* [5; *pl. st.*: мётлы, мётел; мётлам] broom; **~ну́ть** *s.* мета́ть.
ме́тод *m* [1] method; **~и́ческий** [16] methodic(al), systematic(al).
метр *m* [1] meter, *Brt.* metre.
ме́трика *f* [5] certificate of birth; metrics.
метро́ *n* [*ind.*], **~полите́н** (-ˈtɛn) *m* [1] subway, *Brt.* tube, underground.
мех *m* [1] **1.** [*pl. e.*] (*often pl.*) bellows *pl.*; **2.** [*pl.*: -ха́, *etc.*, *e.*] fur; (wine)skin; на ~у́ fur-lined.
механ|изи́ровать [7] (*im*)*pf.* mechanize; **~и́зм** *m* [1] mechanism; **¿ик**

m [1] mechanic(ian); **∠ика** *f* [5] mechanics; **~и́ческий** [16] mechanical propelling (*pencil*).
мехов|о́й [14] fur...; **~щи́к** *m* [1 *e*.] furrier.
меч *m* [1 *e*.] sword.
мече́ть *f* [8] mosque.
мечта́ *f* [5] dream, daydream, reverie; **~ние** *n* [12] **1.** = ~; **2.** dreaming; **~тель** *m* [4] (day)dreamer; **~тельный** [14; -лен, -льна] dreamy; **~ть** [1] dream (of о П).
меша́|ть [1], ⟨раз-⟩ stir; ⟨с-, пере-⟩ mix, mingle; † confuse; ⟨по-⟩ (Д) disturb; hinder, impede, prevent; вам не ~ет (~ло бы) you'd better; **-ся** meddle, interfere (with в В); не ~йтесь не в своё де́ло! mind your own business!
ме́шк|ать F [1], ⟨про-⟩ = ме́длить; **~ова́тый** [14 *sh*.] baggy; clumry.
мешо́к *m* [1; -шка́] sack, bag.
мещан|и́н *m* [1; *pl*.: -а́не, -а́н], **∠ский** [16] (petty) bourgeois, Philistine; **∠ство** *n* [9] petty bourgeoisie, lower-middle class; Philistinism, Babbittry.
миг *m* [1] moment, instant; ∠ом F in a trice (flash); **~а́ть** [1], *once* ⟨~ну́ть⟩ [20] blink, wink; twinkle.
мигре́нь *f* [8] sick headache.
мизе́рный [14; -рен, -рна] paltry.
мизи́нец *m* [1; -нца] little finger.
ми́ленький F [16] lovely; dear; darling.
милици|оне́р *m* [1] militiaman; policeman (*Sov*.); **'~я** *f* [7] militia; police (*Sov*.).
милли|а́рд *m* [1] billion, *Brt*. milliard; **~ме́тр** *m* [1] millimeter (*Brt*. -tre); **~о́н** *m* [1] million.
ми́ловать [7] pardon; spare.
мило|ви́дный [14; -ден, -дна] lovely, sweet; **~се́рдие** *n* [12] charity, mercy; **~се́рдный** [14; -ден, -дна] charitable, merciful; **'~стивый** [14 *sh*.] gracious, kind; **'~стыня** *f* [6] alms; **'~сть** *f* [8] mercy; favo(u)r; pardon, ⚔ quarter; kindness; '~сти про́сим! welcome!; *iron*. скажи́(те) на '~сть just imagine.
ми́л|ый [14; мил, -а́, -о] nice, lovely, sweet; (my) dear, darling.
ми́ля *f* [6] mile.
ми́мо (P) past, by; beside (*mark*); бить ~ miss; **~лётный** [14; -тен, -тна] fleeting, passing; **~хо́дом** in passing; incidentally.
ми́на *f* [5] ⚔, ⚒ mine; look, air.
минда́|лина *f* [5] almond; *anat*. tonsil; **~ль** *m* [4 *e*.] almond(s); **~льничать** F [1] spoon; trifle.
минерало́гия *f* [7] mineralogy.
миниатю́рный [14; -рен, -рна] miniature...; *fig*. tiny, diminutive.
минист|е́рство *n* [9] ministry; ~е́рство иностра́нных (вну́тренних) дел Ministry of Foreign (Internal) Affairs (*U.S.S.R.*), State Department (Dept. of the Interior) (*U.S.*), Foreign (Home) Office (*Brt*.); **∠р** *m* [1] minister, secretary.
мин|ова́ть [7] (*im*)*pf*., ⟨~у́ть⟩ [20] pass; leave out *or* aside, not enter into; (P) escape; (Д) ∠уло *s*. испо́лниться; ~у́вший, ~у́вшее *su*. past.
миноно́сец *m* [1; -сца] torpedo boat; эска́дренный ~ destroyer.
ми́нус *m* [1] minus; defect.
мину́т|а *f* [5] minute; moment, instant (at в В; for на В); сию́ ~у at once, immediately; at this moment; с ~ы на ~у (at) any moment; *cf*. пя́тый & пять; **~ный** [14] minute('s); moment('s), momentary; **~ь** *s*. минова́ть.
мир *m* [1] **1.** peace; **2.** [*pl*. *e*.] world, universe; planet; † (peasants') community (meeting); ~ во всём ∠е world peace; ходи́ть (пусти́ть) по́ ~у go begging (bring to beggary).
мир|и́ть [13], ⟨по-, при-⟩ reconcile (to с Т); **-ся** make it up, be(come) reconciled; ⟨при-⟩ resign o.s. to; put up with; **∠ный** [14; -рен, -рна] peace... peaceful.
мировоззре́ние *n* [12] Weltanschauung, world view; ideology.
мирово́й [14] world('s), world-wide, universal; peaceful, peaceable, of peace; F *su*. *f* arrangement.
миро|люби́вый [14 *sh*.] peaceful; peace loving; **~созерца́ние** *n* [12] world view, outlook.
мирско́й [16] worldly; common.
ми́ска *f* [5; *g*/*pl*.: -сок] dish, tureen; bowl.
мисси|оне́р *m* [1] missionary; **'~я** *f* [7] mission; legation.
ми́стика *f* [5] mysticism.
Ми́тя *m* [6] *dim*. *of* Дми́трий.
миф *m* [1] myth; **~и́ческий** [16] mythic(al); **~оло́гия** *f* [7] mythology.
Ми|ха́ил *m* [1] Michael; **∠ша** *m* [5] (*dim*. *of* ~ха́ил) Mike.
мише́нь *f* [8] target.
мишура́ *f* [5] tinsel, spangle.
младе́н|ец *m* [1; -нца] infant, baby; **~чество** *n* [9] infancy.
мла́дший [17] younger, youngest; junior.
млекопита́ющее *n* [17] mammal.
мле́ть [8] die, faint, sink, droop.
мле́чный [14] milky (*a*. ♀, *ast*.).
мне́ние *n* [12] opinion (in по Д).
мни́|мый [14 *sh*., *no m*] imaginary; supposed, pretended, would-be, sham; **~тельный** [14; -лен, -льна] suspicious; hypochondriac(al).
мно́гие *pl*. [16] many (people, *su*.)
мно́го (P) much, many; a lot (*or* plenty) of; more; ~-~ at (the) most; **~ва́то** F rather much (many) **~во́дный** [14; -ден, -дна] abounding in water, deep; **~гра́нный** [14; -а́нен, -а́нна] many-sided

~жёнство *n* [9] polygamy; **~значи́тельный** [14; -лен, -льна] significant; **~зна́чный** [14; -чен, -чна] of many places (⅄) *or* meanings; **~кра́тный** [14; -тен, -тна] repeated, frequent(ative *gr.*); ⅄ multiple; **~ле́тний** [15] longstanding, of many years; long-lived; long-term ...; ⚘ perennial; **~лю́дный** [14; -ден, -дна] crowded; populous; mass ...; **~обеща́ющий** [17] (very) promising; **~обра́зный** [14; -зен, -зна] varied, manifold; **~речи́вый** [14 *sh.*], **~сло́вный** [14; -вен, -вна] talkative; wordy; **~сторо́нний** [15; -о́нен, -о́ння] many-sided; **~страда́льный** [14; -лен, -льна] long-suffering; **~то́чие** *n* [12] dots *pl.*; **~уважа́емый** [14] dear (*address*); **~цве́тный** [14; -тен, -тна] multicolo(u)red; **~числе́нный** [14 *sh.*] numerous; **~эта́жный** [14] many-storied (*Brt.*-reyed); **~язы́чный** [14; -чен, -чна] polyglot.

мно́ж|ественный [14 *sh.*] plural; **~ество** *n* [9] multitude; **~имое** *n* [14] multiplicand; **~итель** *m* [4] multiplier; **~ить,** ⟨по-⟩ *s.* умножа́ть.

мобилизова́ть [7] (*im*)*pf.* mobilize.

моги́л|а *f* [5] grave; **~ьный** [14] tomb...; **~ьщик** *m* [1] grave digger.

могу́|чий [17 *sh.*], **~щественный** [14 *sh.*] mighty, powerful; **~щество** *n* [9] might.

мо́д|а *f* [5] fashion, vogue; **~е́ль** (-ˈdɛl) *f* [8] model; ⊕ mo(u)ld; **~ернизи́ровать** (-dɛr-) [7] (*im*)*pf.* modernize; **~и́стка** *f* [5; *g*/*pl.*: -ток] milliner; **~ифици́ровать** [7] (*im*-)*pf.* modify; **~ный** [14; -ден, -дна́, -о] fashionable, stylish; [*no sh.*] fashion...

мо́ж|ет быть perhaps, maybe; **~но** (мне, *etc.*) one (I, *etc.*) can *or* may; it is possible; *cf.* как.

моза́ика *f* [5] mosaic.

мозг *m* [1; -а (-у); в -у́; *pl. e.*] brain; marrow; (*spinal*) cord; **~ово́й** [14] cerebral.

мозо́|листый [14 *sh.*] horny, callous; **~лить** [13]: ~лить глаза́ (Д) F be an eyesore to; **~ль** *f* [8] callosity; corn.

мо|й *m*, ~я́ *f*, ~ё *n*, ~и́ *pl.* [24] my; mine; *pl. su.* F my folks; *s.* ваш.

мо́кко *m* [*ind.*] mocha.

мо́к|нуть [21], ⟨про-⟩ become wet; soak; **~ро́та**[1] *f* [5] phleghm; **~рота́**[2] F *f* [5] wet(ness), humidity; **~рый** [14; мокр, -а́, -о] wet; moist.

мол *m* [1] jetty, mole.

молв|а́ *f* [5] rumo(u)r; talk; **~́ить** † [14] (*im*)*pf.*, ⟨про-⟩ say, utter.

молдава́н|ин *m* [1; *pl.*: -ва́не, -а́н], **~ка** *f* [5; *g*/*pl.*: -нок] Moldavian.

моле́бен *m* [1; -бна] thanksgiving (service), Te Deum.

моле́кул|а *f* [5] molecule; **~я́рный** [14] molecular.

моли́т|ва *f* [5] prayer; **~венник** *m* [1] prayer book; **~ь** [13; молю́, мо́лишь] (о П) implore (s. th.), entreat, beseech (for); **~ься,** ⟨по-⟩ pray (to Д; for о П).

молни|ено́сный [14; -сен, -сна] flash-like; blazing; thunder (*cloud*); violent; ⚔ blitz...; **ʹ~я** *f* [7] lightning; flash; zipper, zip fastener.

молод|ёжь *f* [8] youth, young people *pl.*; **~е́ть** [8], ⟨по-⟩ grow (look) younger; **~е́ц** F *m* [1; -дца́] fine fellow, brick; well done!; **~е́цкий** F [16] brave, valiant; smart; **~и́ть** [15 *e.*; -ложу́, -лоди́шь] rejuvenate; **~ня́к** *m* [1 *e.*] offspring; underwood; saplings *pl.*; **~ожёны** *m*/*pl.* [1] newly wedded couple; **~о́й** [14; мо́лод, -а́, -о; *comp.*: моло́же] young; new; *pl. a.* = ~ожёны; **ʹ~ость** *f* [8] youth, adolescence; **~цева́тый** [14 *sh.*] smart.

моложа́вый [14 *sh.*] youthful, young-looking.

моло́к|и *f*/*pl.* [5] milt; **~о́** *n* [9] milk; **~осо́с** F *m* [1] greenhorn.

мо́лот *m* [1] (large) hammer; **~и́лка** *f* [5; *g*/*pl.*: -лок] threshing machine; **~и́ть** [15], ⟨с-⟩ thresh; **~о́к** *m* [1; -тка́] hammer; с ~ка́ by auction; **~́ь** [17; мелю́, ме́лешь; меля́], ⟨пере-, с-⟩ grind; P *impf.* talk; **~ьба́** *f* [5] threshing (time).

моло́чн|ая *f* [14] dairy, creamery; **~ик** *m* [1] milk jug; F milkman; **~ый** [14] milk...; dairy...

мо́лча silently, tacitly; **~ли́вый** [14 *sh.*] taciturn; **~́ние** *n* [12] silence; **~́ть** [4 *e.*; мо́лча], be (*or* keep) silent; (за)молчи́! shut up!

моль *f* [8]moth; [*ind. adj.*] ♪ minor.

мольба́ *f* [5] entreaty; prayer.

моме́нт *m* [1] moment, instant (at в В); **~а́льный** [14] momentary, instantaneous; snap (*shot*).

мона́рхия *f* [7] monarchy.

мона|сты́рь *m* [4 *e.*] monastery, convent; **~́х** *m* [1] monk; **~́хиня** *f* [6] nun (*a.*, F, **~́шенка** *f* [5; *g*/*pl.*: -нок]); **~́шеский** [16] monastic; monk's.

монго́льский [16] Mongolian.

моне́т|а *f* [5] coin; money, cash; той же ~ой in a p.'s own coin; за чи́стую ~у in good faith; **~ный** [14] monetary; ~ный двор *m* mint.

моно|ло́г *m* [1] monologue; **~полизи́ровать** [7] (*im*)*pf.* monopolize; **~по́лия** *f* [7] monopoly; **~то́нный** [14; -то́нен, -то́нна] monotonous.

монт|а́ж *m* [1] assembling, assemblage; cutting (*film*); montage; **~ёр** *m* [1] assembler, mechanic(ian); electrician; **~и́ровать** [7], ⟨с-⟩ assemble, install; cut (*film*).

мора́ль *f* [8] morals *pl.*; morality; moral; F lecture, lecturing; **~ный**

[14; -лен, -льна] moral; ~ное состояние *n* morale.
морг|áть [1], ‹~нýть› [20] blink} **мóрда** *f* [5] muzzle, snout. [(T).}
мóре *n* [10; *pl. e.*] sea; seaside (at на П); ~м by sea; зá ~м overseas; **~плáвание** *n* [12] navigation; **~плáватель** *m* [4] seafarer.
морж *m* [1 *e.*], **~óвый** [14] walrus.
мори́ть [13], ‹за-, у-› exterminate; ~ гóлодом starve; torment, exhaust.
моркóвь *f* [8] carrot(s).
морóженое *n* [14] ice cream.
морóз *m* [1] frost; **~ить** [15], ‹за-› freeze; **~ный** [14; -зен, -зна] frosty.
мороси́ть [15; -си́т] drizzle.
морóчить F [16] fool, beguile.
морск|óй [14] sea..., maritime; naval; nautical; seaside...; ~óй волк *m* old salt; ~óй флот *m* navy.
мóрфий *m* [3] morphine, morphia.
морфолóгия *f* [7] morphology.
морщи́|на *f* [5] wrinkle; **~нистый** [14 *sh.*] wrinkled; **'~ть** [16], ‹на-, с-› wrinkle, frown (*v/i.* **-ся**); distort.
моря́к *m* [1 *e.*] seaman, sailor.
москатéльный [14] drug(gist's).
Москв|á *f* [5] Moscow; **♀ви́ч** *m* [1 *e.*] **♀ви́чка** *f* [5; *g/pl.*: -чек] Moscower; **♀óвский** [16] Moscow...
моски́т *m* [1] mosquito.
мост *m* [1 & 1 *e.*; на -ý; *pl. e.*] bridge; **~и́ть** [15 *e.*; мощý, мости́шь; мощённый], ‹вы́-› pave; **~ки́** *m/pl.* [1 *e.*] planked footway, footbridge; **~овáя** *f* [14] pavement; **~овóй** [14] bridge...; **~овщи́к** *m* [1 *e.*] pavio(u)r.
мот *m* [1] spendthrift, prodigal.
мот|áть [1], ‹на-, с-› reel, wind; F ‹по-›, *once* ‹~нýть› shake, wag; beckon, point; jerk; F ‹про-› squander, waste; **-ся** F *impf* dangle; P knock about.
моти́в *m* [1] motiv, motif; **~и́ровать** [7] (*im*)*pf.* motivate.
мотовствó *n* [9] extravagance.
motóк *m* [1; -ткá] skein.
motóр *m* [1] motor, engine; **~изовáть** [7] (*im*)*pf.* motorize.
мотоци́кл, ~éт *m* [1], motorcycle; **~и́ст** *m* [1] motorcyclist.
моты́га *f* [8] hoe, mattock.
мотылёк [1; -лькá] butterfly.
мох *m* [1; мха & мóха, во (на) мхý; *pl.*: мхи, мхов] moss.
мохнáтый [14 *sh.*] shaggy, hairy.
моховóй [14] mossy.
моч|á *f* [5] urine; **~áлка** *f* [5; *g/pl.*: -лок] bast whisp; **~евóй** [14]: ~евóй пузы́рь *m* (urinary) bladder; **~и́ть** [16], ‹на-, за-› wet, moisten; soak, step (*v/i.* **-ся**; *a.* urinate); **~ка** *f* [5; *g/pl.*: -чек] lobe (*of the ear*).
мочь[1] [26 г/ж: могý, мóжешь, мóгут; мог, -лá; могýщий], ‹с-› can, be able; may; я не могý не + *inf.* I can't help ...ing; не могý знать ... I don't know (,sir); не мóжет быть! that's impossible!
моч|ь[2] P *f* [8]: во всю ~ь, изо всей ~и, что есть ~и with all one's might ~и нет impossible, I, *etc.*, can't awfully.
мошéнни|к *m* [1] swindler, chea(-er); **~чать** [1], ‹с-› swindle; **~ческий** [16] fraudulent; **~чество** [9] swindle, fraud.
мóшка *f* [5; *g/pl.*: -шек] midge.
мощёный [14] paved.
мóщи *f/pl.* [*gen.*: -щéй, *etc. e.*] relics
мóщ|ность *f* [8] power; **~ный** [14 мóщен, -щнá, -o] powerful, mighty **~ь** *f* [8] power, might; strength.
м. пр. *abbr.*: мéжду прóчим.
мрак *m* [1] dark(ness); gloom.
мракобéс *m* [1] obscurant; **~ие** [12] obscurantism.
мрáмор *m* [1] marble.
мрачн|éть [8], ‹по-› darken; **~ый** [14; -чен, -чнá, -o] dark; obscure gloomy, somber (*Brt.*-bre).
мсти́|тель *m* [4] avenger; **~тельный** [14; -лен, -льна] revengeful **~ть** [15], ‹ото-› revenge o.s., take revenge (on Д); (за В) avenge a p.
МТС (маши́нно-трáкторная стáнция) machine and tractor station.
мудр|ёный F [14; -ён, -енá; -енée difficult, hard, intricate; fanciful queer; ~ёного нет (it's) no wonder **~éц** *m* [1 *e.*] sage; **~и́ть** F [13], ‹на-, с-› subtilize; quibble; trick; (на Т) bully; **~ость** *f* [8] wisdom; зу ~ости wisdom tooth; F trick; **~ствовать** F [7] *s.* ~и́ть; **~ый** [14; мудр -á, -o] wise, sage.
муж *m* **1.** [1; *pl.*: -жья́, -жéй -жья́м] husband; **2.** † [1; *pl.*: -жи́ -жéй, -жáм] man; **~áть** [1], ‹воз-› mature, grow; **-ся** *impf.* take courage; **~ественный** [14 *sh.*] courageous; manly; **~ество** *n* [9] courage spirit; **~и́к** † *m* [1 *e.*] peasant; boor; man; **~и́цкий** [16], P **~и́чий** [18] peasant's, rustic; **~скóй** [16 male, (*a. gr.*) masculine; (gentleman('s); **~чи́на** *m* [5] man.
музéй *m* [3] museum.
мýзык|а *f* [5] music; P business **~áльный** [14; -лен, -льна] musical; **~áнт** *m* [1] musician.
мýка[1] *f* [5] pain, torment, suffering torture(s); F harassment.
мукá[2] *f* [5] flour; meal.
мул *m* [1] mule.
мýмия *f* [7] mummy.
мунди́р *m* [1] uniform; картóшка в ~е F potatoes in their jackets *or* skin
мундштýк (-nʃ-) *m* [1 *e.*] cigarette holder; tip; mouthpiece.
муравá *f* [5] (young) grass; glaze.
мурав|éй *m* [3; -вья́; *pl.*: -вьи́ -вьёв] ant; **~éйник** *m* [1] ant hill **~ьи́ный** [14] ant...
мурáшки: (от P) ~ бéгают по спин (у P) F (s. th.) gives (a p.) the shivers
мурлы́кать [3 & 1] purr; F hum.
мускáт *m* [1], **~ный** [14] nutmeg.

му́скул *m* [1] muscle; **~истый** [14 *sh.*], **~ьный** [14] muscular.
му́скус *m* [1] musk.
му́сор *m* [1] rubbish, refuse; **~ный** [14]: ~ный я́щик *m* ash can, *Brt.* dust bin; **~щик** *m* [1] ashman.
муссо́н *m* [1] monsoon.
мусульма́н|ин *m* [1; *pl.*: -а́не, -а́н], **~ка** *f* [5; *g/pl.:* -нок] Moslem.
мут|и́ть [15; мучу́, му́ти́шь], ⟨вз-, по-⟩ trouble, muddle; fog; меня́ ~и́т F I feel sick; **-ся** = **~не́ть** [8], ⟨по-⟩ grow turbid; blur; **~́ный** [14; -тен, -тна́, -о] muddy, (*a. fig.*) troubled (*waters*); dull; blurred; foggy; uneasy; **~о́вка** *f* [5; *g/pl.*: -вок] twirling stick; **~ь** *f* [8] dregs *pl.*; mud; blur; haze; dazzle.
му́фта *f* [5] muff; ⊕ socket, sleeve.
му́х|а *f* [5] fly; **~оло́вка** *f* [5; *g/pl.*: -вок] flycatcher; **~омо́р** *m* [1] toadstool.
муч|е́ние *n* [12] *s.* му́ка; **~́еник** *m* [1] martyr; **~и́тель** *m* [4] tormentor; **~и́тельный** [14; -лен, -льна] painful, agonizing; **~́ить** [16], P **~́ать** [1], ⟨за-, из-⟩ torment, torture; vex, worry; **-ся** agonize, suffer torments; toil; **~но́й** [14] flour(y), mealy.
му́шка *f* [5; *g/pl.*: -шек] midge; beauty spot; speck; (Spanish) fly; (fore)sight (*gun*).
муштр(о́вк)а́ ⚔ *f* [5] drill.
мчать(ся) [4], ⟨по-⟩ rush, whirl *or* speed (along).
мши́стый [14 *sh.*] mossy.
мще́ние *n* [12] vengeance.
мы [20] we; ~ с ним he and I.
мы́л|ить [13], ⟨на-⟩ soap; ~ить го́лову (Д) F blow up, scold; **~о** *n* [9; *pl. e.*] soap; lather; **~оваре́ние** *n* [12] soap boiling; **~ьница** *f* [5] soap dish; **~ьный** [14] soap(y).
мыс *m* [1] cape.
мысл|енный [14] mental; **~имый** [14 *sh.*] conceivable; **~и́тель** *m* [4] thinker; **~ить** [13] think (of, about о П); imagine; **~ь** *f* [8] thought, idea (of о П); intention.
мыта́рство *n* [9] toil, drudgery.
мыть(ся) [22], ⟨по-, у-, вы́-⟩ wash.
мыча́ть [4 *e.*; -чу́, -чи́шь] moo, low; F mumble.
мышело́вка *f* [5; *g/pl.*: -вок] mouse trap.
мы́шечный [14] muscular.
мы́шка *f* [5; *g/pl.*: -шек] **1.** armpit; arm; **2.** *dim. of* мышь.
мышле́ние *n* [12] thougt, thinking.
мы́шца *f* [5] muscle.
мышь *f* [8; *from g/pl. e.*] mouse.
мышья́к *m* [1 *e.*] arsenic.
мя́гк|ий (-xk-) [16; -гок, -гка́, -о; *comp.*: мя́гче] soft; smooth, sleek; tender; mild, gentle; lenient; easy (*chair*); ~ий ваго́н 🚂 first-class coach *or* car(riage); **~осерде́чный** [14; -чен, -чна] soft-hearted; **~ость** *f* [8] softness; **~оте́лый** [14] chubby; *fig.* fladdy, spineless.
мягчи́|тельный (-xtʃ-) [14] lenitive; **~ть** [16; -чи́т] soften.
мяк|и́на *f* [5] chaff; **~́иш** *m* [1] crumb; **~́нуть** [21], ⟨на-, раз-⟩ become soft; **~́оть** *f* [8] flesh, pulp.
мя́млить P [13] mumble; dawdle.
мяс|и́стый [14 *sh.*] fleshy, pulpy; F fat, chubby; **~ни́к** *m* [1 *e.*] butcher; **~но́й** [14] meat...; butcher's; **~́о** *n* [9] meat; flesh, pulp; (*cannon*) fodder; **~oру́бка** *f* [5; *g/pl.*: -бок] mincing machine; *fig.* slaughter.
мя́та *f* [8] mint.
мяте́ж *m* [1 *e.*] rebellion, mutiny; **~ник** *m* [1] rebel; **~ный** [14] rebellious.
мять [мну, мнёшь; мя́тый], ⟨с-, по-, из-⟩ [сомну́; изомну́] (c)rumple, press; knead, wrinkle; trample; **-ся** F waver.
мяу́к|ать [1], *once* ⟨~нуть⟩ mew.
мяч *m* [1 *e.*] ball; **~́ик** [1] *dim. of* ~.

Н

на¹ 1. (В): (*direction*) on, onto; to, toward(s); into, in; (*duration, value, purpose, etc.*) for; till; ✗ by; ~ что? what for?; **2.** (П): (*position*) on, upon; in, at; with; for; ~ ней ... she has ... on.
на́² F there, here (you are, *a.* ~́ тебе).
наба́в|ка F = надба́вка; **~ля́ть** [28], ⟨~ить⟩ [14] raise; add.
наба́т *m* [1] alarm bell, tocsin.
набе́|г *m* [1] incursion, raid; **~га́ть** [1], ⟨~жа́ть⟩ [4; -егу́, -ежи́шь, -егу́т; -еги́(те)!] run (against *or* on на В); cover; gather.
набекре́нь F aslant, cocked.
на́бело (*make*) a fair copy.
на́бережная *f* [14] quay, wharf.
наби|ва́ть [1], ⟨~́ть⟩ [-бью́, -бьёшь; *cf.* бить] stuff, fill; fix on (*a.* many, much); shoot; print (*calico*); **~́вка** *f* [5; *g/pl.:* -вок] stuffing, padding.
набира́ть [1], ⟨набра́ть⟩ [-беру́, -рёшь; *cf.* брать] gather; enlist, recruit; *teleph.* dial; *typ.* set; take (too many, much); gain (*speed, height*); be, have; **-ся** *a.*, (P), pluck *or* screw up; F catch; acquire.
наби́|тый [14 *sh.*] (T) packed; P arrant (*fool*); битко́м ~тый F crammed full; **~ть** *s.* ~ва́ть.
наблюд|а́тель *m* [4] observer; **~а́тельный** [14; -лен, -льна] observant, alert; observation (*post*); **~а́ть** [1] (*v/t.* & за Т) observe; watch;

see after *or* to (it that); **\~éние** *n* [12] observation; supervision.
нáбожный [14; -жен, -жна] pious, devout.
нáбок to *or* on one side.
наболéвший [16] sore; burning.
набóр *m* [1] enlistment, levy; enrol(l)ment; set; typesetting; taking; **\~щик** *m* [1] typesetter, compositor.
набр|áсывать [1] **1.** ⟨\~осáть⟩ [1] sketch, design, draft; throw (up); **2.** ⟨\~óсить⟩ [15] throw over, on (на В); **-ся** fall (up)on.
набрáть *s.* набирáть.
набрести́ F [25] *pf.* come across (на В).
набрóсок *m* [1; -ска] sketch, draft.
набух|áть [1], ⟨\~нуть⟩ [21] swell.
навáл|ивать [1], ⟨\~и́ть⟩ [13; -алю́, -áлишь; -áленный] heap; load; **-ся** press; fall (up)on, go at.
навéд|ываться, ⟨\~аться⟩ F [1] call on (к Д); inquire after, about (о П).
навéк, \~и forever, for good.
навéрн|о(е) probably; for certain, definitely; (*a.*, F, **\~якá**) without fail.
навёрстывать, ⟨наверстáть⟩ [1] make up for.
навéрх up(ward[s]); upstairs; **\~ý** above, on high; upstairs.
навéс *m* [1] awning; shed.
навеселé F tipsy, drunk.
навести́ *s.* наводи́ть.
навести́ть *s.* навещáть.
навéтренный [14] windward.
навéчно forever, for good.
наве|щáть[1], ⟨\~сти́ть⟩[15*e.*; -ещý, -ести́шь; -ещённый] call on.
нáвзничь on one's back.
навзры́д: плáкать \~ sob.
навис|áть [1], ⟨\~нуть⟩ [21] hang (over); impend; \~ший beetle (*brow*).
навле|кáть [1], ⟨\~чь⟩ [26] incur.
наводи́ть [15], ⟨навести́⟩ [25] (на В) direct (to); point (at), turn (to); lead (to), bring on *or* about, cause, raise (*cf.* нагоня́ть); apply (*paint, etc.*); make; construct; \~ спрáвки inquire (after о П).
наводн|éние *n* [12] flood, inundation; **\~я́ть** [28], ⟨\~и́ть⟩ [13] flood, inundate.
наводя́щий [17] leading.
навóз *m* [1], **\~ить** [15], ⟨у-⟩ dung, manure; **\~ный** [14] dung...; \~ная жи́жа *f* liquid manure.
нáволочка *f* [5; *g/pl.*: -чек] pillowcase.
навостри́ть [13] *pf.* prick up (*one's ears*).
навря́д (ли) F hardly, scarcely.
навсегдá forever; (*once*) for all.
навстрéчу toward(s); идти́ \~ (Д) go to meet; *fig.* meet halfway.
навы́ворот P topsy-turvy, inside out, wrongly; дéлать ши́ворот-\~ put the cart before the horse.
нáвык *m* [1] experience, skill (in к Д, на В, в П); habit.
навы́кат(е) goggle (*eye*[*d*]).
навы́лет (*shot*) through.
навы́тяжку at attention.
навя́з|ывать [1], ⟨\~áть⟩ [3] tie (to on на В), fasten; knit; impose obtrude ([up]on Д; *v/i.* **-ся**); **\~чивый** [14 *sh.*] obtrusive; fixed.
нагáйка *f* [5; *g/pl.*: -гáек] whip.
нагáр *m* [1] snuff (*candle*).
наг|ибáть [1], ⟨\~нýть⟩ [20] bend bow, stoop (*v/i.* **-ся**).
нагишóм F naked, nude.
наглáзник *m* [1] blinder.
нагл|éц *m* [1 *e.*] impudent fellow **\~ость** *f* [8] impudence, insolence **\~ухо** tightly; **\~ый** [14; нагл, -á, -о] impudent, insolent, F cheeky.
нагляд|éться [11] *pf.* (на В) feast one's eyes (upon); не \~éться never get tired of looking (at); **\~ный** [14 -ден, -дна] vivid, graphic; obvious direct; object (*lesson*); visual (*aid*).
нагнáть *s.* нагоня́ть.
нагнетá|тельный [14] force (*pump*); **\~ть** [1], ⟨нагнести́⟩ [25 -т-] pump.
нагноéние *n* [12] suppuration.
нагнýть *s.* нагибáть.
нагов|áривать [1], ⟨\~ори́ть⟩ [13] say, tell, talk ([too] much *or* many ...); F slander (a p. на В, о П); conjure; record; **\~ори́ться** *pf.* talk one's fill; не \~ори́ться never get tired of talking. [bare.]
нагóй [14; наг, -á, -о] nude, naked,
нáгол|о clean(-*shaven*); **\~ó** naked.
нáголову (*defeat*) totally.
нагон|я́й F *m* [3] blowup; **\~я́ть** [28] ⟨нагнáть⟩ [-гоню́, -гóнишь; *cf* гнать] overtake, catch up (with), make up (for); drive (together); F \~я́ть страх, скýку, *etc.* (на В) frighten, bore, *etc.*
наготá *f* [5] nudity; bareness.
нагот|áвливать [1] [28], ⟨\~óвить⟩ [14] prepare; lay in; **\~óве** (at the) ready.
нагрáбить [14] *pf.* rob, plunder (a lot of).
награ́|да *f* [5] reward (as a в В), recompense; decoration; **\~ждáть** [1], ⟨\~ди́ть⟩ [15 *e.*; -ажý, -ади́шь; -аждённый] (Т) reward; decorate *fig.* endow.
нагревáт|ельный [14] heating; **\~ь** [1], *s.* греть.
нагромо|ждáть [1], ⟨\~зди́ть⟩ [15 *e.*; -зжý, -зди́шь; -ождённый] pile up.
нагрýдник *m* [1] bib; plastron.
нагру|жáть [1], ⟨\~зи́ть⟩ [15 & 15 *e.*; -ужý, -ýзи́шь; -ужённый] load (with Т); F *a.* burden, busy, assign (*work to*); **\~зка** *f* [5; *g/pl.*: -зок] load(ing); F *a.* burden, job, assignment.
нагря́нуть [20] *pf.* appear, come (upon) suddenly, unawares; break out (*war*); take by surprise (на В).

ад, ~о (Т) over, above; at; about; with.

адáв|ливать [1], ⟨~и́ть⟩ [14] (*a.* на В) press; push; press out (much).

адбáв|ка *f* [5; *g/pl.:* -вок] raise, increase; extra charge; **~ля́ть** [28], ⟨~ить⟩ [14] F, *s.* набавля́ть.

адви|гáть [1], ⟨∠нуть⟩ [20] push; pull; **-ся** approach, draw near; cover.

áдвое in two (parts *or* halves).

адгрóбный [14] tomb..., grave...

аде|вáть [1], ⟨∠ть⟩ [-éну, -éнешь; -éтый] put on.

адéжд|а *f* [5] hope (of на В); подавáть ~ы show promise; ♀а *fem. name, cf.* Hope.

адёжный [14; -жен, -жна] reliable, dependable; firm; safe; sure.

адéл ⚒ *m* [1] lot, plot, allotment.

адéл|ать [1] *pf.* make; do, cause, inflict; **~я́ть** [28], ⟨~и́ть⟩ [13] allot (s. th. to Т/В); give; endow.

адéть *s.* надевáть.

адéяться [27] (на В) hope (for); rely (on).

адзéмный [14] overground; 🚃 elevated, *Brt.* high-level...

адз|ирáтель *m* [4] supervisor; inspector; jailer; **~óр** *m* [1] supervision; surveillance.

адл|áмывать, ⟨~омáть⟩ [1] F, ⟨~оми́ть⟩ [14] crack, break; shatter.

адлежá|ть [4; *impers.*] (Д) have to, be to be + *p. pt.*; **~щий** [17] appropriate, suitable: ~щим óбразом properly, duly.

адлóм *m* [1] crack, fissure; *fig.* crisis; **~áть, ~и́ть** *s.* надлáмывать.

адмéнный [14; -éнен, -éнна] haughty.

áдо it is necessary (for Д); (Д) (one) must (*go, etc.*); need; want; так емý и ~ it serves him right; **~бность** *f* [8] need (of, for в П), necessity; affair, matter (in по Д).

адо|едáть [1], ⟨~éсть⟩ [-éм, -éшь, *etc., s.* есть[1]] (Д/Т) tire; bother, molest; мне ~éл ... I'm tired (of), fed up (with); **~éдливый** [14 *sh.*] tiresome; troublesome, annoying.

адóлго for (a) long (time).

адорвáть *s.* надрывáть.

адпи́|сывать [1], ⟨~сáть⟩ [3] superscribe; ☿ endorse; **'~сь** *f* [8] inscription; ☿ endorsement.

адрéз *m* [1] cut, incision; **~áть** & **~ывать** [1], ⟨~ать⟩ [3] cut, incise.

адругáтельство *n* [9] outrage.

адры́в *m* [1] rent, tear; strain, burst; **~áть** [1], ⟨надорвáть⟩ [-вý, -вёшь; надорвáл, -á, -о; -óрванный] tear; shatter, break, undermine; injure; (over)strain (o. s. себя́, **-ся**; be[come] worn out, exhausted; labo[u]r); **~áть** живóтики, **~áться** (có смеху) split one's sides (with laughing).

адсмóтр *m* [1] supervision (of над, за Т); **~щик** *m* [1] supervisor.

надстр|áивать [1], ⟨~óить⟩ [13] overbuild; raise; **~óйка** *f* [5; *g/pl.:* -póек] superstructure.

наду|вáть [1], ⟨∠ть⟩ [18] inflate, swell; drift, blow; F dupe; ∠ть гýбы pout; **-ся** *v/i.*; **~нóй** [14] inflatable, air...; ∠ть *s.* ~вáть.

надýм|анный [14] far-fetched, strained; **~ать** F [1] *pf.* think (of, out), devise; make up one's mind.

надýтый [14] swollen; sulky.

Нáдя *f* [6] *dim. of* Надéжда.

наедáться [1], ⟨наéсться⟩ [-éмся, -éшься, *etc., s.* есть[1]] eat one's fill.

наединé alone, in private; tête-à-tête.

наéзд *m* [1] (~ом on) short *or* flying visit(s), run; **~ник** *m* [1] horseman, equestrian; (*horse*) trainer.

нае|зжáть [1], ⟨∠хать⟩ [5] (на В) run into, knock against; come across; F come (occasionally), call on (к Д); run (up, down to в В).

наём *m* [1; нáйма] hire; rent; **~ник** *m* [1] hireling, mercenary; **~ный** [14] hired, rent(ed); hackney, mercenary.

наé|сться *s.* ~дáться; **∠хать** *s.* ~зжáть.

нажáть *s.* ~имáть.

наждá|к *m* [1*e.*], **~чный** [14] emery.

нажи́|ва *f* [5] profit(s), gain(s); *a.* = ~вка; **~вáть** [1], ⟨~ть⟩ [-живý, -вёшь; нáжил, -á, -о; нажи́вший; нáжитый (нáжит, -á, -о)] earn, gain, profit(eer), amass; make (*a fortune; enemies*); get, catch; **~вка** *f* [5; *g/pl.:* -вок] bait.

нажи́м *m* [1] pressure; stress, strain; **~áть** [1], ⟨нажáть⟩ [-жмý, -жмёшь; -жáтый] (*a.* на В) press, push (*a.*, F, *fig.* = urge, impel; influence); stress.

нажи́ть *s.* наживáть.

назáвтра F the next day; tomorrow.

назáд back(ward[s]); ~! get back!; томý ~ ago; **~и́** F behind.

назвá|ние *n* [12] name; title; **~ть** *s.* называ́ть.

назéмный [14] land..., ground...

нáземь F to the ground (*or* floor).

назидá|ние *n* [12] edification (for p.'s в В/Д); instruction; **~тельный** [14; -лен, -льна] edifying, instructive.

нáзлó (Д) to (*or* for) spite (s. b.).

назнач|áть [1], ⟨∠ить⟩ [16] appoint (p. s. th. В/Т), designate; fix, settle; prescribe; destine; F assign; **∠ение** *n* [12] appointment; assignment; prescription; destination.

назóйливый [14 *sh.*] importunate.

назре|вáть [1], ⟨∠ть⟩ [8] ripen; swell; ⚕ gather; *fig.* mature; be imminent *or* impending.

назубóк F by heart, thoroughly.

называ́|ть [1], ⟨назвáть⟩ [-зовý, -зовёшь; -звáл, -á, -о; нáзван-

ный (на́зван, -á, -о)] call, name; mention; ~ть себя́ introduce o. s.; F invite; ~ть ве́щи свои́ми имена́ми call a spade a spade; **-ся** call o. s., be called; как ~ется ...? what is (*or* do you call) ...?
наи... *in compds.* ... of all, very; **~бо́лее** most, ...est of all.
наи́вн|ость *f* [12] naïveté; **~ый** [14; -вен, -вна] naïve, ingenuous; unsophisticated.
наизна́нку inside out.
наизу́сть by heart.
наиме́нее least... of all.
наименова́ние *n* [12] name; title.
на́искос|ь, F **~о́к** obliquely, aslant.
наи́тие *n* [12] inspiration; intuition.
найдёныш *m* [1] foundling.
наймит *m* [1] hireling, mercenary.
найти́ *s.* находи́ть.
нака́з *m* [1] order; mandate.
наказ|а́ние *n* [12] punishment (as a в В); penalty; F nuisance; **~у́емый** [14 *sh.*] punishable; **~ы́вать** [1], ⟨~а́ть⟩ [3] punish; † order.
нака́л *m* [1] incandescence; **~ивать** [1], ⟨~и́ть⟩ [13] incandesce; ~ённый incandescent, red-hot.
нак|а́лывать [1], ⟨~оло́ть⟩ [17] pin, fix; chop, break; prick; kill.
накану́не the day before; ~ (P) on the eve (of).
нак|а́пливать [1] & **~опля́ть** [28], ⟨~опи́ть⟩ [14] accumulate, amass; collect, gather.
наки́|дка *f* [5; *g/pl.:* -док] cape, cloak; **~дывать** [1] **1.** ⟨~да́ть⟩ [1] throw (up); **2.** ⟨~нуть⟩ [20] throw upon; F add; raise; **-ся** (на В) F fall (up)on.
на́кипь *f* [8] scum; scale, deposit.
наклад|на́я *f* [14] waybill; **~но́й** [14] laid on; plated; false; ✝ overhead; **~ывать & налага́ть** [1], ⟨наложи́ть⟩ [16] (на В) lay (on), apply (to); put (on), set (to); impose; leave (*trace*); fill; pack, load.
накле́|ивать [1], ⟨~ить⟩ [13; -е́ю] glue *or* paste on; stick on, affix; **~йка** *f* [5; *g/pl.*: -е́ек] label.
накло́н *m* [1] inclination; slope; **~е́ние** *n* [12] *s.* ~; *gr.* mode, mood; **~и́ть** *s.* ~я́ть; **~ный** [14] inclined, slanting; **~я́ть** [28], ⟨~и́ть⟩ [13; -оню́, -о́нишь; -онённый] bend, tilt; bow, stoop; † incline; **-ся** *v/i.*
накова́льня *f* [6; *g/pl.:* -лен] anvil.
нако́жный [14] skin..., cutaneous.
наколо́ть *s.* нака́лывать.
наконе́|ц (~ц-то oh) at last, finally; at length; **~чник** *m* [1] ferrule; tip, point.
накоп|ле́ние *n* [12] accumulation; ⚔ concentration; **~ля́ть, ~и́ть** *s.* нака́пливать.
накра|хма́ленный [14] starched; **~шенный** [14] painted, rouged.
на́крепко fast, tightly, firmly.
на́крест crosswise.
накры|ва́ть [1], ⟨~ть⟩ [22] cover; (*a.* на) lay (*the table*); serve (*meal*); ⚔ hit; P catch, trap; dupe.
накуп|а́ть [1], ⟨~и́ть⟩ [14] (P) buy.
наку́р|ивать [1], ⟨~и́ть⟩ [13; -урю́, -у́ришь; -у́ренный] (fill with) smoke *or* perfume, scent.
налага́ть *s.* накла́дывать.
нала́|живать [1], ⟨~дить⟩ [15] put right *or* in order, get straight, fix; set going; establish; tune.
нале́во to *or* on the left; *s.* напра́во.
нале|га́ть [1], ⟨~чь⟩ [26 г/ж: -ля́гу, -ля́жешь, -ля́гут; -лёг, -легла́; -ля́г(те)!] (на В) press (against, down), *fig.* opress; apply o. s. (to); lie; sink, cover; F stress.
налегке́ F (-xk-) with light *or* no baggage (luggage); lightly dressed.
налёт *m* [1] flight; blast; ⚔, ✈ raid, attack; ⚘ fur; (*a. fig.*) touch; с ~а on the wing, with a swoop; *cf.* лёт; **~а́ть** [1], ⟨~е́ть⟩ [11] (на В) fly (at, [*a.* knock, strike] against); swoop down; raid, attack; fall ([up]on); rush, squall; **~чик** *m* [1] bandit.
нале́чь *s.* налега́ть.
нали|ва́ть [1], ⟨~ть⟩ [-лью́, -льёшь; -ле́й(те)!; на́ли́л, -а́, -о; -ли́вший; на́ли́тый (на́ли́т, -а́, -о)] pour (out); fill; ripen; *p.pt.p.* (*a.* ~то́й) ripe; plump; sappy; (**-ся** *v/i.*; *a.* swell; ~ться кро́вью become bloodshot); **~вка** *f* [5; *g/pl.*: -вок] (fruit) liqueur; **~вно́й** [14] *s.* ~ва́ть *p.pt.p.*; ~вно́е су́дно *n* tanker; **~м** *m* [1] burbot.
налито́й, нали́ть *s.* налива́ть.
налицо́ present, on hand.
нали́ч|ие *n* [12] presence; **~ность** *f* [8] stock; cash; *a.* = ~ие; в ~ности = налицо́; **~ный** [14] (*a. pl., su.*) cash (*a.* down T), ready (*money*); present, on hand; за ~ные (against) cash (down).
нало́г *m* [1] tax, duty, levy; **~оплате́льщик** *m* [1] taxpayer.
нало́ж|енный [14]: ~енным платежо́м cash (*or* collect) on delivery; **~и́ть** *s.* накла́дывать.
налюбова́ться [7] *pf.* (T) admire to one's heart's content; не ~ never get tired of admiring (o. s. собо́й).
нама́|зывать [1] *s.* ма́зать; **~тывать** [1] *s.* мота́ть.
наме́дни P recently, the other day.
нам|ёк *m* [1] (на В) allusion (to), hint (at); **~ека́ть** [1], ⟨~екну́ть⟩ [20] (на В) allude (to), hint (at).
намер|ева́ться [1] intend = (я I, *etc.*) **~ен**(а); **~ение** *n* [12] intention, design, purpose (on с T); **~енный** [14] intentional, deliberate.
наме́стник *m* [1] governor.
намета́ть *s.* намётывать.
наме́тить *s.* намеча́ть.
нам|ётка *f* [5; *g/pl.:* -ток], **~ёты-**

[н]ать [1], ⟨~етáть⟩ [3] draft, plan; [t]ack; *s. a.* метáть.
[н]аме|чáть [1], ⟨~тить⟩ [15] mark, [t]race; design, plan; select; nominate.
[н]амнóго much, (by) far.
[н]амок|áть [1], ⟨~нуть⟩ [21] get wet.
[н]амóрдник *m* [1] muzzle.
[н]анести́ *s.* наноси́ть.
[н]ани́з|ывать [1], ⟨~áть⟩ [3] string.
[н]ан|имáть [1], ⟨~я́ть⟩ [найму́, [най]мёшь; нáнял, -á, -o; -я́вший; [н]áнятый (нáнят, -á, -o)] hire, [e]ngage, rent; F lodge; **-ся** *a.* hire [o]ut (as в И*pl. or* T).
[н]áново anew, (over) again.
[н]анóс *m* [1] alluvium; **~и́ть** [15], ⟨нанести́⟩ [24 -c-: -несу́, -сёшь; [на]нёс, -неслá] bring (much, many); [c]arry, waft, deposit, wash ashore; [h]eap; enter, mark; lay on, apply; [i]nflict (on Д), cause; pay (*visit*); [d]eal (*blow*); **~ный** [14] alluvial; *fig.* [c]asual, assumed.
[н]аня́ть(ся) *s.* нанимáть(ся).
[н]аоборóт the other way round, vice [v]ersa, conversely; on the contrary.
[н]аобу́м F at random, haphazardly.
[н]аотрéз bluntly, categorically.
[н]апа|дáть [1], ⟨~сть⟩ [25; *pt. st.:* [-на]пáл, -a; -пáвший] (на B) attack, [f]all (up)on; come across *or* upon; [h]it on; overcome; **~дáющий** *m* [17] [a]ssailant; (*sport*) forward; **~дéние** [*n*] [12] attack; aggression; forwards [*p*]*l.*; **~дки** *f*/*pl.* [5; *gen.:* -док] accu[s]ations, cavils; carping, faultfinding [*f*]*g.*
[н]ап|áивать [1], ⟨~ои́ть⟩ [13] give [t]o drink; make drunk; imbue.
[н]апá|сть **1.** F *f* [8] misfortune, bad [l]uck; **2.** *s.* ~дáть.
[н]апé|в *m* [1] melody, tune; **~вáть** [1] **1.** hum, sing; **2.** ⟨~ть⟩ [-пою́, [-]поёшь; -пéтый] record.
[н]апере|бóй F vying with each [o]ther; **~вéс** atilt; **~гóнки́** F: бе-[г]áть ~гóнки́ (run a) race; chase [e]ach other; **~д** (-ˈt͡ɕɔt) F *s.* вперёд; **~ди́** P *s.* спéреди; **~кóр** (Д) in [s]pite *or* defiance (of), contrary (to); **~рéз** (in a) short cut, cutting (across [o]r s.b.'s way Д, P); **~ры́в** F = [~]бóй; **~чёт** each and all; few.
[н]апéрсник *m* [1] favo(u)rite; pet.
[н]апёрсток *m* [1; -тка] thimble.
[н]апи|вáться [1], ⟨~ться⟩ [-пью́сь, [-]пьёшься; -пи́лся, -пилáсь; -пéй[-]ся, -пéйтесь!] drink, quench one's [t]hirst, have enough (P); get drunk.
[н]апи́льник *m* [1] file.
[н]апи́|ток *m* [1; -тка] drink, bever[a]ge; **~ться** *s.* ~вáться.
[н]апи́т|ывать, ⟨~áть⟩ [1] (T) (**-ся** [b]ecome) saturate(d), soak(ed), im[b]ue(d).
[н]апи́х|ивать, ⟨~áть⟩ F [1] cram.
[н]аплы́|в *m* [1] rush; deposit; ex[c]rescence; **~вáть** [1], ⟨~ть⟩ [23] [s]wim (against на B), run (on); flow; deposit; approach, cover; waft, reach; gather; **~внóй** [14] *s.* нанóсный.
напова́л (*kill, etc.*) outright.
наподóбие (P) like, resembling.
напои́ть *s.* напáивать.
напокáз for show; *cf.* выставля́ть.
наполн|я́ть [28], ⟨~ить⟩ [13] (T) fill; crowd; imbue; *p.pt.p.* a. full.
наполови́ну half; (*do*) by halves.
напом|инáние *n* [12] reminder; dun(ning); **~инáть** [1], ⟨~нить⟩ [13] remind (a p. of Д/о П), dun.
напóр *m* [1] pressure; charge; F rush, push, vigo(u)r.
напослéдок F ultimately.
напр. *abbr.*: напримéр.
напрáв|ить(ся) *s.* ~ля́ть(ся); **~лéние** *n* [12] direction (in в П, по Д); trend; *fig.* current, school; assignment; **~ля́ть** [28], ⟨~ить⟩ [14] direct; refer; send; assign, detach; **-ся** go, head for; turn (to на B).
напрáво (от P) to *or* on the (s.b.'s) right; ~! ⚔ right face!
напрáсн|ый [14; -сен, -сна] vain; groundless, idle; ~o in vain, wrongly.
напр|áшиваться [1], ⟨~оси́ться⟩ [15] (на B) (pr)offer (o.s. for), solicit; provoke; fish (for); suggest o.s.
напримéр for example *or* instance.
напро|кáт for hire; **~лёт** F (all) ... through[out]; on end; **~лóм** F: идти́ ~лóм force one's way.
напроси́ться *s.* напрáшиваться.
напрóтив (P) opposite; on the contrary; *s. a.* наперекóр & наоборóт.
напря|гáть [1], ⟨~чь⟩ (-ˈpr̥e-) [26 г/ж: ягу́, -яжёшь; -пря́г (-ˈpr̥ɔk), -яглá; -яжённый] strain (*a. fig.*); exert; stretch; bend (*bow*); **~жéние** *n* [12] tension (*a.* ⚡; voltage), strain, exertion; effort; close attention; **~жённый** [14 *sh.*] strained; (in-) tense; keen, close.
напрями́к F straight on; outright.
напря́чь *s.* напрягáть.
напу́ганный [14] scared, frightened.
напус|кáть [1], ⟨~ти́ть⟩ [15] let in, fill; set at (на B); fall; F (~кáть на себя́) put on (*airs*); P cause; **-ся** F fall (up)on (на B); **~кнóй** [14] affected.
напу́тств|енный [14] farewell..., parting; **~ие** *n* [12] parting words.
напы́щенный [14 *sh.*] pompous.
наравнé (с T) on a level with; equally; together (*or* along) with.
нараспáшку F unbuttoned; (душá) ~ frank, candid; in grand style.
нараспéв with a singing accent.
нараст|áть [1], ⟨~и́⟩ [24; -стёт; *cf.* расти́] grow; accrue.
нарасхвáт F greedily; like hot cakes.
нарез|áть [1], ⟨~ать⟩ [3] cut; carve; ⊕ thread; **~ка** *f* [5; *g*/*pl.*: -зок] ⊕ thread; **~ывать** = ~áть.
нарекáние *n* [12] blame, censure.

наре́чие *n* [12] dialect; *gr.* adverb.
нар|ица́тельный [14] *gr.* common; ⚕ nominal; **~ко́з** *m* [1] narcosis.
наро́д *m* [1] people, nation; **~ность** *f* [8] nationality; **~ный** [14] people's, popular, folk...; national; public; **~онаселе́ние** *n* [12] population.
наро|жда́ться [1], ⟨**~ди́ться**⟩ [15] arise, spring up; F be born; grow.
наро́ст *m* [1] (out)growth.
нароч|и́тый [14 *sh.*] deliberate, intentional; *adv.* = **⁓но** (-ʃn-) *a.* on purpose; specially, expressly; F in fun; F*a.* = на́зло́; **ʼ~ный** [14] courier.
на́рты *f*/*pl.* [5] sledge.
нару́ж|ность *f* [8] appearance; exterior; **~ный** [14] external, outward; outdoor, outside; **~у** out (-side), outward(s), (*get*) abroad *fig.*
наруш|а́ть [1], ⟨⁓ить⟩ [16] disturb; infringe, violate; break (*oath*; *silence*); **~е́ние** *n* [12] violation, transgression, breach; disturbance; **~и́тель** *m* [4] trespasser; disturber; **⁓ить** *s.* ~а́ть.
на́ры *f*/*pl.* [5] plank bed.
нары́в *m* [1] abcess; *cf.* гнои́ть.
наря́|д *m* [1] attire, dress; assignment, commission, order; ⚔ fatigue (on в П); detachment; **~ди́ть** *s.* ~жа́ть; **~дный** [14; -ден, -дна] smart, trim, elegant; order...
наряду́ (с Т) together *or* along with, beside(s); side by side; *s. a.* наравне́.
наря|жа́ть [1], ⟨~ди́ть⟩ [15 & 15 *e.*; -яжу́, -я́ди́шь; -я́женный & -яжённый] dress (up) (*v*/*i.* **-ся**); disguise; ⚔ detach; assign; † set up.
наса|жда́ть [1], ⟨~ди́ть⟩ [15] (im)plant (*a. fig.*); *cf. a.* ⁓живать; **~жде́ние** *n* [12] planting; (im-) plantation; trees, plants *pl.*; **⁓живать,** ⟨~жа́ть⟩ [1], ⟨~ди́ть⟩ [15] plant (many); F set, put, place.
насви́стывать [1] whistle.
насе|да́ть [1], ⟨⁓сть⟩ [25; -ся́ду, -ся́дешь; *cf.* сесть] set; sit down; cover; press; **⁓дка** *f* [5; *g*/*pl.*: -док] brood hen.
насеко́мое *n* [14] insect.
насел|е́ние *n* [12] population; **~я́ть** [28], ⟨~и́ть⟩ [13] people, populate; *impf.* inhabit, live in.
насе́|ст *m* [1] roost; **~сть** *s.* ~да́ть; **~чка** *f* [5; *g*/*pl.*: -чек] notch, cut.
наси́|живать [1], ⟨~де́ть⟩ [11] brood, hatch; ~женный *a.* snug, habitual, long-inhabited.
наси́|лие *n* [12] violence, force, coercion; rape; **~ловать** [7], ⟨из-⟩ violate, force; rape; **~лу** F *s.* е́ле; **~льно** by force; forcedly; **~льственный** [14] forcible, forced; violent.
наск|а́кивать [1], ⟨~очи́ть⟩ [16] (на В); fall (up)on; run *or* strike against, come across.

наскво́зь through(out); F throug[h] and through.
наско́лько as (far as); how (much
на́скоро F hastily, in a hurry.
наскочи́ть *s.* наска́кивать.
наску́чить F [16] *pf.*, *s.* надоеда́т[ь]
насла|жда́ться [1], ⟨~ди́ться [15 *e.*; -ажу́сь, -ади́шься] (T) enj[oy] (o.s.), (be) delight(ed); **~жде́ние** [12] enjoyment; delight; pleasur[e]
насле́д|ие *n* [12] heritage, legac[y] *s. a.* ~ство; **~ник** *m* [1] heir; **~ни[ца]** *f* [5] heiress; **~ный** [14] crown.. *s. a.* ~ственный; **~овать** [7] (*im*)*p*[*f*.] ⟨у-⟩ inherit; (Д) succed; **~стве[н]ность** *f* [8] heredity; **~ственны[й]** [14] hereditary, inherited; **~ство** [9] inheritance; *s. a.* ~ие; *vb.* + ~ство (*or* по ~ству) inherit.
наслое́ние *n* [12] stratification.
насл|у́шаться [1] *pf.* (P) listen [to] one's heart's content; не мочь ~[слу]шаться never get tired of listenin[g] to; *a.* = **~ы́шаться** F [4] (P) he[ar] a lot (of), much; *cf.* понаслы́шк[е]
на́смерть to death; mortal(ly *fi*[*g*.] P).
насме|ха́ться [1] mock, jeer; sne[er] (at над T); **⁓шка** *f* [5; *g*/*pl.*: -шек] mockery, sneer; **⁓шливый** [14 *sh*.] (fond of) mocking; **⁓шник** *m* [1] **⁓шница** *f* [5] scoffer, mocker.
на́сморк *m* [1] cold (in the head).
насмотре́ться [9; -отрю́сь, -о́тришься] *pf.* = нагляде́ться, *cf.*
насо́с *m* [1] pump.
на́спех hurriedly, in a hurry.
наста|ва́ть [5], ⟨⁓ть⟩ [-ста́не[т]] come; **~ви́тельный** [14; -ле[н], -льна] instructive; preceptive; [~ста]вить *s.* ~вля́ть; **~вле́ние** *n* [12] instruction; admonition; lectur[e], lesson *fig.*; **~вля́ть** [28], ⟨⁓вит[ь]⟩ [14] put, place, set (many P); pie[ce] (on), add; aim, level (at на В); i[n]struct; teach (s. th. Д, в П); **⁓вни[к]** *m* [1] tutor, mentor, preceptor; [~ста]ивать [1], ⟨настоя́ть⟩ [-сто[ю́], -стои́шь] insist (on на П); dra[w], extract; настоя́ть на своём ha[ve] one's will; **⁓ть** *s.* ~ва́ть.
на́стежь wide (open).
насти|га́ть [1], ⟨⁓гнуть⟩ & ⟨⁓ч[ь]⟩ [21 -г-: -и́гну] overtake; find, catc[h]
наст|ила́ть [1], ⟨~ла́ть⟩ [-тел[ю́], -те́лешь; на́стланный] lay, sprea[d], plank, pave.
насто́й *m* [3] infusion, extract; **~[ка]** *f* [5; *g*/*pl.*: -óек] liqueur; *a.* = ~..
насто́йчивый [14 *sh.*] perseverin[g], pertinacious; persistent; obstinat[e]
насто́ль|ко so (*or* as [much]); **~ны[й]** [14] table...; reference...
настор|а́живаться [1], ⟨~ожи́т[ь]ся⟩ [16 *e.*; -жу́сь, -жи́шься] pri[ck] up one's ears; **~оже́** on the ale[rt], on one's guard.
настоя́|ние *n* [12] insistence, u[r]gent request (at по Д); **~тельны[й]**

.4; -лен, -льна] urgent, pressing, ıstant; **~ть** *s.* настáивать.
стоя́щ|ий [17] present (*a. gr.*; : ... *time* в В); true, real, genuine; э- ~ему properly.
стр|áивать [1], ⟨~óить⟩ [13] uild (many P); tune (up, in); set gainst; *s. a.* налáживать; **∠ого** F ıost strictly; **~оéние** *n* [12] mood, pirits *pl.*, frame (of mind); disposion; **~óить** *s.* ~áивать; **~óйка** *f* [5; *pl.*: -óек] superstructure; tuning.
ступ|áтельный [14] offensive; **áть** [1], ⟨~и́ть⟩ [14] tread *or* step n на В); come, set in; *impf.* attack, dvance; press (hard); approach; **лéние** *n* [12] offensive, attack, dvance; beginning, ...break, ...fall t с Т).
сýпить(ся) [14] *pf.* frown.
.сухо *adv.* dry.
.сýщный [14; -щен, -щна] vital; aily.
.счёт (P) F concerning, about.
.счи́т|ывать, ⟨~áть⟩ [1] count, umber; **-ся** *impf.* there is/are.
.сып|áть [1], ⟨∠ать⟩ [2] pour; rew, scatter; fill; throw up, raise; **.ь** *f* [8] embankment, mound.
.сы|щáть [1], ⟨∠тить⟩ [15] satis-/; saturate; **~щéние** *n* [12] saturation.
.т|áлкивать [1], ⟨~олкнýть⟩ [20] на В) push (against, on); F prompt, ıggest; **-ся** strike against; come cross.
.творúть F [13] *pf.* do, cause.
.тéльный [14] under(*clothes*).
.т|ирáть [1], ⟨~ерéть⟩ [12] (T) ıb (*a.* sore); get (*corn*); wax, polish.
т|иск *m* [1] press(ure), rush; onaught, charge; urge.
.ткнýться *s.* натыкáться.
.толкнýть(ся) *s.* натáлкиваться.
.тощáк on an empty stomach.
.трáв|ливать [1], ⟨~и́ть⟩ [14] et (on, at на В), incite.
.трий *m* [3] natrium.
.тý|га F *f* [5] strain, effort; **′~го** F ight(ly); **~живать** F [1], ⟨~жить⟩ 6] strain, exert (o.s. **-ся**).
.тýр|а *f* [5] nature; model (= **щик** *m* [1], **~щица** *f* [5]); ~ой, в e in kind; с ~ы from nature *or* life; **áльный** [14; -лен, -льна] natural.
.т|ыкáться [1], ⟨~кнýться⟩ [20] на В) run against, (*a.* come) across.
.тя́|гивать [1], ⟨~нýть⟩ [19] tretch, (*a. fig.*) strain; pull (on на); draw in (*reins*); **~жка** *f* [5; *pl.*: -жек] strain(ing); affectation, rced *or* strained argument(ation), etail, trait, *etc.*; с ~жкой *a.* with reat reserve; **~нутый** [14] strained, rced, affected, far-fetched; tense, ad; **~нýть** *s.* ~гивать.
.у|гáд, ~дáчу at random.
.ýка *f* [5] science; lesson.
.утёк F (*take*) to one's heels.

наýтро the next morning.
науч|áть [1], ⟨~и́ть⟩ [16] teach (a p. s.th. В/Д); **-ся** learn (s.th. Д).
наýчный [14; -чен, -чна] scientific.
наýшник F *m* [1] informer; **~и** *m/pl.* [1] earflaps; headphones.
нахáл *m* [1] impudent fellow; **~ьный** [14; -лен, -льна] impudent, insolent; **~ьство** *n* [12] impudence, insolence.
нахвáт|ывать, ⟨~áть⟩ F [1] (P) snatch (up), pick up (a lot of, a smattering of; hoard; *a.* **-ся**).
нахлы́нуть [20] *pf.* rush (up [to]).
нахмýривать [1] = хмýрить, *cf.*
наход|и́ть [15], ⟨найти́⟩ [найдý, -дёшь; нашёл, -шлá; -шéдший; нáйденный; *g. pt.*: найдя́] find (*a. fig.* = think, consider); come (across на В); cover; be seized (F wrong) with; *impf.* take (*pleasure*); (**-ся,** ⟨найти́сь⟩) be (found, there, [*impf.*] situated, located); happen to have; not to be at a loss; **∠ка** *f* [5; *g/pl.*: -док] find; F discovery; бюрó ∠ок lost-property office; **∠чивый** [14 *sh.*] resourceful; ready-witted, smart.
национал|из(и́р)овáть [7] (*im*)*pf.* nationalize (*Brt.* -ise); **∠ьность** *f* [8] nationality; **~ьный** [14; -лен, -льна] national.
начá|ло *n* [9] beginning (at в П); source, origin; basis; principle; *pl.* rudiments; **~льник** *m* [1] chief, superior; ⚔ commander; 🚂 (*station*) master, agent; **~льный** [14] initial, first; opening; elementary, primary; **~льство** *n* [9] command(er[s], chief[s], superior[s]); authority, -ties *pl.*; **~льствовать** [7] (над Т) command; manage; **~тки** *m/pl.* [1] *s.* ~ло *pl.*; **~ть(ся)** *s.* начинáть(ся).
начекý on the alert, on one's guard.
нáчерно roughly, (in) a draft.
начертá|ние *n* [12] tracing; pattern; outline; **~тельный** [14] descriptive; **~ть** [1] *pf.* trace, design.
начинá|ние *n* [12] undertaking; † beginning; **~ть** [1], ⟨начáть⟩ [-чнý, -чнёшь; нáчал, -á, -о; начáвший; нáчатый (нáчат, -á, -о)] begin, start (with с Р, Т); **-ся** *v/i.*; **~ющий** [17] beginner.
начи́н|ка *f* [5; *g/pl.*: -нок] filling; **~я́ть** [28], ⟨~и́ть⟩ [13] fill (with Т).
начислéние *n* [12] extra fee.
нáчисто clean; *s.* нáбело; outright.
начи́т|анный [14 *sh.*] well-read; **~áться** [1] (P) read (a lot of); have enough (of); не мочь ~áться never get tired of reading.
наш *m*, **∠а** *f*, **∠е** *n*, **∠и** *pl.* [25] our; ours; по-∠ему in our way *or* opinion *or* language; ∠а взялá! we've won!
нашаты́р|ный [14]: ~ный спирт *m* aqueous ammonia; **~ь** *m* [4 *e.*] sal ammoniac, ammonium chloride.
нашéствие *n* [12] invasion, inroad.

наши|ва́ть [1], ⟨**∠ть**⟩ [-шью́, -шьёшь; *cf.* шить] sew on (на В *or* П) *or* many ...; **∠вка** *f* [5; *g/pl.:* -вок] galloon, braid; ⚔ stripe.

нащу́п|ывать, ⟨**~ать**⟩ [1] grope, fumble; *fig.* sound; detect, find.

наяву́ in reality; waking.

не not; no; ~ то F (or) else.

неаккура́тный [14; -тен, -тна] careless; inaccurate; unpunctual.

небез... rather ..., not without ...

небе́сный [14] celestial, heavenly; of heaven; divine; *cf.* небосво́д.

неблаго|ви́дный [14; -ден, -дна] unseemly; **~да́рность** *f* [8] ingratitude; **~да́рный** [14; -рен, -рна] ungrateful; **~надёжный** [14; -жен, -жна] unreliable; **~полу́чный** [14; -чен, -чна] unfortunate, adverse, bad; *adv.* not well, wrong; **~прия́тный** [14; -тен, -тна] unfavo(u)rable, negative; **~разу́мный** [14; -мен, -мна] imprudent; unreasonable; **~ро́дный** [14; -ден, -дна] ignoble; indelicate; **~скло́нный** [14; -о́нен, -о́нна] unkindly; unfavo(u)rable.

не́бо¹ *n* [9; *pl.:* небеса́, -е́с] sky (in на П); heaven(s); air (in the *open* под Т).

нёбо² *n* [9] palate.

небога́тый [14 *sh.*] (of) modest (means); poor.

небольш|о́й [17] small; short; ... с ~и́м ... odd.

небо|сво́д *m* [1] firmament; *a.* **~скло́н** *m* [1]; horizon; **~скрёб** *m* [1] skyscraper.

небо́сь F I suppose; sure.

небре́жный [14; -жен, -жна] careless, negligent.

небы|ва́лый [14] unheard-of, unprecedented; **~ли́ца** *f* [5] tale, fable, invention.

небью́щийся [17] unbreakable.

Нева́ *f* [5] Neva.

нева́жный [14; -жен, -жна́, -о] unimportant, trifling; F poor, bad.

невдалеке́ not far off, *or* from (от Р).

неве́|дение *n* [12] ignorance; **~до́мый** [14 *sh.*] unknown; **~жа** *m/f* [5] boor; **~жда** *m/f* [5] ignoramus; **~жество** *n* [9] ignorance; **~жливость** *f* [8] incivility; **~жливый** [14 *sh.*] impolite, uncivil.

неве́р|ие *n* [12] unbelief; **~ный** [14; -рен, -рна́, -о] incorrect; false; unfaithful; unsteady; *su.* infidel; **~оя́тный** [14; -тен, -тна] incredible; **~ующий** [17] unbelieving.

невесо́мый [14 *sh.*] imponderable.

неве́ст|а *f* [5] fiancée, bride; F marriageable girl; **~ка** *f* [5; *g/pl.:* -ток] daughter-in-law; sister-in-law (*brother's wife*).

невз|го́да *f* [5] adversity, misfortune; affliction; **~ира́я** (на В) in spite of, despite; without respect (of p.'s); **~нача́й** F unexpected by chance; **~ра́чный** [14; -ч -чна] plain, homely, mean; **~ыск** тельный [14; -лен, -льна] u pretentious.

неви́д|анный [14] singular, u precedented; **~имый** [14 *sh.*] inv ible.

неви́нный [14; -и́нен, -и́нна] nocent; virgin. [insipi

невку́сный [14; -сен, -сна́, -

невме|ня́емый [14 *sh.*] irrespo sible; **~ша́тельство** *n* [9] n intervention.

невнима́тельный [14; -лен, -ль inattentive.

невня́тный [14; -тен, -тна] distinct, inarticulate; unintelligi

не́вод *m* [1] seine.

невоз|врати́мый [14 *sh.*], **~вра** ный [14; -тен, -тна] irretrievab irreparable; **~вращéнец** *n* -нца] non-returnee; **~де́ржанн** [14 *sh.*] intemperate; unbridl uncontrolled; **~мо́жный** [-жен, -жна] impossible; **~мут** мый [14 *sh.*] imperturbable.

нево́л|ить [13] force, compel; ~ ник *m* [1] slave; captive; **~ьн** [14; -лен, -льна] involunta forced; **~я** *f* [6] captivity; bonda need, necessity.

невоо|брази́мый [14 *sh.*] uni aginable; **~ружённый** [14] u armed.

невоспи́танный [14 *sh.*] ill-br

невпопа́д F *s.* некста́ти.

невреди́мый [14 *sh.*] sound, u hurt.

невы́|годный [14; -ден, -дна] u profitable; disadvantageous; **~де** жанный [14 *sh.*] unbalanc uneven; unseasoned; **~носи́м** [14 *sh.*] unbearable, intolerable; полне́ние *n* [12] nonfulfillme **~полни́мый** *s.* неисполни́мы **~рази́мый** [14 *sh.*] inexpressib ineffable; **~рази́тельный** [-лен, -льна] inexpressive; **~со́к** [16; -со́к, -а́, -со́ко́] low, sma short; inferior, slight.

не́га *f* [5] luxury, comfort; bl delight; affection.

не́где there is no(where *or* room place to [... from] *inf.*; Д for).

негла́сный [14; -сен, -сна] sec private.

него́д|ный [14; -ден, -дна́, -о] u less; unfit; F nasty; **~ова́ние** *n* [indignation; **~ова́ть** [7] be ind nant (with на В); **~я́й** *m* [3] scou drel, rascal.

негр *m* [1] Negro; **~а́мотност** безгра́мотность; **~а́мотный** безгра́мотный; **~итя́нка** *f* *g/pl.:* -нок] Negress; **~итя́нск** [16] Negro...

неда́|вний [15] recent; с **~вн** (**~вней**) пор(ы́) of late; **~в**

:cently; ~лёкий [16; -ёк, -ека́, :ко́ & -ёко] near(by), close; short; ot far (off); recent; dull, stupid; льнови́дный [14; -ден, -дна] ıort-sighted; ~ром not in vain, ot without reason; justly.
движи́мый [14 sh.] immovable.
де|йстви́тельный [14; -лен, льна] invalid, void; ineffective, effectual; ~ли́мый [14] indivisle.
це́л|ьный [14] a week's, weekly; я f [6] week; в ~ю a or per week; а э́той (про́шлой, бу́дущей) ~е ıis (last, next) week.
добро|жела́тельный [14; -лен, льна] unkindly, ill-natured; ~ка́ественный [14 sh.] inferior, offrade; ~со́вестный [14; -тен, тна] unfair; unprincipled; careless.
до́брый [14; -до́бр, -а́, -о] unind(ly), hostile; evil, bad, ill(-bodg).
дове́р|ие n [12] distrust; ~чиый [14 sh.] distrustful (of к Д).
дово́ль|ный [14; -лен, -льна] Г) dissatisfied, discontented; ~тво n [9] discontent, dissatisfacon.
дога́дливый [14 sh.] slow-witted.
доеда́|ние n [12] malnutrition; ть [1] not eat enough (or one's l). [arrears.
до́имки f/pl. [5; gen.: -мок]
до́лго not long, short; F easily.
домога́ть [1] be unwell, sick.
домо́лвка f [5; g/pl.: -вок] mission.
доно́сок m [1; -ска] abortion.
дооце́н|ивать [1], ⟨~и́ть⟩ [13] nderestimate, undervalue.
до|пусти́мый [14 sh.] inadmisble; intolerable, impossible; ~ра́витый [14 sh.] underdeveloped; разуме́ние n [12] misundertanding (through по Д); ~рого́й 16; -до́рог, -а́, -о] inexpensive.
до|росль m [4] greenhorn; ignoamus; ~слы́шать [1] pf. fail to ear.
досмо́тр m [1] oversight, inadertence (through по Д); ~е́ть [9; отрю́, -о́тришь; -о́тренный] pf. verlook (s. th.).
дост|ава́ть [5], ⟨~а́ть⟩ [-ста́нет] npers.: (Д) (be) lack(ing), want -ing), be short or in want of (Р); miss; э́того ещё ~ава́ло! and that oo!; ~а́ток m [1; -тка] want (for а Т, по Д), lack, shortage (of Р, в I); deficiency; defect, shortcomng; privation; ~а́точный [14; чен, -чна] insufficient, deficient, nadequate; gr. defective; ~а́ть s. ава́ть.
до|стижи́мый [14 sh.] unattainble; ~сто́йный [14; -о́ин, -о́йна] nworthy; ~сту́пный [14; -пен, пна] inaccessible.

недосу́г F m [1] lack of time (for за Т, по Д); мне ~ I have no time.
недо|сяга́емый [14 sh.] unattainable; ~у́здок m [1; -дка] halter.
недоум|ева́ть [1] (be) puzzle(d, perplexed); ~е́ние n [12] bewilderment; в ~е́нии at a loss.
недочёт m [1] deficit; defect.
не́дра n/pl. [9] bosom, entrails.
недружелю́бный [14; -бен, -бна] unfriendly.
неду́г m [1] ailment, infirmity.
недурно́й [14; -ду́рен & -рён, -рна́, -о] not bad, pretty, nice, handsome.
недю́жинный [14] remarkable.
неесте́ственный [14 sh.] unnatural; affected, forced.
нежела́|ние n [12] unwillingness; ~тельный [14; -лен, -льна] undesirable.
не́жели † = чем than.
нежена́тый [14] single, unmarried.
нежи́зненный [14 sh.] impracticable; unreal.
нежило́й [14] uninhabited; deserted, desolate; store...
не́ж|ить [16] coddle, pamper, fondle; -ся loll, lounge; ~ничать F [1] indulge in caresses; ~ность f [8] tenderness; fondness; civility; ~ный [14; -жен, -жна́, -о] tender, fond; delicate; soft; sentimental.
незаб|ве́нный [14 sh.], ~ыва́емый [14 sh.] unforgettable; ~у́дка f [5; g/pl.: -док] forget-me-not.
незави́сим|ость f [8] independence; ~ый [14 sh.] independent.
незада́чливый F [14 sh.] unlucky.
незадо́лго shortly (before до Р).
незако́нный [14; -о́нен, -о́нна] illegal, unlawful, illegitimate; illicit.
незаме|ни́мый [14 sh.] irreplaceable; ∠тный [14; -тен, -тна] imperceptible, unnoticeable; plain, ordinary, humdrum; ∠ченный [14] unnoticed.
неза|мыслова́тый F [14 sh.] simple, plain; dull; ~па́мятный [14] immemorial; ~те́йливый [14 sh.] plain, simple; ~уря́дный [14; -ден, -дна] remarkable.
не́зачем there is no need or point.
незва́ный [14] uninvited.
нездоро́в|иться [14]: мне ~ится I feel (am) sick or ill, unwell; ~ый [14 sh.] sick; morbid.
незло́бивый [14 sh.] gentle, placid.
незнако́м|ец m [1; -мца], ~ка f [5; g/pl.: -мок] stranger; a., F, ~ый [14], unknown, strange; unacquainted.
незна́|ние n [12] ignorance; ~чи́тельный [14; -лен, -льна] insignificant.
незр|е́лый [14 sh.] unripe; immature; ~и́мый [14 sh.] invisible.
незы́блемый [14 sh.] firm; unshakable.
неиз|бе́жный [14; -жен, -жна] inevitable; ~ве́данный [14 sh.] s.

~ве́стный [14; -тен, -тна] unknown; *su. a.* stranger; **~гладúмый** [14 *sh.*] indelible; **~лечúмый** [14 *sh.*] incurable; **~ме́нный** [14; -е́нен, -е́нна] invariable; permanent; true; **~мерúмый** [14 *sh.*] immense; **~ъяснúмый** [14 *sh.*] inexplicable.

неим|е́ние *n* [12]: за ~е́нием (P) for want of; **~ове́рный** [14; -рен, -рна] incredible; **~у́щий** [17] poor.

нейс|кренний [15; -енен, -енна] insincere; **~ку́сный** [14; -сен, -сна] unskillful; **~полне́ние** *n* [12] nonfulfillment; **~полнúмый** [14 *sh.*] impracticable.

неиспр|авúмый [14 *sh.*] incorrigible; **~а́вность** *f* [8] ⊕ disrepair; **~а́вный** [14; -вен, -вна] out of repair *or* order, broken, defective; careless, faulty; inaccurate; unpunctual.

неиссяка́емый [14 *sh.*] inexhaustible.

нейстов|ство *n* [9] rage, frenzy; atrocity; **~ствовать** [7] rage; **~ый** [14 *sh.*] frantic, furious.

неис|тощúмый [14 *sh.*] inexhaustible; **~требúмый** [14 *sh.*] ineradicable; **~целúмый** [14 *sh.*] incurable; **~черпа́емый** [14 *sh.*] *s.* ~тощúмый; **~числúмый** [14 *sh.*] innumerable.

нейтрал|ите́т *m* [1] neutrality; **~ьный** [14; -лен, -льна] neutral.

неказúстый F [14 *sh.*] = невзра́чный.

не́|кий [24 *st.*] a certain, some; **~когда** there is (мне ~когда I have) no time; once; **~кого** [23] there is (мне ~кого I have) nobody *or* no one (to *inf.*); **~который** [14] some (*pl.* of из P); **~красúвый** [14 *sh.*] homely, ugly; mean.

некроло́г *m* [1] obituary.

некста́ти inopportunely; inappropriately, malapropos, off the point.

не́кто somebody, -one; a certain.

не́куда there is no(where *or* room *or* place to *inf.*; Д for); *s. a.* не́зачем; F could not be (*better, etc.*).

неку|льту́рный [14; -рен, -рна] uncultured; ill-mannered; **~ря́щий** [17] nonsmoker, nonsmoking.

нел|а́дный F [14; -ден, -дна] wrong, bad; **~ега́льный** [14; -лен, -льна] illegal; **~е́пый** [14 *sh.*] absurd; F awkward.

нело́вкий [16; -вок, -вка́, -о] awkward, clumsy; inconvenient, embarrassing.

нельзя́ (it is) impossible, one (мне I) cannot, must not; ~! no!; как ~ лу́чше in the best way possible, excellently; ~ не *s.* (не) мочь.

нелюдúмый [14 *sh.*] unsociable.

нема́ло (P) a lot, a great deal (of).

неме́дленный [14] immediate.

неме́ть [8], ‹о-› grow dumb, numb.

не́м|ец *m* [1; -мца], **~е́цкий** [1… **~ка** *f* [5; *g/pl.*: -мок] German.

немилосе́рдный [14; -ден, -дн… unmerciful, ruthless.

немúлост|ивый [14 *sh.*] ungr… cious; **~ь** *f* [8] disgrace.

немину́емый [14 *sh.*] inevitable.

немно́|гие *pl.* [16] (a) few, som… **~го** a little; slightly, somewhat; *a.* ~гие; **~гое** *n* [16] little; ~гим… little; **~ж(еч)ко** F a (little) bit.

немо́й [14; нем, -а́, -о] dumb, mu…

немо|лодо́й [14; -мо́лод, -а́, -… elderly; **~та́** *f* [5] muteness.

не́мощный [14; -щен, -щна] i… firm.

немы́слимый [14 *sh.*] inconcei… able.

ненавú|деть [11], ‹воз-› hate; … **стный** [14; -тен, -тна] hatef… odious; **~сть** (ˈne-) *f* [8] hatr… (against к Д).

нена|гля́дный [14] dear, belove… **~дёжный** [14; -жен, -жна] unr… liable; unsafe, insecure; **~до́лго** f… a short while; **~ме́ренный** [1… unintentional; **~паде́ние** *n* [1… nonagression; **~рушúмый** [14 *s*… inviolable; **~́стный** [14; -тен, -т… rainy, foul; **~́стье** *n* [10] fo… weather; **~сы́тный** [14; -тен, -т… insatiable.

нен|орма́льный [14; -лен, -льн… abnormal; F (mentally) derange… **~у́жный** [14; -жен, -жна́, -… unnecessary.

необ|ду́манный [14 *sh.*] ras… hasty; **~ита́емый** [14 *sh.*] uni… habited; desert; **~озрúмый** [… *sh.*] immense, vast; **~осно́ванн…** [14 *sh.*] unfounded; **~рабо́та… ный** [14] uncultivated; crude, u… polished; **~у́зданный** [14 *sh.*] u… bridled, unruly.

необходúм|ость *f* [8] necessity … по Д), need (of, for P, в П); **~…** [14 *sh.*] necessary (for Д; для … essential; *cf.* ну́жный.

необ|щúтельный [14; -ле… -льна] unsociable, reserved; **~ъя… нúмый** [14 *sh.*] inexplicable; … **ъя́тный** [14; -тен, -тна] immens… vast, huge; **~ыкнове́нный** [1… -е́нен, -е́нна], **~ы́ч(а́й)ный** [1… -ч(а)ен, ч(а́й)на] unusual, uncon… mon; **~яза́тельный** [14; -ле… -льна] optional.

неограни́ченный [14 *sh.*] unr… stricted.

неод|нокра́тный [14] repeate… **~обре́ние** *n* [12] disapproval; … **обрúтельный** [14; -лен, -льн… disapproving; **~олúмый** *s.* непр… одолúмый; **~ушевлённый** [1… inanimate.

неожúданн|ость *f* [8] surpris… **~ый** [14 *sh.*] unexpected, sudde…

нео́н *m* [1] neon; **~овый** [14] neo…

…

ɪоп|исýемый [14 *sh.*] indescribable; ~лáченный [14 *sh.*] unpaid, ɪnsettled; ~рáвданный [14] unjustified; ~ределённый [14; -ёнен, ённа] indefinite (*a. gr.*), uncertain, ɪague; *gr.* (*vb.*) infinitive; ~роɪержи́мый [14 *sh.*] irrefutable; ытный [14; -тен, -тна] inexperienced.

ɪос|лáбный [14; -бен, -бна] unremitting, unabated; ~мотри́ɪельный [14; -лен, -льна] imprudent; ~новáтельный [14; лен, -льна] unfounded, baseless; ɪпори́мый [14 *sh.*] incontestable; торóжный [14; -жен, -жна] careless, incautious; imprudent; уществи́мый [14 *sh.*] impracticable; ~язáемый [14 *sh.*] intangible.

ɪот|врати́мый [14 *sh.*] unavoidable; fatal; ~вя́зный [14; -зен, зна], ~вя́зчивый [14 *sh.*] obtrusive, importunate; ~ёсанный 14 *sh.*] unhewn; F rude; '~куда нéгде; ~лóжный [14; -жен, жна] pressing, urgent; ~лýчный неразлýчный & постоя́нный; рази́мый [14 *sh.*] irresistible; стýпный [14; -пен, -пна] persistent; importunate; ~чётливый 14 *sh.*] indistinct; ~ъéмлемый 14 *sh.*] integral; inalienable.

ɪохóт|а *f* [5] listlessness; reluctance; (мне) ~а F I (*etc.*) am not in the mood; ~но unwillingly.

ɪ|оцени́мый [14 *sh.*] invaluable; переходный [14] intransitive; платёж *m* [1 *e.*] nonpayment; платёжеспосóбный [14; -бен, бна] insolvent.

ɪпо|беди́мый [14 *sh.*] invincible; ворóтливый [14 *sh.*] clumsy, low; ~гóда *f* [5] foul weather; ~реши́мый [14 *sh.*] infallible; далёку not far (away *or* off); ~áтливый [14 *sh.*] unyielding, efractory.

под|ви́жный [14; -жен, -жна] motionless, (*a. ast.*) fixed; sluggish; дéльный [14; -лен, -льна] genuine, true; sincere; ~кýпный [14; пен, -пна] incorruptible; ~обáющий [17] improper, unbecoming; undue; ~ражáемый [14 *sh.*] inimitable; ~ходя́щий [17] unsuitable; ~чинéние *n* [12] insubordination.

ɪпо|зволи́тельный [14; -лен, льна] improper, unbecoming; колеби́мый [14 *sh.*] firm, steadfast; unflinching; imperturbable; кóрный [14; -рен, -рна] intractable; ~лáдка F *f* [5; *g/pl.:* -док] defect, trouble; strife; ~лный [14; лон, -лнá, -о] incomplete; short; мéрный [14; -рен, -рна] excessive, exorbitant.

понят|ливый [14 *sh.*] slow-witted; ~ный [14; -тен, -тна] unintelligible, incomprehensible; strange, odd.

непо|прави́мый [14 *sh.*] irreparable; ~рóчный [14; -чен, -чна] chaste, immaculate; virgin...; ~ря́дочный [14; -чен, -чна] dishono(u)rable, disreputable; ~сéдливый [14 *sh.*] fidgety; ~си́льный [14; -лен, -льна] beyond one's strength; ~слéдовательный [14; -лен, -льна] inconsistent; ~слýшный [14; -шен, -шна] disobedient.

непо|срéдственный [14 *sh.*] immediate, direct; spontaneous; ~стижи́мый [14 *sh.*] inconceivable; ~стоя́нный [14; -я́нен, -я́нна] inconstant, unsteady, fickle; ~хóжий [17 *sh.*] unlike, different (from на В).

неправ|да *f* [5] untruth, lie; (it is) not true; ... и ~дами (*by hook*) or by crook; ~доподóбный [14; -бен, -бна] improbable; ~едный [14; -ден, -дна] unjust; sinful; ~ильный [14; -лен, -льна] incorrect, wrong; irregular (*a. gr.*); improper (*a.* ⅍); ~отá *f* [5] wrong(fulness); ~ый [14; неправ, -á, -о] wrong; unjust.

непре|взойдённый [14 *sh.*] unsurpassed; ~ви́денный [14] unforeseen; ~дубеждённый [14] unbias(s)ed; ~клóнный [14; -óнен, -óнна] uncompromising; steadfast; ~лóжный [14; -жен, -жна] inviolable, invariable; incontestable; ~мéнный [14; -éнен, -éнна] indispensable; permanent; ~мéнно *s.* обязáтельно; ~одоли́мый [14 *sh.*] insuperable; irresistible; ~рекáемый [14 *sh.*] indisputable; ~рывный [14; -вен, -вна] continuous; ~стáнный [14; -áнен, -áнна] incessant.

непри|вычный [14; -чен, -чна] unaccustomed; unusual; ~гля́дный [14; -ден, -дна] homely, mean; ~гóдный [14; -ден, -дна] unfit; useless; ~éмлемый [14 *sh.*] unacceptable; ~косновéнный [14; -éнен, -éнна] inviolable; untouched, untouchable; ~крáшенный [14] unvarnished; ~ли́чный [14; -чен, -чна] indecent, unseemly; ~мéтный [14; -тен, -тна] imperceptible, unnoticeable; plain; ~мири́мый [14 *sh.*] irreconcilable, implacable; ~нуждённый [14 *sh.*] (free and) easy, at ease; ~стóйный [14; -óен, -óйна] obscene, indecent; ~стýпный [14; -пен, -пна] inaccessible; impregnable; unapproachable, haughty; ~твóрный [14; -рен, -рна] sincere, unfeigned; ~тязáтельный [14; -лен, -льна] unpretentious, modest, plain.

неприя́|зненный [14 *sh.*] hostile, unkind(ly); ~знь *f* [8] dislike; ~тель *m* [4] enemy; ~тельский

[16] enemy('s); **~тность** *f* [8] trouble; **~тный** [14; -тен, -тна] disagreeable, unpleasant.

непро|гля́дный [14; -ден, -дна] pitch-dark; **~должи́тельный** [14; -лен, -льна] short, brief; **~е́зжий** [17] impassable; **~зра́чный** [14; -чен, -чна] opaque; **~изводи́тельный** [14; -лен, -льна] unproductive; **~изво́льный** [14; -лен, -льна] involuntary; **~мока́емый** [14 *sh.*] waterproof; **~ница́емый** [14 *sh.*] impenetrable, impermeable, impervious; **~сти́тельный** [14; -лен, -льна] unpardonable; **~ходи́мый** [14 *sh.*] impassable; F complete; **~́чный** [14; -чен, -чна́, -o] flimsy, unstable.

нера́бочий [17] free, off (*day*).

нера́в|енство *n* [9] inequality; **~номе́рный** [14; -рен, -рна] uneven; **~ный** [14; -вен, -вна́, -o] unequal.

неради́вый [14 *sh.*] careless, listless.

нераз|бери́ха F *f* [5] mess; **~бо́рчивый** [14 *sh.*] illegible; unscrupulous; **~вито́й** [14; -ра́звит, -á, -o] undeveloped; **~де́льный** [14; -лен, -льна] indivisible, integral; undivided; **~личи́мый** [14 *sh.*] indistinguishable; **~лу́чный** [14; -чен, -чна] inseparable; **~реши́мый** [14 *sh.*] insoluble; **~ры́вный** [14; -вен, -вна] indissoluble; **~у́мный** [14; -мен, -мна] injudicious.

нерас|положе́ние *n* [12] dislike; **~суди́тельный** [14; -лен, -льна] imprudent.

нерв *m* [1] nerve; **~и́ровать** [7] make nervous; **~́ничать** [1] be nervous; **~нобольно́й** [14] neurotic; **~́(о́з)ный** [14; -вен, -вна́, -o (-зен, -зна)] nervous; high-strung.

нереши́тельн|ость *f* [8] indecision; в **~ости** at a loss; **~ый** [14; лен, -льна] irresolute.

неро́|бкий [16; -бок, -бка́, -o] brave; **~вный** [14; -вен, -вна́, -o] uneven.

неруши́мый [14 *sh.*] inviolable.

неря́|ха *m/f* [5] sloven; **~шливый** [14 *sh.*] slovenly; careless.

несамостоя́тельный [14; -лен, -льна] dependent (on, *or* influenced by, others).

несбы́точный [14; -чен, -чна] unrealizable.

не|све́дущий [17 *sh.*] ignorant (of в П); **~своевре́менный** [14; -енен, -енна] untimely; tardy; **~свя́зный** [14; -зен, -зна] incoherent; **~сгора́емый** [14] fireproof; **~сде́ржанный** [14 *sh.*] unrestrained; **~серьёзный** [14; -зен, -зна] frivolous; **~сказа́нный** [14 *sh.*, *no m*] indescribable; **~скла́дный** [14; -ден, -дна] ungainly, unwieldy; incoherent; **~склоня́емый** [14 *sh.*] indeclinabl

не́сколько [32] a few, some, seve al; somewhat.

не|скро́мный [14; -мен, -мна́, - immodest; **~слы́ханный** [14 *sh* unheard-of; awful; **~слы́шны** [14; -шен, -шна] inaudible, nois less; **~сме́тный** [14; -тен, -тн innumerable.

несмотря́ (на В) in spite of, despit notwithstanding; (al)though.

несно́сный [14; -сен, -сна] i tolerable.

несо|блюде́ние *n* [12] nonobser ance; **~вершенноле́тие** *n* [1 minority; **~верше́нный** [1 -е́нен, -е́нна] imperfect(ive *gr.* **~верше́нство** *n* [8] imperfectio **~вмести́мый** [14 *sh.*] incompat ble; **~гла́сие** *n* [12] disagreemen **~гла́сный** [14; -сен, -сна] di cordant; inconsistent; **~измер мый** [14 *sh.*] incommensurable; **круши́мый** [14 *sh.*] indestructib **~мне́нный** [14; -е́нен, -е́нн doubtless; ~мне́нно *a.* undoubted without doubt; **~обра́зный** [1 -зен, -зна] incompatible; absur foolish; **~отве́тствие** *n* [12] di crepancy; **~разме́рный** [14; -ре -рна] disproportionate; **~сто тельный** [14; -лен, -льна] need insolvent; unsound, baseless.

несп|око́йный [14; -о́ен, -о́йн restless, uneasy; **~осо́бный** [1 -бен, -бна] incapable (of к Д, на В unfit (for); **~раведли́вость** *f* [injustice; wrong; **~раведли́вы** [14 *sh.*] unjust, wrong; **~роста́** F неда́ром.

несравне́нный [14; -е́нен, -е́нн incomparable.

нестерпи́мый [14 *sh.*] intolerab

нести́ [24 -с-: -су́], ‹по-› (be) ca ry(ing, *etc.*); bear; bring; suf (*loss*); do (*duty*); drift, waft, spe (along) (**-сь** *v/i.*; *a.* be hear spread); ‹с-› lay (eggs **-сь**); F t (*nonsense*); smell (of T); нес there's a draught.

не|строево́й [14] noncombatan **~стро́йный** [14; -о́ен, -ойна́, - ungainly; discordant; disorder **~сура́зный** F [14; -зен, -зна] foo ish, absurd; ungainly; **~схо́дны** [14; -ден, -дна] unlike, differe (from с T).

несча́ст|ный [14; -тен, -тна] u happy, unlucky; F paltry; **~ье** [12] misfortune; disaster; accide к **~ью** *or* на **~ье** unfortunately.

несчётный [14; -тен, -тна] i numerable.

нет 1. *part.:* no; ~ ещё not y **2.** *impers. vb.* [*pt.* не́ было, *ft.* бу́дет] (P): there is (are) no; у ме (*etc.*) ~ I (*etc.*) have no(ne); его́ (~ (s)he is not (t)here *or* in.

нетерп|ели́вый [14 *sh.*] impatien

.ение *n* [12] impatience; **.и́мый** 14 *sh.*] intolerant; intolerable.
е|**тле́нный** [14; -е́нен, -е́нна] mperishable; **.тре́звый** [14; трезв, -а́, -о] drunk (*a.* в .тре́з-ом ви́де); **.тро́нутый** [14 *sh.*] ntouched; **.трудоспосо́бный** 14; -бен, -бна] disabled.
ет|**то** ('nɛ-) [*ind.*] net; **.у** F = нет 2.
еу|**важе́ние** *n* [12] disrespect (for : Д); **.ве́ренный** [14 *sh.*] uncerain; **.вяда́емый** [14 *sh.*] unading; **.гаси́мый** [14 *sh.*] inexinguishable; **.гомо́нный** [14; о́нен, -о́нна] restless, unquiet; ntiring.
еуда́ч|**а** *f* [5] misfortune; failure; **.ливый** [14 *sh.*] unlucky; **.ник** *m* 1] unlucky fellow; **.ный** [14; чен, -чна] unsuccessful, unfortuate.
еуд|**ержи́мый** [14 *sh.*] irrepressble; **.иви́тельно** (it is) no wonler.
еудо́б|**ный** [14; -бен, -бна] inonvenient; uncomfortable; improper; **.ство** *n* [9] inconvenience.
еудов|**летвори́тельный** [14; лен, -льна] unsatisfactory; **.о́льствие** *n* [12] displeasure.
еуже́ли really?, is it possible?
еу|**жи́вчивый** [14 *sh.*] unsociable, naccomodating; **.кло́нный** [14; о́нен, -о́нна] unswerving, firm; **.клю́жий** [17 *sh.*] clumsy, awkward; **.кроти́мый** [14 *sh.*] indomitable; **.лови́мый** [14 *sh.*] elusive; imperceptible; **.ме́лый** 14 *sh.*] unskillful, awkward; **.ме́ние** *n* [12] inability; **.ме́ренный** [14 *sh.*] intemperate, immoderate; **.ме́стный** [14; -тен, -тна] nappropriate; **.моли́мый** [14 *sh.*] nexorable; **.мы́шленный** [14 *sh.*] unintentional; **.потреби́тельный** 14; -лен, -льна] not in use; **.рожа́й** *m* [3] bad harvest; **.ро́чный** [14] unseasonable; **.спе́х** *m* 1] failure; **.ста́нный** [14; -а́нен, а́нна] incessant; constant; *s. a.* .томи́мый; **.сто́йка** *f* [5; *g/pl.*: ое́к] forfeit; **.сто́йчивый** [14 *sh.*] unstable; unsteady; **.страши́мый** 14 *sh.*] intrepid, dauntless; **.сту́пчивый** [14 *sh.*] uncomplying, enacious; **.сы́пный** [14; -пен, пна] incessant, unremitting; *s. a.* .томи́мый; **.те́шный** [14; -шен, шна] disconsolate, inconsolable; **.толи́мый** [14 *sh.*] unquenchable; nsatiable; **.томи́мый** [14 *sh.*] tireess, indefatigable, untiring.
е́уч F *m* [1] ignoramus; **.ёный** [14] lliterate; **.е́нье** *n* [10] ignorance.
еу|**чти́вый** [14 *sh.*] uncivil; **.ю́тный** [14; -тен, -тна] uncomfortable; **.язви́мый** [14 *sh.*] invulnerable.
ефт|**еналивно́й** *s.* наливно́й; **.епрово́д** *m* [1] pipe line; **.ь** *f* [8] (mineral) oil; **.яно́й** [14] oil...
не|хва́тка F *f* [5; *g/pl.*: -ток] shortage; **.хоро́ший** [17; -ро́ш, -а́] bad; **.хотя** unwillingly; **.цензу́рный** [14; -рен, -рна] *s.* .присто́йный; **.ча́янный** [14] unexpected; accidental, casual.
не́чего [23]: (мне, *etc.*) ~ + *inf.* (there is *or* one can) (I have) nothing to ...; (one) need not, (there is) no need; (it is) no use; stop ...ing.
не|челове́ческий [16] inhuman; superhuman; **.чести́вый** [14 *sh.*] ungodly; **.че́стность** *f* [8] dishonesty; **.че́стный** [14; -тен, -тна́, -о] dishonest; **.чет** F *m* [1] *s.* нечётный; **.чётный** [14] odd (*number*).
нечист|опло́тный [14; -тен, -тна] uncleanly, dirty; **.ота́** *f* [5; *pl. st.*: -о́ты] unclean(li)ness; *pl.* sewage; **.ый** [14; -чи́ст, -а́, -о] unclean, dirty; impure; evil, vile, bad, foul.
не́что something.
не|чувстви́тельный [14; -лен, -льна] insensitive; insensible; **.ща́дный** [14; -ден, -дна] unmerciful; **.я́вка** *f* [5] nonappearance; **.я́ркий** [16; -я́рок, -ярка́, -о] dull, dim; mediocre; **.я́сный** [14; -сен, -сна́, -о] not clear; *fig.* vague.
ни not a (single оди́н); ~ ..., ~ neither ... nor; ... ever (*e. g.* кто [бы] ~ whoever); кто (что, когда́, где, куда́) бы то ~ был(о) whosoever (what-, when-, wheresoever); как ~ + *vb. a.* in spite *or* for all + *su.*; как бы (то) ~ было be that as it may; ~ за что ~ про что for nothing.
ни́ва *f* [5] field (*a. fig.*; in на П).
нигде́ nowhere.
Нидерла́нды *pl.* [1] The Netherlands.
ни́ж|е below, beneath, under; lower; shorter; **.еподписа́вшийся** *m* [17] the undersigned; **.ний** [15] lower; under...; ground *or* first (*floor*).
низ *m* [1; *pl. e.*] bottom, lower part; *pl. a.* masses; **.а́ть** [3], ⟨на-⟩ string.
низвер|га́ть [1], ⟨.гнуть⟩ [21]; **.же́ние** *n* [12] (over)throw.
низи́на *f* [5] hollow, lowland.
ни́зк|ий [16; -зок, -зка́, -о; *comp.*: ни́же] low; mean, base; short; **.опокло́нник** *m* [1] groveler; **.опокло́нничать** [1] grovel, fawn, cringe.
ни́зменн|ость *f* [8] lowland, plain; **.ый** [14 *sh.*] low(er).
низо|во́й [14] lower; local; **.вье** *n* [10; *g/pl.*: -ьев] lower (course); **.йти́** *s.* нисходи́ть; **'.сть** *f* [8] meanness.
ника́к by no means, not at all; **.о́й** [16] no (at all F); ни в како́м слу́чае on no account; *s. a.* ~.
ни́кел|евый [14], **.ь** *m* [4] nickel.
никогда́ never.
Никола́й [3] Nicholas.

ни|кой *s.* никак(ой); **~кто́** [23] nobody, no one, none; **~куда́** nowhere; *cf. a.* годи́ться, го́дный; **~кчёмный** F [14] good-for-nothing; **~ма́ло** *s.* ~ско́лько; **~отку́да** from nowhere; **~почём** F very cheap, easy, *etc.*; **~ско́лько** not in the least, not at all.
нисходя́щий [17] descending.
ни́т|ка *f* [5; *g/pl.:* -ток], **~ь** [8] thread; string; cotton; ~ь *a.* filament; до (после́дней) ~ки F to the skin; (как) по ~ке straight; ши́то бе́лыми ~ками be transparent, на живу́ю ~ку carelessly, superficially.
ниц: па́дать ~ prostrate o. s.
ничего́ (-ˈvɔ) nothing; ~ (себе́) not bad; so-so; no(t) matter; ~! never mind!, that's all right!
нич|е́й *m*, ~ья́ *f*, ~ьё *n*, ~ьи́ *pl.* [26] nobody's; *su. f* draw (*games*).
ничко́м prone; *s. a.* ниц.
ничто́ [23] nothing; *s.* ничего́; **~жество** *n* [9], **~жность** *f* [8] nothingness, vanity, nonentity; **~жный** [14; -жен, -жна] insignificant, tiny; vain.
нич|у́ть F *s.* нисколько; **~ья́** *s.* ~е́й.
ни́ша *f* [5] niche.
ни́щ|ая *f* [17], **~енка** F [5; *g/pl.*: -нок] beggar woman; **~енский** [16] beggarly; **~енство** *n* [9] begging; beggary; **~енствовать** [7] beg; **~ета́** *f* [5] poverty, destitution; **~ий** **1.** [17; нищ, -á, -е] beggarly; **2.** *m* [17] beggar.
НКВД (Наро́дный комиссариа́т вну́тренних дел) People's Commissariat of Internal Affairs (*1935 to 1946*; *since 1946* МВД, *cf.*).
но but, yet.
нова́тор *m* [1] innovator.
нове́лла *f* [5] short story.
но́в|енький [16; -нек] (brand-) new; **~изна́** *f* [5], **~и́нка** [5; *g/pl.:* -нок] novelty; news; **~ичо́к** *m* [1; -чка́] novice, tyro; newcomer.
ново|бра́нец *m* [1; -нца] recruit; **~бра́чный** [14] newly married; **~введе́ние** *n* [12] innovation; **~го́дний** [15] New Year's (Eve ~го́дний ве́чер *m*); **~лу́ние** *n* [12] new moon; **~прибы́вший** [17] newly arrived; newcomer; **~рождённый** [14] newborn (child); **~се́лье** *n* [10] new home; housewarming; **~стро́йка** *f* [5; *g/pl.*: -о́ек] new building (project).
но́в|ость *f* [8] (piece of) news; novelty; **~шество** *n* [9] innovation, novelty; **~ый** [14; нов, -á, -о] new; novel; recent; modern; Ձый год *m* New Year's Day; с Ձым го́дом! a happy New Year!; ~ый ме́сяц *m* crescent; что ~ого? what's (the) new(s *Brt.*)?; **~ь** *f* [8] virgin soil.
ног|а́ *f* [5; *ac/sg.*: но́гу; *pl.*: но́ги, ног, нога́м, *etc. e.*] foot, leg; идти́ в ∠у march in (*or* keep) step; со всех ~ with all one's might, at fu[ll] speed; стать на́ ~и recover; becom[e] independent; положи́ть ∠у на́ ~ cross one's legs; на ... ~е́ *or* ∠у on ... terms *or* a ... footing; in (*gran*[d]) style; ни ~о́й (к Д) not visit (a p.); (е́ле) ∠и унести́ (have a narrow) escape; в ~а́х at the foot (*cf.* го-лова́); под ~а́ми underfoot.
но́готь *m* [4; -гтя; *from g/pl. e*] nail.
нож *m* [1 *e.*] knife; на ~а́х at dagge[rs] drawn; **∠ик** *m* [1] F = нож; **∠ка** [5; *g/pl.*: -жек] *dim. of* нога́, *s.*; le[g] (*chair, etc.*); **∠ницы** *f/pl.* [5] (pa[ir] of) scissors; disproportion; **~но́**[й] [14] foot...; **∠ны́** *f/pl.* [5; *g/pl.*; -же[н] & -жо́н] sheath.
ноздря́ [6; *pl.*: но́здри, ноздре́[й] *etc. e.*] nostril.
ноль & **нуль** *m* [4 *e.*] naught; zer[o].
но́мер *m* [1; *pl.*: -pá, *etc. e.*] numb[er] ([with] за Т); size; (*hotel*) room; item, turn, trick; (*a., dim.,* **~о́к** *m* [... -рка́]) tag, plate.
номина́льный [14; -лен, -льн[а]] nominal.
нора́ *f* [5; *ac/sg.*: -ру́; *pl.st.*] hol[e], burrow.
Норве́|гия *f* [7] Norway; **Ձжец** [*m*] [1; -жца], **Ձжка** *f* [5; *g/pl.*: -жек]; **Ձжский** [16] Norwegian.
но́рка *f* [5; *g/pl.*: -рок] **1.** *dim.* [of] нора́; **2.** *zo.* mink.
но́рм|а *f* [5] norm, standard; rat[e]; **~а́льный** [14; -лен, -льна] norma[l]; **~ирова́ть** [7] (*im*)*pf.* standardize.
нос *m* [1; в, на носу́; *pl. e.*] nose; beak; prow; F spout; в ~ (*spea*[k]) through one's nose; за́ ~ (*lead*) b[y] the nose; на ~у́ (*time*) at hand; меня́ идёт кровь ∠ом my nose [is] bleeding; **∠ик** *m* [1] *dim. of* ~; spou[t].
носи́|лки *f/pl.* [5; *gen.*: -ло[к]] stretcher, litter; **~льщик** *m* [...] porter; **~тель** *m* [4] bearer; carrie[r]; **~ть** [15] carry, bear, *etc.*, *s.* нест[и]; wear (*v/i.* **-ся**); F **-ся** (с Т) *a.* hav[e] one's mind occupied with.
носово́й [14] nasal; prow ...; ~ пла[-] то́к *m* handkerchief.
носо́к *m* [1; -ска́] sock; toe; *a.* [...] но́сик.
носоро́г *m* [1] rhinoceros.
но́та *f* [5] note; *pl. a.* music.
нота́риус *m* [1] notary (public).
нота́ция *f* [7] reprimand, lecture.
ноч|ева́ть [7], ⟨пере-⟩ pass (*or*) spend) the night; **~ёвка** *f* [5; *g/pl*: -вок] overnight stop (*or* stay [or] rest); *a.* = ~ле́г; **~ле́г** *m* [1] night lodging, night quarters; *a.* = ~ёвк[а]; **~но́й** [14] night(ly), (*a.* ♀, *zo*[.]) nocturnal; ~на́я ба́бочка *f* mot[h]; **~ь** *f* [8; в ночи́; *from g/pl. e.*] nigh[t]; ∠ью at (*or* by) night (= *a.* в ~ь, [по] ~а́м); ~ь под ... (В) ... night.
но́ша *f* [5] load, burden.
ноя́брь *m* [4 *e.*] November.

-ав *m* [1] disposition, temper; *pl.* -ustoms; (не) по ~у (Д) (not) to -ne's liking; **~иться** [14], ⟨по-⟩ -lease (a p. Д); он мне ~ится I like -im; **~оучение** *n* [12] moral(ity), -noral teaching; **~оучительный** [14] moral(izing); **~ственность** *f* [8] morals *pl.*, morality; **~ствен-ный** [14 *sh.*] moral.

(*a.* ~-ка) well *or* now (then же)!, -ome (on)!, why!, what!; the deuce -take him *or* it ~ его́)!; (*a.* да ~?) -ndeed?, really?, you don't say!; -a?; ~ да of course, sure; ~ + *inf.* -egin to; ~ так что́ же? what -bout it? [tedious, humdrum.

-дный F [14; ну́ден, -дна́, -о]

-жд|а́ *f* [5; *pl. st.*] need, want (of П); necessity (of из Р, по Д); F -equest; concern; ~ы́ нет it doesn't -matter; **~а́ться** [1] (в П) (be in) -eed (of), be hard up, needy.

-жн|ый [14; ну́жен, -жна́, -о, ну́жны́] necessary (for Д); (Д) ~о + *inf.* must (*cf.* на́до).

нуль = ноль.

ну́мер = но́мер; **~а́ция** *f* [7] numeration; **~ова́ть** [7], ⟨за-, про-⟩ number.

ны́н|е now(adays), today; **~ешний** F [15] present, this; actual, today's; **~че** F = ~е.

ныр|я́ть [28], *once* ⟨~ну́ть⟩ [20] dive.

ныть [22] ache; whimper; F lament.

Нью-Йо́рк *m* [1] New York.

н. э. (на́шей э́ры) A. D.

нэп (но́вая экономи́ческая поли́тика) NEP (New Economic Policy. *Sov., from 1922 to 1928*).

нюх *m* [1] flair, scent; **~ательный** [14]: ~ательный таба́к *m* snuff; **~ать** [1], ⟨по-⟩ smell; scent; snuff.

ня́н|чить [16] nurse, tend (*a.* **-ся**; F fuss over, busy o. s. with [с Т]); **~я** *f* [6] (F **~ька** [5; *g/pl.*: -нек]) nurse, *Brt. a.* nanny.

О

-об, обо **1.** (П) about, of; on; with; (В) against, (up)on; by, in. -oh!, o!

-а *m & n*, **~е** *f* [37] both.

-агр|я́ть [28], ⟨~и́ть⟩ [13] redden, -urple; stain (with Т); steep.

-анкро́титься *s.* банкро́титься.

-ая́|ние *n* [12] spell, charm; **-тельный** [14; -лен, -льна] fasci-nating.

-ва́л *m* [1] collapse; landslide; -valanche; **~иваться** [1], ⟨~и́ться⟩ [13; обва́лится] fall in *or* off; **~я́ть** [1] *pf.* roll.

-вари́ть [13; -арю́, -а́ришь] -ald.

-вёр|тывать [1], ⟨~ну́ть⟩ [20] -rap (up), envelop.

-ве́|сить [15] F = ~шать.

-вести́ *s.* обводи́ть.

-ве́тренный [14 *sh.*] weather-eaten.

-ветша́лый [14] decayed.

-ве́ш|ивать, ⟨~ать⟩ [1] hang (with -).

-ви|ва́ть [1], ⟨~ть⟩ [обовью́, -ьёшь; *cf.* вить] wind round; -nbrace (with Т).

-вин|е́ние *n* [12] accusation, -arge; indictment; prosecution; **-и́тель** *m* [4] accuser; prosecutor; **-и́тельный** [14] accusatory; of -uilty'; ~и́тельный акт *m* indict-ment; **~я́ть** [28], ⟨~и́ть⟩ [13] (в П) -ccuse (of), charge (with); find -uilty; ~я́емый accused; defendant.

-ви́слый F [14] flabby.

-ви́|ть *s.* ~ва́ть.

-води́ть [13], ⟨обвести́⟩ [25] lead, - *or* look (round, about); enclose, encircle *or* border (with Т); draw out; F turn (*a p. round one's finger*).

обвор|а́живать [1], ⟨~ожи́ть⟩ [16 *e.*; -жу́, -жи́шь; -жённый] charm, fascinate; **~ожи́тельный** [14; -лен, -льна] charming, fascinating; **~ожи́ть** *s.* ~а́живать.

обвя́з|ывать [1], ⟨~а́ть⟩ [3] tie up *or* round; dress; hang.

обгоня́ть [28], ⟨обогна́ть⟩ [обгоню́, -о́нишь; обогна́л, -а́, -о; обо́гнанный] (out)distance, outstrip.

обгор|а́ть [1], ⟨~е́ть⟩ [9] scorch.

обгрыз|а́ть [1], ⟨~ть⟩ [24; *pt. st.*] gnaw (at, round, away).

обда|ва́ть [5], ⟨~ть⟩ [-а́м, -а́шь; *cf.* дать; о́бдал, -а́, -о; о́бданный (о́бдан, -а́, -о)] pour over; scald; bespatter; wrap up; seize.

обде́л|ать *s.* ~ывать; **~и́ть** *s.* ~я́ть; **~ывать**, ⟨~ать⟩ [1] work; lay out; cut (*gem*); F manage, wangle; **~я́ть** [28], ⟨~и́ть⟩ [13; -елю́, -е́лишь] deprive of one's due share (of Т).

обдира́ть [1], ⟨ободра́ть⟩ [обдеру́, -рёшь; ободра́л, -а́, -о; обо́дранный] bark, peel; tear (off).

обду́м|ать *s.* ~ывать; **~анный** [14 *sh.*] deliberate; **~ывать,** ⟨~ать⟩ [1] consider, think over.

обе́д *m* [1] dinner (at за Т; for на В, к Д), lunch; F noon; до (по́сле) ~а in the morning (afternoon); **~ать** [1], ⟨по-⟩ have dinner (lunch), dine; **~енный** [14] dinner..., lunch...

обедне́вший [17] impoverished.

обе́дня *f* [6; *g/pl.*: -ден] mass.

обез|бо́ливание *n* [12] an(a)esthetization; **~вре́живать** [1], ⟨~вре́дить⟩ [15] neutralize; **~гла́вли-**

вать [1], ⟨~гла́вить⟩ [14] behead; **~до́ленный** [14] wretched, miserable; **~зара́живание** *n* [12] disinfection; **~ли́чивать** [1], ⟨~ли́чить⟩ [16] deprive of personal character, assignment *or* responsibility; **~лю́деть** [8] *pf.* become deserted; **~надёживать** [1], ⟨~надёжить⟩ [16] bereave of hope; **~обра́живать** [1], ⟨~обра́зить⟩ [15] disfigure; **~опа́сить** [15] *pf.* secure (against от P); **~ору́живать** [1], ⟨~ору́жить⟩ [16] disarm; **~у́меть** [8] *pf.* lose one's senses, go mad.

обезья́н|а *f* [5] monkey; ape; **~ий** [18] monkey('s); apish, apelike; **~ничать** F [1] ape.

обер|ега́ть [1], ⟨~е́чь⟩ [26 г/ж: -гу́, -жёшь] guard (*v/i.* **-ся**), protect (o. s.; against, from от P).

оберну́ть(ся) *s.* обёртывать(ся).

обёрт|ка *f* [5; *g/pl.*: -ток] cover; (book) jacket; **~очный** [14] wrapping (*or* brown *paper*); **~ывать** [1], ⟨оберну́ть⟩ [20] wrap (up); wind; turn (*a.* F, *cf.* обводи́ть F); **-ся** turn (round, F back); F wangle.

обескура́ж|ивать [1], ⟨~ить⟩ [16] discourage, dishearten.

обеспе́ч|ение *n* [12] securing; security (on под B), guarantee; maintenance; (*social*) security; **~енность** *f* [8] (adequate) provision; prosperity; **~енный** [14] well-to-do; **~ивать** [1], ⟨~ить⟩ [16] provide (for; with T); secure, guarantee; protect.

обесси́л|еть [8] *pf.* become enervated; **~ивать** [1], ⟨~ить⟩ [13] enervate.

обессме́ртить [13] *pf.* immortalize.

обесцве́|чивать [1], ⟨~тить⟩ [15] discolo(u)r, make colo(u)rless.

обесце́н|ивать [1], ⟨~ить⟩ [13] depreciate.

обесче́стить [15] *pf.* dishono(u)r.

обе́т *m* [1] vow, promise; **~ова́нный** [14] Promised (*Land*).

обеща́|ние *n* [12], **~ть** [1] (*im*)*pf.*, F *a.* ⟨по-⟩ promise.

обжа́лование ⚖ *n* [12] appeal.

обж|ига́ть [1], ⟨~е́чь⟩ [26 г/ж: обожгу́, -жжёшь, обожгу́т; обжёг, обожгла́; обожжённый] burn; scorch; ⊕ bake, calcine (*cf.* ~ига́тельная печь *f* kiln); **-ся** burn o. s. (F one's fingers).

обжо́р|а F *m/f* [5] glutton; **~ливый** F [14 *sh.*] gluttonous; **~ство** F *n* [9] gluttony.

обзав|оди́ться [15], ⟨~ести́сь⟩ [25] provide o. s. (with T), acquire, get.

обзо́р *m* [1] survey; review.

обзыва́ть [1], ⟨обозва́ть⟩ [обзову́, -ёшь; обозва́л, -а́, -о; обо́званный] call (*names* T).

оби|ва́ть [1], ⟨~ть⟩ [обобью́, обобьёшь; *cf.* бить] upholster; strike off; F wear out; ~ва́ть поро́ги (у importune; **~вка** *f* [5] upholste[ry]

оби́|да *f* [5] insult; не в ~ду бу[дь] ска́зано no offence meant; не да[й] в ~ду let not be offended; **~де[ть]** (**-ся**) *s.* ~жа́ть(ся); **~дный** [1… -ден, -дна] offensive, insultin[g]; (мне) ~дно it is a shame *or* vexi[ng] (it offends *or* vexes me; I am sor[ry] [for за B]); **~дчивый** [14 *sh.*] touch[y]; **~дчик** F *m* [1] offender; **~жа́ть** [… ⟨~деть⟩ [11] (**-ся** be) offend(e[d]), hurt (*a.* be angry with *or* at на [B]) wrong; overreach (*cf. a.* обделя́т[ь]); **~женный** [14 *sh.*] offended (*s.* ~жа́ть[ся]).

оби́л|ие *n* [12] abundance, weal[th]; **~ьный** [14; -лен, -льна] abunda[nt] (in T), plentiful, rich.

обиня́к *m* [1 *e.*]: говори́ть ~á[ми] speak in a roundabout way.

обира́ть F [1], ⟨обобра́ть⟩ [обер[у́], -ёшь; обобра́л, -á, -о; обо́бра[н]ный] rob; P gather.

обита́|емый [14 *sh.*] inhabite[d]; **~тель** *m* [4] inhabitant; **~ть** [… live, dwell, reside.

оби́ть *s.* обива́ть.

обихо́д *m* [1] use, custom, wa[y]; дома́шний ~ household; **~ный** [1… -ден, -дна] everyday; colloquial

обкла́д|ка *f* [5] facing; **~ывать** [… ⟨обложи́ть⟩ [16] lay round; fa[ce], cover; ✂ fur; *pf.* besiege; *s.* облага́[ть]

обко́м *m* [1] (областно́й комит[ет]) regional committee *Sov.*).

обкра́дывать [1], ⟨обокра́сть⟩ [… обкраду́, -дёшь; *pt. st.* обкра́де[н]ный] rob.

обла́ва *f* [5] battue; raid.

облага́ть [1], ⟨обложи́ть⟩ [… impose (*tax, fine* T); tax; fine.

облагор|а́живать [1], ⟨~оди[ть]⟩ [15] ennoble, refine; finish.

облада́|ние *n* [12] possession (of … **~ть** [1] (T) possess; comma[nd]; (*health*) be in; ~ть собо́й cont[rol] o. s.

о́блако *n* [9; *pl.*: -ка́, -ко́в] clou[d]

обл|а́мывать [1], ⟨~ома́ть⟩ [1] ⟨~оми́ть⟩ [14] break off.

обласка́ть [1] *pf.* treat kindly.

област|но́й [14] regional; **'~ь** *f* … *from g/pl. e.*] region; provin[ce]; sphere, field (*fig.*).

обла́тка *f* [5; *g/pl.*: -ток] waf[er]; capsule.

облa|че́ние *n* [12] *eccl.* vestmen[t]

о́блачный [14; -чен, -чна] clou[dy]

обле|га́ть [1], ⟨~чь⟩ [26 г/ж; … лечь] cover; fit (*close*).

облегч|а́ть (-xtʃ-) [1], ⟨~и́ть⟩ [1… -чу́, -чи́шь; -чённый] lighten; [fa]cilitate; ease, relieve.

обледене́лый [14] ice-covered.

обле́злый F [14] mangy, shabby

обле|ка́ть [1], ⟨~чь⟩ [26] dre[ss], invest (with T); put, express; … put on (в B); be(come) invested

блеп|ля́ть [28], ⟨**~и́ть**⟩ [14] stick ll over (*or* round); besiege.
блет|а́ть [1], ⟨**~е́ть**⟩ [11] fly round *or: all over*, past, in); fall.
бле́чь [1], *s.* облега́ть & облека́ть.
бли|ва́ть [1], ⟨**~ть**⟩ [оболью, льёшь; облей!; о́блил, -á, -о; об-итый (о́бли́т, -á, -о)] pour (s. th. Т) over, wet; flood; soak; **-ся** [*pf.*: ился, -ила́сь, -и́ло́сь] (Т) pour over o. s.; shed (*tears*); be dripping *with sweat*) *or* covered (*with blood*); leed (*heart*).
блига́ция *f* [7] bond.
бли́з|ывать [1], ⟨**~а́ть**⟩ [3] lick off); **-ся** lick one's lips (*or* o. s.).
блик *m* [1] face, look; figure.
бли́|ть(ся) *s.* **~ва́ть(ся)**; **~цо́вы-вать** [1], ⟨**~цева́ть**⟩ [7] face.
блич|а́ть [1], ⟨**~и́ть**⟩ [16 *e.*; -чу́, чи́шь; -чённый] unmask; reveal; onvict (of в П); **~е́ние** *n* [12] ex-osure; conviction; **~и́тельный** 14; -лен, -льна] accusatory, in-riminating; **~и́ть** *s.* **~а́ть**.
блож|е́ние *n* [12] taxation; ⚔ iege; **~и́ть** *s.* обкла́дывать & блага́ть; **~ка** [5; *g/pl.*: -жек] over, (book) jacket.
блок|а́чиваться [1], ⟨**~оти́ться**⟩ 15 & 15 *e.*; -кочу́сь, -ко́ти́шься] ean one's elbows (on на В).
блом|а́ть, ~и́ть *s.* обла́мывать; **~ок** *m* [1; -мка] fragment; *pl.* ebris, wreckage.
блуч|а́ть [1], ⟨**~и́ть**⟩ [16 *e.*; -чу́, чи́шь; -чённый] ray.
блучо́к *m* [1; -чка́] (coach) box.
блюбова́ть [7] *pf.* take a fancy to.
бма́з|ывать [1], ⟨**~ать**⟩ [3] be-smear; plaster, coat, cement.
бма́к|ивать [1], ⟨**~ну́ть**⟩ [20] dip.
бма́н *m* [1] deception; deceit, raud; ~ зре́ния optical illusion; **~ный** [14] deceitful, fraudulent; **~у́ть(ся)** *s.* **~ывать(ся)**; **~чивый** 14 *sh.*] deceptive; **~щик** *m* [1], **~щица** *f* [5] cheat, deceiver; **~ы-вать** [1], ⟨**~у́ть**⟩ [20] (**-ся** be) de-ceive(d), cheat; (be mistaken in в П).
бм|а́тывать, ⟨**~ота́ть**⟩ [1] wind round): **~а́хивать** [1], ⟨**~ахну́ть**⟩ 19] wipe, dust; fan.
бме́н *m* [1] exchange (in/for в В/на В); interchange (of Т, Р); **~ивать** 1], ⟨**~я́ть**⟩ [28] & F ⟨**~и́ть**⟩ [13; еню́, -е́нишь; ~енённый] exchange for на В; **-ся** s.th. Т).
бм|ере́ть *s.* **~ира́ть**; **~ета́ть** [1], **~ести́**⟩ [25 -т-: обмету́] sweep off), dust; **~ира́ть** F [1], ⟨**~ере́ть**⟩ 12; обомру́, -рёшь; о́бмер, -рла́, о; обме́рший] be struck *or* stunned with *fear* от Р).
бмо́лв|иться [14] *pf* make a slip in speaking); (Т) mention, say; **~ка** *f* [5; *g/pl.*: -вок] slip of the ongue.
обмоло́т *m* [1] thresh(ing).
обморо́зить [15] *pf.* frostbite.
о́бморок *m* [1] faint, swoon (*vb.*: па́дать, *pf.* упа́сть в ~).
обмот|а́ть *s.* обма́тывать; **~ка** *f* [5; *g/pl.*: -ток] ⚡ winding; *pl.* put-tees.
обмундирова́|ние *n* [12], **~ть** [7] *pf.* uniform, outfit.
обмы|ва́ть [1], ⟨**~ть**⟩ [22] wash (off); **~ва́ние** *n* [12] *a.* ablution.
обнадёж|ивать [1], ⟨**~ить**⟩ [16] (re)assure, encourage, raise hopes.
обнаж|а́ть [1], ⟨**~и́ть**⟩ [16 *e.*; -жу́, -жи́шь; -жённый] bare, strip; lay bare; uncover; unsheathe.
обнаро́довать [7] *pf.* promulgate.
обнару́ж|ивать [1], ⟨**~ить**⟩ [16] disclose, show, reveal; discover, detect; **-ся** appear, show; come to light; be found, discovered.
обнести́ *s.* обноси́ть.
обн|има́ть [1], ⟨**~я́ть**⟩ [обниму́, обни́мешь; о́бнял, -á, -о; о́бнятый (о́бнят, -á, -о)] embrace, hug, clasp.
обнища́лый [14] impoverished.
обно́в|(к)а F *f* [5; (*g/pl.*: -вок)] new thing, novelty; **~и́ть** *s.* **~ля́ть**; **~ле́-ние** *n* [12] renewal; renovation; **~-ля́ть** [28], ⟨**~и́ть**⟩ [14 *e.*; -влю́, -ви́шь; -влённый] renew; renovate.
обн|оси́ть [15], ⟨**~ести́**⟩ [24 -с-: -су́] carry (round); serve; pass by; (Т) fence in, enclose; **-ся** F *impf.* wear out one's clothes.
обню́х|ивать, ⟨**~ать**⟩ [1] smell at.
обня́ть *s.* обнима́ть.
обобра́ть *s.* обира́ть.
обобщ|а́ть [1], ⟨**~и́ть**⟩ [16 *e.*; -щу́, -щи́шь; -щённый] generalize; **~-ествля́ть** [28], ⟨**~естви́ть**⟩ [14 *e.*; -влю́, -ви́шь; -влённый] socialize; **~и́ть** *s.* **~а́ть**.
обога|ща́ть [1], ⟨**~ти́ть**⟩ [15 *e.*; -ащу́, -ти́шь; -ащённый] enrich.
обогна́ть *s.* обгоня́ть.
обогну́ть *s.* огиба́ть.
обоготворя́ть [28] *s.* боготвори́ть.
обогрева́ть [1] *s.* греть.
о́бод *m* [1; *pl.*: обо́дья, -дьев] rim, felloe; **~о́к** *m* [1; -дка́] rim.
обо́др|анный F [14 *sh.*] ragged, shabby; **~а́ть** *s.* обдира́ть; **~е́ние** *n* [12] encouragement; **~я́ть** [28], ⟨**~и́ть**⟩ [13] encourage; **-ся** take courage.
обожа́ть [1] adore, worship.
обожда́ть F = подожда́ть.
обожеств|ля́ть [28], ⟨**~и́ть**⟩ [14 *e.*; -влю́, -ви́шь; -влённый] deify.
обожжённый [14; -ён, -ена́] burnt.
обо́з *m* [1] train (*a.* ⚔), carts *pl.*
обозва́ть *s.* обзыва́ть.
обознач|а́ть [1], ⟨**~ить**⟩ [16] denote, designate, mark; **-ся** appear; **~е́ние** *n* [12] designation.
обозр|ева́ть [1], ⟨**~е́ть**⟩ [9], **~е́ние** *n* [12] survey; review.
обо́|и *m/pl.* [3] wallpaper; **~йти́(сь)**

s. обходи́ть(ся); **~йщик** *m* [1] upholsterer; **~кра́сть** *s.* обкра́дывать.
оболо́чка *f* [5; *g/pl.*: -чек] cover(-ing), envelope; *anat.* membrane; ⊕ jacket, casing; ра́дужная ~ iris.
оболь|сти́тель *m* [4] seducer; **~сти́тельный** [14; -лен, -льна] seductive; **~щать** [1], ⟨~сти́ть⟩ [15 *e.*; -льщу́, -льсти́шь; -льщённый] seduce; (**-ся** be) delude(d; flatter o. s.); **~ще́ние** *n* [12] seduction; delusion.
обомле́ть F [8] *pf.* be stupefied.
обоня́ние *n* [12] (sense of) smell.
обора́чивать(ся) *s.* обёртывать(-ся).
оборв|а́нец F *m* [1; -нца] ragamuffin; **∠анный** [14 *sh.*] ragged; **~а́ть** *s.* обрыва́ть.
обо́рка *f* [5; *g/pl.*: -рок] frill, ruffle.
оборо́н|а *f* [5] defense (*Brt.* defence); **~и́тельный** [14] defensive, defense...; **~ный** [14] defense..., armament...; **~оспосо́бность** *f* [8] defensive capacity; **~я́ть** [28] defend.
оборо́т *m* [1] revolution; rotation; circulation; turn; turnover; transaction; back, reverse; (см.) на ~е p.t.o.; в ~ F (*take*) to task; **~и́ть(ся)** P [15] *pf. s.* оберну́ть(ся); **~ливый** F [14 *sh.*] sharp, smart; **~ный** [14] back, reverse, seamy (*side*); ⚕ circulating.
обору́дова|ние [12] equipment; **~ть** [7] (*im*)*pf.* equip; fit out.
обосн|ова́ние *n* [12] substantiation; ground(s); **~о́вывать** [1], ⟨~ова́ть⟩ [7] prove, substantiate; **-ся** settle down.
обос|обля́ть [28], ⟨~о́бить⟩ [14] segregate, isolate, detach.
обостр|я́ть [28], ⟨~и́ть⟩ [13] (**-ся** become) aggravate(d), strain(ed); refine(d).
обою́д|ный [14; -ден, -дна] mutual; **~оо́стрый** [14 *sh.*] double-edged.
обраб|а́тывать, ⟨~о́тать⟩ [1] work, process; ⚒ till; elaborate, finish, polish; treat; adapt; F work; *p. pr. a.* ⊕ manufacturing; **~о́тка** *f* [5; *g/pl.*: -ток] processing; ⚒ cultivation; elaboration; adaptation.
о́браз *m* [1] manner, way (in Т), mode; form; figure, character; image; [*pl.*: ~а́, *etc. e.*] icon; каки́м (таки́м) ~ом how (thus); нико́им ~ом by no means; **~е́ц** *m* [1; -зца́] specimen, sample; model, example; pattern; fashion, way (in на В); **~ный** [14; -зен, -зна] graphic, vivid; **~ова́ние** *n* [12] formation; constitution; education; **~о́ванный** [14 *sh.*] educated; **~ова́тельный** [14; -лен, -льна] (in)formative; **~о́вывать** [1], ⟨~ова́ть⟩ [7] form (*v/i.* **-ся**; arise); constitute; educate; cultivate; **~у́мить(ся)** F [14] *pf.* bring (come) to one's senses; **~цо́вый** [14] exemplary, model...; **~чик** *m* [1] *s.* ~е́ц.
обрам|ля́ть [28], ⟨∠ить⟩ [14 *st.*; *fig.* ⟨~и́ть⟩ [14 *e.*; -млю́, -ми́шь; -млённый] frame.
обраст|а́ть [1], ⟨~и́⟩ [24 -ст-: -сту; обро́с, -ла́] overgrow; be overgrown.
обра|ти́ть *s.* ~ща́ть; **∠тный** [14] back, return...; reverse, (*a.* ⚗) inverse; ⚖ retroactive; ∠тно back; conversely; **~ща́ть** [1] ⟨~ти́ть⟩ [15 *e.*; -ащу́, -ати́шь; -ащённый] turn; direct; convert; employ; draw or pay *or* (на себя́) attract (*attention* to на В); не ~ща́ть внима́ния (на В) disregard; **-ся** turn (to в В); address o. s. (to к Д), apply (to; for за Т); appeal; take (to *flight* в В); *impf.* (с Т) treat, handle; circulate; **~ще́ние** *n* [12] conversion; transformation; circulation; (с Т) treatment (of), management; manner *pl.*; address; appeal.
обре́з *m* [1] edge; **~а́ть** [1], ⟨~ать⟩ [3] cut off; cut short; **~ок** *m* [1; -зка] scrap; **~ывать** [1] *s.* ~а́ть.
обре|ка́ть [1], ⟨∠чь⟩ [26] doom (to на В, Д).
обремен|и́тельный [14; -лен, -льна] burdensome; **~я́ть** [28], ⟨~и́ть⟩ [13] burden.
обре|чённый [14] doomed (to на В); **∠чь** *s.* ~ка́ть.
обрисо́в|ывать [1], ⟨~а́ть⟩ [7] outline, sketch; **-ся** loom, appear.
обро́к *m* [1] (quit)rent, tribute.
обро́сший [17] overgrown.
обруб|а́ть [1], ⟨~и́ть⟩ [14] hew (off), lop; **∠ок** *m* [1; -бка] stump, block.
о́бруч *m* [1; *from g/pl. e.*] hoop; **~а́льный** [14] engagement...; **~а́ть** [1], ⟨~и́ть⟩ [16 *e.*; -чу́, -чи́шь; -чённый] affiance, betroth; **-ся** be(come) engaged (to с Т); **~е́ние** *n* [12] betrothal; **~ённый** [14] fiancé(e ~ённая *f*).
обру́ш|ивать [1], ⟨~ить⟩ [16] demolish; cast; **-ся** fall in, collapse; fall (up)on (на В).
обры́в *m* [1] precipice, steep; **~а́ть** [1], ⟨оборва́ть⟩ [-ву́, -вёшь; -ва́л, -вала́, -о; обо́рванный] tear or pluck (off, round); break off, cut short; **-ся** *a.* fall (from с Р); **~истый** [14 *sh.*] steep; abrupt; **~ок** *m* [1; -вка] scrap, shred; **~очный** [14; -чен, -чна] scrappy.
обры́зг|ивать, ⟨~ать⟩ [1] sprinkle.
обрю́зглый [14] flabby, bloated.
обря́д *m* [1] ceremony, rite.
об|са́живать [1], ⟨~сади́ть⟩ [15] plant (with Т); **~сева́ть** [1], ⟨~се́ять⟩ [27] sow; stud (with Т).
обсервато́рия *f* [7] observatory.
обсле́дова|ние *n* [12] (P) inspection (of), inquiry (into), investiga-

tion (of); **~ть** [7] (*im*)*pf.* inspect, examine, investigate.
обслу́ж|ивание *n* [12] service; operation; **~ивать** [1], ⟨~и́ть⟩ [16] serve, attend; operate; supply (В/Т).
обсо́хнуть *s.* обсыха́ть.
обста|вля́ть [28], ⟨**~**вить⟩ [14] surround; furnish, fit out (with Т); F arrange, settle; **~но́вка** *f* [5; *g*/*pl.*: -вок] furniture; *thea.* scenery; situation, conditions *pl.*
обстоя́тель|ный [14; -лен, -льна] detailed, circumstantial; F solid, thorough; **~ственный** [14] adverbial; **~ство** *n* [9] circumstance (under, in при П, в П; for по Д); *gr.* adverb.
обстоя́ть [-ои́т] be, stand; как обстои́т де́ло с (Т)? what about ...?
обстре́л *m* [1] bombardment, fire; **~ивать** [1], ⟨~я́ть⟩ [28] fire on, shell; *p. pt. p.* F tried.
обступ|а́ть [1], ⟨~и́ть⟩ [14] surround.
об|сужда́ть [1], ⟨~суди́ть⟩ [15; -ждённый] discuss; **~сужде́ние** *n* [12] discussion; **~суши́ть** [16] *pf.* dry; **~счита́ть** [1] *pf.* cheat; **-ся** miscalculate.
обсып|а́ть [1], ⟨**~**ать⟩ [2] strew.
обс|ыха́ть [1], ⟨~о́хнуть⟩ [21] dry.
обт|а́чивать [1], ⟨~очи́ть⟩[16] turn; **~ека́емый** [14] streamline...; **~ере́ть** *s.* ~ира́ть; **~ёсывать** [1], ⟨~еса́ть⟩ [3] hew; **~ира́ть** [1], ⟨~ере́ть⟩ [12; оботру́; обтёр; *ger. pt. a.*: -тёрши & -терёв] rub off *or* down, wipe (off), dry; F fray.
обточи́ть *s.* обта́чивать.
обтрёпанный [14] shabby, frayed.
обтя́|гивать [1], ⟨~ну́ть⟩ [19] cover (with Т); *impf.* fit close; **~жка** *f* [5]: в ~жку close-fitting.
обу|ва́ть [1], ⟨**~**ть⟩ [18] put (-ся one's) shoes on; F shoe; **'~вь** *f* [8] footwear, shoes *pl.*
обу́гл|ивать [1], ⟨~ить⟩ [13] char.
обу́за *f* [5] burden, load.
обузд|ывать [1], ⟨~а́ть⟩ [1] bridle.
обусло́в|ливать [1], ⟨~ить⟩ [14] condition (on Т); cause.
обу́ть(ся) *s.* обува́ть(ся).
о́бух *m* [1] butt; F thunder(*struck*).
обуч|а́ть [1], ⟨~и́ть⟩ [16] teach (s. th. Д), train; **-ся** (Д) learn, be taught; **~е́ние** *n* [12] instruction, training; education.
обхва́т *m* [1] arm's span; circumference; **~ывать** [1], ⟨~и́ть⟩ [15] clasp (in Т), embrace, infold.
обхо́|д *m* [1] round, beat (be on де́лать); detour; *vb.* + в ~д *s.* ~ди́ть; evasion; **~ди́тельный** [14; -лен, -льна] affable, amiable; **~ди́ть** [15], ⟨обойти́⟩ [обойду́, -дёшь; *cf.* идти́] go *or* pass round; travel through (many) *or* over; visit (all [one's]); ⚔ outflank; avoid; pass over (in Т); (**-ся**, ⟨-сь⟩) cost (me мне); manage; do without (без Р); there is (*no ... without*); treat (s.b. с Т); **~дный** [14] roundabout; **~жде́ние** *n* [12] treatment, manners *pl.*
обш|а́ривать [1], ⟨~а́рить⟩ [13] rummage (around); **~ива́ть** [1], ⟨~и́ть⟩ [обошью́, -шьёшь; *cf.* шить] sew round, border (with Т); plank, face, sheath; F clothe; **~и́вка**; *f* [5] trimming, *etc.* (*s. vb.*).
обши́|рный [14; -рен, -рна] vast, extensive; numerous; **~ть** *s.* ~ва́ть.
обща́ться [1] associate (with с Т).
обще|досту́пный [14; -пен, -пна] popular; *s. a.* досту́пный; **~жи́тие** *n* [12] hostel, home; social intercourse *or* (way of) life; **~изве́стный** [14; -тен, -тна] well-known.
обще́ние *n* [12] intercourse.
общепри́нятый [14 *sh.*] generally accepted, common.
обще́ств|енность *f* [8] community, public (opinion); **~енный** [14] social, public; common; **'~о** *n* [9] society; company; association; community; **~ове́дение** *n* [12] social science.
общеупотреби́тельный [14; -лен, -льна] current, common, widespread.
о́бщ|ий [17; общ, -а́, -е] general; common (in ~его); public; total, (в ~ем on the) whole; (*table*) d'hôte; **~ина** *f* [5] community; † *a.* = ~ество; **~и́тельный** [14; -лен, -льна] sociable, affable; **~ность** *f* [8] community; commonness.
объе|да́ть [1], ⟨**~**сть⟩ [-е́м, -е́шь, *etc. s.* есть[1]] eat *or* gnaw round, away; **-ся** overeat o.s.
объедин|е́ние *n* [12] association, union; unification; **~я́ть** [28], ⟨~и́ть⟩ [13] unite (*cf. a.* ООН), join (**-ся** *v*/*i.*); rally.
объе́дки F *m*/*pl.* [1] leavings.
объе́|зд *m* [1] detour, by-pass; *vb.* + в ~зд = **~зжа́ть** [1] **1.** ⟨~хать⟩ [-е́ду, -е́дешь] go, drive round; travel through *or* over; visit (all [one's]); **2.** ⟨~здить⟩ [15] break in; F *s.* 1.; **~кт** *m* [1] object; **~кти́вный** [14; -вен, -вна] objective.
объём *m* [1] volume; size; extent, range; **~истый** [14 *sh.*] voluminous,
объе́сть(ся) *s.* объеда́ть(ся).
объе́хать *s.* объезжа́ть 1.
объяв|и́ть *s.* ~ля́ть; **~ле́ние** *n* [12] announcement, notice; advertisement; declaration; **~ля́ть** [28], ⟨~и́ть⟩ [14] declare (s.th. *a.* о П; s.b. [to be] s.th. В/Т), tell; announce, proclaim; advertise; express.
объясн|е́ние *n* [12] explanation; declaration (of *love* в П); **~и́мый** [14 *sh.*] explicable, accountable; **~и́тельный** [14] explanatory; **~я́ть** [28], ⟨~и́ть⟩ [13] explain, illustrate; account for; **-ся** explain o.s.; be

accounted for; declare o.s.; *impf.* make o.s. understood (by T).
объя́тия *n/pl.* [12] embrace (*vb.*: заключи́ть в ~); (*with open*) arms.
обыва́тель *m* [4], inhabitant; Philistine; **~ский** [16] Philistine...
обы́гр|ывать, ⟨~а́ть⟩ [1] beat; win.
обы́денный [14] everyday, ordinary.
обыкнове́н|ие *n* [12] habit; по ~ию as usual; **~ный** [14; -е́нен, -е́нна] ordinary, usual, habitual.
о́быск *m* [1], **∠ивать** [1], ⟨~а́ть⟩ [3] search
обы́ч|ай *m* [3] custom; F habit; **~ный** [14; -чен, -чна] customary, usual, habitual.
обя́занн|ость *f* [8] duty; ⚔ service; исполня́ющий ~ости (P) acting; **~ый** [14 *sh.*] obliged; indebted, owe; responsible.
обяза́тель|ный [14; -лен, -льна] obligatory, compulsory; **~но** without fail, certainly; **~ство** *n* [9] obligation; liability; engagement.
обя́з|ывать [1], ⟨~а́ть⟩ [3] oblige; bind, commit; **-ся** engage, undertake, pledge o s.
овдове́вший [17] widowed.
овёс *m* [1; овса́] oats *pl.*
ове́чий [18] sheep('s).
овлад|ева́ть [1], ⟨~е́ть⟩ [8] (T) seize, take possession of; get control over; master.
о́вощ|и *m/pl.* [1; *gen.*: -ще́й, *etc. e.*] vegetables; **~но́й** [14]: ~но́й магази́н *m* greengrocery.
овра́г *m* [1] ravine.
овся́нка *f* [5; *g/pl.*: -нок] oatmeal.
овц|а́ *f* [5; *pl. st.*; *g/pl.*: ове́ц] sheep; **~ево́дство** *n* [9] sheep breeding.
овча́рка *f* [5; *g/pl.*: -рок] sheep dog.
овчи́на *f* [5] sheepskin.
ога́рок *m* [1; -рка] candle end.
огиба́ть [1], ⟨обогну́ть⟩ [20] turn *or* bend (round); ⚓ double.
оглавле́ние *n* [12] table of contents.
огла́|ска *f* [5] publicity; **~ша́ть** [1], ⟨~си́ть⟩ [15 *e.*; -ашу́, -аси́шь -ашённый] announce; divulge; publish (the banns of); fill, resound; **-ся** ring; **~ше́ние** [12] announcement; publication; banns *pl.*
огло́бля *f* [6; *g/pl.*: -бель] shaft.
оглуш|а́ть [1], ⟨~и́ть⟩ [16 *e.*; -шу́, -ши́шь; -шённый] deafen, stun; **~и́тельный** [14; -лен, -льна] deafening, stunning.
огля́|дка F *f* [5]: без ~дки headlong, hastily; **~дывать** [1], ⟨~де́ть⟩ [11] examine, take a view of; **-ся 1.** look round; **2.** *pf.*: ⟨~ну́ться⟩ [20] look back (at на В).
огне|во́й [14] fire...; fiery; **~ды́шащий** [17] volcanic; **~мёт** *m* [1] flame thrower; **'~нный** [14] fiery; **~опа́сный** [14; -сен, -сна] inflammable; **~сто́йкий** [16; -о́ек, -о́йка] *s.* ~упо́рный; **~стре́льный** [14] fire(*arm*); **~туши́тель** *m* [4] fire extinguisher; **~упо́рный** [14; -рен, -рна] fireproof; fire (*clay, etc.*)
огни́во *n* [9] (fire) steel, stone.
огов|а́ривать [1], ⟨~ори́ть⟩ [13] slander; stipulate; *a.* = **-ся** make reservation; *s. a.* обмо́лвиться; **~о́р** F *m* [1] slander; **~о́рка** *f* [5; *g/pl.*: -рок] reservation, reserve proviso; *a.* = обмо́лвка, *cf.*
огол|я́ть [28], ⟨~и́ть⟩ [13] bare.
огонёк *m* [1; -нька́] light; spark.
ого́нь *m* [4; огня́] fire (*a. fig.*) light; из огня́ да в по́лымя out of the frying pan into the fire; сквозь ~ и во́ду through thick & thin.
огор|а́живать [1], ⟨~оди́ть⟩ [15 & 15 *e.*; -ожу́, -о́ди́шь; -о́женный] enclose, fence (in); **~о́д** *m* [1] kitchen garden; **~о́дник** *m* [1] trucker market *or* kitchen gardener; **~о́дничество** *n* [9] trucking, market gardening.
огорч|а́ть [1], ⟨~и́ть⟩ [16 *e.*; -чу́, -чи́шь; -чённый] grieve (**-ся** *v/i.*) (be) afflict(ed), vex(ed), distress(ed) with T); **~е́ние** *n* [9] grief, affliction, trouble; **~и́тельный** [14; -лен, -льна] grievous; vexatious.
огра|бле́ние *n* [12] robbing, robbery; **∠да** *f* [5] fence; wall; **~жда́ть** [1], ⟨~ди́ть⟩ [15 *e.*; -ажу́, -ади́шь -аждённый] enclose; guard, protect; **~жде́ние** *n* [12] enclosure protection.
огранич|е́ние *n* [12] limitation restriction; **∠енный** [14 *sh.*] confined; limited; narrow(-minded); **∠ивать** [1], ⟨∠ить⟩ [16] confine limit, restrict (o.s. **-ся**; to T; content o.s. with; not go beyond); **~и́тельный** [14]; -лен, -льна] restrictive.
огро́мный [14; -мен, -мна] huge vast; enormous, tremendous.
огрубе́лый [14] coarse, hardened.
огрыз|а́ться F [1], *once* ⟨~ну́ться⟩ [20] snap; **∠ок** *m* [1; -зка] bit, end stump, stub.
огу́льный F [14; -лен, -льна] wholesale, indiscriminate; unfounded *adv. a.* in the lump.
огуре́ц *m* [1; -рца́] cucumber.
ода́лживать [1], ⟨одолжи́ть⟩ [16 *e.*; -жу́, -жи́шь] lend (a. p. s. th Д/В); borrow; oblige (a p. by В/Т).
одар|ённый [14 *sh.*] gifted; **∠ивать** [1], ⟨~и́ть⟩ [13] present, gift; (with Т); *fig.* (*impf.* **~я́ть** [28]) endow (with T).
оде|ва́ть [1], ⟨∠ть⟩ [-е́ну, -е́нешь -е́тый) dress (**-ся** *v/i.*); **∠жда** *f* [5] clothes *pl.*, clothing.
одеколо́н *m* [1] cologne. [вать.]
одел|я́ть [28], ⟨~и́ть⟩ [13] *s.* ода́ри-
одеревене́лый [14] numb.
оде́рж|ивать [1], ⟨~а́ть⟩ [4] gain

win; **~имый** [14 *sh.*] (Т) obsessed (by), afflicted (with).
одéть(ся) *s.* одевáть(ся).
одеяло *n* [9] blanket, cover(let).
один *m*, однá *f*, однó *n*, одни́ *pl.* [33] one; alone; only; a, a certain, some; однó *su.* one thing, thought, *etc.*; ~ на ~ face to face; tête-à-tête; hand to hand; все до одногó (*or* все как ~) all to a (*or* the last) man; *cf.* пять & пятый.
один|áковый [14 *sh.*] equal, identical, the same; **~ёшенек** [-нька] F quite alone; **~надцатый** [14] eleventh; *cf.* пятый; **~надцать** [35] eleven; *cf.* пять; **~óкий** [16 *sh.*] lonely; single; lonesome; **~óчество** *n* [9] solitude, loneliness; **~óчка** *m/f* [5; *g/pl.*: -чек] lone person; individualist; one-man boat (*or* F cell); ~óчкой, в ~óчку alone; **~óчный** [14] single, solitary; individual; one-man...
одичáлый [14] (run) wild.
однáжды once, one day.
однáко, (*a.* ~ ж[е]) however, yet, still.
однó... : **~бóртный** [14] single-breasted; **~временный** [14] simultaneous; **~глáзый** [14] one-eyed; **~днéвный** [14] one-day; **~звýчный** [14; -чен, -чна] monotonous; **~знáчный** [14; -чен, -чна] synonymous (*a.* **~знáчащий** [17]); & simple, of one place; **~имённый** [14; -ёнен, -ённа] of the same name; **~клáссник** *m* [1] classmate; **~колéйный** [14] single-track; **~крáтный** [14; -тен, -тна] occuring once, single; *gr.* momentary; **~лéтний** [15] one-year(-old); ⚘ annual; **~лéток** *m* [1; -тка] coeval; **~мéстный** [14] single-seated; **~образный** [14; -зен, -зна] monotonous; **~рóдный** [14; -ден, -дна] homogeneous; **~рýкий** [16] one-armed; **~слóжный** [14; -жен, -жна] monosyllabic; **~сторóнний** [15; -óнен, -óння] one-sided (*a. fig.*); unilateral; **~фами́лец** *m* [1; -льца] namesake; **~цвéтный** [14; -тен, -тна] monochromatic; plain; **~этáжный** [14] one-storied (*Brt.* -reyed).
одобр|éние *n* [12] approval, approbation; **~ительный** [14; -лен, -льна] approving; **~ять** [28], ‹~ить› [13] approve (of).
одол|евáть [1], ‹~éть› [8] overcome, defeat; F exhaust; master.
одолж|éние *n* [12] favo(u)r; **~ить** *s.* одáлживать.
одр † *m* [1 *e.*] bed, couch; bier.
одувáнчик *m* [1] dandelion.
одýм|ываться, ‹~аться› [1] change one's mind.
одур|мáнивать [1], ‹~мáнить› [13] stupefy; **'~ь** F [8] stupor; **~ять** F [28] stupefy.
одутловáтый [14 *sh.*] puffed up.
одухотвор|ять [28], ‹~ить› [13] inspire.
одушев|лённый [14] *gr.* animate; **~лять** [28], ‹~ить› [14 *e.*; -влю, -вишь; -влённый] animate, inspire.
оды́шка *f* [5] short wind.
ожерéлье *n* [10] necklace.
ожесточ|áть [1], ‹~ить› [16 *e.*; -чý, чи́шь; чённый] harden; exasperate; **~éние** *n* [12] exasperation; bitterness; **~ённый** [14 *sh.*] *a.* violent, fierce, bitter.
ожи|вáть [1], ‹~ть› [-ивý, -ивёшь; óжил, -á, -о] revive; **~вить(ся)** *s.* ~влять(ся); **~влéние** *n* [12] animation; **~влённый** [14 *sh.*] animated, lively; bright; **~влять** [28], ‹~вить› [14 *e.*; -влю, -вишь, -влённый] enliven, animate, resuscitate; **-ся** quicken, revive; brighten.
ожидá|ние *n* [12] expectation; зал ~ния waiting room; **~ть** [1] wait (for Р); expect, await.
ожи́ть *s.* оживáть.
ожóг *m* [1] burn; scald.
озабó|чивать [1], ‹~тить› [15] disquiet, alarm; **-ся** attend to (Т); **~ченный** [14 *sh.*] anxious, solicitous (about Т); preoccupied.
озаглáв|ливать [1], ‹~ить› [14] entitle, supply with a title.
озадáч|ивать [1], ‹~ить› [16] puzzle, perplex.
озар|ять [28], ‹~ить› [13] (**-ся** be[come]) illuminate(d), light (lit) up; brighten, lighten.
озверéть [8] *pf.* become brutal.
оздоров|лять [1], ‹~ить› [14] reorganize, reform, improve (the health of).
óзеро *n* [9; *pl.*: озёра, -ёр] lake.
ози́мый [14] winter (*crops*).
озирáться [1] look (round *or* back).
озлоб|лять [28], ‹~ить› [14] (**-ся** become) exasperate(d), embitter(ed); **~лéние** *n* [12] exasperation.
ознак|омлять [28], ‹~óмить› [14] familiarize (o.s. **-ся**, с Т with).
ознамен|овáние *n* [12] commemoration (in в В); **~óвывать** [1], ‹~овáть› [7] mark, commemorate, celebrate.
означáть [1] signify, mean.
озноб *m* [1] chill.
озор|ни́к *m* [1 *e.*], **~ни́ца** *f* [5] F *s.* шалýн(ья); Р ruffian; **~ничáть** [1] F *s.* шали́ть; Р behave outrageously; **~нóй** F [14] mischievous, naughty; **~ствó** F *n* [9] mischief; outrage, excess.
ой oh! o dear!; ~ какóй F awful.
окáз|ывать [1], ‹~áть› [3] show; render, do; exert (*influence*); give (*preference*); **-ся** (Т) turn out (to be), be found; find o.s.; be (shown, rendered, given).
окайм|лять [1], ‹~ить› [14 *e.*; -млю, -ми́шь, -млённый] border.
окаменéлый [14] petrified.

ока́нчивать [1], ⟨око́нчить⟩ [16] finish end (**-ся** *v/i.*).
ока́пывать [1], ⟨окопа́ть⟩ [1] dig round; entrench (o.s. **-ся**).
окая́нный [14] damned, cursed.
океа́н *m* [1], **~ский** [16] ocean.
оки́|дывать [1], ⟨~нуть⟩ [20] (взгля́дом) take a view of, look at.
окис|ля́ть [28],⟨~ли́ть⟩[13] oxidize; **′~ь** *f* [8] oxide.
оккуп|ацио́нный [14] occupation-...; **~и́ровать** [7] (*im*)*pf.* occupy.
окла́д *m* [1] salary; tax rate.
окла́дистый [14 *sh.*] full (*beard*).
окле́и|вать [1], ⟨~ть⟩ [13] paste; paper.
о́клик *m* [1], **~а́ть** [1], ⟨**∠**нуть⟩ [20] call, hail.
окно́ *n* [9; *pl. st.:* о́кна, о́кон, о́кнам] window (*look* through в В).
о́ко ✎ [9; *pl.*: о́чи, оче́й, *etc. e.*] eye.
оков|а́ть *s.* **∠**ывать; **∠ы** *f/pl.* [5] fetters; **∠ывать** [1], ⟨~а́ть⟩ [7 *e.*; окую́, окуёшь; око́ванный] bind; fetter.
околдова́ть [7] *pf.* bewitch.
окол|ева́ть [1], ⟨~е́ть⟩ [8] die.
око́лица *f* [5] *s.* окра́ина & обиня́к.
о́кол|о (Р) about, around; by, at, near(ly); nearby; **∠ыш** *m* [1] cap-band; **∠ьный** [14] roundabout.
око́нный [14] window...
оконч|а́ние *n* [12] end(ing *gr.*), close, termination, completion ([up]on по П), conclusion; **~а́тельный** [14; -лен, -льна] final, definitive; **∠ить** *s.* ока́нчивать.
око́п *m* [1] trench; **~а́ть(ся)** *s.* ока́пывать(ся).
о́корок *m* [1; *pl.:* -ка́, *etc. e.*] ham.
око|стене́лый [14] ossified; hardened; *a.* = **~ченéлый** [14] numb (with cold).
око́ш|ечко *n* [9; *g/pl.*: -чек], **~ко** *n* [9; *g/pl.:* -шек] *dim. of* окно́.
окра́ина *f* [5] outskirts *pl.*
окра́|ска *f* [5] painting; dyeing; tinge; **~шивать** [1], ⟨~сить⟩ [15] paint; dye; tinge.
окре́стн|ость (*often pl.*) *f* [8] environs *pl.*, neighbo(u)rhood; **~ый** [14] surrounding; in the vicinity.
окрова́вленный [14] bloodstained.
о́круг *m* [1; *pl.*: -га́, *etc. e.*] district; избира́тельный ~ constituency.
округл|я́ть [28], ⟨~и́ть⟩ [13] round (off); **∠ый** [14 *sh.*] roundish.
окруж|а́ть [1], ⟨~и́ть⟩ [16 *e.*; -жу́, -жи́шь; -жённый] surround; **~а́ющий** [17] surrounding; **~е́ние** *n* [12] environment; environs *pl.*, neighbo(u)rhood; encirclement; circle company; **~и́ть** *s.* **~**а́ть; **~но́й** [14] district...; circular; **∠ность** *f* [8] circumference; circle; † vicinity.
окрыл|я́ть [28], ⟨~и́ть⟩ [13] *fig.* wing, encourage.
октя́брь *m* [4 *e.*], **~ский** [16] October.
окули́ровать [7] (*im*)*pf.* graft.
окун|а́ть [1], ⟨~у́ть⟩ [20] dip, plunge (*v/i.* **-ся**; dive, *a. fig.*).
о́кунь *m* [4; *from g/pl. e.*] perch.
окуп|а́ть [1],⟨~и́ть⟩[14] (**-ся** be) offset, recompense(d), compensate(d).
оку́рок *m* [1; -рка] cigarette end, cigar stub.
оку́т|ывать, ⟨~ать⟩ [1] wrap (up).
ола́дья *f* [6; *g/pl.:* -дий] fritter.
оледене́лый [14] frozen, iced.
оле́нь *m* [4] deer; се́верный ~ reindeer.
оли́в|а *f* [5], **~ка** *f* [5; *g/pl.*: -вок], **~ковый** [14] olive.
олимп|иа́да *f* [5] Olympiad; **~и́йский** [16] Olympic.
олицетвор|е́ние *n* [12] personification, embodiment; **~я́ть** [28], ⟨~и́ть⟩ personify, embody.
о́лов|о *n* [8], **~я́нный** [14] tin.
о́лух P *m* [1] blockhead, dolt.
ольх|а́ *f* [5], **~о́вый** [14] alder.
ома́р *m* [1] lobster.
оме́ла *f* [5] mistletoe.
омерз|е́ние *n* [12] abhorrence, loathing; **~и́тельный** [14; -лен, -льна] abominable, detestable, loathsome; F lousy.
омертве́лый [14] numb; dead.
омле́т *m* [1] omelet(te).
омоложе́ние *n* [12] rejuvenation.
омо́ним *m* [1] *ling.* homonym.
омрач|а́ть [1], ⟨~и́ть⟩ [16 *e.*; -чу́, -чи́шь; -чённый] darken, sadden (*v/i.* **-ся**).
о́мут *m* [1] whirlpool, vortex; deep.
омы|ва́ть [1], ⟨**∠**ть⟩ [22] wash.
он *m*, **~á** *f*, **~ó** *n*, **~и́** *pl.* [22] he, she, it, they.
онеме́лый [14] numb; F dumb.
оне́жск|ий [16]: ≗ое о́зеро *n* Lake Onega.
ону́ча *f* [5] *s.* портя́нка.
ООН (Организа́ция Объединённых На́ций) U.N.O. (United Nations Organization).
опа|да́ть [1], ⟨**∠**сть⟩ [25; *pt. st.*] fall (off); diminish, decrease.
опа́|здывать, ⟨опозда́ть⟩ [1] be late (for на В, к Д), arrive (5 min. late (на пять мину́т); miss (*train* на В); **~ла** *f* [5] disgrace, ban; **~льный** [14] disgraced.
опал|я́ть [28], ⟨~и́ть⟩ [13] singe.
опас|а́ться [1] (Р) fear, apprehend; beware (of); **~е́ние** *n* [12] fear, apprehension, anxiety; **∠ливый** [14 *sh.*] wary; anxious; **∠ность** *f* [8] danger, peril, jeopardy; risk (at/of с Т/для Р); **∠ный** [14; -сен, -сна] dangerous (to для Р); **∠ть** *s.* опада́ть.
опе́к|а *f* [5] guardianship, (*a. fig.*) tutelage; trusteeship; **~а́ть** [1] be guardian (trustee) to; patronize; **~а́емый** [14] ward; **~у́н** *m* [1 *e.*], **~у́нша** *f* [5] guardian; trustee.
опер|ати́вный [14] operative; surgical; executive; ⚔ front..., war.

~áтор *m* [1] operator (*a.* ⚕ = surgeon); **~ацио́нный** [14] operating.

пере|жáть [1], ⟨~ди́ть⟩ [15] outstrip (*a. fig.* = outdo, surpass); **~ние** *n* [12] plumage; **~ться** *s.* опирáться.

пери́ровать [7] (*im*)*pf.* operate.

перный [14] opera(tic).

пер|я́ться [28], ⟨~и́ться⟩ [13] fledge.

печáт|ка *f* [5; *g/pl.*: -ток] misprint, erratum; **~ывать,** ⟨~ать⟩ [1] seal (up).

пи́лки *f/pl.* [5; *gen.*: -лок] sawdust.

пирáться [1], ⟨оперéться⟩ [12; обопру́сь, -рёшься; опёрся, оперлáсь] lean (against, on на В), *a. fig* = rest, rely ([up]on).

пис|áние *n* [12] description; **~áтельный** [14] descriptive; **~áть** *s.* ~ывать; **~ка** *f* [5; *g/pl.*: -сок] slip of the pen; **~ывать** [1], ⟨~áть⟩ [3] describe (*a.* ⚹); make (*an inventory* [of]); distrain (upon); **-ся** make a slip of the pen; **'~сь** *f* [8] list, inventory; distraint.

плáк|ивать [1], ⟨~ать⟩ [3] bewail, deplore, mourn (over).

плá|та *f* [5] pay(ment); settlement; **~чивать** [1], ⟨~ти́ть⟩ [15] pay (for); remunerate; settle.

плеу́ха F *f* [5] box on the ear.

плодотвор|éние *n* [12] fertilization; **~я́ть** [28], ⟨~и́ть⟩ [13 [fertilize, fecundate.

плóт *m* [1] bulwark, stronghold.

плóшность *f* [8] blunder.

пове|щáть [1], ⟨~сти́ть⟩ [15 *e.*; -ещу́, -ести́шь; -ещённый] notify; inform, ✝ *a.* advise (of о П).

поздá|ние *n* [12] delay; *vb.* + с ~нием = **~ть**, *s.* опáздывать.

позн|авáтельный [14] distinctive; **~авáть** [5], ⟨~áть⟩ [1] identify.

ползень *m* [4; -зня] landslide.

полч|áться [1], ⟨~и́ться⟩ [16 *e.*; -чу́сь, -чи́шься; -чённый] rise in arms; **~éние** *n* [12] militia; Territorial Army; **~éнец** *m* [1; -нца] militiaman.

пóмниться [13] *pf.* come to *or* recover one's senses, come round.

пóр *m* [1]: во весь ~ at full speed, at a gallop; **~а** *f* [5] support, prop, rest; **~ный** [14] strong, of support.

порó|жнить [13] *pf* empty; **~жнивать** [1] ⟨~чить⟩ [16] defile.

пошл|я́ть [28], ⟨~ить⟩ [13] vulgarize.

поя́с|ывать [1], ⟨~ать⟩ [3] gird.

ппозиционный [14] opposition...

ппони́ровать [7] (Д) oppose.

прáва *f* [5] setting; rim, frame.

правд|áние *n* [12] justification, excuse; ⚖ acquittal; **~áтельный** [14] justificatory; of 'not guilty'; ~áтельный докумéнт *m* voucher; **~ывать** [1], ⟨~áть⟩ [1] justify, excuse; acquit; **-ся** *a.* prove (*or* come) true.

оправ|ля́ть [28], ⟨~ить⟩ [14] put in order; set; **-ся** recover (*a.* o.s.); put one's dress, hair in order.

опрáшивать [1], ⟨опроси́ть⟩ [15] interrogate, question.

определ|éние *n* [12] determination; definition; designation (to. for на В); ⚖ decision; *gr.* attribute; **~ённый** [14; -ёнен, -ённа] definite; fixed; certain, positive; **~я́ть** [28], ⟨~и́ть⟩ [13] determine; define; designate (to, for на В к Д); appoint, fix; **-ся** take shape; enter, enlist (in[to] на В).

опров|ергáть [1], ⟨~éргнуть⟩ [21] refute; deny; **~ержéние** *n* [12] refutation; denial.

опроки́|дывать [1], ⟨~нуть⟩ [20; overturn, upset, capsize (**-ся** *v/i.*)] overthrow, throw (down, over).

опро|мéтчивый [14 *sh.*] rash, precipitate; **'~метью** headlong, at top speed.

опрóс *m* [1] interrogation, inquiry; **~и́ть** *s.* опрáшивать; **~ный** [14]: ~ный лист *m* questionnaire.

опры́ск|ивать, ⟨~ать⟩ [1] sprinkle.

опря́тный [14; -тен, -тна] tidy.

óптик *m* [1] optician; **~а** *f* [5] optics.

оптó|вый [14], **'~м** *adv.* wholesale.

опубликов|áние *n* [12] publication; **~ывать** [1] *s.* публиковáть.

опус|кáть [1], ⟨~ти́ть⟩ [15] lower; cast down; hang; drop; draw (down); ~ти́ть ру́ки lose heart; **-ся** sink; fall; go down; *fig.* come down (in the world); *p.pt a.* down & out.

опуст|éлый [14] deserted; **~и́ть** (**-ся**) *s.* опускáть(ся); **~ошáть** [1], ⟨~оши́ть⟩[16 *e.*; -шу́, -ши́шь; -шённый] devastate; **~ошéние** *n* [12] devastation; **~оши́тельный** [14; -лен, -льна] devastating.

опу́т|ывать, ⟨~ать⟩ [1] wrap (up), muffle (in); *fig.* entangle.

опух|áть [1], ⟨~нуть⟩ [21] swell; **'~оль** *f* [8] swelling, tumo(u)r.

опу́|шка *f* [5; *g/pl.*: -шек] edge, border; **~щéние** *n* [12] ommission.

опыл|я́ть [28], ⟨~и́ть⟩ [13] pollinate.

óпыт *m* [1] experiment; attempt; essay; [*sg., pl.* †] experience; **~ный** [14] experiment(al); empirical; [-тен, -тна] experienced.

опьянéние *n* [12] intoxication.

опя́ть again (*a.*, F, ~-таки; and ..., too).

орáва P *f* [5] gang, horde, mob.

орáкул *m* [1] oracle.

орáнже|вый [14] orange...; **~рéя** *f* [6] greenhouse.

орáть F [ору́, орёшь] yell, bawl.

орби́та *f* [5] orbit.

óрган[1] *m* [1] organ.

оргáн[2] ♪ *m* [1] organ.

организ|áтор *m* [1] organizer; **~м** *m* [1] organism; constitution; **~овáть** [7] (*im*)*pf.* (*impf. a.* **~óвывать** [1]) organize (*v/i.* **-ся**).

органи́ческий [16] organic.
о́ргия *f* [7] orgy.
орда́ *f* [5; *pl. st.*] horde.
о́рден *m* [1; *pl.*: -на́, *etc. e.*] order, decoration.
о́рдер *m* [1; *pl.*: -ра́, *etc. e.*] warrant.
ордина́р|ец ⚔ *m* [1; -рца] orderly.
орёл *m* [1; орла́] eagle; ~ или ре́шка? heads or tails?
орео́л *m* [1] halo, aureole.
оре́х *m* [1] nut; лесно́й ~ hazel (-nut); **~овый** [14] (wal)nut...
оригина́льный [14; -лен, -льна] original.
ориенти́р|оваться [7] (*im*)*pf.* orient o. s. (to на В), take one's bearings; familiarize o. s.; **~о́вка** *f* [5; *g/pl*: -вок] orientation, bearings *pl.*; **~о́вочный** [14; -чен, -чна] approximate, tentative.
орке́стр *m* [1] orchestra; band.
орли́ный [14] aquiline.
оро|ша́ть [1], ⟨~си́ть⟩ [15 *e.*; -ошу́, -оси́шь; -ошённый] irrigate; **~ше́ние** *n* [12] irrigation.
ору́д|ие *n* [12] tool, instrument, implement; ⚔ gun; **~ийный** [14] gun...; **~овать** F [7] (T) handle, operate.
оруж|е́йный [14] arms...; **∠ие** *n* [12] weapon(s), arm(s); (*cold*) steel.
орфогра́ф|ия *f* [7] spelling; **~и́ческий** [16] orthographic(al).
орхиде́я *f* [6] orchid.
оса́ *f* [5; *pl. st.*] wasp.
оса́|да *f* [5] siege; **~ди́ть** *s.* ~жда́ть & ~живать; **~дный** [14] of siege *or* martial law; **~док** *m* [1; -дка] sediment; *fig.* aftertaste; ~дки *pl.* precipitations; **~жда́ть** [1], ⟨~ди́ть⟩ [15 & 15 *e.*; -ажу́, -а́ди́шь; -аждённый] besiege; ⚗ precipitate; F importune; **~живать** [1], ⟨~ди́ть⟩ [15] check, snub.
оса́н|истый [14 *sh.*] dignified, stately; **~ка** *f* [5] bearing.
осв|а́ивать [1], ⟨~о́ить⟩ [13] master; open up; ⚘ acclimate (*Brt.* -tize); **-ся** accustom o. s. (to в П); familiarize o. s. (with с T).
осведом|ля́ть [28], ⟨'~ить⟩ [14] inform (of о П); **-ся** inquire (after, for; about о П); **~лённый** [14] informed; versed.
освеж|а́ть [1], ⟨~и́ть⟩ [16 *e.*; -жу́, -жи́шь; -жённый] refresh; freshen *or* touch up; brush up; **~и́тельный** [14; -лен, -льна] refreshing.
осве|ща́ть [1], ⟨~ти́ть⟩ [15 *e.*; -ещу́, -ети́шь; -ещённый] light (up), illuminate; *fig.* elucidate, illustrate.
освиде́тельствова|ние *n* [12] examination; **~ть** [7] *pf.* examine.
осви́ст|ывать [1], ⟨~а́ть⟩ [3] hiss.
освобо|ди́тель *m* [4] liberator; **~ди́тельный** [14] emancipatory; **~жда́ть** [1], ⟨~ди́ть⟩ [15*e.*; -ожу́, -оди́шь; -ождённый] (set) free, release; liberate, deliver; emancipate; exempt, excuse; clear; vacate, quit; **~жде́ние** *n* [12] liberation; release; emancipation; exemption.
осво|е́ние *n* [12] mastering; opening up; **∠ить(ся)** *s.* осва́ивать(ся).
освя|ща́ть [1], ⟨~ти́ть⟩ [15 *e.*; -ящу́, -яти́шь; -ящённый] consecrate.
осе|да́ть [1], ⟨∠сть⟩ [25; ося́дет; осе́л; *cf.* сесть] subside, settle; **∠длый** [14] settled.
осёл *m* [1; осла́] donkey, (*a. fig.*) ass.
осени́ть *s.* осеня́ть.
осе́н|ний [15] autumnal, fall...; **'~ь** *f* [8] fall, *Brt.* autumn (in [the] T).
осен|я́ть [28], ⟨~и́ть⟩ [13] shade; invest; bless, make (*cross*); flash on.
осе́сть *s.* оседа́ть.
осётр *m* [1 *e.*] sturgeon.
осе́чка *f* [5; *g/pl.*: -чек] misfire.
оси́ли|вать [1], ⟨~ть⟩ [13] *s.* одолева́ть.
оси́н|а *f* [5] asp[en]; **~овый** [14] asp(en).
оси́пнуть [21] *pf.* grow hoarse.
осироте́лый [14] orphan(ed).
оска́ли|вать [1], ⟨~ть⟩ [13] show.
оскверн|я́ть [28] ⟨~и́ть⟩ [13] profane, desecrate, defile.
оско́лок *m* [1; -лка] splinter.
оскорб|и́тельный [14; -лен, -льна] offensive, insulting; **~ле́ние** *n* [12] insult, offence; **~ля́ть** [28], ⟨~и́ть⟩ [14 *e.*; -блю́, -би́шь; -блённый] (**-ся** feel) offend(ed), insult.
оскуд|ева́ть [1], ⟨~е́ть⟩ [8] become poor *or* scanty.
ослаб|ева́ть [1], ⟨~е́ть⟩ [8] grow weak *or* feeble, languish; slacken; abate; **∠ить** *s.* ~ля́ть; **~ле́ние** *n* [12] weakening; relaxation; **~ля́ть** [28], ⟨∠ить⟩ [14] weaken, enfeeble; relax, slacken, loosen.
ослеп|и́тельный [14; -лен, -льна] dazzling; **~ля́ть** [28], ⟨~и́ть⟩ [14 *e.*; -плю́, -пи́шь; -плённый] blind; dazzle.
осложн|е́ние *n* [12] complication; **~я́ть** [28] ⟨~и́ть⟩ [13] (**-ся** be[come]) complicate(d).
ослу́ш|иваться, ⟨~аться⟩ [1] disobey; **~ник** *m* [1] disobedient p.
ослы́шаться [4] *pf.* hear amiss.
осм|а́тривать [1], ⟨~отре́ть⟩ [9; -отрю́, -о́тришь; -о́тренный] view, examine; inspect; see (*sights*); **-ся** look round; take a view of (в П).
осме́|ивать [1], ⟨~я́ть⟩ [27 *e.*; -ею́, -еёшь; -е́янный] laugh at, ridicule, deride.
осме́ли|ваться [1], ⟨~ться⟩ [13] dare, venture; beg *to*.
осмея́|ние *n* [12] ridicule, derision; **~ть** *s.* осме́ивать.
осмо́тр *m* [1] examination, inspection; (*sight*)seeing; visit (to P); **~е́ть(ся)** *s.* осма́тривать(ся); **~и́тельность** *f* [8] circumspection, prudence; **~и́тельный** [14; -лен, -льна] circumspect, prudent.

смысл|енный [14 *sh.*] sensible; intelligent; **~ивать** [1] *&* **~ять** [28], ⟨~ить⟩ [13] comprehend, conceive; grasp, make sense of.
сна́|стка *f* [5] rigging (out, up); **~ща́ть** [1], ⟨~сти́ть⟩ [15 *e.*; -ащу́, -асти́шь; -ащённый] rig (out, up); **~ще́ние** *n* [12] equipment.
снов|а *f* [5] basis, foundation; fundamental, essential principle; *gr* stem; *text.* warp; **~а́ние** *n* [12] foundation, basis; ⚗, △, ⚒ base; fundamental; ground(s), reason; argument; **~а́тель** *m* [4] founder; **~а́тельный** [14; -лен, -льна] valid; sound, solid; thorough; **~а́ть** *s.* ~ывать; **~но́й** [14] fundamental, basic, principal, primary; ✝ original (*stock*); **~ополо́жник** *m* [1] founder; **~ывать** [1], ⟨~а́ть⟩ [7] found; establish; **-ся** be based, rest; settle.
со́ба *f* [5] person; personage.
со́бенн|ость *f* [8] peculiarity; **~ый** [14] (e)special, particular, peculiar.
собня́к *m* [1 *e.*] villa, private residence; **~о́м** apart; aloof; separate (-ly).
со́б|ый [14] *s.* ~енный; separate.
созн|ава́ть [5], ⟨~а́ть⟩ [1] realize.
со́ка *f* [5] sedge.
сп|а *f* [5] smallpox; **~опривива́ние** *n* [12] vaccination.
сп|а́ривать [1], ⟨~о́рить⟩ [13] contest, dispute; contend (for).
става́ться [5], ⟨оста́ться⟩ [-а́нусь, -а́нешься] (T) remain, stay; be left; keep; stick (to); be(come); have to; go, get off; ~ (за T) get, win; reserve, take; owe; ~ без (P) lose, have no (left); ~ с но́сом F get nothing.
став|ля́ть [28], ⟨∠ить⟩ [14] leave; give up; drop, stop; let (*alone*); keep; ~ля́ть за собо́й reserve to o.s.
стально́|й [14] remaining; *pl. a.* the others; *n & pl. a. su.* the rest (в ~м as for the rest).
стан|а́вливать [1], ⟨~ови́ть⟩ [14] stop, bring to a stop; fix; **-ся** stop; put up (at в П); dwell (on на П); **∠ки** *m/pl.* [1] remains; **~ови́ть(ся)** *s.* ~а́вливать(ся); **~о́вка** *f* [5; *g/pl.*: -вок] stop(page); break; ~о́вка за ... (T) (*only*) ... is wanting.
ста́|ток *m* [1; -тка] remainder (*a.* ⚗), rest; remnant; *pl.* remains; **~ться** *s.* ~ва́ться.
стекл|я́ть [28], ⟨~и́ть⟩ [13] glaze.
стервене́лый [14] furious.
стер|ега́ться [1], ⟨~е́чься⟩ [26 г/ж: -регу́сь, -ежёшься, -егу́тся] (P) beware of, be careful of.
сто́в *m* [1] skeleton, framework.
столбене́лый F [14] stunned.
столо́п F *contp.* *m* [1] dolt, dunce.
сторо́жн|ость *f* [8] caution, heed; **~ый** [14; -жен, -жна] cautious, careful, wary; prudent; ~о! look out!; with care!
стри|га́ть [1], ⟨∠чь⟩ [26 г/ж: -игу́, -ижёшь, -игу́т] (-**ся** have one's hair) cut; crop; shear; pare; **~ё** *n* [12; *g/pl.*: -иёв] point; edge; **∠ть** [13], ⟨за-⟩ sharpen; ⟨с-⟩ joke, be witty; **∠чь(ся)** *s.* ~га́ть(ся).
о́стров *m* [1; *pl.*: -ва́, *etc. e.*] island; isle; **~итя́нин** *m* [1; *pl.*: -я́не, -я́н] islander; **~о́к** *m* [1; -вка́] islet.
остро́г *m* [1] prison; *hist.* burg.
остро|гла́зый F [14 *sh.*] sharp-sighted; **~коне́чный** [14; -чен, -чна] pointed; **~та́** *f* [5; *pl. st.*: -о́ты] sharpness, keenness, acuteness; witticism; joke; **~у́мие** *n* [12] wit; sagacity; **~у́мный** [14; -мен, -мна] witty; ingenious.
о́стр|ый [14; остр (F *a.* остёр), -а́, -о] sharp, pointed; keen; acute; critical; **~я́к** *m* [1 *e.*] wit(ty fellow).
оступ|а́ться [1], ⟨~и́ться⟩ [14] stumble.
остыва́ть [1] *s.* сты́нуть.
осу|жда́ть [1], ⟨~ди́ть⟩ [15; -уждённый] condemn; doom (to на В); **~жде́ние** *n* [12] condemnation; conviction.
осу́нуться [20] *pf.* grow lean.
осуш|а́ть [1], ⟨~и́ть⟩ [16] drain; dry (up); empty.
осуществ|и́мый [14 *sh.*] practicable; **~ля́ть** [28], ⟨~и́ть⟩ [14 *e.*; -влю́, -ви́шь; -влённый] realize; **-ся** be carried out; come true; **~ле́ние** *n* [12] realization.
осчастли́вить [14] *pf.* make happy.
осып|а́ть [1], ⟨∠ать⟩ [2] strew (over); stud; *fig.* heap; **-ся** crumble; fall.
ось *f* [8; *from g/pl. e.*] axis; axle.
осяза́|емый [14 *sh.*] tangible; **~ние** *n* [12] sense of touch; **~тельный** [14] of touch; [-лен, -льна] palpable; **~ть** [1] touch, feel.
от, ото (P) from; of; off; against; for, with; in; on behalf
ота́пливать [1], ⟨отопи́ть⟩ [14] heat.
отбав|ля́ть [28], ⟨∠ить⟩ [14] take away *or* off; diminish.
отбе|га́ть [1], ⟨~жа́ть⟩ [4; -бегу́, -бежи́шь, -бегу́т] run off.
отби|ва́ть [1], ⟨∠ть⟩ [отобью́, -бьёшь; *cf.* бить] beat, strike (*or* kick) off; ⚔ repel; deliver; snatch away (from у P); break off; **-ся** ward off (от P); get lost, drop behind; break off; F get rid.
отбира́ть [1], ⟨отобра́ть⟩ [отберу́, -рёшь; отобра́л, -а́, -о; ото́бранный] take away *or* off; select, pick out; collect.
отби́ть(ся) *s.* отбива́ть(ся).
о́тблеск *m* [1] reflection; vestige.
отбо́й *m* [3] ⚔ retreat; all clear (*signal*); *teleph.* ring off.
отбо́р *m* [1] selection, choice; **~ный** [14] select, choice, picked.
отбр|а́сывать [1], ⟨~о́сить⟩ [15] throw off *or* away; ⚔ throw back; reject; **~о́сы** *m/pl.* [1] refuse, waste.
отбы|ва́ть [1], ⟨∠ть⟩ [-бу́ду, -бу́-

дешь; о́тбыл, -а́, -о] **1.** *v/i.* leave, depart (for в В); **2.** *v/t.* serve; do; **ˏтие** *n* [12] departure.

отва́|га *f* [5] bravery, valo(u)r; **~живаться** [1], ⟨**~житься**⟩ [16] venture, dare; **~жный** [14; -жен, -жна] valiant, brave.

отва́л: до ~а F one's fill; **~иваться** [1], ⟨**~и́ться**⟩ [13; -а́лится] fall off.

отварно́й [14] boiled.

отве́|дывать, ⟨**~дать**⟩ [1] (*a.* Р) taste; **~зти́** *s.* отвози́ть.

отверг|а́ть [1], ⟨**ˏнуть**⟩ [21] reject, repudiate.

отвердева́ть [1] *s.* тверде́ть.

отве́рженный [14] outcast.

отверну́ть(ся) *s.* отвёртывать & отвора́чивать(ся).

отвёр|тка [5; *g/pl.*: -ток] screwdriver; **~тывать** [1], ⟨отверну́ть⟩ [20; отвёрнутый], ⟨отверте́ть⟩ F [10] turn off.

отве́с *m* [1] plummet; **~ить** *s.* отве́шивать; **~ный** [14; -сен, -сна] plumb; sheer; **~ти́** *s.* отводи́ть.

отве́т *m* [1] answer, reply (в ~ на В in reply to); responsibility.

ответвл|е́ние *n* [12] branch, offshoot; **~я́ться** [28] branch off.

отве́|тить *s.* ~ча́ть; **~тственность** *f* [8] responsibility; **~тственный** [14 *sh.*] responsible (to пе́ред Т); **~тчик** *m* [1] defendant; **~ча́ть** [1], ⟨~тить⟩ [15] (на В) answer, reply (to); (за В) answer, account (for); (Д) answer, suit.

отве́|шивать [1], ⟨**~сить**⟩ [15] weigh out; make (*a bow*).

отви́н|чивать [1], ⟨**~ти́ть**⟩ [15 *e.*; -нчу́, -нти́шь; -и́нченный] unscrew, unfasten.

отвис|а́ть [1], ⟨**ˏнуть**⟩ [21] hang down, lop; **ˏлый** [14] loppy.

отвле|ка́ть [1], ⟨**ˏчь**⟩ [26] divert, distract; abstract; **~чённый** [14 *sh.*] abstract.

отво́д *m* [1] allotment; rejection; **~и́ть** [15], ⟨отвести́⟩ [25] lead, get, take (off); turn off, avert; parry; reject; allot; ~и́ть ду́шу F unburden one's heart; **~ный** [14] drain ...

отво|ёвывать [1], ⟨**~ева́ть**⟩ [6] (re)conquer, win; **~зи́ть** [15], ⟨отвезти́⟩ [24] take, get, drive (off).

отвора́чивать [1], ⟨отверну́ть⟩ [20] turn off; **-ся** turn away.

отвори́ть(ся) *s.* отворя́ть(ся).

отворо́т *m* [1] lapel; (*boot*) top.

отвор|я́ть [28], ⟨**~и́ть**⟩ [13; -орю́, -о́ришь; -о́ренный] open (*v/i.* **-ся**).

отвра|ти́тельный [14; -лен, -льна] disgusting, abominable; **~ща́ть** [1], ⟨~ти́ть⟩ [15 *e.*; -ащу́, -ати́шь; -ащённый] avert; **~ще́ние** *n* [12] aversion, disgust (for, at к Д).

отвык|а́ть [1], ⟨**ˏнуть**⟩ [21] (от Р) wean (from), leave off, become disaccustomed (to).

отвя́з|ывать [1], ⟨**~а́ть**⟩ [3] (**-ся** [be]come) untie(d), undo(ne); F get rid of (от Р); let a person alone.

отга́д|ывать, ⟨**~а́ть**⟩ [1] guess; **~ка** *f* [5; *g/pl.*: -док] solution.

отгиба́ть [1], ⟨отогну́ть⟩ [20] unbend; turn up (*or* back).

отгов|а́ривать [1], ⟨**~ори́ть**⟩ [13] dissuade (from от Р); **-ся** pretend (s. th. Т), extricate o. s.; **~о́рка** [5; *g/pl.*: -рок] excuse, pretext.

отголо́сок *m* [1; -ска] *s.* о́тзвук.

отгоня́ть [28], ⟨отогна́ть⟩ [отгоню́, -о́нишь; ото́гнанный; *cf.* гнать] drive (*or* frighten) away; *fig.* banish.

отгор|а́живать [1], ⟨**~оди́ть**⟩ [15 & 15 *e.*; -ожу́, -о́ди́шь; -о́женный] fence in; partition off.

отгру|жа́ть [1], ⟨**~зи́ть**⟩ [15 & 15 *e.*; -ужу́, -у́зи́шь; -у́женный & -ужённый] load, ship.

отгрыз|а́ть [1], ⟨**ˏть**⟩ [24; *pt. st.*] gnaw (off), pick.

отда|ва́ть [5], ⟨**ˏть**⟩ [-да́м, -да́шь *etc.*, *cf.* дать; о́тдал, -а́, -о] give back, return; give (away); send (to в В); devote; deliver, (*baggage*) check, *Brt.* book; put; pay; marry; make (*bow*); cast (*anchor*); recoil (*gun*); ~ва́ть честь (Д) ⚔ salute; F sell; *impf.* smell *or* taste (of Т); **-ся** devote o.s.; surrender, give o.s. up; resound; be reflected.

отда́в|ливать [1], ⟨**~и́ть**⟩ [14] crush.

отдал|е́ние *n* [12] removal; estrangement; distance; **~ённый** [14 *sh.*] remote; **~я́ть** [28], ⟨**~и́ть**⟩ [13] move away, remove; put off, postpone; alienate; **-ся** move away (from от Р); become estranged.

отда́|ть(ся) *s.* ~ва́ть(ся); **~ча** *f* [5] delivery; recoil; return.

отде́л *m* [1] department; office, section; **~ать(ся)** *s.* ~ывать(ся); **~е́ние** *n* [12] separation; secretion; department, division; branch (office); ⚔ squad; compartment; (police) station; **~и́мый** [14 *sh.*] separable; **~и́ть(ся)** *s.* ~я́ть(ся); **~ка** *f* [5; *g/pl.*: -лок] finishing, trimming; **~ывать,** ⟨**~ать**⟩ [1] finish, put the final touches on; trim; **-ся** get rid of (от Р); get off, escape (with Т); **~ьность** *f* [8]: в ~ьности individually; **~ьный** [14] separate; individual, single; **~я́ть** [28], ⟨**~и́ть**⟩ [13; -елю́, -е́лишь] separate (*v/i.* **-ся** from от Р; come off); secrete.

отдёр|гивать [1], ⟨**~нуть**⟩ [20] draw back; draw open.

отдира́ть [1], ⟨отодра́ть⟩ [отдеру́, -рёшь; отодра́л, -а́, -о; ото́дранный] tear (off); *pf.* F thrash; pull.

отдохну́ть *s.* отдыха́ть.

отду́шина *f* [5] vent (*a. fig.*).

о́тдых *m* [1] rest, relaxation; дом ~а rest home, sanatorium; **~а́ть** [1], ⟨отдохну́ть⟩ [20] rest, relax.

отдыша́ться [4] *pf.* recover breath.

тёк *m* [1] edema.
те|ка́ть [1], ⟨**∠чь**⟩ [26] swell; become dropsical.
те́ц *m* [1; отца́] father.
те́че|ский [16] fatherly; paternal; **∠ственный** [14] native, home...; patriotic (*war*); **∼ство** *n* [9] motherland, fatherland, one's (native) country.
те́чь *s.* отека́ть.
тжи|ва́ть [1], ⟨**∠ть**⟩ [-живу́, -вёшь; о́тжил, -а́, -о; о́тжитый (о́тжи́т, -а́, -о)] (have) live(d, had) one's time *or* day); become obsolete, die out.
тзвук *m* [1] echo, repercussion; response; reminiscence.
тзыв *m* [1] response; opinion (in по Д *pl.*), reference; comment, review; recall; password; **∼а́ть** [1], ⟨отозва́ть⟩ [отзову́, -вёшь; отозва́л, -а́, -о; ото́званный] take aside; recall; **-ся** respond, answer; speak (of о П); (re)sound; call forth (s. th. Т); affect (s. th. на П); *impf.* smack (of Т); **∠чивый** [14 *sh.*] responsive, sympathetic.
тка́з *m* [1] refusal, denial, rejection (of в П, Р); renunciation (of от Р); ⊕ breakdown; ♪ natural; без **∼а** smoothly; до **∼а** to the full; получить **∼** be refused; **∼ывать** [1], ⟨**∼а́ть**⟩ [3] refuse, deny (a p. s. th. Д/в П); (от Р) dismiss; ⊕ break; **-ся** (от Р) refuse, decline, reject; renounce, give up; would(*n't*) mind.
тка́|лывать [1], ⟨отколо́ть⟩ [17] cut *or* chop off; unfasten; **-ся** come off; secede; **∼пывать,** ⟨откопа́ть⟩ [1] dig up, unearth; **∼рмливать** [1], ⟨откорми́ть⟩ [14] feed, fatten; **∼тывать** [1], ⟨**∼ти́ть**⟩ [15] roll (aside, away) (**-ся** *v/i.*); **∼чивать,** ⟨**∼ча́ть**⟩ [1] pump out; **∼шливаться** [1], ⟨**∼шляться**⟩ [28] clear one's throat.
тки|дно́й [14] folding, tip-up; **∠дывать** [1], ⟨**∠нуть**⟩ [20] throw off; back); turn down; drop, leave; **-ся** recline.
ткла́|дывать [1], ⟨отложи́ть⟩ [16] lay aside; save; put off, defer, postpone; **∼няться** [28] *pf.* take one's leave.
ткле́|ивать [1], ⟨**∼ить**⟩ [13] unstick; **-ся** come unstuck.
тклик *m* [1] response; comment; suggestion; *s. a.* о́тзвук; **∼а́ться** [1], ⟨**∠нуться**⟩ [20] (на В) respond (to), answer; comment (on).
тклон|е́ние *n* [12] deviation, deflection; digression; rejection; **∼я́ть** [28], ⟨**∼и́ть**⟩ [13; -оню́, -о́нишь] deflect; decline, reject; divert, dissuade; **-ся** deviate, deflect; digress.
тк|оло́ть *s.* **∼а́лывать**; **∼опа́ть** *s.* **∼а́пывать**; **∼орми́ть** *s.* **∼а́рмливать.**
ткос *m* [1] slope, slant, (e)scarp.
кровен|ие *n* [12] revelation; **∼ный** [14; -е́нен, -е́нна] frank, candid, open(-hearted), outspoken.
откры|ва́ть [1], ⟨**∠ть**⟩ [22] open; turn on; discover; disclose; reveal; unveil; inaugurate; **-ся** open; declare *or* unbosom o. s.; **∠тие** *n* [12] opening; discovery; revelation; inauguration; unveiling; **∠тка** *f* [5; *g/pl.*: -ток] (с ви́дом picture) post card; **∠тый** [14] open; public; **∠ть(ся)** *s.* **∼ва́ть(ся).**
отку́да where from?; wherefrom; F why; *a.*, F, = **∼-нибудь, ∼-то** (from) somewhere *or* anywhere.
о́ткуп *m* [1; *pl.*: -па́, *etc. e.*] *hist.* lease; **∼а́ть** [1], ⟨**∼и́ть**⟩ [14] buy (up); take on lease; **-ся** ransom o. s.
отку́пори|вать [1], ⟨**∼ть**⟩ [13] uncork; open.
отку́с|ывать [1], ⟨**∼и́ть**⟩ [15] bite off; pinch off.
отлага́тельство *n* [9] delay.
отлага́ться [1], ⟨отложи́ться] [16] be deposited; secede, fall away.
отла́мывать, ⟨отлома́ть⟩ [1], ⟨отломи́ть⟩ [14] break off (*v/i.* **-ся**).
отл|епи́ть(ся) [14] *pf.*, *s.* откле́ить (-ся); **∼ёт** *m* [1] ✈ start; **∼ета́ть** [1], ⟨**∼ететь**⟩ [11] fly away *or* off; F come off.
отли́|в *m* [1] ebb (tide); shimmer; **∼ва́ть** [1], ⟨**∼ть**⟩ [отолью́, -льёшь; о́тли́л, -а́, -о; *cf.* лить] pour off, in, out (some ... Р); ⊕ found, cast; *impf.* (Т) shimmer, play.
отлич|а́ть [1], ⟨**∼и́ть**⟩ [16 *e.*; -чу́, -чи́шь; -чённый] distinguish (from от Р); decorate; **-ся** *a.*, *impf.*, differ; be noted (for Т); **∠ие** *n* [12] distinction, difference; в **∠ие** от (Р) as against; зна́ки **∠ия** decorations; **∼и́тельный** [14] distinctive; **∠ник** *m* [1], **∠ница** *f* [5] excellent pupil, *etc.*; **∠ный** [14; -чен, -чна] excellent, perfect; different; *adv. a.* very good, A (*mark*, *cf.* пятёрка).
отло́гий [16 *sh.*] sloping.
отлож|е́ние *n* [12] deposit; **∼и́ть** (**-ся**) *s.* откла́дывать отлага́ться; **∼но́й** [14] turndown (*collar*).
отлом|а́ть, ∼и́ть *s.* отла́мывать.
отлуч|а́ть [1], ⟨**∼и́ть**⟩ [16 *e.*; -чу́, -чи́шь; -чённый] separate; wean; **∼и́ть** от це́ркви excommunicate; **-ся** (из Р) leave, absent o. s. (from); **∠ка** *f* [5] absence.
отма́лчиваться [1] keep silence.
отма́|тывать [1], ⟨отмота́ть⟩ [1] wind *or* reel off, unwind; **∼хивать** [1], ⟨**∼хну́ть**⟩ [20] drive (*or* brush) away (aside) (*a.* **-ся** от Р; F disregard, dismiss).
о́тмель *f* [8] shoal, sandbank.
отме́н|а *f* [5] abolition; cancellation; countermand; **∼ный** [14; -е́нен, -е́нна] *s.* отли́чный; **∼я́ть** [28], ⟨**∼и́ть**⟩ [13; -еню́, -е́нишь] abolish; cancel; countermand.
отмер|е́ть *s.* отмира́ть; **∼за́ть** [1], ⟨отмёрзнуть⟩ [21] be frostbitten.

отмéр|ивать [1] & **~я́ть** [28], ⟨~ить⟩ [13] measure (off).

отмéстк|а F *f* [5]: в ~у in revenge.

отмé|тка *f* [5; *g/pl.*: -ток] mark, grade; **~ча́ть** [1], ⟨~тить⟩ [15] mark, note.

отмира́ть [1], ⟨отмерéть⟩ [12; отомрёт; óтмер,- рлá, -о; отмéрший] die away *or* out; fade; mortify.

отмор|а́живать [1], ⟨~óзить⟩ [15] frostbite.

отмота́ть *s.* отмáтывать.

отмы|ва́ть [1], ⟨*´*ть⟩ [22] wash (off); **~ка́ть** [1], ⟨отомкну́ть⟩ [20] unlock, open; **´чка** *f* [5; *g/pl.*: -чек] picklock.

отнéкиваться F [1] deny, disavow.

отнести́(сь) *s.* относи́ть(ся).

отнима́ть [1], ⟨отня́ть⟩ [-ниму́, -ни́мешь; óтнял, -á, -о; óтнятый (óтнят, -á, -о)] take away (from у Р); take (*time, etc.*); F amputate; ~ от груди wean; **-ся** grow numb.

относи́тельн|ый [14; -лен, -льна] relative; ~о (Р) concerning, about.

отно|си́ть [15], ⟨отнести́⟩ [24 -с-: -есу́; -ёс, -еслá] take (to Д, в В); carry (off, away); put; refer to; ascribe; **-ся**, ⟨отнести́сь⟩ (к Д) treat, be; show; speak (of о П); *impf.* concern; refer; belong; date from; be relevant; **~шéние** *n* [12] attitude (toward[s] к Д); treatment; relation; ratio; (official) letter; respect (in, with в П, по Д); по ~шéнию (к Д) as regards, to (-ward[s]); имéть ~шéние concern.

отны́не henceforth, henceforward.

отню́дь: ~ не by no means.

отня́|тие *n* [12] taking (away); amputation; weaning; **~ть(ся)** *s.* отнимáть(ся).

отобра|жа́ть [1], ⟨~зи́ть⟩ [15 *e.*; -ажу́, -ази́шь] (**-ся** be) reflect(ed); **~жéние** *n* [12] reflection.

ото|бра́ть *s.* отбирáть; **~всю́ду** from everywhere; **~гна́ть** *s.* отгонять; **~гну́ть** *s.* отгибáть; **~грева́ть** [1], ⟨~грéть⟩ [8; -грéтый] warm (up); **~двига́ть** [1], ⟨~дви́нуть⟩ [20 *st.*] move aside, away (*v/i.* **-ся**); F put off.

отодра́ть *s.* отдирáть.

отож(д)еств|ля́ть [28], ⟨~и́ть⟩ [14 *e.*; -влю́, -ви́шь; -влённый] identify.

ото|зва́ть(ся) *s.* отзывáть(ся); **~йти́** *s.* отходи́ть; **~мкну́ть** *s.* отмыкáть; **~мсти́ть** *s.* мстить.

отоп|и́ть [28] *s.* отáпливать; **~лéние** *n* [12] heating.

оторва́ть(ся) *s.* отрывáть(ся).

оторопéть F [8] *pf.* be struck dumb.

отосла́ть *s.* отсылáть.

отпа|да́ть [1], ⟨*´*сть⟩ [25; *pt. st.*] (от Р) fall off; fall away, secede, desert; be dropped; pass.

отпе|ва́ние *n* [12] burial service; **´тый** F [14] inveterate, incorrigible; **~ре́ть(ся)** *s.* отпирáть(ся).

отпеча́т|ок *m* [1; -тка] (im)print; mark; stamp; **~ывать**, ⟨~ать⟩ [1] print; type; imprint, impress.

отпи|ва́ть [1], ⟨*´*ть⟩ [отопью́, -пьёшь; óтпил, -á, -о; -пéй(те)!] drink (some ... Р); **´ливать** [1], ⟨~ли́ть⟩ [13] saw off.

отпира́т|ельство *n* [9] disavowel; **~ь** [1], ⟨отперéть⟩ [12; отопру́, -прёшь; óтпер, -рлá, -о; отпёрший; óтпертый (-ерт, -á, -о)] unlock, unbar, open; **-ся** open; (от Р) disavow.

отпи́ть *s.* отпивáть.

отпи́х|ивать F [1], *once* ⟨~нуть⟩ [20] push off, away, aside, back.

отпла́|та *f* [5] repayment, requital; **~чивать** [1], ⟨~ти́ть⟩ [15] (re)pay, requite.

отплы|ва́ть [1], ⟨*´*ть⟩ [23] sail, leave; swim (off); **´тие** *n* [12] sailing off, departure.

óтповедь *f* [8] rebuff, snub.

отпóр *m* [1] repulse, rebuff.

отпоро́ть [17] *pf.* rip (off).

отправ|и́тель *m* [4] sender; **´ить (-ся)** *s.* ~ля́ть(ся); **´ка** F *f* [5] dispatch; **~лéние** *n* [12] dispatch; departure; exercise, practice; function; **~ля́ть** [28], ⟨*´*ить⟩ [14] send, dispatch, forward; mail, *Brt.* post; exercise, perform; **-ся** go; leave, set off (for в, на В); *impf.* (от Р) start from (*fig.*); **~нóй** [14] starting

отпра́шиваться [1], ⟨отпроси́ться⟩ [15] ask (and get) leave (*to go* ...)

отпры́г|ивать [1], *once* ⟨~нуть⟩ [20] jump back (*or* aside); rebound

óтпрыск *m* [1] offshoot.

отпря|га́ть [1], ⟨*´*чь⟩ [26 г/ж: -ягу́, -яжёшь] unharness; **´нуть** [20 *st.*] *pf.* recoil.

отпу́г|ивать [1], ⟨~ну́ть⟩ [20] scare

óтпуск *m* [1; *pl.* -кá, *etc. e.*] leave, vacation (on: *go* в В; *be* в П: *a.*, в ~у́); sale; supply; allotment; **~а́ть** [1], ⟨отпусти́ть⟩ [15] let go; release, set free; dismiss; sell; provide; allot; slacken; remit; grow; F crack; **~ни́к** *m* [1 *e.*] vacationist; **~нóй** [14] vacation..., holiday...; selling (*price*).

отпущéн|ие *n* [12] remission; козёл ~ия scapegoat.

отраб|а́тывать, ⟨~óтать⟩ [1] work off; finish work; *p. pt. p. a.* waste.

отра́в|а *f* [5] poison; *fig.* bane; **~лéние** *n* [12] poisoning; **~ля́ть** [28], ⟨~и́ть⟩ [14] poison; spoil.

отра́д|а *f* [5] comfort, joy, pleasure; **~ный** [14; -ден, -дна] pleasant, gratifying, comforting.

отра|жа́ть [1], ⟨~зи́ть⟩ [15 *e.*; -ажу́, -ази́шь; -ажённый] repel, ward off; refute; reflect, mirror (*v/i.* **-ся**; на П affect; show).

óтрасль *f* [8] branch.

отра|ста́ть [1], ⟨~сти́⟩ [24 -ст-

:тý; *cf.* расти́] grow; grow again; :цивать [1], ⟨~сти́ть⟩ [15 *e.*; ащý, -асти́шь; -ащённый] grow.
рéбье *n* [10] rubbish; rabble.
рéз *m* [1] pattern, length (*of aterial*); **~áть** & ~ывать [1], ~ать⟩ [3] cut off; F cut short.
резв|ля́ть [28], ⟨~и́ть⟩ [14 *e.*; влю, -ви́шь; -влённый] sober; *g.* disillusion.
рéз|ок *m* [1; -зка] piece; stretch; segment; **~ывать** *s.* ~áть.
ре|кáться [1], ⟨~чься⟩ [26] (от) disown, disavow; renounce; чься от престóла abdicate.
рéпье *n* [10] *coll.* rags *pl.*
ре|чéние *n* [12] (от P) disavowal; enunciation; abdication; **~чься** *s.* кáться; **~шать** [1], ⟨~ши́ть⟩ [16 ; -шý, -ши́шь; -шённый] disiss; release; **-ся** relinquish; **~шéние** *n* [12] dismissal, removal; renunciation (of от P).
рицá|ние *n* [12] negation, denial; **тельный** [14; -лен, -льна] negave; **~ть** [1] deny.
рó|г *m* [1] spur; **'~ду** F from irth; in one's life; **~дье** F *n* [10] awn; **'~к** † *m* [1] boy; **~сток** *m* ; -тка] ♀ shoot; *anat.* appendix; **чество** *n* [9] boyhood; adolesence.
руб|áть [1], ⟨~и́ть⟩ [14] cut off.
руби *f/pl.* [8; *from g/pl. e.*] bran.
ры́в *m* [1] separation; disengageent (*a.* ⚔); alienation; interrupon; **~áть** [1] **1.** ⟨оторвáть⟩ [-вý, вёшь; -вáл, -á, -о; отóрванный] ar (*or* pull, turn) off, away; seprate; **-ся** (от P) come off; turn ear o. s.) away; lose contact vith); ⚔ disengage; не ~áясь withut rest; **2.** ⟨оты́ть⟩ [22] dig up, ut, away; F disinter; **~истый** 4 *sh.*] abrupt; **~нóй** [14] sheet *or* lock (*calendar*); **~ок** *m* [1; -вка] ragment; extract, passage; **~очый** [14; -чен, -чна] fragmentary; crappy.
ры́жка *f* [5; *g/pl.*: -жек] belch ing); F survival.
ры́ть *s.* отрывáть.
ря́|д *m* [1] detachment; squadron; roop; ♀, *zo.* class; **~жáть** [1], ~ди́ть⟩ [15 *e.*; -яжý, -яди́шь; яжённый] detach; **~хивать** [1], *ice* ⟨~хнýть⟩ [20] shake off.
свéчивать [1] shimmer (with T).
сé|ивать [1], ⟨~ять⟩ [27] sift; *g.* eliminate; **~кáть** [1], ⟨~чь⟩ 26; *pt.*: -сéк, -секлá; -сечённый] ut off; **~чéние** *n* [12] cutting off.
ск|áкивать [1], ⟨~очи́ть⟩ [16] ump off, back; rebound; F fall off.
слýж|ивать [1], ⟨~и́ть⟩ [16] erve (one's time); be worn out; old.
совéт|овать [1] *pf.* dissuade from).

отсохнýть *s.* отсыхáть.
отсрóч|ивать [1], ⟨~ить⟩ [16] postpone; respite; **~ка** *f* [5; *g/pl.*: -чек] delay; respite; prolongation.
отста|вáть [5], ⟨~ть⟩ [-áну, -áнешь] (от P) lag, fall *or* remain behind; *clock*: be slow (5 min. на пять минýт); desert; leave off; come (*or* fall) off; F *pf.* leave alone.
отстáв|ка *f* [5] resignation, retirement; dismissal; в ~ке = ной; **~ля́ть** [28], ⟨~ить⟩ [14] remove, set aside; dismiss; F countermand; **~нóй** [14] retired.
отст|áивать [1], ⟨~оя́ть⟩ [-ою́, -ои́шь] defend, save; maintain, assert; push; F stand; tire; *pf.* be away; **-ся** settle.
отстá|лость *f* [8] backwardness; **~лый** [14] backward; **~ть** *s.* ~вáть.
отстёгивать [1], ⟨отстегнýть⟩ [20; -ёгнутый] unbutton, unfasten.
отстоя́ть(ся) *s.* отстáивать(ся).
отстр|áивать [1], ⟨~óить⟩ [13] build (up); **~аня́ть** [28], ⟨~ани́ть⟩ [13] push aside, remove; dismiss; debar; **-ся** (от P) dodge; shirk; **~óить** *s.* ~áивать.
отступ|áть [1], ⟨~и́ть⟩ [14] step back; retreat, fall back; recoil; *fig.* recede; deviate; indent; **-ся** renounce (s. th. от P); **~лéние** *n* [12] retreat; deviation; digression; **~ник** *m* [1] apostate; **~нóе** *n* [14] smart money.
отсýтств|ие *n* [12] absence (in в B; in the/of за T/P); lack; в ~ии absent; **~овать** [7] be absent; be lacking.
отсчи́т|ывать, ⟨~áть⟩ [1] count.
отсыл|áть [1], ⟨отослáть⟩ [-ошлю́, -шлёшь; отóсланный] send (off, back); refer (to к Д); **~ка** *f* [5; *g/pl.*: -лок] dispatch; reference.
отсып|áть [1], ⟨~ать⟩ [2] pour (out).
отсы|рéлый [14] damp; **~хáть** [1], ⟨отсóхнуть⟩ [21] wither (off).
отсю́да from here; hence.
оттá|ивать [1], ⟨~ять⟩ [27] thaw; **~лкивать** [1], ⟨оттолкнýть⟩ [20] push off, away, aside; repel; **~лкивающий** [17] repellent; **~скивать** [1], ⟨~щи́ть⟩ [16] pull off, away, aside; **~чивать** [1], ⟨отточи́ть⟩ [16] sharpen; **~ять** *s.* ~ивать.
оттéн|ок *m* [1; -нка] shade, nuance, tinge; **~я́ть** [28], ⟨~и́ть⟩ [13] shade; set off, emphasize.
óттепель *f* [8] thaw.
оттесн|я́ть [28], ⟨~и́ть⟩ [13] push off, aside; ⚔ drive back; F oust.
óттис|к *m* [1] impression, reprint; **~кивать** [1], ⟨~нуть⟩ [20] print (off).
отто|гó therefore. (*a.* ~гó и) that's why; ~гó что because; **~лкнýть** *s.* оттáлкивать; **~пы́рить** F [13] *pf.* bulge, protrude (*v/i.* **-ся**); **~чи́ть** *s.* оттáчивать.
оттýда from there.

оття́|гивать [1], ‹~ну́ть› [20; -я́нутый] draw off (back); delay.
отуч|а́ть [1], ‹~и́ть› [16] disaccustom (to от Р), cure (of); **-ся** leave off.
отхлы́нуть [20] *pf.* rush away, back.
отхо́д *m* [1] departure; ⚔ withdrawal; deviation; rupture; **~и́ть** [15], ‹отойти́› [-ойду́, -дёшь; отошёл, -шла́; отоше́дший; отойдя́] go (away, aside); leave; deviate; ⚔ withdraw; turn away; come (*or* fall) off; thaw; recover; expire; *impers.* be relieved; **~ы** *m/pl.* [1] waste.
отцве|та́ть [1], ‹~сти́› [25 -т-: -ету́] fade, wither.
отцеп|ля́ть [28], ‹~и́ть› [14] unhook; uncouple; F remove.
отцо́в|ский [16] paternal; fatherly; **~ство** *n* [9] paternity.
отча́|иваться [1], ‹~яться› [27] despair (of в П), despond.
отча́ли|вать [1], ‹~ть› [13] unmoor; push off; sail away.
отча́сти partly, in part.
отча́я|ние *n* [12] despair; **~нный** [14 *sh.*] desperate; **~ться** *s.* отча́иваться.
о́тче: ~ наш Our Father; Lord's Prayer.
отчего́ why; ~-то for some reason.
отчека́н|ивать [1], ‹~ить› [13] coin; say distinctly.
о́тчество *n* [9] patronymic.
отчёт *m* [1] account (of о, в П), report (on); return; (от)дава́ть себе́ ~ в П realize *v/t.*; **~ливый** [14 *sh.*] distinct, clear; precise; **~ность** *f* [8] accounting; F accounts *pl.*; **~ный** [14] of account.
отчи́|зна *f* [5] fatherland; **'~й** [17] paternal; **'~м** *m* [1] stepfather.
отчисл|е́ние *n* [12] deduction; subscription; dismissal; **~я́ть** [28], ‹′~ить› [13] deduct; allot; dismiss.
отчи́т|ывать F, ‹~а́ть› [1] blow up, rebuke; **-ся** give *or* render an account (to пе́ред Т).
от|чужда́ть [1] alienate, expropriate; **~шатну́ться** [20] *pf.* start *or* shrink back; **~швырну́ть** F [20] *pf.* hurl (away); **~ше́льник** *m* [1] hermit.
отшиб|а́ть F [1], ‹~и́ть› [-бу́, -бёшь; -ши́б(ла); -ши́бленный] strike (off).
отщепе́нец *m* [1; -нца] renegade.
отъе́|зд *m* [1] departure; **~зжа́ть** [1], ‹′~хать› [-е́ду, -е́дешь] drive (off), depart.
отъя́вленный [14] notorious, arch.
оты́гр|ывать, ‹~а́ть› [1] win back, regain (one's [lost] money **-ся**).
оты́ск|ивать [1], ‹~а́ть› [3] find.
отяго|ща́ть [1], ‹~ти́ть› [15 *e.*; -щу́, -оти́шь; -ощённый] (over-) burden.
офиц|е́р *m* [1] officer; **~е́рск**[ий] [16] offi e(r's, -s'); **~иа́льный** [14; -лен, -льна] official; **~иа́нт** *m* [1] waiter; **~ио́зный** [14; -зен, -зна] semiofficial.
оформ|ля́ть [28], ‹′~ить› [14] form, shape; get up (*book*); mount (*play*); legalize; adjust.
ох oh!, ah!; **′~анье** *n* [10] groan(s).
оха́пка *f* [5; *g/pl.*: -пок] armful; fagot.
о́х|ать [1], *once* ‹~нуть› [20] groan.
охва́т|ывать [1], ‹~и́ть› [15] seize, grasp; embrace; envelop.
охла|дева́ть, ‹~де́ть› [8] cool down; **~жда́ть** [1], ‹~ди́ть› [15 *e.*; -ажу́, -ади́шь; -аждённый] cool; **~жде́ние** *n* [12] cooling.
охмел|я́ть [28], ‹~и́ть› [13] (**~еть** [8] become) intoxicate(d).
о́хнуть *s.* о́хать.
охо́т|а *f* [5] (на В, за Т) hunt(ing) (of, for); chase (after); (к Д) F desire (for), mind (to); ~а Д + *inf.*! why do(es) ... want + *inf.* for?; **~ить** [15] (на В, за Т) hunt; chase (after); **~ник** *m* [1] hunter; volunteer; lover (of до Р); **~ничий** [17] hunting, shooting; hunter's (-s'); **~но** willingly, gladly, with pleasure; ~нее rather; ~нее всего́ best of all.
охра́н|а *f* [5] guard(s); protection; **~е́ние** *n* [12] protection; ⚔ outpost(-s); **~я́ть** [28], ‹~и́ть› [13] guard, protect (from, against от Р).
охри́п|лый F [14], **~ший** [17] hoarse.
оце́н|ивать [1], ‹~и́ть› [13; -еню́, -е́нишь] value (at в В), appraise; estimate; appreciate; **~ка** *f* [5; *g/pl.*: -нок] valuation, appraisal; estimation, appreciation; mark.
оцепене́|лый [14] benumbed; stupefied; **~ние** *n* [12] numbness.
оцеп|ля́ть [28] ‹~и́ть› [14] encircle.
оча́г *m* [1 *e.*] fireplace, (*a. fig.* home) hearth; *fig.* center (-tre), seat.
очаров|а́ние *n* [12] charm, fascination; **~а́тельный** [14; -лен, -льна] charming; **′~ывать** [1], ‹~а́ть› [7] charm, fascinate, enchant.
очеви́д|ец *m* [1; -дца] eyewitness; **~ный** [14; -ден, -дна] evident.
о́чень very, (very) much.
очередно́й [14] next (in turn); regular; foremost; latest.
о́черед|ь *f* [8; *from g/pl. e.*] turn (in, by turns по ~ди); order, succession; line (*Brt.* queue); ⚔ volley; ва́ша ~ь *or* ~ь за ва́ми it is your turn; ~и next; в свою́ ~ь in (for) my, etc., turn (part).
о́черк *m* [1] sketch; outline; essay.
очерня́ть [28] *s.* черни́ть.
очерстве́лый [14] hardened.
очер|та́ние *n* [12] outline, contour; **′~чивать** [1], ‹~ти́ть› [15] outline, sketch; ~тя́ го́лову F headlong.
очи́|стка *f* [5; *g/pl.*: -ток] clean(ing)

ng; clearance; *pl.* peelings; **~щáть** 1], ⟨~стить⟩ [15] clean(se); clear; eel; purify; evacuate, quit; empty.
к|и́ *n/pl.* [1] spectacles, glasses; **ó** *n* [9; *pl.*: -кú, -кóв] *sport*: point; *ards*: spot, *Brt.* pip; ⚘, ⊕ eye; **~о-тирáтель-сгво** F *n* [9] eyewash, umbug.
ну́ться [20] *pf.*, *s.* опóмниться.
умéлый P [14] crazy, mad.
утúться [15; *1st. p. sg. not used*] et, find o. s.
палéлый F [14] crazy, mad.
шéйник *m* [1] collar (*on a dog only*).
шелом|ля́ть [28], ⟨~úть⟩ [14 *e.*; млю́, -мúшь; -млённый] stun, tupefy.
ошиб|áться [1], ⟨~úться⟩ [-бу́сь, -бёшься; -úбся, -úблась] be mistaken, make a mistake (-s), err; miss; **∠ка** *f* [5; *g/pl.*: -бок] mistake (by по Д), error, fault; **∠очный** [14; -чен, -чна] erroneous, mistaken.
ошпáр|ивать [1], ⟨~ить⟩ [13] scald.
ощу́п|ывать, ⟨~ать⟩ [1] feel, touch; **'~ь** *f* [8]: на '~ь to the touch; **'~ью** *adv.* gropingly.
ощу|тúмый [14 *sh.*], **~тúтельный** [14; -лен, -льна] palpable, tangible; felt; not(ice)able; **~щáть** [1], ⟨~тúть⟩ [15 *e.*; -ущу́, -утúшь; -ущённый] feel, sense; **-ся** be felt; **~щéние** *n* [12] sensation; feeling.

П

áвел *m* [1; -вла] Paul.
авиáн *m* [1] baboon.
авильóн *m* [1] pavilion; (*fair*) hall; *film*) studio.
авлúн *m* [1], **~ий** [18] peacock.
áводок *m* [1; -дка] flood.
á|губный [14; -бен, -бна] pernicious; **~даль** *f* [8] carrion.
áда|ть [1] **1.** ⟨упáсть⟩ [25; *pt. st.*] all; **2.** ⟨пасть⟩ *fig.* fall; die; **~ть** ду́хом lose courage (*or* heart).
ад|ёж[1] *m* [1 *e.*] *gr.* case; **~ёж**[2] *m* 1 *e.*] (*cattle*) plague, rinderpest; **~éние** *n* [12] fall; downfall, overthrow; ⚕ slump; **∠кий** [16; -док, дка] (на В) greedy (of, for), mad after); **~у́чая** *f* [17] epilepsy.
áдчерица *f* [5] stepdaughter.
аёк *m* [1; пайкá] ration.
áзуха *f* [5] bosom (in за В); cavity.
ай *m* [3; *pl. e.*: паú, паёв] share; **∠щик** *m* [1] shareholder.
акéт *m* [1] parcel, package, packet; dispatch; paper bag.
áкля *f* [6] tow, oakum.
аковáть [7], ⟨у-, за-⟩ pack.
áк|ость *f* [8] filth, smut, dirt(y trick); **~т** *m* [1] pact, treaty.
алáт|а *f* [5] chamber; *parl.* house; board; ward; оружéйная ~а armo(u)ry; **~ка** *f* [5; *g/pl.*: -ток] tent; booth.
алáч *m* [1 *e.*] hangman, executioner.
алестúна *f* [5] Palestine.
áл|ец *m* [1; -льца] finger; toe; смотрéть сквозь ~ьцы wink (at на В); знать как свой пять ~ьцев have at one's fingertips; **~исáдник** *m* [1] (small) front garden
алúтра *f* [5] palette.
алúть [13] **1.** ⟨с-⟩ burn, scorch; **2.** ⟨о-⟩ singe; **3.** ⟨вы́-⟩ fire, shoot.
áл|ка *f* [5; *g/pl.*: -лок] stick; cane; club; из-под ~ки F under *or* in constraint; **~очка** *f* [5; *g/pl.*: -чек] (small) stick; ♪ baton; wand; ⚘ bacillus.
палóмни|к *m* [1] pilgrim; **~чество** *n* [9] pilgrimage.
пáлуба *f* [5] deck.
пальбá *f* [5] firing, fire.
пáльма *f* [5] palm (tree).
пальтó *n* [*indecl.*] (over)coat.
пáмят|ник *m* [1] monument; memorial; **~ный** [14; -тен, -тна] memorable; unforgettable; **~ь** *f* [8] memory (in/of на В/о П); remembrance; recollection (of о П); на ~ь *a.* by heart; без ~и unconscious; F mad (about от Р).
Панáмский [16]: ~ пролúв *m* Panama Canal.
панéль *f* [8] pavement; wainscot.
пáника *f* [5] panic.
панихúда *f* [5] requiem, dirge.
пансиóн *m* [1] boarding house; boarding school.
панталóны *m/pl.* [5] drawers, pants.
пантéра *f* [5] panther.
пáнцирь *m* [4] coat of mail.
пáпа[1] F *m* [5] papa; dad(dy).
пáпа[2] *m* [5] pope.
пáперть *f* [8] porch (*of a church*).
папильóтка *f* [5; *g/pl.*: -ток] hair curler.
папирóса *f* [5] cigarette.
пáпка *f* [5; *g/pl.*: -пок] folder; cardboard.
пáпоротник *m* [1] fern.
пар *m* [1; в -у́; *pl. e.*] **1.** steam; **2.** fallow; **∠а** *f* [5] pair; couple.
Парагвáй *m* [4] Paraguay.
парáграф *m* [1] paragraph.
парáд *m* [1] parade; **~ный** [14] full (dress); front (door).
парашю́т (-'ʃut) *m* [1] parachute; **~úст** *m* [1] parachutist; ⚔ paratrooper.
парéние *n* [12] soar(ing), hover.
пáрень *m* [4; -рня; *from g/pl. e.*] lad, guy.

пари́ *n* [*indecl.*] bet, wager (*vb.*: держа́ть ~); (идёт) ~? what do you bet?
Пари́ж *m* [1] Paris; ≗а́нин *m* [1; *pl.*: -а́не, -а́н], ≗а́нка *f* [5; *g/pl.*: -нок] Parisian.
пари́к *m* [1 *e.*] wig; **~ма́хер** *m* [1] hairdresser, barber; **~ма́херская** *f* [16] hairdressing saloon, barber's (shop).
пари́|ровать [7] (*im*)*pf.*, *a.* ⟨от-⟩ parry; **~ть**[1] [13] soar, hover.
па́рить[2] [13] steam (*in a bath*: **-ся**).
парла́мент *m* [1] parliament; **~а́рий** *m* [3] parliamentarian; **~ский** [16] parliamentary.
парни́к *m* [1 *e.*], **~о́вый** [14] hotbed.
парни́шка F *m* [5; *g/pl.*: -шек] guy, lad, youngster.
парно́й [14] fresh (*milk, meat*).
па́рный [14] paired; twin...
паро|во́з *m* [1] 🚂 engine; **~во́й** [14] steam...; **~ди́ровать** [7] (*im*)*pf.*, **∠дия** *f* [7] parody.
паро́ль *m* [4] password, parole.
паро́м *m* [1] ferry(boat); **~щик** *m* [1] ferryman.
парохо́д *m* [1] steamer; **~ный** [14] steamship...; **~ство** *n* [9] (steamship) line.
па́рт|а *f* [5] (*school*) bench, *Brt. a.* form; **~акти́в** *m* [1] = ~и́йный акти́в; **~би́лет** *m* [1] = ~и́йный биле́т; **~е́р** (-'tɛr) *m* [1] parterre, *Brt.* pit; **~и́ец** F *m* [1; -и́йца] Party man *or* member (*Sov.*); **~иза́н** *m* [1] guerilla, partisan; **~и́йность** *f* [8] Party membership; partisanship; Party discipline (*Sov.*); **~и́йный** [14] party...; *su.* = ~и́ец; **~иту́ра** *f* [5] ♪ score; **~ия** *f* [7] party; ☤ parcel, lot, consignment; ⚔ detachment; batch; game, set; match; ♪ part; ☤ ~иями in lots; **~нёр** *m* [1], **~нёрша** *f* [5] partner; **~о́рг** *m* [1] Party organizer (*Sov.*).
па́рус *m* [1; *pl.*: -са́, *etc. e.*] sail; на всех ~а́х under full sail; **~и́на** *f* [5] sailcloth, canvas, duck; **~и́новый** [14] canvas...; **~ник** *m* [1] = ~ное су́дно *n* [14/9] sailing ship.
парфюме́рия *f* [7] perfumery.
парч|а́ *f* [5] brocade; **~о́вый** [14] brocade(d).
парши́вый [14 *sh.*] mangy.
пас *m* [1] pass (*sport, cards*).
па́сквиль *m* [4] lampoon.
паску́дный P [14; -ден, -дна] foul, filthy.
па́смурный [14; -рен, -рна] dull; gloomy.
пасова́ть [7] pass (*sport*; *cards*, ⟨с-⟩); F yield (to пе́ред T).
па́спорт *m* [1; *pl.*: -та́, *etc. e.*], **~ный** [14] passport.
пассажи́р *m* [1], **~ка** *f* [5; *g/pl.*: -рок], **~ский** [16] passenger.
пасси́в *m* [1] ☤ liabilities *pl.*; **~ный** [14; -вен, -вна] passive.
па́ста *f* [5] paste.
па́ст|бище *n* [11] pasture; **~ва** [5] *eccl.* flock; **~и́** [24 -с-] graze (*v*, **-сь**), pasture; **~у́х** *m* [1 *e.*] herd (*Brt.* herdsman), shepherd; **~у́шк** *f* [5; *g/pl.*: -шек] shepherdes **~у́ший** [18] shepherd's; **~ырь** [4] pastor; **~ь 1.** *s.* па́дать; **2.** [8] jaws *pl.*, mouth.
па́сха *f* [5] Easter (for на В; on П); Easter cake; Passover; **∠льны** [14] Easter...
па́сынок *m* [1; -нка] stepson.
пате́нт *m* [1], **~ова́ть** [7] (*im*)*pf.*, ⟨за-⟩ patent.
патефо́н *m* [1] record player.
па́тока *f* [5] molasses, *Brt.* treacle.
патр|ио́т *m* [1]; patriot; **~иоти ческий** [16] patriotic; **~о́н** *m* [**1.** cartridge, shell; (lamp) socket; patron; **3.** pattern; **~онта́ш** *m* [cartridge belt, pouch; **~ули́рова** [7], **~у́ль** *m* [4 *e.*] patrol.
па́уза *f* [5] pause.
пау́к *m* [1 *e.*] spider.
паути́на *f* [5] cobweb.
па́фос *m* [1] pathos; verve, vim.
пах *m* [1; в -у́] *anat.* groin; **∠арь** [4] plowman, *Brt.* ploughman; **~а́т** [3], ⟨вс-⟩ plow (*Brt.* plough), ti
па́хн|уть[1] [20] smell (of T); **~у́т** F [20] *pf.* puff.
па́хот|а *f* [5] tillage; **~ный** [1 arable.
паху́чий [17 *sh.*] fragrant.
пацие́нт *m* [1], **~ка** *f* [5; *g/pl.*: -тс patient.
па́че F: тем ~ all the more.
па́чка *f* [5; *g/pl.*: -чек] pack(e package; batch.
па́чкать [1], ⟨за-, ис-, вы́-⟩ so
па́шня *f* [6; *g/pl.*: -шен] tillage [field
паште́т *m* [1] pie.
пая́льник *m* [1] soldering iron.
пая́сничать F [1] play the fool.
пая́ть [28], ⟨за-⟩ solder.
пая́ц *m* [1] buffoon, merry-andre
ПВО = противовозду́шная обор на.
пев|е́ц *m* [1; -вца́], **~и́ца** *f* singer; **~у́чий** [17 *sh.*] melodiou **∠чий** [17] singing (*bird*); *su.* cho ister, choirboy.
пе́гий [16 *sh.*] piebald.
педаго́г *m* [1] pedagogue, teach **~ика** *f* [5] pedagogics; **~и́ческ** [16], **~и́чный** [14; -чен, -чн pedagogic(al).
педа́ль *f* [8] treadle, pedal.
педа́нт *m* [1] pedant, **~и́чный** [-чен, -чна] pedantic(al).
пейза́ж *m* [1] landscape.
пека́р|ня *f* [6; *g/pl.*: -рен] baker **'~ь** *m* [4; *pl. a.* -ря́, *etc. e.*] bak
пелен|а́ *f* [5] shroud; **~а́ть** [⟨за-, с-⟩ swaddle; **~ка** (-'lɔn-) [5; *g/pl.*: -нок] swaddling band (clothes), diaper, *Brt. a.* napkin.

ельмéни *m/pl.* [*gen.:* -ней] ravioli.
éна *f* [5] foam, froth; lather.
енáл *m* [1] pen case.
éние *n* [12] singing; crow.
éн|истый [14 *sh.*] foamy, frothy; **~иться** [13], ⟨вс-⟩ foam, froth; sparkle, mantle; **~ка** *f* [5; *g/pl.:* -нок] scum; froth.
éнсия *f* [7] pension.
енснé (-ˈnɛ) *n* [*indecl.*] pince-nez, eyeglasses *pl.*
éнь *m* [4; пня] stump; blockhead.
еньк|á *f* [5] hemp; **~óвый** [14] hemp(en).
éня *f* [6; *g/pl.:* -ней] fine.
еня́ть F [28], ⟨по-⟩ blame (a p. for Д *or* на В/за В).
éпел *m* [1; -пла] ashes *pl.*; **~и́ще** *n* [11] the ashes; *s. a.* пожáрище; **~ьница** *f* [5] ash tray; **~ьный** [14] ashy.
éрвен|ец *m* [1; -нца] first-born; **~ство** *n* [9] primogeniture; superiority; championship.
ерви́чный [14; -чен, -чна] primary.
ерво|бы́тный [14; -тен, -тна] primitive, primeval; **~истóчник** *m* [1] (first) source, origin; **~клáссный** [14] first-rate *or* -class; **~кýрсник** *m* [1] freshman; **~-нá-перво** P first of all; **~начáльный** [14; -лен, -льна] original; primary; **~óбраз** *m* [1] prototype; **~оснóвы** *f/pl.* [5] elements; **~очереднóй** [14] top-priority; **~сóртный** = ~клáссный; **~степéнный** [14; -éнен, -éнна] paramount, supreme.
éрв|ый [14] first; chief, main; *Brt.* ground (*floor*); *thea.* dress (*circle*); ~ое *n* first course (*meal*; for на В); ~ым дéлом (дóлгом) *or* в ~ую óчередь first of all, first thing; ~éйший the very first; first-rate; *cf.* пя́тый.
ергáмент *m* [1] parchment.
ереб|егáть [1], ⟨~ежáть⟩ [4; -егý, -ежи́шь, -егýт] run over (*or* across); desert; **~éжчик** *m* [1] deserter; turncoat; **~ивáть** [1], ⟨~и́ть⟩ [-бью, -бьёшь, *cf.* бить] interrupt; break; kill; **-ся** break; F rough it.
ереб|ирáть [1], ⟨~рáть⟩ [-берý, -рёшь; -брáл, -á, -о; -éбранный] look a th. over; sort (out); *impf.* ♪ finger; tell (one's beads); **-ся** move (into на, в В); cross (*v/t.* чéрез В).
ереб|и́ть *s.* ~ивáть; **~óй** *m* [3] stoppage, break; irregularity; **~-орóть** [17] *pf.* overcome, master.
еребр|áнка F *f* [5; *g/pl.:* -нок] wrangle; **~áсывать** [1], ⟨~óсить⟩ [15] throw over; ⚔, ✝ transfer, shift; lay (*bridge*); **-ся** exchange (*v/t.* Т); **~áть(ся)** *s.* перебирáть (-ся); **~óска** *f* [5; *g/pl.:* -сок] transference.
еревáл *m* [1] pass; **~ивать** [1], ⟨~и́ть⟩ [13; -алю́, -áлишь; -áленный] tumble, turn (over; *v/i.* **-ся**; *impf.* waddle); F pass; *impers.* (Д) ~и́ло за (В) (р.) is past ...
перевáр|ивать [1], ⟨~и́ть⟩ [13; -арю́, -áришь; -áренный] digest.
пере|везти́ *s.* ~вози́ть; **~вёртывать** [1], ⟨~вернýть⟩ [20; -вёрнутый] turn over (*v/i.* **-ся**); overturn; turn; **~вéс** *m* [1] preponderance; **~вести́(сь)** *s.* переводи́ть(ся); **~вéшивать** [1], ⟨~вéсить⟩ [15] hang (elsewhere); reweigh; outweigh; **-ся** hang *or* bend over; **~вирáть** F [1], ⟨~врáть⟩ [-врý, -врёшь; -éвранный] misquote, distort.
перевóд *m* [1] transfer(ence); translation (from/into с Р/на В); remittance; (*money*) order; **~и́ть** [15], ⟨перевести́⟩ [25] lead; transfer; translate (from/into с Р/на В), turn; interpret; remit; set (*watch, clock*; *usu.* стрéлку); ~и́ть дух take breath; (**-ся**, ⟨-сь⟩) transfer; die out; (у Р/И) run out/of; **~ный** [14] translated; (*a.* ✝) transfer...; ~ный вéксель *m* draft; **~чик** *m* [1], **~чица** *f* [5] translator; interpreter.
перевóз *m* [1] ferriage, ferry; *a.* = ~ка; **~и́ть** [15], ⟨перевезти́⟩ [24] transport, convey; remove; ferry (over); **~ка** *f* [5; *g/pl.:* -зок] transport(ation), conveyance; **~чик** *m* [1] ferryman.
пере|вооружéние *n* [12] rearmament; **~ворáчивать** [1] = ~вёртывать; **~ворóт** *m* [1] revolution; **~воспитáние** *n* [12] reëducation; **~врáть** *s.* ~вирáть; **~вы́боры** *m/pl.* [1] reëlection.
перевыполн|éние *n* [12] overful-fil(l)ment (*Sov.*); **~я́ть** [28], ⟨ˈ~ить⟩ [13] exceed, surpass.
перевя́з|ка *f* [5; *g/pl.:* -зок] dressing, bandage; **~очный** [14] dressing; **~ывать** [1], ⟨~áть⟩ [3] tie up; dress, bandage.
перереги́б *m* [1] bend, fold; dog-ear; **~áть** [1], ⟨перегнýть⟩ [20] bend; **-ся** lean over.
перегля́|дываться [1], *once* ⟨~нýться⟩ [19] exchange glances.
пере|гнáть *s.* ~гоня́ть; **~гнóй** *m* [3] humus; **~гнýть(ся)** *s.* ~гибáть(ся).
перегов|áривать [1], ⟨~ори́ть⟩ [13] talk (s. th.) over (о Т), discuss; **~óры** *m/pl.* [1] negotiations; ⚔ parley.
перег|óнка *f* [5] distillation; **~оня́ть** [28], ⟨~нáть⟩ [-гоню́, -гóнишь; -гнáл, -á, -о; -éгнанный] (out)distance, outstrip; surpass, outdo; ⚗ distil.
перегор|áживать [1], ⟨~оди́ть⟩ [15 & 15 *e.*; -рожý, -рóдишь] partition (off); **~áть** [1], ⟨~éть⟩ [9] (*lamp*) burn out; (*fuse, etc.*) blow

(out); **~о́дка** *f* [5; *g/pl.:* -док] partition.
перегр|ева́ть [1], ⟨**~е́ть**⟩ [8; -е́тый] overheat; **~ужа́ть** [1], ⟨**~узи́ть**⟩ [15 & 15 *e.*; -ужу́, -у́зи́шь], **~у́зка** *f* [5; *g/pl.:* -зок] overload; overwork; **~уппирова́ть** [7] *pf.* regroup; **~уппиро́вка** *f* [5; *g/pl.:* -вок] regrouping; **~ыза́ть** [1], ⟨**~ы́зть**⟩ [24; *pt. st.*; -ы́зенный] gnaw through.
пе́ред[1], ~о (T) before, in front of.
перёд[2] *m* [1; пе́реда; *pl.:* -да́, *etc. e.*] front.
перед|ава́ть [5], ⟨**~а́ть**⟩ [-да́м, -да́шь, *etc., cf.* дать; *pt.* пе́редал, -а́, -о] pass, hand (over), deliver; give (*a.* regards); broadcast; transmit; reproduce; render; tell; take a message (for Д, *on the phone*); ☤ endorse; **-ся** ⚕ be communicated; **~а́точный** [14] transmissive; **~а́тчик** *m* [1] transmitter; **~а́ть(ся)** *s.* ~ава́ть(ся); **~а́ча** *f* [5] delivery, handing over; transfer; broadcast, (*a.* ⊕) transmission; gear; ⚕ communication; reproduction; package.
передв|ига́ть [1], ⟨**~и́нуть**⟩ [20] move, shift; **~иже́ние** *n* [12] movement; transportation; **~и́жка** *f* [5; *g/pl.:* -жек], **~ижно́й** [14] travel(l)ing, mobile, itinerant.
переде́л *m* [1] repartition; **~ка** *f* [5; *g/pl.:* -лок] alteration; recast; F mess; **~ывать**, ⟨**~ать**⟩ [1] recast; make over, alter.
пере́дн|ий [15] front..., fore...; **~ик** *m* [1] apron; **~яя** *f* [15] hall, antechamber.
передов|и́к *m* [1 *e.*] best worker *or* farmer (*Sov.*); **~и́ца** *f* [5] leading article, editorial; **~о́й** [14] progressive; leading, foremost; front (*line*); ~о́й отря́д *m* vanguard.
пере|до́к *m* [1; -дка́] front; ⚔ limber; **~дохну́ть** [20] *pf.* take breath *or* rest; **~дра́знивать** [1], ⟨**~дразни́ть**⟩ [13; -азню́, -а́знишь] mimic; **~дря́га** F *f* [5] fix, scrape; **~ду́мывать**, ⟨**~ду́мать**⟩ [1] change one's mind; F *s.* обду́мать; **~ды́шка** *f* [5; *g/pl.:* -шек] respite.
перее́|зд *m* [1] passage; crossing; move, removal (в, на В [in]to); **~зжа́ть** [1], ⟨**~хать**⟩ [-е́ду, -е́дешь; -езжа́й] **1.** *v/i.* cross (*v/t.* че́рез В); (re)move (в, на В [in]to); **2.** *v/t.* run over.
переж|да́ть *s.* ~ида́ть; **~ёвывать** [1], ⟨**~ева́ть**⟩ [7 *e.*; -жую́, -жуёшь] chew (well); F repeat over and over again; **~ива́ние** *n* [12] experience; **~ива́ть** [1], ⟨**~и́ть**⟩ [-живу́, -вёшь; пе́режи́л, -а́, -о; пе́режи́тый (пе́режи́т, -а́, -о)] experience; go through, endure; survive, outlive; **~ида́ть** [1], ⟨**~да́ть**⟩ [-жду́, -ждёшь; -жда́л, -а́, -о] wait (till *s. th.* is over); **~и́ток** *m* [1; -тк...] survival.
перезре́лый [14] overripe.
переиз|бира́ть [1], ⟨**~бра́т...**⟩ [-беру́, -рёшь; -бра́л, -а́, -о; -и...бранный] reëlect; **~бра́ние** *n* [...] reëlection; **~дава́ть** [5], ⟨**~да́т...**⟩ [-да́м, -да́шь, *etc. cf.* дать; -да́л, ... -о] republish; **~да́ние** *n* [12] reë...ition: **~да́ть** *s.* ~дава́ть.
переименова́ть [7] *pf.* rename.
переина́чи|вать F [1], ⟨**~ть**⟩ [...] alter, modify; distort.
перейти́ *s.* переходи́ть.
переки́|дывать [1], ⟨**~нуть**⟩ [2...] throw over (че́рез В); upset; -... exchange (*v/t.* Т).
переки|па́ть [1], ⟨**~пе́ть**⟩ [10 ... 3rd. p. only] boil over; **~сь** ('pe-... [8] peroxide.
перекла́д|ина *f* [5] crossbar, cro... beam; **~ывать** [1], ⟨переложи́т...⟩ [16] put, lay *or* pack (elsewher... shift; interlay (with T); *cf.* перел... га́ть.
перекл|ика́ться [1], ⟨**~и́кнутьс...**⟩ [20] shout to o.a.; reëcho (*v/t.* с Т...); **~и́чка** *f* [5; *g/pl.:* -чек] roll call.
переключ|а́ть [1], ⟨**~и́ть**⟩ [16 ... -чу́, -чи́шь; -чённый] switch o... (*v/i.* **-ся**); **~е́ние** *n* [12] switchi... over; **~и́ть** *s.* ~а́ть.
перекова́ть [7 *e.*; -кую́, -куёш...] *pf.* shoe over again; *fig.* reëduca... remake.
переко́шенный [14] wry.
перекр|а́ивать [1], ⟨**~ои́ть**⟩ [1... -о́енный] cut again; remake.
перекрёст|ный [14] cross (*fi... -examination*); **~ок** *m* [1; -тк...] crossroad(s).
перекрои́ть *s.* перекра́ивать.
перекр|ыва́ть [1], ⟨**~ы́ть**⟩ [2...] (re-)cover; exceed, surpass; **~ы́т...** *n* [12] covering.
переку́с|ывать [1], ⟨**~и́ть**⟩ [1...] bite through; F take a bite.
перел|ага́ть [1], ⟨**~ожи́ть**⟩ [1...] transpose; arrange.
перел|а́мывать [1] **1.** ⟨**~оми́т...**⟩ [14] break in two; overcom... **2.** ⟨**~ома́ть**⟩ [1] break to pieces.
перел|еза́ть [1], ⟨**~е́зть**⟩ [24 *s...* -ле́з] climb over (че́рез В).
перел|ёт *m* [1] passage (*birds*); ... flight; **~ета́ть** [1], ⟨**~ете́ть**⟩ [1...] fly (across); pass, migrate; f... **~ётный** [14] (*bird*) of passage.
перели́|в *m* [1] ♪ run, roulade; pl... (*colo[u]rs*); **~ва́ние** ⚕ *n* [12] tra... fusion; **~ва́ть** [1], ⟨**~ть**⟩ [-ль... -льёшь, *etc., cf.* лить] decant, po... ⚕ transfuse; ~ва́ть из пусто́го... поро́жнее mill the wind; **-ся** ov... flow; *impf.* ♪ warble, roll; (*colo[u]...*) play, shimmer.
перели́ст|ывать, ⟨**~а́ть**⟩ [1] tu... over (*pages*); look through.
перели́ть *s.* перелива́ть.

ерелицева́ть [7] *pf.* turn (*clothes*).
ерелож|е́ние *n* [12] transposition; rrangement; setting to music; **~и́ть** *s.* перекла́дывать & перелаа́ть.
ерело́м *m* [1] fracture; crisis, turning point; **~а́ть, ~и́ть** *s.* перела́мывать.
ерем|а́лывать [1], ⟨**~оло́ть**⟩ [17; -мелю́, -ме́лешь; -меля́] grind, mill; **~ежа́ть(ся)** [1] alternate; intermit.
ереме́н|а *f* [5] change; recess, reak (*school*); **~и́ть(ся)** *s.* **~я́ться**; **~ный** [14] variable; ⚡ alternating; **~чивый** F [14] changeable, variable; **~я́ть** [28], ⟨**~и́ть**⟩ [13; -еню́, -е́нишь] change (*v/i.* **-ся**); exchange.
ереме|сти́ть(ся) *s.* **~ща́ть(ся)**; **~шивать,** ⟨**~ша́ть**⟩ [1] mix (up); confuse; **~ща́ть** [1], ⟨**~сти́ть**⟩ [15 *e.*; -ещу́, -ести́шь; -ещённый] move, shift (*v/i.* **-ся**); **~щённый** [14]: **~щённые ли́ца** *pl.* displaced persons.
ереми́рие *n* [12] armistice, truce.
еремоло́ть *s.* перема́лывать.
еренаселе́ние *n* [12] overpopulation.
еренести́ *s.* переноси́ть.
ерен|има́ть [1], ⟨**~я́ть**⟩ [-ейму́, -мёшь; пе́ренял, -а́, -о; пе́ренятый (пе́ренят, -а́, -о)] adopt, take over.
ерено́с *m* [1] transfer, carrying over; sum carried over; syllabification; **~и́ть** [15], ⟨перенести́⟩ [24 -с-] transfer, carry over; bear, endure, stand; postpone, put off (till на В); **~ица** *f* [5] bridge (*of nose*).
ерено́с|ка *f* [5; *g/pl.:* -сок] carrying, transport(ation); **~ный** [14] portable; figurative.
ереня́ть *s.* перенима́ть.
ереобору́дова|ть [7] (*im*)*pf.* reëquip; **~ние** *n* [12] reëquipment.
ереод|ева́ться [1], ⟨**~е́ться**⟩ [-е́нусь, -нешься] change (one's clothes); **~е́тый** [14 *sh.*] *a.* disguised.
ереоце́н|ивать [1], ⟨**~и́ть**⟩ [13; -еню́, -е́нишь] overestimate, overrate; revalue; **~ка** *f* [5; *g/pl.:* -нок] overestimation; revaluation.
е́репел *m* [1; *pl.*: -ла́, *etc. e.*] quail.
ерепеча́т|ка *f* [5; *g/pl.:* -ток] reprint; **~ывать,** ⟨**~ать**⟩ [1] reprint; type.
ерепи́с|ка *f* [5; *g/pl.:* -сок] copying; typing; correspondence; **~чик** *m* [1] copyist; **~ывать** [1], ⟨**~а́ть**⟩ [3] copy; type; list; enumerate; **-ся** *impf.* correspond (with с Т); **~ь** ('pe-) *f* [8] census.
ерепла́|чивать [1], ⟨**~ти́ть**⟩ [15] overpay.
ерепл|ета́ть [1], ⟨**~ести́**⟩ [25 -т-] bind (*book*); interlace, intertwine (*v/i.* **-ся**, ⟨-сь⟩); **~ёт** *m* [1] binding, book cover; **~ётчик** *m* [1] bookbinder; **~ыва́ть** [1], ⟨**~ы́ть**⟩ [23] swim *or* sail (across че́рез В).
перепол|за́ть [1], ⟨**~ти́**⟩ [24] creep, crawl (over).
перепо́лн|енный [14 *sh.*] overcrowded; overflowing; **~я́ть** [28], ⟨**~ить**⟩ [13] overfill (*v/i.* **-ся**), cram; overcrowd.
перепо́ло|х *m* [1] tumult, turmoil; dismay, fright; **~ши́ть** F [16 *e.*; -шу́, -ши́шь; -шённый] *pf.* (**-ся** get) alarm(ed), perturb(ed).
перепо́нка *f* [5; *g/pl.:* -нок] membrane; web.
перепра́в|а *f* [5] crossing, passage; ford; temporary bridge; **~ля́ть** [28], ⟨**~ить**⟩ [14] carry (over), convey; **-ся** cross, pass.
перепрод|ава́ть [5], ⟨**~а́ть**⟩ [-да́м, -да́шь, *etc.*, *cf.* дать; *pt.:* -о́да́л, -ла́, -о] resell; **~а́жа** *f* [5] resale.
перепры́г|ивать [1], ⟨**~нуть**⟩ [20] jump (over).
перепу́г F *m* [1] fright (for с **~у**); **~а́ть** [1] *pf.* (**-ся** get) frighten(ed).
перепу́тывать [1] *s.* пу́тать.
перепу́тье *n* [10] crossroad(s).
перераб|а́тывать, ⟨**~о́тать**⟩ [1] work (up), process; remake; **~о́тка** *f* [5; *g/pl.:* -ток] working (up), processing; remaking.
перерас|та́ть [1], ⟨**~ти́**⟩ [24 -ст-; -ро́с, -сла́] grow, develop; overgrow; **~хо́д** *m* [1] excess expenditure.
перерез|а́ть & **~ывать** [1], ⟨**~ать**⟩ [3] cut (through); cut off; kill.
переро|жда́ться [1], ⟨**~ди́ться**⟩ [15 *e.*; -ожу́сь, -оди́шься; -ождённый] regenerate; degenerate.
переруб|а́ть [1], ⟨**~и́ть**⟩ [14] hew *or* cut through.
переры́в *m* [1] interruption; stop, break, interval; (*lunch*) time.
переса́|дка *f* [5; *g/pl.:* -док] transplanting; grafting; 🚂 change; **~живать** [1], ⟨**~ди́ть**⟩ [15] transplant; graft; make change seats; **-ся,** ⟨пересе́сть⟩ [25; -ся́ду, -дешь; се́л] take another seat, change seats; change (*trains*).
пересд|ава́ть [5], ⟨**~а́ть**⟩ [-да́м, -да́шь, *etc.*, *cf.* дать] repeat (*exam.*).
пересе|ка́ть [1], ⟨**~чь**⟩ [26; *pt.* -се́к, -секла́] cut (through, off); intersect, cross (*v/i.* **-ся**).
пересел|е́нец *m* [1; -нца] (re-) settler; **~е́ние** *n* [12] (e)migration; removal, move; **~я́ть** [28], ⟨**~и́ть**⟩ [13] (re)move (*v/i.* **-ся**; [e]migrate).
пересе́сть *s.* переса́живаться.
пересе|че́ние *n* [12] intersection; **~чь** *s.* **~ка́ть**.
переси́ли|вать [1], ⟨**~ть**⟩ [13] overpower, master, subdue.
переска́з *m* [1] retelling; **~ывать** [1], ⟨**~а́ть**⟩ [3] retell.
переск|а́кивать [1], ⟨**~очи́ть**⟩ [16] jump (over че́рез В); skip.

пересла́ть *s.* пересыла́ть.
пересм|а́тривать [1], ⟨**~отре́ть**⟩ [9; -отрю́, -о́тришь; -о́тренный] reconsider, revise; ⚖ review; **~о́тр** *m* [1] reconsideration, revision; ⚖ review.
пересо|ли́ть [13; -солю́, -о́ли́шь] *pf.* oversalt; **~хнуть** *s.* пересыха́ть.
переспр|а́шивать [1], ⟨**~оси́ть**⟩ [15] repeat one's question.
пересо́риться [13] *pf.* quarrel.
перест|ава́ть [5], ⟨**~а́ть**⟩ [-а́ну, -а́нешь] stop, cease, quit; **~авля́ть** [28], ⟨**~а́вить**⟩ [14] put (elsewhere), (*a. clock*) set, move; rearrange; transpose; convert (into на В); 🝖 permute; **~ано́вка** *f* [5; *g/pl.:* -вок] shift, move; rearrangement; transposition; conversion (into на В); 🝖 permutation; **~а́ть** *s.* **~ава́ть**.
перестр|а́ивать [1], ⟨**~о́ить**⟩ [13] rebuild, reconstruct; reorganize; regroup (*v/i.* **-ся**; adapt o. s., change one's views); **~е́ливаться** [1], **~е́лка** *f* [5; *g/pl.:* -лок] skirmish; **~о́ить** *s.* **~а́ивать**; **~о́йка** *f* [5; *g/pl.:* -оек] rebuilding, reconstruction; reorganization.
переступ|а́ть [1], ⟨**~и́ть**⟩ [14] step over, cross; *fig.* transgress.
пересу́ды F *m/pl.* [1] gossip.
пересчи́т|ывать, ⟨**~а́ть**⟩ [1] re-count; (*a.* ⟨перече́сть⟩ [-чту́, -чтёшь; -чёл, -чла́]) count (down).
перес|ыла́ть [1], ⟨**~ла́ть**⟩ [-ешлю́, -шлёшь; -е́сланный] send (over), transmit; forward; **~ы́лка** *f* [5; *g/pl.:* -лок] consignment, conveyance; carriage; **~ыха́ть** [1], ⟨**~о́хнуть**⟩ [21] dry up; parch.
перета́|скивать [1], ⟨**~щи́ть**⟩ [16] drag *or* carry (over, across че́рез В).
пере́т|ь F [12] press, push; **~яги-ва́ть** [1], ⟨**~яну́ть**⟩ [19] draw (*fig.* win) over; outweigh; cord.
переубе|жда́ть [1], ⟨**~ди́ть**⟩ [15 *e.*; *no 1st p. sg.*; -ди́шь; -еждённый] make s. o. change his mind.
переу́лок *m* [1; -лка] lane, alleyway, side street.
переутомл|е́ние *n* [12] overfatigue; **~ённый** [14 *sh.*] overtired.
переучёт *m* [1] inventory; stock-taking.
перехва́т|ывать [1], ⟨**~и́ть**⟩ [15] intercept; embrace; F borrow.
перехитри́ть [13] *pf.* outwit.
перехо́д *m* [1] passage; crossing; ⚔ march; *fig.* transition; conversion; **~и́ть** [15], ⟨перейти́⟩ [-йду́, -дёшь; -шёл, -шла́; *cf.* идти́] cross, go over; pass (on), proceed (to); turn ([in]to); exceed, transgress; **~ный** [14] transitional; *gr.* transitive; **~я́щий** [17] challenge (*cup, etc.*).
пе́рец *m* [1; -рца] pepper; paprika.
пе́речень *m* [4; -чня] list; index.
пере|чёркивать [1], ⟨**~черкну́ть**⟩ [20] cross out; **~че́сть** *s.* **~счи́тывать** & **~чи́тывать**; **~числя́ть** [28], ⟨**~чи́слить**⟩ [13] enumerate; **~чи́тывать**, ⟨**~чита́ть**⟩ [1] & ⟨**~че́сть**⟩ [-чту́, чтёшь; -чёл, -чла́] reread; read (many, all ...); **~чить** F [16] contradict, oppose; **~шагну́ть** [20] *pf.* step over, cross; transgress; **~ше́ек** *m* [1; -ше́йка] isthmus; **~шёптываться** [1] whisper (to one another); **~шива́ть** [1], ⟨**~ши́ть**⟩ [-шью́, -шьёшь, *etc., cf.* шить] make over, alter; **~щеголя́ть** F [28] *pf.* outdo.
пери́ла *n/pl.* [9] railing; banisters.
пери́на *f* [5] feather bed.
пери́од *m* [1] period; epoch, age; **~и́ческий** [16] periodic(al); 🝖 circulating.
перифери́я *f* [7] circumference, periphery; outskirts *pl.* (in на П).
перламу́тр *m* [1] mother-of-pearl.
перло́вый [14] pearl (*barley*).
пермане́нт *m* [1] permanent wave.
перна́тый [14 *sh.*] feathered, feathery.
перо́ *n* [9; *pl.:* пе́рья, -ьев] feather, plume; pen; ве́чное ~ fountain pen; **~чи́нный** [14]: ~чи́нный но́ж(ик) *m* penknife.
перро́н *m* [1] 🚂 platform.
перс *m* [1], **~и́дский** [16] Persian; **~ик** *m* [1] peach; **~ия́нин** *m* [1; *pl.:* -я́не, -я́н], **~ия́нка** *f* [5; *g/pl.:* -нок] Persian; **~о́на** *f* [5] person; **~она́л** *m* [1] personnel; **~пекти́ва** *f* [5] perspective; *fig.* prospect, outlook.
пе́рстень *m* [4; -тня] (*finger*) ring.
пе́рхоть *f* [8] dandruff.
перча́тка *f* [5; *g/pl.:* -ток] glove.
пёс *m* [1; пса] dog; F cur.
пе́сенка *f* [5; *g/pl.:* -нок] ditty.
песе́ц *m* [1; песца́] Arctic fox.
песка́рь *m* [4 *e.*] gudgeon.
песн|ь *f* [8] (*poet., eccl.*), **~я** *f* [6; *g/pl.:* -сен] song; F story.
песо́|к *m* [1; -ска́] sand; granulated sugar; **~чный** [14] sand(y).
пессимисти́ч|еский [16], **~ный** [14; -чен, -чна] pessimistic.
пестр|е́ть [8] grow (*or* appear, *a.* **~и́ть** [13]) variegated; gleam, glisten; **~ота́** *f* [5] motley; gayness; **~ый** ('pɔ-) [14; пёстр, пестра́, пёстро & пестро́] variegated, parti-colo(u)red, motley (*a. fig.*); gay.
песч|а́ный [14] sand(y); **~и́нка** *f* [5; *g/pl.:* -нок] grain (of sand).
петли́ца *f* [5] buttonhole; tab.
пе́тля *f* [6; *g/pl.:* -тель] loop (*a.* ✈, мёртвая ~); eye; mesh; stitch; hinge.
Пётр *m* [1; Петра́] Peter.
Петру́шка [5; *g/pl.:* -шек] **1.** *m* Punch (and Judy); **2.** ♀ *f* parsley.
пету́|х *m* [1 *e.*] rooster, cock; **~ши́ный** [14] cock(s)...
петь [пою́, поёшь; пе́тый] **1.** ⟨с-про-⟩ sing; **2.** ⟨про-⟩ crow.

пехо́т|а *f* [5], **~ный** [14] infantry; **~и́нец** *m* [1; -нца] infantryman.
печа́л|ить [13], ⟨о-⟩ grieve (*v/i.* **-ся**); **~ь** *f* [8] grief, sorrow; F business, concern; **~ьный** [14; -лен, -льна] sad, grieved, sorrowful.
печа́т|ать [1], ⟨на-⟩ print; type; **-ся** *impf.* be in the press; write for, appear in (в П); **~ник** *m* [1] printer; **~ный** [14] printed; printing; **~ь** *f* [8] seal, stamp (*a. fig.*); press; print, type.
печён|ка *f* [5; *g/pl.:* -нок] liver (*food*); **~ый** [14] baked.
пе́чень *f* [8] liver (*anat.*); **∠е** *n* [10] pastry; cookie, biscuit.
пе́чка *f* [5; *g/pl.:* -чек] *s.* печь[1].
печь[1] *f* [8; в -чи́; *from g/pl. e.*] stove; oven; furnace; kiln.
печь[2] [26], ⟨ис-⟩ bake; scorch (*sun*).
пе́чься [26] care (for о П).
пеш|ехо́д *m* [1] pedestrian; **∠ий** [17] unmounted; **∠ка** *f* [5; *g/pl.:* -шек] pawn (*a. fig.*); **~ко́м** on foot.
пеще́ра *f* [5] cave.
пиани́но *n* [*indecl.*] piano.
пивна́я *f* [14] alehouse, bar, saloon.
пи́во *n* [9] beer; ale; **~ва́р** *m* [1] brewer; **~ва́ренный** [14]: ~ва́ренный заво́д *m* brewery.
пиджа́к *m* [1 *e.*] coat, jacket.
пижа́ма *f* [5] pajamas (*Brt.* py-) *pl.*
пик *m* [1] peak.
пи́ка *f* [5] pike, lance; **∠нтный** [14; -тен, -тна] piquant, spicy (*a. fig.*).
пи́ки *f/pl.* [5] spades (*cards*).
пики́ровать ✈ [7] (*im*)*pf.* dive.
пи́кнуть [20] *pf.* peep; F stir.
пил|а́ *f* [5; *pl. st.*], **~и́ть** [13; пилю́, пи́лишь] saw; **~о́т** *m* [1] pilot.
пилю́ля *f* [6] pill.
пингви́н *m* [1] penguin.
пино́к *m* [1; -нка́] kick.
пинце́т *m* [1] tweezers *pl.*
пионе́р *m* [1] pioneer (*a. member of Communist youth organization in the U.S.S.R.*); **~ский** [16] pioneer…
пир *m* [1; в -у́; *pl. e.*] feast.
пирами́да *f* [5] pyramid.
пирова́ть [7] feast, banquet.
пиро́|г *m* [1 *e.*] pie; **~жник** *m* [1] pastry cook; **~жное** *n* [14] pastry; fancy cake; **~жо́к** *m* [1; -жка́] patty.
пир|у́шка *f* [5; *g/pl.:* -шек] carousal, revel(ry); **∠шество** *n* [9] feast, banquet.
писа́|ние *n* [12] writing; (*Holy*) Scripture; **ˈ~рь** *m* [4; *pl.:* -ря́, *etc.* *e.*] clerk; **~тель** *m* [4] writer, author; **~тельница** *f* [5] authoress; **~ть** [3], ⟨на-⟩ write; type(write); paint.
писк *m* [1] squeak; **~ли́вый** [14 *sh.*] squeaky; **∠нуть** *s.* пища́ть.
пистоле́т *m* [1] pistol.
писч|ебума́жный [14] stationery (*store, Brt. shop*); **∠ий** [17] note (*paper*).
пи́сьмен|ность *f* [8] literature; **~ный** [14] written; in writing; writing (*a. table*).
письмо́ *n* [9; *pl. st., gen.:* пи́сем] letter; writing (in на П); **~но́сец** *m* [1; -сца] postman, mailman.
пита́|ние *n* [12] nutrition; nourishment, food; board; ⊕ feeding; **~тельный** [14; -лен, -льна] nutritious, nourishing; **~ть** [1] nourish (*a. fig.*), feed (*a.* ⊕); cherish (*hope, etc.*), bear (*hatred, etc.*, against к Д); **-ся** feed *or* live (on T).
питóм|ец *m* [1; -мца], **~ица** *f* [5] pupil; nursling; **~ник** *m* [1] nursery.
пить [пью, пьёшь; пил, -á, -o; пéй (-те)!; пи́тый (пит, -á, -o)], ⟨вы́-⟩ drink (*pf. a.* up; to за В); have, take; **~ё** *n* [10] drink(ing); **~ево́й** [14] drinking (*water*), drinkable.
пих|а́ть F [1], ⟨~ну́ть⟩ [20] shove.
пи́хта *f* [5] fir.
пи́чкать F [1], ⟨на-⟩ stuff (with T).
пи́шущ|ий [17] writing; **~ая** машинка *f* typewriter.
пи́ща *f* [5] food; fare, board.
пища́ть [4 *e.*; -щу́, -щи́шь], ⟨за-⟩, *once* ⟨пи́скнуть⟩ [20] peep, squeak, cheep.
пище|варе́ние *n* [12] digestion; **~во́д** *m* [1] *anat.* gullet; **~во́й** [14] food(*stuffs*).
пия́вка *f* [5; *g/pl.:* -вок] leech.
пла́ва|ние *n* [12] swimming; navigation; voyage, trip; **~ть** [1] swim; float; sail, navigate.
плав|и́льный [14] melting; **~и́льня** *f* [6; *g/pl.:* -лен] foundry; **∠ить** [14], ⟨рас-⟩ smelt, fuse; **∠ка** *f* [5] fusion; **~ни́к** *m* [1 *e.*] fin.
пла́вный [14; -вен, -вна] fluent, smooth; *gr.* liquid.
плагиа́т *m* [1] plagiarism.
плака́т *m* [1] poster, placard, bill.
пла́к|ать [3] weep (for от P; о П), cry; **-ся** F complain (of на В); **~са** F *m/f* [5] crybaby; **~си́вый** F [14 *sh.*] whining.
плам|ене́ть [8] flame; **∠енный** [14] flaming, fiery; *fig. a.* ardent; **∠я** *n* [13] flame; blaze.
план *m* [1] plan; draft; plane; пéрвый, перéдний (зáдний) ~ fore- (back)ground (in на П).
планёр ✈ *m* [1] glider.
плане́та *f* [5] planet.
плани́ров|ать[1] [7] **1.** ⟨за-⟩ plan; **2.** ⟨с-⟩ ✈ glide; **~а́ть**[2], ⟨рас-⟩ level; **∠ка** *f* [5; *g/pl.:* -вок] planning; level(l)ing.
пла́нка *f* [5; *g/pl.:* -нок] lath.
пла́но|вый [14] planned; plan(-ning); **~ме́рный** [14; -рен, -рна] systematic, planned.
планта́тор *m* [1] planter.
пласт *m* [1 *e.*] layer, stratum; **∠ика** *f* [5] plastic arts *pl.*; plastic figure; **~и́нка** *f* [5; *g/pl.:* -нок] plate; (*gramophone*) record; **~ма́сса** *f* [5] plastic; **∠ырь** *m* [4] plaster.

плáт|а *f* [5] pay(ment); fee; wages *pl.*; fare; rent; **~ёж** *m* [1 *e.*] payment; **~ёжеспосóбный** [14; -бен, -бна] solvent; **~ёжный** [14] of payment; **~éльщик** *m* [1] payer; **~ина** *f* [5] platinum; **~ить** [15], ⟨за-, у-⟩ pay (in Т; for за В); settle (*account* по Д); **-ся**, ⟨по-⟩ *fig.* pay (with Т); **~ный** [14] paid; to be paid for.

платóк *m* [1; -ткá] (hand)kerchief.

платфóрма *f* [5] platform.

плáт|ье *n* [10; *g/pl.*: -ьев] dress, gown; **~янóй** [14] clothes...

плáха *f* [5] block.

плац|дáрм *m* [1] base; bridgehead; **~кáрта** *f* [5] reserved seat (ticket).

пла|ч *m* [1] weeping; **~чéвный** [14; -вен, -вна] deplorable, pitiable, lamentable; plaintive; **~шмя́** flat.

плащ *m* [1 *e.*] raincoat; cloak.

плебисци́т *m* [1] plebiscite.

плевá *f* [5] membrane; pleura.

плевáт|ельница *f* [5] cuspidor, spittoon; **~ь** [6 *e.*; плюю́, плюёшь], *once* ⟨плю́нуть⟩ [20] spit (out); F not care (for на В).

плéвел *m* [1] weed.

плевóк *m* [1; -вкá] spit(tle).

плеври́т *m* [1] pleurisy.

плед *m* [1] plaid, travel(l)ing rug.

плем|еннóй [14] tribal; brood..., stud...; **∠я** *n* [13] tribe; race; family; generation; breed; F brood.

племя́нни|к *m* [1] nephew; **~ца** *f* [5] niece.

плен *m* [1; в -ý] captivity; взять (попáсть) в ~ (be) take(n) prisoner; **~áрный** [14] plenary; **~и́тельный** [14; -лен, -льна] captivating, fascinating; **~и́ть(ся)** *s.* ~я́ть(ся).

плён|ка *f* [5; *g/pl.*: -нок] film; pellicle.

плéн|ник *m* [1], **~ный** *m* [14] captive, prisoner; **~я́ть** [28], ⟨~и́ть⟩ [13] (**-ся** be) captivate(d).

плéнум *m* [1] plenary session.

плéсень *f* [8] mo(u)ld.

плеск *m* [1], **~áть** [3], *once* ⟨плеснýть⟩ [20], **-ся** *impf.* splash.

плéсневеть [8], ⟨за-⟩ get mo(u)ldy.

пле|сти́ [25 -т-: плетý], ⟨с-, за-⟩ braid, plait; weave; spin; F twaddle; lie; **-сь** F drag, lag; **~тёный** [14] wicker...; **~тéнь** *m* [4; -тня́] wicker fence.

плётка *f* [5; *g/pl.*: -ток], **плеть** *f* [8; *from g/pl. e.*] lash, scourge.

плеч|ó *n* [9; *pl.*: плéчи, плеч, -чáм] shoulder; back; ⊕ arm; с ~ долóй F be rid of s. th.; с(о всегó) ~á with all one's might; straight from the shoulder; (И) не по ~ý (Д) not be equal to a th.; на ~ó! shoulder arms!; прáвое ~ó вперёд! ⚔ left turn (*Brt.* wheel)!; *cf. a.* горá F.

плеш|и́вый [14 *sh.*] bald; **~ь** *f* [8] bald patch.

плит|á *f* [5; *pl.st.*] slab, (flag-, *grave*) stone; plate; (*kitchen*) range; (*ga*[s]) stove; **∠ка** *f* [5; *g/pl.*: -ток] table[t], cake, bar; hot plate.

плов|éц *m* [1; -вцá] swimmer; **~[у]чий** [17] floating (*dock*); **~ýч[ий]** маяк *m* lightship; *s. a.* льди́на.

плод *m* [1 *e.*] fruit; **~и́ть** [15 *e.*; пл[о]жý, -ди́шь], ⟨рас-⟩ propagate, mu[l]tiply (*v/i.* **-ся**); **~ови́тый** [14 *sh.*] fruitful, prolific; **~овóдство** *n* [...] fruit growing; **~óвый** [14] fruit...; **~онóсный** [14; -сен, -сна] fru[c]tiferous; **~орóдие** *n* [12] fertilit[y]; **~орóдный** [14; -ден, -дна] ferti[le], fruitful, fecund; **~отвóрный** [1[4]; -рен, -рна] fruitful, productiv[e], profitable; favo(u)rable.

плóмб|а *f* [5] (lead) seal; (*tooth*) filling; **~ировáть** [7], ⟨о-⟩ sea[l]; ⟨за-⟩ fill, stop.

плóск|ий [16; -сок, -скá, -о; *comp.* плóще] flat (*a. fig.* = stale, trit[e]); plain, level; **~огóрье** *n* [10] platea[u], tableland; **~огýбцы** *pl.* [1] plie[rs]; **~ость** *f* [8; *from g/pl. e.*] flatnes[s]; plane; level (on в П); angle (und[er]) в П); platitude.

плот *m* [1 *e.*] raft; **~и́на** *f* [5] da[m], dike; **∠ник** *m* [1] carpenter.

плóтн|ость *f* [8] density; solidit[y]; **~ый** [14; -тен, -тнá, -о] compa[ct], solid; dense; close, thick; thicks[et].

плот|оя́дный [14; -ден, -дна] ca[r]nivorous; **∠ский** [16] carnal, fles[h]ly; **~ь** *f* [8] flesh.

плох|óй [16; плох, -á, -о] bad; bad(ly); bad, F (*mark*; *cf.* двóй[ка] & едини́ца).

плошáть F [1], ⟨с-⟩ blunder.

площáд|ка *f* [5; *g/pl.*: -док] grou[nd], playground; (*tennis*) court; pl[at]form; landing; **~нóй** [14] vulgar; [~ь] *f* [8; *from g/pl. e.*] square; area (&); (*living*) space, *s.* жилпл[о]щадь.

плуг *m* [1; *pl. e.*] plow, *Brt.* ploug[h].

плут *m* [1 *e.*] rogue; trickster, che[at]; **~áть** F [1] stray; **~овáть** [7], ⟨с[-]⟩ trick, cheat; **~овскóй** [16] roguis[h], rogue...; **~овствó** *n* [9] roguery.

плыть [23] (be) swim(ming); fl[oat] (-ing), sail(ing); *cf.* плáвать.

плюгáвый F [14 *sh.*] shabby.

плю́нуть *s.* плевáть.

плюс (*su. m* [1]) plus; F advanta[ge].

плюш *m* [1] plush.

плющ *m* [1 *e.*] ivy.

пляж *m* [1] beach.

пляс|áть [3], ⟨с-⟩ dance; **∠ка** *f* [5; *g/pl.*: -сок] (folk) dance; dancin[g]; **~овóй** [14] dance..., dancing.

пневмати́ческий [16] pneumati[c].

по 1. (Д) on, along; through; over; in; by; according to, aft[er]; through; owing to; for; over; acro[ss]; upon; each, at a time (*2, 3, 4 with* пó два); **2.** (В) to, up to; t[ill]; through; for; **3.** (П) (up)on; ~ м[...]

for all I care; ~часу в день an hour a day.
о- (in *compds.*): *cf.* ру́сский; ваш.
оба́иваться [1] be (a little) afraid of (Р).
обе́г *m* [1] escape, flight; ⚘ shoot, sprout; **~у́шки:** быть на ~у́шках F run errands (for у Р).
обе́|да *f* [5] victory; **~ди́тель** *m* [4] victor; winner; **~ди́ть** *s.* ~жда́ть; **~дный** [14], **~доно́сный** [14; -сен, -сна] victorious; **~жда́ть** [1], ⟨~ди́ть⟩ [15 *e.*; *1st p. sg. not used*; -ди́шь; -еждённый] be victorious (over В), win (a victory), conquer, vanquish, defeat; overcome; beat.
обере́жье *n* [10] shore, coast.
обла́жка F *f* [5; *g/pl.*: -жек] indulgence.
обли́зости close by; (от Р) near.
обо́и *m/pl.* [3] beating; **~ще** *n* [11] (great) battle.
обо́р|ник *m* [1] advocate; **~о́ть** [17] *pf.* conquer; overcome; beat.
обо́чный [14] accessory, incidental, casual; secondary; subsidiary; by-(*product*); illegitimate.
обу|ди́тельный [14]: ~ди́тельная причи́на *f* motive; **~жда́ть** [1], ⟨~ди́ть⟩ [15 *e.*; -ужу́, -уди́шь; -уждённый] induce, prompt, impel; **~жде́ние** *n* [12] motive, impulse, incentive.
обы́вка F *f* [5; *g/pl.*: -вок] stay, visit (for, on на В [*or* П]).
ова́д|иться F [15] *pf.* fall into the habit (of [visiting] *inf.*); **~ка** *f* [5; *g/pl.*: -док] F habit; P encouragement.
ова́льный [14] epidemic; general.
о́вар *m* [1; *pl.*: -pá, *etc. e.*] cook; **~енный** [14] culinary; cook(*book*, *Brt.* cookery book); kitchen (*salt*); **~и́ха** *f* [5] cook.
ове|де́ние *n* [12] behavio(u)r, conduct; **~лева́ть** [1] (Т) rule; ⟨~ле́ть⟩ [9] (Д) order; command; **~ли́тельный** [14; -лен, -льна] imperative (*a. gr.*).
оверг|а́ть [1], ⟨~нуть⟩ [21] throw *or* cast (down); put into (в В).
ове́р|енный [14] confidant; plenipotentiary; charge (d'affaires в дела́х); **~ить** *s.* ~я́ть & ве́рить; **~ка** *f* [5; *g/pl.*: -рок] check(up); roll call; **~ну́ть(ся)** *s.* повора́чивать (-ся).
ове́рх (Р) over, above; **~ностный** [14; -тен, -тна] superficial; surface...; **~ность** *f* [8] surface.
ове́р|ье *n* [10] legend, popular belief; **~я́ть** [28], ⟨~ить⟩ [13] entrust, confide (to Д); check (up).
ове́с|а F *m* [5] scapegrace; **~ить** (-ся) *s.* ве́шать(ся); **~ничать** F [1] romp, play pranks.
овествова́|ние *n* [12] narration, narrative; **~тель** *m* [4] narrator; **~тельный** [14] narrative; ~тельное предложе́ние *n gr.* statement; **~ть** [7] narrate (*v/t.* о П).
пове́ст|ка *f* [5; *g/pl.*: -ток] summons; notice; ~ка дня agenda; **'~ь** *f* [8; *from g/pl. e.*] story, tale; narrative.
пове́шение *n* [12] hanging.
по-ви́димому apparently.
пови́дло *n* [9] jam, fruit butter.
пови́н|ность *f* [8] duty; **~ный** [14; -и́нен, -и́нна] guilty; owing; ~ная *f* confession; **~ова́ться** [7] (*pt. a. pf.*) (Д) obey; submit (to); **~ове́ние** *n* [12] obedience.
по́вод *m* **1.** [1] cause; occasion (on по Д); по ~у (Р) *a.* concerning; **2.** [1; в -ду́; *pl.*: -о́дья, -о́дьев] rein; на ~у́ (у Р) in (s.b.'s) leading strings.
пово́зка *f* [5; *g/pl.*: -зок] cart; wag(g)on.
Пово́лжье *n* [10] Volga region.
повор|а́чивать [1], ⟨поверну́ть⟩ [20], F ⟨~оти́ть⟩ [15] turn (*v/i.* **-ся**; ~а́чивайся! come on!); **~о́т** *m* [1] turn; **~о́тливый** [14 *sh.*] nimble, agile; **~о́тный** [14] turning.
повре|жда́ть [1], ⟨~ди́ть⟩ [15 *e.*; -ежу́, -еди́шь; -еждённый] damage; injure, hurt; spoil; **~жде́ние** *n* [12] damage; injury.
поврем|ени́ть F [13] *pf* wait a little; **~е́нный** [14] periodical; time...
повсе|дне́вный [14; -вен, -вна] everyday, daily; **~ме́стный** [14; -тен, -тна] general, universal; ~ме́стно everywhere.
повста́н|ец *m* [1; -нца] rebel, insurgent; **~ческий** [16] rebel(lious).
повсю́ду everywhere.
повтор|е́ние *n* [12] repetition; review; **~и́тельный** [14] repetitive; **~ный** [14] repeated, second; **~я́ть** [28], ⟨~и́ть⟩ [13] repeat (o.s. **-ся**); review (*lessons, etc.*).
повы|ша́ть [1], ⟨~сить⟩ [15] raise; promote; **-ся** rise; advance; **~ше́ние** *n* [12] rise; promotion; **~шенный** [14] increased, higher.
повя́з|ка *f* [5; *g/pl.*: -зок] bandage; band, armlet; **~ывать** [1], ⟨~а́ть⟩ [3] bind (up); put on.
пога|ша́ть [1], ⟨~си́ть⟩ [15] put out, extinguish; discharge (*debt*).
погиб|а́ть [1], ⟨~нуть⟩ [21] perish; **~ель** † *s.* ги́бель; **~ший** [17] lost.
погло|ща́ть [1], ⟨~ти́ть⟩ [15; -ощу́: -още́нный] swallow up, devour; absorb; **~ще́ние** *n* [12] absorption.
погля́дывать [1] look (F *a.* after).
погов|а́ривать [1] speak; say; **~о́рка** [5; *g/pl.*: -рок] saying, proverb.
пого́|да *f* [5] weather (in в В, при П); **~ди́ть** F [15 *e.*; -гожу́, -годи́шь] *pf.* wait; **~дя́** later; **~ло́вный** [14] general, universal; ~ло́в-

но without exception; ~ло́вье n [10] livestock.
пого́н m [1] epaulet, shoulder strap; **~щик** m [1] drover; **~я** f [6] pursuit (of за T); pursuers pl.; **~я́ть** [28] drive or urge (on), hurry (up).
пого|ре́лец m [1; -льца] burnt down p.; **∠ст** [1] churchyard.
пограни́чн|ый [14] frontier...; **~ик** m [1] frontier guard.
по́гре|б m [1; pl.: -ба́, etc. e.] cellar; (powder) magazine; **~ба́льный** [14] funeral; **~ба́ть** [1], ⟨**~сти́**⟩ [24 -б-: -бу́] bury, inter; **~бе́ние** n [12] burial; funeral; **~му́шка** f [5; g/pl.: -шек] rattle; **∠шность** f [8] error, fault.
погру|жа́ть [1], ⟨**~зи́ть**⟩ [15 & 15 e.; -ужу́, -у́зи́шь; -у́женный & -ужённый] immerse; sink, plunge, submerge (v/i. **-ся**); ~жённый a. absorbed, lost (in в B); load, ship; **~же́ние** n [12] immersion; **∠зка** [5; g/pl.: -зок] loading, shipment.
погряз|а́ть [1], ⟨∠нуть⟩ [21] sink.
под[1], **~о 1.** (B): (direction) under; toward(s), to; (age, time) about; on the eve of; à la, in imitation of; for, suitable as; **2.** (T): (position) under, below, beneath; near, by, (battle) of; (used) for, with; по́ле ~ ро́жью rye field; **~**[2] m [1; на -у́] hearth, floor.
подава́льщица f [5] waitress.
пода|ва́ть [5], ⟨∠ть⟩ [-да́м, -да́шь, etc., cf. дать] give; serve (a. sport); drive up, get ready; move (in); hand (or send) in; lodge (complaint), bring (action); set (example); render; raise (voice); не ~ва́ть ви́ду s. пока́зывать; **-ся** move; yield.
подав|и́ть s. ~ля́ть; **~и́ться** pf. choke, suffocate; **~ле́ние** n [12] suppression; **~ля́ть** [28], ⟨~и́ть⟩ [14] suppress; repress; depress; crush; ~ля́ющий a. overwhelming.
пода́вно F so much or all the more.
пода́гра f [5] gout; podagra.
пода́льше F rather far off.
пода́|рок m [1; -рка] present, gift; **~тель** m [4] bearer; petitioner; **~тливый** [14 sh.] (com)pliant; **'~ть** f [8; from g/pl. e.] tax; **~ть(ся)** s. ~ва́ть(ся); **~ча** f [5] giving; serving; serve; presentation; rendering; supply; ~ча го́лоса voting; **~чка** f [5; g/pl.: -чек] charity, gift; **~я́ние** n [12] alms.
подбе|га́ть [1], ⟨**~жа́ть**⟩ [4; -бегу́, -бежи́шь, -бегу́т] run up (to к Д).
подби|ва́ть [1], ⟨∠ть⟩ [подобью́, -бьёшь, etc., cf. бить] line, fur; (re)sole; hit, injure; F instigate, incite; ∠тый F black (eye).
под|бира́ть [1], ⟨~обра́ть⟩ [подберу́, -рёшь; подобра́л, -а́, -о; подо́бранный] pick up; tuck up; draw in; pick out, select; **-ся** sneak up (to к Д); **~би́ть** s. ~бива́ть; **~бо́р** m [1] picking up or out; selection; assortment; на ~бо́р chosen, select.
подборо́док m [1; -дка] chin.
подбр|а́сывать [1], ⟨~о́сить⟩ [15] throw (up); jolt; add; foist, palm (on Д).
подва́л m [1] basement; cellar.
подвезти́ s. подвози́ть.
подвер|га́ть [1], ⟨∠гнуть⟩ [21] subject, expose; **-ся** undergo; be exposed; run (risk); **∠женный** [14 sh.] subject; **~же́ние** n [12] subjection.
подве́с|ить s. подве́шивать; **~но́й** [14] hanging (lamp); ⊕ suspension.
подвести́ s. подводи́ть.
подве́тренный [14] leeward.
подве́|шивать [1], ⟨~сить⟩ [15] hang (under; on); fix.
по́двиг m [1] feat, exploit, deed.
подви|га́ть [1], ⟨∠нуть⟩ [20] move (v/i. **-ся**; advance, get on); push (on, ahead); **~жно́й** [14] mobile; movable; nimble; 🚂 rolling (stock); **∠жность** f [8] mobility; agility; **~за́ться** [1] be active; **∠нуть(ся)** s. ~га́ть(ся).
подв|ла́стный [14; -тен, -тна] subject; **~о́да** f [5] cart; wag(g)on.
подводи́ть [15], ⟨подвести́⟩ [25] lead ([up] to); bring, get; lay; build; make (up); F let a p. down.
подво́дн|ый [14] submarine ~ая ло́дка f submarine; ~ый ка́мень m reef.
подво́з m [1] supplies pl.; **~и́ть** [15], ⟨подвезти́⟩ [24] bring, get; give a p. a lift.
подвы́пивший F [17] tipsy, drunk.
подвя́з|ка f [5; g/pl.: -зок] garter; **~ывать** [1], ⟨~а́ть⟩ [3] tie (up).
под|гиба́ть [1], ⟨~огну́ть⟩ [20] tuck (under); bend; **-ся** fail.
подгля́д|ывать [1], ⟨~е́ть⟩ [11] peep, spy.
подгов|а́ривать [1], ⟨~ори́ть⟩ [13] instigate, talk a p. into.
под|гоня́ть [28], ⟨~огна́ть⟩ [подгоню́, -го́нишь; cf. гнать] drive or urge on, hurry (up); fit, adapt.
подгор|а́ть [1], ⟨~е́ть⟩ [9] burn.
подготов|и́тельный [14] preparatory; **∠ка** f [5; g/pl.: -вок] preparation (for к Д); training; ⚔ drill; **~ля́ть** [28], ⟨∠ить⟩[14] prepare.
подда|ва́ться [5], ⟨∠ться⟩ [-да́мся, -да́шься, etc., cf. дать] yield; не ~ва́ться (Д) defy (description).
подда́к|ивать F [1], ⟨~нуть⟩ [20] say yes (to everything), consent.
по́дда|нный m [14] subject; **~нство** n [9] nationality, citizenship; **∠ться** s. ~ва́ться.
подде́л|ка f [5; g/pl.: -лок] forgery, counterfeit; **~ывать**, ⟨~ать⟩ [1] forge; **~ьный** [14] counterfeit... sham...
подде́рж|ивать [1], ⟨~а́ть⟩ [4] support; back up; uphold; maintain

ка *f* [5; *g/pl.*: -жек] support; pproval.
дéл|ать F [1] *pf.* do; ничегó не аешь there's nothing to be done; *f. a.* дéлать F; **~óм** F rightly; ~óм мý it serves him right; **~ывать** [1]: что (вы) ~ываете? what are ou doing (now)?
дéржанный [14] second-hand; vorn, used.
джáр|ивать [1], ⟨~ить⟩ [13] oast, brown; toast; **~ый** [14 *sh.*] ean.
джáть *s.* поджимáть.
д|жéчь *s.* ~жигáть; **~жигáтель** *n* [4] incendiary; **~жигáть** [1], ~жéчь⟩ [26; подожгý, -жжёшь; оджёг, подожглá; подожжён-ый] set on fire (*or* fire to).
д|жидáть [1], ⟨~ождáть⟩ [-дý, дёшь; -áл, -á, -о] wait (for P, B).
д|жимáть [1], ⟨~жáть⟩ [подо-кмý, -мёшь; поджáтый] cross *legs* under под B); purse (*lips*); raw in (*tail*).
джóг *m* [1] arson; burning.
дзаголóвок *m* [1; -вка] subtitle.
дзадóр|ивать F [1], ⟨~ить⟩ [13] nstigate, incite (to на B).
дза|тыльник *m* [1] cuff on the ape; **~щúтный** *m* [14] ⚖ client.
дзем|éлье *n* [10] (underground) ault, cave; dungeon; **∠ный** [14] nderground, subterranean; *cf.* етрó.
дзóрная [14]: ~ трубá *f* spyglass.
д|зывáть [1], ⟨~озвáть⟩ [под-овý, -ёшь; подозвáл, -á -о; по-óзванный] call, beckon; **~ú** P come now); go; try; I suppose.
д|кáпываться [1], ⟨~копáться⟩ ndermine (*v/t.* под B); **~караýли-ать** F [1], ⟨~караýлить⟩ [13] *s.* одстерегáть; **~кáрмливать** [1], ~кормúть⟩ [14] feed, fatten; **кáтывать** [1], ⟨~катúть⟩ [15] oll *or* drive up (under); **~кáши-аться** [1], ⟨~косúться⟩ [15] fail.
дкú|дывать [1], ⟨~нуть⟩ [20] *s.* одбрáсывать; **~дыш** *m* [1] oundling.
дклáд|ка *f* [5; *g/pl.*: -док] lining; ⊕ support; **~ывать** [1], ⟨под-ожúть⟩ [16] lay (under); add; nclose; foist (on Д).
дклé|ивать [1], ⟨~ить⟩ [13] glue, aste (under).
дкóв|а *f* [5] horseshoe; **~ывать** 1], ⟨~áть⟩ [7 *e.*; -кую, -куёшь] hoe; ~анный *a.* versed.
дкóжный [14] hypodermic.
дкóп *m* [1] sap, mine; **~áться** *s.* одкáпываться
дкосúться *s.* подкáшиваться.
дкрá|дываться [1], ⟨~сться⟩ 25] steal *or* sneak up (to к Д); шивать [1], ⟨~сить⟩ [15] touch p; make up.
дкреп|лáть [28], ⟨~úть⟩ [14 *e.*; -плю, -пúшь; -плённый] reinforce, fortify; corroborate; refresh; **~лéние** *n* [12] reinforcement; corroboration; refreshment.
пóдкуп *m* [1] bribery; **~áть** [1], ⟨~úть⟩ [14] bribe; win, prepossess; **~нóй** [14] corrupt.
подлá|живаться F [1], ⟨~диться⟩ [15] adapt o. s.; make up to.
пóдле (P) beside, by (the side of); nearby.
подлеж|áть [4 *e.*; -жý, -жúшь] be subject to; be to be; (И) не ~úт (Д) there can be no (*doubt* about); **~áщий** [17] subject (to Д); ...able; ~áщее *n gr.* subject.
подле|зáть [1], ⟨∠зть⟩ [24 *st.*] creep (under; up); **~тáть** [1], ⟨~тéть⟩ [11] fly (up).
подлéц *m* [1 *e.*] scoundrel, rascal.
подли|вáть [1], ⟨∠ть⟩ [подолью, -льёшь; подлéй!; пóдлúл, -á, -о; пóдлúтый (-лúт· -á, -о)] pour, add; **∠вка** *f* [5; *g/pl.*: -вок] gravy; sauce.
подлúз|а *m/f* [5] toady; **~ываться** F [1], ⟨~áться⟩ [3] flatter, insinuate o. s. (with к Д).
пóдлинн|ик *m* [1] original; **~ый** [14; -инен, -инна] original; authentic, genuine; true; pure.
подлúть *s.* подливáть.
пóдличать F [1], ⟨с-⟩ act meanly.
подлó|г *m* [1] forgery; **~жúть** *s.* подкладывать; **~жный** [14; -жен, -жна] spurious, false.
пóдл|ость *f* [8] meanness; low act; **~ый** [14; подл, -á, -о] mean, base, low.
подмáз|ывать [1], ⟨~ать⟩ [3] grease (*a.*, F, *fig.*), smear; F make up; **-ся** F insinuate o. s. (with к Д).
подмáн|ивать [1], ⟨~úть⟩ [13; -аню, -áнишь] beckon.
подмастéрье *m* [10; *g/pl.*: -ьев] journeyman.
подмéн|а *f* [5] substitution, exchange; **~ивать** [1], ⟨~úть⟩ [13; -еню, -éнишь] substitute (s.th./for T/B) (ex)change.
подме|тáть [1], ⟨~стú⟩ [25 -т-: -метý] sweep; **∠тить** *s.* подмечáть.
подмётка *f* [5; *g/pl.*: -ток] sole.
подме|чáть [1], ⟨∠тить⟩ [15] notice, observe, perceive.
подмéш|ивать, ⟨~áть⟩ [1] mix (s. th. with s. th. P/в B), adulterate.
подмúг|ивать [1], ⟨~нýть⟩ [20] wink (at Д).
подмóга F *f* [5] help, assistance.
подмок|áть [1], ⟨∠нуть⟩ get wet.
подмóстки *m/pl.* [1] scaffold; stage.
подмóченный [14] wet; F stained.
подмы|вáть [1], ⟨∠ть⟩ [22] wash (*a.* out, away); F press.
подне|бéсье *n* [10] firmament; **~вóльный** [14; -лен, -льна] dependent; forced; **~стú** *s.* подносúть.
поднимáть [1], ⟨поднять⟩ [-нимý, -нúмешь; пóднял, -á, -о; пóдня-

тый (-нят, -á, -o)] lift; pick up (from с Р); elevate; set (up; off); take up (*arms*); hoist (*flag*); weigh (*anchor*); set (*sail*); give (*alarm*); make (*noise*); scare (*game*); plow (*Brt.* plough) up; ~ нос assume airs; ~ нá ноги alarm; ~ нá смех ridicule; **-ся** [*pt.:* -нялся́, -ла́сь] (с Р from) rise; arise; go up(*stairs* по Д); climb (*hill* на В); set out; get agitated.
подного́тная F *f* [14] ins & outs *pl.*
подно́ж|ие *n* [12] foot, bottom (at у Р); pedestal; **~ка** *f* [5; *g/pl.*: -жек] footboard; *mot.* running board; trip; **~ный** [14] green (*fodder*).
подно́|с *m* [1] tray; **~си́ть** [15], ⟨поднести́⟩ [24 -с-] bring, carry; offer, present (Д); **~ше́ние** *n* [12] gift.
подня́т|ие *n* [12] raise, raising; rise; elevation, *etc.*, *cf.* поднима́ть(ся); **~ь(ся)** *s.* поднима́ть(ся).
подоб|а́ть: ~а́ет it becomes; ought; **∠ие** *n* [12] resemblance; image (*a. eccl.*); ⚐ similarity; **∠ный** [14; -бен, -бна] similar (to Д); such; и тому́ ∠ное and the like; ничего́ ∠ного nothing of the kind; **~о-стра́стный** [14; -тен, -тна] servile.
подо|бра́ть(ся) *s.* подбира́ть(ся); **~гна́ть** *s.* подгоня́ть; **~гну́ть(ся)** *s.* подгиба́ть(ся); **~грева́ть** [1], ⟨~гре́ть⟩ [8; -е́тый] warm up; **~двига́ть** [1], ⟨~дви́нуть⟩ [20] move ([up] to к Д) (*v/i.* **-ся**; draw near); **~жда́ть** *s.* поджида́ть & ждать; **~зва́ть** *s.* подзыва́ть.
подозр|ева́ть [1], ⟨заподо́зрить⟩ [13] suspect (of в П); **~е́ние** *n* [12] suspicion; **~и́тельный** [14; -лен, -льна] suspicious.
подойти́ *s.* подходи́ть.
подоко́нник *m* [1] window sill.
подо́л *m* [1] lap, hem.
подо́лгу (for a) long (time).
подо́нки *m/pl.* [1] dregs (*a. fig.*).
подо́пытный [14] test...
подорва́ть *s.* подрыва́ть.
подоро́жн|ая *f* [14] *hist.* post-horse order; **~ик** *m* [1] plantain, ribwort.
подо|сла́ть *s.* подсыла́ть; **~спе́ть** [8] *pf.* come (in time); **~стла́ть** *s.* подстила́ть.
подотде́л *m* [1] sub-division.
подотчётный [14; -тен, -тна] accountable.
подохо́дный [14] income (*tax*).
подо́шва *f* [5] sole; foot, bottom.
подпа|да́ть [1], ⟨∠сть⟩ [25; *pt. st.*] fall (under); **∠ивать** F [1], ⟨подпои́ть⟩ [13] make drunk; **~ли́ть** [13] *pf.* F = поджéчь; singe; **∠сок** *m* [1; -ска] shepherd boy; **∠сть** *s.* ~да́ть.
подпева́ть [1] *s.* вто́рить.
подпира́ть [1], ⟨подпере́ть⟩ [12; подопру́, -прёшь] support, prop.
подпис|а́ть(ся) *s.* ∠ывать(ся); **∠ка** *f* [5; *g/pl.*: -сок] subscription (to; for на В); pledge (take дать); **~но́й** [14] subscription...; **∠чик** *m* [1] subscriber; **∠ывать(ся)** [1], ⟨~а́ть(-ся)⟩ [3] sign; subscribe (to; for на В); **'~ь** *f* [8] signature (for на В) за '~ью (Р) signed by.
подплы|ва́ть [1], ⟨∠ть⟩ [23] swim (under *or* up [to к Д]).
подпо|и́ть *s.* подпа́ивать; **~лза́ть** [1], ⟨~лзти́⟩ [24] creep *or* crawl (under *or* up [to к Д]); **~лко́вник** *m* [1] lieutenant colonel; **∠лье** *n* [10; *g/pl.*: -ьев], **∠льный** [14] underground; **∠р(к)а** *f* [5 (*g/pl.* -рок)] prop; **∠чва** *f* [5] subsoil; **~я́сывать** [1], ⟨~я́сать⟩ [3] gird.
подпр|у́га *f* [5] girth; **~ы́гивать** [1], *once* ⟨~ы́гнуть⟩ [20] jump up.
подпус|ка́ть [1], ⟨~ти́ть⟩ [15] allow to approach; admit; F add.
подр|а́внивать [1], ⟨~овня́ть⟩ [28] straighten; level; clip.
подража́|ние *n* [12] imitation (in /of в В/Д); **~тель** *m* [4] imitator (of Д); **~ть** [1] imitate, copy (*v/t* Д); counterfeit.
подраздел|е́ние *n* [12] subdivision; ⚔ unit; **~я́ть** [28], ⟨~и́ть⟩ [13] (**-ся** be) subdivide(d) (into на В).
подра|зумева́ть [1] mean (by под Т), imply; **-ся** be implied; ✝ be understood; **~ста́ть** [1], ⟨~сти́⟩ [24 -ст-; -ро́с, -ла́] grow (up); rise.
подрез|а́ть & **∠ывать** [1], ⟨∠ать⟩ [3] cut; crop, clip.
подро́бн|ость *f* [8] detail; **~ый** [14; -бен, -бна] detailed, full-length; ~о in detail, in full.
подровня́ть *s.* подра́внивать.
подро́сток *m* [1; -стка] teenager, youth, juvenile. [hem.]
подруб|а́ть [1], ⟨~и́ть⟩ [14] cut;
подру́га [5] (girl) friend; playmate.
по-дру́жески (in a) friendly (way).
подружи́ться [16 *e.*; -жу́сь, -жи́шься] *pf.* make friends (with с Т).
подрумя́нить [13] *pf.* redden.
подру́чный [14] assistant; helper.
подры́|в *m* [1] undermining; blowing up; **~ва́ть** [1] **1.** ⟨~ть⟩ [22] sap, undermine; **2.** ⟨подорва́ть⟩ [-рву́, -рвёшь; -рва́л, -á, -o; подо́рванный] blow up, blast, spring; *fig.* undermine; **~вно́й** [14] blasting, explosive; subversive.
подря́д **1.** *adv.* successive(ly), running; one after another; **2.** *m* [1] contract; **~чик** *m* [1] contractor.
подс|а́живать [1], ⟨~ади́ть⟩ [15] help; plant; **-ся**, ⟨~е́сть⟩ [25; -ся́ду, -ся́дешь; -се́л] sit down (by к Д).
подсве́чник *m* [1] candlestick.
подсе́сть *s.* подса́живаться.
подска́з|ывать [1], ⟨~а́ть⟩ [3] prompt; **~ка** F *f* [5] prompting.
подскак|а́ть [3] *pf.* gallop (up to к Д); **∠ивать** [1], ⟨подскочи́ть⟩ [16] run ([up] to к Д); jump up.

од|сла́щивать [1], ‹~сласти́ть› 15 *e.*; -ащу́, -асти́шь; -ащённый] weeten; **~сле́дственный** *m* [14] prisoner) on trial; **~слепова́-тый** [14 *sh.*] weak-sighted; **~слу́-шивать,** ‹~слу́шать› [1] eaves-drop, overhear; **~сма́тривать** [1], ‹~смотре́ть› [9; -отрю́, -о́тришь] py, peep; **~сме́иваться** [1] laugh at над Т); **~смотре́ть** *s.* ~сма́три-вать.

одсне́жник *m* [1] snowdrop.

одсо́|бный [14] subsidiary, by-..., ide..., subordinate; **~вывать** [1], ‹подсу́нуть› [20] push, shove; resent; F palm ([off] on Д); **~зна́-тельный** [14; -лен, -льна] sub-conscious; **~лнечник** *m* [1] sun-flower; **~хнуть** *s.* подсыха́ть.

одспо́рье F *n* [10] help, support.

одста́в|ить *s.* ~ля́ть; **~ка** *f* [5; *g/pl.*: -вок] support, prop, stay; stand; saucer; **~ля́ть** [28], ‹~ить› 14] put, place, set (under под В); move up (to [к] Д); expose; ⚗ substitute; ~ля́ть но́гу *or* но́жку Д) trip (a p.) up; **~но́й** [14] false, traw...; ~но́е лицо́ *n* dummy.

одстан|о́вка ⚗ *f* [5; *g/pl.*: -вок] substitution; **~́ция** *f* [7] substation.

одстер|ега́ть [1], ‹~е́чь› [26 г/ж: регу́, -режёшь; -рёг, -регла́] lie n wait of; *pf.* trap.

одстил|а́ть [1], ‹подостла́ть› подстелю́, -е́лешь; подо́стлан-ный & подсте́ленный] spread under под В); **~́ка** *f* [5; *g/pl.*: -лок] edding; spreading.

одстр|а́ивать [1], ‹~о́ить› [13] ⚒ build, add; F ♪ tune (to под В); lot.

одстрек|а́тель *m* [4] instigator, monger; **~а́тельство** *n* [9] insti-gation; **~а́ть** [1], ‹~ну́ть› [20] incite to на В); stir up, provoke.

одстр|е́ливать [1], ‹~ели́ть› 13; -елю́, -е́лишь] hit, wound; **~ига́ть** [1], ‹~и́чь› [26 г/ж: -игу́, ижёшь; -и́г, -и́гла; -и́женный] ut, crop, clip; trim, lop; **~о́ить** *s.* одстра́ивать; **~о́чный** [14] inter-inear; foot(*note*).

одступ *m* [1] approach (*a.* ⚔); **~а́ть** [1], ‹~и́ть› [14] approach (*v/t.* Д); rise; press.

одсуд|и́мый *m* [14] defendant; **~́ность** *f* [8] jurisdiction.

одсу́нуть *s.* подсо́вывать.

одсч|ёт *m* [1] calculation, com-putation, cast; **~и́тывать,** ‹~и-та́ть› [1] count (up), compute.

одсы|ла́ть [1], ‹подосла́ть› -шлю́, -шлёшь; -о́сланный] send secretely); **~па́ть** [1], ‹~́пать› [2] dd, pour; **~ха́ть** [1], ‹подсо́х-нуть› [21] dry (up).

одта́|лкивать [1], ‹подтолк-ну́ть› [20] push; nudge; **~со́вы-вать** [1], ‹~сова́ть› [7] shuffle (trickily); garble; **~чивать** [1], ‹подточи́ть› [16] eat (away); wash (out); sharpen; *fig.* undermine.

подтвер|жда́ть [1], ‹~ди́ть› [15 *e.*; -ржу́, -рди́шь; -рждённый] con-firm, corroborate; acknowledge; **-ся** prove (to be) true; **~жде́ние** *n* [12] confirmation; acknowledg(e)ment.

под|тере́ть *s.* ~тира́ть; **~тёк** *m* [1] bloodshot spot; **~тира́ть** [1], ‹~те-ре́ть› [12; подотру́; подтёр] wipe (up); **~толкну́ть** *s.* ~та́лкивать; **~точи́ть** *s.* ~та́чивать.

подтру́н|ивать [1], ‹~и́ть› [13] tease, banter, chaff (*v/t.* над Т).

подтя́|гивать [1], ‹~ну́ть› [19] pull (up); draw (in *reins*); tighten; raise (*wages*); wind *or* key up, egg on; join in (*song*); **-ся** chin; brace up; improve, pick up; **~жки** *f/pl.* [5; *gen.*: -жек] suspenders, *Brt.* braces.

поду́мывать [1] think (about о П).

подуч|а́ть [1], ‹~и́ть› [16] *s.* учи́ть.

поду́шка *f* [5; *g/pl.*: -шек] pillow; cushion, pad.

подхали́м *m* [1] toady, lickspittle.

подхва́т|ывать [1], ‹~и́ть› [15] catch; pick up; take up; join in.

подхо́д *m* [1] approach (*a. fig.*); **~и́ть** [15], ‹подойти́› [-ойду́, -дёшь; -ошёл; -шла́; *g. pt.* -ойдя́] (к Д) approach, go (up to); arrive, come; (Д) suit, fit; **~я́щий** [17] suitable, fit(ting), appropriate; convenient.

подцеп|ля́ть [28], ‹~и́ть› [14] hook (*a. fig.*); pick up, catch.

подча́с at times, sometimes.

подч|ёркивать [1], ‹~еркну́ть› [20; -ёркнутый] underline; stress.

подчин|е́ние *n* [12] submission; subjection; *gr.* hypotaxis; **~ённый** [14] subordinate; **~я́ть** [28], ‹~и́ть› [13] subject, subdue; subordinate; put under (s.b.'s Д) supervision; **-ся** (Д) submit (to); obey.

под|ше́фный [14] sponsored; **~-шива́ть** [1], ‹~ши́ть› [подошью́, -шьёшь; *cf* шить] sew on (to к Д); hem; file; **~ши́пник** ⊕ *m* [1] bear-ing; **~ши́ть** *s.* ~шива́ть; **~шу́чи-вать** [1], ‹~шути́ть› [15] play a trick (on над Т).

подъе́|зд *m* [1] entrance, porch; drive; approach; **~здно́й** [14] 🚂 branch (*line*); **~зжа́ть** [1], ‹~хать› [-е́ду, -е́дешь] (к Д) drive *or* ride up (to), approach; F drop in (on); make up to.

подъём *m* [1] lift(ing); ascent, rise (*a. fig.*); enthusiasm; instep; лёгок (тяжёл) на ~ nimble (slow); **~ник** *m* [1] elevator, lift, hoist; **~ный** [14]: ~ный мост *m* drawbridge; ~ная си́ла *f* carrying capacity; ~ные (де́ньги) *pl.* travel(l)ing expenses.

подъе́|хать *s.* ~зжа́ть.

под|ыма́ть(ся) *s.* ~нима́ть(ся).

подыск|ивать [1], ‹~а́ть› [3] *impf.* look for; *pf.* find; choose.

подыто́ж|ивать [1], ⟨**~ить**⟩ [16] sum up.
поеда́ть [1], ⟨пое́сть⟩ *cf.* есть[1].
поеди́нок *m* [1; -нка] duel (with *arms* на П).
по́езд *m* [1; *pl.:* -да́, *etc. e.*] train; **∠ка** *f* [5; *g/pl.:* -док] trip, journey; voyage; tour; **~но́й** 🚂 [14] train...
пое́ние *n* [12] watering.
пожа́луй maybe, perhaps; I suppose; **~ста** (pa'ʒałustə) please; *cf. a.* (не́ за) что; скажи́(те) ~ста! I say!; **~те** come in(to в В), please; ~те сюда́! this way, please; *cf.* жа́ловать & добро́[2].
пожа́р *m* [1] fire (to/at на В/П); conflagration; **~ище** *n* [11] scene of conflagration; **~ник** *m* [1] fireman; **~ный** [14] fire...; *su.* = ~ник; *cf.* кома́нда.
пожа́т|ие *n* [12] shake (*of hand*); **~ь** *s.* пожима́ть & пожина́ть.
пожела́ние *n* [12] wish; request.
пожелте́лый [14] yellow, faded.
поже́ртвование *n* [12] donation.
пожи́|ва *f* [5] F = нажи́ва, *s.*; **~ва́ть** [1] F live; как (вы) ~ва́ете? how are you (getting on)?; **~ви́ться** [14*e.*; -влю́сь, -ви́шься] *pf.* F (T) = нажи́ть; **~зненный** [14] life...; **~ло́й** [14] elderly.
пожи|ма́ть [1], ⟨пожа́ть⟩ [-жму́, -жмёшь; -а́тый] *s.* жать[1]; **~ма́ть** плеча́ми shrug one's shoulders; **~на́ть** [1], ⟨пожа́ть⟩ [-жну́, -жнёшь; -жа́тый] *s.* жать[2]; **~ра́ть** P [1], ⟨пожра́ть⟩ [-жру́, -рёшь; -а́л, -а́, -о] eat up; devour; **∠тки** F *m/pl.* [1] belongings, things; со всéми ∠тками with bag & baggage.
по́за *f* [5] pose, posture, attitude.
поза|вчера́ the day before yesterday; **~ди́** (P) behind; past; **~про́шлый** [14] the ... before last.
позвол|е́ние *n* [12] permission (with с P), leave (by); **~и́тельный** [14; -лен, -льна] permissible; ~и́тельно one may; **~я́ть** [28], ⟨**∠ить**⟩ [13] allow (*a.* of), permit (Д); ~я́ть себе́ venture, presume; ✝ beg *to*; afford; ∠ь(те) may I; let; I say.
позвоно́|к *m* [1; -нка́] *anat.* vertebra; **~чник** *m* [1] spinal (*or* vertebral) column, spine, backbone; **~чный** [14] vertebral; vertebrate.
по́здн|ий [15] (-ʐŋ-) (~о *a.* it is) late.
поздоро́вит|ься F *pf.*: ему́ не ~ся he will (have to) pay for it.
поздрав|и́тель *m* [4] congratulator; **~и́тельный** [14] congratulatory; **∠ить** *s.* ~ля́ть; **~ле́ние** *n* [12] congratulation; *pl.* compliments (of the season с T); **~ля́ть** [28], ⟨**∠ить**⟩ [14] (с T) congratulate (on), wish (many happy returns [of the day]); send (*or* give) one's compliments (of the season).
поземе́льный [14] land..., ground...
по́зже later; не ~ (P) ... at the latest.
позити́вный [14; -вен, -вна] positive.
позици|о́нный [14] trench..., position...; **'~я** *f* [7] position; *pl.* ⚔ line; *fig.* attitude (on по Д).
позна|ва́ть [5], ⟨**∠ть**⟩ [1] perceive (come to) know; **∠ние** *n* [12] perception; *pl.* knowledge.
позоло́та *f* [5] gilding.
позо́р *m* [1] shame, disgrace, infamy; **~ить** [13], ⟨о-⟩ dishono(u)r, disgrace; **~ный** [14; -рен, -рна] shameful, disgraceful, infamous, ignominious; ~ный столб *m* pillory.
позы́в *m* [1] desire; impulse.
поим|ённый [14] of names; by (roll) call; **~енова́ть** [7] *pf.* name; **~у́щественный** [14] property...
по́ис|ки *m/pl.* [1] search (in в П), quest; **∠тине** truly, really.
по|и́ть [13], ⟨на-⟩ water; give to drink (s. th. T); **∠йло** *n* [9] swill.
пой|ма́ть *s.* лови́ть; **~ти́** *s.* идти́.
пока́ for the time being (*a.* ~ что) meanwhile; while; ~ (не) until; ~ F so long!, (I'll) see you later.
пока́з *m* [1] demonstration; showing; **~а́ние** (*usu. pl.*) *n* [12] evidence; ⊕ indication; **~а́тель** *m* [4] *β* exponent; index; figure; **~а́тельный** [14; -лен, -льна] significant, demonstrative; model; show (*trial*); **~а́ть(ся)** *s.* ~ывать(ся); **~но́й** [14] ostentatious; sham...; **~ывать** [1], ⟨~а́ть⟩ [3] show; demonstrate; point (at на В); ⚖ testify, depose (against на В); ⊕ read; ~а́ть себя́ (T) prove; и ви́ду не ~ывать seem to know nothing; look unconcerned; **-ся** appear (*a.* = seem, T), turn up.
пока́мест P, *s.* пока́.
пока́т|ость *f* [8] declivity; slope, slant; **~ый** [14 *sh.*] slanting, sloping; retreating (*forehead*).
покая́н|ие *n* [12] penance (do быть на П); penitence; repentance.
поквита́ться F [1] *pf.* settle accounts.
поки|да́ть [1], ⟨**∠нуть**⟩ [20] leave, quit; abandon, desert.
покла|да́я: не ~да́я рук unremittingly; **∠дистый** [14 *sh.*] accommodating; **∠жа** *f* [5] load, lading.
покло́н *m* [1] bow; regards *pl.*; **~е́ние** *n* [12] (Д) worship; deference; **~и́ться** *s.* кла́няться; **~ник** *m* [1] worship(p)er; admirer; **~я́ться** [28] (Д) worship; bow (to).
поко́иться [13] rest, lie; be based
поко́й *m* [3] rest; repose, peace, calm; † apartment; (оста́вить в let) alone; **~ник** *m* [1], **~ница** *f* [5] the deceased; ⚖ decedent; **~ницкая** *f* [14] mortuary; **~ный** [14; -о́ен, -о́йна] quiet; calm; easy; the late; *su.* = ~ник, ~ница; *cf.* спокойный.
поколе́ние *n* [12] generation.
поко́нчить [16] *pf.* ([с] T) finish

: Т) do away with; commit (suicide с собой).
покор|е́ние *n* [12] conquest; subjugation; **~и́тель** *m* [4] conqueror; **~и́ть(ся)** *s.* ~я́ть(ся); **~́ность** *f* [8] submission, obedience; **~́ный** [14; -рен, -рна] obedient; humble, submissive; ~́но *a.* (*thank*) very much; **~я́ть** [28], ‹~и́ть› [13] conquer, subdue; **-ся** submit; resign o. s.
поко́с *m* [1] (hay)mowing; meadow.
покри́кивать F [1] shout (at на В).
покро́в *m* [1] cover; hearse cloth.
покрови́тель *m* [4] patron, protector; **~ница** *f* [5] patroness, protectress; **~ственный** [14] patronizing; ✝ protective; **~ство** *n* [9] protection (of Д); patronage; **~ствовать** [7] (Д) patronize; protect.
покро́й *m* [3] cut; kind, breed.
покры|ва́ло *n* [9] coverlet; veil; **~ва́ть** [1], ‹~́ть› [22] (Т) cover (*a.* = defray); coat; beat, trump; P call *or* run down; **-ся** cover o. s.; be(come) covered; **~́тие** *n* [12] cover(ing); coat(ing); defrayal; **~́шка** *f* [5; *g/pl.*: -шек] (tire) cover; F lid.
покуп|а́тель *m* [4], **~а́тельница** *f* [5] buyer; customer; **~а́тельный** [14] purchasing; **~а́ть** [1], ‹купи́ть› [14] buy, purchase (from у Р); **~́ка** *f* [5; *g/pl.:* -пок] purchase; package; за ~́ками (*go*) shopping; **~но́й** [14] purchasing; purchase(d).
покуш|а́ться [1], ‹~си́ться› [15 *e.*; -ушу́сь, -уси́шься] attempt (*v/t.* на В); encroach ([up]on); **~е́ние** *n* [12] attempt ([up]on на В).
пол[1] *m* [1; на́ ~; на -у́; *pl. e.*] floor.
пол[2] *m* [1; *from g/pl. e.*] sex.
пол[3](...) [*g/sg., etc.*: ~(у)...] half (...).
пола́ *f* [5; *pl. st.*] skirt, tail.
полага́|ть [1], ‹положи́ть› [16] put; decide; ♪ set (to на В); *impf.* think, suppose, guess; fancy; на́до ~ть probably; поло́жим, что ... suppose, let's assume that; **-ся** rely (on на В); (Д) ~ется must; be due *or* proper; как ~ется properly.
по́л|день *m* [*gen.:* -(у́)дня; *g/pl.:* -дён] noon (at в В); *cf.* обе́д; **~дне́вный** [14] midday...; **~доро́ги** *f*. ~пути́; **~дю́жины** [*gen.:* -удю́жины] half (a) dozen.
по́ле *n* [10; *pl. e.*] field (*a. fig.*; on на, в П; across по́ Д; Т); ground; *mst. pl.* margin; **~во́й** [14] field...; **поле́зный** [14; -зен, -зна] useful, of use; helpful; wholesome; ⊕ effective; net.
полем|изи́ровать [7] polemize; **~́ика** *f* [5], **~и́ческий** [16] polemic.
поле́но *n* [9; -нья, -ньев] log.
полёт *m* [1] flight; бре́ющий ~ low-level flight; слепо́й ~ blind flying.
по́лз|ать [1], **~ти́** [24] creep, crawl; **~ко́м** on all fours; **~у́чий** [17]: ~у́чее расте́ние *n* creeper, climber.
поли|ва́ть [1], ‹~́ть› [-лью́, -льёшь; *cf.* лить] water; *pf.* start raining (*or* pouring); **~́вка** *f* [5] watering; flushing.
полиго́н *m* [1] (target) range.
полиня́лый [14] faded.
поли|рова́ть [7], ‹от-› polish, burnish; **~ро́вка** *f* [5; *g/pl.*: -вок] polish(ing); **'~с** *m* [1] (*insurance*) policy.
Полит|бюро́ *n* [*indecl.*] Politburo (*Sov.*), Political Bureau; **♀гра́мота** *f* [5] political primer (*Sov.*); **♀е́хникум** *m* [1] polytechnic; **♀заключённый** *m* [14] political prisoner.
поли́т|ик *m* [1] politician; **~ика** *f* [5] policy; politics *pl.*; **~и́ческий** [16] political; **~ру́к** *m* [1] political instructor (*or* commissar[y]) (*Sov.*); **~у́ра** *f* [5] polish; **~учёба** *f* [5] political instruction (*Sov.*); **~ь** *s.* полива́ть; **~эконо́мия** *f* [7] political economy, economics.
полиц|е́йский [16] police(man *su.*); **~́ия** *f* [7] police.
поли́чн|ое *n* [14] corpus delicti; с ~ым (*catch*) red-handed.
полк *m* [1 *e.*; в -у́] regiment; **~́а** *f* [5; *g/pl.:* -лок] shelf; pan (*gun*).
полко́в|ник *m* [1] colonel; **~о́дец** *m* [1; -дца] commander, general; **~о́й** [14] regimental.
полне́ть [8], ‹по-› grow stout.
по́лно 1. full, to the brim; **2.** F (*a.* ~те) okay, all right; never mind; enough *or* no more (of this); (*a.* ~ Д + *inf.*) stop, quit (that) (...ing)!; **~ве́сный** [14; -сен, -сна] weighty; **~вла́стный** [14; -тен, -тна] absolute; **~во́дный** [14; -ден, -дна] deep; **~кро́вный** [14; -вен, -вна] full-blooded; ⚕ plethoric; **~лу́ние** *n* [12] full moon; **~мо́чие** *n* [12] (full) power; **~мо́чный** [14; -чен, -чна] plenipotentiary; *cf.* полпре́д (-ство); **~пра́вный** [14; -вен, -вна]: ~пра́вный член *m* full member; **~стью** completely, entirely; **~та́** *f* [5] fullness, plenitude; completeness; corpulence; **~це́нный** [14; -е́нен, -е́нна] full (value)...; *fig.* full-fledged.
по́лночь *f* [8; -(у́)ночи] midnight.
по́лн|ый [14; по́лон, полна́, по́лно́; полне́е] full (of Р *or* Т); complete, absolute; perfect (*a. right*); stout; chubby; ~ы́м-~ы́й F full up, packed (with Р).
полови́к *m* [1 *e.*] mat.
полови́н|а *f* [5] half (by на В); ~а (в ~е) пя́того (at) half past four; два с ~ой two & a half; **~ка** *f* [5; *g/pl.:* -нок] half; leaf (*door*); **~чатый** [14] *fig.* vague, evasive.
полови́ца *f* [5] deal, board. [*spring*).]
полово́дье *n* [10] high water (*in*)
полов|о́й[1] [14] floor...; ~а́я тря́пка *f* mop; **~о́й**[2] [14] sexual; ~а́я зре́лость *f* puberty; ~ы́е о́рганы *m/pl.* genitals.

пóлог *m* [1] bed curtain.
полóгий [16; *comp.*: полóже] slightly sloping, flat.
полож|éние *n* [12] position, location; situation; state, condition; standing; regulations *pl.*; thesis; в (интерéсном) ~éнии F in the family way; **~и́тельный** [14; -лен, -льна] positive; affirmative; **~и́ть** (**-ся**) *s.* класть 1. & полагáть(ся).
пóлоз *m* [1; *pl.*: -лóзья, -лóзьев] runner.
полóмка *f* [5; *g/pl.*: -мок] breakage.
полосá *f* [5; *ac/sg.*: пóлосу́; *pl.*: пóлосы, полóс, -сáм] stripe, streak; strip; belt, zone; bar; field; period; **~тый** [14 *sh.*] striped.
полоскáть [3], ⟨про-⟩ rinse; gargle; **-ся** paddle; flap (*flag, etc.*).
пóлость *f* [8; *from g/pl. e.*] cavity.
полотéнце *n* [11; *g/pl.*: -нец] towel (on T); мохнáтое ~ Turkish towel.
полóтн|ище *n* [11] width; **~ó** *n* [9; *pl.*: -óтна, -óтен, -óтнам] linen; bunting; 🚂 roadbed; embankment; (*saw*) blade; **~я́ный** [14] linen...
полóть [17], ⟨вы́-, про-⟩ weed.
пол|пре́д *m* [1] ambassador; **~пре́дство** *n* [9] embassy (*Sov., till 1941*); **~пути́** halfway (*a.* на ~пути́); **~слóва** [9; *gen.*: -(у)слóва] half a word; (a few) word(s); на ~(у)слóве (*stop*) short; **~сóтни** [6; *g/sg.*: -(у)сóтни; *g/pl.*: -лусóтен] fifty; **~ти́нник** F *m* [1], P **~ти́на** *f* [5] half (a) ruble, 50 kopecks.
полтор|á *m & n*, ~ы́ *f* [*gen.*: -ýтора; -ры (*f*)] one and a half; **~áста** [*obl. cases*; -ýтораста] a hundred and fifty.
полу|боти́нки *m/pl.* [1; *g/pl.*: -нок] (low) shoes; **~глáсный** [14] semivowel; **~гóдие** *n* [12] half year, six months; **~годи́чный**, **~годовóй** [14] semiannual, half-yearly; **~грáмотный** [14; -тен, -тна] semiliterate; **∠денный** [14] midday...; meridional; **~живóй** [14; -жив, -á, -о] half dead; **~защи́тник** *m* [1] halfback; **~кру́г** *m* [1] semicircle; **~мéсяц** *m* [1] half moon, crescent; **~мрáк** *m* [1] twilight, semi-darkness; **∠ночный** [14] midnight...; **~оборóт** *m* [1] half-turn; **~óстров** *m* [1; *pl.*: -вá, *etc. e.*] peninsula; **~свéт** *m* [1] twilight; demimonde; **~спу́щенный** [14] half-mast; **~стáнок** *m* [1; -нка] 🚂 stop, substation; **~тьмá** *f* [5] = ~мрáк.
получ|áтель *m* [4] addressee, recipient; **~áть** [1], ⟨~и́ть⟩ [16] receive, get; obtain; catch; have; **-ся** come in, arrive; result; prove, turn out; **~чéние** *n* [12] receipt; getting; **∠чка** F *f* [5; *g/pl.*: -чек] pay (day).
полу|шáрие *n* [12] hemisphere; **~шу́бок** *m* [1; -бка] short fur coat.
пол|фу́нта [*g/sg.*: -уфу́нта] half pound; **~цены́**: за ~цены́ at half price; **~часá** *m* [1; *g/sg.*: -учá… half (an) hour.
пóлчище *n* [11] horde; mass.
пóлый [14] hollow; high; iceless.
полы́нь *f* [8] wormwood.
полынья́ *f* [6] ice-hole (*on froz… river etc.*).
пóльз|а *f* [5] use; benefit (for … в В, для Р); profit; advantag… utility; в ~у (Р) in favo(u)r of; **~вать** [7] treat; **-ся**, ⟨вос~оватьс…⟩ (Т) use, make use of; avail o. s. … enjoy, have; take (*opportunity*).
пóль|ка *f* [5; *g/pl.*: -лек] **1.** Pol… **2.** polka; **~ский** [16] Polish; **Ωш…** [5] Poland.
полюбóвный [14] amicable.
пóлюс *m* [1] pole; ⚡ *a.* terminal.
поля́|к *m* [1] Pole; **~на** *f* [5] glad… meadow; **~рный** [14] polar.
помáда *f* [5] pomade; (*lip*)stick.
помáз|ание *n* [12] unction; **~…вать** [1], ⟨~ать⟩ [3] anoint; *s.* мáза…
помалéньку F so-so; little by litt…
помáлкивать F [1] keep silent.
помá|рка *f* [5; *g/pl.*: -рок] bl… erasure; **~хивать** [1] wag; flouris…
поместúт|ельный [14; -лен, -л…на] spacious; **~ь(ся)** *s.* помещáт… [(-ся)]
помéстье *n* [10] estate.
пóмесь *f* [8] cross breed, mongr…
помéсячный [14] monthly.
помёт *m* [1] dung; litter, brood.
помé|тить *s.* ~чáть; **~тка** *f* [5; *g/p…* -ток] mark, note; **~ха** *f* [5] hi… drance; trouble, disturbance (*a.* ⊕…); **~чáть** [1], ⟨∠тить⟩ [15] mark, no…
помéш|анный [14 *sh.*] crazy; m… (about на П); **~áтельство** *n* [… insanity; **~áть** *s.* мешáть; **-ся** … go mad (*a.* ~áться в умé); F be m… (about на П).
поме|щáть [1], ⟨~сти́ть⟩ [15 … -ещу́, -ести́шь; -ещённый] plac… lodge, accommodate; settle; inves… insert, publish; **-ся** settle (o. s… locate; lodge; find room; hold; … placed *or* invested; *impf.* be (loca…ed); **~щéние** *n* [12] lodg(e)me… premise(s), room; investment; … **щик** *m* [1] landowner, landlord.
помидóр *m* [1] tomato.
поми́л|ование *n* [12], **~овать** [… *pf.* pardon; **~уй(те)**! for goodnes… sake; good gracious; ~уй бог! G… forbid!; гóсподи ~уй! God, ha… mercy upon us.
поми́мо (Р) besides; in spite … ~ негó without his knowledge.
поми́н *m* [1] mention (of о П); **~á…** [1], ⟨помянýть⟩ [19] recollect, r… member; speak about, mentio… pray for (*a.* о П); commemorat… ~áй, как звáли (be) off and awa… не ~áть ли́хом bear no ill will (t… ward[s] a p. В); **~ки** *f/pl.* [5; *gen…* -нок] commemoration (for t… dead); **~ýтно** every minute; co… stantly.

•мнит|ь [13], ⟨вс-⟩ remember, ecollect, think of (*a.* о П); мне ~ся as far as) I remember.
•мо|гáть [1], ⟨∠чь⟩ [26 г/ж: огý, -óжешь, -óгут; -óг, -оглá] Д) help; aid, assist; avail.
•мó|и *m/pl.* [3] slops; ~йный [14] op, garbage, dust (*hole* =, F, ~йка [5; *g/pl.*: -óек]).
•мóл *m* [1] grind(ing); ~вить [14] *f.* affiance (to с Т); ~вка *f* [5; *g/pl.*: вок] betrothal, engagement.
•мóст *m* [1] dais; rostrum; scaffold.
•моч|и F *f/pl.* [8; *from gen. e.*] leadng strings (in на П); = подтя́жки; ь *s.* помогáть.
•мóщ|ник *m* [1], ~ница *f* [5] asistant; deputy (s. th. P); helper, id; ʹ~ь *f* [8] help, aid, assistance with с Т *or* при П; to one's на /Д; *call* for на В, о П); ⚕ treatnent; relief; карéта скóрой ʹ~и mbulance.
•мпа *f* [5] pomp; ⊕ pump.
•мрачáть *s.* омрачáть.
•мутнéние *n* [12] turbidity.
•мы|сел *m* [1; -сла] thought; esign; ~шля́ть [28] think (of о П).
мянýть *s.* поминáть.
мя́тый [14] (c)rumpled; trodden.
нá|добиться [14] *pf.* (Д) need, ant; ~пра́сну F = напрáсно; слы́шке F by hearsay.
не|вóле F willy-nilly; against one's ill; ~дéльник *m* [1] Monday (on: В, *pl.*: по Д).
немнó|гу, F ~жку (a) little; little y little, gradually; F *a.* so-so.
ни|жáть [1], ⟨∠зить⟩ [15] lower, educe (*v/i.* -ся; fall, sink); ~жé-ие *n* [12] fall; reduction; decrease; egradation.
ник|áть [1], ⟨∠нуть⟩ [21] hang one's head головóй); droop; wilt.
нимá|ние *n* [12] comprehension, nderstanding; conception; ~ть [1], поня́ть⟩ [поймý, -ёшь; пóнял, -á, ; пóнятый (пóнят, -á, -о)] underand, comprehend, see; realize; ppreciate; ~ю (~ешь, ~ете [ли]) I ou) see.
номáрь *m* [4 *e.*] sexton.
нó|с *m* [1] diarrhea; ~си́ть [15], шéние *n* [12] abuse.
нóшенный [14 *sh.*[worn, shab-.
нтóн *m* [1], ~ный [14] pontoon.
ну|ждáть [1], ⟨∠дить⟩ [15; -у-дённый] force, compel; ~ждé-ие *n* [12] compulsion.
нукáть [1] urge on, spur.
нýр|ить [13] hang; ~ый [14 *sh.*] owncast.
нчик *m* [1] doughnut.
ны́не until now.
ня́т|ие *n* [12] idea, notion; con-pt(ion); comprehension; ~ливый 4 *sh.*] quick-witted, bright; ~ный 4; -тен, -тна] intelligible, understandable; clear, plain; ~но *a.*, F, = конéчно; ~ь *s.* понимáть.
поó|даль at some distance; ~ди-нóчке one by one; ~черёдный [14] alternate.
поощр|éние *n* [12] encouragement; ~я́ть [28], ⟨~и́ть⟩ [13] encourage.
поп F *m* [1 *e.*] priest.
попа|дáние *n* [12] hit; ~дáть [1], ⟨∠сть⟩ [25; *pt. st.*] (в *or* на В) get, come (*a.* across), fall, find o. s.; hit; catch (*train*); become (в И *pl.*); F (Д *impers.*) get it; не ∠сть miss; как ∠ло anyhow, at random, haphazard; комý ∠ло to the first comer (= пéр-вому ∠вшемуся); -ся (в В) be caught; fall (into a trap на ýдочку); F (Д + *vb.* + И) come across, chance (up)on, meet; occur, there is (are); strike (a p.'s eye Д на глазá; не ~дáться be out of a p.'s sight).
попадья́ *f* [6] priest's wife.
попáрно by pairs, in couples.
попáсть(ся) *s.* попадáть(ся).
попер|ёк (P) across, crosswise; in (*a p.'s way*); ~емéнно by turns; ~éчный [14] transverse, transversal; cross...
попеч|éние *n* [12] care, charge (in на П); ~и́тель *m* [4] curator, trustee.
попирáть [1] trample (on) (*fig.*).
пóпка F *m* [5; *g/pl.*: -пок] parrot.
поплавóк *m* [1; -вкá] float (*a.* ⊕).
попóйка F *f* [5; *g/pl.*: -óек] booze.
попол|áм in half; half & half; fifty--fifty; ~зновéние *n* [12] mind; pretension (to на В); ~ня́ть [28], ⟨∠нить⟩ [13] replenish, supplement; enrich; reman, reinforce.
пополýдни in the afternoon, p. m.
попóна *f* [5] horsecloth.
попрáв|ить(ся) *s.* ~ля́ть(ся); ~ка *f* [5; *g/pl.*: -вок], ~лéние *n* [12] correction; amendment; improvement; recovery; repair; ~ля́ть [28], ⟨~ить⟩ [14] repair; adjust; correct, (a)mend; improve; recover (*v/i.* -ся; put on weight, look better).
по-прéжнему (now) as before.
попрек|áть [1], ⟨~нýть⟩ [20] reproach (with Т).
пóприще *n* [11] field (in на П).
пóпро|сту plainly, unceremoniously; downright; ~шáйка F *m/f* [5; *g/pl.*: -áек] beggar.
попугáй *m* [3] parrot.
популя́рн|ость *f* [8] popularity; ~ый [14; -рен, -рна] popular.
попус|ти́тельство *n* [9] connivance; ʹ~т(óм)у F in vain, to no purpose.
попýт|ный [14] fair, favo(u)rable (*wind*); (~но in) passing, incidental(ly); ~чик *m* [1] fellow travel-(l)er.
попыт|áть F [1] *pf.* try (one's luck счáстья); ∠ка *f* [5; *g/pl.*: -ток] attempt.

Ф*

пор|á[1] *f* [5; *ac/sg.*: пóру; *pl. st.*] time; season; weather (in в В); period; F prime; (давнó) ~á it's (high) time (for Д); в (сáмую) ~у in the nick of time; до ~ы́, до врéмени not last forever; *wait* for one's opportunity; до (с) какúх ~? how long (since when)?; до сих ~ hitherto, so far, up to now (here); до тех ~ (, покá) so (*or* as) long (as); с тех ~ (как) since then (since); на пéрвых ~áх at first, in the beginning; ~óй at times; вечéрней ~óй = вéчером.

пóра[2] *f* [5] pore.

порабо|щáть [1], ‹~тúть› [15 *e.*; -ощý, -отúшь; -ощённый] enslave, subjugate.

поравня́ться [28] *pf.* overtake (с Т).

пора|жáть [1], ‹~зúть› [15 *e.*; -ажý, -азúшь; -ажённый] strike (*a. fig.* = amaze, & ⚕ = affect); defeat; **~жéнец** *m* [1; -нца] defeatist; **~жéние** *n* [12] defeat; ⚕ affection; ⚖ deprivation; striking; **~жéнчество** *n* [9] defeatism; **~зúтельный** [14; -лен, -льна] striking; **~зúть** *s.* ~жáть; **~нить** [13] *pf.* wound, cut.

порвáть(ся) *s.* порывáть(ся).

порéз *m* [1], **~ать** [3] *pf.* cut.

порéй *m* [3] leek.

пóристый [14 *sh.*] porous.

порицá|ние *n* [12], **~ть** [1] censure.

пóровну (in) equal parts.

порóг *m* [1] threshold; *pl.* rapids.

порó|да *f* [5] breed, species, race; stock; ⚒ rock; layer; **~дистый** [14 *sh.*] thoroughbred; racy; **~ждáть** [1], ‹~дúть› [15 *e.*; -ожý, -одúшь; -ождённый] cause, give rise to, entail; **~ждéние** *n* [12] brood; production.

порóжний F [15] empty.

пóрознь F separately; one by one.

порóк *m* [1] vice; defect; disease.

поросёнок *m* [2] young pig.

порó|ть [17] **1.** ‹рас-› undo, unpick; *impf.* F talk (*nonsense*); **2.** F ‹вы́-› whip, flog; **'~х** *m* [1] gunpowder; **~ховóй** [14] (gun)powder...

порóч|ить [16], ‹о-› discredit; defile; **~ный** [14; -чен, -чна] vicious.

порошóк *m* [1; -шкá] powder.

порт *m* [1; в -ý; *from g/pl. e.*] port; harbo(u)r; **~атúвный** [14; -вен, -вна] portable; **~ить** [15], ‹ис-› spoil (*v/i.* **-ся**; break down).

портн|úха *f* [5] dressmaker; **~óй** *m* [14] tailor.

портов|úк *m* [1 *e.*] longshoreman, *Brt. a.* docker; **~ый** [14] port..., dock...; ~ый гóрод *m* seaport.

портсигáр *m* [1] cigar(ette) case.

португáл|ец *m* [1; -льца] Portuguese; **Ωия** *f* [7] Portugal; **~ка** *f* [5; *g/pl.*: -лок], **~ьский** [16] Portuguese.

порт|упéя *f* [6] sword knot; **~фéль** *m* [4] brief case; portfolio; **~я́нка** [5; *g/pl.*: -нок] foot wrap (rag).

поругáние *n* [12] abuse, affront.

порý|ка *f* [5] bail (on на В *p*... security; guarantee; responsibilit... **~чáть** [1], ‹~чúть› [16] charge (a... with Д/В); commission, bid, ... (+ *inf.*); entrust; **~чéние** *n* [1... commission; instruction; me... sage; mission; (*a.* ✝) order (by Д; *a.* on behalf); **~чик** † *m* [1] (fir... lieutenant; **~чúтель** *m* [4] ba... surety; **~чúть** *s.* ~чáть.

порх|áть [1], *once* ‹~нýть› [20] f...

пóрция *f* [7] portion, helping.

пóр|ча *f* [5] spoiling, spoilage; da... age; **~шень** *m* [4; -шня] piston.

поры́в *m* [1] gust, squall; fit, ou... burst; impulse; **~áть** [1], ‹п... рвáть› [-вý, -вёшь; -áл, -á, -... пóрванный] tear; break (off; w... с Т); **-ся** *v/i.*; *impf.* jerk; striv... *s. a.* рвáть(ся); **~истый** [14 *s.*... gusty; jerky; impulsive.

поря́дко|вый [14] current; ... ordinal; **~м** F rather; properly.

поря́д|ок *m* [1; -дка] order; w... (by в П; in Т), form; course; ... conditions; kind; ~ок дня agend... по ~ку one after another; curre... (*no.*); **~очный** [14; -чен, -чна] ... derly, decent; fair(ly large *or* grea...

посáд|ить *s.* сажáть & садúть; ... *f* [5; *g/pl.*: -док] planting; embark... tion, (*a.* 🚂) boarding; ✈ landi... alighting; **~очный** [14] landing...

по-свóему in one's own way.

посвя|щáть [1], ‹~тúть› [15 ... -ящý, -ятúшь; -ящённый] dev... ([o.s.] to [себя́] Д); dedicate; ini... ate (into в В); (в И *pl.*) ordai... knight; **~щéние** *n* [12] dedicatio... initiation.

посéв *m* [1] sowing; crop; **~нóй** [... sowing (campaign *su. f*).

поседéлый [14] (turned) gray, *B*... grey.

посел|éнец *m* [1; -нца] settl... **~éние** *n* [12] colony (*a.* **посёл**... *m* [1; -лка]); **~я́ть** [28], ‹~úт... [13] settle (*v/i.* **-ся**; put up [at... П]); inspire.

посерединé in the middle *or* mid...

посе|тúтель *m* [4], **~тúтельни...** *f* [5] visitor, caller; **~тúть** *s.* ... щáть; **~щáемость** *f* [8] atten... ance; **~щáть** [1], ‹~тúть› [15 ... -ещý, -етúшь; -ещённый] vis... call on; *impf.* attend; **~щéние** ... [12] visit (to Р), call.

посúльный [14; -лен, -льна] ... cording to one's strength *or* pos... bilities, adequate, equal to.

поскользнýться [20] *pf.* slip.

поскóльку inasmuch as, as.

послаблéние *n* [12] indulgence.

послá|ние *n* [12] message; epist... **~нник** *m* [1] envoy; messeng... **~ть** *s.* посылáть.

осле 1. (P) after (*a.* ~ того́ как + *b.*); ~ чего́ whereupon; **2.** *adv.* fter(ward[s]), later (on); **~вое́нный** [14] postwar.
осле́дний [15] last; latest; ultimate, final; latter; worst; highest.
осле́д|ователь *m* [4] follower; **~овательный** [14; -лен, -льна] consistent; successive; **~ствие** *n* [12] consequence; **~ующий** [17] following.
осле|за́втра the day after tomorrow; **~сло́вие** *n* [12] epilogue.
осло́вица *f* [5] proverb.
ослуш|а́ние *n* [12] obedience; **~ник** *m* [1] novice; **∠ный** [14; -шен, -шна] obedient; docile.
осм|а́тривать [1] (keep) look -ing); **~е́иваться** [1] chuckle; augh (in one's sleeve в кула́к; at над T); **~е́ртный** [14] posthumous; **~е́шище** *n* [11] laughing-stock; **~ея́ние** *n* [12] ridicule.
осо́б|ие *n* [12] grant; relief, dole, benefit; aid, means; textbook, manual; **~ля́ть** P [28], ⟨~и́ть⟩ [14 *e.*; блю́, -би́шь] (Д) help, remedy.
осо́л *m* [1; -сла́] ambassador; **~ьство** *n* [9] embassy.
осох *m* [1] staff, stick.
оспа́ть [-сплю́, -спи́шь; -спа́л, а́, -о] *pf.* (have a) nap.
оспе|ва́ть [1], ⟨∠ть⟩ [8] ripen; F = успева́ть; be done; get ready.
оспе́шн|ость *f* [8] haste; **~ый** 14; -шен, -шна] hasty, hurried; ash.
осред|и́(не) (P) amid(st), in the niddle; **∠ник** *m* [1] mediator, internediary, middleman; **∠ничество** *n* [9] mediation; **∠ственность** *f* 8] mediocrity; **∠ственный** [14 *sh.*] niddling; mediocre; **∠ственно** *a.* air, satisfactory, C (*mark*; *cf.* тро́йка); **∠ство** *n* [9]: при ∠стве, че́рез ∠ство =**~ством** (P) by means f.
ост *m* [1 *e.*] **1.** post; на ~у́ ⚔ *stand* entinel; **2.** fast; вели́кий ~ Lent.
оста́в|ить *s.* ~ля́ть & ста́вить; **~ка** *f* [5; *g*/*pl.*: -вок] delivery (on при П); supply; **~ля́ть** [28], ⟨~ить⟩ [14] deliver (*v*/*t.*; p. Д); upply, furnish; **~щи́к** *m* [1 *e.*] upplier.
останов|и́ть *s.* ~овля́ть; **~о́вка** *f* 5; *g*/*pl.*: -вок] erection; staging, production; performance; position; organization; **~овле́ние** *n* [12] resolution, decision; decree; **~овля́ть** 28], ⟨~ови́ть⟩ [14] decide; decree; **~о́вщик** *m* [1] stage manager, director.
осте|ли́ть *s.* стлать; **∠ль** *f* [8] bed; **~пе́нный** [14; -е́нен, -е́нна] gradual.
ости|га́ть [1], ⟨∠гнуть⟩ & ⟨∠чь⟩ 21] comprehend, grasp; overtake; **~жи́мый** [14 *sh.*] conceivable.

пост|ила́ть [1] *s.* стлать; **~и́ться** [15 *e.*; пощу́сь, пости́шься] fast; **~и́чь** *s.* ~ига́ть; **∠ный** [14; -тен, -тна́, -о] fast...; vegetable (*oil*); F lean (*meat*); *fig.* sour; sanctimonious; **~ово́й** *m* [14] sentry; **~о́й** *m* [3] quarters, billets *pl.*
посто́льку insomuch.
посторо́нний [15] strange(r *su.*), outside(r), foreign (*a. body*); unauthorized; accessory, secondary.
постоя́лый [14]: ~ двор *m* inn.
постоя́н|ный [14; -я́нен, -я́нна] constant, permanent; continual, continuous; steady; ⚔ standing; ⚡ direct; **~ство** *n* [9] constancy.
пострада́вший [17] injured.
постре́л F *m* [1] scapegrace, rogue.
постри|га́ть [1] ⟨∠чь⟩ [26 г/ж: -игу́, -ижёшь, -игу́т] (-**ся** have one's hair) cut; make (become) a monk *or* nun.
постро|е́ние [12], **∠йка** *f* [5; *g*/*pl.*: -о́ек] construction; building.
поступ|а́тельный [14] progressive; **~а́ть** [1], ⟨~и́ть⟩ [14] act; (с T) treat, deal (with), handle; (в, на В) enter, join, matriculate; become; come in, be received (for на В); **-ся** (T) renounce; **~ле́ние** *n* [12] entrance, entry; matriculation; receipt; **∠ок** *m* [1; -пка] act; behavio(u)r, conduct; **′~ь** *f* [8] gait, step.
посты́|дный [14; -ден, -дна] shameful; **~лый** [14 *sh.*] odious.
посу́д|а *f* [5] crockery; (*tea*) service, F things *pl.*; F vessel; **~ный** [14] cup(*board*); dish (*towel*).
посу́точный [14] daily; 24 hours'.
посчастли́ви|ться [14; *impers.*] *pf.*: ему́ ~лось he succeeded (in *inf.*) *or* was lucky (enough).
посыл|а́ть [1], ⟨посла́ть⟩ [пошлю́, -шлёшь; по́сланный] send (for за T); dispatch; **∠ка** *f* [5; *g*/*pl.*: -лок] dispatch, sending; package, parcel; premise; *cf. a.* побегу́шки; **∠ьный** *m* [14] messenger.
посып|а́ть [1], ⟨∠ать⟩ [2] (be)strew (over; with T); sprinkle; **∠аться** *pf.* fall down; F shower (down).
посяг|а́тельство *n* [9] encroachment; **~а́ть** [1], ⟨~ну́ть⟩ [20] encroach (on на В), attempt.
пот *m* [1] sweat; весь в ~у́ sweating all over.
пота|йно́й [14] secret; **~ка́ть** F [1] connive (at Д); **~со́вка** F *f* [5; *g*/*pl.*: -вок] scuffle; thrashing; **∠ш** *m* [1] potash.
потво́рство *n* [9] indulgence, connivance; **~вать** [7] indulge, connive (at Д).
пот|ёмки *f*/*pl.* [5; *gen.*: -мок] darkness; **~енциа́л** (-tɛ-) *m* [1] potential.
потерпе́вший [17] (*ship*)wrecked.
потёртый [14 *sh.*] shabby, worn.

потéря *f* [6] loss; waste.
потéть [8], ⟨вс-⟩ sweat (*a.* F = toil; *pane:* ⟨за-⟩), perspire.
потé|ха *f* [5] fun, F lark; **~шáть** [1], ⟨~шить⟩ [16] entertain, amuse; **~шный** [14; -шен, -шна] funny, amusing.
поти|рáть F [1] rub; **~хóньку** F slowly; silently; secretly, on the sly.
пóтный [14; -тен, -тнá; -о] sweaty.
потóк *m* [1] stream; torrent; flow.
потолóк *m* [1; -лкá] ceiling (*a.* ✈).
потóм afterward(s); then; **~ок** *m* [1; -мка] descendant, offspring; **~ственный** [14] hereditary; **~ство** *n* [9] posterity, descendants *pl.*
потомý therefore; ~ что because.
потóп *m* [1] flood, deluge.
потреб|ѝтель *m* [4] consumer; buyer; **~ѝть** *s.* ~лять; **~лéние** *n* [12] consumption; use; **~лять** [28], ⟨~ѝть⟩ [14 *e.*; -блю́, -бѝшь; -блён-ный] consume; use; **ʼность** *f* [8] need, want (of в П), requirement; **ʼбный** [14; -бен, -бна] necessary.
потрёпанный F [14] shabby, worn.
потро|хá *m/pl.* [1 *e.*] giblets; bowels; **~шѝть** [16 *e.*; -шу́, -шѝшь; -шён-ный], ⟨вы́-⟩ draw, disembowel.
потряс|áть [1], ⟨~тѝ⟩ [24 -с-] shake (*a. fig.*); **~áющий** [17] tremendous; **~éние** *n* [12] shock, shake; **~тѝ** *s.* ~áть.
потý|ги *f/pl.* [5] travail, labo(u)r; **~плять** [28], ⟨~пить⟩ [14] cast down (*eyes*); hang (*head*); **~хáние** *n* [12] extinction; **~хáть** [1] *s.* тýхнуть.
пóтчевать [7], ⟨по-⟩ F = угощáть.
потягивать(ся) *s.* тянýть(ся).
поутрý F early in the morning.
поуч|áть [1] teach (s. th. Д); **~ѝтельный** [14; -лен, -льна] instructive; edifying.
похáбный P [14; -бен, -бна] obscene, smutty.
похвал|á *f* [5] praise; commendation; **ʼьный** [14; -лен, -льна] laudable, commendable, praiseworthy; laudatory.
похи|щáть [1], ⟨ʼтить⟩ [15; -ѝщу; -ѝщенный] purloin; kidnap; **~ѝщéние** *n* [12] kidnap(p)ing, abduction.
пох|лёбка *f* [5; *g/pl.*: -бок] soup; skilly; **~мéлье** *n* [10] hang-over.
похóд *m* [1] campaign; march; cruise; крестóвый ~ crusade; **~ѝть** [15] (на В) be like, resemble; **~ка** *f* [5] gait; **~ный** [14] marching; camp-...; battle...
похождéние *n* [12] adventure.
похóж|ий [17 *sh.*] (на В) like, resembling; similar (to); быть ~им look like; ни на что не ~е F shocking.
похо|рóнный [14] funeral...; dead (*march*); undertaker's (*office*); **ʼ~**-**роны** *f/pl.* [5; -óн, -онáм] funer… burial (at на П); **~тлѝвый** [14 *sh*…] lustful, lewd; **ʼ~ть** *f* [8] lust.
поцелýй *m* [3] kiss (on в В).
почáсно hourly.
пóчва *f* [5] soil, (*a. fig.*) ground.
почём F how much (is); how shoul…
почемý why; ~-то for some reaso…
пóчерк *m* [1] handwriting.
почерп|áть [1], ⟨~нýть⟩ [20; -ép…нутый] gather, derive; obtain.
пóчесть[1] *f* [8] hono(u)r.
почéсть[2] *s.* почитáть 2.
почёт *m* [1] hono(u)r, esteem; **~ны…** [14; -тен, -тна] honorary; hono(u)…able; (*e. g. guard*) of hono(u)r.
почи|вáть [1], ⟨ʼть⟩ [-ѝю, -ѝеш…] rest, repose; F sleep.
почѝн *m* [1] initiative; F ☤ sta…
почѝн|ка *f* [5; *g/pl.*: -нок] repa… (for в В); **~ять** [28] *s.* чинѝть 1
поч|итáть[1] [1] **1.** ⟨~тѝть⟩ [-чт… -тѝшь; -чтённый] esteem, respec… hono(u)r; worship; ☤ favo(u)r (wi… Т); **2.** ⟨~éсть⟩ [25; -чтý, -тёш… -члá; -чтённый] (Т, за В) esteem… consider; **-ся** be held *or* reputed (… be Т); **~итáть**[2] [1] *pf.* read … while); **~ѝть** *s.* почивáть; **ʼка** *f* [… *g/pl.*: -чек] ⚘ bud; *anat.* kidney.
пóчт|а *f* [5] mail, *Brt.* post (by по … Т); post; *a.* = ~áмт; **~альóн** [1] mailman, postman; **~áмт** *m* [… post office (at на П).
почтéн|ие *n* [12] respect (for к Д… esteem, obeisance; F compliment… с совершéнным ~ием respectful… yours, yours faithfully; **~ный** [1… -éнен, -éнна] respectable; vene…able.
почтѝ almost, nearly, all but; **~…тельность** *f* [8] respect; **~тел…ный** [14; -лен, -льна] respectfu… respectable; **~ть** *s.* почитáть.
почтóв|ый [14] post(al), mail… post-office; note (*paper*); **~ы…** ящик *m* mail (*Brt.* letter) bo… (*abbr.*: п/я) Post Office Box (POB… ~ая мáрка *f* (postage) stamp.
пóшл|ина *f* [5] custom, dut… **~ость** *f* [8] platitude; **~ый** [1… пошл, -á, -о] common(place), trit… stale.
поштýчный [14] (by the) piece.
пощáда *f* [5] mercy; ⚔ quarter.
пощёчина *f* [5] slap in the face.
поэ́|зия *f* [7] poetry; **~тѝчески…** [16] poetic(al); **~тому** therefore.
появ|ѝться *s.* ~ляться; **~лéние** … [12] appearance; **~ляться** [28… ⟨~ѝться⟩ [14] appear; emerge.
пóяс *m* [1; *pl.*: -cá, *etc. e.*] belt; zon…
поясн|éние *n* [12] explanatio… **~ѝтельный** [14] explanatory; **~ѝт…** *s.* ~ять; **~ѝца** *f* [5] small of th… back; **~óй** [14] belt...; zone… half-length; **~ять** [28], ⟨~ѝть⟩ [1… explain. [great-grandmother
прабáбушка *f* [5; *g/pl.*: -шек]

ҏáвд|а *f* [5] truth; (э́то) ~а it is ·ue; ва́ша ~а you are right; не а ли? isn't it, (s)he?, aren't you, ·ey?, do(es)n't ... (*etc.*)?; **~и́вый** 4 *sh.*] truthful; **~оподо́бный** 4; -бен, -бна] likely, probable, ·erisimilar.
ҏа́ведн|ик *m* [1] (*pl.* the) right·ous (man); **~ый** [14; -ден, -дна] ·st, righteous, godly.
ҏа́вил|о *n* [9] rule; principle; *pl.* ·gulations; **~ьный** [14; -лен, ·льна] correct, right; regular.
ҏави́тель *m* [4] ruler; regent; **·ственный** [14] governmental; **·ство** *n* [9] government.
ҏа́в|ить [14] (Т) govern, rule; ·rive; ⚓ steer; (В) (proof)read; ·rop; perform; **~ка** *f* [5] proof·eading; stropping; **~ле́ние** *n* [12] ·overnment; board of directors, ·anaging *or* executive committee; administration.
ҏа́внук *m* [1] great-grandson.
ҏа́во 1. *n* [9; *pl. e.*] right (to на В; ·, by по Д); law; justice; *pl.* F ·cense; **2.** *adv.* F indeed, really; **·вéд** *m* [1] jurist; **~вéдение** *n* [12] ·risprudence; **~ве́рный** [14; -рен, ·рна] orthodox; **~во́й** [14] legal; **·мо́чный** [14; -чен, -чна] author·ed; **~писа́ние** *n* [12] orthography, ·pelling; **~сла́вие** *n* [12] Orthodoxy; **·сла́вный** [14] Orthodox; **~су́дие** [12] (administration of) justice; **·та́** *f* [5] right(fulness), rectitude.
ҏа́вый [14; *fig.* прав, -á, -о] right ·. *fig.*; *a. side*, on *a.* с Р), right·and.
ҏа́вящий [17] ruling.
ҏа́га *f* [5] Prague.
ҏа́дед *m* [1] (great-)grandfather.
ҏа́здн|ик *m* [1] holiday; festival; ~иком! compliments *pl.* (of the ·eason)!; **~ичный** [14] festive, ·oliday...; **~ование** *n* [12] celebra·on; **~овать** [7], ⟨от-⟩ celebrate; **·осло́вие** *n* [12] idle talk; **~ость** *f* ·] idleness; **~ый** [14; -ден, -дна] ·le.
ҏа́кти|к *m* [1] practical man; ex·ert; **~ка** *f* [5] practice (in на П); **·кова́ть** [7] practice, -ise (*v/i.* **-ся**; be practiced); **∠ческий** [16], **·чный** [14; -чен, -чна] practical.
ҏа́порщик † *m* [1] ensign.
ҏах *m* [1] dust; ashes *pl.* (*fig.*).
ҏа́ч|ечная (-ʃn-) *f* [14] laundry; **·ка** *f* [5; *g/pl.*: -чек] laundress.
ҏаща́ *f* [5; *g/pl.*: -щéй] sling.
ҏебыва́|ние *n* [12], **~ть** [1] stay.
ҏевзойти́ *s.* превосходи́ть.
ҏевоз|мога́ть [1], ⟨~мо́чь⟩ [26 ·ж: -огу́, -о́жешь, -о́гут; -о́г, ·ла́] overcome, subdue; **~носи́ть** ·5], ⟨~нести́⟩ [24 -с-] extol, exalt.
ҏевосх|оди́тельство *n* [9] Ex·ellency; **~оди́ть** [15], ⟨превзой·ти́⟩ [-йду́, -йдёшь, *etc.*, *cf.* идти́; -йдённый] excel, surpass; **~о́дный** [14; -ден, -дна] excellent, splendid; superior; *gr.* superlative; **~о́дство** *n* [9] superiority.
превра|ти́ть(ся) *s.* ~ща́ть(ся); **∠тность** *f* [8] vicissitude; wrongness; **∠тный** [14; -тен, -тна] wrong, mis...; adverse, changeful; **~ща́ть** [1], ⟨~ти́ть⟩ [15 *e.*; -ащу́, -ати́шь; -ащённый] change, turn, transform (into в В) (*v/i.* **-ся**); **~ще́ние** *n* [12] change; transformation; conversion.
превы|ша́ть [1], ⟨∠сить⟩ [15] exceed; **~ше́ние** *n* [12] excess.
прегра́|да *f* [5] barrier; obstacle; **~жда́ть** [1], ⟨~ди́ть⟩ [15 *e.*; -ажу́, -ади́шь; -аждённый] bar, block (up).
прегреш|а́ть [1], ⟨~и́ть⟩ [16] sin.
пред = пéред.
преда|ва́ть [5], ⟨∠ть⟩ [-да́м, -да́шь, *etc.*, *cf.* -дать; пре́дал, -á, -о; -да́й (-те)!; пре́данный (-ан, -á, -о)] betray; subject, expose; ∠ть забвéнию bury in oblivion; **-ся** (Д) indulge (in); devote o. s., give o. s. up (to); **∠ние** *n* [12] legend; tradition; **'~нный** [14 *sh.*] devoted, faithful, true; *cf.* и́скренний; **∠тель** *m* [4] traitor; **∠тельский** [16] treacherous; **∠тельство** *n* [9] treason, treachery; **∠ть(ся)** *s.* ~ва́ть(ся).
предвар|и́тельно previously, before(hand); **~и́тельный** [14] preliminary; ⚖ *a.* on remand; **~я́ть** [28], ⟨~и́ть⟩ [13] (В) forestall; advise (of о П).
предвé|стие = предзнаменова́ние; **~стник** *m* [1] harbinger; **~ща́ть** [1] forebode, presage.
предвзя́тый [14 *sh.*] preconceived.
предви́деть [11] foresee.
предвку|ша́ть [1], ⟨~си́ть⟩ [15] foretaste; **~ше́ние** *n* [12] foretaste.
предводи́тель *m* [4] (ring)leader; † marshal; **~ство** *n* [9] leadership.
предвосх|ища́ть [1], ⟨~и́тить⟩ [15; -и́щу] anticipate, forestall.
предвы́борный [14] election...
предéл *m* [1] limit, bound(ary) (within в П); border; *pl.* precincts; **~ьный** [14] limit..., maximum...; utmost, extreme.
предзнаменова́|ние *n* [12] omen, presage, portent; **~ть** [7] *pf.* portend, presage.
предисло́вие *n* [12] preface.
предл|ага́ть [1], ⟨~ожи́ть⟩ [16] offer (a p. s. th. Д/В); propose; suggest; order.
предло́|г *m* [1] pretext (on, under под Т), pretense (under); *gr.* preposition; **~же́ние** *n* [12] offer; proposal, proposition, suggestion; *parl.* motion; ⚕ supply; *gr.* sentence, clause (*cf.* пя́тый); **~жи́ть** *s.* предлага́ть; **~жный** [14] *gr.* prepositional (*case*).
предме́стье *n* [10] suburb.

предмéт *m* [1] object; subject (matter); ✝ article; на ~ (P) for the purpose of; **~ный** [14] subject...; [-тен, -тна] objective.
предназн|ачáть [1], ⟨~áчить⟩ [16] (**-ся** be) destine(d).
предна|мéренный [14 *sh.*] premeditated, deliberate; **~чертáть** [1] *pf.* predetermine.
прéдок *m* [1; -дка] ancestor.
предопредел|éние *n* [12] predestination; **~я́ть** [28], ⟨~и́ть⟩ [13] predetermine.
предост|авля́ть [28], ⟨~áвить⟩ [14] (Д) let (a p.) have; leave (to); give, render; grant; place (at a p.'s disposal).
предостер|егáть [1], ⟨~éчь⟩ [26 г/ж] warn (of от P); **~ежéние** *n* [12] warning.
предосторóжност|ь *f* [8] precaution(ary measure мéра ~и).
предосуди́тельный [14; -лен, -льна] reprehensible, scandalous.
предотвра|щáть [1], ⟨~ти́ть⟩ [15 *e.*; -ащý, -ати́шь; -ащённый] avert, prevent; **~щéние** *n* [12] prevention,
предохран|éние *n* [12] protection (from, against от P); **~и́тельный** [14] precautionary; ⚕ preventive; ⊕ safety...; **~я́ть** [28], ⟨~и́ть⟩ [13] guard, preserve (from от P).
предпис|áние *n* [12] order, instruction, direction; **~ывать** [1], ⟨~áть⟩ [3] order, prescribe.
предпол|агáть [1], ⟨~ожи́ть⟩ [16] suppose, assume; *impf.* intend, plan; presuppose; **~ожи́тельный** [14; -лен, -льна] presumable; **~ожи́ть** *s.* ~агáть.
предпо|слáть *s.* ~сылáть; **~слéдний** [15] last but one; **~сылáть** [1], ⟨~слáть⟩ [-шлю, -шлёшь; *cf.* слать] premise; **~сы́лка** *f* [5; *g/pl.:* -лок] (pre)supposition; (pre-)condition, prerequisite.
предпоч|итáть [1], ⟨~éсть⟩ [25 -т-: -чтý, -чтёшь; -чёл, -члá; -чтённый] prefer; *pt.* + бы would rather; **~тéние** *n* [12] preference; favo(u)r; отдáть ~тéние (Д) prefer; **~ти́тельный** [14; -лен, -льна] preferable.
предпри|и́мчивость *f* [8] enterprise; **~и́мчивый** [14 *sh.*] enterprising; **~ни́матель** *m* [4] employer; industrialist, businessman; **~нимáть** [1], ⟨~ня́ть⟩ [-имý, -и́мешь; -и́нял, -á, -o; -и́нятый (-и́нят, -á, -o)] undertake; **~я́тие** *n* [12] undertaking, enterprise; business; plant, works, factory (at на П).
предраспол|агáть [1], ⟨~ожи́ть⟩ [16] predispose; **~ожéние** *n* [12] predisposition.
предрассýдок *m* [1; -дка] prejudice.
председáтель *m* [4] chairman, president; **~ство** *n* [9] presidency; **~ствовать** [7] preside (over П), be in the chair.
предсказ|áние *n* [12] predictio forecast; prophecy; **~ывать** [⟨~áть⟩ [3] foretell, predict; for cast; prophesy.
предсмéртный [14] death..., d ing.
представи́тель *m* [4] represent tive; *cf. a.* полпрéд; advoca **~ный** [14; -лен, -льна] represent tive; stately, imposing; **~ство** *n* representation; *cf. a.* полпрéдств
предстáв|ить(ся) *s.* ~ля́ть(ся); **лéние** *n* [12] presentation; perfor ance; introduction; idea, notio application (for на B); **~ля́ть** [2 ⟨~ить⟩ [14] present (o.s., occ offer **-ся**); produce; introdu (o.s.); (*a.* собóй) represent, be; (*a.* = feign -ся [T]); (*esp.* ~ля себé) imagine; propose (for к Д *refl. a.* appear; seem.
предст|авáть [5], ⟨~áть⟩ [-áн -áнешь] appear; **~оя́ть** [-ойт] in store (of Д), expect; (will) ha to; **~оя́щий** [17] (forth)coming.
преду|беждéние *n* [12] prejudi bias; **~ведомля́ть** [28], ⟨~вéд мить⟩ [14] advise (of о П); **~г дывать** [1], ⟨~гадáть⟩ [1] gu (beforehand), foresee; **~мы́шле ный** [14] *s.* преднамéренный.
предупре|ди́тельный [14; -ле -льна] preventive; obliging; ~ дáть [1], ⟨~ди́ть⟩ [15 *e.*; -еж -еди́шь; -еждённый] foresta anticipate (*p.*), prevent (*th.*); wa (of о П); give notice (of); **~ждéн** *n* [12] warning; notice; notificatio prevention.
предусм|áтривать [1], ⟨~отрé [9; -отрю́, -óтришь] foresee; pr vide (for), stipulate; **~отри́тел ный** [14; -лен, -льна] prudent.
предчýвств|ие *n* [12] presen ment; **~овать** [7] have a presen ment (of).
предшéств|енник *m* [1] predec sor; **~овать** [7] (Д) precede.
предъяв|и́тель *m* [4] beare **~ля́ть** [28], ⟨~и́ть⟩ [14] prese produce, show; ⚖ bring (*acti* against к Д); assert (*claim*).
пре|дыдýщий [17] preceding, pr vious; **~éмник** *m* [1] successor.
прéж|де formerly; (at) first; before (*a.* ~де чем); **~девремé ный** [14; -енен, -енна] prematu early; **~ний** [15] former, previo
презид|éнт *m* [1] president; **~иу** *m* [1] presidium (*Sov.*).
през|ирáть [1] despise; ⟨~рéть⟩ scorn, disdain; **~рéние** *n* [12] co tempt (for к Д); **~рéнный** [14 *s.* contemptible, despicable; **~рéть** ~ирáть; **~ри́тельный** [14; -ле -льна] contemptuous, scornful.
преимýществ|енно predomina

у, mainly; **~о** *n* [9] advantage; reference; privilege; по ~у = ~нно.
рейскурант *m* [1] price list.
реклон|éние *n* [12] inclination; dmiration (of пéред Т); **~йться** ~яться; **∠ный** [14] old, advanced; senile; **~яться** [28], ⟨~йться⟩ [13] bow (to, before пéред Т); dmire.
рекословить [14] contradict.
рекрáсный [14; -сен, -сна] beautiful; fine, splendid, excellent; *a.* ery well.
рекра|щáть [1], ⟨~тить⟩ [15 *e.*; ащý, -атишь; -ащённый] stop, cease, end (*v/i.* **-ся**); break off; **щéние** *n* [12] cessation, stoppage.
релéст|ный [14; -тен, -тна] lovely, charming, delightful; **'~ь** *f* [8] harm; F *s.* ~ный.
релом|лéние *n* [12] refraction; **лять** [28], ⟨~ить⟩ [14; -млённый] **-ся** be) refract(ed).
рéлый [14 *sh.*] rotten, putrid.
рель|щáть [1], ⟨~стить⟩ [15 *e.*; льщý, -льстишь; -льщённый] (-**ся** e) charm(ed), tempt(ed), entice(d), educe(d).
релюдия *f* [7] prelude.
реми|нуть [19] *pf.* fail; **~ровáть** 7] (*im*)*pf.* award a prize (to B); **'~я** [7] prize; bonus; premium; rate.
ремьéр *m* [1] premier, (*usu.* ~-министр) prime minister; **~а** *f* [5] première, first night.
ренебр|егáть [1], ⟨~éчь⟩ [26 г/ж], **~ежéние** *n* [12] (Т) neglect, disregard, disdain, scorn, slight; **ежительный** [14; -лен, -льна] slighting, scornful, disparaging; **~éчь** *s.* ~егáть.
рéния *n/pl.* [12] debate, discussion.
реобладá|ние *n* [12] predominance; **~ть** [1] prevail, predominate.
реобра|жáть [1], ⟨~зить⟩ [15 *e.*; ажý, -азишь; -ажённый] change, transform (*v/i.* **-ся**); **~жéние** *n* [12] transformation; *eccl.* Transfiguration; **~зить(ся)** *s.* ~жáть(ся); **зовáние** *n* [12] transformation; reorganization; reform; **~зовáтель** *m* [4] reformer; **~зóвывать** [1], ⟨~зовáть⟩ [7] reform, reorganize; transform.
реодол|евáть [1], ⟨~éть⟩ [8] overcome, subdue; surmount.
репарáт *m* [1] preparation.
репирáтельство *n* [9] wrangle.
реподавá|ние *n* [12] teaching, instruction; **~тель** *m* [4], **~тельница** *f* [5] teacher, instructor; **~ть** [5] teach.
реподн|осить [15], ⟨~ести⟩ [24 -с-] present, offer.
репрово|ждáть [1], ⟨~дить⟩ [15 *e.*; -ожý, -одишь; -ождённый] forward, send; spend, pass.
препя́тств|ие *n* [12] obstacle, hindrance; бег (*or* скáчки) с ~иями steeplechase; **~овать** [7], ⟨вос-⟩ hinder, prevent (a p. from Д/в П).
прер|вáть(ся) *s.* ~ывáть(ся); **~екáние** *n* [12] squabble; **~ывáть** [1], ⟨~вáть⟩ [-вý, -вёшь; -áл, -á, -о; прéрванный (-ан, -á, -о)] interrupt; break (off), *v/i.* **-ся**; **~ывистый** [14 *sh.*] broken, faltering.
пресе|кáть [1], ⟨∠чь⟩ [26] cut short; suppress; **-ся** break; stop.
преслéдов|ание *n* [12] pursuit; persecution; ⚖ prosecution; **~ать** [7] pursue; persecute; haunt; ⚖ prosecute.
пресловýтый [14] notorious.
пресмыкá|ться [1] creep, crawl; *fig.* cringe (to пéред Т); **~ющиеся** *n/pl.* [17] reptiles.
прéсный [14; -сен, -снá, -о] fresh (*water*); unleavened (*bread*); stale.
пресс *m* [1] ⊕ press; **∠а** *f* [5] press; **~-конферéнция** *f* [7] press conference; **~-папьé** *n* [*ind.*] paperweight.
престарéлый [14] aged.
престóл *m* [1] throne; altar.
преступ|áть [1], ⟨~йть⟩ [14] break, infringe; **~лéние** *n* [12] crime; на мéсте ~лéния red-handed; **∠ник** *m* [1] criminal, delinquent; **∠ность** *f* [8] criminality, delinquency.
пресы|щáть [1], ⟨∠тить⟩ [15] surfeit (*v/i.* **-ся**), satiate; **~щéние** *n* [12] satiety.
претвор|я́ть [28], ⟨~йть⟩ [13] change, transform; ~я́ть в жизнь put into practice, realize.
претен|довáть [7] (на В) (lay) claim (to); **∠зия** *f* [7] claim, pretension, title (to на В, к Д); быть в ∠зии (на В [за В]) take (a p.'s [th.]) amiss *or* ill.
преувел|ичéние *n* [12] exaggeration; **~йчивать** [1], ⟨~ичить⟩ [16] exaggerate.
преусп|евáть [1], ⟨~éть⟩ [8] succeed; thrive, prosper.
при (П) by, at, near; (*battle*) of; under, in the time of; in a p.'s presence; about (one ~ себé), with; in (*health, weather, etc.*); for (all that ~ всём том); when, on (*-ing*); быть ~ have; be attached to; ~ э́том at that; ✝ ~ сём herewith; быть ни ~ чём F have nothing to do with (it тут), not be p.'s fault.
прибáв|ить(ся) *s.* ~ля́ть(ся); **~ка** *f* [5; *g/pl.:* -вок], **~лéние** *n* [12] increase, raise; addition; addendum; **~ля́ть** [28], ⟨~ить⟩ [14] (B *or* P) add; increase; put on (*weight* в П); mend (one's pace ~ля́ть шáгу) **-ся** increase; be added; (a)rise; grow longer; **~очный** [14] additional; surplus...
прибалтийский [16] Baltic.

прибау́тка F *f* [5; *g/pl.:* -ток] byword, saying.
прибе|га́ть [1] **1.** ⟨⁓жа́ть⟩ [4; -егу́, -ежи́шь, -егу́т] come running; **2.** ⟨⁓́гнуть⟩ [20] resort, have recourse (to к Д); **⁓рега́ть** [1], ⟨⁓ре́чь⟩ [26 г/ж] save, reserve.
приби|ва́ть [1], ⟨⁓́ть⟩ [-бью́, -бьёшь, *etc., cf.* бить] fasten, nail; beat (down); throw (*ashore*); **⁓ра́ть** [1], ⟨прибра́ть⟩ [-беру́, -рёшь; -бра́л, -а́, -о; при́бранный] tidy *or* clean (up); прибра́ть к рука́м appropriate; **-ся** F make o.s. up; **⁓́ть** *s.* ⁓ва́ть.
прибли|жа́ть [1], ⟨⁓́зить⟩ [15] approach, draw near (к Д; *v/i.* **-ся**); approximate; **⁓же́ние** *n* [12] approach(ing); approximation; **⁓жённый** [14] confidant; *a.* = **⁓зи́тельный** [14; -лен, -льна] approximate; **⁓́зить(ся)** *s.* ⁓жа́ть(ся).
прибо́й *m* [3] surf.
прибо́р *m* [1] apparatus, instrument; set; cover; service; (*table*)ware; utensils *pl.*, (*shaving*) things *pl.*
прибра́ть *s.* прибира́ть.
прибре́жный [14] littoral.
прибы|ва́ть [1], ⟨⁓́ть⟩ [-бу́ду, -дешь; при́был, -а́, -о] arrive (in, at в В); increase, rise; **'⁓ль** *f* [8] profit, gains *pl.*; rise; **'⁓льный** [14; -лен, -льна] profitable; **⁓́тие** *n* [12] arrival (in, at в В; upon по П); **⁓́ть** *s.* ⁓ва́ть.
прива́л *m* [1] halt, rest.
приве|де́ние *n* [12] putting (*in order* в В); ♃ reduction; **⁓сти́** *s.* привози́ть; **⁓ре́дливый** [14 *sh.*] fastidious.
приве́ржен|ец *m* [1; -нца] adherent; **⁓ный** [14 *sh.*] attached.
привести́ *s.* приводи́ть.
приве́т *m* [1] greeting(s); *esp.* ⚔ salute; regards, compliments *pl.*; F hello!, hi!; **⁓ливый** [14 *sh.*] affable; **⁓ственный** [14] of welcome; **⁓ствие** *n* [12] greeting, welcome; **⁓ствовать** [7; *pt. a. pf.*] greet, salute; welcome.
приви|ва́ть [1], ⟨⁓́ть⟩ [-вью́, -вьёшь, *etc., cf.* вить] inoculate, vaccinate; ⚘ (en)graft; **-ся** take; **⁓́вка** *f* [5; *g/pl.:* -вок] inoculation, vaccination; grafting; **⁓де́ние** *n* [12] ghost, specter (*Brt.*-tre), apparition; **⁓легиро́ванный** [14] privileged; **⁓ле́гия** *f* [7] privilege; **⁓́нчивать** [1], ⟨⁓нти́ть⟩ [15 *e.*; -нчу́, -нти́шь] screw on; **⁓́ть(ся)** *s.* ⁓ва́ть(ся).
при́вкус *m* [1] smack (*a. fig.*).
привле|ка́тельный [14; -лен, -льна] attractive; **⁓ка́ть** [1], ⟨⁓́чь⟩ [26] draw, attract; engage (in к Д); call (*to account*); bring (*to trial*); **⁓че́ние** *n* [12] attraction; calling.
приво́д *m* [1] bringing; ⊕ drive; **⁓и́ть** [15], ⟨привести́⟩ [25] bring; lead; result (in к Д); quote, cite; ♃ reduce; put, set; drive, throw; **-ся**, ⟨-сь⟩ Д + *vb.* F happen; have to; **⁓но́й** [14] driving (*belt, etc.*).
привоз|и́ть [15], ⟨привезти́⟩ [2...] bring; import; **⁓но́й** & **⁓́ный** [1...] imported.
приво́лье *n* [10] open (space), expanse; freedom; ease, comfort; в ⁓ *a.* in clover.
привы|ка́ть [1], ⟨⁓́кнуть⟩ [21] get *or* be(come) accustomed *or* used (to к Д); **⁓́чка** *f* [5; *g/pl.:* -чек] habit; custom; **⁓́чный** [14; -чен, -чна] habitual.
привя́з|анность *f* [8] attachment; **⁓а́ть(ся)** *s.* ⁓ывать(ся); **⁓чивый** [14 *sh.*] affectionate; captious; obtrusive; **⁓ывать** [1], ⟨⁓а́ть⟩ [3] (к Д) tie, attach (to); **-ся** become attached; F run after; intrude (upon); cavil; **'⁓ь** *f* [8] leash.
пригла|си́тельный [14] invitation...; **⁓ша́ть** [1], ⟨⁓си́ть⟩ [15 *e.*; -ашу́, -аси́шь; -ашённый] invite (to *mst* на В), ask; call (*doctor*); **⁓ше́ние** *n* [12] invitation.
пригна́ть *s.* пригоня́ть.
пригов|а́ривать [1], ⟨⁓ори́ть⟩ [1...] sentence; condemn; *impf.* F say (at the same time); **⁓о́р** *m* [1] sentence, verdict (*a. fig.*); **⁓ори́ть** *s.* ⁓а́ривать.
приго́дный [14; -ден, -дна] ...го́дный.
пригоня́ть [28], ⟨пригна́ть⟩ [-гоню́, -го́нишь; -гна́л, -а́, -о; при́гнанный] drive; fit, adjust.
пригор|а́ть [1], ⟨⁓е́ть⟩ [9] burn; **'⁓од** *m* [1] suburb; **'⁓одный** [1...] suburban; **'⁓́шня** *f* [6; *g/pl.:* -ней & -шен] hand(ful).
пригот|а́вливать(ся) [1] *s.* ⁓овля́ть(ся); **⁓ови́тельный** [14] preparatory; **⁓о́вить(ся)** *s.* ⁓овля́ть(-ся); **⁓овле́ние** *n* [12] preparation (for к Д); **⁓овля́ть** [28], ⟨⁓о́вить⟩ [14] prepare (*v/i.*, o.s. **-ся**) (for к Д).
прида|ва́ть [5], ⟨⁓́ть⟩ [-да́м, -да́шь, *etc., cf.* дать; при́да́л, -а́, -о; при́данный (-ан, -а́, -о)] add; give; attach; **⁓́ное** *n* [14] dowry; **⁓́ток** *m* [1; -тка] appendage; *anat.* appendix; **⁓́точный** [14] *gr.* subordinate (*clause*); **⁓́ть** *s.* ⁓ва́ть; **⁓́ча** *f* [5]: в ⁓́чу to boot.
придви|га́ть [1], ⟨⁓́нуть⟩ [20] move up (*v/i.* **-ся**; draw near).
придво́рный [14] court(ier *su. m*).
приде́л|ывать, ⟨⁓ать⟩ [1] fasten, fix (to к Д).
приде́рж|ивать [1], ⟨⁓а́ть⟩ [4...] hold (back); **-ся** *impf.* (P) adhere to; F hold (on [to]).
приди́р|аться [1], ⟨придра́ться⟩ [-деру́сь, -рёшься; -дра́лся, -а́ла́сь, -а́ло́сь] (к Д) find fault (with), carp *or* cavil (at); seize; **⁓ка** *f* [5; *g/pl.:* -рок] cavil; **⁓чивый** [1... *sh.*] captious.

идра́ться *s.* придира́ться.
идум|ывать, ⟨~ать⟩ [1] think ut, devise, contrive.
идыха́ние *n* [12] aspiration.
иéз|д *m* [1] arrival (in в В; upon о П); **~жа́ть** [1], ⟨приéхать⟩ -éду, -éдешь] arrive (in, at в В); жий [17] visitant..., guest...
иём *m* [1] reception; acceptance, dmission; consultation; engagement, ⚔ enlistment; taking; dose; novement (with в В); draught; itting (at в В); device, trick; nethod, way; **~ник** *m* [1] receiver, eceiving set; *s.* радиоприёмник; ный [14] reception (*day*; *room*: *a.* vaiting, *usu. su. f* ~ная), receiving, onsultation..., office (*hours*); entrance (*examination*); foster (*father*, *tc.*; foster child *a.* **~ыш** *m* [1]).
и|éхать *s.* ~езжа́ть; **~жа́ть(ся)** ~жима́ть(ся); **~жига́ть** [1], ~жéчь⟩ [26 г/ж: -жгу́, -жжёшь; *f.* жечь] cauterize; **~жима́ть** [1], ~жа́ть⟩ [-жму́, -жмёшь; -а́тый] ress (to, on к Д); **-ся** press; nestle; з *m* [1] prize; **~заду́м(ыв)аться** заду́м(ыв)аться.
изва́|ние *n* [12] vocation, calling; ть *s.* призыва́ть.
иземл|я́ться ✈ [28], ⟨~и́ться⟩ 13] land; **~éние** *n* [12] landing.
и́зма *f* [5] prism.
изна|ва́ть [5], ⟨~ть⟩ [1] (Т; *a.* В) recognize, acknowledge (as); ee, admit, own; find, consider, eclare; **-ся** confess (s. th. в П), vow, admit; ~ться *or* ~ю́сь to tell he truth, frankly speaking; **'~к** *m* 1] sign; feature, characteristic; ние *n* [12] acknowledg(e)ment, ecognition; confession; declaration of love в любви́); **~тельность** *f* 8] gratitude; **~тельный** [14; -лен, льна] grateful, thankful (for за В); ть(ся) *s.* ~ва́ть(ся).
и́зра|к *m* [1] phantom, specter *Brt.* -tre); **~чный** [14; -чен, -чна] hostly; illusive.
изы́в *m* [1] appeal, call (for на В), immons; ⚔ draft, conscription; а́ть [1], ⟨призва́ть⟩ [-зову́, вёшь; -зва́л, -а́, -о; при́званный] all (for на В; to witness в свидéели), appeal; ⚔ draft, call out *or* p (for на В); при́званный *a.* ualified; **~ни́к** *m* [1 *e.*] draftee, onscript; **~но́й** [14] ⚔ draft(ee)...
и́иск *m* [1] mine, field.
ийти́(сь) *s.* приходи́ть(ся).
ика́з *m* [1] order, command; *hist.* ffice, board; **~а́ть** *s.* ~ывать; **~ик** *m* [1] † *s.* продавéц; steward; ывать [1], ⟨~а́ть⟩ [3] order, command; tell; F should, ought; *s. a.* го́дно.
и|ка́лывать [1], ⟨~коло́ть⟩ [17] in, fasten; stab; **~каса́ться** [1], ~косну́ться⟩ [20] (к Д, † Р) touch;

~ки́дывать [1], ⟨~ки́нуть⟩ [20] weigh; calculate; estimate; **-ся** F pretend *or* feign to be, act (the T).
прикла́д *m* [1] (*rifle*) butt; **~но́й** [14] applied; **~ывать** [1], ⟨приложи́ть⟩ [16] (к Д) apply (to), pu (on); enclose (with); affix (*seal*); **-ся** kiss; F level; apply (s. th. to Т/к Д).
приклéи|вать [1], ⟨~ть⟩ [13] paste.
приключ|а́ться F [1], ⟨~и́ться⟩ [16 *e.*; *3rd p. only*] happen, occur; **~éние** *n* [12] (**~éнческий** [16] of) adventure.
прико́|вывать [1], ⟨~ва́ть⟩ [7 *e.*; -кую́, -куёшь] chain, fetter; arrest, captivate; **~ла́чивать** [1], ⟨~лоти́ть⟩ [15] nail (on, to к Д), fasten; **~ло́ть** *s.* прика́лывать; **~мандирова́ть** [7] *pf.* attach; **~сновéние** *n* [12] touch, contact; **~сну́ться** *s.* прикаса́ться.
прикра́|са F *f* [5] embellishment; **~шивать** [1], ⟨~сить⟩ [15] embellish.
прикреп|и́ть(ся) *s.* ~ля́ть(ся); **~лéние** *n* [12] fastening; attaching; **~ля́ть** [28], ⟨~и́ть⟩ [14 *e.*; -плю́, -пи́шь; плённый] fasten; attach; **-ся** register (with к Д).
прикри́к|ивать [1], ⟨~нуть⟩ [20] shout (at на В).
прикры|ва́ть [1], ⟨~ть⟩ [22] cover; protect; **~тие** *n* [12] cover (*a.* ⚔); convoy; *fig.* cloak.
прила́вок *m* [1; -вка] counter.
прилага́|тельное *n* [14] adjective (*a.* и́мя ~тельное); **~ть** [1], ⟨приложи́ть⟩ [16] (к Д) enclose (with); apply (to); take (*pains*), make (*efforts*); ~емый enclosed.
прила́|живать [1], ⟨~дить⟩ [15] fit.
приле|га́ть [1] **1.** (к Д) (ad)join, border; **2.** ⟨~чь⟩ [26 г/ж: -ля́гу, -ля́жешь, -ля́гут; -лёг, -легла́; -ля́г(те)!] lie down (for a while); fit (closely); **~жа́ние** *n* [12] diligence; **~жный** [14; -жен, -жна] diligent, industrious; **~пля́ть** [28], ⟨~пи́ть⟩ [14] stick; **~та́ть** [1], ⟨~тéть⟩ [11] arrive, fly; **~чь** *s.* ~га́ть 2.
прили́|в *m* [1] flood, flow; *fig.* rush; **~ва́ть** [1], ⟨~ть⟩ [-лью́, -льёшь; *cf.* лить] rush; add; **~па́ть** [1], ⟨~пнуть⟩ [21] stick; **~ть** *s.* ~ва́ть.
прили́ч|ие *n* [12] decency (for d.'s sake из *or* для Р), decorum; **~ный** [14; -чен, -чна] decent, proper; F respectable.
прилож|éние *n* [12] enclosure; supplement; application; *gr.* apposition; *seal*: affixture; **~и́ть** *s.* прикла́дывать & прилага́ть.
прима́нка *f* [5; *g/pl.*: -нок] bait, lure.
примен|éние *n* [12] application; use; adaptation; **~и́мый** [14 *sh.*] applicable; **~я́ть** [28], ⟨~и́ть⟩ [13;

-еню́, -е́нишь; -енённый] apply (to к Д); use, employ; **-ся** adapt o.s.
приме́р *m* [1] example (в ~ *cite* as an example); не в ~ F far + *comp.*; к ~у F = наприме́р; **~ивать** [1], ⟨~ить⟩ [13] try *or* fit on; **~ка** *f* [5; *g/pl.*: -рок] trying *or* fitting on; **~ный** [14; -рен, -рна] exemplary; approximate; **~я́ть** [28] = ~ивать.
при́месь *f* [8] admixture.
приме́|та *f* [5] mark, sign, token; omen; *pl.* signalment, description; на ~те in view; **~тить** *s.* ~ча́ть; **~тный** *s.* заме́тный; **~ча́ние** *n* [12] (foot)note; notice; **~ча́тельный** [14; -лен, -льна] notable, remarkable; **~ча́ть** F [1], ⟨~тить⟩ [15] notice; **~шивать** [1], ⟨~ша́ть⟩ [1] add, (ad)mix.
примир|е́ние *n* [12] reconciliation; **~и́тельный** [14; -лен, -льна] (re-) conciliatory; arbitration...; **~и́ть** (**-ся**) [28] *s.* мири́ть(ся).
примити́вный [14; -вен, -вна] primitive.
прим|кну́ть *s.* ~ыка́ть; **~о́рский** [16] coastal, seaside...; **~о́чка** *f* [5; *g/pl.*: -чек] lotion; **~ула** *f* [5] primrose; **~ус** *m* [1] kerosene stove; **~ча́ться** [4 *e.*; -мчу́сь, -чи́шься] *pf.* come in a great hurry; **~ыка́ть** [1], ⟨~кну́ть⟩ [20] join (*v/t.* к Д); *impf.* adjoin.
принадл|ежа́ть [4 *e.*; -жу́, -жи́шь] belong (to [к] Д), pertain; **~е́жность** *f* [8] accessory; material, implement; *pl.* *a.* equipment; membership.
принести́ *s.* приноси́ть.
принима́ть [1], ⟨приня́ть⟩ [приму́, -и́мешь; при́нял, -а́, -о; при́нятый (-ят, -а́, -о)] take (*a.* over; for за В; *measures*); accept; receive; admit ([in]to в, на В); pass (*law, etc.*); adopt; assume; ~ на себя́ take (up)on o.s., undertake; ~ на свой счёт feel hurt; ~ пара́д review troops; **-ся** [-нялся́, -ла́сь] (за В) set about *or* to, start; F take to task; ⚘, ⚕ take.
принорови́ть F [14 *e.*; -влю́, -ви́шь] *pf.* adapt; fit.
прин|оси́ть [15], ⟨~ести́⟩ [24 -с-: -есу́; -ёс, -есла́] bring (*a.* forth, in); yield (*a. profit, thanks*); make (*sacrifice* в В); ~оси́ть в дар *s.* дари́ть.
прину|ди́тельный [14; -лен, -льна] forced, compulsory, coercive; **~жда́ть** [1], ⟨~дить⟩ [15] force, compel, constrain, oblige; **~жде́ние** *n* [12] compulsion, coercion, constraint (under по Д); **~ждённый** [14] forced, constrained, obliged.
при́нцип *m* [1] principle; (on в П, ~иа́льно); **~иа́льный** [14; -лен, -льна] of principle(s) (*a.* из ~а).
приня́|тие *n* [12] taking (over); acceptance; admission ([in]to в, на В); passing (*law, etc.*); adoptio assumption; **'~тый** [14] customar *cf. a.* **~ть(ся)** → принима́ть(ся).
приобре|та́ть [1], ⟨~сти́⟩ [25 -т acquire, obtain, get; buy; **~те́ние** [12] acquisition.
приобщ|а́ть [1], ⟨~и́ть⟩ [16 *e.*; -щ -щи́шь; -щённый] (к Д) join, ad **-ся** join.
приостан|а́вливать [1], ⟨~ови́т [14] stop (*v/i.* **-ся**); ⚖ suspend.
припа́док *m* [1; -дка] fit, attack.
припа́сы *m/pl.* [1] supplies, stor
припая́ть [28] *pf.* solder (on to Д).
припе́|в *m* [1] refrain; **~ва́ть** F [sing; ~ва́ючи F in clover; **~ка́** [1], ⟨~чь⟩ [26] burn, be hot.
припи́с|ка *f* [5; *g/pl.*: -сок] pos script; addition; **~ывать** [1], ⟨~а́т [3] ascribe, attribute (to к Д); ad
припла́та *f* [5] extra payment.
припло́д *m* [1] increase, offspring
приплы|ва́ть [1], ⟨~ть⟩ [23] com arrive, swim *or* sail (up to к Д).
приплю́снутый [14] flat (*nose*).
приподн|има́ть [1], ⟨~я́ть⟩ [-н му́, -ни́мешь; -по́днял, -а́, -по́днятый (-ят, -а́, -о)] lift raise (**-ся** rise) (a little); **~ятı** [14] high (*spirits*); elevated (*style*
приполз|а́ть [1], ⟨~ти́⟩ [24] cre
припом|ина́ть [1], ⟨~нить⟩ [1 remember (*a. impers.* Д **-ся** И).
припра́в|а *f* [5] seasoning; **~ля́** [28], ⟨~ить⟩ [14] season, dress.
припух|а́ть [1], ⟨~нуть⟩ [21] sw
приравн|ивать [1], ⟨~я́ть⟩ [compare (to к Д); level.
прира|ста́ть [1], ⟨~сти́⟩ [24 -с -стёт; -ро́с, -сла́] take; grow (t Д); increase (by на В); **~ще́ни** [12] increase; taking.
приро́|да *f* [5] nature (by, *a.* bi от Р [*a.* in]; по Д); **~дный** [natural; *a.* = **~ждённый** [(in)born; **~ст** *m* [1] increase.
прируч|а́ть [1], ⟨~и́ть⟩ [16 *e.*; - -чи́шь; -чённый] tame.
при|са́живаться [1], ⟨~се́сть⟩ [-ся́ду; -се́л] sit down (a while).
присв|а́ивать [1], ⟨~о́ить⟩ [appropriate; adopt; confer ([up] Д); **~ое́ние** *n* [12] appropriatio adoption; conferment.
присе|да́ть [1], ⟨~сть⟩ [25; -ся́ -се́л] squat; curts(e)y; **~ст** *m* sitting (at, in в В); **~сть** *s.* ~да́ть присаживаться.
приска́к|ивать [1], ⟨~а́ть⟩ come, arrive (at full gallop; lea ing).
приско́рб|ие *n* [12] regret; **~н** [14; -бен, -бна] deplorable, pitiab
присла́ть *s.* присыла́ть.
прислон|я́ть [28], ⟨~и́ть⟩ [13] le (*v/i.* **-ся**; against к Д).
прислу́|га *f* [5] servant(s); ⚔ cre gunners *pl.*; **~живать** [1] w

up)on (Д), serve; **-ся** (Д) be subservient (to), ingratiate o. s. (with); **шиваться,** ⟨~шаться⟩ [1] listen to к Д).
рисм|áтривать [1], ⟨~отрéть⟩ 9; -отрю́, -óтришь; -óтренный] ook after (за Т); F find; **-ся** (к Д) eer, look narrowly (at); examine closely); familiarize o.s., get acquainted (with, *or* accustomed to); **óтр** *m* [1] care, supervision; **~отрéть(ся)** *s.* ~áтривать(ся).
рисовокуп|ля́ть [28], ⟨~и́ть⟩ [14 .; -плю́, -пи́шь; -плённый] add; nclose (with к Д).
рисоедин|éние *n* [12] joining; onnection; annexation; **~я́ть** [28], ~и́ть⟩ [13] (к Д) join (*a.* **-ся**); onnect, attach (to); annex, incorporate.
риспéшник *m* [1] accomplice.
риспосóб|ить(ся) *s.* ~ля́ть(ся); **лéние** *n* [12] adaptation; device; **ля́ть** [28], ⟨~ить⟩ [14] fit, adapt o.s. **-ся**; to, for к Д, под В).
ри́став *m* [1] (*form.*) police officer.
риста|вáть [5], ⟨~ть⟩ [-áну, áнешь] (к Д) stick (to); importune, ester; join; ⚓ land; F become; efit; ⚘ be taken (with); **∠вить** *s.* вля́ть; **∠вка** *f* [5; *g/pl.*: -вок] refix; **~вля́ть** [28], ⟨∠вить⟩ [14] к Д) set, put (to), lean (against); dd, piece on; appoint (to look after); **~льный** [14; -лен, -льна] steadfast; **~нь** *f* [8; *from g/pl. e.*] quay, wharf, ier; **∠ть** *s.* ~вáть.
ристёгивать [1], ⟨пристегну́ть⟩ 20] button *or* fasten (to).
ристр|áивать [1], ⟨~óить⟩ [13] к Д) add *or* attach (to); settle; lace; provide; **-ся** F = устрáиваться; join.
ристрáст|ие *n* [12] predilection for к Д); bias; **~ный** [14; -тен, тна] bias(s)ed, partial (to к Д).
ристрéли|вать [1], ⟨∠ть⟩ [13; стрелю́, -éлишь] shoot.
ристр|óить(ся) *s.* ~áивать(ся); **óйка** *f* [5; *g/pl.*: -óек] addition; nnex.
ри́ступ *m* [1] assault, onset, onslaught, storm (by Т); ⚘ & *fig.* fit, ttack; F access; **~áть** [1], ⟨~и́ть⟩ 14] set about, start, begin; proceed to); approach (*a.*, F, **-ся**).
рису|ждáть [1], ⟨~ди́ть⟩ [15; ужденный] (к Д) sentence, condemn (to); award; **~ждéние** *n* [12] awarding.
рису́тств|ие *n* [12] presence (in в П; of mind ду́ха); † office (hours); **овать** [7] be present (at на, в, ри П); **~ующий** [17] present.
рису́щий [17 *sh.*] peculiar (to Д).
рис|ылáть [1], ⟨~лáть⟩ [-шлю́, шлёшь; при́сланный] send (for за Т); **~ыпáть** [1], ⟨~ы́пать⟩ [2] be)strew.

прися́|га *f* [5] oath (upon под Т); **~гáть** [1], ⟨~гну́ть⟩ [20] swear; **~жный** [14] juror; суд ~жных jury.
прита|и́ть [13] *pf.* F *s.* затаи́ть; **-ся** hold (*breath*); hide; keep quiet; **∠скивать** [1], ⟨~щи́ть⟩ [16] drag (o.s. **-ся** F; [up] to к Д); F bring (come).
притвор|и́ть(ся) *s.* ~я́ть(ся); **∠ный** [14; -рен, -рна] feigned, pretended, sham; **∠ство** *n* [9] pretense, dissimulation; **~я́ть** [28], ⟨~и́ть⟩ [13; -орю́, -óришь; -óренный] close; leave ajar; **-ся** [13] feign, pretend (to be Т).
притесн|éние *n* [12] oppression; **~и́тель** *m* [4] oppressor; **~я́ть** [28], ⟨~и́ть⟩ [13] oppress; † press.
притих|áть [1], ⟨∠нуть⟩ [21] become silent, stop; abate (*wind*).
прито́к *m* [1] tributary; afflux.
притóм besides; to that *or* it.
притóн *m* [1] den, nest.
при́торный [14; -рен, -рна] sugary, luscious.
притр|áгиваться [1], ⟨~óнуться⟩ [20] touch (slightly; *v/t.* к Д).
притуп|ля́ть [28], ⟨~и́ть⟩ [14] (**-ся** become) blunt, dull.
при́тча *f* [5] parable.
притя́|гивать [1], ⟨~ну́ть⟩ [19] draw, pull; attract; F *s.* привлекáть; **~жáтельный** [14] possessive; **~жéние** *n* [12] attraction; **~зáние** *n* [12] claim, pretension (to на В); **~ну́ть** *s.* ~гивать.
приу|рóчить [16] *pf.* time, date (for к Д); **~чáть** [1], ⟨~чи́ть⟩ [16] accustom, habituate; train.
при|хвáрывать F [1], ⟨~хворну́ть⟩ [20] be(come *pf.*) unwell *or* sickly.
прихóд *m* [1] arrival, coming; † receipt(s), credit; parish; **~и́ть** [15], ⟨прийти́⟩ [приду́, -дёшь; пришёл, -шлá; -шéдший; *g. pt.*: придя́] come (to), arrive (in, at в, на В; for за Т); *fig.* fall, get, fly (into в В); (Д) ~и́ть в гóлову, на ум, *etc.* think of, hit on (the idea), take into one's head; *not: a.* dream; ~и́ть в себя́ (*or* чу́вство) come to (o.s.); **-ся,** ⟨~сь⟩ suit, fit ([p.'s] s. th. [Д] по Д), be (to; Т p.'s *aunt, etc.*); fall (on в В; to на В); мне ~ится I have to, must; придётся *a.* = попáло, *s.* попáсть; **~ный** [14] receipt...; **~о-расхóдный** [14] cash(*book*); **~ский** [16] parish...; **~я́щий** [17] day (*servant*); ⚘ ambulatory.
прихож|áнин *m* [1; *pl.* -áне, -áн] parishioner; **∠ая** *f* [17] *s.* перéдняя.
прихот|ли́вый [14 *sh.*] freakish; fastidious; **'~ь** *f* [8] whim, freak.
прихрáмывать [1] limp slightly.
прицéл *m* [1] sight; *a.* = **~ивание** *n* [12] (taking) aim; **~иваться** [1], ⟨~иться⟩ [13] (take) aim (at в В).
прицéп *m* [1] trailer; **~ка** *f* [5; *g/pl.*:

-пок] coupling; **~ля́ть** [28], ⟨**~и́ть**⟩ [14] hook (on; to к Д); couple; **-ся** stick, cling; *s. a.* приста́(ва́)ть; **~но́й** [14]: ~но́й ваго́н *m* = ~.

прича́л *m* [1] mooring(s); **~ивать** [1], ⟨~ить⟩ [13] moor; land.

прича́|стие *n* [12] *gr.* participle; *eccl.* Eucharist; F = ~щение; **~стный** [14; -тен, -тна] participating *or* involved (in к Д); **~ща́ть** [1], ⟨~сти́ть⟩ [15 *e.*; -ащу́, -асти́шь; -ащённый] administer (**-ся** receive) the Lord's Supper *or* Sacraments; **~ще́ние** *n* [12] administration of the Lord's Supper.

причём: ... ~ изве́стно, что ... = ... it being known that ...

причёс|ка *f* [5; *g/pl.*: -сок] hairdo (*Brt.* -dress), coiffure; **~ывать** [1], ⟨причеса́ть⟩ [3] do, brush, comb (one's hair **-ся**).

причи́н|а *f* [5] cause; reason (for по Д); по ~е because of; **~ность** *f* [8] causality; **~ный** [14] causal; **~я́ть** [28], ⟨~и́ть⟩ [13] cause, do.

причи|сля́ть [28], ⟨**~**сли́ть⟩ [13] rank, number (among к Д); ⚔ assign; F add; **~та́ние** *n* [12] lamentation; **~та́ть** [1] lament; **~та́ться** [1] be due, (p.: с Р) have to pay.

причу́д|а *f* [5] whim, freak; **~ливый** [14 *sh.*] freakish; cranky.

при|ше́лец *m* [1; -льца] newcomer, arrival; **~ши́бленный** F [14] dejected; **~шива́ть** [1], ⟨~ши́ть⟩ [-шью́, -шьёшь, *etc.*, *cf.* шить] (к Д) sew ([on] to); F involve (in), impose ([up]on); **~шпо́рить** [13] *pf.* spur on; **~щемля́ть** [28], ⟨~щеми́ть⟩ [14 *e.*; -млю́, -ми́шь; -млённый] pinch, squeeze in; **~щу́ривать** [1], ⟨~щу́рить⟩ [13] *s.* жму́рить.

прию́т *m* [1] refuge, shelter; asylum, orphanage; **~и́ть** [15 *e.*; -ючу́, -юти́шь] *pf.* shelter (*v/i.* **-ся**).

прия́|тель *m* [4], **~тельница** *f* [5] friend; **~тельский** [16] friendly; **~тный** [14; -тен, -тна] pleasant, pleasing, agreeable.

про F (В) about, of; ~ себя́ to o.s., (*read*) silently.

про́ба *f* [5] trial (on [= probation] на В), test; ⊕ assay, sample; standard, hallmark.

пробе́|г *m* [1] run, race; **~га́ть** [1], ⟨~жа́ть⟩ [4 *e.*; -егу́, -ежи́шь, -гу́т] run (through, over), pass (by); cover; skim.

пробе́л *m* [1] blank, gap; defect.

проби|ва́ть [1], ⟨**~**ть⟩ [-бью́, -бьёшь; -бе́й(те)!; проби́л, -а, -о] break through; pierce, punch; *s. a.* бить 2.; **-ся** fight (*or* make) one's way (through сквозь В); *fig.* F rough it; ⚘ come up; shine through; *pf.* toil (at над Т); **~ра́ть** [1], ⟨пробра́ть⟩ [-беру́, -рёшь; *cf.* брать] F scold; blow up, upbraid; **-ся** [-бра́лся, -ла́сь, -ло́сь] make one's way (through сквозь В); ste[al] *or* slip; **~рка** *f* [5; *g/pl.*: -рок] te[st] tube; **~ть(ся)** *s.* ~ва́ть(ся).

про́бк|а *f* [5; *g/pl.*: -бок] cork; sto[p]per, plug; ⚡ fuse; *traffic*: ja[m]; **~овый** [14] cork...

пробле́ма *f* [5] problem; **~ти́ческий** [16], **~ти́чный** [14; -чен, -чна] problematic(al).

про́блеск *m* [1] gleam; flash.

про́б|ный [14] trial..., test...; spe[ci]men..., sample...; touch(*stone*); p[i]lot (*balloon*); **~овать** [7], ⟨по-⟩ t[ry,] taste.

пробо́ина *f* [5] hole; ⚓ leak.

пробо́р *m* [1] (hair) parting.

про́бочник *m* [1] corkscrew.

пробра́ться *s.* пробира́ть(ся).

пробу|жда́ть [1], ⟨~ди́ть⟩ [1... -уждённый] waken, rouse; -[ся] awake, wake up; **~жде́ние** *n* [1...] awakening.

пробы́ть [-бу́ду, -бу́дешь; про́бы[л,] -а́, -о] *pf.* stay.

прова́л *m* [1] collapse; *fig.* failu[re]; **~ивать** [1], ⟨~и́ть⟩ [13; -алю́, -...лишь; -а́ленный] wreck; fail; [re]ject; *thea.* damn; ~ивай(те)! F ... camp; **-ся** break *or* fall in; fa[il,] flunk; *thea.* be damned; disappea[r;] ~и́сь! F the deuce take you!

прова́нский [16] olive (*oil*).

прове́|дать F [1] *pf.* visit; find ou[t;] **~де́ние** *n* [12] carrying out, re[al]ization; construction, installatio[n;] **~зти́** *s.* провози́ть; **~рить** *s.* ~ря́[ть;] **~рка** *f* [5; *g/pl.*: -рок] check(up), examination, control; **~ря́ть** [2...] ⟨~рить⟩ [13] examine, check (up), control; **~сти́** *s.* проводи́ть; **~тривать** [1], ⟨~трить⟩ [13] air, ven[ti]late.

прови|а́нт *m* [1] *s.* ~зия; **~зия** *f* [...] provisions, foodstuffs, victuals *p[l.];* **~ни́ться** [13] *pf.* commit offen[ce,] be guilty (of в П), offend (p. пе́р[ед] Т; with в П); **~нциа́льный** [1...; -лен, -льна] provincial; **~нция** [...] [7] province.

про́во|д *m* [1; *pl.*: -да́, *etc. e.*] wi[re,] line; cable; lead; **~ди́мость** *f* [...] conductivity; **~ди́ть** [15] **1.** ⟨пр[о]вести́⟩ [25] lead, *a.* ⚡, *impf.* co[n]duct, guide; carry out (*or* through), realize, put (*into practice*); put [through,] get through; pass; spend (*time*; за Т); draw (*line, etc.*); lay, co[n]struct; develop (*idea*); purs[ue] (*policy*); hold (*meeting*); ✝ ente[r,] book; *pf.* F trick, cheat; **2.** *s.* ~жа́т[ь;] **~дка** *f* [5; *g/pl.*: -док] constructio[n,] installation; ⚡ lead; *tel.* line, wire(s); **~дни́к** *m* [1 *e.*] guide; 🚂, ⚡ co[n]ductor (*Brt.* 🚂 guard); **~жа́ть** [1...] ⟨~ди́ть⟩ [15] see (off), accompan[y,] follow; **~з** *m* [1] transport(ation).

провозгла|ша́ть [1], ⟨~си́ть⟩ [1... *e.*; -ашу́, -аси́шь; -ашённый] pr[o]claim; propose (*toast*).

ɔовози́ть [15], ⟨провезти́⟩ [24] lrive, convey; take, get, carry.
ɔовока́|тор *m* [1] agent provocaeur; **~ция** *f* [7] provocation.
ɔóвол|ока *f* [5] wire; **~óчка** F *f* 5; *g*/*pl*.: -чек] delay (in с T), proraction.
ɔовóр|ный [14; -рен, -рна] quick, iimble, deft; **~ство** *n* [9] quickness, iimbleness, deftness.
ɔовоци́ровать [7] (*im*)*pf*., *a*. ⟨c-⟩ rovoke (to на B).
ɔогада́ть F [1] *pf*. lose (by на I).
ɔога́лина *f* [5] glade; patch, spot.
ɔогл|а́тывать [1], ⟨~оти́ть⟩ [15] wallow, gulp; F lose (*tongue*);
я́дывать [1] 1. ⟨~ядéть⟩ [11] verlook; look over (*or* through); . ⟨~яну́ть⟩ [19] peep out, appear.
ɔогн|а́ть *s*. прогоня́ть; **~óз** *m* [1] orecast; ⚕ prognosis.
ɔого|ва́ривать [1], ⟨~вори́ть⟩ 13] say; talk; **-ся** blab (*v*/*t*. о П);
лода́ться [1] *pf*. get *or* feel ungry; **~ня́ть** [28], ⟨прогна́ть⟩ гоню́, -гóнишь; -гна́л, -á, -o; рóгнанный] drive (away); F *fig*. anish; F fire; run (the gantlet квозь строй); **~ра́ть** [1], ⟨~рéть⟩)] burn through; F smash (up).
ɔогра́мма *f* [5] program(me *Brt*.).
ɔогрéсс *m* [1] progress; **~и́вный** 14; -вен, -вна] progressive; **~и́роать** [7] (make) progress.
ɔогрыз|а́ть [1], ⟨**∠ть**⟩ [24; *pt*. *st*.] naw *or* bite through.
ɔогу́л *m* [1] truancy; **~ивать** [1], ~я́ть⟩ [28] shirk (work), play ruant; **-ся** take (*or* go for a) walk;
ка *f* [5; *g*/*pl*.: -лок] walk (for на B), roll, ride; **~ьщик** *m* [1] shirker, uant; **~я́ть(ся)** *s*. ~ивать(ся).
ɔода|ва́ть [5], ⟨**∠ть**⟩ [-да́м, -да́шь, c., *cf*. дать; прóдал, -á, -o; прóанный (прóдан, -á, -o)] sell (*v*/*i*. ся; *a*. = be for *or* on sale); **~вéц** *m* ; -вцá], **~вщи́ца** *f* [5] seller, les(wo)man, (store) clerk, *Brt*. op assistant; **∠жа** *f* [5] sale (on в ; for в B); **∠жный** [14] for sale; жен, -жна] venal, corrupt; **∠ть ся)** *s*. ~ва́ть(ся).
одви|га́ть [1], ⟨**∠нуть**⟩ [20] ove, push (ahead); **-ся** advance; жéние *n* [12] advance(ment).
одéл|ать *s*. ~ывать; **~ка** *f* [5; *pl*.: -лок] trick, prank; **~ывать**, ~ать⟩ [1] break through, make; rry through *or* out, do; F play rick).
одéть [-дéну, -дéнешь; -дéнь те)!; -дéтый] *pf*. pass through, read.
одл|ева́ть [1], ⟨~и́ть⟩ [13] prong; **~éние** *n* [12] prolongation.
одовóльств|енный [14] food...; ocery...; **~ие** *n* [12] food(stuffs), ovisions *pl*.

продол|гова́тый [14 *sh*.] oblong; **~жа́тель** *m* [4] continuator; **~жа́ть** [1], ⟨**∠жить**⟩ [16] continue, go on; lengthen; prolong; **-ся** last; **~жéние** *n* [12] continuation; sequel; course (in в B); ~жéние слéдует to be continued; **~жи́тельность** *f* [8] duration; **~жи́тельный** [14; -лен, -льна] long; **∠жить (-ся)** *s*. ~жа́ть(ся); **∠ьный** [14] longitudinal.
продрóгнуть [21] *pf*. be chilled (to the marrow).
проду́к|т *m* [1] product; material; *pl*. *a*. (food)stuffs; **~ти́вный** [14; -вен, -вна] productive; **~тóвый** [14] grocery (*store*); **~ция** *f* [7] production (= product[s]), output.
проду́м|ывать, ⟨~ать⟩ [1] think over.
про|еда́ть [1], ⟨~éсть⟩ [-éм, -éшь, *etc*., *cf*. есть[1]] eat away *or* through; F spend (on eating); eat.
проéз|д *m* [1] passage, thoroughfare (no t.! ~а нет!); ~ом on the way, in passing; transient(ly); **~дить** *s*. ~жа́ть; **~днóй** [14]: ~днóй билéт *m* ticket; ~дная пла́та *f* fare; **~жа́ть** [1] 1. ⟨проéхать⟩ [-éду, -éдешь; -езжа́й(те)!] pass, drive *or* ride through (*or* past, by); travel; **-ся** F take a drive *or* ride; 2. ⟨~дить⟩ [15] break in (*horse*); F spend (on fare *or* in driving, riding); **~жий** [17] (through) traveller, transient; ~жая дорóга *f* highway.
проéк|т *m* [1] project, plan, scheme; draft; **~ти́ровать** [7], ⟨c-⟩ project, plan: **~циóнный** [14]: ~циóнный аппара́т *m* projector.
проé|сть *s*. ~да́ть; **~хать** *s*. ~зжа́ть.
прожéктор *m* [1] searchlight.
прожи|ва́ть [1], ⟨**∠ть**⟩ [-иву́, -ивёшь; прóжил, -á, -o; прóжитый (прóжит, -á, -o)] live; F spend; **~га́ть** [1], ⟨прожéчь⟩ [26 г/ж: -жгу́, -жжёшь] burn (through); ~га́ть жизнь F live fast; **∠точный** [14]: ∠точный ми́нимум *m* living wage; **∠ть** *s*. ~ва́ть.
прожóрлив|ость *f* [8] gluttony, voracity; **~ый** [14 *sh*.] gluttonous.
прóза *f* [5] prose; **∠ик** *m* [1] prose writer; **~и́ческий** [16] prosaic.
прó|звище *n* [11] nickname; по ~звищу nicknamed; **~зва́ть** *s*. ~зыва́ть; **~зева́ть** F [1] *pf*. miss; let slip; **~зорли́вый** [14 *sh*.] perspicacious; **~зра́чный** [14; -чен, -чна] transparent; **~зрéть** [9] *pf*. recover one's sight: see, perceive; **~зыва́ть** [1], ⟨~зва́ть⟩ [-зову́, -вёшь; -зва́л, -á, -o; прóзванный] (T) nickname; **~зяба́ть** [1] vegetate; **~зя́бнуть** F [21] *s*. продрóгнуть.
проигр|ывать [1], ⟨~а́ть⟩ [1] lose (at play); F play; **-ся** lose all one's money; **'~ыш** *m* [1] loss (в П lose).

произв|еде́ние *n* [12] work, product(ion); **~ести́** *s.* ~оди́ть; **~оди́тель** *m* [4] producer; **~оди́тельность** *f* [8] productivity; output; **~оди́тельный** [14; -лен, -льна] productive; **~оди́ть** [15], ⟨~ести́⟩ [25] (**-ся** *impf.* be) make (made), carry (-ried) out, execute(d), effect (-ed); (⊕ *usu. impf.*) produce(d); bring forth; promote(d [to the rank of] [в И *pl.*]); *impf.* derive(d; from от Р); **~о́дный** [14] derivative (*a. su. f* Ꭿ); **~о́дственный** [14] production...; manufacturing; works...; industrial; **~о́дство** *n* [9] production, manufacture; plant, works, factory (at на П); execution; promotion.

произ|во́л *m* [1] arbitrariness; mercy; despotism, tyranny; **~во́льный** [14; -лен, -льна] arbitrary; **~носи́ть** [15], ⟨~нести́⟩ [24 -с-] pronounce; deliver, make (*speech*); utter; **~ноше́ние** *n* [12] pronunciation; **~ойти́** *s.* происходи́ть.

про́ис|ки *m/pl.* [1] intrigues; **~ходи́ть** [15], ⟨произойти́⟩ [-зойдёт; -зошёл, -шла́; *g. pt.*: произойдя́] take place, happen; arise, originate (from от Р); descend (from от, из Р); **~хожде́ние** *n* [12] origin (by [= birth] по Д), descent; **~ше́ствие** *n* [12] incident, occurrence, event.

про|йти́(сь) *s.* ~ходи́ть & ~ха́живаться).

прок F *m* [1] *s.* по́льза & впрок.

прока́з|а *f* [5] prank, mischief; ⚕ leprosy; **~ник** *m* [1], **~ница** *f* [5] F *s.* шалу́н(ья); **~ничать** [1] F *s.* шали́ть.

прока́|лывать [1], ⟨проколо́ть⟩ [17] pierce, stick, stab; **~пывать** [1], ⟨прокопа́ть⟩ [1] dig (through); **~рмливать** [1], ⟨прокорми́ть⟩ [14] support, nourish; feed; **-ся** F subsist (on, by T).

прока́т *m* [1] hire (for на В), lease; (*film, etc.*) distribution; отда́ть в ~ hire out; **~и́ть(ся)** [15] *pf.* give (take) a drive *or* ride; **~ный** [14] rolled (*iron*); rolling (*mill*); for hire; lending; **~ывать,** ⟨~а́ть⟩ [1] mangle; ⊕ roll; ride; **-ся** F *s.* ~и́ться.

прокла́д|ка *f* [5; *g/pl.*: -док] laying; construction; packing; lining; **~ывать** [1], ⟨проложи́ть⟩ [16] lay (*a.* = build); *fig.* pave; force (one's *way* себе́), interlay; draw.

проклама́ция *f* [7] leaflet.

прокл|ина́ть [1], ⟨~я́сть⟩ [-яну́, -янёшь; про́клял, -а́, -о; про́клятый (про́клят, -а́, -о)] curse, damn; **~я́тие** *n* [12] damnation; **~я́тый** [14] cursed, damned.

проко́|л *m* [1] perforation; **~ло́ть** *s.* прока́лывать; **~па́ть** *s.* прока́пывать; **~рми́ть(ся)** *s.* прока́рмливать(ся); **~рмле́ние** *n* [12] support.

прокра́|дываться [1], ⟨~стьс[я]⟩ [25; *pt. st.*] steal; go stealthily.

прокуро́р *m* [1] public prosecut[or]

про|лага́ть *s.* ~кла́дывать; **~л[а]мывать,** ⟨~лома́ть⟩ [1] & ⟨~л[о]ми́ть⟩ [14] break (through; *v*[/*i.*] **-ся**); fracture; **~лега́ть** [1] ru[n] **~леза́ть** [1], ⟨~ле́зть⟩ [24 *st.*] cre[ep] *or* get (in[to]); **~лёт** *m* [1] passag[e] flight; ⚠ span; well; **~летари[ат]** *m* [1] proletariat; **~лета́рий** *m* [...] **~лета́рский** [16] proletarian; [~]**лета́ть** [1], ⟨~лете́ть⟩ [11] fly (pa[st,] by, over), pass (by, quickly); **~лё[т]ка** *f* [5; *g/pl.*: -ток] droshky.

проли́|в *m* [1] strait (*e.g.* Strait [of] Dover ~в Па-де-Кале́); **~ва́ть** [...] ⟨~ть⟩ [-лью́, -льёшь; -ле́й(те)...] про́ли́л, -а́, -о; про́ли́тый (пр[о-]ли́т, -а́, -о)] spill (*v/i.* **-ся**); she[d]; **~вно́й** [14]: ~вно́й дождь *m* dow[n]pour, cloudburst; **~ть** *s.* ~ва́ть.

проло́|г *m* [1] prologue; **~жи́ть** [*s.*] прокла́дывать; **~м** *m* [1] brea[ch,] fracture; **~ма́ть, ~ми́ть** *s.* пр[о-]ла́мывать.

про́мах *m* [1] miss; blunder (ma[ke]: дать *or* сде́лать; *a.* miss, fail; [...] fool); **∠иваться** [1], ⟨~ну́тьс[я]⟩ [20] miss; blunder.

промедле́ние *n* [12] delay.

промежу́то|к *m* [1; -тка] inter[val] (at в П; ... of в В); period; **~чн[ый]** [14] intermediate.

проме|лькну́ть *s.* мелька́ть; **∠н[и-]вать** [1], ⟨~ня́ть⟩ [28] exchan[ge] (for на В); **~рза́ть** [1], ⟨промёр[з-]нуть⟩ [21] freeze (through); F продрогнуть.

промо|ка́тельный [14]: ~ка́те[ль-]ная бума́га *f* blotting paper; **~ка́[ть]** [1], ⟨∠кнуть⟩ [21] get wet [...] drenched; **~лча́ть** [4 *e.*; -[чу́,] -чи́шь] *pf.* keep silent; **~чи́ть** [...] *pf.* wet, drench.

промтова́ры *m/pl.* [1] *s.* шир[о-]тре́б.

промча́ться [4] *pf.* dash *or* fly (pa[st,] by).

промы|ва́ть [1], ⟨∠ть⟩ [22] wa[sh] (out, away); ⚕ irrigate.

про́мы|сел *m* [1; -сла] trade, (l[ine] of) business; (*oil, gold*) field; (*s[alt] etc.*) works; **~сло́вый** [14] trade ...; **∠ть** *s.* ~ва́ть.

промы́шлен|ник *m* [1] indust[ri]alist; **~ность** *f* [8] industry; **~н[ый]** [14] industrial.

пронести́(сь) *s.* проноси́ть(ся).

прон|за́ть [1], ⟨~зи́ть⟩ [15*e.*; -нж[у́,] -нзи́шь; -нзённый] pierce, st[ab]; **~зи́тельный** [14; -лен, -ль[на]] shrill, piercing, penetrating; **~и́з[ы]вать** [1], ⟨~иза́ть⟩ [3] penetra[te,] pierce.

прони|ка́ть [1], ⟨∠кнуть⟩ [...] penetrate; permeate; get (i[n]); spread; **-ся** be imbued *or* inspi[red] (with T); **~кнове́ние** *n* [12] pe[...]

ation; fervo(u)r; ~кнове́нный
4; -е́нен, -е́нна] feeling, heart-
lt, pathetic; ~ца́емый [14 *sh.*]
ermeable; ~ца́тельный [14; -лен,
ьна] penetrating, searching;
cute, shrewd; ~ца́ть *s.* ~ка́ть.
о|носи́ть [15] **1.** ⟨~нести́⟩ [24
-: -есу́; -ёс, -есла́] carry (through,
y, away); speed; **-ся**, ⟨-сь⟩ fly
ast, by), pass *or* spread (swiftly);
pf. F wear out; **~ны́рливый** [14
] crafty; **~ню́хать** P [1] smell
t.
оо́браз *m* [1] prototype.
опага́нд|и́ровать [7] propagan-
ze; **~и́стский** [16] propagan-
ist...; propaganda...
опа|да́ть [1], ⟨~́сть⟩ [25; *pt. st.*]
t *or* be lost, be gone (wasted); be
issing; *a.* ~́сть бе́з вести); lose,
il; vanish; perish, die; **~́жа** *f* [5]
ss; **~́сть**[1] *s.* ~да́ть; **'~сть**[2] *f* [8]
recipice, abyss; chasm, gap; dis-
ster; F lots *or* a lot (of).
опи|ва́ть [1], ⟨~́ть⟩ [-пью́,
ьёшь; -пе́й(те)!; про́пи́л, -а́, -о;
ро́пи́тый (про́пи́т, -а́, -о)] spend
n drinking); drink.
опис|а́ть(ся) *s.* ~́ывать(ся); **~́ска**
[5; *g/pl.*: -сок] registration; **~но́й**
4] capital, *cf.* бу́ква; common;
egistration...; **~́ывать** [1], ⟨~а́ть⟩
] prescribe (for Д), order; register
/i. **-ся**); **'~ью** (*write*) in full.
опи|та́ние *n* [12] livelihood,
ving (*earn* one's себе́ на В); **~́ты-
вать**, ⟨~та́ть⟩ [1] (**-ся** be[come])
npregnate(d), imbue(d; with Т);
ть *s.* ~ва́ть.
оплы|ва́ть [1], ⟨~́ть⟩ [23] swim
sail (by, under); pass; strut.
опове́д|ник *m* [1] preacher;
овать [1] preach; **~ь** ('prɔ-) *f* [8]
cl. sermon; propagation.
опол|за́ть [1], ⟨~зти́⟩ [24] creep
y, through, under); **~́ка** *f* [5]
eeding.
опорциона́льный [14; -лен,
ьна] proportional, proportionate.
о́пус|к *m* [1] **1.** ommission, blank;
sence; **2.** [*pl.*: -ка́, *etc. e.*] passage); ⚔ password; **~ка́ть** [1],
~ти́ть⟩ [15] let pass (*or* through);
ass; omit; miss; let slip; *impf.*
ak; **~кно́й** [14] blotting (*paper*).
ора|ба́тывать, ⟨~бо́тать⟩ F, [1]
udy; **~ста́ть** [1], ⟨~сти́⟩ [24 -ст-:
стёт; -рос, -росла́] grow (through);
ome up.
орва́ть(ся) *s.* прорыва́ть(ся).
орез|а́ть [1], ⟨~́ать⟩ [3] cut
hrough); **-ся** cut (*teeth*); **~и́нен-
ный** [14] gummed.
оре́ха *f* [5] slit, hole, tear.
оро́|к *m* [1] prophet; **~ни́ть** [13;
оню́, -о́нишь; -о́ненный] *pf.* utter;
ческий [16] prophetic(al); **~че-
ство** *n* [9] prophecy; **~чить** [16]
rophesy.

проруб|а́ть [1], ⟨~и́ть⟩ [14] cut (through); **'~ь** *f* [8] ice-hole.
прор|ы́в *m* [1] break; breach; gap, arrear(s), hitch; **~ыва́ть** [1] **1.** ⟨~ва́ть⟩ [-ву́, -вёшь; -ва́л, -а́, -о; про́рванный (-ан, -а́, -о)] tear; break through (*v/i.* **-ся**; burst open; force one's way); **2.** ⟨~ы́ть⟩ [22] dig (through).
про|са́чиваться [1], ⟨~сочи́ться⟩ [16 *e.*; *3rd p. only*] ooze (out), percolate; **~сверли́ть** [13] *pf.* bore (through).
просве́|т *m* [1] gleam, glimpse; chink; ⩓ bay, opening; *fig.* hope; **~ти́тельный** [14] of enlightenment; educational; **~ти́ть** *s.* ~ща́ть & ~чивать **2.**; **~тле́ть** [8] *pf.* clear up, brighten; **~чивать** [1] **1.** shine through, be seen; **2.** ⟨~ти́ть⟩ [15] radiograph, X-ray; test (*egg*); **~ща́ть** [1], ⟨~ти́ть⟩ [15 *e.*; -ещу́, -ети́шь; -ещённый] enlighten, educate, instruct; **~ще́ние** *n* [12] enlightenment, education, instruction.
про́|седь *f* [8] grayish (*Brt.* greyish), grizzly (hair); **~се́ивать** [1], ⟨~се́ять⟩ [27] sift; **~се́ка** *f* [5] glade; **~сёлок** *m* [1; -лка] = ~сёлочная доро́га; **~сёлочный** [14]: ~сёлочная доро́га *f* by-road, field path; **~се́ять** *s.* ~се́ивать.
проси́|живать [1], ⟨~де́ть⟩ [11] sit (up); stay, remain; spend; F wear out; **~тель** *m* [4], **~тельница** *f* [5] petitioner, applicant; **~ть** [15], ⟨по-⟩ ask (p. for В/о П; у Р/Р, *a.* beg p.'s), request; entreat; invite; intercede (for за В); прошу́, про́сят *a.* please; **-ся** (в, на В) ask (for; leave [to enter, go]; F suggest o. s.; **~я́ть** [28] *pf.* shine forth, brighten.
проск|ользну́ть [20] *pf.* slip (into в В); **~очи́ть** [16] *pf.* jump *or* slip (by, through, in[to]).
просл|авля́ть [28], ⟨~а́вить⟩ [14] glorify, make (**-ся** become) famous; **~еди́ть** [15 *e.*; -ежу́, -еди́шь; -е́женный] *pf.* follow up; **~ези́ться** [15 *e.*; -ежу́сь, -ези́шься] *pf.* shed tears.
просло́йка *f* [5; *g/pl.*: -оек] streak, layer.
про|слу́шать [1] *pf.* hear; ⚕ auscultate; F miss; **~сма́тривать** [1], ⟨~смотре́ть⟩ [9; -отрю́, -о́тришь; -о́тренный] look through *or* over; overlook; **~смо́тр** *m* [1] examination, review, revision; oversight; **~сну́ться** *s.* ~сыпа́ться; **~́со** *n* [9] millet; **~со́вывать** [1], ⟨~су́нуть⟩ [20] pass *or* push (through); **~со́хнуть** *s.* ~сыха́ть; **~сочи́ться** *s.* ~са́чиваться; **~спа́ть** *s.* ~сыпа́ть.
проспе́кт *m* [1] avenue; prospectus.
просро́ч|ивать [1], ⟨~ить⟩ [16] let lapse, expire; exceed; **~ка** *f* [5; *g/pl.*: -чек] expiration; exceeding.
прост|а́ивать [1], ⟨~оя́ть⟩ [-ою́,

-ойшь] stand; stay; **~áк** *m* [1 *e.*] simpleton; **~éнок** *m* [1; -нка] pier.

прост|ирáть [1], ‹**~ерéть**› [12] stretch (out; *v/i.* **-ся**), extend.

простительный [14; -лен, -льна] pardonable, excusable, venial.

проститýтка *f* [5; *g/pl.*: -ток] prostitute.

простить(ся) *s.* прощáть(ся).

простодýш|ие *n* [12] naïveté; **~ный** [14; -шен, -шна] simple-minded, ingenuous, artless.

простóй 1. [14; прост, -á, -о; *comp.*: прóще] simple, plain; easy; artless, unsophisticated; ordinary, common; prime (*number*); **2.** *m* [3] stoppage, standstill.

простоквáша *f* [5] curdled milk.

простó|р *m* [1] open (space); freedom (in на П); scope; **~рéчие** *n* [12] language of the (uneducated) people; vernacular; **~рный** [14; -рен, -рна] spacious, roomy; **~сердéчный** [14; -чен, -чна] *s.* ~дýшный; **~тá** *f* [5] simplicity; naïveté; silliness; **~фи́ля** *m/f* F [6] ninny; **~я́ть** *s.* простáивать.

простра́н|ный [14; -áнен, -áнна] vast; diffuse; **~ство** *n* [9] space; room; area.

прострéл *m* [1] lumbago; **~ивать** [1], ‹**~и́ть**› [13; -елю́, -éлишь; -éленный] shoot (through).

простý|да *f* [5] cold; **~живать** [1], ‹**~ди́ть**› [15] chill; **-ся** catch a cold.

простýпок *m* [1; -пка] offence.

простыня́ *f* [6; *pl.*: прóстыни, -ы́нь, *etc. e.*] (*bed*) sheet.

просý|нуть *s.* просóвывать; **~шивать** [1], ‹**~ши́ть**› [16] dry (up).

просфорá *f* [5; *pl.*: прóсфоры, -фóр, *etc. e.*] *eccl.* Host.

просчитáться [1] *pf.* miscalculate.

просыпáть [1], ‹проспáть› [-плю́, -пи́шь; -спáл, -á, -о] oversleep; sleep; F miss (by sleeping); **~ся**, ‹проснýться› [20] awake, wake up.

прос|ыхáть [1], ‹**~óхнуть**› [21] dry.

прóсьба *f* [5] request (at по П; for о П); entreaty; † petition; please (don't не + *inf.*); (у Р/к Д) ~ (may p.) ask (p.) a favo(u)r.

про|тáлкивать [1], *once* ‹**~толкнýть**› [20], F ‹**~толкáть**› [1] push (through); **-ся** force one's way (through); **~тáптывать** [1], ‹**~топтáть**› [3] tread (out); F wear out *or* down; **~тáскивать** [1], ‹**~тащи́ть**› [16] carry *or* drag (past, by); F smuggle in.

протéз (-ˈtɛs) *m* [1] artificial limb.

проте|кáть [1], ‹**~чь**› [26] flow (by); leak; pass, elapse; take a ... course; **~кция** *f* [7] patronage; **~рéть** *s.* протирáть; **~ст** *m* [1], **~стовáть** [7], *v/t.* (*im*)*pf.* & ‹о-› protest; **~чь** *s.* ~кáть.

прóтив (Р) against (*a.* as against); opposite; быть *or* имéть ~ (have) object(ion; to), mind; **~иться** [1 ‹вос-› (Д) oppose, object; **~ник** [1] opponent, adversary; enem **~ный** [14; -вен, -вна] repugna disgusting, offensive, nasty; opp site, contrary; мне ~но *a.* I hate ~ном слýчае otherwise, faili which.

противо|вéс *m* [1] counterbalanc **~воздýшный** [14] anti-aircr (*defense*), air-raid (*precautions*, *p tection*); **~гáз** *m* [1] gas mas **~дéйствие** *n* [12] counteractio resistance; **~дéйствовать** counteract; resist; **~естéстве ный** [14 *sh.*] unnatural; **~закó ный** [14; -óнен, -óнна] unlawf illegal; **~общéственный** [14] a tisocial; **~полóжность** *f* [8] co trast, opposition (in в В); antithes **~полóжный** [14; -жен, -жн opposite; contrary, opposed; **поставля́ть** [28], ‹~постáвит [14] oppose; **~поставлéние** *n* [opposition; **~рéчие** *n* [12] contr diction; **~речи́вый** [14 *sh.*] contr dictory; **~рéчить** [16] (Д) co tradict; **~стоя́ть** [-ою́, -ои́шь] (withstand; stand against; **~тáнк вый** [14] antitank...; **~хими́ч ский** [16] (anti)gas...; **~я́дие** *n* [antidote.

про|тирáть [1], ‹**~терéть**› [12] r (through); wipe; **~ткнýть** *s.* ~т кáть; **~токóл** *m* [1] (**~токоли́р вать** [7] [*im*]*pf.*, *a.* ‹за-› take do the) minutes *pl.*, record; *su. a.* pr tocol; **~толкáть, ~толкнýть** *s.* тáлкивать; **~топтáть** *s.* ~тáпт вать; **~торённый** [14] beat (*path*), trodden; **~роти́п** *m* [1] pr totype; **~тóчный** [14] flowin running; **~трезвля́ться** [2 ‹~трезви́ться› [14 *e.*; -влю́ -ви́шься; -влённый] (becom sober; **~тыкáть** [1], *once* ‹~ткнýт [20] pierce.

протя́|гивать [1], ‹**~нýть**› [stretch (out), extend, hold ou pass; drawl; P turn up (one's to нóги); **~жéние** *n* [12] exte stretch (at на П); course (in на П **~жный** [14; -жен, -жна] drawlin lingering; **~нýть** *s.* ~гивать.

проучи́ть F [16] *pf.* teach a lesso

професс|ионáльный [14] profe sional; trade (*union*, *cf.* профсою **~ия** *f* [7] profession (by по Д), c ling, trade; **~ор** *m* [1; *pl.*: -рá, *e.*] professor; **~ýра** *f* [5] professo ship; professorate.

прóфиль *m* [4] profile.

профóрма F *f* [5] formality.

профсою́з *m* [1], **~ный** [14] tra union.

про|хáживаться [1], ‹**~йтис** [-йдýсь, -йдёшься; -ошёло -шлáсь] (go for a) walk, stroll; pass; mock (at насчёт Р); **~хвáт**

ать F [1], ⟨~хвати́ть⟩ [15] pierce; low up; **~хво́ст** F *m* [1] scoundrel.
охла́д|а *f* [5] cool(ness); **~и́ельный** [14; -лен, -льна] refreshing, cooling; **~ный** [14; -ден, дна] cool (*a. fig.*), fresh.
охо́|д *m* [1] passage, pass; *anat.* uct (за́дний ~д anus); **~ди́мец** *m* ; -мца] impostor, villain; **~ди́мость** *f* [8] passableness; maeuverability; **~ди́ть** [15], ⟨пройи⟩ [пройду́, -дёшь; прошёл, шла́; -ше́дший; про́йденный; *g. t.*: пройдя́] pass, go (by, through, ver, along); take a ... course, be; pread; **~дно́й** [14] (with a) hrough passage; **~жде́ние** *n* [12] assing *or* going (through, over); **жий** *m* [17] passer-by; traveller.
оцвета́ть [1] prosper, thrive.
оце|ду́ра *f* [5] procedure; **∠жи-ать** [1], ⟨~ди́ть⟩ [15] filter; **∠нт** *m*] percent(age) (by на В); (*usu. pl.*) nterest; **∠сс** *m* [1] process; ⚖ trial t на П); **∠ссия** *f* [7] procession.
оче́сть *s.* прочи́тывать.
оч|ий [17] other; *n & pl. a. su.* e rest; и ~ее and so on *or* forth, c.; ме́жду ~им by the way, incientally; among other things.
очи́|стить *s.* ~ща́ть; **~тывать,** ~та́ть⟩ [1] & ⟨проче́сть⟩ [25 -т-: тý, -тёшь; -чёл, -чла́; *g. pt.*: тя́; -чтённый] read (through); cite; **'~ть** [16] designate (to в В); **ща́ть** [1], ⟨~стить⟩ [15] clean.
о́чн|ость *f* [8] durability; **~ый** 4; -чен, -чна́, -о] firm, solid, rong; lasting.
очте́ние *n* [12] reading, perusal.
очь away, off (with you поди́[те] ; *cf.* доло́й; я не ~ + *inf.* F I ouldn't mind ...ing.
ош|е́дший [17] past (*a. su. n* ~е́дee), *a. gr.*, last; **~е́ние** *n* [12] petion, application (for о П; on по Д); **е́ствие** *n* [12] *s.* истече́ние; **~ло́дний** [15] last year's; **∠лый** [14] ast (*a. su. n* ∠лое), last; **~мыгну́ть** [20] *pf.* slip, whisk.
ощ|а́й(те)! farewell!, goodby(e)!, dieu!; **~а́льный** [14] farewell...; arting; **~а́ние** *n* [12] parting when, at при П; на В), leaveaking, farewell; **~а́ть** [1], ⟨проти́ть⟩ [15 *e.*; -ощу́, ости́шь; ощённый] forgive (р. Д), excuse, ardon; прости́(те) *a.* = ~а́й(те), ; **-ся** (с Т) take leave (of), say oodby (to); **~е́ние** *n* [12] forgiveess; pardon.
оявл|и́тель *m* [4] *phot.* developer; **ить(ся)** *s.* ~ля́ть(ся); **~ле́ние** *n* 2] manifestation, display, demstration; *phot.* development; **ля́ть** [28], ⟨~и́ть⟩ [14] show, disay, evince, manifest; *phot.* develop.
оясн|я́ться [28], ⟨~и́ться⟩ [13] ear up, brighten.

пруд *m* [1 *e.*; в -ý] pond.
пружи́на *f* [5] spring; motive.
прусс|а́к *m* [1*e.*], **∠кий** [16] Prussian.
прут *m* [1; *a. e.*; *pl.*: -ья, -ьев] rod, switch.
пры́|гать [1], *once* ⟨~гнуть⟩ [20] jump, spring, leap; **~гу́н** *m* [1 *e.*] jumper; **~жо́к** *m* [1; -жка́] jump, leap, bound; dive; **~ткий** [16; -ток, -тка́, -о] nimble, quick; **~ть** F *f* [8] agility; speed (at full во всю); **~щ** *m* [1 *e.*], **~щик** *m* [1] pimple.
пряди́ль|ный [14] spinning; **~щик** *m* [1], **~щица** *f* [5] spinner.
пря|дь *f* [8] lock, tress, strand; **∠жа** *f* [5] yarn; **∠жка** *f* [5; *g/pl.*: -жек] buckle **∠лка** *f* [*g/pl.*: -лок] spinning wheel.
прям|изна́ *f* [5] straightness; **~оду́шие** *n* [12] *s.* ~ота́; **~оду́шный** [14; -шен, -шна] *s.* ~о́й *fig.*; **~о́й** [14; прям, -á, -о] straight (*a.* [= bee] line ~а́я *su. f*); direct (*a. gr.*); 🚃 through...; ⊿ right; *fig.* straight (-forward), downright, outspoken, frank; ~а́я кишка́ *f* rectum; **~олине́йный** [14; -е́ен, -е́йна] rectilinear; *fig. s.* ~о́й *fig.*; **~ота́** *f* [5] straightforwardness, frankness; **~оуго́льник** *m* [1] rectangle; **~оуго́льный** [14] rectangular.
пря́н|ик *m* [1] gingerbread; **~ость** *f* [8] spice, *pl.* spicery; spiciness; **~ый** [14 *sh.*] spicy, piquant.
прясть [25; -ял, -á, -о], ⟨с-⟩ spin.
пря́т|ать [3], ⟨с-⟩ hide (*v/i.* **-ся**), conceal; **~ки** *f/pl.* [5; gen.: -ток] hide-and-seek.
пря́ха *f* [5] spinner.
псал|о́м *m* [1; -лма́] psalm; **~о́мщик** *m* [1] *s.* дьяк; **~ты́рь** *f* [8] Psalter.
пса́рня *f* [6; *g/pl.*: -рен] kennel(s).
псевдони́м *m* [1] pseudonym.
псих|иа́тр *m* [1] psychiatrist; **∠ика** *f* [5] mind, psyche; mentality; **~и́ческий** [16] mental, psychic(al); **~о́лог** *m* [1] psychologist; **~оло́гия** *f* [7] psychology.
птене́ц [1; -нца́] nestling.
пти́|ца *f* [5] bird; дома́шняя ~ца poultry; **~чий** [18] bird('s); poultry...; вид с ~чьего полёта bird's-eye view; **~чка** *f* [5; *g/pl.*: -чек] birdie.
пу́бли|ка *f* [5] audience; public; **~ка́ция** *f* [7] publication; advertisement; **~кова́ть** [7], ⟨о-⟩ publish; **~ци́ст** *m* [1] publicist; **∠чность** *f* [8] publicity; **∠чный** [14] public; ∠чная же́нщина *f* prostitute.
пу́г|ало *n* [9] scarecrow; **~а́ть** [1], ⟨ис-, на-⟩, *once* ⟨~ну́ть⟩ [20] (**-ся** be) frighten(ed; of P), scare(d); **~ли́вый** [14 *sh.*] timid, fearful.
пу́говица *f* [5] button.
пуд *m* [1; *pl. e.*] pood (= *36 lbs.*); **∠ель** *m* [4; *pl. a.* -ля́, *etc. e.*] poodle.

пу́др|а *f* [5] powder; са́харная **~а** powdered sugar; **~еница** *f* [5] powder box; **~ить** [13], ⟨на-⟩ powder.
пуз|а́тый P [14 *sh.*] paunchy; **∠о** P *n* [9] paunch.
пузыр|ёк [1; -рька́] vial; *a. dim. of* **∠ь** *m* [4 *e.*] bubble; *anat.* bladder; F blister; kid.
пук *m* [1; *pl. e.*] wisp; bunch, bundle.
пулемёт *m* [1] machine gun; **~ный** [14] machine-gun; cartridge (*belt*); **~чик** *m* [1] machine gunner.
пуль|веризáтор *m* [1] spray(er); **~с** *m* [1] pulse; **~си́ровать** [7] puls(at)e; **~т** *m* [1] desk, stand.
пу́ля *f* [6] bullet.
пункт *m* [1] point (at *all* по Д); station; place, spot; item, clause, article; **~и́р** *m* [1] dotted line; **~и́рный** [14] dotted; **~уа́льность** *f* [8] punctuality; accuracy; **~уа́льный** [14; -лен, -льна] punctual; accurate.
пунцо́вый [14] crimson.
пунш *m* [1] punch (*drink*).
пуп|о́к *m* [1; -пка́], F **~** *m* [1 *e.*] navel.
пурга́ *f* [5] blizzard, snowstorm.
пу́рпур *m* [1], **∠ный, ∠овый** [14] purple.
пуск *m* [1] (*a.* **~** в ход) start(ing), setting in operation; **~а́й** F *s.* пусть; **~а́ть** [1], ⟨пусти́ть⟩ [15] let (go; in[to]), set (free; going, in motion *or* operation [*a.* **~**а́ть в ход]); start; launch, throw; release; allow; put (forth); send; force; take (*root*); **~**а́ть под отко́с derail; **-ся** (+ *inf.*) start (...ing; *v/t.* в В), set out (on в В); enter *or* engage (into), begin, undertake.
пуст|е́ть [8], ⟨о-, за-⟩ become empty *or* deserted; **~и́ть** *s.* пуска́ть.
пуст|о́й [14; пуст, -á, -о] empty; void; vain, idle (talk **~**óе *n su.*; *s. a.* **~**я́к); vacant; blank; dead (*rock*); F hollow; **~ота́** *f* [5; *pl. st.*: -óты] emptiness; void; *phys.* vacuum; vacancy.
пусты́|нный [14; -ы́нен, -ы́нна] desert, desolate; **~ня** *f* [6] desert, waste, wilderness; **~рь** *m* [4 *e.*] waste ground; **~шка** F *f* [5; *g/pl.*: -шек] blank; nonentity.
пусть let (him, *etc.*, + *vb.*; **~** [он] + *vb. 3rd. p.*), may; even (if).
пустя́|к F *m* [1 *e.*] trifle; *pl.* nonsense; (it's) nothing; **~ко́вый, ~чный** (-ʃn-) F [14] trifling.
пу́та|ница *f* [5] confusion, muddle, mess; **~ть** [1], ⟨за-, с-, пере-⟩ (**-ся** get) confuse(d), muddle(d), mix(ed) up, entangle(d; interfere in в В).
путёвка *f* [5; *g/pl.*: -вок] pass (*Sov.*), permit.
путе|води́тель *m* [4] guide(book) (to по Д); **~во́дный** [14] lode..., pole(*star*); **~во́й** [14] travelling; traveller's; road...
путеше́ств|енник *m* [1] travel(l)er; **~ие** *n* [12] journey, trawel, tour (on в В *or* П); voyage; **~овать** [7] trav (through по Д).
пу́т|ник *m* [1] travel(l)er; **~ный** [14] *s.* де́льный; **~ы** *pl.* [9] shackle
пут|ь *m* [8 *e.*; *instr/sg.*: -тём] way (*fig.*: [in] *that* way **~**ём, *a.* by mea of P), road, path; 🚂 track (*a. fig* line; means; trip, journey (on в *or* П); route; в *or* по **~**и́ on the wa in passing; нам по **~**и́ I (we) ha the same way (as с Т); F *s.* толк.
пух *m* [1; в -хý] down; в **~** (и пра (*smash*) to pieces; (*defeat*) utter totally; F over(*dress*); **∠ленький** [16], **∠лый** [14; пухл, -á, -о] chubb plump; **∠нуть** [21], ⟨рас-⟩ swe **~о́вка** *f* [5; *g/pl.*: -вок] powd puff; **~о́вый** [14] down...
пучи́на *f* [5] gulf, abyss; eddy.
пучо́к *m* [1; -чкá] *dim. of* пук, *s.*
пу́ш|ечный [14] gun..., cannon. **~и́нка** *f* [5; *g/pl.*: -нок] down, flu **~и́стый** [14 *sh.*] downy, fluffy; **~** *f* [5; *g/pl.*: -шек] gun, cannon; hoax; **~ни́на** *f* [5] furs *pl.*; **~н** [14] fur...; **~о́к** F *m* [1; -шкá] dow
пу́ще P more (than P).
пчел|á *f* [5; *pl. st.*: пчёлы] bee; **~ово́д** *m* [1] beekeeper; **~ово́дст** *n* [9] beekeeping; **∠ьник** *m* apiary.
пшен|и́ца *f* [5] wheat; **~и́чн** [14] wheaten; **∠ный** (ˈpʃɔ-) [millet...; **~о́** *n* [9] millet.
пыл *m* [1] ardo(u)r, zeal, blaze; в in the thick (*of the fight*); **~а́ть** [⟨вос-, за-⟩ blaze, flare (up), (i flame; glow, burn; (en)rage (w Т); **~есо́с** *m* [1] vacuum clean **~и́нка** *f* [5; *g/pl.*: -нок] mote; **~и́** [13], ⟨за-⟩ dust; **-ся** be(come) dus **∠кий** [16; -лок, -лкá, -о] arde fiery.
пыль *f* [8; в -ли́] dust; **∠ный** [-лен, -льнá, -о] dusty (*a.* = в -л **~цá** *f* [5] pollen.
пыт|а́ть [1] torture; **~а́ться** ⟨по-⟩ try, attempt; **∠ка** *f* [5; *g/* -ток] torture; **~ли́вый** [14 *sh.*] quisitive, searching.
пыхте́ть [11] puff, pant; F sweat
пы́шн|ость *f* [8] splendo(u pomp; **~ый** [14; -шен, -шнá, magnificent, splendid, sumptuo luxuriant, rich.
пьедеста́л *m* [1] pedestal.
пье́са *f* [5] *thea.* play; ♪ piece.
пьян|е́ть [8], ⟨о-⟩ get drunk (*a.* with от Р); **∠ица** *m/f* [5] dru ard; **∠ство** *n* [9] drunkenne **∠ствовать** [7] drink, F boo **∠ый** [14; пьян, -á, -о] drunk(*a. fig.* (with от Р).
пюре́ (-ˈrɛ) *n* [*ind.*] mashed pota *pl.* [inc
пядь *f* [8; *from g/pl. e.*] span; *f*
пята́ *f* [5; *nom/pl. st.*] heel (on Д).
пят|а́к F *m* [1 *e.*], **~ачо́к** F *m* [1; -ч

ıve-kopeck coin; ~ёрка *f* [5; *g/pl.*: рок] five (*cf.* двойка); F (*mark*) = тлично, *cf.*; five-ruble note; ∠еро 37] five (*cf.* двое).
ıти|десятый [14] fiftieth; ~деся-ые годы *pl.* the fifties; *cf.* пятый;
конечный [14] five-pointed *star*); ~**летка** *f* [5; *g/pl.*: -ток] five-year plan (*Sov.*); ~**летний** [15] ıve-year (old), of five; ~**сотый** [14] ıve hundredth.
ıтиться [15], ⟨по-⟩ (move) back.
ıтка *f* [5; *g/pl.*: -ток] heel (take to ne's heels показать ~и).
ıтнадцат|ый [14] fifteenth; *cf.* ıятый; ~**ь** [35] fifteen; *cf.* пять.
пятнистый [14 *sh.*] spotty, spotted.
пятн|ица *f* [5] Friday (on: в B, *pl.*: по Д); ~**о** *n* [9; *pl. st.*; *g/pl.*: -тен] spot, stain, blot(ch) (with *pl.* в П); родимое ~о birthmark, mole.
пят|ый [14] fifth; (*page*, *chapter*, *year*, *etc.*, *sentence or lesson no.*) five; ~ая *f su.* ♄ fifth (*part*); ~ое *n su.* fifth (*date*; on P: ~ого; *cf.* число); ~ь (минут) ~ого five (minutes) past four; ~**ь** [35] five; без ~и (минут) час (два, *etc.*, [часа], ~ь, *etc.* [часов]) five (minutes) to one (two, *etc.* [o'clock]); ~**ьдесят** [35] fifty; ~**ьсот** [36] five hundred; ~**ью** five times.

Р

abbr.: **1.** рубль, -ля, -лей; **2.** река.
аб *m* [1 *e.*], ~**а** *f* [5] slave; ~**овла-делец** *m* [1; -льца] slaveholder; ~**олепство** *n* [9] servility, ~**олепст-вовать** [7] cringe (to перед T).
абот|а *f* [5] work (at за T; на П); abo(u)r, toil; assignment, task; ~**ать** [1] work (on th. над T; for p. на B; as T), function; labo(u)r, toil; be open; ~**ник** *m* [1], ~**ница** *f* [5] worker, working (wo)man; (day) labo(u)rer, (farm)hand; (*house*)maid; official, functionary; employee; member; clerk; ~**одатель** *m* [4] employer, F boss; ~**оспособный** [14; -бен, -бна] able to work, able-bodied; hard-working, efficient.
абоч|ий *m* [17] (*esp. industrial*) worker; *adj.*: working, work (*a. day*); workers', labo(u)r...; ~ая сила *f* man power; labo(u)r.
аб|ский [16] slave...; slavish, servile; ~**ство** *n* [9] slavery; ~**ыня** *f* [6] *s.* ~а.
ав|енство *n* [9] equality; ~**нение** *n* [12] ⚔ eyes (*right!*); ~**нина** *f* [5] plain; ~**но** equal(ly); as well (as); всё ~но it's all the same, it doesn't matter; anyway, in any case.
авно|весие *n* [12] balance (*a. fig.*), equilibrium; ~**душие** *n* [12] indifference (to к Д) ~**душный** [14; -шен, -шна] indifferent (to к Д); ~**значный** [14; -чен, -чна] equivalent; ~**мерный** [14; -рен, -рна] uniform, even, equal; ~**правие** *n* [12] equality (of rights); ~**правный** [14; -вен, -вна] (enjoying) equal (rights); ~**сильный** [14; -лен, -льна] equivalent; ~**ценный** [14; -енен, -енна] equal (in value).
авн|ый [14; равен, -вна] equal; (*a. su.*); ~ым образом *s.* ~о; ему нет ~ого he has no match; ~**ять** [28], ⟨с-⟩ equalize; ⚔ dress (*ranks*); F compare; (*v/i.* -**ся**; *a.* be [equal to Д]).
рад [14; рада] (be) glad (at, of Д; *a.* to see p.), pleased, delighted; would like; (be) willing; не ~ (be) sorry; ~ не ~ willy-nilly; ~**ар** *m* [1] radar; ∠и (P) for the sake of (*or*... ['s] sake); for.
радиатор *m* [1] radiator.
радий *m* [3] radium.
радикал *m* [1], ~**ьный** [14; -лен, льна] radical.
радио *n* [*ind.*] radio, *Brt. a.* wireless (on по Д); ~**активность** *f* [8] radioactivity; ~**активный** [14; -вен, -вна] radioactive; ~**аппарат** *m* [1] *s.* ~приёмник; ~**вещание** *n* [12] broadcasting (system); ∠**ла** *f* [5] radio-gramophone; ~**любитель** *m* [4] radiofan; ~**передача** *f* [5] (radio)broadcast, transmission; ~**приёмник** *m* [1] receiving set, radio, *Brt.* wireless (set); ~**слуша-тель** *m* [4] listener; ~**станция** *f* [7] radio station; ~**узел** [1; -зла] radio center (*Brt.*: -tre); ~**установка** *f* [5; *g/pl.*: -вок] radio plant.
ради|ст *m* [1] radio (wireless) operator; ′~**ус** *m* [1] radius.
радо|вать [7], ⟨об-, по-⟩ (B) gladden, please, rejoice; -**ся** (Д) rejoice (at), be glad *or* pleased (of, at); look forward (to); ~**стный** [14; -тен, -тна] joyful, glad; merry; ~**сть** *f* [8] joy, gladness; pleasure.
раду|га *f* [5] rainbow; ~**жный** [14] iridescent, rainbow...; *fig.* rosy.
радуш|ие *n* [12] kindliness; hospitality; ~**ный** [14; -шен, -шна] kindly, hearty; hospitable.
раз *m* [1; *pl. e.*, *gen.* раз] time (*this*, *etc.* [в] B); one; (один) ~ once; два ∠а twice; ни ∠у not once, never; не ~ repeatedly; как ~ just (in time F в самый ~; *s. a.* впору), the very; вот тебе ~ F *s.* на[2].
разба|влять [28], ⟨∠вить⟩ [14] dilute; ∠**лтывать** F, ⟨разболтать⟩ [1] let out.

разбе́|г *m* [1] start, run (with, at с Р); **~га́ться** [1], ⟨~жа́ться⟩ [4; -егу́сь, -ежи́шься, -егу́тся] take a run; scatter; disperse.

разби|ва́ть [1], ⟨∠ть⟩ [разобью́, -бьёшь; разбе́й(те)!; -и́тый] break (to pieces), crash, crush; defeat; divide (into на В); lay out (*park*); pitch (*tent*); knock; **-ся** break; crash; split; come to nothing; **~ра́тельство** *n* [9] trial; **~ра́ть** [1], ⟨разобра́ть⟩ [разберу́, -рёшь; разобра́л, -а́, -о; -о́бранный] take to pieces, dismantle, pull down; investigate, inquire into; review; analyze (*Brt.* -se), parse; make out, decipher, understand; sort out; ⚖ try; buy up; F take; *impf.* be particular; **-ся** F (в П) grasp, understand; unpack; **∠тие** *n* [12] crash, defeat (*cf.* ~ва́ть); **∠тый** [14 *sh.*] broken; F jaded; **∠ть(ся)** *s.* ~ва́ть(ся).

разбо́й *m* [3] robbery; **~ник** *m* [1] robber; **~ничать** [1] rob; pirate; **~нический** [16], **~ничий** [18] predatory; of robbers *or* brigands.

разболта́ть *s.* разба́лтывать.

разбо́р *m* [1] analysis; review, critique; investigation, inquiry (into); ⚖ trial; без ~а, ~у F indiscriminately; **~ка** *f* [5] taking to pieces, dismantling; sorting (out); **~ный** [14] folding, collapsible; **~чивость** *f* [8] legibility; scrupulousness; **~чивый** [14 *sh.*] legible; discerning; scrupulous, fastidious.

разбр|а́сывать, ⟨~оса́ть⟩ [1] scatter, throw about, strew; F squander; **~еда́ться** [1], ⟨~ести́сь⟩ [25] disperse; **~о́д** *m* [1] disorder, mess; **~о́санный** [14] scattered; **~оса́ть** *s.* ~а́сывать.

разбух|а́ть [1], ⟨∠нуть⟩ [21] swell.

разва́л *m* [1] collapse, breakdown; chaos; **~ивать** [1], ⟨~и́ть⟩ [13; -алю́, -а́лишь] pull (*or* break) down; disorganize; **-ся** fall to pieces, collapse; F sprawl; **~ины** *f/pl.* ruins (F *a. sg* = *p.*).

ра́зве really; perhaps; only; F unless.

развева́ться [1] flutter; stream.

разве́д|ать *s.* ~ывать; **~е́ние** *n* [12] breeding; cultivation; **~ённый** [14] divorced, divorcé(e) *su.*; **~ка** *f* [5; *g/pl.*: -док] reconnaissance; intelligence service; **~очный** [14] reconnaissance...; **~чик** *m* [1] scout; intelligence officer; reconnaissance plane; **~ывательный** [14] *s.* ~очный; **~ывать,** ⟨~ать⟩ [1] reconnoiter (*Brt.* -tre); F find out.

разве|сти́ *s.* разводи́ть; **~нча́ть** [1] *pf.* uncrown, dethrone; unmask.

развёр|нутый [14] large-scale; **~тывать** [1], ⟨развернуть⟩ [20] unfold, unroll, unwrap; open; ⚔ deploy; *fig.* develop; (**-ся** *v/i.*; *a.* turn).

разве|сно́й [14] weighed out; ... **сить** *s.* ∠шивать; **~сти́(сь)** *s.* ра... води́ть(ся); **~твле́ние** *n* [12] ram... fication, branching; **~твля́ть...** [28], ⟨~тви́ться⟩ [14 *e.*; *3rd p. on...* ramify, branch; **∠шивать** [... ⟨∠сить⟩ [15] weigh (out); ha... (out); **∠ять** [27] *pf.* disperse, disp...

разви|ва́ть [1], ⟨∠ть⟩ [разовь... -вьёшь; разве́й(те)!; разви́л, -а́, -... -ви́тый (ра́звит, -а́, -о]) devel... (*v/i.* **-ся**); evolve; untwist; **∠нчи...** **вать** [1], ⟨~нти́ть⟩ [15 *e.*; -нч... -нти́шь; -и́нченный] unscrew; ... **тие** *n* [12] development; evolutio... **~то́й** [14; ра́звит, -а́, -о] develope... intelligent; advanced; **∠ть(ся)** ~ва́ть(ся).

развле|ка́ть [1], ⟨∠чь⟩ [26] ente... tain, amuse (o.s. **-ся**); divert; ... **че́ние** *n* [12] entertainment, amus... ment, diversion.

разво́д *m* [1] divorce; ⚔ reli... mounting; **~и́ть** [15], ⟨развести... [25] take (along), bring; divor... (from с Т); separate; dilute; mi... rear, breed; plant, cultivate; ligh... make; ⚔ mount, relieve; **-ся,** ⟨-с... get divorced (from с Т); F multipl... grow *or* increase in number.

раз|вози́ть [15], ⟨~везти́⟩ [2... deliver, carry; **~вора́чивать** F ... ~вёртывать.

развра́|т *m* [1] debauch; depravit... **~ти́ть(ся)** *s.* ~ща́ть(ся); **~тник** ... [1] libertine, debauchee, rake; ~... **ничать** F [1] (indulge in) debauc... **~тный** [14; -тен, -тна] dissolu... licentious; **~ща́ть** [1], ⟨~ти́ть⟩ [... *e.*; -ащу́; -ати́шь; -щённый] (-... become) deprave(d), debauch(e... corrupt; **~ще́ние** *n* [12], **~щё...** **ность** *f* [8] depravity.

развяз|а́ть *s.* ∠ывать; **∠ка** *f* [... *g/pl.*: -зок] denouement; outcom... conclusion, head; **∠ный** [14; -зе... -зна] forward, (free &) easy; **∠ы...** **вать** [1], ⟨~а́ть⟩ [3] untie, und... *fig.* unleash; F loosen; **-ся** co... untied; F get rid (of с Т).

разгад|а́ть *s.* ∠ывать; **∠ка** *f* [... *g/pl.*: -док] solution; **∠ыва...** ⟨~а́ть⟩ [1] solve, unriddle.

разга́р *m* [1] (в П *or* В) heat, thi... (in), height (at), (in full) swing.

раз|гиба́ть [1], ⟨~огну́ть⟩ [20] u... bend, straighten (o.s. **-ся**).

разгла́|живать [1], ⟨~дить⟩ [1... smooth; iron, press; **~ша́ть** [... ⟨~си́ть⟩ [15 *e.*; -ашу́, -аси́шь; -ашё... ный] divulge; trumpet.

разгляд|е́ть [11] *pf.* make ou... **∠ывать** [1] examine, view.

разгне́ванный [14] angry.

разгов|а́ривать [1] talk (to, wi... с Т; about, of о П), converse, spea... **~о́р** *m* [1] talk, conversation; ... речь; **~о́рный** [14] colloquial; **~о́...** **чивый** [14 *sh.*] talkative.

разгóн *m* [1] dispersal; *a.* = разбéг; в **~**е out; **~я́ть** [28], ⟨разогна́ть⟩ [разгоню́, -óнишь; разогна́л, -á, -о; разóгнанный] disperse, scatter; dispel; F drive away; **-ся** take a run.
разгор|а́ться [1], ⟨**~**éться⟩ [9] kindle (*a. fig.*), (in)flame, blaze up.
разгра|бля́ть [28], ⟨**~**бить⟩ [14], **~блéние** *n* [12] plunder, pillage, loot; **~ничéние** *n* [12] delimitation; **~ни́чивать** [1], ⟨**~**ни́чить⟩ [16] demarcate, delimit.
разгрóм *m* [1] rout; debacle, destruction, ruin, chaos.
разгру|жа́ть [1], ⟨**~**зи́ть⟩ [15 & 15 *e.*; -ужу́, -у́зи́шь; -у́женный & -ужённый] (**-ся** be) unload(ed); F relieve(d); **~зка** *f* [5; *g/pl.*: -зок] unloading.
разгу́л *m* [1] revelry, carouse; debauch(ery), licentiousness; **~ивать** F [1] stroll, saunter; **-ся**, ⟨**~**я́ться⟩ [28] clear up; F have a good walk *or* run, move without restraint; **~ьный** F [14; -лен, -льна] dissolute; loose, easy.
разда|ва́ть [5], ⟨**~**ть⟩ [-да́м, -да́шь, *etc.*, *s.* дать; рóздал, раздала́, рóздало; рóзданный (-ан, раздана́, рóздано)] distribute; play (*cards:* deal) out; **-ся** (re)sound, be heard; give way; split, separate; F expand; **~вливать** [1] *s.* дави́ть 2.; **~ть(ся)** *s.* **~**ва́ть(ся); **~ча** *f* [5] distribution.
раздвáиваться *s.* двои́ться.
раздви|га́ть [1], ⟨**~**нуть⟩ [20] part, separate, move apart; pull out; **~жнóй** [14] sash...; telescope, -pic.
раздвоéние *n* [12] bifurcation.
раздева́|лка F *f* [5; *g/pl.*: -лок], F **~льня** *f* [6; *g/pl.*: -лен] checkroom, cloakroom; **~ть** [1], ⟨раздéть⟩ [-дéну, -дéнешь; -дéтый] undress (*v/i.* **-ся**), take off; F strip (of).
раздéл *m* [1] division; section; **~аться** F [1] *pf.* get rid *or* be quit (of с T); **~éние** *n* [12] division (into на B); *eccl.* schism; **~и́тельный** [14] dividing; *gr.* disjunctive; **~и́ть(ся)** *s.* **~**я́ть(ся) & дели́ть(ся); **~ьный** [14] separate; distinct; **~я́ть** [28], ⟨**~**и́ть⟩ [13; елю́, -éлишь; -елённый] divide (into на B; *a.* [-ed] by); separate; share; **-ся** (be) divide(d), fall.
раздéть(ся) *s.* раздева́ть(ся).
раз|дира́ть F [1], ⟨**~**одра́ть⟩ [раздеру́, -рёшь; разодра́л, -á, -о; -óдранный] *impf.* rend; *pf.* F tear; **~добы́ть** F [-бу́ду, -бу́дешь] *pf.* get, procure.
раздóлье *n* [10] *s.* привóлье.
раздóр *m* [1] discord, contention.
раздоса́дованный F [14] angry.
раздраж|а́ть [1], ⟨**~**и́ть⟩ [16 *e.*; -жу́, -жи́шь; -жённый] irritate, provoke; vex, annoy; **-ся** lose one's temper; **~éние** *n* [12] irritation; temper; **~и́тельный** [14; -лен, -льна] irritable, touchy; **~и́ть(ся)** *s.* **~**а́ть(ся).
раздробл|éние *n* [12] breaking; smashing; **~я́ть** [28] *s.* дроби́ть.
разду|ва́ть [1], ⟨**~**ть⟩ [18] fan; blow (away); swell; puff up, exaggerate; **-ся** swell, inflate.
разду́м|ывать, ⟨**~**ать⟩ [1] change one's mind; *impf.* deliberate, consider; **~ье** *n* [10] thought(s), meditation; doubt(s).
разду́ть(ся) *s.* раздува́ть(ся).
раз|ева́ть F [1], ⟨**~**и́нуть⟩ [20] open wide; **~**ева́ть рот gape; **~жа́лобить** [14] *pf.* move to pity; **~жа́ловать** [7] *pf.* degrade (to в И *pl.*); **~жа́ть** *s.* **~**жима́ть; **~жёвывать** [1], ⟨**~**жева́ть⟩ [7 *e.*; -жую́, -жуёшь] chew; **~жига́ть** [1], ⟨**~**жéчь⟩ [г/ж: -зожгу́, -жжёшь, -жгу́т; разжёг, -зожгла́; разожжённый] kindle (*a. fig.*); heat; rouse; unleash; **~жима́ть** [1], ⟨**~**жа́ть⟩ [разожму́, -мёшь; разжа́тый] unclench, open; **~и́нуть** *s.* **~**ева́ть; **~и́ня** F *m/f* [6] gawk, gaper; **~и́тельный** [14; -лен, -льна] striking.
раз|лага́ть [1], ⟨**~**ложи́ть⟩ [16] analyze (*Brt.* -yse); decompose; (*v/i.* **-ся**); (become) demoralize(d), corrupt(ed; decay); **~ла́д** *m* [1] dissension, discord, dissonance; disturbance; **~ла́мывать** [1], ⟨**~**лома́ть⟩ [1], ⟨**~**ломи́ть⟩ [14] break; pull down; **~лета́ться** [1], ⟨**~**летéться⟩ [11] fly (away, asunder); F break (to pieces); come to naught; take a sweep.
разли́|в *m* [1] flood; **~ва́ть** [1], ⟨**~**ть⟩ [разолью́, -льёшь; *cf.* лить; -лéй(те)!; -и́л, -á, -о; -и́тый (-и́т, -á, -о)] spill; pour out; bottle; ladle; flood, overflow; spread; bestow; (*v/i.* **-ся**).
различ|а́ть [1], ⟨**~**и́ть⟩ [16 *e.*; -чу́, -чи́шь; -чённый] distinguish; **-ся** *impf.* differ (in T, по Д); **~ие** *n* [12] distinction, difference; **~и́тельный** [14] distinctive; **~и́ть** *s.* **~**а́ть; **~ный** [14; -чен, -чна] different (from от P); different, various, diverse.
разлож|éние *n* [12] analysis; decomposition, decay; corruption, degeneration; **~и́ть(ся)** *s.* разлага́ть(ся) & раскла́дывать.
разлом|а́ть, ~и́ть *s.* разла́мывать.
разлу́|ка *f* [5] separation (from с T), parting; **~ча́ть** [1], ⟨**~**чи́ть⟩ [16 *e.*; -чу́, -чи́шь; -чённый] separate (*v/i.* **-ся**; from с T), part.
разма́|зывать [1], ⟨**~**зать⟩ [3] smear, spread; **~тывать** [1], ⟨размота́ть⟩ unwind, wind off; **~х** *m* [1] swing, brandish (with [*a.* might] с **~**ху); span (✈ & *fig.*), sweep; amplitude; *fig.* vim, verve, élan; scope; **~хивать** [1], *once* ⟨**~**хну́ть⟩ [20] (T) swing, sway,

dangle; brandish; gesticulate; **-ся** lift (one's hand T); **~шистый** F [14 *sh.*] wide; diffuse.

разме|жева́ть [7] *pf.* mark off, demarcate; **~льча́ть** [1], ‹~льчи́ть› [16 *e.*; чу́, -чи́шь; -чённый] pound, crush.

разме́н *m* [1], **~ивать** [1], ‹~я́ть› [28] (ex)change (for на В); **~ный** [14]: ~ная моне́та *f* change.

разме́р *m* [1] size; dimension(s), measure(ment); rate (at в П), amount; scale; *poetic.*, ♪ meter (*Brt.* -tre; in T), ♪ *a.* time, measure (of в В); **~енный** [14 *sh.*] measured; **~я́ть** [28], ‹~ить› [13] measure (off).

разме|сти́ть *s.* ~ща́ть; **~ча́ть** [1], ‹~тить› [15] mark; **~шивать** [1], ‹~ша́ть› [1] stir (up); knead; **~ща́ть** [1], ‹~сти́ть› [15 *e.*; -ещу́, -ести́шь; -ещённый] place; lodge, accommodate (in, at, with в П, по Д); distribute; **~ще́ние** *n* [12] distribution; accomodation; arrangement, order.

размин|а́ть [1], ‹размя́ть› [разомну́, -нёшь; размя́тый] knead; F stretch (*limbs*); **~у́ться** F *pf.* [20] cross; miss o. a.

размнож|а́ть [1], ‹~ить› [16] multiply (*v/i.* **-ся**); mimeograph; **~е́ние** *n* [12] multiplication; propagation, reproduction; **~ить(ся)** *s.* ~а́ть(ся).

размо|зжи́ть [16 *e.*; -жу́, -жи́шь; -жённый] *pf.* smash, crush; **~ка́ть** [1], ‹~кнуть› [21] soak, swell; **~лвка** *f* [5; *g/pl.*: -вок] tiff, quarrel; **~ло́ть** [17; -мелю́, -ме́лешь] *pf.* grind, crush; **~та́ть** *s.* разма́тывать; **~чи́ть** [16] *pf.* soak.

размы|ва́ть [1], ‹~ть› [22] wash out *or* away; **~ка́ть** [1], ‹разомкну́ть› [20] open (⚡, ⊕); **~ть** *s.* ~ва́ть.

размышл|е́ние *n* [12] reflection (for на В), thought; **~я́ть** [28] reflect, meditate (on о П).

размягч|а́ть (-xtʃ-) [1], ‹~и́ть› [16 *e.*; -чу́, -чи́шь; -чённый] soften, mollify.

раз|мя́ть *s.* ~мина́ть; **~на́шивать,** ‹~носи́ть› [15] tread out, wear to shape; **~нести** *s.* ~носи́ть 1.; **~нима́ть** [1], ‹~ня́ть› [-ниму́, -ни́мешь; -ня́л & ро́зняли, -а́, -о; -ня́тый (-ня́т, -а́, -о)] part; take to pieces.

ра́зница *f* [5] difference.

разно|ви́дность *f* [8] variety, sort; **~гла́сие** *n* [12] discord, disagreement, difference, variance; discrepancy; **~кали́берный** F [14], **~ма́стный** [14; -тен, -тна] *s.* ~ше́рстный; **~обра́зие** *n* [12] variety, diversity, multiplicity; **~обра́зный** [14; -зен, -зна] manifold, multifarious, various; **~реч...** *s.* противоре́ч...; **~ро́дный** [14; -ден, -дна] heterogeneous.

разно́с *m* [1] delivery; peddlery; **~и́ть** [15] **1.** ‹разнести́› [25 -с-] deliver (to, at по Д), carry; hawk, peddle; F spread; smash, destroy; blow up; scatter; swell; **2.** *s.* разна́шивать; **~ка** *f* [5] *s.* ~; **~ный** [14] peddling.

разно|сторо́нний [15; -о́нен, -о́нняя] many-sided; **'~сть** *f* [8] difference; **~счик** *m* [1] peddler, hawker; (*news*)boy, man; messenger; **~цве́тный** [14; -тен, -тна] multicolo(u)red; **~ше́рстный** [14; -тен, -тна] variegated; F motley, mixed.

разну́зданный [14 *sh.*] unbridled.

ра́зн|ый [14] various, different, diverse; **~я́ть** *s.* ~има́ть.

разо|блача́ть [1], ‹~блачи́ть› [16 *e.*; -чу́, -чи́шь; -чённый] expose, disclose, unmask; **~блаче́ние** *n* [12] exposure, disclosure, unmasking; **~бра́ть(ся)** *s.* разбира́ть(ся); **~гна́ть(ся)** *s.* разгоня́ть(ся); **~гну́ть(ся)** *s.* разгиба́ть(ся); **~грева́ть** [1], ‹~гре́ть› [8; -е́тый] warm (up); **~де́тый** F [14 *sh.*] dressed up; **~дра́ть** *s.* раздира́ть; **~йти́сь** *s.* расходи́ться; **~мкну́ть** *s.* размыка́ть; **~рва́ть(ся)** *s.* разрыва́ть(-ся).

разор|е́ние *n* [12] ruin, destruction, devastation; **~и́тельный** [14; -лен, -льна] ruinous; **~и́ть(ся)** *s.* ~я́ть(ся); **~ужа́ть** [1], ‹~ужи́ть› [16 *e.*; -жу́, -жи́шь; -жённый] disarm (*v/i* **-ся**); **~уже́ние** *n* [12] disarmament; **~я́ть** [28], ‹~и́ть› [13] (**-ся** be[come]) ruin(ed), destroy(ed), ravage(d).

разосла́ть *s.* рассыла́ть.

разостла́ть *s.* расстила́ть.

разочар|ова́ние *n* [12] disappointment; **~о́вывать** [1], ‹~ова́ть› [7] (**-ся** be) disappoint(ed) (in в П).

разра|ба́тывать, ‹~бо́тать› [1] work up (into на В), process; work out, elaborate; ⚒ till; ⚒ exploit; **~бо́тка** *f* [5; *g/pl.*: -ток] working (out); elaboration; ⚒ tillage; ⚒ exploitation; **~жа́ться** [1], ‹~зи́ться› [15 *e.*; -ажу́сь, -ази́шься] burst out (into T); **~ста́ться** [1], ‹~сти́сь› [24; *3rd p. only*: -тётся; -ро́сся, -сла́сь] grow; enlarge, expand.

разрежённый [14] rarefied.

разре́з *m* [1] cut; section; angle (from в П); **~а́ть** [1], ‹~ать› [3] cut (up), slit; **~но́й** [14]: ~но́й нож *m* paper knife; **~ывать** [1] *s.* ~а́ть.

разреш|а́ть [1], ‹~и́ть› [16 *e.*; -шу́, -ши́шь; -шённый] permit, allow; (re)solve; release (for к Д); absolve; settle; **-ся** be (re)solved; end, burst (in[to] T); be delivered (of T); **~е́ние** *n* [12] permission (with с P); licence (for на В); (re)solution; settlement; absolution; delivery; **~и́ть(ся)** *s.* ~а́ть(ся).

раз|рисова́ть [7] *pf.* ornament

рóзненный [14] odd; isolated;
рубáть [1], ⟨~рубить⟩ [14] split.
зрý|ха f [5] ruin; ~шáть [1], ~шить⟩ [16] destroy, demolish; uin; frustrate; -ся (fall or come o) ruin; ~шéние n [12] destruction, lemolition, devastation; ~шить -ся) s. ~шáть(ся).
зры́|в m [1] breach, break, rupure; explosion; gap; ⊕ на ~в tenile; ~вáть [1] 1. ⟨разорвáть⟩ [-вý, вёшь; -вáл, -á, -о; -óрванный] ear (to pieces на В); break (off); mpers. burst, explode; (-ся v/i.); . ⟨~ть⟩ [22] dig up; ~внóй [14] xplosive; ~дáться [1] pf. break nto sobs; ~ть s. ~вáть 2.; ~хлять 28] s. рыхлить.
зря́|д m [1] category, class; disharge; unloading; ~дить s. ~жáть; дка f [5; g/pl.: -док] spacing, pace; slackening; disengagement; жáть [1], ⟨~дить⟩ [15 e. & 15; яжý, -яди́шь; -яжённый & я́женный] unload; discharge; reluce, disengage (tension); typ. space; 15] F dress up.
зу|беждáть [1], ⟨~бедить⟩ [15 .; -ежý, -еди́шь; -еждённый] (в I) dissuade (from); -ся change ne's mind (about); ~вáться [1], ~ться⟩ [18] take off one's shoes; верять [28], ⟨~вéрить⟩ [13] (в П) -ся be) undeceive(d), disabuse(d) of); disappoint(ed); ~знавáть F 5], ⟨~знáть⟩ [1] find out (about о I, В); ~крáшивать [1], ⟨~крáить⟩ [15] decorate; embellish; ~крупнять [28], ⟨~крупнить⟩ [14] liminish; decentralize.
áзум m [1] reason; sense(s); ~éть 8] understand; know; mean, imply by под Т); -ся be meant or undertood; ~éется of course; ∠ный [14; мен, -мна] rational; reasonable, ensible; clever, wise.
азý|ться s. ~вáться; ~чивать [1], ~чить⟩ [16] study, learn; -ся orget, unlearn.
азъе|дáть [1] s. есть[1] 2; ~динять 28], ⟨~динить⟩ [13] separate; ⚡ lisconnect; ∠зд m [1] trip, journey on в П); setting out, departure; ⚔ orse patrol; 🚃 siding; ~зжáть [1] lrive, ride, go about; be on a jourey or trip; -ся, ⟨∠хаться⟩ [-éдусь, éдешься; -езжáйтесь!] leave (for о Д); separate; pass o. a. (с Т).
азъярённый [14] enraged, furious.
азъясн|éние n [12] explanation; larification; ~ять [28], ⟨~ить⟩ [13] xplain, elucidate.
азы́|грывать, ⟨~грáть⟩ [1] play; affle (off); -ся break out; run high; appen; ~скивать [1], ⟨~скáть⟩ 3] seek, search (for; pf. out = find).
ай m [3; в раю́] paradise.
ай|кóм m [1] (райóнный комитéт) listrict committee (Sov.); ~óн m [1] district; region, area; ~óнный [14] district...; regional; ~совéт m [1] (райóнный совéт) district soviet (or council).
рак m [1] crawfish, Brt. crayfish; морскóй ~ lobster; ⚕, ast. (♋) cancer.
ракéт|а f [5] (a. sky) rocket; ~ка f [5; g/pl.: -ток] racket (sport); ~ный [14] rocket...
рáковина f [5] shell; sink; bowl.
рáм|(к)а f [5; (g/pl.: -мок)] frame (-work, a. fig. = limits; within в П); ~па f [5] footlights pl.; stage.
рáн|а f [5] wound; ~г m [1] rank; ~éние n [12] wound(ing); ~еный [14] wounded (a. su.); ~ец m [1; -нца] satchel; ⚔ knapsack; ~ить [13] (im)pf. wound, injure (in в В).
рáн|ний [15] early (adv. ~о); morning...; spring...; ~о или пóздно sooner or later; ~овáто F rather early; ~ьше earlier; formerly; first; (P) before.
рап|и́ра f [5] rapier; ∠орт m [1], ~ортовáть [7] (im)pf. report; ~с m [1] ⚘ rape; ~сóдия f [7] rhapsody.
рáса f [5] race.
раскá|иваться [1], ⟨~яться⟩ [27] repent (v/t., of в П); ~лённый [14], ~лить(ся) s. ~лять(ся); ~лывать [1], ⟨расколóть⟩ [17] split, cleave; crack; (v/i. -ся); ~лять [28], ⟨~лить⟩ [13] make (-ся become) red-hot, white-hot; ~пывать [1], ⟨раскопáть⟩ [1] dig out or up; ~т m [1] roll, peal; ~тистый [14 sh.] rolling; ~тывать, ⟨~тáть⟩ [1] (un-) roll; v/i. -ся; ⟨~титься⟩ [15] gain speed; roll (off); ~чивать, ⟨~чáть⟩ [1] swing; shake; F bestir; ~яние n [12] repentance (of в П); ~яться s. ~иваться.
расквартировáть [7] pf. quarter.
раски́|дывать [1], ⟨~нуть⟩ [20] spread (out); throw out; pitch (tent), set up.
раскла|днóй [14] folding, collapsible; ∠дывать [1], ⟨разложить⟩ [16] lay or spread out, display; lay; set up; make, light; apportion, repartition; ∠ниваться [1], ⟨∠няться⟩ [28] (с Т) bow (to), greet; take leave (of).
раскó|л m [1] split, schism; ~лóть (-ся) s. раскáлывать(ся); ~пáть s. раскáпывать; ~пка f [5; g/pl.: -пок] excavation.
раскр|áшивать [1] s. крáсить; ~епощáть [1], ⟨~епостить⟩ [15 e.; -ощý, -ости́шь; -ощённый] emancipate, liberate; ~епощéние n [12] emancipation, liberation; ~итиковáть [7] pf. scarify; ~ичáться [4e.; -чýсь, -чи́шься] pf. shout, bawl (at на В); ~ывáть [1], ⟨~ы́ть⟩ [22] open (v/i. -ся); uncover; disclose, reveal; put one's cards on the table.
раску|лáчить [16] pf. dispossess or oust (the kulak[s]) ~пáть [1],

⟨~пи́ть⟩ [14] buy up; **∠поривать** [1], ⟨∠порить⟩ [13] uncork; open; **∠сывать** [1], ⟨~си́ть⟩ [15] crack; F see through, get (the hang of); **∠тывать**, ⟨∠тать⟩ [1] unwind, un-wrap.

ра́совый [14] racial.

распа́д *m* [1] disintegration; decay.

распа|да́ться [1], ⟨∠сться⟩ [25; -пался, -лась; -павшийся] fall to pieces; decay; disintegrate; break up (into на В), split; **~ко́вывать** [1], ⟨~кова́ть⟩ [7] unpack; **∠рывать** [1] *s.* поро́ть; **∠сться** *s.* ~да́ться; **∠хивать** [1] **1.** ⟨~ха́ть⟩ [3] plow (*Brt.* plough) up; **2.** ⟨~хну́ть⟩ [20] throw *or* fling open (*v/i.* **-ся**); **~я́ть** [24] *pf.* (**-ся** come) unsolder(ed).

распе|ва́ть [1] sing; **~ка́ть** F [1], ⟨∠чь⟩ [26] dress down, scold, call down, blow up; **~ча́тывать**, ⟨~ча́тать⟩ [1] unseal; open.

распи́|ливать [1], ⟨~ли́ть⟩ [13; -илю́, -и́лишь; -и́ленный] saw; **~на́ть** [1], ⟨распя́ть⟩ [-пну, -пнёшь; -пя́тый] crucify.

распис|а́ние *n* [12] timetable (🚂 ~а́ние поездо́в; *school:* ~а́ние уро́ков), schedule (on по Д); **~а́ть(ся)** *s.* ∠ывать(ся); **∠ка** *f* [5; *g/pl.*: -сок] receipt (against под В); **∠ывать** [1], ⟨~а́ть⟩ [3] write, enter; paint; ornament; **-ся** sign (one's name); (acknowledge) receipt (в П); F register one's marriage.

распл|авля́ть [28] *s.* пла́вить; **~а́каться** [3] *pf.* burst into tears; **~а́та** *f* [5] payment; requital; **~а́чиваться** [1], ⟨~ати́ться⟩ [15] (с Т) pay off, settle accounts (with); pay (for за В); **~еска́ть** [3] *pf.* spill.

распле|та́ть [1], ⟨~сти́⟩ [25 -т-] (**-ся**, ⟨-сь⟩ get) unbraid(ed); untwist.

расплы|ва́ться [1], ⟨∠ться⟩ [23] spread; run; swim about; blur; swell; F grow fat; **∠вчатый** [14 *sh.*] blurred, diffuse, vague.

расплю́щить [16] *pf.* flatten.

распозн|ава́ть [5], ⟨~а́ть⟩ [1] perceive, discern; find out.

распол|ага́ть [1], ⟨~ожи́ть⟩ [16] dispose (*a. fig.* = incline), arrange; place, lodge; *impf.* (Т) dispose (of), have (at one's disposal); **-ся** settle; encamp; *pf.* be situated; **~ага́ющий** [17] engaging; **~за́ться** [1], ⟨~зти́сь⟩ [24] creep *or* crawl (away); **~оже́ние** *n* [12] arrangement, order, (dis)position (toward[s] к Д); situation; inclination, favo(u)r; mind; ~оже́ние ду́ха mood; **~о́женный** [14 *sh.*] *a.* situated; (well-) disposed (toward[s] к Д); inclined; **~ожи́ть(ся)** *s.* ~ага́ть(ся).

распор|яди́тельность *f* [8] administrative ability, management; **~яди́тельный** [14; -лен, -льна] circumspect, efficient; **~яди́ться** *s.* ~яжа́ться; **~я́док** *m* [1; -дка] order, rule, (*office, etc.*) regulatio[ns] *pl.*; **~яжа́ться** [1], ⟨~яди́тьс[я]⟩ [15 *e.*; -яжу́сь, -яди́шься] give o[r]ders; (Т) dispose (of); take charge [of], care (of); *impf.* manage, direct; **~[я]же́ние** *n* [12] order(s), instru[c]tion(s); decree; disposal (at в [П]), в П); charge, command (to в [В]).

распра́в|а *f* [5] punishment ([with] с Т); massacre; *short* work (of с Т); **~ля́ть** [28], ⟨~ить⟩ [14] straighte[n]; smooth; spread, stretch; **-ся** (с [Т]) punish, avenge o.s. (on).

распредел|е́ние *n* [12] distributio[n]; **~и́тельный** [14] distributing; control...; ⚡ switch...; **~я́ть** [28], ⟨~и́ть⟩ [13] distribute; allot; assi[gn] (to по Д); arrange, classify.

распрод|ава́ть [5], ⟨~а́ть⟩ [-да́м, -да́шь, *etc.*, *s.* дать; -про́дал, -а́, -; -про́данный] sell out (*or* off); **~а́ж[а]** *f* [5] (clearance) sale.

распрост|ира́ть [1], ⟨~ере́ть⟩ [1[2]] spread, stretch; extend; (*v/i.* **-ся**); ~ёртый *a.* open (arms объя́тия *pl*); **~и́ться** [15 *e.*; -ощу́сь, -ости́шьс[я]] (с Т) bid farewell (to); give u[p], abandon.

распростран|е́ние *n* [12] sprea[d](-ing), expansion; disseminatio[n], propagation; circulation; **~ённы[й]** [14] widespread; **~я́ть** [28], ⟨~и́т[ь]⟩ [13] spread, extend (*v/i.* **-ся**); prop[agate], disseminate; diffuse; -ся enlarge upon.

распро|ща́ться [1] F = ~сти́тьс[я].

ра́спря *f* [6; *g/pl.*: -рей] strife, co[n]tention, conflict; **~га́ть** [1], ⟨∠ч[ь]⟩ [26 г/ж: -ягу́, -яжёшь] unharne[ss].

распу|ска́ть [1], ⟨~сти́ть⟩ [1[5]] dismiss, disband, dissolve, bre[ak] up; unfurl; undo; loosen; sprea[d]; melt; *fig.* spoil; **-ся** open; expan[d]; loosen, untie; dissolve; F beco[me] spoiled; **∠тать** *s.* ∠тывать; **∠тиц[а]** [5] impassability of roads; **∠тн[ик]** *s.* развра́тник; **∠тывать**, ⟨∠тат[ь]⟩ [1] untangle; **∠тье** *n* [10] cros[s]road(s); **~ха́ть** [1], ⟨∠хнуть⟩ [2[1]] swell; **∠хший** [17] swollen; **∠ще[н]ный** [14 *sh.*] spoiled, undisciplined, dissolute.

распыл|и́тель *m* [4] spray(e[r]), atomizer; **~я́ть** [28], ⟨~и́ть⟩ [1[3]] spray, atomize; scatter.

распя́|тие *n* [12] crucifixion; **~ть** распина́ть.

расса́|да *f* [5] sprout(s); **~ди́ть** ~живать; **~дник** *m* [1] nursery; *f*[ig.] hotbed; **~живать** [1], ⟨~ди́ть⟩ [1[5]] transplant; seat; **-ся**, ⟨рассе́стьс[я]⟩ [расся́дусь, -дешься; -се́лся, -[се́]лась] sit down, take seats; F sit [at] ease.

рассве́|т *m* [1] dawn (at на П), da[y]break; **~та́ть** [1], ⟨~сти́⟩ [25 -т-; -светёт; -свело́] dawn.

рассе|дла́ть [1] *pf.* unsaddle; **∠[и]ва́ть** [1], ⟨∠ять⟩ [27] dissemina[te] atter, disperse (*v/i.* **-ся**); dissipate, spel; divert (*usu.* **-ся** o.s.); **~ка́ть**], ⟨∠чь⟩ [26] cut (up), dissect, :w, cleave; swish; **~ля́ть** [28], лить⟩ [13] settle (*v/i.* **-ся**); parate; **∠ся** *s.* рассáживать-; **∠янность** *f* [8] absent-minded-:ss; **∠янный** [14 *sh.*] absent-ıinded; dissipated; scattered; *phys.* ffused; **∠ять(ся)** *s.* ∠ивать(ся).

:ска́з *m* [1] story, tale, narrative; ort novel (*or* story); **~а́ть** *s.* ~ы-ть; **~чик** *m* [1] narrator; story-ller; **~ывать** [1], ⟨~а́ть⟩ [3] tell; late, narrate.

сслаб|ля́ть [28], ⟨∠ить⟩ [14] eaken, enervate (*v/i.* **~е́ть** [8] *pf.*).

ссл|е́дование *n* [12] investiga-on, inquiry into; **~е́довать** [7] *n)pf.* investigate, inquire into; **е́ние** *n* [12] stratification; **~ы́-ать** [16] *pf.* hear distinctly; не ішать not (quite) catch.

ссм|а́тривать [1], ⟨~отре́ть⟩ отрю́, -о́тришь; -о́тренный] :amine, view; consider; discern, stinguish; **~ея́ться** [27 *e.*; -ею́сь, ёшься] *pf.* burst out laughing; **~-тре́ние** *n* [12] examination (at ри П); consideration; **~отре́ть** *s.* трривать.

ссо́л *m* [1] brine, pickle.

сспр|а́шивать [1], ⟨~оси́ть⟩ [15] quire, ask; **~о́сы** *pl.* [1] inquiries.

ссро́чка *f* [5] (payment by) in-al(l)ments (by в В *sg.*).

сста|ва́ние *s.* проща́ние; **~ва́ть-я** [5], ⟨∠ться⟩ [-а́нусь, -а́нешься] ırt, separate (from с Т); leave; **~-ля́ть** [28], ⟨∠вить⟩ [14] place; range; set (up); move apart; **~-о́вка** *f* [5; *g/pl.*: -вок] arrange-ent; distribution; order; punctu-ion; drawing up; pause; **∠ться** *s.* а́ться.

сст|ёгивать [1], ⟨~егну́ть⟩ [20] ıbutton; unfasten (*v/i.* **-ся**); **~и-а́ть** [1], ⟨разостла́ть⟩ [расстелю́, лешь; разо́стланный] spread *v/i.* **-ся**); **~оя́ние** *n* [12] distance t на П).

сстр|а́ивать [1], ⟨~о́ить⟩ [13] oset, derange; disorganize; dis-ırb, spoil; shatter; frustrate; ♪ put ıt of tune (*or* humo[u]r, *fig.*); **:я** be(come) upset, *etc.*; fail.

сстре́л *m* [1] (death by) shooting, :ecution; **~ивать** [1], ⟨~я́ть⟩ [28] ıoot, execute.

сстро́|ить(ся) *s.* расстра́ивать ся); **~йство** *n* [9] disorder, con-ısion; disturbance, derangement; ustration.

сступ|а́ться [1], ⟨~и́ться⟩ [14] ve way, part; open, split.

ссу|ди́тельность *f* [8] judicious-:ss; **~ди́тельный** [14; -лен, -ль-ı] judicious, wise; **~ди́ть** [15] *pf.* dge; decide (*a. issue*); consider; **∠док** *m* [1; -дка] reason, sense(s); judg(e)ment, mind (of в П); **∠доч-ный** [14; -чен, -чна] rational; **~-жда́ть** [1] argue, reason; talk; **~жде́ние** *n* [12] reasoning, argu-ment(ation); objection; treatise, essay (on о П).

рассчи́т|ывать [1], ⟨~а́ть⟩ [1] & ⟨расче́сть⟩ [25; разочту́, -тёшь; расчёл, разочла́; разочтённый; *g. pt.*: разочтя́]; (не mis)calculate, estimate; judge; dismiss, pay off; *impf.* count *or* reckon (on на В); expect; intend; **-ся** settle accounts, get even (with с Т), pay off; count off.

рассыл|а́ть [1], ⟨разосла́ть⟩ [-ошлю́, -ошлёшь; -о́сланный] send out (*or* round); **∠ка** *f* [5] distribu-tion, dispatch.

рассып|а́ть [1], ⟨∠ать⟩ [2] scatter, spill; spread; (*v/i.* **-ся**; crumble, fall to pieces; break up; fail; shower [s.th. on в П/Д]; resound; burst out).

раста́|лкивать, ⟨растолка́ть⟩ [1] push aside; push; **~пливать** [1], ⟨растопи́ть⟩ [14] light, kindle; melt; (*v/i.* **-ся**); **~птывать** [1], ⟨растоп-та́ть⟩ [3] tread down; **~скивать** [1], ⟨~щи́ть⟩ [16], F ⟨~ска́ть⟩ [1] pilfer; take to pieces; F separate.

раство́р *m* [1] solution; mortar; **~и́мый** [14 *sh.*] soluble; **~я́ть** [28], ⟨~и́ть⟩ **1.** [13] dissolve; **2.** [13; -орю́, -о́ришь; -о́ренный] open.

расте́|ние *n* [12] plant; **~ре́ть** *s.* растира́ть; **~рза́ть** [1] *pf.* tear to pieces; lacerate; **~рянный** [14 *sh.*] confused, perplexed, bewildered; **~ря́ть** [28] *pf.* lose (one's head **-ся**; be[come] perplexed *or* puzzled).

расти́ [24 -ст-: -сту́, -стёшь; рос, -сла́; ро́сший], ⟨вы́-⟩ grow, in-crease.

раст|ира́ть [1], ⟨~ере́ть⟩ [12; разо-тру́, -трёшь] pound, pulverize; rub; smear.

расти́тельн|ость *f* [8] vegetation, flora; hair; **~ый** [14] vegetable; vegetative.

расти́ть [15 *e.*; ращу́, расти́шь] rear; F grow.

расто|лка́ть *s.* раста́лкивать; **~л-кова́ть** [7] *pf.* expound, explain; **~пи́ть** *s.* раста́пливать; **~пта́ть** *s.* раста́птывать; **~пы́рить** F [13] *pf.* spread; **~рга́ть** [1], ⟨∠ргнуть⟩ [21] break (off), annul; dissolve, sever; **~ржéние** *n* [12] breaking off; an-nulment; dissolution; **~ро́пный** [14; -пен, -пна] deft, quick; **~ча́ть** [1], ⟨~чи́ть⟩ [16 *e.*; -чу́, -чи́шь; -чённый] squander, waste, dissi-pate; lavish (on Д); **~чи́тель** *m* [4], **~чи́тельный** [14; -лен, -льна] prodigal, spendthrift, extravagant.

растра|вля́ть [28], ⟨~ви́ть⟩ [14] irritate; fret, stir (up); **∠та** *f* [5] waste; embezzlement; **∠тчик** *m* [1] embezzler; **∠чивать** [1], ⟨∠тить⟩ [15] spend, waste; embezzle.

растр|епа́ть [2] *pf.* (**-ся** be[come]) tousle(d, **~ёпанный** [14]), dishevel (-[1]ed); tear (torn), thumb(ed).

растро́гать [1] *pf.* move, touch.

растя́|гивать [1], ⟨~ну́ть⟩ [19] stretch (*v/i.* **-ся**; F fall flat); ⚕ strain; drawl; extend, prolong; **~же́ние** *n* [12] stretching; strain(ing); **~жи́мый** [14 *sh.*] extensible, elastic; *fig.* vague; **~нутый** [14] long-drawn; **~ну́ть(ся)** *s.* ~гивать(ся).

рас|формирова́ть [8] *pf.* disband; **~ха́живать** [1] walk about *or* up & down, pace; **~хва́ливать** [1], ⟨~хвали́ть⟩ [13; -алю́, -а́лишь; -а́ленный] extol(l *Brt.*), praise (highly); **~хва́тывать** F, ⟨~хвата́ть⟩ [1] snatch away; buy up (quickly).

расхи|ща́ть [1], ⟨∠тить⟩ [15] plunder; **~ще́ние** *n* [12] plunder.

расхо́|д *m* [1] expenditure (for на В), expense(s); ✝ *a.* debit; consumption; sale; **~и́ться** [15], ⟨разойти́сь⟩ [-ойду́сь, -ойдёшься; -ошёлся, -ошла́сь; -ошéдшийся; *g. pt.*: -ойдя́сь] disperse; break up; differ (from с Т); diverge; part, separate, get divorced (from с Т); pass *or* miss o.a., (*letters*) cross; be sold out, sell; be spent, (у Р) run out of; melt, dissolve; ramify; radiate; F spread; become enraged; get excited *or* animated; **~довать** [7], ⟨из-⟩ spend, expend; *pf. a.* use up; **~жде́ние** *n* [12] divergence, difference (of в П); radiation.

расцара́п|ывать, ⟨~ать⟩ [1] scratch.

расцве́|т *m* [1] blossom, (*a. fig.*) bloom; prime; prosperity; **~та́ть** [1], ⟨~сти́⟩ [25 -т-] blo(ss)om; flourish, thrive; **~тка** *f* [5; *g/pl.*: -ток] colo(u)ring.

расце́|нивать [1], ⟨~ни́ть⟩ [13; -еню́, -е́нишь; -енённый] estimate, value, rate; **~нка** *f* [5; *g/pl.*: -нок] valuation; rate, tariff; **~пля́ть** [28], ⟨~пи́ть⟩ [14] uncouple, unhook.

рас|чеса́ть *s.* ~чёсывать; **~чёска** *f* [5; *g/pl.*: -сок] comb; **~че́сть** *s.* рассчита́ть; **~чёсывать** [1], ⟨~чеса́ть⟩ [3] comb (one's hair **-ся** F).

расчёт *m* [1] calculation; estimation; settlement (of accounts); payment; dismissal, *Brt.* F *a.* sack; account, consideration; intention; providence; F use; ⚔ gunners *pl.*; из ~а on the basis (of); в ~е quits; **~ливый** [14 *sh.*] provident, thrifty; circumspect.

рас|чища́ть [1], ⟨~чи́стить⟩ [15] clear (away); **~членя́ть** [28], ⟨~члени́ть⟩ [13] dismember; **~ша́тывать**, ⟨~шата́ть⟩ [1] loosen (*v/i.* **-ся**); (be[come]) shatter(ed); **~шевели́ть** F [13] *pf.* stir (up).

расши|ба́ть F *s.* ушиба́ть; **~ва́ть** [1], ⟨∠ть⟩ [разошью́, -шьёшь; *cf.* шить] embroider; undo, rip; **~ре́ние** *n* [12] widening, enlargement; expansion; **~ря́ть** [28], ⟨∠рить⟩ [13] widen, enlarge; extend, expand; ⚕ dilate; **∠ть** *s.* ~ва́ть; **~фро́вывать** [1], ⟨~фрова́ть⟩ [7] decipher, decode.

рас|шнурова́ть [7] *pf.* untie; **~щéлина** *f* [5] crevice, cleft, crack; **~щепле́ние** *n* [12] splitting; fission; **~щепля́ть** [28], ⟨~щепи́ть⟩ [14 *e.*; -плю́, -пи́шь; -плённый] split.

ратифи|ка́ция *f* [7] ratification; **~ци́ровать** [7] (*im*)*pf.* ratify.

ра́товать [7] fight, struggle.

рафина́д *m* [1] lump sugar.

рахи́т *m* [1] rickets.

рацион|ализи́ровать [7] (*im*)*pf.* rationalize; **~а́льный** [14; -лен, -льна] rational (*a.* ♇, *no sh.*).

рвану́ть [20] *pf.* jerk; **-ся** dart.

рвать [рву, рвёшь; рвал, -а́, -о] **1.** ⟨разо-, изо-⟩ [-о́рванный] tear (to, in *pieces* на, в В), *v/i.* **-ся**; **2.** ⟨со-⟩ pluck; **3.** ⟨вы-⟩ pull out; *impers.* (В) vomit, spew; **4.** ⟨пре-⟩ break off; **5.** ⟨взо-⟩ blow up; ~ и мета́ть F be in a rage; **-ся** break; strive *or* long (eagerly).

рве́ние *n* [12] zeal; eagerness.

рво́т|а *f* [5] vomit(ing); **~ный** [14] emetic (*a. n, su.*).

рдеть [8] redden, flush.

реа|билити́ровать [7] (*im*)*pf.* rehabilitate; **~ги́ровать** [7] (на В) react (upon); respond (to); **~кти́вный** [14] reactive; jet (*plane*); **~кционе́р** *m* [1], **~кцио́нный** [14] reactionary.

реал|и́зм *m* [1] realism; **~изова́ть** [7] (*im*)*pf.* realize; ✝ *a.* sell; **~исти́ческий** [16] realistic; **∠ьность** *f* [8] reality; **∠ьный** [14; -лен, -льна] real; realistic.

ребёнок *m* [2; *pl. a.* де́ти, *s.*] child, baby, F kid; грудно́й ~ suckling.

ребро́ *n* [9; *pl.*: рёбра, рёбер, рёбрам] rib; edge (on ~м); ~м *fig.* point-blank.

ребя́|та *pl. of* ребёнок; F boys; **~ческий** [16], **~чий** F [18] childish; **~чество** F [9] childishness; **~читься** F [16] behave childishly.

рёв *m* [1] roar; bellow; howl.

рев|а́нш *m* [1] revenge; return match; **~е́нь** *m* [4 *e.*] rhubarb; **~е́ть** [-ву, -вёшь] roar; bellow; howl, cry.

реви́з|ия *f* [7] inspection; auditing; revision; **~о́р** *m* [1] inspector; auditor.

ревмати́|зм *m* [1] rheumatism; [**~ческий** [16] rheumatic

ревн|и́вый [14 *sh.*] jealous; **~ова́ть** [7], ⟨при-⟩ be jealous (of [p.'s] к [В]); **∠ость** *f* [8] jealousy; zeal, eagerness; **∠остный** [14; -тен, -тна] zealous, eager.

ол|ьвéр *m* [1] revolver; ~люцио-
р *m* [1], ~люциóнный [14] rev-
utionary; ~люция *f* [7] revolution.
и́стр *m* [1], ~и́ровать [7], ⟨за-⟩
gister (*v/i.* -ся; *a.* get married *in*
civil ceremony); index.
|ла́мент *m* [1] order, regula-
ns *pl.*; ~ре́сс *m* [1] retrogression.
гул|и́ровать [7], ⟨у-⟩ regulate;
p. pf.) settle; ~я́рный [14; -рен,
на] regular; ~я́тор *m* [1] regu-
tor.
цак|ти́ровать [7], ⟨от-⟩ edit,
dact; ~тор *m* [1] editor; ~ция *f*
] editorial staff; editorship; edi-
r's office; wording, text, version;
daction; (*radio*) desk.
д|éть [8], ⟨по-⟩ (grow) thin; ~-
ска *f* [5; *g/pl.*: -сок] (*red*) radish.
дк|ий [16; -док, -дка́, -о; *comp.*:
е́же] rare; thin, sparse; scarce;
lv. a. seldom; ~ость *f* [8] rarity,
riosity; sparsity, thinness; un-
mmon (thing); на ~ость F extrem-
y, awfully.
дька *f* [5; *g/pl.*: -дек] radish.
жи́м *m* [1] regime(n); conditions
.; regulations *pl.*, order.
жисс|ёр *m* [1] stage manager;
irector, producer; ~и́ровать [7]
age.
зать [3] **1.** ⟨раз-⟩ cut (up, open);
rve (*meat*); **2.** ⟨за-⟩ slaughter,
ll; **3.** ⟨вы́-⟩ carve, cut (in *wood*
› Д, на П); **4.** ⟨с-⟩ cut off; F fail;
npf. hurt; F say; P talk; **5.** -ся F
it (one's teeth); gamble.
зв|и́ться [14 *e.*; -влю́сь, -ви́шься]
olic, frisk, gambol; ~ый [14;
эзв, -á, -о] frisky, sportive, frolic-
me; quick; lively.
зéрв *m* [1], reserve(s); ~и́ст *m* [1]
eservist; ~ный [14] reserve...
зéц *m* [1; -зца́] incisor.
зи́н|а *f* [5] rubber; ~овый [14]
ıbber...; ~ка *f* [5; *g/pl.*: -нок]
raser, (india) rubber; elastic.
з|кий [16; -зок, -зка́, -о; *comp.*:
е́зче] sharp, keen; biting, piercing;
cute; harsh, shrill; glaring; rough,
brupt; ~кость *f* [8] sharpness, *etc.*,
~кий; harsh word; ~но́й [14] carv-
d; ~ня́ *f* [6] slaughter; ~олю́ция
[7] resolution; decision; ~о́н *m* [1]
eason; ~она́нс *m* [1] resonance;
о́нный F [14; -о́нен, -о́нна] rea-
onable; ~ульта́т *m* [1] result (as a
П); ~ьба́ *f* [5] carving.
зюм|é *n* [*ind.*] summary; ~и́ро-
ать [7] (*im*)*pf.* summarize.
йд *m* [1] ⚓ road(stead); ⚔ raid.
йн *m* [1] Rhine.
йс *m* [1] trip; voyage; flight.
ка́ *f* [5; *ac/sg. a. st.*; *pl. st.*; *from*
at/pl. a. e.] river, stream.
кла́м|а *f* [5] advertising; adver-
isement; publicity; ~и́ровать [7]
m)*pf.* advertise; boost; (re-)claim,
omplain; ~ный [14] advertising.

реко|менда́тельный [14] of rec-
ommendation; ~менда́ция *f* [7]
recommendation; reference; ~мен-
дова́ть [7] (*im*)*pf.*, *a.* ⟨по-⟩ recommend, advise; † introduce; ~н-
струи́ровать [7] (*im*)*pf.* reconstruct; ~рд *m* [1] record; ~рдный
[14] record...; ~рдсме́н *m* [1],
~рдсме́нка *f* [5; *g/pl.*: -нок] champion.
ре́ктор *m* [1] president, (*Brt.* vice-)-
chancellor, rector (*univ.*).
рели|гио́зный [14; -зен, -зна]
religious; ~гия *f* [7] religion; ~к-
вия *f* [7] relic.
рельс *m* [1], ~овый [14] rail; track.
реме́нь *m* [4; -мня́] strap; belt.
реме́сл|енник *m* [1] (handi)crafts-
man, artisan; *fig.* bungler; ~енный
[14] trade...; handicraft...; home-
-made; bungling; ~о́ *n* [9; *pl.*:
-мёсла, -мёсел, -мёслам] trade,
(handi)craft; occupation.
ремо́нт *m* [1] repair(s); remount
(-ing); ~и́ровать [7] (*im*)*pf.*, ~ный
[14] repair.
ре́нта *f* [5] rent; revenue; (*life*) annuity; ~бельный [14; -лен, -льна]
profitable.
рентге́новск|ий [16]: ~ий сни́мок
m roentgenogram; ~ие лучи́ *m/pl.*
X-rays.
реорганизова́ть [7] (*im*)*pf.* reor-
ganize (*Brt.* -se).
ре́па *f* [5] turnip.
репа|рацио́нный [14] reparation...;
~трии́ровать [7] (*im*)*pf.* repatriate.
репе́йник *m* [1] bur(dock); agri-
mony.
репертуа́р *m* [1] repertoire, re-
pertory.
репети́|ровать [7], ⟨про-⟩ re-
hearse; ~ция *f* [7] rehearsal.
ре́плика *f* [5] retort; *thea.* cue.
репорта́ж *m* [1] report(ing).
репортёр *m* [1] reporter.
репре́сс(а́л)ия *f* [7] reprisal.
репроду́ктор *m* [1] loud-speaker.
ресни́ца *f* [5] eyelash.
респу́блик|а *f* [5] republic; ~а́нец
m [1; -нца], ~а́нский [16] repub-
lican.
рессо́ра *f* [5] spring.
рестора́н *m* [1] restaurant (at в П).
ресу́рсы *m/pl.* [1] resources.
рети́вый [14] zealous; mettlesome.
ре|туши́ровать [7] (*im*)*pf.*, ⟨от-⟩
retouch; ~фера́т *m* [1] report, paper.
рефо́рм|а *f* [5], ~и́ровать [7]
(*im*)*pf.* reform; ~а́тор *m* [1] re-
former.
реценз|е́нт *m* [1] reviewer; ~и́ро-
вать [7], ⟨про-⟩, ~ия *f* [7] review.
реце́пт *m* [1] recipe.
рециди́в *m* [1] relapse.
речево́й [14] speech...
ре́ч|ка *f* [5; *g/pl.*: -чек] (small)
river; ~но́й [14] river...
реч|ь *f* [8; *from g/pl. e.*] speech;

discourse, talk, conversation; word; об э́том не мо́жет быть и ∠и that is out of the question; *cf.* идти́.

реш|а́ть [1], ⟨**~и́ть**⟩ [*e.*; -шу́, -ши́шь; -шённый] solve; decide, resolve (*a.* **-ся** [on, to на В]; make up one's mind); dare, risk; не ~а́ться hesitate; **~а́ющий** [17] decisive; **~е́ние** *n* [12] decision; (re)solution; **~ётка** *f* [5; *g/pl.*: -ток] grating; lattice; trellis; grate; **~ето́** *n* [9; *pl. st.*: -шёта] sieve; **~ётчатый** [14] trellis(ed); **~и́мость** *f* [8] determination; **~и́тельный** [14; -лен, -льна] resolute, firm; decisive; definite; absolute; **~и́ть(ся)** *s.* ~а́ть(ся).

ре́ять [27] soar, fly.

ржа́|веть [8], ⟨за-⟩, **~вчина** *f* [5] rust; **~вый** [14] rusty; **~но́й** [14] rye...; **~ть** [ржёт], ⟨за-⟩ neigh.

ри́за *f* [5] chasuble; robe.

Рим *m* [1] Rome; **'**2**ля́нин** *m* [1; *pl.*: -я́не, -я́н], **'**2**ля́нка** *f* [5; *g/pl.*: -нок], **'**2**ский** [14] Roman.

ри́нуться [20] *pf.* rush; plunge.

рис *m* [1] rice.

риск *m* [1] risk (at на В); **~о́ванный** [14 *sh.*] risky; **~ова́ть** [7], ⟨**~ну́ть**⟩ [20] (*usu.* Т) risk, venture.

рисова́|ние *n* [12] drawing; designing; **~ть** [7], ⟨на-⟩ draw; design; **-ся** appear, loom; pose, mince.

ри́совый [14] rice...

рису́нок *m* [1; -нка] drawing, design; picture, illustration (in на П).

ритм *m* [1] rhythm; **~и́чный** [14; -чен, -чна] rhythmical.

риф *m* [1] reef; **∠ма** *f* [5] rhyme.

роб|е́ть [8], ⟨о-⟩ be timid, quail; не ~е́й! courage!; **∠кий** [16; -бок, -бка́, -о; *comp.*: ро́бче] shy, timid; **∠ость** *f* [8] shyness, timitidy.

ров *m* [1; рва; во рву] ditch.

рове́сник *m* [1] coeval, of the same age.

ро́вн|ый [14; -вен, -вна́, -о] even, level, flat; straight; equal; equable; ~о precisely, exactly, *time a.* sharp; F absolutely; **∠я́** F *f* [5] equal.

рог *m* [1; *pl. e.*: -га́] horn; antler; bugle; **~а́тый** [14*sh.*] horned; **~ови́ца** *f* [5] cornea; **~ово́й** [14] horn ...

рого́жа *f* [5] (bast) mat.

род *m* [1; в, на -у́; *pl. e.*] genus; race; generation; kind; way; *gr.* gender; birth (by Т); F class; ∠ом из, с Р come *or* be from; о́т ~у (Д) *be* ... old; с ∠у in one's life.

роди́|льный [14] maternity (hospital дом *m*); **~мый** [14] *s.* родно́й & '~нка; **'~на** *f* [5] native land, home(land) (in на П); **'~нка** *f* [5; *g/pl.*: -нок] birthmark, mole; **~тели** *m/pl.* [4] parents; **~тельный** [14] genitive (*case*); **~тельский** [16] parental.

роди́ть [15 *e.*; рожу́, роди́шь; -и́л, -а (*pf.*: -а́), -о; рождённый] (*im-*) *pf.*, (*impf. a.* **рожда́ть**, F **рожа́ть** [1]) bear, give birth to; beget; bring forth, produce; **-ся** [*pf.* -и- ся́] be born; arise; come up, gr

родн|и́к *m* [1 *e.*] spring; **~о́й** [own; native; (my) dear; *pl.* = *f* [6] relative(s), relation(s).

родо|во́й [14] patrimonial; gene **~нача́льник** *m* [1] ancestor, *fig.*) father; **~сло́вный** [14] ge alogical; ~сло́вная *f* family tree.

ро́дствен|ник *m* [1], **~ница** *f* relative, relation; **~ный** [14 related, kindred, cognate; of blo

родств|о́ *n* [9] relationship; cog tion; F relatives; в ~е́ related (to c

ро́ды *pl.* [1] (child)birth.

ро́жа *f* [5] ⚕ erysipelas; P mug.

рожд|а́емость *f* [8] birth ra **~а́ть(ся)** *s.* роди́ть(ся); **~е́ние** [12] birth (by от Р); день ~е́н birthday (on в В); **~е́ственск** [16] Christmas...; **~ество́** *n* [9] 2ество́ [Христо́во]) Christmas на В); поздра́вить с 2ество́м Х сто́вым wish a Merry Xmas; (по́сле) Р.Хр. В. С. (A. D.).

рож|о́к *m* [1; -жка́] *dim. of* p ear trumpet; feeding bottle; (burner; shoehorn; **~ь** *f* [8; рж *instr/sg.*: ро́жью] rye.

ро́за *f* [5] rose.

ро́зга *f* [5; *g/pl.*: -зог] rod.

розе́тка *f* [5; *g/pl.*: -ток] rose ⚡ (*plug*) socket.

ро́зн|ица *f* [5]: в ~ицу by ret **~ичный** [14] retail...; **~ь** F *f* discord; И/Д ~ь th. *or* p. & th are not the same *or* different.

ро́зовый [14 *sh.*] pink, rosy.

ро́зыгрыш *m* [1] draw; dra game; drawing of a lottery; ~ пе венства play(s) for championshi

ро́зыск *m* [1] search (in/of в *pl.*/Р); ⚖ preliminary trial; у ло́вный ~ criminal investigat department.

ро|и́ться [13], **~й** *m* [3; в рою́; *e.*: рой, роёв] swarm.

рок *m* [1] fate; **~ово́й** [14] fat **∠от** *m* [1], **~ота́ть** [3] roll.

ро́лик *m* [1] roller (skates *pl.*).

роль *f* [8; *from g/pl. e.*] part, r

ром *m* [1] rum.

рома́н *m* [1] novel; F (love) aff romance; **~и́ст** *m* [1] novelist; **ти́зм** *m* [1] romanticism; **~ти́ч ский** [16], **~ти́чный** [14; -ч -чна] romantic.

ром|а́шка *f* [5; *g/pl.*: -шек] ca mile; **~б** *m* [1] rhombus.

роня́ть [28], ⟨урони́ть⟩ [13; -он -о́нишь; -о́ненный] drop; dro lose; shed; *fig.* disparage, discre

ро́п|от *m* [1], **~та́ть** [3; -п ро́пщешь] murmur, grumble, gro (at на В).

роса́ *f* [5; *pl. st.*] dew.

роско́ш|ный [14; -шен, -ш luxurious; magnificent, splend

...mptuous; F luxuriant, exuberant; ...ь f [8] luxury; magnificence, ...mptuousness; luxuriance.
...слый [14] big, tall.
...спись f [8] list; fresco.
...спуск m [1] dissolution; dismiss-...; disbandment; breaking up.
...сси́|я f [7] Russia; ♀йский [16] ...ussian; cf. РСФСР.
...ст m [1] growth; increase; stat-...re, size; ... высо́кого ∠а tall ...
...стовщи́к m [1 e.] usurer.
...с|то́к m [1; -тка́] sprout, shoot; ...черк m [1] flourish; stroke.
...т m [1; рта; во рту́] mouth; ∠а [5] company; ∠ный [14] company ...ommander); ~озе́й F [3] gaper.
...ща f [5] grove.
...я́ль m [4] (grand) piano.
...ФСР (Росси́йская Сове́тская ...едерати́вная Социалисти́ческая ...еспу́блика) Russian Soviet Fed-...ative Socialist Republic.
...у́ть f [8] mercury.
...ба́|нок m [1; -нка] plane; ~шка [5; g/pl.: -шек] shirt; chemise.
...бе́ж m [1 e.] boundary; border ...ine), frontier; за ~о́м abroad.
...бе́ц m [1; -бца́] hem; scar, ...ake.
...би́ть [14] 1. ⟨на-⟩ chop, cut, hew, ...ack; mince; 2. ⟨с-⟩ fell; F impf. ...eak bluntly; -ся fight (hand to ...and).
...бка f [5] felling; ⚓ cabin.
...бленый [14] chopped, minced.
...бль m [e.] r(o)uble.
...б|рика f [5] heading; column;
...чатый [14] ribbed.
...га|нь f [8] abuse; ∠тельный ...4] abusive; ∠тельство n [9] curse, ...th; ∠ть [1], ⟨вы́-⟩ abuse, scold; ...я swear, curse; abuse o. a.
...д|а́ f [5; pl. st.] ore; ~ни́к m [1 e.] ...ine, pit; ~ни́чный [14] mine(r's); ...e(damp); ~око́п m [1] miner.
...ж|е́йный [14] gun...; ~ьё n [10; ... st.; g/pl.: -жей] gun, rifle.
...к|а́ f [5; ac/sg.: ру́ку; pl.: ру́ки, ...к, -ка́м] hand; arm; ~а́ в ∠у (or ... ~у) hand in hand (arm in arm; ... под ~у); из ~ вон (пло́хо) F ...ite wretched(ly); быть на́ ~у (Д) ...it a p. (well); на́ ~у нечи́ст light-...ngered; от ~и́ in handwriting; ... ~а́м! it's bargain!; под ~о́й at ...nd, within reach; ~о́й пода́ть ...s no distance (a stone's throw); ... P) ∠и ко́ротки́ F it's not in (p.'s) ...wer; из пе́рвых ~ at first hand; ...иложи́ть ∠у sign.
...ка́в m [1 e.; pl.: -ва́, -во́в] sleeve; ...anch; hose; ~и́ца f [5] mitten; ...untlet; ~чик m [1] cuff.
...ковод|и́тель m [4] leader; chief; ...anager; teacher; ~и́ть [15] (Т) ...ad; direct, manage; -ся follow, ...nform (to); ∠ство n [9] leader-...ip; guidance; instruction; text-book, guide; ∠ствовать(ся) [7] s. ~и́ть(ся); ~я́щий [17] leading.
руко|де́лие n [12] needlework; ~мо́йник m [1] washstand; ~па́шный [14] hand-to-hand; '~пись f [8] manuscript; ~плеска́ние n [12] (mst pl.) applause; ~пожа́тие n [12] hand shake; ~я́тка f [5; g/pl.: -ток] handle, gripe; hilt.
рул|ево́й [14] steering; control...; su. steersman, helmsman; ~ь m [4 e.] rudder; helm; steering wheel; handle bar; ~ь высоты́ ✈ elevator.
румы́н m [1], ~ка f [5; g/pl.: -нок]; ~ский [16] R(o)umanian.
румя́н|а n/pl. [9] rouge; ~ец m [1; -нца] ruddiness; blush; ~ить [13] 1. ⟨за-⟩ redden; 2. ⟨на-⟩ rouge; ~ый [14 sh.] ruddy, rosy; red, scarlet.
ру|но́ n [9; pl. st.] fleece; ∠пор m [1] megaphone; mouthpiece.
руса́лка f [5; g/pl.: -лок] mermaid.
ру́сло n [9] bed, (a. fig.) channel.
ру́сский [16] Russian (a. su.); adv. по-ру́сски (in) Russian.
ру́сый [14sh.] fair(-haired), blond(e).
Русь f [8; -си́] hist., poet. Russia.
рути́н|а f [5], ~ный [14] routine.
ру́хлядь F f [8] lumber, stuff.
ру́хнуть [20] pf. crash down; fail.
руча́|тельство n [9] guarantee; ~ться [1], ⟨поручи́ться⟩ [16] (за В) warrant, guarantee, vouch for.
руче́й m [3 e.; -чья́] brook, stream.
ру́чка f [5; g/pl.: -чек] (small) hand; handle, knob; chair arm; lever; pen(holder).
ручно́й [14] hand...; manual; handmade; small; ⚔ a. light; tame; wrist (watch).
ру́шить(ся) [16] (im)pf. collapse, break down.
ры́б|а f [5] fish; ~а́к m [1 e.] fisherman; ~ий [18] fish...; cod-liver (oil); ~ный [14] fish(y); ~ный про́мысел m fishery.
рыболо́в m [1] angler; ~ный [14] fishing; fish...; ~ство n [9] fishery.
рыво́к m [1; -вка́] jerk.
рыг|а́ть [1], ⟨~ну́ть⟩ [20] belch.
рыда́|ние n [12] sob(bing); ~ть [1] sob.
ры́жий [17; рыж, -а́, -е] red; sorrel.
ры́ло n [9] snout; P mug.
ры́но|к m [1]; -нка] market (in на П); ~чный [14] market...
рыс|а́к m [1 e.] trotter; ∠кать [3] rove, run about; ~ь f [8] trot (at, in в В, на ~си́, Т); zo. lynx.
ры́твина f [5] rut, groove, hole.
рыть [22], ⟨вы́-⟩ dig; burrow, mine; ~ся rummage.
рыхл|и́ть [13], ⟨вз-, раз-⟩ loosen (soil); ∠ый [14; рыхл, -а́, -о] friable, crumbly, loose.

ры́цар|ский [16] knightly, chivalrous; knight's; **~ь** *m* [4] knight.
рыча́г *m* [1 *e.*] lever.
рыча́ть [4 *e.*; -чу́, -чи́шь] growl.
рья́ный [14 *sh.*] zealous; mettlesome.
рю́мка *f* [5; *g/pl.:* -мок] (wine-) glass.
ряби́на *f* [5] mountain ash; F pit.
ряби́ть [14 *e.*; -и́т] ripple; mottle; *impers.* flicker (before p.'s *eyes* в П/у Р).
рябо́й [14; ряб, -а́, -о] pockmarked; piebald, spotted; freckled.
ря́б|чик *m* [1] hazel grouse; **~ь** *f* ripples *pl.*; flicker.
ря́вк|ать F [1], *once* ⟨~нуть⟩ [20] bellow, bawl; snap (at на В).
ряд *m* [1; в -у́; *pl. e.*; *after 2,3,4,* ряда́] row; line; file; series; [в -е] number, several; *pl.* ranks; *thea. a.* tier; **~а́ми** in rows; из **~а** вон выходя́щий remarkable, outstanding; **~ово́й** [14] ordinary; *su.* ⚔ private; **~ом** side by side; (с Т) beside, next to; next door; close by.
ря́женый [14] disguised, masked; [masker.]
ря́са *f* [5] cassock.

С

с. *abbr.*: село́.
с, со: 1. (Р) from; since; with; for; **2.** (В) about; **3.** (Т) with; of; to.
са́бля *f* [6; *g/pl.*: -бель] saber (*Brt.* -bre).
сабот|а́ж *m* [1], sabotage; **~а́жник** *m* [1] saboteur; **~и́ровать** [7] (*im*)*pf.* sabotage.
са́ван *m* [1] shroud.
савра́сый [14] roan.
сад *m* [1; в -у́; *pl. e.*] garden.
сади́ть [15], ⟨по-⟩ *s.* сажа́ть; **~ся**, ⟨сесть⟩ [25; ся́ду, -дешь; сел, -а; се́вший] (на, в В) sit down; get in(to) *or* on, board; ⚓ embark, 🚂 entrain; mount (*horse*); alight (*bird*); ✈ land; set (*sun*); settle; sink; shrink (*fabric*); set (to *work* за В); run (aground на мель).
садо́в|ник *m* [1] gardener; **~о́дство** *n* [9] gardening, horticulture.
са́ж|а *f* [5] soot; в **~е** sooty.
сажа́ть [1] (*iter. of* сади́ть) seat; put; plant; ⚓ embark, 🚂 entrain.
са́же́нь *f* [8] *Russ.* fathom (= 7*ft.*).
саквоя́ж *m* [1] travel(l)ing bag.
сала́зки *f/pl.* [5; *gen.*: -зок] sled.
сала́т *m* [1] salad; lettuce.
са́ло *n* [9] bacon; suet, tallow.
салфе́тка *f* [5; *g/pl.*: -ток] napkin.
са́льдо *n* [*ind.*] † balance.
са́льный [14; -лен, -льна] greasy; obscene.
салю́т *m* [1], **~ова́ть** [7] (*im*)*pf.* salute.
сам *m*, **~а́** *f*, **~о́** *n*, **~и** *pl.* [30] -self: я **~(а́)** I ... myself; мы **~и** we ... ourselves; **~е́ц** *m* [1; -мца́] *zo.* male; **~ка** *f* [5; *g/pl.*: -мок] *zo.* female.
само|бы́тный [14; -тен, тна] original; **~ва́р** *m* [1] samovar; **~вла́стный** [14; -тен, -тна] autocratic; **~во́льный** [14; -лен, льна] arbitrary; **~го́н** *m* [1] home-brew; **~де́льный** [14]homemad, self-made.
самодержа́в|ие *n* [12] autocracy; **~ный** [14; -вен, -вна] autocratic.
само|де́ятельность *f* [8] amateur performance(s); **~дово́льный** [14; -лен, -льна] self-satisfied, self-complacent; **~ду́р** *m* [1] despot; **~защи́та** *f* [5] self-defense; **~зва́нец** *m* [1; -нца] impostor, usurper; pseudo...; **~ка́т** *m* [1] scooter; **~кри́тика** *f* [5] self-criticism.
самолёт *m* [1] airplane (*Brt.* aeroplane), aircraft; пассажи́рский ~ air liner; **~-снаря́д** *m* guided missile.
само|люби́вый [14 *sh.*] ambitious, vain, conceited; **~лю́бие** *n* [12] ambition; vanity; **~мне́ние** *n* [12] self-conceit; **~наде́янный** [14 *sh.*] self-confident, self-assertive; **~облада́ние** *n* [12] self-control; **~обма́н** *m* [1] self-deception; **~оборо́на** *f* [5] self-defense; **~обслу́живание** *n* [12] self-service; **~определе́ние** *n* [12] self-determination; **~отве́рженный** [14 *sh.*] self-denying, self-sacrificing; **~пи́шущий** [17] fountain (*pen*); **~поже́ртвование** *n* [12] self-sacrifice; **~ро́дный** [14; -ден, -дна] nativ[e] pure; original; **~сохране́ние** [12] self-preservation.
самостоя́тельн|ость *f* [8] independence; **~ый** [14; -лен, -льн[а]] independent.
само|су́д *m* [1] lynch law; **~уби́йство** *n* [9], **~уби́йца** *m/f* [5] su[i]cide; **~уве́ренный** [14 *sh.*] se[lf]-confident; **~управле́ние** *n* [1[2]] self-government; **~у́чка** *m/f* [5; *g/pl.*: -чек] self-taught p.; **~хвал[ь]ство** F *n* [9] boasting; **~хо́дны[й]** [14] self-propelled; **~це́ль** *f* [8] e[nd] in itself; **~чу́вствие** *n* [12] (sta[te] of) health.
са́м|ый [14] the most, ...est; t[he] very; the (self)same; just, righ[t] early *or* late; **~ое** бо́льшее (ма́ло[е]) F at (the) most (least).
сан *m* [1] dignity.
санато́рий *m* [3] sanatorium.
санда́лии *f/pl.* [7] sandals.
са́ни *f/pl.* [8; *from g/pl. e.*] sled(g[e])
санита́р *m* [1], **~ка** *f* [5; *g/*

ок] nurse; *m a.* hospital attend-
t, orderly; **~ный** [14] sanitary.
ı|**кционировать** [7] *(im)pf.*
nction; **~овник** *m* [1] dignitary.
нтиметр *m* [1] centimeter.
пёр *m* [1] engineer, *Brt.* sapper.
пóг *m* [1 *e.*; *g/pl.:* сапóг] boot.
пóжник *m* [1] shoemaker.
рáй *m* [3] shed; barn.
ранчá *f* [5; *g/pl.:* -чéй] locust.
рафáн *m* [1] sarafan (*long sleeve-*
ss gown of countrywomen).
рд|éлька *f* [5; *g/pl.:* -лек] wiener
hick variety); **~ина** *f* [5] sardine.
танá *m* [8] Satan.
теллит *m* [1] satellite.
тин *m* [1] sateen, glazed cotton.
тир|а *f* [5] satire; **~ик** *m* [1]
tirist; **~ический** [16] satirical.
фьян *m* [1] morocco.
кар *m* [1; *part. g.*: -у] sugar; **~и-**
стый [14 *sh.*] sugary; **~ница** *f* [5]
gar bowl; **~ный** [14] sugar...;
ная болéзнь *f* diabetes.
чóк *m* [1; -чкá] butterfly net.
ш([ень]к)а *m/f* [5] *dim. of* Алек-
ндр, -а.
áв|ить *s.* ~лять; **~ка** *f* [5; *g/pl.:*
вок] reduction; **~лять** [28],
~ить⟩ [14] reduce.
е|гáть[1] [1], ⟨~жáть⟩ [4; -егý,
жишь, -егýт] run down; *pf.* run
way, escape, flee; **-ся** come run-
ing; **∠гать**[2] [1] *pf.* run (for за Т).
ере|гáтельный [14] savings
ank)...; **~гáть** [1], ⟨∠чь⟩ [26 г/ж:
егý, -режёшь, -регýт] save; pre-
rve; **~жéние** *n* [12] saving; pre-
rvation.
еркáсса *f* [5] savings bank.
и|вáть [1], ⟨~ть⟩ [собью, -бьёшь;
бей!; сбитый] knock down (*or* off);
verthrow (*a.* с ног); shoot down;
hip (*cream*), beat up (*eggs*), churn
utter); mix; lead (astray с пути;
ся lose one's way); (-ся be[come]
onfus(ed) *or* puzzl(ed) (с тóлку);
fl. a. run o.s. off (one's legs с ног);
ock; **∠вчивый** [14 *sh.*] confused;
neven; **∠ть(ся)** *s.* ~вáть(ся).
ли|жáть [1], ⟨∠зить⟩ [15] bring
draw together; **-ся** become
iends (with с Т); **~жéние** *n* [12]
. pol.) rapprochement; approach
es).
óку sideways; next to it.
ор *m* [1] collection; gathering;
arvest; levy; tax; duty; receipts
.; ⚔ muster; *pl.* preparations; в ∠е
ssembled; **∠ище** *n* [11] concourse,
rowd; **∠ка** *f* [5; *g/pl.:* -рок] pleat,
ıck; ⊕ assemblage; **∠ник** *m* [1]
ollection; symposium; **∠ный** [14]
assembly (*point*); *sport:* select
eam); **∠очный** [14] assembling.
р|áсывать [1], ⟨~óсить⟩ [15]
hrow off, drop, shed; discard; **~од**
[1] rabble, riff-raff; **~óсить** *s.*
áсывать; **~ýя** *f* [6] harness.

сбы|вáть [1], ⟨~ть⟩ [сбýду, -дешь; сбыл, -á, -о] sell, market; get rid of (*a.* с рук); fall; **-ся** come true; **~т** *m* [1] sale; **~ть(ся)** *s.* ~вáть(ся).
свáд|ебный [14], **~ьба** *f* [5; *g/pl.:* -деб] wedding.
свáл|ивать [1], ⟨~ить⟩ [13; -алю, -áлишь] knock down, overthrow; fell; dump; heap up; shift (off) (to на В); **-ся** fall down; **~ка** *f* [5; *g/pl.:* -лок] dump; brawl.
свáр|ивать [1], ⟨~ить⟩ [13; сварю, свáришь; свáреннный] weld; **~ка** *f* [5], **~очный** [14] welding.
сварливый [14 *sh.*] quarrelsome.
сва|т *m* [1] matchmaker; **∠тать** [1], ⟨по-⟩ seek (**-ся** ask) in marriage (for за В); **∠ха** *f* [5] matchmaker.
свáя *f* [6; *g/pl.:* свай] pile.
свéд|ение *n* [12] information; принять к ~ению take notice (of В); **~ущий** [17 *sh.*] expert, versed.
свéж|есть *f* [8] freshness; **~éть** [8], ⟨по-⟩ freshen, become fresh; **~ий** [15; свеж, -á, -ó, свéжи] fresh; cool; latest; new.
свезти *s.* свозить.
свёкла *f* [5; *g/pl.:* -кол] beet.
свёкор *m* [1; -кра] (**свекрóвь** *f* [8]) father-(mother-)in-law (*husband's father or mother resp.*).
свер|гáть [1], ⟨∠гнуть⟩ [21] overthrow; dethrone (с трóна); shake off (*yoke*); **~жéние** *n* [12] overthrow; **∠ить** *s.* ~ять.
сверк|áть [1], *once* ⟨~нýть⟩ [20] sparkle, glitter; flash; мóлния ~áет it lightens.
сверл|éние *n* [12], **~ильный** [14] drilling; **~ить** [13], ⟨про-⟩, **~ó** *n* [9; *pl. st.*: свёрла] drill.
свер|нýть(ся) *s.* свёртывать(ся) & сворáчивать; **∠стник** *s.* ровéсник.
свёрт|ок *m* [1; -тка] roll; parcel; **~ывать** [1], ⟨свернýть⟩ [20] roll (up); turn; curtail; break up (*camp*); twist; **-ся** coil up; curdle; coagulate.
сверх (Р) above, beyond; over; besides; ~ тогó moreover; **~звуковóй** [14] supersonic; **~прибыль** *f* [8] surplus profit; **∠у** from above; **~урóчный** [14] overtime; **~штáтный** [14] supernumerary; **~ъестéственный** [14 *sh.*] supernatural.
сверчóк *m* [1; -чкá] *zo.* cricket.
свер|ять [28], ⟨∠ить⟩ [13] compare, collate.
свéсить *s.* свéшивать.
свести(сь) *s.* сводить(ся).
свет *m* [1] light; world (in на П); day(light); (high) society; P dear, darling; чуть ~ at dawn; **~áть** [1] dawn; **~ило** *n* [9] star; (*celestial*) body; **~ить(ся)** [15] shine.
светл|éть [8], ⟨по-⟩ brighten; grow light(er); **~о...** light...; **∠ый** [14; -тел, -тлá, -о] light, bright; serene; **~як** *m* [1 *e.*], **~ячóк** [1 *e.*; -чкá] glowworm.

свето|во́й [14] light...; **~маскиро́вка** *f* [5; *g/pl.*: -вок] blackout; **~фо́р** *m* [1] traffic light.
све́тский [16] secular, worldly; of high society.
светя́щийся [17] luminous.
свеча́ *f* [5; *pl.*: све́чи, -е́й, -а́м] candle; ⚡ plug.
све́|шивать [1], ‹~сить› [15] hang down; dangle; **-ся** hang over.
сви|ва́ть [1], ‹~ть› [совью́, -вьёшь; *cf.* вить] braid, plait; build (*nest*).
свида́ни|е *n* [12] appointment, meeting (at на П); до ~я good-by(e).
свиде́тель *m* [4], **~ница** *f* [5] witness; **~ство** *n* [9] evidence; certificate; licence; **~ствовать** [7], ‹за-› testify; *impf.* (о П) show.
свина́рник *m* [1] pigsty.
свине́ц *m* [1; -нца́] lead.
свин|и́на *f* [5] pork; **∠ка** *f* [5; *g/pl.*: -нок] mumps; морска́я ∠ка guinea pig; **~о́й** [14] pig...; pork...; **∠ство** *n* [9] dirty *or* rotten act, smut; **~цо́вый** [14] lead(en).
сви́н|чивать [1], ‹~ти́ть› [15 *e.*; -нчу́, -нти́шь; сви́нченный] screw together, fasten with screws.
свинья́ *f* [6; *pl. st.*, *gen.*: -не́й; *a.* -нья́м] pig, hog, swine.
свире́ль *f* [8] pipe, reed.
свире́п|ствовать [7] rage; **~ый** [14 *sh.*] fierce, furious, grim.
свиса́ть [1] hang down; slouch.
свист *m* [1] whistle; hiss; **~а́ть** [3] & **~е́ть** [11], *once* ‹∠нуть› [20] whistle; *pf.* P pilfer; **~о́к** *m* [1; -тка́] whistle.
сви́т|а *f* [5] retinue, suite; **~ер** (-tɛr) *m* [1] sweater; **~ок** *m* [1; -тка] roll; **~ь** *s.* свива́ть. [mad.
свихну́ть F [20] *pf.* sprain; **-ся** go
свищ *m* [1 *e.*] fistula; crack.
свобо́д|а *f* [5] freedom, liberty; на ~у (*set*) free; **~ный** [14; -ден, -дна] free (from, of от Р); vacant (*seat, etc.*); spare (*time, etc.*); ready (*money*); easy; loose; fluent; exempt (from от Р); **~омы́слящий** [17] freethinking; *su.* freethinker, liberal.
свод *m* [1] ⚠ vault; ⚖ code.
своди́ть [15], ‹свести́› [25] lead, take (down); bring (together); close (*vault*); reduce (to в В); square (*accounts*); contract; remove; drive (mad с ума́); ~ на нет bring to nought; **-ся**, ‹-сь› (к Д) come *or* amount (to), result (in); turn (into на В).
сво́д|ка *f* [5; *g/pl.*: -док] summary; report, communiqué; *typ.* revise; **~ный** [14] summary; step...; **~ча́тый** [14] vaulted.
свое|во́льный [14; -лен, -льна] self-willed, wil(l)ful; **~вре́менный** [14; -менен, -менна]] timely; **~нра́вный** [14; -вен, -вна] capricious; **~обра́зный** [14; -зен, -зна] original; peculiar.
свози́ть [15], ‹свезти́› [24] ta
сво|й *m*, ~я́ *f*, ~ё *n*, ~и́ *pl.* [24] m his, her, its, our, your, their (*ref.* one's own; peculiar; *su. pl.* on people, folks, relations; не ~й fran (*voice* in Т); **∠йственный** [14 *s.* peculiar (to Д); (р.'s Д) usual; ∠ **ство** *n* [9] property, quality; F kir
сво́|лочь *f* [8] rabble, riff-raff; rasc **~ра** *f* [5] pack; **~ра́чивать** [‹сверну́ть› [20] &, Р, ‹~роти́т [15] turn (off с Р); **~я́ченица** *f* sister-in-law (*wife's sister*).
свы|ка́ться [1], ‹∠кнуться› [2 get used (to с Т); **~сока́** haughti **∠ше** from above; (Р) over; beyor
связ|а́ть(ся) *s.* ∠ывать(ся); **~и́ст** [1] signalman; **∠ка** *f* [5; *g/p* -зок] bunch; *anat.* ligament; (*voc* cord; *gr.* copula; **∠ный** [16; -зе -зна] coherent; **∠ывать** [1], ‹~а́т [3] tie (together), bind; conne join; unite; associate; *teleph.* p through, connect; **-ся** get in touch, contact; associate (with с Т **~ь** *f* [8; в -зи́] tie, bond; connecti (*Brt.* connexion); relation; conta liaison; ⚔ signal (*service, etc.*); co munication; post(al system).
свят|и́ть [15 *e.*; -ячу́, -яти́шь], ‹о consecrate, hallow; **∠ки** *f/pl.* *gen.*: -ток] Christmastide (at на П **~о́й** [14; свят, -а́, -о] holy; sacre godly; solemn; Easter (week *f*); *su.* saint; **∠ость** *f* [8] holine sanctity; **~ота́тство** *n* [9] sacrileg **~о́ша** *m/f* [5] hypocrite; **~ы́ня** *f* relic; sanctuary.
свяще́нн|ик *m* [1] priest; **~ый** [*sh.*] holy; sacred.
с. г. *abbr.*: сего́ го́да; *cf.* сей.
сгиб *m* [1], **~а́ть** [1], ‹согну́ть› [2 bend, curve, fold; *v/i.* **-ся**.
сгла́|живать [1], ‹~дить› [1 smooth; **-ся** be smoothed (out).
сгнива́ть [1] *s.* гнить.
сго́вор *m* [1] F *s.* угово́р; **~и́ть** [13] *pf.* agree; come to terms; **∠ч вый** [14 *sh.*] compliant, amenab
сго|ня́ть [28], ‹согна́ть› [сгон сго́нишь; согна́л, -а́, -о; со́гна ный] drive (off); **~ра́ние** *n* [1 combustion; **~ра́ть** [1], ‹~ре́т [9] burn down; perish; die (of от Р); **~ряча́** in a temper.
сгр|еба́ть [1], ‹~ести́› [24-б-: сгр бу́; сгрёб, сгребла́] rake up; shov (down); **~ужа́ть** [1], ‹~узи́ть› [& 15 *e.*; -ужу́, -у́зишь; -у́женны & -ужённый] unload.
сгу|сти́ть *s.* ~ща́ть; **∠сток** *m* [-тка] clot; **~ща́ть** [1], ‹~сти́т [15 *e.*; -ущу́, -усти́шь; -ущённы thicken; condense; ~ща́ть кра́с exaggerate.
сда|ва́ть [5], ‹~ть› [сдам, сдаш *etc. s.* дать] deliver, hand in (over); surrender; check, registe rent, let (out); deal (*cards*); retu

(change); pass (examination); yield; P seem; -ся surrender; ~ётся ... ... for rent (Brt. to let); ~вливать [1], ⟨~вить⟩ [14] squeeze; ~ть(ся) s. ~вать(ся); ~ча f [5] surrender; delivery; deal; change; check, register.
двиг m [1] shift; (land)slide; ~ать [1], ⟨сдвинуть⟩ [20] move (v/i. -ся); join; knit (brow).
дел|ка f [5; g/pl.: -лок] bargain, transaction, deal; arrangement, settlement; ~ьный [14] piece(-work).
держ|анный [14 sh.] reserved, (self-)restrained; ~ивать [1], ⟨~áть⟩ [4] check, restrain; suppress; keep (word, etc.); -ся control o.s.
дирáть [1], ⟨содрáть⟩ [сдеру́, -рёшь; содрáл, -á, -о; сóдранный] tear off (or down), strip; flay (a. fig).
добн|ый [14]: ~ая бу́л(оч)ка f bun.
дружи́ться s. подружи́ться.
ду|вáть [1], ⟨~ть⟩ [16], once ⟨~нуть⟩ [20] blow off (or away); ~ру F foolishly.
еáнс m [1] sitting; cinema: show.
ебестóимость f [8] prime cost.
еб|я́ [21] myself, yourself, himself, herself, itself, ourselves, yourselves, themselves (refl.); oneself; к ~é home; into one's room; от ~я́ on o.'s behalf; тáк ~é so-so; ~ялюби́вый [14 sh.] selfish, self-loving.
ев m [1] sowing.
евастóполь m [4] Sevastopol.
éвер m [1] north; cf. востóк; ~ный [14] north(ern); northerly; arctic; ~ный Ледови́тый океáн m Arctic Ocean; ~о-востóк m [1] northeast; ~о-востóчный [14] northeast...; ~о-зáпад m [1] northwest; ~о-зáпадный [14] northwest...
егóдня today; ~ у́тром this morning; ~шний [15] today's; this (day).
ед|éть [8], ⟨по-⟩ turn gray (Brt. grey); ~инá f [5] gray hair; pl. a. fig. great age.
едл|áть [1], ⟨о-⟩, ~ó n [9; pl. st.: сёдла, сёдел, сёдлам] saddle.
едо|волóсый [14 sh.], ~й [14; сед, -á, -о] gray(-haired, -headed), Brt. grey.
едóк m [1 e.] horseman; passenger.
едьмóй [14] seventh; cf. пя́тый.
езóн m [1] season; ~ный [14] seasonal.
ей m, сия́ f, сиé n, сии́ pl. † [29] this; сим herewith, hereby; при сём enclosed; сегó гóда (мéсяца) of this year (month); cf. порá.
ейчáс now, at present; presently, (a. ~ же) immediately, at once; just now).
екрéт m [1] secret (in по Д, под T); ~ариáт m [1] secretariat; ~áрь m [4 e.] secretary; ~ничать F [1] be secretive, act secretely; whisper; ~ный [14; -тен, -тна] secret; confidential.
ек|суáльный [14; -лен, -льна] sexual; ~та f [5] sect; ~тор m [1] sector; sphere, branch.
секу́нд|а f [5] second; ~ный [14] second...; ~омéр m [1] stop watch.
селёдка f [5; g/pl.: -док] herring.
селез|ёнка f [5; g/pl : -нок] anat. spleen; '~ень m [4; -зня] drake.
селéние n [12] settlement, colony.
сели́т|ра f [5] saltpeter, niter, Brt. nitre; ~ь(ся) [13] s. поселя́ть(ся).
сел|ó n [9; pl. st.: сёла] village (in в or на П); на ~é a. in the country; ни к ~у́ ни к гóроду F without rhyme or reason.
сельд|ерéй m [3] celery; ~ь f [8; from g/pl. e.] herring.
сéль|ский [16] rural, country..., village...; ~ское хозя́йство n agriculture; ~скохозя́йственный [14] agricultural; farming; ~совéт m [1] village soviet.
сéльтерская f [16] Seltzer.
сёмга f [5] salmon.
семéй|ный [14] family...; married; ~ство n [9] family.
Семён m [1] Simeon.
семен|и́ть F [13] trip, mince; ~нóй [14] seed...; seminal.
семёрка f [5; g/pl.: -рок] seven; cf. двóйка.
сéмеро [37] seven; cf. двóе.
семé|стр m [1] term, semester; '~чко n [9; pl.: -чки, -чек, -чкам] seed.
семи|деся́тый [14] seventieth; cf. пя́(тидеся́)тый; ~лéтка f [5; g/pl.: -ток] seven-year school (or plan); ~лéтний [15] seven-year (old), of seven.
семинáр m [1], ~ий m [3] seminar; ~ия f [7] seminary.
семисóтый [14] seven hundredth.
семнáдцат|ый [14] seventeenth; cf. пя́тый; ~ь [35] seventeen; cf. пять.
семь [35] seven; cf. пять & пя́тый; ~десят [35] seventy; ~сóт [36] seven hundred; ~ю seven times.
семья́ f [6; pl.: сéмьи, семéй, сéмьям] family; ~ни́н m [1] family man.
сéмя n [13; pl.: -менá, -мя́н, -менáм] seed (a. fig.).
сенáт m [1] senate; ~ор m [1] senator.
сéни f/pl. [8; from gen. e.] hall(way).
сéно n [9] hay; ~вáл m [1] hayloft; ~кóс m [1] haymaking; cf. коси́лка.
сен|сациóнный [14; -óнен, -óнна] sensational; ~тиментáльный [14; -лен, -льна] sentimental.
сентя́брь m [4 e.] September.
сень † f [8; в -ни́] shade; shelter.
сепарáтный [14] separate.
сéра f [5] sulfur; F earwax.
серб m [1], ~(ия́н)ка f [5; g/pl.: -б(ия́н)ок] Serb(ian); ~ский [16] Serbian.
серви́|з m [1] service, set; ~ровáть [7] (im)pf. serve.
Сергéй m [3] Sergius, Serge.

серде́чный [14; -чен, -чна] heart('s); hearty, cordial; intimate; dear; best.
серди́|тый [14 *sh.*] angry, mad (with, at на В), wrathful; irascible, fretful; spiteful, vicious; **~ть** [15], ⟨рас-⟩ annoy, vex, fret, anger; **-ся** be(come) angry (with на В).
се́рдц|е *n* [11; *pl. e.*: -дца́, -де́ц, -дца́м] heart; temper; anger; darling, love, sweetheart (*address*); от всего́ ~а whole-heartedly; по́ ~у (Д) to one's liking; положа́ ру́ку на́ ~е F (quite) frankly; **~ебие́ние** *n* [12] palpitation; **~еви́на** *f* [5] core, heart.
серебр|и́стый [14 *sh.*] silvery; **~и́ть** [13], ⟨по-, вы́-⟩ silver; **-ся** glisten like silver; **~о́** *n* [9] silver; **~яный** [14] silver(y).
середи́на *f* [5] middle; center (*Brt.* -tre); mean.
Сер|ёж([ень]к)а *m* [5] *dim. of* Серге́й; **~е́ть** [8], ⟨по-⟩ turn (*impf.* show) gray (*Brt.* grey).
сержа́нт *m* [1] sergeant; мла́дший ~ corporal.
сери́|йный [14] serial; multiple; **'~я** *f* [7] series.
се́рна *f* [5] chamois.
се́р|ный [14] sulfuric; sulfur...; **~ова́тый** [14 *sh.*] grayish, Brt. greyish.
серп *m* [1 *e.*] sickle; crescent.
се́рый [14; сер, -а́, -о] gray, *Brt.* grey; dull (*a. fig.* = humdrum).
се́рьги *f/pl.* [5; серёг, серьга́м; *sg. e.*] earrings.
серьёзн|ый [14; -зен, -зна] serious, grave; earnest (in ~о); ~о *a.* indeed, really.
се́ссия *f* [7] session (in на П).
сестра́ *f* [5; *pl.*: сёстры, сестёр, сёстрам] sister; nurse; на́ша ~ F (such as) we.
сесть *s.* сади́ться.
се́т|ка *f* [5; *g/pl.*: -ток] net; ⚡ grid; scale; **~овать** [1] complain (about на В); **~ча́тка** *f* [5; *g/pl.*: -ток] retina; **~ь** *f* [8; в сети́; *from g/pl. e.*] net; network.
сече́ние *n* [12] section.
сечь[1] [26; *pt. e.*; сек, секла́] cut (up), chop, hew; cleave; **-ся** split; ravel; **~**[2] [26: *pt. st.*; сек, се́кла], ⟨вы́-⟩ whip, flog.
се́ялка *f* [5; *g/pl.*: -лок] seeder.
се́ять [27], ⟨по-⟩ sow (*a. fig.*).
сжа́литься [13] *pf.* (над Т) have *or* take pity (on), pity.
сжа́т|ие *n* [12] pressure; compression; **~ый** [14] compressed; compact, concise, terse; **~ь(ся)** *s.* сжима́ть(ся) & жать[1], жать[2].
сжига́ть [1], ⟨сжечь⟩ *cf.* жечь.
сжима́ть [1], ⟨сжать⟩ [сожму́, -мёшь; сжа́тый] (com)press, squeeze; clench; **-ся** contract; shrink; become clenched.
сза́ди (from) behind (*as prp.*: Р).
сзыва́ть *s.* созыва́ть.
Сиби́р|ь *f* [8] Siberia; **~ский** [1… **~я́к** *m* [1 *e.*], **~я́чка** *f* [5; *g/pl.*: -че… Siberian.
си́вый [14; сив, -а́, -о] (ash) gr… (grey).
сига́р(е́т)а *f* [5] cigar(ette).
сигна́л *m* [1], **~изи́ровать** … (*im*)*pf.*, **~ьный** [14] signal; alarm…
сиде́лка *f* [5; *g/pl.*: -лок] nurse.
сиде́|нье *n* [10] seat; **~ть** [11; сиж… sit (at, over за Т); be, stay; fit (a… на П); **-ся**: ему́ не сиди́тся … can't sit still.
сидр *m* [1] cider.
сидя́чий [17] sedentary; sitting.
си́зый [14; сиз, -а́, -о] (bluish) gr… *Brt.* grey; dove-colo(u)red.
си́л|а *f* [5] strength; force; pow… might; vigo(u)r; intensity; efficac… energy; volume; свои́ми ~ами … o. s.; в ~у (Р) by virtue (of); не… ~ах unable; не по ~ам above on… strength; ~ нет F awfully; изо вс… ~ F with all one's might; **~а́ч** *m* … *e.*] athlete; **~иться** [13] try, endea… o(u)r; **~ово́й** [14] power...
сило́к *m* [1; -лка́] snare, noose.
си́льн|ый [14; си́лен & силе… -льна́, -о, си́льны́] strong; powerf… mighty; intense; heavy (*rain*); b… (*cold*); great; ⚡ power...; ~о *a.* ve… much; hard.
си́мвол *m* [1] symbol; **~и́ческ…** [16], **~и́чный** [14; -чен, -чна] sy… bolic(al).
симметри́|чный [14; -чен, -ч… symmetrical; **~я** *f* [7] symmetry.
симпат|изи́ровать [7] sympath… (with Д); **~и́чный** [14; -чен, -ч… nice, sympathetic; он мне **~и́ч…** I like him; **~тия** *f* [7] sympathy.
симул|и́ровать [7] (*im*)*pf.* feig… sham; malinger; **~я́нт** *m* [… **~я́нтка** *f* [5; *g/pl.*: -ток] simulat…
симфони́|ческий [16] symphon… symphony...; **'~я** *f* [7] symphony…
синдика́т *m* [1] syndicate.
син|ева́ *f* [5] blue; **~ева́тый** [14 *s…* bluish; **~е́ть** [8], ⟨по-⟩ turn (*im…* show) blue; **~ий** [15; синь, си… си́не] blue; **~и́льный** [14] hyd… cyanic, prussic (*acid*); **~и́ть** [1… ⟨под-⟩ blue; **~и́ца** *f* [5] titmous…
син|о́д *m* [1] synod; **~о́ним** *m* … synonym; **~таксис** *m* [1] synt… **~тез** *m* [1] synthesis; **~тети́ческ…** [16] synthetic(al); **~хронизи́р…вать** [7] (*im*)*pf.* synchronize.
синь *f* [8], **~ка** *f* [5; *g/pl.*: -не… blue.
синя́к *m* [1 *e.*] livid spot, bruise.
си́плый [14; сипл, -а́, -о] hoarse…
сире́на *f* [5] siren.
сире́н|евый [14], **~ь** *f* [8] lilac.
сиро́п *m* [1] syrup.
сирота́ *m/f* [5; *pl. st.*: сиро́… orphan.
систе́ма *f* [5] system; **~ти́ческ…**

[16], ~ти́чный [14; -чен, -чна] [s]ystematic(al).
[с]итец m [1; -тца] chintz, cotton.
[с]ито n [9] sieve.
[С]ици́лия f [7] Sicily.
[с]ия́|ние n [12] radiance; light, shine; [h]alo; ~ть [28] shine, beam; radiate.
[с]каз|а́ние n [12] legend; saga; [s]tory; ~а́ть s. говори́ть; ∠ка f [5; [g]/pl.: -зок] fairy tale; tale, fib; ∠оч[н]ый [14; -чен, -чна] fabulous, [f]antastic; fairy (tale)...
[с]казу́емое n [14] gr. predicate.
[с]как|а́ть [3] skip, hop, leap; gal[l]op; race; ~ово́й [14] race...; racing.
[с]кал|а́ f [5; pl. st.] rock, cliff, crag; [~]и́стый [14 sh.] rocky, cliffy; ∠ить [13], ⟨о-⟩ show, bare (one's teeth); impf. grin; jeer; ∠ка f [5; g/pl.: [-]лок] rolling pin; ∠ывать [1], ⟨ско[л]о́ть⟩ [17] pin together; split (off); [b]rick.
[с]кам|е́ечка f [5; g/pl.: -чек] foot[s]tool; a. dim. of ~е́йка f [5; g/pl.: [-]е́ек], ~ья́ f [6; nom/pl. a. st.] bench; [~]ья́ подсуди́мых dock.
[с]канда́л m [1] scandal; row; F shame; [~]ить [13], ⟨на-⟩ row; ~ьный [14; [-]лен, -льна] scandalous; F wretch[e]d.
[с]кандина́вский [16] Scandinavian.
[с]ка́пливать(ся) [1] s. скопля́ть [(]-ся).
[с]кар|б F [1] belongings, things pl.; [~]е́дный F [14; -ден, -дна] stingy; [~]лати́на f [5] scarlet fever.
[с]кат m [1] slope, pitch.
[с]кат|а́ть s. ска́тывать 2; ∠ерть f [8; from g/pl. e.] tablecloth.
[с]ка́т|ывать [1] 1. ⟨~и́ть⟩ [15] roll [(]or slide) down (v/i. -ся); 2. ⟨~а́ть⟩ [1] roll (up); P copy.
[с]ка́ч|ка f [5; g/pl.: -чек] gallop; [p]l. horse race(s); ~о́к s. прыжо́к.
[с]ка́шивать [1], ⟨скоси́ть⟩ [15] mow [o]ff or down; slope; bevel.
[с]ква́жина f [5] chink, crack; pore; [⊕] hole; замо́чная ~ keyhole.
[с]квер m [1] square, park; ~носло́[в]ить [14] talk smut; ∠ный [14; [-]рен, -рна́, -о] nasty, foul.
[с]квоз|и́ть [15; -и́т] shine through, [a]ppear; ~и́т there is a draft, Brt. [d]raught; ~но́й [14] through...; [t]horough...; transparent; ~ня́к m [1 e.] draft, Brt. draught; ~ь (В) [t]hrough.
[с]кворе́|ц m [1; -рца́] starling; ~ч[н]ица (-ʃn-) f [5] nestling box.
[с]келе́т m [1] skeleton.
[с]епти́ческий [16] skeptic(al).
[с]ки́|дка f [5; g/pl.: -док] discount, [r]ebate; ~дывать [1], ⟨~нуть⟩ [20] [t]hrow off or down; take or put off; [d]iscount, reduce; ~петр m [1] scep[t]er, Brt. -tre; ~пида́р m [1] tur[p]entine; ~рд m [1 e.] haystack.
[с]кис|а́ть [1], ⟨∠нуть⟩ [21] turn [s]our.

скита́|лец m [1; -льца] wanderer; ~ться [1] wander, rove.
склад m [1] warehouse, storehouse (in на П); ⚔ depot; constitution, disposition, turn; breed; way (of life); F harmony; sense; ∠ка f [5; g/pl.: -док] pleat, fold; crease; wrinkle; ~но́й [14] fold(ing), collapsible; camp...; falt(boat); ∠ный [14; -ден, -дна́, -о] harmonious; coherent; fluent, smooth; P well-made (or -built); accommodating; ∠чина f [5]: в ~чину by clubbing (together); ∠ывать [1], ⟨сложи́ть⟩ [16] lay or put (together, up, down); pile up; pack (up); fold; add; compose; lay down (arms; one's life); сложа́ ру́ки idle; -ся (be) form (-ed), develop; F club (together).
скле́и|вать [1], ⟨~ть⟩ [13; -е́ю] stick together (v/i. -ся).
склеп m [1] crypt, vault.
скло́ка f [5] squabble.
склон m [1] slope; ~е́ние n [12] inclination; gr. declension; ast. declination; ~и́ть(ся) s. ~я́ть(ся); ∠ность f [8] inclination (fig.; to, for к Д), disposition; ∠ный [14; -о́нен, -онна́, -о] inclined (to к Д), disposed; ~я́ть [28] 1. ⟨~и́ть⟩ [13; -оню́, -о́нишь; -онённый] bend, incline (a. fig.; v/i. -ся; sink); persuade; 2. ⟨просклоня́ть⟩ gr. (-ся be) decline(d).
скоб|а́ f [5; pl.: ско́бы, скоб, скоба́м] cramp (iron); ∠ка f [5; g/pl.: -бок] cramp; gr., typ. bracket, parenthesis; ~ли́ть [13; -облю́, -о́бли́шь; -о́бленный] scrape; ~яно́й [14] hard(ware).
скова́ть s. ско́вывать.
сковорода́ f [5; pl.: ско́вороды, -ро́д, -да́м] frying pan.
ско́в|ывать [1], ⟨~а́ть⟩ [7 e.; скую́, скуёшь] forge (together); weld; fetter, chain; bind; arrest.
сколо́ть s. ска́лывать.
скольз|и́ть [15 e.; -льжу́, -льзи́шь], once ⟨~ну́ть⟩ [20] slide, glide, slip; ∠кий [16; -зок, -зка́, -о] slippery.
ско́лько [32] how (or as) much, many; ~ лет, ~ зим s. ве́чность F.
сконча́ться [1] pf. die, expire.
скоп|ля́ть [28], ⟨~и́ть⟩ [14] accumulate, gather (v/i. -ся), amass; save; ~ле́ние n [12] accumulation; gathering, crowd.
скорб|е́ть [10 e.; -блю́, -би́шь] grieve (over о П); ∠ный [14; -бен, -бна] mournful, sorrowful; ~ь f [8] grief, sorrow.
скорлупа́ f [5; pl. st.: -лу́пы] shell.
скорня́к m [1 e.] furrier.
скоро|гово́рка f [5; g/pl.: -рок] tongue twister; rapid speech, sputter; ∠мный [14; -мен, -мна] meat, milk (food, forbidden in Lent); ~пости́жный [14; -жен, -жна] sudden; ~спе́лый [14 sh.] early; pre-

cocious; **~стной** [14] (high-)speed-...; **'~сть** *f* [8; *from g/pl. e.*] speed; rate; *mot.* gear; груз большо́й (ма́лой) '~сти express (ordinary) freight; **~те́чный** [14; -чен, -чна] transient; ⚕ galloping.

ско́р|ый [14; скор, -á, -o] quick, fast, rapid, swift; speedy, prompt; first (*aid*); near (*future*); early (*reply*); ~о *a.* soon; ~ée всегó F most probably; на ~ую ру́ку F in haste, offhand, anyhow.

скоси́ть *s.* ска́шивать.

скот *m* [1 *e.*] cattle, livestock; **~и́на** *f* [5] F cattle; P brute; dolt, boor; **∠ный** [14]: ∠ный двор cattle yard; **~обо́йня** *f* [6; *g/pl.*: -óен] slaughterhouse; **~ово́дство** *n* [9] cattle breeding; **~ский** [16] brutish, bestial, swinish.

скребо́к *m* [1; -бкá] scraper.

скре́жет *m* [1], **~áть** [3] (T) gnash.

скре́п|а *f* [5] cramp, clamp; **~и́ть** *s.* ~ля́ть; **~ка** *f* [5; *g/pl.*: -пок] (paper) clip; **~ле́ние** *n* [12] fastening; **~ля́ть** [28], ⟨~и́ть⟩ [14 *e.*; -плю́, -пи́шь; -плённый] fasten; tighten; corroborate; validate; countersign; ~я́ сéрдце reluctantly.

скрести́ [24 -б-: скребу́; скрёб] scrape; scratch.

скре́щива|ть [1], ⟨скрести́ть⟩ [15 *e.*; -ещу́, -ести́шь; -ещённый] cross (*v/i.* **-ся**); **~ние** *n* [12] crossing.

скрип *m* [1] creak; scratch; **~áч** *m* [1 *e.*] violinist; **~е́ть** [10 *e.*; -плю́, -пи́шь], ⟨про-⟩, *once* ⟨∠нуть⟩ [20] creak; scratch; grit, gnash; **∠ка** *f* [5; *g/pl.*: -пок] violin.

скро́мн|ость *f* [8] modesty; **~ый** [14; -мен, -мнá, -o] modest; frugal.

скру́|чивать [1], ⟨~ти́ть⟩ [15] braid; roll; bind; P bend.

скры|ва́ть [1], ⟨~ть⟩ [22] hide, conceal (from от P); **-ся** disappear; hide; **∠тность** *f* [8] reserve; **∠тный** [14; -тен, -тна] reserved, reticent; **∠тый** [14] concealed; latent; secret; **∠ть(ся)** *s.* ~ва́ть(ся).

скря́га *m/f* [5] miser.

ску́дный [14; -ден, -днá, -o] scanty, poor.

ску́ка *f* [5] boredom, ennui.

скула́ *f* [5; *pl. st.*] cheekbone; **~стый** [14 *sh.*] with high cheek-bones.

скули́ть [13] whimper.

скульпту́ра *f* [5] sculpture.

ску́мбрия *f* [7] mackerel.

скуп|áть [1], ⟨~и́ть⟩ [14] buy up.

скуп|и́ться [14], ⟨по-⟩ be stingy (*or* sparing), stint (in, of на В); **~о́й** [14; скуп, -á, -o] avaricious, stingy; sparing (in на В); scanty, poor; taciturn (на словá); *su.* miser; **∠ость** *f* [8] avarice.

скуч|áть [1] be bored; (по П *or* Д) long (for), miss; **∠ный** (-ʃn-) [14; -чен, -чнá, -o] boring, tedious, dull; sad; (Д) ~но feel bored.

слаб|е́ть [8], ⟨о-⟩ weaken, slacken; **~и́тельный** [14] laxative (*n a. su.*); **~ово́льный** [14; -лен, -льна] weak-willed (*or* -minded); **~оси́льный** [14; -лен, -льна] *s.* ∠ый; **∠ость** *f* [8] weakness (*a. fig.* = foible; for к Д); infirmity; **~оу́мный** [14; -мен, -мна] feeble-minded; **~охара́ктерный** [14; -рен, -рна] flabby; **∠ый** [14; слаб, -á, -o] weak (a. ⚡), feeble; faint; infirm; delicate; flabby; poor.

сла́в|а *f* [5] glory; fame, renown; reputation, repute; (Д) hail; long live; ~а бо́гу! God be praised! thank goodness!; на ~у F first-rate, A-one; **~ить** [14], ⟨про-⟩ glorify, praise, extol; **-ся** be famous (for T); **~ный** [14; -вен, -внá, -o] famous, glorious; F nice; capital, dandy.

славян|и́н *m* [1; *pl.*: -я́не, -я́н], **∠ка** *f* [5; *g/pl.*: -нок] Slav; **∠ский** [16] Slavic, *Brt.* Slavonic.

слага́ть [1], ⟨сложи́ть⟩ [16] compose; lay down; resign (from), exonerate; relieve o.s. (of); *cf.* складывать(ся); **-ся** *a.* be composed.

сла́д|кий [16; -док, -дкá, -o; *comp.* сла́ще] sweet; sugary; ~ое *su.* dessert (for на В); **~остный** [14; -тен, -тна] sweet, delightful; **~острастие** *n* [12] voluptuousness; **~острастный** [14; -тен, -тна] voluptuous; **~ость** *f* [8] sweetness; delight; *cf.* сла́сти.

сла́женный [14 *sh.*] harmonious.

сла́нец *m* [1; -нца] slate.

сла́сти *f/pl.* [8; *from gen. e.*] candy *sg.*, *Brt. a.* sweets.

слать [шлю, шлёшь], ⟨по-⟩ send.

слаща́вый [14 *sh.*] sugary.

сле́ва on, to (*or* from) the left.

слегка́ (-xk-) slightly; in passing.

след *m* [1; *g/sg. e.* & -ду; на -ду́; *pl. e.*] trace (*a. fig.*), track; footprint, footstep; print; scent; **∠ом** (right) behind; его́ и ~ просты́л F he was off and away; **~и́ть** [15 *e.*; -ежу́, -еди́шь] (за T, † B) watch, follow; look after; shadow; trace.

сле́доват|ель *m* [4] examining magistrate; **~ельно** consequently, therefore; so; **~ь** [7] (за T; Д) follow; ensue (from из P); go, move; (Д) *impers.* should, ought to; be to be; как сле́дует properly, duly; downright, thoroughly; as it should be; кому́ *or* куда́ сле́дует to the proper p. *or* quarter; ско́лько с меня́ сле́дует? how much do I have to pay?

сле́дствие *n* [12] consequence; inquest, trial.

сле́дующий [17] following, next.

сле́жка *f* [5; *g/pl.*: -жек] shadowing.

слез|á *f* [5; *pl.*: слёзы, слёз, слезáм] tear; **~áть** [1], ⟨~ть⟩ [24 *st.*] climb *or* get down; dismount, alight

get out; F come off; ~**иться** [15; -ится] water; ~**ливый** [14 *h.*] tearful, lachrymose; ~**оточивый** [14] tear (*gas*); watering; ~**ть** *s.* ~ать.
слеп|ень *m* [4; -пня] gadfly; ~**ец** *m* [1; -пца] blind man; ~**ить** **1.** [14 *e.*; -плю, -пишь], ‹о-› [ослеплённый] blind; dazzle; **2.** [14] *pf.*; *impf.*: ~**лять** [28] stick together (*v/i.* **-ся**); *s. a.* лепить; ∠**нуть** [21], ‹о-› grow (*or* become) blind; ~**ой** [14; слеп, -а, -о] blind (in, *Brt.* of *one eye* на В); dull (*glass*); indistinct; *su.* blind man; ∠**ок** *m* [1; -пка] mould, cast; ~**ота** *f* [5] blindness.
слесар|ь *m* [4; *pl.*: -ря, *etc. e.*, & -ри] locksmith; fitter, mechanic.
слёт *m* [1] flight; rally, meeting (at на П).
слет|ать [1], ‹~еть› [11] fly (down, off); F fall (down, off); **-ся** fly together; F gather.
слечь F [26 г/ж: слягу, сляжешь; сляг(те)!] *pf.* fall ill.
слива *f* [5] plum.
сли|вать [1], ‹~ть› [солью, -льёшь; *cf.* лить] pour (off, out, together); fuse, merge, amalgamate (*v/i.* **-ся**).
сливк|и *f/pl.* [5; *gen.*: -вок] cream (*a. fig.* = elite); ~**очный** [14] creamy; (*ice*) cream.
слиз|истый [14 *sh.*] mucous; slimy; ~**ь** *f* [8] slime; mucus, phlegm.
слипаться [1] stick together; close.
слит|ный [14] conjoint; continuous; ~но *a.* together; in one word; ~**ок** *m* [1; -тка] ingot; ~**ь(ся)** *s.* сливать(ся).
слич|ать [1], ‹~ить› [16 *e.*; -чу, -чишь; -чённый] compare, collate.
слишком too, too much; это (уж) ~ F that beats everything.
слияние *n* [12] confluence; fusion, amalgamation; blending.
словак *m* [1] Slovak.
словар|ный [14]: ~ный состав *m* stock of words; ~**ь** *m* [4 *e.*] dictionary; vocabulary, glossary; lexicon.
слов|ацкий [16], ~**ачка** *f* [5; *g/pl.*: -чек] Slovak; ~**енец** *m* [1; -нца], ~**енка** *f* [5; *g/pl.*: -нок], ~**енский** [16] Slovene.
словесн|ость *f* [8] literature; (*folk-*)lore; philology; ~**ый** [14] verbal, oral; literary; philologic(al).
словно as if; like; F as it were.
слово *n* [9; *pl. e.*] word (in a T; ... or ... И/в В); term; speech; к слову сказать by the way; на словах by word of mouth, orally; по словам according to; просить (предоставить Д) ~ ask (give p.) permission to speak; ~**изменение** *n* [12] inflection (*Brt.* -xion); ~**охотливый** [14 *sh.*] talkative.
слог *m* [1; *from g/pl. e.*] syllable; style.
слоёный [14] puff (*paste*).
слож|ение *n* [12] addition; composition; constitution, build; laying down; resignation; ~**ить(ся)** *s.* складывать(ся), слагать(ся) & класть 2.; ∠**ность** *f* [8] complexity, complicacy, complication; ∠**ный** [14; -жен, -жна, -о] complicated, complex, intricate; compound.
сло|истый [14 *sh.*] stratiform; flaky; ~**й** *m* [3; *pl. e.*: слои, слоёв] layer, stratum (in T *pl.*); coat(ing).
слом *m* [1] demolition, destruction; ~**ить** [14] *pf.* break, overcome; overpower; ~я голову F headlong.
слон *m* [1 *e.*] elephant; bishop (*chess*); ~**овый** [14]: ~овая кость *f* ivory.
слоняться F [28] linger, loaf.
слу|га *m* [5; *pl. st.*] servant; ∠**жащий** *m* [17] employee; ∠**жба** *f* [5] (на П) service (in); employment, job; office, work (at); duty (on); ~**жебный** [14] office...; official; secondary, subordinate, subservient; *gr.* relational; ~**жение** *n* [12] service; ~**жить** [16], ‹по-› serve (a p./th. Д); work (as T); be.
слух *m* [1] hearing; ear (by на В; по Д); rumo(u)r, hearsay; news, sign; ~**овой** [14] of hearing; acoustic(al); ear...; dormer (*window*).
случа|й *m* [3] case; occurrence, event; occasion (on по Д; при П), opportunity, chance, (*a.* несчастный ~й) accident; на всякий (пожарный F) ~й to be on the safe side; по ~ю second hand; (P) on account of; ∠**йность** *f* [8] chance, fortuity; ∠**йный** [14; -аен, -айна] accidental, casual, chance (by ∠йно); ∠**ться** [1], ‹случиться› [16 *e.*; *3rd p. or impers.*] happen (to с T); come; take place; F be.
слуша|тель *m* [4] listener, hearer; student; *pl.* audience; ~**ть** [1], ‹по-› listen (to B), hear; attend; ⚕ auscultate; ~й! *a.*, ⚔, attention!; ~ю! *teleph.*: hullo!; ~ю(сь)! yes (, sir); **-ся** obey (p. P); take (*advice*).
слыть [23], ‹про-› (T, за B) pass for, have the reputation of.
слыхать, ‹у-› *s.* слышать.
слы|шать [4] (F ~хать [*no pr.*]), ‹у-› hear (of, about о П); F feel, notice; ~**шаться** [4] be heard; ~**шимость** *f* [8] audibility; ~**шно** it can be heard (of о П); it is said; (мне) ~шно one (I) can hear; что ~шно? what is the news?; ~**шный** [14; -шен, -шна, -о] audible.
слюда *f* [5] mica.
слюн|а *f* [5], ∠**и** F *pl.* [8; *from gen. e.*] saliva, spittle; ∠**ки** F *f/pl.*: ∠ки текут mouth waters; ~**явый** F [14 *sh.*] slobbery.
слякоть *f* [8] slush.
см. *abbr.*: смотри see, v(ide).
с. м. *abbr.*: сего месяца; *cf.* сей.
смаз|ать *s.* ~ывать; ~**ка** *f* [5 *g/pl.*: -зок] greasing, oiling, lubrication; ~**очный** [14] lubricant; ~**ывать**

[1], ⟨~ать⟩ [3] grease, oil, lubricate; F blur.
сма́|нивать [1], ⟨~ни́ть⟩ [13; сманю́, -а́нишь; -а́ненный & -анённый] lure away, entice; **~тывать,** ⟨смота́ть⟩ [1] reel on *or* off; **~хивать** [1], ⟨~хну́ть⟩ [20] brush off (*or* aside); *impf.* F have a likeness (with на В); **~чивать** [1], ⟨смочи́ть⟩ [16] moisten.
сме́жный [14; -жен, -жна] adjacent.
сме́л|ость *f* [8] boldness; courage; **~ый** [14; смел, -á, -о] courageous, bold; **~о** *a.* F easily; offhand.
сме́н|а *f* [5] shift (in в В); ⚔ relief; change; supersession; successors *pl.*; прийти́ на **~у** *s.* **~и́ться**; **~я́ть** [28], ⟨~и́ть⟩ [13; -еню́, -е́нишь; -енённый] (**-ся** be) supersede(d; o. a.), ⚔ relieve(d), replace(d; by T), substitute(d; for); change.
смерк|а́ться [1], ⟨**∠**нуться⟩ [20] grow dusky *or* dark.
смерт|е́льный [14; -лен, -льна] mortal, fatal, (*a. adv.*) deadly; **∠ность** *f* [8] mortality, death rate; **∠ный** [14; -тен, -тна] mortal (*a. su.*), deadly, fatal; (a. ⚖) death ...; ⚖ capital; **~ь** *f* [8; *from g/pl. e.*] death; F (*a.* **~ь** как, до́ **~и**, на́ **~ь**) deadly, utterly; при́ **~и** at death's door.
смерч *m* [1] waterspout; tornado.
смести́ *s.* смета́ть; **~ть** *s.* смеща́ть.
сме|сь *f* [8] mixture; blend; alloy; miscellanies *pl.*; **∠та** *f* [5] estimate.
смета́на *f* [5] sour cream.
сме|та́ть [1], ⟨~сти́⟩ [25 -т-] sweep away; sweep together; wipe off
сме́тливый [14 *sh.*] sharp(-witted).
сметь [8], ⟨по-⟩ dare, venture; beg.
смех *m* [1] laughter (with со́ **~у**); joke, fun (for ра́ди Р, в *or* на В); *cf.* шу́тка.
сме́ш|анный [14] mixed; **~а́ть(ся)** *s.* **~ивать(ся)**; **~е́ние** *n* [12] mixture; confusion; **~ивать,** ⟨~а́ть⟩ [1] mix (up), mingle, blend (*v/i.* **-ся**; get *or* be[come]) confuse(d).
смеш|и́ть [16 *e.*; -шу́, -ши́шь], ⟨рас-⟩ [-шённый] make laugh; **~но́й** [14; -шо́н, -шна́] laughable, ludicrous, ridiculous; funny; (Д) **~но́** amuse (p.).
сме|ща́ть [1], ⟨~сти́ть⟩ [15 *e.*; -ещу́, -ести́шь; -ещённый] displace, shift, dislocate; **~ще́ние** *n* [12] displacement.
смея́ться [27 *e.*; -ею́сь, -еёшься], ⟨за-⟩ laugh (at *impf.* над T); mock (at); deride; F joke.
смир|е́ние *n* [12], **~е́нность** *f* [8] humility; meekness; **~е́нный** [14 *sh.*] humble; meek; **~и́ть(ся)** *s.* **~я́ть(ся)**; **∠ный** [14; -рен (F -рён), -рна́, -о] quiet, still; meek, gentle; **∠но**! ⚔ (at) attention!; **~я́ть** [28], ⟨~и́ть⟩ [13] subdue; restrain, check; **-ся** humble o.s.
смо́кинг *m* [1] tuxedo, dinner jacket.
смол|а́ *f* [5; *pl. st.*] resin; pitch; tar; **~и́стый** [14 *sh.*] resinous; **~и́ть** [13], ⟨вы́-, за-⟩ pitch, tar; **~ка́ть** [1], ⟨**∠**кнуть⟩ [21] grow silent; cease; **∠оду** F from one's youth; **~яно́й** [14 pitch..., tar...
сморка́ться [1], ⟨вы́-⟩ blow one's nose.
сморо́дина *f* [5] currant(s *pl.*).
смота́ть *s.* сма́тывать.
смотр *m* [1; ⚔ на -у́ & *pl. e.*] review; parade, show; inspection; **~е́ть** [9; -отрю́, -о́тришь; -о́тренный], ⟨по-⟩ look (at на В; after за Т), gaze; (re)view, see, watch; examine, inspect; mind (*v/t.* на В); look out; **~я́** it depends (on по Д), according (to); **~е́ть** в о́ба be all eyes; **~и́тель** *m* [4] inspector; (*post*)master.
смочи́ть *s.* сма́чивать.
смрад *m* [1] stench; **∠ный** [14; -ден, -дна] stinking.
сму́глый [14; смугл, -á, -о] swarthy
смут|и́ть(ся) *s.* смуща́ть(ся); **∠ный** [14; -тен, -тна́, -о] vague, dim; restless, uneasy; of unrest.
смущ|а́ть [1], ⟨смути́ть⟩ [15 *e.*; -ущу́, -ути́шь; -ущённый] (**-ся** be[come]) embarrass(ed), confuse(d), perplex(ed); **~е́ние** *n* [12] embarrassment, confusion; **~ённый** [14] embarrassed.
смы|ва́ть [1], ⟨**~ть**⟩ (22) wash off (*or* away); **~ка́ть** [1], ⟨сомкну́ть⟩ [20] close (*v/i.* **-ся**); **~сл** *m* [1] sense, meaning; respect; F use; **∠слить** F [13] understand; **~ть** *s.* **~ва́ть**; **~чко́вый** [14] ♪ stringed; **~чо́к** *m* [1; -чка́] ♪ bow; **~шлёный** F [14 *sh.*] clever, bright.
смягч|а́ть (-xtʃ-) [1], ⟨~и́ть⟩ [16 *e.*; -чу́, -чи́шь; -чённый] soften (*v/i.* **-ся**); mitigate, alleviate; extenuate; *phon.* palatalize; **-ся** *a.* relent; **~а́ющий** ⚖ extenuating; **~е́ние** *n* [12] mitigation; extenuation; palatalization; **~и́ть(ся)** *s.* **~а́ть(ся)**.
смяте́ние *n* [12] confusion.
снаб|жа́ть [1], ⟨~ди́ть⟩ [15 *e.*; -бжу́, -бди́шь; -бжённый] supply, furnish, provide (with T); **~же́ние** *n* [12] supply, provision; purchasing (*dept.*).
сна́йпер *m* [1] sharpshooter.
снару́жи from (the) outside.
снаря́|д shell; missile, projectile; apparatus; tool, equipment; tackle; **~жа́ть** [1], ⟨~ди́ть⟩ [15 *e.*; -яжу́, -яди́шь; -яжённый] equip, fit out (with T); **~же́ние** *n* [12] equipment; munitions *pl.*
снасть *f* [8; *from g/pl. e.*] tackle; rigging.
снача́ла at first; first; over again.
снег *m* [1; в -у́; *pl. e.*: -á] snow; идёт it is snowing; **~и́рь** *m* [4 *e.*] bullfinch; **~опа́д** *m* [1] snowfall.

снеж|и́нка *f* [5; *g/pl.*: -нок] snowflake; **∠ный** [14; -жен, -жна] snow(y); **~о́к** *m* [1; -жка́] *dim. of* снег; snowball.

снести́(сь) *s.* сноси́ть(ся).

сни|жа́ть [1], ⟨**∠зить**⟩ [15] lower; reduce, decrease; (-**ся** *v/i.*; *a.* fall; ✈ land); **~же́ние** *n* [12] lowering; reduction, decrease; fall; landing; **~зойти́** *s.* ~сходи́ть; **∠зу** from below.

сним|а́ть [1], ⟨снять⟩ [сниму́, сни́мешь; снял, -а́, -о; сня́тый (снят, -а́, -о)] take (off, away *or* down); remove, discard, dismiss; withdraw; cut (off); rent; (take a) photograph (of); reap, gather cancel, strike off; deprive (of); release (from с Р); raise (*siege*); strike (*camp*); make (*copy, etc.*); ~а́ть сли́вки skim; -**ся** take off; weigh (*anchor* с Р); have a picture of o.s. taken; be struck off (*a list*); **∠ок** *m* [1; -мка] photograph, picture (in на П).

сни́ск|ивать [1], ⟨~а́ть⟩ [3] get, win.

снисхо|ди́тельный [14; -лен, -льна] indulgent; condescending; **~ди́ть** [15], ⟨снизойти́⟩ [-ойду́, -ойдёшь; *cf.* идти́] condescend; **~жде́ние** *n* [12] indulgence, leniency; condescension.

сни́ться [13], ⟨при-⟩ *impers.*: (Д) dream (of И).

сно́ва (over) again, anew.

сно|ва́ть [7 *e.*] scurry, whisk; **~виде́ние** *n* [12] vision, dream.

сноп *m* [1 *e.*] sheaf.

сноро́вка *f* [5] knack, skill.

снос|и́ть [15], ⟨снести́⟩ [24 -с-: снесу́; снёс] carry (down, away *or* off, together), take; pull down, demolish; endure, bear, tolerate; *cf.* *a.* нести́; -**ся**, ⟨-сь⟩ communicate (with с Т); get in touch, contact; **∠ка** *f* [5; *g/pl.*: -сок] footnote; **∠ный** [14; -сен, -сна] tolerable.

сноха́ [5; *pl. st.*] daughter-in-law.

сноше́ние *n* [12] (*usu. pl.*) intercourse; relations.

сня́т|ие *n* [12] taking down; raising; removal; dismissal; **~о́й** [14] skim (*milk*); **~ь(ся)** *s.* снима́ть(ся).

соба́|ка *f* [5] dog; hound; **~чий** [18] dog('s).

собесе́дник *m* [1] interlocutor.

собира́т|ель *m* [4] collector; **~ельный** [14] *gr.* collective; **~ь** [1], ⟨собра́ть⟩ [-беру́, -рёшь; -а́л, -а́, -о; со́бранный (-ан, -а́, -о)] gather, collect; ⊕ assemble; prepare; -**ся** gather, assemble; prepare, make o.s. *or* be ready to start (*or* set out *or* go; on a journey в путь); be going, intend, collect (*one's thoughts* с Т); brace up (с си́лами).

собла́зн *m* [1] temptation; **~и́тель** *m* [4] seducer, temper; **~и́тельный** [14; -лен, -льна] tempting, seductive; **~я́ть** [28], ⟨~и́ть⟩ [13] (-**ся** be) tempt(ed); seduce(d).

соблю|да́ть [1], ⟨~сти́⟩ [25] observe, obey, adhere (to); maintain (*order*); **~де́ние** *n* [12] observance; maintenance; **~сти́** *s.* ~да́ть.

соболе́знова|ние *n* [12] condolence; **~ть** [7] condole (with Д).

со́бо|ль *m* [4; *pl. a.* -ля́, *etc. e.*] sable; **∠р** *m* [1] cathedral; council; diet; **∠ровать(ся)** [7] administer (receive) extreme unction.

собра́|ние *n* [12] meeting (at, in на П), assembly; collection; **~ть(ся)** *s.* собира́ть(ся).

со́бственн|ик *m* [1] owner, proprietor; **~ость** *f* [8] property; **~ый** [14] own; proper; personal; dead (*weight*).

собы́тие *n* [12] event, occurrence.

сова́ *f* [5; *pl. st.*] owl.

сова́ть [7 *e.*; сую́, суёшь], ⟨су́нуть⟩ [20] put; F slip, give; poke (one's nose -**ся**; *a.* butt in).

соверш|а́ть [1], ⟨~и́ть⟩ [16 *e.*; -шу́, -ши́шь; -шённый] accomplish; commit; make (*a. trip*); strike (*bargain*), effect; celebrate, do; -**ся** happen, take place; be effected, *etc.*; **~еннoléтие** *n* [12] majority, full age; **~еннoléтний** [15] (стать Т come) of age; **~е́нный** [14; -е́нен, -е́нна] perfect(ive *gr.*); absolute, complete; *adv. a.* quite; **~е́нство** *n* [9] perfection; в ~е́нстве *a.* perfectly; **~е́нствовать** [7], ⟨у-⟩ perfect (o.s. -**ся**), improve, polish up; **~и́ть(ся)** *s.* соверша́ть(ся).

со́вест|ливый [14 *sh.*] conscientious; **~но** (р. Д) ashamed; **~ь** *f* [8] conscience; по ~и honestly.

сове́т *m* [1] advice, counsel; council, board; *USSR a.* soviet; Верхо́вный ♀ Supreme Soviet; **~ник** *m* [1] council(l)or; **~овать** [7], ⟨по-⟩ advise (р. Д); -**ся** consult, deliberate (on о П); **~ский** [16] Soviet; **~чик** *m* [1] adviser.

совеща́|ние *n* [12] conference (at на П), meeting (*a.* in); deliberation, consultation (for на В); **~тельный** [14] advisory, consultative; **~ться** [1] confer, consult, deliberate.

совлада́ть F [1] *pf.* (с Т) master.

совме|сти́мый [14 *sh.*] compatible; **~сти́ть** *s.* ~ща́ть; **∠стный** [14] joint, combined; co(*education*); **∠стно** together, conjointly; **~ща́ть** [1], ⟨~сти́ть⟩ [15 *e.*; -ещу́, ести́шь; -ещённый] combine; unite; reconcile.

сово́к *m* [1; -вка́] scoop.

совоку́пн|ость *f* [8] total(ity), aggregate, whole; **~ый** [14] joint.

совпа|да́ть [1], ⟨**∠сть**⟩ [25; *pt. st.*] coincide; agree; A be congruent; **~де́ние** *n* [12] coincidence, *etc. s. vb.*

совреме́нн|ик *m* [1] contemporary; **~ый** [14; -е́нен, -е́нна] modern; present-day, up-to-date; *s. a.* ~ик.

совсе́м quite, entirely; at all.

совхо́з *m* [1] (сове́тское хозя́йство) state farm; *cf.* колхо́з.

согла́|сие *n* [12] consent (to на В; with с Р); agreement (by по Д); harmony, concord; accordance; **~си́ться** *s.* ~ша́ться; **~сно** (Д) according to, in accordance with; **~сный** [14; -сен, -сна] agreeable, accordant; harmonious; я ~сен (*f* ~сна) I agree (with с Т; to на В); (*a. su.*) consonant; **~сова́ние** *n* [12] coördination; *gr.* agreement, concord; **~сова́ть** *s.* ~со́вывать; **~сова́ться** [7] (*im*)*pf.* (с Т) conform (to); agree (with); **~со́вывать** [1], ‹~сова́ть› [7] coördinate; adjust; (*a. gr.*) make agree; **~ша́тельский** [16] conciliatory; **~ша́ться** [1], ‹~си́ться› [15 *e.*; -ашу́сь, -аси́шься] agree (with с Т; to на В), consent (to), assent; F admit; **~ше́ние** *n* [12] agreement, understanding; consent.

согна́ть *s.* сгоня́ть.

согну́ть(ся) *s.* сгиба́ть(ся).

согре|ва́ть [1], ‹**~**ть› [8] warm, heat.

соде́йств|ие *n* [12] assistance, help; **~овать** [7] (*im*)*pf.*, *a.* ‹по-› (Д) assist, help, coöperate; contribute (to), further, promote.

содерж|а́ние *n* [12] content(s); maintenance, support, upkeep; cost (at на П); salary; **~а́тель** *m* [4] holder, owner; **~а́тельный** [14; -лен, -льна] pithy, substantial; **~а́ть** [4] contain, hold; maintain, support; keep; **-ся** be contained, *etc.*; **~и́мое** *n* [14] contents *pl.*

содра́ть *s.* сдира́ть.

содрог|а́ние *n* [12], **~а́ться** [1], *once* ‹~ну́ться› [20] shudder.

содру́жество *n* [9] community.

соедин|е́ние *n* [12] union, junction, (at *a.* на П), connection; combination; ⚗ compound; ⚒ formation; **~и́тельный** [14] connective; *gr. a.* copulative; **~я́ть** [28], ‹~и́ть› [13] unite, join; (*a. teleph.*) connect; (*a.* ⚗) combine; (*v/i.* **-ся**); *cf.* США.

сожал|е́ние *n* [12] regret (for о П); pity (on к Д); к ~е́нию unfortunately, to (p.'s) regret; **~е́ть** [8] (о П) regret.

сожже́ние *n* [12] burning.

сожи́тельство *n* [9] cohabitation.

созв|а́ть *s.* созыва́ть; **~е́здие** *n* [12] constellation; **~они́ться** F [13] *pf.* (с Т) phone; **~у́чный** [14; -чен, -чна] conformable, accordant; concordant.

созда|ва́ть [5], ‹**~**ть› [-да́м, -да́шь *etc.*, *cf.* дать; со́здал, -а́, -о; со́зданный (-ан, -а́, -о)] create; produce; build up; prepare; **-ся** arise, form; **~ние** *n* [12] creation; creature; **~тель** *m* [4] creator; founder; **~ть (-ся)** *s.* ~вать(ся).

созерца́т|ельный]14; -лен, -льна] contemplative; **~ь** [1] contemplate.

созида́тельный [14; -лен, -льна] creative.

созна|ва́ть [5], ‹**~**ть› [1] realize (*Brt.* realise), see; **-ся** (в П) confess, avow, own; **~ние** *n* [12] consciousness; realization, perception, awareness; confession (of в П); без ~ния unconscious; **~тельный** [14; -лен, -льна] conscious; class conscious; conscientious; **~ть(ся)** *s.* ~ва́ть(ся).

созы́в *m* [1] convocation; **~а́ть** [1], ‹созва́ть› [созову́, -вёшь; -зва́л, -а́, -о; со́званный] call, invite; convoke, convene, summon.

соизмери́мый [14 *sh.*] commensurable.

сойти́(сь) *s.* сходи́ть(ся).

сок *m* [1; в -у́] juice; sap.

со́кол *m* [1] falcon.

сокра|ща́ть [1], ‹~ти́ть› [15 *e.*; -ащу́, -ати́шь; -ащённый] shorten; abbreviate; abridge; reduce, curtail; *p. pt. p. a.* short, brief; **-ся** decrease, shorten; contract; **~ще́ние** *n* [12] abbreviation; reduction, curtailment; abridg(e)ment; contraction.

сокров|е́нный [14 *sh.*] secret; **~ище** *n* [11] treasure; F darling; **~ищница** *f* [5] treasury, thesaurus.

сокруш|а́ть [1], ‹~и́ть› [16 *e.*; -шу́, -ши́шь; -шённый] smash, break; distress, afflict; **-ся** *impf.* grieve, be distressed; **~е́ние** *n* [12] destruction distress, contrition; **~и́тельный** [14; -лен, -льна] shattering; **~и́ть** *s.* ~а́ть.

солда́т *m* [1; *g/pl.*: солда́т] soldier **~ский** [16] soldier's.

сол|е́ние *n* [12] salting; **~ёный** [14 со́лон, -а́, -о] salt(y); saline; pickled; corned; *fig.* spicy.

солида́рн|ость *f* [8] solidarity **~ый** [14; -рен, -рна] solidary; in sympathy with.

соли́дн|ость *f* [8] solidity; **~ый** [14; -ден, -дна] solid, firm, sound respectable.

соли́ст *m* [1], **~ка** *f* [5; *g/pl.*: -ток soloist.

солитёр *m* [1] tapeworm.

соли́ть [13; солю́, со́ли́шь; со́лен ный] **1.** ‹по-› salt; **2.** ‹за-› pickl

со́лн|ечный [14; -чен, -чна] su (-ny); solar; **~це** (ˈsɔn-) *n* [11] su (*lie* in на П).

со́лод *m* [1], **~о́вый** [14] malt.

солове́й *m* [3; -вья́] nightingale.

соло́м|а *f* [5] straw; thatch; **~ен ный** [14] straw...; thatched; gras (*widow*[*er*]); **~инка** *f* [5; *g/pl.*: -но straw.

солони́на *f* [5] corned beef.

соло́нка *f* [5; *g/pl.*: -нок] saltcella

сол|ь *f* [8; *from g/pl. e.*] salt (*a. fig.* F point; **~яно́й** [14] salt...; hydr chloric (*acid*).

сом *m* [1 *e.*] catfish, sheatfish.

ікнýть(ся) s. смыкáть(ся).
ин|евáться [1], ⟨усомни́ться⟩
3] (в П) doubt; ~éние n [12]
ubt (about в П); question (in под
); ~и́тельный [14; -лен, -льна]
ubtful; dubious.
m [1; сна] sleep; dream (in во
); ~ли́вый [14 sh.] sleepy; ∠ный
4] sleeping (a. ...); sleepy, drowsy;
porific; ∠я F m/f [6; g/pl.: -ней]
epyhead; '♀я f [6] dim. of Сóфья.
бра|жáть [1], ⟨~зи́ть⟩ [15 e.;
ку́, -зи́шь; -жённый] consid-
weigh, think (over); grasp, un-
rstand; ~жéние n [12] considera-
n; reason; grasp, understanding;
и́тельный [14; -лен, -льна]
arp, quick-witted; ~зи́ть s. ~-
áть; ∠зный [14; -зен, -зна] con-
rmable (to с T); adv. a. according
); ~зовáть [7] (im)pf. (make)
nform, adapt (to с T), coördinate
ith); -ся conform (to с T).
бщá together, conjointly.
бщ|áть [1], ⟨~и́ть⟩ [16 e.; -щу́,
и́шь; -щённый] communicate
/i. -ся impf.), report; inform (p. of
o П); impart; ~éние n [12] com-
unication; report, statement, an-
uncement, information; ∠ество
[9] community; company; ~и́ть
~áть; ∠ник m [1], ∠ница f [5]
complice.
ору|жáть [1], ⟨~ди́ть⟩ [15 e.;
жу́, -уди́шь; -ужённый] build,
nstruct, erect, raise; ~жéние n
2] construction, building, struc-
re.
ответств|енный [14 sh.] corre-
onding; adv. a. according(ly) (to
), in accordance (with); ~ие n [12]
nformity. accordance; ~овать [7]
) correspond, conform (to), agree,
mply (with); ~ующий [17] cor-
sponding, respective; suitable.
отéчественни|к m [1], ~ца f [5]
mpatriot, fellow country(wo)man.
отношéние n [12] correlation.
пéрни|к m [1] rival; ~чать [1]
mpete, rival, vie; be a match (for
T); ~чество n [9] rivalry.
п|éть [10 e.; соплю́, сопи́шь]
heeze; ∠ли P pl. [6; gen.: -лéй,
c. e.] snot; ~ля́к P m [1 e.] snot
se.
постав|лéние n [12] comparison;
ля́ть [28], ⟨∠вить⟩ [14] compare.
при|касáться [1], ⟨~коснýться⟩
0] (с T) adjoin; (get in) touch
ith); ~коснове́ние n [12] con-
ct, touch.
прово|ди́тельный [14] covering
etter); ~ждáть [1] 1. accompany;
cort; 2. ⟨~ди́ть⟩ [15 e.; -ожу́,
оди́шь; -ождённый] provide (with
); -ся impf. be accompanied (by
); entail; ~ждéние n [12] accom-
animent; в ~ждéнии (P) accom-
nied (by).

сопротивл|éние n [12] resistance;
~я́ться [28] (Д) resist, oppose.
сопряжённый [14; -жён, -женá]
connected.
сопу́тствовать [7] (Д) accompany.
сор m [1] rubbish, litter.
соразмéрно in proportion (to Д).
сорáтник m [1] brother-in-arms.
сорв|анéц F m [1; -нцá] madcap
(fellow); ~áть(ся) s. срывáть(ся);
~иголовá F m/f [5; ac/sg.: сорви-
головýу; pl. s. головá] daredevil.
соревновá|ние n [12] competition;
contest; emulation; ~ться [7] (с T)
compete (with); emulate.
сор|и́ть [13], ⟨на-⟩ litter; make
dirty; ∠ный [14]: ∠ная травá f =
~ня́к m [1 e.] weed.
сóрок [35] forty; ∠а f [5] magpie.
сороко|вóй [14] fortieth; cf. пя́т(и-
деся́т)ый; ~нóжка f [5; g/pl.:
-жек] centipede.
сорóчка f [5; g/pl.: -чек] (under-)
shirt.
сорт m [1; pl.: -тá, etc. e.] sort;
quality; ~ировáть [7], ⟨рас-⟩ (as-)
sort; ~ирóвка f [5] (as)sorting;
~ирóвочный [14] ... switching.
сосáть [-сý, -сёшь; сóсанный] suck.
сосéд m [sg.: 1; pl.: 4], ~ка f [5;
g/pl.: -док] neighbo(u)r; ~ний [15]
neighbo(u)ring, adjoining; ~ский
[16] neighbo(u)r's; ~ство n [9]
neighbo(u)rhood.
соси́ска f [5; g/pl.: -сок] sausage.
сóска f [5; g/pl.: -сок] (baby's)
dummy.
соск|áкивать [1], ⟨~очи́ть⟩ [16]
jump or spring (off, down); ~áль-
зывать [1], ⟨~ользнýть⟩ [20] slide
(down, off); slip (off); ~у́читься
[16] pf. become bored; s. скучáть.
сосл|агáтельный [14] gr. sub-
junctive; ~áть(ся) s. ссылáть(ся);
~óвие n [12] estate, class; ~ужи́-
вец m [1; -вца] colleague.
соснá f [5; pl. st.: сóсны, сóсен,
сóснам] pine.
сосóк m [1; -скá] nipple, teat.
сосредотóч|ение n [12] concentra-
tion; ~ивать [1], ⟨~ить⟩ [16] concentrate (v/i. -ся); p. pt. p. a. intent.
состáв m [1] composition, structure;
body; (ли́чный ~) staff; рядовóй
~ rank & file; strength (of в П);
thea. cast; ... stock; ... facts pl.; ...
solution, mixture; в ~е (P) a. con-
sisting of; ~и́тель m [4] compiler,
author; ~ить s. ~ля́ть; ~лéние n
[12] composition; compilation;
drawing up; ~ля́ть [28], ⟨~ить⟩
[14] compose, make (up); put together, arrange; draw up, work out;
compile; form, constitute; amount
(or come) to; ~нóй [14] composite,
compound; component, constituent (part; ~нáя часть f a. ingredient).
состоя́|ние n [12] state, condition;
status, station; position; fortune;

быть в ~нии ... *a.* be able to ...; **~тельный** [14; -лен, -льна] well-to-do, well-off; solvent; valid, sound, well-founded; **~ть** [-ою́, -ои́шь] consist (of из Р; in в П); be (*a.* Т); occupy (*position* в П), work (with при П); **-ся** *pf.* take place; come about.
сострада́ние *n* [12] compassion.
состяза́|ние *n* [12] contest, competition; match; **~ться** [1] compete, vie, contend.
сосу́д *m* [1] vessel.
сосу́лька *f* [5; *g/pl.*: -лек] icicle.
сосуществова́|ние *n* [12] coexistence; **~ть** [7] coexist.
сотворе́ние *n* [12] creation.
со́тня *f* [6; *g/pl.*: -тен] a hundred.
сотру́дни|к *m* [1] collaborator; employee, member; *pl.* staff; contributor; colleague; **~чать** [1] collaborate, coöperate; **~чество** *n* [9] collaboration, coöperation.
сотрясе́ние *n* [12] concussion.
со́ты *m/pl.* [1] honeycomb(s); **~й** [14] hundredth; *cf.* пя́тый; две це́лых и два́дцать пять ~х 2.25.
со́ус *m* [1] sauce; gravy.
соуча́ст|ие *n* [12] complicity; **~ник** *m* [1] accomplice.
соучени́к *m* [1 *e.*] schoolmate.
Со́фья *f* [6] Sophia.
соха́ *f* [5; *pl. st.*] (wooden) plow, plough.
со́хнуть [21] **1.** ⟨вы́-⟩ dry; **2.** ⟨за-⟩ fade, wither; **3.** F *impf.* pine away.
сохран|е́ние *n* [12] preservation, conservation; charge (*give* into, *take* ... of на В); **~и́ть(ся)** *s.* ~я́ть (-ся); **∠ность** *f* [8] safety; integrity; в ∠ности *a.* safe; **~я́ть** [28], ⟨~и́ть⟩ [13] keep; preserve; retain; maintain; reserve (to o.s. за собо́й); (*God*) forbid!; **-ся** be preserved; keep (safe, *etc.*).
социа́л|-демокра́т *m* [1] Social Democrat; **~-демократи́ческий** [16] Social Democrat(ic); **~и́зм** *m* [1] socialism; **~и́ст** *m* [1] socialist; **~исти́ческий** [16] socialist(ic); **~ьный** [14] social.
соц|соревнование *n* [12] socialist competition (*Sov.*); **~стра́х** *m* [1] social insurance (*Sov.*).
соче́льник *m* [1] (Xmas) Eve.
сочета́|ние *n* [12] combination; union; **~ть** [1] combine (*v/i.* **-ся**); unite (in Т).
сочин|е́ние *n* [12] composition; writing, work; thesis; *gr.* parataxis, coördination; **~и́тель** *m* [4] author; **~я́ть** [28], ⟨~и́ть⟩ [13] compose, write; invent; *gr.* coördinate.
соч|и́ться [16 *e.*; *3rd. p. only*] ooze (out); ~и́ться кро́вью bleed; **∠ный** [14; -чен, -чна́, -о] juicy; rich.
сочу́вств|енный [14 *sh.*] sympathetic, sympathizing; **~ие** *n* [12] sympathy (with, for к Д); **~овать** [7] (Д) sympathyze, feel with; prove (of); **~ующий** *m* [17] sym thizer.
сою́з *m* [1] union; alliance; c federacy; league; *gr.* conjuncti Сове́тский ∠ Soviet Union; СССР; **~ник** *m* [1] ally; **~ный** allied; (of the) Union (*Sov.*).
со́я *f* [6] soy(bean).
спа|да́ть [1], ⟨~сть⟩ [25; *pt.* fall (down); **∠ивать 1.** ⟨~я́ть⟩ solder; **2.** F ⟨спои́ть⟩ [13] m drunk; **∠йка** *f* [5] solder(ing); **зывать** *s.* сполза́ть.
спа́льн|ый [14] sleeping; bed...; *f* [6; *g/pl.*: -лен] bedroom.
спа́ржа *f* [5] asparagus.
спас|а́тельный [14] life...; **~** [1], ⟨~ти́⟩ [24 -с-] save, resc redeem; **-ся,** ⟨-сь⟩ *a.* escape (от Р); **~е́ние** *n* [12] rescue; reden tion.
спаси́бо (вам) thank you (very m большо́е ~), thanks (for за В, на
спаси́тель *m* [4] savio(u)r, rescu **~ный** [14] saving.
спас|ти́ *s.* ~а́ть; **~ть** *s.* спада́ть.
спать [сплю, спишь; спал, -а́, sleep; (*a.* идти́, ложи́ться ~) to bed; мне не спи́тся F **I** ca sleep.
спая́ть *s.* спа́ивать 1.
спека́ться [1] F *s.* запека́ться; conglomerate.
специа́кль *m* [4] performance.
спекул|и́ровать [7] speculate (w Т); **~я́нт** *m* [1] speculator.
спе́лый [14; спел, -á, -о] ripe.
сперва́ F (at) first.
спе́реди in (from) front (*as prp.*:
спёртый F [14 *sh.*] stuffy, close.
спеси́вый [14 *sh.*] haughty.
спеть [8], ⟨по-⟩ ripen; *s. a.* петь
спех F *m* [1] haste, hurry.
специ|ализи́роваться [7] (*im*) specialize (in в П, по Д) **~али́** *m* [1] specialist, expert (in по **~а́льность** *f* [8] special(i)ty, li profession (by по Д); **~а́льный** [-лен, -льна] special; express; **фи́ческий** [16] specific.
спецоде́жда *f* [5] overalls *pl.*
спеш|и́ть [16 *e.*; -шу́, -ши́шь] hu (up), hasten; *clock*: be fast (5 m на 5 мину́т); **∠иться** [16] *pf.* d mount; **∠ка** F *f* [5] haste, hurry; **ный** [14; -шен, -шна] urge pressing; special, express.
спин|а́ *f* [5; *ac/sg.*: спи́ну; *pl.* back; **∠ка** *f* [5; *g/pl.*: -нок] ba (*of chair, etc.*); **~но́й** [14] spi (cord мозг *m*); vertebral (colu хребе́т *m*), back(*bone*).
спира́ль *f* [8], **~ный** [14] spiral.
спирт *m* [1; *a.* в -у́; *pl. e.*] spiri *pl.*), alcohol; **~но́й** [14] alcoho strong (*drink*).
спис|а́ть *s.* ∠ывать; **∠ок** *m* [1; -сі list, register; copy; **∠ывать** [

,ать› [3] copy; write (off); plagia-
ze, crib; ⚓ pay off.
áх|ивать [1], *once* ‹~нýть› F [20]
ısh (down, aside).
úца *f* [5] spoke; knitting needle.
áчка *f* [5; *g/pl.*: -чек] match.
лав *m* [1] alloy; float(ing); **~ля́ть**
8], ‹~ить› [14] float; alloy.
лáчивать [1], ‹сплоти́ть› [15 *e.*;
чý, -оти́шь; -очённый] rally (*v/i.*
:я); fasten.
лет|áть [1], ‹сплести́› [25 -т-]
ait, braid; (inter)lace; F invent;
:ние *n* [12] interlacement, tex-
ıre; **∠ник** *m* [1], **∠ница** *f* [5]
andalmonger; **∠ничать** [1], ‹на-›
ssip; **∠ня** *f* [6; *g/pl.*: -тен] gossip;
. scandal.
ло|ти́ть(ся) *s.* сплáчивать(ся);
кова́ть F [7] *pf.* blunder; **~че́ние**
[12] rallying; **~шно́й** [14] solid,
mpact; sheer, complete; continu-
ıs; **~шь** throughout, entirely,
erywhere; quite often.
люшить [16] *pf.* flatten.
одви́жник *s.* сорáтник.
ои́ть *s.* спáивать 2.
око́й|ный [14; -óен, -óйна] calm,
iet, tranquil; composed; ~но F *s.*
ıéло F; ~ной нóчи! good night!;
ýдьте ~ны! don't worry!; **~ствие**
[12] calm(ness), tranquility; com-
osure; peace, order.
олз|áть [1], ‹~ти́› [24] climb *or*
p (down, off).
олнá ... wholly, whole ..., total ...
олоснýть [20] *pf.* rinse.
ор *m* [1] dispute, controversy,
gument; wrangle, quarrel; ∠у нет
doubt; **∠ить** [13], ‹по-› dispute,
gue, debate; quarrel; F bet; *poet.*
ght; **∠иться** F [13] succeed, get
ong; **∠ный** [14; -рен, -рна] dis-
ıtable, questionable.
орт *m* [1] sport; лы́жный ~ skiing;
и́вный [14] sporting, athletic;
ort(s)...; **~смéн** *m* [1] sportsman;
смéнка *f* [5; *g/pl.*: -нок] sports-
oman.
óсоб *m* [1] method, means; man-
er, way (in T); directions *pl.* (for
se P); **∠ность** *f* [8] (cap)ability
or к Д), talent; faculty; capacity;
ower; quality; **∠ный** [14; -бен,
бна] (к Д) able, talented, clever
t); capable (of; *a.* на В); **∠ство-
вать** [7], ‹по-› (Д) promote,
rther, contribute to.
от|ыкáться [1], ‹~кнýться› [20]
umble (over o B).
охвáт|ываться [1], ‹~и́ться›
5] bethink o.s.
рáва on, to (*or* from) the right.
раведли́в|ость *f* [8] justice;
uth; по ~ости by rights; **~ый** [14
.] just, fair; true, right.
рáв|ить(ся) *s.* ~ля́ть(ся); **~ка** *f*
; *g/pl.*: -вок] inquiry (make на-
оди́ть); information; certificate;
~ля́ть [28], ‹~ить› [14] F celebrate;
make (*holiday*); **-ся** inquire (after,
about o П); consult (*v/t.* в П); (c Т)
manage, cope with; **~очник** *m* [1]
reference book, vade mecum;
directory; guide; **~очный** [14] (of)
information, inquiry; reference...
спрáшива|ть [1], ‹спроси́ть› [15]
ask (p. *a.* y P; for, s.th. *a.* P), inquire; demand; (c P) be taken to
account; **-ся** *s.* проси́ться; ~ется
one may ask.
спрос *m* [1] demand (for на В);
без ∠а *or* ∠у F without permission;
~и́ть(ся) *s.* спрáшивать(ся).
спросóнок F half asleep.
спростá F unintentionally, innocently.
спры́|гивать [1], *once* ‹~гнуть› [20]
jump down (*or* off); **~скивать** [1],
‹~снуть› [20] sprinkle; F wet.
спря|гáть [1], ‹про-› *gr.* (**-ся** *impf.*
be) conjugate(d); **~жéние** *n* [12] *gr.*
conjugation.
спус|к *m* [1] lowering; descent;
slope; launch(ing); drain(ing); *fig.* F
quarter; **~кáть** [1], ‹~ти́ть› [15]
lower, let down; launch; drain;
unchain, set free; pull (*trigger*);
slacken; F pardon; lose, gamble
away; **-ся** go (*or* come) down(*stairs*
по Д), descend; slip down, sink;
~тя́ (B) later, after.
спýтни|к *m* [1], **~ца** *f* [5] fellow
travel(l)er; (*life's*) companion; ~к
ast. satellite.
спя́чка *f* [5] hibernation; sleep.
ср. *abbr.:* сравни́ compare, cf.
сравн|éние *n* [12] comparison (in/
with по Д/с Т); compare; simile;
∠ивать [1] **1.** ‹~и́ть› [13] compare
(to, with с Т; *v/i.* **-ся**); **2.** ‹~я́ть›
[28] level; equalize; **~и́тельный**
[14] comparative; **~и́ть(ся)** *s.* ∠и-
вать(ся); **~я́ть** *s.* ∠ивать 2.
сра|жáть [1], ‹~зи́ть› [15 *e.*; -ажý,
-ази́шь; -ажённый] smite; over-
whelm; overtake; **-ся** fight, battle;
F contend, play; **~жéние** *n* [12]
battle; **~зи́ть(ся)** *s.* ~жáть(ся).
срáзу at once; at one stroke.
срам *m* [1] shame, disgrace; **~и́ть**
[14 *e.*; -млю́, -ми́шь], ‹о-› [осрам-
лённый] disgrace, shame, compromise; **-ся** bring shame upon o.s.
сраст|áться [1], ‹~и́сь› [24 -ст-;
срóсся, срослáсь] grow together,
knit.
сред|á *f* **1.** [5; *ac/sg.*: срéду; *nom/pl.*
st.] Wednesday (on: в В, *pl.*: по Д);
2. [5; *ac/sg.*: -дý; *pl. st.*] environ-
ment, surroundings *pl.*, sphere;
medium; midst; **~и́** (P) among; in
the middle (of), amid(st); **~изéм-
ный** [14], **~иземномóрский** [16]
Mediterranean; **~невекóвый** [14]
medieval; **∠ний** [15] middle; medium...; central; middling; average... (on в П); ⚹ mean; *gr.* neuter; secondary (*school*).

средото́чие *n* [12] center (*Brt.* -tre).

сре́дство *n* [9] means (within [beyond] one's [не] по Д *pl.*); remedy; ⚗ agent; *pl. a.* facilities.

срез|а́ть & **∠ывать** [1], ⟨∠ать⟩ [3] cut off; F cut short; fail (*v/i.* **-ся**).

сровня́ть *s.* сра́внивать 2.

сро́д|ный [14; -ден, -дна] related, cognate; **~ство́** *n* [9] affinity.

сро|к *m* [1] term (for/of Т/на В), date, deadline; time (in, on в В, к Д), period; **∠чный** [14; -чен, -чна́, -o] urgent, pressing; timed.

сруб|а́ть [1], ⟨~и́ть⟩ [14] cut down, fell; carpenter, build.

сры|в *m* [1] frustration; failure, breakdown; breaking up; **~ва́ть** [1] **1.** ⟨сорва́ть⟩ [-ву́, -вёшь; сорва́л, -а́, -о; со́рванный] tear off; pluck, pick; F break up, disrupt, frustrate; vent; **-ся** (с Р) come off; break away (*or* loose); fall down; F dart off; escape; fail, go wrong; **2.** ⟨~ть⟩ [22] level, raze to the ground.

сса́дин|а *f* [5] graze, abrasion; **∠ть** [15] *pf.* graze; make alight; drop.

ссо́р|а *f* [5] quarrel; altercation; variance (at в П); **~иться** [13], ⟨по-⟩ quarrel, fall out.

СССР (Сою́з Сове́тских Социалисти́ческих Респу́блик) U.S.S.R. (Union of Soviet Socialist Republics).

ссу́д|а *f* [5] loan; **~и́ть** [15] *pf.* lend; **~ный** [14] loan...

ссыл|а́ть [1], ⟨сосла́ть⟩ [сошлю́, -лёшь; со́сланный] exile, banish; **-ся** (на В) refer to, cite; **∠ка** *f* [5; *g/pl.*: -лок] exile; deportation; reference (to на В); **∠ьный** [14] exiled (p.).

ссыпа́|ть [1], ⟨'~ть⟩ [2] pour, sack.

ст. *abbr.*: **1.** столе́тие; **2.** ста́нция; **3.** ста́рший.

стабил|из(и́р)ова́ть [7] (*im*)*pf.* stabilize; **∠ьный** [14; -лен, -льна] stable.

ста́вень *m* [4; -вня] shutter.

ста́в|ить [14], ⟨по-⟩ put, place, set, stand; (*clock, etc.*) set; put (*or* set) up; stake, (на В) back; *thea.* stage; ⚔ billet; make (*conditions, etc.*); drive; cite; impute (в В); bring (to p.'s *notice* В/в В); give; organize; value, esteem; F appoint, engage; **~ка** *f* [5; *g/pl.*: -вок] rate; wage, salary; stake; (head)quarters *pl.*; *fig.* hope; о́чная ~ка confrontation; **~ленник** *m* [1] protegé; **~ня** *f* [6; *g/pl.*: -вен] *s.* ~ень.

стадио́н *m* [1] stadium (in на П).

ста́дия *f* [7] stage.

ста́до *n* [9; *pl. e.*] herd; flock.

стаж *m* [1] length of service.

стака́н *m* [1] glass.

сталелите́йный [14] steel (*mill.*).

ста́лкивать [1], ⟨столкну́ть⟩ [20] push (off, down, together); **-ся** (с Т) collide, run into; come across.

сталь *f* [8] steel; **~но́й** [14] stee

стаме́ска *f* [5; *g/pl.*: -сок] chise

стан *m* [1] figure; camp; ⊕ mill

станда́рт *m* [1] standard; **~ный** [-тен, -тна] standard...; prefab cated.

стани́ца *f* [5] Cossack village.

станови́ться [14], ⟨стать⟩ [ста́ -нешь] stand; (Т) become, gr get; step, place o. s., get, stop; ~ о́чередь line, *Brt.* queue up; begin; will; feel (*better*); во что́ то ни ста́ло at all costs, at any co

стано́к *m* [1; -нка́] machine; lat press; bench; тка́цкий ~ loom.

станци|о́нный [14] station...; wa ing; post(*master*); **'~я** *f* [7] stati (at на П); *teleph.* office, exchan 🚂 *a.* yard; узлова́я '~я junction

ста́птывать [1], ⟨стопта́ть⟩ tread down; wear out.

стара́|ние *n* [12] pains *pl.*, care(effort); endeavo(u)r, trouble; **тельный** [14; -лен, -льна] assic ous, diligent; careful; **~ться** [⟨по-⟩ endeavo(u)r, try (hard); str (for о П).

стар|е́ть [21] **1.** ⟨по-⟩ grow c age; **2.** ⟨у-⟩ grow obsolete; **∠ец** [1; -рца] (old) monk; *a.* = **~и́к** [1 *e.*] old man; **~ина́** *f* [5] old time *or* days (of yore) (in в В) old man; **~и́нный** [14] ancie antique; old; longstanding; **∠и** [13], ⟨со-⟩ make (**-ся** grow) old.

старо|мо́дный [14; -ден, -д old-fashioned, out-of-date; **'~ста** [5] (*village*) elder; (*church*) warde (*class*) monitor; **'~сть** *f* [8] old a (in one's на П лет).

стартова́ть [7] (*im*)*pf.* start.

стар|у́ха *f* [5] old woman; **∠ческ** [16] senile; **∠ший** [17] elder, old senior; eldest, oldest; higher, hig est; fore(*man*); first (*lieutenan* **~шина́** *m* [5] foreman; chairm manager; ⚔ first sergeant (*or*, mate); **~шинство́** *n* [9] seniorit

ста́р|ый [14; стар, -а́, -о] o ancient, antique; olden; **~ьё** *n* [second-hand articles *pl.*; junk, *B* lumber.

ста́|скивать [1], ⟨~щи́ть⟩ [16] p (off, down); take, bring.

стати́ст *m* [1], **~ка** *f* [5; *g/pl.*: -тс *thea.* supernumerary; *film*: ext **~ика** *f* [5] statistics; **~и́ческ** [16] statistical.

ста́т|ный [14; -тен, -тна́, stately, portly; **~уя** [6; *g/pl.*: -у statue; **~ь**[1] *f* [8] build; trait; need, seemly; с како́й ~и? F w (should I, *etc.*).

стать[2] *s.* станови́ться; **~ся** F (*i* *pers.*) happen (to с Т); (*may*)be.

статья́ *f* [6; *g/pl.*: -те́й] artic item, entry; F matter, business (a other осо́бая). [vit

стаха́новец *m* [1; -вца] Stakhano

ационáрный [14] stationary.
áчка *f* [5; *g/pl.*: -чек] strike.
ащи́ть *s.* стáскивать.
áя *f* [6; *g/pl.*: стай] flight, flock; ноal; pack, troop.
áять [27] *pf.* thaw off, melt.
вол *m* [1 *e.*] trunk; barrel.
вóрчатый [14] folding (*doors*).
éбель *m* [4; -бля; *from g/pl. e.*] :alk, stem.
ёганый [14] quilted.
егáть [1] **1.** ⟨вы́-, про-⟩ quilt; **2.** *нсе* ⟨стегну́ть⟩ [20] whip.
е|кáть [1], ⟨~чь⟩ [26] flow lown); **-ся** join; flock, gather.
ек|лó *n* [9; *pl.*: стёкла, стёкол, тёклам] glass; pane; (*lamp*) chimey; **~ля́нный** [14] glass...; glassy; **óльщик** *m* [1] glazier.
ел|и́ть(ся) F *s.* стлать(ся); **~лáж** [1 *e.*] shelf; **~ька** *f* [5; *g/pl.*: -лек] ıner sole; **~ьный** [14]: **~ьная** коóва cow with calf.
ен|á *f* [5; *ac/sg.*: стéну; *pl.*: стéны, ген, стенáм] wall; **~газéта** *f* [5] тенная газéта) wall newspaper; **ка** *f* [5; *g/pl.*: -нок] wall; **~нóй** 4] wall...
еногрá|мма *f* [5] shorthand (veratim) report *or* notes *pl.*; **~фи́ст** [1], **~фи́стка** *f* [5; *g/pl.*: -ток] enographer; **~фия** *f* [7] shorthand.
епáн *m* [1] Stephen.
епéнный [14; -éнен, -éнна] seate, staid, grave, dignified; mature.
éпень *f* [8; *from g/pl. e.*] degree о до Р), extent; *A* power.
еп|нóй [14] steppe...; **~ь** *f* [8; в и́й; *from g/pl. e.*] steppe.
éрва P *contp. f* [5] damned wretch.
ере|оти́пный [14; -пен, -пна] ereotyped; **~ть** *s.* стирáть
ерéчь [26 г/ж: -егу́, -ежёшь; г, -еглá] guard, watch (over).
éржень *m* [4; -жня] core (*a. fig.*); ivot.
ерил|изовáть [7] (*im*)*pf.* sterize; **~ьный** [14; -лен, -льна] sterile.
ерпéть [10] *pf.* endure, bear.
есн|éние *n* [12] constraint, reraint; **~и́тельный** [14; -лен, льна] constraining, embarrassing; **и́ть** [28], ⟨~и́ть⟩ [13] constrain, strain; embarrass, hamper; cramp; ouble, press; **~и́ться,** ⟨по-⟩ feel r be) shy, self-conscious *or* embarssed; (P) be ashamed of; hesitate.
еч|éние *n* [12] confluence; coincience; **~ь(ся)** *s.* стекáть(ся).
иль *m* [4] style; (*Old, New*) Style.
ипéндия *f* [7] scholarship.
ир|áльный [14] washing; **~áть**] **1.** ⟨стерéть⟩ [12; сотру́, -трёшь; ёр(ла); стёрши & стерéв] wipe rub off, out; erase, efface, blot ıt; clean; pulverize; **2.** ⟨вы́-⟩ ash, launder; **~ка** *f* [5] wash(ing), ındry; отдáть в **~ку** send to the ash.

сти́с|кивать [1], ⟨~нуть⟩ [20] clench; grasp, press.
стих (*a.* ~и́ *pl.*) *m* [1 *e.*] verse; *pl. a.* poem(s); **~áть** [1], ⟨~нуть⟩ [21] abate; fall; cease; calm down, (become) quiet; **~и́йный** [14; -и́ен, -и́йна] elemental; spontaneous; natural; **~и́я** *f* [7] element(s); **~нуть** *s.* ~áть.
стихотворéние *n* [12] poem.
стлать & F **стели́ть** [стелю́, -стéлешь], ⟨по-⟩ [пóстланный] spread, lay; make (*bed*); **-ся** *impf.* (be) spread; drift; ♀ creep.
сто [35] hundred.
стог *m* [1; в стóге & в стогу́; *pl.*: -á, *etc. e.*] stack, rick.
стóи|мость *f* [8] cost; value, worth (... Т/в В); **~ть** [13] cost; be worth; pay; take, require; (Д) need, if (*only*); matter; не ~т F = нé за что.
стой! stop!, halt!; **~ка** *f* [5; *g/pl.*: стóек] stand(ard); support; counter; **~кий** [16; стóек, стойкá, -о; *comp.*: стóйче] firm, steadfast, steady; **~кость** *f* [8] firmness; **~ло** *n* [9] box (stall); **~мя́** upright.
сток *m* [1] flowing (off); drain.
Стокгóльм *m* [1] Stockholm.
стокрáтный [14] hundredfold.
стол *m* [1 *e.*] table (at за Т); board, fare; meal; office, bureau; *hist.* throne.
столб *m* [1 *e.*] post, pole; column; pillar; **~енéть** [8], ⟨о-⟩ petrify; **~éц** *m* [1; -бцá], **~ик** *m* [1] column; **~ня́к** *m* [1 *e.*] stupor; tetanus; **~овóй** [14]: ~овáя дорóга *f* highway.
столéтие *n* [12] century; centenary.
стóлик *m* [1] *dim. of* стол; F table.
столи́|ца *f* [5] capital; **~чный** [14] metropolitan.
столкн|овéние *n* [12] collision, clash; **~у́ть(ся)** *s.* стáлкивать(ся).
столóв|ая *f* [14] dining room; restaurant; **~ый** [14] table(*spoon*); dinner (*service*).
столп *m* [1 *e.*] pillar; column.
столь so; **~ко** [32] so much, so many; ~ко же as much *or* many.
столя́р *m* [1 *e.*] joiner; cabinetmaker; **~ный** [14] joiner's (*shop, etc.*).
стон *m* [1], **~áть** [-ну́, стóнешь; стонáя], ⟨про-⟩ groan, moan.
стоп! stop!; **~á** *f* **1.** [5 *e.*] foot; footstep (with Т; in по Д); **2.** [5; *pl. st.*] foot (*verse*); pile; **~ка** *f* [5; *g/pl.*: -пок] cup; roll, rouleau; **~орить** [13], ⟨за-⟩ stop; **~тáть** *s.* стáптывать.
стóрож *m* [1; *pl.*: -á, *etc. e.*] guard, watchman; **~евóй** [14] watch...; on duty; sentry (*box*); observation (*post*); ⚓ patrol...; **~и́ть** [16 *e.*; -жу́, -жи́шь] guard, watch (over).
сторон|á *f* [5; *ac/sg.*: стóрону; *pl.*: стóроны, сторóн, -нáм] side (on *a.* по Д; с Р); direction; part (on с[о]

P); place, region, country; party; distance (at в П; from с P); в '~у aside, apart (*a.* joking шу́тки); в ~е́ aloof, apart; на́ ~у abroad; с одно́й ~ы́ on the one hand; ... с ва́шей ~ы́ *a.* ... of you; **~и́ться** [13; -оню́сь, -о́нишься], ⟨по-⟩ make way, step aside; (P) avoid, shun; ~и́сь! look out!; **∠ник** *m* [1] adherent, follower, supporter; partisan.

сто́чный [14] waste..., soil...

стоя́|лый [14] stale; **~нка** *f* [5; *g/pl.*: -нок] stop (at на П); stand, station, (fixed) quarters *pl.*; parking place *or* lot; ⚓ anchorage.

стоя́|ть [стою́, стои́шь; сто́я] stand; be; stop; lodge, quarter; stand up (for за В), defend; insist (on на П); сто́й(те)! stop!; F wait!; **~чий** [17] standing; stagnant; stand-up (*collar*); standard (*lamp*).

стр. *abbr.*: страни́ца page, p.

страда́|лец *m* [1; -льца] martyr; **~ние** *n* [12] suffering; **~тельный** [14] *gr.* passive; **~ть** [1], ⟨по-⟩ suffer (from от P, T; for за B); F be poor.

страж *m* [1] guard; **∠а** *f* [5] guard(s); watch; custody (in[to] под T [B]).

стран|а́ *f* [5; *pl. st.*] country; **~и́ца** *f* [5] page (*cf.* пя́тый); column (in на П); **∠ник** *m* [1] wanderer, travel(l)er; pilgrim; **∠ность** *f* [8] strangeness, oddity; **∠ный** [14; -а́нен, -анна́, -о] strange, odd; **∠ств(ован)ие** *n* [12] wandering, travel; **∠ствовать** [7] wander, travel; ∠ствующий *a.* (*knight*-)errant.

страст|но́й (-sn-) [14] Holy; Good (*Friday*); **∠ный** (-sn-) [14; -тен, -тна́, -о] passionate, fervent; **~ь** *f* [8; *from g/pl. e.*] passion (for к Д); P awfully.

стратег|и́ческий [16] strategic(al); **∠ия** *f* [7] strategy.

стратосфе́ра *f* [5] stratosphere.

стра́ус *m* [1] ostrich.

страх *m* [1] fear (for от, со P); risk, peril (at на B); F awfully; **~ка́сса** *f* [5] insurance office; **~ова́ние** *n* [12] insurance (*fire* ... от P); **~ова́ть** [7], ⟨за-⟩ insure (against от P); **~о́вка** *f* [5; *g/pl.*: -вок] insurance (rate); **~ово́й** [14] insurance...

страш|и́ть [16 *e.*; -шу́, -ши́шь], ⟨у-⟩ [-шённый] (**-ся** be) frighten (-ed; at P; fear, dread, be afraid of); **∠ный** [14; -шен, -шна́, -о] terrible, frightful, dreadful; Last (*Judg*[*e*]*ment*); F awful; мне ∠но I'm afraid, I fear.

стрекоза́ *f* [5; *pl. st.*: -о́зы, -о́з, -о́зам] dragonfly.

стрел|а́ *f* [5; *pl. st.*] arrow(like T); ⚘ shaft; **∠ка** *f* [5; *g/pl.*: -лок] hand, pointer, indicator; needle; arrow (*drawing, etc.*); clock (*stocking*); tongue (*land*); 🚂 switch, *Brt.* point; **~ко́вый** [14] shooting...; (of) rifles

pl.; **~о́к** *m* [1; -лка́] marksma[n] shot; ⚔ rifleman; **∠очник** 🚂 *m* switchman, *Brt.* pointsman; **~ьба́** [5; *pl. st.*] shooting, fire; **~я́ть** [2 ⟨вы́стрелить⟩ [13] shoot, fire в В, по Д; *gun* из P); F *impers.* f[eel] acute pains *pl.*; **-ся** *impf.* (fight [a] duel.

стрем|гла́в headlong, headfir[st]; **~и́тельный** [14; -лен, -льна] i[m]petuous, violent, rash; **~и́ть** [14 *e.*; -млю́сь, -ми́шься] (к Д) [as]pire (to, after), strive (for, afte[r]) rush; **~ле́ние** *n* [12] aspirati[on], striving, urge; tendency.

стре́мя *n* [13; *pl.*: -мена́, -мя́н, -м[е]на́м] stirrup.

стриж *m* [1 *e.*] sand martin.

стри́|женый [14] bobbed, sho[rt]-haired; shorn; trimmed; **~жк[а]** [5] haircut(ting); shearing; tri[m]ming; **~чь** [26 г/ж: -игу́, -ижё[шь]; *pt. st.*], ⟨по-, о(б)-⟩ cut; shear; c[lip], trim; **-ся** have one's hair cut.

строга́ть [1], ⟨вы́-⟩ plane.

стро́г|ий [16; строг, -а́, -о; *com[p].*: стро́же] severe; strict; auste[re], stern; **~ость** *f* [8] severity, aust[er]ity, strictness.

строе|во́й [14] fighting, front(lin[e]); ~во́й лес *m* timber; **∠ние** *n* [...] construction, building; structure.

строи́тель *m* [4] builder, constr[uc]tor; **~ный** [14] building...; **~ств[о]** [9] construction.

стро́ить [13] **1.** ⟨по-⟩ build (u[p]), construct; make, scheme; play ... (из P); **2.** ⟨вы́-⟩ ⚔ draw up, for[m]; **-ся**, ⟨вы́-, по-⟩ be built; buil[d a] house; ⚔ fall in.

строй *m* **1.** [3; в строю́; *pl.* строи́, строёв] order, array; li[ne]; **2.** [3] system, order, regime; ♪ tu[ne]; **∠ка** *f* [5; *g/pl.*: -о́ек] constructi[on]; **∠ность** *f* [8] harmony; slenderne[ss]; **∠ный** [14; -о́ен, -ойна́, -о] slend[er], slim; harmonious; symmetri[c], well-shaped, well-disposed.

строка́ *f* [5; *ac/sg.*: стро́ку́; *p[l.]*: стро́ки, строк, строка́м] line.

стропи́ло *n* [9] rafter. [refractor[y]]

стропти́вый [14 *sh.*] obstina[te].

строфа́ *f* [5; *nom/pl. st.*] stanza.

строч|и́ть [16 & 16 *e.*; -очу́, -о́чи́шь; -о́ченный & -очённ[ый]] stitch, sew; F scribble, write; cra[w]le; **∠ка** *f* [5; *g/pl.*: -чек] line; sea[m].

стру́|жка *f* [5; *g/pl.*: -жек] shavi[ng]; **~и́ться** [13] stream, flow, run; p[our]; **~йка** *f* [5; *g/pl.*: -у́ек] *dim. of* ~[я].

структу́ра *f* [5] structure.

струн|а́ ♪ *f* [5; *pl. st.*], **∠ный** [...] string.

струч|ко́вый *s.* бобо́вый; **~о́к** [*m*] [1; -чка́] pod, husk.

струя́ *f* [6; *pl. st.*: -у́и] stream (T); jet; current; flood.

стря́|пать F [1], ⟨со-⟩ cook; **~х[ивать]** [1], ⟨~хну́ть⟩ [20] shake o[ff]

студе́н|т *m* [1], **~тка** *f* [5; *g*/*pl.*: -ток] student, undergraduate; **~ческий** [16] students'.
студёный F [14 *sh.*] (icy) cold.
сту́день *m* [4; -дня] jellied meat.
сту́дия *f* [7] studio, atelier.
стук *m* [1] knock; rattle, clatter, noise; **∠нуть** *s.* стуча́ть.
стул *m* [1; *pl.*: сту́лья, -льев] chair; seat; ⚕ stool.
сту́па *f* [5] mortar (*vessel*).
ступ|а́ть [1], ⟨**~и́ть**⟩ [14] step, tread, go; **~е́нчатый** [14 *sh.*] (multi)graded; **~е́нь** *f* **1.** [8; *pl.*: ступе́ни, ступе́ней] step; **2.** [8; *pl.*: ступе́ни, -не́й, *etc. e.*] stage, grade; **~е́нька** *f* [5; *g*/*pl.*: -нек] step; rung; **~и́ть** *s.* **~а́ть**; **∠ка** *f* [5; *g*/*pl.*: -пок] (small) mortar; **~ня́** *f* [6; *g*/*pl.*: -не́й] foot; sole.
сту|ча́ть [4 *e.*; -чу́, -чи́шь] ⟨по-⟩, *once* ⟨**∠кнуть**⟩ [20] knock (at *door* в В; *a.* **-ся**); rap, tap; throb; chatter; clatter, rattle; **~ча́т** there's a knock at the door; **∠кнуть** F *s.* испо́лниться.
стыд *m* [1 *e.*] shame; **~и́ть** [15 *e.*; -ыжу́, -ыди́шь], ⟨при-⟩ [пристыжённый] shame, make ashamed; **-ся**, ⟨по-⟩ be ashamed (of P); **~ли́вый** [14 *sh.*] shy, bashful; **∠ный** F [14; -ден, -дна́, -о] shameful; **∠но!** (for) shame!; мне **∠но** I am ashamed (for p. за B).
стык *m* [1] joint, juncture (at на П).
сты́(ну)ть [21], ⟨о-⟩ (become) cool.
сты́чка *f* [5; *g*/*pl.*: -чек] skirmish.
стя́|гивать [1], ⟨**~ну́ть**⟩ [19] draw *or* pull together (off, down); tie up; ⚔ concentrate; F pilfer; **~жа́ть** [1] gain, acquire; **~ну́ть** *s.* **~гивать**.
суб|бо́та *f* [5] Saturday (on: в B, *pl.*: по Д); **~си́дия** *f* [7] subsidy.
субтропи́ческий [16] subtropical.
субъе́кт *m* [1] subject; F fellow; **~и́вный** [14; -вен, -вна] subjective.
суверен|ите́т *m* [1] sovereignty; **∠ный** [14; -е́нен, -е́нна] sovereign.
суг|ро́б *m* [1] snowdrift, bank; **~у́бый** [14 *sh.*] especial, exceptional.
суд *m* [1 *e.*] judg(e)ment (to на B); court (of justice); tribunal; trial put on отда́ть под B; bring to преда́ть Д); justice; полево́й ~ court martial; **~а́к** *m* [1 *e.*] pike perch.
суда́р|ыня *f* [6] madam; **'~ь** *m* [4] sir.
суд|е́бный [14] judicial, legal; law-...; (of the) court; **~е́йский** [16] judicial; referee's; **~и́ть** [15; суждённый] **1.** ⟨по-⟩ judge *fig.* (of о П; by по Д); **2.** (*im*)*pf.* try, judge; destine; **∠я** по (Д) judging by; **-ся** be at law (with с T).
су́д|но *n* **1.** [9; *pl.*: суда́, -о́в] ⚓ ship, vessel; **2.** [9; *pl.*: су́дна, -ден] vessel; **~омо́йка** *f* [5; *g*/*pl.*: -о́ек] scullery *or* kitchen maid.

су́доро|га *f* [5] cramp, spasm; **~жный** [14; -жен, -жна] convulsive.
судо|строе́ние *n* [12] shipbuilding; **~строи́тельный** [14] shipbuilding...; ship(*yard*); **~хо́дный** [14; -ден, -дна] navigable; **~хо́дство** *n* [9] navigation.
судьба́ *f* [5; *pl.*: су́дьбы, су́деб, су́дьбам] fate.
судья́ *m* [6; *pl.*: су́дьи, суде́й, су́дьям] judge; arbitrator, referee, umpire.
суеве́р|ие *n* [12] superstition; **~ный** [14; -рен, -рна] superstitious.
сует|а́ *f* [5] vanity; fuss; **~и́ться** [15 *e.*; суечу́сь, суети́шься] fuss; **~ли́вый** [14 *sh.*] fussy.
суж|де́ние *n* [12] judg(e)ment; **~е́ние** *n* [12] narrowing; ⚕ constriction; **∠ивать** [1], ⟨су́зить⟩ [15] narrow (*v*/*i.* **-ся**; taper).
сук *m* [1 *e.*; на -у́; *pl.*: су́чья, -ьев & -и́, -о́в] bough, branch; knot; **∠а** *f* [5] bitch; **∠ин** [19] of a bitch.
сукно́ *n* [9; *pl. st.*; су́кна, су́кон, су́кнам] cloth.
суко́нный [14] cloth...
сули́ть [13], ⟨по-⟩ promise.
султа́н *m* [1] sultan; plume.
сумасбро́д *m* [1] madman; crank; **~ный** [14; -ден, -дна] crazy, cranky, foolish; **~ство** *n* [9] folly, madness.
сумасше́|дший [17] mad, insane; *su.* madman; lunatic (asylum дом *m*); **~ствие** *n* [12] madness, insanity.
сумато́ха *f* [5] turmoil, fuss.
сум|бу́р *m* [1] *s.* пу́таница; **∠ерки** *f*/*pl.* [5; *gen.*: -рек] dusk, twilight; **∠ка** *f* [5; *g*/*pl.*: -мок] (hand)bag; pouch; satchel; wallet; **∠ма** *f* [5] sum (for/of на B/в B), amount; **~ма́рный** [14; -рен. -рна] summary; **~ми́ровать** [7] (*im*)*pf.* sum up.
су́мочка *f* [5; *g*/*pl.*: -чек] handbag.
су́мра|к *m* [1] twilight, dusk; gloom; **~чный** [14; -чен, -чна] gloomy.
сунду́к *m* [1 *e.*] trunk, chest.
су́нуть(ся) *s.* сова́ть(ся).
суп *m* [1; *pl. e.*], **~ово́й** [14] soup.
супру́|г *m* [1] husband; **~га** *f* [5] wife; **~жеский** [16] matrimonial, conjugal; married; **~жество** *n* [9] matrimony, wedlock.
сургу́ч *m* [1 *e.*] sealing wax.
суро́в|ость *f* [8] severity; **~ый** [14 *sh.*] harsh, rough; severe, austere; stern; rigorous.
суррога́т *m* [1] substitute.
сурьма́ *f* [5] antimony.
суста́в *m* [1] joint.
су́тки *f*/*pl.* [5; *gen.*: -ток] 24 hours, day (and night); кру́глые ~ round the clock.
су́толока *f* [5] turmoil.
су́точный [14] day's, daily, 24 hours'; *pl. su.* daily allowance.

суту́лый [14 *sh.*] round-shouldered.
сут|ь *f* [8] essence, core, main point; по ∠и (де́ла) at bottom.
суфл|ёр *m* [1] prompter; **~и́ровать** [7] prompt (p. Д).
сух|а́рь *m* [4 *e.*] cracker, zwieback, *Brt.* biscuit; **~ожи́лие** *n* [12] sinew; **~о́й** [14; сух, -á, -o; *comp.*: су́ше] dry; arid; lean; land...; *fig.* cool, cold; boring, dull; **~опу́тный** [14] land...; **∠ость** *f* [8] dryness, *etc.*, *s.* ~о́й; **~оща́вый** [14 *sh.*] lean, meager.
сучи́ть [16] twist; roll.
сучо́к *m* [1; -чкá] *dim. of* сук, *cf.*
су́ш|а *f* [5] (main)land; **~е́ние** *n* [12] drying; **~ёный** [14] dried; **~и́лка** *f* [5; *g/pl.*: -лок] drying apparatus; *a.* = **~и́льня** *f* [6; *g/pl.*: -лен] drying room; **~и́ть** [16] **1.** ⟨вы́-⟩ dry; air; **2.** ⟨ис-⟩ wear out, emaciate; **~ка** *f* [5; *g/pl.*: -шек] drying; ring-shaped cracknel.
суще́ств|енный [14 *sh.*] essential, substantial; **~и́тельное** *n* [14] noun, substantive (*a.* и́мя ~и́тельное); **~о́** *n* [9] creature, being; essence; по ~у́ at bottom; to the point; **~ова́ние** *n* [12] existence, being; subsistence; **~ова́ть** [7] exist, be; live.
су́щ|ий [17] existing; F plain (*truth*), quite (*true* or *right*), sheer, downright; **~ность** *f* [8] essence, substance; в ~ности at bottom, properly.
суэ́цкий [16]: ♀ кана́л Suez Canal.
сфе́ра *f* [5] sphere; field, realm.
с.-х. *abbr.*: сельскохозя́йственный.
схват|и́ть(ся) *s.* ∠ывать(ся); **∠ка** *f* [5; *g/pl.*: -ток] skirmish, fight, combat; scuffle; *pl. a.* (*childbirth*) labo(u)r; **∠ывать** [1], ⟨~и́ть⟩ [15] seize (by за В), grasp (*a. fig.*), grab; snatch; catch; **-ся** seize, lay hold of; F grapple.
схе́ма *f* [5] diagram, scheme (in на П); **~ти́ческий** [16] schematic.
сход|и́ть [15], ⟨сойти́⟩ [сойду́, -дёшь; сошёл, -шлá; с(о)ше́дший; *g. pt.*: сойдя́] go (*or* come) down, descend (from с Р); get off (out); come off (out); run off; leave; disappear; F pass (for за В); P do; pass off; ~и́ть *pf.* go (& get, fetch за Т); *cf.* ум; **-ся**, ⟨-сь⟩ meet; gather; become friends; agree (upon в П); harmonize (in Т); coincide; approximate; F click; **∠ка** *f* [5; *g/pl.*: -док] meeting (at на П); **∠ни** *f/pl.* [6; *gen.*: -ней] gangplank, gangway; **∠ный** [14; -ден, -днá, -o] similar (to с Т), like; F reasonable; **∠ство** *n* [9] similarity (to с Т), likeness.
сцеди́ть [15] *pf.* draw off.
сце́н|а *f* [5] stage; scene (*a. fig.*); **~а́рий** *m* [3] scenario, script; **~и́ческий** [16] stage..., scenic.
сцеп|и́ть(ся) *s.* ~ля́ть(ся); **∠ка** *f* [5; *g/pl.*: -пок] coupling; **~ле́ние** *n* [12] *phys.* cohesion; ⊕ coupling; *fig.* concatenation; **~ля́ть** [28], ⟨~и́ть⟩ [14] link; ⊕ couple (*v/i.* **-ся**; concatenate; F grapple).
счаст|ли́вец *m* [1; -вца] lucky man; **~ли́вый** [14; сча́стли́в, -a, -o] happy; fortunate, lucky; ~ли́вого пути́ bon voyage!; ~ли́во F bye-bye, so long: ~ли́во отде́латься have a narrow escape; **∠ье** *n* [10] happiness; good luck; fortune; к, по ∠ью fortunately.
счесть(ся) *s.* счита́ть(ся).
счёт *m* [1; на -е & счету́; *pl.*: счета́, *etc. e.*] count, calculation; account (on в В; на В); bill; invoice; *sport* score; в коне́чном ~е ultimately; за ~ (Р) at the expense (of); на э́тот ~ in this respect, as for this; ска́зано на мой ~ aimed at me; быть на хоро́шем ~у́ (у Р) stand high (in p.'s) favo(u)r; у него́ ~у нет (Д) he has lots (of); **~ный** [14] calculating (*machine*, calculator); slide (*rule*).
счетово́д *m* [1] accountant.
счёт|чик *m* [1] meter; counter; **~ы** *pl.* [1] abacus *sg.*; accounts *fig.*
счисле́ние *n* [12] calculation.
счита́|ть [1], ⟨со-⟩ & ⟨счесть⟩ [25 сочту́, -тёшь; счёл, сочлá; сочтённый; *g. pt.*: сочтя́] count; (*pf.* счесть) (Т, за В) consider, regard (*a.* as), hold, think; ~я *a.* including; '~нные *pl.* very few; **-ся** count; settle accounts; (Т) be considered (*or* reputed) to be, pass for; (с Т) consider, regard.
США (Соединённые Шта́ты Аме́рики) U.S.A. (United States of America).
сши|ба́ть [1], ⟨~би́ть⟩ [-бу́, -бёшь; *cf.* ушиби́ть] F *s.* сби(ва́)ть; **~ва́ть** [1], ⟨~ть⟩ [сошью́, -шьёшь; сше́й(-те)!; сши́тый] sew (together).
съед|а́ть [1], ⟨съесть⟩ *s.* есть[1]; **~о́бный** [14; -бен, -бна] edible.
съез|д *m* [1] congress (at на П); **∠дить** [15] *pf.* go; (за Т) fetch; (к Д) visit; **~жа́ть** [1], ⟨съе́хать⟩ [съе́ду, -дешь] go, drive (*or* slide) down; move; **-ся** meet; gather.
съёмка *f* [5; *g/pl.*: -мок] survey; shooting.
съестно́й [14] food...
съе́хать(ся) *s.* съезжа́ть(ся).
сы́|воротка *f* [5; *g/pl.*: -ток] whey; serum; **~гра́ть** *s.* игра́ть.
сы́знова F anew, (once) again.
сын *m* [1; *pl.*: сыновья́, -ве́й, -вья́м; *fig. pl.*: сыны́] son; *fig.* child; **~о́вний** [15] filial; **~о́к** F [1; -нкá] sonny.
сы́п|ать [2], ⟨по-⟩ strew, scatter; pour; F (Т, В) sputter, pelt, (*jokes*) crack, (*money*) squander; **-ся** pour; F spatter, hail, pelt; **~но́й** [14]: ~но́й тиф spotted fever; **~у́чий** [17 *sh.*] dry; quick(*sand*); **~ь** *f* [8] rash.

m [1; *pl. e.*] cheese; как ~ в
сле (*live*) in clover; ~**е́ть** [8],
с-⟩ dampen; ~**е́ц** *m* [1; -рца́]:
лк-~е́ц raw silk; ∠**ник** *m* [1]
ese cake; ∠**ный** [14] cheese...;
eous; ~**ова́тый** [14 *sh.*] dampish;
e, *Brt.* underdone; ~**о́й** [14; сыр,
-o] damp; moist; raw; crude;
aked; ∠**ость** *f* [8] dampness;
isture; ~**ьё** *n* [10] *coll.* raw ma-
ial.

сыск|а́ть F [3] *pf.* find; **-ся** be found; ~**но́й** [14] detective.
сы́т|ный [14; сы́тен, -тна́, -o] substantial, rich; F fat; ~**ый** [14; сыт, -а́, -o] satisfied; fat.
сыч *m* [1 *e.*] horned owl.
сы́щик *m* [1] detective, policeman.
сюда́ here, hither; this way.
сюже́т *m* [1] subject; plot.
сюрпри́з *m* [1] surprise.
сюрту́к *m* [1 *e.*] frock coat.

T

bbr.: **1.** това́рищ; **2.** том; **3.** то́н-
; **4.** ты́сяча.
а́|к *m* [1 *e.*; *part. g.*: -у́] tobacco;
е́рка *f* [5; *g/pl.*: -рок] snuffbox;
ный [14] tobacco...
|**ель** *m* [4] time sheet; ~**ле́тка** *f*
g/pl.: -ток] tablet; ~**ли́ца** *f* [5]
le, schedule, list; scale; *gr.* para-
m; ~**ор** *m* [1] (*gipsy's*) camp; ⚔
у́н *m* [1 *e.*] herd, drove. [party.]
уре́тка *f* [5; *g/pl.*: -ток] stool.
жи́к *m* [1], ~**ский** [16] Tajik.
m [1; в -у́; *pl. e.*] basin; *anat.*
vis.
нств|енный [14 *sh.*] mysterious;
ret(ive); ′~**о** *n* [9] sacrament.
ть [13] conceal; **-ся** hide.
га́ *f* [5] taiga.
ко́м secretly; behind (one's)
k (от P); ∠**на** *f* [5] secret; mys-
y; ~**ни́к** *m* [1 *e.*] hiding (place);
most) recess; ∠**ный** [14] secret;
althy; vague; privy.
so, thus; like that; (~ же just)
so much; just so; then; well; yes;
way ...; *s. a.* пра́вда; F prop-
y; не ~ wrong(ly); ~ и (*both*...)
l; F downright; ∠ как as, since;
without that; ∠**же** also, too; ∠же
neither, nor; а ∠же as well as;
F all the same; indeed; ~ **наз.**
r.: ~ называ́емый so-called;
ged; ~**ово́й** [14; -ко́в, -кова́]
h; (a)like; same; был(а́) ~о́в(а́)
appeared, vanished; ~**о́й** [16]
h; so; ~**о́е** *su.* such things; ~о́й
the same; as ...; ~о́й-то such-
d-such; so-and-so; что (э́то)
? F what's the matter?, what's
?; кто вы ~о́й (~а́я)? = кто́ вы?
са *f* [5] (fixed) rate.
си́ *n* [*ind.*] taxi(cab).
си́ровать [7] (*im*)*pf.* rate.
т *m* [1] ♪ time, measure, bar;
tact; ∠**ика** *f* [5] tactics *pl.* & *sg.*;
ческий [16] tactical; ~**и́чность**
8] tactfulness; ~**и́чный** [14;
н, -чна] tactful.
а́нт *m* [1] talent, gift (for к Д);
ивый [14 *sh.*] talented, gifted.
ия *f* [7] waist.
о́н *m* [1] coupon.

та́лый [14] thawed; slushy.
там there; F then; ~ же in the same place; ibidem; ~ и сям F here and there.
тамо́ж|енный [14] custom(s)...; ~**ня** *f* [6; *g/pl.*: -жен] custom house.
та́мошний [15] of that place, there.
та́н|ец *m* [1; -нца] dance (*go* dancing на B *pl.*); ~**к** *m* [1] tank; ~**ковый** [14] armo(u)red...; tank...
танц|ева́льный [14] dancing...; ~**ева́ть** [7], ⟨с-⟩ dance; ~**о́вщик** *m* [1], ~**о́вщица** *f* [5] (ballet) dancer; ~**о́р** *m* [1], ~**о́рка** *f* [5; *g/pl.*: -рок] dancer.
Та́ня *f* [6] *dim. of* Татья́на.
та́почка *f* [5; *g/pl.*: -чек] sport slipper.
та́ра *f* [5] tare; packing.
тарака́н *m* [1] cockroach.
тара́нить [13], ⟨про-⟩ ram.
тарахте́ть F [11] rumble.
тара́щить [16], ⟨вы́-⟩: ~ глаза́ stare (at на B; with *surprise* от P).
таре́лка *f* [5; *g/pl.*: -лок] plate.
тари́ф *m* [1] tariff; ~**ный** [14] tariff...; standard (*wages*).
таска́ть [1] carry; drag, pull; F steal; P wear; **-ся** F roam; go; frequent; gad about.
тасова́ть [7], ⟨с-⟩ shuffle.
ТАСС (Телегра́фное Аге́нтство Сове́тского Сою́за) TASS (Telegraph Agency of the U.S.S.R.).
тата́р|ин *m* [1; *pl.*: -ры, -р, -рам], ~**ка** *f* [5; *g/pl.*: -рок], ~**ский** [16] Tartar.
Татья́на *f* [5] Tatyana.
тафта́ *f* [5] taffeta.
тача́ть [1], ⟨с-, вы́-⟩ seam, sew.
тащи́ть [16] **1.** ⟨по-⟩ drag, pull; carry, bring; **2.** F ⟨с-⟩ steal, pilfer; ~**ся** F trudge, drag (o.s.) along.
та́ять [27], ⟨рас-⟩ thaw, melt; fade, die (away); languish, pine.
тварь *f* [8] creature; F wretch.
тверде́ть [8], ⟨за-, о-⟩ harden.
тверди́ть F [15 *e.*; -ржу́, -рди́шь] reiterate, repeat (over & over again); talk; practice; ⟨за-, вы́-⟩ learn.
твёрд|ость *f* [8] firmness; hardness; ~**ый** [14; твёрд, тверда́, -o] hard;

solid; firm (*a. fig.*); (stead)fast, steady; fixed (*a. prices*); sound, good; F sure; ~о *a.* well, for sure.
твердыня *f* [6] stronghold.
тво|й *m*, **~я́** *f*, **~ё** *n*, **~и́** *pl.* [24] your; yours; *pl. su.* F your folks; *cf.* ваш.
твор|е́ние *n* [12] work; creature; **~е́ц** *m* [1; -рца́] creator; author; **~и́тельный** [14] *gr.* instrumental (*case*); **~и́ть** [13], ⟨со-⟩ create, do; perform; **-ся** F be (going) on; **~о́г** *m* [1 *e.*] curd(s).
тво́рче|ский [16] creative; **~ство** *n* [9] work(s), creation.
т. е. *abbr.:* то́ есть, *cf.*
теа́тр *m* [1] theater (*Brt.* -tre; at в П); house; stage; **~а́льный** [14; -лен, -льна] theatrical; theater...
тёзка *m/f* [5; *g/pl.*: -зок] namesake.
тексти́ль *m* [4] *coll.* textiles *pl.*; **~ный** [14] textile; cotton (*mill*).
теку́|чий [17 *sh.*] fluid; fluctuating; **~щий** [17] current; instant; present; miscellaneous.
телеви́|дение *n* [12] television (on по Д); **~зио́нный** [14] TV; **~зор** *m* [1] TV set.
теле́га *f* [5] cart, telega.
телегра́мма *f* [5] telegram, wire.
телегра́ф *m* [1] telegraph (office); wire (by по Д); **~и́ровать** [7] (*im*)*pf.* telegraph, wire, cable; **~ный** [14] telegraph(ic); telegram..., by wire.
теле́жка *f* [5; *g/pl.*: -жек] handcart.
телёнок *m* [2] calf.
телепереда́ча *f* [5] telecast.
телеско́п *m* [1] telescope.
теле́сный [14] corporal; corporeal; flesh-colo(u)red.
телефо́н *m* [1] telephone (by по Д); **~и́ровать** [7] (*im*)*pf.* (Д) telephone, F phone; **~и́ст** *m* [1], **~и́стка** *f* [5; *g/pl.*: -ток] operator; **~ный** [14] tele(phone)...; call (*box*).
тели́ться [13; те́лится], ⟨о-⟩ calve.
тёлка *f* [5; *g/pl.*: -лок] heifer.
те́ло *n* [9; *pl. e.*] body; *phys.* solid; иноро́дное ~ foreign matter; всем ~м all over; **~сложе́ние** *n* [12] build; constitution; **~храни́тель** *m* [4] bodyguard.
теля́|тина *f* [5], **~чий** [18] veal.
тем *s.* тот.
те́м(а́тик)а *f* [5] subject, theme(s).
тембр (tɛ-) *m* [1] timbre.
Те́мза *f* [5] Thames.
темн|е́ть [8] **1.** ⟨по-⟩ darken; **2.** ⟨с-⟩ grow *or* get dark; **3.** (*a.* **-ся**) appear *or* show dark; loom; **~и́ца** *f* [5] prison, dungeon.
тёмно... (*in compds.*) dark...
темнота́ *f* [5] darkness; obscurity.
тёмн|ый [14; тёмен, темна́] dark; *fig.* obscure; gloomy; shady, dubious; evil, malicious; ignorant, slow, backward.
темп (tɛ-) *m* [1] tempo; rate, pace.
темпера́мент *m* [1] temperament; spirits *pl.*; **~ный** [14; -тен, -...] temperamental.
температу́ра *f* [5] temperatur...
те́мя *n* [13] crown.
тенденци|о́зный (tɛndɛ-) [14; -зна] tendentious; **'~я** (tɛn'dɛ...) [7] tendency.
те́ндер 🚂, ⚓ ('tɛnder) *m* [1] ten...
тени́стый [14 *sh.*] shady.
те́ннис ('tɛ-) *m* [1] tennis.
те́нор ♪ *m* [1; *pl.*: -ра́, *etc. e.*] te...
тень *f* [8; в тени́; *pl.*: те́ни, те... *etc. e.*] shade; shadow.
теор|е́тик *m* [1] theorist; **~ети... ский** [16] theoretical; **~ия** ... theory; **~ия** позна́ния epistemol...
тепе́р|ешний [15] present, ac... **~ь** now, at present.
тепл|е́ть [8; *3rd p. only*], ⟨... grow warm; **~и́ться** [13] b... glimmer; **~и́ца** *f* [5], **~и́чный** hothouse; **~о́ 1.** *n* [9] warmth; ... heat; warm weather; **2.** *adv.*, *s.* ...лый; **~ово́й** [14] (of) heat, ther... **~ота́** *f* [5] warmth; *phys.* hea... **~охо́д** *m* [1] motor ship; **~у́ш...** [5; *g/pl.*: -шек] heatable boxca...
тёплый [14; тёпел, тепла́, -... тёпло] warm (*a. fig.*); hot (... (мне) тепло́ it is (I am) warm.
терапи́я *f* [7] therapy.
тере|би́ть [14 *e.*; -блю́, -би́шь] tousle; twitch; F pester; **'~м** ... *pl.*: -а́, *etc. e.*] attic; (tower-)ch... ber; **~ть** [12] rub; grate; **-ся** F ... about.
терза́|ние *n* [12] torment, ag... **~ть** [1] **1.** ⟨ис-⟩ torment, tor... **2.** ⟨рас-⟩ tear to pieces.
тёрка *f* [5; *g/pl.*: -рок] grater.
те́рмин *m* [1] term; **~оло́гия** ... terminology.
термо́|метр *m* [1] thermom... **'~с** ('tɛ-) *m* [1] vacuum *or* the... bottle.
терни́стый [14 *sh.*] thorny.
терп|ели́вый [14 *sh.*] patient; **~е...** *n* [12] patience; **~е́ть** [10], ⟨... suffer, endure; tolerate, bear, s... not press, permit of delay; (Д... **-ся** *impf.* be impatient *or* e... **~и́мость** *f* [8] tolerance (towa... к Д); **~и́мый** [14 *sh.*] tole... bearable. [те́рпче] ...
те́рпкий [16; -пок, -пка́, -о; *com...*
терра́са *f* [5] terrace.
террит|ориа́льный [14] territ... **~о́рия** *f* [7] territory.
терро́р *m* [1] terror; **~изи́ро...** & **~изова́ть** [7] *im*(*pf.*) terro...
тёртый F [14] cunning, sly.
теря́ть [28], ⟨по-⟩ lose; waste; (*leaves*); give up (*hope*); **-ся** be... disappear, vanish; become em... rassed, be at a loss.
теса́ть [3], ⟨об-⟩ hew, cut.
тесн|и́ть [13], ⟨с-⟩ press; opp... **-ся** crowd, throng; jostle; **~о...** [5] narrowness; throng; **~ый** ...

тéсен, теснá, -о] narrow; tight; clore; intimate.
éст|о *n* [9] dough, paste; ⁓ь *m* [4] father-in-law (*wife's father*).
есьмá *f* [5; *g*/*pl*.: -сём] tape.
éтер|ев *m* [1; *pl*.: -á, *etc. e.*] black grouse, blackcock; ⁓я P *f* [6]: глухáя ⁓я deaf fellow; сóнная ⁓я sleepyhead.
етивá *f* [5] bowstring.
ётка *f* [5; *g*/*pl*.: -ток] aunt.
етрáд|ь *f* [8], ⁓ка *f* [5; *g*/*pl*.: -док] exercise book, notebook, copybook.
ётя F *f* [6; *g*/*pl*.: -тей] aunt.
éхн|ик *m* [1] technician; ⁓ика *f* [5] technics; technique; equipment; F skill; ⁓икум *m* [1] technical school; ⁓и́ческий [16] technical; ⁓ологи́ческий [16] technological; ⁓олóгия *f* [7] technology.
еч|éние *n* [12] current; stream up- [down-] вверх [вниз] по Д); course (in в В; in/of *time* с Т/Р); *fig.* trend; movement; ⁓ь [26] 1. flow, run; stream; move; leak; 2. *f* [8] leak (spring дать).
шить [16], ⟨по-⟩ amuse; please; ся amuse o. s.; take comfort; banter.
ща *f* [5] mother-in-law (*wife's mother*).
ибéтец *m* [1; -тца] Tibetan.
игр *m* [1] tiger; ⁓и́ца *f* [5] tigress.
ка|нье *n* [10], ⁓ть [1] tick.
имофéй *m* [3] Timothy.
ин|а *f* [5] ooze; ⁓истый [14 *sh.*] oozy.
ип *m* [1] type; F character; ⁓и́чный [14; -чен, -чна] typical;
ография *f* [7] printing plant *or* office; ⁓огрáфский [16] printing (*press*); printer's (ink крáска *f*).
ир *m* [1] shooting gallery, rifle range.
рáда *f* [5] tirade.
рáж *m* [1 *e.*] circulation; drawing of a lottery).
рáн *m* [1] tyrant; ⁓ить [13] tyrannize; ⁓и́я *f* [7], ⁓ство *n* [9] tyranny.
ре́ *n* [*ind.*] dash.
с|кать [1], ⟨⁓нуть⟩ [20] squeeze, press; print; ⁓ки́ *m*/*pl*. [1 *e.*] vice, grip; F fix; ⁓нёный [14] (im-)printed.
гул *m* [1], ⁓ьный [14] title.
ф *m* [1] typhus.
хий [16; тих, -á, -о; *comp*.: ти́ше] quiet, still; calm; soft, gentle; slow; dull, flat; *cap.* Pacific; ⁓хомóлком F on the quiet; ⁓ше! silence!;
шинá *f* [5] silence, stillness, calm (ness); ⁓шь *f* [8; в тиши́] calm; silence.
т. *abbr.*: тáк как, *cf.* так.
|нь *f* [8] fabric, cloth; *biol.* tissue; ⁓ть [тку, ткёшь; ткал, ткáлá, ⟨со-⟩ [сóтканный] weave; ⁓цкий [16] weaver's; weaving; ⁓ч *m* [1 *e.*], ⁓чи́ха *f* [5] weaver.
нуть(ся) *s.* ты́кать(ся).
|ние *n* [12] decay, putrefaction; smo(u)ldering; ⁓ть [8], ⟨ис-⟩ (s)mo(u)lder, decay, rot, putrefy; glimmer.
то 1. [28] that; ⁓ же the same; к ⁓му́ (же) in addition (to that), moreover; add to this; ни ⁓ ни сё F neither fish nor flesh; ни с ⁓гó ни с сегó F all of a sudden, without any visible reason; до ⁓гó so much; **2.** (*cj.*) then; ⁓ ... ⁓ now ... now; не ⁓ ... не ⁓ *or* ⁓ ли ... ⁓ ли either ... or, half ... half; не ⁓, чтóбы not that; а не ⁓ (or) else; **3.** ⁓ -⁓ just, exactly; although; oh ...
тов. *abbr.*: товáрищ.
товáр *m* [1] commodity, article (of trade); *pl.* goods, wares.
товáрищ *m* [1] comrade, friend; mate, companion (in *arms* по Д); colleague; assistant; ⁓ по шкóле schoolmate; ⁓ по университéту fellow student; ⁓еский [16] friendly; companionable; ⁓ество *n* [9] comradeship, fellowship; partnership; association, company.
товáр|ный [14] ware(*house*); goods-...; 🚂 freight..., *Brt.* goods...; ⁓ообмéн *m* [1] barter; ⁓оборóт *m* [1] commodity circulation.
тогдá then, at that time; ⁓ как whereas, while; ⁓шний [15] of that (*or* the) time, then.
тó есть that is (to say), i. e.
тождéств|енный [14 *sh.*] identical; '⁓о *n* [9] identity.
тóже also, too, as well; *cf.* тáкже.
ток *m* **1.** [1] current; **2.** [1; на -ý; *from g*/*pl. e.*] (threshing) floor.
токáр|ный [14] turner's; turning (*lathe*); '⁓ь *m* [4] turner.
толк *m* [1; бéз -у] sense; use; judg(e)-ment; F talk, rumo(u)r; † doctrine; sect; знать ⁓ в (П) be a judge of; ⁓áть [1], *once* ⟨⁓нýть⟩ [20] push, shove, thrust; *fig.* induce, prompt; F urge on, spur; -ся push (o. a.); F knock (at в В; about); ⁓овáть [7] **1.** ⟨ис-⟩ interpret, expound, explain; comment; take (in ... part в ... стóрону); **2.** ⟨по-⟩ F talk (to с Т); speak, tell, say; ⁓óвый [14] explanatory, commenting; F [*sh.*] sensible, smart, wise; ⁓ом = ⁓óво; *a.* in earnest; ⁓отня́ F *f* [6] crush, crowd; ⁓ýчка P *f* [5; *g*/*pl*.: -чек] second-hand market.
толо|кнó *n* [9] oat flour; ⁓чь [26; -лкý, -лчёшь, -лкýт; -лóк, -лклá; -лчённый], ⟨рас-, ис-⟩ pound; ⁓чься P hang about.
толп|á *f* [5; *pl. st.*], ⁓и́ться [14 *e.*; *no 1st. & 2nd p. sg.*], ⟨с-⟩ crowd, throng; mob; swarm.
толст|éть [8], ⟨по-, рас-⟩ grow stout; ⁓окóжий [17 *sh.*] thick-skinned; ⁓ый [14; толст, -á, -о; *comp*.: тóлще] thick; large, big; stout, fat; ⁓я́к F *m* [1 *e.*] fat man.
толч|ёный [14] pounded; ⁓ея́ F *f*

[6] crush, crowd; **~о́к** *m* [1; -чка́] push; shock; jolt; *fig.* impulse.
толщин|á *f* [5] thickness; stoutness; ~о́й в (B), ... в ~у́ ... thick.
толь *m* [4] roofing felt.
то́лько only, but; как ~ as soon as; лишь (*or* едва́) ~ no sooner ... than; ~ бы if only; ~ что just (now); ~-~ F barely.
том *m* [1; *pl.*: -á, *etc. e.*] volume.
том|и́тельный [14; -лен, -льна] painful, tormenting; oppressive; **~и́ть** [14 *e.*; томлю́, томи́шь, томлённый], ⟨ис-⟩ torment, plague, harass, pester; pinch, oppress; **-ся** pine (for T), languish (with; be tormented, *etc.*, *s.* ~и́ть); **~ле́ние** *n* [12], **∠ность** *f* [8] languor; **∠ный** [14; -мен, -мна́, -о] languishing.
тон *m* [1; *pl.*: -á, *etc. e.*] tone.
то́нк|ий [16; -нок, -нка́, -о; *comp.*: то́ньше] thin; slim, slender; small; fine; delicate, subtle; keen; light (*sleep*); high (*voice*); F cunning; **~ость** *f* [8] thinness, *etc. s.* ~ий; delicacy, subtlety; *pl.* details (go into вдава́ться в B; F split hairs).
то́нна *f* [5] ton; **∠ж** *m* [1] tonnage.
тону́ть [19] *v/i.* **1.** ⟨по-, за-⟩ sink; submerge; **2.** ⟨у-⟩ drown.
То́ня *f* [6] *dim. of* Антони́на.
то́п|ать [1], *once* ⟨~нуть⟩ [20] stamp; **~и́ть** [14] *v/t.* **1.** ⟨за-, по-⟩ sink; flood; **2.** ⟨за-, ис-, на-⟩ heat; light a fire; **3.** ⟨рас-⟩ melt; **4.** ⟨у-⟩ drown; **~ка** *f* [5; *g/pl.*: -пок] heating; furnace; **~кий** [16; -пок, -пка́, -о] boggy, marshy; **~лёный** [14] melted; molten; **~ливо** *n* [9] fuel; **~нуть** *s.* ~ать.
топогра́фия *f* [7] topography.
то́поль *m* [4; *pl.*: -ля́, *etc. e.*] poplar.
топо́р *m* [1 *e.*] ax(e); **~ный** [14; -рен, -рна] coarse.
то́пот *m* [1] stamp(ing), tramp(ing).
топта́ть [3], ⟨по-, за-⟩ trample, tread; ⟨вы́-⟩ press; ⟨с-⟩ wear out; **~ся** tramp(le); F hang about; mark time (на ме́сте).
топь *f* [8] marsh, mire, bog, fen.
торг *m* [1; на -у́; *pl.*: -и́, *etc. e.*] bargaining, chaffer; *pl.* auction (by с P; at на П); **~а́ш** *contp. m* [1 *e.*] dealer; **~ова́ть** [8] trade, deal (in T); sell; be open; **-ся,** ⟨с-⟩ (strike a) bargain (for о П); **~о́вец** *m* [1; -вца] dealer, trader, merchant; **~о́вка** *f* [5; *g/pl.*: -вок] market woman; **~о́вля** *f* [6] trade, commerce; traffic; business; **~о́вый** [14] trade..., trading, commercial, of commerce; ⚓ mercantile, merchant...; **~пре́д** *m* [1] Soviet trade representative; **~пре́дство** *n* [9] trade agency of the U.S.S.R.
торже́ств|енность *f* [8] solemnity; **~енный** [14 *sh.*] solemn; festive; triumphant; **~о́** *n* [9] triumph; festivity celebration; **~ова́ть** [7], ⟨вос-⟩ triumph (over над T); *i*
celebrate.
то́рмо|з *m* **1.** [1; *pl.*: -á, *etc. e.*] br
2. [1] *fig.* drag; **~зи́ть** [15 *e.*; -о
-ози́шь; -ожённый], ⟨за-⟩
the) brake(s on); *fig.* hamper; *ps*
curb, restrain; **~ши́ть** F [16
-шу́, -ши́шь] *s.* теребить.
то́рный [14] beaten (*road, a. fi*
тороп|и́ть [14], ⟨по-⟩ hasten, h
up (*v/i.* **-ся**; *a.* be in a hurry); ~
вый [14 *sh.*] hasty, hurried.
торпе́д|а *f* [5], **~и́ровать** [7] (*im*
torpedo; **~ный** [14] torpedo...
торт *m* [1] pie; fancy cake.
торф *m* [1] peat; **~яно́й** [14] pe
торча́ть [4 *e.*; -чу́, чи́шь] stick
F hang about.
тоск|á *f* [5] melancholy; anx
grief; yearning; boredom, en
~á по ро́дине homesickness; ~
вый [14 *sh.*] melancholy; sad, dre
~ова́ть [7] grieve, feel sad (*or* l
ly); feel bored; yearn *or* long
по П *or* Д); be homesick (по
дине).
тот *m*, та *f*, то *n*, те *pl.* [28] that
those; the one; the other;
wrong; (н)и тот (н)и друго́й
(neither); тот же (са́мый) the sa
тем бо́лее the more so; тем лу́
so much the better; тем са́
thereby; *cf. a.* то.
то́тчас (же) immediately, at on
точи́|льный [14] grinding; ~
щик *m* [1] grinder; **~ть** [16
⟨на-⟩ whet, grind; sharpen; **2.** ⟨в
turn; **3.** ⟨ис-⟩ eat (*or* gnaw) a
gnaw at; perforate; wear; weat
то́чк|а *f* [5; *g/pl.*: -чек] point;
typ., *gr.* period, full stop; вы́с
~а zenith, climax (at на П); ~а
пято́й *gr.* semicolon; ~а! F enou
s. a. точь.
то́чн|о *adv. of* ~ый; *a.* = сло́
indeed; так ~о! ⚔ yes, sir!; **~о**
f [8] accuracy, exactness, precis
в ~ости *s.* ~о; **~ый** [14; -чен,
-о] exact, precise, accurate; p
tual; (of) precision.
точь: ~ в ~ F exactly.
тошн|и́ть [13]; меня́ ~и́т I feel
I loathe; **~ота́** *f* [5] nausea; F lo
ing; **∠ый** [14; -шен, -шна́, -о] lo
some, nauseous; мне ∠о *s.* ~и́ть
то́щий [17; тощ, -á, -е] lean,
gaunt; F empty; scanty, poor.
трава́ *f* [5; *pl. st.*] grass; h
weed.
трав|и́ть [14] **1.** ⟨за-⟩ bait, c
course; *fig.* attack; **2.** ⟨с-, в
corrode, stain; exterminate; **3**
⟨вы́-⟩ loosen; **∠ля** *f* [6; *g/pl.*: -
baiting; *fig.* defamation.
травян|и́стый [14 *sh.*], **~о́й**
grass(y).
траг|е́дия *f* [7] tragedy; **∠ик** *m*
tragedian; **~и́ческий** [16], ~
ный [14; -чен, -чна] tragic(al)

радицио́нный [14; -о́нен, -о́нна] traditional.
ракт *m* [1] highway; *anat.* tract; **~а́т** *m* [1] treatise; **~и́р** *m* [1] inn, tavern, *Brt.* public house, F pub; **~и́рщик** *m* [1] innkeeper; **~ова́ть** [7] treat; **~о́вка** *f* [5; *g/pl.*: -вок] treatment; **~ори́ст** *m* [1] tractor operator; **~о́рный** [14] tractor...
ра́льщик *m* [1] trawler; ⚔ mine sweeper.
рамбова́ть [7], ⟨у-⟩ ram.
рамва́й *m* [3] streetcar, *Brt.* tramway, tram(car) (by T, на П).
рампли́н *m* [1] springboard.
ранзи́т *m* [1], **~ный** [14] transit.
ранс|криби́ровать [7] (*im*)*pf.* transcribe; **~ли́ровать** [7] (*im*)*pf.* transmit; relay; **~ля́ция** *f* [7] transmission; **~пара́нт** *m* [1] transparency.
ра́нспорт *m* [1] transport(ation; *a.* system [of]); **~и́ровать** [7] (*im*)*pf.* transport, convey; **~ный** [14] (of) transport(ation).
рансформа́тор *m* [1] transformer.
раншея́ *f* [6; *g/pl.*: -е́й] trench.
рап *m* [1] gangway; **~е́ция** *f* [7] trapeze; ⩲ trapezium.
ра́сса *f* [5] route. line.
ра́т|а *f* [5] expenditure; expense; waste; **~ить** [15], ⟨ис-, по-⟩ spend; waste; **~та** ✝ *f* [5] draft.
ра́ур *m* [1] mourning; **~ный** [14] mourning...; funeral...
трафаре́т *m* [1] cliché (*a. fig.*).
трах! crack!
тре́бова|ние *n* [12] demand (on по Д); requirement; claim; order; **~тельный** [14; -лен, -льна] exacting; particular; pretentious; **~ть** [7], ⟨по-⟩ (P) demand; require; claim; cite, summon; call; **-ся** be required (*or* wanted); be necessary.
трево́|га *f* [5] alarm; warning, alert; anxiety; **~жить** [16] **1.** ⟨вс-, рас-⟩ alarm, disquiet; **2.** ⟨по-⟩ disturb, trouble; **-ся** be anxious; worry; **~жный** [14; -жен, -жна] restless, uneasy; alarm(ing), disturbing.
тре́зв|ость *f* [8] sobriety; **~ый** [14; трезв, -á, -o] sober (*a. fig.*).
трель *f* [8] trill, shake; warble.
тре́нер *m* [1] trainer, coach.
тре́ние *n* [12] friction (*a. fig.*).
тренир|ова́ть [7], ⟨на-⟩ train, coach; *v/i.* **-ся**; **~о́вка** *f* [5] training.
трепа́ть [2] **1.** ⟨по-⟩ tousle; twitch; flutter; F tap (on по Д); wear out, fray; harass; prate; **2.** ⟨вы́-⟩ scutch.
тре́пет *m* [1] tremor; quiver; **~а́ть** [3], ⟨за-⟩ tremble (with от P); quiver, shiver; flicker; palpitate; **~ный** [14; -тен, -тна] quivering; flickering.
треск *m* [1] crack, crash; **~á** *f* [5] cod; **~аться** [1], ⟨по-, тре́снуть⟩ [20] burst; crack, split; chap; **~отня́** *f* [6] crackle; rattle; chirp; gabble
~у́чий [17 *sh.*] hard, ringing (*frost*); *fig.* bombastic.
тре́снуть *s.* тре́скаться & треща́ть.
трест *m* [1] trust.
трет|е́йский [16] of arbitration; **~ий** [18] third; **~ьего дня** = позавчера́; *cf.* пя́тый; **~и́ровать** [7] (mal)treat; **~ь** *f* [8; *from g/pl. e.*] (one) third.
треуго́льн|ик *m* [1] triangle; **~ый** [14] triangular; three-cornered (*hat*).
тре́фы *f/pl.* [5] clubs (*cards*).
трёх|годи́чный [14] three years'; triennial; **~дне́вный** [14] three days'; **~колёсный** [14] three-wheeled; **~ле́тний** [15] three-years(-old)'; **~со́тый** [14] three hundredth; **~цве́тный** [14] three-colo(u)r; tricolor(ed); **~эта́жный** [14] three-storied (*Brt.* -reyed).
трещ|а́ть [4 *e.*; -щу́, -щи́шь] **1.** ⟨за-⟩ crack; **2.** ⟨про-⟩ crackle; rattle; chirp; F prattle; **3.** ⟨тре́снуть⟩ [20] burst; **~ина** *f* [5] split (*a. fig.*), crack, cleft, crevice, fissure; chap; **~о́тка** *f* [5; *g/pl.*: -ток] rattle; F chatterbox.
три [34] three; *cf.* пять.
трибу́н|а *f* [5] tribune, platform; stand; **~а́л** *m* [1] tribunal.
тригономе́трия *f* [7] trigonometry.
тридца́|тый [14] thirtieth; *cf.* пятидеся́тый; **'~ть** [35 *e.*] thirty.
три́жды three times, thrice.
трико́ *n* [*ind.*] tights *pl.*; **~та́ж** *m* [1] hosiery; jersey.
трило́гия *f* [7] trilogy.
трина́дца|тый [14] thirteenth; *cf.* пя́тый; **~ть** [35] thirteen; *cf.* пять.
три́ста [36] three hundred.
триу́мф *m* [1] triumph; **~а́льный** [14] triumphal; triumphant.
тро́га|тельный [14; -лен, -льна] touching, moving; **~ть** [1], *once* ⟨тро́нуть⟩ [20] touch (*a. fig.* = move); F pester; **~й**! go!; **-ся** start; set out (on a journey в путь); move; be touched.
тро́е [37] three (*cf.* дво́е); **~кра́тный** [14; -тен, -тна] repeated three times.
тро́иц|а *f* [5] Trinity; Whitsunday.
тро́й|ка *f* [5; *g/pl.*: тро́ек] three (*cf.* дво́йка); troika (*team of 3 horses abreast* [+ *vehicle*]); triumvirate; F (*mark* =) посре́дственно, *cf.*; **~но́й** [14] threefold, triple, treble; **~ня** *f* [6; *g/pl.*: тро́ен] triplets *pl.*
тролле́йбус *m* [1] trolley bus.
трон *m* [1] throne; **~ный** [14] *Brt.* King's (Queen's) (*speech*).
тро́нуть(ся) *s.* тро́гать(ся).
троп|а́ *f* [5; *pl.*: тро́пы, троп, -па́м] path, track; **~и́нка** [5; *g/pl.*: -нок] (small) path.
тропи́ческий [16] tropic(al).
трос *m* [1] hawser, cable.
трост|ни́к *m* [1 *e.*] reed; cane; **~ни-**

ко́вый [14] reed...; cane...; **∠очка** *f* [5; *g/pl.*: -чек], **~ь** *f* [8; *from g/pl. e.*] cane, *Brt. a.* walking stick.
тротуа́р *m* [1] sidewalk, *Brt.* pavement, footpath, footway.
трофе́й *m* [3], **~ный** [14] trophy.
тро|ю́родный [14] second (cousin брат *m*, сестра́ *f*); **~я́кий** [16 *sh.*] threefold, triple.
труб|а́ *f* [5; *pl. st.*] pipe, (*a. anat.*) tube; chimney; 🚂, ⚓ smokestack, funnel; (*fire*) engine; ♪ trumpet; **~а́ч** *m* [1 *e.*] trumpeter; **~и́ть** [14 *e.*; -блю́, -би́шь], ⟨про-⟩ blow (the в В); **∠ка** *f* [5; *g/pl.*: -бок] tube; pipe (*to smoke*); *teleph.* receiver; roll; **~опрово́д** *m* [1] pipe line; **~очи́ст** *m* [1] chimney sweep; **∠чатый** [14] tubular.
труд *m* [1 *e.*] labo(u)r, work; pains *pl.*, trouble; difficulty (with с Т; *a.* hard[ly]); *pl. a.* transactions; F service; **~и́ться** [15], ⟨по-⟩ work; toil, exert o.s.; trouble; **∠ность** *f* [8] difficulty; **∠ный** [14; -ден, -дна́, -o] difficult, hard; F heavy; **~ово́й** [14] labo(u)r...; working; workman's; earned; service...; **~олюби́вый** [14 *sh.*] industrious; **~оспосо́бный** [14; -бен, -бна] able-bodied, able to work; **~я́щийся** [17] working; *su.* worker.
тру́женик *m* [1] toiler, worker.
труни́ть [13] make fun (of над Т).
труп *m* [1] corpse, body.
тру́ппа *f* [5] company, troupe.
трус *m* [1] coward; **∠ики** *m/pl.* [1] trunks, shorts; **∠ить** [15], ⟨с-⟩ be afraid (of Р); **~и́ха** F *f* [5] *f of* ~; **~ли́вый** [14 *sh.*] cowardly; **∠ость** *f* [8] cowardice; **~ы́** *s.* ∠ики.
трут *m* [1] tinder.
тру́тень *m* [4; -тня] drone.
трущо́ба *f* [5] slum, den, nest.
трюк *m* [1] trick, F stunt.
трюм ⚓ *m* [1] hold.
трюмо́ *n* [*ind.*] pier glass.
тряп|и́чник *m* [1] ragpicker; **∠ка**; [5; *g/pl.*: -пок] rag; duster; patch; F milksop; **~ьё** *n* [10] rag(s).
тряси́на *f* [5] bog, fen, quagmire.
тря́с|ка *f* [5] jolting; **~кий** [16; -сок, -ска] shaky; jolty; **~ти́** [24 -с-], *once* ⟨тряхну́ть⟩ [20] shake (a p.'s Д *hand*; *head*, *etc.* Т; *a. fig.*); F (*impers.*) jolt; **~ти́сь** shake; shiver (with от Р).
тряхну́ть *s.* трясти́.
тсс! hush!
тт. *abbr.*: **1.** това́рищи; **2.** тома́.
туале́т *m* [1] toilet.
туберкулёз *m* [1] tuberculosis; **~ный** [14] tubercular; tuberculous (patient).
туго́|й [14; туг, -а́, -o; *comp.*: ту́же] tight, taut; stiff; crammed; F stingy; slow, hard (*a.* of hearing на́ ухо); *adv. a.* hard put to it; hard up; hard, with difficulty.
туда́ there, thither; that way.
тужи́ть F [16] grieve; long for (П).
тужу́рка *f* [5; *g/pl.*: -рок] jacket.
туз *m* [1 *e.*] ace; F boss.
тузе́м|ец *m* [1; -мца] native; **~ный** [14] native.
ту́ловище *n* [11] trunk.
тулу́п *m* [1] sheepskin coat.
тума́н *m* [1] fog, mist; haze; smog **~ный** [14; -а́нен, -а́нна] foggy misty; *fig.* hazy, vague.
ту́мб|а *f* [5] curbstone (*Brt.* kerb-) pedestal; **~очка** *f* [5; *g/pl.*: -чек bedside table.
тунея́дец *m* [1; -дца] parasite.
Туни́с *m* [1] Tunisia; Tunis.
тунне́ль (-'nɛ-) *m* [4] tunnel.
туп|е́ть [8], ⟨(п)о-⟩ grow blunt **~и́к** *m* [1 *e.*] blind alley, dead end (*a. fig.*) impasse; nonplus, tight corner; ста́вить в ~и́к baffle; стат в ~и́к be at one's wit's end; **~о́й** [14; туп, -а́, -o] blunt; ⟁ obtuse *fig.* dull, stupid; apathetic; **∠ость** [8] bluntness; dullness; **~оу́мный** [14; -мен, -мна] stupid.
тур *m* [1] round; tour; *zo.* aurochs
тура́ *f* [5] rook, castle (*chess*).
турби́на *f* [5] turbine.
туре́цкий [16] Turkish.
тури́|зм *m* [1] tourism; **~ст** *m* [1 tourist.
туркме́н *m* [1] Turk(o)man; **~ский** [16] Turkmen(ian).
турне́ (-'nɛ) *n* [*ind.*] tour.
турни́к *m* [1 *e.*] horizontal bar.
турни́р *m* [1] tournament (in на П)
ту́р|ок *m* [1; -рка; *g/pl.*: ту́рок] **~ча́нка** *f* [5; *g/pl.*: -нок] Turk **♀ция** *f* [7] Turkey.
ту́ск|лый [14; тускл, -а́, -o] dim dull; dead (*gold*, *etc.*); **~не́ть** [8] ⟨по-⟩ & **~нуть** [20] grow dim or dull.
тут F here; there; then; ~! present! ~ же there & then, on the spot; как ~ already there.
ту́тов|ый [14]: ~ое де́рево *n* mulberry. [per.
ту́фля *f* [6; *g/pl.*: -фель] shoe; slip-
ту́х|лый [14; тухл, -а́, -o] bad (*egg*) rotten; **~нуть** [21] **1.** ⟨по-⟩ go out, die out, expire; **2.** ⟨про-⟩ go bad
ту́ч|а *f* [5] cloud; *dim.* **~ка** *f* [5, *g/pl.*: -чек]; **~ный** [14; -чен, -чна́, -o] corpulent, obese, stout, fat; fertile (*soil*).
туш ♪ *m* [1] flourish.
ту́ша *f* [5] carcass.
туш|ёный [14] stewed; **~и́ть** [16] ⟨по-, F за-⟩ put out, extinguish; *impf.* stew; *fig.* subdue.
тушь *f* [8] Indian ink.
тща́тельн|ость *f* [8] care(fulness); **~ый** [14; -лен, -льна] careful.
тще|ду́шный [14; -шен, -шна] sickly; **~сла́вие** *n* [12] vanity; **~сла́вный** [14; -вен, -вна] vain

glorious); ∠тный [14; -тен, -тна] in, futile; ∠тно in vain.
[21] you, † thou; быть на ~ (с thou (p.), be familiar (with).
кать [3], ⟨ткнуть⟩ [20] poke, jab, rust (*v/i.* -ся); F (thee &) thou.
ква *f* [5] pumpkin.
л *m* [1; в -ý; *pl. e.*] rear, base; убóкий ~ hinterland.
сяч|а *f* [5] thousand; ~елéтие *n* 2] millenium; ~ный [14] thoundth; of thousand(s).
ма *f* [5] dark(ness); F lots of.
фу! F fie!, for shame!
бик *m* [1] tube.
к *m* [1 *e.*] bale, pack.
лéнь *m* [4] seal; F lout.
ль *m* [4] tulle.
льпáн *m* [1] tulip.
р|éмный [14] prison ...; ~éмик *m* [1] jailer, *Brt.* gaoler, ward-; ~ьмá *f* [5; *pl.*: тю́рьмы, -рем, ьмам] prison, jail, *Brt.* gaol.
фя́к *m* [1 *e.*] mattress.
вкать F [1] yap, yelp.
|а *f* [5] draft, *Brt.* draught; traction; *fig.* bent (for к Д), desire (of);
ться F [1] (с Т) be a match (for), pe, vie (with); be at law (with);
стный [14; -тен, -тна] burdensome; painful; ~ость *f* [8] burden (*be* ... to в В/Д); ~отéние *n* [12] gravitation; *a.* = ∠а *fig.*; ~отéть [8] gravitate (toward[s] к Д); weigh (upon над Т); ~оти́ть [15 *e.*; -ощу́, -оти́шь] weigh upon, be a burden to; -ся feel the burden (of Т); ~у́чий [17 *sh.*] viscous; ductile; drawling, lingering.
тя́ж|ба *f* [5] action, lawsuit; **~еловéс** *m* [1] heavyweight; **~еловéсный** [14; -сен -сна] heavy, ponderous; **~ёлый** [14; -жёл, -желá] heavy; difficult, hard; laborious; serious (*wound, etc.*); (*a.* ⚕) severe, grave; grievous, sad, oppressive, painful; close (*air*); (Д) ~ело́ feel sad; **~есть** *f* [8] heaviness; weight; load; burden; gravity; seriousness; painfulness; **~кий** [16; тя́жек, тяжкá, -о] heavy (*fig.*), *etc.*, *cf.* ~ёлый.
тян|у́ть [19] pull, draw; ⚓ tow; draw in (out = delay); protract; drawl (out); attract; gravitate; drive at; long; have a mind to; would like; waft; ∠ет there is a draft (*Brt.* draught) (of Т); F drag (on); steal; take (from с Р); **-ся** stretch (*a.* = extend); last; drag, draw on; reach out (for к Д).

У

P) at, by, near; with; (at) ...'s; p.'s place; у меня́ (был, -á ...) have (had); my; (*borrow, learn*, .) from; of; off (*coast*); in; у себя́ (at) one's home *or* room, office.
в|ля́ть [28], ⟨∠ить⟩ [14] lower, duce, diminish, decrease; *v/i.* -ся.
|гáть [1], ⟨~жáть⟩ [4; -егу́, жи́шь, -гу́т] run away; escape.
|ди́тельный [14; -лен, -льна] nvincing; urgent (*request*); ~дáть [1], ⟨~ди́ть⟩ [15 *e.*; *no 1st sg.*; -еди́шь; -еждённый] conce (of в П), persuade (*impf. a.* to ...); ~ждéние *n* [12] persion; conviction.
ж|áть *s.* убегáть; ∠ище *n* [11] elter, refuge; asylum.
р|егáть [1], ⟨~éчь⟩ [26 г/ж] save, feguard.
|вáть [1], ⟨∠ть⟩ [убью́, -ьёшь; и́тый] kill; murder; beat (*card*); ive into despair; blight; F waste.
й|ственный [14 *sh.*] killing; urderous; F deadly, terrible; ~во *n* [9] murder; покушéние на тво murderous assault; ~ца *m/f* murderer; assassin.
рá|ть [1], ⟨убрáть⟩ [уберу́, ёшь; убрáл, -á, -о; у́бранный] ke (*or* put, clear) away (in); gather, rvest; tidy up; decorate, adorn, im; dress up; -ся F clear off, away; ~йся (вон)! get out of here!
уби́ть *s.* убивáть.
убо́|гий [16 *sh.*] needy, poor; wretched, miserable; scanty; crippled; **~жество** *n* [9] poverty.
убо́й *m* [3] slaughter (for на В).
убо́р *m* [1] attire; (*head*)gear; **~истый** [14 *sh.*] close: **~ка** *f* [5; *g/pl.*: -рок] harvest, gathering; tidying up; **~ная** *f* [14] lavatory, toilet, water closet; dressing room; **~очный** [14] harvest(ing); **~щица** *f* [5] charwoman.
убрá|нство *n* [9] attire; furniture; **~ть(ся)** *s.* убирáть(ся).
убы|вáть [1], ⟨∠ть⟩ [убу́ду, убу́дешь; у́был, -á, -о] subside, fall; decrease; leave; fall out; **′~ль** *f* [8] decrease, fall; loss; **∠ток** *m* [1; -тка] loss, damage; disadvantage (*be* at в П); **∠точный** [14; -чен, -чна] unprofitable; **∠ть** *s.* ~вáть.
уваж|áемый [14] dear (*address*); **~áть** [1], **~éние** *n* [12] respect, esteem (*su.* for к Д); **~и́тельный** [14; -лен, -льна] valid.
уведом|ля́ть [28], ⟨′~ить⟩ [14] inform, notify, advise (of о П); **~лéние** *n* [12] notification, ☤ advice.
увезти́ *s.* увози́ть.
увековéчи|вать [1], ⟨~ть⟩ [16] immortalize.
увелич|éние *n* [12] increase; en-

largement; **∠ивать** [1], ⟨∠ить⟩ [16] increase; enlarge; magnify; *v/i.* **-ся**; **~ительный** [14] *opt.* magnifying; *gr.* augmentative.

увенча́ться [1] *pf.* (T) be crowned.

увер|е́ние *n* [12] assurance (of в П); **∠енность** *f* [8] firmness, assurance; certainty; confidence (in в П); **∠енный** [14 *sh.*] firm, steady; confident (of в П); positive, sure, certain; бу́дьте **∠ены** I assure you, you may depend on it; **∠ить** *s.* **~я́ть**.

увёрт|ка F *f* [5; *g/pl.*: -ток] subterfuge, dodge; **~ливый** [14 *sh.*] evasive.

увертю́ра *f* [5] overture.

увер|я́ть [28], ⟨∠ить⟩ [13] assure (of в П); make believe (sure **-ся**), persuade.

увесел|е́ние *n* [12] amusement; **~и́тельный** [14] pleasure...; **~я́ть** [[28] amuse.

увести́ *s.* уводи́ть.

уве́ч|ить [16], ⟨из-⟩ mutilate; **~ный** [14] crippled; **~ье** *n* [10] mutilation.

увещ(ев)а́|ние *n* [12] admonition; **~ть** [1] admonish.

уви́л|ивать [1], ⟨~ьну́ть⟩ [20] shirk.

увлажн|я́ть [28], ⟨~и́ть⟩ [13] wet, dampen.

увле|ка́тельный [14; -лен, -льна] fascinating; **~ка́ть** [1], ⟨∠чь⟩ [26] carry (away; *a. fig.* = transport, captivate); **-ся** (T) be carried away (by), be(come) enthusiastic (about); be(come) absorbed (in); take to; fall (*or* be) in love (with); **~че́ние** *n* [12] enthusiasm, passion (for T).

уво́|д *m* [1] ⚔ withdrawal; theft; **~ди́ть** [15], ⟨увести́⟩ [25] take, lead (away, off); steal; ⚔ withdraw; **~зи́ть** [15], ⟨увезти́⟩ [24] take, carry, drive (away, off); F steal, kidnap.

уво́л|ить *s.* **~ьня́ть**; **~ьне́ние** *n* [12] dismissal (from с Р); granting (of *leave* в В); **~ьня́ть** [28], ⟨~ить⟩ [13] dismiss (from с Р); give (leave of absence в о́тпуск); (от Р) dispense (with), spare.

увы́! alas!

увя|да́ние *n* [12] withering; **~да́ть** [1], ⟨∠нуть⟩ [20] wither, fade; **∠дший** [17] withered.

увяз|а́ть [1] **1.** ⟨∠нуть⟩ [21] stick, sink; **2.** *s.* **∠ывать(ся)**; **∠ка** *f* [5] coördination; **∠ывать** [1], ⟨~а́ть⟩ [3] tie up; coördinate (*v/i.* **-ся**).

уга́д|ывать [1], ⟨~а́ть⟩ [1] guess.

уга́р *m* [1] coal gas; poisoning by coalgas; *fig.* frenzy, intoxication; **~ный** [14] full of coal gas; charcoal...

угас|а́ть [1], ⟨∠нуть⟩ [21] die (*or* fade) out, away, expire, become extinct.

угле|кислота́ *f* [5] carbonic acid; **~ки́слый** [14] carbon(ic); chokedamp...; **~ко́п** *m* [1] *s.* шахтёр; **~ро́д** *m* [1] carbon.

углово́й [14] corner...; angle...

углуб|и́ть(ся) *s.* **~ля́ть(ся)**; **~ле́[ние]** *n* [12] deepening; hollow, cav[ity]; absorption; extension; **~лённ[ый]** [14 *sh.*] profound; *a. p.pt.p.* o[f] [угл]уби́ть(ся); **~ля́ть** [28], ⟨~и́ть⟩ [14; -блю́, -би́шь; блённый] dee[pen] (*v/i.* **-ся**); make (become) m[ore] profound, extend; -ся *a.* go d[eep] (into в В), be(come) absorbed (i[n])

угна́ть *s.* угоня́ть.

угнет|а́тель *m* [4] oppressor; **~[а́ть]** [1] oppress; depress; **~е́ние** *n* [12] oppression; (*a.* **~ённость** *f* [8]) depression; **~ённый** [14; -т[ён], -тена́] oppressed; depressed.

угов|а́ривать [1], ⟨~ори́ть⟩ [13] (В) (*impf.* try to) persuade; [-ся] arrange, agree; **~о́р** *m* [1] agreem[ent], arrangement (by по Д); condi[tion] (on с Т); *pl.* persuasion(s); **~ори́ть(ся)** *s.* **~а́ривать(ся)**.

уго́д|а *f* [5]: в **~у** (Д) for p.'s s[ake], to please s. o.; **~и́ть** *s.* угожда́[ть]; **~ливый** [14 *sh.*] complaisant; ob[lig]ing; ingratiating, toadyish; **~ни[к]** [1] saint; **~но** please; как (ч[то]) вам **~но** just as (whatever) [you] like; что вам **~но**? what can I [do] for you?; не **~но** ли вам [...] wouldn't you like ...; ско́лько ([душе́]) **~но** *s.* вдо́воль & вла́сть.

уго|жда́ть [1], ⟨~ди́ть⟩ [15 *e.*; -о[жу́], -оди́шь] (Д, на В) please; *pf.* F [be]come; (в В) hit.

у́гол *m* [1; угла́; в, на углу́] co[rner] (at на П); ⚔ angle; nook; ho[me]; **~о́вный** [14] criminal.

уголо́к *m* [1; -лка́] nook, corne[r].

у́голь *m* [4; у́гля] coal; как на [угля́х] F on tenterhooks; **~ный**[1] [14] c[oal] ...; carbonic; **∠ный**[2] F [14] corn[er]...

угомони́ть(ся) [13] *pf.* calm (dow[n]).

угоня́ть [28], ⟨угна́ть⟩ [уго[ню́], уго́нишь; угна́л, -а́, -о; у́гнанн[ый]] drive (away, off); steal; **-ся** F c[atch] up (with за Т).

угор|а́ть [1], ⟨~е́ть⟩ [9] be [poi]soned by coal gas; F go mad.

у́горь *m* [4 *e.*; угря́] eel; blackh[ead].

уго|ща́ть [1], ⟨~сти́ть⟩ [15 *e.*; -о[щу́], -ости́шь; -ощённый] treat (with[...]), entertain; **~ще́ние** *n* [12] entert[ain]ment; food, drinks *pl.*

угро|жа́ть [1] threaten (p. w[ith] Д/Т); **∠за** *f* [5] threat, menace.

угрызе́ни|е *n* [12]; **~я** *pl.* со́ве[сти] remorse.

угрю́мый [14 *sh.*] morose, gloo[my].

уда́в *m* [1] boa.

уда|ва́ться [5], ⟨∠ться⟩ [уда́с[тся], -аду́тся; уда́лся, -ла́сь] succe[ed]; мне **~ётся** (**~ло́сь**) (+ *inf.*) I succ[eed] (-ed) (in ...ing).

удал|е́ние *n* [12] removal; ext[rac]tion; **~и́ть(ся)** *s.* **~я́ть(ся)**; **~[ой]**, **∠ый** [14; уда́л, -а́, -о] b[old], daring; **'~ь** *f* [8], F **~ьство́** *n* boldness, daring; **~я́ть** [28], ⟨~и́[ть]⟩

[13] remove; extract (*tooth*); **-ся** retire, withdraw; move away.
удáр *m* [1] blow (*a. fig.*); (*a.* ⚕) stroke; ⚡, *fig.* shock; impact; slash; (*thunder*)clap; F form; **~éние** *n* [12] stress, accent; **~ить(ся)** *s.* ~ять(ся); **~ник** *m* [1] shock worker, Stakhanovite (*Sov.*); **~ный** [14] shock...; impact...; foremost; **~ять** [28], ⟨~ить⟩ [13] strike (on по Д), hit; knock; beat, sound; punch (кулакóм); butt (головóй); kick (ногóй); set about, start (...ing в В *pl.*); attack (*v/t.* на В; with в В *pl.*); go (to *head* в В); F set in; stir; **-ся** strike *or* knock (with/against Т/о В); hit (в В); F fall into; throw o.s., plunge.
удáться *s.* удавáться.
удáч|а *f* [5] (good) luck; **~ник** F *m* [1] lucky man; **~ный** [14; -чен, -чна] successful; good.
удв|áивать [1], ⟨~óить⟩ [13] double (*v/i.* **-ся**).
удéл *m* [1] lot, destiny; appanage; **~ить** *s.* ~ять; **~ьный** [14] specific (*gravity, a. fig.*); **~ять** [28], ⟨~ить⟩ [13] devote; spare; allot.
удéрж|ивать [1], ⟨~áть⟩ [4] withhold, restrain; keep, retain; suppress; deduct; **-ся** hold (on; to за В; *a.* out); refrain (from от Р).
удешев|лять [28], ⟨~ить⟩ [14 *e.*; -влю, -вишь; -влённый] cheapen.
удив|ительный [14; -лен, -льна] wonderful, marvel(l)ous; miraculous; amazing, strange; (не) ~ительно it is a (no) wonder **~ить(ся)** *s.* ~лять(ся); **~лéние** *n* [12] astonishment, surprise; **~лять** [28], ⟨~ить⟩ [14 *e.*; -влю, -вишь; -влённый] (**-ся** be) astonish(ed at Д), surprise(d, wonder).
удилá *n/pl.* [9; -ил, -илáм] bit.
удирáть F [1], ⟨удрáть⟩ [удерý, -рёшь; удрáл, -á, -о] run away.
удить [15] angle (for *v/t.*), fish (рыбу).
удлин|éние *n* [12] lengthening; **~ять** [28], ⟨~ить⟩ [13] lengthen.
удóб|ный [14; -бен, -бна] convenient; comfortable; **~о...** easily ...; **~оваримый** [14 *sh.*] digestible; **~рéние** *n* [12] manure, fertilizer; fertilization; **~рять** [28], ⟨~рить⟩ [13] fertilize, manure, dung; **~ство** *n* [9] convenience; comfort; *pl.* facilities.
удовлетвор|éние *n* [12] satisfaction; **~ительный** [14; -лен, -льна] satisfactory; *adv. a.* D (*mark*); **~ять** [28], ⟨~ить⟩ [13] satisfy; grant; (Д) meet; **-ся** content o.s. (with Т).
удо|вóльствие *n* [12] pleasure; **~рожáть** [1], ⟨~рожить⟩ [16] raise the price of.
удост|áивать [1], ⟨~óить⟩ [13] (**-ся** be) hono(u)r(ed), (*a.* ✝) favo(u)r(ed) (with Р, Т); bestow, confer (on); award; deign (to look at р. взглядa, -ом В); **~оверéние** *n* [12] certificate, certification; (*identity*) card; corroboration (in в В); **~оверять** [28], ⟨~овéрить⟩ [13] certify, attest; prove (*one's identity*); convince (of в П; o.s. **-ся**; *a.* make sure); **~óить(ся)** *s.* ~áивать(ся).
удосýжиться F [16] find time.
ýдочк|а *f* [5; *g/pl.*: -чек] fishing tackle; *fig.* trap; закинуть ~у F *fig.* drop a hint.
удрáть *s.* удирáть.
удружить [16 *e.*; -жý, -жишь] F *s.* услужить.
удруч|áть [1], ⟨~ить⟩ [16 *e.*; -чý, -чишь; -чённый] deject, depress.
удуш|éние *n* [12] suffocation; poisoning; **~ливый** [14 *sh.*] stifling, suffocating; oppressive (*heat*); poison (*gas*); **~ье** *n* [10] asthma.
уедин|éние *n* [12] solitude; **~ённый** [14 *sh.*] retired, secluded, lonely, solitary; **~яться** [28], ⟨~иться⟩ [13] retire, seclude o.s.
уéзд † *m* [1], **~ный** [14] district.
уезжáть [1], ⟨уéхать⟩ [уéду, -дешь] (в В) leave (for), go (away; to).
уж 1. *m* [1 *e.*] grass snake; **2.** = ужé; F indeed, well; *do, be* (+ *vb.*).
ýжас *m* [1] horror; terror, fright; F = ~ный, ~но; **~áть** [1], ⟨~нýть⟩ [20] horrify; **-ся** be horrified *or* terrified (at Р, Д); **~áющий** [17] horrifying; **~ный** [14; -сен, -сна] terrible, horrible, dreadful; F awful.
ужé already; as early as; ~ не not ... any more; (вóт) ~ for (*time*).
ужéние *n* [12] angling, fishing.
ужи|вáться [1], ⟨~ться⟩ [-ивýсь, -вёшься; -ился, -илáсь] get accustomed (to в П); live in harmony (with с Т); **~вчивый** [14 *sh.*] sociable, accomodating; **~мка** *f* [5; *g/pl.*: -мок] grimace; gesture.
ýжин *m* [1] supper (at за Т; for на В, к Д); **~ать** [1], ⟨по-⟩ have supper.
ужиться *s.* уживáться.
узакон|éние *n* [12] legalization; statute; **~ивать** & **~ять** [28], ⟨~ить⟩ [13] legalize.
узбéк *m* [1], **~ский** [16] Uzbek.
узд|á *f* [5; *pl. st.*], **~éчка** *f* [5; *g/pl.*: -чек] bridle.
ýзел *m* [1; узлá] knot; 🚂 junction; center, *Brt.* centre; *anat.* ganglion; bundle; **~óк** *m* [1; -лкá] knot; packet.
ýзк|ий [16; ýзок, узкá, -о; *comp.*: ýже] narrow (*a. fig.*); tight; ~ое мéсто *n* bottleneck; weak point; **~околéйный** [14] narrow-gauge.
узлов|áтый [14 *sh.*] knotty; **~óй** [14] knot(ty); central, chief; 🚂 *s.* узел.
узна|вáть [5], ⟨~ть⟩ [1] recognize (by по Д); learn (from: р. от Р; th. из Р), find out, (get to) know, hear; позвóльте ~ть tell me, please.

ýзник *m* [1] prisoner.
узóр *m* [1] pattern, design; с ~ами = **~чатый** [14 *sh.*] figured; pattern.
ýзость *f* [8] narrow(-minded)ness.
ýзы *f/pl.* [5] bonds, ties.
ýйма F *f* [5] a great lot.
уйтú *s.* уходúть.
укáз *m* [1] decree, edict, ukase; **~áние** *n* [12] instruction (by по Д), direction; indication (of Р, на В); **~áтель** *m* [4] index; indicator; guide; **~áтельный** [14] indicatory; fore(*finger*), index; *gr.* demonstrative; **~áть** *s.* ∠ывать; **~ка** *f* [5] pointer; F order (by по Д); **~ывать** [1], ⟨~áть⟩ [3] point out; point (to на В); show; indicate.
укáч|ивать, ⟨~áть⟩ [1] rock to sleep, lull; *impers.* make (sea)sick.
уклáд *m* [1] mode, way (*of life*); form; **~ка** *f* [5] packing; laying; **~ывать** [1], ⟨уложúть⟩ [16] put (to bed); lay; pack (up F **-ся**); place; cover; -ся *a.* find room; F manage.
уклóн *m* [1] slope, incline; slant (*a. fig.* = bias, bent, tendency); *pol.* deviation; **~éние** *n* [12] swerve, deviation; evasion; **~úться** *s.* ~я́ться; **~чивый** [14 *sh.*] evasive; **~я́ться** [28], ⟨~úться⟩ [13; -оню́сь, -óнишься] deviate; evade (*v/t.* от Р); swerve; digress.
уклю́чина *f* [5] oarlock (*Brt.* row-).
укóл *m* [1] prick; ⚕ injection.
укомплектóв|ывать [1], ⟨~áть⟩ [7] complete, fill; supply (fully; with Т).
укóр *m* [1] reproach; **~áчивать** [1], ⟨~отúть⟩ [15 *e.*; -очý, -отúшь; -óченный] shorten; **~ени́ть** [28], ⟨~енúть⟩ [13] implant; -ся take root; **~úзна** *f* [5] *s.* ~; **~úзненный** [14] reproachful; **~úть** *s.* ~я́ть; **~отúть** *s.* ~áчивать; **~я́ть** [28], ⟨~úть⟩ [13] reproach, blame (of в П, за В).
укрáдкой furtively.
Украúн|а *f* [5] Ukraine (in на П); **⁓ец** *m* [1; -нца], **⁓ка** *f* [5; *g/pl.:* -нок], **⁓ский** [16] Ukrainian.
укра|шáть [1], ⟨∠сить⟩ [15] adorn; (**-ся** be) decorate(d); trim; embellish; **~шéние** *n* [12] adornment; decoration; ornament; embellishment.
укреп|úть(ся) *s.* ~ля́ть(ся); **~лéние** *n* [12] strengthening; consolidation; ⚔ fortification; **~ля́ть** [28], ⟨~úть⟩ [14 *e.*; -плю́, -пúшь; -плённый] strengthen; fasten; consolidate; ⚔ fortify; ~ля́ющий *a.* ⚕ restorative; **-ся** strengthen, become stronger; ⚔ entrench.
укрó|мный [14; -мен, -мна] secluded; **~п** *m* [1] fennel.
укро|тúтель *m* [4], **~тúтельница** [5] tamer; **~щáть** [1], ⟨~тúть⟩ [15 *e.*; -ощý, -отúшь; -ощённый] tame; break (*horse*); subdue, restrain; **~щéние** *n* [12] taming; subdual.
укрупн|я́ть [28], ⟨~úть⟩ [13] enlarge, extend; centralize.
укры|вáтель *m* [4] receiver; **~вáть** [1], ⟨∠ть⟩ [22] cover; shelter; conceal, harbo(u)r; **-ся** cover o.s.; hide; take shelter *or* cover; **∠тие** *n* [12] cover, shelter.
ýксус *m* [1] vinegar.
укýс *m* [1] bite; **~úть** *s.* кусáть.
укýт|ывать, ⟨~ать⟩ [1] wrap up
ул. *abbr.*: ýлица.
улá|вливать [1], ⟨уловúть⟩ [14] catch, seize; grasp; **~живать** [1], ⟨~дить⟩ [15] settle, arrange; reconcile.
ýлей *m* [3; ýлья] beehive.
улет|áть [1], ⟨~éть⟩ [11] fly (away)
улетýчи|ваться [1], ⟨~ться⟩ [16] volatilize; F disappear, vanish.
улéчься [26 г/ж: уля́гусь, уля́жешься, уля́гутся] lie down, go (to bed); settle; calm down, abate
улúка *f* [5] corpus delicti, proof
улúтка *f* [5; *g/pl.:* -ток] snail; *anat.* cochlea.
ýлиц|а *f* [5] street (in, on на П); на ~е *a.* outside, outdoors.
улич|áть [1], ⟨~úть⟩ [16 *e.*; -чý, -чúшь; -чённый] (в П) detect, catch (in the act [of]); convict (of); give (a p. *the lie*).
ýличный [14] street...
улóв *m* [1] catch; **~úмый** [14 *sh.*] perceptible; **~úть** *s.* улáвливать; **~ка** *f* [5; *g/pl.*: -вок] trick, ruse.
уложúть(ся) *s.* уклáдывать(ся).
улуч|áть F [1], ⟨~úть⟩ [16 *e.*; -чý, -чúшь; -чённый] find.
улучш|áть [1], ⟨∠ить⟩ [16] improve; *v/i.* **-ся**; **~éние** *n* [12] improvement; ∠ить(ся) *s.* ~áть(ся).
улыб|áться [1], ⟨~нýться⟩ [20]; **∠ка** *f* [5; *g/pl.*: -бок] smile (at Д).
ультракорóткий [16] very-high-frequency (*radio*).
ум *m* [1 *e.*] intellect; mind; sense(s); head (off не в П); без ~á mad (about от Р); зáдним ~óм крéпок *be* wise after the event; быть на ~é (у Р) have in mind; не егó ~á дéло beyond his reach; сойтú (F спя́тить) с ~á go mad; сходúть с ~á F *a.* be mad (about по П); (у Р) ~ за рáзум захóдит F *be* crazy; (у Р) ~ корóток F *be* dull *or* dense.
умал|éние *n* [12] belittling; **~úть(-ся)** *s.* ~я́ть(ся); **~ишённый** [14] *s.* сумасшéдший; **∠чивать** [1] ⟨умолчáть⟩ [4 *e.*; -чý, -чúшь] (о П) pass (th.) over in silence; **~я́ть** [28], ⟨~úть⟩ [13] belittle, derogate, disparage; curtail; **-ся** decrease, lessen.
умé|лый [14] skil(l)ful, skilled; **~ние** *n* [12] skill, faculty, knowhow.
уменьш|áть [1], ⟨∠úть⟩ [16 & 16 *e.*; -éньшý, -éньшúшь; -éньшенный & -шённый] reduce, diminish

decrease (*v/i.* **-ся**); **\~éние** *n* [12] decrease, reduction; **\~и́тельный** [14] diminutive; **\~и́ть(ся)** *s.* \~áть (-ся).
мéренн|ость *f* [8] moderation, moderateness; **\~ый** [14 *sh.*] moderate, (*a. geogr.* [*no sh.*]) temperate.
мер|éть *s.* умирáть; **\~ить** *s.* \~я́ть; **\~тви́ть** *s.* \~щвля́ть; **\~ший** [17] dead; **\~щвля́ть** [28], ⟨\~тви́ть⟩ [14 *e.*; -рщвлю́, -ртви́шь; -рщвлённый] kill, destroy; mortify; **\~я́ть** [28], ⟨\~ить⟩ [13] moderate.
ме|сти́ть(ся) *s.* \~щáть(ся); **\~стный** (-ˈmesn-) [14; -тен, -тна] appropriate; **\~ть** [8], ⟨с-⟩ can; know how; **\~щáть** [1], ⟨\~сти́ть⟩ [15 *e.*; -ещу́, -ести́шь; -ещённый] get (into в В); **-ся** find room; sit down.
мил|éние *n* [12] deep emotion, affection; **\~ённый** [14] affected; affectionate; **\~я́ть** [28], ⟨\~и́ть⟩ [13] (**-ся** be) move(d), touch(ed).
мирáть [1], ⟨умерéть⟩ [12; *pt.*: у́мер, умерлá, -о; умéрший] die (of, from от, с Р).
мн|éть [8], ⟨по-⟩ grow wiser; **\~ик** F *m* [1], **\~ица** *m/f* [5] clever (*or* good) boy, girl, (wo)man; **\~ичать** F [1] *s.* мудри́ть.
множ|áть [1], ⟨\~ить⟩ [16] multiply (by на В); *v/i.* **-ся**; **\~жéние** *n* [12] multiplication.
м|ный [14; умён, умнá, у́мно́] clever, smart, wise; **\~озаключéние** *n* [12] conclusion; **\~озри́тельный** [14; -лен, -льна] speculative.
мол|и́ть *s.* \~я́ть; **'\~к**: без '\~ку incessantly; **\~кáть** [1], ⟨\~кнуть⟩ [21] stop, become silent; subside; **\~чáть** *s.* умáлчивать; **\~я́ть** [28], ⟨\~и́ть⟩ [13; -олю́, -óлишь] implore (*v/t.*), beseech, entreat (for о П).
умопо|мешáтельство *n* [9], **\~мрачéние** *n* [12] (mental) derangement.
умóр|а F *f* [5], **\~и́тельный** F [14; -лен, -льна] side-splitting, awfully funny; **\~и́ть** F [13] *pf.* kill; exhaust, fatigue (*a.* with laughing со́ смеху).
у́мственный [14] intellectual, mental; brain (*work*[*er*]).
умудр|я́ть [28], ⟨\~и́ть⟩ [13] make wise; **-ся** F contrive, manage.
умывá|льная *f* [14] washroom; **\~льник** *m* [1] wash(ing) stand; washbowl, *Brt.* wash-basin; **\~ние** *n* [12] washing; wash; **\~ть** [1], ⟨умы́ть⟩ [22] (**-ся**) wash (*a.* o.s.).
у́мы|сел *m* [1; -сла] design, intent(ion); с \~слом (без \~ла) (un-) intentionally; **\~ть(ся)** *s.* \~вáть(ся); **\~шленный** [14] deliberate; intentional.
унавóживать [1], *s.* навóзить.
унести́(сь) *s.* уноси́ть(ся).
универ|мáг *m* [1] (\~сáльный магази́н) department store, *Brt.* stores *pl.*; **\~сáльный** [14; -лен, -льна] universal; *cf. a.* универмáг; **\~ситéт** *m* [1] university (at, in в П).
уни|жáть [1], ⟨\~зить⟩ [15] humble, humiliate, abase; **\~жéние** *n* [12] humiliation; **\~жённый** [14 *sh.*] humble; **\~зи́тельный** [14; -лен, -льна] humiliating; **\~зить** *s.* \~жáть.
унимáть [1], ⟨уня́ть⟩ [уйму́, уймёшь; уня́л, -á, -о; -я́тый (-я́т, -á, -о)] appease, soothe; still (*pain*); stanch (*blood*); **-ся** calm *or* quiet down; subside.
уничижи́тельный [14] *ling.* pejorative.
уничт|ожáть [1], ⟨\~óжить⟩ [16] annihilate; destroy; abolish, annul; **\~ожéние** *n* [12] annihilation; **\~óжить** *s.* \~ожáть.
уноси́ть [15], ⟨унести́⟩ [24 -с-] carry, take (away, off); **-ся**, ⟨-сь⟩ speed away.
у́нтер-офицéр *m* [1] corporal.
уны|вáть [1] despond; **\~лый** [14 *sh.*] sad, dejected; **\~ние** *n* [12] despondency; ennui.
уня́ть(ся) *s.* унимáть(ся).
упáдо|к *m* [1; -дка] decay, decadence; \~к ду́ха dejection; \~к сил collapse; **\~чный** [14; -чен, -чна] decadent; depressive.
упаков|áть *s.* \~ывать; **\~ка** *f* [5; *g/pl.*: -вок] packing; wrappings *pl.*; **\~щик** *m* [1] packer; **\~ывать** [1], ⟨\~áть⟩ [7] pack (up).
упáсть *s.* пáдать.
упирáть [1], ⟨уперéть⟩ [12] prop, stay (against в В); rest (*a.*, F, *eyes* on в В); P steal; **-ся** lean, prop (s.th. Т; against в В); F rest (on в В); insist on; be obstinate.
упи́танный [14 *sh.*] well-fed, fat.
уплá|та *f* [5] payment (in в В); **\~чивать** [1], ⟨\~ти́ть⟩ [15] pay; meet (*bill*).
уплотн|я́ть [28], ⟨\~и́ть⟩ [13] condense, compact; fill up (with work).
уплы|вáть [1], ⟨\~ть⟩ [23] swim *or* sail (away, off); pass (away), vanish.
уповáть [1] (на В) trust (in), hope (for).
упод|обля́ть [28], ⟨\~óбить⟩ [14] liken; assimilate (*v/i.* **-ся**).
упо|éние *n* [12] rapture, ecstasy; **\~ённый** [14; -ён, -енá] enraptured; **\~и́тельный** [14; -лен, -льна] rapturous, delightful; intoxicating.
уползти́ [24] *pf.* creep away.
уполномóч|енный *m* [14] plenipotentiary; **\~ивать** [1], ⟨\~ить⟩ [16] authorize, empower (to на В).
упоминá|ние *n* [12] mention (of о П); **\~ть** [1], ⟨упомяну́ть⟩ [19] mention (*v/t.* В, о П).

упо́р *m* [1] rest; support, prop; 🚂 buffer stop; ⊕ stop, catch; де́лать ~ lay stress *or* emphasis (on на В); в ~ point-blank, straightforward (*a. look* at на В); **~ный** [14; -рен, -рна] pertinacious, persistent, persevering; stubborn, obstinate; **~ство** *n* [9] persistence, perseverance; obstinacy; **~ствовать** [7] persevere, persist (in в П).

употреб|и́тельный [14; -лен, -льна] common, customary; current; **~и́ть** *s.* ~ля́ть; **~ле́ние** *n* [12] use; usage; **~ля́ть** [28], ⟨~и́ть⟩ [14 *e.*; -блю́, -би́шь; -блённый] (*impf.* **-ся** be) use(d), employ(ed); take (*medicine*); make (*efforts*); ~и́ть во зло abuse.

управ|до́м *m* [1] (управля́ющий до́мом) manager of the house; **∠иться** *s.* ~ля́ться; **~ле́ние** *n* [12] administration (of P; T), management; direction; board; ⊕ control; *gr.* government; **~ля́ть** [28] (T) manage, operate; rule; govern (*a. gr.*); drive; ⚓ steer; ⊕ control; guide; ♪ conduct; **-ся,** ⟨∠иться⟩ F [14] (с T) manage; finish; **~ля́ющий** *m* [17] manager; steward.

упражн|е́ние *n* [12] exercise; practice; **~я́ть** [28] exercise (*v/t.*, *v/refl.* **-ся**; в П: practise s.th.).

упраздн|е́ние *n* [12] abolition; **~я́ть** [28], ⟨~и́ть⟩ [13] abolish.

упра́шивать [1], ⟨упроси́ть⟩ [15] (*impf.* try to) persuade.

упрёк *m* [1] reproach, blame.

упрек|а́ть [1], ⟨~ну́ть⟩ [20] reproach, blame (with в П).

упро|си́ть *s.* упра́шивать; **~сти́ть** *s.* ~ща́ть; **∠чение** *n* [12] consolidation; **∠чивать** [1], ⟨∠чить⟩ [16] consolidate (*v/i.* **-ся**), stabilize; **~ща́ть** [1], ⟨~сти́ть⟩ [15 *e.*; -ощу́, -ости́шь; -ощённый] simplify; **~ще́ние** *n* [12] simplification.

упру́г|ий [16 *sh.*] elastic, resilient; **~ость** *f* [8] elasticity.

у́пряжь *f* [8] harness.

упря́м|иться [14] be obstinate; persist; **~ство** *n* [9] obstinacy, stubbornness; **~ый** [14 *sh.*] obstinate, stubborn.

упря́т|ывать [1], ⟨~ать⟩ [3] hide.

упу|ска́ть [1], ⟨~сти́ть⟩ [15] let go; let escape; miss; *cf.* вид); **~ще́ние** *n* [12] neglect, ommission.

ура́! hurrah!

уравн|е́ние *n* [12] equation; **∠ивать** [1] **1.** ⟨уровня́ть⟩ [28] level; **2.** ⟨~я́ть⟩ [28] equalize, level *fig.*; **~и́тельный** [14] level(l)ing; **~ове́шивать** [1], ⟨~ове́сить⟩ [15] balance; *p.pt.p. a.* well-balanced, composed, calm; **~я́ть** *s.* ∠ивать 2.

урага́н *m* [1] hurricane.

Ура́л *m* [1], **♀ьский** [16] Ural.

ура́н *m* [1], **~овый** [14] uranium.

урегули́рование *n* [12] settlement; regulation; *vb. cf.* регули́ровать.

урез|а́ть & ∠ывать F [1], ⟨∠ать⟩ [3] cut (down), curtail; **~о́нить** [13] *pf.* bring to reason.

у́рна *f* [5] urn; (*voting*) box.

у́ров|ень *m* [4; -вня] level (at, on на П; в В); standard; gauge; rate; **~ня́ть** *s.* ура́внивать 1.

уро́д *m* [1] monster; F ugly creature; **~и́ться** [15 *e.*; -и́тся; -ождённый] *pf.* grow, be born; F be like (p. в В); **~ливый** [14 *sh.*] deformed; ugly, abnormal; **~овать** [7], ⟨из-⟩ deform, disfigure; mutilate; spoil; **~ство** *n* [9] deformity; ugliness, abnormity.

урож|а́й *m* [3] harvest, (abundant) crop; **~а́йность** *f* [8] yield (heavy высо́кая), productivity; **~а́йный** [14] fruitful; **~дённая** [14] née; **~е́нец** *m* [1; -нца], **~е́нка** *f* [5; *g/pl* -нок] native.

уро́|к *m* [1] lesson (in на П); task; **~н** *m* [1] loss(es); injury; **~ни́ть** *s.* роня́ть; **~чный** [14] set, fixed.

Уругва́й *m* [4] Uruguay.

урча́ть [4 *e.*; -чу́, -чи́шь] (g)rumble, murmur.

уры́вками F by fits (& starts).

ус *m* [1; *pl. e.*] (*mst pl.*) m(o)ustache; кито́вый ~ whalebone.

уса|ди́ть *s.* ∠живать; **∠дьба** *f* [5; *g/pl.*: -деб] farm (land); manor; **∠живать** [1], ⟨~ди́ть⟩ [15] seat, set; plant (with T); **-ся,** ⟨усе́сться⟩ [25; уся́дусь, -дешься; уся́дься, -дьтесь!; усе́лся, -лась] sit down, take a seat; settle down.

уса́тый [14] with a m(o)ustache.

усв|а́ивать [1], ⟨~о́ить⟩ [13] adopt, acquire, assimilate; master, learn; **~о́ение** *n* [12] adoption; acquirement, assimilation; mastering, learning.

усе́|ивать [1], ⟨~ять⟩ [27] stud.

усе́рд|ие *n* [12] zeal, eagerness (for к Д); assiduity; **~ный** [14; -ден, -дна] eager, zealous; assiduous.

усе́сться *s.* уса́живаться.

усе́ять *s.* усе́ивать.

усид|е́ть [11] *pf.* remain seated; sit still, (can) sit; hold out; **∠чивый** [14 *sh.*] assiduous, persevering.

у́сик *m* [1] *dim. of* ус; *zo.* feeler.

усил|е́ние *n* [12] strengthening, reinforcement; intensification; amplification; **∠енный** [14] intens(iv)e, substantial; pressing; **∠ивать** [1], ⟨∠ить⟩ [13] strengthen, reinforce; intensify; (*sound*) amplify; aggravate; **-ся** increase; **∠ие** *n* [12] effort, strain, exertion; **~и́тель** *m* [4] amplifier (*radio*); **∠ить(ся)** *s.* ∠ивать(ся).

ускака́ть [3] *pf.* leap *or* gallop (away).

ользз|ать [1], ⟨**~**нýть⟩ [20] slip
f, away), escape (from от Р).
ор|éние *n* [12] acceleration;
ть [28], ⟨**~**ить⟩ [13] speed up,
celerate; *v/i.* **-ся.**
á|вливаться F *s.* услóвливать-
; **~ждáть** [1], ⟨**~**дить⟩ [15 *e.*;
кý, -адишь; -аждённый] sweet-
, soften; delight, **~ть** *s.* усы-
ть.
óв|ие *n* [12] condition (on с Т,
и П; under на П), term; stipula-
n; proviso; agreement, contract;
ться *s.* **~**ливаться; **~ленный**
sh.] agreed upon, fixed; **~ли-
ться** [1], ⟨**~**иться⟩ [14] arrange,
agree (upon о П); **~ность** *f* [8]
nvention; **~ный** [14; -вен, -вна]
nditional; conventional; relative;
probational; **~**ные знáки *pl.*
nditional signes.
ожн|ять [28], ⟨**~**ить⟩ [13] (**-ся**
come) complicate(d).
ý|га *f* [5] service (at к Д *pl.*),
o(u)r; **~живать** [1], ⟨**~**жить⟩
5] do (р. Д) a service *or* favo(u)r;
кливый [14 *sh.*] obliging.
|áтривать [1], ⟨**~**отрéть⟩ [9;
трю, -óтришь; -óтренный] see
ter за Т); **~ехáться** [1], ⟨**~**ех-
ться⟩ [20], **~éшка** *f* [5; *g/pl.:*
ек] smile, grin; **~ирéние** *n* [12]
ppression; **~ирять** [28], ⟨**~**и-
ть⟩ [13] pacify; suppress; **~от-
ние** *n* [12] discretion (at по Д;
на В), judg(e)ment; **~отрéть** *s.*
тривать
ýть [20] *pf.* fall asleep;
ep.
вершéнствован|ие *n* [12] im-
ovement, perfection; **~ный** [14]
proved, perfected.
мниться *s.* сомневáться.
пший [17] deceased.
е|вáемость *f* [8] progress; **~-
áть** [1], ⟨**~**ть⟩ [8] have (*or* find)
ne, manage, succeed; arrive, be
time (for к Д, на В); catch
ain на В); *impf.* get on, make
ogress, learn; не **~**л(а) (+ *inf.*),
к no sooner + *pt.* than; **~вáю-
щий** [17] advanced; **~х** *m* [1]
ccess; result; *pl. a.* progress;
шный [14; -шен, -шна] success-
l; **~**шно *a.* with success.
ок|áивать [1], ⟨**~**óить⟩ [13]
lm, soothe; reassure; satisfy; **-ся**
lm down; subside; become quiet;
ntent o.s. (with на П); **~оéние** *n*
2] peace; calm; **~оительный**
4; -лен, -льна] soothing, reas-
ring; **~óить(ся)** *s.* **~**áивать(ся).
СР (Украинская Совéтская
оциалистическая Респýблика)
krainian Soviet Socialist Repub-
.
тá † *n/pl.* [9] mouth, lips *pl.*
тáв *m* [1] statute(s); regulations
.; charter (*a. UNO*).

уста|вáть [5], ⟨**~**ть⟩ [-áну, -áнешь]
get tired; **~влять** [28], ⟨**~**вить⟩ [14]
place; cover (with Т), fill; fix (*eyes*
on на В); **-ся** stare (at, на *or* в В);
~лость *f* [8] weariness, fatigue;
~лый [14] tired, weary; **~нáв-
ливать** [1], ⟨**~**новить⟩ [14] set *or*
put up; mount; arrange; fix;
establish; find out, ascertain; adjust (to на В); **-ся** be established;
form; set in; **~нóвка** *f* [5; *g/pl.:*
-вок] mounting, installation; ⊕
plant; *fig.* orientation (toward[s] на
В); **~новлéние** *n* [12] establishment; **~рéлый** [14] obsolete,
out-of-date; **~ть** *s.* **~**вáть.
устилáть [1], ⟨устлáть⟩ [-телю,
-тéлешь; ýстланный] cover, lay
out (with Т).
ýстный [14] oral, verbal.
устó|и *m/pl.* [3] foundations; **~йчи-
вость** *f* [8] stability; **~йчивый**
[14 *sh.*] stable; **~ять** [-ою, -оишь]
keep one's balance; hold one's
ground; resist (*v/t.* прóтив Р,
пéред Т).
устр|áивать [1], ⟨**~**óить⟩ [13] ar-
range; organize, set up; furnish;
construct; make (*scene, etc.*); provide (*job* на В, place in в В); F suit;
-ся be settled; settle; get a job (*a.*
на В); **~анéние** *n* [12] removal;
elimination; **~анять** [28], ⟨**~**анить⟩
[13] remove; eliminate; **~ашáть
(-ся)** [1], *s.* страшить(ся); **~ем-
лять** [28], ⟨**~**емить⟩ [14 *e.*; -млю,
-мишь; -млённый] (на В) direct
(to, at), fix (on); **-ся** rush; be di-
rected; **~ица** *f* [5] oyster; **~óить
(-ся)** *s.* **~**áивать(ся); **~óйство** *n* [9]
arrangement; establishment; equip-
ment; installation; organization;
system; mechanism.
устýп *m* [1] ledge; projection; step;
terrace; **~áть** [1], ⟨**~**ить⟩ [14] cede,
let (р. Д) have; yield; be inferior to
(Д); sell; abate (*v*/t. с Р, в П); **~-
áть** дорóгу (Д) let p. pass, give
way; **~ительный** [14] *gr.* conces-
sive; **~ка** *f* [5; *g/pl.*: -пок] concession; cession; † abatement, reduction; **~чивый** [14 *sh.*] compliant,
pliant.
усты|жáть [1], ⟨**~**дить⟩ [15 *e.*;
-ыжý, -ыдишь; -ыжённый] (**-ся**
be) ashame(d; of Р).
ýстье *n* [10; *g/pl.:* -ьев] mouth (at
в П).
усугуб|лять [28], ⟨**~**ить⟩ [14 & 14
e.; -гублю, -гýбишь; -гýблен-
ный & -гублённый] increase, redouble.
усы *s.* ус; **~лáть** [1], ⟨услáть⟩
[ушлю, ушлёшь; ýсланный] send
(away); **~новлять** [28], ⟨**~**новить⟩
[14 *e.*; -влю, -вишь; -влённый]
adopt; **~пáть** [1], ⟨**~**пать⟩ [2]
(be)strew (with Т); **~пительный**
[14; -лен, -льна] soporific; drowsy;

~пля́ть [28], ⟨~пи́ть⟩ [14 *e.*; -плю́, -пи́шь; -плённый] lull (to sleep); ⚕ narcotize.
ута́|ивать [1], ⟨~и́ть⟩ [13] conceal, hide; embezzle; **~йка** F: без ~йки frankly; **~птывать** [1], ⟨утопта́ть⟩ [3] tread *or* trample (down); **~скивать** [1], ⟨~щи́ть⟩ [16] carry, drag *or* take (off, away); F pilfer.
у́тварь *f* [8] implements, utensils *pl.*
утвер|ди́тельный [14; -лен, -льна] affirmative (in the -но); **~жда́ть** [1], ⟨~ди́ть⟩ [15 *e.*; -ржу́, -рди́шь; -рждённый] confirm; consolidate (*v/i.* **-ся**); *impf.* affirm, assert, maintain; **~жде́ние** *n* [12] confirmation; affirmation, assertion; consolidation.
уте|ка́ть [1], ⟨~́чь⟩ [26] flow (away); F escape; **~ре́ть** *s.* утира́ть; **~рпе́ть** [10] *pf.*: не ~рпе́л, что́бы не (+ *inf. pf.*) could not help ...ing.
утёс *m* [1] cliff, rock.
уте́|чка *f* [5] leakage, escape; **~чь** *s.* ~ка́ть; **~ша́ть** [1], ⟨~шить⟩ [16] console, comfort; **-ся** *a.* take comfort (in T); **~ше́ние** *n* [12] comfort, consolation; **~ши́тельный** [14; -лен, -льна] comforting, consolatory.
ути́|ль *m* [4], **~льсырьё** *n* [10] scrap(s); **~ра́ть** [1], ⟨утере́ть⟩ [12] wipe; **~ха́ть** [1], ⟨~хнуть⟩ [21] subside, abate; cease; calm down.
у́тка *f* [5; *g/pl.*: у́ток] duck; canard.
уткну́ть(ся) F [20] *pf.* thrust; hide; put; be(come) engrossed.
утол|и́ть *s.* ~я́ть; **~ща́ть** [1], ⟨~сти́ть⟩ [15 *e.*; -лщу́, -лсти́шь; -лщённый] thicken; **~ще́ние** *n* [12] thickening; **~я́ть** [28], ⟨~и́ть⟩ [13] quench; appease; allay, still.
утом|и́тельный [14; -лен, -льна] wearisome, tiresome; **~и́ть(ся)** *s.* ~ля́ть(ся); **~ле́ние** *n* [12] fatigue, exhaustion; **~лённый** [14; -лён, -ена́] tired, weary; **~ля́ть** [28], ⟨~и́ть⟩ [14 *e.*; -млю́, -ми́шь; -млённый] tire, weary (*v/i.* **-ся**; *a.* get tired).
утонч|а́ть [1], ⟨~и́ть⟩ [16 *e.*; -чу́, -чи́шь; -чённый] thin; *fig.* refine; (*v/i.* **-ся**).
утоп|а́ть [1] **1.** ⟨утону́ть⟩ *s.* тону́ть 2.; **2.** overflow (with в П); wallow, revel; **~́ленник** *m* [1] drowned man; **~́ленница** *f* [5] drowned woman; **~та́ть** *s.*ута́птывать.
уточн|е́ние *n* [12] specification; **~я́ть** [28], ⟨~и́ть⟩ [13] specify.
утра́|ивать [1], ⟨утро́ить [13] treble; *v/i.* **-ся**; **~мбова́ть** [7] *pf.* ram; stamp; **~та** *f* [5] loss; **~чивать** [1], ⟨~тить⟩ [15] lose.
у́тренн|ий [15] morning; **~ик** *m* matinee; morning frost.
у́тр|о *n* [9; с, до -а́; к -у́] morn (in the ~ом; по ~́ам);... ~а́ *a.* ... a (*cf.* день); **~о́ба** *f* [5] womb; **~о́** (-**ся**) *s.* ~а́ивать(ся); **~ужда́ть** ⟨~уди́ть⟩ [15 *e.*; -ужу́, -уди -уждённый] trouble, bother.
утю́|г *m* [1 *e.*] (flat)iron; **~жи** [16], ⟨вы́-, от-⟩ iron; stroke.
уха́ *f* [5] fish soup; **~б** *m* [1] h **~би́стый** [14 *sh.*] bumpy.
уха́живать [1] (за T) nurse, l after; (pay) court (to), woo.
у́харский F [16] dashing.
у́хать [1], *once* ⟨у́хнуть⟩ [20] bo
ухва́т|ывать [1], ⟨~и́ть⟩ [15] B) seize, grasp; **-ся** snatch; c to.
ухи|тря́ться [28], ⟨~три́ться⟩ [contrive, manage; **~щре́ние** *n* [**~щря́ться** [28] shift.
ухмыл|я́ться F [28], ⟨~ьну́ть [20] grin, smile (contentedly).
у́хнуть *s.* у́хать.
у́хо *n* [9; *pl.*: у́ши, уше́й, *etc. e.*] (in на́ B); по́ уши over head ears; пропуска́ть ми́мо уше́й t a deaf ear (to B); держа́ть ~ вос *s.* насторо́же.
ухо́д *m* [1] departure; (за T) c tendance; nursing; **~и́ть** [⟨уйти́⟩ [уйду́, уйдёшь; уш ушла́; уше́дший; *g.pt.*: уйдя́] le (*v/t.* из, от P), depart (from), (away); pass; escape; evade; resi retire; be lost; fail; take; si plunge; F be spent (for на B).
ухудш|а́ть [1], ⟨~́ить⟩ [16] dete rate (*v/i.* **-ся**); **~е́ние** *n* [12] det oration; change for the worse.
уцеле́ть [8] *pf.* escape; be spare
уцепи́ться [14] F *s.* ухвати́ться.
уча́ст|вовать [7] participate, t part (in в П); **~вующий** [17 ~ник; **~ие** *n* [12] (в П) partici tion (in); interest (in), sympa (with); **~и́ть(ся)** *s.* учаща́ть(с **~ливый** [14 *sh.*] sympathizi sympathetic; **~ник** *m* [1], **~ниц** [5] participant, participator; co petitor (*sports*); member; **~ок** [1; -тка] (p)lot; section; regi district; site; *fig.* field, branch (police) station; **'~ь** *f* [8] fate, lo
уча|ща́ть [1], ⟨~сти́ть⟩ [15 *e.*; -аı -асти́шь; -ащённый] make (become) more frequent; speed u
уч|а́щийся *m* [17] schoolboy, pu student; **~ёба** *f* [5] studies study; training; drill; **~е́бник** [1] textbook; **~е́бный** [14] schoo educational; text(*book*), exercise training; ⚔ drill...; ~е́бный пл *m* curriculum.
уче́н|ие *n* [12] learning; instructi apprenticeship; ⚔ drill; teachi doctrine; **~и́к** *m* [1 *e.*] schoolb (**~и́ца** *f* [5] schoolgirl), pu

student; apprentice; disciple; ~и́ческий [16] pupils', students'.
учён|ость f [8] learning; ~ый [14 sh.] learned; su. scholar.
уч|е́сть s. учи́тывать; ~ёт m [1] calculation; registration; inventory; discount; list(s); fig. consideration, regard; вести́ ~ёт keep books pl.; взять на ~ёт register.
учи́лище n [11] school (at в П).
учини́ть [28] s. чини́ть 2.
учи́тель m [4; pl.: -ля́, etc. e.; fig. ...], ~ница f [5] teacher, instructor; ~ский [16] (of) teachers(').
учи́тывать [1], ⟨уче́сть⟩ [25; учту́, учтёшь; учёл, учла́; g. pt.: учтя́; учтённый] take into account, consider; calculate; register; ✝ take note; stock; discount.
учи́ть [16] 1.⟨на-, об-, вы́-⟩ teach(p. s.th. В/Д), instruct; ⚔ drill; train; (v. -ся Д); 2. ⟨вы́-⟩ learn, study.
учреди́тель m [4] founder; ~ный [14] constituent.
учре|жда́ть [1], ⟨~ди́ть⟩ [15 e.; -ежу́, -еди́шь; -еждённый] found, constitute; establish, introduce; ~жде́ние n [12] foundation, constitution; institution; institute, office (at в П).
учти́вый [14 sh.] polite; obliging.
уша́т m [1] tub, bucket.
ушй́б m [1] bruise; injury; ~а́ть [1], ⟨~и́ть⟩ [-бу́, -бёшь; -и́б(ла); уши́бленный] hurt, bruise (o.s. -ся).
ушко́ n [9; pl.: -ки́, -ко́в] eye.
ушно́й [14] ear...
уще́лье n [10] gorge, ravine.
ущем|ля́ть [28], ⟨~и́ть⟩ [14 e.; -млю́, -ми́шь; -млённый] pinch, jam; fig. restrain; F wound, impair.
ущёрб m [1] damage; wane.
ущи́пнуть [20] s. щипа́ть.
Уэ́льс m [1] Wales.
ую́т m [1] coziness; ~ный [14; -тен, -тна] snug, cozy, comfortable.
уязв|и́мый [14 sh.] vulnerable; ~ля́ть [28], ⟨~и́ть⟩ [14 e.; -влю́, -ви́шь; -влённый] wound, sting; fig. hurt.
уясн|я́ть [28], ⟨~и́ть⟩ [13] comprehend; make clear, clear up.

Ф

фабзавко́м m [1] s. завко́м.
фа́брик|а f [5] factory (in на П); mill; ~а́нт m [1] manufacturer; ~а́т m [1] product; ~чный [14] factory (a. worker); trade(mark).
фа́була f [5] plot.
фа́з|а f [5], ~ис m [1] phase.
фаза́н m [1] pheasant.
фа́кел m [1] torch.
факт m [1] fact; ~ тот the matter is; ~и́ческий [16] (f)actual, real; adv. in fact; ~у́ра f [5] invoice.
факульте́т m [1] faculty (in на П).
фаль|сифици́ровать [7] (im)pf. falsify, forge; adulterate; ~ши́вить [14], ⟨с-⟩ sing out of tune, play falsely; F cheat, be false; ~ши́вка f [5; g/pl.: -вок] forgery; ~ши́вый [14 sh.] false; forged, counterfeit; base (coin); ~шь f [8] falseness; hypocrisy; deceit(fulness).
фами́л|ия f [7] surname, family name; как ва́ша ~ия? what is your name?; ~ья́рный [14; -рен, -рна] familiar.
фанати́|зм m [1] fanaticism; ~ческий [16], ~чный [14; -чен, -чна] fanatical.
фане́ра f [5] plywood; veneer.
фанта|зёр m [1] visionary; ~зи́ровать [7] indulge in fancies, dream; ⟨с-⟩ invent; ~зия f [7] imagination; fancy; invention, fib; ♪ fantasia; F whim, freak; ~сти́ческий [16], ~сти́чный [14; -чен, -чна] fantastic.
фа́р|а f [5] headlight; ~ва́тер m [1] waterway, fairway; fig. track; ~маце́вт m [1] pharmac(eut)ist; ~тук m [1] apron; ~фо́р m [1], ~фо́ровый [14] china, porcelain; ~ш m [1] stuffing; forcemeat; ~широва́ть [7] stuff.
фасо́|ль f [8] string (Brt. runner) bean(s); ~н m [1] cut, style.
фат m [1] dandy, fop, dude.
фата́льный [14; -лен, -льна] fatal.
фаши́|зм m [1] fascism; ~ст m [1] fascist; ~стский [16] fascist...
фая́нс m [1], ~овый [14] faïence.
февра́ль m [4 e.] February.
федера́|льный [14] federal; ~ти́вный [14] federative, federal.
Фёдор m [1] Theodore; dim. Фе́дя [m [6].]
феери́ческий [16] fairylike.
фейерве́рк m [1] firework.
фельд|ма́ршал m [1] field marshal; ~фе́бель m [4] sergeant; ~шер m [1] medical assistant.
фельето́н m [1] feuilleton.
фено́мен m [1] phenomenon.
феода́льный [14] feudal.
ферзь m [4 e.] queen (chess).
фе́рм|а f [5] farm; ~ер m [1] farmer.
фестива́ль m [4] festival.
фетр m [1] felt; ~овый [14] felt...
фехтова́|льщик m [1] fencer; ~ние n [12] fencing; ~ть [7] fence.
фиа́лка f [5; g/pl.: -лок] violet.
фи́бра f [5] fiber, Brt. fibre.
фи́г|а f [5], ~овый [14] fig.
фигу́р|а f [5] figure; (chess)man;

~а́льный [14; -лен, -льна] figurative; **~и́ровать** [7] figure, appear; **~ный** [14] figured; trick..., stunt...
фи́зи|к *m* [1] physicist; **~ка** *f* [5] physics; **~оло́гия** *f* [7] physiology; **~оно́мия** *f* [7] physiognomy; **∠ческий** [16] physical; manual.
физкульту́р|а *f* [5] physical culture; gymnastics; **~ник** *m* [1], **~ница** *f* [5] sports(wo)man, gymnast.
фик|са́ж *m* [1] fixative; **~си́ровать** [7], ⟨за-⟩ fix; **~ти́вный** [14; -вен, -вна] fictitious.
фила|нтро́п *m* [1] philanthropist; **~рмони́ческий** [16] philharmonic.
филе́ *n* [*ind.*] tenderloin, fillet.
филиа́л *m* [1] branch (office); **~ьный** [14] branch...
фи́лин *m* [1] eagle owl.
Филиппи́ны *f/pl.* [5] Philippines.
фило́л|ог *m* [1] philologist; **~оги́ческий** [16] philological; **~о́гия** *f* [7] philology.
фило́с|оф *m* [1] philosopher; **~о́фия** *f* [7] philosophy; **~о́фский** [16] philosophical; **~о́фствовать** [7] philosophize.
фильм *m* [1] film (*vb.*: снима́ть ~).
фильтр *m* [1], **~ова́ть** [7] filter.
фимиа́м *m* [1] incense.
фина́л *m* [1] final; ♪ finale.
финанс|и́ровать [7] (*im*)*pf.* finance; **∠овый** [14] financial; **∠ы** *m/pl.* [1] finance(s).
фи́ник *m* [1] date; **~овый** [14] date...
фин|ля́ндец *m* [1; -дца], **~н** *m* [1], **∠(ля́нд)ка** *f* [5; *g/pl.*: -н(ля́нд)ок] Finn; **♀ля́ндия** *f* [7] Finland; **∠(ля́нд)ский** [16] Finnish.
фиоле́товый [14] violet.
фи́рма *f* [5] firm.
фити́ль *m* [4 *e.*] wick; match.
флаг *m* [1] flag, colo(u)rs *pl.*; banner.
фланг *m* [1], **∠овый** [14] flank.
Фла́ндрия *f* [7] Flanders.
флане́л|евый [14], **~ь** *f* [8] flannel.
фле́гма *f* [5] phlegm; **~ти́чный** [14; -чен, -чна] phlegmatic(al).
фле́йта *f* [5] flute.
фли́|гель △ *m* [4; *pl.*: -ля́, *etc. e.*] wing; **~рт** *m* [1] flirtation; **~ртова́ть** [7] flirt.
флот *m* [1] fleet; marine; navy; (*air*) force; **∠ский** [16] naval; *su.* F sailor.
флю|гер *m* [1] weathercock, weather vane; **~с** *m* [1] gumboil.
фля́|га, **~жка** *f* [5; *g/pl.*: -жек] flask; canteen, *Brt.* water bottle.
фойе́ *n* [*ind.*] *thea.* lobby, foyer.
фокстро́т *m* [1] fox trot.
фо́кус *m* [1] hocus-pocus, (juggler's) trick, sleight of hand; F trick; freak, whim; **~ник** *m* [1] juggler, conjurer; **~ничать** F [1] trick.
фо́льга *f* [5] foil.
фолькло́р *m* [1], **~ный** [14] folklore.
Фо|ма́ *m* [5] Thomas; **♀н** *m* [1] background (against на П).
фона́р|ик *m* [1] flashlight, *B* (electric) torch; **~ь** *m* [4 *e.*] lante (street) lamp; (head)light; F *s.* синя
фонд *m* [1] fund.
фоне́т|ика *f* [5] phonetics; **~и́ческий** [16] phonetic(al).
фонта́н *m* [1] fountain.
форе́ль *f* [8] trout.
фо́рм|а *f* [5] form, shape; model; mo(u)ld; ⚔ uniform; dress (*sport* **~а́льность** *f* [8] formality; **~а́льный** [14; -лен, -льна] formal; ~ *m* [1] size; form; **~енный** [formal; F downright; ~енная оде́ж *f* uniform; **~ирова́ть** [7], ⟨с-⟩ (- be) form(ed); **~ова́ть** [7], ⟨ от-⟩ mo(u)ld, model; **~ули́рова** [7] (*im*)*pf.* & ⟨с-⟩ formulate; **~ули́ро́вка** *f* [5; *g/pl.*: -вок] formulatic **~уля́р** *m* [1] form.
форпо́ст *m* [1] advanced post.
форси́ровать [7] (*im*)*pf.* force.
фо́|рточка *f* [5; *g/pl.*: -чек] wind leaf; **~сфор** *m* [1] phosphorus.
фото|аппара́т *m* [1] camera; **граф** *m* [1] photographer; **~графи́ровать** [7], ⟨с-⟩ photograp **~графи́ческий** [16] photograp ic; *cf.* ~аппара́т; **~гра́фия** *f* photograph; photography; photo rapher's.
фра́за *f* [5] phrase; empty talk.
фрак *m* [1] dress coat.
фра́кция *f* [7] faction.
франки́ровать [7] (*im*)*pf.* stamp
франт *m* [1] dandy, fop; **~и́ть** [15 *e.*; -нчу́, -нти́шь] overdre **~овско́й** [16] dandyish, dudish.
Фра́нц|ия *f* [7] France; **♀у́жен** *f* [5; *g/pl.*: -нок] Frenchwoma **♀у́з** *m* [1] Frenchman; **♀у́зск** [16] French.
фрахт *m* [1], **~ова́ть** [7] freight.
ФРГ *cf.* Герма́ния.
фре́зер *m* [1] milling cutter.
френч *m* [1] (army-type) jacket.
фре́ска *f* [5] fresco.
фронт *m* [1] front; **~ово́й** [14] fron
фрукт *m* [1] (*mst pl.*) fruit; **~о́в** [14] fruit...; ~о́вый сад *m* orchar
фу! fie!, ugh!
фуга́сный [14] demolition (*bomb*
фунда́мент *m* [1] foundation; ba **~а́льный** [14; -лен, -льна] fun mental.
функциони́ровать [7] function.
фунт *m* [1] pound (= *409.5 g*).
фур|а́ж *m* [1 *e.*] fodder; **~а́жк** [5; *g/pl.*: -жек] (service) cap; **~г** *m* [1] van; **∠ия** *f* [7] fury; **~о́р** *m* furor; **~у́нкул** *m* [1] furunc boil.
футбо́л *m* [1] soccer, *Brt. a.* assoc tion football; **~и́ст** *m* [1] soc player; **~ьный** [14] soccer..., fo ball...
футля́р *m* [1] case; sheath; box.
фуфа́йка *f* [5; *g/pl.*: -а́ек] jersey
фы́рк|ать [1], ⟨~нуть⟩ [20] snor

Х

ха́ки [*ind.*] khaki.
халáт *m* [1] dressing gown, bathrobe; smock; **~ный** F [14; -тен, -тна] careless, negligent; sluggish.
халту́ра F *f* [5] botch, bungle.
хам F *m* [1] cad, boor, churl.
хандр|á *f* [5] melancholy, blues *pl.*; **~и́ть** [13] be in the dumps.
ханж|á F *m/f* [5; *g/pl.*: -жéй] hypocrite; **~ествó** *n* [9] hypocrisy, bigotry.
хаó|с *m* [1] chaos; **~ти́ческий** [16], **~ти́чный** [14; -чен, -чна] chaotic.
харáктер *m* [1] character, nature; temper, disposition; principles *pl.*; **~изовáть** [7] (*im*)*pf.* & ‹о-› characterize, mark; **~и́стика** *f* [5] character(istic); characterization; **~ный** [14; -рен, -рна] characteristic (of для Р).
хáрк|ать F [1], ‹~нуть› [20] spit.
харч|éвня *f* [6; *g/pl.*: -вен] tavern; **~и́** P *m/pl.* [1 *e.*] food, grub; board.
хáря P *f* [6] mug, phiz.
хáта *f* [5] (peasant's) hut.
хвал|á *f* [5] praise; **~éбный** [14; -бен, -бна] laudatory; **~и́ть** [13; хвалю́, хвáлишь] praise; **-ся** boast of T).
хвáст|аться &, F, **~ать** [1], ‹по-› boast, brag (of T); **~ли́вый** [14 *sh.*] boastful; **~овствó** *n* [9] boasting; **~у́н** *m* [1 *e.*] boaster, braggart.
хват|áть [1] **1.** ‹(с)хвати́ть› [15] (за В) snatch (at); grasp, seize (by); *a.*, (-ся за В; lay hold of); **2.** ‹~и́ть› (*impers.*) (P) suffice, be sufficient; (P. Д, у P) have enough; last (*v/t.* на В); (э́того мне) **~ит** (that's) enough (for me); F hit, knock, strike; drink, eat; take; go.
хво́йный [14] coniferous.
хворáть F [1] be sick *or* ill.
хво́рост *m* [1] brushwood.
хвост *m* [1 *e.*] tail; brush (*fox*); F train; line, *Brt.* queue; в ~сте́ (*lag*) behind; поджáть ~ F come down a peg (or two).
хво́я *f* [6] (pine) needle(s *or* branches).
хижина *f* [5] hut, cabin.
хи́лый [14; хил, -á, -о] sickly.
хими|к *m* [1] (*Brt.* analytical) chemist; **~ческий** [16] chemical; indelible *or* copying-ink (*pencil*); **~я** *f* [7] chemistry.
хини́н *m* [1] quinine.
хирéть [8] weaken, grow sickly.
хиру́рг *m* [1] surgeon; **~и́ческий** [16] surgical; **~и́я** *f* [7] surgery.
хитр|éц *m* [1 *e.*] cunning fellow, dodger; **~и́ть** [13], ‹с-› dodge; fox; quibble; *cf.* мудри́ть; **~ость** *f* [8] craft(iness), cunning; artifice, ruse, trick; stratagem; **~ый** [14; -тёр, -трá, хи́тро] cunning, crafty, sly, artful; ingenious.
хихи́кать [1] chuckle, giggle, titter.
хищéние *n* [12] embezzlement.
хи́щн|ик *m* [1] beast (*or* bird) of prey; **~ый** [14; -щен, -щна] rapacious, predatory; of prey.
хладнокро́в|ие *n* [12] composure; **~ный** [14; -вен, -вна] cool(-headed), calm.
хлам *m* [1] trash, stuff, lumber.
хлеб *m* **1.** [1] bread; loaf; **2.** [1; *pl.*: -бá, *etc. e.*] grain, *Brt.* corn; livelihood; *pl.* cereals; **~áть** [1], *once* ‹~ну́ть› [20] drink, sip; P eat; **~ный** [14] grain..., corn..., cereal; bread...; baker's; F profitable; **~опекáрня** *f* [6; *g/pl.*: -рен] bakery; **~осо́льный** [14; -лен, -льна] hospitable; **~осо́льство** *n* [9], F **~-со́ль** *f* [1/8] hospitality.
хлев *m* [1; в -е & -у́; *pl.*: -á, *etc. e.*] shed; cote; sty.
хлест|áть [3], *once* ‹~ну́ть› [20] lash, whip, beat; splash; gush, spurt; pour.
хли́пать F [1] sob.
хлоп! crack!, plop!; *cf. a.* **~ать** [1], ‹по-›, *once* ‹~нуть› [20] slap; clap; bang, slam (*v/t.* T); crack; pop (*cork*); detonate; resound; blink.
хло́пок *m* [1; -пка] cotton.
хлопот|áть [3], ‹по-› (о П) strive (for), endeavo(u)r; exert o. s. (on behalf of о П, за В); apply (for); *impf.* bustle (about); **~ли́вый** [14 *sh.*] troublesome; busy, fussy; **'~ы** *f/pl.* [5; *gen.*: -по́т] trouble(s), cares; business, commissions.
хлопу́шка *f* [5; *g/pl.*: -шек] fly flap; cracker.
хлопчатобумáжный [14] cotton...
хло́пья *n/pl.* [10; *gen.*: -ьев] flakes.
хлор *m* [1] chlorine; **~истый** [14] ... chloride; **~ный** [14] chloric; **~офо́рм** *m* [1], **~оформи́ровать** [7] (*im*)*pf.* chloroform.
хлы́нуть [20] *pf.* gush (forth); rush; (begin to) pour in torrents.
хлыст *m* [1 *e.*] horsewhip; switch.
хлю́пать F [1] squelch.
хмел|ь *m* [4] hop; intoxication; во ~ю́ drunk; **~ьно́й** F [14; -лён, -льнá] intoxicated; intoxicating.
хму́р|ить [13], ‹на-› knit (*the brow*); **-ся** frown, scowl; be(come) overcast; **~ый** [14; хмур, -á, -о] gloomy, sullen; cloudy.
хны́кать F [3] whine, snivel.
хо́бот *m* [1] *zo.* trunk.
ход *m* [1; в (на) -у́ & -е; *pl.*: хо́ды] motion; speed (at на П), pace; course; passage; walk; ⊕ *a.* action, movement; stroke (*piston*); entrance; access; lead (*cards*); move (*chess, etc.*); turn; vogue, currency;

в ~у́ *a.* = ~кий; на ~у́ *a.* while walking, *etc.*; F in progress; пусти́ть в ~ start, set going *or* on foot, circulate; все ~ы́ и вы́ходы the ins and outs.

ходáтай *m* [3] intercessor, advocate; **~ство** *n* [9] intercession; petition; **~ствовать** [7], ⟨по-⟩ intercede (with/for у Р/за В); petition (for о П).

ход|и́ть [15] go (to в, на В); walk; sail; run, ply; move; visit, attend (*v/t.* в, на В; р. к Д); circulate; (в П) wear; (за Т) look after, take care of, nurse; tend; (на В) hunt; lead (*cards*); F be current; ease o. s.; **~кий** [16; хо́док, -дка́, -о; *comp.*: хо́дче] marketable, sal(e)able; current; F quick, easygoing; ~кая кни́га *f* best seller; **~у́льный** [14; -лен, -льна] stilted; **~ьба́** *f* [5] walking; walk; **~я́чий** [17] current; trivial; F walking.

хожде́ние *n* [12] going, walking; circulation.

хозя́|ин *m* [1; *pl.*: хозя́ева, хозя́ев] master, owner; boss, principal; landlord; host; innkeeper; manager; farmer; ~ева = ~ин & ~йка; **~йка** *f* [5; *g/pl.*: -я́ек] mistress; landlady; hostess; housewife; **~йничать** [1] keep house; manage (at will); make o. s. at home; **~йственный** [14 *sh.*] economic(al); thrifty; **~йство** *n* [9] economy; household; farm.

хокке́й *m* [3] hockey.

холе́ра *f* [5] cholera.

хо́лить [13] groom, care for, fondle.

хо́л|ка *f* [5; *g/pl.*: -лок] withers; **~м** *m* [1 *e.*] hill; **~ми́стый** [14 *sh.*] hilly.

хо́лод *m* [1] cold (in на П); chill (*a. fig.*); *pl.* [-а́, *etc. e.*] cold (weather) (in в В); **~е́ть** [8], ⟨по-⟩ grow cold, chill; **~е́ц** *m* [1; -дца́] = сту́день; **~и́льник** *m* [1] refrigerator; **~ность** *f* [8] coldness; **~ный** [14; хо́лоден, -дна́, -о] cold (*a. fig.*); *geogr.* & *fig.* frigid; (мне) ~но it is (I am) cold.

холо́п *m* [1] bondman; F toady.

холост|о́й [14; хо́лост] single, unmarried; bachelor('s); blank (*cartridge*); ⊕ idle (*motion*); **~я́к** *m* [1 *e.*] bachelor.

холст *m* [1 *e.*] linen; canvas.

холу́й P *m* [3] cad; toady.

хому́т *m* [1 *e.*] (horse) collar.

хомя́к *m* [1 *e.*] hamster.

хор *m* [1] chorus; choir.

хорва́т *m* [1], **~ка** *f* [5; *g/pl.*: -ток] Croat; **~ский** [16] Croatian.

хорёк *m* [1; -рька́] polecat, fitch.

хорово́д *m* [1] round dance.

хорони́ть [13; -оню́, -о́нишь], ⟨по-⟩ bury.

хоро́ш|енький [16] pretty; **~е́нько** F properly; **~е́ть** [8], ⟨по-⟩ grow prettier; **~ий** [17; хоро́ш, -а́; *comp.*: лу́чше] good; fine, nice; (*a.* собо́й) pretty, good-looking, handso[me]; **~о́** well; *mark*: good, B (*cf.* четв[ёр]ка); all right!, O.K.!, good!; ~о́ I am well off; ~о́ вам (+ *inf.*) is very well for you to ...

хоте́|ть [хочу́, хо́чешь, хо́чет, [хо]ти́м, хоти́те, хотя́т], ⟨за-⟩ (Р) w[ant,] wish; я ~л(а) бы I would (or should) like; я хочу́, что́бы вы [+] *pt.* I want you to ...; хо́чешь [не] хо́чешь willy-nilly; **-ся** (*imper[s.]*) мне хо́чется I'd like; *a.* = ~ть.

хоть (*a.* ~ бы) at least; even (i[f]; though); if only; ~ ... ~ whethe[r ...] whether, (either ...) or; if you ple[ase;] so much, *etc.*, that; any ...; I wi[sh I] could (*or* you'd); ~ бы и так eve[n if] it be so; ~ убей for the life of [me]; *s. a.* хотя́.

хотя́ although, though (*a.* ~ и); ~ even though; if; *s. a.* хоть.

хохо́л *m* [1; хохла́] tuft; crest; f[or]lock; *contp.* Ukrainian (*man*).

хо́хот *m* [1] (loud) laughter, r[oar;] **~а́ть** [3], ⟨за-⟩ roar (with laugh[ter]).

храбр|е́ц *m* [1 *e.*] brave; **~ость** *f* valo(u)r, bravery; **~ый** [14; хра[бр], -а́, -о] brave, valient.

храм *m* [1] *eccl.* temple.

хран|е́ние *n* [12] keeping; stor[age;] ка́мера ~е́ния ручно́го бага́жа cloackroom, *Brt.* left-luggage of[fice;] **~и́лище** *n* [11] storehouse; arch[ive(s)] *pl.*; **~и́тель** *m* [4] keeper, guard[ian;] custodian; **~и́ть** [13], ⟨со-⟩ k[eep;] store; preserve; observe; guard.

храп *m* [1], **~е́ть** [10 *e.*; -п[лю́],] -пи́шь] snore; snort.

хребе́т *m* [1; -бта́] *anat.* spine; ra[nge].

хрен *m* [1] horseradish.

хрип *m* [1], **~е́ние** *n* [12] ra[ttle;] **~е́ть** [10 *e.*; -плю́, -пи́шь] ra[ttle;] be hoarse; F speak hoarsely; **~л[ый]** [14; хрипл, -а́, -о] hoarse, hu[sky;] **~нуть** [21], ⟨о-⟩ become ho[arse;] **~ота́** *f* [5] hoarseness; husky v[oice].

христ|иани́н *m* [1; *pl.*: -а́не, -[а́н]] **~иа́нка** *f* [5; *g/pl.*: -нок], **~и[а́н]ский** [16] Christian; **~иа́нств[о]** [9] Christianity; 2**о́в** [19] Chri[st's;] 2**о́с** *m* [Христа́] Christ.

хром *m* [1] chromium; chrome.

хром|а́ть [1] limp; be lame; [**~о́й**] [14; хром, -а́, -о] lame; **~ота́** [*f* [5]] lameness.

хро́н|ика *f* [5] chronicle; cu[rrent] events; newsreel; **~и́ческий** chronic(al); **~ологи́ческий** chronological; **~оло́гия** *f* [7] c[hro]nology.

хру́|пкий [16; -пок, -пка́, -о; *co[mp.]*: хру́пче] brittle, fragile; frail, inf[irm;] **~ста́ль** *m* [4 *e.*] crystal; **~ста[ль]ный** [14] crystal...; **~сте́ть** [...] crunch; **~щ** *m* [1 *e.*] cockchafe[r].

хрю́к|ать [1], *once* ⟨~нуть⟩ grunt.

хрящ *m* [1 *e.*] cartilage.

худе́ть [8], ⟨по-⟩ grow thin.

о *n* [9] evil; *s. a.* худо́й.
о́ж|ественный [14 *sh.*] artistic; (s)...; of art; belles(-*lettres*); ap-ied (*arts*); **~ество** *n* [9] (applied) t; **~ник** *m* [1] artist; painter.
|о́й [14; худ, -á, -о; *comp.*: худе́е] thin, lean, scrawny (*a.* **~оща́вый** [14 *sh.*]); [*comp.*: ху́же] bad, evil; **´~ший** [16] worse, worst; *cf.* лу́чший.
ху́же worse; *cf.* лу́чше & тот.
хулига́н *m* [1] rowdy, hooligan.
ху́тор *m* [1] farm(stead); hamlet.

Ц

|ать F [1], *once* ⟨~нуть⟩ [20] atch.
ля *f* [6; *g/pl.*: -пель] heron.
а́п|ать [1], ⟨(п)о-⟩, *once* ⟨~нуть⟩ 0], **~ина** *f* [5] scratch.
|е́вич *m* [1] czarevitch; prince;
вна *f* [5; *g/pl.*: -вен] princess;
ть [13] reign; prevail; **~и́ца** *f* czarina; empress; *fig.* queen;
кий [16] of the czar(s), czarist; perial; **´~ство** *n* [9] empire; king-m (*a. fig.*); rule; *a.* = **´~ствова-**ие *n* [12] reign (in в В); **´~ство-**ть [7] reign, rule; prevail; **~ь** *m e.*] czar, (Russian) emperor; king.
сти́ [25 -т-] bloom, blossom.
т *m* [1] **1.** [*pl.*: -á, *etc. e.*] col-u)r; ~ лица́ complexion; защи́т-го **´~а** khaki; **2.** [*only pl.*: -ы́, *etc.* flowers; **3.** [*no pl.*; в -у́; *fig.* в(о) е́те] blossom, bloom; *fig. a.* prime;
ние *n* [12] flowering; **~и́стый** 4 *sh.*] florid; **~ни́к** *m* [1 *e.*] flower d; **~но́й** [14] colo(u)red; varie-ted; nonferrous (*metals*); techni-lor (*film*); **~на́я капу́ста** *f* cauli-wer; **~о́к** *m* [1; -тка́; *pl. usu.* = ~ flower (*a. fig.*); **~о́чник** *m* [1] rist; **~о́чница** *f* [5] florist, *Brt.* wer girl; **~о́чный** [14] flower...;
щий [17 *sh.*] flowering; flourish-g; prime (*of life*).
ди́ть [15] **1.** ⟨про-⟩ strain, pass, ter; F murmur, utter (between e's teeth); **2.** ⟨вы́-⟩ draw (off).
йло́н *m* [1] Ceylon.
йхга́уз (сеjˈха-) *m* [1] arsenal.
е́|бный [14; -бен, -бна] cura-e, medicinal; **~во́й** [14] special, a specified purpose, purposeful; incipal; **~сообра́зный** [14; -зен, на] expedient; **~устремлённый** 4 *sh.*] purposeful.
и|ко́м entirely, wholly; **~на́** *f*] virgin soil; **´~тельный** [14; ен, -льна] salutary, curative; **ˈ~ть** ся) [13], ⟨при-⟩ aim (at в В).
люло́за *f* [5] cellulose.
ова́ть(ся) [7], ⟨по-⟩ kiss.
|ое *n* [14] whole (on the в П; the lump); **~ому́дренный** [14 .] chaste; **~ому́дрие** *n* [12] chas-y; **~ость** *f* [8] integrity; в ~ости tact; **~ый** [14; цел, -á, -о] whole; tire; safe, sound; intact; ~ое число́ integer; *cf.* деся́тый & со́тый.
ь *f* [8] aim, end, goal, object; target; purpose (for с Т, в П *pl.*); име́ть **´~ю** aim at; **´~ность** *f* [8] in-tegrity; **´~ный** [14; це́лен, -льна́, -о] entire, whole; righteous; [*no sh.*] rich (*milk*).
цеме́нт *m* [1], **~и́ровать** [7] cement.
цен|а́ *f* [5; *ac/sg.*: це́ну; *pl. st.*] price (of Р, на В, Д; at/of по Д/в В), cost (at Т); value (of *or* one's Д); **~ы́ нет** (Д) be invaluable; любо́й **~о́й** at any price; **~зу́ра** *f* [5] censorship.
цен|и́тель *m* [4] judge, connoisseur; **~и́ть** [13; ценю́, це́нишь], ⟨о-⟩ value, estimate, appreciate; **´~ность** *f* [8] value; *pl.* valuables; **´~ный** [14; -е́нен, -е́нна] valuable; money (*letter*); **´~ные бума́ги** *pl.* securities.
це́нтнер *m* [1] centner (= *100 kg*).
центр *m* [1] center, *Brt.* centre; **~ализова́ть** [7] (*im*)*pf.* centralize; **~а́льный** [14] central; *cf.* ЦИК & ЦК; **~обе́жный** [14] centrifugal.
цеп *m* [1 *e.*] flail.
цеп|ене́ть [8], ⟨о-⟩ grow numb, stiffen; be transfixed; **´~кий** [16; -пок, -пка́, -о] clinging; tenacious; **~ля́ться** [28] cling (to за В); **~но́й** [14] chain(ed); **~о́чка** *f* [5; *g/pl.*: -чек] chain; **~ь** *f* [8; в, на -и́; *from g/pl. e.*] chain (*a. fig.*); ⚔ line; ⚡ circuit.
церемо́н|иться [13], ⟨по-⟩ stand on ceremony, be ceremonious; **~ия** *f* [7] ceremony; **~ный** [14] ceremonious.
церко́в|ный [14] church...; **ˈ~ь** *f* [8; -кви; *instr/sg.*: -ковью; *pl.*: -кви, -ве́й, -ва́м] church.
цех *m* [1] shop, section; † guild.
цивилиз|ова́ть [7] (*im*)*pf.* civilize; **~о́ванный** [14] civilized.
ЦИК (Центра́льный Исполни́тельный Комите́т) Central Executive Committee (*Sov.*); *cf.* ЦК.
цикл *m* [1] cycle; course, set; **~о́н** *m* [1] cyclone.
цико́рий *m* [3] chicory.
цили́ндр *m* [1] cylinder; top (*or* high) hat; **~и́ческий** [16] cylindrical.
цинга́ *f* [5] scurvy.
цини́|зм *m* [1] cynicism; **ˈ~к** *m* [1] cynic; **~чный** [14; -чен, -чна] cynical.
цинк *m* [1] zinc; **´~овый** [14] zinc ...
цино́вка *f* [5; *g/pl.*: -вок] mat.
цирк *m* [1], **~ово́й** [14] circus.
циркул|и́ровать [7] circulate; **ˈ~ь**

m [4] (оди́н a pair of) compasses *pl.*; **~я́р** *m* [1] circular.
цисте́рна *f* [5] cistern, tank.
цитаде́ль (-ˈdɛ-) *f* [8] citadel; stronghold.
цита́та *f* [5] quotation.
цити́ровать [7], ⟨про-⟩ quote.
циф|ербла́т *m* [1] dial, face (*watch, etc.*); **ˆра** *f* [5] figure.

ЦК (Центра́льный Комите́т) C tral Committee (*Sov.*); *cf.* ЦИК
цо́коль *m* [4] ⚠ socle; ⊕ socket
цыга́н *m* [1; *nom/pl.*: -е & -ы; g цыга́н], **~ка** *f* [5; *g/pl.*: -нок] **ский** [16] Gypsy, *Brt.* Gipsy.
цыплёнок *m* [2] chicken.
цы́почк|и: на ~ах (*or* ~и) on toe.

Ч

ч. *abbr.*: **1.** час; **2.** часть.
чад *m* [1; в -у́] smoke, fume(s); *fig.* daze; frenzy; **~и́ть** [15 *e.*; чажу́, чади́шь], ⟨на-⟩ smoke.
ча́до † & *iron. n* [9] child.
чаевы́е *pl.* [14] tip.
чай[1] *m* [3; *part. g.*: -ю; в -е & -ю́; *pl. e.*: чаи́, чаёв] tea; tea party; дать на ~ tip; **~**[2] P perhaps, I suppose.
ча́йка *f* [5; *g/pl.*: ча́ек] (sea) gull, mew.
ча́йн|ик *m* [1] teapot; teakettle; **~ый** [14] tea(*spoon, etc.*).
чалма́ *f* [5] turban.
чан *m* [1; *pl. e.*] tub, vat.
ча́р|ка *f* [5; *g/pl.*: -рок] (*wine-etc.*) glass; **~ова́ть** [20] charm; **~оде́й** *m* [3] magician.
час *m* [1; в -е & -у́; *after 2, 3, 4*: -а́; *pl. e.*] hour (by the по ~а́м; for *pl.* ~а́ми); (one) o'clock (at в В); time, moment (at в В); an hour's ...; второ́й ~ (it is) past one; в пя́том ~у́ between four & five; (*cf.* пять & пя́тый); ~ о́т ~у *or* с ˆу на ~ hourly; на ~а́х (*stand*) sentinel; **~о́вня** *f* [6; *g/pl.*: -вен] chapel; **~ово́й** [14] hour's; by the hour; watch..., clock-...; *su.* sentry, sentinel; ~ово́й ма́стер *m* = **~овщи́к** [1 *e.*] watchmaker.
част|и́ца *f* [5] particle; **~и́чный** [14; -чен, -чна] partial; **ˆное** *n* [14] quotient; **ˆность** *f* [8] particular; **ˆный** [14] private; particular; individual; **~око́л** *m* [1] palisade; **~ота́** *f* [5; *pl. st.*: -о́ты] frequency; **~у́шка** *f* [5; *g/pl.*: -шек] couplet; **ˆый** [14; част, -а́, -о; *comp.*: ча́ще] frequent (*adv. a.* often); thick(-set), dense; close; quick, rapid; **~ь** *f* [8; *from g/pl. e.*] part (in Т; *pl. a.* по Д); share; piece; department, section (in *a.* по Д), F line, branch; ⚔ unit; † police station; бо́льшей ˆью, по бо́льшей ˆи for the most part, mostly.
час|ы́ *m/pl.* [1] watch; clock; (*sun*)dial; на мои́х ~а́х by my watch.
ча́х|лый [14 *sh.*] sickly; stunted; **~нуть** [21], ⟨за-⟩ wither, shrivel; grow stunted; **~о́тка** *f* [5] consumption; **~о́точный** [14; -чен, -ч consumptive.
ча́ша *f* [5] cup, chalice; bowl.
ча́шка *f* [5; *g/pl.*: -шек] cup; p cap; надколе́нная ~ kneecap.
ча́ща *f* [5] thicket.
ча́ще more (~ всего́ most) ofter
ча́я|ние *n* [12] expectation (c trary to па́че *or* сверх Р), h dream.
чва́н|иться F [13], **~ство** *n* [9] b blow, swagger.
чей *m*, чья *f*, чьё *n*, чьи *pl.* whose; ~ э́то дом? whose hous this?
чек *m* [1] check, *Brt.* cheque; **нить** [13], ⟨вы́-⟩ mint, coin; ch **~а́нка** *f* [5; *g/pl.*: -нок] mint coinage; chase; **~и́ст** *m* [1] mem of ЧК, *cf.*; **ˆовый** [14] check...
чёлн *m* [1 *e.*; челна́] boat; canoe
челно́к *m* [1 *e.*] *dim. of* чёлн shuttle.
чело́ † *n* [9; *pl. st.*] foreh brow.
челове́|к *m* [1; *pl.*: лю́ди, *cf.*; *etc.* -е́к] man, human being; son, individual; one; † serv waiter; ру́сский ~к Russian; **~** лю́бие *n* [12] philanthropy; **~** ский [16] human(e); **~честв** [9] mankind, humanity; **~чн** [14; -чен, -чна] humane.
че́люсть *f* [8] jaw; (full) dentur
че́лядь *f* [8] servants *pl.*
чем than; F instead of; ~ ..., те the ... the ...; **~ода́н** *m* [1] s case.
чемпио́н *m* [1] champion; **~а́т** *m* championship.
чепе́ц *m* [1; -пца́] cap.
чепуха́ F *f* [5] nonsense; trifle.
че́пчик *m* [1] cap.
че́рв|и *f/pl.* [4; *from gen. e.*] & *f/pl.* [5] hearts (*cards*).
черви́вый [14 *sh.*] worm-eaten.
черво́нец *m* [1; -нца] 10 rubles
черв|ь *m* [4 *e.*; *nom/pl. st.*: че́р черве́й], **~я́к** *m* [1 *e.*] worm.
черда́к *m* [1 *e.*] garret, attic, loft
черёд F *m* [1 *e.*] turn; course.
чередова́|ние *n* [12] alternati **~ть(ся)** [7] alternate.
че́рез (В) through; across, o

time: in, after; *go*: via; with (the help of); because of; ~ день *a.* every other day.
черёмуха *f* [5] bird cherry.
че́реп *m* [1; *pl.*: -á, *etc. e.*] skull.
черепа́|ха *f* [5] tortoise; turtle; tortoise shell; **~ховый** [14] tortoise(-shell)...; **~ший** [18] tortoise's, snail's (pace шаг *m*; at T).
череп|и́ца *f* [5] tile (*of roof*); **~и́чный** [14] tiled; **~о́к** *m* [1; -пка́] fragment, piece.
чере|счу́р too, too much; **~́шня** *f* [6; *g*/*pl.*: -шен] (sweet) cherry.
черкну́ть F [20] *pf.*: ~ па́ру (*or* не́сколько) слов drop a line.
черн|е́ть [8], ‹по-› blacken, grow black; *impf.* (*a.* -ся) show black; **~е́ц** *m* [1 *e.*] monk; **~и́ка** *f* [5] bilberry, -ries *pl.*; **~и́ла** *n*/*pl.* [9] ink; **~и́льница** *f* [5] inkwell (*Brt.* inkpot), inkstand; **~и́льный** [14] ink...; **~и́ть** [13] **1.** ‹на-› blacken; **2.** ‹о-› blacken (*fig.*), denigrate, slander.
черно|ви́к *m* [1 *e.*] rough copy; draft; **~во́й** [14] draft...; rough; waste (*book*); **~воло́сый** [14 *sh.*] black-haired; **~гла́зый** [14 *sh.*] black-eyed; **~го́рец** *m* [1; -рца] Montenegrin; **~зём** *m* [1] chernozem, black earth; **~ко́жий** [17 *sh.*] Negro; **~ма́зый** [14 *sh.*] swarthy; **~мо́рский** [16] Black Sea ...; **~рабо́чий** *m* [17] unskilled worker; **~сли́в** *m* [1] prune(s); **~та́** *f* [5] blackness.
чёрн|ый [14; чёрен, черна́] black (*a. fig.*); brown (*bread*); ferrous (*metals*); rough (*work*); back(*stairs, etc.*); leafy (*wood*); на ~ый день for a rainy day; ~ым по бе́лому in black & white.
чернь *f* [8] mob, rabble.
че́рп|ать [1], ‹~ну́ть› [20] scoop, draw; gather (from из P, в П).
черст|ве́ть [8], ‹за-, по-› grow stale; harden; **~́вый** (ˈtʃɔ-) [14; чёрств, -á, -о] stale, hard; callous.
чёрт *m* [1; *pl.* 4 че́рти, -те́й, *etc. e.*] devil; F the deuce (go: *a.* ступа́й, убира́йся; take: возьми́, побери́, [по]дери́; *a.* confound; blast, damn it!); к ~у, на кой ~ F *a.* the deuce; ни черта́ F nothing at all; never mind!
черт|á *f* [5] line; trait, feature (*a.* ~ы лица́); precincts *pl.* (within в П); term.
чертёж *m* [1 *e.*] (mechanical) drawing, draft (*Brt.* draught), design; **~ник** *m* [1] draftsman, *Brt.* draughtsman; **~ный** [14] drawing (*board, etc.*).
черт|и́ть [15], ‹на-› draw, design; **~о́вский** [16] devilish.
чёрточка *f* [5; *g*/*pl.*: -чек] hyphen.
черче́ние *n* [12] drawing.
чеса́ть [3] **1.** ‹по-› scratch; **2.** ‹при› F comb; **3.** *impf.* hackle, card; **-ся** *a.*, F, itch (my у меня́).
чесно́к *m* [1 *e.*] garlic.
чесо́тка *f* [5] itch.
че́ст|вование *n* [12] celebration; **~вовать** [7] celebrate, hono(u)r; **~ность** *f* [8] honesty; **~ный** [14; че́стен, -тна́, -о] honest, of hono(u)r; fair; **~олюби́вый** [14 *sh.*] ambitious; **~олю́бие** *n* [12] ambition; **~ь** *f* [8] hono(u)r (in в B); credit; по ~и F honestly; ~ь ~ью F properly, well.
чета́ *f* [5] couple, pair; F match.
четве́р|г *m* [1 *e.*] Thursday (on: в B, *pl.*: по Д); **~е́ньки** F *f*/*pl.* [5] all fours (on на B, П); **~ка** (-ˈɣɔr-) *f* [5; *g*/*pl.*: -рок] four (*cf.* тро́йка); F (*mark*) = хорошо́, *cf.*; **'~о** [37] four (*cf.* дво́е); **~оно́гий** [16] four-footed; **~тый** (-ˈɣɔr-) [14] fourth; *cf.* пя́тый; **'~ть** *f* [8; *from g*/*pl. e.*] (one) fourth; quarter (to без P; past one второ́го).
чёткий [16; чёток, четка́, -о] distinct, clear; legible; exact, accurate.
чётный [14] even.
четы́ре [34] four; *cf.* пять; **~жды** four times; **~ста** [36] four hundred.
четырёх|ле́тний [15] four-years(-old)'; **~ме́стный** [14] four-seated; **~со́тый** [14] four hundredth; **~уго́льник** *m* [1] quadrangle; **~уго́льный** [14] quadrangular; **~эта́жный** [14] four-storied (*Brt.* -storeyed).
четы́рнадца|тый [14] fourteenth; *cf.* пя́тый; **~ть** [35] fourteen; *cf.* пять.
чех *m* [1] Czech.
чехарда́ *f* [5] leapfrog.
чехо́л *m* [1; -хла́] case, cover.
Чехослова́|кия *f* [7] Czechoslovakia: **~цкий** [16] Czechoslovak.
чечеви́ца *f* [5] lentil(s).
че́ш|ка *f* [5; *g*/*pl.*: -шек] Czech (woman); **~ский** [16] Czech(ic).
чешуя́ *f* [6] scales *pl.*
чи́бис *m* [1] lapwing.
чиж *m* [1 *e.*], F **~́ик** *m* [1] siskin.
Чи|ка́го *n* [*ind.*] Chicago; **~́ли** *n* [*ind.*] Chile; **~ли́ец** *m* [1; -и́йца] Chilean.
чин *m* [1; *pl. e.*] rank, grade; station; order, ceremony; official; **~и́ть** **1.** [13; чиню́, чи́нишь] a) ‹по-› mend, repair; b) ‹о-› sharpen, point; **2.** [13], ‹у-› raise, cause; administer; **~́ный** [14; чи́нен, чинна́, чи́нно] proper; sedate; **~о́вник** *m* [1] official; bureaucrat.
чири́к|ать [1], ‹~нуть› [20] chirp.
чи́рк|ать [1], ‹~нуть› [20] strike.
чи́сл|енность *f* [8] number; ⚔ strength (of/of T/в B); **~енный** [14] numerical; **~и́тель** ℞ *m* [4]

numerator; **~и́тельное** *n* [14] *gr.* numeral (*a.* и́мя ~и́тельное); **~иться** [13] be on the ... list (в П *or* по Д/Р); **~о́** *n* [9; *pl. st.*: чи́сла, чи́сел, чи́слам] number; date; day (in в П; on Р); кото́рое (како́е) сего́дня ~о́? what date is today? (*cf.* пя́тый); в ~е́ (Р), в том ~е́ including.

чи́стильщик *m* [1] (*boot*)black.

чи́ст|ить [15] **1.** ⟨по-, вы́-⟩ clean(se); brush; polish; **2.** ⟨о-⟩ peel; *pol.* purge; **~ка** *f* [5; *g/pl.*: -ток] clean(s)ing; polish(ing); *pol.* purge; **~окро́вный** [14; -вен, -вна] thoroughbred; *fig.* genuine; **~опло́тный** [14; -тен, -тна] cleanly; *fig.* clean; **~осерде́чный** [14; -чен, -чна] open-hearted, frank, sincere; **~ота́** *f* [5] clean(li)ness; purity; **~ый** [14; чист, -а́, -о; *comp.*: чи́ще] clean; pure; neat, cleanly; clear; net; blank (*sheet*); fine, faultless; genuine; sheer; plain (*truth*); mere (*chance*); hard (*cash*); free, open (*field*).

чита́|льный [14]: ~льный зал *m*, **~льня** *f* [6; *g/pl.*: -лен] reading room; **~тель** *m* [4] reader; **~ть** [1], ⟨про-⟩ & ⟨проче́сть⟩ F [25; -чту́, -чтёшь; -чёл, -чла́; -чтённый] read, recite; give (*lecture* on о П), deliver, lecture; teach; ~ть по склада́м spell.

чи́тка *f* [5; *g/pl.*: -ток] reading.

чих|а́ть [1], *once* ⟨~ну́ть⟩ [20] sneeze.

ЧК (Чрезвыча́йная коми́ссия ...) Cheka (*predecessor, 1917—22, of the* ГПУ, *cf.*).

член *m* [1] member; limb; *gr.* article; part; **~ора́зде́льный** [14; -лен, -льна] articulate; **∠ский** [16] member(-ship)...; **∠ство** *n* [9] membership.

чмо́к|ать F [1], *once* ⟨~нуть⟩ [20] smack.

чо́к|аться [1], *once* ⟨~нуться⟩ [20] touch (glasses T) (with с T).

чо́|порный [14; -рен, -рна] prim, prudish; **~рт** *s.* чёрт.

чрев|а́тый [14 *sh.*] pregnant (*a. fig.*); **∠о** *n* [9] womb.

чрез *s.* че́рез; **~выча́йный** [14; -а́ен, -а́йна] extraordinary; extreme; special; **~ме́рный** [14; -рен, -рна] excessive.

чте́|ние *n* [12] reading; recital; **~ц** *m* [1 *e.*] reader.

чтить *s.* почита́ть[1].

что [23] **1.** *pron.* what (*a.* ~ за); that, which; how; (*a.* а ~?) why (so?); (*a.* а ~) what about; what's the matter; F а ~? well?; how (*or* as) much, how many; во́т ~ the following; listen; that's it; ~ до меня́ as for me; ~ вы (ты)! you don't say!, what next!; не́ за ~ (you are) welcome, *Brt.* don't mention it; ни за ∠ not for the world; ну ~ же? what of that?; (уж) на ~ F however; с чего́? F why?, wherefore?; ~ и говори́ть F sure; *cf.* ни; F *s.* ∠-нибудь, ∠-то; **2.** *cj.* that; like, as if; ~ (ни) ..., то ... every ... (a)...

что́б(ы) (in order) that *or* to (*a.* с тем, ~); ~ не lest, for fear that; вме́сто того́ ~ + *inf.* instead of ...ing; скажи́ ему́, ~ он + *pt.* tell him to *inf.*

что́|-либо, ~-нибудь, ~-то [23] something; anything; ~-то *a.* F somewhat; somehow, for some reason or other.

чу́вств|енный [14 *sh.*] sensuous; sensual; material; **~и́тельность** *f* [8] sensibility; **~и́тельный** [14; -лен, -льна] sensitive; sentimental; sensible (*a.* = considerable, great, strong); biting (*cold*); grievous (*loss*); **~о** *n* [9] sense; feeling; sensation; F love; без ~ unconscious, senseless; **~овать** [7], ⟨по-⟩ feel (*a.* себя́ [T s. th.]); **-ся** be felt.

чугу́н *m* [1 *e.*] cast iron; **~ный** [14] cast-iron; **~олите́йный** [14]: ~олите́йный заво́д *m* iron foundry.

чуд|а́к *m* [1 *e.*] crank, character; **~а́чество** *n* [9] eccentricity; **~е́сный** [14; -сен, -сна] wonderful, marvel(l)ous; miraculous; **~и́ть** [15 *e.*] F *s.* дури́ть; **∠иться** [15] F = мере́щиться; **~но́й** F [14; -дён, -дна́] queer, odd, strange; funny; **∠ный** [14; -ден, -дна] wonderful, marvel(l)ous; **∠о** *n* [9; *pl.*: чудеса́, -е́с, -еса́м] miracle, marvel; wonder; *a.* = ∠но; **~о́вище** *n* [11] monster; **~о́вищный** [14; -щен, -щна] monstrous; **~отво́рец** *m* [1; -рца] wonderworker.

чуж|би́на *f* [5] foreign country (in на П; *a.* abroad); **~да́ться** [1] (Р) shun, avoid; **∠дый** [14; чу́жд, -а́, -о] foreign; strange, alien; free (from Р); **~езе́мец** *m* [1; -мца] foreigner; **~о́й** [14] someone else's, alien; strange, foreign; *su. a.* stranger, outsider.

чул|а́н *m* [1] closet; pantry; **~о́к** *m* [1; -лка́; *g/pl.*: -ло́к] stocking.

чума́ *f* [5] plague, pestilence.

чума́зый F [14 *sh.*] dirty.

чурба́н *m* [1] block; blockhead.

чу́тк|ий [16; -ток, -тка́, -о; *comp.*: чу́тче] sensitive (to на В), keen; light (*sleep*); vigilant, watchful; wary; quick (of hearing); responsive; sympathetic; **~ость** *f* [8] keenness; delicacy (of feeling).

чу́точку F a bit.

чуть hardly, scarcely; a little; ~ не nearly, almost; ~ ли не F seem(-ingly); ~ что F on the least occasion; ~-~ *s.* ~; **~ё** *n* [10] instinct (for на В); scent, flair.

чу́чело *n* [9] stuffed animal *or* bird; scarecrow; ~ горо́ховое F dolt.

чушь F *f* [8] bosh, baloney.

чу́ять [27], ⟨по-⟩ scent, feel.

Ш

шаба́ш F **1.** *m* [1] (knocking-)off-time; **2.** *int.* enough!, no more!; **~ить** F [16], ‹по-› knock off.
шабло́н *m* [1] stencil, pattern, cliché; **~ный** [14] trite, hackneyed.
шаг *m* [1; *after 2, 3, 4*: -á; в -ý; *pl. e.*] step (by step ~ за T) (*a. fig.*); pace (at T); stride; démarche; ни **~у** (да́льше) no step further; на ка́ждом ~ý everywhere, on end; **~а́ть** [1], *once* ‹~ну́ть› [20] step, stride; march; walk; advance; (че́рез) cross; *pf. a.* take a step; далеко́ ~ну́ть *fig.* make great progress; **~ом** at a slow pace, slowly.
ша́йба *f* [5] disk.
ша́йка *f* [5; *g/pl.*: ша́ек] gang.
шака́л *m* [1] jackal.
шала́ш *m* [1] hut; tent.
шал|и́ть [13] be naughty, frolic, romp; fool (about), play (pranks); be up to mischief; buck; ~и́шь! P fiddlesticks!, on no account!; **~овли́вый** [14 *sh.*] frolicsome, playful; **~опа́й** F *m* [3] good-for-nothing; **~ость** *f* [8] prank; **~у́н** *m* [1 *e.*] naughty boy; **~у́нья** *f* [6; *g/pl.*: -ний] tomboy, madcap.
шаль *f* [8] shawl.
шально́й [14] mad, crazy; stray...
ша́мкать [1] mumble.
шампа́нское *n* [16] champagne.
шампу́нь *m* [4] shampoo.
шанс *m* [1] chance, prospect (of на B).
шанта́ж *m* [1], **~и́ровать** [7] blackmail.
ша́пка *f* [5; *g/pl.*: -пок] cap; heading.
шар *m* [1; *after 2, 3, 4*: -á; *pl. e.*] sphere; ball; возду́шный ~ balloon; земно́й ~ globe.
шара́х|аться F [1], ‹~нуться› [20] rush (aside), recoil; shy; plop.
шарж *m* [1] cartoon, caricature.
ша́рик *m* [1] *dim. of* шар; corpuscle; **~овый** [14] ball (point *pen*); **~оподши́пник** *m* [1] ball bearing.
ша́рить [13], ‹по-› rummage.
ша́р|кать [1], *once* ‹~кнуть› [20] scrape; bow; **~ма́нка** *f* [5; *g/pl.*: -нок] hand organ.
шарни́р *m* [1] hinge, joint.
шаро|ва́ры *f/pl.* [5] baggy trousers; **~ви́дный** [14; -ден, -дна] **~обра́зный** [14; -зен, -зна] spherical, globular.
шарф *m* [1] scarf, neckerchief.
шасси́ *n* [*ind.*] chassis; ✈ undercarriage.
шат|а́ть [1], *once* ‹(по)шатну́ть› [20] (**-ся** be[come]) shake(n); rock; **-ся** *a.* stagger, reel, totter; F lounge loaf, gad about.
шатёр *m* [1; -тра́] tent.
ша́т|кий [16; -ток, -тка] shaky, rickety, tottering; *fig.* unsteady, fickle; **~ну́ть(ся)** *s.* ~а́ть(ся).
ша́|фер *m* [1; *pl.*: -á, *etc. e.*] best man; **~х** *m* [1] shah; check (*chess*).
шахмат|и́ст *m* [1] chess player; **'~ный** [14] chess...; **'~ы** *f/pl.* [5] chess (*play v/t.* в B).
ша́хт|а *f* [5] mine, pit; **~ёр** *m* [1] miner, pitman; **~ёрский** [16] miner's.
ша́шка *f* [5; *g/pl.*: -шек] saber, *Brt.* sabre; checker, draughtsman; *pl.* checkers, *Brt.* draughts.
швед *m* [1], **~ка** *f* [5; *g/pl.*: -док] Swede; **~ский** [16] Swedish.
шве́йный [14] sewing (*machine*).
швейца́р *m* [1] doorman, doorkeeper, porter; **~ец** *m* [1; -рца], **~ка** *f* [5; *g/pl.*: -рок] Swiss; **Ꞩия** *f* [7] Switzerland; **~ский** [16] Swiss; doorman's, porter's.
Шве́ция *f* [7] Sweden.
швея́ *f* [6] seamstress.
швыр|я́ть [28], *once* ‹~ну́ть› [20] hurl, fling (*a.* T); squander.
шеве|ли́ть [13; -елю́, -е́ли́шь], ‹по-›, *once* ‹(по)~льну́ть› [20] stir, move (*v/i.* **-ся**); turn (*hay*).
шеде́вр (-ˈdɛvr) *m* [1] masterpiece.
ше́йка *f* [5; *g/pl.*: ше́ек] neck.
ше́лест *m* [1], **~е́ть** [11] rustle.
шёлк *m* [1; *g/sg. a.* -у; в шелку́; *pl.*: шелка́, *etc. e.*] silk.
шелкови́|стый [14 *sh.*] silky; **~ца** *f* [5] mulberry (tree); **~чный** [14]: ~чный червь *m* silkworm.
шёлковый [14] silk(en).
шел|охну́ться [20] *pf.* stir; **~уха́** *f* [5], **~уши́ть** [16 *e.*; -шу́, -ши́шь] peel, husk; **~ьма** F *f* [5] rascal, rogue.
шепеля́в|ить [14] lisp; **~ый** [14 *sh.*] lisping.
шёпот *m* [1] whisper (in a T).
шеп|та́ть [3], ‹про-›, *once* ‹~ну́ть› [20] whisper (*v/i. a.* **-ся**).
шере́нга *f* [5] file, rank.
шерохова́тый [14 *sh.*] rough.
шерст|ь *f* [8; *from g/pl. e.*] wool; coat; fleece; **~яно́й** [14] wool([l]en).
шерша́вый [14 *sh.*] rough; shaggy.
шест *m* [1 *e.*] pole.
ше́ств|ие *n* [12] procession; **~овать** [7] step, stride, go, walk.
шест|ёрка [5; *g/pl.*: -рок] six (*cf.* тро́йка); **~ерня́** ⊕ *f* [6; *g/pl.*: -рён] pinion; cogwheel; **~еро** [37] six (*cf.* дво́е); **~идеся́тый** [14] sixtieth; *cf.* пят(идеся́т)ый; **~име́сячный** [14] six-months(-old)'; **~исо́тый** [14] six hundredth; **~иуго́льник** *m* [1] hexagon; **~на́дцатый** [14] sixteenth; *cf.* пя́тый; **~на́дцать** [35] sixteen; *cf.* пять;

~о́й [14] sixth; *cf.* пя́тый; **~ь** [35 *e.*] six; *cf.* пять; **~ьдеся́т** [35] sixty; **~ьсо́т** [36] six hundred; **́~ью** six times.
шеф *m* [1] chief, head, F boss; patron, sponsor; **́~ство** *n* [9] patronage, sponsorship.
шея́ *f* [6; *g/pl.*: шей] neck; back.
ши́|бко P swiftly; very; **~ворот**: взять за ~ворот collar.
шик|а́рный [14; -рен, -рна] chic, smart; **́~ать** F [1], *once* ⟨́~нуть⟩ [20] hiss.
ши́ло *n* [1; *pl.*: -лья, -льев] awl.
ши́на *f* [5] tire, *Brt.* tyre; ⚕ splint.
шине́ль *f* [8] greatcoat, overcoat.
шинкова́ть [7] chop, shred.
шип *m* [1 *e.*] thorn; (dowel) pin.
шипе́|ние *n* [12] hiss(ing); **~ть** [10], ⟨про-⟩ hiss; spit; whiz.
шипо́вник *m* [1] dogrose.
шип|у́чий [17 *sh.*] sparkling, fizzy; **~я́щий** [17] sibilant.
шири|на́ *f* [5] width, breadth; ~но́й в (B) *or* ... в ~ну́ ... wide; **'~ть** [13], (**-ся**) widen, spread.
ши́рма *f* [5] (*mst pl.*) screen.
широ́к|ий [16; широ́к, -ока́, -о́ко́; *comp.*: ши́ре] broad; wide; vast; (at) large; great; mass...; large-scale; *phon.* open; на ~ую но́гу in grand style; **~овеща́тельный** [14] broadcasting; [-лен, -льна] promising; **~оплечий** [17 *sh.*] broad-shouldered.
шир|ота́ *f* [5; *pl. st.*: -о́ты] breadth; *geogr.* latitude; **~потре́б** F *m* [1] consumers' goods; **~ь** *f* [8] breadth, width; open (space).
шить [шью, шьёшь; ше́й(те)!; ши́тый], ⟨с-⟩ [сошью́, -ьёшь; сши́тый] sew (*pf. a.* together); embroider; have made; **~ё** *n* [10] sewing; embroidery.
шифр *m* [1] cipher, code; pressmark; **~ова́ть** [7], ⟨за-⟩ cipher, code.
шиш F *m* [1 *e.*] fig; **́~ка** *f* [5; *g/pl.*: -шек] bump, lump; ⚘ cone; knot; F bigwig.
шка|ла́ *f* [5; *pl. st.*] scale; **~ту́лка** *f* [5; *g/pl.*: -лок] casket; **~ф** *m* [1; в -у́; *pl. e.*] cupboard; wardrobe; (*book*)case; несгора́емый ~ф safe.
шквал *m* [1] squall, gust.
шкив ⊕ *m* [1] pulley.
шко́л|а *f* [5] school (*go* to в B; *be* at, in в П); вы́сшая ~а academy; university; **~ьник** *m* [1] schoolboy; **~ьница** *f* [5] schoolgirl; **~ьный** [14] school...
шку́р|а *f* [5] skin (*a.* **~ка** *f* [5; *g/pl.*: -рок]), hide; **~ник** F *m* [1] self-seeker.
шлагба́ум *m* [1] barrier, turnpike.
шлак *m* [1] slag, scoria; cinder.
шланг *m* [1] hose.
шлем *m* [1] helmet.
шлёп F crack!; **~ать** [1], *once* ⟨~нуть⟩ [20] slap; shuffle; plump (*v/i.* F **-ся**; plop).
шлифова́ть [7], ⟨от-⟩ grind; p ish.
шлю|з *m* [1] sluice, lock; **́~пка** *f* *g/pl.*: -пок] boat; launch.
шля́п|а *f* [5] hat; F milksop; ~ [5; *g/pl.*: -пок] *dim. of.* ~а; (*lad* hat; head (*nail*); **~очник** *m* hatter; **~ный** [14] hat...; hatte milliner's.
шля́ться P [1] *s.* шата́ться.
шмель *m* [4 *e.*] bumblebee.
шмыг quick!; **́~ать** F [1], *o* ⟨~ну́ть⟩ [20] whisk, scurry, slip.
шни́цель *m* [4] cutlet.
шнур *m* [1 *e.*] cord; **~ова́ть** ⟨за-⟩ lace (*or* tie) up; **~о́к** *m* -рка́] shoestring, (shoe) lace.
шныря́ть F [28] poke about.
шов *m* [1; шва] seam; ⊕ *a.* join
шокола́д *m* [1] chocolate.
шо́мпол *m* [1; *pl.*: -а́, *etc. e.*] ram
шо́пот *m* [1] *s.* шёпот.
шо́рник *m* [1] saddler.
шо́рох *m* [1] rustle.
шоссе́ (-ˈsɛ) *n* [*ind.*] high road.
шотла́нд|ец *m* [1; -дца] Scot man, *pl.* the Scotch; **~ка** *f* [5; *g* -док] Scotchwoman; **Ωия** *f* Scotland; **~ский** [16] Scotch, S tish.
шофёр *m* [1] driver, chauffeur.
шпа́га *f* [5] sword.
шпага́т *m* [1] packthread, strin
шпа́л|а 🚂 *f* [5] cross tie, *Brt.* sle er; **~е́ра** *f* [5] trellis; lane.
шпа|рга́лка F *f* [5; *g/pl.*: -л pony, *Brt.* crib; **~т** *m* [1] *min.* s
шпигова́ть [7], ⟨на-⟩ lard.
шпик *m* [1] slab bacon, fat; F sle
шпи́|лька *f* [5; *g/pl.*: -лек] hair hat pin; tack; *fig.* taunt, twit (пусти́ть B); **~на́т** *m* [1] spinach
шпио́н *m* [1], **~ка** *f* [5; *g/pl.*: -н spy; **~а́ж** *m* [1] espionage; ~ [13] spy.
шпиц *m* [1] Pomeranian (*dog*).
шпо́р|а *f* [5], **~ить** [13] spur.
шприц *m* [1] syringe, squirt.
шпрот *m* [1] sprat, brisling.
шпу́лька *f* [5; *g/pl.*: -лек] sp bobbin.
шрам *m* [1] scar.
шрифт *m* [1] type, print.
штаб ⚔ *m* [1] staff; headquarte
шта́бель *m* [4; *pl.*: -ля́, *etc. e.*] p
штабно́й ⚔ [14] staff...
штамп *m* [1], **~ова́ть** [7], ⟨ stamp.
шта́нга *f* [5] ⊕ pole; *sport*: wei
штаны́ F *m/pl.* [1 *e.*] pants, t sers.
штат *m* [1] state; staff; *cf.* CI **~и́в** *m* [1] support; *phot.* trip **́~ный** [14] (on the) staff; **́~ск** [16] civil; civilian; plain (*clothes*
штемпел|ева́ть (ʃtɛ-) [6], **'~ь** *m* *pl.*: -ля́, *etc. e.*] stamp; postmar
ште́псель (ˈʃtɛ-) *m* [4; *pl.*: -ля́, *e.*] plug; jack.

шти|ль *m* [4] calm; **~фт** *m* [1 *e.*] pin.
што́п|ать [1], ⟨за-⟩ darn; **~ка** *f* [5] darning.
што́пор *m* [1] corkscrew; ✈ spin.
што́|ра *f* [5] blind; curtain; **~рм** *m* [1] storm; **~ф** *m* [1] quart, bottle; damask.
штраф *m* [1] fine, penalty, mulct; **~но́й** [14] fine...; penalty...; convict...; **~ова́ть** [7], ⟨о-⟩ fine.
штрейкбре́хер *m* [1] strikebreaker.
штрих *m* [1 *e.*] stroke; trait; touch; **~ова́ть** [7], ⟨за-⟩ hatch; shade.
штуди́ровать [7], ⟨про-⟩ study.
шту́ка *f* [5] piece; F thing; fish; trick; story; business; point.
штукату́р|ить [13], ⟨о-⟩, **~ка** *f* [5] plaster.
штурва́л *m* [1] steering wheel.
штурм *m* [1] storm, onslaught; **∠ан** *m* [1] navigator; **~ова́ть** [7] storm, assail; **~ови́к** *m* [1 *e.*] battleplane.
шту́чный [14] (by the) piece.
штык *m* [1 *e.*] bayonet.
шу́ба *f* [5] fur (coat).
шу́лер *m* [1; *pl.*: -á, *etc. e.*] sharper.
шум *m* [1] noise; din; rush; bustle; buzz; F hubbub, row, ado; ~ и гам hullabaloo; наде́лать ∠у cause a sensation; **~е́ть** [10 *e.*; шумлю́, шуми́шь] make a noise; rustle; rush; roar; bustle; buzz; **~и́ха** F *f* [5] sensation, clamo(u)r; **~ли́вый** [14 *sh.*] clamorous; **∠ный** [14; -мен, -мна́, -о] noisy, loud; sensational; **~ово́й** [14] noise...; jazz...; **~о́к** *m* [1; -мка́]: под ~о́к F on the sly.
Шу́ра *m/f* [5] *dim. of* Алекса́ндр(а).
шу́р|ин *m* [1] brother-in-law (*wife's brother*); **~ша́ть** [4 *e.*; -шу́, ши́шь], ⟨за-⟩ rustle.
шу́стрый F [14; -тёр, -тра́, -о] nimble.
шут *m* [1 *e.*] fool, jester, clown, buffoon; F deuce; **~и́ть** [15], ⟨по-⟩ joke, jest; make fun (of над T); **∠ка** *f* [5; *g/pl.*: -ток] joke, jest (in в В); fun (for ра́ди P); trick (*play:* on с T); F trifle (it's no ∠ка ли); кро́ме ∠ок joking apart; are you in earnest?; не на ∠ку serious(ly); (Д) не до ∠ок be in no laughing mood; **~ли́вый** F [14 *sh.*] jocose, playful; **~ни́к** *m* [1 *e.*] joker, wag; **∠очный** [14] jocose, sportive, comic; laughing (*matter*); **~я́** jokingly (не in earnest).
шушу́кать(ся) F [1] whisper.
шху́на *f* [5] schooner.
ш-ш hush!

Щ

щаве́ль *m* [4 *e.*] ⚘ sorrel.
щади́ть [15 *e.*; щажу́, щади́шь], ⟨по-⟩ [-щажённый], spare.
ще́бень *m* [4; -бня] road metal.
щебета́ть [3] chirp, twitter.
щего́л *m* [1; -гла́] goldfinch; **~ева́тый** [14 *sh.*] stylish, smart; **′~ь** ('ʃtʃɔ-) *m* [4] dandy, fop; **~ьско́й** [16] foppish; **~я́ть** [28] flaunt, parade.
ще́др|ость *f* [8] liberality; **~ый** [14; щедр, -á, -о] liberal, generous.
щека́ *f* [5; *ac/sg.*: щёку; *pl.*: щёки, щёк, щека́м, *etc. e.*] cheek.
щеко́лда *f* [5] latch.
щекот|а́ть [3], ⟨по-⟩, **∠ка** *f* [5] tickle; **~ли́вый** [14 *sh.*] ticklish.
щёлк|ать [1], *once* ⟨~нуть⟩ [20] **1.** *v/i.* click (*one's tongue* T), snap (*one's fingers* T), crack (*whip* T); chatter (*one's teeth* T); warble, sing (*birds*); **2.** *v/t.* fillip (on по Д); crack (*nuts*).
щёло|к *m* [1] lye; **~чь** *f* [8; *from g/pl. e.*] alkali; **~чно́й** [14] alkaline.
щелчо́к *m* [1; -чка́] fillip; crack.
щель *f* [8; *from g/pl. e.*] chink, crack, crevice; slit; голосова́я ~ glottis.
щеми́ть [14 *e.*; *3rd. p., a. impers.*] press; *fig.* oppress.
щено́к *m* [1; -нка́; *pl.*: -нки́ & (2) -ня́та] puppy, whelp.
щеп|ети́льный [14; -лен, -льна] scrupulous, punctilious, squeamish, fancy...; **∠ка** *f* [5; *g/pl.*: -пок] chip; *fig.* lath
щепо́тка *f* [5; *g/pl.*: -ток] pinch.
щети́н|а *f* [5] bristle(s); **~истый** [14 *sh.*] bristly; **~иться** [13], ⟨о-⟩ bristle up.
щётка *f* [5; *g/pl.*: -ток] brush.
щи *f/pl.* [5; *gen.*: щей] cabbage soup.
щи́колотка *f* [5; *g/pl.*: -ток] ankle.
щип|а́ть [2], *once* ⟨(у)~ну́ть⟩ [20] pinch, tweak (*v/t.* за В), (*a. cold*) nip; bite; twitch; pluck; browse; **~цы́** *m/pl.* [1 *e.*] tongs, pliers, pincers, nippers; ⚕ forceps; (nut)crackers; **∠чики** *m/pl.* [1] tweezers.
щит *m* [1 *e.*] shield; buckler; screen, guard, protection; (snow)shed; (⚡ switch)board; sluice gate; (tortoise) shell.
щитови́дный [14] thyroid (*gland*).
щу́ка *f* [5] pike (*fish*).
щу́п|альце *n* [11; *g/pl.*: -лец] feeler, tentacle; **~ать** [1], ⟨по-⟩ feel; touch; *fig.* sound; **~лый** F [14; щупл, -á, -о] puny.
щу́рить [13] screw up (one's eyes **-ся**).

Э

эвакуи́ровать [7] (*im*)*pf*. evacuate.
эволюцио́нный [14] evolution(ary).
эгои́|зм *m* [1] ego(t)ism, selfishness; **~ст** *m* [1], **~стка** *f* [5; *g*/*pl*.: -ток] egoist; **~сти́ческий** [16], **~сти́чный** [14; -чен, -чна] selfish.
Эдинбу́рг *m* [1] Edinburgh.
эй! halloo!, hullo!, hey!
эквивале́нт *m* [1], **~ный** [14; -тен, -тна] equivalent.
экза́м|ен *m* [1] examination (in ... на П; ... in по Д); **~ена́тор** *m* [1] examiner; **~енова́ть** [7], ⟨про-⟩ examine; **-ся** be examined (by у Р), have one's examination (with); *p. pr. p.* examinee.
экземпля́р *m* [1] copy; specimen.
экзоти́ческий [16] exotic.
э́кий F [16; *sh*.: *no m*, -а] what (a).
экип|а́ж *m* [1] carriage; ⚓, ✈ crew; **~ирова́ть** [7] (*im*)*pf*. fit out, equip.
эконо́м|ика *f* [5] economy; economics; **~ить** [14], ⟨с-⟩ save; economize; **~и́ческий** [16] economic; **~ия** *f* [7] economy; saving (of Р, в П); **~ный** [14; -мен, -мна] economical, thrifty.
экра́н *m* [1] screen.
экскава́тор *m* [1] dredge(r *Brt*.).
экскурс|а́нт *m* [1] excursionist; **~ия** *f* [7] excursion, outing, trip; **~ово́д** *m* [1] guide.
экспеди́|тор *m* [1] forwarding agent(s); **~цио́нный** [14] forwarding...; expedition...; **~ция** *f* [7] dispatch (office); forwarding agency; expedition.
экспер|имента́льный [14] experimental; **~т** *m* [1] expert (in по Д); **~ти́за** *f* [5] examination; (expert) opinion.
эксплуа|та́тор *m* [1] exploiter; **~та́ция** *f* [7] exploitation; ⊕ operation; **~ти́ровать** [7] exploit; sweat; ⊕ operate, run.
экспон|а́т *m* [1] exhibit; **~и́ровать** [7] (*im*)*pf*. exhibit; *phot*. expose.
э́кспорт *m* [1], **~и́ровать** [7] (*im*)*pf*. export; **~ный** [14] export...
экс|про́мт *m* [1] impromptu; **~про́мтом** *a*. extempore; **~та́з** *m* [1] ecstasy; **~тра́кт** *m* [1] extract; **~тренный** [14 *sh*.] special; extra; urgent; **~центри́чный** [14; -чен, -чна] eccentric.
эласти́чн|ость *f* [8] elasticity; **~ый** [14; -чен, -чна] elastic.
элега́нтн|ость *f* [8] elegance; **~ый** [14; -тен, -тна] elegant, stylish.
эле́ктр|ик *m* [1] electrician; **~ифици́ровать** [7] (*im*)*pf*. electrify; **~и́ческий** [16] electric(al); **~и́чество** *n* [9] electricity; **~ово́з** *m* [1] electric locomotive; **~о́д** *m* [1] electrode; **~омонтёр** *s*. **~ик**; **~о́[н]** *m* [1], electron; **~оста́нция** *f* [7] power station; **~оте́хник** *m* [1] electrical engineer; **~оте́хника** [5] electrical engineering.
элеме́нт *m* [1] element; **~а́рны[й]** [14; -рен, -рна] elementary.
эма́л|евый [14], **~ирова́ть** [7], **~[ь]** *f* [8] enamel.
эмбле́ма *f* [5] emblem.
эмигр|а́нт *m* [1], **~а́нтка** *f* [5; *g*/*pl*.: -ток], **~а́нтский** [16] emigran[t], emigre; **~и́ровать** [7] (*im*)*pf*. emigrate.
эмоциона́льный [14; -лен, -льн[а]] emotional.
эмпири́зм *m* [1] empiricism.
энерг|и́чный [14; -чен, -чна] energetic; drastic; **~ия** *f* [7] energy.
энтузиа́зм *m* [1] enthusiasm.
энциклопе́д|ия *f* [7] (*a*. **~и́ческий** словáрь *m*) encyclop(a)edia.
эпи|гра́мма *f* [5] epigram; **~де́ми́ческий** [16], **~де́мия** *f* [7] epidemic; **~зо́д** *m* [1] episode; **~ле́псия** *f* [7] epilepsy; **~ло́г** *m* [1] epilogue; **~тет** *m* [1] epithet.
э́по|с *m* [1] epic (poem), epos; **~ха** *f* [5] epoch, era, period (in в В).
эроти́ческий [16] erotic.
эска́др|а *f* [5] ⚓ squadron; **~и́лья** *f* [6; *g*/*pl*.: -лий] ✈ squadron.
эс|кала́тор *m* [1] escalator; **~и́[з]** *m* [1] sketch; **~кимо́с** *m* [1] Eskimo; **~корти́ровать** [7] escort; **~ми́нец** *m* [1; -нца] ⚓ destroyer; **~се́нция** *f* [7] essence; **~тафе́та** *f* [5] relay race; **~тети́ческий** [16] aesthetic.
эсто́н|ец *m* [1; -нца], **~ка** *f* [5; *g*/*pl*.: -нок], **~ский** [16] Estonian.
эстра́да *f* [5] platform; *s*. варьете́.
эта́ж *m* [1 *e*.] floor, stor(e)y; дом в три **~а́** three-storied (*Brt*. -reyed) house; **~е́рка** *f* [5; *g*/*pl*.: -рок] whatnot; bookshelf.
э́так(ий) F *s*. так(о́й).
эта́п *m* [1] stage; base; transport(s).
э́тика *f* [5] ethics (*a*. *pl*.).
этике́тка *f* [5; *g*/*pl*.: -ток] label.
этимоло́гия *f* [7] etymology.
этногра́фия *f* [7] ethnography.
э́т|от *m*, **~а** *f*, **~о** *n*, **~и** *pl*. [27] this, *pl*. these; *su*. this one; that; it; the[y] (-*in*, *etc*.); **~о** *a*. well, then, as a matter of fact.
этю́д *m* [1] study, étude; sketch.
эф|е́с *m* [1] (*sword*) hilt; **~и́р** *m* [1] ether; **~и́рный** [14; -рен, -рна] ethereal.
эффект|и́вность *f* [8] efficacy; **~и́вный** [14; -вен, -вна] efficacious; **~ный** [14; -тен, -тна] effective.
эх ah!
эшафо́т *m* [1] scaffold.
эшело́н *m* [1] echelon; troop train.

Ю

билǀе́й *m* [3] jubilee; ~е́йный 14] jubilee...; ~я́р *m* [1] p. celeorating his jubilee.
бка *f* [5; *g/pl.*: ю́бок] skirt.
велир *m* [1] jeweller(' ~ный [14]).
г *m* [1] south; е́хать на ~ travel outh; *cf.* восто́к; ~о-восто́к *m* 1] southeast; ~о-восто́чный [14] outheast...; ~о-за́пад *m* [1] southvest; ~о-за́падный [14] southvest...; ♀осла́вия *f* [7] Yugoslavia.
огу́рт *m* [1] yogurt.
Эжно-Африка́нский Сою́з *m* 16/1] Union of South Africa.
жный [14] south(ern); southerly.
ла́ *f* [5] humming top; F fidgety p.
мор *m* [1] humo(u)r; ~исти́ческий [16] humorous; comic.
нга *m* [5] cabin boy.
ю́ность *f* [8] youth (*age*).
ю́ношǀа *m* [5; *g/pl.*: -шей] youth (*young man*); ~ество *n* [9] youth.
ю́ный [14; юн, -á, -о] young, youthful.
юриǀди́ческий [16] juridical; of law; ~скóнсульт *m* [1] legal adviser.
ˈЮрий *m* [3] George.
юри́ст *m* [1] lawyer; F law student.
ю́ркǀий [16; ю́рок, юрка́, -о] nimble, quick; ~ну́ть [20] *pf.* vanish (quickly).
юрǀо́дивый [14] fool(ish) „in Christ"; ∠та *f* [5] nomad's tent.
юсти́ция *f* [7] justice.
юти́ться [15 *e.*; ючу́сь, юти́шься] nestle; be cooped.
юфть *f* [8] Russia leather.

Я

[20] I; э́то я it's me.
бедǀа F *f* [5] slander, talebearing; ~ник *m* [1] slanderer, informer; ~ничать [1] slander (*v/t.* на В).
блоǀко *n* [9; *pl.*: -ки, -к] apple; (*eye*)ball; ~ня *f* [6] apple tree.
вǀи́ть(ся) *s.* ~ля́ть(ся); ∠ка *f* [5] appearance; presence, attendance; submission, presentation; place of secret meeting; ~ле́ние *n* [12] phenomenon; occurrence, event; *thea.* scene; appearance, apparition; ~ля́ть [28], ⟨~и́ть⟩ [14] present, submit; do; show; -ся appear, turn up; come; (T) be; ∠ный [14; я́вен, я́вна] open; obvious, evident; avowed; ∠ствовать [7] follow.
гнёнок *m* [2] lamb.
годǀа *f* [5], ~ный [14] berry.
годица *f* [5] buttock.
д *m* [1] poison; *fig. a.* venom.
дерный [14] nuclear.
дови́тый [14 *sh.*] poisonous; venomous.
дрǀёный F [14 *sh.*] strong, stalwart, solid; pithy; fresh; ~о́ *n* [9; *pl. st.*; *g/pl.*: я́дер] kernel; *phys.*, ⚘ nucleus; cannon ball; *fig.* core, pith.
звǀа *f* [5] ulcer; plague; wound; ~и́тельный [14; -лен, -льна] venomous; caustic.
зы́к *m* [1 *e.*] tongue; language (in на П); speech; на ру́сском ~е́ *speak* (*text, etc.* in) Russian; держа́ть ~ за зуба́ми hold one's tongue; ~ове́д *m* [1] linguist; ~ово́й [14] language...; ~о́вый [14] tongue...; ~озна́ние *n* [12] linguistics.
зы́чǀеский [16] pagan; ~ество *n* [9] paganism; ~ник *m* [1] pagan.
зычо́к *m* [1; -чка́] uvula; tongue.
и́чнǀица (-ʃn-) *f* [5] (scrambled *or* fried) eggs *pl.*; ~ый [14] egg...
яйцо́ *n* [9; *pl.*: я́йца, яи́ц, я́йцам] egg.
я́кобы allegedly; as it were.
ˈЯков *m* [1] Jakob.
я́корǀь *m* [4; *pl.*: -ря́, *etc. e.*] anchor (at на П); стоя́ть на ~е anchor.
я́лик *m* [1] jolly boat.
я́мǀа *f* [5] hole, pit; F dungeon; ~(оч)ка *f* [5; *g/pl.*: я́мо(че)к] dimple.
ямщи́к *m* [1 *e.*] coachman, driver.
янва́рь *m* [4 *e.*] January.
янта́рь *m* [4 *e.*] amber.
япо́нǀец *m* [1; -нца], ~ка *f* [5; *g/pl.*: -нок], ~ский [16] Japanese; ♀ия *f* [7] Japan.
я́ркий [16; я́рок, ярка́, -о; *comp.*: я́рче] bright; glaring; vivid, rich (*colo[u]r*); blazing; *fig.* striking, outstanding.
ярǀлы́к *m* [1 *e.*] label; ∠марка *f* [5; *g/pl.*: -рок] fair (at на П).
ярмо́ *n* [9; *pl.*: я́рма, *etc. st.*] yoke.
ярово́й [14] summer, spring (*crops*).
я́ростǀный [14; -тен, -тна] furious, fierce; ~ь *f* [8] fury, rage.
я́рус *m* [1] circle (*thea.*); layer.
я́рый [14 *sh.*] fierce, violent; ardent.
я́сень *m* [4] ash (*tree*).
я́сли *m/pl.* [4; *gen.*: я́слей] crib, manger; day nursery, *Brt.* crèche.
яснǀови́дец *m* [1; -дца] clairvoyant; ∠ость *f* [8] clarity; ∠ый [14; я́сен, ясна́, -о] clear; bright; fine; limpid; distinct; evident; plain (*answer*).
я́стреб *m* [1; *pl.*: -ба́ & -бы] hawk.
я́хта *f* [5] yacht.
яче́ǀйка *f* [5; *g/pl.*: -е́ек], ~я́ *f* [6; *g/pl.*: яче́й] cell; mesh.
ячме́нь *m* [4 *e.*] barley; ⚕ sty.
ˈЯш(к)а *m* [5] *dim.* of ˈЯков.
я́щерица *f* [5] lizard.
я́щик *m* [1] box, case, chest; drawer; откла́дывать в до́лгий ~ shelve; *cf.* для.

PART TWO

ENGLISH-RUSSIAN VOCABULARY

A

ei, ə] неопределённый арти́кль; ıк пра́вило, не перево́дится; table стол; 10 roubles a dozen ;сять рубле́й дю́жина.
[ei'wʌn] **1.** F первокла́ссный; прекра́сно.
ack [ə'bæk] *adv.* наза́д.
andon [ə'bændən] отка́зываться за́ться] от (Р); оставля́ть [-а́вить], ›кида́ть [-и́нуть]; **~ed** поки́нуй; распу́тный; **~ment** [-mənt] ставле́ние.
ase [ə'beis] унижа́ть [уни́зить]; **nent** [-mənt] униже́ние.
ash [ə'bæʃ] смуща́ть [смути́ть]; **nent** [-mənt] смуще́ние.
ate [ə'beit] *v/t.* уменьша́ть е́ньши́ть]; *v/i.* утиха́ть [ути́хнуть] бу́ре и т. п.); **~ment** [-mənt] леньше́ние; ски́дка.
attoir ['æbətwa:] скотобо́йня.
b|ess ['æbis] настоя́тельница онастыря́; **~ey** ['æbi] монасты́рь ; **~ot** ['æbət] абба́т, настоя́тель *m.*
breviat|e [ə'bri:vieit] сокра-а́ть [-рати́ть]; **~ion** [əbri:vi'eiʃən] краще́ние.
dicat|e ['æbdikeit] отрека́ться : престо́ла; отка́зываться [-за́ть-] от (Р); **~ion** [æbdi'keiʃən] от-ече́ние от престо́ла.
domen [æb'doumen] живо́т; ›ю́шная по́лость *f.*
duct [æb'dʌkt] похища́ть и́тить] (же́нщину).
erration [æbə'reiʃən] заблуж-е́ние; *ast.* аберра́ция.
et [ə'bet] *v/t.* подстрека́ть [-к-у́ть]; [по]соде́йствовать (дур-о́му); **~tor** [-ə] подстрека́тель ница *f*) *m.*
eyance [ə'beiəns] состоя́ние не-зве́стности; in **~** без владе́льца; ре́менно отменённый (зако́н).
hor [əb'hɔ:] ненави́деть; **~rence** b'hɔrəns] отвраще́ние; **~rent** ənt] □ отврати́тельный.
ide [ə'baid] [*irr.*] *v/i.* пребыва́ть; by твёрдо держа́ться (Р); *v/t.* ot **~** не терпе́ть.
ility [ə'biliti] спосо́бность *f.*
ject ['æbdʒekt] □ презре́нный, а́лкий.
jure [əb'dʒuə] отрека́ться [-е́чь-я] от (Р).
le ['eibl] □ спосо́бный; be **~** очь, быть в состоя́нии; **~-bodied** bɔdid] здоро́вый; го́дный.
negat|e ['æbnigeit] отка́зывать за́ть] себе́ в (П); отрица́ть; **~ion** ebni'geiʃən] отрица́ние; (само-) рече́ние.

abnormal [æb'nɔ:məl] □ ненорма́льный.
aboard [ə'bɔ:d] ⚓ на кора́бль, на корабле́.
abode [ə'boud] **1.** *pt.* от abide; **2.** местопребыва́ние; жили́ще.
aboli|sh [ə'bɔliʃ] отменя́ть [-ни́ть]; упраздня́ть [-ни́ть]; **~tion** [æbo'liʃən] отме́на.
abomina|ble [ə'bɔminəbl] □ отврати́тельный; **~te** [-neit] *v/t.* пита́ть отвраще́ние к (Д); **~tion** [əbɔmi'neiʃən] отвраще́ние.
aboriginal [æbə'ridʒənəl] **1.** тузе́мный; **2.** тузе́мец.
abortion [ə'bɔ:ʃən] вы́кидыш, або́рт.
abound [ə'baund] изоби́ловать (in (Т).
about [ə'baut] **1.** *prp.* вокру́г (Р); о́коло (Р); о (П), об (П), обо (П), насчёт (Р); у (Р); про (В); I had no money **~** me у меня́ не́ было с собо́й де́нег; **2.** *adv.* вокру́г, везде́; приблизи́тельно; be **~** to do собира́ться де́лать.
above [ə'bʌv] **1.** *prp.* над (Т); вы́ше (Р); свы́ше (Р); **~** all гла́вным о́бразом; **2.** *adv.* наверху́, наве́рх; вы́ше; **3.** *adj.* вышеска́занный.
abreast [ə'brest] в ряд.
abridg|e [ə'bridʒ] сокраща́ть [-рати́ть]; **~(e)ment** [-mənt] сокраще́ние.
abroad [ə'brɔ:d] за грани́цей, за грани́цу; there is a report **~** хо́дит слух.
abrogate ['æbrogeit] *v/t.* отменя́ть [-ни́ть]; аннули́ровать (*im*)*pf.*
abrupt [ə'brʌpt] □ обры́вистый; внеза́пный; ре́зкий.
abscond [əb'skɔnd] *v/i.* скры́(ва́)ться.
absence ['æbsns] отсу́тствие; отлу́чка; **~** of mind рассе́янность *f.*
absent **1.** ['æbsnt] □ отсу́тсвующий; **2.** [æb'sent] **~** o. s. отлуча́ться [-чи́ться]; **~-minded** □ рассе́янный.
absolut|e ['æbsəlu:t] □ абсолю́тный; беспример́ный; **~ion** [æbsə'lu:ʃən] отпуще́ние грехо́в.
absolve [əb'zɔlv] проща́ть [прости́ть]; освобожда́ть [-боди́ть] (from от Р).
absorb [əb'sɔ:b] впи́тывать [впита́ть]; абсорби́ровать (*im*)*pf.*
absorption [əb'sɔ:pʃən] вса́сывание, впи́тывание; *fig.* погружённость *f* (в ду́мы).
abstain [əbs'tein] возде́рживаться [-жа́ться] (from от Р).

abstemious [əbs'ti:miəs] □ воздéржанный, умéренный.
abstention [æbs'tenʃən] воздержáние.
abstinen|ce ['æbstinəns] умéренность *f*; трéзвость *f*; **~t** [-nənt] □ умéренный, воздéржанный; непью́щий.
abstract 1. ['æbstrækt] □ отвлечённый, абстрáктный; **2.** конспéкт; извлечéние; *gr.* отвлечённое и́мя существи́тельное **3.** [æbs'trækt] отвлекáть [-éчь]; резюми́ровать (*im*)*pf*.; **~ed** [-id] □ отвлечённый; **~ion** [-kʃən] абстрáкция.
abstruse [æbs'tru:s] □ *fig.* непоня́тный, тёмный.
abundan|ce [ə'bʌndəns] избы́ток, изоби́лие; **~t** [-dənt] □ оби́льный, богáтый.
abus|e 1. [ə'bju:s] злоупотреблéние; оскорблéние; брань *f*; **2.** [ə'bju:z] злоупотребля́ть [-би́ть] (Т); [вы́]ругáть; **~ive** [ə'bju:siv] □ оскорби́тельный.
abut [ə'bʌt] грани́чить (upon с Т).
abyss [ə'bis] бéздна.
academic|(al □) [ækə'demik(əl)] академи́ческий; **~ian** [əkædə'miʃən] акадéмик.
accede [æk'si:d]: **~** to вступáть [-пи́ть] в (В).
accelerat|e [æk'seləreit] ускоря́ть [-óрить]; **~or** [æk'seləreitə] ускори́тель *m*.
accent 1. ['æksənt] ударéние; произношéние, акцéнт; **2.** [æk'sent] *v/t.* дéлать и́ли стáвить ударéние на (П); **~uate** [æk'sentjueit] дéлать и́ли стáвить ударéние на (П); *fig.* подчёркивать [-черкну́ть].
accept [ək'sept] принимáть [-ня́ть]; соглашáться [-гласи́ться] с (Т); **~able** [ək'septəbl] □ приéмлемый; прия́тный; **~ance** [ək'septəns] приём, приня́тие; ⚓ акцéпт.
access ['ækses] дóступ; прохóд; ⚕ при́ступ; easy of **~** досту́пный; **~ary** [æk'sesəri] соучáстник (-ица); **~ible** [æk'sesəbl] □ досту́пный, достижи́мый; **~ion** [æk'seʃən] вступлéние (to в В); дóступ (to к Д); **~** to the throne вступлéние на престóл.
accessory [æk'sesəri] □ **1.** добáвочный, второстепéнный; **2.** *pl.* принадлéжности *f*/*pl*.
accident ['æksidənt] случáйность *f*; катастрóфа, авáрия; **~al** [æksi'dentl] □ случáйный.
acclaim [ə'kleim] шу́мно привéтствовать (В); аплоди́ровать (Д).
acclamation [æklə'meiʃən] шу́мное одобрéние.
acclimatize [ə'klaimətaiz] акклиматизи́ровать(ся) (*im*)*pf*.
acclivity [ə'kliviti] подъём (дорóги).
accommodat|e [ə'kɔmədeit] приспособля́ть [-пособить]; дав… жильё (Д); **~ion** [əkɔmə'deiʃ… прию́т; помещéние.
accompan|iment [ə'kʌmpənimə… аккомпанемéнт; сопровождéн… **~y** [-pəni] *v/t.* аккомпани́ров… (Д); сопровождáть [-води́ть].
accomplice [ə'kɔmplis] соучáстн… (-ица).
accomplish [-pliʃ] выполня́ть [в… полнить]; достигáть [-и́гнуть] (… **~ment** [-mənt] выполнéние; … стижéние; **~s** *pl.* образóванно… *f.*
accord [ə'kɔ:d] **1.** соглашéн… гармóния; with one **~** единоду́… но; **2.** *v/i.* соглacóвываться [-… вáться] (с Т); гармони́ровать … Т); *v/t.* предоставля́ть [-стáвит… **~ance** [-əns] соглáсие; **~ant** [-ə… □ соглáсный (с Т); **~ing** [-iŋ] … to соглáсно (Д); **~ingly** [-iŋli] *a*… соотвéтственно; таки́м óбразом…
accost [ə'kɔst] заговáривать [-… ри́ть] с (Т).
account [ə'kaunt] **1.** счёт; отч… of no **~** незначи́тельный; on n… ни в кóем слу́чае; on **~** of из-за (… take into **~**, take **~** of принимáть … внимáние; turn to **~** испóльзов… (*im*)*pf*.; call to **~** призывáть к … вéту; make **~** of придавáть зна… ние (Д); **2.** *v/i.* **~** for отвечá… [-éтить] за (В); объясня́ть [-ни́т… be much **~ed** of имéть хорóш… репутáцию; *v/t.* считáть [счес… (В/Т); **~able** [ə'kauntəbl] □ об… ясни́мый; **~ant** [-ənt] счетов… (chartered, *Am.* certified public… прися́жный) бухгáлтер; **~ing** [-… отчётность *f*; учёт.
accredit [ə'kredit] аккредитов… (*im*)*pf*.; припи́сывать [-сáть].
accrue [ə'kru:] накопля́ться [-пи́… ся]; происходи́ть [произойт… (from из Р).
accumulat|e [ə'kju:mjuleit] накá… ливать(ся) [-копи́ть(ся)]; ско… ля́ть(ся) [-пи́ть(ся)]; **~ion** [əkj… mju'leiʃən] накоплéние; ско… лéние.
accura|cy ['ækjurəsi] тóчность … тщáтельность *f*; **~te** [-rit] □ тó… ный; тщáтельный.
accurs|ed [ə'kə:sid], **~t** [-st] пр… кля́тый.
accus|ation [ækju'zeiʃən] обвин… ние; **~e** [ə'kju:z] *v/t.* обвиня́… [-ни́ть]; **~er** [-ə] обвини́тель(ни… *f*) *m*.
accustom [ə'kʌstəm] приучá… [-чи́ть] (to к Д); get **~ed** прив… кáть [-вы́кнуть] (to к Д); **~ed** [-… привы́чный; приу́ченный.
ace [eis] туз; *fig.* первоклáссн… лётчик.
acerbity [ə'sə:biti] тéрпкость *f*.
acet|ic [ə'si:tik] у́ксусный; **~i…** [ə'setifai] окисля́ть(ся) [-ли́ть(ся…

che [eik] **1.** боль *f*; **2.** *v/i.* болéть (о чáсти тéла).

chieve [ə'tʃi:v] достигáть [-и́гнуть] (Р); **~ment** [-mənt] достижéние.

cid ['æsid] ки́слый; éдкий; **~ity** [ə'siditi] кислотá; éдкость *f*.

cknowledg|e [ək'nɔlidʒ] *v/t.* подтверждáть [-ерди́ть]; признá(вá)ть; **~(e)ment** [-mənt] признáние; распи́ска.

cme ['ækmi] вы́сшая тóчка (Р); кри́зис.

corn ['eikɔ:n] ⚘ жёлудь *m*.

coustics [ə'kaustiks] акýстика.

cquaint [ə'kweint] *v/t.* [по]знакóмить; be ~ed with быть знакóмым с (Т); **~ance** [-əns] знакóмство; знакóмый.

cquiesce [ækwi'es] мóлча и́ли неохóтно соглашáться (in на В); **~ment** [-mənt] молчали́вое и́ли неохóтное соглáсие.

cquire [ə'kwaiə] *v/t.* приобретáть [-ести́]; достигáть [-и́гнуть] (Р); **~ment** [-mənt] приобретéние.

cquisition [ækwi'ziʃən] приобретéние.

cquit [ə'kwit] *v/t.* опрáвдывать [-дáть]; ~ of освобождáть [-боди́ть] от (Р); выполня́ть [вы́полнить] (обя́занности); ~ o. s. well хорошó справля́ться с рабóтой; **~tal** [-l] оправдáние; **~tance** уплáта (дóлга и т. п.).

cre ['eikə] акр (0,4 га).

crid ['ækrid] óстрый, éдкий.

cross [ə'krɔs] **1.** *adv.* поперёк; на ту стóрону; крестóм; **2.** *prp.* сквозь (В), чéрез (В).

ct [ækt] **1.** *v/i.* дéйствовать; поступáть [-пи́ть]; *v/t. thea.* игрáть [сыгрáть] **2.** дéло; постановлéние; акт; **~ing** [-iŋ] **1.** исполня́ющий обя́занности; **2.** дéйствия *n/pl.*; *thea.* игрá.

ction ['ækʃən] постýпок; дéйствие (*a. thea.*); дéятельность *f*; ⚔ бой; иск; take ~ принимáть мéры.

ctiv|e ['æktiv] □ акти́вный; энерги́чный; дéятельный; **~ity** [æk'tiviti] дéятельность *f*; акти́вность *f*; энéргия.

ct|or ['æktə] актёр; **~ress** [-tris] актри́са.

ctual ['æktjuəl] □ действи́тельный.

ctuate ['æktjueit] приводи́ть в дéйствие.

cute [ə'kju:t] □ óстрый; проницáтельный.

damant ['ædəmənt] *fig.* несокруши́мый.

dapt [ə'dæpt] приспособля́ть [-пособить] (to, for к Д); **~ation** [ædæp'teiʃən] приспособлéние; передéлка; аранжирóвка.

dd [æd] *v/t.* прибавля́ть [-áвить]; Ⱥ склáдывать [сложи́ть]; *v/i.* увели́чи(ва)ть (to В).

addict ['ædikt] наркомáн; **~ed** [ə'diktid] склóнный (to к Д).

addition [ə'diʃən] Ⱥ сложéние; прибавлéние; in ~ крóме тогó, к томý же; in ~ to вдобáвок к (Д); **~al** [-l] □ добáвочный, дополни́тельный.

address [ə'dres] *v/t.* **1.** адресовáть (*im*)*pf.*; обращáться [обрати́ться] к (Д); **2.** áдрес; обращéние; речь *f*; **~ee** [ædre'si] адресáт.

adept ['ædept] адéпт.

adequa|cy ['ædikwəsi] соразмéрность *f*; **~te** [-kwit] □ достáточный; адеквáтный.

adhere [əd'hiə] прилипáть [-ли́пнуть] (to к Д); *fig.* придéрживаться (to Р); **~nce** [-rəns] привéрженность *f*; **~nt** [-rənt] привéрженец (-нка).

adhesive [əd'hi:siv] □ ли́пкий, клéйкий; ~ plaster, ~ tape ли́пкий плáстырь *m*.

adjacent [ə'dʒeisənt] □ смéжный (to с Т), сосéдний.

adjoin [ə'dʒɔin] примыкáть [-мкнýть] к (Д); грани́чить с (Т).

adjourn [ə'dʒə:n] *v/t.* отклáдывать [отложи́ть]; отсрóчи(ва)ть; *parl.* дéлать переры́в; **~ment** [-mənt] отсрóчка; переры́в.

adjudge [ə'dʒʌdʒ] выноси́ть пригóвор (Д).

administ|er [əd'ministə] управля́ть (Т); ~ justice отправля́ть правосýдие; **~ration** [ədminis'treiʃən] администрáция; **~rative** [əd'ministrətiv] администрати́вный; исполни́тельный; **~rator** [əd'ministreitə] администрáтор.

admir|able ['ædmərəbl] □ превосхóдный; восхити́тельный; **~ation** [ædmi'reiʃən] восхищéние; **~e** [əd'maiə] восхищáться [-ити́ться] (Т); [по]любовáться (Т *or* на В).

admiss|ible [əd'misəbl] □ допусти́мый, приéмлемый; **~ion** [əd'miʃən] вход; допущéние; признáние.

admit [əd'mit] *v/t.* допускáть [-сти́ть]; **~tance** [-əns] дóступ, вход.

admixture [əd'mikstʃə] при́месь *f*.

admon|ish [əd'mɔniʃ] увещ(ев)áть *impf.*; предостерегáть [-рéчь] (of от Р); **~ition** [ædmo'niʃən] увещáние; предостережéние.

ado [ə'du:] суетá; хлóпоты *f/pl.*

adolescen|ce [ædo'lesns] ю́ность *f*; **~t** [-snt] ю́ный, ю́ношеский.

adopt [ə'dɔpt] *v/t.* усыновля́ть [-ви́ть]; усвáивать [усвóить]; **~ion** [ə'dɔpʃən] усыновлéние; усвáивание.

ador|ation [ædo'reiʃən] обожáние; **~e** [ə'dɔ:] *v/t.* обожáть.

adorn [ə'dɔ:n] украшáть [укрáсить]; **~ment** [-mənt] украшéние.

adroit [ə'drɔit] □ лóвкий; находчи́вый.

adult ['ædʌlt] взро́слый, совершеннолéтний.

adulter|ate [ə'dʌltəreit] фальсифици́ровать (*im*)*pf*.; **~er** [ə'dʌltərə] наруша́ющий супру́жескую вéрность; **~ess** [-ris] наруша́ющая супру́жескую вéрность; **~y** [-ri] нарушéние супру́жеской вéрности.

advance [əd'vɑ:ns] **1.** *v/i*. подвига́ться вперёд; ⚔ наступа́ть [-пи́ть]; продвига́тся [-и́нуться]; дéлать успéхи; *v/t*. продвига́ть [-и́нуть]; выдвига́ть [вы́двинуть]; плати́ть ава́нсом; **2.** ⚔ наступлéние; успéх (в учéнии); прогрéсс; **~d** [-t] передово́й; **~ment** [-mənt] успéх; продвижéние.

advantage [əd'vɑ:ntidʒ] преиму́щество; вы́года; take ~ of [вос-]по́льзоваться (Т); **~ous** [ædvən'teidʒəs] □ вы́годный.

adventur|e [əd'ventʃə] приключéние; **~er** [-rə] искáтель приключéний; авантюри́ст; **~ous** [-rəs] □ предприи́мчивый; авантю́рный.

advers|ary ['ædvəsəri] проти́вник (-ица); сопéрник (-ица); **~e** ['ædvə:s] □ враждéбный; **~ity** [əd'və:siti] бéдствие, несча́стье.

advertis|e ['ædvətaiz] реклами́ровать (*im*)*pf*.; объявля́ть [-ви́ть]; **~ement** [əd'və:tismənt] объявлéние; рекла́ма; **~ing** ['ædvətaiziŋ] рекла́мный.

advice [əd'vais] совéт.

advis|able □ [əd'vaizəbl] желáтельный; **~e** [əd'vaiz] *v/t*. [по]совéтовать (Д); *v/i*. [по]совéтоваться (with с Т; on, about о П); **~er** [-ə] совéтник (-ица), совéтчик (-ица).

advocate **1.** ['ædvəkit] защи́тник (-ица); сторо́нник (-ица); адвокáт; **2.** [-keit] отстáивать [отстоя́ть].

aerial ['ɛəriəl] **1.** □ возду́шный; **2.** антéнна; outdoor ~ нару́жная антéнна.

aero... ['ɛərou] аэро...; **~drome** ['ɛərədroum] аэродро́м; **~naut** [-nɔ:t] аэронáвт; **~nautics** [-'nɔ:tiks] аэронáвтика; **~plane** [-plein] самолёт, аэроплáн; **~stat** [-stæt] аэростáт.

aesthetic [i:s'θetik] эстети́чный; **~s** [-s] эстéтика.

afar [ə'fɑ:] *adv*. вдалекé, вдали́; from ~ издалекá.

affable ['æfəbl] привéтливый.

affair [ə'fɛə] дéло.

affect [ə'fekt] *v/t*. [по]дéйствовать на (В); задé(вá)ть; ⚕ поражáть [-рази́ть]; **~ation** [æfek'teiʃən] жемáнство; **~ed** [ə'fektid] □ жемáнный; **~ion** [ə'fekʃən] привя́занность *f*; заболевáние; **~ionate** □ нéжный.

affidavit [æfi'deivit] пи́сьменное показáние под прися́гой.

affiliate [ə'filieit] *v/t*. присоеди́нять [-ни́ть] (как филиáл).

affinity [ə'finiti] сродство́.

affirm [ə'fə:m] утверждá[ть] [-рди́ть]; **~ation** [æfə:'meiʃə[n]] утверждéние; **~ative** [ə'fə:məti[v]] □ утверди́тельный.

affix [ə'fiks] прикрепля́ть [-пи́т[ь]] (to к Д).

afflict [ə'flikt] *v/t*. огорчáть [-чи́ть] be ~ed страдáть (with от Р); **~io[n]** [ə'flikʃən] гóре; болéзнь *f*.

affluen|ce ['æfluens] изоби́ли[е] богáтство; **~t** [-ənt] **1.** □ оби́ль[ный], богáтый; **2.** прито́к.

afford [ə'fɔ:d] позволя́ть [-во́лит[ь]] себé; I can ~ it я могу́ себé э́то по[-] зво́лить; предоставля́ть [-áвить]

affront [ə'frʌnt] **1.** оскорбля́[ть] [-би́ть]; **2.** оскорблéние.

afield [ə'fi:ld] *adv*. вдалекé; [в] по́ле; на войнé.

afloat [ə'flout] ⚓ на водé; в мо́р[е]; в ходу́.

afraid [ə'freid] испу́ганный; be [afraid] of боя́ться (Р).

afresh [ə'freʃ] *adv*. сно́ва, сы́знов[а].

African ['æfrikən] **1.** африкáне[ц] (-нка); **2.** африкáнский.

after ['ɑ:ftə] **1.** *adv*. пото́м, по́сл[е], затéм; позади́; **2.** *prp*. за (Т), по[-] зади́ (Р); чéрез (В); по́сле (Р); [3.] *cj*. с тех пор, как; по́сле тогó, как; **4.** *adj*. послéдующий; **~crop** вто[-] ро́й урожáй; **~math** [-mæθ] отáв[а]; *fig*. послéдствия *n*/*pl*.; **~noo[n]** [-'nu:n] врéмя по́сле полу́дня; **~-taste** (остаю́щийся) при́вкус; **~thought** мысль, пришéдшая позд[-] но; **~wards** [-wədz] *adv*. пото́м.

again [ə'gein *Am*. ə'gen] *adv*. сно́в[а], опя́ть; ~ and ~, time and ~ то [же] дéло; as much ~ ещё сто́лько же.

against [ə'geinst] *prp*. про́тив (Р); о, об (В); на (В); as ~ про́тив (Р); ~ the wall у стены́; к стенé.

age [eidʒ] во́зраст; годá *m*/*pl*; эпо́ха; of ~ совершеннолéтни[й]; under ~ несовершеннолéтний; **~[d]** ['eidʒid] стáрый, постарéвши[й]; ~ twenty двадцати́ лет.

agency ['eidʒənsi] дéйствие; агéн[т]ство.

agent ['eidʒənt] фáктор; агéн[т]; довéренное лицо́.

agglomerate [ə'glɔməreit] *v/t*. с[о]б(и)рáть; *v/i*. скопля́ться [-пи́т[ь]ся].

agglutinate [ə'glu:tineit] скл[е]и(ва)ть.

aggrandize ['ægrəndaiz) увели́ч[и]-(ва)ть; возвели́чи(ва)ть.

aggravate ['ægrəveit] усугубля́[ть] [-би́ть]; ухудшáть [уху́дшить]; раздражáть [-жи́ть].

aggregate **1.** ['ægrigeit] собирá[ть] (-ся) в одно́ цéлое; **2.** □ [-git] с[о]воку́пный; **3.** [-git] совоку́пнос[ть] *f*; агрегáт.

gress|ion [əˈgreʃən] нападе́ние; гре́ссия; **~or** [əˈgresə] агре́ссор.
hast [əˈgɑ:st] ошеломлённый, оражённый у́жасом.
il|e [ˈædʒail] □ прово́рный, живо́й; **~ity** [əˈdʒiliti] прово́рство, ки́вость *f*.
itat|e [ˈædʒiteit] *v/t.* [вз]волнова́ть, возбужда́ть [-уди́ть]; *v/i.* агити́ровать (for за В); **~ion** [ædʒiˈteiʃən] волне́ние; агита́ция.
nail [ˈægneil] ⚕ заусе́ница.
o [əˈgou]: a year ~ год тому́ наза́д.
onize [ˈægənaiz] быть в аго́нии; и́льно му́чить(ся).
ony [ˈægəni] аго́ния; боль *f*.
ree [əˈgri:] *v/i.* соглаша́ться -ласи́ться] (to с Т, на В); ~ up]on усла́вливаться [усло́виться] о (П); **~able** [-əbl] согла́сный о с Т, на В); прия́тный; **~ment** -mənt] согла́сие; соглаше́ние, оговор.
ricultur|al [ægriˈkʌltʃərəl] сельскохозя́йственный; **~e** [ˈægrikʌlʃə] се́льское хозя́йство; земледе́лие; агроно́мия; **~ist** [ægriˈkʌlʃərist] агроно́м; земледе́лец.
ue [ˈeigju:] лихора́дочный озно́б.
head [əˈhed] вперёд, впереди́; traight ~ пря́мо, вперёд.
d [eid] **1.** по́мощь *f*; помо́щник -ица); **2.** помога́ть [помо́чь] (Д).
l [eil]: what ~s him? что его́ беспоко́ит?; **~ing** [ˈeiliŋ] больно́й, ездоро́вый; **~ment** [ˈeilmənt] ездоро́вье.
m [eim] **1.** *v/i.* прице́ли(ва)ться at в В); *fig.* ~ at име́ть в виду́; /*t.* направля́ть [-ра́вить] (at на В); . цель *f*, наме́рение; **~less** [eimlis]] бесце́льный.
r¹ [ɛə] **1.** во́здух; by ~ самолётом; оздушной по́чтой; *Am.* be on the ~ рабо́тать (о радиоста́нции); *Am.* ut on the ~ передава́ть по ра́дио; *Am.* be off the ~ не рабо́тать (о радиоста́нции); **2.** прове́три(ва)ть.
r² [~] *mst pl.* аффекта́ция, ва́жничанье; give o.s. ~s ва́жничать.
r³ [~] ♪ мело́дия; пе́сня; а́рия.
r|-base авиаба́за; **~-brake** возду́шный то́рмоз; **~conditioned** с кондициони́рованным во́здухом; **craft** самолёт; **~field** аэродро́м; **force** вое́нно-возду́шный флот; **-jacket** надувно́й спаса́тельный нагру́дник; **~-lift** «возду́шный мост», возду́шная перево́зка; **~-liner** ре́йсовый самолёт; **~-mail** возду́шная по́чта; **~man** лётчик, авиа́тор; **~plane** *Am.* самолёт; **~-port** аэропо́рт; **~-raid** возду́шный налёт; ~ precautions *pl.* противовозду́шная оборо́на; **~-route** возду́шная тра́сса; **~shelter** бомбоубе́жище; **~ship** дирижа́бль *m*; **~-tight** гермети́ческий; **~-tube** ка́мера ши́ны; *anat.* трахе́я; **~way** возду́шная тра́сса.
airy [ˈɛəri] □ возду́шный; легкомы́сленный.
aisle [ail] ⛪ приде́л (хра́ма); прохо́д.
ajar [əˈdʒɑ:] приотво́ренный.
akin [əˈkin] ро́дственный, бли́зкий (to Д).
alarm [əˈlɑ:m] **1.** трево́га; страх; **2.** [вс]трево́жить], [вз]волнова́ть; **~-clock** буди́льник.
albuminous [ælˈbju:minəs] содержа́щий бело́к; альбуми́нный.
alcohol [ˈælkəhɔl] алкого́ль *m*; спирт; **~ic** [ælkəˈhɔlik] **1.** алкого́льный; **2.** алкого́лик; **~ism** [ˈælkəhɔlizm] алкоголи́зм.
alcove [ˈælkouv] алько́в, ни́ша.
ale [eil] пи́во, эль *m*.
alert [əˈlə:t] **1.** □ живо́й, прово́рный; **2.** (возду́шная) трево́га; on the ~ настороже́.
alien [ˈeiliən] **1.** иностра́нный; чу́ждый; **2.** иностра́нец, чужестра́нец; **~able** [-əbl] отчужда́емый; **~ate** [-eit] отчужда́ть [-уди́ть]; **~ist** [ˈeiliənist] психиа́тр.
alight [əˈlait] **1.** сходи́ть [сойти́] (с Р); приземля́ться [-ли́ться]; **2.** *adj. predic.* зажжённый, в огне́; освещённый.
align [əˈlain] выра́внивать(ся) [вы́ровнять(ся)].
alike [əˈlaik] **1.** *adj. pred.* одина́ковый; похо́жий; **2.** *adv.* то́чно так же; подо́бно.
aliment [ˈælimənt] пита́ние; **~ary** [æliˈmentəri] пищево́й; пита́тельный; ~ canal пищево́д.
alimony [ˈæliməni] алиме́нты *m/pl.*
alive [eˈlaiv] живо́й, бо́дрый; чу́ткий (to к Д); киша́щий (with Т); be ~ to я́сно понима́ть.
all [ɔ:l] **1.** *adj.* весь *m*, вся *f*, всё *n*, все *pl*; вся́кий; всевозмо́жный; for ~ that несмотря́ на то; **2.** всё, все; at ~ вообще́; not at ~ во́все не; for ~ (that) I care мне безразли́чно; for ~ I know поско́льку я зна́ю; **3.** *adv.* вполне́, всеце́ло, соверше́нно; ~ at once сра́зу; ~ the better тем лу́чше; ~ but почти́; ~ right хорошо́, ла́дно.
allay [əˈlei] успока́ивать [-ко́ить].
alleg|ation [æleˈgeiʃən] заявле́ние; голосло́вное утвержде́ние; **~e** [əˈledʒ] ссыла́ться [сосла́ться] на (В); утвержда́ть (без основа́ния).
allegiance [əˈli:dʒəns] ве́рность *f*, пре́данность *f*.
alleviate [əˈli:vieit] облегча́ть [-чи́ть].
alley [ˈæli] алле́я; переу́лок.
alliance [əˈlaiəns] сою́з.
allocat|e [ˈælokeit] размеща́ть [-мести́ть]; распределя́ть [-ли́ть]; **~ion** [æloˈkeiʃən] распределе́ние.

allot [ə'lɔt] *v/t.* распределя́ть [-ли́ть]; разда́(ва́)ть.
allow [ə'lau] позволя́ть [-о́лить]; допуска́ть [-сти́ть]; *Am.* утвержда́ть; **~able** [-əbl] □ позволи́тельный; **~ance** [-əns] (материа́льное) содержа́ние; ски́дка; разреше́ние; make ~ for принима́ть во внима́ние.
alloy [ə'lɔi] **1.** при́месь *f*; сплав; **2.** сплавля́ть [-а́вить].
all-round всесторо́нний.
allude [ə'lu:d] ссыла́ться [сосла́ться] (to на В); намека́ть [-кну́ть] (to на В).
allure [ə'ljuə] завлека́ть [-е́чь]; **~ment** [-mənt] обольще́ние.
allusion [ə'luʒən] намёк; ссы́лка.
ally 1. [ə'lai] соединя́ть [-ни́ть] (to, with с Т); **2.** ['ælɑi] сою́зник.
almanac ['ɔ:lmənæk] календа́рь *m*, альмана́х.
almighty [ɔ:l'maiti] всемогу́щий.
almond ['ɑ:mənd] **1.** минда́ль *m*; минда́лина (*a.* ⚘); **2.** минда́льный.
almost ['ɔ:lmoust] почти́, едва́ не.
alms [ɑ:mz] *sg. a. pl.* ми́лостыня; **~-house** богаде́льня.
aloft [ə'lɔft] наверху́, наве́рх.
alone ['loun] оди́н *m*, одна́ *f*, одно́ *n*, одни́ *pl.*; одино́кий (-кая); let (и́ли leave) ~ оста́вить в поко́е; let ~ ... не говоря́ уже́ о ... (П).
along [ə'lɔŋ] **1.** *adv.* вперёд; all ~ всё вре́мя; ~ with вме́сте с (Т); F get ~ with you! убира́йтесь!; **2.** *prp.* вдоль (Р), по (Д); **~side** [-said] бок-о́-бок, ря́дом.
aloof [ə'lu:f] по́одаль, в стороне́; stand ~ держа́ться в стороне́.
aloud [ə'laud] гро́мко, вслух.
alp [ælp] го́рное па́стбище; ♀s 'Альпы *f/pl.*
already [ɔ:l'redi] уже́.
also ['ɔ:lsou] та́кже, то́же.
alter ['ɔ:ltə] изменя́ть(ся) [-ни́ть (-ся)]; **~ation** [ɔ:ltə'reiʃən] переме́на, измене́ние, переде́лка (to Р).
alternat|e 1. ['ɔ:ltə:neit] чередова́ть(ся); **2.** □ [ɔ:l'tə:nit] переме́нный; ⚡ alternating current переме́нный ток; **~ion** [ɔ:ltə:'neiʃən] чередова́ние; **~ive** [ɔ:l'tə:nətiv] **1.** □ взаимоисключа́ющий, альтернати́вный; переме́нно де́йствующий; **2.** альтернати́ва; вы́бор, возмо́жность *f*.
although [ɔ:l'ðou] хотя́.
altitude ['æltitju:d] высота́; возвы́шенность *f*.
altogether [ɔ:ltə'geðə] вполне́, всеце́ло; в о́бщем.
alumin(i)um [ælju'minjəm] алюми́ний.
always ['ɔ:lwəz] всегда́.
am [æm; в предложе́нии: əm] [*irr.*] *1. pers. sg. prs.* от be.
amalgamate [ə'mælgəmeit] амальгами́ровать (*im*)*pf*.
amass [ə'mæs] соб(и)ра́ть; накопля́ть [-пи́ть].
amateur ['æmətə:, -tjuə] любитель(ница *f*) *m*; дилета́нт(ка).
amaz|e [ə'meiz] изумля́ть [-ми́ть] поража́ть [порази́ть]; **~emen** [-mənt] изумле́ние; **~ing** [ə'meizi удиви́тельный, изуми́тельный.
ambassador [æm'bæsədə] посо́л посла́нец.
amber ['æmbə] янта́рь *m*.
ambigu|ity [æmbi'gjuiti] двусмы́сленность *f*; **~ous** [-'bigjuə □ двусмы́сленный; сомни́телный.
ambitio|n [æm'biʃən] честолю́би **~us** [-ʃəs] □ честолюби́вый.
amble ['æmbl] **1.** и́ноходь *f*; **2.** идт и́ноходью.
ambulance ['æmbjuləns] каре́т ско́рой по́мощи.
ambuscade [æmbəs'keid], **ambus** ['æmbuʃ] заса́да.
ameliorate [ə'mi:liəreit] улу ша́ть(ся) [улу́чшить(ся)].
amend [ə'mend] исправля́ть(с [-а́вить(ся)]; *parl.* вноси́ть попра́ ки в (В); **~ment** [-mənt] испрале́ние; *parl.* попра́вка (к резол ции, законопрое́кту); **~s** [ə'mend компенса́ция.
amenity [ə'mi:niti] прия́тность
American [ə'merikən] **1.** амер ка́нец (-нка); **2.** америка́нски **~ism** [-izm] американи́зм; **~iz** [-aiz] американизи́ровать (*im*)*pf*
amiable ['eimjəbl] □ дружелю ный; доброду́шный.
amicable ['æmikəbl] □ дру́же кий, дру́жественный.
amid(st) [ə'mid(st)] среди́ (Р), п среди́ (Р), ме́жду (Т *sometimes* Р
amiss [ə'mis] *adv.* пло́хо, непр вильно; некста́ти; несвоевре́ме но; take ~ обижа́ться [оби́деться]
amity ['æmiti] дру́жба.
ammonia [ə'mounjə] ⚗ аммиа́
ammunition [æmju'niʃən] боепр па́сы *m/pl.*
amnesty ['æmnesti] **1.** амни́сти **2.** амнисти́ровать (*im*)*pf*.
among(st) [ə'mʌŋ(st)] среди́ (Р ме́жду (Т *sometimes* Р).
amorous ['æmərəs] □ влюблё ный (of в В); влю́бчивый.
amount [ə'maunt] **1.** ~ to равня́т ся (Д); **2.** су́мма; коли́чество.
ample ['æmpl] □ доста́точны оби́льный; просто́рный.
ampli|fication [æmplifi'keiʃə расшире́ние; увеличе́ние; усил ние; **~fier** ['æmplifaiə] *phys.* ус ли́тель *m*; **~fy** ['æmplifai] ус ли(ва)ть; распространя́ть(с [-ни́ть(ся)]; **~tude** [-tju:d] ши рота́, разма́х (мы́сли); *phys., ast* амплиту́да.
amputate ['æmpjuteit] ампути́р вать (*im*)*pf.*, отнима́ть [-ня́ть].

ause [ə'mju:z] забавля́ть, поза-
а́вить *pf.*, развлека́ть [-е́чь]: **~-
ent** [-mənt] развлече́ние, заба́ва.
[æn, ən] неопределённый
лен.
(a)esthetic [æni:s'θetik] нарко́-
ик.
alog|ous [ə'næləgəs] □ аналоги́ч-
ый, схо́дный; **~y** [ə'nælədʒi] ана-
о́гия, схо́дство.
alys|e ['ænəlaiz] анализи́ровать
m)pf., *pf. a.* [про-]; **~is** [ə'næləsis]
на́лиз.
archy ['ænəki] ана́рхия.
atom|ize [ə'nætəmaiz] анатоми́-
овать (*im*)*pf.*; [про]анализи́ро-
ать (*im*)*pf.*; **~y** анато́мия.
cest|or ['ænsistə] пре́док; **~ral**
en'sestrəl] насле́дственный, ро-
ово́й; **~ress** ['ænsistris] прароди́-
ельница; **~ry** ['ænsistri] проис-
ожде́ние; пре́дки *m/pl.*
chor ['æŋkə] **1.** я́корь *m*; at ~
а я́коре; **2.** ста́вить (стать) на
корь.
chovy [æn'tʃouvi] анчо́ус.
cient ['einʃənt] **1.** дре́вний; ан-
и́чный; **2.** the ~s *pl. hist.* дре́вние
аро́ды *m/pl.*
d [ænd, ənd, ꟳ ən] и; а.
ew [ə'nju:] *adv.* сно́ва, сы́знова;
о-но́вому.
gel ['eindʒəl] а́нгел; **~ic(al** □)
en'dʒelik(əl)] а́нгельский.
ger ['æŋgə] **1.** гнев; **2.** [рас]сер-
и́ть.
gle ['æŋgl] **1.** у́гол; то́чка зре́-
ия; **2.** уди́ть (for В); уди́ть ры́бу;
g. заки́дывать у́дочку.
nglican ['æŋglikən] **1.** член ан-
лика́нской це́ркви; **2.** англи-
а́нский.
nglo-Saxon ['æŋglou'sæksn] **1.**
нглоса́кс; **2.** англосаксо́нский.
gry ['æŋgri] серди́тый (with на
).
guish ['æŋgwiʃ] му́ка.
gular ['æŋgjulə] углово́й, уго́ль-
ый; *fig.* углова́тый; нело́вкий.
imal ['æniməl] **1.** живо́тное; **2.**
живо́тный; ско́тский.
imat|e ['ænimeit] оживля́ть
-ви́ть]; воодушевля́ть [-ви́ть];
ion [æni'meiʃən] жи́вость *f*;
оживле́ние.
imosity [æni'mɔsiti] вражде́б-
ость *f.*
kle ['æŋkl] лоды́жка.
nals ['ænlz] *pl.* ле́топись *f.*
nex **1.** [ə'neks] аннекси́ровать
im)pf.; присоединя́ть [-ни́ть]; **2.**
'æneks] пристро́йка; приложе́ние;
ation [ænek'seiʃən] анне́ксия.
nihilate [ə'naiəleit] уничтожа́ть
-о́жить], истребля́ть [-би́ть].
niversary [æni'və:səri] годов-
ци́на.
notat|e ['ænouteit] аннoти́ро-
ать (*im*)*pf.*; снабжа́ть примеча́ни-
ями; **~ion** [ænou'teiʃən] приме-
ча́ние.
announce [ə'nauns] объявля́ть
[-ви́ть]; дава́ть знать; заявля́ть
[-ви́ть]; **~ment** [-mənt] объявле́-
ние; **~r** [-ə] *radio* ди́ктор.
annoy [ə'nɔi] надоеда́ть [-е́сть] (Д);
досажда́ть [досади́ть] (Д); **~ance**
[-əns] доса́да; раздраже́ние; не-
прия́тность *f.*
annual ['ænjuəl] **1.** □ ежего́дный;
годово́й; **2.** ежего́дник; однолет-
нее расте́ние.
annuity [ə'njuiti] годова́я ре́нта.
annul [ə'nʌl] аннули́ровать (*im*)*pf.*;
отменя́ть [-ни́ть]; **~ment** [-mənt]
аннули́рование.
anoint [ə'nɔint] нама́з(ыв)ать; *eccl.*
пома́з(ыв)ать.
anomalous [ə'nɔmələs] □ ано-
ма́льный, непра́вильный.
anonymous [ə'nɔniməs] □ анони́м-
ный.
another [ə'nʌðə] друго́й; ещё
оди́н.
answer ['ɑ:nsə] **1.** *v/t.* отвеча́ть
[-е́тить] (Д); удовлетворя́ть
[-ри́ть]; ~ the bell *or* door откры-
ва́ть дверь на звоно́к; *v/i.* отвеча́ть
[-е́тить] (to a p. Д, to a question на
вопро́с); ~ for отвеча́ть [-е́тить] за
(В); **2.** отве́т (to на В); **~able**
['ɑ:nsərəbl] □ отве́тственный.
ant [ænt] мураве́й.
antagonis|m [æn'tægənizm] анта-
гони́зм, вражда́; **~t** [-ist] антаго-
ни́ст, проти́вник.
antecedent [ænti'si:dənt] **1.** □
предше́ствующий, предыду́щий
(to Д); **2.** ~s *pl.* про́шлое (челове́-
ка).
anterior [æn'tiriə] предше́ствую-
щий (to Д); пере́дний.
ante-room ['æntirum] пере́дняя.
anthem ['ænθəm] гимн.
anti... [ænti...] противо..., анти...;
~-aircraft [ænti'ɛəkra:ft] проти-
вовозду́шный; ~ alarm возду́ш-
ная трево́га; ~ defence проти-
вовозду́шная оборо́на (ПВО).
antic ['æntik] **1.** □ шутовско́й; **2.**
гроте́ск; ~s *pl.* ужи́мки *f/pl.*;
ша́лости *f/pl.*
anticipat|e [æn'tisipeit] предвку-
ша́ть [-уси́ть]; предчу́вствовать;
предупрежда́ть [-реди́ть]; **~ion**
[æntisi'peiʃən] ожида́ние; пред-
чу́вствие; in ~ зара́нее.
antidote ['æntidout] противо-
я́дие.
antipathy [æn'tipəθi] антипа́тия.
antiqua|ry ['æntikwəri] антиква́р;
~ted [-kweitid] устаре́лый; ста-
ромо́дный.
antiqu|e [æn'ti:k] **1.** □ анти́чный;
стари́нный; **2.** анти́чное произ-
веде́ние иску́сства; антиква́рная
вещь *f*; **~ity** [æn'tikwiti] дре́в-
ность *f*; старина́; анти́чность *f.*

antlers ['æntləz] *pl.* олéньи porá *m/pl.*

anvil ['ænvil] наковáльня.

anxiety [æŋ'zaiəti] беспокóйство; стрáстное желáние; опасéние.

anxious ['æŋkʃəs] □ озабóченный; беспокóящийся (about, for o П).

any ['əni] **1.** *pron.* какóй-нибудь; всякий, любóй; not ~ никакóй; **2.** *adv.* скóлько-нибудь; нéсколько; **~body, ~one** ктó-нибудь; всякий; **~how** кáк-нибудь; так или ńначе, во всяком слýчае; **~thing** чтó-нибудь; ~ but далéко не ..., совсéм не ...; **~where** гдé--нибудь, кудá-нибудь.

apart [ə'pɑ:t] отдéльно; пóрознь; ~ from крóме (Р); **~ment** [-mənt] кóмната (меблирóванная); **~s** *pl.* квартира; *Am.* ~ house многоквартирный дом.

ape [eip] **1.** обезьяна; **2.** подражáть (Д), [с]обезьянничать.

aperient [ə'piəriənt] слабительное срéдство.

aperture ['æpətjuə] отвéрстие; проём. [ство.]

apiculture ['eipikʌltʃə] пчеловóд-

apiece [ə'pi:s] за штýку; за кáждого, с человéка.

apish ['eipiʃ] □ обезьяний; глýпый.

apolog|etic [əpɔlə'dʒetik] (**~ally**) извинительный; извиняющийся; защитительный; **~ize** [ə'pɔlədʒaiz] извиняться [-нйться] (for за В; to пéред Т); **~y** [-dʒi] извинéние.

apoplexy ['æpopleksi] удáр, паралич.

apostate [ə'pɔstit] отстýпник.

apostle [ə'pɔsl] апóстол.

apostroph|e [ə'pɔstrefi] апострóфа; апострóф; **~ize** [-faiz] обращáться [обратиться] к (Д).

appal [ə'pɔ:l] [ис]пугáть; устрашáть [-шить].

apparatus [æpə'reitəs] прибóр; аппаратýра, аппарáт.

apparel [ə'pærəl] одéжда, плáтье.

appar|ent [ə'pærənt] □ очевидный, несомнéнный; **~ition** [æpə'riʃən] появлéние; призрак.

appeal [ə'pi:l] **1.** апеллировать (*im*)*pf.*; подавáть жáлобу; обращáться [обратиться] (to к Д); привлекáть [-éчь] (to B); **2.** воззвáние, призыв; апелляция; привлекáтелность *f*; **~ing** [-iŋ] трóгательный; привлекáтельный.

appear [ə'piə] появляться [-вйться]; покáзываться [-зáться]; выступáть [вы́ступить] (на концéрте и т. п.); **~ance** [ə'piərəns] появлéние; внéшний вид, нарýжность *f*; **~s** *pl.* прилйчия *n/pl.*

appease [ə'pi:z] умиротворять [-рить]; успокáивать [-кóить].

appellant [ə'pelənt] апеллянт.

append [ə'pend] прилагáть [-л жить] (к Д), прибавлять [-áвит (к Д); **~age** [-idʒ] придáток; ~ [ə'pendiks] приложéние.

appertain [æpə'tein] принадл жáть; относиться (to к Д).

appetite ['æpitait] аппетит (for В); *fig.* влечéние, склóнность (for к Д).

appetizing ['æpitaiziŋ] аппети ный.

applaud [ə'plɔ:d] *v/t.* аплодир вать (Д); одобрять [одóбрить].

applause [ə'plɔ:z] аплодисмéнт *m/pl.*; одобрéние.

apple [æpl] яблоко; **~sauce** ябло ный мусс; *sl.* лесть *f*; ерундá.

appliance [ə'plaiəns] приспосо лéние, прибóр.

applica|ble ['æplikəbl] примен мый, подходящий (to к Д); ~ [-kənt] просйтель(ница *f*) кандидáт (for на В); **~tion** [æp 'keiʃən] применéние; заявлéни прóсьба (for o П).

apply [ə'plai] *v/t.* прилагáть [-л жить] (to к Д); применять [-нйт (to к Д); ~ o. s. to заниматься [з няться] (Т); *v/i.* обращáться [обр титься] (for за Т; to к Д); отн ситься.

appoint [ə'pɔint] назначáть [-н чить]; определять [-лйть]; сн ряжáть [-ядйть]; well ~ed хорош оборýдованный; **~ment** [-mən назначéние; свидáние; ~s оборýдование; обстанóвка.

apportion [ə'pɔ:ʃən] [по]делйт разделять [-лйть]; **~ment** [-mər пропорционáльное распредел ние.

apprais|al [ə'preizəl] оцéнка; [ə'preiz] оцéнивать [-нйть], ра цéнивать [-нйть].

apprecia|ble [ə'pri:ʃəbl] □ замé ный, ощутимый; **~te** [-ieit] *v* оцéнивать [-нйть]; [о]ценйть; п нимáть [-нять]; *v/i.* повышáться цéнности; **~tion** [əpri:ʃi'eiʃə оцéнка; понимáние.

apprehen|d [æpri'hend] предчý ствовать; боя́ться; задéржива [-жáть], арестóвывать [-овáть **~sion** [-'henʃən] опасéние, пре чýвствие; арéст; **~sive** [-'hensi □ озабóченный; понятливый.

apprentice [ə'prentis] **1.** подма тéрье, ученик; **2.** отдавáть учéние; **~ship** [-ʃip] учéние, уч ничество.

approach [ə'proutʃ] **1.** прибли жáться [-блйзиться] к (Д); обр щáться [обратиться] к (Д); приближéние; пóдступ; *fig.* по хóд.

approbation [æpro'beiʃən] одо рéние; сáнкция.

appropriat|e 1. [ə'prouprieit] пр свáивать [-свóить]; *parl.* пре

назначáть [-знáчить]; **2.** [-it] □ подходя́щий; соотвéтствующий; **~ion** [əproupri'eiʃən] присвоéние; *parl.* ассигновáние.
approv|al [ə'pru:vəl] одобрéние; утверждéние; **~e** [ə'pru:v] одобря́ть [одóбрить]; утверждáть [-рди́ть]; санкциони́ровать *(im)pf.*
approximate **1.** [ə'prɔksimeit] приближáть(ся) [-бли́зить(ся)] к (Д); **2.** [-mit] □ приблизи́тельный.
apricot ['eiprikɔt] абрикóс.
April ['eiprəl] aпрéль *m.*
apron ['eiprən] перéдник, фáртук.
apt [æpt] □ подходя́щий; спосóбный; ~ to склóнный к (Д); **~itude** ['æptitju:d], **~ness** [-nis] спосóбность *f*; склóнность *f* (for, to к Д); умéстность *f.*
aquatic [ə'kwætik] **1.** водянóй; вóдный; **2.** **~s** *pl.* вóдный спорт.
aque|duct ['ækwidʌkt] акведу́к; **~ous** ['eikwiəs] водяни́стый.
Arab ['ærəb] ара́б(ка); **~ic** ['ærəbik] **1.** ара́бский язы́к; **2.** ара́бский.
arable ['ærəbl] пáхотный.
arbit|er ['ɑbitə] арби́тр, третéйский судья́ *m*; *fig.* верши́тель сýдеб; **~rariness** ['ɑ:bitrərinis] произвóл; **~rary** [-trəri] □ произвóльный; **~rate** ['ɑ:bitreit] решáть третéйским судóм; **~ration** [ɑ:bi'treiʃən] третéйское решéние; **~rator** ['ɑ:bitreitə] ⚖ арби́тр, третéйский судья́ *m.*
arbo(u)r ['ɑ:bə] бесéдка.
arc [ɑ:k] *ast.*, ⩓, ⚡ дугá; **~ade** [ɑ:'keid] пассáж; свóдчатая галерéя.
arch¹ [ɑ:tʃ] **1.** áрка; свод; дугá; **2.** придавáть фóрму áрки; изгибáть(ся) дугóй.
arch² [~] **1.** хи́трый, лукáвый; **2.** *pref.* архи... (выражéние превосхóдной стéпени).
archaic [ɑ:'keiik] (~ally) устарéлый.
archbishop ['ɑ:tʃbiʃəp] архиепи́скоп.
archery ['ɑ:tʃəri] стрельбá из лýка.
architect ['ɑ:kitekt] архитéктор; **~onic** [-'ɔnik] (~ally) архитектýрный, конструкти́вный; **~ure** ['ɑ:kitektʃə] архитектýра.
archway ['ɑ:tʃwei] свóдчатый прохóд.
arc-lamp ['ɑ:klæmp] ⚡ дуговáя лáмпа.
arctic ['ɑ:ktik] поля́рный, аркти́ческий.
arden|cy ['ɑ:dənsi] жар, пыл; рвéние; **~t** ['ɑ:dənt] □ *mst fig.* горя́чий, пы́лкий; рéвностный.
ardo(u)r ['ɑ:də] рвéние; пыл.
arduous ['ɑ:djuəs] □ трýдный.
are [ɑ:; в предложéнии: ɑ] *s.* be.
area ['ɛəriə] плóщадь *f*; óбласть *f*, райóн.
Argentine ['ɑ:dʒəntain] **1.** аргенти́нский; **2.** аргенти́нец (-и́нка).
argue ['ɑ:gju:] *v/t.* обсуждáть [-уди́ть]; докáзывать [-зáть]; ~ a p. into убеждáть [убеди́ть] в (П); *v/i.* [по]спóрить (с Т).
argument ['ɑ:gjumənt] дóвод, аргумéнт; спор; **~ation** [ɑ:gjumen'teiʃən] аргументáция.
arid ['ærid] сухóй (*a. fig.*), безвóдный.
arise [ə'raiz] [*irr.*] *fig.* возникáть [-ни́кнуть] (from из Р); восст(ав)áть; **~n** [ə'rizn] *p. pt.* от arise.
aristocra|cy [æris'tɔkrəsi] аристокрáтия; **~t** ['æristəkræt] аристокрáт; **~tic(al** □) [æristə'krætik, -ikəl] аристократи́ческий.
arithmetic [ə'riθmətik] арифмéтика.
ark [ɑ:k] ковчéг.
arm¹ [ɑ:m] рукá; рукáв (реки́).
arm² [~] **1.** орýжие; род войск; **2.** вооружáть(ся) [-жи́ть(ся)].
arma|ment ['ɑ:məmənt] вооружéние; **~ture** ['ɑ:mətjuə] броня́; ⊕ арматýра.
armchair крéсло.
armistice ['ɑ:mistis] переми́рие.
armo(u)r ['ɑ:mə] **1.** доспéхи *m/pl.*; броня́, пáнцирная обши́вка; **2.** покрывáть бронëй; **~y** [-ri] арсенáл.
armpit [ɑ:mpit] подмы́шка.
army ['ɑ:mi] áрмия; *fig.* мнóжество.
arose [ə'rouz] *pt.* от *arise.*
around [ə'raund] **1.** *adv.* всюду, кругóм; **2.** *prp.* вокрýг (Р).
arouse [ə'rauz] [раз]буди́ть; возбуждáть [-уди́ть]; вызывáть [вы́звать].
arraign [ə'rein] привлекáть к судý; *fig.* находи́ть недостáтки в (П).
arrange [ə'reindʒ] приводи́ть в поря́док; устрáивать [-рóить]; классифици́ровать *(im)pf.*; уславливаться [услóвиться]; ♪ аранжи́ровать *(im)pf.*; **~ment** [-mənt] устрóйство; расположéние; соглашéние; мероприя́тие; ♪ аранжирóвка.
array [ə'rei] **1.** боевóй поря́док; *fig.* мнóжество, цéлый ряд; **2.** одé(вá)ть; украшáть [укрáсить]; выстрáивать в ряд.
arrear [ə'riə] *mst. pl.* задóлженность *f*, недои́мка.
arrest [ə'rest] **1.** арéст, задержáние; **2.** арестóвывать [-овáть], задéрживать [-жáть].
arriv|al [ə'raivəl] прибы́тие, приéзд; **~s** *pl.* прибы́вшие *pl.*; **~e** [ə'raiv] прибы́(вá)ть; приезжáть [-éхать] (at в, на В).
arroga|nce ['ærəgəns] надмéн-

ность *f*, высокоме́рие; **~nt** □ надме́нный, высокоме́рный; **~te** [-geit] де́рзко тре́бовать (Р).
arrow ['ærou] стрела́.
arsenal ['ɑ:sinl] арсена́л.
arsenic ['ɑ:snik] мышья́к.
arson ['ɑ:sn] ⚖ поджо́г.
art [ɑ:t] иску́сство; *fig.* хи́трость *f.*
arter|ial [ɑ'tiəriəl]: ~ road магистра́ль *f*; **~y** ['ɑ:təri] арте́рия; гла́вная доро́га.
artful ['ɑ:tful] ло́вкий; хи́трый.
article ['ɑ:tikl] статья́; пара́граф; *gr.* арти́кль *m*, член; ~d to о́тданный (в уче́ние) к (Д).
articulat|e **1.** [ɑ:'tikjuleit] отчётливо, я́сно произноси́ть; **2.** [-lit] отчётливый; членоразде́льный; коле́нчатый; **~ion** [ɑ:tikju'leiʃən] артикуля́ция; членоразде́льное произноше́ние; *anat.* сочлене́ние.
artific|e ['ɑ:tifis] ло́вкость *f*; изобрете́ние, вы́думка; **~ial** [ɑ:ti'fiʃəl] □ иску́сственный.
artillery [ɑ:'tiləri] артилле́рия; **~man** [-mən] артиллери́ст.
artisan [ɑ:ti'zæn] реме́сленник.
artist ['ɑ:tist] худо́жник (-ица); актёр, актри́са; **~e** [ɑ:'tist] эстра́дный (-ная) арти́ст(ка); **~ic(al** □) [ɑ:'tistik, -tikəl] артисти́ческий, худо́жественный.
as [æz] *cj. a. adv.* когда́; в то вре́мя как; та́к как; хотя́; ~ it were ка́к бы; ~ well та́к же; в тако́й же ме́ре; such ~ тако́й как; как наприме́р; ~ well ~ и ... и ...; *prp.* ~ for, ~ to что каса́ется (Р); ~ from с (Р).
ascend [ə'send] поднима́ться [-ня́ться]; всходи́ть [взойти́] на (В); восходи́ть (to к Д); ✈ наб(и)ра́ть высоту́.
ascension [ə'senʃən] восхожде́ние; ♀ (Day) вознесе́ние.
ascent [ə'sent] подъём; крутизна́.
ascertain [æsə'tein] удостоверя́ться [-ве́риться] в (П).
ascribe [ə'skraib] припи́сывать [-са́ть] (Д/В).
aseptic [ei'septik] ⚕ стери́льный.
ash¹ [æʃ] ♀ я́сень *m*; mountain ~ ряби́на.
ash² [~], *mst pl.* **~es** [æʃiz] зола́, пе́пел.
ashamed [ə'ʃeimd] пристыжённый.
ash-can *Am.* ведро́ для му́сора.
ashen [æʃn] пе́пельный (цвет).
ashore [ə'ʃɔ:] на́ берег, на берегу́; run ~, be driven ~ наскочи́ть на мель.
ash-tray пе́пельница.
ashy ['æʃi] пе́пельный; бле́дный.
Asiatic [eiʃi'ætik] **1.** азиа́тский; **2.** азиа́т(ка).
aside [ə'said] в сто́рону, в стороне́; отде́льно.

ask [ɑ:sk] *v/t.* [по]проси́ть (a th. of, from a p. что́-нибудь у кого́-нибудь); ~ that проси́ть, что́бы ...; спра́шивать [спроси́ть]; ~ (a p.) a question задава́ть вопро́с (Д); *v/i.* ~ for [по]проси́ть (В *or* Р *or* о П).
askance [əs'kæns], **askew** [əs'kju:] и́скоса, ко́со; кри́во.
asleep [ə'sli:p] спя́щий; be ~ спать.
aslope [ə'sloup] *adv.* пока́то; на склоне, на ска́те.
asparagus [əs'pærəgəs] ♀ спа́ржа.
aspect ['æspekt] вид (*a. gr.*); аспе́кт; сторона́.
asperity [æs'periti] стро́гость *f*; суро́вость *f.*
asphalt ['æsfælt] **1.** асфа́льт; **2.** покрыва́ть асфа́льтом.
aspir|ant [əs'paiərənt] кандида́т; **~ate** ['æspəreit] произноси́ть с придыха́нием; **~ation** [æspə'reiʃən] стремле́ние; *phon.* придыха́ние; **~e** [əs'paiə] стреми́ться (to, after, at к Д); домога́ться (Р).
ass [æs] осёл.
assail [ə'seil] напада́ть [-па́сть] на (В), атакова́ть (В) (*im*)*pf.*; *fig.* энерги́чно бра́ться за (де́ло); **~ant** [-ənt] проти́вник; напада́ющий.
assassin [ə'sæsin] уби́йца *m/f*; **~ate** [-ineit] уби́(ва́)ть; **~ation** [əsæsi'neiʃən] уби́йство.
assault [ə'sɔ:lt] **1.** нападе́ние, ата́ка; ⚖ слове́сное оскорбле́ние; физи́ческое наси́лие; **2.** напада́ть [напа́сть], набра́сываться [-ро́ситься] на (В).
assay [ə'sei] **1.** испыта́ние, опро́бование (мета́ллов); **2.** [ис]про́бовать, испы́тывать [испыта́ть].
assembl|age [ə'semblidʒ] собра́ние; скопле́ние; сбор; ⊕ монта́ж, сбо́рка; **~e** [ə'sembl] соз(ы)ва́ть; ⊕ [с]монти́ровать; **~y** [-... собра́ние; ассамбле́я; ⊕ сбо́рка часте́й.
assent [ə'sent] **1.** согла́сие; **2.** соглаша́ться [-ласи́ться] (to на В; с Т).
assert [ə'sə:t] утвержда́ть [-рди́ть]; **~ion** [ə'sə:ʃən] утвержде́ние.
assess [ə'ses] облага́ть нало́гом; оце́нивать иму́щество (Р); **~able** [-əbl] □ подлежа́щий обложе́нию; **~ment** [-mənt] обложе́ние; оце́нка.
asset ['æset] це́нное ка́чество; статья́ дохо́да; **~s** *pl.* ✝ акти́в.
assiduous [ə'sidjuəs] □ приле́жный.
assign [ə'sain] определя́ть [-ли́ть]; назнача́ть [-на́чить]; ассигно́вывать, ассигнова́ть (*im*)*pf*; поруча́ть [-чи́ть]; **~ment** [ə'sainmənt] назначе́ние; ⚖ переда́ча; зада́ние.
assimilat|e [ə'simileit] ассимили́ровать(ся) (*im*)*pf.*; осва́ивать [осво́ить]; прира́внивать [-ня́ть]

~ion [əsimi'leiʃən] уподобле́ние; ассимиля́ция; усвое́ние.
ssist [ə'sist] помога́ть [-мо́чь] (Д), [по]соде́йствовать (*im*)*pf.* (Д); **~ance** [-əns] по́мощь *f*; **~ant** [-ənt] ассисте́нт(ка); помо́щник (-ица).
ssocia|te 1. [ə'souʃieit] обща́ться (with с Т); ассоции́ровать(ся) (*im*)*pf.*; присоединя́ть(ся) [-ни́ть(-ся)] (with к Д); **2.** [-ʃiit] a) свя́занный; объединённый; b) това́рищ, колле́га; соуча́стник; **~tion** [əsousi'eiʃən] ассоциа́ция; соедине́ние; о́бщество.
ssort [ə'sɔ:t] [рас]сортирова́ть; подбира́ть [подобра́ть]; снабжа́ть ассортиме́нтом; **~ment** [-mənt] сортиро́вка.
ssum|e [ə'sju:m] принима́ть [-ня́ть] (на себя́); предполага́ть [-ложи́ть]; **~ption** [ə'sʌmpʃən] предположе́ние; присвое́ние; *eccl.* 2 успе́ние.
ssur|ance [ə'ʃuərəns] увере́ние; уве́ренность *f*; страхо́вка; **~e** [ə'ʃuə] уверя́ть [уве́рить]; обеспе́чи(ва)ть; [за]страхова́ть; **~edly** [-ridli] *adv.* коне́чно, несомне́нно.
stir [əs'tə:] в движе́нии; на нога́х
tonish [əs'tɔniʃ] удивля́ть [-ви́ть], изумля́ть [-ми́ть]; be ~ed удивля́ться [-ви́ться] (at Д); **~ing** [-iʃiŋ] □ удиви́телный, изуми́тельный; **~ment** [əs'tɔniʃmənt] удивле́ние, изумле́ние.
stound [əs'taund] поража́ть [порази́ть].
tray [əs'trei]: go ~ заблуди́ться, би́ться с пути́.
tride [əs'traid] верхо́м (of на Т).
tringent [əs'trindʒənt] □ ⚕ вя́жущий (о сре́дстве).
tro|logy [əs'trɔlədʒi] астроло́гия; **nomer** [əs'trɔnəmə] астроно́м; **nomy** [əs'trɔnəmi] астроно́мия.
tute [əs'tju:t] □ хи́трый; проница́тельный; **~ness** [-nis] хи́трость; проница́тельность *f*.
under [ə'sʌndə] по́рознь, отде́льно; в куски́, на ча́сти.
ylum [ə'sailəm] прию́т; убе́жище.
[æt] *prp.* в (П, В); у (Р); при (П); на (П, В); о́коло (Р); за (Т); ~ school в шко́ле; ~ the age of в во́зрасте (Р).
e [et, eit] *pt.* от eat.
heism ['eiθiizm] атеи́зм.
hlet|e ['æθli:t] атле́т; **~ic(al** □) [æθ'letik(əl)] атлети́ческий; **~ics** *pl.* [æθ'letiks] атле́тика.
lantic [ət'læntik] **1.** атланти́ческий; **2.** (*a.* ~ Ocean) Атланти́ческий океа́н.
mospher|e ['ætməsfiə] атмосфе́ра; **~ic(al** □) [ætməs'ferik(əl)] атмосфе́рный, атмосфери́ческий.

atom ['ætəm] 🕮 а́том; ~ (*a.* ~ic) bomb а́томная бо́мба; **~ic** [ə'tɔmik] а́томный; ~ pile а́томный реа́ктор; ~ smashing расщепле́ние а́тома; **~izer** ['ætəmaizə] распыли́тель *m*.
atone [ə'toun]: ~ for загла́живать [-ла́дить], искупа́ть [-пи́ть]; **~ment** [-mənt] искупле́ние.
atroci|ous [ə'trouʃəs] □ зве́рский, ужа́сный; **~ty** [ə'trɔsiti] зве́рство.
attach [ə'tætʃ] *v/t. com.* прикрепля́ть [-пи́ть]; прикомандиро́вывать [-рова́ть] (к Д); прид(ав)а́ть; ⚖ налага́ть аре́ст на (В); аресто́вывать [-ова́ть]; ~ o. s. to привя́зываться [-за́ться] к (Д); **~ment** [-mənt] привя́занность *f*; прикрепле́ние; наложе́ние аре́ста.
attack [ə'tæk] **1.** ата́ка, наступле́ние; припа́док; **2.** *v/t.* атакова́ть (*im*)*pf.*; напада́ть [напа́сть] на (В); набра́сываться [-ро́ситься] на (В); ⚕ поража́ть [порази́ть] (о боле́зни).
attain [ə'tein] *v/t.* достига́ть [-и́гнуть] (Р), доби́(ва́)ться (Р); **~ment** [-mənt] приобрете́ние; достиже́ние; ~s *pl.* зна́ния *n/pl.*; на́выки *m/pl.*
attempt [ə'tempt] **1.** попы́тка; покуше́ние; **2.** [по]пыта́ться; покуша́ться [-уси́ться] на (В).
attend [ə'tend] обслу́живать [-жи́ть]; посеща́ть [-ети́ть]; ⚕ ходи́ть, уха́живать за (Т); прислу́живать (to Д); прису́тствовать (at на П); быть внима́тельным; **~ance** [ə'tendəns] прису́тствие (at на П); обслу́живание; пу́блика; посеща́емость *f*; ⚕ ухо́д (за Т); **~ant** [-ənt] **1.** сопровожда́ющий (on В); прису́тствующий (at на П); **2.** посети́тель(ница *f*) *m*; спу́тник (-ица); ⚕ санита́р; служи́тель *m*.
attent|ion [ə'tenʃən] внима́ние; **~ive** [-tiv] □ внима́тельный.
attest [ə'test] [за]свиде́тельствовать; удостоверя́ть [-ве́рить]; *part.* ⚔ приводи́ть к прися́ге.
attic ['ætik] черда́к; манса́рда.
attire [ə'taiə] **1.** наря́д; **2.** оде́(ва́)ть, наряжа́ть [-яди́ть].
attitude ['ætitju:d] отноше́ние; пози́ция; по́за, оса́нка; *fig.* то́чка зре́ния.
attorney [ə'tə:ni] пове́ренный; power of ~ полномо́чие; ♀ General *Am.* мини́стр юсти́ции.
attract [ə'trækt] *v/t.* привлека́ть [-вле́чь] (*a. fig.*); притя́гивать [-яну́ть]; *fig.* прельща́ть [-льсти́ть]; **~ion** [ə'trækʃən] притяже́ние, тяготе́ние; *fig.* привлека́тельность *f*; *thea.* аттракцио́н; **~ive** [-tiv] привлека́тельный; зама́нчивый; **~iveness** [-tivnis] привлека́тельность *f*.
attribute 1. [ə'tribju:t] припи́сывать [-са́ть] (Д/В); относи́ть [от-

нести́] (к Д); **2.** ['ætribju:t] сво́йство, при́знак; *gr.* определе́ние.
attune [ə'tju:n] приводи́ть в созву́чие.
auction ['ɔ:kʃən] **1.** аукцио́н, торги́ *m/pl.*; sell by ~, put up for ~ продава́ть с аукцио́на; **2.** продава́ть с аукцио́на (*mst* ~ off); **~eer** [ɔ:kʃə'niə] аукциони́ст.
audaci|ous [ɔ:'deiʃəs] □ сме́лый; де́рзкий; *b. s.* на́глый; **~ty** [ɔ:'dæsiti] сме́лость *f*; де́рзость *f*; *b.s.* на́глость *f*.
audible ['ɔ:debl] □ вня́тный, слы́шный.
audience ['ɔ:djəns] слу́шатели *m/pl.*, зри́тели *m/pl.*, пу́блика; аудие́нция (of, with у Р).
audit ['ɔ:dit] **1.** прове́рка, реви́зия (бухга́лтерских книг); **2.** проверя́ть [-е́рить] (отчётность); **~or** ['ɔ:ditə] слу́шатель *m*; ревизо́р, (фина́нсовый) контролёр.
auger ['ɔ:gə] ⊕ сверло́, бура́в.
augment [ɔ:g'ment] увели́чи(ва)ть; **~ation** [ɔ:gmen'teiʃən] увеличе́ние, приро́ст, приращéние.
augur ['ɔ:gə] **1.** авгу́р, прорица́тель *m*; **2.** предска́зывать [-за́ть] (well хоро́шее, ill плохо́е); **~y** предзнаменова́ние.
August ['ɔ:gəst] а́вгуст.
aunt [ɑ:nt] тётя, тётка.
auspic|e ['ɔ:spis] до́брое предзнаменова́ние; ~s *pl.* покрови́тельство; **~ious** [ɔ:s'piʃəs] □ благоприя́тный.
auster|e [ɔ:s'tiə] □ стро́гий, суро́вый; **~ity** [ɔ:s'teriti] стро́гость *f*, суро́вость *f*.
Australian [ɔ:s'treiljən] **1.** австрали́ец (-и́йка); **2.** австрали́йский.
Austrian ['ɔ:striən] **1.** австри́ец (-и́йка); **2.** австри́йский.
authentic [ɔ:'θentik] (~ally) по́длинный, достове́рный.
author ['ɔ:θə] а́втор; **~itative** [ɔ:'θɔriteitiv] □ авторите́тный; **~ity** [ɔ:'θɔriti] авторите́т; полномо́чие; власть *f* (over над Т); on the ~ of на основа́нии (Р); по утвержде́нию (Р); **~ize** ['ɔ:θəraiz] уполномо́чи(ва)ть; санкциони́ровать (*im*)*pf*.
autocar ['ɔ:təkɑ:] автомоби́ль *m*.
autocra|cy [ɔ:'tɔkrəsi] самодержа́вие, автокра́тия; **~tic(al** □) [ɔ:tə'krætik(əl)] самодержа́вный; деспоти́ческий.
autogyro ['ɔ:tou'dʒaiərou] ✈ автожи́р.
autograph ['ɔ:təgrɑ:f] авто́граф.
automat|ic [ɔ:tə'mætik] (~ally) автомати́ческий; ~ machine автома́т; **~on** [ɔ:'tɔmətən] автома́т.
automobile ['ɔtəməbi:l] *part. Am.* автомоби́ль *m*.
autonomy [ɔ:'tɔnəmi] автоно́мия, самоуправле́ние.

autumn ['ɔ:təm] о́сень *f*; ... [ɔ:'tʌmnəl] осе́нний.
auxiliary [ɔ:g'ziljəri] вспомо...тельный; доба́вочный.
avail [ə'veil] **1.** помога́ть [помо́...] (Д); ~ o. s. of [вос]по́льзоват... (Т); **2.** по́льза, вы́года; of no... бесполе́зный; **~able** [ə'veiləbl] досту́пный; нали́чный.
avalanche ['ævəlɑ:nʃ] лави́на.
avaric|e ['ævəris] ску́пость *f*; жа...ность *f*; **~ious** [ævə'riʃəs] □ ск...по́й; жа́дный.
aveng|e [ə'vendʒ] [ото]мсти́ть ... за В); **~er** [-ə] мсти́тель(ница *f*).
avenue ['ævinju:] алле́я; *Am.* ш...ро́кая у́лица, проспе́кт; *fig.* п... *m.*
aver [ə'və:] утвержда́ть.
average ['ævəridʒ] **1.** сре́д... число́; at an ~ в сре́днем; **2.** ср...ний; **3.** выводи́ть сре́днее числ...
avers|e [ə'və:s] □ нерасполо́ж...ный (to, from к Д); неохо́тны... **~ion** отвраще́ние, антипа́тия.
avert [ə'və:t] отвраща́ть [-рати́ть]
aviat|ion [eivi'eiʃən] авиа́ция; ~... ['eivietə] лётчик, авиа́тор.
avoid [ə'vɔid] избега́ть [-ежа́...] (Р); **~ance** [-əns] избежа́ние.
avow [ə'vau] призн(ав)а́ть; ~ ones... призн(ав)а́ться; **~al** [-əl] призн...ние.
await [ə'weit] ожида́ть (Р).
awake [ə'weik] **1.** бо́дрствующ...; be ~ to я́сно понима́ть; **2.** [*irr.*] ... (*mst* **~n** [ə'weikən]) [раз]буди́... пробужда́ть [-уди́ть] (созна́н... интере́с) (к Д); *v/i.* просыпа́ть... [просну́ться]; ~ to a th. осозн... в)а́ть (В).
aware [ə'wɛə]: be ~ of знать (В... о П), созн(ав)а́ть (В); become ~ отдава́ть себе́ отчёт в (П).
away [ə'wei] прочь; далеко́.
awe [ɔ:] **1.** благогове́ние, тре́пет ... пе́ред Т); **2.** внуша́ть благо...ве́ние, страх (Д).
awful [ɔ:ful] □ внуша́ющий бла...гове́ние; стра́шный; F ужа́сны... чрезвыча́йный.
awhile [ə'wail] на не́которое вре́м... ненадо́лго.
awkward ['ɔ:kwəd] неуклю́ж... нело́вкий; неудо́бный.
awl [ɔ:l] ши́ло.
awning ['ɔ:niŋ] наве́с, тент.
awoke [ə'wouk] *pt.* и *p. pt.* ... awake.
awry [ə'rai] ко́со, на́бок; *fig.* ... пра́вильно.
ax(e) [æks] топо́р, колу́н.
axis ['æksis], *pl.* axes [-si:z] ось *f*
axle ['æksl] ⊕ ось *f*; ~-tree кол... ный вал.
ay(e) [ai] да; *parl.* утверди́тельн... го́лос (при голосова́нии).
azure ['æʒə] **1.** лазу́рь *f*; **2.** лазу...ный.

B

ble ['bæbl] 1. лéпет; болтовня́; [по]болта́ть; [за]лепета́ть.
oon [bə'bu:n] *zo.* бабуи́н.
y ['beibi] 1. младéнец, ребёнок, тя́ *n*; 2. небольшо́й, ма́лый;
ood ['beibihud] младéнчество.
helor ['bætʃələ] холостя́к; *univ.* калáвр.
k [bæk] 1. спина́; спи́нка у́ла, пла́тья и т. п.); изна́нка тéрии); *football* защи́тник; 2. за́дний; обра́тный; отда- нный; 3. *adv.* наза́д, обра́тно; му́ наза́д; 4. *v/t.* поддéрживать ка́ть]; подкрепля́ть [-епи́ть];]пя́тить; держа́ть пари́ на (В),]ста́вить на (ло́шадь); † индос- ровать; *v/i.* отступа́ть [-пи́ть];]пя́титься; ~bone позвоно́ч- к, спинно́й хребéт; *fig.* опо́ра;
r ['bækə] † индосса́нт; ~- ound за́дний план, фон; ~ing ддéржка; † индоссамéнт; ~side няя, ты́льная сторона́; зад;
ide [*irr.* (slide)] отпада́ть [от- сть] (от вéры); ~stairs чёрная стница; ~stroke пла́вание на инé; ~-talk *Am.* дéрзкий отвéт;
ard ['bækwəd] 1. *adj.* обра́т- й; *fig.* отста́лый; 2. *adv.* (*a.* ~- rds [-z]) наза́д; за́дом; наобо- т; обра́тно; ~water за́водь *f*;
heel за́днее колесо́.
on ['beikən] бекóн, копчёная уди́нка.
teri|ologist [bæktiəri'ɔlədʒist] ктерио́лог; ~um [bæk'tiəriəm], ~a [-riə] бактéрия.
[bæd] □ плохо́й, дурно́й, вéрный; he is ~ly off его́ дела́ о́хи́; ~ly wounded тяжелора́- ный; F want ~ly о́чень хотéть.
le [beid, bæd] *pt.* от bid.
ge [bædʒ] значо́к.
ger ['bædʒə] 1. *zo.* барсу́к; [за]трави́ть; изводи́ть [из- сти́].
ness ['bædnis] него́дность *f*; éдность *f*.
fle ['bæfl] расстра́ивать [-ро́ить]; ива́ть с то́лку.
[bæg] 1. мешо́к; су́мка; класть в мешо́к; *hunt.* уби́- á)ть.
gage ['bægidʒ] бага́ж; ~-check *n.* бага́жная квита́нция.
gpipe ['bægpaip] волы́нка.
l [beil] 1. поруча́тельство; mit to ~ ⚖ выпуска́ть на по- ки; 2. ~ out ⚖ брать на пору́ки.
liff ['beilif] судéбный при́став; равля́ющий (имéнием).
t [beit] 1. прима́нка, нажи́вка; искушéние; 2. прима́нивать и́ть]; *hunt.* трави́ть соба́ками; *fig.* преслéдовать насмéшками, изводи́ть [-вести́].
bak|e [beik] [ис]пéчь(ся); обжи- га́ть [обжéчь] (кирпичи́); ~er ['beikə] пéкарь *m*, бу́лочник; ~ery [-ri] пека́рня; ~ing-powder пе- ка́рный порошо́к.
balance ['bæləns] 1. весы́ *m/pl.*; равновéсие; противовéс; балан- си́р; † бала́нс; са́льдо *n indecl.*; *sl.* оста́ток; ~ of power полити́ческое равновéсие; ~ of trade акти́вный бала́нс; 2. [с]баланси́ровать (В); сохраня́ть равновéсие; † подво- ди́ть бала́нс; взвéшивать [-éсить] (в умé); быть в равновéсии.
balcony ['bælkəni] балко́н.
bald [bɔ:ld] лы́сый, плеши́вый; *fig.* просто́й; бесцвéтный (стиль).
bale [beil] † ки́па, тюк.
balk [bɔ:k] 1. межа́; брус; ба́лка; 2. *v/t.* [вос]препя́тствовать (Д), [по]меша́ть (Д); [за]арта́читься (*a. fig.*).
ball[1] [bɔ:l] 1. мяч; шар; клубо́к (шéрсти); keep the ~ rolling под- дéрживать разгово́р; 2. соби- ра́ть(ся) в клубо́к; сви́(ва́)ть(ся).
ball[2] [~] бал, танцева́льный вéчер.
ballad ['bæləd] балла́да.
ballast ['bæləst] 1. щéбень *m*; 🚂, ⚓ балла́ст; 2. грузи́ть балла́стом.
ball-bearing(s *pl.*) шарикопод- ши́пник.
ballet ['bælei] балéт.
balloon [bə'lu:n] возду́шный шар, аэроста́т; ~ist [-ist] аэрона́вт, пи- ло́т аэроста́та.
ballot ['bælət] 1. баллотиро́вка, голосова́ние; 2. [про]голосова́ть; ~-box избира́тельная у́рна.
ball-point (*a.* ~ pen) ша́риковая ру́чка.
ball-room ба́льный зал.
balm [bɑ:m] бальза́м; *fig.* уте- шéние.
balmy [bɑ:mi] □ арома́тный.
baloney [bə'louni] *Am. sl.* вздор.
balsam ['bɔ:lsəm] бальза́м; ✿ бальзами́н.
balustrade [bæləstreid] балю- стра́да.
bamboo [bæm'bu:] бамбу́к.
bamboozle F [-zl] наду́(ва́)ть, об- ма́нывать [-ну́ть].
ban [bæn] 1. запрещéние, запрéт; 2. налага́ть запрещéние на (В).
banana [bə'nɑ:nə] бана́н.
band [bænd] 1. лéнта, тесьма́; о́бод; ба́нда; отря́д; ♪ оркéстр; 2. свя́зывать [-за́ть]; ~ o. s. объ- единя́ться [-ни́ться].
bandage ['bændidʒ] 1. бинт, бан- да́ж; 2. [за]бинтова́ть, перевя́зы- вать [-за́ть].
bandbox ['bændbɔks] карто́нка (для шляп).

bandit ['bændit] банди́т.
band-master ['bændmɑ:stə] капельме́йстер.
bandy ['bændi] обме́ниваться [-ня́ться] (слова́ми, мячо́м и т. п.).
bane [bein] *fig.* отра́ва.
bang [bæŋ] **1.** уда́р, стук; **2.** ударя́ть(ся) [уда́рить(ся)]; сту́кать(ся) [-кнуть(ся)].
banish ['bæniʃ] изгоня́ть [изгна́ть]; высыла́ть [вы́слать]; **~ment** [-mənt] изгна́ние.
banisters ['bænistəz] *pl.* пери́ла *n/pl.*
bank [bæŋk] **1.** бе́рег; на́сыпь *f*; банк; ~ of issue эмиссио́нный банк; **2.** *v/t.* окружа́ть ва́лом; запру́живать [-уди́ть]; ✝ класть (де́ньги) в банк; *v/i.* быть банки́ром; ✈ де́лать вира́ж, накреня́ться [-ни́ться]; ~ on полага́ться [-ложи́ться] на (В); **~er** ['bæŋkə] банки́р; **~ing** ['bæŋkiŋ] ба́нковое де́ло; **~rupt** ['bæŋkrʌpt] **1.** банкро́т; **2.** обанкро́тившийся; **3.** де́лать банкро́том; **~ruptcy** ['bæŋkrʌptsi] банкро́тство.
banner ['bænə] зна́мя *n*, стяг.
banns [bænz] *pl.* оглаше́ние (вступа́ющих в брак).
banquet ['bæŋkwit] **1.** банке́т, пир; **2.** дава́ть банке́т; пирова́ть.
banter ['bæntə] подшу́чивать [-ути́ть], поддра́знивать [-ни́ть].
baptism [bæp'tizm] креще́ние.
baptize [bæp'taiz] [о]крести́ть.
bar [bɑ:] **1.** брусо́к; засо́в; о́тмель *f*; бар; сто́йка; ♪ такт; *fig.* прегра́да, препя́тствие; ⚖ адвокату́ра; **2.** запира́ть на засо́в; прегражда́ть [-ради́ть]; исключа́ть [-чи́ть].
barb [bɑ:b] колю́чка; зубе́ц; **~ed** wire колю́чая про́волока.
barbar|ian [bɑ:'bɛəriən] **1.** ва́рвар; **2.** ва́рварский; **~ous** ['bɑ:bərəs] □ ди́кий; гру́бый, жесто́кий.
barbecue ['bɑ:bikju:] **1.** целико́м жа́рить (ту́шу); **2.** целико́м зажа́ренная ту́ша.
barber ['bɑ:bə] парикма́хер.
bare [bɛə] **1.** го́лый, обнажённый; пусто́й; **2.** обнажа́ть [-жи́ть], откры́(ва́)ть; **~faced** ['bɛəfeist] □ бессты́дный; **~-foot** босико́м; **~-footed** босо́й; **~-headed** с непокры́той голово́й; **~ly** ['bɛəli] едва́.
bargain ['bɑ:gin] **1.** сде́лка, вы́годная поку́пка; **2.** [по]торгова́ться (о П, с Т).
barge [bɑ:dʒ] ба́ржа; **~man** ['bɑ:dʒmən] ло́дочник с ба́ржи.
bark[1] [bɑ:k] **1.** кора́; **2.** сдира́ть кору́ с (Р).
bark[2] [~] **1.** лай; **2.** [за]ла́ять.
bar-keeper буфе́тчик.
barley ['bɑ:li] ячме́нь *m.*
barn [bɑ:n] амба́р.
baron ['bærən] баро́н; **~ess** бароне́сса. [каза́р...
barrack(s *pl.*) ['bærək(s)] бар...
barrage ['bærɑ:ʒ] загражде́ние; заградительный ого́нь *m.*
barrel ['bærəl] **1.** бо́чка, бочо́н...; ствол (ружья́); ⊕ цили́ндр; ба...ба́н; вал; **2.** разлива́ть по бо́ч...
barren ['bærən] □ неплодор...ный, беспло́дный.
barricade [bæri'keid] **1.** барр...да; **2.** [за]баррикади́ровать.
barrier ['bæriə] барье́р, заст...препя́тствие, поме́ха.
barrister ['bæristə] адвока́т.
barrow ['bærou] та́чка.
barter ['bɑ:tə] **1.** товарообм...менова́я торго́вля; **2.** [по]мен...обме́нивать [-ня́ть] (for на В).
base[1] [beis] □ по́длый, ни́зк...
base[2] [~] **1.** осно́ва, ба́зис, фун...мент; ⚗ основа́ние; **2.** осно́...вать [-ова́ть] (В на П), ба...рова́ть.
base|-ball *Am.* бейсбо́л; **~...** ['beislis] без основа́ний; **~m...** [-mənt] подва́л, подва́льный эт...
baseness ['beisnis] ни́зость *f.*
bashful ['bæʃful] □ засте́нчив...ро́бкий.
basic ['beisik] (**~ally**) основно́й; осно́вный.
basin [beisn] таз, ми́ска; бассе́...
bas|is ['beisis], *pl.* **~es** [-i:z] ос...ва́ние, исхо́дный пункт; ⚔, ба́за.
bask [bɑ:sk] гре́ться (на со́лнце...
basket ['bɑ:skit] корзи́на; **~-...** баскетбо́л.
bass [beis] ♪ **1.** бас; **2.** басо́вый
basso ['bæsou] ♪ бас.
bastard ['bæstəd] **1.** □ внебр...ный; подде́льный; ло́маный ...языке́); **2.** внебра́чный ребён...
baste[1] [beist] полива́ть жарко́е ...ком (во вре́мя жа́рения).
baste[2] [~] намётывать [намета́...
bat[1] [bæt] летучая мышь *f.*
bat[2] [~] **1.** бита́ (в крике́те); **2.** б...ударя́ть в мяч.
bath [bɑ:θ] **1.** ва́нна; купа́ль...**2.** [вы́-, по]мы́ть, [вы́]купа́ть.
bathe [beið] [вы́]купа́ться.
bathing ['beiðiŋ] купа́ние; **~-...** каби́на; **~-suit** купа́льный кост...
bath|-room ва́нная ко́мна...; **~-sheet** купа́льная просты...; **~-towel** купа́льное полоте́нце.
batiste [bæ'ti:st] ✝ бати́ст.
baton ['bætən] жезл; дирижёрс...па́лочка; полице́йская дуби́н...
battalion [bə'tæljən] батальо́н.
batter ['bætə] **1.** взби́тое те́с...**2.** си́льно бить, [по]колоти́ть, [...дуба́сить; ~ down и́ли in взла́м...вать [взлома́ть]; **~y** [-ri] батар...assault and ~ оскорбле́ние де́й...вием.
battle ['bætl] **1.** би́тва, сраже́...

of под T); **2.** сражáться [сразúть-я]; борóться; **~-ax(e)** *hist.* боевóй опóр; *Am. fig.* бой-бáба.
ttle|-field пóле бúтвы; **~-plane** ; штурмовúк; **~-ship** ⚔ линéй-ый корáбль *m.*
wdy ['bɔ:di] непристóйный.
wl [bɔ:l] кричáть [крúкнуть], а]орáть; ~ out выкрúкивать [вы́-рикнуть].
y¹ [bei] **1.** гнедóй; **2.** гнедáя лó-шадь *f.*
y² [~] залúв, бýхта.
y³ [~] лáвровое дéрево.
y⁴ [~] **1.** лай; **2.** [за]лáять; bring ~ *fig.* приперéть к стенé; заго-ять [загнáть] (звéря).
yonet ['beiənit] ⚔ **1.** штык; **2.** олóть штыкóм.
y-window ['bei'windou] ⌂ э́р-ер; *Am.* брюшкó.
za(a)r [bə'zɑ:] базáр.
[bi:, bi] [*irr.*]: a) быть, бывáть; ить; находúться; поживáть, ýвствовать себя́; there is, are сть; ~ about соб(и)рáться (+ *inf.*); at s. th. быть зáнятым (T); ~ off правля́ться [-áвиться]; ~ on ыть в дéйствии; b) *v/aux.* (для бразовáния длúтельной фóрмы): reading читáть; c) *v/aux.* (для бразовáния пассúва): ~ read итáться, быть чúтанным (чи-емым).
ach [bi:tʃ] **1.** пляж, взмóрье; ⚓ вы́тащить на бéрег; посадúть мель.
acon ['bi:kən] сигнáльный огóнь ; бáкен; буй.
ad [bi:d] бýсина, бúсерина; áпля; **~s** *pl. a.* чётки *f/pl.*; бýсы *pl.*; бúсер.
ak [bi:k] клюв; нóсик (сосýда).
am [bi:m] **1.** бáлка, брус; луч; сия́ть; излучáть [-чúть].
an [bi:n] боб.
ar¹ [bεə] медвéдь *m* (-вéдица *f*); *sl.* спекуля́нт, игрáющий на онижéние.
ar² [~] [*irr.*] *v/t.* носúть [нестú]; ы]терпéть, выдéрживать [вы́-ержать]; рождáть [родúть]; ~ own преодолé(вá)ть; ~ out под-верждáть [-рдúть]; ~ o. s. дер-áться, вестú себя́; ~ up поддéр-ивать [-жáть]; ~ (up)on касáться оснýться] (P); имéть отношéние (Д); bring to ~ употребля́ть бúть].
ard [biəd] **1.** бородá; зубéц; ⚘ сть *f* (кóлоса); **2.** *v/t.* смéло вы-упáть прóтив (P).
arer ['bεərə] носúльщик; по-тель(ница *f*) *m*, предъявúтель ница *f*) *m*.
aring ['bεəriŋ] ношéние; тер-ние; манéра держáть себя́; де-рождéние.
ast [bi:st] зверь *m*; скотúна; **~ly** i] грýбый, ужáсный.

beat [bi:t] **1.** [*irr.*] *v/t.* [по]бúть; ударя́ть [ударúть]; [по]колотúть; ~ a retreat отступáть [-пúть]; ~ up избú(вá)ть; взбú(вá)ть; ~ about the bush подходúть к дéлу издалекá; *v/i.* бить; бúться; [по]стучáться; **2.** удáр; бой; биéние; ритм; **~en** [bi:tn] **1.** *p. pt.* от beat; **2.** бúтый, побеждённый; проторённый (путь).
beatitude [bi'ætitju:d] блажéнство.
beau [bou] щёголь *m*; кавалéр.
beautiful ['bju:tiful] □ прекрáс-ный, красúвый.
beautify ['bju:tifai] украшáть [укрáсить].
beauty ['bju:ti] красотá; красáвица.
beaver ['bi:və] бобр.
became [bi'keim *pt.* от become.
because [bi'kɔz] потомý что, тáк как; ~ of из-за (P).
beckon ['bekən] [по]манúть.
becom|e [bi'kʌm] [*irr.* (come)] *v/i.* [с]дéлаться; становúться [стать]; *v/t.* быть к лицý, идтú (об одéжде) (Д); подобáть (Д); **~ing** [-iŋ] □ к лицý (одéжда).
bed bed] **1.** постéль *f*; кровáть *f*; ✓ гря́дка, клýмба; **2.** класть úли ложúться в постéль; высáжи-вать [вы́садить] (цветы́).
bed-clothes *pl.* постéльное бельё.
bedding ['bediŋ] постéльные при-надлéжности *f/pl.*
bedevil [bi'devl] [ис]терзáть, [из-]мýчить; околдóвывать [-довáть].
bed|rid(den) прикóванный к по-стéли (болéзнью); **~room** спáль-ня; **~spread** покрывáло (на кро-вáть); **~stead** кровáть *f*; **~time** врéмя ложúться спать.
bee [bi:] пчелá; have a ~ in one's bonnet F быть с причýдой.
beech [bi:tʃ] ⚘ бук, бýковое дéре-во; **~nut** бýковый орéшек.
beef [bi:f] говя́дина; **~-tea** крéп-кий бульóн; **~y** [bi:fi] мýскули-стый; мясúстый.
bee|hive ýлей; **~-line** прямáя лúния.
been [bi:n, bin] *p. pt.* от be.
beer [biə] пúво; small ~ слáбое пúво.
beet [bit] ⚘ свёкла.
beetle [bi:tl] жук.
befall [bi'fɔ:l] [*irr.* (fall)] *v/t.* по-стигáть [-úгнуть, -úчь] (о судьбé) (B); *v/i.* случáться [-чúться].
befit [bi'fit] прилúчествовать (Д), подходúть [подойтú] (Д).
before [bi'fɔ:] **1.** *adv.* вперéдú, вперёд; рáньше; long ~ задóлго; **2.** *cj.* прéжде чем; скорéе чем; **3.** *prp.* пéред (T); впередú (P); до (P); **~hand** зарáнее, заблаго-врéменно.
befriend [bi'frend] относúться по-дрýжески к (Д).
beg [beg] *v/t.* [по]просúть (P);

умоля́ть [-ли́ть] (for о П); выпра́шивать [вы́просить] (of у Р); *v/i.* ни́щенствовать.
began [bi'gæn] *pt.* от begin.
beget [bi'get] [*irr.* (get)] рожда́ть [роди́ть], производи́ть [-вести́].
beggar ['begə] **1.** ни́щий, ни́щенка; **2.** разоря́ть [-ри́ть], доводи́ть до нищеты́; *fig.* превосходи́ть [-взойти́]; it **~s** all description не поддаётся описа́нию.
begin [bi'gin] [*irr.*] нач(ин)а́ть (with с Р); **~ner** [-ə] начина́ющий, новичо́к; **~ning** [-iŋ] нача́ло.
begot(ten) [bi'gɔt(n)] *pt.* от beget.
begrudge [bi'grʌdʒ] [по]зави́довать (Д в П).
beguile [bi'gail] обма́нывать [-ну́ть]; [с]корота́ть (вре́мя).
begun [bi'gʌn] *pt.* от begin.
behalf [bi'hɑ:f] : on *or* in ~ of для (Р), ра́ди (Р); от и́мени (Р).
behav|e [bi'heiv] вести́ себя́; поступа́ть [-пи́ть]; **~iour** [-jə] поведе́ние.
behead [bi'hed] обезгла́вливать [-гла́вить].
behind [bi'haind] **1.** *adv.* по́сле; позади́, сза́ди; **2.** *prp.* за (Т); позади́ (Р), сза́ди (Р); по́сле (Р).
behold [bi'hould] [*irr.* (hold)] **1.** замеча́ть [-е́тить], [у]ви́деть; **2.** смотри́!, вот!
behoof [bi'hu:f]: to (for, on) (the) ~ of в по́льзу (Р), за (В).
being ['bi:iŋ] бытие́, существова́ние.
belated [bi'leitid] запозда́лый.
belch [beltʃ] **1.** отры́жка; столб (огня́, ды́ма); **2.** рыга́ть [рыгну́ть]; изверга́ть [-е́ргнуть].
belfry ['belfri] колоко́льня.
Belgian ['beldʒən] **1.** бельги́ец (-и́йка); **2.** бельги́йский.
belief [bi'li:f] ве́ра (in в В); убежде́ние.
believable [bi'li:vəbl] правдоподо́бный.
believe [bi'li:v] [по]ве́рить (in в В); **~r** [-ə] ве́рующий.
belittle [bi'litl] *fig.* умаля́ть [-ли́ть]; принижа́ть [-ни́зить].
bell [bel] ко́локол; звоно́к.
belle [bel] краса́вица.
belles-lettres ['be'letr] *pl.* худо́жественная литерату́ра, беллетри́стика.
belligerent [bi'lidʒərənt] **1.** вою́ющая сторона́; **2.** вою́ющий.
bellow ['belou] **1.** мыча́ние; рёв (бу́ри); **2.** [за]мыча́ть; [за]реве́ть, [за]бушева́ть; **~s** [-z] *pl.* кузне́чные мехи́ *m/pl.*
belly ['beli] **1.** живо́т, брю́хо; **2.** наду́(ва́)ть(ся).
belong [bi'lɔŋ] принадлежа́ть (Д); относи́ться (к Д); **~ings** [-iŋz] *pl.* принадле́жности *f/pl.*; пожи́тки *m/pl.*
beloved [bi'lʌvid, *pred.* bi'lʌ… возлю́бленный, люби́мый.
below [bi'lou] **1.** *adv.* внизу́; ни́ж… **2.** *prp.* ни́же (Р); под (В, Т).
belt [belt] **1.** по́яс; зо́на; ⊕ прив… но́й реме́нь *m*; ⚔ портупе́я; подпоя́с(ыв)ать; поро́ть ремн…
bemoan [bi'moun] опла́к(ив)а…
bench [bentʃ] скамья́; ⊕ верст…
bend [bend] **1.** сгиб; изги́б (… ро́ги); излу́чина (реки́); ⚓ у́з… шпанго́ут; **2.** [*irr.*] сгиба́ть(… [согну́ть(ся)]; направля́ть [-… вить]; покоря́ть [-ри́ть].
beneath [bi'ni:θ] *s.* below.
benediction [beni'dikʃən] бла… слове́ние.
benefact|ion [-'fækʃən] благоде… ние; **~or** ['benifæktə] благоде́т… *m.*
beneficе|nce [bi'nefisns] бла… твори́тельность *f*; **~nt** □ благо… тельный.
beneficial [beni'fiʃə] □ благотв… ный, поле́зный.
benefit ['benifit] **1.** вы́года, по́… за; посо́бие; *thea.* бенефи́с; **2.** п… носи́ть по́льзу; извлека́ть по́ль…
benevolen|ce [bi'nevələns] бла… жела́тельность *f*; **~t** [-ənt] благожела́тельный.
benign [bi'nain] □ до́брый, ми́… стивый; ⚕ доброка́чественный
bent [bent] **1.** *pt.* и *p. pt.* от be… ~ on поме́шанный на (П); скло́нность *f.*
benz|ene [ben'zi:n] ⚗ бензо́л; ~… [~] бензи́н.
bequeath [bi'kwi:ð] завещ… *(im)pf.*
bequest [bi'kwest] насле́дство.
bereave [bi'ri:v] [*irr.*] лиш… [-ши́ть] (Р); отнима́ть [-ня́ть].
berry ['beri] я́года.
berth [bə:θ] ⚓ яко́рная стоя́н… ко́йка; *fig.* (вы́годная) до́лжно… *f.*
beseech [bi'si:tʃ] [*irr.*] умол… [-ли́ть], упра́шивать [упроси́… (+ *inf.*).
beset [bi'set] [*irr.* (set)] окруж… [-жи́ть]; осажда́ть [осади́ть].
beside [bi'said] *prp.* ря́дом с (… о́коло (Р), близ (Р); ми́мо (… ~ o. s. вне себя́ (with от Р); ~ … question некста́ти, не по существ… **~s** [-z] **1.** *adv.* кро́ме того́, св… того́; **2.** *prp.* кро́ме (Р).
besiege [bi'si:dʒ] осажда́ть [о… ди́ть].
besmear [bi'smiə] [за]па́чкать, [… мара́ть.
besom ['bi:zəm] метла́, ве́ник.
besought [bi'sɔ:t] *pt.* от beseech.
bespatter [bi'spætə] забры́зг… в)ать.
bespeak [bi'spi:k] [*irr.* (spea… зака́зывать [-за́ть]; bespoke ta… портно́й, рабо́тающий по зака́…

t [best] **1.** *adj.* лучший; ~ man ıфер; **2.** *adv.* лучше всего́, всех; са́мое лу́чшее; to the ~ of ... на- ɔлько ...; по ме́ре ...; make the ıf испо́льзовать наилу́чшим об- зом; at ~ в лу́чшем слу́чае.
tial ['bestjəl] □ ско́тский, жи- тный.
tow [bi'stou] дарова́ть ([up]on В *or* В/Т), награжда́ть [-ра- ть].
[bet] **1.** пари́ *n indecl.*; **2.** [*irr.*] ɔжа́ть пари́; би́ться об закла́д.
ake [bi'teik] [*irr.* (take)]: ~ o. s. отправля́ться [-а́виться] в (В); прибега́ть [-е́гнуть] к (Д).
hink [bi'θiŋk] [*irr.* (think)]: ~ s. вспомина́ть [вспо́мнить]; ду́- ть (of о П); ~ o. s. to *inf.* заду́- ıв)ать.
ray [bi'trei] преда́(ва́)ть; вы́- (ва́)ть; **~er** [-ə] преда́тель(ница *m.*
rothal [bi'trouðəl] помо́лвка, ɔруче́ние.
ter ['betə] **1.** *adj.* лу́чший; he is ɛму́ лу́чше; **2.** преиму́щество; *pl.* лица стоя́щие вы́ше; get ~ of взять верх над (Т); **3.** *v.* лу́чше; бо́льше; so much the тем лу́чше; you had ~ go вам бы чше пойти́; **4.** *v/t.* улучша́ть лу́чшить]; поправля́ть [-а́вить]; . поправля́ться [-а́виться];
nent [-mənt] улучше́ние.
ween [bi'twi:n] **1.** *adv.* ме́жду ıми; **2.** *prp.* ме́жду (Т).
erage ['bevəridʒ] напи́ток.
y ['bevi] стая (птиц); ста́до; у́ппа, толпа́ (де́вушек).
vail [bi'weil] скорбе́ть о (П), лáк(ив)ать.
vare [bi'wɛə] оберега́ться ре́чься] (Р).
vilder [bi'wildə] смуща́ть [сму- ть]; ста́вить в тупи́к; сбива́ть то́лку; **~ment** [-mənt] смуще́- ɛ, замеша́тельство; пу́таница.
vitch [bi'witʃ] околдо́вывать цова́ть]; очаро́вывать [-рова́ть].
ond [bi'jɔnd] **1.** *adv.* вдали́, на сстоя́нии; **2.** *prp.* за (В, Т); вне); сверх (Р); по ту сто́рону (Р).
s ['baiəs] предубежде́ние (про́- в Р); склон, укло́н; **2.** склоня́ть ни́ть]; **3.** ко́со.
[bib] де́тский нагру́дник.
le [baibl] би́блия.
lical ['biblikəl] □ библе́йский.
arbonate [bai'kɑ:bənit] ⚗: ~ of da двууглеки́слый на́трий.
ker ['bikə] пререка́ться (с Т).
ycle ['baisikl] **1.** велосипе́д; е́здить на велосипе́де.
[bid] **1.** [*irr.*] прика́зывать за́ть]; предлага́ть [-ложи́ть] е́ну); ~ fair [по]сули́ть, [по]обе- а́ть; ~ farewell [по]проща́ться рости́ться]; **2.** предложе́ние (цены́), зая́вка (на торга́х); *Am.* F приглаше́ние; **~den** [bidn] *p. pt.* от bid.
bide [baid] : ~ one's time ожида́ть благоприя́тного слу́чая.
biennial [bai'enjəl] двухле́тний.
bier [biə] похоро́нные дро́ги *f/pl.*
big [big] большо́й, кру́пный; взро́слый; F *fig.* ва́жный, ва́ж- ничающий; F *fig.* ~ shot ва́жная «ши́шка»; talk ~ [по]хва́статься.
bigamy ['bigəmi] бига́мия, двое- бра́чие.
bigot ['bigət] слепо́й приве́рже- нец; **~ry** [-ri] слепа́я приве́ржен- ность *f.*
bigwig ['bigwig] F ва́жная «ши́шка».
bike [baik] F велосипе́д.
bile [bail] жёлчь *f*; *fig.* раздражи́- тельность *f.*
bilious ['biljəs] □ жёлчный.
bill[1] [bil] клюв; носо́к я́коря.
bill[2] [~] **1.** законопрое́кт, билль *m*; счёт; афи́ша; ✝ ве́ксель *m*; ~ of fare меню́; ~ of lading коносаме́нт; ~ of sale ⚖ закладна́я; **2.** объ- явля́ть [-ви́ть] (афи́шей).
billfold бума́жник.
billiards ['biljədz] *pl.* билья́рд.
billion ['biljən] биллио́н; *Am.* мил- лиа́рд.
billow ['bilou] больша́я волна́; **2.** вздыма́ться (во́лна́ми), [вз]вол- нова́ться (о мо́ре); **~y** ['biloui] вздыма́ющийся (о во́лна́х).
bin [bin] за́кром; ларь *m;* му́сор- ное ведро́.
bind [baind] [*irr.*] **1.** *v/t.* [с]вяза́ть; свя́зывать [-за́ть]; обя́зывать [-за́ть]; переплета́ть [-плести́]; **2.** *v/i.* затверде́(ва́)ть; **~er** ['baində] переплётчик; **~ing** [-iŋ] **1.** пере- плёт; **2.** связу́ющий.
binocular [bai'nɔkjulə] бино́кль *m.*
biography [bai'ɔgrəfi] биогра́фия.
biology [bai'ɔlədʒi] биоло́гия.
birch [bə:tʃ] **1.** ⚘ (и́ли **~-tree**) бе- рёза, берёзовое де́рево; ро́зга; **2.** сечь ро́згой.
bird [bə:d] пти́ца; **~'s-eye** ['bə:d- zai]: ~ view вид с пти́чьего полёта.
birth [bə:θ] рожде́ние; происхож- де́ние; bring to ~ порожда́ть [-ро- ди́ть]; **~day** день рожде́ния; **~-place** ме́сто рожде́ния.
biscuit ['biskit] пече́нье.
bishop ['biʃəp] епи́скоп; *chess* слон; **~ric** [-rik] епа́рхия.
bison ['baisn] *zo.* бизо́н, зубр.
bit [bit] **1.** кусо́чек, части́ца; не- мно́го; удила́ *n/pl.*; боро́дка (клю- ча́); **2.** *pt.* от **~e.**
bitch [bitʃ] су́ка.
bite [bait] **1.** уку́с; клёв (ры́бы); кусо́к; острота́; **2.** [*irr.*] куса́ть [укуси́ть]; клева́ть [клю́нуть] (о ры́бе); жечь (о пе́рце); щипа́ть (о моро́зе); ⊕ брать [взять]; *fig.* [съ]язви́ть.

bitten ['bitn] *pt.* от bite.
bitter ['bitə] □ го́рький; ре́зкий; *fig.* го́рький, мучи́тельный; **~s** *pl.* [-z] го́рький лека́рственный напи́ток.
blab [blæb] F разба́лтывать [-болта́ть].
black [blæk] **1.** □ чёрный; тёмный, мра́чный; **2.** [по]черни́ть; *fig.* [о]позо́рить; ~ out затемня́ть [-ни́ть]; **3.** чернота́; чёрный цвет; черноко́жий (негр); **~berry** ежеви́ка; **~bird** чёрный дрозд; **~board** кла́ссная доска́; **~en** ['blækn] *v/t.* [на]черни́ть; *fig.* [о]черни́ть; *v/i.* [по]черне́ть; **~-guard** ['blægɑ:d] **1.** негодя́й, подле́ц; **2.** □ по́длый; **~head** ⚕ угри́ *m/pl.*; **~ing** [blækiŋ] ва́кса; **~ish** ['blækiʃ] □ чернова́тый; **~leg** моше́нник; штрейкбре́хер; **~-letter** *typ.* стари́нный готи́ческий шрифт; **~mail 1.** вымога́тельство, шанта́ж; **2.** вымога́ть де́ньги у (Р); **~ness** [-nis] чернота́; **~out** затемне́ние; **~smith** кузне́ц.
bladder ['blædə] *anat.* пузы́рь *m.*
blade [bleid] ло́пасть *f; anat.* лопа́тка; ле́звие; клино́к; ⚘ лист; сте́бель *m,* были́нка.
blame [bleim] **1.** упрёк; вина́; порица́ние; **2.** порица́ть; обвиня́ть [-ни́ть]; be to ~ for быть винова́тым в (П); **~ful** ['bleimful] заслу́живающий порица́ния; **~less** ['bleimlis] □ безупре́чный.
blanch [blɑ:ntʃ] [вы́]бели́ть; [вы́-]чи́стить (мета́лл); ~ over обеля́ть [-ли́ть], опра́вдывать [-да́ть].
bland [blænd] □ ве́жливый; мя́гкий.
blank [blæŋk] **1.** □ пусто́й; бессодержа́тельный; невырази́тельный; ✝ незапо́лненный; ~ cartridge ⚔ холосто́й патро́н; **2.** бланк; пробе́л; пустота́ (душе́вная).
blanket [blæŋkit] **1.** шерстяно́е одея́ло; **2.** покрыва́ть одея́лом.
blare [blɛə] [за]труби́ть.
blasphem|e [blæs'fi:m] богоху́льствовать; поноси́ть (against В); **~y** ['blæsfimi] богоху́льство.
blast [blɑ:st] **1.** си́льный поры́в ве́тра; звук (духово́го инструме́нта); взрывна́я волна́; подрывно́й заря́д; ⚘ головня́; ⊕ дутьё; *fig.* па́губное влия́ние; **2.** взрыва́ть [взорва́ть]; проклина́ть [-кля́сть]; **~-furnace** ⊕ до́мна, до́менная печь *f.*
blaze [bleiz] **1.** я́ркое пла́мя *n;* вспы́шка (огня́, стра́сти); **2.** *v/i.* горе́ть; пыла́ть; сверка́ть [-кну́ть]; *v/t.* разглаша́ть [-гласи́ть]; **~r** ['bleizə] спорти́вная ку́ртка.
blazon ['bleizn] герб.
bleach [bli:tʃ] [вы́]бели́ть.
bleak [bli:k] □ го́лый, пусты́нный; суро́вый (по кли́мату).
blear [bliə] **1.** затума́ненный, нея́[сный]; **2.** затума́ни(ва)ть; **~-eye[d]** ['bliəraid] с затума́ненными глаз[а]ми.
bleat [bli:t] **1.** бле́яние; **2.** [за]бле́ять.
bleb [bleb] волды́рь *m;* пузыр[ёк] во́здуха (в воде́).
bled [bled] *pt.* и *p. pt.* от bleed.
bleed [bli:d] [*irr.*] **1.** *v/i.* кровото[чить]; истека́ть кро́вью; **2.** *v*[*/t.*] пуска́ть кровь (Д); **~ing** ['bli:di[ŋ]] кровотече́ние; кровопуска́ние.
blemish ['blemiʃ] **1.** недоста́то[к]; пятно́; позо́р; **2.** [за]пятна́[ть]; [ис]по́ртить; [о]позо́рить.
blench [blentʃ] отступа́ть [-пи́[ть]] (пе́ред Т).
blend [blend] **1.** сме́шивать(с[я]) [-ша́ть(ся)]; разбавля́ть [-ба́вит[ь]]; сочета́ть(ся) *(im)pf.*; **2.** сме́шив[а]ние; смесь *f.*
bless [bles] благословля́ть [-ви́т[ь]]; осчастли́вливать [-тли́вить]; ~ (*pt.* blest; *adj.* 'blesid) □ счастл[и]вый, блаже́нный; **~ing** ['bles[iŋ]] благослове́ние.
blew [blu:] *pt.* от blow², ³.
blight [blait] **1.** ⚘ ми́лдью *n inde[cl.]* (и други́е боле́зни расте́ний); *[f]* ги́бель *f;* **2.** приноси́ть вр[ед] (расте́ниям); разби́(ва́)ть (наде́[ж]ды и т. п.).
blind [blaind] □ **1.** слепо́й (*fig.* ~ к Д); нечёткий, нея́сный; ~ all[ey] тупи́к; **~ly** *fig.* науга́д, наобу́[м]; **2.** што́ра; марки́за; жалю[зи] *n indecl.;* **3.** ослепля́ть [-пи́ть]; [~-]**fold** ['blaindfould] завя́зыва[ть] глаза́ (Д).
blink [bliŋk] **1.** мерца́ние; морг[а]ние; миг; **2.** *v/i.* мига́ть [мигну́т[ь]], морга́ть [-гну́ть]; прищу́ри(ва)[ть]ся; *v/t.* закрыва́ть глаза́ на (В).
bliss [blis] блаже́нство.
blister ['blistə] **1.** волды́рь *m;* **2.** [по]крыва́ться пузыря́ми.
blizzard ['blizəd] бура́н, си́льн[ая] мете́ль *f.*
bloat [blout] распуха́ть [-пу́хнут[ь]], разду́(ва́)ться; **~er** ['bloutə] ко[п]чёная сельдь *f.*
block [blɔk] **1.** коло́да, чурба́[н]; пла́ха; глы́ба; кварта́л (го́род[а]); **2.** ~ in набра́сывать вчерне́; (*[a.]* ~ up) блоки́ровать *(im)pf.*
blockade [blɔ'keid] **1.** блока́[да]; **2.** блоки́ровать *(im)pf.*
blockhead ['blɔkhed] болва́н.
blond [blɔnd] **1.** белоку́рый; [2.] блонди́нка.
blood [blʌd] кровь *f;* in cold [~] хладнокро́вно; **~-horse** чист[о]кро́вная ло́шадь *f;* **~shed** кров[о]проли́тие; **~shot** нали́тый кро́в[ью] (о глаза́х); **~thirsty** кровожа́[д]ный; **~-vessel** кровено́сный [со]су́д; **~y** ['blʌdi] □ окрова́вле[н]ный; крова́вый.

m [blu:m] **1.** цветóк; цвете́
:; расцве́т (*a. fig.*); **2.** цвести́,
ть в цвету́.
som ['blɔsəm] **1.** цветóк (фрук-
ого де́рева); расцве́т; **2.** цве-
, расцвета́ть [-ести́].
[blɔt] **1.** пятно́, кля́кса; *fig.*
гно́; **2.** [за]па́чкать; промока́ть
ну́ть]; вычёркивать [вы́черк-
ь].
ch [blɔtʃ] прыщ; пятно́; кля́кса.
ter ['blɔtə] пресс-папье́
idecl.
ting-paper промока́тельная
ага.
se [blauz] блу́за; блу́зка.
[1] [blou] уда́р.
[2] [~] [*irr.*] **1.** цвести́; **2.** цвете́ние.
[3] [~] [*irr.*] **1.** [по]ду́ть; ве́ять;
пыхте́ть; игра́ть на (духо-
инструме́нте); ~ up взрыва́ть
) [взорва́ть(ся)]; разду́(ва́)ть
о́нь); гна́ть (ту́чи); ~ one's nose
]сморка́ться; **2.** дунове́ние; **~er**
ouə] труба́ч; **~n** [-n] *p. pt.* от
w[2,3]; **~-out** *mot.* разры́в ши́ны;
ipe пая́льная тру́бка.
lgeon ['blʌdʒən] дуби́на.
[blu:] **1.** □ голубо́й; лазу́р-
й; си́ний; F уны́лый, пода́в-
ный; **2.** си́няя кра́ска; си́ний
т; голуба́я кра́ска; си́нька; ~s
меланхо́лия, хандра́; **3.** окра́-
вать в си́ний, голубо́й цвет;
]сини́ть (бельё).
f [blʌf] **1.** □ ре́зкий; грубова́-
й; обры́вистый; **2.** обма́н, блеф;
апу́гивать [-га́ть]; обма́нывать
у́ть].
sh ['blu:iʃ] синева́тый, голубо-
ый.
der ['blʌndə] **1.** гру́бая оши́б-
2. де́лать гру́бую оши́бку.
t [blʌnt] **1.** □ тупо́й; ре́зкий;
притупля́ть [-пи́ть].
[blə:] **1.** нея́сное очерта́ние;
кса, пятно́; **2.** *v/t.* [за]мара́ть,
па́чкать, [за]пятна́ть (*a. fig.*);
затемня́ть [-ни́ть] (созна́ние).
h [blʌʃ] **1.** кра́ска стыда́; **2.**
покрасне́ть.
ter ['blʌstə] **1.** хвастовство́,
охва́льство; пусты́е угро́зы
.; **2.** грози́ться; [по]хва́статься.
[bɔ:] бо́ров; *hunt.* каба́н.
rd [bɔ:d] **1.** доска́; стол (пита́-
); ⚓ борт; сце́на, подмо́стки
l.; правле́ние; ♀ of Trade
инисте́рство торго́вли; *Am.* тор-
ая пала́та; **2.** *v/t.* наст(и)ла́ть
л); ⚓ брать на аборда́ж; *v/i.*
лова́ться; сади́ться [сесть] на
езд, кора́бль); **~er** [ˌbɔ:də] пан-
не́р(ка); **~ing-house** меблиро́-
нные ко́мнаты со столо́м.
t [boust] **1.** хвастовство́; **2.** (of,
ut) горди́ться (Т); [по]хва́-
ться (Т); **~ful** ['boustful] □
стли́вый.

boat [bout] ло́дка; су́дно; **~ing** ['boutiŋ] ката́ние на ло́дке.
bob [bɔb] **1.** ги́ря (ма́ятника); ры-во́к; ко́ротко подстри́женные во́лосы *m/pl.*; **2.** *v/t.* стри́чь ко́ротко; *v/i.* подпры́гивать [-гнуть].
bobbin ['bɔbin] кату́шка; шпу́лька.
bode [boud] предвеща́ть [-ести́ть], предска́зывать [-за́ть].
bodice ['bɔdis] лиф, ли́фчик.
bodily ['bɔdili] теле́сный.
body ['bɔdi] те́ло; труп; *mot.* ку́зов; ⚔ войскова́я часть *f.*
bog [bɔg] **1.** боло́то, тряси́на; **2.** be ~ed увя́за́ть [увя́знуть] (в тряси́не).
boggle ['bɔgl] [ис]пуга́ться (at P); неуме́ло рабо́тать.
bogus ['bougəs] подде́льный.
boil [bɔil] **1.** кипе́ние; фуру́нкул, нары́в; **2.** [с]вари́ть(ся); [вс]кипяти́ть(ся); кипе́ть; **~er** ['bɔilə] котёл; куб, бак (для кипяче́ния).
boisterous ['bɔistərəs] □ бу́рный, шу́мный.
bold [bould] □ сме́лый; самоуве́ренный; на́глый; *typ.* жи́рный, отчётливый (шрифт); **~ness** ['bouldnis] сме́лость *f*; на́глость *f.*
bolster ['boulstə] **1.** (дива́нный) ва́лик; поду́шка; **2.** подде́рживать [-жа́ть].
bolt [boult] **1.** болт; засо́в, задви́жка; мо́лния; **2.** *v/t.* запира́ть на засо́в; *v/i.* нести́сь стрело́й; убега́ть [убежа́ть]; понести́ *pf.* (о лошадя́х).
bomb [bɔm] **1.** бо́мба; **2.** бомби́ть.
bombard [bɔm'bɑ:d] бомбардирова́ть.
bombastic [bɔm'bæstik] напы́щенный.
bomb-proof непробива́емый бо́мбами.
bond [bɔnd] *pl.*: ~s у́зы *f/pl.*; око́вы *f/pl.*; ♱ долгово́е обяза́тельство; **~age** ['bɔndidʒ] ра́бство; зави́симость *f*; **~(s)man** ['bɔnd(z)-mən] раб.
bone [boun] **1.** кость *f*; ~ of contention я́блоко раздо́ра; make no ~s about F не церемо́ниться с (Т); **2.** вынима́ть, выреза́ть ко́сти.
bonfire ['bɔnfaiə] костёр.
bonnet ['bɔnit] че́пчик; ка́пор; шля́пка; *mot.* капо́т.
bonus ['bounəs] ♱ пре́мия; тантье́ма.
bony ['bouni] костля́вый; кости́стый.
booby ['bu:bi] болва́н, дура́к.
book [buk] **1.** кни́га; **2.** заноси́ть в кни́гу; регистри́ровать (*im*)*pf.*, *pf. a.* [за-]; зака́зывать и́ли брать (биле́т в теа́тр, на по́езд и т. п.); приглаша́ть [-ласи́ть] (арти́стов); **~-case** кни́жный шкаф; **~ing-clerk** ['bukiŋklɑ:k] касси́р; **~ing-office** биле́тная ка́сса; **~-keeping**

счетово́дство; **~let** ['buklit] брошю́ра; **~seller** книгопрода́вец; букини́ст.

boom[1] [bu:m] **1.** ✝ бум; **2.** производи́ть сенса́цию, шум вокруг (P).

boom[2] [~] **1.** гул; гуде́ние; **2.** [за-] гуде́ть; [за]жужжа́ть.

boon[1] [bu:n] благодея́ние.

boon[2] [~] благотво́рный; прия́тный.

boor [buə] гру́бый, невоспи́танный челове́к; **~ish** ['buəriʃ] □ гру́бый, невоспи́танный.

boost [bu:st] поднима́ть [-ня́ть] (торго́влю).

boot[1] [bu:t]: to ~ в прида́чу, вдоба́вок *adv.*

boot[2] [~] сапо́г.

booth [bu:ð] пала́тка; кио́ск.

bootlegger ['bu:tlegə] *Am.* торго́вец контраба́ндными напи́тками.

booty ['bu:ti] добы́ча; награ́бленное добро́.

border ['bɔ:də] **1.** грани́ца; край; кайма́ (на ска́терти и т. п.); **2.** грани́чить (upon с T); окаймля́ть [-ми́ть].

bore[1] [bɔ:] **1.** вы́сверленное отве́рстие; кали́бр; *fig.* ску́чный челове́к; **2.** [про]сверли́ть; [про-] бура́вить; надоеда́ть [-е́сть] (Д).

bore[2] [~] **1.** *pt.* от bear[2].

born [bɔ:n] рождённый; прирождённый; **~e** [~] *p. pt.* от bear[2].

borough ['bʌrə] небольшо́й го́род; municipal ~ го́род, име́ющий самоуправле́ние.

borrow ['bɔrou] занима́ть [-ня́ть] (from, of у P).

bosom ['buzəm] грудь *f*; па́зуха; *fig.* ло́но; не́дра *n/pl.*

boss F [bɔs] **1.** хозя́ин; предпринима́тель(ница *f*) *m*; *pol. Am.* руководи́тель полити́ческой па́ртии; **2.** распоряжа́ться [-яди́ться] (T), быть хозя́ином (P); **~y** *Am.* ['bɔsi] лю́бящий распоряжа́ться.

botany ['bɔtəni] бота́ника.

botch [bɔtʃ] **1.** гру́бая запла́та; плоха́я почи́нка; **2.** де́лать гру́бые запла́ты на (П); пло́хо чини́ть.

both [bouθ] о́ба, о́бе; и тот и друго́й; ~ ... and ... как ... так и ...; и ... и ...

bother ['bɔðə] F **1.** беспоко́йство; oh ~! кака́я доса́да!; **2.** надоеда́ть [-е́сть] (Д); [по]беспоко́ить.

bottle [bɔtl] **1.** буты́лка; **2.** разлива́ть по буты́лкам.

bottom ['bɔtəm] **1.** дно, дни́ще; ни́жняя часть *f*; грунт, по́чва; F зад; *fig.* осно́ва, суть *f*; at the ~ внизу́; *fig.* в су́щности; на дне (о́бщества); **2.** са́мый ни́жний.

bough [bau] ве́тка, ветвь *f*.

bought [bɔ:t] *pt.* и *p. pt.* от buy.

boulder ['bouldə] валу́н.

bounce [bauns] **1.** прыжо́к, скачо́к; **2.** подпры́гивать [-гнуть]; отска́кивать [отскочи́ть] (о мяче́); преувеличе́ние.

bound[1] [baund] **1.** преде́л; огра... че́ние; **2.** ограни́чи(ва)ть; с... живать [-жа́ть].

bound[2] [~] ⚔ гото́вый к отпра... нию, направля́ющийся (for в...

bound[3] [~] **1.** прыжо́к, ска... **2.** пры́гать [-гнуть], [по]скак... отска́кивать [отскочи́ть].

bound[4] [~] **1.** *pt.* и *p. pt.* от b... **2.** свя́занный; обя́занный; п... плетённый.

boundary ['baundəri] грани́ца

boundless [-lis] □ безграни́чн...

bounteous ['bauntiəs] □, **bount...** ['bauntiful] □ ще́дрый (челов... оби́льный.

bounty ['baunti] ще́дрость *f*... прави́тельственная пре́мия.

bouquet ['bukei] буке́т; ар... (вина́).

bout [baut] черёд; раз; ⚕ пр... док; *sport*: схва́тка.

bow[1] [bau] **1.** покло́н; ⚓ нос; **2.** [со]гну́ться; кла́няться [по... ни́ться]; подчиня́ться [-ни́т... (Д); *v/t.* [со]гну́ть.

bow[2] [bou] **1.** лук; дуга́; бан... смычо́к; rain~ ра́дуга; **2.** ♪ ... де́ть смычко́м.

bowels ['bauəlz] *pl.* кишки́ *f*... вну́тренности *f/pl.*; не́дра ... (земли́); *fig.* сострада́ние.

bower ['bauə] бесе́дка.

bowl[1] [boul] ку́бок, ча́ша; ва́...

bowl[2] [~] **1.** шар; **2.** *v/t.* [по]кат... *v/i.* игра́ть в шары́; ~ along ... ти́ться бы́стро.

box[1] [bɔks] **1.** коро́бка; я́щик; ... ду́к; ⊕ бу́кса; вту́лка; ⚘ б... *thea.* ло́жа; **2.** вкла́дыват... я́щик.

box[2] [~] **1.** *sport* бокс; ~ on ... ear пощёчина.

box|-keeper капельди́нер; **~-o...** театра́льная ка́сса.

boy [bɔi] ма́льчик; молодо́й ч... ве́к; **~hood** ['bɔihud] о́трочес... **~ish** ['bɔiiʃ] □ мальчи́шеский, ... роческий.

brace [breis] **1.** ⊕ связь *f*; ско́... па́ра (о ди́чи); **~s** *pl.* подтя́... *f/pl.*; **2.** свя́зывать [-за́ть]; ... пира́ть [-пере́ть]; ~ up подба́... вать [-бодри́ть].

bracelet ['breislit] брасле́т.

bracket ['brækit] **1.** △ кроншт... консо́ль *f*; га́зовый рожо́к; ско́бка; **2.** заключа́ть в ско́... *fig.* ста́вить на одну́ до́ску с ...

brag [bræg] **1.** [по]хва́статься... хвастовство́.

braggart ['brægət] **1.** хвас... **2.** □ хвастли́вый.

braid [breid] **1.** коса́ (вол... тесьма́; галу́н; **2.** запле... [-ести́]; обшива́ть тесьмо́й.

brain [brein] **1.** мозг; голова́;

st ~s) рассу́док, ум; у́мствен-
ıе спосо́бности *f/pl.*; **2.** размоз-
ить го́лову (Д).
ake [breik] **1.** ⊕ то́рмоз; **2.** [за-]
рмози́ть.
amble ['bræmbl] ⚘ ежеви́ка.
an [bræn] о́труби *f/pl.*
anch [brɑːntʃ] **1.** ветвь *f*, ве́тка,
к (*pl.*: су́чья); о́трасль *f* (нау́ки);
илиа́л; **2.** разветвля́ть(ся) [-ет-
ть(ся)]; расширя́ться [-ши́рить-
].
and [brænd] **1.** вы́жженное
леймо́, тавро́; ⊕ фабри́чное
леймо́; сорт; **2.** выжига́ть клей-
; *fig.* [за]клейми́ть, [о]позо́рить.
andish ['brændiʃ] разма́хивать
кну́ть] (Т).
an(d)new ['brænd'njuː] F со-
ршённо но́вый, «с иго́лочки».
andy ['brændi] конья́к.
ass [brɑːs] лату́нь *f*, жёлтая
едь *f*; F бессты́дство; ~ band
уховой орке́стр.
assiere ['bræsiɛə] бюстга́льтер.
ave [breiv] **1.** хра́брый, сме́лый;
брави́ровать; хра́бро встреча́ть
па́сность и т. п.); **~ry** ['breivəri]
а́брость *f*, сме́лость *f*.
awl [brɔːl] **1.** шу́мная ссо́ра,
ичный сканда́л; **2.** [по]ссо́рить-
(с Т).
awny ['brɔːni] си́льный; му́ску-
истый.
ay¹ [brei] **1.** крик осла́; **2.** [за-]
ича́ть (об осле́).
ay² [~] [ис]толо́чь.
azen ['breizn] □ ме́дный, бро́н-
овый; бессты́дный, на́глый (*a.*
faced).
azilian [brə'ziljən] **1.** брази́ль-
кий; **2.** брази́лец, бразилья́нка.
each [briːtʃ] **1.** проло́м; *fig.* раз-
ы́в (отноше́ний); наруше́ние; ⚔
решь *f*; **2.** пробива́ть брешь в (П).
ead [bred] хлеб.
eadth [bredθ] ширина́; широта́
ругозо́ра); широ́кий разма́х.
eak [breik] **1.** переры́в; па́уза;
ассве́т; тре́щина; F a bad ~ неу-
а́ча; **2.** [*irr.*] *v/t.* [с]лома́ть; раз-
и́(ва́)ть; разруша́ть [-ру́шить];
ер(ы)ва́ть; взла́мывать [взло-
а́ть]; ~ up разла́мывать [-лома́ть];
зби́(ва́)ть; *v/i.* пор(ы)ва́ть (с Т);
о]лома́ться, разби́(ва́)ться; ~
way отделя́ться [-ли́ться] (от Р);
down потерпе́ть ава́рию, неу-
а́чу; **~able** ['breikəbl] ло́мкий,
у́пкий; **~age** ['breikidʒ] по-
о́мка; **~-down** разва́л, расстро́й-
во; *mot.* ава́рия; **~fast** ['breik-
st] **1.** за́втрак; **2.** [по]за́втра-
ать; **~-up** распа́д, разва́л; **~water**
ол; волноре́з.
east [brest] грудь *f*; make a clean
of a th. чистосерде́чно созна-
а́ться в чём-либо; **~-stroke** брасс.
eath [breθ] дыха́ние; вздох; **~e**
[briːð] *v/i.* дыша́ть [дохну́ть]; перевести́ дух; **~less** ['breθlis] □ запыха́вшийся; безве́тренный.

bred [bred] **1.** вско́рмленный; воспи́танный; **2.** *pt.* и *p. pt.* от breed.

breeches ['bretʃiz] *pl.* бри́джи *pl.*, штаны́ *m/pl.*

breed [briːd] **1.** поро́да; **2.** [*irr.*] *v/t.* выводи́ть [вы́вести]; разводи́ть [-вести́]; выси́живать [вы́сидеть]; вска́рмливать [вскорми́ть]; *v/i.* размножа́ться [-о́житься]; [вы́]расти́; **~er** ['briːdə] производи́тель *m*; скотово́д; **~ing** [-diŋ] разведе́ние (живо́тных); хоро́шие мане́ры *f/pl.*; воспита́ние.

breez|e [briːz] лёгкий ветеро́к, бриз; **~y** ['briːzi] све́жий, живо́й, весёлый.

brethren ['breðrin] собра́тья *m/pl.*, бра́тия.

brevity ['breviti] кра́ткость *f*.

brew [bruː] *v/t.* [с]вари́ть (пи́во); зава́ривать [-ри́ть] (чай); приготовля́ть [-то́вить]; *fig.* затева́ть [зате́ять]; **~ery** ['bruəri] пивова́ренный заво́д.

brib|e [braib] **1.** взя́тка; по́дкуп; **2.** подкупа́ть [-пи́ть]; дава́ть взя́тку (Д); **~ery** ['braibəri] взя́точничество.

brick [brik] **1.** кирпи́ч; *fig.* сла́вный па́рень *m*; **2.** класть кирпичи́; облицо́вывать кирпича́ми; **~layer** ка́менщик.

bridal ['braidl] □ сва́дебный; ~ procession сва́дебная проце́ссия.

bride [braid] неве́ста; новобра́чная; **~groom** жени́х; новобра́чный; **~smaid** подру́жка неве́сты.

bridge [bridʒ] **1.** мост; **2.** соединя́ть мосто́м; наводи́ть мост че́рез (В); *fig.* преодоле́(ва́)ть (препя́тствия).

bridle ['braidl] **1.** узда́; по́вод; **2.** *v/t.* взну́здывать [-да́ть]; *v/i.* [за]арта́читься; задира́ть нос (*a.* ~ up); **~-path** верхова́я тропа́.

brief [briːf] **1.** □ коро́ткий, кра́ткий, сжа́тый; **2.** ⚖ резюме́ де́ла для защи́тника; hold a ~ for принима́ть на себя́ веде́ние де́ла (Р); **~-case** портфе́ль *m*.

brigade [bri'geid] ⚔ брига́да.

bright [brait] □ я́ркий; све́тлый, я́сный; **~en** ['braitn] *v/t.* [на]полирова́ть; придава́ть блеск (Д); *v/i.* проясня́ться [-ни́ться]; **~ness** [-nis] я́ркость *f*; блеск.

brillian|ce, ~cy ['briljəns, -si] я́ркость *f*; блеск; великоле́пие; **~t** [-jənt] **1.** □ блестя́щий (*a. fig.*); сверка́ющий; **2.** бриллиа́нт.

brim [brim] **1.** край; поля́ *n/pl.* (шля́пы); **2.** наполня́ть(ся) до краёв.

brine [brain] рассо́л; морска́я вода́.

bring [briŋ] [*irr.*] приноси́ть [-нести́]; доставля́ть [-а́вить];

привози́ть [-везти́]; приводи́ть [-вести́]; ~ about осуществля́ть [-ви́ть]; ~ down снижа́ть [сни́зить] (це́ны); ~ forth производи́ть [-вести́]; ~ home to дава́ть по- ня́ть (Д); ~ round приводи́ть [-вести́] в себя́ (по́сле о́бморока); ~ up воспи́тывать [-та́ть].

brink [briŋk] край (обры́ва); (кру- то́й) бе́рег.

brisk [brisk] □ живо́й, оживлён- [ный.

bristl|e ['brisl] **1.** щети́на; **2.** [о]ще- ти́ниться; [рас]серди́ться; ~ with изоби́ловать (Т); **~ed** [-d], **~y** [-i] щети́нистый, колю́чий.

British ['britiʃ] брита́нский; the ~ англича́не *m/pl.*

brittle ['britl] хру́пкий, ло́мкий.

broach [broutʃ] поч(ин)а́ть; под- нима́ть [-ня́ть] (вопро́с); на- ч(ин)а́ть (разгово́р).

broad [brɔ:d] □ широ́кий; обши́р- ный; грубова́тый; **~cast** **1.** раз- бра́сывать [-роса́ть] (семена́); рас- пространя́ть [-ни́ть]; передава́ть по ра́дио, веща́ть; **2.** радиопере- да́ча; радиовеща́ние; **~cloth** то́н- кое сукно́; бума́жная ткань *f.*

brocade [bro'keid] парча́.

broil [brɔil] **1.** жа́реное мя́со; **2.** жа́рить(ся) на огне́; F жа́риться на со́лнце.

broke [brouk] *pt.* от break.

broken ['broukən] **1.** *p. pt.* от break; **2.** разби́тый, раско́лотый; ~ health надло́мленное здоро́вье.

broker ['broukə] ма́клер.

bronc(h)o ['brɔŋkou] *Am.* полуди́- кая ло́шадь *f.*

bronze [brɔnz] **1.** бро́нза; **2.** бро́н- зовый; **3.** бронзирова́ть (*im*)*pf.*; загора́ть на со́лнце.

brooch [broutʃ] бро́шка.

brood [bru:d] **1.** вы́водок; ста́я; **2.** сиде́ть на я́йцах; *fig.* гру́стно размышля́ть.

brook [bruk] руче́й.

broom [bru:m, brum] метла́, ве́- ник; **~stick** метлови́ще.

broth [brɔ:θ, brɔθ] бульо́н.

brothel ['brɔθl] публи́чный дом.

brother [brʌðə] брат; собра́т; **~hood** [-hud] бра́тство; **~-in-law** [-rinlɔ] шу́рин; зять *m*; де́верь *m*; своя́к; **~ly** [-li] бра́тский.

brought [brɔ:t] *pt.* и *pt.* от bring.

brow [brau] бровь *f*; вы́ступ (скалы́); **~beat** ['braubi:t] [*irr.* (beat)] запу́гивать [-га́ть].

brown [braun] **1.** кори́чневый цвет; **2.** кори́чневый; сму́глый; загоре́лый; **3.** загора́ть [-ре́ть].

browse [brauz] **1.** ощи́пывать, объеда́ть ли́стья; *fig.* чита́ть бес- поря́дочно; **2.** молоды́е побе́ги *m/pl.*

bruise [bru:z] **1.** синя́к, кровопод- тёк; **2.** ушиба́ть [-би́ть]; подстав- ля́ть синяки́.

brunt [brʌnt] гла́вный уд вся тя́жесть *f.*

brush [brʌʃ] **1.** щётка; кисть чи́стка щёткой; *Am.* ~wo за́росль *f*; **2.** *v/t.* чи́стить щётк причёсывать щёткой (во́лос ~ up приводи́ть в поря́док; освежа́ть в па́мяти; *v/i.* ~ by п шмы́гивать [-гну́ть]; ~ against слегка́ заде́ть кого́-либо (прох ми́мо); **~wood** [brʌʃwud] хво́р валёжник.

brusque [brusk] □ гру́бый; р кий.

brut|al ['bru:tl] □ гру́бый; жес кий; **~ality** [bru:'tæliti] гру́бо *f*; жесто́кость *f*; **~e** [bru:t] жесто́кий; бессозна́тельный; живо́тное; F скоти́на (руга́тел во).

bubble ['bʌbl] **1.** пузы́рь *m*; пузы́риться; кипе́ть; бить к чо́м.

buccaneer [bʌkə'niə] пира́т.

buck [bʌk] **1.** *zo.* саме́ц (оле́нь, з и др.); **2.** станови́ться на ды брыка́ться [-кну́ться]; ~ up встряхну́ться *pf.*; оживля́т [-ви́ться].

bucket ['bʌkit] ведро́; бадья́.

buckle ['bʌkl] **1.** пря́жка; **2.** застёгивать [-тегну́ть] (пря́жк *v/i.* ⊕ сгиба́ться [согну́ться] давле́ния); ~ to *fig.* подтя́гива ся [-тяну́ться]; принима́ться эн ги́чно за де́ло.

buckshot ['bʌkʃɔt] *hunt.* кру́п дробь *f.*

bud [bʌd] **1.** по́чка, буто́н; заро́дыш; **2.** *v/i.* ↗ дава́ть по́ч пуска́ть ростки́; *fig.* разви́(ва́ ся.

budge ['bʌdʒ] шевели́ть(ся) [- ну́ть(ся)]; сдвига́ть с ме́ста.

budget ['bʌdʒit] бюдже́т; фин совая сме́та; draft ~ прое́кт гс да́рственного бюдже́та.

buff [bʌf] **1.** бу́йволовая ко́ **2.** тёмно-жёлтый.

buffalo ['bʌfəlou] *zo.* бу́йвол.

buffer ['bʌfə] 🚂 бу́фер; аморти то́р, де́мпфер.

buffet[1] ['bʌfit] **1.** уда́р (рукс толчо́к; **2.** наноси́ть уда́р (Д).

buffet[2] **1.** [~] буфе́т; **2.** ['bu буфе́тная сто́йка.

buffoon [bʌ'fu:n] шут, фигля́р.

bug [bʌg] клоп; *Am.* насеко́м

bugle ['bju:gl] рожо́к, горн.

build [bild] **1.** [*irr.*] [по]стро́ить; оружа́ть [-руди́ть]; [с]вить (гн до́); ~ on полага́ться [положи́ ся] на (В); **2.** констру́кция; ст *m*; телосложе́ние; **~er** ['bi строи́тель *m*; подря́дчик; пл ник; **~ing** [-iŋ] зда́ние; постр ка; строи́тельство.

built [bilt] *pt.* и *p. pt.* от build.

bulb [bʌlb] ⚘ лу́ковица; ла́мпоч

lge [bʌldʒ] **1.** вы́пуклость *f*; **2.** ыпя́чиваться [вы́пятиться], вы- ава́ться [вы́даться].
lk [bʌlk] объём; ⚓ вмести́мость , in ~ в нава́лку; in the ~ в це́лом;
y [bʌlki] громо́здкий.
ll¹ [bul] бык; ☿ *sl.* спекуля́нт, гра́ющий на повыше́ние; *Am. sl.* еле́пость *f*; противоре́чие.
ll² [~] па́пская бу́лла.
lldog ['buldɔg] бульдо́г.
llet ['bulit] пу́ля; ядро́.
lletin ['bulitin] бюллете́нь *m.*
llion ['buljən] сли́ток зо́лота ли серебра́.
lly ['buli] **1.** зади́ра *m*, забия́ка ; **2.** задира́ть; запу́гивать [-га́ть]; . *Am.* F первокла́ссный, вели- оле́пный; хвастли́вый.
lwark ['bulwək] ⚔ вал; *mst fig.* плот, защи́та.
m [bam] *Am.* F **1.** за́д(ница); о́дырь *m*, безде́льник, лентя́й; . ло́дырничать.
mble-bee ['bʌmblbi] шмель *m.*
mp [bʌmp] **1.** столкнове́ние; глухо́й уда́р; ши́шка; *fig.* спосо́б- ость *f* (of к Д); **2.** ударя́ть(ся) уда́рить(ся)].
mper ['bʌmpə] **1.** бока́л, по́л- ый до краёв; ~ crop F *sl.* небы- а́лый урожа́й; **2.** *Am. mot.* амор- иза́тор.
n [bʌn] бу́лочка (с изю́мом).
nch [bʌntʃ] **1.** свя́зка; пучо́к; а́чка; **2.** свя́зывать в пучо́к.
ndle ['bʌndl] **1.** у́зел; вяза́нка; . *v/t.* собира́ть вме́сте (ве́щи); вя́зывать в у́зел (*a.* ~ up).
ngalow ['bʌŋgəlou] одноэта́ж- ая да́ча, бу́нгало *n indecl.*
ngle ['bʌŋgl] **1.** (плоха́я) неб- е́жная рабо́та; оши́бка; пу́тани- а; **2.** неуме́ло, небре́жно рабо́- ать; по́ртить рабо́ту.
nk¹ [bʌŋk] *Am.* вздор.
nk² [~] ложи́ться спать.
nny ['bʌni] кро́лик.
oy [bɔi] ⚓ **1.** ба́кен, буй; **2.** ста́- ить ба́кены; подде́рживать на ове́рхности; (*mst* ~ up) *fig.* под- е́рживать [-жа́ть]; **~ant** ['bɔiənt]] плаву́чий; жизнера́достный; о́дрый.
rden ['bə:dn] **1.** но́ша; тя́жесть ; бре́мя *n*; груз; **2.** нагружа́ть -рузи́ть]; обременя́ть [-ни́ть]; **~-** **ome** [-səm] обремени́тельный.
reau [bjuə'rou, 'bjuərou] конто́р- а; конто́ра; бюро́ *n indecl.*; отде́л;
cracy [bjuə'rɔkrəsi] бюрокра́тия.
rglar ['bə:glə] вор-взло́мщик;
y [-ri] кра́жа со взло́мом.
rial ['beriəl] по́хороны *f/pl.*
rlesque [bə:'lesk] **1.** коми́чный; . карикату́ра, паро́дия; **3.** паро- и́ровать (*im*)*pf.*
rly ['bə:li] доро́дный.
rn [bə:n] **1.** ожо́г; клеймо́; **2.** [*irr.*] *v/i.* горе́ть; подгора́ть [-ре́ть] (о пи́ще); же́чь; *v/t.* [с]жечь; сжи- га́ть [сжечь]; **~er** ['bə:nə] горе́лка.
burnish ['bə:niʃ] **1.** полиро́вка; блеск (мета́лла); **2.** [от]полиро- ва́ть (мета́лл); блесте́ть.
burnt [bə:nt] *pt.* и *p. pt.* от burn.
burrow ['bʌrou] **1.** нора́; **2.** рыть нору́; [по]ры́ться в (кни́гах и т. п.).
burst [bə:st] **1.** разры́в (снаря́да); взрыв *a. fig.*; вспы́шка (гне́ва, пла́мени); **2.** [*irr.*] *v/i.* взрыва́ться [взорва́ться] (о котле́, бо́мбе); прор(ы)ва́ться (о плоти́не); ло́- паться [ло́пнуть] (with от Р); ~ forth и́ли out вспы́хивать [-хнуть] (о вражде́, войне́); ~ into tears залива́ться слеза́ми; *v/t.* взры- ва́ть [взорва́ть]; разруша́ть [-ру́- шить].
bury ['beri] [по]хорони́ть; зары́- (ва́)ть.
bus [bʌs] F авто́бус.
bush ['buʃ] куст, куста́рник.
bushel ['buʃl] бу́шель *m* (ме́ра ём- кости сыпу́чих тел в 'Англии [= 36,3 л] и в США [=35,2 л]).
bushy ['buʃi] густо́й.
business ['biznis] де́ло, заня́тие; профе́ссия; ☿ фи́рма; торго́вое предприя́тие; ~ of the day пове́ст- ка дня; ~ (*or* professional) discre- tion служе́бная обя́занность хра- ни́ть молча́ние; have no ~ to *inf.* не име́ть пра́ва (+ *inf.*); **~-like** [-laik] делово́й; практи́чный.
bust [bʌst] бюст; же́нская грудь *f.*
bustle ['bʌsl] **1.** сумато́ха; суета́; **2.** *v/i.* [по]торопи́ться, [за]суе- ти́ться; *v/t.* [по]торопи́ть.
busy ['bizi] **1.** □ де́ятельный; заня- то́й (at T); за́нятый; *Am. teleph.* за́нятая (ли́ния); **2.** (*mst* ~ o. s.) занима́ться [заня́ться] (with T).
but [bʌt] **1.** *cj.* но, а; одна́ко; тем не ме́нее; е́сли бы не (*a.* ~ that) **2.** *prp.* кро́ме (Р), за исключе́нием (Р); the last ~ one предпосле́дний; ~ for без (Р); **3.** *adv.* то́лько, лишь; ~ just то́лько что; ~ now лишь те- пе́рь; all ~ едва́ не ...; nothing ~ ни- чего́ кро́ме, то́лько; I cannot ~ *inf.* не могу́ не (+ *inf.*).
butcher ['butʃə] **1.** мясни́к; *fig.* уби́йца *m*; **2.** бить (скот); уби́(ва́)ть; **~y** [-ri] скотобо́йня; резня́.
butler ['bʌtlə] дворе́цкий.
butt [bʌt] **1.** уда́р; прикла́д (ружья́); (*a.* ~ end) то́лстый коне́ц; **~s** *pl.* стре́льбище, полиго́н; *fig.* посме́шище; **2.** ударя́ть голово́й; бода́ть(ся) [боднуть]; натыка́ться [наткну́ться].
butter ['bʌtə] **1.** ма́сло; **2.** нама́- зывать ма́слом; **~cup** ⚘ лю́тик; **~fly** ба́бочка; **~y** ['bʌtəri] **1.** кла- дова́я; **2.** ма́сляный.
buttocks ['bʌtəks] *pl.* я́годицы *f/pl.*

button ['bʌtn] **1.** пу́говица; кно́пка; буто́н (цветка́); **2.** застёгивать [-тегну́ть] (на пу́говицу).
buttress ['bʌtris] **1.** подпо́ра, усто́й; бык (моста́); *fig.* опо́ра, подде́ржка; **2.** подде́рживать [-жа́ть]; служи́ть опо́рой (Д).
buxom ['bʌksəm] здоро́вый; миловидный.
buy [bai] [*irr.*] *v/t.* покупа́ть [купи́ть] (from у Р); **~er** ['baiə] покупа́тель(ница *f*) *m*.
buzz [bʌz] **1.** жужжа́ние; гул; **2.** *v/i.* [за]жужжа́ть; [за]гуде́ть.
buzzard ['bʌzəd] сары́ч.
by [bai] **1.** *prp.* у (Р), при (П), о́коло (Р); вдоль (Р); ~ the dozen дю́жинами; ~ o. s. оди́н *m*, одна́ ~ land сухи́м путём; ~ rail по ж лéзной доро́ге; day ~ day изо д в де́нь; **2.** *adv.* бли́зко, ря́до ми́мо; ~ and ~ вско́ре; ~ the ме́жду про́чим; ~ and large *A* вообще́ говоря́; **~-election** ['ba 'lekʃən] дополни́тельные вы́бор *m/pl.*; **~-gone** про́шлый; **~-la** постановле́ние ме́стной власт **~-path** обхо́д, обхо́дная доро́г **~-product** побо́чный проду́к **~-stander** свиде́тель(ница *f*) зри́тель(ница *f*) *m*; **~-street** гл ха́я у́лица; переу́лок; **~-w** малопрое́зжая доро́га; **~-wo** погово́рка.

C

cab [kæb] экипа́ж; такси́ *n indecl.*; 🚂 бу́дка (на парово́зе).
cabbage ['kæbidʒ] капу́ста.
cabin ['kæbin] **1.** хи́жина; бу́дка; ⚓ каю́та; **2.** помеща́ть в те́сную ко́мнату и т. п.
cabinet ['kæbinit] кабине́т; го́рка; я́щик; ♀ Council сове́т мини́стров; **~-maker** столя́р.
cable ['keibl] **1.** ка́бель *m*; кана́т; **2.** *tel.* телеграфи́ровать (*im*)*pf.*; **~gram** [-græm] телегра́мма.
cabman ['kæbmən] изво́зчик.
cacao [kə'kɑ:ou] кака́овое де́рево; кака́о *n indecl.*
cackle ['kækl] **1.** куда́хтанье; гогота́нье; **2.** [за]куда́хтать; [за]гогота́ть.
cad [kæd] F невоспи́танный, гру́бый челове́к.
cadaverous [kə'dævərəs] □ исхуда́лый как труп; тру́пный.
cadence ['keidəns] ♪ каде́нция; модуля́ция.
cadet [kə'det] каде́т.
café ['kæfei] кафе́ *n indecl.*, кафе́-рестора́н.
cafeteria [kæfi'tiəriə] кафете́рий, кафе́-заку́сочная.
age [keidʒ] **1.** кле́тка; лифт; ⚒ склеть *f* (в ша́хтах); **2.** сажа́ть в кле́тку.
cajole [kə'dʒoul] [по]льсти́ть (Д).
cake [keik] **1.** торт; кекс; пиро́жное; **2.** спека́ться [спе́чься].
calami|tous [kə'læmitəs] □ па́губный; бе́дственный; **~ty** [-ti] бе́дствие.
calcify ['kælsifai] превраща́ться в и́звесть.
calculat|e ['kælkjuleit] *v/t.* вычисля́ть [вы́числить]; подсчи́тывать [-ита́ть]; [с]калькули́ровать; *v/i.* рассчи́тывать (on на В); **~ion** [kælkju'leiʃən] вычисле́ние; калькуля́ция; расчёт.
caldron ['kɔ:ldrən] котёл.
calendar ['kælində] **1.** календа́ *m*; рее́стр; **2.** составля́ть и́нде (Р); [за]регистри́ровать.
calf[1] [kɑ:f], *pl.* calves [kɑ:vz] тел нок (*pl.*: теля́та); (и́ли **~-ski** теля́чья ко́жа, опо́ек.
calf[2] [~], *pl.* calves [~] икра́ (ноги
calibre ['kælibə] кали́бр.
calico ['kælikou] † коленко́р; *A* си́тец.
call [kɔ:l] **1.** зов, о́клик; *telep* вы́зов; *fig.* предложе́ние (ме́ст ка́федры и т. п.); призы́в; сигна́ тре́бование; спрос (for на В); в зи́т, посеще́ние; on ~ по тре́бов нию; **2.** *v/t.* [по]зва́ть; соз(ы)ва́т вызыва́ть [вы́звать]; [раз]буди́т приз(ы)ва́ть; ~ in тре́бовать наз (долг); ~ over де́лать перекли́ч (Р); ~ up призыва́ть на вое́нну слу́жбу; *teleph.* вызыва́ть [в звать]; *v/i.* крича́ть [кри́кнут *teleph.* [по]звони́ть; заходи́ть [за ти́] (at в В; on a p. к Д); ~ for [п тре́бова́ть; [по]зва́ть на (В); ~ a p. заходи́ть [зайти́] за (Т); ~ F забега́ть [-ежа́ть] (к Д); ~ on н веща́ть [-ести́ть] (В); взыва́ [воззва́ть] к (Д) (for о П); пр з(ы)ва́ть (to do *etc.* сде́лать и т. д **~-box** ['kɔ:lbɔks] телефо́нная бу ка; **~er** ['kɔ:lə] го́сть(я *f*) *m*.
calling ['kɔ:liŋ] призва́ние; пр фе́ссия.
call-office ['kɔ:lɔfis] телефо́нн ста́нция.
callous ['kæləs] □ огрубе́лый, м зо́листый; *fig.* бессерде́чный.
calm [kɑ:m] **1.** □ споко́йный; бе ве́тренный; **2.** тишина́; штиль споко́йствие; **3.** ~ down успока́ вать(ся) [-ко́ить(ся)].
calori|c [kə'lɔrik] **1.** *phys.* тепло **2.** теплово́й; **~e** ['kæləri] *ph* кало́рия.

lumn|iate [kəˈlʌmnieit] [о]клеве-тать; **~iation** [kəlʌmniˈeiʃən], **~y** kæləmni] клевета́.
lve [kɑːv] [о]тели́ться; **~s** *pl.* от alf.
mbric [ˈkeimbrik] ✝ бати́ст.
me [keim] *pt.* от come.
mera [ˈkæmərə] фотографи́че-ский аппара́т; in ~ ⚖ в кабине́те удьи́.
momile [ˈkæməmail] ⚘ рома́шка.
mouflage [ˈkæmuːflɑːʃ] ⚔ маски-о́вка; **2.** [за]маскирова́ть(ся).
mp [kæmp] **1.** ла́герь *m*; ~ bed охо́дная крова́ть *f*; **2.** располага́ться ла́герем; ~ out ночева́ть на ткры́том во́здухе.
mpaign [kæmˈpein] **1.** ⚔ похо́д; ампа́ния; **2** уча́ствовать в по-хо́де; проводи́ть кампа́нию.
mphor [ˈkæmfə] камфара́.
n¹ [kæn] [*irr.*] могу́ и т. д.; *inf.*: e able = [с]мочь, быть в состо-янии; [с]уме́ть.
n² [~] **1.** бидо́н; ба́нка; **2.** *Am.* онсерви́ровать (*im*)*pf.*, *pf. a.* [за-].
nal [kəˈnæl] кана́л.
nard [kəˈnɑː] «у́тка», ло́жный лух.
nary [kəˈnɛəri] канаре́йка.
ncel [ˈkænsəl] вычёркивать [вы́-черкнуть]; аннули́ровать (*im*)*pf.*; огаша́ть [погаси́ть] (ма́рки); A *.* ~ out) сокраща́ть [-рати́ть].
ncer [ˈkænsə] *ast.* созве́здие а́ка; ⚕ рак; **~ous** [-rəs] ра́ковый.
ndid [ˈkændid] □ и́скренний, рямо́й.
ndidate [ˈkændidit] кандида́т(ка) for на В).
ndied [ˈkændid] заса́харенный.
ndle [ˈkændl] свеча́; **~stick** [-stik] одсве́чник.
ndo(u)r [ˈkændə] и́скренность *f*.
ndy [ˈkændi] **1.** леденец; *Am.* онфе́ты *f/pl.*, сла́сти *f/pl.*; **2.** *v/t.* аса́хари(ва)ть.
ne [kein] **1.** ⚘ камы́ш; тростни́к; рость *f*; **2.** бить па́лкой.
nker [ˈkæŋkə] ⚕ гангрено́зный томати́т; ⚘ рак.
nned [kænd] *Am.* консерви́ро-анный (проду́кт).
nnibal [ˈkænibəl] каннибал.
nnon [ˈkænən] пу́шка; ору́дие.
nnot [ˈkænɔt] не в состоя́нии, can.
noe [kəˈnuː] челно́к; байда́рка.
non [ˈkænən] ♪ кано́н; пра́вило; крите́рий.
nopy [ˈkænəpi] по́лог; *fig.* небе́с-ный свод; △ наве́с.
nt¹ [kænt] **1.** кося́к, накло́н; **2.** ка́шивать [скоси́ть]; наклоня́ть -ни́ть].
nt² [~] **1.** плакси́вый тон; хан-жество́; **2.** говори́ть на распе́в; ханжи́ть.
n't [kɑːnt] F не в состоя́нии.

canteen [kænˈtiːn] ⚔ ла́вка; сто-ло́вая; похо́дная ку́хня.
canton 1. [ˈkæntɔn] канто́н; **2.** [kənˈtuːn] ⚔ расквартиро́вывать [-ова́ть] (во́йска́).
canvas [ˈkænvəs] холст; канва́; *paint.* карти́на.
canvass [~] **1.** обсужде́ние; **2.** *v/t.* обсужда́ть [-уди́ть]; *v/i.* собира́ть голоса́; иска́ть зака́зов.
caoutchouc [ˈkautʃuk] каучу́к.
cap [kæp] **1.** ке́пка, фура́жка, ша́п-ка; ⊕ колпачо́к, голо́вка; шля́пка (гриба́); писто́н; set one's ~ at a p. заи́грывать с ке́м-либо (о же́н-щине); **2.** присужда́ть учёную сте́-пень (Д); *fig.* заверша́ть [-ши́ть]; F перещеголя́ть.
capab|ility [keipəˈbiliti] спосо́б-ность *f*; **~le** [ˈkeipəbl] □ спосо́б-ный (of на В), одарённый.
capaci|ous [kəˈpeiʃəs] □ просто́р-ный; объёмистый; **~ty** [kəˈpæsiti] объём, вмести́тельность *f*; спо-со́бность *f* ; in the ~ of в ка́честве (Р).
cape¹ [keip] плащ; пелери́на.
cape² [~] мыс.
caper [ˈkeipə] скачо́к; ша́лость *f*, прока́за; cut ~s дура́читься.
capital [ˈkæpitl] **1.** □ основно́й, капита́льный; (*crime*) уголо́вный; (*sentence, punishment*) сме́ртный; **2.** столи́ца; капита́л; (или ~ letter) прописна́я бу́ква; **~ism** [ˈkæpitə-lizm] капитали́зм; **~ize** [kəˈpitəlaiz] капитализи́ровать (*im*)*pf*.
capitulate [kəˈpitjuleit] сд(ав)а́ться (to Д).
capric|e [kəˈpriːs] капри́з, причу́-да; **~ious** [kəˈpriʃəs] □ капри́зный.
capsize [kæpˈsaiz] *v/i.* ⚓ опроки́-дываться [-ки́нуться]; *v/t.* опро-ки́дывать [-ки́нуть] (ло́дку и т. п.).
capsule [ˈkæpsjuːl] ка́псюль *m*; ⚕ ка́псула.
captain [ˈkæptin] ⚔ капита́н; руко-води́тель(ница *f*) *m*; ⚓ капита́н, команди́р.
caption [ˈkæpʃən] *part. Am.* заго-ло́вок (статьи́, главы́); (кино́) на́дпись на экра́не.
captious [ˈkæpʃəs] □ приди́рчи-вый.
captiv|ate [ˈkæptiveit] пленя́ть [-ни́ть]; очаро́вывать [-ова́ть]; **~e** [ˈkæptiv] **1.** пле́нник; пле́нный; **2.** взя́тый в плен; **~ity** [kæpˈtiviti] плен.
capture [ˈkæptʃə] **1.** захва́тывать си́лой; брать в плен; **2.** по́имка; захва́т; добы́ча; ⚓ приз.
car [kɑː] ваго́н; автомоби́ль *m*.
caramel [ˈkærəmel] караме́ль *f*.
caravan [kærəˈvæn] карава́н; дом-автоприце́п.
caraway [ˈkærəwei] ⚘ тмин.
carbine [ˈkɑːbain] караби́н.
carbohydrate [ˈkɑːbouˈhaidreit] ⚗ углево́д.

carbon ['kɑ:bən] ⚗ углерóд; (или ~ paper) копи́рка.
carburet(t)or ['kɑ:bjuretə] *mot.* карбюрáтор.
carcas|e, *mst* **~s** ['kɑ:kəs] труп; тýша.
card ['kɑ:d] кáрта; кáрточка; **~board** [kɑ:dbɔ:d] картóн.
cardigan ['kɑ:digən] шерстянóй джéмпер.
cardinal ['kɑ:dinl] **1.** □ глáвный, основнóй; кардинáльный; ~ number коли́чественное числи́тельное; **2.** кардинáл.
card-index ['kɑ:dindeks] картотéка.
card-sharp(er) [kɑ:dʃɑ:pə] шýлер
care [kɛə] **1.** забóта; попечéние; внимáние; ~ of (*abbr.* c/o) по áдресу (Р); take ~ of [с]берéчь (В); [по-] смотрéть за (Т); with ~! осторóжно!; **2.** имéть желáние, [за-] хотéть (to: + *inf.*); ~ for: a) [по]заботиться о (П); b) люби́ть (В); питáть интерéс к (Д); F I don't ~! мне всё равнó!; well ~d-for вы́холенный; хорошó обеспéченный.
career [kə'riə] **1.** карьéр; *fig.* карьéра, успéх; **2.** бы́стро продвигáться.
carefree ['kɛəfri:] беззабóтный.
careful ['kɛəful] □ забóтливый (for о П); аккурáтный; внимáтельный (к Д); **~ness** [-nis] забóтливость *f.*
careless [-lis] □ легкомы́сленный; небрéжный; **~ness** [-nis] небрéжность *f.*
caress [kə'res] **1.** лáска; **2.** ласкáть; [по]глáдить.
caretaker ['kɛəteikə] двóрник; стóрож.
carfare ['kɑ:fɛə] *Am.* проездны́е (дéньги).
cargo ['kɑ:gou] ⚓ груз.
caricature ['kærikə'tjuə] **1.** карикатýра; **2.** изображáть в карикатýрном ви́де.
carn|al ['kɑ:nl] □ чýвственный, плóтский; **~ation** [kɑ:'neiʃən] ♀ гвозди́ка.
carnival ['kɑ:nivəl] карнавáл.
carnivorous [kɑ:'nivərəs] плотоя́дный.
carol ['kærəl] **1.** рождéственский гимн; **2.** воспé(вá)ть, слáвить.
carous|e [kə'rauz] **1.** *a.* **~al** [-əl] пирýшка, попóйка; **2.** пировáть.
carp[1] [kɑ:p] *zo.* карп.
carp[2] [~] прид(и)рáться (at к Д).
carpent|er ['kɑ:pintə] плóтник; **~ry** [-tri] плóтничное дéло.
carpet [kɑ:pit] **1.** ковёр; **2.** устилáть коврóм.
carriage ['kæridʒ] экипáж; перевóзка; трáнспорт; **~-drive** подъéзд; **~ free, ~ paid** пересы́лка бесплáтно.
carrier ['kæriə] посы́льный; носи́льщик; ⚔ транспортёр.
carrot ['kærət] морκóвь *f.*
carry ['kæri] **1.** *v/t.* носи́ть, [по-] нести́; вози́ть, [по]везти́; ~ o. s. держáться, вести́ себя́; be carried быть при́нятым; ✝ ~ forward или over переноси́ть на другýю страни́цу; ~ on продолжáть [-дóлжить]; вести́ (дéло, борьбý и т. п.); ~ out или through доводи́ть до концá; выполня́ть [вы́полнить]; *v/i.* доноси́ться [донести́сь]; ⚔ долетáть [долетéть] (о снаря́де); **2.** ⚔ дальнобóйность *f*; дáльность полёта (снаря́да).
cart [kɑ:t] **1.** телéга, повóзка; **2.** везти́ в телéге; **~age** ['kɑ:tidʒ] перевóзка, стóимость перевóзки.
carter ['kɑ:tə] вóзчик.
cartilage ['kɑ:tilidʒ] хрящ.
carton ['kɑ:tən] картóн.
cartoon [kɑ:'tu:n] карикатýра; ⊕ картóн.
cartridge ['kɑ:tridʒ] патрóн; заря́д.
carve [kɑ:v] рéзать (по дéреву); [вы́]гравировáть; нарезáть [нарéзать] (мя́со); **~r** ['kɑ:və] рéзчик (по дéреву); гравёр; нож для раздéлки мя́са.
carving ['kɑ:viŋ] резьбá (по дéреву).
case[1] [keis] **1.** я́щик; футля́р; сýмка; витри́на; *typ.* набóрная кáсса; **2.** класть в я́щик.
case[2] [~] слýчай; положéние; обстоя́тельство; ⚖ судéбное дéло
case-harden ['keishɑ:dn] ⊕ цементи́ровать (сталь) (*im*)*pf.*; *fig.* дéлать нечувстви́тельным.
casement ['keismənt] створны́й окóнный переплёт.
cash [kæʃ] **1.** дéньги; нали́чные дéньги *f/pl.*; ~ down, for ~ за нали́чный расчёт; ~ on delivery налóженным платежóм; ~ register кáссовый аппарáт; **2.** получáть дéньги по (Д); **~-book** кáссовая кни́га; **~-ier** [kæ'ʃiə] касси́р(ша)
casing ['keisiŋ] опрáва; рáма; обши́вка, оби́вка.
cask [kɑ:sk] бóчка, бочóнок.
casket ['kɑ:skit] шкатýлка; *Am.* гроб.
casserole ['kæsəroul] кастрю́ля.
cassock ['kæsək] ря́са, сутáна.
cast [kɑ:st] **1.** бросóк, метáние; ги́псовый слéпок; ⚓ бросáние (я́коря); *thea.* распределéние ролéй; состáв исполни́телей; **2.** [*irr.*] *v/t.* бросáть [брóсить]; кидáть [ки́нуть]; метáть [-тнýть]; ⊕ отли́(вá)ть (метáллы); *thea.* распределя́ть [-ли́ть] (рóли); ~ iron чугýн; ~ lots бросáть жрéбий; be ~ down быть в уны́нии; *v/i.* ~ about for обдýм(ыв)ать (В).
castaway ['kɑ:stəwei] **1.** пáриа, отвéрженец; ⚓ потерпéвший крушéние; **2.** отвéрженный
caste [kɑ:st] кáста.

astigate ['kæstigeit] нака́зывать -за́ть]; *fig.* жесто́ко критикова́ть.
ast-iron чугу́нный.
astle ['kɑ:sl] за́мок; *chess* ладья́.
astor[1] ['kɑ:stə]: ~ oil касто́ровое ма́сло.
astor[2] [~] колёсико (на но́жке ме́бели).
astrate [kæs'treit] кастри́ровать (*im*)*pf*.
asual ['kæʒjuəl] □ случа́йный; небре́жный; **~ty** [-ti] несча́стный слу́чай; *pl.* ⚔ поте́ри (на войне́) *f/pl.*
at [kæt] ко́шка.
atalog, *Brt.* **~ue** ['kætəlɔg] **1.** катало́г; прейскура́нт; **2.** каталогизи́ровать (*im*)*pf.*, вноси́ть в катало́г.
ataract ['kætərækt] водопа́д; ⚕ катара́кта.
atarrh [kə'tɑ:] ката́р.
atastrophe [kə'tæstrəfi] катастро́фа.
atch [kætʃ] **1.** пои́мка; захва́т; уло́в; добы́ча; лову́шка; ⊕ задви́жка; шпингале́т; **2.** [*irr.*] *v/t.* лови́ть [пойма́ть]; схва́тывать [схвати́ть]; заража́ться [зарази́ться] (Т); поспе́(ва́)ть к (по́езду и т. п.); ~ cold простужа́ться [-уди́ться]; ~ a p. 's eye улавливать взгляд (P); ~ up догоня́ть [догна́ть]; F поднима́ть [-ня́ть]; **3.** *v/i.* зацепля́ться [-пи́ться]; F ~ on станови́ться мо́дным; ~ up with догоня́ть [догна́ть] (B); **~er** ['kætʃə] лове́ц; **~ing** ['kætʃiŋ] *fig.* зарази́тельный (смех); привлека́тельный; ⚕ зарази́тельный; **~word** мо́дное слове́чко; загла́вное сло́во.
atechism ['kætikizm] катехи́зис.
ategor|ical [kæti'gɔrikəl] □ категори́ческий; реши́тельный; **~y** ['kætigəri] катего́рия, разря́д.
ater ['keitə]: ~ for поставля́ть прови́зию (Д); *fig.* [по]забо́титься о (П).
aterpillar *zo.*, ⊕ ['kætəpilə] гу́сеница.
atgut ['kætgʌt] кише́чная струна́.
athedral [kə'θi:drəl] собо́р.
atholic ['kæθəlik] **1.** като́лик; **2.** католи́ческий.
attle [kætl] кру́пный рога́тый скот; **~-breeding** скотово́дство; **~-plague** чума́.
aught [kɔ:t] *pt.* и *pt.* от catch.
auldron ['kɔ:ldrən] котёл.
auliflower ['kɔliflauə] ⚘ цветна́я капу́ста.
aulk [kɔ:k] ⚓ [про]конопа́тить.
aus|al ['kɔ:zəl] □ причи́нный; **~e** [kɔ:z] **1.** причи́на, основа́ние; по́вод; ⚖ де́ло, проце́сс; **2.** причиня́ть [-ни́ть]; вызыва́ть [вы́звать]; **~eless** ['kɔ:zlis] □ беспричи́нный, необосно́ванный.
aution ['kɔ:ʃən] **1.** (пред)осторо́жность *f*; предостереже́ние; ~ money зало́г; **2.** предостерега́ть [-ре́чь] (against от P).
cautious ['kɔ:ʃəs] □ осторо́жный; предусмотри́тельный; **~ness** [-nis] осторо́жность *f*; предусмотри́тельность *f*.
cavalry ['kævəlri] ⚔ ко́нница.
cave ['keiv] **1.** пеще́ра; **2.** ~ in: *v/i.* оседа́ть [осе́сть], опуска́ться [-сти́ться].
cavil ['kævil] **1.** приди́рка; **2.** прид(и)ра́ться (at, about к Д, за В).
cavity ['kæviti] впа́дина; по́лость *f*.
caw [kɔ:] **1.** ка́рканье; **2.** [за]ка́ркать.
cease [si:s] *v/i.* перест(ав)а́ть; *v/t.* прекраща́ть [-крати́ть]; приостана́вливать [-нови́ть]; **~less** ['si:slis] □ непреры́вный, непреста́нный.
cede [si:d] уступа́ть [-пи́ть] (B).
ceiling ['si:liŋ] потоло́к; *attr.* максима́льный; ~ price преде́льная цена́.
celebrat|e ['selibreit] [от]пра́здновать; **~ed** [-id] знамени́тый; **~ion** [seli'breiʃən] торжества́ *n/pl.*; пра́зднование.
celebrity [si'lebriti] знамени́тость *f*.
celerity [-riti] быстрота́.
celery ['seləri] ⚘ сельдере́й.
celestial [si'lestjəl] □ небе́сный.
celibacy ['selibəsi] целиба́т; обе́т безбра́чия.
cell [sel] яче́йка; тюре́мная ка́мера; ке́лья; ⚡ элеме́нт.
cellar ['selə] подва́л; ви́нный по́греб.
cement [si'ment] **1.** цеме́нт; **2.** цементи́ровать (*im*)*pf*.
cemetery ['semitri] кла́дбище.
censor ['sensə) **1.** це́нзор; **2.** подверга́ть цензу́ре; **~ious** [sen'sɔ:riəs] □ стро́гий, критику́ющий; **~ship** ['sensəʃip] цензу́ра.
censure [senʃə] **1.** осужде́ние, порица́ние; **2.** осужда́ть [осуди́ть], порица́ть.
census ['sensəs] пе́репись *f*.
cent [sent] со́тня *f*; *Am.* цент (0,01 до́ллара); per ~ проце́нт.
centennial [sen'tenjəl] столе́тний; происходя́щий раз в сто лет.
center *s.* centre.
centi|grade ['sentigreid] стогра́дусный; **~metre** [-mi:tə] сантиме́тр; **~pede** [-pi:d] *zo.* сороконо́жка.
central ['sentrəl] □ центра́льный; гла́вный; ~ office центра́льная конто́ра; ~ station гла́вный вокза́л; **~ize** [-laiz] централизова́ть (*im*)*pf*.
centre ['sentə] **1.** центр; средото́чие; **2.** [с]концентри́ровать(ся); сосредото́чи(ва)ть(ся).
century ['sentʃəri] столе́тие, век.
cereal ['siəriəl] хле́бный злак; *Am.* ка́ша.
ceremon|ial [seri'mounjəl] □ фор-

ма́льный; церемониа́льный; **~ious** [-njəs] церемо́нный; жема́нный; **~y** [ˈseriməni] церемо́ния.

certain [ˈsəːtn] □ определённый; уве́ренный; не́кий; не́который; **~ty** [-ti] уве́ренность *f*; определённость *f*.

certi|ficate 1. [səˈtifikit] свиде́тельство; сертифика́т; ~ of birth свиде́тельство о рожде́нии, ме́трика; **2.** [-keit] вы́дать пи́сьменное удостовере́ние (Д); **~fication** [səːtifiˈkeiʃən] удостовере́ние; **~fy** [ˈsəːtifai] удостоверя́ть [-е́рить]; **~tude** [-tjuːd] уве́ренность *f*.

cessation [seˈseiʃən] прекраще́ние.

cession [ˈseʃən] усту́пка, переда́ча.

cesspool [ˈsespuːl] выгребна́я я́ма; сто́чный коло́дец.

chafe [tʃeif] *v/t.* натира́ть [натере́ть]; нагре́(ва́)ть; *v/i.* раздража́ться [-жи́ться], не́рвничать.

chaff [tʃɑːf] **1.** мяки́на; отбро́сы *m/pl.*; F подшу́чивание, поддра́знивание; **2.** ме́лко наре́зать (соло́му и т. п.); F подшу́чивать [-шути́ть] над (Т), поддра́знивать [-зни́ть].

chagrin [ˈʃægrin] **1.** доса́да, огорче́ние; **2.** досажда́ть [досади́ть] (Д); огорча́ть [-чи́ть].

chain [tʃein] **1.** цепь *f*; ~s *pl. fig.* око́вы *f/pl.*; у́зы *f/pl.*; **2.** ско́вывать [скова́ть]; держа́ть в цепя́х; *fig.* прико́вывать [-ова́ть].

chair [tʃɛə] стул; ка́федра; председа́тельское ме́сто; be in the ~ председа́тельствовать; **~man** [ˈtʃɛəmən] председа́тель *m*.

chalk [tʃɔːk] **1.** мел; **2.** писа́ть, рисова́ть ме́лом; (*mst* ~ up) запи́сывать [-иса́ть] (долг) ~ out набра́сывать [-броса́ть]; намеча́ть [-е́тить].

challenge [ˈtʃælindʒ] **1.** вы́зов; ⚔ о́клик (часово́го); *part.* ⚖ отво́д (присяжных); **2.** вызыва́ть [вы́звать]; оспа́ривать [оспо́рить]; [по]тре́бовать (внима́ния).

chamber [ˈtʃeimbə] ко́мната; пала́та; ~s *pl.* конто́ра адвока́та; ка́мера судьи́; **~maid** го́рничная.

chamois [ˈʃæmwɑː] **1.** се́рна; [ˈʃæmi] за́мша; **2.** жёлто-кори́чневый.

champion [ˈtʃæmpjən] **1.** чемпио́н (-ка); победи́тель(ница *f*) *m*; защи́тник (-ница); **2.** защища́ть [-ити́ть]; боро́ться за (В).

chance [tʃɑːns] **1.** случа́йность *f*; риск (в игре́); уда́ча; удо́бный слу́чай; шанс (of на В); by ~ случа́йно; take a ~ рискова́ть [-кну́ть]; **2.** случа́йный; **3.** *v/i.* случа́ться [-чи́ться]; ~ upon случа́йно найти́ *pf.*; *v/t.* F про́бовать наудачу.

chancellor [ˈtʃɑːnsələ] ка́нцлер.

chandelier [ʃændiˈliə] лю́стра.

chandler [ˈtʃɑːndlə] ла́вочник.

change [ˈtʃeindʒ] **1.** переме́на, изменение; сме́на (белья́); ме́лочь сда́ча (о деньга́х); **2.** *v/t.* [по меня́ть; изменя́ть [-ни́ть], пер меня́ть [-ни́ть]; обме́нивать [-ня́ть разме́нивать [-ня́ть] (де́ньги); *v.* [по]меня́ться; изменя́ться [-ни́т ся]; переменя́ться [-ни́ться переоде́(ва́)ться; обме́нивать [-ня́ться]; 🚃 переса́живать [-се́сть]; **~able** [ˈtʃeindʒəbl] □ н посто́янный, переме́нчивый; **~les** [-lis] □ неизме́нный, посто́янны

channel [ˈtʃænl] ру́сло; фарва́те проли́в; *fig.* путь *m*; исто́чник.

chant [tʃɑːnt] **1.** песнь *f*; песноп ние; **2.** петь моното́нно; *fig.* вос

chaos [ˈkeiɔs] хао́с. [пе́(ва́)ть

chap¹ [tʃæp] **1.** щель *f*; тре́щин **2.** [по]тре́скаться.

chap² [~] F ма́лый, па́рень *m*.

chapel [ˈtʃæpəl] часо́вня; капе́лл

chaplain [ˈtʃæplin] свяще́нник.

chapter [ˈtʃæptə] глава́.

char [tʃɑː] обжига́ть [обже́чь]; о у́гли(ва)ть(ся).

character [ˈkæriktə] хара́кте ли́чность *f*; *thea.* де́йствующ лицо́; бу́ква; **~istic** [kæriktəˈristi **1.** (~ally) характе́рный; типи́ ный (of для Р); **2.** характе́рн осо́бенность *f*; **~ize** [ˈkæriktərai характеризова́ть (*im*)*pf.*; изобр жа́ть [-рази́ть].

charcoal [ˈtʃɑːkoul] древе́сны у́голь *m*.

charge [tʃɑːdʒ] **1.** заря́д; нагру́зк поруче́ние; цена́; обвине́ни ата́ка; *fig.* попече́ние, забо́та; *pl.* ☤ расхо́ды *m/pl.*; издержк *f/pl.*; be in ~ of заве́довать (Т); *v/t.* заряжа́ть [-яди́ть]; нагружа [-узи́ть]; поруча́ть [-чи́ть] (Д обвиня́ть [-ни́ть] (with в П); н знача́ть [-на́чить] (це́ну) (to на В *Am.* утвержда́ть [-рди́ть].

charitable [ˈtʃæritəbl] □ благотв ри́тельный; милосе́рдный.

charity [ˈtʃæriti] милосе́рдие; бл готвори́тельность *f*.

charlatan [ˈʃɑːlətən] шарлата́н.

charm [tʃɑːm] **1.** амуле́т; *fig.* ча́р *f/pl.*; обая́ние, очарова́ние; **2.** з колдо́вывать [-дова́ть]; *fig.* оч ро́вывать [-ова́ть]; **~ing** [ˈtʃɑːmi □ очарова́тельный, обая́тельны

chart [tʃɑːt] **1.** ⚓ морска́я ка́рт **2.** нанос́ить на ка́рту; черти́ ка́рту.

charter [ˈtʃɑːtə] **1.** ха́ртия; пра́в привиле́гия; **2.** дарова́ть прив ле́гию (Д); ⚓ [за]фрахтова́ (су́дно).

charwoman [ˈtʃɑːwumən] подё щица.

chary [ˈtʃɛəri] □ осторо́жны скупо́й (на слова́ и т. п.).

chase [tʃeis] **1.** пого́ня *f*; охо́т **2.** охо́титься за (Т); пресле́доват прогоня́ть [-гна́ть].

hasm [kæzm] бе́здна, про́пасть *f.*
haste [tʃeist] □ целому́дренный.
hastity ['tʃæstiti] целому́дрие; де́вственность *f.*
hat [tʃæt] **1.** бесе́да; **2.** [по]болта́ть, [по]бесе́довать.
hattels ['tʃætlz] *pl.* (*mst* goods and ~) иму́щество, ве́щи *f/pl.*
hatter [tʃætə] **1.** болтовня́ *f*; щебета́ние) **2.** [по]болта́ть; **~er** [-rə] болту́н(ья).
hatty ['tʃæti] болтли́вый.
hauffeur ['ʃoufə] води́тель *m*, шофёр.
heap [tʃi:p] □ дешёвый; *fig.* плохо́й; **~en** ['tʃi:pən] [по]дешеве́ть; снижа́ть це́ну (В); *fig.* унижа́ть [уни́зить].
heat [tʃi:t] **1.** обма́нщик, плут; обма́н; **2.** обма́нывать [-ну́ть].
heck [tʃek] **1.** *chess* шах; препя́тствие; остано́вка; контро́ль *m* (on над Т), прове́рка (on P); *Am.* бага́жная квита́нция; *Am.* ☨ чек; клётчатая ткань *f*; **2.** проверя́ть [-ве́рить]; [про]контроли́ровать; остана́вливать [-нови́ть]; препя́тствовать; **~er** ['tʃekə] контролёр; **~s** *pl. Am.* ша́шки *f/pl.*; **~ing-room** *Am.* ка́мера хране́ния (багажа́); **~mate** **1.** шах и мат; **2.** де́лать мат; **~-up** *Am.* стро́гая прове́рка.
heek [tʃi:k] щека́ (*pl.*: щёки); F на́глость *f*, де́рзость *f.*
heer [tʃiə] **1.** весе́лье; одобри́тельные во́згласы *m/pl.*; **2.** *v/t.* ободря́ть [-ри́ть]; поощря́ть [-ри́ть]; приве́тстсвовать гро́мкими во́згласами; *v/i.* ликова́ть; **~ful** ['tʃiəful] □ бо́дрый, весёлый; **~less** [-lis] □ уны́лый, мра́чный; **~y** [-ri] □ живо́й, весёлый, ра́достный.
heese [tʃi:z] сыр.
hemical ['kemikəl] **1.** □ хими́ческий; **2.** **~s** [-s] *pl.* хими́ческие препара́ты *m/pl.*, химика́лии *f/pl.*
hemist ['kemist] хи́мик; апте́карь *m*; **~ry** ['kemistri] хи́мия.
heque [tʃek] ☨ ба́нковый чек.
hequer ['tʃekə] **1.** *mst* **~s** *pl.* клётчатый узо́р; **2.** графи́ть в клётку.
herish ['tʃeriʃ] леле́ять (наде́жду); храни́ть (в па́мяти); не́жно любить.
herry ['tʃeri] ви́шня.
hess [tʃes] ша́хматы *f/pl.*; **~board** ша́хматная доска́; **~man** ша́хматная фигу́ра.
hest [tʃest] я́щик, сунду́к; грудна́я клётка; ~ of drawers комо́д.
hestnut ['tʃesnʌt] **1.** кашта́н; F изби́тый анекдо́т; **2.** кашта́новый; гнедо́й (о ло́шади).
hevy ['tʃevi] *Brit.* F **1.** охо́та; пого́ня; **2.** гна́ться за (Т); уд(и)ра́ть.
hew [tʃu:] жева́ть; размышля́ть; **~ing-gum** ['tʃu:iŋgʌm] жева́тельная рези́нка.
hicane [ʃi'kein] **1.** приди́рка; **2.** прид(и)ра́ться к (Д).

chick [tʃik], **~en** ['tʃikin] цыплёнок; птене́ц; **~en-pox** ⚕ ве́тряная о́спа.
chief [tʃi:f] **1.** □ гла́вный; руководя́щий; ~ clerk нача́льник отде́ла; **2.** глава́, руководи́тель (-ница *f*) *m*; ...-in-~ гла́вный ...; **~tain** ['tʃi:ftən] вождь *m* (кла́на); атама́н.
chilblain ['tʃilblein] отморо́женное ме́сто.
child [tʃaild] ребёнок, дитя́ *n* (*pl.*: де́ти); from a ~ с де́тства; with ~ бере́менная; **~birth** ро́ды *m/pl.*; **~hood** [-hud] де́тство; **~ish** ['tʃaildiʃ] □ де́тский; **~like** [-laik] как ребёнок; неви́нный; **~ren** ['tʃildrən] *pl.* от child.
chill [tʃil] **1.** хо́лод; хо́лодность *f*; ⚕ просту́да; **2.** холо́дный; расхола́живающий; **3.** *v/t.* охлажда́ть [-лади́ть]; [о]студи́ть; *v/i.* охлажда́ться [-лади́ться]; **~y** ['tʃili] зя́бкий; холо́дный.
chime [tʃaim] **1.** звон колоколо́в; бой часо́в; *fig.* гармони́чное сочета́ние; **2.** [по]звони́ть (о колокола́х); [про]би́ть (о часа́х); *fig.* соотве́тствовать; гармони́ровать.
chimney ['tʃimni] дымова́я труба́; ла́мповое стекло́.
chin [tʃin] подборо́док.
china ['tʃainə] фарфо́р.
Chinese ['tʃai'ni:z] **1.** кита́ец (-ая́нка); **2.** кита́йский.
chink [tʃiŋk] щель *f*, сква́жина.
chip [tʃip] **1.** ще́пка, лучи́на; стру́жка; оско́лок (стекла́); **2.** *v/t.* отбива́ть края́ (посу́ды и т. п.); *v/i.* отла́мываться [отлома́ться].
chirp [tʃə:p] **1.** чири́канье; щебета́ние; **2.** чири́кать [-кнуть]; [за-] щебета́ть.
chisel ['tʃizl] **1.** долото́, стаме́ска; **2.** [из]вая́ть; *sl.* наду́(ва́)ть, обма́нывать [-ну́ть].
chit-chat ['tʃit-tʃæt] болтовня́.
chivalr|ous ['ʃivəlrəs] □ ры́царский; **~y** [-ri] ры́царство.
chlor|ine ['klɔ:ri:n] ⚗ хлор; **~oform** ['klɔrəfɔ:m] **1.** хлорофо́рм; **2.** хлороформи́ровать (*im*)*pf.*
chocolate ['tʃɔkəlit] шокола́д.
choice [tʃɔis] **1.** вы́бор; отбо́р; альтернати́ва; **2.** □ отбо́рный.
choir ['kwaiə] хор.
choke [tʃouk] **1.** *v/t.* [за]души́ть; засоря́ть [-ри́ть]; ⚡ дроссели́ровать; (*mst* ~ down) глота́ть с трудо́м; дави́ться (with от P); задыха́ться [-дохну́ться]; **2.** припа́док уду́шья; ⊕ заслонка.
choose [tʃu:z] [*irr.*] выбира́ть [вы́брать]; предпочита́ть [-че́сть]; ~ to *inf.* хоте́ть (+ *inf.*).
chop [tʃɔp] **1.** отбивна́я котле́та; **~s** *pl.* че́люсть *f*; **2.** *v/t.* ⊕ стёсывать [стеса́ть]; долби́ть; [на]руби́ть; [на]кроши́ть; *v/i.* колеба́ть-

ся; меня́ться, перемени́ться *pf.* (о ве́тре); **~per** ['tʃɔpə] коса́рь (нож) *m*; лесору́б; колу́н; **~py** ['tʃɔpi] неспоко́йный (о мо́ре).

choral ['kɔrəl] □ хорово́й; **~(e)** [kɔ'rɑ:l] ♪ хора́л.

chord [kɔ:d] струна́; ♪ акко́рд; созву́чие.

chore [tʃɔ:] *Am.* подённая рабо́та; рути́нная дома́шняя рабо́та.

chorus ['kɔ:rəs] **1.** хор; му́зыка для хо́ра; **2.** петь хо́ром.

chose [tʃouz] *pt.* от choose; **~n** (~n) **1.** *p. pt.* от choose; **2.** и́збранный.

Christ [kraist] Христо́с.

christen ['krisn] [о]крести́ть; **~ing** [-iŋ] крести́ны *f/pl.*; креще́ние.

Christian ['kristjən] **1.** христиа́нский; ~ name и́мя (в отли́чие от фами́лии); **2.** христиани́н (-а́нка); **~ity** [kristi'æniti] христиа́нство.

Christmas ['krisməs] рождество́.

chromium ['kroumiəm] ⚗ хром; **~-plated** покры́тый хро́мом.

chronic ['krɔnik] (**~ally**) хрони́ческий; ⚕ застаре́лый; P отврати́тельный; **~le** [~l] **1.** хро́ника, ле́топись *f*; **2.** вести́ хро́нику (P).

chronolog|ical [krɔnə'lɔdʒikəl] □ хронологи́ческий; **~y** [krə'nɔlədʒi] хроноло́гия.

chubby ['tʃʌbi] F по́лный, то́лстый.

chuck[1] [tʃʌk] **1.** куда́хтанье; цыплёнок; my ~! голу́бчик !; **2.** [за-] куда́хтать.

chuck[2] [~] **1.** броса́ть [бро́сить]; F швыря́ть [-ну́ть]; **2.** F увольне́ние.

chuckle ['tʃʌkl] посме́иваться.

chum [tʃʌm] F **1.** това́рищ; закады́чный друг; **2.** быть в дру́жбе.

chump [tʃʌmp] коло́да, чурба́н; F «башка́».

chunk [tʃʌŋk] F ломо́ть *m*; болва́н.

church [tʃə:rʃ] це́рковь *f*; ~ service богослуже́ние; **~yard** кла́дбище.

churl [tʃə:l] гру́бый челове́к; **~ish** ['tʃə:liʃ] □ скупо́й; гру́бый.

churn [tʃə:n] **1.** маслобо́йка; **2.** сбива́ть ма́сло; *fig.* взба́лтывать [взболта́ть]; вспе́ни(ва)ть.

cider ['saidə] сидр.

cigar [si'gɑ:] сига́ра.

cigarette [sigə'ret] папиро́са, сигаре́та; **~-case** портсига́р.

cigar-holder мундшту́к.

cinch [sintʃ] *Am. sl.* не́что надёжное, ве́рное.

cincture ['siŋktʃə] по́яс; опоя́сывание.

cinder ['sində] шлак; ока́лина; ~s *pl.* зола́; **~-path** *sport*: гарева́я доро́жка.

cinema ['sinimə] кинемато́граф, кино́ *n indecl.*

cinnamon ['sinəmən] кори́ца.

cipher ['saifə] **1.** шифр; ци́фра; нуль *m or* ноль *m*; **2.** зашифро́вывать [-ова́ть]; вычисля́ть [вы́числить]; высчи́тывать [вы́считать].

circle ['sə:kl] **1.** круг; окру́жност *f*; орби́та; кружо́к; сфе́ра; *thea* я́рус; **2.** враща́ться вокру́г (Р); соверша́ть круги́, кружи́ть(ся).

circuit ['sə:kit] кругооборо́т; объ езд; о́круг (суде́бный); ⚡ цепь *j* ко́нтур; ⚡ short ~ коро́ткое замыка́ние; ✈ кругово́й полёт.

circular ['sə:kjulə] **1.** □ кру́глый кругово́й; ~ letter циркуля́р, циркуля́рное письмо́; ~ note † ба́нковый аккредити́в; **2.** циркуля́р проспе́кт.

circulat|e ['sə:kjuleit] *v/i.* распространя́ться [-ни́ться]; име́ть круговое движе́ние; циркули́ровать **~ing** [-iŋ]: ~ library библиоте́ка с вы́дачей книг на́ дом; **~ion** [sə:kju'leiʃən] кровообраще́ние; циркуля́ция; тира́ж (газе́т и т. п.); *fig* распростране́ние (слу́хов и т. п.)

circum... ['sə:kəm] *pref.* (в сло́жных слова́х) вокру́г, круго́м **~ference** [sə'kʌmfərəns] окру́жность *f*; перифери́я; **~jacent** [sə:kəm'dʒeisnt] окружа́ющий; **~locution** [-lə'kju:ʃən] многоречи́вость *f*; **~navigate** [-'nævigeit] соверша́ть пла́вание вокру́г (Р) **~scribe** ['sə:kəmskraib] ⚹ опи́сывать [описа́ть] (круг); *fig.* ограни́чи(ва)ть (права́ и т. п.); **~spect** [-spekt] □ осмотри́тельный, осторо́жный; **~stance** ['sə:kəmstəns обстоя́тельство; **~stantial** [sə:kəm'stænʃəl] □ обстоя́тельный, подро́бный; **~vent** [-'vent] обходи́ть [обойти́] (зако́н и т. п.).

cistern ['sistən] бак; водоём цисте́рна.

cit|ation [sai'teiʃən] цита́та, ссы́лка; цити́рование; **~e** [sait] ссыла́ться [сосла́ться] на (В).

citizen ['sitizn] граждани́н (-да́нка); **~ship** [-ʃip] гражда́нство.

citron ['sitrən] цитро́н.

city ['siti] го́род; *attr.* городско́й **2.** the ♀ делово́й кварта́л в Ло́ндоне; ♀ article биржево́й бюллете́нь *m*; статья́ в газе́те по фина́нсовым и комме́рческим вопро́сам

civic ['sivik] гражда́нский; **~s** [-s] *pl.* ⚖ гражда́нские дела́ *n/pl.*; осно́вы гражда́нственности.

civil ['sivil] □ гражда́нский; шта́тский; ве́жливый; ⚖ гражда́нский (противополо́жный уголо́вному); ~ servant чино́вник; ~ service госуда́рственная слу́жба; **~ian** [si'viljən] ⚔ шта́тский; **~ity** [si'viliti] ве́жливость *f*; **~ization** [sivilai'zeiʃən] цивилиза́ция; **~ize** ['sivilaiz] цивилизова́ть *(im)pf.*

clad [klæd] *pt.* и *p. pt.* от clothe.

claim [kleim] **1.** предъявля́ть прете́нзию на (В); [по]тре́бовать; заявля́ть права́; утвержда́ть [-рди́ть]; заявля́ть права́ на (В); **2.** тре́бование; иск; прете́нзия; ~ to be

ыдавать себя за (В); **~ant** ['klei-
ənt] претендент; ⚖ истец.
ıirvoyant [klɛə'vɔiənt] ясновй-
ец.
ımber ['klæmbə] [вс]карабкать-
ı.
ımmy ['klæmi] □ клейкий, лип-
ий; холодный и влажный.
ımo(u)r ['klæmə] **1.** шум, крики
/pl.; протесты m/pl. (шумные);
шумно требовать (P).
ımp [klæmp] ⊕ скоба; скрепа;
ıжим; **2.** скреплять [-пить]; за-
(им)ать; смыкать [сомкнуть].
ındestine [klæn'destin] □ тай-
ый.
ıng [klæŋ] **1.** лязг, звон (оружия,
олоколов, молота); **2.** лязгать
гнуть].
ınk [klæŋk] **1.** звон, лязг (цепей,
елеза и т. п.), бряцание; **2.** бря-
ать, [за]греметь.
ıp [klæp] **1.** хлопок; хлопанье;
дар (грома); **2.** хлопать (в ла-
оши); **~trap** погоня за эффек-
м.
ırify ['klærifai] *v/t.* очищать
чистить]; делать прозрачным;
g. выяснять [выяснить]; *v/i.* де-
ться прозрачным, ясным.
ırity ['klæriti] ясность *f*.
ısh [klæʃ] **1.** столкновение;
отиворечие; конфликт; **2.** стал-
иваться [столкнуться]; расхо-
иться [разойтись] (о взглядах).
ısp [klɑ:sp] **1.** пряжка, застёжка;
g. объятия *n/pl.*; **2.** *v/t.* застёги-
ть [застегнуть]; сж(им)ать; *fig.*
ключать в объятия; *v/i.* обви-
а)ться (о растении).
ıss [klɑ:s] **1.** класс (школы);
щественный класс; **2.** класси-
ицировать (*im*)*pf*.
ıssic ['klæsik] **1.** классик; **2.** ~(al
) [~, -ikəl] классический.
ıssi|fication [klæsifi'keiʃən] клас-
фикация; **~fy** [klæ'sifai] класси-
ицировать (*im*)*pf*.
ıtter ['klætə] **1.** звон (посуды);
охот (машин); болтовня; топот;
[за]греметь; [за]топать; *fig.*
о]болтать.
ıuse [klɔ:z] пункт; статья; клау-
ла (в договоре).
ıw [klɔ:] **1.** коготь *m*; клешня
ака); **2.** разрывать, терзать
огтями.
ıy [klei] глина; *fig.* прах.
ıan [kli:n] **1.** *adj.* □ чистый; оп-
тный; чистоплотный; **2.** *adv.*
чисто; совершенно, полностью;
[вы]чистить; прочищать [-чис-
ть]; счищать [счистить]; ~ up
(и)рать; приводить в порядок;
ng ['kli:niŋ] чистка; уборка;
истка; **~liness** ['klenlinis] чисто-
отность *f*; **~ly 1.** *adv.* ['kli:nli]
сто; целомудренно; **2.** *adj.*
lenli] чистоплотный; **~se** [klenz]
очищать [очистить]; дезинфици-
ровать (*im*)*pf*.
clear [kliə] **1.** □ ясный, светлый;
прозрачный; *fig.* свободный
(from, of от P); ✝ чистый (вес,
доход и т. п.); **2.** *v/t.* очищать
[очистить] (from, of от P); рас-
чищать [-истить]; распрод(ав)ать
(товар); ⚖ оправдывать [-дать]
(обвиняемого); *v/i.* (*a.* ~ up) рас-
сеиваться [-еяться] (о тумане);
проясняться [-ниться]; **~ance**
['kliərəns] очистка; устранение
препятствий; очистка от тамо-
женных пошлин; расчистка (под
пашню); **~ing** ['kliəriŋ] проясне-
ние; просека; клиринг (между
банками); ♀ House расчётная палата.
cleave[1] [kli:v] [*irr.*] раскалывать
(-ся) [-колоть(ся)]; рассекать
[-ечь] (волны, воздух).
cleave[2] [~] *fig.* оставаться верным
(to Д).
cleaver ['kli:və] большой нож мяс-
clef [klef] ♪ ключ. [ника.
cleft [kleft] **1.** расселина; **2.** раско-
лотый.
clemen|cy ['klemənsi] милосердие;
снисходительность *f*; **~t** ['klemənt]
□ милосердный, милостивый.
clench [klentʃ] заж(им)ать; сж(и-
м)ать (кулаки); стискивать [стис-
нуть] (зубы); *s.* clinch.
clergy ['klə:dʒi] духовенство; **~-
man** [-mən] священник.
clerical ['klerikəl] **1.** □ клерикаль-
ный; канцелярский; **2.** клерикал.
clerk [klə:k] чиновник; контор-
ский служащий; *Am.* приказчик.
clever ['klevə] □ умный; даровй-
тый, одарённый; ловкий.
clew [klu:] **1.** клубок; **2.** сматывать
в клубок.
click [klik] **1.** щёлканье; ⊕ защёлка, собачка; **2.** щёлкать [-кнуть]
(замком); прищёлкивать [-кнуть]
(языком); *Am.* иметь успех.
client ['klaiənt] клиент(ка); постоянный (-ная) покупатель(ница *f*)
m; **~èle** [kli:ɑn'teil] клиентура.
cliff [klif] утёс, скала.
climate ['klaimit] климат.
climax ['klaimæks] **1.** кульмина-
ционный пункт; **2.** достигать куль-
минационного пункта.
climb [klaim] [*irr.*] влез(а)ть на
(В); подниматься [-няться] (на
гору); **~er** ['klaimə] альпинист;
fig. честолюбец; ⚘ вьющееся растение.
clinch [klintʃ] **1.** ⊕ зажим; скоба;
2. *v/t.* заклёпывать [-лепать]; ~ a
bargain заключать сделку; *s.*
clench.
cling [kliŋ] [*irr.*] (to) [при]льнуть к
(Д); ~ together держаться вместе.
clinic ['klinik] **1.** клиника; **2.** = **~al**
[-ikəl] клинический.

clink [kliŋk] **1.** звон (мета́лла, стекла́); **2.** [за]звене́ть; [за]звуча́ть.
clip[1] [klip] **1.** стри́жка; **2.** обреза́ть [обре́зать]; [о]стри́чь.
clip[2] [~] скре́пка.
clipp|er ['klipə]: (a pair of) ~s *pl.* но́жницы *f/pl.*; сека́тор; ⚓ кли́ппер (па́русное су́дно); (flying ~) самолёт гражда́нской авиа́ции; **~ings** [-iŋz] *pl.* газе́тные вы́резки *f/pl.*; обре́зки *m/pl.*
cloak [klouk] **1.** плащ; ма́нтия; покро́в; *fig.* предло́г; **2.** покры́(ва́)ть (плащо́м и т. п.); *fig.* прикры́(ва́)ть; **~-room** раздева́льня; 🚂 ка́мера хране́ния.
clock [klɔk] часы́ *m/pl.* (стенны́е, насто́льные, ба́шенные).
clod [klɔd] ком (гря́зи); ду́рень *m*, о́лух.
clog [klɔg] **1.** препя́тствие; пу́ты *f/pl.*; деревя́нный башма́к; **2.** [вос]препя́тствовать (Д); засоря́ть(ся) [-ри́ть(ся)].
cloister ['klɔistə] монасты́рь *m*; кры́тая арка́да.
close 1. [klous] □ закры́тый; бли́зкий; те́сный; ду́шный, спёртый (во́здух); скупо́й; ~ by *adv.* ря́дом, побли́зости; ~ to о́коло (Р); ~ fight, ~ quarters *pl.* рукопа́шный бой; *hunt.* ~ season, ~ time запре́тное вре́мя охо́ты; **2.** a) [klouz] коне́ц; заключе́ние; b) [klous] огоро́женное ме́сто; **3.** [klouz] *v/t.* закры́(ва́)ть; зака́нчивать [-ко́нчить]; конча́ть [ко́нчить]; заключа́ть [-чи́ть] (речь); *v/i.* закры́(ва́)ться; конча́ться [ко́нчиться]; ~ in приближа́ться [-ли́зиться]; наступа́ть [-пи́ть]; ~ on (*prp.*) замыка́ться вокру́г (Р); **~ness** ['klousnis] бли́зость *f*; ску́пость *f*.
closet ['klɔzit] **1.** чула́н; убо́рная; стенно́й шкаф; **2.** be ~ed with совеща́ться наедине́ с (Т).
closure ['klouʒə] закры́тие; *parl.* прекраще́ние пре́ний.
clot [klɔt] **1.** сгу́сток (кро́ви); комо́к; **2.** сгуща́ться [сгусти́ться], свёртываться [сверну́ться].
cloth [klɔ:θ, klɔθ], *pl.* ~s [klɔ:ðz, klɔθs] ска́терть *f*; ткань *f*; сукно́; F the ~ духове́нство; ~ binding тка́невый переплёт.
clothe [klouð] [*a. irr.*] оде́(ва́)ть; *fig.* облека́ть [-е́чь].
clothes [klouðz] *pl.* оде́жда, пла́тье; бельё; **~-basket** бельева́я корзи́на; **~-line** верёвка для су́шки белья́; **~-peg** зажи́мка для разве́шенного белья́.
clothier ['klouðiə] фабрика́нт суко́н.
clothing ['klouðiŋ] оде́жда, пла́тье.
cloud [klaud] **1.** о́блако, ту́ча; **2.** покрыва́ть(ся) ту́чами, облака́ми; омрача́ть(ся) [-чи́ть(ся)]; **~-burst** ли́вень *m*; **~less** ['klaudlis] □ безо́блачный; **~y** [-i] □ о́блачн… му́тный (о жи́дкости); тума́нн… (о мы́сли).
clove[1] [klouv] гвозди́ка (пря́ност…
clove[2] [~] *pt.* от cleave; **~n** ['klou… *p. pt.* от cleave.
clover ['klouvə] ⚘ кле́вер.
clown [klaun] кло́ун.
cloy [klɔi] пресыща́ть [-сы́тить].
club [klʌb] **1.** клуб; дуби́на; A… па́лка полице́йского; ~s *pl.* тре́… *f/pl.* (ка́рточная масть); **2.** … [по]би́ть (па́лкой и т.п.); *v/i.* со… ра́ться вме́сте; устра́ивать скла… чину.
clue [klu:] ключ к разга́дке; пу… во́дная нить *f*.
clump [klʌmp] **1.** комо́к; гру́п… (дере́вьев); **2.** тяжело́ ступа́ть.
clumsy ['klʌmzi] □ неуклю́жи… нело́вкий; беста́ктный.
clung [klʌŋ] *pt.* и *p. pt.* от cling.
cluster ['klʌstə] **1.** кисть *f*; пучо… гроздь *f*; **2.** расти́ гро́здья… пучка́ми.
clutch [klʌtʃ] **1.** сжа́тие; захв… ⊕ зажи́м; защёлка; му́фта сц… ле́ния; **2.** схва́тывать [-ти́т… заж(им)а́ть.
clutter ['klʌtə] **1.** сумато́ха; ха… **2.** приводи́ть в беспоря́док.
coach [koutʃ] **1.** экипа́ж; тре́н… инстру́ктор; 🚂 пассажи́рск… ваго́н; **2.** е́хать в каре́те; [на]т… нирова́ть; ната́скивать к экза́ме… **~man** ку́чер.
coagulate [kou'ægjuleit] сгуща́т… [сгусти́ться].
coal [koul] **1.** у́голь *m* (ка́менны… **2.** ⚓ грузи́ть(ся) у́глем.
coalesce [kouə'les] сраста́т… [срасти́сь].
coalition [kouə'liʃən] коали́ц… сою́з.
coal-pit у́гольная ша́хта, копь…
coarse [kɔ:s] □ гру́бый; кру́пн… неотёсанный.
coast [koust] **1.** морско́й бе́р… побере́жье; **2.** плыть вдоль … бере́жья; **~er** ['koustə] ⚓ ка… та́жное су́дно.
coat [kout] **1.** пиджа́к; пальто́ *indecl.*; мех, шерсть *f* (у жив… ных); слой; ~ of arms ге́рбов… щит; **2.** покры́(ва́)ть (кра́ск… пы́лью и т. п.); облицо́выв… [-цева́ть]; **~-hanger** ве́шалка; **~i…** ['koutiŋ] слой (кра́ски и т. п.).
coax [kouks] угова́ривать [уго… ри́ть].
cob [kɔb] ком; *Am.* поча́ток ку… ру́зы.
cobbler ['kɔblə] сапо́жник; … халту́рщик, плохо́й ма́стер.
cobweb ['kɔbweb] паути́на.
cock [kɔk] **1.** пету́х; кран; флю́г… куро́к; **2.** (*a.* ~ up) насторажив… [-рожи́ть] (у́ши).
cockade [kɔ'keid] кока́рда.

'katoo [kɔkə'tu:] какаду́ *m indecl.*
kboat ['kɔkbout] ⚓ судова́я
шлюпка.
:kchafer ['kɔktʃeifə] ма́йский
ук.
:k-eyed ['kɔkaid] *sl.* косогла́зый;
•сой; *Am.* пья́ный.
'kpit ['kɔkpit] ме́сто петуши́ных
ёв; ⚓ ку́брик; ✈ каби́на.
kroach ['kɔkroutʃ] *zo.* тарака́н.
k|sure F самоуве́ренный; ~tail
•ктейль *m*; *fig.* вы́скочка; ~y
:ɔki] □ F наха́льный; де́рзкий.
:o ['koukou] коко́совая па́льма.
'oa ['koukou] кака́о (порошо́к,
пи́ток) *n indecl.*
o-nut ['koukənʌt] коко́совый
•е́х.
:oon [kɔ'ku:n] ко́кон.
[kɔd] треска́.
ldle ['kɔdl] изне́жи(ва)ть; [из-]
лова́ть.
le [koud] 1. ко́декс; *telegr.* код;
кодиро́вать (*im*)*pf.*
lger ['kɔdʒə] F чуда́к.
l-liver: ~ oil ры́бий жир.
rc|e [kou'ə:s] принужда́ть [-ну́-
ть]; ~ion [-ʃən] принужде́ние.
val [kou'i:vəl] □ совреме́нный.
xist ['kouig'zist] сосуществo-
ть (с T).
fee ['kɔfi] ко́фе *m indecl.*; ~-pot
фе́йник; ~-room столо́вая в
сти́нице; ~-set кофе́йный сер-
з.
fer ['kɔfə] металли́ческий сун-
к.
fin ['kɔfin] гроб.
ent ['koudʒənt] □ неоспори́-
ий; убеди́тельный.
:itate ['kɔdʒiteit] *v/i.* размыш-
ть; *v/t.* обду́м(ыв)ать.
nate ['kɔgneit] ро́дственный;
о́дный.
nition [kɔg'niʃən] зна́ние; по-
а́ние.
eir ['kou'ɛə] сонасле́дник.
eren|ce [kou'hiərəns] связь *f*;
я́зность *f*; согласо́ванность *f*; ~t
эnt] □ свя́зный; согласо́ван-
ий.
esi|on [kou'hi:ʒən] связь *f*;
лочённость *f*; ~ve [-siv] связу́ю-
ий; спосо́бный к сцепле́нию.
ff|eur [kwɑ:'fə:] парикма́хер;
re [-'fjuə] приче́ска.
[kɔil] 1. кольцо́ (верёвки, змеи́
т. п.); ⚡ кату́шка; ⊕ змееви́к;
(*a.* ~ up) свёртываться кольцо́м
сира́лью).
n [kɔin] 1. моне́та; 2. [вы́]чека́-
ть (моне́ты); вы́би(ва́)ть (ме-
ли); ~age ['kɔinidʒ] чека́нка
оне́т).
ncide [kouin'said] совпада́ть
а́сть]; ~nce [kou'insidəns] сов-
де́ние; *fig.* случа́йное стече́ние
стоя́тельств.
[kouk] 1. кокс; 2. коксова́ть.

cold [kould] **1.** □ холо́дный; не-приве́тливый; **2.** хо́лод; просту́да; **~ness** ['kouldnis] хо́лодность *f*; равноду́шие.

colic ['kɔlik] ⚕ ко́лики *f/pl.*

collaborat|e [kə'læbəreit] сотру́дничать; **~ion** [kəlæbə'reiʃən] сотру́дничество; in ~ в сотру́дничестве (с T).

collapse [kə'læps] **1.** обва́л; разруше́ние; упа́док сил; **2.** обру́ши(ва)ться; обва́ливаться [-ли́ться]; си́льно слабе́ть.

collar ['kɔlə] **1.** воротни́к; оше́йник; хому́т; ⊕ вту́лка; о́бруч; ша́йба; **2.** схвати́ть за во́рот; *sl.* завладе́(ва́)ть (T); захва́тывать [-ти́ть] (си́лой).

collate [kɔ'leit] слича́ть [-чи́ть]; сопоставля́ть [-ста́вить].

collateral [kɔ'lætərəl] **1.** □ побо́чный; ко́свенный; **2.** родство́ по боково́й ли́нии.

colleague ['kɔli:g] колле́га *f/m*, сослужи́вец (-вица).

collect 1. ['kɔlekt] *eccl.* кра́ткая моли́тва; **2.** [kə'lekt] *v/t.* соб(и-)ра́ть; коллекциони́ровать; заходи́ть [зайти́] за (T); *v/i.* соб(и)ра́ться; овладева́ть собо́й; **~ed** [kə'lektid] □ *fig.* хладнокро́вный; споко́йный; **~ion** [kə'lekʃən] колле́кция; собра́ние; **~ive** [-tiv] □ коллекти́вный; совоку́пный; **~or** [-tə] коллекционе́р; сбо́рщик.

college ['kɔlidʒ] колле́дж; сре́дняя шко́ла.

collide [kə'laid] ста́лкиваться [столкну́ться].

collie ['kɔli] ко́лли *m/f indecl.* (шотла́ндская овча́рка).

collier [kɔliə] шахтёр; ⚓ у́гольщик (су́дно); **~y** [kɔ'ljəri] каменноуго́льный рудни́к.

collision ['kəliʒən] столкнове́ние.

colloquial [kə'loukwiəl] □ разгово́рный.

colloquy ['kɔləkwi] разгово́р, собесе́дование.

colon ['koulən] *typ.* двоето́чие.

colonel ['kə:nl] ⚔ полко́вник.

coloni|al [kə'lounjəl] **1.** колониа́льный; **2.** жи́тель(ница *f*) *m* коло́ний; **~ze** ['kɔlənaiz] колонизи́ровать (*im*)*pf.*; заселя́ть [-ли́ть].

colony ['kɔləni] коло́ния.

colo(u)r ['kʌlə] **1.** цвет; кра́ска; румя́нец (на лице́); *fig.* колори́т; ~s *pl.* знамя́ *n*; **2.** *v/t.* [по]кра́сить; окра́шивать [окра́сить]; *fig.* прикра́шивать [-кра́сить]; *v/i.* [по-]красне́ть; [за]рде́ться (о лице́, плоде́ и т. п.); **~ed** [-d] окра́шенный; цветно́й; **~ful** [-ful] я́ркий; **~ing** [-riŋ] окра́ска, раскра́ска; *fig.* прикра́шивание; **~less** [-lis] □ бесцве́тный.

colt [koult] жеребёнок (*pl.* жеребя́та); *fig.* нович́ок.

column ['kɔləm] △, ⚔ коло́нна; столб; *typ.* столбе́ц.
comb [koum] **1.** гре́бень *m*, гребёнка; со́ты *m/pl.*; ⊕ бёрдо, чеса́лка; **2.** *v/t.* расчёсывать [-чеса́ть]; чеса́ть (*a.* ⊕); трепа́ть (лён и т. п.).
combat ['kɔmbət, 'kʌm-] **1.** бой, сраже́ние; **2.** сража́ться [срази́ться]; **~ant** [-ənt] бое́ц.
combin|ation [kɔmbi'neiʃən] соедине́ние; сочета́ние; *mst* **~s** *pl.* комбина́ция (бельё); **~e** [kəm'bain] объединя́ть(ся) [-ни́ть(ся)]; сочета́ть(ся) (*im*)*pf.*
combusti|ble [kəm'bʌstəbl] **1.** горю́чий, воспламеня́емый; **2.** **~s** *pl.* то́пливо; *mot.* горю́чее; **~on** [-tʃən] горе́ние, сгора́ние.
come [kʌm] [*irr.*] приходи́ть [прийти́]; приезжа́ть [прие́хать]; to ~ бу́дущий; ~ about случа́ться [-чи́ться], происходи́ть [произойти́]; ~ across a p. встреча́ться [-ре́титься] с (Т), ната́лкиваться [натолкну́ться] на (В); ~ at доб(и)ра́ться до (Р); ~ by дост(ав)а́ть (случа́йно); ~ off отде́л(ыв)аться; сходи́ть [сойти́]; ~ round приходи́ть в себя́; F заходи́ть [зайти́] (к Д); *fig.* идти́ на усту́пки; ~ to доходи́ть [дойти́] до (Р); ⚓ останови́ть су́дно; равня́ться (Д), сто́ить (В *or* Р); ~ up to соотве́тствовать (Д).
comedian [kə'mi:diən] актёр-ко́мик; а́втор коме́дии.
comedy ['kɔmidi] коме́дия.
comeliness ['kʌmlinis] милови́дность *f.*
comfort ['kʌmfət] **1.** комфо́рт, удо́бство; *fig.* утеше́ние; подде́ржка; **2.** утеша́ть [уте́шить]; успока́ивать [-ко́ить]; **~able** [-əbl] □ удо́бный, комфорта́бельный; *Am.* F доста́точный; **~er** [-ə] утеши́тель *m*; *Am.* стёганое одея́ло; **~less** [-lis] □ неую́тный.
comic(al □) ['kɔmik(əl)] коми́ческий, смешно́й; юмористи́ческий.
coming ['kʌmiŋ] **1.** прие́зд, прибы́тие; **2.** бу́дущий; ожида́емый.
command [kə'mɑ:nd] **1.** кома́нда, прика́з; кома́ндование; have at ~ име́ть в своём распоряже́нии; **2.** прика́зывать [-за́ть] (Д); владе́ть (Т); ⚔ кома́ндовать; **~er** [kə'mɑ:ndə] ⚔ команди́р; ⚓ капита́н; ♀**er-in-Chief** [-rin'tʃi:f] главнокома́ндующий; **~ment** [-mənt] прика́з; *eccl.* за́поведь *f.*
commemora|te [kə'meməreit] [от]пра́здновать (годовщи́ну); отмеча́ть [отме́тить] (собы́тие); **~tion** [kəmemə'reʃən] пра́зднование (годовщи́ны).
commence [kə'mens] нач(ин)а́ть (-ся); **~ment** [-mənt] нача́ло.
commend [kə'mend] рекомен… ва́ть (*im*)*pf.*
comment ['kɔment] **1.** толкова́н… коммента́рий; **2.** (upon) комм… ти́ровать (*im*)*pf.*; объясн… [-ни́ть]; **~ary** ['kɔməntəri] комм… та́рий; **~ator** ['kɔmenteitə] комм… та́тор.
commerc|e ['kɔməs, -ə:s] торг… ля; обще́ние; **~ial** [kə'mə:ʃəl] торго́вый, комме́рческий.
commiseration [kəmizə'rei… сочу́вствие, соболе́знование.
commissary ['kɔmisəri] комисс… уполномо́ченный; ⚔ интенда́…
commission [kə'miʃən] **1.** ком… сия; полномо́чие; поруче́н… ⚔ пате́нт на офице́рский чин… назнача́ть на до́лжность; уп… номо́чи(ва)ть; ⚓ гото́вить (… ра́бль) к пла́ванию; **~er** [kə'miʃ… уполномо́ченный; комисса́р.
commit [kə'mit] поруча́ть [-чи́… вверя́ть [вве́рить]; преда́(в… (огню́, земле́, суду́ и т.п.); сов… ша́ть [-ши́ть] (преступле́ние)… (o. s.) [с]компромети́ровать (се… обя́зывать(ся) [-за́ть(ся)]; ~ … prison) заключа́ть [-чи́ть] (в тю… му́); **~ment** [-mənt], **~tal** [-l] п… да́ча; обяза́тельство; **~tee** [-i] … ми́ссия; комите́т.
commodity [kə'mɔditi] то… предме́т потребле́ния.
common ['kɔmən] **1.** □ о́бщ… просто́й; гру́бый; обыкнове́нн… зауря́дный; ♀ Council муни… па́льный сове́т; ~ law обы́ч… пра́во; ~ sense здра́вый смы… in ~ совме́стно, сообща́; **2.** о́бщ… ная земля́; вы́гон; **~place** … бана́льность *f*; **2.** бана́льный… изби́тый; **~s** [-z] *pl.* о́бщий ст… (*mst* House of) ♀ пала́та о́бщ… **~wealth** [-welθ] содру́жест… федера́ция; the British ♀ of Nat… Брита́нское Содру́жество На́…
commotion [kə'mouʃən] волне́… смяте́ние.
communal ['kɔmjunl] □ ком… на́льный; о́бщи́нный; коллект… ный.
communicat|e [kə'mju:nikeit] сообща́ть [-щи́ть]; перед(ав)… *v/i.* сообща́ться; **~ion** [kəmju… 'keiʃən] сообще́ние; коммуни… ция; связь *f*; **~ive** [kə'mju:nike… □ общи́тельный, разгово́рчив…
communion [kə'mju:njən] об… ние; *eccl.* прича́стие.
communis|m ['kɔmjunizm] к… муни́зм; **~t** **1.** коммуни́ст(ка)… коммунисти́ческий.
community [kə'mju:niti] о́бщ… о́бщество.
commutation [kɔmju'teiʃən] … ме́на; ⚖ смягче́ние наказа́… ⚡ коммута́ция; переключе́ни…
compact **1.** ['kɔmpækt] догово́…

əm'pækt] *adj.* компа́ктный; ло́тный; сжа́тый (о сти́ле); **3.** *t.* сж(им)а́ть; уплотня́ть [-ни́ть].
mpanion [kəm'pænjən] това́ищ; спу́тник; собесе́дник; **~ship** ʃip] компа́ния; това́рищеские тноше́ния *n/pl.*
mpany ['kʌmpəni] о́бщество; омпа́ния, това́рищество; го́сти .; ⚓ экипа́ж (су́дна); *thea.* тру́п- а; have ~ име́ть госте́й; keep ~ ith подде́рживать знако́мство с Т).
mpar|able ['kɔmpərəbl] □ срав- и́мый; **~ative** [kəm'pærətiv] □ равни́тельный; **~e** [kəm'pɛə] **1.** eyond ~, without ~, past ~ вне я́кого сравне́ния; **2.** *v/t.* сра́в- ивать [-ни́ть], слича́ть [-чи́ть], о с Т); уподобля́ть [-до́бить] /Д); *v/i.* сра́вниваться [-ни́ться]; **son** [kəm'pærisn] сравне́ние.
npartment [kəm'pɑːtmənt] от- еле́ние; перегоро́дка; 🚃 купе́ *n decl.*
mpass ['kʌmpəs] **1.** ко́мпас; ъём; окру́жность *f*; ♪ диапа- н; (a pair of) ~es *pl.* ци́ркуль *m*; достига́ть [дости́гнуть] (Р); за- ышля́ть [-ы́слить] (дурно́е).
npassion [kəm'pæʃən] состра- ние, жа́лость *f*; **~ate** [-it] □ страда́тельный, жа́лостливый.
mpatible [kəm'pætəbl] □ сов- ести́мый.
mpatriot [-triət] сооте́чествен- ник (-ица).
mpel [kəm'pel] заставля́ть а́вить]; принужда́ть [-ну́дить].
mpensat|e ['kɔmpenseit] *v/t.* ознагражда́ть [-ради́ть]; возме- а́ть [-ести́ть] (убы́тки); **~ion** ompen'seiʃən] вознагражде́ние; омпенса́ция.
mpete [kəm'piːt] состяза́ться; онкури́ровать (with с Т, for ра́ди .
npeten|ce, ~cy ['kɔmpitəns, -i] осо́бность *f*; компете́нтность *f*; [-tənt] □ компете́нтный.
npetit|ion [kɔmpi'tiʃən] состя- ние; соревнова́ние; ⚖ конку- е́нция; **~or** [kəm'petitə] конку- е́нт(ка); сопе́рник (-ица).
npile [kəm'pail] [с]компили́ро- ть; составля́ть [-а́вить] (from из .
nplacen|ce, ~cy [kəm'pleisns, nsi] самодово́льство.
nplain [kəm'plein] [по]жа́ло- аться (of на В); подава́ть жа́ло- ; **~t** жа́лоба; ⚕ боле́знь *f*; **~ant** ənt] исте́ц.
nplement ['kɔmplimənt] **1.** до- олне́ние; компле́кт; **2.** дополня́ть опо́лнить]; [у]комплектова́ть.
nplet|e [kəm'pliːt] **1.** □ по́лный; ко́нченный; **2.** зака́нчивать [за- ончить]; дополня́ть [-о́лнить]; **on** [-ʃən] оконча́ние.

*

complex ['kɔmpleks] **1.** □ сло́ж- ный; ко́мплексный, составно́й; *fig.* сло́жный, запу́танный; **2.** ко́м- плекс; **~ion** [kəm'plekʃən] цвет лица́; **~ity** [-siti] сло́жность *f*.
compliance [kəm'plaiəns] согла́сие; in ~ with в соотве́тствии с (Т).
complicate ['kɔmplikeit] услож- ня́ть(ся) [-ни́ть(ся)].
compliment 1. ['kɔmplimənt] ком- плиме́нт; приве́т; **2.** [-'ment] *v/t.* говори́ть комплиме́нты (Д); по- здравля́ть [-а́вить] (on с Т).
comply [kəm'plai] соглаша́ться [-ласи́ться] (with с Т); подчиня́ть- ся [-ни́ться] (with Д).
component [kəm'pounənt] **1.** ком- поне́нт; составна́я часть *f*; **2.** составно́й.
compos|e [kəm'pouz] составля́ть [-а́вить]; сочиня́ть [-ни́ть]; писа́ть му́зыку; успока́иваться [-ко́иться]; *typ.* наб(и)ра́ть; **~ed** [-d] □ спо- ко́йный, сде́ржанный; **~er** [-ə] компози́тор; **~ition** [kɔmpə'ziʃən] компози́ция; соста́в; сочине́ние; ⚖ полюбо́вная сде́лка; **~ure** [kəm- 'pouʒə] самооблада́ние.
compound 1. ['kɔmpaund] соста́в, соедине́ние; **2.** составно́й; сло́ж- ный; ~ interest сло́жные про- це́нты *m/pl.*; **3.** [kəm'paund] *v/t.* сме́шивать [-ша́ть]; соединя́ть [-ни́ть]; ула́живать [ула́дить]; *v/i.* приходи́ть к компроми́ссу.
comprehend [kɔmpri'hend] пости- га́ть [пости́гнуть]; обхва́тывать [обхвати́ть].
comprehen|sible [kɔmpri'hensəbl] □ поня́тный, постижи́мый; **~sion** [-ʃən] понима́ние; поня́тливость *f*; **~sive** [-siv] □ объе́млющий; ис- че́рпывающий.
compress [kəm'pres] сж(им)а́ть; сда́вливать [сдави́ть]; ~ed air сжа́тый во́здух; **~ion** [kəm'preʃən] *phys.* сжа́тие; ⊕ компре́ссия; на- би́вка; прокла́дка.
comprise [kəm'praiz] содержа́ть; заключа́ть в себе́.
compromise ['kɔmprəmaiz] **1.** ком- проми́сс; **2.** *v/t.* [с]компромети́ро- вать; подверга́ть ри́ску; *v/i.* пойти́ на компроми́сс.
compuls|ion [kəm'pʌlʃən] принуж- де́ние; **~ory** [-səri] принуди́тель- ный; обяза́тельный.
comput|ation [kɔmpju'teiʃən] вы- числе́ние; вы́кладка; расчёт; **~e** [kəm'pjuːt] вычисля́ть [вы́чис- лить]; де́лать вы́кладки.
comrade ['kɔmrid] това́рищ.
con [kɔn] = contra про́тив.
conceal [kən'siːl] скры(ва́)ть;ута́и- вать [-и́ть], ума́лчивать [умол- ча́ть].
concede [kən'siːd] уступа́ть [-пи́ть]; допуска́ть [-сти́ть].
conceit [kən'siːt] самомне́ние; тще-

сла́вие; ~**ed** [-id] □ самодово́льный; тщесла́вный.
conceiv|able [kən'si:vəbl] мы́слимый; постижи́мый; ~**e** [kən'si:v] *v/i.* представля́ть себе́; *v/t.* постига́ть [пости́гнуть]; понима́ть [-ня́ть]; заду́м(ыв)ать.
concentrate ['kɔnsentreit] сосредото́чи(ва)ть(ся).
conception [kən'sepʃən] поня́тие; конце́пция; за́мысел; *biol.* зача́тие; оплодотворе́ние.
concern [kən'sə:n] **1.** де́ло; уча́стие; интере́с; забо́та; ✝ предприя́тие; **2.** каса́ться [косну́ться] (P); име́ть отноше́ние к (Д); ~ o. s. about, for [за]интересова́ться, занима́ться [заня́ться] (T); ~**ed** [-d] □ заинтересо́ванный; име́ющий отноше́ние; озабо́ченный; ~**ing** [-iŋ] *prp.* относи́тельно (P), каса́тельно (P).
concert 1. ['kɔnsət] конце́рт; согла́сие, соглаше́ние; **2.** [kən'sə:t] сгова́риваться [сговори́ться]; ~ed согласо́ванный.
concession [kən'seʃən] усту́пка; конце́ссия.
conciliat|e [kən'silieit] примиря́ть [-ри́ть]; ~**or** [-ə] посре́дник.
concise [kən'sais] □ сжа́тый, кра́ткий; ~**ness** [-nis] сжа́тость *f*, кра́ткость *f*.
conclude [kən'klu:d] заключа́ть [-чи́ть]; зака́нчивать [зако́нчить]; to be ~d оконча́ние сле́дует.
conclusi|on [kən'klu:ʒən] оконча́ние; заключе́ние; вы́вод; ~**ve** [-siv] □ заключи́тельный; реша́ющий; убеди́тельный.
concoct [kən'kɔkt] [со]стря́пать (*a. fig.*); *fig.* приду́м(ыв)ать; ~**ion** [kən'kɔkʃən] стряпня́; *fig.* небыли́ца.
concord ['kɔŋkɔ:d] согла́сие; соглаше́ние; догово́р, конве́нция; ♪ гармо́ния; ~**ant** [kən'kɔ:dənt] □ согла́сный; согласу́ющийся; ♪ гармони́чный.
concrete ['kɔnkri:t] **1.** □ конкре́тный; **2.** бето́н; **3.** [за]бетони́ровать; [kən'kri:t] сгуща́ть(ся) [сгусти́ть(ся)]; [за]тверде́ть.
concur [kən'kə:] соглаша́ться [-ласи́ться]; совпада́ть [-па́сть]; [по]соде́йствовать; ~**rence** [kən'kʌrəns] совпаде́ние; согла́сие.
condemn [kən'dem] осужда́ть [осуди́ть]; пригова́ривать [-вори́ть] (к Д); [за]бракова́ть; ~**ation** ['kəndem'neiʃən] осужде́ние.
condens|ation ['kɔnden''seiʃən] конденса́ция, уплотне́ние, сгуще́ние; ~**e** [kən'dens] сгуща́ть(ся); ⊕ конденси́ровать (*im*)*pf.*; *fig.* сокраща́ть [-рати́ть].
condescen|d [kɔndi'send] снисходи́ть [снизойти́]; удоста́ивать [-сто́ить]; ~**sion** [-'senʃən] снисхожде́ние; снисходи́тельность *f*.
condiment ['kɔndimənt] припра́
condition [kən'diʃən] **1.** усло́ви состоя́ние; ~s *pl.* обстоя́тельст *n/pl.*; усло́вия *n/pl.*; **2.** ста́ви усло́вия; обусло́вливать [-о́вит ~**al** [-l] □ усло́вный.
condol|e [kən'doul] соболе́знов (with Д); ~**ence** [-əns] соболе́зн вание.
conduc|e [kən'dju:s] спосо́бств вать (to Д); ~**ive** [-iv] спос ствующий.
conduct 1. ['kɔndəkt] поведе́н **2.** [kən'dʌkt] вести́ себя́; руко ди́ть (де́лом); ♪ дирижи́рова ~**ion** [-kʃən] ⊕ проводи́мость ~**or** [kəndʌktə] конду́ктор (тра ва́я и т. п.); *Am.* 🚃 вагоно жа́тый; ♪ дирижёр.
conduit ['kɔndjuit, 'kɔndit] тру прово́д.
cone [koun] ко́нус; ⚘ ши́шка.
confabulation [kənfæbju'leiʃ болтовня́.
confection [kən'fekʃən] сласти *f*/ ~**er** [-ə] конди́тер; ~**ery** [-əri] к ди́терская; конди́терские из лия *n/pl.*
confedera|cy [kən'fedərəsi] к федера́ция; сою́з; ~**te 1.** [-rit] дерати́вный, сою́зный; **2.** [- член конфедера́ции, сою́зник; [-reit] объединя́ться в со ~**tion** [kənfedə'reiʃən] конфеде ция; сою́з.
confer [kənfə:] *v/t.* дарова́ть; п сужда́ть [-уди́ть]; *v/i.* совеща́ть ~**ence** ['kɔnfərəns] конфере́нц съезд; совеща́ние.
confess [kən'fes] призн(ав)а́ть созн(ав)а́ться в (П); испове́д в)ать(ся); ~**ion** [-ʃən] призна́н и́споведь *f*; вероиспове́дание; **ional** [-ʃənl] исповеда́льня *f*; [-sə] испове́дник.
confide [kən'faid] доверя́ть (in вверя́ть [вве́рить]; полага́т [положи́ться] (in на В); ~ ['kɔnfidəns] дове́рие; уве́ренно *f*; ~**nt** ['kɔnfidənt] □ уве́ренн ~**ntial** [kɔnfi'denʃəl] □ конфид циа́льный; секре́тный.
confine [kən'fain] ограни́чи(ва) заключа́ть [-чи́ть] (в тюрьму́); ~d рожа́ть [роди́ть] (of В); ~**m** [-mənt] ограниче́ние; заклю ние; ро́ды *m/pl.*
confirm [kən'fə:m] подтвержд [-рди́ть]; подде́рживать [-жа́т ~**ation** [kɔnfə'meiʃən] подтвер де́ние; *eccl.* конфирма́ция.
confiscat|e ['kɔnfiskeit] конфис ва́ть (*im*)*pf.*; ~**ion** [kɔnfis'kei конфиска́ция.
conflagration [kɔnflə'greiʃən] с жéние; бушу́ющий пожа́р.
conflict 1. ['kɔnflikt] конфли́ столкнове́ние; **2.** [kən'flikt] б в конфли́кте.

nflu|ence ['kɔnfluəns] слия́ние ɔек); стече́ние наро́да; **~ent** ·fluənt] **1.** слива́ющийся; **2.** при- ɔк (реки́).
nform [kən'fɔ:m] согласо́вы- аться [-сова́ться] (to с T); под- иня́ться [-ни́ться] (to Д); **~able** ·əbl] □ (to) соотве́тствующий Д); подчиня́ющийся (Д); **~ity** iti] соотве́тствие; подчине́ние.
nfound [kən'faund] [с]пута́ть; оража́ть [порази́ть], приводи́ть смуще́ние.
nfront [kən'frʌnt] стоя́ть лицо́м лицу́ с (T); слича́ть [-чи́ть] (with T).
nfus|e [kən'fju:z] сме́шивать ·ша́ть]; смуща́ть [-ути́ть]; **~ion** ɔn'fju:ʒən] смуще́ние; беспо- я́док.
nfut|ation [kɔnfju:teiʃən] опро- ерже́ние; **~e** [kən'fju:t] опровер- а́ть [-ве́ргнуть].
ngeal [kən'dʒi:l] засты́(ва́)ть.
ngenial [kən'dʒi:niəl] □ бли́зкий о ду́ху; благоприя́тный.
ngestion [kən'dʒestʃən] перегру́- кенность *f*; перенаселённость *f*.
nglomeration [kɔn'glɔmə''rei- ·n]накопле́ние, скопле́ние.
ngratulat|e [kən'grætjuleit] по- дравля́ть [-а́вить] (on с T); **~ion** ɔngrætju'leiʃən] поздравле́ние.
ngregat|e ['kɔŋgrigeit] соб(и)- а́ть(ся); **~ion** [kɔŋgri'geiʃən] соб- а́ние; *eccl.* прихожа́не *m/pl.*.
ngress ['kɔŋgres] конгре́сс; ьезд.
ngruous ['kɔŋgruəs] □ соот- е́тствующий; гармони́рующий o с T).
nifer ['kounifə] хво́йное де́рево.
njecture [kən'dʒektʃə] **1.** дога́дка, редположе́ние; **2.** предполага́ть ·ложи́ть].
njoin [kən'dʒɔin] соединя́ть(ся) ·ни́ть(ся)]; сочета́ть(ся) (*im*)*pf.*; **t** [-t] о́бщий; объединённый.
njugal ['kɔndʒugəl] □ супру́же- кий, бра́чный.
njunction [kən'dʒʌŋkʃən] соеди- е́ние, связь *f*.
njur|e **1.** ['kʌndʒə] *v/t.* вызыва́ть ы́звать], заклина́ть [-ля́сть] ду́хов); изгоня́ть ду́хов; ~ up *fig.* ызыва́ть в воображе́нии; *v/i.* анима́ться ма́гией; пока́зывать о́кусы; **2.** [kən'dʒuə] умоля́ть ли́ть], заклина́ть; **~er, ~or** [-rə] олшебник; фо́кусник.
nnect [kə'nekt] соединя́ть(ся) ·ни́ть(ся)]; свя́зывать(ся) [-за́ть ся)]; ⚡ соединя́ть [-ни́ть]; **~ed** id] □ свя́занный; свя́зный (о е́чи); be ~ with име́ть свя́зи (с); **~ion** *s.* connexion.
nnexion [kə'nekʃən] связь *f*; со- ине́ние; родство́.
nnive [kə'naiv]: ~ at потво́рство- вать (Д), смотре́ть сквозь па́льцы на (B).
connoisseur [kɔni'sə:] знато́к.
connubial [kə'nju:biəl] □ бра́чный.
conquer ['kɔŋkə] завоёвывать [-оева́ть]; побежда́ть [победи́ть]; **~able** [-rəbl] победи́мый; **~or** [-rə] победи́тель(ница *f*) *m*; за- воева́тель(ница *f*) *m*.
conquest ['kɔŋkwest] завоева́ние; побе́да.
conscience ['kɔnʃəns] со́весть *f*.
conscientious [kɔnʃi'enʃəs] □ доб- росо́вестный; **~ness** [-nis] доб- росо́вестность *f*.
conscious ['kɔnʃəs] □ созна́тель- ный; сознаю́щий; **~ness** [-nis] созна́ние; созна́тельность *f*.
conscript ['kɔnskript] ⚔ призыв- ни́к; **~ion** [kən'skripʃən] ⚔ во́ин- ская пови́нность *f*.
consecrat|e ['kɔnsikreit] освяща́ть [-яти́ть]; посвящать [-яти́ть]; **~ion** [kɔnsi'kreiʃən] освяще́ние; посвяще́ние.
consecutive [kən'sekjutiv] □ после́- довательный.
consent [kən'sent] **1.** согла́сие; **2.** соглаша́ться [-ласи́ться].
consequen|ce ['kɔnsikwəns] (по-) сле́дствие; вы́вод, заключе́ние; **~t** [-kwənt] **1.** после́довательный; **2.** (по)сле́дствие; **~tial** [kɔnsi- 'kwenʃəl] □ логи́чески вытека́ю- щий; ва́жный; **~tly** ['kɔnsikwəntli] сле́довательно; поэ́тому.
conserv|ation [kɔnsə'veiʃən] со- хране́ние; **~ative** [kən'sə:vətiv] **1.** □ консервати́вный; охрани́тель- ный; **2.** *pol.* консерва́тор; **~atory** [-tri] оранжере́я; ♪ консервато́- рия; **~e** [kən'sə:v] сохраня́ть [-ни́ть].
consider [kən'sidə] *v/t.* обсужда́ть [-уди́ть]; обду́м(ыв)ать; полага́ть, счита́ть; счита́ться с (T); *v/i.* со- обража́ть [-рази́ть]; **~able** [-rəbl] □ значи́тельный; ва́жный; боль- шо́й; **~ate** [-rit] □ внима́тельный (к Д); **~ation** [kənsidə'reiʃən] об- сужде́ние; соображе́ние; внима́- ние; on no ~ ни под каки́м ви́дом; **~ing** [kən'sidəriŋ] *prp.* учи́тывая (B), принима́я во внима́ние (B).
consign [kən'sain] перед(ав)а́ть; поруча́ть [-чи́ть]; ☤ посыла́ть (груз) на консигна́цию; **~ment** [-ment] па́ртия това́ров; коно- саме́нт.
consist [kən'sist] состоя́ть (of из P); заключа́ться (in в П); **~ence, ~ency** [-əns, -ənsi] логи́чность *f*; пло́тность *f*; **~ent** [-ənt] □ пло́т- ный; после́довательный; согла- су́ющийся (with с T).
consol|ation [kɔnsə'leiʃən] уте- ше́ние; **~e** [kən'soul] утеша́ть [уте́шить].
consolidate [kən'sɔlideit] под-

твержда́ть [-рди́ть]; объединя́ть (-ся) [-ни́ть(ся)]; консолиди́ровать (за́ймы) (*im*)*pf*.

consonan|ce ['kɔnsənəns] созву́чие; согла́сие; **~t** [-nənt] □ согла́сный (*a.* noun); совмести́мый.

consort ['kɔnsɔ:t] супру́г(а).

conspicuous [kən'spikjuəs] □ заме́тный, броса́ющийся в глаза́.

conspir|acy [kən'spirəsi] за́говор; **~ator** [-tə] загово́рщик (-ица); **~e** [kən'spaiə] устра́ивать за́говор; сгова́риваться [-вори́ться].

constab|le ['kʌnstəbl] консте́бль *m*, полице́йский; **~ulary** [kən'stæbjuləri] поли́ция.

constan|cy ['kɔnstənsi] постоя́нство; ве́рность *f*; **~t** ['kɔnstənt] □ постоя́нный; ве́рный.

consternation [kɔnstə'neiʃən] оцепене́ние (от стра́ха).

constipation [kɔnsti'peiʃən] ⚕ запо́р.

constituen|cy [kən'stitjuənsi] избира́тельный о́круг; избира́тели *m/pl.*; **~t** [-ənt] суще́ственный; учреди́тельный; **2.** избира́тель *m*; составна́я часть *f*.

constitut|e ['kɔnstitju:t] составля́ть [-а́вить]; осно́вывать [-нова́ть]; **~ion** [kɔnsti'tju:ʃn] конститу́ция; учрежде́ние; телосложе́ние; соста́в; **~ional** [-l] □ конституцио́нный; органи́ческий.

constrain [kən'strein] принужда́ть [-ну́дить]; сде́рживать [-жа́ть]; **~t** [-t] принужде́ние; принуждённость *f*.

constrict [kən'strikt] стя́гивать [стяну́ть]; сж(им)а́ть; **~ion** [kən'strikʃən] сжа́тие; стя́гивание.

construct [kən'strʌkt] [по]стро́ить; сооружа́ть [-уди́ть]; *fig.* созд(ав)а́ть; **~ion** [-kʃən] строи́тельство, стро́йка; строе́ние; **~ive** [-tiv] конструкти́вный; строи́тельный; тво́рческий; **~or** [-tə] строи́тель *m*.

construe [kən'stru:] истолко́вывать [-кова́ть]; *gr.* де́лать синтакси́ческий разбо́р.

consul ['kɔnsəl] ко́нсул; ~ general генера́льный ко́нсул; **~ate** ['kɔnsjulit] ко́нсульство.

consult [kən'sʌlt] *v/t.* спра́шивать сове́та у (Р); *v/i.* [по]сове́товаться, совеща́ться; **~ation** [kɔnsəl'teiʃən] консульта́ция; конси́лиум (враче́й); **~ative** [kən'sʌltətiv] совеща́тельный.

consum|e [kən'sju:m] *v/t.* потребля́ть [-би́ть]; [из]расхо́довать; **~er** [-ə] потреби́тель *m*.

consummate 1. [kən'sʌmit] □ соверше́нный, зако́нченный; **2.** ['kɔnsʌmeit] доводи́ть до конца́; заверша́ть [-ши́ть].

consumpti|on [kən'sʌmpʃən] потребле́ние, расхо́д; ⚕ туберкулёз лёгких; **~ve** [-tiv] □ туберкул... ный, чахо́точный.

contact ['kɔntækt] конта́кт; сопр... косновéние.

contagi|on [kən'teidʒən] ⚕ зара́... инфе́кция; **~ous** [-dʒəs] □ зар... зи́тельный, инфекцио́нный.

contain [kən'tein] содержа́ть ... себе́), вмеща́ть [-вести́ть]; ~ o... сде́рживаться [-жа́ться]; **~er** [-... вмести́лище; конте́йнер.

contaminate [kən'tæmineit] ... грязня́ть [-ни́ть]; *fig.* заража́... [зарази́ть]; оскверня́ть [-ни́ть].

contemplat|e ['kɔntempleit] созе... ца́ть; обду́м(ыв)ать; **~ion** [kɔ... tem'pleiʃən] созерца́ние; размы... ле́ние; **~ive** [kən'templətiv] ... созерца́тельный.

contempora|neous [kəntempə'rei... jəs] □ совреме́нный; одновре́ме... ный; **~ry** [kən'tempərəri] **1.** сов... ме́нный; одновре́ме́нный; **2.** ... вре́менник (-ица).

contempt [kən'tempt] презре́н... (for к Д); **~ible** [-əbl] □ презре́... ный; **~uous** [-juəs] □ презри́те... ный.

contend [kən'tend] *v/i.* боро́тьс... сопе́рничать; *v/t.* утвержда́ть.

content [kən'tent] **1.** дово́льны... **2.** удовлетворя́ть [-ри́ть]; **3.** ... во́льство; **4.** ['kɔntent] соде... жа́ние; объём; **~ed** [kən'tent... □ дово́льный, удовлетворённы...

contention [kən'tenʃən] спор, ссо́...

contentment [kən'tentmənt] ... во́льство.

contest 1. ['kɔntest] соревнова́н... **2.** [kən'test] оспа́ривать [осп... рить]; доби́(ва́)ться (ме́ста); ... ста́ивать [отстоя́ть] (террито́ри...

context ['kɔntekst] конте́кст.

contiguous [kən'tiguəs] □ сме́... ный, соприкаса́ющийся (to с ...

continent ['kɔntinənt] **1.** □ сде́... жанный; целому́дренный; **2.** м... тери́к, контине́нт.

contingen|cy [kən'tindʒənsi] с... ча́йность *f*; непредви́денное ... стоя́тельство; **~t** [-dʒənt] **1.** ... случа́йный, непредви́денный; ... ⚔, ⚓ континге́нт.

continu|al [kən'tinjuəl] □ бесп... ры́вный, беспреста́нный; **~an...** [-juəns] продолжи́тельность ... **~ation** [kəntinju'eiʃən] прод... же́ние; **~e** [kən'tinju:] *v/t.* продо... жа́ть [-до́лжить]; to be ~d продо... же́ние сле́дует; *v/i.* продолжа́ть... [-до́лжиться]; простира́ться; **~...** [kɔntin'juiti] непреры́вность ... **~ous** [kən'tinjuəs] □ непреры́... ный; сплошно́й.

contort [kən'tɔ:t] искажа́ть [иск... зи́ть] **~ion** [kən'tɔ:ʃən] искаже́н... искривле́ние.

contour ['kɔntuə] ко́нтур, очер... ние.

ntraband ['kɔntrəbænd] контра-
анда.
ntract 1. [kən'trækt] *v/t.* сокра-
(ать [-рати́ть]; сж(им)а́ть; заклю-
а́ть [-чи́ть] (сде́лку, дру́жбу); за-
оди́ть [-вести́](знако́мство); всту-
а́ть [-пи́ть] в (брак); *v/i.* сокра-
(а́ться [-рати́ться]; сж(им)а́ть
ся); **2.** ['kɔntrækt] контра́кт, до-
овóр; **~ion** [kən'trækʃən] сжа́тие;
окраще́ние; **~or** [-tə] подря́дчик.
ntradict [kɔntrə'dikt] противо-
е́чить (Д); **~ion** [kɔntrə'dikʃən]
ротиворе́чие; **~ory** [-təri] □
ротиворечи́вый.
ntrar|iety [kɔntrə'raiəti] разно-
ла́сие, противоре́чие; **~y** ['kɔn-
əri] **1.** противополо́жный; ~ to
rp. вопреки́ (Д), про́тив (Р); **2.**
бра́тное; on the ~ наоборо́т.
ntrast 1. ['kɔntræst] противопо-
о́жность *f*, контра́ст; **2.** [kən-
ræst] сопоставля́ть [-а́вить], про-
ивополага́ть [-ложи́ть]; состав-
я́ть контра́ст.
ntribut|e [kən'tribju:t] соде́йст-
овать, спосо́бствовать; [по]же́рт-
овать; сотру́дничать (to в П);
ion [kɔntri'bju:ʃən] вклад; взнос;
татья́; сотру́дничество; **~or** [kən-
ribjutə] сотру́дник (-ица); **~ory**
-təri] соде́йствующий; сотру́дни-
ающий.
ntrit|e ['kɔntrait] □ сокруша́ю-
ийся, ка́ющийся; **~ion** [kən'tri-
ən] раска́яние.
ntriv|ance [kən'traivəns] вы́-
умка; изобрете́ние; **~e** [kən'traiv]
/t. приду́м(ыв)ать; изобрета́ть
ести́]; затева́ть [-е́ять]; *v/i.* ухит-
я́ться [-ри́ться]; умудря́ться
ри́ться]; **~er** [-ə] изобрета́тель
ница *f*) *m.*
ntrol [kən'troul] **1.** руково́дство;
адзо́р; контро́ль *m*; **2.** управля́ть
Г); [про]контроли́ровать, регу-
и́ровать (*im*)*pf.*; сде́рживать
-жа́ть] (чу́вства, слёзы); **~ler** [-ə]
онтролёр, инспе́ктор.
ntrover|sial [kɔntrə'və:ʃəl] □
по́рный; **~sy** ['kɔntrəvə:si] спор,
иску́ссия, поле́мика; **~t** ['kɔntrə-
ə:t] оспа́ривать [оспо́рить].
ntumacious [kɔntju'meiʃes] □
по́рный; непоко́рный; ⚖ непод-
иня́ющийся распоряже́нию су-
а́.
ntumely ['kɔntjum(i)li] оскорб-
е́ние; де́рзость *f*; бесче́стье.
nvalesce [kɔnvə'les] выздора́в-
ивать [вы́здороветь]; **~nce** [-ns]
ыздоровле́ние; **~nt** [-nt] □ вы-
дора́вливающий.
nvene [kən'vi:n] соз(ы)ва́ть;
об(и)ра́ть(ся); ⚖ вызыва́ть [вы́-
ва́ть] (в суд).
nvenien|ce [kən'vi:njəns] удо́б-
тво; at your earliest как мо́жно
коре́е; **~t** [-jənt] □ удо́бный.

convent ['kɔnvənt] монасты́рь *m*; **~ion** [kən'venʃən] собра́ние; съезд; соглаше́ние; обы́чай.
converge [kən'və:dʒ] сходи́ться [сойти́сь]; сводить в одну́ то́чку.
convers|ant ['kɔnvəsnt] све́дущий; **~ation** [kɔnvə'seiʃn] разгово́р, бесе́да; **~ational** [-l] разгово́рный; **~e** [kən'və:s] разгова́ривать, бесе́довать; **~ion** [kən'və:ʃən] превраще́ние; измене́ние; ⊕ перерабо́тка, превра́щение; ⚡ трансформи́рование; *eccl.* обраще́ние в другу́ю ве́ру; ⚕ конве́рсия.
convert 1. ['kɔnvə:t] новообращённый; **2.** [kən'və:t] превраща́ть [-ати́ть]; ⊕ перераба́тывать [-бо́тать]; ⚡ трансформи́ровать (*im*)*pf.*; *eccl.* обраща́ть [-рати́ть] (в другу́ю ве́ру); ⚕ конверти́ровать (*im*)*pf.*; **~er** [-ə] ⚡ конве́ртер; **~ible** [-əbl] □ изменя́емый; обрати́мый; ⚕ подлежа́щий конве́рсии.
convey [kən'vei] перевози́ть [-вез-ти́], переправля́ть [-пра́вить]; перед(ав)а́ть; **~ance** [-əns] перево́зка; доста́вка; **~or** [-ə] ⊕ (или ~ belt) конве́йер; транспортёр.
convict 1. ['kɔnvikt] осуждённый; ка́торжник; **2.** [kən'vikt] признава́ть вино́вным; изоблича́ть [-чи́ть]; **~ion** [kən'vikʃən] ⚖ осужде́ние; убежде́ние.
convince [kən'vins] убежда́ть [убеди́ть] (of в П).
convocation [kɔnvo'keiʃən] созы́в; собра́ние.
convoke [kən'vouk] соз(ы)ва́ть.
convoy 1. ['kɔnvɔi] конво́й; сопровожде́ние; **2.** [kən'vɔi] сопровожда́ть; конвои́ровать.
convuls|ion [kən'vʌlʃən] колеба́ние (по́чвы); су́дорога; **~ive** [-siv] □ су́дорожный.
coo [ku:] воркова́ть.
cook [kuk] **1.** куха́рка, по́вар; **2.** [со]стря́пать, [при]гото́вить; **~ery** ['kukəri] кулина́рия; стряпня́; **~ie**, **~y** ['kuki] *Am.* пече́нье.
cool [ku:l] **1.** прохла́дный; *fig.* хладнокро́вный; невозмути́мый; *b. s.* де́рзкий, наха́льный; **2.** прохла́да; хладнокро́вие; **3.** охлажда́ть(ся) [охлади́ть(ся)]; осты́(ва́)ть.
coolness ['ku:lnis] холодо́к; прохла́да; хладнокро́вие.
coop [ku:p] **1.** куря́тник; **2.** ~ up или in держа́ть взаперти́.
cooper ['ku:pə] бо́ндарь *m.*
co-operat|e [kou'ɔpəreit] сотру́дничать; **~ion** [kouɔpə'reiʃən] коопера́ция; сотру́дничество; **~ive** [kou'ɔpərətiv] совме́стный, объединённый; ~ society кооперати́вное о́бщество; **~or** [-eitə] сотру́дник; коопера́тор.
co-ordinat|e 1. [kou'ɔ:dnit] □ неподчинённый; ра́вный; **2.** [-neit]

координи́ровать (*im*)*pf.*; согласо́вывать [-ова́ть]; **~ion** [kouˈɔːdiˈˈneiʃən] координа́ция.
cope [koup]: ~ with справля́ться [-а́виться] с (Т).
copious [ˈkoupjəs] □ оби́льный; **~ness** [-nis] оби́лие.
copper [ˈkɔpə] **1.** медь *f*; ме́дная моне́та; **2.** ме́дный; **~y** [-ri] цве́та ме́ди.
coppice, copse [ˈkɔpis, kɔps] ро́ща.
copy [ˈkɔpi] **1.** ко́пия; ру́копись *f*; экземпля́р; **2.** переписывать [-са́ть]; снима́ть ко́пию с (Р); **~-book** тетра́дь *f*; **~ing** [ˈkɔpiiŋ] перепи́сывание; **~ist** [ˈkɔpiist] перепи́счик; подража́тель *m*; **~-right** [-rait] а́вторское пра́во.
coral [ˈkɔrəl] кора́лл.
cord [kɔːd] **1.** верёвка, шнуро́к; *anat.* свя́зка; **2.** свя́зывать [-за́ть]; **~ed** [ˈkɔːdid] ру́бчатый (о мате́рии).
cordial [ˈkɔːdiəl] **1.** □ серде́чный, и́скренний; **2.** стимули́рующее (серде́чное) сре́дство; **~ity** [kɔːdiˈæliti] серде́чность *f*, раду́шие.
cordon [ˈkɔːdən] **1.** кордо́н; **2.** ~ off отгора́живать [-роди́ть].
corduroy [ˈkɔːdərɔi, -dju] ру́бчатый плис, вельве́т; **~s** *pl.* пли́совые (*or* вельве́товые) штаны́ *m/pl.*
core [kɔː] **1.** сердцеви́на; вну́тренность *f*; ядро́; *fig.* суть *f*; **2.** выре́зывать сердцеви́ну из (Р).
cork [kɔːk] **1.** про́бка; **2.** затыка́ть про́бкой; **~-jacket** спаса́тельный жиле́т; **~-screw** што́пор.
corn [kɔːn] зерно́; хлеба́ *m/pl.*; *Am.* кукуру́за, маи́с; ⚕ мозо́ль *f*.
corner [ˈkɔːnə] **1.** у́гол; **2.** ✝ ску́пка това́ра; **3.** *fig.* загна́ть в тупи́к; припере́ть к стене́; ✝ скупа́ть това́р.
cornet [ˈkɔːnit] ♪ корне́т, корне́т-а-писто́н.
cornice [ˈkɔːnis] ⟁ карни́з.
coron|ation [kɔrəˈneiʃən] корона́ция; **~et** [ˈkɔrənit] коро́на, диаде́ма.
corpor|al [ˈkɔːpərəl] **1.** □ теле́сный; **2.** ⚔ капра́л; **~ation** [kɔːpəˈreiʃən] корпора́ция; муниципалите́т; *Am.* акционе́рное о́бщество.
corpse [kɔːps] труп.
corpulen|ce, ~cy [ˈkɔːpjuləns] доро́дность *f*, ту́чность *f*; **~t** [-lənt] доро́дный, ту́чный.
corral *Am.* [kɔˈrɑːl] **1.** заго́н (для скота́); **2.** загоня́ть [загна́ть].
correct [kəˈrekt] **1.** □ пра́вильный, ве́рный, то́чный; **2.** *v/t.* исправля́ть [-а́вить], [про]корректи́ровать; **~ion** [kəˈrekʃən] исправле́ние, попра́вка; house of ~ исправи́тельный дом.
correlate [ˈkɔrileit] устана́вливать соотноше́ние.
correspond [kɔrisˈpɔnd] соотве́тсвовать (with, to Д); согласо́вываться [-сова́ться] (с Т); перепи́сываться (с Т); **~ence** [-əns] соотве́тствие, соотноше́ние; перепи́ска; **~ent** [-ənt] **1.** □ соотве́тствующий; **2.** корреспонде́нт(ка).
corridor [ˈkɔridɔː] коридо́р; ~ train по́езд, состоя́щий из вагонов, соединённых та́мбурами.
corroborate [kəˈrɔbəreit] подде́рживать [-жа́ть]; подтвержда́ть [-рди́ть].
corro|de [kəˈroud] разъеда́ть [-е́сть]; [за]ржаве́ть; **~sion** [kəˈrouʒən] корро́зия; ржа́вчина; окисле́ние; **~sive** [-siv] **1.** □ е́дкий; **2.** е́дкое вещество́.
corrugate [ˈkɔrugeit] смо́рщи(ва)ть(ся); ⊕ де́лать рифлёным, волни́стым; **~d** iron рифлёное желе́зо.
corrupt [kəˈrʌpt] **1.** □ испо́рченный; искажённый; развращённый; **2.** *v/t.* искажа́ть [-зи́ть]; развраща́ть [-рати́ть]; подкупа́ть [-пи́ть]; *v/i.* [ис]по́ртиться; искажа́ться [-зи́ться]; **~ible** [kəˈrʌptəbl] □ подкупно́й; **~ion** [-ʃən] по́рча; искаже́ние; прода́жность *f*.
corsage [kɔːˈsɑːʒ] корса́ж.
corset [ˈkɔːsit] корсе́т.
co-signatory [ˈkouˈsignətəri] лицо́, подписа́вшее соглаше́ние совме́стно с други́ми; **2.** подпи́сывающий соглаше́ние совме́стно с други́ми.
cosmetic [kɔzˈmetik] **1.** космети́ческий; **2.** косме́тика.
cosmopolit|an [kɔzmoˈpɔlitən] космополити́ческий; **~e** [kɔzˈmɔpəlait] **1.** космополи́т(ка); **2.** космополити́ческий.
cost [kɔst] **1.** цена́, сто́имость *f*; first и́ли prime ~ фабри́чная себесто́имость *f*; **2.** [*irr.*] сто́ить.
costl|iness [ˈkɔstlinis] дорогови́зна; **~y** [-li] дорого́й, це́нный.
costume [ˈkɔstjuːm] (национа́льный и́ли маскара́дный) костю́м.
cosy [ˈkouzi] **1.** □ ую́тный; **2.** стёганый чехо́л (для ча́йника).
cot [kɔt] де́тская крова́ть *f*; ⚓ ко́йка.
cottage [ˈkɔtidʒ] котте́дж; изба́; *Am.* ле́тняя да́ча; ~ piano небольшо́е пиани́но *n indecl.*
cotton [ˈkɔtn] **1.** хло́пок; хлопча́тая бума́га; ✝ си́тец; ни́тка; **2.** хлопчатобума́жный; ~ wool ва́та; **3.** сдружи́ться (to с Т) *pf.*
couch [kautʃ] **1.** куше́тка; ло́говище; **2.** *v/t.* излага́ть [изложи́ть]; [с]формули́ровать; *v/i.* лежа́ть; притаи́ться *pf.* (о звеpя́х).
cough [kɔːf, kɔf] **1.** ка́шель *m*; **2.** ка́шлять [кашляну́ть].
could [kud] *pt.* от can.

ouncil ['kaunsl] совéт; **~(l)or** [-silə] член совéта; совéтник.
ounsel ['kaunsəl] **1.** обсуждéние, совещáние; ⚖ адвокáт; ~ for the prosecution обвинúтель *m*; **2.** давáть совéт (Д); **~(l)or** [-ə] советник; *Am.* адвокáт.
ount¹ [kaunt] **1.** счёт, подсчёт; итóг; ⚖ статья́ в обвинúтельном акте; **2.** *v/t.* [со]считáть; подсчúтывать [-итáть]; зачисля́ть [-úслить]; *v/i.* считáться; имéть значéние.
ount² [~] граф (не англúйский).
ountenance ['kauntinəns] **1.** лицó; самообладáние; поддéржка; **2.** поддéрживать [-жáть], поощря́ть [-рúть].
ounter¹ ['kauntə] прилáвок; стóйка; таксóметр; счётчик; фúшка.
ounter² [~] **1.** противополóжный (to Д); встрéчный; **2.** *adv.* обрáтно; напрóтив; **3.** [вос]протúвиться (Д); (в бóксе) наносúть встрéчный удáр.
ounteract [kauntə'rækt] противодéйствовать (Д); нейтрализовáть (*im*)*pf*.
ounterbalance **1.** ['kauntəbæləns] противовéс; **2.** [kauntə'bæləns] уравновéшивать [-вéсить]; служúть противовéсом (Д).
ounter-espionage ['kauntər'espiənɑ:ʒ] контрразвéдка.
ounterfeit ['kauntəfit] **1.** поддéльный, подлóжный; **2.** поддéлка; **3.** поддéл(ыв)ать; обмáнывать [-нýть].
ountermand **1.** ['kauntə'mɑ:nd] контрприкáз; **2.** [kauntə'mɑ:nd] отменя́ть [-нúть] (закáз, прикáз); отзывáть [отозвáть] (лицó, вóинскую часть).
ounter-move ['kauntəmu:v] *fig.* отвéтная мéра.
ounterpane [-pein] покрывáло; стёганое одея́ло.
ounterpart [-pɑ:t] кóпия; двойник; **~s** лúца úли вéщи, взаúмно дополня́ющие друг дрýга.
ounterpoise [-pɔiz] **1.** противовéс; равновéсие; **2.** держáть равновéсие; (*a. fig.*) уравновéшивать [-éсить].
ountersign [-sain] **1.** контрасигнóвка; ⚔ парóль *m*; **2.** скрепля́ть [-пúть] (пóдписью).
ountervail [-veil] противостоя́ть (Д); уравновéшивать [-éсить].
ountess ['kauntis] графúня.
ounting-house ['kauntiŋhaus] контóра.
ountless ['kauntlis] бесчúсленный, несчётный.
ountry ['kʌntri] **1.** странá; мéстность *f*; дерéвня; **2.** деревéнский; **man** [-mən] крестья́нин; земля́к; **side** [-'said] сéльская мéстность *f*; сéльское населéние.

county ['kaunti] грáфство; *Am.* óкруг.
coup [ku:] удáчный ход (удáр и т. п.).
couple [kʌpl] **1.** пáра; свóра; **2.** соединя́ть [-нúть]; ассоциúровать (*im*)*pf*.; ⊕ сцепля́ть [-пúть]; **~r** [-ə] *radio* устрóйство связи.
coupling ['kʌpliŋ] совокуплéние; ⊕ мýфта; сцеплéние; *radio* связь *f*.
coupon ['ku:pɔn] купóн, талóн.
courage ['kʌridʒ] мýжество, смéлость *f*, хрáбрость *f*, отвáга; **~ous** [kə'reidʒəs] □ мýжественный, смéлый, хрáбрый.
courier ['kuriə] курьéр, нарóчный.
course [kɔ:s] **1.** направлéние, курс; ход; течéние; блю́до (за обéдом); of ~ конéчно; **2.** *v/t.* гнáться за (Т); охóтиться (с гóнчими) на (В) *or* за (Т); *v/i.* бéгать, [по]бежáть.
court [kɔ:t] **1.** двор (*a. fig.*); суд; pay (one's) ~ ухáживать (to за Т); **2.** ухáживать за (Т); искáть располóжения (Р); **~eous** ['kə:tiəs] □ вéжливый, учтúвый; **~esy** ['kə:tisi] учтúвость *f*, вéжливость *f*; **~ier** ['kɔ:tjə] придвóрный; **~ly** [-ly] вéжливый; **~-martial** ⚔ **1.** воéнный трибунáл; **2.** судúть воéнным судóм; **~ship** [-ʃip] ухáживание; **~yard** двор.
cousin ['kʌzn] двою́родный брат, двою́родная сестрá.
cove [kouv] (мáленькая) бýхта; *fig.* убéжище.
covenant ['kʌvinənt] **1.** ⚖ договóр; завéт; **2.** соглашáться [-ласúться].
cover ['kʌvə] **1.** крышка; обёртка; покрывáло; переплёт; конвéрт; ⚔ укрытие; *fig.* покрóв; ⊕ кожýх; *mot.* покрышка; **2.** покры(вá)ть (*a.* ✝); прикры(вá)ть; скры(вá)ть; **~ing** [-riŋ] (по)крышка; обшúвка; облицóвка.
covert ['kʌvət] **1.** □ прикрытый, тáйный; **2.** убéжище для дúчи.
covet ['kʌvit] жáждать (Р); **~ous** [-əs] □ жáдный, áлчный; скупóй.
cow¹ [kau] корóва.
cow² [~] запýгивать [-гáть]; терроризовáть (*im*)*pf*.
coward ['kauəd] **1.** □ труслúвый; малодýшный, рóбкий; **2.** трус (-úха); **~ice** [-is] трýсость *f*; малодýшие; **~ly** [-li] труслúвый.
cowboy ['kaubɔi] пастýх; *Am.* ковбóй.
cower ['kauə] съёжи(ва)ться.
cowl [kaul] капюшóн.
coxcomb ['kɔkskoum] ⚘ петýший гребешóк; фат.
coxswain ['kɔkswein, *mst* 'kɔksn] рулевóй.
coy [kɔi] □ застéнчивый, скрóмный.
crab [kræb] *zo.* краб; ⊕ лебёдка, вóрот; F ворчлúвый человéк.
crab-louse ['kræblaus] площúца.

crack ['kræk] **1.** треск; тре́щина; щель *f*; рассе́лина; F уда́р; *Am.* саркасти́ческое замеча́ние; *Am.* at ~ of day на заре́; **2.** F перво-кла́ссный; **3.** *v/t.* раска́лывать [-коло́ть], коло́ть; ~ a joke отпусти́ть шу́тку; *v/i.* производи́ть треск, шум; тре́скаться [тре́снуть], раска́лываться [-коло́ться]; лома́ться (о го́лосе); **~ed** [krækt] тре́снувший; F вы́живший из ума́; **~er** ['krækə] хлопу́шка-конфе́та; *Am.* то́нкое сухо́е пече́нье; **~le** ['krækl] потре́скивание; треск.
cradle ['kreidl] **1.** колыбе́ль *f*; *fig.* нача́ло; младе́нчество; **2.** убаю-к(ив)ать.
craft [krɑːft] ло́вкость; сноро́вка; ремесло́; су́дно (*pl.* суда́); **~sman** ['krɑːftsmən] ма́стер; ремéсленник; **~y** ['krɑːfti] □ ло́вкий, иску́сный; хи́трый.
crag [kræg] скала́, утёс.
cram [kræm] впи́хивать [-хну́ть]; переполня́ть [-о́лнить]; [на]пи́чкать; F [за]зубри́ть.
cramp [kræmp] **1.** су́дорога, спа́змы *f/pl.*; ⊕ зажи́м, скоба́; **2.** вызыва́ть су́дорогу у (Р); стесня́ть [-ни́ть] (разви́тие); су́живать [су́зить] (по́ле де́йствия).
cranberry ['krænbəri] клю́ква.
crane [krein] **1.** жура́вль *m*; ⊕ подъёмный кран; **2.** поднима́ть кра́ном; вытя́гивать ше́ю.
crank [kræŋk] **1.** рукоя́тка; причу́да; челове́к с причу́дами; **2.** заводи́ть рукоя́тью (автомоби́ль и т. п.); **~-shaft** ⊕ колéнчатый вал; **~y** [kræŋki] неиспра́вный (механи́зм); капри́зный; эксцентри́чный.
cranny ['kræni] щель *f*, тре́щина.
crape [kreip] креп; тра́ур.
crash [kræʃ] **1.** гро́хот, треск; ✈ ава́рия; 🚂 круше́ние; ✝ крах; **2.** па́дать, ру́шиться с тре́ском; разби́(ва́)ть(ся); ✈ потерпе́ть ава́рию.
crater ['kreitə] кра́тер; ⚔ воро́нка.
crave [kreiv] *v/t.* настоя́тельно проси́ть; *v/i.* стра́стно жела́ть, жа́ждать (for P).
crawfish ['krɔːfiʃ] речно́й рак.
crawl [krɔːl] **1.** по́лзание; *fig.* пресмыка́тельство; **2.** пресмыка́ться; по́лзать, [по]ползти́.
crayfish ['kreifiʃ] речно́й рак.
crayon ['kreiən] цветно́й каранда́ш; пасте́ль *f* (каранда́ш); пасте́льный рису́нок.
craz|e [kreiz] **1.** ма́ния; F мо́да, пова́льное увлече́ние; be the ~ быть в мо́де; **2.** своди́ть с ума́; сходи́ть с ума́; **~y** ['kreizi] □ поме́шанный; ша́ткий.
creak [kriːk] **1.** скрип; **2.** [за]скрипе́ть.
cream [kriːm] **1.** сли́вки *f/pl.*; крем; са́мое лу́чшее; **2.** снима́ сли́вки с (Р); **~ery** ['kriːməri] ма лобо́йня; моло́чная; **~y** ['kriːm □ сли́вочный; кре́мовый.
crease [kriːs] **1.** скла́дка; сгиб; [с]мя́ть(ся); загиба́ть [загну́т
creat|e [kri'eit] [со]твори́ть; со д(ав)а́ть; **~ion** [-ʃən] создáни (со)творе́ние; **~ive** [-tiv] тво́рч ский; **~or** [-tə] созда́тель *m*, тв ре́ц; **~ure** ['kriːtʃə] созда́ние; с щество́; тварь *f*.
creden|ce ['kriːdəns] ве́ра, дов рие; **~tials** [kriː'denʃəlz] *pl.* в ри́тельные гра́моты *f/pl.*, док ме́нты *m/pl.*
credible ['kredəbl] □ заслу́жи ва́ющий дове́рие; вероя́тный.
credit ['kredit] **1.** дове́рие; хор шая репута́ция; ✝ креди́т; ве́рить, доверя́ть (Д); ✝ кредит ва́ть (*im*)*pf.*; ~ a p. with a th. пр пи́сывать кому́-либо что-либ **~able** ['kreditəbl] □ похва́льны **~or** [-tə] кредито́р.
credulous ['kredjuləs] □ легкове́ ный, дове́рчивый.
creed [kriːd] вероуче́ние; кре́ *indecl. n.*
creek [kriːk] бу́хта; зали́в; рук реки́; *Am.* прито́к; руче́й.
creep [kriːp] [*irr.*] по́лзать, [по ползти́; ви́ться (о расте́ниях кра́сться; *fig.* ~ in вкра́дывать [вкра́сться]; **~er** ['kriːpə] вьющ еся расте́ние.
crept [krept] *pt.* и *p. pt.* от creep
crescent ['kresnt] **1.** расту́щи ['kreznt] серпови́дный; **2.** пол ме́сяц.
crest [krest] гребешо́к (петуха́ хохоло́к (пти́цы); гре́бень (волны́, горы́, шле́ма); **~-fall** ['krestfɔːlən] упа́вший ду́хо уны́лый.
crevasse [kri'væs] рассе́лина (в ле нике́); *Am.* проры́в плоти́ны.
crevice ['krevis] щель *f*, расще́л на, тре́щина.
crew[1] [kruː] брига́да, арте́ль раб чих; ⚓ судова́я кома́нда.
crew[2] [~] *pt.* от crow.
crib [krib] **1.** я́сли *m/pl.*, корму́шк де́тская крова́тка; *school*: шпа га́лка; **2.** помеща́ть в те́сное п меще́ние; F спи́сывать тайко́м.
cricket ['krikit] *zo.* сверчо́к; кр ке́т (игра́); F not ~ не по пра́в лам, нече́стно.
crime [kraim] преступле́ние.
crimina|l ['kriminəl] **1.** престу́ ник; **2.** престу́пный; кримина́л ный, уголо́вный; **~lity** [krimi'n liti] престу́пность *f*; вино́вность
crimp [krimp] гофрирова́ть (*im*)
crimson ['krimzn] **1.** багро́вы мали́новый **2.** [по]красне́ть.
cringe [krindʒ] раболе́пствова
crinkle ['kriŋkl] **1.** скла́дка; мо

ина; **2.** [с]мо́рщиться; за-
й(ва́)ться; [по]мя́ться.
ipple ['kripl] **1.** кале́ка *m/f*, ин-
али́д; **2.** [ис]калéчить, [из]уро́до-
ать; *fig.* парализова́ть (*im*)*pf.*
isp [krisp] **1.** кудря́вый; хрус-
ящий; све́жий (о во́здухе); **2.**
ави́(ва́)ть(ся); хрусте́ть [хру́ст-
уть]; покрыва́ться ря́бью (о ре-
é и т. п.).
iss-cross ['kriskrɔs] **1.** *adv.* крест-
на́крест; вкось; **2.** перекре́щи-
ать [-крести́ть].
iteri|on [krai'tiəriən], *pl.* **~a** [-riə]
рите́рий, мери́ло.
iti|c ['kritik] кри́тик; **~cal** ['kri-
kəl] □ крити́ческий; разбо́рчи-
ый; **~cism** [-sizm], **~que** [kriti:k]
ри́тика; реце́нзия; **~cize** [k'riti-
aiz] [рас]критикова́ть; осужда́ть
осуди́ть].
oak [krouk] [за]ка́ркать; [за-]
ва́кать.
ochet ['krouʃei] **1.** вяза́ние (крюч-
о́м); **2.** вяза́ть (крючко́м).
ock [krɔk] гли́няный кувши́н;
ery ['krɔkəri] посу́да.
one [kroun] F стару́ха; ста́рая
арга́. [друг.
ony ['krouni] F закады́чный
ook [kruk] **1.** по́сох; крюк; пово-
о́т; заги́б; *sl.* обма́нщик, плут; **2.**
гиба́ть(ся) [согну́ть(ся)]; ис-
ривля́ть(ся) [-ви́ть(ся)]; **~ed**
'krukid] изо́гнутый; криво́й; не-
е́стный.
oon [kru:n] **1.** моното́нное пе́ние;
. напева́ть.
op [krɔp] **1.** урожа́й; хлеба́ на
орню́; кнутови́ще; зоб; **2.** засе-
а́ть [засе́ять]; собира́ть урожа́й;
одстрига́ть [-ри́чь]; **~** up (вне-
а́пно) появля́ться [-ви́ться].
oss [krɔs, krɔ:s] **1.** крест; рас-
я́тие; **2.** □ попере́чный; серди́-
ый; **3.** *v/t.* [о]крести́ть; скре́щи-
ать [-ести́ть] (ру́ки и т. п.); пе-
еходи́ть [перейти́], переезжа́ть
перее́хать]; *fig.* противоде́йст-
овать (Д); противоре́чить (Д); **~**
. s. [пере]крести́ться; *v/i.* разми-
ну́ться *pf.*; **~-bar** попере́чина;
-breed по́месь *f*; гибри́д; **~-**
examination перекрёстный до-
про́с; **~-eyed** косо́й, косогла́зый;
ing ['krɔsiŋ] перекрёсток; пере-
пра́ва; перее́зд, перехо́д; **~-road**
опере́чная доро́га; **~s** *pl.* или *sg.*
ерекрёсток; **~-section** попере́ч-
ое сече́ние; **~wise** крестообра́з-
о; кресто́м.
rotchet ['krɔtʃit] крючо́к; при-
у́да; ♪ четвертна́я но́та.
rouch [krautʃ] раболе́пствовать;
ритаи́ться *pf.*
row [krou] **1.** воро́на; пе́ние пе-
уха́; ра́достный крик (младе́н-
а); **2.** [*irr.*] [про]пе́ть (о петухе́);
икова́ть; **~-bar** лом, ва́га.

crowd [kraud] **1.** толпа́; мно́жество,
ма́сса; толкотня́, да́вка; F компа́-
ния; **2.** собира́ться толпо́й, тол-
пи́ться; набива́ться битко́м.
crown [kraun] **1.** вене́ц, коро́на;
fig. заверше́ние; кро́на (де́рева);
маку́шка (головы́); коро́нка (зу́ба);
2. [у]венча́ть; коронова́ть (*im*)*pf.*;
fig. заверша́ть [-ши́ть]; поста́вить
коро́нку (на зуб).
cruci|al ['kru:ʃiəl] □ крити́ческий;
реша́ющий; **~ble** [-sibl] ти́гель *m*;
~fixion [kru:si'fikʃən] распя́тие;
~fy ['kru:sifai] распина́ть [-пя́ть].
crude [kru:d] □ сыро́й; необрабо́-
танный; незре́лый; гру́бый.
cruel ['kru:əl] □ жесто́кий; *fig.*
мучи́тельный; **~ty** [-ti] жесто́-
кость *f*.
cruet-stand ['kruitstænd] судо́к.
cruise [kru:z] ⚓ **1.** морско́е путе-
ше́ствие; **2.** крейси́ровать; соверш-
ша́ть ре́йсы; **~r** ['kru:zə] ⚓ кре́й-
сер.
crumb [krʌm] **1.** кро́шка; **2.** (= **~le**
['krʌmbl]) [рас-, ис]кроши́ть(ся).
crumple ['krʌmpl] [с]мя́ть(ся);
[с]ко́мкать(ся).
crunch [krʌntʃ] разжёвывать [-же-
ва́ть]; хрусте́ть [хру́стнуть].
crusade [kru:'seid] кресто́вый по-
хо́д; кампа́ния; **~r** [-ə] крестоно́сец.
crush [krʌʃ] **1.** да́вка; толкотня́; **2.**
v/t. [раз]дави́ть; выжима́ть [вы́-
жать]; уничтожа́ть [-о́жить].
crust [krʌst] **1.** ко́рка; кора́; **2.**
покрыва́ть(ся) ко́ркой, коро́й; **~y**
['krʌsti] □ покры́тый ко́ркой, ко-
ро́й.
crutch [krʌtʃ] косты́ль *m*.
cry [krai] **1.** крик; вопль *m*;
плач; **2.** [за]пла́кать; восклица́ть
[-и́кнуть]; крича́ть [кри́кнуть];
~ for [по]тре́бовать (P).
crypt [kript] склеп; **~ic** ['kriptik]
таи́нственный; сокрове́нный.
crystal ['kristl] хруста́ль *m*; кри-
ста́лл; *Am.* стекло́ для часо́в;
~line [-təlain] хруста́льный;
~lize [-təlaiz] кристаллизова́ть(ся)
(*im*)*pf*.
cub [kʌb] **1.** детёныш (зве́ря); *Am.*
новичо́к; **2.** [о]щени́ться.
cub|e [kju:b] ⅋ **1.** куб; **~** root куби́-
ческий ко́рень *m*; **2.** возводи́ть в
куб; **~ic**(**al** □) ['kju:bik, -ikəl]
куби́ческий.
cuckoo ['kuku:] куку́шка.
cucumber ['kju:kəmbə] огуре́ц.
cud [kʌd] жва́чка; chew the **~** же-
ва́ть жва́чку.
cuddle ['kʌdl] *v/t.* прижима́ть к
себе́; *v/i.* приж(им)а́ться (друг к
дру́гу). [ба́сить дуби́ной.
cudgel ['kʌdʒəl] **1.** дуби́на; **2.** ду-
cue [kju:] (билья́рдный) кий;
намёк; *thea.* ре́плика.
cuff [kʌf] **1.** манже́та, обшла́г; **2.**
[по]би́ть (руко́й), [по]колоти́ть.

culminate ['kʌlmineit] достигáть вы́сшей тóчки (и́ли стéпени).
culpable ['kʌlpəbl] □ винóвный; престу́пный.
culprit ['kʌlprit] престу́пник; винóвный.
cultivat|e ['kʌltiveit] обрабáтывать [-бóтать]; воздéл(ыв)ать; культиви́ровать; **~ion** [kʌlti'veiʃən] воздéлывание (земли́); разведéние, культу́ра (растéний); **~or** ['kʌltiveitə] культивáтор (⛏ ору́дие); землёдéлец.
cultural ['kʌltʃərəl] □ культу́рный.
culture ['kʌltʃə] культу́ра; разведéние, воздéлывание; **~d** [-d] культу́рный; культиви́рованный.
cumber ['kʌmbə] затрудня́ть [-ни́ть]; стесня́ть [-ни́ть]; **~some** [-səm], **cumbrous** ['kʌmbrəs] громóздкий; обремени́тельный.
cumulative ['kju:mjulətiv] □ совоку́пный; кумуляти́вный; накóпленный.
cunning ['kʌniŋ] **1.** лóвкий; хи́трый; ковáрный; *Am.* изя́щный; прелéстный; **2.** лóвкость *f*; хи́трость *f*; ковáрство.
cup [kʌp] чáшка; чáша; ку́бок; **~board** ['kʌbəd] шкаф.
cupidity [kju'piditi] áлчность *f*, жáдность *f*, скáредность *f*.
cupola ['kju:pələ] ку́пол.
cur [kə:] дворня́жка (собáка).
curate ['kjuərit] помóщник прихóдского свящéнника.
curb [kə:b] **1.** мундшту́чная уздéчка; уздá (*a. fig.*); (*a.* ~-stone) обóчина тротуáра; **2.** обу́здывать [-дáть] (*a. fig.*).
curd [kə:d] **1.** творóг; **2.** (*mst* **~le,** [kə:dl]) свёртываться [сверну́ться] (о молокé, крóви).
cure [kjuə] **1.** лечéние; срéдство; **2.** [вы́]лечи́ть, исцеля́ть [-ли́ть]; заготовля́ть [-тóвить], консерви́ровать (*im*)*pf*.
curio ['kjuəriou] рéдкая антиквáрная вещь *f*; **~sity** [kjuəri'ɔsiti] любопы́тство; рéдкость *f*; **~us** ['kjuəriəs] □ любопы́тный; пытли́вый; стрáнный.
curl [kə:l] **1.** лóкон; завитóк; спирáль *f*; **2.** ви́ться; клуби́ться; **~y** ['kə:li] кудря́вый; курчáвый; вью́щийся.
currant ['kʌrənt] сморóдина; (*a.* dried ~) кори́нка.
curren|cy ['kʌrənsi] ☤ дéньги *f*/*pl.*, валю́та; дéнежное обращéние; **~t** [-ənt] **1.** □ теку́щий; ходя́чий; ☤ находя́щийся в обращéнии; **2.** потóк; течéние; ⚡ ток.
curse [kə:s] **1.** проклятие; ругáтельство; бич, бéдствие; **2.** проклинáть [-кля́сть]; ругáться; **~d** ['kə:sid] □ прокля́тый.
curt [kə:t] □ крáткий.
curtail [kə:'teil] укорáчивать [-роти́ть]; урéз(ыв)ать; *fig.* сокращ[áть] [сократи́ть].
curtain ['kə:tn] **1.** занавéска; [...] навес; **2.** занавéшивать [-вéси[ть]]
curts(e)y ['kə:tsi] **1.** реверáнс; [...] клóн; **2.** дéлать реверáнс (to [...])
curv|ature ['kə:vətʃə] искрив[лé]ние; **~e** [kə:v] **1.** △ кривáя; изг[иб]; кривизнá; **2.** [со]гну́ть; изгиб[áть] (-ся) [изогну́ть(ся)].
cushion ['kuʃin] **1.** поду́шка; б[орт] (бильярдного столá); **2.** подк[лá]дывать поду́шку под (B).
custody ['kʌstədi] опéка, попе[чé]ние; заточéние.
custom ['kʌstəm] обы́чай; пр[и]вы́чка; клиенту́ра; **~s** *pl.* тамóж[ен]ные пóшлины *f*/*pl.*; **~ary** [-əri] обы́чный; **~er** [-ə] постоя́нн[ый] (-ная) покупáтель(ница *f*) *m*; кл[и]éнт(ка); **~-house** тамóжня; **~-ma[de]** *Am.* изготóвленный на закáз.
cut [kʌt] **1.** разрéз, порéз; зару́б[ка]; засéчка; отрéз (матéрии); покр[ой] (плáтья); (*mst* short-~) сокращ[ён]ный путь *m*; **2.** [*irr.*] *v*/*t.* рéза[ть]; разрезáть [-рéзать]; [по]стри́[чь]; [от]шлифовáть; [с]коси́ть (трав[у]); прорéз(ыв)аться (о зубáх); ~ sh[ort] прер(ы)вáть; ~ down сокращ[áть] [-рати́ть] (расхóды); ~ out выр[е]зáть [вы́резать]; [с]крои́ть; в[ы]ключáть [вы́ключить]; *fig.* выт[ес]ня́ть [вы́теснить]; be ~ out for бы[ть] слóвно сóзданным для (P); [...] рéзать; ~ in вмéшиваться [-шá[ться]] ся].
cute [kju:t] □ F хи́трый; *Am.* [ми]лы́й, привлекáтельный. [*n*/*p*...]
cutlery ['kʌtləri] ножевы́е издéли[я]
cutlet ['kʌtlit] котлéта.
cut|-out ⚡ автомати́ческий в[ы]ключáтель *m*, предохрани́тель [...] **~ter** ['kʌtə] рéзчик (по дéрев[у]); закрóйщик; ⊕ рéжущий инстр[у]мéнт; ⚓ кáтер; **~-throat** голов[о]рéз; уби́йца *m*; **~ting** ['kʌtiŋ] □ óстрый, рéзкий; язви́тельн[ый]; **2.** рéзание; закрóйка; ⊕ фрезер[о]вáние; гранéние; ⚘ побéг, че[ре]нóк; **~s** *pl.* обрéзки *m*/*pl.*; (газ[ет]ные) вы́резки *f*/*pl.*; ⊕ стру́ж[ки] *f*/*pl.*
cycl|e ['saikl] **1.** цикл; круг; [ве]лосипéд; ⊕ круговóй процéсс; [...] éздить на велосипéде; **~ist** [-i...] велосипеди́ст(ка).
cyclone ['saikloun] циклóн.
cylinder ['silində] цили́ндр (*geom*[...]) ⊕ барабáн; вáлик.
cymbal ['simbəl] ♪ тарéлки *f*/[*pl.*]
cynic ['sinik] **1.** (*a.* ~al □, -ikəl) [ци]ни́чный; **2.** ци́ник.
cypress ['saipris] ⚘ кипари́с.
Czech [tʃək] **1.** чех, чéшка; [...] чéшский.
Czecho-Slovak ['tʃekou'slouva[k]] **1.** жи́тель(ница) Чехословáки[и]; **2.** чехословáцкий.

D

dab [dæb] **1.** шлепо́к; мазо́к; пятно́ (кра́ски); **2.** слегка́ тро́гать (В); де́лать лёгкие мазки́ на (П).
dabble [ˈdæbl] плеска́ть(ся); бара́хтаться (в воде́ и т. п.); халту́рить, занима́ться че́м-либо пове́рхностно.
dad [dæd] F, **~dy** [ˈdædi] F па́па.
daffodil [ˈdæfədil] жёлтый нарци́сс.
dagger [ˈdægə] кинжа́л; be at **~s** drawn быть на ножа́х (с Т).
daily [ˈdeili] **1.** *adv.* ежедне́вно; **2.** ежедне́вный; **3.** ежедне́вная газе́та.
dainty [ˈdeinti] **1.** □ ла́комый; изя́щный; изы́сканный; **2.** ла́комство, деликате́с.
dairy [ˈdɛəri] моло́чная; маслоде́льня.
daisy [ˈdeizi] маргари́тка.
dale [deil] доли́на, дол.
dall|iance [ˈdæliəns] несерьёзное заня́тие; флирт; **~y** [ˈdæli] зря теря́ть вре́мя; флиртова́ть.
dam [dæm] **1.** ма́тка (живо́тных); да́мба, плоти́на; **2.** запру́живать [-уди́ть].
damage [ˈdæmidʒ] **1.** вред; поврежде́ние; убы́ток; **~s** *pl.* ⚖ убы́тки *m/pl.*; компенса́ция за убы́тки; **2.** поврежда́ть [-еди́ть], [ис]по́ртить.
damask [ˈdæməsk] камка́.
damn [dæm] **1.** проклина́ть [-ля́сть]; осужда́ть [осуди́ть]; руга́ться; **2.** прокля́тие; руга́тельство; **~ation** [dæmˈneiʃən] прокля́тие; осужде́ние.
damp [dæmp] **1.** сы́рость *f*, вла́жность *f*; **2.** вла́жный, за́тхлый; **3.** *a.* **~en** [ˈdæmpən] [на]мочи́ть; [от-]сыре́ть; *fig.* обескура́жи(ва)ть.
danc|e [dɑːns] **1.** та́нец; бал; **2.** танцева́ть; **~er** [ˈdɑːnsə] танцо́р, танцо́вщик (-ица); **~ing** [-iŋ] та́нцы *m/pl.*; пля́ска; *attr.* танцева́льный.
dandelion [ˈdændilaiən] ⚘ одува́нчик.
dandle [ˈdændl] [по]кача́ть (на рука́х).
dandruff [ˈdændrəf] пе́рхоть *f*.
dandy [ˈdændi] **1.** щёголь *m*; *sl.* первокла́ссная вещь *f*; **2.** *Am. sl.* первокла́ссный.
Dane [dein] датча́нин (-ча́нка).
danger [ˈdeindʒə] опа́сность *f*; **~ous** [ˈdeindʒrəs] □ опа́сный.
dangle [ˈdæŋgl] висе́ть, свиса́ть [сви́снуть]; болта́ть (Т).
Danish [ˈdeiniʃ] да́тский.
dapple [ˈdæpl] испещря́ть [-ри́ть]; **~d** [-d] испещрённый, пёстрый; **~-grey** се́рый в я́блоках (конь).
dar|e [dɛə] *v/i.* [по]сме́ть; отва́жи(ва)ться; *v/t.* вызыва́ть [вы́звать]; **~e-devil** смельча́к, сорвиголова́ *m*; **~ing** [dɛəriŋ] **1.** □ сме́лый, отва́жный; де́рзкий; **2.** сме́лость *f*, отва́жность *f*.
dark [dɑːk] **1.** тёмный; сму́глый; та́йный; мра́чный; **~** horse „тёмная лоша́дка"; **~** lantern потайно́й фона́рь *m*; **2.** темнота́, тьма; неве́дение; **~en** [ˈdɑːkən] затемня́ть(ся) [-ни́ть(ся)]; **~ness** [ˈdɑːknis] темнота́, тьма; **~y** [ˈdɑːki] F черноко́жий, чёрный (о не́гре).
darling [ˈdɑːliŋ] **1.** люби́мец (-мица); ба́ловень *m*; **2.** люби́мый.
darn [dɑːn] [за]што́пать.
dart [dɑːt] **1.** стрела́; дро́тик; прыжо́к; **2.** *v/t.* мета́ть [метну́ть] (стре́лы, взгля́ды и т. п.); *v/i. fig.* мча́ться стрело́й.
dash [dæʃ] **1.** поры́в; уда́р; взмах; плеск (воды́); *fig.* при́месь *f*, чу́точка; набро́сок; штрих; тире́ *n indecl.* **2.** *v/t.* броса́ть [бро́сить]; разби́(ва́)ть; разбавля́ть [-а́вить]; *v/i.* ри́нуться; броса́ться [бро́ситься]; **~-board** *mot.*, ✈ прибо́рная доска́; **~ing** [ˈdæʃiŋ] □ лихо́й.
data [ˈdeitə] *pl.*, *Am. a. sg.* да́нные *n/pl.*; но́вости *f/pl.*; фа́кты *m/pl.*
date [deit] **1.** да́та, число́; F свида́ние; out of **~** устаре́лый; up to **~** нове́йший; совреме́нный; **2.** дати́ровать *(im)pf.*; *Am.* F усло́вливаться [-о́виться] с (Т) (о встре́че); име́ть свида́ние.
daub [dɔːb] [по]ма́зать; [на]малева́ть.
daughter [ˈdɔːtə] дочь *f*; **~-in-law** [-rinlɔː] неве́стка, сноха́.
daunt [dɔːnt] устраша́ть [-ши́ть], запу́гивать [-га́ть]; **~less** [ˈdɔːntlis] неустраши́мый, бесстра́шный.
dawdle [ˈdɔːdl] F безде́льничать.
dawn [dɔːn] **1.** рассве́т, у́тренняя заря́; *fig.* зача́тки *m/pl.*; про́блески *m/pl.*; **2.** света́ть.
day [dei] день *m*; (*mst* **~s** *pl.*) жизнь *f*; **~** off выходно́й день *m*; the other **~** на дня́х; неда́вно; **~break** рассве́т; **~-labo(u)rer** подёнщик (-ица); **~-star** у́треняя звезда́.
daze [deiz] ошеломля́ть [-ми́ть]; ослепля́ть [-пи́ть].
dazzle [ˈdæzl] ослепля́ть [-пи́ть]; ⚓ маскирова́ть окра́ской.
dead [ded] **1.** мёртвый; увя́дший (о цвета́х); онеме́вший (о па́льцах); неподви́жный; безразли́чный; **~** bargain дешёвка; **~** letter письмо́, недоста́вленное по а́дресу; a **~** shot стрело́к, не даю́щий про́маха; **~** wall глуха́я стена́; **2.** *adv.* по́лно, соверше́нно; **~** against реши́тельно про́тив; **3.** the **~** по-

ко́йники *m/pl.*; **~en** [dedn] лища́ть (-ся) си́лы; заглуша́ть [-ши́ть]; **~-lock** *fig.* мёртвая то́чка; засто́й; **~ly** [-li] смерте́льный; смертоно́сный.

deaf [def] □ глухо́й; **~en** [defn] оглуша́ть [-ши́ть].

deal [di:l] **1.** коли́чество; соглаше́ние; обхожде́ние; F сде́лка; a good ~ весьма́ мно́го; a great ~ о́чень мно́го; **2.** [*irr.*] *v/t.* разд(ав)а́ть; распределя́ть [-ли́ть]; *v/i.* торгова́ть; ~ with обходи́ться [обойти́сь] *or* поступа́ть [-пи́ть] с (T); име́ть де́ло с (T); **~er** ['di:lə] торго́вец; **~ing** ['di:liŋ] (*mst* ~s *pl.*) торго́вые дела́ *n/pl.*; **~t** [delt] *pt.* и *p. pt.* от ~.

dean [di:n] настоя́тель собо́ра; дека́н (факульте́та).

dear [diə] **1.** □ дорого́й, ми́лый; **2.** прекра́сный челове́к; **3.** F o(h) ~!, ~ me! го́споди!

death [deθ] смерть *f*; **~-bed** сме́ртное ло́же; **~-duty** нало́г на насле́дство; **~less** ['deθlis] бессме́ртный; **~ly** [-li] смерте́льный; **~-rate** проце́нт сме́ртности; **~-warrant** сме́ртный пригово́р.

debar [di'bɑ:] исключа́ть [-чи́ть]; лиша́ть пра́ва.

debase [di'beis] унижа́ть [уни́зить]; понижа́ть ка́чество (P).

debat|able [di'beitəbl] □ спо́рный, дискуссио́нный; **~e** [di'beit] **1.** диску́ссия; пре́ния *n/pl.*, деба́ты *m/pl.*; **2.** обсужда́ть [-уди́ть]; [по-] спо́рить; обду́м(ыв)ать.

debauch [di'bɔtʃ] **1.** распу́тство; попо́йка; **2.** развраща́ть [-рати́ть]; обольща́ть [-льсти́ть].

debilitate [di'biliteit] ослабля́ть [-а́бить]; расслабля́ть [-а́бить].

debit ['debit] ☦ **1.** де́бет; **2.** дебетова́ть (*im*)*pf.*, вноси́ть в де́бет.

debris ['debri:] разва́лины *f/pl.*; обло́мки *m/pl.*

debt [det] долг; **~or** ['dətə] должни́к (-и́ца).

decade ['dekəd] дека́да; десятиле́тие.

decadence ['dekədəns] упа́док; декаде́нтство.

decamp [di'kæmp] снима́ться с ла́геря; уд(и)ра́ть; **~ment** [-mənt] выступле́ние из ла́геря; бы́стрый ухо́д.

decant [di'kænt] [про]фильтрова́ть; сце́живать [сцеди́ть]; **~er** [-ə] графи́н.

decapitate [di'kæpiteit] обезгла́вливать [-ла́вить].

decay [di'kei] **1.** гние́ние; разложе́ние; **2.** [с]гнить; разлага́ться [-ложи́ться].

decease [di'si:s] *part.* ⚖ **1.** смерть *f*, кончи́на; **2.** умира́ть [умере́ть], сконча́ться *pf.*

deceit [di'si:t] обма́н; **~ful** [-ful] □ обма́нчивый.

deceiv|e [di'si:v] обма́нывать [-ну́ть]; **~er** [-ə] обма́нщик (-ица).

December [di'sembə] дека́брь *m.*

decen|cy ['di:snsi] прили́чие; благопристо́йность *f*; **~t** [-t] □ прили́чный; сла́вный.

deception [di'sepʃən] обма́н; ложь *f.*

decide [di'said] реша́ть(ся) [реши́ть(ся)]; принима́ть реше́ние; **~d** [-id] □ реши́тельный; определённый; бесспо́рный.

decimal ['desiməl] **1.** десяти́чный; **2.** десяти́чная дробь *f.*

decipher [di'saifə] расшифро́вывать [-ова́ть]; разбира́ть [разобра́ть].

decisi|on [di'siʒən] реше́ние; реши́тельность *f*; ⚖ пригово́р; **~ve** [di'saisiv] реша́ющий.

deck [dek] **1.** ⚓ па́луба; *Am.* коло́да (карт); **2.** украша́ть [укра́сить]; уб(и)ра́ть (цвета́ми и т. п.); **~-chair** складно́й стул.

declaim [di'kleim] произноси́ть [-нести́] (речь); [про]деклами́ровать.

declar|able [di'klɛərəbl] подлежа́щий деклара́ции; **~ation** [deklə'reiʃən] заявле́ние; деклара́ция (*a.* ☦); **~e** [di'klɛə] объявля́ть [-ви́ть]; заявля́ть [-ви́ть]; выска́зываться [вы́сказаться] (for за В, against про́тив Р); предъявля́ть [-ви́ть] (ве́щи в тамо́жне).

declin|ation [dekli'neiʃən] отклоне́ние; накло́н; **~e** [di'klain] **1.** склон, укло́н; паде́ние; упа́док (сил); сниже́ние (цен); ухудше́ние (здоро́вья); зака́т (жи́зни); **2.** *v/t.* отклоня́ть [-ни́ть] (предложе́ние); *gr.* [про]склоня́ть; *v/i.* приходи́ть в упа́док; ухудша́ться [уху́дшиться] (о здоро́вье и т. п.)

declivity [di'kliviti] пока́тость *f*, отло́гий спуск.

decode [di:'koud] *tel.* расшифро́вывать [-рова́ть].

decompose [di:kəm'pouz] разлага́ть(ся) [-ложи́ть(ся)]; [с]гнить.

decontrol ['di:kən'troul] освобожда́ть от контро́ля (торго́влю и т. п.).

decorat|e ['dekəreit] украша́ть [укра́сить]; награжда́ть зна́ком отли́чия; **~ion** [dekə'reiʃən] украше́ние; о́рден, знак отли́чия; **~ive** ['dekərətiv] декорати́вный.

decor|ous ['dekərəs] □ присто́йный; **~um** [di'kɔ:rəm] этике́т.

decoy [di'kɔi] **1.** прима́нка, мано́к; **2.** прима́нивать [-ни́ть]; завлека́ть [-е́чь].

decrease 1. ['di:kri:s] уменьше́ние, убыва́ние, пониже́ние; **2.** [di'kri:s] уменьша́ть(ся) [уме́ньшить(-ся)], убы́(ва́)ть.

decree [di'kri:] **1.** ука́з, декре́т, прика́з; ⚖ постановле́ние **2.** издава́ть декре́т.

crepit [di'krepit] дряхлый; ветий.
dicat|e ['dedikeit] посвящать ятить]; **~ion** [dedi'keiʃən] посвящение.
duce [di'dju:s] выводить [вывести] (заключение, формулу и п.).
duct [di'dʌkt] вычитать [вычесть]; **~ion** [di'dʌkʃən] вычет; вывод, заключение; скидка.
ed [di:d] **1.** действие; поступок; подвиг; документ; **2.** *Am.* передавать по акту.
em [di:m] *v/t.* считать [счесть]; *'i.* полагать; [по]думать (of о П).
ep [di:p] **1.** □ глубокий; хитрый; устой (о краске); **2.** бездна; *poet.* море, океан; **~en** ['di:pən] углублять(ся) [-бить(ся)]; сгущать(ся) сгустить(ся)] (о красках, тенях); **ness** [-nis] глубина.
er [diə] *coll.* красный зверь *m*; олень *m*; лань *f*.
face [di'feis] искажать [исказить]; стирать [стереть].
fam|ation [defə'meiʃən] диффамация; клевета; **~e** [di'feim] поносить; [о]клеветать.
fault [di'fɔ:lt] **1.** невыполнение обязательств; неявка в суд; in ~ of за неимением (Р); **2.** не выполнять обязательств; прекращать платежи; не являться по вызову суда.
feat [di'fi:t] **1.** поражение; расстройство (планов); **2.** ⚔ побеждать [-едить]; расстраивать [-роить] (планы).
fect [di'fekt] недостаток; неисправность *f*, дефект; изъян; **~ive** [-tiv] □ недостаточный; дефектный, повреждённый.
fence, *Am.* **defense** [di'fens] оборона, защита; **~less** [-lis] беззащитный.
fend [di'fend] оборонять(ся), [-нить(ся)], защищать(ся) [-итить(ся)]; защищать на суде; **ant** [-ənt] подсудимый; **~er** [-ə] защитник.
fensive [di'fensiv] **1.** оборона; **2.** оборонный, оборонительный.
fer [di'fə] откладывать [отложить]; отсрочи(ва)ть; *Am.* ⚔ давать отсрочку от призыва.
fian|ce [di'faiəns] вызов; неповиновение; пренебрежение; **~t** [-ənt] □ вызывающий.
ficien|cy [di'fiʃənsi] недостаток; дефицит; **~t** [-ənt] недостаточный; несовершенный.
ficit ['defisit] недочёт, дефицит.
file [di'fail] [про]дефилировать.
fin|e [di'fain] определять [-лить]; давать характеристику (Р); устанавливать значение (Р); **~ite** ['definit] □ определённый; точный; **~ition** [defi'niʃən] определение; **~itive** [di'finitiv] □ определительный.
deflect [di'flekt] отклонять(ся) [-нить(ся)].
deform [di'fɔ:m] [из]уродовать; искажать [исказить] (мысль); **~ed** изуродованный; искажённый (о мысли); **~ity** [di'fɔmiti] уродство.
defraud [di'frɔ:d] обманывать [-нуть]; выманивать [выманить] (of В). [тить].
defray [di'frei] оплачивать [опла-]
deft [deft] □ ловкий, искусный.
defy [di'fai] вызывать [вызвать] (на спор, борьбу); пренебрегать [-бречь] (Т).
degenerate 1. [di'dʒenəreit] вырождаться [выродиться]; **2.** [-rit] □ вырождающийся.
degrad|ation [degrə'deiʃən] понижение, деградация; **~e** [di'greid] *v/t.* понижать [понизить]; разжаловать *pf.*; унижать [унизить].
degree [di'gri:] градус; ступень *f*; уровень *m*; степень *f*; звание; by ~s *adv.* постепенно; in no ~ *adv.* ничуть, нисколько.
deify ['di:ifai] боготворить.
deign [dein] соизволять [-олить]; удостаивать [-стоить].
deity ['di:iti] божество.
deject [di'dʒekt] удручать [-чить]; угнетать [-ести]; **~ed** [-id] □ удручённый; угнетённый; **~ion** [di'dʒekʃən] уныние.
delay [di'lei] **1.** задержка; отсрочка; замедление; **2.** *v/t.* задерживать [-жать]; откладывать [отложить]; медлить с (Т); *v/i.* медлить, мешкать.
delega|te 1. ['deligit] делегат, представитель(ница *f*) *m*; **2.** [-geit] делегировать (*im*)*pf.*, поручать [-чить]; **~tion** [deli'geiʃən] делегация, депутация.
deliberat|e 1. [di'libəreit] *v/t.* обдум(ыв)ать; взвешивать [-есить]; обсуждать [обсудить]; *v/i.* совещаться; **2.** [-rit] □ преднамеренный, умышленный; **~ion** [dilibə'reiʃən] размышление; обсуждение; осмотрительность *f*.
delica|cy ['delikəsi] деликатность *f*; лакомство; утончённость *f*; нежность *f*; чувствительность *f*; **~te** [-kit] □ деликатный; хрупкий; изящный; искусный (о работе); чувствительный; щепетильный; **~tessen** *Am.* [delikə'tesn] гастрономический магазин.
delicious [di'liʃəs] восхитительный; очень вкусный.
delight [di'lait] **1.** удовольствие; восторг; наслаждение; **2.** восхищать [-итить]; доставлять наслаждение (Д); наслаждаться (in Т); ~ to *inf.* иметь удовольствие (+*inf.*); **~ful** [-ful] □ очаровательный; восхитительный.

delineate [di'linieit] обрисо́вывать [-ова́ть]; опи́сывать [-са́ть].
delinquent [di'liŋkwənt] **1.** правонаруши́тель(ница *f*) *m*; престу́пник (-ица); **2.** престу́пный.
deliri|ous [di'liriəs] находя́щийся в бреду́, вне себя́, в исступле́нии; **~um** [-əm] бред; исступле́ние.
deliver [di'livə] освобожда́ть [-боди́ть]; доставля́ть [-а́вить]; разноси́ть [-нести́] (газе́ты и т. п.); произноси́ть [-нести́] (речь); сда(ва́)ть (зака́з); наноси́ть [нанести́] (уда́р); be **~ed** ⚕ разреши́ться от бре́мени, роди́ть; **~ance** [-rəns] освобожде́ние; **~er** [-rə] освободи́тель *m*; поставщи́к; **~y** [-ri] ⚕ ро́ды *m/pl.*; 📯 разно́ска; ⚚ доста́вка.
dell [del] ле́си́стая доли́на.
delude [di'lu:d] вводи́ть в заблужде́ние; обма́нывать [-ну́ть].
deluge ['delju:dʒ] **1.** наводне́ние; пото́п; **2.** затопля́ть [-пи́ть]; наводня́ть [-ни́ть] *(a. fig.)*.
delus|ion [di'lu:ʒən] заблужде́ние; иллю́зия; **~ive** [-siv] □ обма́нчивый; иллюзо́рный.
demand [di'ma:nd] **1.** тре́бование (*a.* ⚖); запро́с; потре́бность *f*; ⚚ спрос (на това́р); **2.** [по]тре́бовать (Р).
demean [di'mi:n] вести́ себя́; **~** o.s. роня́ть своё досто́инство; **~o(u)r** [-ə] поведе́ние.
demented [di'mentid] сумасше́дший.
demilitarize [di:'militəraiz] демилитаризова́ть (*im*)*pf.*
demobilize [di:'moubilaiz] демобилизова́ть (*im*)*pf.*
democra|cy [di'mɔkrəsi] демокра́тия; **~tic(al** □) [demɔ'krætik(əl)] демократи́ческий.
demolish [di'mɔliʃ] разруша́ть [-ру́шить]; сноси́ть [снести́].
demon ['di:mən] де́мон, дья́вол.
demonstrat|e ['demənstreit] [про-] демонстри́ровать; дока́зывать [-за́ть]; **~ion** [deməns'treiʃən] демонстра́ция; демонстри́рование; доказа́тельство; **~ive** [di'mɔnstrətiv] □ убеди́тельный; демонстрати́вный; экспанси́вный; *gr.* указа́тельный.
demote [di:'mout] снижа́ть в до́лжности.
demur [di'mə:] **1.** [по]колеба́ться; возража́ть [-рази́ть]; **2.** колеба́ние; возраже́ние.
demure [di'mjuə] □ серьёзный; чо́порный.
den [den] ло́говище; берло́га; *sl.* прито́н.
denial [di'naiəl] отрица́ние; опроверже́ние; отка́з.
denominat|e [di'nɔmineit] наз(ы)ва́ть; дава́ть и́мя (Д); **~ion** [dinɔmi'neiʃn] наименова́ние; се́кта.
denote [di'nout] означа́ть [-н чить], обознача́ть [-на́чить].
denounce [di'nauns] обвиня [-ни́ть]; поноси́ть; денонси́рова (догово́р) (*im*)*pf.*
dens|e [dens] □ густо́й; пло́тны *fig.* глу́пый, тупо́й; **~ity** ['densi густота́; пло́тность *f*.
dent [dent] **1.** вы́боина, вда́вле ное ме́сто; **2.** вда́вливать [вд ви́ть].
dentist ['dentist] зубно́й врач.
denunciat|ion [dinʌnsi'eiʃən] д но́с; обличе́ние, обвине́ние; **~** [di'nʌnsieitə] обвини́тель *m*; д но́счик (-ица).
deny [di'nai] отрица́ть; отка́зі ваться [-за́ться] от (Р); отка́зі вать [-за́ть] в (П).
depart [di'pa:t] *v/i.* уходи́ть [уйті уезжа́ть [уе́хать]; отбы́(ва́)ть, о правля́ться [-а́виться]; отступа́ [-пи́ть] (from от Р); **~ment** [-mə ве́домство; департа́мент; о́трас *f* (нау́ки); отде́л, отделе́ние; о ласть *f*; *Am.* министе́рство; Sta ♀ министе́рство иностра́нных де **~** store универма́г; **~ure** [di'pa:t отхо́д, отбы́тие, отъе́зд; ухо́ отправле́ние; отклоне́ние.
depend [di'pend]: **~** (up)on зав сеть от (Р); F it **~**s смотря́ по о стоя́тельствам; **~able** [-əbl] н дёжный; **~ant** [-ənt] подчинё ный; иждиве́нец; **~ence** [-ə зави́симость *f*; дове́рие; **~en** [-ənsi] зави́симость *f*; коло́ни **~ent** [-ənt] □ (on) зави́сящий (Р); подчинённый (*a. gr.*).
depict [di'pikt] изобража́ть [-р зи́ть]; *fig.* опи́сывать [-са́ть].
deplete [di'pli:t] опорожня́ [-ни́ть]; *fig.* истоща́ть [-щи́ть].
deplor|able [di'plɔ:rəbl] □ плаче́ ный; заслу́живающий сожал ния; **~e** [di'plɔ:] опла́к(ив)а сожале́ть о (П).
deport [di'pɔ:t] высыла́ть [ві слать]; ссыла́ть [сосла́ть]; **~** o. вести́ себя́; **~ment** [-mənt] м не́ры *f/pl.*, уме́ние держа́ть себя́.
depose [di'pouz] смеща́ть [сме ти́ть]; сверга́ть [све́ргнуть] престо́ла); ⚖ дать показа́ния п прися́гой.
deposit [di'pɔzit] **1.** отложе́ние; з лежь *f*; ⚚ вклад (в банк); деп зи́т; зало́г; **2.** класть [положи́ть депони́ровать (*im*)*pf.*; дава́ть ос док; **~ion** [depə'ziʃən] сверже́н (с престо́ла); показа́ние под пр ся́гой; оса́док; **~or** [di'pɔzit вкла́дчик (-ица).
depot **1.** ['depou] 🚂 депо́ *n indecl* склад; сара́й; **2.** ['di:po] *Am.* ста́нция.
deprave [di'preiv] развраща́т [[-рати́ть]
depreciate [di'pri:ʃieit] обесц ни(ва)ть; недооце́нивать [-и́ть].

press [di'pres] угнета́ть [-ести́]; одавля́ть [-ви́ть]; унижа́ть [-и́-ть]; **~ed** [-t] *fig.* уны́лый; **~ion** i'preʃən] сниже́ние; впа́дина; ска́; ⚕ депре́ссия.
prive [di'praiv] лиша́ть [лиши́ть] f P).
pth [depθ] глубина́.
put|ation [depju'teiʃən] депута́-ия, делега́ция; **~e** [di'pju:t] де-эги́ровать (*im*)*pf*.; **~y** ['depjuti] елега́т(ка); депута́т(ка); замести́-ль(ница *f*) *m*.
rail [di'reil] 🚂 *v/i*. сходи́ть с е́льсов; *v/t*. устро́ить круше́ние оезда).
range [di'reindʒ] расстра́ивать ро́ить] (мы́сли, пла́ны); приво-ить в беспоря́док.
relict ['derilikt] поки́нутый (ко-а́бль, дом), (за)бро́шенный; **~ion** eri'likʃən] забро́шенность *f*.
ri|de [di'raid] осме́ивать [-ея́ть], ысме́ивать [вы́смеять]; **~sion** i'riʒən] высме́ивание; **~sive** i'raisiv] □ насме́шливый.
riv|ation [deri'veiʃən] исто́чник; роисхожде́ние; **~e** [di'raiv] про-ходи́ть [-изойти́]; извлека́ть влёчь] (по́льзу) (from от P); танавливать происхожде́ние).
rogat|e ['derogeit] умаля́ть ли́ть] (from B); **~ion** [dero'geiʃən] иале́ние.
rrick ['derik] ⊕ де́ррик-кран; бурова́я вы́шка; ⚓ подъёмная ре́ла́.
scend [di'send] спуска́ться [спу-и́ться]; сходи́ть [сойти́]; ✈ ижа́ться [сни́зиться]; **~** (up)on ру́ши(ва)ться на (B); происхо-и́ть [-изойти́] (*from* из P); **~ant** эnt] пото́мок.
scent [di'sent] спуск; сниже́ние; лон; скат; происхожде́ние.
scribe [dis'kraib] опи́сывать са́ть].
scription [dis'kripʃən] описа́ние; ображе́ние.
sert 1. ['dezət] a) пусты́нный; бро́шенный; b) пусты́ня; **2.** i'zə:t] a) *v/t*. броса́ть [бро́сить]; кида́ть [-ки́нуть]; *v/i*. дезерти́-вать (*im*)*pf*.; b) заслу́га; **~er** [-ə] зерти́р; **~ion** [-ʃən] дезерти́р-во; оставле́ние.
serv|e [di'zə:v] заслу́живать жи́ть]; име́ть заслу́ги (of пе́ред); **~ing** [-iŋ] заслу́живающий; сто́йный (of P).
sign [di'zain] **1.** за́мысел; про-т; план; рису́нок; узо́р; наме́-ние; **2.** предназнача́ть [-зна́-ить]; заду́м(ыв)ать; составля́ть ан (P); [на]рисова́ть.
signat|e ['dezigneit] определя́ть ли́ть]; обознача́ть [-зна́чить]; редназнача́ть [-зна́чить]; **~ion** [dezig'neiʃən] указа́ние; назначе́-ние.
designer [di'zainə] констру́ктор; чертёжник; *fig*. интрига́н.
desir|able [di'zaiərəbl] □ жела́-тельный; **~e** [di'zaiə] **1.** жела́ние; тре́бование; **2.** [по]жела́ть (P); [по]тре́бовать (P); **~ous** [-rəs] □ жела́ющий, жа́ждущий (of P).
desist [di'zist] отка́зываться [-за́ть-ся] (from от P).
desk [desk] конто́рка; пи́сьменный стол.
desolat|e 1. ['desoleit] опустоша́ть [-ши́ть]; разоря́ть [-ри́ть]; **2.** [-lit] □ опустошённый; несча́стный; одино́кий; **~ion** [deso'leiʃən] опустоше́ние; одино́чество.
despair [dis'pɛə] **1.** отча́яние; без-надёжность *f*; **2.** отча́иваться [-ча́яться]; теря́ть наде́жду (of на B); **~ing** [-riŋ] □ отча́ивающийся.
despatch *s*. dispatch.
desperat|e ['despərit] □ отча́ян-ный; безнадёжный; отъя́влен-ный; *adv*. отча́янно; стра́шно; **~ion** [despə'reiʃən] отча́яние; без-рассу́дство.
despise [dis'paiz] презира́ть.
despite [dis'pait] **1.** зло́ба; in **~** of вопреки́ (Д); несмотря́ на (B); на́-зло́ (Д); **2.** *prp*. (*a*. **~** of) несмотря́ на (B).
despoil [dis'pɔil] [о]гра́бить; ли-ша́ть [лиши́ть] (of P).
despond [dis'pɔnd] уныва́ть; теря́ть наде́жду; па́дать ду́хом; **~ency** [-ənsi] уны́ние; упа́док ду́ха; **~ent** [-ənt] □ пода́вленный; уны́лый.
dessert [di:'zə:t] десе́рт.
destin|ation [desti'neiʃən] назна-че́ние; ме́сто назначе́ния, цель *f* (путеше́ствия); **~e** ['destin] пред-назнача́ть [-зна́чить]; предопре-деля́ть [-ли́ть]; **~y** [-tini] судьба́; уде́л.
destitute ['destitju:t] □ нужда́ю-щийся; лишённый (of P).
destroy [dis'trɔi] уничтожа́ть [-о́жить]; истребля́ть [-би́ть]; раз-руша́ть [-у́шить].
destruct|ion [dis'trʌkʃən] разру-ше́ние; уничтоже́ние; разоре́ние; **~ive** [-tiv] □ разруши́тельный; па́губный; вре́дный.
detach [di'tætʃ] отделя́ть [-ли́ть]; отвя́зывать [-за́ть]; разъединя́ть [-ни́ть]; ⚔, ⚓ отряжа́ть [-яди́ть], пос(ы)ла́ть; **~ed** [-t] отде́льный; беспристра́стный; **~ment** [-mənt] разъедине́ние; ⚔ командирова́-ние; ⚔ отря́д.
detail 1. ['di:teil] подро́бность *f*, дета́ль *f*; ⚔ наря́д, кома́нда; in **~** в подро́бностях, подро́бно; **2.** [di'teil] входи́ть в подро́бности; ⚔ откомандиро́вывать [-рова́ть].
detain [di'tein] заде́рживать [-жа́ть]; содержа́ть под стра́жей.

detect [di'tekt] обнару́жи(ва)ть; ⚡ детекти́ровать; **~ion** [di'tekʃən] обнару́жение; ⚡ детекти́рование; **~ive** [-tiv] **1.** сы́щик, аге́нт сыскно́й поли́ции; **2.** сыскно́й, детекти́вный.

detention [di'tenʃən] задержа́ние, содержа́ние под аре́стом.

deter [di'tə:] отпу́гивать [-гну́ть] (from от P).

deteriorat|e [di'tiəriəreit] ухудша́ть(ся) [уху́дшить(ся)]; [ис]по́ртить(ся); **~ion** [ditiəriə'reiʃən] ухудше́ние; по́рча.

determin|ation [ditə:mi'neiʃən] определе́ние; установле́ние (грани́ц); калькуля́ция (цен); реши́тельность *f*; **~e** [di'tə:min] *v/t.* устана́вливать [-нови́ть]; определя́ть [-ли́ть]; реша́ть [реши́ть]; *v/i.* реша́ться [реши́ться]; **~ed** [-d] реши́тельный; твёрдый (хара́ктер).

detest [di'test] ненави́деть; пита́ть отвраще́ние к (Д); **~able** [-əbl] □ отврати́тельный; **~ation** [dites'teiʃən] отвраще́ние.

dethrone [di'θroun] сверга́ть с престо́ла.

detonate ['di:touneit] детони́ровать; взрыва́ть(ся) [взорва́ть(ся)].

detour [di'tuə] **1.** око́льный путь *m*; *Am.* объе́зд; make a ~ де́лать крюк.

detract [di'trækt] умаля́ть [-ли́ть], уменьша́ть [уме́ньшить]; **~ion** [di'trækʃən] умале́ние (досто́инства); клевета́.

detriment ['detrimənt] уще́рб, вред.

devaluate [di:'væljueit] обесце́ни(ва)ть.

devastat|e ['devəsteit] опустоша́ть [-ши́ть]; разоря́ть [-ри́ть]; **~ion** [devəs'teiʃən] опустоше́ние.

develop [di'veləp] разви́(ва́)ть(ся); излага́ть [изложи́ть] (пробле́му); *phot.* проявля́ть [-ви́ть]; *Am.* обнару́жи(ва)ть; **~ment** [-mənt] разви́тие; эволю́ция; рост; расшире́ние; собы́тие.

deviat|e ['di:vieit] отклоня́ться [-ни́ться]; уклоня́ться [-ни́ться]; **~ion** [di:vi'eiʃən] отклоне́ние; девиа́ция (ко́мпаса); *pol.* укло́н.

device [di'vais] приспособле́ние, изобрете́ние; деви́з, эмбле́ма; leave a p. to his own ~s предоставля́ть челове́ка самому́ себе́.

devil [devl] **1.** дья́вол, чёрт, бес; **2.** *v/i.* исполня́ть черново́ю рабо́ту для како́го-либо литера́тора; **~ish** [-iʃ] □ дья́вольский; а́дский; **~(t)ry** чёрная ма́гия; чертовщи́на.

devious ['di:viəs] □ блужда́ющий.

devise [di'vaiz] **1.** ⚖ завеща́ние; **2.** приду́м(ыв)ать; изобрета́ть [-рести́]; ⚖ завеща́ть (*im*)*pf*.

devoid [di'vɔid] (of) лишённый (P).

devot|e [di'vout] посвяща́ть [-ти́ть] (В/Д); отд(ав)а́ть; **~ed** [-… □ пре́данный; привя́занны… **~ion** [di'vouʃən] пре́данность … привя́занность *f*; ~s *pl.* религио́… ные обря́ды *m/pl.*, моли́твы *f/…*

devour [di'vauə] пож(и)ра́ть.

devout [di'vaut] □ благогове́йны… на́божный, благочести́вый.

dew [dju:] **1.** роса́; *poet.* све́жес… *f*; **2.** ороша́ть [ороси́ть]; **~y** п… кры́тый росо́й; вла́жный.

dexter|ity [deks'teriti] прово́рств… ло́вкость *f*; **~ous** ['dekstərəs] … ло́вкий; прово́рный.

diabolic(al □) [daiə'bɔlik(əl)] ди… вольский; *fig.* жесто́кий; злой.

diagram ['daiəgræm] диагра́мм… схе́ма.

dial ['daiəl] **1.** цифербла́т; со́лне… ные часы́ *m/pl.*; *teleph.* диск; … *teleph.* набира́ть но́мер.

dialect ['daiəlekt] диале́кт, на… чие.

dialogue ['daiəlɔg] диало́г; р… гово́р.

diameter [dai'æmitə] диа́метр.

diamond ['daiəmənd] алма́з; бри… лиа́нт; ромб; ~s *pl. cards*: бу́бн…

diaper ['daiəpə] пелёнка. [*f/…*

diaphragm ['daiəfræm] диафра́… *a. opt.*; *teleph.* мембра́на.

diary ['daiəri] дневни́к.

dice [dais] **1.** (*pl.* от die²) ко́с… *f/pl.*; **2.** игра́ть в ко́сти; **~-b…** стака́нчик для игра́льных кост…

dicker ['dikə] *Am.* торгова́ться … мелоча́м.

dictat|e **1.** ['dikteit] предписа́н… веле́ние; *pol.* дикта́т; **2.** [dik't… [про]диктова́ть (*a. fig.*); предп… сывать [-са́ть]; **~ion** [dik'teiʃ… дикто́вка, дикта́нт; предписа́н… **~orship** [dik'teitəʃip] диктату́р…

diction ['dikʃən] ди́кция; **~ary** [-… слова́рь *m*.

did [did] *pt.* от do.

die¹ [dai] умира́ть [умере́ть]; ско… ча́ться *pf.*; F томи́ться жела́ние… ~ away, ~ down замира́ть [-мере́… (о зву́ке); затиха́ть [-и́хнуть] … ве́тре); увяда́ть [-я́нуть]; угаса́… [уга́снуть].

die² [~] (*pl.* dice) игра́льная кост… (*pl.* dies [daiz]) ⊕ штамп; чека́… lower ~ ма́трица.

diet ['daiət] **1.** пи́ща, стол; дие́… **2.** *v/t.* держа́ть на дие́те; *v/i.* бь… на дие́те.

differ ['difə] различа́ться, отл… ча́ться; не соглаша́ться [-ласи́… ся], расходи́ться [разойти́сь] (*fr…* с Т, in в П); **~ence** ['difrəns] р… ница; разли́чие; разногла́сие; ра́зность *f*; **~ent** [-t] □ ра́зны… друго́й, не тако́й (from как), ин… **~entiate** [difə'renʃieit] различа… (-ся) [-чи́ть(ся)], отлича́ть(… [-чи́ть(ся)].

ficult ['difikəlt] □ тру́дный; ебовательный; **~y** тру́дность *f*; трудне́ние.
fiden|ce ['difidəns] неуве́ренсть *f*; засте́нчивость *f*; **~t** [-dənt] неуве́ренный; засте́нчивый.
fus|e 1. [di'fju:z] *fig.* распростраіть [-ни́ть]; разглаша́ть [-ласи́ть]; [di'fju:s] □ распространённый; ссе́янный (о све́те); **~ion** [di'f-:ʒən] распростране́ние; расивание.
; [dig] 1. [*irr.*] копа́ться; [вы́]коть; ры́ться; [вы́]рыть; **2.** F толк, тычо́к.
est 1. [di'dʒest] перева́ривать ри́ть] (пи́щу); усва́ивать [усво́ь]; *v/i.* перева́риваться [-ри́ть-]; усва́иваться [усво́иться]; **2.** laidʒest] о́черк, резюме́ *n indecl.*; свод зако́нов; **~ible** [di'dʒeəbl] удобовари́мый; *fig.* легко́ ва́иваемый; **~ion** [-tʃən] пищере́ние.
nif|ied ['dignifaid] досто́йный; ли́чественный; **~y** [-fai] возвоть в сан; *fig.* облагора́живать ро́дить].
nit|ary ['dignitəri] сано́вник; [-ti] досто́инство; сан.
ress [dai'gres] отступа́ть [-пи́ть]; клоня́ться [-ни́ться] (от те́мы).
e [daik] **1.** да́мба; плоти́на; гать **2.** ока́пывать рвом; защища́ть мбой; осуша́ть кана́вами.
apidate [di'læpideit] приходи́ть упа́док; приводи́ть в упа́док.
at|e [dai'leit] расширя́ть(ся) ши́рить(ся)]; **~ory** ['dilətəri] □ дленный; запозда́лый.
igen|ce ['dilidʒəns] прилежа́ние, е́рдие; **~t** □ приле́жный, усе́рдий.
ute [dai'lju:t] разбавля́ть [-ба́ть]; разводи́ть [-вести́].
n [dim] **1.** □ ту́склый, нея́сный вет); сла́бый (о зре́нии); сму́тый (о воспомина́ниях); **2.** [по-] скне́ть; [за]тума́нить(ся).
ne [daim] *Am.* моне́та в 10 це́нв (= 0,1 до́ллара).
nin|ish [di'miniʃ] уменьша́ть(ся) ме́ньши́ть(ся)]; убы́(ва́)ть; **~ion** [dimi'nju:ʃən] уменьше́ние; авле́ние; **~utive** [di'minjutiv] □ ниатю́рный.
nple ['dimpl] я́мочка (на щеке́).
[din] шум; гро́хот.
e [dain] [по]обе́дать; угоща́ть е́дом; **~r** ['dainə] обе́дающий; (*part. Am.*) ваго́н-рестора́н.
gle ['diŋgl] глубо́кая лощи́на.
gy ['dindʒi] □ гря́зный; ту́склый.
ing|-car 🚃 ваго́н-рестора́н; [**~-room** столо́вая.]
ner ['dinə] обе́д; **~-party** го́сти зва́ном обе́де.
t [dint]: by ~ of посре́дством).

dip [dip] **1.** *v/t.* погружа́ть [-узи́ть]; окуна́ть [-ну́ть]; обма́кивать [-кну́ть]; *v/i.* погружа́ться [-узи́ться], окуна́ться [-ну́ться]; салютова́ть (фла́гом) (*im*)*pf.*; спуска́ться [-сти́ться]; **2.** погруже́ние; отко́с; F карма́нник.
diploma [di'ploumə] дипло́м; свиде́тельство; **~cy** [-si] диплома́тия; **~t** *s.* **~tist**; **tic(al** □) [diplo'mætik, -ikəl] дипломати́ческий; **~tist** [di'ploumətist] диплома́т.
dipper ['dipə] ковш; черпа́к.
dire ['daiə] ужа́сный.
direct [di'rekt] **1.** □ прямо́й; непосре́дственный; диаметра́льный; я́сный; откры́тый; ~ current ⚡ постоя́нный ток; ~ train беспереса́дочный по́езд; **2.** *adv.* = **~ly**: непосре́дственно; пря́мо, неме́дленно; **3.** руководи́ть (Т); управля́ть (Т); направля́ть [-а́вить]; ука́зывать доро́гу (Д); **~ion** [di'rekʃən] руково́дство; указа́ние; инстру́кция; направле́ние; **~ion-finder** радиопеленга́тор; **~ive** [di'rektiv] директи́вный; направля́ющий; **~ly** [-li] **1.** *adv.* пря́мо, непосре́дственно; неме́дленно; **2.** *cj.* как то́лько.
director [di'rektə] руководи́тель *m*, дире́ктор; *films* режиссёр; board of ~s наблюда́тельный сове́т; **~ate** [-rit] дире́кция; правле́ние; дире́кторство; **~y** [-ri] а́дресная (и́ли телефо́нная) кни́га.
dirge [də:dʒ] погреба́льная песнь *f*.
dirigible ['diridʒəbl] дирижа́бль *m*.
dirt [də:t] грязь *f*; нечисто́ты *f/pl.*; **~-cheap** F деше́вле па́реной ре́пы; **~y** ['də:ti] **1.** □ гря́зный; неприли́чный, скабрёзный; нена́стный (о пого́де); **2.** загрязня́ть [-ни́ть].
disability [disə'biliti] неспосо́бность *f*, бесси́лие.
disable [dis'eibl] де́лать неприго́дным; [ис]кале́чить; **~d** [-d] искале́ченный; ~ veteran инвали́д войны́.
disadvantage [disəd'va:ntidʒ] невы́года; уще́рб; неудо́бство.
disagree [disə'gri:] расходи́ться во взгля́дах; противоре́чить друг дру́гу; быть вре́дным (with для Р); **~able** [-əbl] □ неприя́тный; **~ment** [-mənt] разла́д, разногла́сие.
disappear [disə'piə] исчеза́ть [-е́знуть]; скры́(ва́)ться; **~ance** [-rəns] исчезнове́ние.
disappoint [disə'pɔint] разочаро́вывать [-рова́ть]; обма́нывать [-ну́ть]; **~ment** разочарова́ние.
disapprov|al [disə'pru:vəl] неодобре́ние; **~e** ['disəpru:v] не одобря́ть [одо́брить] (Р); неодобри́тельно относи́ться (of к Д).
disarm [dis'a:m] *v/t.* обезору́жи(ва)ть; разоружа́ть [-жи́ть];

v/i. разоружáться [-жи́ться]; **~ament** [dis'ɑːməmənt] разоружéние.
disarrange ['dise'reindʒ] расстрáивать [-рóить]; приводи́ть в беспоря́док.
disast|er [di'zɑːstə] бéдствие; катастрóфа; **~rous** [-rəs] □ бéдственный; катастрофи́ческий.
disband [dis'bænd] распускáть [-усти́ть].
disbelieve [disbi'liːv] не [по]вéрить; не доверя́ть (Д).
disburse [dis'bəːs] расплáчиваться [-лати́ться].
disc [disk] *s.* disk.
discard [dis'kɑːd] отбрáсывать [-рóсить] (за ненáдобностью); отвергáть [-éргнуть].
discern [di'səːn] различáть [-чи́ть]; распознá(ав)áть; разглядéть *pf.*; отличáть [-чи́ть]; **~ing** [-iŋ] □ проницáтельный; **~ment** [-mənt] распознавáние; проницáтельность *f.*
discharge [dis'tʃɑːdʒ] **1.** *v/t.* разгружáть [-узи́ть]; освобождáть [-боди́ть]; увольня́ть [увóлить]; уплáчивать [уплати́ть] (долги́); выполня́ть [вы́полнить] (обязáтельства); *v/i.* разряжáться [-ряди́ться]; гнои́ться; **2.** разгру́зка; вы́стрел; освобождéние; увольнéние; разря́д; выполнéние.
disciple [di'saibl] учени́к (-и́ца); послéдователь(ница *f*) *m.*
discipline ['disiplin] **1.** дисципли́на, поря́док; **2.** дисциплини́ровать (*im*)*pf.*
disclose [dis'klouz] обнару́жи(ва)ть; разоблачáть [-чи́ть]; раскры́(вá)ть.
discolo(u)r [dis'kʌlə] обесцвéчивать(ся) [-éтить(ся)].
discomfort [dis'kʌmfət] **1.** неудóбство; беспокóйство; **2.** причиня́ть неудóбство (Д).
discompose [diskəm'pouz] расстрáивать [-рóить]; [вз]волновáть, [вс]тревóжить.
disconcert [diskən'səːt] смущáть [смути́ть]; приводи́ть в замешáтельство.
disconnect [diskə'nekt] разъединя́ть [-ни́ть] (*a.* ⚡); разобщáть [-щи́ть]; расцепля́ть [-пи́ть]; **~ed** [-id] □ бессвя́зный; отры́вистый.
disconsolate [dis'kɔnsəlit] □ неутéшный.
discontent ['diskən'tent] недовóльство; неудовлетворённость *f*; **~ed** [-id] □ недовóльный; неудовлетворённый.
discontinue ['diskən'tinjuː] прер(ы)вáть; прекращáть [-рати́ть].
discord ['diskɔːd], **~ance** [dis'kɔːdəns] разноглáсие; разлáд; ♪ диссонáнс.
discount **1.** ['diskaunt] ⚕ дискóнт, учёт векселéй; ски́дка; **2.** [d 'kaunt] ⚕ дисконти́ровать (*im*); учи́тывать [учéсть] (вексел дéлать ски́дку.
discourage [dis'kʌridʒ] обеску жи(ва)ть; отбивáть охóту (Д; fr к Д); **~ment** [-mənt] обескурáж ность *f*, упáдок ду́ха.
discourse [dis'kɔːs] **1.** рассуж ние; речь *f*; бесéда, разгов **2.** орáторствовать; вести́ бесé
discourte|ous [dis'kəːtiəs] □ вéжливый, неучти́вый; **~sy** [-t невéжливость *f*, неучти́вость *f.*
discover [dis'kʌvə] дéлать крь́тие (Р); обнару́жи(ва)ть, р кры́(вá)ть; **~y** [-ri] откры́тие.
discredit [dis'kredit] **1.** дискре тáция; **2.** дискредити́ров (*im*)*pf.*; [о]позóрить.
discreet [dis'kriːt] □ осторóжны не болтли́вый.
discrepancy [dis'krepənsi] р ноглáсие; рáзница; несхóдство
discretion [dis'kreʃən] благора мие; осторóжность *f*; усмотрéн
discriminat|e [dis'krimineit] в деля́ть [вы́делить]; относи́т по-рáзному; умéть распознав различáть; ~ against стáвить неблагоприя́тные услóвия (. **~ing** [-iŋ] □ умéющий различá распознавáть; **~ion** [-'neiʃən] п ницáтельность *f*; дискриминáц
discuss [dis'kʌs] обсуждáть [ди́ть], дискути́ровать; **~ion** [-ʃ обсуждéние, диску́ссия; прé *n/pl.*
disdain [dis'dein] **1.** презир [-зрéть]; считáть ни́же своегó , стóинства; **2.** презрéние; пре брежéние. [больнó
disease [di'ziːz] болéзнь *f*; **~d** [-
disembark ['disim'bɑːk] сходи нá берег (с су́дна); выгруж [вы́грузить] (товáры).
disengage ['disin'geidʒ] высвобо дáть(ся) [вы́свободить(ся)]; р общáть [-щи́ть]; ⊕ разъедин [-ни́ть].
disentangle ['disin'tæŋgl] рас т(ыв)ать(ся); *fig.* выпу́тыват [вы́путать(ся)] (из затруднéни
disfavo(u)r ['dis'feivə] **1.** нем лость *f*; **2.** не одобря́ть [одóбри
disfigure [dis'figə] обезобрáж вать [-рáзить]; искажáть [ис зи́ть].
disgorge [dis'gɔːdʒ] изверг [-éргнуть] (лáву); изрыг [-гну́ть] (пи́щу).
disgrace [dis'greis] **1.** неми́лост позóр, бесчéстие; **2.** [о]позóри подвéргнуть неми́лости; **~ful** [- □ посты́дный, позóрный.
disguise [dis'gaiz] **1.** маскирóв переодевáние; мáска; **2.** [за]мас ровáть(ся); переодé(вá)ть(с скры(вá)ть.

sgust [dis'gʌst] **1.** отвращéние; . внушáть отвращéние (Д); **~ing** -iŋ] □ отвратúтельный.
sh [diʃ] **1.** блю́до, тарéлка, мú-а; ~s *pl.* посу́да; блю́до, ку́шанье; . класть на блю́до; (*mst* ~ up) по-авáть на стол.
shearten [dis'hɑ:tn] приводúть уны́ние.
shevel(l)ed [di'ʃevəld] растрёпан-ый, взъерóшенный.
shonest [dis'ɔnist] □ нечéстный; едобросóвестный; **~y** [-i] не-обросóвестность *f*; обмáн.
shono(u)r [dis'ɔnə] **1.** бесчéстие, озóр; **2.** [о]бесчéстить, [о]позó-ить; **~able** [-rəbl] □ бесчéстный; íзкий.
sillusion [disi'lu:ʒən] **1.** разоча-ование; **2.** (*a.* **~ize** [-aiz]) разру-áть иллю́зии (Р); открывáть рáвду (Д).
sinclined ['disin'klaind] нерас-олóженный.
sinfect ['disin'fekt] дезинфицú-овать (*im*)*pf.*; **~ant** [-ənt] дезин-ицúрующее срéдство.
sintegrate [dis'intigreit] распа-áться [-пáсться]; разрушáться у́шиться].
sinterested [dis'intristid] □ бес-оры́стный; беспристрáстный.
sk [disk] диск.
slike [dis'laik] **1.** не любúть; пи-áть отвращéние к (Д); **2.** нелю-óвь *f* (for к Д); антипáтия.
slocate ['dislokeit] вывúхивать вы́вихнуть]; нарушáть [нару́-ить]; расстрáивать [-рóить].
slodge [dis'lɔdʒ] смещáть [сме-тúть]; изгоня́ть [изогнáть].
sloyal [dis'lɔiəl] □ нелоя́льный; еролóмный,
smal ['dizməl] □ мрáчный; ны́лый; гнету́щий.
smantl|e [dis'mæntl] ⚓ расснá-цивать [-настúть]; ⊕ демонтú-овать (*im*)*pf.*; **~ing** [-iŋ] демон-áж.
smay [dis'mei] **1.** уны́ние; грах; **2.** *v/t.* приводúть в уны́-ие.
smiss [dis'mis] *v/t.* отпускáть -стúть]; увольня́ть [увóлить]; свобождáть [-бодúть]; ⚖ пре-ращáть [-ратúть] (дéло); откло-я́ть [-нúть] (иск); **~al** [-əl] рóс-уск; увольнéние; освобождéние; ⚖ отклонéние.
smount ['dis'maunt] *v/t.* раз-имáть [-ня́ть]; ⊕ разбирáть [ра-обрáть]; *v/i.* слезáть с лóшади, пéши(ва)ться.
sobedien|ce [diso'bi:dʒəns] не-ослушáние, неповиновéние; **~t** -t] □ непослу́шный, непокóр-ый.
sobey ['diso'bei] ослу́шаться *pf.* Р), не повиновáться (*im*)*pf.* (Д).

disorder [dis'ɔ:də] **1.** беспоря́док; ⚕ расстрóйство; **~s** *pl.* мáссовые волнéния *n/pl.*; **2.** приводúть в беспоря́док; расстрáивать [-рóить] (здорóвье); **~ly** [-li] беспоря́доч-ный; беспокóйный; распу́щен-ный.
disorganize [dis'ɔ:gənaiz) дезор-ганизовáть (*im*)*pf.*, расстрáивать [-рóить].
disown [dis'oun] не призн(ав)áть; откáзываться [-зáться] от (Р).
dispassionate [dis'pæʃnit] □ бес-пристрáстный; бесстрáстный.
dispatch [dis'pætʃ] **1.** отпрáвка; отправлéние; депéша; донесéние; by ~ с курьéром **2.** пос(ы)лáть; от-правля́ть [-áвить].
dispel [dis'pel] рассéивать [-сéять]; разгоня́ть [разогнáть].
dispensa|ry [dis'pensəri] аптéка; амбулатóрия; **~tion** [dispen'seiʃən] раздáча; разделéние; велéние (судьбы́); освобождéние.
dispense [dis'pens] *v/t.* освобож-дáть [-бодúть]; приготовля́ть и распределя́ть (лекáрства); от-правля́ть [-áвить] (правосу́дие).
disperse [dis'pə:s] разгоня́ть [ра-зогнáть]; рассéивать(ся) [-éять (-ся)]; распространя́ть [-нúть].
dispirit [dis'pirit] удручáть [-чúть]; приводúть в уны́ние.
displace [dis'pleis] смещáть [смес-тúть]; переставля́ть [-áвить]; пе-рекладывать [переложúть]; вы-тесня́ть [вы́теснить].
display [dis'plei] **1.** выставля́ть [вы́ставить] (в витрúне); про-являть [-вúть]; выставля́ть на-покáз; **2.** вы́ставка; проявлéние.
displeas|e [dis'pli:z] не [по]нра-виться (Д); быть не по вку́су (Д); **~ed** [-d] □ недовóльный; **~ure** [dis'pleʒə] недовóльство.
dispos|al [dis'pouzəl] расположé-ние; распоряжéние; употреблé-ние; удалéние (нечистóт и т. п.); **~e** [dis'pouz] *v/t.* располагáть [-ло-жúть] (В); склоня́ть [-нúть]; *v/i.* ~ of распоряжáться [-ядúться] (Т); отдéл(ыв)аться от (Р); **~ed** [-d] □ располóженный; настрóен-ный; **~ition** [dispə'ziʃən] располо-жéние; распоряжéние; предрас-положéние (к Д), склóнность (к Д).
disproof ['dis'pru:f] опровержéние.
disproportionate [disprə'pɔ:ʃənit] □ непропорционáльный, несораз-мéрный.
disprove ['dis'pru:v] опровергáть [-вéргнуть].
dispute [dis'pju:t] **1.** оспáривать [оспóрить]; пререкáться; [по]спó-рить; **2.** дúспут; дебáты *m/pl.*; по-лéмика.
disqualify [dis'kwɔlifai] дисквали-фицúровать (*im*)*pf.*; лишáть прáва.

disregard ['disri'gɑ:d] **1.** пренебрежение; игнорирование; **2.** игнорировать (*im*)*pf.*; пренебрегать [-бречь] (Т).
disreput|able [dis'repjutəbl] □ дискредитирующий; пользующийся дурной репутацией; **~e** ['disri'pju:t] дурная слава.
disrespect ['disris'pekt] неуважение, непочтительность *f*; **~ful** [-ful] □ непочтительный.
dissatis|faction ['dissætis'fækʃən] недовольство; **~factory** [-təri] неудовлетворительный; **~fy** ['dis'sætisfai] не удовлетворять [-рить].
dissect [di'sekt] рассекать [-ечь]; вскры(ва)ть (труп).
dissemble [di'sembl] *v/t.* скры(ва)ть; *v/i.* притворяться [-риться], лицемерить.
dissen|sion [di'senʃən] разногласие; распря, разлад; **~t** [-t] **1.** несогласие; **2.** расходиться во взглядах, мнениях.
dissimilar ['di'similə] □ непохожий, несходный, разнородный.
dissimulation [disimju'leiʃən] симуляция; притворство, обман, лицемерие.
dissipat|e ['disipeit] рассеивать [-еять]; расточать [-чить], растрачивать [-тратить]; **~ion** [disi'peiʃən] рассеяние; расточение; беспутный образ жизни.
dissoluble [di'sɔljubl] ⚗ растворимый; расторжимый (о браке, договоре).
dissolut|e ['disəlu:t] □ распущенный; беспутный; **~ion** [disə'lu:ʃən] расторжение (брака, договора); роспуск (парламента).
dissolve [di'zɔlv] *v/t.* распускать [-устить] (парламент и т. п.); расторгать [-оргнуть]; аннулировать (*im*)*pf.*; *v/i.* растворяться [-риться]; разлагаться [-ложиться].
dissonant ['disonənt] ♪ нестройный, диссонирующий.
dissuade [di'sweid] отговаривать [-ворить] (from от Р).
distan|ce ['distəns] **1.** расстояние; даль *f*; промежуток, период (времени); at a ~ на известном расстоянии; **2.** оставлять далеко позади себя; размещать на равном расстоянии; **~t** [-t] □ дальний, далёкий; отдалённый; сдержанный, холодный.
distaste ['dis'teist] отвращение; **~ful** [-ful] □ противный, неприятный (на вкус, вид; to Д).
distemper [dis'tempə] нездоровье; собачья чума.
distend [dis'tend] наду(ва)ть(ся).
distil [dis'til] сочиться, капать; гнать (спирт и т. п.); ⚗ перегонять [-гнать], дистиллировать (*im*)*pf.*; **~lery** [-əri] винокуренный завод.

distinct [dis'tiŋkt] □ особый, ин[ди]видуальный; отчётливый; оп[ре]делённый; **~ion** [dis'tiŋkʃən] р[аз]личение; отличие; отличите[ль]ная особенность *f*; знак отличи[я]; **~ive** [-tiv] □ отличительны[й]; характерный.
distinguish [dis'tiŋgwiʃ] различ[ать] [-чить]; разглядывать [-де...]; выделять [выделить]; **~ed** выдающийся, известный.
distort [-'tɔ:t] искажать [ис[ка]зить]; искривлять [-вить]; ... вращать [-ратить].
distract [dis'trækt] отвлекать [... влечь], рассеивать [-еять]; **~...** [dis'trækʃən] развлечение; ... влечение (внимания).
distress [dis'tres] **1.** горе; б... ствие; страдание; нужда, ни[ще]та; **2.** причинять горе, страда[ние] (Д); **~ed** [-t] нуждающийся; ст[ра]дающий.
distribut|e [dis'tribju:t] расп[ре]делять [-лить]; разд(ав)ать; р[ас]пространять [-нить]; **~ion** [d[is]tri'bju:ʃən] распределение; р[аз]дача; распространение.
district ['distrikt] район; окр[уг]; область *f*.
distrust [dis'trʌst] **1.** недовер[ие]; подозрение; **2.** не доверять (...); **~ful** [-ful] □ недоверчивый; ... дозрительный; ~ (of o. s.) ... уверенный в себе.
disturb [dis'tə:b] [по]беспокои[ть]; [по]мешать (Д); нарушать [...шить]; **~ance** [-əns] нарушени[е]; тревога, волнение.
disunite ['disju:'nait] раздел[ять] [-лить]; разъединять(ся) [-н[ить]] (-ся)].
disuse ['dis'ju:z] изъять из у[по]требления.
ditch [ditʃ] канава, ров.
ditto ['ditou] то же; столько ...
dive [daiv] **1.** нырять [нырну[ть]]; погружаться [-узиться]; б[ро]саться в воду; ✈ пикиров[ать] (*im*)*pf.*; **2.** ныряние; погружени[е]; пикирование; *Am.* притон; ... ['daivə] водолаз; ныряльщ[ик] (-ица).
diverge [dai'və:dʒ] расходит[ься] [разойтись]; отклоняться [-ни[ть]ся], уклоняться [-ниться]; **~...** [-əns] расхождение; отклонен[ие]; уклонение; **~nt** [-ənt] □ расхо[дя]щийся; отклоняющийся.
divers|e [dai'və:s] □ различны[й]; разнообразный; иной; **~ion** [d[ai]'və:ʃən] развлечение; **~ity** [-s...] разнообразие; различие.
divert [dai'və:t] отводить в сто[ро]ну (дорогу и т. п.); отвлекать [-е...] (внимание); развлекать [-ечь].
divest [dai'vest] разде(ва)ть; ... лишать [-шить] (of P).
divid|e [di'vaid] *v/t.* [раз]дели...

разделя́ть [-ли́ть]; *v/i.* [раз]делиться; разделя́ться [-ли́ться]; ⩘ дели́ться без оста́тка; **~end** ['dividend] дивиде́нд; ⩘ дели́мое.
ivine [di'vain] **1.** □ боже́ственный; ~ service богослуже́ние; **2.** уга́дывать [-да́ть].
iving ['daiviŋ] ныря́ние; *sport* прыжки́ в во́ду.
ivinity [di'viniti] богосло́вие; божество́; боже́ственность *f.*
ivis|ible [di'vizəbl] □ дели́мый; **~ion** [di'viʃən] деле́ние; разделе́ние; перегоро́дка; ⚔ диви́зия; ⩘ деле́ние без оста́тка.
ivorce [di'vɔ:s] **1.** разво́д; разры́в; **2.** расторга́ть брак (Р); разводи́ться [-вести́сь] с (Т).
ivulge [dai'vʌldʒ] разглаша́ть [-ласи́ть] (та́йну).
izz|iness ['dizinis] головокруже́ние; **~y** ['dizi] □ чу́вствующий головокруже́ние; головокружи́тельный.
o [du:] [*irr.*] (*s. a.* done) **1.** *v/t.* [с]де́лать; выполня́ть [вы́полнить]; устра́ивать [-ро́ить]; приготовля́ть [-то́вить]; ~ London осма́тривать Ло́ндон; have done reading ко́нчить чита́ть; F ~ in обма́нывать [-ну́ть]; уби́(ва́)ть; ~ into переводи́ть [-вести́]; ~ over переде́л(ыв)ать; покры́(ва́)ть; обма́з(ыв)ать; ~ up завора́чивать [заверну́ть]; приводи́ть в поря́док; уб(и)ра́ть; **2.** *v/i.* [с]де́лать; поступа́ть [-пи́ть], де́йствовать; ~ so as to ... устра́ивать так, что́бы ...; that will ~ доста́точно, дово́льно; сойдёт; how ~ you ~? здра́вствуй(те)!; как вы пожива́ете?; ~ well успева́ть; хорошо́ вести́ де́ло; ~ away with уничтожа́ть [-о́жить]; I could ~ with ... мне мог бы пригоди́ться (И); ~ without обходи́ться [обойти́сь] без (Р); ~ be quick поспеши́те!, скоре́й!; ~ you like London? — I do вам нра́вится Ло́ндон? — Да.
ocil|e ['dousail] послу́шный; поня́тливый; **~ity** [dou'siliti] послуша́ние; поня́тливость *f.*
ock¹ [dɔk] обруба́ть [-уби́ть] (хвост); ко́ротко стричь (во́лосы); *fig.* сокраща́ть [сократи́ть].
ock² [~] **1.** ⚓ док; ⚖ скамья́ подсуди́мых; **2.** ⚓ ста́вить су́дно в док; входи́ть в док.
ockyard ['dɔkjɑ:d] верфь *f.*
octor ['dɔktə] **1.** врач; до́ктор (учёная сте́пень); **2.** F лечи́ть.
octrine ['dɔktrin] уче́ние, доктри́на.
ocument **1.** ['dɔkjumənt] докуме́нт; свиде́тельство; **2.** [-'mənt] подтвержда́ть докуме́нтами.
odge [dɔdʒ] **1.** увёртка, уло́вка, хи́трость *f*; **2.** увиливать [-льну́ть]; [с]хитри́ть; избега́ть [-ежа́ть] (Р).
doe [dou] са́мка (оле́ня, за́йца, кры́сы, кро́лика).
dog [dɔg] **1.** соба́ка, пёс; **2.** ходи́ть по пята́м (Р); высле́живать [вы́следить].
dogged ['dɔgid] □ упря́мый, упо́рный, насто́йчивый.
dogma ['dɔgmə] до́гма; до́гмат; **~tic(al** □) [dɔg'mætik, -ikəl] догмати́ческий; **~tism** ['dɔgmətizm] догмати́зм.
dog's-ear F заги́б (за́гнутый у́гол страни́цы).
dog-tired ['dɔg'taiəd] уста́лый как соба́ка.
doings ['du:iŋz] де́йствия *n/pl.*, посту́пки *m/pl.*
dole [doul] **1.** *Brt.* посо́бие (безрабо́тным); **2.** выдава́ть ску́по.
doleful ['doulful] □ ско́рбный, печа́льный.
doll [dɔl] ку́кла.
dollar ['dɔlə] до́ллар.
dolly ['dɔli] ку́колка.
dolt [doult] ду́рень *m*, болва́н.
domain [do'mein] владе́ние; име́ние; террито́рия; *fig.* о́бласть *f*, сфе́ра.
dome [doum] ку́пол; свод.
domestic [do'mestik] **1.** (**~al**) дома́шний; семе́йный; домосе́дливый; **2.** дома́шняя рабо́тница; слуга́ *m*; **~ate** [-tikeit] привя́зывать к семе́йной жи́зни; приуча́ть [-чи́ть] (живо́тное).
domicile ['dɔmisail] постоя́нное местожи́тельство; **~d** [-d] осе́длый; прожива́ющий.
domin|ant ['dɔminənt] госпо́дствующий, преоблада́ющий; **~ate** [-neit] госпо́дствовать, преоблада́ть; **~ation** [dɔmi'neiʃən] госпо́дство, преоблада́ние; **~eer** [dɔmi'niə] де́йствовать деспоти́чески; влады́чествовать; **~eering** [-riŋ] □ деспоти́ческий, вла́стный.
dominion [də'minjən] доминио́н; владе́ние.
don [dɔn] наде́(ва́)ть.
donat|e [dou'neit] *Am.* [по]же́ртвовать; **~ion** [-ʃən] поже́ртвование.
done [dʌn] **1.** *p. pt.* от do; **2.** *adj.* гото́вый; уста́лый; обма́нутый; well ~ хорошо́ пригото́вленный; прожа́ренный.
donkey ['dɔŋki] осёл.
donor ['dounɔ:] же́ртвователь(ница *f*) *m*; ⚕ до́нор.
doom [du:m] **1.** рок, судьба́; **2.** осужда́ть [осуди́ть]; обрека́ть [-е́чь] (to на В).
door [dɔ:] дверь *f*; next ~ ря́дом; (with)in ~s внутри́, в до́ме; **~-handle** ру́чка две́ри; **~-keeper**, *Am.* **~man** швейца́р, привра́тник; **~way** вход; пролёт две́ри.
dope [doup] **1.** нарко́тик; F дурма́н; **2.** дава́ть нарко́тики (Д).
dormant ['dɔ:mənt] *mst fig.* безде́йствующий, спя́щий.

dormer(-window) ['dɔ:mə('windou)] слуховóе окнó.
dormitory ['dɔ:mitəri] дортуáр, óбщая спáльня; *Am.* общежи́тие.
dose [dous] **1.** дóза, приём; **2.** дози́ровать (*im*)*pf.*; давáть дóзами.
dot [dɔt] **1.** тóчка; крóшечная вещь *f*; **2.** стáвить тóчки над (Т); отмечáть пункти́ром.
dot|e [dout]: ~ (up)on люби́ть до безýмия; **~ing** [dəutiŋ] безýмно лю́бящий.
double ['dʌbl] □ двойнóй; двоя́кий; двули́чный; **2.** двойни́к; двойнóе коли́чество; пáрная игрá; *thea.* дублёр; **3.** *v/t.* удвáивать [удвóить]; склáдывать вдвóе; ~d up скрю́чившийся; *v/i.* удвáиваться [удвóиться]; **~-breasted** двубóртный (пиджáк); **~-dealing** двурýшничество; **~-edged** обоюдоóстрый; **~ entry** ⚕ двойнáя бухгалтéрия.
doubt [daut] **1.** *v/t.* сомневáться [усомни́ться] в (П); не доверя́ть (Д); подозревáть; *v/i.* имéть сомнéния; **2.** сомнéние; no ~ без сомнéния; **~ful** ['dautful] □ сомни́тельный; **~fulness** [-nis] сомни́тельность *f*; **~less** ['dautlis] несомнéнно; вероя́тно.
douche [du:ʃ] **1.** душ; обливáние; **2.** принимáть душ; обливáть(ся) водóй.
dough [dou] тéсто; **~nut** ['dounʌt] [пóнчик.]
dove [dʌv] гóлубь *m*; *fig.* голýбчик (-бушка).
dowel ['dauəl] ⊕ дю́бель *m*, штифт.
down[1] [daun] пух; холм; безлéсная возвы́шенность *f*.
down[2] [~] **1.** *adv.* вниз, внизý; ~ to вплоть до (Р); F be ~ upon нападáть [напáсть] на (В); **2.** *prp.* вниз по (Д); вдоль по (Д); ~ the river вниз по рекé; **3.** *adj.* напрáвленный вниз; ~ platform перрóн для поездóв, идýщих из столи́цы (и́ли большóго гóрода); **4.** *v/t.* опускáть [опусти́ть]; сби(вá)ть (самолёт); одолé(вá)ть; **~cast** ['daunka:st] удручённый; **~fall** падéние; **~-hearted** пáвший дýхом; **~hill** вниз; пóд гору; **~pour** ли́вень *m*; **~right 1.** *adv.* совершéнно; прямо; **2.** *adj.* прямóй; откровéнный, чéстный; **~stairs** ['daun'stɛəz] вниз, внизý; **~stream** вниз по течéнию; **~town** *part. Am.* в деловýю часть гóрода, в деловóй чáсти гóрода; **~ward**(s) [-wəd(z)] вниз, книзу.
downy ['dauni] пуши́стый, мя́гкий как пух; *sl.* хи́трый.
dowry ['dauəri] придáное.
doze [douz] **1.** дремóта; **2.** дремáть, «клевáть нóсом».
dozen ['dʌzn] дю́жина.
drab [dræb] желтовáто-сéрый; однообрáзный.
draft [dra:ft] **1.** = draught; че[к]; сýмма, полýченная по чéку; пополнéние, подкреплéние; набрáсывать [-росáть].
drag [dræg] **1.** обýза, брéмя; дрáга; боронá; **2.** *v/t.* [по]тяну[ть]; [по]волочи́ть; чи́стить дно (ре[ки] и т. п.); *v/i.* [по]волочи́ться; ~ тянýться (о врéмени).
dragon ['drægən] дракóн; ~-f[ly] стрекозá.
drain [drein] **1.** дренáж; канал[и]зáция; водостóк; **2.** *v/t.* дрени́р[о]вать (*im*)*pf.*; истощáть [-щи́ть]; осушáть [-ши́ть]; **~age** ['dreinid[ʒ]] дренáж; сток; канализáция.
drake [dreik] сéлезень *m*.
drama|tic [drə'mætik] (~ally) др[а]мати́ческий; драмати́чный; **~ti[st]** ['dræmətist] драматýрг; **~ti[ze]** [-taiz] драматизи́ровать (*im*)*pf.*
drank [dræŋk] *pt.* от drink.
drape [dreip] [за]драпировáт[ь]; располагáть склáдками; **~ry** ['dr[ei]pəri] драпирóвка; ткáни *f*/*pl.*
drastic ['dræstik] (~ally) решител[ь]ный, крутóй (о мéрах).
draught [dra:ft] тя́га; сквозня́[к]; глотóк; чернови́к, набрóсок; водоизмещéние; ~s *pl.* шáшки *f*/*p[l.]*; *s.* draft; ~ beer пи́во в бóчке; [~]-**horse** ломовáя лóшадь *f*; **~sm[an]** [-smən] чертёжник.
draw [drɔ:] **1.** [*irr.*] [на]рисовáт[ь]; [по]тянýть; [по]тащи́ть; выр[ы]вáть [вы́рвать]; чéрпать (вóду); привлекáть [-éчь] (внимáние); в[ы]води́ть [вы́вести] (заключéние); кончáть (игрý) вничью́; ~ ne[ar] приближáться [-ли́зиться]; ~ o[ut] вытя́гивать [вы́тянуть]; ~ up с[о]ставля́ть [-ави́ть] (докумéнт) [ост]анáвливаться [-нови́ться]; ~ (up)[on] ⚕ вы́ставить вéксель на (В); тя́га; жеребьёвка; F гвоздь *m* (с[е]зóна, вéчера и т. п.); **~back** ['drɔ:bæk] помéха; недостáток; ⚕ во[з]врáтная пóшлина; **~er 1.** ['drɔ:ə] чертёжник; ⚕ трассáнт; **2.** [drɔ:] вы́движной я́щик; (a pair of) ~s *pl.* кальсóны *f*/*pl.*
drawing ['drɔ:iŋ] рисýнок; рис[о]вáние; чертёж; черчéние; ~-**board** чертёжная доскá; **~-roo[m]** гости́ная.
drawn [drɔ:n] *p. pt.* от draw.
dread [dred] **1.** боя́ться, страши́т[ь]ся (Р); **2.** страх, боя́знь *f*; **~f[ul]** ['dredful] □ ужáсный, стрáш[ный].
dream [dri:m] **1.** сон, сновидéни[е]; мечтá; грёза; **2.** [*a. irr.*] ви́деть в[о] снé; мечтáть; грéзить; вообр[а]жáть [-рази́ть]; **~er** ['dri:mə] ме[ч]тáтель(ница *f*) *m*, фантазёр(ка); **~y** [-i] □ мечтáтельный.
dreary ['driəri] □ тосkли́вый; скýчный.
dredge [dredʒ] **1.** землечерпáлк[а]

ра́га, экскава́тор; **2.** драги́ро-
ать (*im*)*pf.*; углубля́ть фарва́тер.
egs [dregz] *pl.* оса́док; неболь-
іо́й оста́ток; подо́нки *m/pl.*
ench [drentʃ] **1.** промока́ние (под
южде́м); **2.** прома́чивать на-
кво́зь.
ess [dres] **1.** оде́жда, пла́тье;
дея́ние; *thea.* ~ rehearsal гене-
а́льная репети́ция; **2.** оде́(ва́)ть
-ся); украша́ть(ся) [укра́сить(ся)];
е́лать причёску; ⚔ равня́ться
вы́ровняться]; выра́внивать [вы́-
овнять]; ⚕ перевя́зывать [-за́ть];
-circle *thea.* бельэта́ж; **~er**
'dresə] ку́хонный шкаф; *Am.*
уале́тный сто́лик.
essing ['dresiŋ] перевя́зочный
атериа́л; перевя́зка; *cook.* при-
ра́ва; ~ down вы́говор, голово-
о́йка; **~-gown** хала́т; **~table**
уале́тный сто́лик.
ess|maker портни́ха; **~-parade**
ы́ставка мод.
ew ['dru:] *pt.* от draw.
ibble ['dribl] ка́пать; пуска́ть
люни.
ied [draid] сухо́й; вы́сохший.
ift [drift] **1.** дрейф; сугро́б (сне́-
а); нано́с (песка́); *fig.* стремле́-
ие; тенде́нция; **2.** *v/t.* относи́ть
отнести́]; наноси́ть [нанести́];
нести́ (сне́г, о ве́тре); *v/i.* дрейфо-
а́ть (*im*)*pf.*; скопля́ться ку́чами
о ли́стьях и т. п.); *fig.* безде́йст-
овать, быть пасси́вным, не со-
ротивля́ться.
ill [dril] **1.** сверло́; бура́в; коло-
оро́т; физи́ческое упражне́ние;
борозда́; ⚔ строево́е обуче́ние;
. [на]тренирова́ть; ⚔ проводи́ть
троево́е обуче́ние.
ink [driŋk] **1.** питьё; напи́ток;
. [*irr.*] [вы́]пить; пья́нствовать.
ip [drip] **1.** ка́пание; **2.** ка́пать.
ive [draiv] **1.** ката́нье, езда́;
одъездна́я алле́я (к до́му); ⚔
да́р, ата́ка; ⊕ переда́ча, приво́д;
ig. эне́ргия; си́ла; **2.** [*irr.*] *v/t.*
по]гнать; вби(ва́)ть (гвоздь и т.
.); вози́ть, [по]везти́ (в автомо-
и́ле, экипа́же и т. п.); пра́вить (ло-
адьми́ и т. п.); управля́ть (ма-
и́ной); *v./i.* е́здить, [по]е́хать;
ата́ться; [по]нести́сь; ~ at [на-]
е́тить на (В).
ivel ['drivl] **1.** распуска́ть слю́ни;
ести́ вздор; **2.** бессмы́слица,
епуха́.
iven ['drivn] *p. pt.* от drive.
iver ['draivə] пого́нщик (скота́);
ot. шофёр, води́тель *m*; 🚂 ма-
ини́ст; ⊕ веду́щее колесо́.
izzle ['drizl] **1.** ме́лкий дождь *m*,
зморось *f*; **2.** мороси́ть.
one [droun] **1.** *zo.* тру́тень *m*;
g. безде́льник, лентя́й; **2.** [за-]
ужжа́ть; [за]гуде́ть.
oop [dru:p] *v/t.* склоня́ть [-ни́ть]
(го́лову); *v/i.* свиса́ть [сви́снуть],
поника́ть [-и́кнуть]; увяда́ть [увя́-
нуть] (о цвета́х).
drop [drɔp] **1.** ка́пля; ледене́ц;
паде́ние, пониже́ние; *thea.* за́-
навес; **2.** *v/t.* роня́ть [урони́ть];
броса́ть [бро́сить] (привы́чку); ~
a p. a line черкну́ть кому́-либо сло-
ве́чко; *v/i.* ка́пать [ка́пнуть]; спа-
да́ть [спасть]; па́дать [упа́сть]; по-
нижа́ться [-и́зиться]; ~ in захо-
ди́ть [зайти́], загля́дывать [загля-
ну́ть].
drought [draut] за́суха.
drove [drouv] **1.** гурт, ста́до; **2.** *pt.*
от drive.
drown [draun] *v/t.* затопля́ть
[-пи́ть]; *fig.* заглуша́ть [-ши́ть]
(звук); *v/i.* [у]тону́ть = be ~ed; ~
o. s. [у]топи́ться.
drows|e [drauz] [за]дрема́ть; **~y**
['drausi] со́нный.
drudge [drʌdʒ] исполня́ть ску́ч-
ную, тяжёлую рабо́ту, «тяну́ть
ля́мку».
drug [drʌg] **1.** лека́рство, медика-
ме́нт; нарко́тик; **2.** употребля́ть
нарко́тики; дава́ть нарко́тики (Д);
~gist ['drʌgist] апте́карь *m.*
drum [drʌm] **1.** бараба́н; бараба́н-
ный бой; *anat.* бараба́нная пере-
по́нка; **2.** бить в бараба́н, бараба́-
нить.
drunk [drʌŋk] **1.** *p. pt.* от drink;
2. пья́ный; get ~ напива́ться
пья́ным; **~ard** ['drʌŋkəd] пья́ница
m/f; **~en** ['drʌŋkən] пья́ный.
dry [drai] **1.** □ сухо́й, вы́сохший;
F жа́ждущий; F антиалкого́ль-
ный; ~ goods *pl. Am.* мануфакту́-
ра; галантере́я; **2.** [вы́]суши́ть;
[вы́]со́хнуть; ~ up высу́шивать
[вы́сушить]; высыха́ть [вы́сох-
нуть], пересыха́ть [-со́хнуть] (о
реке́ и т. п.); **~-clean** чи́стить
хими́чески; **~-nurse** ня́ня.
dual ['dju:əl] □ двойственный;
двойно́й.
dubious ['dju:biəs] □ сомни́тель-
ный, подозри́тельный.
duchess ['dʌtʃis] герцоги́ня.
duck [dʌk] **1.** у́тка; наклоне́ние го-
ловы́; ныря́ние; F ду́шка; **2.** ны-
ря́ть [нырну́ть]; окуна́ться [-ну́ть-
ся]; увёртываться [уверну́ться].
duckling ['dʌkliŋ] утёнок.
dudgeon ['dʌdʒən] оби́да.
due [dju:] **1.** до́лжный, надлежа́-
щий; обя́занный; ожида́емый;
in ~ time в своё вре́мя; it is his ~
ему́ э́то полага́ется; **2.** *adv.* ⚓ то́ч-
но, пря́мо (о стре́лке ко́мпаса); **3.**
до́лжное; то, что причита́ется;
mst ~s *pl.* сбо́ры *m/pl.*, нало́ги
m/pl.; по́шлины *f/pl.*; чле́нский
взнос.
duel ['dju:əl] **1.** дуэ́ль *f*; **2.** дра́ться
на дуэ́ли.
dug [dʌg] *pt.* и *p. pt.* от dig.

duke [dju:k] гéрцог; **~dom** ['dju:-kdəm] гéрцогство.
dull [dʌl] **1.** □ тупóй (*a. fig.*); скýчный; ☤ вя́лый; пáсмурный (день); **2.** притупля́ть(ся) [-пи́ть (-ся)]; *fig.* дéлать(ся) тупы́м, скýчным; **~ness** ['dʌlnis] скýка; вя́лость *f*; тýпость *f*.
duly ['dju:li] дóлжным óбразом.
dumb [dʌm] □ немóй; глýпый.
dummy ['dʌmi] манекéн, кýкла; ⚔ макéт; *fig.* фикти́вное лицó.
dump [dʌmp] **1.** свáлка; ⚔ полевóй склад; **2.** сбрáсывать [сбрóсить]; навáливать [-ли́ть]; свáливать [-ли́ть] (мýсор); **~s** *pl.* плохóе настроéние; **~ing** ☤ дéмпинг.
dun [dʌn] настóйчиво трéбовать уплáты дóлга.
dunce [dʌns] тупи́ца *m/f*.
dune [dʒu:n] дю́на.
dung [dʌŋ] **1.** навóз; **2.** унавáживать [унавóзить].
dungeon ['dʌndʒən] подзéмная тюрьмá.
duplic|ate 1. ['dju:plikit] a) двойнóй; запаснóй; b) дубликáт, кóпия; **2.** [-keit] снимáть, дéлать кóпию с (Р); удвáивать [удвóить]; **~ity** [dju:'plisiti] двули́чность *f*.
dura|ble ['djuərəbl] □ прóчный; долговрéменный; **~tion** [djuə'rei-ʃən] продолжи́тельность *f*.
duress(**e**) [djuə'res] принуждéние.
during ['djuəriŋ] *prp.* в течéние (Р), во врéмя (Р).
dusk [dʌsk] сýмерки; **~y** ['dʌski] сýмеречный; смýглый.
dust [dʌst] **1.** пыль *f*; **2.** [за-, на] пыли́ть; вытирáть пыль; **~-b** мýсорный я́щик; **~er** ['dʌs пы́льная тря́пка; **~y** ['dʌsti] пы́льный.
Dutch [dʌtʃ] **1.** голлáндец (-дка **2.** голлáндский; the ~ голлáнд *pl.*
duty ['dju:ti] долг, обя́занность дежýрство; пóшлина; off ~ св бóдный от дежýрства; **~-free** *ad* беспóшлинно.
dwarf [dwɔ:f] **1.** кáрлик; **2.** мешá рóсту, останáвливать разви́т (Р).
dwell [dwel] [*irr.*] жить, преб вáть; ~ (up)on задéрживать [-жáться] на (П); **~ing** ['dwel жили́ще, дом.
dwelt [dwelt] *pt.* и *p. pt.* от dwell
dwindle ['dwindl] уменьшáть [умéньши́ться], сокращáться [-р ти́ться].
dye [dai] **1.** крáска; окрáска; *f* of deepest ~ настоя́щий; **2.** [п крáсить, окрáшивать [окрáсит
dying ['daiiŋ] (*s.* die[1]) **1.** □ умирá щий; предсмéртный; **2.** умир ние.
dynam|ic [dai'næmik] динами́ч ский; акти́вный; энерги́чны **~ics** [-iks] *mst sg.* динáмика; **~i** ['dainəmait] **1.** динами́т; **2.** взр вáть динами́том.

E

each [i:tʃ] кáждый; ~ other друг другá.
eager [i:gə] □ стремя́щийся; усéрдный; энерги́чный; **~ness** [-nis] пыл, рвéние.
eagle [i:gl] орёл, орли́ца.
ear [iə] ýхо (*pl.*: ýши); **~-drum** барабáнная перепóнка.
earl [ə:l] граф ((англи́йский).
early ['ə:li] **1.** рáнний; преждеврéменный; **2.** *adv.* рáно; заблаговрéммено; as ~ as ужé.
ear-mark ['iəmɑ:k] отмечáть [-éтить].
earn [ə:n] зарабáтывать [-бóтать]; заслýживать [-жи́ть].
earnest ['ə:nist] **1.** □ серьёзный; убеждённый; и́скренний; **2.** серьёзность *f*.
earnings ['ə:niŋz] зáработок.
ear|piece рáковина телефóнной трýбки; **~-shot** предéлы слы́шимости.
earth [ə:θ] **1.** земля́, земнóй шар; земля́, пóчва; **2.** *v/t.* зары́(вá)ть; закáпывать [закопáть]; ↯ заземля́ть [-ли́ть]; **~en** ['ə:θən] земляной; **~enware** [-wɛə] гли́нян посýда; **~ing** ['ə:θiŋ] ↯ заземлéни **~ly** ['ə:θli] земнóй; *fig.* сýетны **~quake** [-kweik] землетрясéни **~worm** земляно́й червь *m*.
ease [i:z] **1.** покóй; лёгкость *f*; н принуждённость *f*; at ~ свобóд удóбно; **2.** облегчáть [-чи́ть]; у покáивать [-кóить].
easel ['i:zl] мольбéрт.
easiness ['i:zinis] *s.* ease 1.
east [i:st] **1.** востóк; **2.** востóчны **3.** *adv.* на востóк; к востóку от Р).
Easter ['i:stə] пáсха.
easter|ly ['i:stəli], **~n** ['i:stən] в стóчный.
eastward(**s**) ['i:stwəd(z)] на востó
easy [i:zi] лёгкий; спокóйный; н принуждённый; take it ~! не тор пи́(те)сь!; спокóйнее!; **~-cha** крéсло; **~-going** *fig.* добродý ный; беззабóтный.
eat [i:t] **1.** [*irr.*] [съ]есть; разъедá [-éсть] **2.** [et] *pt.* от eat 1; **~abl** ['i:təblz] *pl.* съестнóе; **~en** ['i: *p. pt.* от eat 1.

.ves [i:vz] *pl.* карниз; стреха; .drop подслуш(ив)ать.
.b [eb] **1.** (*a.* ~-tide) отлив; *fig.* перемена к худшему; **2.** отли(ва)ть, убы(ва)ть (о воде); *fig.* слабе(ва)ть.
.ony ['ebəni] чёрное дерево.
.ullition [ebə'liʃən] кипение; скипание.
.centric [ik'sentrik] **1.** эксцентричный; ⚙ эксцентрический; **2.** чудак.
.clesiastic [ikli:zi'æstik] **1.** ⚒, *mst* ~al □ [-tikəl] духовный, церковный; **2.** духовное лицо.
.ho ['ekou] **1.** эхо; *fig.* отголосок; **2.** отдаваться как эхо.
.lipse [i'klips] **1.** затмение; **2.** затмевать [-мить]; заслонять [-нить].
.onom|ic(al □) [i:kə'nɔmik(əl)] экономический; экономный, бережливый; ~ics [-iks] *pl.* экономика; народное хозяйство; ~ist [i:'kɔnəmist] экономист; ~ize [-maiz] [с]экономить; ~y [-mi] хозяйство; экономия; бережливость *f*; political ~ политическая экономия.
.sta|sy ['ekstəsi] экстаз; ~tic [eks-tætik] (~ally) исступлённый.
.dy ['edi] **1.** водоворот; **2.** кружиться в водовороте.
.ge [edʒ] **1.** край; лезвие, остриё; кряж, хребет (гор); кромка (материи); обрез (книги); be on ~ быть как на иголках; **2.** обрезать края; окаймлять [-мить]; натачивать [наточить]; ~ways, ~wise [-weiz, -waiz] краем, боком.
.lging ['edʒiŋ] край, кайма, бордюр.
.ible ['edibl] съедобный.
.ifice ['edifis] здание.
.it ['edit] изд(ав)ать; [от]редактировать; ~ion [i'diʃən] издание; ~or ['editə] издатель *m*; редактор; ~orial [edi'tɔ:riəl] **1.** редакторский; редакционный; **2.** передовая статья; ~orship ['editəʃip] редакторство.
.ucat|e ['edju:keit] давать образование (Д); воспитывать [-тать]; ~ion [edju'keiʃən] образование; воспитание; Board of ♀ министерство просвещения; ~ional [-ʃnl] □ педагогический; учебный; ~or ['edjukeitə] педагог.
.l [i:l] угорь *m*.
.face [i'feis] стирать [стереть]; вычёркивать [вычеркнуть]; *fig.* ~ o. s. стушёвываться [-шеваться].
.fect [i'fekt] **1.** следствие; результат; ⊕ производительность *f*; действие; ~s *pl.* имущество; пожитки *m/pl.*; take ~, be of ~ вступать в силу; in ~ в действительности; to the ~ следующего содержания; **2.** производить [-вести]; выполнять [выполнить]; совершать [-шить]; ~ive [-iv] □ эффективный, действительный; имеющий силу; ⊕ полезный; ~ date дата вступления в силу (P); ~ual [juəl] □ действительный; ⚖ имеющий силу.

effeminate [i'feminit] □ женоподобный.
effervesce [efə'ves] [вс]пениться; играть (о вине).
effete [e'fi:t] истощённый; бесплодный.
efficacy ['efikəsi] действительность *f*, сила.
efficien|cy [i'fiʃənsi] эффективность *f*; умелость *f*; ~t [-ənt] □ умелый, квалифицированный; эффективный.
efflorescence [əflɔ:'resns] расцвет.
effluence ['efluəns] истечение; эманация.
effort ['efət] усилие; достижение.
effrontery [e'frʌntəri] бесстыдство.
effulgent [e'fʌldʒənt] □ лучезарный.
effus|ion [i'fju:ʒən] излияние; ~ive [i'fju:siv] □ экспансивный; несдержанный.
egg[1] [eg] подстрекать [-кнуть] (*mst* ~ *on*).
egg[2] [~] яйцо; buttered, scrambled ~s *pl.* яичница-болтунья; fried ~s *pl.* яичница-глазунья.
egotism ['egoutizm] эготизм; самомнение.
egress ['i:gres] выход; исток, истечение.
Egyptian [i'dʒipʃən] **1.** египтянин (-янка); **2.** египетский.
eight [eit] **1.** восемь; **2.** восьмёрка; ~een ['ei'ti:n] восемнадцать; ~eenth [-θ] восемнадцатый; ~h [eitθ] **1.** восьмой; **2.** восьмая часть *f*; ~ieth ['eitiiθ] восьмидесятый; ~y ['eiti] восемьдесят.
either ['aiðə] **1.** *pron.* один из двух; тот или другой; и тот и другой, оба; **2.** *cj.* ~ ... or ... или ... или ...; либо ... либо ...; not (...) ~ также не.
ejaculate [i'dʒækjuleit] восклицать [-ликнуть]; извергать [-ергнуть].
eject [i'dʒekt] изгонять [изгнать]; выселять [выселить]; извергать [-ергнуть]; выпускать [выпустить] (дым).
eke [i:k]: ~ out восполнять [-полнить]; ~ out one's existence перебиваться кое-как.
elaborat|e **1.** [i'læbərit] □ сложный; тщательно выработанный; **2.** [-reit] разрабатывать [-ботать]; разви(ва)ть; ~eness [-ritnis], ~ion [ilæbə'reiʃən] разработка; развитие; уточнение.
elapse [i'læps] проходить [пройти], пролетать [-лететь] (о времени).
elastic [i'læstik] **1.** [~ally] эластич-

ный; упру́гий; **2.** рези́нка (шнур); **~ity** [elæs'tisiti] эласти́чность *f.*
elate [i'leit] **1.** □ лику́ющий; **2.** поднима́ть настрое́ние (Р).
elbow ['elbou] **1.** ло́коть *m*; ⊕ коле́но; уго́льник; at one's ~ под руко́й, ря́дом; **2.** толка́ть локтя́ми; ~ out выта́лкивать [вы́толкнуть].
elder ['eldə] **1.** ста́рший; **2.** ♀ бузина́; **~ly** ['eldəli] пожило́й.
eldest ['eldist] (са́мый) ста́рший.
elect [i'lekt] **1.** изб(и)ра́ть; выбира́ть [вы́брать]; назнача́ть [-на́чить]; **2.** и́збранный; **~ion** [i'lekʃən] вы́боры *m/pl.*; **~or** [-tə] избира́тель *m*; **~oral** [-tərəl] избира́тельный; **~orate** [-tərit] континге́нт избира́телей.
electri|c [i'lektrik] электри́ческий; ~ circuit электри́ческая цепь *f*; **~cal** [-trikəl] □ электри́ческий; ~ engineering электроте́хника; **~cian** [ilek'triʃən] электромонтёр.
electri|city [ilek'trisiti] электри́чество; **~fy** [i'lektrifai], **~ze** [i'lektraiz) электрифици́ровать (*im*)*pf.*; [на-] электризова́ть.
electro|cute [i'lektrəkju:t] казни́ть на электри́ческом сту́ле.
electron [i'lektrɔn] электро́н; ~-ray tube опти́ческий индика́тор настро́йки, «маги́ческий глаз».
electro|plate гальванизи́ровать (*im*)*pf.*; **~type** гальванопла́стика.
elegan|ce ['eligəns] элега́нтность *f*, изя́щество; **~t** ['eligənt] □ элега́нтный, изя́щный.
element ['elimənt] элеме́нт; стихи́я; ~s *pl.* осно́вы *f/pl.*; **~al** [eli'mentl] □ основно́й; стихи́йный; **~ary** [-təri] □ элемента́рный; elementaries *pl.* осно́вы *f/pl.* (како́й-либо нау́ки).
elephant ['elifənt] слон.
elevat|e ['eliveit] поднима́ть [-ня́ть], повыша́ть [-вы́сить]; *fig.* возвыша́ть [-вы́сить]; **~ion** [eli'veiʃən] возвыше́ние, возвы́шенность *f*; высота́ (над у́ровнем мо́ря); **~or** ['eliveitə] ⊕ элева́тор, грузоподъёмник; *Am.* лифт; ✈ руль высоты́.
eleven [i'levn] оди́ннадцать; **~th** [-θ] **1.** оди́ннадцатый; **2.** оди́ннадцатая часть *f.*
elf [elf] эльф; прока́зник.
elicit [i'lisit] извлека́ть [-е́чь]; вызыва́ть [вы́звать].
eligible ['elidʒəbl] □ могу́щий быть и́збранным; подходя́щий.
eliminat|e [i'limineit] устраня́ть [-ни́ть]; уничтожа́ть [-то́жить]; **~ion** [ilimi'neiʃən] выключе́ние; уничтоже́ние.
elk [elk] *zo.* лось *m.*
elm [elm] ♀ вяз.
elocution [elə'kju:ʃən] ора́торское иску́сство.
elope [i'loup] [у]бежа́ть (с возлю́ленным).
eloquen|ce ['elokwəns] красн[оречие]; **~t** [-t] □ красноречивы[й].
else [els] ещё; кро́ме; и́наче; ино́[й], друго́й; or ~ а то; и́ли же; [~]where ['els'wɛə] где́-нибудь [в] друго́м ме́сте.
elucidat|e [i'lu:sideit] разъясня́[ть] [-ни́ть]; **~ion** [ilu:si'deiʃən] раз[ъ]ясне́ние.
elude [i'lu:d] избега́ть [-ежа́ть] (Р); уклоня́ться [-ни́ться] от (Р).
elus|ive [i'lu:siv] неуловимы[й]; **~ory** [-səri] ускольза́ющий.
emaciate [i'meiʃieit] истоща́[ть] [-щи́ть], изнуря́ть [-ри́ть].
emanat|e ['eməneit] истека́[ть] [-е́чь]; происходи́ть [произойт[и́]] (from от Р); **~ion** [emə'neiʃə[n]] эмана́ция; испуска́ние; *fig.* изл[у]че́ние.
emancipat|e [i'mænsipeit] освоб[о]ди́ть от ограниче́ний; **~ion** [imæn]si'peiʃən] освобожде́ние.
embalm [im'bɑ:m] [на]бальзами́[]ровать.
embankment [im'bæŋkmənt] да́м[]ба, на́сыпь *f*; на́бережная.
embargo [em'bɑ:gou] эмба́рго *indecl.*; запреще́ние.
embark [im'bɑ:k] [по]грузи́ть(ся); сади́ться [сесть] (на кора́бль); *fi[g.]* ~ in, (up)on нач(ин)а́ть (В).
embarras [im'bærəs] затрудня́[ть] [-ни́ть]; смуща́ть [смути́ть]; сте[с]ня́ть [-ни́ть]; **~ing** [-iŋ] □ затру[д]ни́тельный; неудо́бный; стесн[и́]тельный; **~ment** [-mənt] затру[д]не́ние; смуще́ние; замеша́тел[ь]ство.
embassy ['embəsi] посо́льство.
embellish [im'beliʃ] украша́[ть] [укра́сить].
embers ['embəz] *pl.* после́дни[е] тле́ющие уго́льки́ *m/pl.*
embezzle [im'bezl] растра́чива[ть] [-а́тить] (чужи́е де́ньги); **~me[nt]** [-mənt] растра́та.
embitter [im'bitə] озлобля́ть [о[з]]ло́бить].
emblem ['embləm] эмбле́ма, си́[м]вол.
embody [im'bɔdi] воплоща́ть [-л[о]]ти́ть]; олицетворя́ть [-ри́ть]; включа́ть [-чи́ть] (в соста́в).
embosom [im'buzəm] обнима́[ть] [обня́ть]; ~ed with окружённ[ый] (Т).
emboss [im'bɔs] выбива́ть вы́пу[к]лый рису́нок на (П), [от-, вы́]ч[е]ка́нить; лепи́ть релье́ф.
embrace [im'breis] **1.** объя́тие; [2.] обнима́ть(ся) [-ня́ть(ся)]; прин[и]ма́ть [-ня́ть] (ве́ру и т. п.); обхв[а́]тывать [обхвати́ть].
embroider [im'brɔidə] вы́ш[и]- (ва́)ть; **~y** [-ri] вышива́ние; в[ы́]шивка.

nbroil [im'brɔil] запу́т(ыв)ать делá); впу́т(ыв)ать (в неприят- ıости).
nerald ['emərəld] изумру́д.
nerge [i'mə:dʒ] появля́ться -ви́ться]; всплы(вá)ть; **~ncy** -ənsi] непредви́денный слу́чай; *ttr.* запасно́й, вспомогáтельный; call *teleph.* сро́чный вы́зов по елефо́ну; **~nt** [-ənt] непредви́ценный; сро́чный.
nigra|nt ['emigrənt] **1.** эмигрáнт, тереселе́нец; **2.** эмигри́рующий, тереселе́нческий; **~te** [-greit] эмигри́ровать *(im)pf.*, переселя́ться -ли́ться]; **~tion** [emi'greiʃən] эмигрáция, переселе́ние.
ninen|ce ['eminəns] высотá; вы- óкое положе́ние; **2ce** высоко- преосвяще́нство; **~t** [-ənt] □ *fig.* ыдаю́щийся, замечáтельный; *dv.* замечáтельно.
nit [i'mit] изд(ав)áть, испускáть -усти́ть] (зáпах, звук, крик); вы- целя́ть [вы́делить].
noti|on [i'mouʃən] душе́вное олне́ние, возбужде́ние; эмо́ция; **onal** [-l] □ взволно́ванный; олну́ющий (о му́зыке и т. п.).
nperor ['empərə] императо́р.
npha|sis ['emfəsis] вырази́тель- ость *f*; ударе́ние, акце́нт; **~size** -saiz] подчёркивать [-черкну́ть]; **tic** [im'fætik] (**~ally**) вырази́тель- ый; подчёркнутый; настóйчи- ый.
npire ['empaiə] импе́рия.
nploy [im'plɔi] **1.** употребля́ть -би́ть], применя́ть [-ни́ть], ис- о́льзовать *(im)pf.*; давáть рабо́ту Д); **2.** in the ~ of на рабо́те у (P), абóтающий у (P); **~ee** [emplɔiə] лу́жащий (-щая), рабо́тник -ница); **~er** [im'plɔiə] нанимáтель -ница *f*) *m*, работодáтель(ница *f*) ı; ⚕ закáзчик (-ица); **~ment** -mənt] примене́ние; рабо́та, за- я́тие; 2 Exchange би́ржа трудá.
npower [im'pauə] уполномо́чи- вa)ть.
npress ['empris] императри́ца.
npt|iness ['emptinis] пустотá; **~y** -ti] **1.** □ пусто́й, поро́жний; F оло́дный; **2.** опорожня́ть(ся) -ни́ть ся)]; [о]пусте́ть.
nul|ate ['emjuleit] соревновáть- я с (Т); **~ation** [emju'leiʃən] со- евновáние.
able [i'neibl] давáть возмо́ж- ость и́ли прáво (Д).
act [i'nækt] предпи́сывать -сáть]; поставновля́ть [-ви́ть]; *hea.* игрáть роль; стáвить на сце́не.
amel [i'næml] **1.** эмáль *f*; **2.** малировáть *(im)pf.*; покрывáть мáлью.
amo(u)red [i'næməd]: ~ of} [влюблённый в (В).}
camp [in'kæmp] ⚔ располагáть- я лáгерем.
enchain [in'tʃein] закóвывать [-овáть]; прикóвывать [-овáть].
enchant [in'tʃɑ:nt] очарóвывать [-овáть]; **~ment** [-ment] очаровáние; **~ress** [-ris] чароде́йка.
encircle [in'sə:kl] окружáть [-жи́ть].
enclos|e [in'klouz] заключáть [-чи́ть]; огорáживать [-роди́ть]; прилагáть [-ложи́ть]; **~ure** [-ʒə] огоро́женное ме́сто; вложе́ние, приложе́ние.
encompass [in'kʌmpəs] окружáть [-жи́ть].
encore [ɔŋ'kɔ:] *thea.* **1.** бис!; **2.** кричáть «бис»; вызывáть [вы́звать].
encounter [in'kauntə] **1.** встре́ча; столкнове́ние; **2.** встречáть(ся) [-е́тить(ся)]; натáлкиваться [натолкну́ться] на (тру́дности и т. п.).
encourage [in'kʌridʒ] ободря́ть [-ри́ть]; поощря́ть [-ри́ть]; **~ment** [-mənt] ободре́ние; поощре́ние.
encroach [in'kroutʃ]: ~ (up)on вторгáться [вто́ргнуться] в (В); **~ment** [-mənt] вторже́ние.
encumb|er [in'kʌmbə] обременя́ть [-ни́ть]; загромождáть [-мозди́ть]; затрудня́ть [-ни́ть]; [вос]препя́тствовать (Д); **~rance** [-brəns] бре́мя *n*; обу́за; *fig.* препя́тствие.
encyclop(a)edia [ensaiklo'pi:diə] энциклопе́дия.
end [end] **1.** коне́ц, окончáние; цель *f*; результáт; no ~ of безме́рно, бесконе́чно мно́го (P); in the ~ в конце́ концо́в; on ~ стоймя́; ды́бом; беспреры́вно, подря́д; **2.** кончáть(ся) [ко́нчить(ся)].
endanger [in'deindʒə] подвергáть опáсности.
endear [in'diə] внушáть любо́вь, заставля́ть полюби́ть; **~ment** [-mənt] лáска, выраже́ние не́жности.
endeavo(u)r [in'devə] **1.** [по]пытáться, прилагáть уси́лия, [по-] старáться; **2.** попы́тка, старáние.
end|ing ['endiŋ] окончáние; **~less** ['endlis] □ бесконе́чный.
endorse [in'dɔ:s] ⚕ индосси́ровать *(im)pf.*; одобря́ть [одо́брить]; **~-ment** [in'dɔ:smənt] ⚕ индоссаме́нт.
endow [in'dau] одаря́ть [-ри́ть] (умо́м и т. п.); наделя́ть [-ли́ть]; **~ment** [-mənt] наде́л.
endue [in'dju:] облекáть [-е́чь].
endur|ance [in'djuərəns] выно́сливость *f*; про́чность *f*; **~e** [in'djuə] выноси́ть [вы́нести], терпе́ть.
enema ['enimə] кли́зма.
enemy ['enimi] враг; неприя́тель *m*; проти́вник.
energ|etic [enə'dʒetik] (**~ally**) энерги́чный; **~y** ['enədʒi] эне́ргия.
enervate ['enə:veit] обесси́ли(ва)ть, ослабля́ть [-áбить].

enfold [inˈfould] обнима́ть [обня́ть], обхва́тывать [обхвати́ть].

enforce [inˈfɔːs] навя́зывать [-за́ть] (upon Д); наста́ивать [настоя́ть] на (П); добива́ться (Р) си́лой; уси́ли(ва)ть; **~ment** [-mənt] принужде́ние.

engage [inˈgeidʒ] *v/t.* нанима́ть [наня́ть]; зака́зывать [-за́ть]; занима́ть [заня́ть]; привлека́ть [-е́чь]; завладе́(ва́)ть; *fig.* привя́зывать [-за́ть]; вовлека́ть [-е́чь]; ⚔ вводи́ть в бой; be **~d** быть за́нятым; быть помо́лвленным; *v/i.* обя́зываться [-за́ться]; занима́ться [заня́ться] (in Т); ⚔ вступа́ть в бой; **~ment** [-mənt] обяза́тельство; свида́ние; приглаше́ние; помо́лвка; ⚔ бой.

engaging [-iŋ] □ очарова́тельный.

engender [inˈdʒendə] *fig.* порожда́ть [породи́ть].

engine [ˈendʒin] маши́на; ⊕ мото́р; 🚂 парово́з; **~-driver** машини́ст.

engineer [endʒiˈniə] **1.** инжене́р; меха́ник; машини́ст; **2.** сооружа́ть [-ди́ть]; [за]проекти́ровать; **~ing** [-riŋ] те́хника.

English [ˈiŋgliʃ] **1.** англи́йский; **2.** англи́йский язы́к; the **~** англича́не *pl.*; **~man** [-mən] англича́нин; **~woman** [-ˈwumən] англича́нка.

engrav|e [inˈgreiv] [вы́]гравирова́ть; *fig.* запечатле́(ва́)ть (в па́мяти); **~er** [-ə] граве́р; **~ing** [-iŋ] гравирова́ние; гравю́ра.

engross [inˈgrous] поглоща́ть [-лоти́ть] (внима́ние).

engulf [inˈgʌlf] *fig.* поглоща́ть [-лоти́ть] (о пучи́не).

enhance [inˈhɑːns] повыша́ть [повы́сить]; уси́ли(ва)ть.

enigma [iˈnigmə] зага́дка; **~tic(al** □) [enigˈmætik, -ikəl] зага́дочный.

enjoin [inˈdʒɔin] втолко́вывать [-кова́ть] (Д).

enjoy [inˈdʒɔi] наслажда́ться [наслади́ться] (Т); **~** o. s. забавля́ться [заба́виться]; **~able** [-əbl] прия́тный; **~ment** [-mənt] наслажде́ние, удово́льствие.

enlarge [inˈlɑːdʒ] увели́чи(ва)ть (-ся); распростроня́ться (on о П); **~ment** [-mənt] расшире́ние; увеличе́ние.

enlighten [inˈlaitn] *fig.* озаря́ть [-ри́ть]; просвеща́ть [-ети́ть]; **~ment** просве́щение; просвещённость *f.*

enlist [inˈlist] *v/t.* ⚔ вербова́ть на вое́нную слу́жбу; **~ed man** ⚔ рядово́й.

enliven [inˈlaivn] оживля́ть [-ви́ть].

enmity [ˈenmiti] вражда́, неприя́знь *f.*

ennoble [iˈnoubl] облагора́живать [-ро́дить].

enorm|ity [iˈnɔːmiti] чудо́вищность *f*; **~ous** [-əs] □ огро́мный, грома́дный; чудо́вищный.

enough [iˈnʌf] доста́точно, д… во́льно.

enquire [inˈkwaiə] *s.* inquire.

enrage [inˈreidʒ] [вз]беси́ть, пр… води́ть в я́рость.

enrapture [inˈræptʃə] восхища́… [-ити́ть], очаро́вывать [-ова́ть].

enrich [inˈritʃ] обогаща́ть [-гати́т…

enrol(l) [inˈroul] *v/t.* [за]регистр… ровать; ⚔ [за]вербова́ть; *v/i.* п… ступа́ть на вое́нную слу́жбу; … **ment** [-mənt] регистра́ция; ве… бо́вка.

ensign [ˈensain] значо́к, эмбле́м… зна́мя, флаг; *Am.* ⚓ мла́дш… лейтена́нт.

enslave [inˈsleiv] порабоща́ть [-б… ти́ть]; **~ment** [-mənt] порабощ… ние.

ensnare [inˈsnɛə] зама́нива… [-ни́ть].

ensue [inˈsjuː] [по]сле́довать; п… луча́ться в результа́те.

entail [inˈteil] влечь за собо́… вызыва́ть [вы́звать] (что́-либо…

entangle [inˈtæŋgl] запу́т(ыв)ат… **~ment** [-mənt] ⚔ (про́волочно… загражде́ние.

enter [ˈentə] *v/t.* вступа́ть [-пи́т… в (В); поступа́ть [-пи́ть] в (В); … вноси́ть [внести́] (в кни́гу); вх… ди́ть [войти́] в (В); проника́… [-ни́кнуть] в (В); *v/i.* входи́… [войти́], вступа́ть [-пи́ть]; **~** (up)… ⚖ вступа́ть во владе́ние (Т).

enterpris|e [ˈentəpraiz] предпри… тие; предприи́мчивость *f*; **~in…** [-iŋ] □ предприи́мчивый.

entertain [entəˈtein] угоща́ть [уго… ти́ть]; развлека́ть [-ле́чь], зан… ма́ть [заня́ть]; **~ment** [-mənt] ра… влече́ние; приём (госте́й).

enthrone [inˈθroun] возводи́ть … престо́л.

enthusias|m [inˈθjuːziæzm] во… то́рг; энтузиа́зм; **~t** [-æst] энт… зиа́ст(ка); **~tic** [inθjuːziˈæsti… (**~ally**) восто́рженный; по́лны… энтузиа́зма.

entic|e [inˈtais] зама́нивать [-ни́ть… соблазня́ть [-ни́ть]; **~eme…** [-mənt] собла́зн, прима́нка.

entire [inˈtaiə] □ це́лый, це́льны… сплошно́й; **~ly** [-li] всеце́ло; с… верше́нно; **~ty** [-ti] полнота́, це́л… ность *f*; о́бщая су́мма.

entitle [inˈtaitl] озагла́вливать [-л… ви́ть]; дава́ть пра́во (Д).

entity [ˈentiti] бытие́; су́щность …

entrails [ˈentreilz] *pl.* вну́тре… ности *f/pl.*; не́дра *n/pl.* (земли́).

entrance [ˈentrəns] вход, въез… вы́ход (актёра на сце́ну); до́сту…

entrap [inˈtræp] пойма́ть в л… ву́шку; запу́т(ыв)ать.

entreat [inˈtriːt] умоля́ть; **~y** [-… мольба́, про́сьба.

entrench [inˈtrentʃ] ⚔ окружа́… око́пами.

trust [in'trʌst] поруча́ть [-чи́ть], веря́ть [вве́рить].
try ['entri] вход, вступле́ние, ьезд; *thea.* вы́ход (на сце́ну); ; вступле́ние во владе́ние; *sport*: я́вка.
umerate [i'nju:məreit] пере- исля́ть [-и́слить].
unciate [i'nʌnsieit] хорошо́ про- зноси́ть; [с]формули́ровать.
velop [in'veləp] заку́т(ыв)ать; ювора́чивать [заверну́ть]; ⚔ кружа́ть [-жи́ть]; **~e** ['enviloup] онве́рт; оболо́чка.
vi|able ['enviəbl] □ зави́дный; **ous** □ зави́стливый.
viron [in'vaiərən] окружа́ть жи́ть]; **~ment** [-mənt] окружа́- щая обстано́вка; **~s** ['envirənz] '. окре́стности *f/pl.*
voy ['envɔi] посла́нник.
vy ['envi] **1.** за́висть *f*; **2.** [по]за- и́довать (Д).
ic ['epik] **1.** эпи́ческая поэ́ма; эпи́ческий.
icure ['epikjuə] эпикуре́ец.
idemic [epi'demik] 🕮 **1.** (~ally) лидеми́ческий; **2.** эпиде́мия.
ilogue ['epilɔg] эпило́г.
iscopa|cy [i'piskəpəsi] еписко- а́льная систе́ма церко́вного правле́ния; **~l** [-pəl] епи́скоп- кий.
ist|le [i'pisl] посла́ние; **~olary** təlәri] эпистоля́рный.
itaph ['epitɑ:f] эпита́фия.
itome [i'pitəmi] конспе́кт, о́черк.
och ['i:pɔk] эпо́ха.
uable ['ekwəbl] □ равноме́рный, о́вный; *fig.* уравнове́шенный.
ual ['i:kwəl] **1.** □ ра́вный; оди- а́ковый; ~ to *fig.* спосо́бный на 3); **2.** равня́ться (Д); **~ity** 'kwɔliti] ра́венство; **~ization** kwəlai'zeiʃən] ура́внивание; **~- :e** [-aiz] ура́внивать [-ня́ть].
uat|ion [i'kweiʃən] ⅍ уравне́ние; **or** [-tə] эква́тор.
uestrian [i'kwestriən] **1.** ко́нный; . вса́дник.
uilibrium [i:kwi'libriəm] рав- ове́сие.
uip [i'kwip] снаряжа́ть [-яди́ть]; набжа́ть [-бди́ть]; **~ment** [-mənt] наряже́ние; обмундирова́ние; боруд́ование.
uipoise ['ekwipɔiz] равнове́сие; ротивове́с. [*f.*
uity ['ekwiti] беспристра́стность
uivalent [i'kwivələnt] **1.** эквива- е́нт (to Д); **2.** равноце́нный; авнозна́чащий.
uivoca|l [i'kwivəkəl] □ дву- мы́сленный; сомни́тельный; **~te** 'kwivəkeit] говори́ть двусмы́с- енно.
a ['iərə] э́ра; эпо́ха.
adicate [i'rædikeit] искореня́ть ни́ть].

eras|e [i'reiz] стира́ть [стере́ть]; подчища́ть [-и́стить]; **~er** [-ə] рези́нка; **~ure** [i'reiʒə] подчи́стка; стёртое рези́нкой.
ere [ɛə] **1.** *cj.* пре́жде чем, скоре́е чем; **2.** *prp.* до (Р); пе́ред (Т).
erect [i'rekt] **1.** □ прямо́й; по́дня- тый; **2.** сооружа́ть [-уди́ть], воз- двига́ть [-и́гнуть]; **~ion** [i'rekʃən] сооруже́ние, строе́ние.
eremite ['erimait] отше́льник.
ermine ['ə:min] *zo.* горноста́й.
erosion [i'rouʒən] эро́зия; разъ- еда́ние.
erotic [i'rɔtik] эроти́ческий.
err [ə:] ошиба́ться [-би́ться], за- блужда́ться.
errand ['erənd] поруче́ние; **~boy** ма́льчик на посы́лках.
errant ['erənt] □ стра́нствующий; блужда́ющий (о мы́слях).
errat|ic [i'rætik] (~ally) неусто́йчи- вый; **~um** [i'reitəm], *pl.* **~a** [-tə] опеча́тка, опи́ска.
erroneous [i'rounjəs] □ оши́боч- ный.
error ['erə] оши́бка, заблужде́ние; ~s excepted исключа́я оши́бки.
erudit|e ['erudait] □ учёный; **~ion** [eru'diʃən] эруди́ция, учёность *f.*
eruption [i'rʌpʃən] изверже́ние; ⚕ высыпа́ние (сы́пи, прыще́й).
escalator ['eskəleitə] эскала́тор.
escap|ade [eskə'peid] сме́лая про- де́лка; побе́г (из тюрьмы́); **~e** [is- 'keip] **1.** *v/i.* бежа́ть (из тюрьмы́) (*im*)*pf.*; спаса́ться [спасти́сь]; *v/t.* избега́ть [-ежа́ть] (опа́сности и т. п.); ускольза́ть [-зну́ть] от (Р); **2.** бе́гство; спасе́ние.
escort **1.** ['eskɔ:t] эско́рт, конво́й; **2.** [is'kɔ:t] конвои́ровать, сопро- вожда́ть.
escutcheon [is'kʌtʃən] щит герба́.
especial [is'peʃəl] осо́бенный; спе- циа́льный; **~ly** [-i] осо́бенно.
espionage [espiə'nɑ:ʒ] шпиона́ж.
essay **1.** ['esei] о́черк; попы́тка; сочине́ние; **2.** [e'sei] подверга́ть испыта́нию; [по]пыта́ться.
essen|ce ['esns] су́щность *f*; су- щество́; эссе́нция; **~tial** [i'senʃəl] **1.** □ суще́ственный (to для Р), ва́жный; **2.** су́щность *f.*
establish [is'tæbliʃ] устана́вливать [-нови́ть]; учрежда́ть [-еди́ть], осно́вывать [-ова́ть]; ~ o. s. по- селя́ться [-ли́ться], устра́иваться [-ро́иться] (в П); ℒed Church го- суда́рственная це́рковь *f*; **~ment** [-mənt] учрежде́ние, заведе́ние; хозя́йство.
estate [es'teit] *pol.* сосло́вие; иму́- щество; име́ние; real ~ недви́- жимость *f.*
esteem [is'ti:m] **1.** уваже́ние; **2.** уважа́ть.
estimable ['estiməbl] досто́йный уваже́ния.

estimat|e 1. [-meit] оцéнивать [-нúть]; **2.** [-mit] смéта, калькуля́ция; оцéнка; **~ion** [esti'meiʃən] оцéнка; мнéние.

estrange [is'treindʒ] отчуждáть [-удúть].

etch [etʃ] гравировáть травлéнием.

etern|al [i'tə:nəl] □ вéчный; неизмéнный; **~ity** [-niti] вéчность *f*.

ether ['i:θə] эфúр; **~eal** [i'θiəriəl] □ эфúрный; воздýшный.

ethic|al ['eθikəl] □ этúчный, этúческий; **~s** ['eθiks] э́тика.

etiquette [eti'ket] этикéт.

etymology [eti'mɔlədʒi] этимолóгия.

eucharist ['ju:kərist] евхарúстия.

European [juərə'piən] **1.** европéец [-пéйка]; **2.** европéйский.

evacuate [i'vækjueit] эвакуúровать (*im*)*pf*.

evade [i'veid] избегáть [-ежáть] (P); ускользáть [-знýть] от (P); обходúть [обойтú] (закóн и т. п.).

evaluate [i'væljueit] оцéнивать [-нúть]; выражáть в чúслах.

evangelic, ~al □ [ivæn'dʒelik, -ikəl] евангелúческий; евáнгельский.

evaporat|e [i'væpəreit] испаря́ть (-ся) [-рúть(ся)]; **~ion** [ivæpə'reiʃən] испарéние.

evasi|on [i'veiʒən] уклонéние, увёртка; **~ve** [-siv] □ уклóнчивый (of от P).

eve [i:v] канýн; on the ~ of накану́не (P).

even ['i:vən] **1.** *adj.* □ рóвный, глáдкий; рáвный, одинáковый; монотóнный; беспристрáстный; чётный (о числé); **2.** *adv.* рóвно; как раз; дáже; not ~ дáже не; ~ though, ~ if хотя́ бы, дáже éсли; **3.** вырáвнивать [вы́ровнять]; сглáживать [сглáдить]; **~-handed** ['hændid] беспристрáстный.

evening ['i:vniŋ] вéчер; вечерúнка; ~ dress вечéрний туалéт, фрак.

evenness ['i:vənnis] рóвность *f*; глáдкость; равномéрность *f*.

evensong вечéрня.

event [i'vent] собы́тие, происшéствие; *fig.* исхóд; нóмер (в прогрáмме); at all ~s во вся́ком слýчае; in the ~ of в слýчае (P); **~ful** [-ful] пóлный собы́тий.

eventual [i'ventjuəl] □ возмóжный; конéчный; **~ly** в концé концóв; со врéменем.

ever ['evə] всегдá; когдá-нибудь, когдá-либо; ~ so óчень; как бы ни; as soon as ~ I can как тóлько я смогý; for ~ навсегдá; yours ~ ваш ... (в концé письмá); **~green** вечнозелёный; **~lasting** [evə'la:stiŋ] □ прóчный; постоя́нный; **~more** ['evəmɔ:] навéки, навсегдá.

every ['evri] кáждый; ~ now and then врéмя от врéмени; ~ other
day чéрез день; **~body** все [...]
кáждый, вся́кий; **~day** ежедне[...]
ный; **~one** кáждый, вся́кий; [...]
pl.; **~thing** всё; **~where** вез[...]
всю́ду.

evict [i'vikt] выселя́ть [вы́селит[...]
оттягáть по судý.

eviden|ce ['evidəns] **1.** очевúднос[...]
f; доказáтельство; ⚖ улúка, св[...]
дéтельское показáние; in ~ в [...]
казáтельство; **2.** служúть дока[...]
тельством; **~t** [-t] □ очевúдны[...]

evil ['i:vl] **1.** □ злой; пáгубны[...]
дурнóй, плохóй; the ♀ One д[...]
вол; **2.** зло; бéдствие.

evince [i'vins] проявля́ть [-вúт[...]

evoke [i'vouk] вызывáть [вы́зва[...]
(воспоминáния и т. п.).

evolution [i:və'lu:ʃən] эволю́ци[...]
развúтие; передвижéние.

evolve [i'vɔlv] развú(вá)ться; эв[...]
люционúровать (*im*)*pf*.

ewe [ju:] овцá.

exact [ig'zækt] **1.** □ тóчный, акк[...]
рáтный; **2.** [по]трéбовать ([...]
взы́скивать [-кáть]; **~ing** [-[...]
трéбовательный, взыскáтельны[...]
~itude [-titju:d], **~ness** [-nis] тó[...]
ность *f*.

exaggerate [ig'zædʒəreit] преув[...]
лúчи(ва)ть.

exalt [ig'zɔ:lt] возвышáть [-ы́сит[...]
превозносúть [-нестú]; **~ati**[...]
[egzɔ:l'teiʃən] возвышéние; во[...]
тóрг.

examin|ation [igzæmi'neiʃən] [...]
мóтр; исслéдование; освидéтел[...]
ствование; экспертúза; экзáме[...]
~e [ig'zæmin] осмáтривать [-мо[...]
рéть]; исслéдовать (*im*)*pf*.; [пр[...]
экзаменовáть.

example [ig'za:mpl] примéр; обр[...]
зéц; for ~ напримéр.

exasperate [ig'za:spəreit] дов[...]
дúть до бéлого калéния; усúл[...]
(ва)ть.

excavate ['ekskəveit] выкáпыва[...]
[вы́копать].

exceed [ik'si:d] превышáть [-в[...]
сить]; переходúть гранúцы ([...]
~ing [-iŋ] □ огрóмный; чрезв[...]
чáйный.

excel [ik'sel] *v/t.* превосходú[...]
[-взойтú] (in, at T); *v/i.* выделя́[...]
ся [вы́делиться]; **~lence** ['eks[...]
ləns] превосхóдство; **~lency** [...]
превосходúтельство; **~lent** ['eks[...]
lənt] □ превосхóдный.

except [ik'sept] **1.** исключá[...]
[-чúть]; **2.** *prp.* исключáя ([...]
крóме (P); ~ for за исключéни[...]
(P); **~ing** [-iŋ] *prp.* за исключ[...]
нием (P); **~ion** [ik'sepʃən] искл[...]
чéние; take ~ to возражáть [-[...]
зúть] прóтив (P); **~ional** [~l] [...]
ключúтельный; **~ionally** [-əli] [...]
ключúтельно.

excess [ik'ses] избы́ток, излúше[...]
эксцéсс; ~ fare доплáта, приплá[...]

, luggage багáж вы́ше нóрмы; ~ive [-iv] □ чрезмéрный.
xchange [iks'tʃeindʒ] 1. обмéниваться [-ня́ться] (T); обмéнивать [-ня́ть], by mistake: [-ни́ть] (for на В); [по]меня́ться (T); 2. обмéн; размéн; (a. ♀) би́ржа; foreign ~(s pl.) инострáнная валю́та; ~ office меня́льная контóра.
xchequer [iks'tʃekə] казначéйство; казнá; Chancellor of the ♀ мини́стр финáнсов Великобритáнии.
xcit|able [ik'saitəbl] возбуди́мый; ~e [ik'sait] возбуждáть [-уди́ть], [вз]волновáть; ~ement [-mənt] возбуждéние, волнéние.
xclaim [iks'kleim] восклицáть [-и́кнуть].
xclamation [ekskla'meiʃən] восклицáние.
xclude [iks'klu:d] исключáть [-чи́ть].
xclusi|on [iks'klu:ʒən] исключéние; ~ve [-siv] □ исключи́тельный; еди́нственный; ~ of за исключéнием (P).
xcommunicat|e [ekskə'mju:nikeit] отлучáть от цéркви; ~ion [ekskəmju:ni'keiʃən] отлучéние от цéркви.
xcrement ['ekskrimənt] экскремéнты m/pl., испражнéния n/pl.
xcrete [eks'kri:t] выделя́ть [вы́делить], извергáть [-éргнуть].
xcruciate [iks'kru:ʃieit] [из-, за-] му́чить; терзáть.
xculpate ['ekskʌlpeit] оправдывать [-дáть].
xcursion [iks'kə:ʃən] экску́рсия.
xcursive [eks'kə:siv] □ отклоня́ющийся (от тéмы).
xcus|able [iks'kju:zəbl] □ извини́тельный, прости́тельный; ~e 1. [iks'kju:z] извиня́ть [-ни́ть], прощáть [прости́ть]; 2. [iks'kju:s] извинéние; оправдáние; отговóрка.
xecra|ble ['eksikrəbl] □ отврати́тельный; ~te ['eksikreit] питáть отвращéние к (Д); проклинáть [-кля́сть].
xecut|e ['eksikju:t] исполня́ть [-óлнить]; выполня́ть [вы́полнить]; казни́ть (im)pf.; ~ion [eksi'kju:ʃən] исполнéние; выполнéние; казнь f; ~ioner [-ə] палáч; ~ive [ig'zekjutiv] 1. □ исполни́тельный; администрати́вный; ~ committee исполни́тельный комитéт; 2. исполни́тельная власть f; ☤ администрáтор; ~or [-tə] душеприкáзчик.
xemplary [ig'zempləri] образцóвый, примéрный.
xemplify [ig'zemplifai] поясня́ть примéром; служи́ть примéром (P).
xempt [ig'zempt] 1. освобождáть [-боди́ть] (от воéнный слу́жбы и т. п.); 2. освобождённый, свобóдный (of от P).
exercise ['eksəsaiz] 1. упражнéние; тренирóвка; моциóн; take ~ дéлать моциóн; 2. упражня́ть(ся); разви́(вá)ть; [на]тренировáть(ся); ⚔ обучáть(ся) [-чи́ть(ся)].
exert [ig'zə:t] напрягáть [-ря́чь] (си́лы); окáзывать [-зáть] (влия́ние и т. п.); ~ o. s. [по]старáться; ~ion [ig'zə:ʃən] напряжéние и т. д.
exhale [eks'heil] выдыхáть [вы́дохнуть]; испаря́ть(ся) [-ри́ть(ся)].
exhaust [ig'zɔ:st] 1. изнуря́ть [-ри́ть], истощáть [-щи́ть]; 2. ⊕ выхлопнáя трубá; вы́хлоп, вы́пуск; ~ion [-ʃən] истощéние, изнурéние; ~ive [-iv] □ истощáющий; исчéрпывающий.
exhibit [ig'zibit] 1. покáзывать [-зáть], проявля́ть [-ви́ть]; выставля́ть [вы́ставить]; 2. экспонáт; ⚖ вещéственное доказáтельство; ~ion [eksi'biʃən] проявлéние, покáз; вы́ставка; ~or [ig'zibitə] экспонéнт.
exhilarate [ig'ziləreit] оживля́ть [-ви́ть]; развеселя́ть [-ли́ть].
exhort [ig'zɔ:t] увещáть, увещевáть.
exigen|ce, ~cy ['eksidʒəns(i)] óстрая необходи́мость f, крáйность f.
exile ['eksail] 1. изгнáние, ссы́лка; изгнáнник; 2. изгоня́ть [изгнáть], ссылáть [сослáть].
exist [ig'zist] существовáть, жить; ~ence [-əns] существовáние, жизнь f; in ~ = ~ent [-ənt] существу́ющий.
exit ['eksit] вы́ход; fig. смерть f; thea. ухóд со сцéны.
exodus ['eksədəs] мáссовый отъéзд; исхóд еврéев из Еги́пта.
exonerate [ig'zɔnəreit] fig. реабили́тировать (im)pf.; снять брéмя (вины́ и т. п.) с (P).
exorbitant [ig'zɔ:bitənt] □ непомéрный, чрезмéрный.
exorci|se, ~ze ['eksɔ:saiz] изгоня́ть [изгнáть] (ду́хов, нечи́стую си́лу); освобождáть [-боди́ть] (of от P).
exotic [eg'zɔtik] экзоти́ческий.
expan|d [iks'pænd] расширя́ть(ся) [-и́рить(ся)], увели́чи(ва)ть(ся); разви́(вá)ть(ся); ~se [iks'pæns], ~sion [-ʃən] прострáнство; протяжéние; экспáнсия; расширéние; ~sive [-siv] □ спосóбный расширя́ться; обши́рный; fig. экспанси́вный.
expatriate [eks'pætrieit] изгоня́ть [из отéчества.]
expect [iks'pekt] ожидáть (P); рассчи́тывать, надéяться; F полагáть, [по]ду́мать; ~ant [-ənt] 1. ~ ожидáющий; ~ mother берéменная жéнщина; 2. кандидáт; ~ation [ekspek'teiʃən] ожидáние; рассчёт; надéжда.

expectorate [eks'pektəreit] отхáркивать [-кнуть]; плевáть [плю́нуть].
expedi|ent [iks'pi:diənt] **1.** подходя́щий, целесообрáзный, соотвéтствующий (обстоя́тельствам); **2.** подру́чное срéдство; улóвка; **~tion** [ekspi'diʃən] экспеди́ция; быстротá; поспéшность *f*.
expel [iks'pel] изгоня́ть [изгнáть] (из P), исключáть [-чи́ть] (из P).
expen|d [iks'pend] [ис]трáтить; [из]расхóдовать; **~diture** [-itʃə] расхóд, трáта; **~se** [iks'pens] расхóд, трáта; ~s *pl.* расхóды *m/pl.*; **~sive** [-siv] □ дорогóй, дóрого стóящий.
experience [iks'piərəns] **1.** óпыт (жи́зненный); переживáние; **2.** испы́тывать [испытáть]; пережи́(вá)ть; **~d** [-t] óпытный.
experiment 1. [iks'perimənt] óпыт, эксперимéнт; **2.** [-'ment] производи́ть óпыты; **~al** [eksperi'mentl] □ экспериментальный, оснóванный на óпыте; прóбный.
expert ['ekspə:t] **1.** □ [*pred.* eks'pə:t] óпытный, искýсный; **2.** экспéрт, знатóк, специали́ст.
expir|ation [ekspai'reiʃən] выдыхáние; окончáние, истечéние (срóка); **~e** [iks'paiə] выдыхáть [вы́дохнуть]; умирáть [умерéть]; ⚕ кончáться [кóнчиться], истекáть [-éчь] (о срóке).
explain [iks'plein] объясня́ть [-ни́ть]; опрáвдывать [-дáть] (поведéние).
explanat|ion [eksplə'neiʃən] объяснéние; толковáние; **~ory** [iks'plænətəri] □ объясни́тельный.
explicable ['eksplikəbl] объясни́мый.
explicit [iks'plisit] □ я́сный, недвусмы́сленный.
explode [iks'ploud] взрывáть(ся) [взорвáть(ся)]; подрывáть [подорвáть]; разражáться [-рази́ться] (with T).
exploit 1. ['eksplɔit] пóдвиг; **2.** [iks'plɔit] эксплуати́ровать; ⚒ разрабáтывать [-бóтать]; **~ation** [eksplɔi'teiʃən] эксплуатáция; ⚒ разрабóтка.
explor|ation [eksplɔ:'reiʃən] исслéдование; **~e** [iks'plɔ:] исслéдовать (*im*)*pf.*; развéд(ыв)ать **~er** [-rə] исслéдователь(ница *f*) *m*.
explosi|on [iks'plouʒən] взрыв; вспы́шка (гнéва); **~ve** [-siv] **1.** □ взры́вчатый; *fig.* вспы́льчивый; **2.** взры́вчатое веществó.
exponent [eks'pounənt] объясни́тель *m*; представи́тель *m*; образéц; ℞ показáтель стéпени.
export 1. ['ekspɔ:t] э́кспорт, вы́воз; **2.** [eks'pɔ:t] экспорти́ровать (*im*)*pf.*, вывози́ть [вы́везти] (товáры); **~ation** [ekspɔ:'teiʃən] вы́воз.

expos|e [iks'pouz] подвергá [-éргнуть] (опáсности и т. п.); бр сáть на произвóл судьбы́; выста ля́ть [вы́ставить]; разоблачá [-чи́ть]; *phot.* экспони́рова (*im*)*pf.*; **~ition** [ekspo'ziʃən] в ставка; изложéние
exposure [iks'pouʒə] подвергáни выставлéние; разоблачéние; *ph* экспози́ция, вы́держка.
expound [iks'paund] излагáть [и ложи́ть]; разъясня́ть [-ни́ть].
express [iks'pres] **1.** □ определё ный, тóчно вы́раженный; спец áльный; срóчный; ~ compa *Am.* трáнспортная контóра; курьéр, нарóчный; (*a.* ~ trai экспрéсс, курьéрский пóезд; *adv.* спéшно; с нарóчным; **4.** вы ражáть [вы́разить]; **~ion** [ik 'preʃən] выражéние; вырази́тел ность *f*; **~ive** [iks'presiv] □ вы рази́тельный; выражáющий.
expropriate [eks'prouprieit] эк проприи́ровать (*im*)*pf.*; лишá сóбственности.
expulsion [iks'pʌlʃən] изгнáни исключéние (из шкóлы и т. п
exquisite ['ekskwizit] **1.** □ изы́ канный, утончённый; прелéс ный; **2.** фат, щёголь *m*.
extant [eks'tænt] сохрани́вшийс
extempor|aneous [ekstempə're njəs] □, **~ary** [iks'tempərəri] н подготóвленный; **~e** [-pəri] *ad* экспрóмтом.
extend [iks'tend] *v/t.* протя́гива [-тянýть]; распространя́ть [-ни́т (влия́ние); продлевáть [-ли́т (срок); ⚔ рассыпáть в цепь; *v* простирáться [простерéться].
extensi|on [iks'tenʃən] вытя́г вание; расширéние; распростр нéние; протяжéние; продлéни University ♀ популя́рные лéкци организýемые университéтом; **~** [-siv] □ обши́рный, простра́нны
extent [iks'tent] протяжéние; ра мéр, стéпень *f*, мéра; to the ~ в размéре (P); to some ~ до и вéстной стéпени.
extenuate [eks'tenjueit] уменьшá [умéньши́ть] (винý); старáть найти́ извинéние; ослабля́ [-áбить].
exterior [eks'tiəriə] **1.** □ внéшни нарýжный; **2.** внéшность *f*, н рýжность *f*.
exterminate [eks'tə:mineit] иск реня́ть [-ни́ть], истребля́ть [-би́ть
external [eks'tə:nl] **1.** □ нарýж ный, внéшний; **2.** ~s *pl.* внé ность *f*, нарýжность *f*; *fig.* внé ние обстоя́тельства.
extinct [iks'tiŋkt] угáсший; вы́ме ший; потýхший.
extinguish [iks'tiŋgwiʃ] [по]гаси́т [по]туши́ть; погашáть [погаси́т (долг).

ktirpate ['ekstə:peit] искоренять -нить], истреблять [-бить].
ktol [iks'tɔl] превозносить [-нести].
ktort [iks'tɔ:t] вымогать (деньги); выпытывать [выпытать] (тайну); **~ion** [iks'tɔ:ʃən] вымогательство.
ktra ['ekstrə] **1.** добавочный, дополнительный; экстренный; **2.** *adv.* особо; особенно; дополнительно; **3.** приплата; *Am.* экстренный выпуск газеты; **~s** *pl.* побочные расходы (доходы).
ktract **1.** ['ekstrækt] экстракт; выдержка, извлечение; **2.** [iks'trækt] удалять [-лить]; извлекать [-ечь]; вырывать [вырвать]; **~ion** [-kʃən] извлечение; происхождение (человека).
ktraordinary [iks'trɔ:dnri] необычайный; удивительный, странный.
ktravagan|ce [iks'trævigəns] расточительность *f*; нелепость *f*; излишество; **~t** [-gənt] □ расточительный; сумасбродный, нелепый.
extrem|e [iks'tri:m] **1.** □ крайний; последний; чрезвычайный; **2.** крайность *f*; **~ity** [iks'tremiti] оконечность *f*; крайность *f*; крайняя нужда; крайняя мера; **~ities** [-z] *pl.* конечности *f/pl.*
extricate ['ekstrikeit] выводить [вывести] (из затруднительного положения).
exuberan|ce [ig'zju:bərəns] изобилие, избыток; **~t** [-t] обильный; пышный; цветистый, многословный.
exult [ig'zʌlt] ликовать; торжествовать.
eye [ai] **1.** глаз, око; взгляд; ушко; with an ~ to с целью (+ *inf.*); **2.** смотреть на (В), пристально разглядывать; **~ball** глазное яблоко; **~brow** бровь *f*; **...~d** [aid] ...глазый; **~-glass** линза; (a pair of) **~es** *pl.* очки *n/pl.*; лорнет; **~lash** ресница; **~lid** веко; **~sight** зрение.

F

ble ['feibl] басня.
bric ['fæbrik] сооружение; структура; выделка; фабрикат; ткань *f*, материя; **~ate** ['fæbrikeit] (*mst fig.*) выдумывать [выдумать]; выделывать [выделать].
bulous ['fæbjuləs] □ баснословный; неправдоподобный.
ce [feis] **1.** лицо, физиономия; гримаса; лицевая сторона (ткани); фасад; on the ~ of it с первого взгляда; **2.** *v/t.* встречать смело; смотреть в лицо (Д): стоять лицом к (Д); выходить на (В) (об окне); ⚒ облицовывать [-цевать]; [на-, от]полировать; *v/i.* ~ about ⚔ поворачиваться кругом.
cetious [fə'si:ʃəs] □ шутливый.
cil|e ['fæsail] лёгкий; свободный (о речи и т. п.); **~itate** [fə'siliteit] облегчать [-чить]; **~ity** [fə'siliti] лёгкость *f*; способность *f*; плавность *f* (речи); облегчение.
cing ['feisiŋ] ⊕ облицовка; **~s** *pl.* отделка мундира.
ct [fækt] факт; дело; явление; истина; действительность *f*.
ction ['fækʃən] фракция; клика.
ctitious [fæk'tiʃəs] □ искусственный.
ctor ['fæktə] фактор; агент; ✝ комиссионер; **~y** [-ri] фабрика, завод.
culty ['fækəlti] способность *f*; *fig.* дар; *univ.* факультет. [чуда.]
d [fæd] F конёк; прихоть *f*, при-
de [feid] увядать [увянуть]; постепенно исчезать.
fag [fæg] *v/i.* потрудиться; корпеть (над Т); *v/t.* утомлять [-мить].
fail [feil] **1.** *v/i.* ослабе(ва)ть; недост(ав)ать; потерпеть неудачу; проваливаться [-литься] (на экзамене); he **~ed** to do ему не удалось сделать (Р); забы(ва)ть; *v/t.* изменять [-нить] (Д), покидать [-инуть]; **2.** *su.*: without ~ наверняка; непременно; **~ing** ['feiliŋ] недостаток; слабость *f*; **~ure** [feiljə] неудача, неуспех; провал (на экзамене); банкротство; неудачник (-ица).
faint [feint] **1.** □ слабый; робкий (голос); тусклый; **2.** [о]слабеть; потерять сознание (with от Р); **3.** обморок, потеря сознания; **~hearted** ['feint'hɑ:tid] малодушный.
fair[1] [fɛə] **1.** *adj* прекрасный, красивый; благоприятный; белокурый; ясный; попутный; справедливый; **2.** *adv.* честно; любезно; прямо, ясно; ~ copy чистовик; ~ play игра по правилам.
fair[2] [~] ярмарка.
fair|ly ['fɛəli] справедливо; довольно; сносно; **~ness** ['fɛənis] справедливость *f*; красота (*s.* fair[1]); **~way** ⚓ фарватер.
fairy ['fɛəri] фея; **~land** сказочная страна; **~-tale** сказка.
faith [feiθ] доверие, вера; вера (религия); **~ful** ['feiθful] □ верный, преданный; правдивый; yours **~ly** уважающий Вас; **~less** ['feiθlis] □ вероломный; неверующий.

fake [feik] *sl.* **1.** подде́лка, фальши́вка; **2.** подде́л(ыв)ать.

falcon [ˈfɔːlkən] со́кол.

fall [fɔːl] **1.** паде́ние; упа́док; обры́в, склон; напо́р; *Am.* о́сень *f*; (*mst* ~s *pl.*) водопа́д; **2.** [*irr.*] па́дать [упа́сть]; спада́ть [спасть]; убы́(ва́)ть (о воде́); обва́ливаться [-ли́ться] (о земле́); ~ back отступа́ть [-пи́ть]; ~ ill *или* sick заболе́(ва́)ть; ~ out [по]ссо́риться; ~ short of не оправда́ть (ожида́ний); не достига́ть [-и́чь] *a.* [-и́гнуть] (це́ли); ~ short не хвата́ть [-ти́ть], конча́ться [ко́нчиться]; ~ to принима́ться [-ня́ться] за (В).

fallacious [fəˈleiʃəs] □ оши́бочный, ло́жный.

fallacy [ˈfæləsi] заблужде́ние, оши́бка.

fallen [ˈfɔːlən] *p. pt.* от fall.

falling [ˈfɔːliŋ] паде́ние; пониже́ние; ~**-sickness** эпиле́псия; ~**-star** метео́р, па́дающая звезда́.

fallow [ˈfælou] *adj.* вспа́ханный под па́р.

false [fɔːls] □ ло́жный, оши́бочный; фальши́вый; вероло́мный; иску́сственный (о зуба́х); ~**hood** [ˈfɔːlshud], ~**ness** [-nis] ложь *f*; фальши́вость *f*; оши́бочность *f*.

falsi|fication [fɔːlsifiˈkeiʃən] подде́лка; ~**fy** [ˈfɔːlsifai] подде́л(ыв)ать; ~**ty** [-ti] ло́жность *f*, оши́бочность *f*; вероло́мство.

falter [ˈfɔːltə] спотыка́ться [-т-кну́ться]; запина́ться [запну́ться]; *fig.* колеба́ться.

fame [feim] сла́ва; молва́; ~**d** [feimd] изве́стный, знамени́тый.

familiar [fəˈmiljə] **1.** □ бли́зкий, хорошо́ знако́мый; обы́чный; **2.** бли́зкий друг; ~**ity** [fəmiliˈæriti] бли́зость *f*; фамилья́рность *f*; осведомлённость *f*; ~**ize** [fəˈmiljəraiz] ознакомля́ть [-ко́мить].

family [ˈfæmili] семья́, семе́йство; in the ~ way в интере́сном положе́нии (бере́менна); ~ tree родосло́вное де́рево.

fami|ne [ˈfæmin] го́лод; голода́ние; ~**sh** голода́ть; мори́ть го́лодом.

famous [ˈfeiməs] □ знамени́тый.

fan [fæn] **1.** ве́ер; вентиля́тор; *sport* боле́льщик (-ица); покло́нник (-ица); **2.** обма́хивать [-хну́ть].

fanatic [fəˈnætik] **1.** (*a.* ~**al** □ [-ikəl]) фанати́ческий; **2.** фана́тик (-ти́чка).

fanciful [ˈfænsiful] □ прихотли́вый, капри́зный, причу́дливый.

fancy [ˈfænsi] **1.** фанта́зия, воображе́ние; при́хоть *f*; пристра́стие; скло́нность *f*; **2.** прихотли́вый; фантасти́ческий; орнамента́льный; ~ ball костюмиро́ванный бал; ~ goods *pl.* мо́дные това́ры *m/pl.*; **3.** вообража́ть [-рази́ть]; представля́ть [-а́вить] себе́; [по]люби́ть; [за]хоте́ть; just ~! предста́вьте себе́!

fang [fæŋ] клык; ядови́тый зу (змей).

fantas|tic [fænˈtæstik] (~ally) при чу́дливый, фантасти́чный; ~ [ˈfæntəsi] фанта́зия, воображе́ни

far [fɑː] *adj.* да́льний, далёки отдалённый; *adv.* далеко́; г ра́здо; as ~ as до (Р); in so ~ as н ско́льку; ~ **away** далеко́.

fare [fɛə] **1.** проездны́е де́ньги *f/p* пассажи́р; съестны́е припа́с *m/pl.*; **2.** быть, пожива́ть; п та́ться; ~**well** [ˈfɛəˈwel] **1.** пр ща́й(те)!; **2.** проща́ние.

far-fetched [ˈfɑːˈfetʃt] *fig.* притя нутый за́ волосы.

farm [fɑːm] **1.** фе́рма; **2.** обраба́ть вать зе́млю; ~**er** [ˈfɑːmə] крест я́нин, фе́рмер; ~**house** жило́й до на фе́рме; ~**ing** **1.** заня́тие се́л ским хозя́йством; **2.** сельскох зя́йственный; ~**stead** [ˈfɑːmste уса́дьба.

far-off [ˈfɑːrɔf] далёкий.

farthe|r [ˈfɑːðə] **1.** *adv.* да́льш **2.** *adj.* отдалённый; ~**st** [-ðist] *adj.* са́мый далёкий, са́мый да́л ний; **2.** *adv.* да́льше всего́.

fascinat|e [ˈfæsineit] очаро́выва [-ова́ть], пленя́ть [-ни́ть]; ~io [fæsiˈneiʃən] очарова́ние, оба ние.

fashion [ˈfæʃn] **1.** мо́да; стиль фасо́н, покро́й; о́браз, мане́ра; (out of) ~ (не)мо́дный; **2.** прид ва́ть фо́рму, вид (Д into Р); ~**ab** [ˈfæʃnəbl] □ мо́дный, фешене́бел ный.

fast¹ [fɑːst] про́чный, кре́пки твёрдый; бы́стрый; легкомы́ ленный.

fast² [~] **1.** *eccl.* пост; **2.** пости́тьс

fasten [ˈfɑːsn] *v/t.* прикрепля́ [-пи́ть]; привя́зывать [-за́ть свинчивать [-нти́ть]; застёгива [-тегну́ть]; *v/i.* запира́ться [за ре́ться]; застёгивать(ся) [-тегну́ (-ся)]; ~ upon *fig.* ухвати́ться (В); ~**er** [-ə] запо́р, задви́жка; з стёжка. [ре́дливый

fastidious [fæsˈtidiəs] □ приве

fat [fæt] **1.** □ жи́рный; са́льны ту́чный; **2.** жир; са́ло; **3.** с ка́рмливать [откорми́ть]; [ра жире́ть.

fatal [ˈfeitl] □ рокова́й, фата́л ный, неизбе́жный; смерте́льны ~**ity** [fəˈtæliti] обречённость *f*; ф та́льность *f*; несча́стье; смерть (от несча́стного слу́чая).

fate [feit] рок, судьба́.

father [ˈfɑːðə] оте́ц; ~**hood** [-hu отцо́вство; ~**-in-law** [ˈfɑːðərinl свёкор; тесть *m*; ~**less** [-lis] оста́ шийся без отца́; ~**ly** [-li] оте́ч ский.

fathom ['fæðəm] **1.** ⚓ морска́я са́жень *f* (= 6 футам = 182 сантиме́трам); **2.** ⚓ измеря́ть глубину́ (Р); *fig.* вника́ть [вни́кнуть] в (В), понима́ть [поня́ть]; **~less** [-lis] неизмери́мый; бездо́нный.
fatigue [fə'ti:g] **1.** утомле́ние, уста́лость *f*; **2.** утомля́ть [-ми́ть], изнуря́ть [-ри́ть].
fat|ness ['fætnis] жи́рность *f*; **~ten** ['fætn] отка́рмливать [откорми́ть] (на убо́й); [раз]жире́ть.
fatuous ['fætjuəs] □ глу́пый, пусто́й.
faucet ['fɔ:sit] *Am.* (водопрово́дный) кран.
fault [fɔ:lt] недоста́ток, дефе́кт; просту́пок, вина́; find ~ with прид(и)ра́ться к (Д); be at ~ потеря́ть след; **~-finder** придира *m/f*; **~less** ['fɔ:ltlis] □ безупре́чный; **~y** ['fɔ:lti] □ име́ющий недоста́ток, дефе́ктный.
favo(u)r ['feivə] **1.** благоскло́нность *f*, расположе́ние; одобре́ние; одолже́ние; your ~ ✝ Ва́ше письмо́; **2.** благоволи́ть к (Д); ока́зывать внима́ние (Д); покрови́тельствовать (Д); **~able** [-rəbl] □ благоприя́тный, удо́бный; **~ite** ['feivərit] **1.** люби́мец (-мица); фаво́рит(ка); **2.** люби́мый.
fawn [fɔ:n] **1.** молодо́й оле́нь *m*; кори́чневый цвет; **2.** подли́зываться [-за́ться] (upon к Д).
fear [fiə] **1.** страх, боя́знь *f*; опасе́ние; **2.** боя́ться (Р); **~ful** ['fiəful] □ стра́шный, ужа́сный; **~less** ['fiəlis] □ бесстра́шный, неустраши́мый.
feasible ['fi:zəbl] возмо́жный, вероя́тный; выполни́мый.
feast [fi:st] **1.** пир, пра́зднество, банке́т; **2.** *v/t.* угоща́ть [угости́ть]; че́ствовать; *v/i.* пирова́ть.
feat [fi:t] по́двиг; трюк.
feather ['feðə] **1.** перо́; опере́ние; show the white ~ F прояви́ть тру́сость; in high ~ в отли́чном настрое́нии; **2.** украша́ть пе́рьями; **~-brained, ~-headed** пусто́й, ве́треный, глу́пый; **~ed** ['feðəd] перна́тый; **~y** [-ri] оперённый; пуши́стый.
feature ['fi:tʃə] **1.** осо́бенность *f*, сво́йство; *Am.* газе́тная статья́; **~s** *pl.* черты́ лица́; **2.** изобража́ть [-рази́ть]; пока́зывать [-за́ть] (на экра́не); выводи́ть в гла́вной ро́ли.
February ['februəri] февра́ль *m*.
fecund ['fekənd] плодоро́дный.
fed [fed] *pt.* и *p. pt.* от feed; I am ~ up with ... мне надое́л (-ла, -ло).
federa|l ['fedərəl] федера́льный; сою́зный; **~tion** [fedə'reiʃən] федера́ция.
fee [fi:] **1.** гонора́р; взнос; пла́та; чаевы́е *pl.* **2.** [за]плати́ть.
feeble ['fi:bl] □ сла́бый, хи́лый.
feed [fi:d] **1.** пита́ние, кормле́ние; пи́ща; ⊕ пода́ча (материа́ла); **2.** [*irr.*] *v/t.* пита́ть, [по]корми́ть; ⊕ снабжа́ть [-бди́ть] (материа́лом); *v/i.* пита́ться, корми́ться; пасти́сь; **~ing-bottle** де́тский рожо́к.
feel [fi:l] **1.** [*irr.*] [по]чу́вствовать (себя́); испы́тывать [-та́ть]; ощуща́ть [ощути́ть], осяза́ть; ~ like doing быть скло́нным сде́лать; **2.** ощуще́ние, осяза́ние; чутьё; **~er** ['fi:lə] щу́пальце; **~ing** ['fi:liŋ] **1.** □ чувстви́тельный; прочу́вствованный; **2.** чу́вство.
feet [fi:t] *pl.* от foot 1.
feign [fein] притворя́ться [-ри́ться], симули́ровать (*im*)*pf*.
feint [feint] притво́рство; манёвр.
felicit|ate [fi'lisiteit] поздравля́ть [-а́вить]; **~ous** [-təs] □ уда́чный; счастли́вый.
fell [fel] **1.** *pt.* от fall; **2.** [с]руби́ть.
felloe ['felou] о́бод (колеса́).
fellow [~] това́рищ, собра́т; челове́к; the ~ of a glove па́рная перча́тка; **~-countryman** соотече́ственник; **~ship** [-ʃip] това́рищество.
felly ['feli] о́бод (колеса́).
felon ['felən] ⚖ уголо́вный престу́пник; **~y** ['feləni] уголо́вное преступле́ние.
felt[1] [felt] *pt.* и *p. pt.* от feel.
felt[2] [~] **1.** во́йлок, фетр; **2.** сбива́ть (*or* сбива́ться в) во́йлок.
female ['fi:meil] **1.** же́нский; **2.** же́нщина.
feminine ['feminin] □ же́нский; же́нственный.
fen [fen] боло́то, топь *f*.
fence [fens] **1.** забо́р, и́згородь *f*, огра́да; sit on the ~ колеба́ться ме́жду двумя́ мне́ниями; занима́ть выжида́тельную пози́цию; **2.** *v/t.* огора́живать [-роди́ть]; защища́ть [-ити́ть]; *v/i.* фехтова́ть; укрыва́ть кра́деное.
fencing ['fensiŋ] **1.** и́згородь *f*, забо́р, огра́да; фехтова́ние; **2.** *attr.* фехтова́льный.
fender ['fendə] ками́нная решётка; *mot. Am.* крыло́.
ferment 1. ['fə:ment] заква́ска, ферме́нт; 🝪 броже́ние; *fig.* возбужде́ние, волне́ние; **2.** [fə'ment] вызыва́ть броже́ние; броди́ть; *fig.* волнова́ться; **~ation** [fə:men'teiʃən] броже́ние, фермента́ция.
fern [fə:n] ⚘ па́поротник.
feroci|ous [fə'rouʃəs] □ жесто́кий, свире́пый; **~ty** [fə'rɔsiti] жесто́кость *f*, свире́пость *f*.
ferret ['ferit] **1.** *zo.* хорёк; **2.** [по-]ры́ться, [по]ша́рить; ~ out выи́скивать [вы́искать]; разве́д(ыв)ать.
ferry ['feri] **1.** перево́з, перепра́ва; паро́м; **2.** перевози́ть [-везти́]; **~man** перево́зчик.

fertil|e ['fə:tail] □ плодоро́дный; изоби́льный; изоби́лующий (T); **~ity** [fə:'tiliti] плодоро́дие; изоби́лие; **~ize** ['fə:tilaiz] удобря́ть [удо́брить]; оплодотворя́ть [-ри́ть]; **~izer** удобре́ние.
ferven|cy ['fə:vənsi] рве́ние, пыл; **~t** [-t] □ горя́чий, пы́лкий.
fervour ['fə:və] жар, пыл.
festal ['festl] □ пра́здничный.
fester [-tə] гнои́ться.
festiv|al ['festəvəl] пра́зднество; фестива́ль *m*; **~e** ['festiv] □ пра́здничный; **~ity** [fes'tiviti] пра́зднество; весе́лье.
fetch [fetʃ] сходи́ть, съе́здить за (T); приноси́ть [-нести́]; **~ing** F □ привлека́тельный.
fetid ['fetid] □ зловóнный, воню́чий.
fetter ['fetə] **1.** *mst* ~s *pl.* пу́ты *f/pl.*; кандалы́ *m/pl.*; *fig.* око́вы *f/pl.*, у́зы *f/pl.*; **2.** зако́вывать [-ова́ть].
feud [fju:d] вражда́; феода́льное поме́стье; **~al** ['fju:dəl] □ феода́льный; **~alism** [-delizm] феодали́зм.
fever ['fi:və] лихора́дка, жар; **~ish** [-riʃ] □ лихора́дочный.
few [fju:] немно́гие; немно́го, ма́ло (P); a ~ не́сколько (P).
fiancé(e) [fi'ɑ:ŋsei] жени́х (неве́ста).
fib [fib] **1.** вы́думка, непра́вда; **2.** прив(и)ра́ть.
fibr|e ['faibə] фи́бра, волокно́, нить *f*; **~ous** ['faibrəs] □ волокни́стый.
fickle ['fikl] непостоя́нный; **~ness** [-nis] непостоя́нство.
fiction ['fikʃən] вы́мысел, вы́думка; беллетри́стика; **~al** [-l] □ вы́мышленный; беллетристи́ческий.
fictitious [fik'tiʃəs] □ вы́мышленный; фикти́вный.
fiddle ['fidl] F **1.** скри́пка; **2.** игра́ть на скри́пке; **~stick** смычо́к.
fidelity [fi'deliti] ве́рность *f*, пре́данность *f*; то́чность *f*.
fidget ['fidʒit] F **1.** беспоко́йное состоя́ние; **2.** ёрзать, быть в волне́нии; приводи́ть в беспоко́йство; **~y** суетли́вый, беспоко́йный, не́рвный.
field [fi:ld] по́ле; луг; простра́нство; hold the ~ уде́рживать пози́ции; **~-glass** полево́й бино́кль *m*; **~-officer** штаб-офице́р; **~ of vision** по́ле зре́ния; **~-sports** *pl.* спорт на откры́том во́здухе.
fiend [fi:nd] дья́вол; злой дух; **~ish** ['fi:ndiʃ] □ дья́вольский; жесто́кий, злой.
fierce [fiəs] □ свире́пый, лю́тый; си́льный; **~ness** ['fiəsnis] свире́пость *f*, лю́тость *f*.
fif|teen ['fif'ti:n] пятна́дцать; **~teenth** [-θ] пятна́дцатый; **~th** [fifθ] **1.** пя́тый; **2.** пя́тая часть *f*; **~tieth** ['fiftiiθ] пятидеся́тый; **~ty** ['fifti] пятьдеся́т.
fig [fig] **1.** ви́нная я́года, инжи́р, смо́ква; **2.** F состоя́ние.
fight [fait] **1.** сраже́ние, бой; дра́ка; спор; борьба́; show ~ быть гото́вым к борьбе́; **2.** [*irr.*] *v/t.* боро́ться про́тив (P); отста́ивать [отстоя́ть]; *v/i.* сража́ться [срази́ться]; воева́ть; боро́ться; **~er** ['faitə] бое́ц; ✈ истреби́тель *m*; **~ing** ['faitiŋ] сраже́ние, бой; дра́ка; *attr.* боево́й.
figurative ['figjurətiv] □ перено́сный, метафори́ческий.
figure ['figə] **1.** фигу́ра; изображе́ние; ци́фра; диагра́мма; F цена́; **2.** *v/t.* изобража́ть [-рази́ть]; представля́ть себе́; вычисля́ть [вы́числить], рассчи́тывать [-ита́ть]; *v/i.* фигури́ровать.
filament ['filəmənt] ⚡ нить нака́ла; волокно́, волосо́к.
filbert ['filbət] ⚘ лесно́й opе́х.
filch [filtʃ] [у]красть, [у-, с]тащи́ть (from у P).
file[1] [fail] **1.** ⊕ напи́льник; пи́лочка (для ногте́й); **2.** пили́ть, подпи́ливать [-ли́ть].
file[2] [~] **1.** регистра́тор; подши́тые бума́ги *f/pl.*; картоте́ка; **2.** регистри́ровать (докуме́нты) (*im*)*pf.*; подшива́ть к де́лу.
filial ['filjəl] □ сыно́вний, доче́рний.
filibuster ['filibʌstə] флибустье́р, пира́т.
fill [fil] **1.** наполня́ть(ся) [-о́лнить (-ся)]; [за]пломбирова́ть (зуб); удовлетворя́ть [-ри́ть]; *Am.* выполня́ть [вы́полнить] (зака́зы); ~ in заполня́ть [-о́лнить]; **2.** доста́ток; сы́тость *f*.
fillet ['filit] повя́зка (на го́лову); филе́(й) (мя́со) *n indecl.*
filling ['filiŋ] наполне́ние; погру́зка; (зубна́я) пло́мба; фарш, начи́нка; *mot.* ~ station бензи́новая коло́нка.
fillip ['filip] щелчо́к; толчо́к.
filly ['fili] молода́я кобы́ла.
film [film] **1.** плёнка; фильм; ды́мка; ~ cartridge кату́шка с плёнками; **2.** производи́ть киносъёмку (P); экранизи́ровать (*im*)*pf.*
filter ['filtə] **1.** фильтр, цеди́лка; **2.** [про]фильтрова́ть, проце́живать [-цеди́ть].
filth [filθ] грязь *f*; **~y** ['filθi] □ гря́зный, нечи́стый.
fin [fin] плавни́к (ры́бы); *sl.* рука́.
final ['fainl] **1.** □ заключи́тельный; оконча́тельный; **2.** *sport* фина́л.
financ|e [fi'næns] **1.** нау́ка о фина́нсах; ~s *pl.* фина́нсы *m/pl.*; **2.** *v/t.* финанси́ровать (*im*)*pf.*; *v/i.* занима́ться фина́нсовыми опера́циями; **~ial** [fi'nænʃəl] □ фина́нсовый; **~ier** [-siə] финанси́ст.
finch [fintʃ] *zo.* зя́блик.

ind [faind] [*irr.*] **1.** находи́ть [найти́]; счита́ть [счесть]; обрета́ть [обрести́]; заст(ав)ля́ть; all found на всём гото́вом; **2.** нахо́дка; **~ing** ['faindiŋ] ⚖ пригово́р; *pl.* вы́воды.

ine¹ [fain] □ то́нкий, изя́щный; прекра́сный; высокопро́бный.

ine² [~] **1.** штраф; in ~ в о́бщем, сло́вом; наконе́ц; **2.** [о]штрафова́ть.

ineness ['fainnis] то́нкость *f*, изя́щество; острота́ (чувств).

inery ['fainəri] пы́шный наря́д; украше́ние.

inger ['fiŋgə] **1.** па́лец; **2.** тро́гать, перебира́ть па́льцами; **~-language** язы́к глухонемы́х; **~-print** дактилоскопи́ческий отпеча́ток.

inish ['finiʃ] **1.** *v/t.* конча́ть [ко́нчить]; заверша́ть [-ши́ть]; отде́л(ыв)ать; доеда́ть [дое́сть], допи́(ва́)ть; *v/i.* конча́ть(ся) [ко́нчить(ся)]; **2.** коне́ц; зако́нченность *f*; отде́лка; *sport* фи́ниш.

inite ['fainait] □ ограни́ченный, име́ющий преде́л.

ir [fəː] ель *f*, пи́хта; **~-cone** ['fəːkoun] ело́вая ши́шка.

ire ['faiə] **1.** ого́нь *m*; be on ~ горе́ть; **2.** *v/t.* зажига́ть [заже́чь], поджига́ть [-же́чь]; [за]топи́ть (пе́чку); обжига́ть [обже́чь] (кирпичи́ и т. п.); *fig.* воспламеня́ть [-ни́ть]; *Am.* F увольня́ть [уво́лить]; *v/i.* стреля́ть [вы́стрелить]; **~-alarm** пожа́рная трево́га; **~-brigade**, *Am.* **~-department** пожа́рная кома́нда; **~-engine** ['ˈfaiər'endʒin] пожа́рная маши́на; **~-escape** ['ˈfaiəris'keip] пожа́рная ле́стница; **~-extinguisher** [-riks'tiŋgwiʃə] огнетуши́тель *m*; **~man** пожа́рный; кочега́р; **~place** ками́н; **~plug** пожа́рный кран, гидра́нт; **~proof** огнеупо́рный; **~-side** ме́сто о́коло ками́на; **~-station** пожа́рная ста́нция; **~wood** дрова́ *n/pl.*; **~works** *pl.* фейерве́рк.

firing ['faiəriŋ] стрельба́; отопле́ние.

firm [fəːm] **1.** □ кре́пкий, пло́тный, твёрдый; сто́йкий; насто́йчивый; **2.** фи́рма; **~ness** ['fəːmnis] твёрдость *f*.

first [fəːst] **1.** *adj.* пе́рвый; ра́нний; выдаю́щийся; ~ cost ✝ себесто́имость *f*; **2.** *adv.* сперва́, снача́ла; впервы́е; скоре́е; at ~ снача́ла; ~ of all пре́жде всего́; **3.** нача́ло; the ~ пе́рвое число́; from the ~ с са́мого нача́ла; **~-born** пе́рвенец; **~-class** первокла́ссный; **~ly** ['fəːstli] во-пе́рвых; **~-rate** первокла́ссный.

fish [fiʃ] **1.** ры́ба; F odd (и́ли queer) ~ чуда́к; **2.** уди́ть ры́бу; выу́живать [вы́удить] (*a. fig.*); **~-bone** ры́бная кость *f*.

fisher|man ['fiʃəmən] рыба́к, рыболо́в; **~y** [-ri] рыболо́вство; ры́бный про́мысел.

fishing ['fiʃiŋ] ры́бная ло́вля; **~-line** ле́са́; **~-tackle** рыболо́вные принадле́жности *f/pl.*

fiss|ion ['fiʃən] ⚛ расщепле́ние; **~ure** ['fiʃə] тре́щина, рассе́лина.

fist [fist] кула́к; по́черк (шутли́во); **~icuffs** ['fistikʌfs] *pl.* кула́чный бой.

fit¹ [fit] **1.** □ го́дный, подходя́щий; здоро́вый; досто́йный; **2.** *v/t.* прила́живать [-ла́дить] (to к Д); подходи́ть [подойти́] к (Д); приспособля́ть [-спосо́бить] (for, to к Д); ~ out снаряжа́ть [-яди́ть]; снабжа́ть [-бди́ть]; ~ up соб(и)ра́ть, [с]монти́ровать; *v/i.* годи́ться; сиде́ть (о пла́тье); прила́живаться [-ла́диться]; приспособля́ться [-посо́биться]; **3.** ⊕ приго́нка; поса́дка.

fit² [fit] ⚕ припа́док, пароксизм, при́ступ; поры́в; by ~s and starts поры́вами, уры́вками; give a p. a ~ поража́ть [порази́ть] (В), возмуща́ть [-ути́ть] (В).

fit|ful ['fitful] □ су́дорожный, поры́вистый; **~ness** [-nis] приго́дность *f*; **~ter** [-ə] меха́ник, монтёр; **~ting** [-iŋ] **1.** □ подходя́щий, го́дный; **2.** устано́вка; сбо́рка, монта́ж; приме́рка (пла́тья); **~s** *pl.* армату́ра.

five [faiv] **1.** пять; **2.** пятёрка.

fix [fiks] **1.** устана́вливать [-нови́ть]; укрепля́ть [-пи́ть]; остана́вливать [-нови́ть] (взгляд, внима́ние) (на П); *Am.* приводи́ть в поря́док; ~ o. s. устра́иваться [-ро́иться]; ~ up реша́ть [реши́ть]; организова́ть (*im*)*pf.*; ула́живать [ула́дить]; устра́ивать [-ро́ить]; *v/i.* затверде́(ва)ть; остана́вливаться [-нови́ться] (on на П); **2.** F диле́мма, затрудни́тельное положе́ние; **~ed** [fikst] (*adv.* **~edly** ['fiksidli]) неподви́жный; **~ture** ['fikstʃə] армату́ра; прибо́р, приспособле́ние; устано́вленная величина́; lighting ~ освети́тельный прибо́р.

fizzle ['fizl] [за]шипе́ть.

flabby ['flæbi] □ вя́лый; *fig.* слабохара́ктерный.

flag [flæg] **1.** флаг, зна́мя *n*; плита́; плитня́к; **2.** сигнализи́ровать фла́гом; украша́ть фла́гами; мости́ть пли́тами.

flagitious [flə'dʒiʃəs] □ престу́пный, гну́сный, позо́рный.

flagrant ['fleigrənt] □ сканда́льный; очеви́дный.

flag|staff флагшто́к; **~-stone** плита́ (для моще́ния).

flair [flɛə] чутьё, нюх.

flake [fleik] **1.** слой; **~s** *pl.* хло́пья *m/pl.*; **2.** па́дать хло́пьями; рассла́иваться [-ло́иться].

flame [fleim] **1.** пла́мя *n*; ого́нь *m*; *fig.* пыл, страсть *f*; **2.** пламене́ть; пыла́ть.
flank [flæŋk] **1.** бок, сторона́; склон (горы́); ⚔ фланг; **2.** быть располо́женым сбо́ку, на фла́нге (P); ~ (on) грани́чить (с T), примыка́ть (к Д).
flannel ['flænl] флане́ль *f*; **~s** [-z] *pl.* флане́левые брю́ки *f/pl.*
flap [flæp] **1.** взмах (кры́льев); хлопо́к, шлепо́к; пола́; дли́нное у́хо (соба́ки и т. п.); **2.** *v/t.* маха́ть [махну́ть] (T); взма́хивать [-хну́ть] (кры́льями); шлёпать [-пнуть], ударя́ть легко́; *v/i.* свиса́ть; развева́ться [-ве́яться].
flare [flɛə] **1.** горе́ть я́рким пла́менем; расширя́ться [-ши́риться]; ~ up вспы́хивать [-хнуть]; *fig.* разрази́ться гне́вом, вспыли́ть *pf.*; **2.** вспы́шка; сигна́льная раке́та; вспы́хивание.
flash [flæʃ] **1.** показно́й, безвку́сный, крича́щий; **2.** вспы́шка; *fig.* про́блеск; in a ~ в мгнове́ние о́ка; **3.** сверка́ть [-кну́ть]; вспы́хивать [-хнуть]; бы́стро пронести́сь; сро́чно передава́ть (по телефо́ну, телегра́фу); **~-light** *phot.* вспы́шка ма́гния; *Am.* карма́нный электри́ческий фона́рь *m*; **~y** □ показно́й, безвку́сный.
flask [flɑːsk] фля́жка; флако́н.
flat [flæt] **1.** □ пло́ский; ро́вный; ску́чный; ✝ вя́лый (о ры́нке); ♪ бемо́льный, мино́рный; прямо́й; ~ price станда́ртная цена́; fall ~ не име́ть успе́ха; sing ~ детони́ровать; **2.** пло́скость *f*; равни́на, низи́на; ♪ бемо́ль *m*; **~-iron** утю́г; **~ness** ['flætnis] пло́скость *f*; безвку́сица; ✝ вя́лость *f*; **~ten** ['flætn] де́лать(ся) пло́ским, ро́вным.
flatter ['flætə] [по]льсти́ть (Д); **~er** [-rə] льстец (льсти́ца); **~y** [-ri] лесть *f*.
flavo(u)r ['fleivə] **1.** прия́тный вкус; арома́т; *fig.* при́вкус; **2.** приправля́ть [-ра́вить] (пи́щу); придава́ть за́пах, вкус (Д); **~less** [-lis] безвку́сный.
flaw [flɔː] **1.** тре́щина, щель *f*; недоста́ток; поро́к; брак (това́ра); ⚓ шквал, поры́в ве́тра; **2.** поврежда́ть [-еди́ть]; [по]тре́скаться; **~less** ['flɔːlis] □ безупре́чный.
flax [flæks] ⚘ лён.
flay [flei] сдира́ть ко́жу с (P).
flea [fliː] блоха́.
fled [fled] *pt.* и *p. pt.* от flee.
flee [fliː] [*irr.*] [по]бежа́ть, спаса́ться бе́гством.
fleec|e [fliːs] **1.** руно́; ове́чья шерсть *f*; **2.** [о]стри́чь (овцу́); *fig.* обдира́ть [ободра́ть]; **~y** ['fliːsi] покры́тый ше́рстью.
fleer [fliə] насмеха́ться [-ея́ться (at над T).
fleet [fliːt] **1.** □ бы́стрый; неглубо кий; **2.** флот.
flesh [fleʃ] **1.** сыро́е мя́со; плоть *f* мя́коть *f* (плода́); *fig.* по́хоть *f*; 2 приуча́ть вку́сом кро́ви (соба́ку охо́те); **~ly** ['fleʃli] пло́тский, те ле́сный; **~y** [-i] мяси́стый; то́л стый.
flew [fluː] *pt.* от fly.
flexib|ility [fleksə'biliti] ги́бкость *f* **~le** ['fleksəbl] □ ги́бкий, гну щийся; *fig.* пода́тливый.
flicker ['flikə] **1.** мерца́ние; трепе та́ние; **2.** мерца́ть; мелька́т [-кну́ть].
flier *s.* flyer лётчик.
flight [flait] полёт, перелёт; ста́ (птиц); ⚔, ✈ звено́; бе́гство; ря ступе́ней; put to ~ обраща́ть бе́гство; **~y** ['flaiti] □ ве́треный капри́зный.
flimsy ['flimzi] непро́чный, то́нкий
flinch [flintʃ] уклоня́ться [-ни́ться (from от P).
fling ['fliŋ] **1.** бросо́к, швыро́к жизнера́достность *f*; весе́лье have one's ~ [по]весели́ться; 2 [*irr.*] *v/i.* кида́ться [ки́нуться] броса́ться [бро́ситься]; *v/t.* кида́т [ки́нуть], броса́ть [бро́сить]; рас пространя́ть [-ни́ть] (арома́т и т п.); ~ open распа́хивать [-хну́т (окно́ и т. п.).
flint [flint] креме́нь *m*.
flip [flip] **1.** щелчо́к; **2.** щёлкат [щёлкнуть].
flippan|cy ['flipənsi] легкомы́слие ве́треность *f*; **~t** □ легкомы́слен ный, ве́треный.
flirt [fləːt] **1.** коке́тка; **2.** флирто ва́ть; коке́тничать; **~ation** [fləː 'teiʃən] флирт.
flit [flit] порха́ть [-хну́ть]; ю́рка [юркну́ть]; (та́йно) переезжа́т [перее́хать].
float [flout] **1.** поплаво́к; буй; па ро́м; плот; пла́вательный по́яс ломова́я теле́га; **2.** *v/t.* затопля́т [-пи́ть]; наводня́ть [-ни́ть]; ⚓ снима́ть с ме́ли; ✝ пуска́ть в хо (предприя́тие); *v/i.* пла́вать, [поплы́ть (о предме́те); держа́ться н воде́.
flock [flɔk] **1.** пуши́нка; клочо́к ста́до (ове́ц); стая́; **2.** стека́тьс [сте́чься]; держа́ться вме́сте.
flog [flɔg] [вы́]поро́ть, [вы́]сечь.
flood [flʌd] **1.** (*a.* ~-tide) прили́в подъём воды́; наводне́ние, поло во́дье, разли́в; **2.** поднима́тьс [-ня́ться] (об у́ровне реки́), вы ступа́ть из берего́в; затопля́т [-пи́ть]; наводня́ть [-ни́ть]; **~-gat** шлюз.
floor [flɔː] **1.** пол; эта́ж; ⚒ гумно́ have the ~ *parl.* взять сло́во; 2 настила́ть пол; вали́ть на́ пол; *fi*

ущать [смутить]; **~ing** ['flɔ:riŋ] стилка полов; пол.
› [flɔp] **1.** шлёпаться [-пнуть-]; плюхать(ся) [-хнуть(ся)]; ть (крыльями); *Am.* потерпеть аско, **2.** шлёпанье.
rid ['flɔrid] □ цветистый (*a.* .).
rin [-in] флорин (монета).
rist ['flɔrist] торговец цветами.
ss [flɔs] шёлк-сырец.
unce¹ [flauns] оборка.
unce² [~] бросаться [броситься], зко двигаться.
under¹ *zo.* ['flaundə] камбала.
under² [~] барахтаться; [за]путься (в словах).
ur ['flauə] мука.
urish ['flʌriʃ] **1.** росчерк; цветое выражение; ♪ туш; **2.** *v/i.* ышно расти; процветать, препевать; *v/t.* размахивать (T).
ut [flaut] насмехаться (at над T).
w [flou] **1.** течение, поток; руя; прилив; изобилие; плавость *f* (речи); **2.** течь; струиться; ться,
wer [flauə] **1.** цветок; цветение; цвет; **2.** цвести; **~y** [-ri] *fig.* етистый (стиль).
wn [floun] *p. pt.* от fly.
[flu:] = influenza F грипп.
ctuat|e ['flʌktjueit] колебаться; ыть неустойчивым; **~ion** [flʌku'eiʃən] колебание; неустойчиость *f.*
e [flu:] дымоход; ⊕ жаровая убá.
en|cy ['flu:ənsi] *fig.* плавность *f*, глость *f* (речи); **~t** [-t] □ плавый, беглый; жидкий; текучий.
ff [flʌf] пух, пушок; **~y** ['flʌfi] ушистый.
id ['flu:id] **1.** жидкость *f*; **2.** идкий; текучий.
ng [flʌŋ] *pt.* и *p. pt.* от fling.
nk [flʌŋk] *Am.* F провалиться а экзамене.
nk(e)y ['flʌŋki] ливрейный лаей.
rry ['flʌri] волнение; суматоха.
sh [flʌʃ] **1.** внезапный приток; рилив крови, краска (на лице); рилив (чувст); **2.** полный (до раёв); изобилующий; **3.** *v/t.* заоплять [-пить]; спускать воду в I); *v/i.* течь; хлынуть *pf.*; [по-] раснеть.
ster ['flʌstə] **1.** суета, волнение; . [вз]волновать(ся); возбуждать ся) [-дить(ся)].
te [flu:t] **1.** ♪ флейта; выемка а колонне); **2.** играть на флейте.
tter ['flʌtə] **1.** порхание; трепет, олнение; **2.** *v/i.* махать крыльяи; развеваться (по ветру); порать [-хнуть].
x [flʌks] *fig.* течение; поток; патологическое истечение.

fly [flai] **1.** муха; **2.** [*irr.*] летать, [по]лететь; пролетать [-ететь]; [по]спешить; поднимать [-нять] (флаг); ✈ управлять (самолётом); ~ at набрасываться [-роситься] (с бранью) на (B); ~ into a passion вспылить *pf.*
flyer ['flaiə] лётчик.
fly-flap ['flaiflæp] хлопушка.
flying ['flaiiŋ] летательный; лётный; летучий; ~ squad выездная полицейская команда.
fly|-weight наилегчайший вес (о боксёре); **~-wheel** маховое колесо.
foal [foul] **1.** жеребёнок; ослёнок; **2.** [о]жеребиться.
foam [foum] **1.** пена; мыло (на лошади); **2.** [вс]пениться; взмыли(ва)ться (о лошади); **~y** ['foumi] пенящийся; взмыленный.
focus ['foukəs] **1.** центр; *phys.*, ⚕ фокус; **2.** помещать, быть в фокусе; сосредоточи(ва)ть (*a. fig.*).
fodder ['fɔdə] фураж, корм (скота).
foe [fou] враг.
fog [fɔg] **1.** густой туман; мгла; замешательство; *phot.* вуаль *f*; **2.** [за]туманить; *fig.* напускать (в глаза) туману; озадачи(ва)ть; **~gy** ['fɔgi] □ туманный.
foible ['fɔibl] *fig.* слабость *f.*
foil¹ [fɔil] фольга; фон.
foil² [~] **1.** ставить в тупик; расстраивать планы (P); **2.** рапира.
fold¹ [fould] **1.** (*mst* sheep-~) загон, овчарня; *fig.* паства; **2.** загонять [загнать] (овец).
fold² [~] **1.** складка, сгиб; **2.** створ (двери); ⊕ фальц; **3.** *v/t.* складывать [сложить]; сгибать [согнуть]; скрещивать [-естить] (руки); **~er** ['fouldə] фальцовщик; *Am.* брошюра.
folding ['fouldiŋ] складной; створчатый; откидной; **~-camera** *phot.* складной аппарат; **~-chair** складной стул; **~-door**(*s pl.*) двустворчатая дверь *f*; **~-screen** ширма.
foliage ['fouliidʒ] листва.
folk [fouk] народ, люди *m/pl.*; **~lore** ['fouklɔ:] фольклор; **~-song** народная песня.
follow ['fɔlou] следовать (за T *or* Д); следить за (T); [по]гнаться за (T); заниматься [-няться] (T); ~ suit следовать примеру; **~er** ['fɔlouə] последователь(ница *f*) *m*; *pol.* попутчик; поклонник; **~ing** ['fɔlouiŋ] следующий; попутный.
folly ['fɔli] безрассудство, глупость *f*, безумие.
foment [fou'ment] класть припарку (Д); подстрекать [-кнуть].
fond [fɔnd] □ нежный, любящий; be ~ of любить (B).
fond|le ['fɔndl] [при]ласкать; **~ness** [-nis] нежность *f*, любовь *f.*

font [fɔnt] купе́ль *f*; исто́чник.
food [fu:d] пи́ща; **~-stuffs** *pl.* съестны́е проду́кты *m/pl.*; **~-value** пита́тельность *f*.
fool [fu:l] **1.** дура́к, глупе́ц; make a ~ of a p. одура́чи(ва)ть кого́-либо; **2.** *v/t.* обма́нывать [-ну́ть]; ~ away упуска́ть [-сти́ть]; *v/i.* [по-]дура́читься; ~ about болта́ться зря.
fool|ery ['fu:ləri] дура́чество; **~-hardy** ['fu:lhɑ:di] □ безрассу́дно хра́брый; **~ish** ['fu:liʃ] □ глу́пый; **~ishness** [-nis] глу́пость *f*; **~-proof** несло́жный, безопа́сный.
foot [fut] **1.** (*pl.* feet) нога́, ступня́; фут (ме́ра); основа́ние; on ~ пешко́м; в ходу́; **2.** *v/t.* (*mst* ~ up) подсчи́тывать [-ита́ть]; ~ the bill заплати́ть по счёту; ~ it идти́ пешко́м; **~boy** паж; **~fall** по́ступь *f*; звук шаго́в; **~-gear** F *coll.* о́бувь *f*; чулки́ *m/pl.*; **~hold** *fig.* то́чка опо́ры.
footing ['futiŋ] опо́ра; основа́ние; ито́г столбца́ цифр; lose one's ~ оступа́ться [-пи́ться].
foot|lights *pl. thea.* ра́мпа; **~man** ['futmən] ливре́йный лаке́й; **~-path** тропи́нка; тротуа́р; **~print** след; **~-sore** со стёртыми нога́ми; **~step** стопа́; след; шаг; **~stool** скаме́ечка для ног; **~wear** *part. Am.* = ~-gear.
fop [fɔp] щёголь *m*, хлыщ.
for [fɔ:; fɔ:r; fɔ, fo, f] *prp. mst* для (Р); ра́ди (Р); за (В); в направле́нии (Р), к (Д); из-за (Р), по причи́не (Р), всле́дствие (Р); в тече́ние (Р), в продолже́ние (Р); ~ three days в тече́ние трёх дне́й; уже́ три дня; вме́сто (Р); в обме́н на (В); **2.** *cj.* так как, потому́ что, и́бо.
forage ['fɔridʒ] **1.** фура́ж; корм; **2.** фуражи́ровать.
foray ['fɔrei] набе́г, мародёрство.
forbad(**e**) [fə'beid] *pt.* от forbid.
forbear[1] [fɔ:'bɛə] [*irr.*] быть терпели́вым; возде́рживаться [-жа́ться] (from от Р).
forbear[2] ['fɔ:bɛə] пре́док; предше́ственник.
forbid [fə'bid] [*irr.*] запреща́ть [-ети́ть]; **~den** [-n] *p. pt.* от forbid; **~ding** [-iŋ] □ отта́лкивающий; угрожа́ющий.
forbor|e [fɔ:'bɔ:] *pt.* от forbear[1]; **~ne** [-n] *p. pt.* от forbear[1].
force [fɔ:s] **1.** си́ла; наси́лие, принужде́ние; смысл, значе́ние; armed ~s *pl.* вооружённые си́лы *f/pl.*; come in ~ вступа́ть в си́лу; **2.** заставля́ть [-а́вить], принужда́ть [-у́дить]; брать си́лой; ~ open взла́мывать [взлома́ть]; **~d** [-t]: ~ loan принуди́тельный заём; ~ landing вы́нужденная поса́дка; ~ march форси́рованный марш
(похо́д); **~ful** □ си́льный, де́й
венный.
forcible ['fɔ:səbl] □ наси́льств
ный; убеди́тельный; эффект
ный. [вбро
ford [fɔ:d] **1.** брод; **2.** переходи́
fore [fɔ:] **1.** *adv.* впереди́; **2.**
пере́дний; **~bode** [fɔ:'boud] пр
веща́ть; предчу́вствовать; **~b**
ing плохо́е предзнаменова́н
предчу́вствие; **~cast 1.** ['fɔ:kɑ
предсказа́ние; **2.** [fɔ:'kɑ:st]
(cast)] предска́зывать [-каза́
~father пре́док; **~finger** ука
тельный па́лец; **~foot** пере́д
нога́; **~go** [fɔ:'gou] [*irr.* (go)] пр
ше́ствовать; **~gone** [fɔ:'gɔn, *a*
'fɔ:gɔn]: ~ conclusion зара́
при́нятое реше́ние; **~ground**
ре́дний план; **~head** ['fɔrid] л
foreign ['fɔrin] иностра́нный;
~ Office министе́рство иностр
ных дел (в Ло́ндоне); ~ po
вне́шняя поли́тика; **~er** [-ə] и
стра́нец (-нка).
fore|leg пере́дняя нога́; **~lock** ч
прядь воло́с на лбу; **~man**
старшина́ прися́жных; деся́тн
прора́б; **~most** пере́дний, пе
дово́й; **~noon** у́тро; **~run**
предве́стник (-ица); **~see** [fɔ:'
[*irr.* (see)] предви́деть; **~si**
['fɔ:sait] предви́дение; предус
три́тельность *f*.
forest ['fɔrist] **1.** лес; **2.** заса́жив
ле́сом.
forestall [fɔ:'stɔ:l] предупрежд
[-упреди́ть]; предвосхища́ть [-
тить].
forest|er ['fɔristə] лесни́к, лес
чий; **~ry** [-tri] лесни́чество; ле
во́дство.
fore|taste ['fɔ:teist] **1.** предвку
ние; **2.** предвкуша́ть [-уси́
~tell [fɔ:'tel] [*irr.* (*tell*)] предс
зывать [-за́ть].
forfeit ['fɔ:fit] **1.** штраф; конф
ка́ция; утра́та (пра́ва); фант;
[по]плати́ться (Т); утра́чив
[-а́тить] (пра́во).
forgave [fə'geiv] *pt.* от forgive.
forge[1] [fɔ:dʒ] (*mst* ~ ahead)
сто́йчиво продвига́ться вперёд
forge[2] [~] **1.** ку́зница; **2.** кова́
подде́л(ыв)ать; **~ry** ['fɔ:dʒəri] п
де́лка, подло́г.
forget [fə'get] [*irr.*] забы́(ва́)
~ful [-ful] □ забы́вчивый; **~-n**
not [-minɔt] незабу́дка.
forgiv|e [fə:giv] [*irr.*] прощ
[прости́ть]; **~en** [fa'givn] *p. pt.*
~e; **~eness** [-nis] проще́ние; **~i**
□ всепроща́ющий, снисходи́те
ный.
forgo [fɔ:'gou] [*irr.* (go)] возде́рж
ваться [-жа́ться] от (Р), отка́з
ваться [-за́ться] от (Р).
forgot, ~ten [fə'gɔt(n)] *pt. a. p.*
от forget.

: [fɔ:k] ви́лка; ви́лы *f/pl.*; ♪
иерто́н; разветвле́ние (доро́ги).
orn [fə'lɔ:n] забро́шенный,
сча́стный.
n [fɔ:m] **1.** фо́рма; фигу́ра;
анк; *school* па́рта; класс; **2.** об-
зо́вывать(ся) [-ова́ть(ся)]; со-
вля́ть [-а́вить]; ⚔ [по]стро́ить
я); [с]формирова́ть.
nal ['fɔ:məl] □ форма́льный,
ициа́льный; **~ity** [fɔ:'mæliti]
рма́льность *f.*
nation [fɔ:'meiʃən] образова́-
е; формирова́ние; ⚔ располо-
ние, строй; систе́ма; строе́ние.
ner ['fɔ:mə] пре́жний, бы́в-
ий; предше́ствующий; **~ly** [-li]
е́жде.
nidable ['fɔ:midəbl] □ стра́ш-
й; грома́дный; тру́днопреодо-
мый (о зада́че).
nula ['fɔ:mjulə] фо́рмула; ⚕
це́пт; **~te** [-leit] формули́ро-
ть (*im*)*pf.*, *pf. a.* [с-].
sake [fə'seik] [*irr.*] оставля́ть
вить], покида́ть [-и́нуть].
wear [fɔ:'swɛə] [*irr.* (swear)]
река́ться [-е́чься] от (Р); ~ o. s.
руша́ть кля́тву.
[fɔ:t] ⚔ форт.
h [fɔ:θ] *adv.* вперёд, да́льше;
редь; **~coming** предстоя́щий,
ду́щий; **~with** *adv.* тотча́с,
ме́дленно.
ieth ['fɔ:tiiθ] сороково́й; соро-
ва́я часть *f.*
i|fication [fɔ:tifi'keiʃən] фор-
фика́ция; укрепле́ние; **~fy** ['fɔ:-
i] ⚔ укрепля́ть [-пи́ть], соору-
ть укрепле́ние (Р); *fig.* подкре-
я́ть [-пи́ть] (фа́ктами); **~tude**
u:d] си́ла ду́ха.
night ['fɔ:tnait] две неде́ли *f/pl.*
ress ['fɔ:tris] кре́пость *f.*
uitous [fɔ:'tjuitəs] □ случа́й-
й.
unate ['fɔ:tʃnit] счастли́вый,
а́чный; **~ly** *adv.* к сча́стью.
une ['fɔ:tʃən] судьба́; бога́т-
во, состоя́ние; **~-teller** гада́лка.
y ['fɔ:ti] со́рок.
vard ['fɔ:wəd] **1.** *adj.* пере́дний;
редово́й; развя́зный, де́рзкий;
ний; **2.** *adv.* вперёд, да́льше;
редь; **3.** *sport* напада́ющий; **4.**
ес(ы)ла́ть; препровожда́ть
оди́ть].
warding-agent экспеди́тор.
went [fɔ:'went] *pt.* от forego.
er ['fɔstə] воспи́тывать [-ита́ть];
ди́ть за (детьми́, больны́ми); *fig.*
а́ть (чу́вство), леле́ять (мысль);
ощря́ть [-ри́ть]; благоприя́т-
овать (Д).
ght [fɔ:t] *pt.* и *p. pt.* от fight.
[faul] **1.** □ гря́зный, отврати́-
льный; бу́рный (о пого́де);
о́йный; зара́зный; бесче́стный;
~ of ста́лкиваться [столкну́ть-

ся] с (Т); **2.** *sport* игра́ про́тив пра́вил; **3.** [за]па́чкать(ся); нече́стно игра́ть.

found [faund] **1.** *pt.* и *p. pt.* от find; **2.** закла́дывать [заложи́ть] (фунда́мент); осно́вывать [основа́ть]; учрежда́ть [-еди́ть]; ⊕ пла́вить; отли́(ва́)ть.

foundation [faun'deiʃən] фунда́мент, осно́ва.

founder ['faundə] **1.** основа́тель(ница *f*) *m*, учреди́тель(ница *f*) *m*; **2.** *v/i.* идти́ ко дну́.

foundry ['faundri] ⊕ лите́йная; литьё.

fountain ['fauntin] исто́чник; фонта́н; **~-pen** авторучка, ве́чное перо́.

four [fɔ:] **1.** четы́ре; **2.** четвёрка; **~-square** квадра́тный; *fig.* усто́йчивый; **~teen** ['fɔ:'ti:n] четы́рнадцать; **~teenth** [-θ] четы́рнадцатый; **~th** [fɔ:θ] **1.** четвёртый; **2.** че́тверть *f.*

fowl [faul] дома́шняя пти́ца.

fox [fɔks] **1.** лиси́ца, лиса́; **2.** [с]хитри́ть; обма́нывать [-ну́ть]; **~y** ['fɔksi] хи́трый.

fraction ['frækʃən] дробь *f*; части́ца.

fracture ['fræktʃə] **1.** тре́щина, изло́м; ⚕ перело́м; **2.** [с]лома́ть (*a.* ⚕); раздробля́ть [-би́ть].

fragile ['frædʒail] хру́пкий, ло́мкий.

fragment ['frægmənt] обло́мок, оско́лок; отры́вок.

fragran|ce ['freigrəns] арома́т; **~t** [-t] □ арома́тный.

frail [freil] □ хру́пкий; хи́лый, боле́зненный; **~ty** *fig.* хру́пкость *f.*

frame [freim] **1.** сооруже́ние; сруб, скеле́т; телосложе́ние; ра́мка, ра́ма; ~ of mind настрое́ние; **2.** сооружа́ть [-уди́ть]; созд(ав)а́ть; вставля́ть в ра́му; **~work** ⊕ ра́ма; сруб, о́стов; *fig.* строй, ра́мки *f/pl.*

franchise ['fræntʃaiz] ⚖ пра́во уча́ствовать в вы́борах; привиле́гия.

frank [fræŋk] □ и́скренний, открове́нный.

frankfurter ['fræŋkfətə] *Am.* соси́ска.

frankness ['fræŋknis] открове́нность *f.*

frantic ['fræntik] (~ally) неи́стовый.

fratern|al [frə'tə:nl] □ бра́тский; *adv.* по-бра́тски; **~ity** [-niti] бра́тство; общи́на; *Am. univ.* студе́нческая организа́ция.

fraud [frɔ:d] обма́н, моше́нничество; **~ulent** ['frɔ:djulənt] □ обма́нный, моше́ннический.

fray [frei] **1.** дра́ка, столкнове́ние; **2.** изна́шивать(ся) [износи́ть(ся)].

freak [fri:k] капри́з, причу́да; уро́дец (в приро́де).

freckle ['frekl] весну́шка.
free [fri:] **1.** □ *com.* свобо́дный, во́льный; незави́симый; неза́нятый; беспла́тный; he is ~ to он во́лен (+ *inf.*); make ~ to *inf.* позволя́ть себе́; set ~ выпуска́ть на свобо́ду; **2.** освобожда́ть [-боди́ть]; **~booter** ['fri:bu:tə] пира́т; **~dom** ['fri:dəm] свобо́да; ~ of a city зва́ние почётного граждани́на; **~holder** земе́льный со́бственник; **~mason** масо́н.
freez|e [fri:z] [*irr.*] *v/i.* замерза́ть [замёрзнуть]; засты́(ва́)ть; мёрзнуть; *v/t.* замора́живать [-ро́зить]; **~er** ['fri:zə] моро́женица; **~ing 1.** □ леденя́щий; **2.** замора́живание; замерза́ние; ~ point то́чка замерза́ния.
freight [freit] **1.** фрахт, груз; сто́имость перево́зки; **2.** [по]грузи́ть; [за]фрахтова́ть; **~-car** *Am.* 🚂 това́рный ваго́н.
French [frentʃ] **1.** францу́зский; take ~ leave уйти́ не прости́вшись; **2.** францу́зский язы́к; the ~ францу́зы *pl.*; **~man** ['frentʃmən] францу́з; **~woman** ['frentʃwumən] францу́женка.
frenz|ied ['frenzid] взбешённый; **~y** [-zi] безу́мие, бе́шенство.
frequen|cy ['fri:kwənsi] частота́ (*a. phys.*); ча́стое повторе́ние; **~t 1.** [-t] □ ча́стый; **2.** [fri'kwent] посеща́ть ча́сто.
fresh [freʃ] □ све́жий; но́вый; чи́стый; *Am.* F де́рзкий; ~ water пре́сная вода́; **~en** ['freʃn] освежа́ть [-жи́ть]; [по]свеже́ть; **~et** ['freʃit] полово́дье; *fig.* пото́к; **~-man** [-mən] *univ. sl.* первоку́рсник; **~ness** [-nis] све́жесть *f.*
fret [fret] **1.** волне́ние, раздраже́ние; ♪ лад (в гита́ре); **2.** [о]беспоко́ить(ся), [вз]волнова́ть(ся); подта́чивать [-точи́ть], разъеда́ть [-е́сть]; ~ted instrument стру́нный щипко́вый инструме́нт.
fretful ['fretful] □ раздражи́тельный, капри́зный.
friar ['fraiə] мона́х.
friction ['frikʃən] тре́ние (*a. fig.*).
Friday ['fraidi] пя́тница.
friend [frend] прия́тель(ница *f*) *m*, друг, подру́га; **~ly** [-li] дру́жеский; **~ship** [-ʃip] дру́жба.
frigate ['frigit] ⚓ фрега́т.
fright [frait] испу́г; *fig.* пу́гало, страши́лище; **~en** ['fraitn] [ис-]пуга́ть; вспу́гивать [-гну́ть]; ~ed at и́ли of испу́ганный (Т); **~ful** [-ful] □ стра́шный, ужа́сный.
frigid ['fridʒid] □ холо́дный.
frill [fril] обо́рка.
fringe [frindʒ] **1.** бахрома́; чёлка; кайма́; **2.** отде́лывать бахромо́й; окаймля́ть [-ми́ть].
frippery ['fripəri] безделу́шки *f/pl.*; мишу́рные украше́ния *n/pl.*
frisk [frisk] **1.** прыжо́к; **2.** резви́ся; **~y** ['friski] □ ре́звый, игри́в
fritter ['fritə] **1.** ола́дья; **2.** ~ а растра́чивать по мелоча́м.
frivol|ity [fri'vɔliti] легкомы́сл фриво́льность *f*; **~ous** ['frivələs легкомы́сленный, пове́рхн ный; пустя́чный.
frizzle ['frizl] жа́рить(ся) с пе́нием.
fro [frou]: to and ~ взад и впе
frock [frɔk] да́мское и́ли дето пла́тье; ря́са; (*mst* ~-coat) сюрт
frog [frɔg] лягу́шка.
frolic ['frɔlik] **1.** ша́лость *f*, весе ре́звость *f*; **2.** резви́ться, [на]п ка́зничать; **~some** [səm] □ иг вый, ре́звый.
from [frɔm, frəm] *prp.* от (Р); (Р); с (Р); по (Д); defend ~ за щи́ть от (Р).
front [frʌnt] **1.** фаса́д; пере́д сторона́; ⚔ фронт; in ~ of пе (Т); впереди́ (Р); **2.** пере́дний выходи́ть на (В) (об окне́) (*a.* ~ towards); **~al** ['frʌntl] *anat.* ный; ⚠ фаса́дный; фронта́льн **~ier** ['frʌntjə] **1.** грани́ца; **2.** грани́чный; **~ispiece** ['frʌntis *typ.* фронтиспи́с; ⚠ фаса́д.
frost [frɔst] **1.** моро́з; **2.** поби моро́зом (расте́ния); **~-bite** ⚕ моро́женное ме́сто; **~y** ['frɔsti моро́зный; *fig.* ледяно́й.
froth [frɔθ] **1.** пе́на; **2.** [вс-, за нить(ся); **~y** ['frɔθi] □ пе́нист *fig.* пусто́й.
frown [fraun] **1.** хму́рый взгл нахму́ренные бро́ви *f/pl.*; **2.** [на]хму́риться; [на]су́питься.
frow|zy, ~sy ['frauzi] за́тхл спёртый; неря́шливый.
froze [frouz] *pt.* от freeze; **~n 1.** *p. pt.* от freeze; **2.** замёрзш заморо́женный.
frugal ['fru:gəl] □ уме́ренн скро́мный.
fruit [fru:t] **1.** плод, фрукт; плодоноси́ть, дава́ть плоды́; **~erer** ['fru:tərə] торго́вец фру ми; **~ful** ['fru:tful] □ плодови́т плодоро́дный; *fig.* плодотв ный; **~less** [-lis] □ беспло́дн
frustrat|e [frʌs'treit] расстраи [-ро́ить] (пла́ны), де́лать т ным; **~ion** [frʌs:'treiʃən] расст ство (пла́нов), круше́ние де́жд).
fry [frai] **1.** жа́реное (ку́шанье [из]жа́рить(ся); **~ing-pan** [' iŋpæn] сковорода́.
fudge [fʌdʒ] **1.** вы́думка; пома́ **2.** де́лать ко́е-ка́к.
fuel ['fjuəl] **1.** то́пливо; **2.** горю́чее.
fugitive ['fju:dʒitiv] бегле́ц; бе нец (-нка); **2.** бе́глый; мимо ный.
fulfil(l) [ful'fil] выполня́ть

лнить], осуществлять [-вить];
nent [-mənt] осуществление,
полнение.
l [ful] 1. □ *com.* полный; целый;
родный; of ~ age совершен-
летний; 2. *adv.* вполне; как
з; очень; 3. полность *f*; in ~
лностью; to the ~ в полной ме-
; **~-dress** парадная форма; **~-**
edged вполне оперившийся,
звитый. [лие.]
l)ness ['fulnis] полнота, оби-
minate ['fʌlmineit] сверкать
кнуть]; [за]греметь; ~ against
аз]громить (В).
nble ['fʌmbl] нащуп(ыв)ать;
ро]мямлить; вертеть в руках.
ne [fju:m] 1. пар, дым; испа-
ние; 2. окуривать [-рить]; ис-
ряться [-риться].
nigate ['fju:migeit] окуривать
рить].
i [fʌn] веселье; забава; make ~
высмеивать [высмеять] (В).
action ['fʌŋkʃən] 1. функция,
значение; 2. функционировать,
йствовать; **~ary** [-əri] долж-
остное лицо.
nd [fʌnd] 1. запас; капитал,
онд; ~s *pl.* государственные
роцентные бумаги *f/pl.*; 2. кон-
лидировать *(im)pf.*; фундиро-
ать *(im)pf.*
ndament|al [fʌndə'mentl] □ ос-
овной, коренной, существен-
ый; **~als** *pl.* основы *f/pl.*
ner|al ['fju:nərəl] 1. похороны
pl.; 2. похоронный; **~eal** [fju:-
iəriəl] □ траурный; мрачный.
n-fair ['fʌnfɛə] ярмарка.
nnel ['fʌnl] воронка; ⚓, 🚂 ды-
овая труба.
nny ['fʌni] □ забавный, смеш-
ой; странный.
r [fə:] 1. мех; шкура; ~s *pl.* меха
/pl., меховые товары *m/pl.*, пуш-
ина; 2. подбивать мехом.
rbish ['fə:biʃ] [от]полировать;
up подновлять [-вить].

furious ['fjuəriəs] □ взбешённый.
furl [fə:l] уб(и)рать (паруса); складывать [сложить] (зонтик).
furlough ['fə:lou] 1. отпуск; 2.
увольнять в отпуск (*mst* о солда-
тах).
furnace ['fə:nis] горн, печь *f*; топ-
ка.
furnish ['fə:niʃ] снабжать [снаб-
дить] (with T); доставлять
[-авить]; обставлять [-авить], ме-
блировать *(im)pf.*
furniture ['fə:nitʃə] мебель *f*, об-
становка; оборудование.
furrier ['fʌriə] меховщик.
furrow ['fʌrou] борозда; колея;
жёлоб; морщина.
further ['fə:ðə] 1. дальше, далее;
затем; кроме того; 2. содейство-
вать, способствовать (Д); **~ance**
[-rəns] продвижение (of P), со-
действие (of Д); **~more** [-mɔ:]
adv. к тому же, кроме того.
furthest ['fə:ðist] самый дальний.
furtive ['fə:tiv] □ скрытый, тай-
ный.
fury ['fjuəri] неистовство, ярость *f*.
fuse [fju:z] 1. плавка; ⚔ взрыватель *m*; ⚡ плавкий предохранитель
m; 2. сплавлять(ся) [-авить(ся)];
⚡ [рас]плавить(ся); ⚔ вставлять
взрыватель в (В).
fusion ['fju:ʒən] плавка; *fig.* слияние.
fuss [fʌs] F 1. суета; возбуждённое
состояние; 2. [за]суетиться; [вз-]
волноваться (about из-за P); на-
доедать с пустяками (Д).
fusty ['fʌsti] затхлый, спёртый;
fig. старомодный, устаревший.
futile ['fju:tail] безполезный, тщетный; пустой.
future ['fju:tʃə] 1. будущий; 2. будущее, будущность *f*; ~s *pl.* ☨
товары, закупаемые заблаговре-
менно.
fuzz [fʌz] 1. пух; пушинка; 2. по-
кры(ва)ться пухом; разлетаться
[-лететься] (о пухе).

G

b [gæb] F болтовня; the gift of
he ~ хорошо подвешенный язык.
bble ['gæbl] 1. бормотание, бес-
вязная речь *f*; 2. [про]бормотать;
за]гоготать.
berdine ['gæbədi:n] габардин.
ble ['geibl] ⚠ фронтон, щипец.
d [gæd]: ~ about шляться, шататься.
d-fly ['gædflai] *zo.* овод, сле-
пень *m*.
g [gæg] 1. затычка, кляп; *parl.*
рекращение прений; *Am.* остро-
а; 2. затыкать рот (Д); заставить

замолчать; *pol.* заж(им)ать (кри-
тику и т. п.).
gage [geidʒ] залог, заклад; вызов.
gaiety ['geiəti] весёлость *f*.
gaily ['geili] *adv.* от gay весело;
ярко.
gain [gein] 1. прибыль *f*; вы-
игрыш; заработок; прирост; 2.
выигривать [выиграть]; приобре-
тать [-ести]; **~ful** ['geinful] □
доходный, выгодный.
gait [geit] походка.
gaiter ['geitə] гамаша, гетра, крага.
gale [geil] шторм, сильный ветер.

gall [gɔ:l] **1.** ⚕ жёлчь *f*; жёлчность *f*; ссáдина; **2.** раздражáть [-жи́ть]; [о]беспоко́ить.
gallant *mst* [gə'lænt] **1.** □ галáнтный; внимáтельный; почти́тельный; **2.** ['gælənt] *adj.* □ хрáбрый, дóблестный; *su.* кавалéр; **~ry** ['gæləntri] хрáбрость *f*; галáнтность *f*.
gallery ['gæləri] галерéя.
galley ['gæli] ⚓ галéра; **~-proof** грáнка.
gallon ['gælən] галлóн (мéра жи́дких и сыпу́чих тел; англ. = 4,54 л; ам. = 3,78 л).
gallop ['gæləp] **1.** галóп; **2.** скакáть (пускáть) галóпом.
gallows ['gælouz] *sg.* ви́селица.
gamble ['gæmbl] **1.** азáртная игрá; рискóванное предприя́тие; **2.** игрáть в азáртные и́гры; спекули́ровать (на би́рже); **~r** [-ə] картёжник, игрóк.
gambol ['gæmbəl] **1.** прыжóк; **2.** пры́гать, скакáть.
game [geim] **1.** игрá; пáртия (игры́); дичь *f*; **~s** *pl.* состязáния *n/pl.*; и́гры *f/pl.*; **2.** F охóтно готóвый (сдéлать чтó-либо); **3.** игрáть на дéньги; **~ster** игрóк, картёжник.
gander ['gændə] гусáк.
gang [gæŋ] **1.** бригáда; артéль *f*; смéна (рабóчих); шáйка, бáнда; **2.** ~ up организовáть шáйку; **~-board** ⚓ схóдни *f/pl.*
gangway [-wei] прохóд мéжду рядáми (крéсел и т. п.); ⚓ схóдни *f/pl.*
gaol [dʒeil] тюрьмá; *s.* jail.
gap [gæp] пробéл; брешь *f*, щель *f*; *fig.* расхождéние (во взгля́дах).
gape [geip] разевáть рот; [по]глазéть; зия́ть.
garb [gɑ:b] наря́д, одея́ние.
garbage ['gɑ:bidʒ] (ку́хонные) отбрóсы *m/pl.*; му́сор.
garden ['gɑ:dn] **1.** сад; огорóд; **2.** занимáться садовóдством; **~er** садóвник, садовóд; **~ing** садовóдство.
gargle ['gɑ:gl] **1.** полоскáть гóрло; **2.** полоскáние для гóрла.
garish ['gɛəriʃ] □ кричáщий (о плáтье, крáсках); я́ркий.
garland ['gɑ:lənd] гирля́нда, венóк.
garlic ['gɑ:lik] ⚘ чеснóк.
garment ['gɑ:mənt] предмéт одéжды; *fig.* покрóв, одея́ние.
garnish ['gɑ:niʃ] **1.** гарни́р; украшéние; **2.** гарни́ровать (*im*)*pf.*; украшáть [укрáсить].
garret ['gærit] мансáрда.
garrison ['gærisn] ⚔ **1.** гарнизóн; **2.** стáвить (полк и т. п.) гарнизóном.
garrulous ['gæruləs] □ болтли́вый.
garter ['gɑ:tə] подвя́зка.
gas [gæs] **1.** газ; F болтовня́; *Am* бензи́н, горю́чее; **2.** выпуск газы; отравля́ть гáзом; F болт бахвáлиться; **~eous** ['geiziəs] зообрáзный.
gash [gæʃ] **1.** глубóкая рáна, р рéз; **2.** наноси́ть глубóкую р (Д).
gas|-lighter гáзовая зажигál **~-mantle** кали́льная сéтка; **olene, ~oline** ['gæsoli:n] *mot.* га ли́н; *Am.* бензи́н.
gasp [gɑ:sp] задыхáться [зад ну́ться]; лови́ть вóздух.
gas|sed [gæst] отрáвленный гáз **~-stove** гáзовая плитá; **~-wo** *pl.* гáзовый завóд.
gate [geit] ворóта *n/pl.*; кали́т **~man** 🚂 стóрож; **~way** вор *n/pl.*, вход; подворóтня.
gather ['gæðə] **1.** *v/t.* соб(и)рá снимáть [снять] (урожáй); [н со]рвáть (о цветáх); *fig.* дéл вы́вод; ~ speed набирáть скóрос ускоря́ть ход; *v/i.* соб(и)рáть **2.** **~s** *pl.* сбóрки *f/pl.*; **~ing** соби ние; сбóрище, собрáние.
gaudy ['gɔ:di] □ я́ркий, кричáщ безвку́сный.
gauge [geidʒ] **1.** мéра; измери́те ный прибóр; масштáб; 🚂 шири колéй; ⊕ шаблóн, лекáло; **2.** мерять [-éрить]; градуи́ров (*im*)*pf.*; выверя́ть [вы́верить]; оцéнивать [-ни́ть] (человéка).
gaunt [gɔ:nt] □ исхудáлый, можденный; мрáчный.
ga(u)ntlet ['gɔ:ntlit] **1.** *hist.* лáтн рукави́ца; рукави́ца (шофё фехтовáльная и т. п.); **2.** run th пройти́ сквозь стрóй; подвергá ся рéзкой кри́тике.
gauze [gɔ:z] газ (матéрия); мáр
gave [geiv] *pt.* от give.
gawk [gɔ:k] F остолóп, рази́ня *m* **~y** [gɔ:'ki] неуклю́жий. [стры
gay [gei] □ весёлый; я́ркий, п
gaze [geiz] **1.** внимáтельн взгляд; **2.** при́стально глядéть.
gazette [gə'zet] **1.** официáльн газéта; **2.** опубликовáть в офи áльной газéте.
gear [giə] **1.** механи́зм; приспосо лéния *n/pl.*; ⊕ шестерня́; зубчáт передáча; *mot.* передáча; скóро *f*; in ~ включённый, дéйству щий; **2.** приводи́ть в движéни включáть [-чи́ть]; **~ing** ⊕ зу чáтая передáча; привóд.
geese [gi:s] *pl.* от goose.
gem [dʒem] драгоцéнный кáме *m*; *fig.* сокрóвище.
gender ['dʒendə] *gr.* род.
general ['dʒenərəl] **1.** □ óбщи оби́чный; повсемéстный; глá ный; генерáльный; ~ electi всеóбщие вы́боры *m/pl.*; **2.** генерáл; **~ity** [dʒenə'ræliti] вс óбщность *f*; примени́мость

емý; большинствó; **~ize** ['dʒenə-aiz] обобщáть [-щи́ть]; **~ly** [-li] общé; обы́чно.
erat|e ['dʒenəreit] порождáть одить]; производи́ть [-вести́]; **on**; [dʒenə'reiʃən] поколéние; рождéние.
er|osity [dʒenə'rɔsiti] велико-шие; щéдрость *f*; **~ous** ['dʒenə-] □ великоду́шный; щéдрый.
ial ['dʒi:njəl] □ тёплый, мяг-й (клúмат); дóбрый, сердéчный.
ius ['dʒi:njəs] гéний; дух; ода-нность *f*, гениáльность *f*.
teel [dʒen'ti:l] свéтский; эле-нтный.
tle ['dʒentl] □ знáтный; мя́гкий; óткий; ти́хий; нéжный; сми́р-й (о живóтных); лёгкий (вé-р); **~man** ['dʒentlmən] джен-льмéн; господи́н; **~manlike**, **manly** [-li] воспи́танный; **~ness** ʒentlnis] мя́гкость *f*; добротá.
try ['dʒentri] мелкопомéстное ворянство.
uine ['dʒenjuin] □ пóдлинный; кренний; неподдéльный.
graphy [dʒi'ɔgrəfi] геогрáфия.
logy [dʒi'ɔlədʒi] геолóгия.
metry [dʒi'ɔmitri] геомéтрия.
m [dʒə:m] **1.** микрóб; зарóдыш; *fig.* зарождáться [-оди́ться].
rman[1] ['dʒə:mən] **1.** гермáн-ий, немéцкий; ~ silver ⊕ ней-льбер; **2.** нéмец, нéмка; немéц-й язы́к.
man[2] [~]: brother ~ роднóй ат; **~e** [dʒə:'mein] умéстный, дходя́щий.
minate ['dʒə:mineit] давáть стки́, прорастáть [-расти́].
ticulat|e [dʒes'tikjuleit] жести-ли́ровать; **~ion** [-'tikju''leiʃən] естикуля́ция.
ture ['dʒestʃə] жест; ми́мика.
[get] [*irr.*] **1.** *v/t.* дост(ав)áть; лучáть [-чи́ть]; зарабáтывать бóтать]; добы́(вá)ть; заставля́ть стáвить]; I have got я имéю; one's hair cut [по]стри́чься; ~ heart учи́ть наизу́сть; **2.** *v/i.* дéлаться, станови́ться [стать]; ready [при]готóвиться; ~ about чинáть ходи́ть (пóсле болéзни); broad распростроня́ться [-ни́ть-] (о слу́хах); ~ ahead продви-ться вперёд; ~ at доб(и)рáться (P); ~ away уд(и)рáть, уходи́ть йти́]; отправля́ться [-áвиться]; in входи́ть [войти́]; ~ on with р. ужи́(вá)ться с кéм-либо; ~ t выходи́ть [вы́йти]; ~ to hear now, learn) узн(ав)áть; ~ up т(ав)áть; **~-up** [get'ʌp] манéра евáться; оформлéние; *Am.* едприи́мчивость *f*.
stly ['gɑ:stli] ужáсный; мéрт-нно-блéдный.
st [goust] при́зрак, привидéние; дух (*a. eccl.*); *fig.* тень *f*, лёгкий след; **~like** ['goustlaik], **~ly** [-li] похóжий на привидéние, при́зрачный.
giant ['dʒaiənt] **1.** великáн, гигáнт, исполи́н; **2.** гигáнтский, исполи́нский.
gibber ['dʒibə] говори́ть невня́тно.
gibbet ['dʒibit] **1.** ви́селица; **2.** вé-шать [повéсить].
gibe [dʒaib] *v/t.* смея́ться над (T); *v/i.* насмехáться (at над T).
gidd|iness ['gidinis] ⚕ головокру-жéние; легкомы́слие; **~y** ['gidi] □ испы́тывающий головокружé-ние; легкомы́сленный.
gift [gift] дар, подáрок; спосóб-ность *f*, талáнт (of к Д); **~ed** ['giftid] одарённый, спосóбный, талáнтливый.
gigantic [dʒai'gæntik] (~ally) ги-гáнтский, громáдный.
giggle ['gigl] **1.** хихи́канье; **2.** хи-хи́кать [-кнуть].
gild [gild] [*irr.*] [по]золоти́ть.
gill [gil] *zo.* жáбра.
gilt [gilt] **1.** позолóта; **2.** позолó-ченный.
gin [dʒin] джин (напи́ток); ⊕ подъ-ёмная лебёдка.
ginger ['dʒindʒə] **1.** имби́рь *m*; F воодушевлéние; **2.** F подстёгивать [-стегну́ть], оживля́ть [-ви́ть]; **~-bread** имби́рный пря́ник; **~ly** [-li] осторóжный, рóбкий.
Gipsy ['dʒipsi] цыгáн(ка).
gird [gə:d] [*irr.*] опоя́сывать(ся) [-сать(ся)]; окружáть [-жи́ть].
girder ['gə:də] ⊕ бáлка, перекла́-дина, подпóрка.
girdle ['gə:dl] **1.** пóяс, кушáк; **2.** подпоя́сывать [-сать].
girl [gə:l] дéвочка, дéвушка; **~hood** ['gə:lhud] деви́чество; **~ish** □ деви́ческий.
girt [gə:t] *pt.* и *p. pt.* от gird.
girth [gə:θ] обхвáт, размéр; под-пру́га.
gist [dʒist] суть *f*, су́щность *f*.
give [giv] [*irr.*] **1.** *v/t.* да(вá)ть; [по]дари́ть; причиня́ть [-ни́ть]; доставля́ть [-áвить]; ~ birth to ро-ди́ть; ~ away отд(ав)áть; F вы́да-(вá)ть, пред(ав)áть; ~ forth изд(а-в)áть (зáпах и т. п.); объявля́ть [-ви́ть]; ~ in под(ав)áть; ~ up от-кáзываться [-зáться] от (P); **2.** *v/i.* ~ (in) уступáть [-пи́ть]; ~ into, ~ (up)on выходи́ть на (B) (об óкнах и т. п.); ~ out кончáться [кóнчить-ся]; обесси́леть *pf.*; [ис]пóртиться; **~n** [givn] **1.** *p. pt.* от give; **2.** *fig.* дáнный; склóнный (to к Д); прé-данный (to Д).
glaci|al ['gleisiəl] □ леднико́вый; ледянóй; леденя́щий; **~er** глéт-чер, ледни́к.
glad [glæd] □ довóльный; рáдост-ный, весёлый; I am ~ я рáд(а);

~ly охóтно, рáдостно; **~den** ['glædn] [об]рáдовать.
glade [gleid] прогáлина, прóсека.
gladness ['glædnis] рáдость *f*.
glamo|rous ['glæmərəs] обаятель-ный, очаровáтельный; **~(u)r** ['glæmə] **1.** очаровáние; **2.** очарó-вывать [-ровáть].
glance [glɑ:ns] **1.** бы́стрый взгляд; **2.** скользи́ть [-зну́ть] (*mst* ~ aside, off); ~ at мéльком взгляну́ть на (В).
gland [glænd] железá.
glare [glɛə] **1.** ослепи́тельно свер-кáть; при́стально смотрéть; **2.** при́-стальный и́ли свирéпый взгляд; ослепи́тельный блеск.
glass [glɑ:s] **1.** стеклó; стакáн, рю́мка; зéркало; (a pair of) ~es *pl.* очки́ *n/pl.*; **2.** *attr.* стекля́нный; **~-shade** (стекля́нный) колпáк; абажу́р; **~y** ['glɑ:si] □ зеркáльный; безжи́зненный; стекля́нный.
glaz|e [gleiz] **1.** глазу́рь *f*, муравá; **2.** глазировáть (*im*)*pf*.; застекля́ть [-ли́ть]; **~ier** ['gleiziə] стекóльщик.
gleam [gli:m] **1.** óтблеск; слáбый свет; *fig.* прóблеск; **2.** мерцáть, слáбо свети́ться.
glean [gli:n] *v/t. fig.* тщáтельно со-бирáть (фáкты, свéдения); *v/i.* подбирáть колóсья (пóсле жáтвы).
glee [gli:] ликовáние; ~ club клуб для хоровóго пéния.
glib [glib] □ глáдкий; бóйкий (о рéчи).
glid|e [glaid] **1.** скользи́ть, плáвно дви́гаться; ✈ [с]плани́ровать; **2.** плáвное движéние; **~er** ['glaidə] ✈ планёр.
glimmer ['glimə] **1.** мерцáние, ту́склый свет; *min.* слюдá; **2.** мер-цáть, ту́скло свети́ть.
glimpse [glimps] **1.** мимолётный взгляд; мимолётное впечатлé-ние (of от Р); **2.** (у)ви́деть мéльком.
glint [glint] **1.** я́ркий блеск; **2.** я́рко блестéть; отражáть свет.
glisten ['glisn], **glitter** ['glitə] блестéть, сверкáть, сия́ть.
gloat [glout]: ~ (up)on, over пожи-рáть глазáми (В).
globe [gloub] шар; земнóй шар; глóбус.
gloom [glu:m], **~iness** ['glu:minis] мрак; мрáчность *f*; **~y** ['glu:mi] □ мрáчный; угрю́мый.
glori|fy ['glɔ:rifai] прославля́ть [-áвить]; восхваля́ть [-ли́ть]; **~ous** ['glɔ:riəs] □ великолéпный, чу-дéсный.
glory ['glɔ:ri] **1.** слáва; **2.** торже-ствовáть; горди́ться (in Т)
gloss [glɔs] **1.** внéшний блеск; глóсса; **2.** наводи́ть гля́нец на (В); ~ over прикрáшивать [-крáсить].
glossary ['glɔsəri] глоссáрий, сло-вáрь *m* (в концé кни́ги).
glossy ['glɔsi] □ глянцеви́тый, ло-щёный.
glove [glʌv] перчáтка.
glow [glou] **1.** накаля́ться дóкр[…] на; горéть; тлеть; сия́ть; **2.** зн[…] накáл; зáрево; жар; румя́нец; […] **worm** светля́к, светлячóк.
glue [glu:] **1.** клей; **2.** [е]клéить.
glut [glʌt] пресыщéние; затовá[…] вание (ры́нка).
glutton ['glʌtn] обжóра *m/f*; ~[…] [-əs] □ обжóрливый; **~y** [-i] жóрство.
gnash [næʃ] [за]скрежетáть ([…] бáми).
gnat [næt] комáр.
gnaw [nɔ:] глодáть.
gnome [noum] гном, кáрлик.
go [gou] **1.** [*irr.*] *com.* ходи́ть, и[…] [пойти́]; проходи́ть [пройт[…] уходи́ть [уйти́]; éздить, [по]éха[…] [с]дéлаться; рабóтать (о маши́[…] сéрдце); let ~ пускáть [пусти́[…] выпускáть из рук; ~ shares ли́ться пóровну; ~ to (*or* and) заходи́ть [зайти́] к [Д], навещ[…] [-ести́ть]; ~ at набрáсыват[…] [-рóситься] на (В); ~ between срéдничать мéжду (Т); ~ by […] ходи́ть [пройти́]; руководи́т[…] (Т); ~ for идти́ [пойти́] за (Т[…] for a walk дéлать прогу́лку; ~ for an examination [про]экзаме[…] вáться; ~ on продолжáть [-д[…] жить]; идти́ дáльше; ~ thro[…] with доводи́ть до концá (В[…] without обходи́ться [обойти́сь] (Р); **2.** ходьбá, движéние; F мó[…] энергия; on the ~ на ходу́; на […] гáх; it is no ~ ничегó не подé[…] ешь; in one ~ срáзу; have a ~ [по]прóбовать (В).
goad [goud] **1.** побуждáть [по[…] ди́ть]; подстрекáть [-кну́ть]; стрекáло; *fig.* сти́мул, возбуди́т[…] *m*.
goal [goul] цель *f*; мéсто назна[…] ния; *sport* ворóта *n/pl.*; гол; […] ниш; **~-keeper** вратáрь *m*.
goat [gout] козёл, козá.
gobble [gɔbl] есть жáдно, бы́ст[…] **~r** [-ə] обжóра *m/f*; индю́к.
go-between ['goubitwi:n] поср[…] ник.
goblin ['gɔblin] гном, домовóй.
god бог (*eccl.*: ♀ Бог); божест[…] *fig.* и́дол, куми́р; **~child** крéст[…] (-ица); **~dess** ['godis] боги́ня; […] **father** крёстный отéц; **~head** […] жествó; **~less** [-'lis] безбóжн[…] **~like** богоподóбный; **~lin**[…] [-linis] набóжность *f*; благочéст[…] **~ly** [-li] благочести́вый; **~moth**[…] крёстная мать *f*.
goggle [gɔgl] **1.** тарáщить гла[…] **2.** (a pair of) ~s *pl.* защи́тные о[…] *n/pl.*
going ['gouiŋ] **1.** иду́щий; дéйст[…] ющий; be ~ to *inf.* намéревать[…] собирáться (+ *inf.*); **2.** ходь[…] ухóд; отъéзд.

old [gould] **1.** зóлото; **2.** золотóй; **~en** ['gouldən] золотóй; **~finch** *zo.* щегóл; **~smith** золотых дел мáстер.

olf [gɔlf] **1.** гольф; **2.** игрáть в гольф.

ondola ['gɔndələ] гондóла.

one [gɔn] *p. pt.* от go; ушéдший, уéхавший; F безнадёжный, потéрянный; умéрший, покóйный.

ood [gud] **1.** *com.* хорóший; дóбрый; гóдный, полéзный; ☤ кредитоспосóбный; ♀ Friday *eccl.* великая страстнáя пятница; be ~ at быть спосóбным к (Д); **2.** добрó, блáго; пóльза; ~s *pl.* товáр; that's no ~ это бесполéзно; for ~ навсегдá; **~by(e)** [gud'bai] **1.** до свидáния!, прощáйте!; **2.** прощáние; **~ly** ['gudli] миловидный, приятный; значительный, изрядный; **~natured** добродýшный; **~ness** [-nis] добротá; *int.* гóсподи!; **~will** доброжелáтельность *f.*

oody ['gudi] конфéта.

oose [gu:s], *pl.* geese [gi:s] гусь *m*, гусыня; портнóвский утюг.

ooseberry ['gu:zbəri] крыжóвник (*no pl.*).

oose|-flesh, *Am.* **~-pimples** *pl. fig.* гусиная кóжа (от хóлода).

ore [gɔ:] **1.** запёкшаяся кровь *f*; **2.** забодáть *pf.*

orge [gɔ:dz] **1.** пасть *f*, глóтка; ýзкое ущéлье; пресыщéние; **2.** [со]жрáть; ~ o. s. наж(и)рáться.

orgeous ['gɔ:dʒəs] □ пышный, великолéпный.

ory ['gɔ:ri] □ окровáвленный; кровопролитный.

ospel ['gɔspəl] евáнгелие.

ossip ['gɔsip] **1.** сплéтни *f/pl.*; сплéтник (-ица); **2.** [на]сплéтничать.

ot [gɔt] *pt.* и *p. pt.* от get.

Gothic ['gɔθik] готический; *fig.* вáрварский.

ouge [gaudʒ] **1.** ⊕ долотó, стамéска; **2.** выдáлбливать [выдолбить]; *Am.* F обмáнывать [-нýть].

ourd [guəd] ⚘ тыква.

out [gaut] ⚕ подáгра.

overn ['gʌvən] *v/t.* прáвить, управлять (Т); *v/i.* госпóдствовать; **~ess** [-is] гувернáнтка; **~ment** [-mənt] правительство; управлéние; губéрния; *attr.* правительственный; **~mental** [gʌvən'mentl] правительственный; **~or** ['gʌvənə] правитель *m*; комендáнт; губернáтор; F отéц.

own [gaun] **1.** (жéнское) плáтье; мáнтия; **2.** одé(вá)ть.

rab [græb] F **1.** схвáтывать [-атить]; **2.** захвáт; ⊕ автоматический ковш, черпáк.

race [greis] **1.** грáция, изящество; любéзность *f*; милость *f*, милосéрдие; Your ♀ Вáша Милость *f*; **2.** *fig.* украшáть [укрáсить]; удостáивать [-стóить]; **~ful** ['greisful] □ грациóзный, изящный; **~fulness** [-nis] грациóзность *f*, изящность *f*.

gracious ['greiʃəs] □ снисходительный; благосклóнный; милостивый.

gradation [grə'deiʃən] градáция, постепéнный перехóд.

grade [greid] **1.** стéпень *f*; грáдус; ранг; кáчество; *Am.* класс (шкóлы); 🚂 уклóн; **2.** [рас]сортировáть; ⊕ нивелировать (*im*)*pf.*

gradua|l ['grædjuəl] □ постепéнный; послéдовательный; **~te** **1.** [-eit] градуировать (*im*)*pf.*, наносить делéния; кончáть университéт; *Am.* кончáть (любóе) учéбное заведéние; **2.** [-it] *univ.* окóнчивший университéт с учёной стéпенью; **~tion** [grædju'eiʃən] градуирóвка (сосýда); *Am.* окончáние учéбного заведéния; *univ.* получéние учёной стéпени.

graft [grɑ:ft] **1.** ⸙ черенóк; прививка (растéния); *Am.* взятка; пóдкуп; **2.** ⸙ приви(вá)ть (растéние); ⚕ пересáживать ткань; *Am.* давáть (брать) взятки.

grain [grein] зернó; хлéбные злáки *m/pl.*; крупинка; *fig.* склóнность *f*, принóда.

gramma|r ['græmə] граммáтика; ~ school срéдняя шкóла; *Am.* стáршие клáссы срéдней шкóлы; **~tical** [grə'mætikəl] □ грамматический.

gram(me) [græm] грамм.

granary ['grænəri] житница; амбáр.

grand [grænd] **1.** □ величественный; грандиóзный; великий; **2.** ♪ (*a.* ~ piano) рояль *m*; **~child** внук, внýчка; **~eur** ['grændʒə] грандиóзность *f*; величие.

grandiose ['grændious] □ грандиóзный; напыщенный.

grandparents *pl.* дéдушка и бáбушка.

grange [greindʒ] фéрма.

grant [grɑ:nt] **1.** предоставлять [-áвить]; допускáть [-стить]; даровáть (*im*)*pf.*; **2.** дар; субсидия; дáрственный акт; take for ~ed считáть докáзанным.

granul|ate ['grænjuleit] [раз]дробить; гранулировать(ся) (*im*)*pf.*; **~e** ['grænju:l] зернó, зёрнышко.

grape [greip] виногрáд; **~-fruit** ⚘ грéйпфрут.

graph [græf] диагрáмма, грáфик; **~ic(al** □) ['græfik, -ikəl] графический; наглядный; ~ arts *pl.* изобразительные искýсства *n/pl.*; **~ite** ['græfait] графит.

grapple ['græpl]: ~ with борóться с (Т); *fig.* пытáться преодолéть (затруднéние).

grasp [grɑ:sp] **1.** хватáть [схватúть] (by за В); заж(им)áть (в рукé); хватáться [схватúться] (at за В); понимáть [понять]; **2.** спосóбность восприятия; схвáтывание, крéпкое сжáтие; власть *f.*
grass [grɑ:s] травá; пáстбище; send to ~ выгонять на поднóжный корм; **~hopper** кузнéчик; **~-widow** F «солóменная» вдовá; **~y** травянúстый; травянóй.
grate [greit] **1.** решётка; ⊕ грóхот; **2.** [на]терéть (тёркой); [за]скрежетáть (зубáми); ~ on *fig.* раздражáть [-жúть] (В).
grateful ['greitful] □ благодáрный.
grater ['greitə] тёрка.
grati|fication [grætifi'keiʃən] вознаграждéние; удовлетворéние; **~fy** ['grætifai] удовлетворять [-рúть].
grating ['greitiŋ] **1.** □ скрипýчий, рéзкий; **2.** решётка.
gratitude ['grætitju:d] благодáрность *f.*
gratuit|ous [grə'tju(:)itəs] □ даровóй, безвозмéздный; **~y** [-i] дéнежный подáрок; чаевы́е.
grave [greiv] **1.** □ серьёзный, вéский; вáжный; тяжёлый; **2.** могúла; **3.** [*irr.*] *fig.* запечатлé(вá)ть; **~-digger** могúльщик.
gravel ['grævəl] **1.** грáвий; ⚕ мочевóй песóк; **2.** посыпáть грáвием.
graveyard клáдбище.
gravitation [grævi'teiʃən] притяжéние; тяготéние (*a. fig.*).
gravity ['græviti] серьёзность *f*, вáжность *f*; тяжесть *f*, опáсность (положéния).
gravy ['greivi] (мяснáя) подлúвка.
gray [grei] сéрый.
graze [greiz] пастú(сь); щипáть травý; задé(вá)ть.
grease [gri:s] **1.** сáло; смáзка, смáзочное веществó; **2.** [gri:z] смáз(ыв)ать.
greasy ['gri:zi] □ сáльный, жúрный; скóльзкий (о грязной дорóге).
great [greit] □ *com.* велúкий; большóй; огрóмный; F восхитúтельный; великолéпный; ~ grandchild прáвнук (-учка); **~coat** ['greit'kout] пальтó *n indecl.*; **~ly** ['greitli] óчень, сúльно; **~ness** [-nis] велúчие, сúла.
greed [gri:d] жáдность *f*, áлчность *f*; **~y** ['gri:di] □ жáдный, áлчный (of, for к Д).
Greek [gri:k] **1.** грек, гречáнка; **2.** грéческий.
green [gri:n] **1.** □ зелёный; незрéлый; *fig.* неóпытный; **2.** зелёный цвет, зелёная крáска; мóлодость *f*; лужáйка; ~s *pl.* зéлень *f*, óвощи *m/pl.*; **~back** *Am.* банкнóта; **~grocer** зеленщúк; **~house** теплúца, оранжерéя; **~ish** ['gri:ni… зеленовáтый; **~sickness** блéдна… нéмочь *f.*
greet [gri:t] привéтствовать; кл…няться [поклонúться] (Д); **~in…** ['gri:tiŋ] привéтствие; привéт.
grenade [gri'neid] ⚔ гранáта.
grew [gru:] *pt.* от grow.
grey [grei] **1.** □ сéрый; седó… **2.** сéрый цвет, сéрая крáска; … дéлать(ся) сéрым; **~hound** борзá… (собáка). [рáшпер…
grid [grid] решётка; сéтка; **~iron…**
grief [gri:f] гóре, печáль *f*; com… to ~ потерпéть неудáчу, попáст… в бедý.
griev|ance ['gri:vəns] обúда; ж… лоба; **~e** [gri:v] горевáть; огор… чáть [-чúть], опечáли(ва)ть; **~ou…** ['gri:vəs] □ гóрестный, печáл… ный.
grill [gril] **1.** рáшпер; жáреное н… рáшпере (мясо и т. п.); **2.** жáри… на рáшпере; **~-room** кóмна… ресторáна, где мясо жáрится пр… пýблике.
grim [grim] □ жестóкий; мрá… ный, зловéщий.
grimace [gri'meis] **1.** гримáс… ужúмка; **2.** гримáсничать.
grim|e [graim] грязь *f*, сáж… (на кóже); **~y** ['graimi] □ запá… канный, грязный.
grin [grin] **1.** усмéшка; **2.** усмехáт… ся [-хнýться].
grind [graind] [*irr.*] **1.** [с]молóт… размáлывать [-молóть]; растирá… [растерéть] (в порошóк); [на]то… чúть; *fig.* зубрúть; **2.** размáлы… вание; тяжёлая, скýчная рабóт… **~stone** точúльный кáмень *m.* жёрнов.
grip [grip] **1.** схвáтывание, зажá… тие, пожáтие; рукоять *f*; *fig.* тиск… *m/pl.*; **2.** схвáтывать [схватúть] (… *fig.*); овладевáть внимáнием (Р).
gripe [graip] зажúм; рукоятка; … *pl.* кóлики *f/pl.*
grisly ['grizli] ужáсный.
gristle ['grisl] хрящ.
grit [grit] **1.** песóк, грáвий; F твёр… дость харáктера, вы́держка; … *pl.* овсяная крупá; **2.** [за]скреже… тáть (Т).
grizzly ['grizli] **1.** сéрый; с прó… седью; **2.** североамерикáнский сé… рый медвéдь *m*, грúзли *m indecl.*
groan [groun] óхать [óхнуть]; [застонáть.
grocer ['grousə] бакалéйщик; **~ie…** [-riz] *pl.* бакалéя; **~y** [-ri] бака… лéйная лáвка; торгóвля бакалéй… ными товáрами.
groggy ['grɔgi] нетвёрдый на но… гáх; шáткий.
groin [grɔin] *anat.* пах.
groom [grum] **1.** грум, кóнюх… женúх; **2.** ходúть за (лóшадью)… хóлить; well- ~ed вы́холенный.

groove [gruːv] **1.** желобо́к, паз; *fig.* рути́на, привы́чка, колея́; **2.** де́лать вы́емку на (П).
grope [group] идти́ о́щупью; нащу́п(ыв)ать (*a. fig.*).
gross [grous] **1.** □ большо́й; ту́чный; гру́бый; † валово́й, бру́тто; **2.** ма́сса; гросс; in the ~ о́птом, гурто́м.
grotto [ˈgrɔtou] пеще́ра, грот.
grouch [grautʃ] *Am.* F **1.** дурно́е настрое́ние; **2.** быть не в ду́хе; **~y** [ˈgrautʃi] ворчли́вый.
ground[1] [graund] *pt.* и *p. pt.* от grind; ~ glass ма́товое стекло́.
ground[2] [graund] **1.** *mst* земля́, по́чва; уча́сток земли́; площа́дка; основа́ние; дно; **~s** *pl.* сад, парк (при до́ме); (кофе́йная) гу́ща; on the ~(s) of на основа́нии (Р); stand one's ~ удержа́ть свои́ пози́ции, прояви́ть твёрдость; **2.** класть на зе́млю; обосно́вывать [-нова́ть]; ⚡ заземля́ть [-ли́ть]; обуча́ть осно́вам предме́та; **~-floor** ни́жний эта́ж; **~less** [-lis] □ беспричи́нный, необосно́ванный; **~-staff** ✈ нелётный соста́в; **~work** фунда́мент, осно́ва.
group [gruːp] **1.** гру́ппа; фра́кция; **2.** (с)группирова́ть(ся); классифици́ровать (*im*)*pf*.
grove [grouv] ро́ща, лесо́к.
grovel [ˈgrɔvl] *mst fig.* по́лзать, пресмыка́ться.
grow [grou] [*irr.*] *v/i.* расти́; выраста́ть [вы́расти]; [с]де́латься, станови́ться [стать]; *v/t.* ⚘ выра́щивать [вы́растить]; культиви́ровать (*im*)*pf*.; **~er** [ˈgrouə] садово́д, плодово́д.
growl [graul] [за]рыча́ть; [за]ворча́ть.
grow|n [groun] *p. pt.* от grow; **~n-up** [ˈgrounˈʌp] взро́слый; **~th** [grouθ] рост.
grub [grʌb] **1.** личи́нка; гу́сеница; **2.** вска́пывать [вскопа́ть]; выкорчёвывать [вы́корчевать]; **~by** [ˈgrʌbi] чума́зый, неря́шливый.
grudge [grʌdʒ] **1.** недово́льство; за́висть *f*; **2.** [по]зави́довать в (П); неохо́тно дава́ть; [по]жале́ть.
gruff [grʌf] □ гру́бый.
grumble [ˈgrʌmbl] [за]ворча́ть; [по]жа́ловаться; [за]грохота́ть; **~r** [-ə] *fig.* ворчу́н(ья).
grunt [grʌnt] хрю́кать [-кнуть].
guarant|ee [gærənˈtiː] **1.** поручи́тель(ница *f*) *m*; гара́нтия; поручи́тельство; **2.** гаранти́ровать (*im*)*pf*., руча́ться за (В); **~or** [gærənˈtɔ] поручи́тель *m*; **~y** [ˈgærənti] гара́нтия.
guard [gɑːd] **1.** стра́жа; ⚔ карау́л; 🚂 конду́ктор; *Am.* тюре́мщик; **~s** *pl.* гва́рдия; be off ~ быть недоста́точно бди́тельным; **2.** *v/t.* охраня́ть [-ни́ть]; сторожи́ть; защища́ть [защити́ть] (from от Р); *v/i.* [по]бере́чься, остерега́ться [-ре́чься] (against Р); **~ian** [ˈgɑːdjən] храни́тель *m*; ⚖ опеку́н; **~ianship** [-ʃip] охра́на; ⚖ опеку́нство.
guess [ges] **1.** дога́дка, предположе́ние; **2.** отга́дывать [-да́ть], уга́дывать [-да́ть]; *Am.* счита́ть, полага́ть.
guest [gest] го́сть(я *f*) *m*.
guffaw [gʌˈfɔː] хо́хот.
guidance [ˈgaidəns] руково́дство.
guide [gaid] **1.** проводни́к, гид; ⊕ переда́точный рыча́г; Girl ♀s *pl.* ска́утки *f/pl.*; **2.** направля́ть [-ра́вить]; руководи́ть (Т); **~-book** путеводи́тель *m*; **~-post** указа́тельный столб.
guild [gild] цех, ги́льдия; организа́ция.
guile [gail] хи́трость *f*, кова́рство; **~ful** [ˈgailful] □ кова́рный; **~less** [-lis] □ простоду́шный.
guilt [gilt] вина́, вино́вность *f*; **~less** [ˈgiltlis] □ невино́вный; **~y** [ˈgilti] □ вино́вный, винова́тый.
guise [gaiz] нару́жность *f*; ма́ска.
guitar [giˈtɑː] ♪ гита́ра.
gulf [gʌlf] зали́в; про́пасть *f*.
gull [gʌl] **1.** ча́йка; глупе́ц; **2.** обма́нывать [-ну́ть]; [о]дура́чить.
gullet [ˈgʌlit] пищево́д; гло́тка.
gulp [gʌlp] **1.** жа́дно глота́ть; **2.** глото́к.
gum [gʌm] десна́; гу́мми *n indecl.*; клей; **~s** *pl. Am.* гало́ши *f/pl.*; **2.** скле́и(ва)ть; гумми́ровать (*im*)*pf*.
gun [gʌn] **1.** ору́дие, пу́шка; ружьё; *Am.* револьве́р; F big ~ *fig.* ва́жная персо́на, «ши́шка»; **2.** *Am.* охо́титься; **~boat** каноне́рка; **~-man** *Am.* банди́т; **~ner** ⚔, ⚓ [ˈgʌnə] артиллери́ст, пулемётчик; **~powder** по́рох; **~smith** оруже́йный ма́стер.
gurgle [ˈgəːgl] [за]журча́ть, [за-]бу́лькать.
gush [gʌʃ] **1.** си́льный пото́к; ли́вень *m*; *fig.* излия́ние; **2.** хлы́нуть *pf.*; ли́ться пото́ком; *fig.* излива́ть чу́вства; **~er** [ˈgʌʃə] *fig.* челове́к, излива́ющий свои́ чу́вства; *Am.* нефтяно́й фонта́н.
gust [gʌst] поры́в (ве́тра).
gut [gʌt] кишка́; **~s** *pl.* вну́тренности *f/pl.*; F си́ла во́ли.
gutter [ˈgʌtə] водосто́чный жёлоб; сто́чная кана́ва.
guy [gai] **1.** пу́гало, чу́чело; *Am.* F па́рень *m*, ма́лый; **2.** издева́ться над (Т), осме́ивать [-е́ять].
guzzle [ˈgʌzl] жа́дно пить; есть с жа́дностью.
gymnas|ium [dʒimˈneizjəm] гимнасти́ческий зал; **~tics** [dʒimˈnæstiks] *pl.* гимна́стика.
gyrate [dʒaiəˈreit] враща́ться по кру́гу, дви́гаться по спира́ли.
gyroplane [ˈdʒaiəroplein] автожи́р.

H

haberdashery ['hæbədæʃəri] галантерея; *Am.* мужское бельё.
habit ['hæbit] **1.** привычка; сложение; свойство; **2.** оде(ва)ть; **~able** ['hæbitəbl] годный для жилья; **~ation** [hæbi'teiʃən] жилище.
habitual [hə'bitjuəl] □ обычный, привычный.
hack [hæk] **1.** тесать; рубить [руб(а)нуть]; разбивать на куски; **2.** наёмная лошадь *f*; мотыга.
hackneyed ['hæknid] *fig.* избитый, банальный.
had [hæd] *pt.* и *p. pt.* от have.
hag [hæg] (*mst fig.* old ~) ведьма.
haggard ['hægəd] □ измождённый, осунувшийся.
haggle [hægl] [с]торговаться.
hail [heil] **1.** град; оклик; **2.** it ~s град идёт; *fig.* сыпаться градом; приветствовать; ~ from происходить из (Р); **~stone** градина.
hair [hɛə] волос; **~-breadth** минимальное расстояние; **~-cut** стрижка; **~-do** причёска; **~dresser** парикмахер; **~less** ['hɛəlis] лысый, безволосый; **~pin** шпилька; **~-raising** страшный; **~splitting** крохоборство; **~y** [-ri] волосатый.
hale [heil] здоровый, крепкий.
half [hɑ:f] **1.** половина; ~ a crown полкроны; by halves кое-как; go halves делить пополам; **2.** полу...; половинный; **3.** почти; наполовину; **~-back** полузащитник; **~-breed** метис; гибрид; **~-caste** человек смешанной расы; **~-hearted** □ равнодушный, вялый; **~-length** (*a.* ~ portrait) поясной портрет; **~penny** ['heipni] полпенни *n indecl.*; **~-time** *sport* тайм, половина игры; **~-way** на полпути; **~witted** слабоумный.
halibut ['hælibət] палтус (рыба).
hall [hɔ:l] зал; холл, вестибюль *m*; *Am.* коридор; *univ.* общежитие для студентов.
halloo [hə'lu:] кричать ату; науськ(ив)ать.
hallow ['hælou] освящать [-ятить]; **~mas** [-mæs] *eccl.* день «всех святых».
halo ['heilou] *ast.* венец; ореол.
halt [hɔ:lt] **1.** привал; остановка; **2.** останавливать(ся) [-новить(ся)]; делать привал; *mst fig.* колебаться; запинаться [запнуться].
halter ['hɔ:ltə] повод, недоуздок.
halve [hɑ:v] **1.** делить пополам; **2.** ~s [hɑ:vz] *pl.* от half.
ham [hæm] окорок, ветчина.
hamburger ['hæmbə:gə] *Am.* (рубленая) котлета.
hamlet ['hæmlit] деревушка.
hammer ['hæmə] **1.** молоток, молот; ♪ молоточек; **2.** ковать молотом; бить молотком; [по]стучать; выковывать [выковать].
hammock ['hæmək] гамак, подвесная койка.
hamper ['hæmpə] **1.** корзина с крышкой; **2.** [вос]препятствовать, [по]мешать (Д).
hand [hænd] **1.** рука; почерк; стрелка (часов); рабочий; at ~ под рукой; a good (poor) ~ at (не-) искусный в (П); ~ and glove в тесной связи; lend a ~ помогать [-мочь]; off ~ экспромтом; on ~ ⚕ имеющийся в продаже, в распоряжении; on the one ~ с одной стороны; on the other ~ с другой стороны; ~-to-~ рукопашный; come to ~ получаться [-читься]; прибы(ва)ть; **2.** ~ down оставлять потомству; ~ in вручать [-чить]; ~ over перед(ав)ать; **~-bag** дамская сумочка; **~bill** рекламный листок; **~-brake** ⊕ ручной тормоз; **~cuff** наручник; **~ful** ['hændful] горсть *f*; F «наказание»; **~-glass** ручное зеркало.
handicap ['hændikæp] **1.** помеха; *sport* гандикап; **2.** ставить в невыгодное положение.
handi|craft [-krɑ:ft] ручная работа, ремесло; **~craftsman** кустарь *m*; ремесленник; **~work** рукоделие; ручная работа.
handkerchief ['hæŋkətʃi(:)f] носовой платок; косынка.
handle [hændl] **1.** ручка, рукоятка; **2.** держать в руках, трогать или брать руками; обходится [обойтись] с (Т).
hand|made ручной работы; **~-set** *Am.* телефонная трубка; **~shake** рукопожатие; **~some** ['hænsəm] □ красивый; порядочный; **~work** ручная работа; **~writing** почерк; **~y** ['hændi] □ удобный; близкий
hang [hæŋ] **1.** [*irr.*] *v/t.* вешать [повесить]; подвешивать [-весить] (*pt.* и *p. pt.* ~ed) вешать [повесить] *v/i.* висеть; ~ about (*Am.* around) слоняться, околачиваться, шляться; ~ on прицепляться -[питься] к (Д); *fig.* упорствовать; **2.** смысл, сущность *f*.
hangar ['hæŋə] ангар.
hang-dog пристыжённый, виноватый (вид).
hanger ['hæŋə] вешалка (платья) крючок, крюк; **~-on** *fig.* прихлебатель *m*.
hanging ['hæŋiŋ] вешание; повешение (казнь); **~s** [-s] *pl.* драпировки *f/pl*.
hangman ['hæŋmən] палач.

hang-over F похмéлье.
hap|hazard ['hæp'hæzəd] **1.** случáйность *f*; at ~ наудáчу; **2.** случáйный; **~less** [-lis] □ злополýчный.
happen ['hæpən] случáться [-чи́ться], происходи́ть [произойти́]; окáзываться [-зáться]; he ~ed to be at home он случáйно оказáлся дóма; ~ (up)on, *Am.* ~ in with случáйно встрéтить; **~ing** ['hæpniŋ] слу́чай, собы́тие.
happi|ly ['hæpili] счастли́во; к счáстью; **~ness** [-nis] счáстье.
happy ['hæpi] □ *com.* счастли́вый; удáчный.
harangue [hə'ræŋ] **1.** речь *f*; **2.** произноси́ть речь.
harass ['hærəs] [вс]тревóжить; изводи́ть [-вести́].
harbo(u)r ['hɑ:bə] **1.** гáвань *f*, порт; **2.** стать на я́корь; дать убéжище (Д); *fig.* затáивать [-и́ть]; **~age** [-ridʒ] убéжище, приют.
hard [hɑ:d] **1.** *adj. com.* твёрдый, жёсткий; крéпкий; трýдный; тяжёлый; *Am.* спиртнóй; ~ cash нали́чные *pl.* (дéньги); ~ currency устóйчивая валюта; ~ of hearing тугóй нá ухо; **2.** *adv.* твёрдо; крéпко; си́льно; упóрно; с трудóм; ~ by бли́зко, ря́дом; ~ up в затрудни́тельном финáнсовом положéнии; **~-boiled** свáренный вкрутýю; бесчýвственный, чёрствый; *Am.* хладнокрóвный; **~en** ['hædn] дéлать(ся) твёрдым; [за-] твердéть; *fig.* закаля́ть(ся) [-ли́ть (-ся)]; **~-headed** практи́чный, трéзвый; **~-hearted** □ бесчýвственный; **~iness** выносливость *f*; **~ly** ['hɑ:dli] с трудóм; едвá; едвá ли; **~ness** [-nis] твёрдость *f* и т. д.; **~ship** [-ʃip] лишéние, нуждá; **~ware** скобянóй товáр; **~y** ['hɑ:di] □ смéлый, отвáжный; выносливый.
hare [hɛə] зáяц; **~-brained** рассéянный.
hark [hɑ:k] прислýш(ив)аться (to к Д); ~! чу!
harlot ['hɑ:lət] проститýтка.
harm [hɑ:m] **1.** вред, зло; оби́да; **2.** [по]вреди́ть (Д); **~ful** ['hɑ:mful] □ врéдный, пáгубный; **~less** [-lis] □ безврéдный, безоби́дный.
harmon|ic [hɑ:'mɔnik] (**~ally**, **~ious** □ [hɑ:'mounjəs]) гармони́чный, стрóйный; **~ize** ['hɑ:mənaiz] *v/t.* гармонизи́ровать (*im*)*pf.*; приводи́ть в гармóнию; *v/i.* гармони́ровать; **~y** [-ni] гармóния, созвýчие; соглáсие.
harness ['hɑ:nis] **1.** ýпряжь *f*, сбрýя; **2.** запрягáть [запря́чь].
harp [hɑ:p] **1.** áрфа; **2.** игрáть на áрфе; ~ (up)on завести́ волы́нку о (П).
harpoon [hɑ:'pu:n] гарпýн, острогá.
harrow ['hærou] **1.** боронá; **2.** [вз]борони́ть; *fig.* [из]мýчить, [ис]терзáть.
harry ['hæri] разоря́ть [-ри́ть], опустошáть [-ши́ть].
harsh [hɑ:ʃ] □ рéзкий; жёсткий; стрóгий, сурóвый; тéрпкий.
hart [hɑ:t] *zo.* олéнь *m.*
harvest ['hɑ:vist] **1.** жáтва, убóрка (хлéба), сбор (я́блок и т. п.); урожáй; **2.** собирáть урожáй.
has [hæz] 3. *p. sg. pres.* от have.
hash [hæʃ] **1.** рýбленое мя́со; *fig.* пýтаница; **2.** [по]руби́ть, [по]кроши́ть (о мя́се).
hast|e [heist] поспéшность *f*, торопли́вость *f*; make ~ [по]спеши́ть; **~en** ['heisn] [по]торопи́ть(ся); **~y** ['heisti] □ поспéшный; вспы́льчивый; необдýманный.
hat [hæt] шля́па.
hatch [hætʃ] **1.** вы́водок; ⚓, ✈ люк; **2.** выси́живать [вы́сидеть] (цыпля́т и т. п.) (*a. fig.*); вылупля́ться из яйцá.
hatchet ['hætʃit] топóрик.
hatchway ['hætʃwei] ⚓ люк.
hat|e [heit] **1.** нéнависть *f*; **2.** ненави́деть; **~eful** ['heitful] □ ненави́стный; **~red** ['heitrid] нéнависть *f*.
haught|iness ['hɔ:tinis] надмéнность *f*, высокомéрие; **~y** [-ti] □ надмéнный, высокомéрный.
haul [hɔ:l] **1.** перевóзка; тя́га; **2.** [по]тянýть; таскáть, [по]тащи́ть; перевози́ть [-везти́].
haunch [hɔ:ntʃ] бедрó, ля́жка; зáдняя ногá.
haunt [hɔ:nt] **1.** появля́ться [-ви́ться] в (П) (о при́зраке); чáсто посещáть (мéсто); **2.** люби́мое мéсто; притóн; ~ed house дом с привидéнием.
have [hæv] **1.** [*irr.*] *v/t.* имéть; I ~ to do я дóлжен сдéлать; ~ one's hair cut стри́чься; he will ~ it that ... он настáивает на том, чтóбы (+ *inf.*); I had better go мне бы лýчше пойти́; I had rather go я предпочёл бы пойти́; ~ about one имéть при себé; **2.** *v/aux.* вспомогáтельный глагóл для образовáния перфéктной фóрмы: I ~ come я пришёл.
haven ['heivn] гáвань *f*; убéжище.
havoc ['hævək] опустошéние.
hawk [hɔ:k] **1.** я́стреб; **2.** торговáть вразнóс.
hawthorn ['hɔ:θɔ:n] ⚘ боя́рышник.
hay [hei] сéно; ~ fever сеннáя лихорáдка; **~cock**, **~stack** копнá сéна; **~loft** сеновáл.
hazard ['hæzəd] **1.** шанс; риск; **2.** рисковáть [-кнýть]; **~ous** ['hæzədəs] □ рискóванный.
haze [heiz] **1.** лёгкий тумáн, ды́мка; **2.** *Am.* зло подшýчивать над (Т).

hazel ['heizl] **1.** ♀ opéшник; **2.** кáрий (цвет); **~-nut** леснóй opéx.

hazy ['heizi] □ тумáнный; *fig.* смýтный.

he [hi:] **1.** *pron. pers.* он; ~ who ... тот, кто ...; **2.** ~-... пéред назвáнием живóтного обозначáет самцá.

head [hed] **1.** *com.* головá; главá; начáльник; вождь *m*; изголóвье; лицевáя сторонá (монéты); come to a ~ назрé(вá)ть (о нарыве); *fig.* достúгнуть критúческой стáдии; get it into one's ~ that ... забрáть себé в гóлову, что ...; **2.** глáвный; **3.** *v/t.* возглавлять; ~ off отклонять [-нúть]; *v/i.* направляться [-áвиться]; ~ for держáть курс на (В); **~ache** ['hedeik] головнáя боль *f*; **~-dress** головнóй убóр; причёска; **~ing** [-iŋ] заголóвок; **~land** мыс; **~light** 🚂 головнóй фонáрь *m*; *mot.* фáра; **~-line** заголóвок; **~long** *adj.* опромéтчивый; *adv.* опромéтчиво; очертя гóлову; **~master** дирéктор шкóлы; **~-phone** наýшник; **~quarters** *pl.* ⚔ штаб-квартúра; **~strong** своевóльный, упрямый; **~waters** *pl.* истóки *m/pl.*; **~way**: make ~ дéлать успéхи; **~y** ['hedi] □ стремúтельный; опьяняющий.

heal [hi:l] излéчивать [-чúть], исцелять [-лúть]; (*a.* ~ up) зажи(вá)ть.

health [helθ] здорóвье; **~ful** ['helθful] □ целéбный; **~-resort** курóрт; **~y** ['helθi] □ здорóвый; полéзный.

heap [hi:p] **1.** кýча, мáсса; грýда; **2.** нагромождáть [-моздúть]; нагружáть [-узúть]; накоплять [-пúть] (*a* ~ up).

hear [hiə] [*irr.*] [у]слышать; [по-]слýшать; **~d** [hə:d] *pt.* и *p. pt.* от hear; **~er** ['hiərə] слýшатель(ница *f*) *m*; **~ing** [-iŋ] слух; ⚖ слýшание, разбóр дéла; **~say** ['hiəsei] слух, молвá.

hearse [hə:s] катафáлк.

heart [hɑ:t] *com.* сéрдце; мýжество; суть *f*; сердцевúна; ~s *pl.* чéрви *f/pl.* (кáрточная масть); *fig.* сéрдце, душá; by ~ наизýсть; out of ~ в унынии; lay to ~ принимáть блúзко к сéрдцу; lose ~ терять мýжество; take ~ собрáться с дýхом; **~ache** ['hɑ:teik] душéвная боль *f*; **~-break** сúльная печáль *f*; **~-broken** убúтый гóрем; **~burn** изжóга; **~en** ['hɑ:tən] ободрять [-рúть]; **~felt** úскренний.

hearth [hɑ:θ] очáг (*a. fig.*).

heart|less ['hɑ:tlis] □ бессердéчный; **~rending** душераздирáющий; **~y** ['hɑ:ti] □ дрýжеский, сердéчный; здорóвый.

heat [hi:t] **1.** *com.* жарá, жар; пыл; *sport* забéг, заплыв, заéзд; **2.** нагрé(вá)ть(ся); топúть; [раз]горячúть; **~er** ['hi:tə] ⊕ нагревáтель *m*; калорúфер, радиáтор.

heath [hi:θ] мéстность, порóсшая вéреском; ♀ вéреск.

heathen ['hi:ðən] **1.** язычник; **2.** языческий.

heating ['hi:tiŋ] нагревáние; отоплéние; накáливание.

heave [hi:v] **1.** подъём; волнéние (мóря); **2.** [*irr.*] *v/t.* поднимáть [-нять]; [по]тянýть (якорь); *v/i.* вздымáться; напрягáться [-ячься].

heaven ['hevn] небесá *n/pl.*, нéбо; **~ly** [-li] небéсный.

heaviness ['hevinis] тяжесть *f*; инéртность *f*; депрéссия.

heavy ['hevi] □ *com.* тяжёлый; обúльный (урожáй); сúльный (вéтер и т. п.); бýрный (о мóре); мрáчный; неуклюжий; ⚡ ~ current ток высóкого напряжéния; **~-weight** *sport* тяжеловéс.

heckle ['hekl] прерывáть замечáниями (орáтора).

hectic ['hektik] ⚕ чахóточный; лихорáдочный, возбуждённый.

hedge [hedʒ] **1.** úзгородь *f*; **2.** *v/t.* огорáживать úзгородью; огранúчи(ва)ть; *fig.* окружáть [-жúть] (with T); *v/i.* уклоняться от прямóго отвéта; **~hog** *zo.* ёж.

heed [hi:d] **1.** внимáние, осторóжность *f*; take no ~ of не обращáть внимáния на (В); **2.** обращáть внимáние на (В); **~less** [-lis] □ небрéжный; необдýманный.

heel [hi:l] **1.** пятка; каблýк; *Am. sl.* хам, подлéц; head over ~s, ~s over head вверх тормáшками; down at ~ *fig.* неряшливый; **2.** прибивáть каблýк к (Д); слéдовать по пятáм за (T).

heifer ['hefə] тёлка.

height [hait] высотá; вышинá; возвышенность *f*; верх; **~en** ['haitn] повышáть [повысить]; усúли(ва)ть.

heinous ['heinəs] □ отвратúтельный, ужáсный.

heir [εə] наслéдник; ~ apparent закóнный наслéдник; **~ess** ['εəris] наслéдница; **~loom** [-lu:m] наслéдство.

held [held] *pt.* и *p. pt.* от hold.

helicopter ['helikɔptə] вертолёт.

hell [hel] ад; *attr.* áдский; raise ~ скандáлить, безобрáзничать; **~ish** ['heliʃ] □ áдский.

hello ['hʌ'lou, hə'lou] аллó!

helm [helm] ⚓ руль *m*, рулевóе колесó, штурвáл; *fig.* кормúло.

helmet ['helmit] шлем.

helmsman ['helmzmən] ⚓ рулевóй; кóрмчий.

help [help] **1.** *com.* пóмощь *f*; спасéние; mother's ~ бóнна **2.** *v/t.* помогáть [помóчь] (Д); угощáть [угостить] (to T); ~ o. s. не церемониться, брать (за столом); I could not ~ laughing я не мог не смеяться; *v/i.* помогать [-мочь]; годиться; **~er** ['helpə] помощник (-ица); **~ful** ['helpful] □ полезный; **~ing** ['helpiŋ] порция; **~less** ['helplis] □ беспомощный; **~lessness** [-nis] беспомощность *f*; **~-mate** ['helpmeit], **~meet** [-mi:t] помощник (-ица); товарищ, подруга; супру́г(а).

helve [helv] ручка, рукоять *f*.

hem [hem] **1.** рубец, кромка; **2.** подрубать [-бить]; ~ in окружать [-жить].

hemisphere ['hemisfiə] полушарие.

hemlock ['hemlɔk] ⚘ болиголов.

hemp [hemp] конопля, пенька.

hemstitch ['hemstitʃ] ажурная строчка.

hen [hen] курица; самка (птица).

hence [hens] отсюда; следовательно; a year ~ через год; **~forth** ['hens'fɔ:θ], **~forward** ['hens'fɔ:wəd] с этого времени, впредь.

henpecked находящийся под башмаком у жены.

her [hə:, hə] её; ей.

herald ['herəld] **1.** вестник; **2.** возвещать [-вестить], объявлять [-вить]; ~ in вводить [ввести].

herb [hə:b] (целебная) трава; (пряное) растение; **~ivorous** [hə:'bivərəs] травоядный.

herd [hə:d] **1.** стадо, гурт; *fig.* толпа; **2.** *v/t.* пасти (скот); *v/i.* (*a.* ~ together) ходить стадом; [с]толпиться; **~sman** ['hə:dzmən] пастух.

here [hiə] здесь, тут; сюда; вот; ~'s to you! за ваше здоровье!

here|after [hiər'ɑ:ftə] **1.** в будущем; **2.** будущее; **~by** этим, настоящим; при сём; таким образом.

heredit|ary [hi'reditəri] наследственный; **~y** [-ti] наследственность *f*.

here|in ['hiər'in] в этом; здесь; при сём; **~of** этого, об этом; отсюда, из этого.

heresy ['herisi] ересь *f*.

heretic ['heritik] еретик (-ичка).

here|tofore ['hiətu'fɔ:] прежде, до этого; **~upon** вслед за этим, после этого; вследствие этого; **~with** настоящим, при сём.

heritage ['heritidʒ] наследство; наследие (*mst fig.*).

hermit ['hə:mit] отшельник, пустынник.

hero ['hiərou] герой; **~ic** [-'rouik] (**~ally**) героический, геройский; **~ine** ['herouin] героиня; **~ism** [-izm] героизм.

heron ['herən] *zo.* цапля.

herring ['heriŋ] сельдь *f*, селёдка.

hers [hə:z] *pron. poss.* её.

herself [hə:'self] сама; себя, -ся, -сь.

hesitat|e ['heziteit] [по]колебаться; запинаться [запнуться]; **~ion** [hezi'teiʃən] колебание; запинка.

hew [hju:] [*irr.*] рубить; разрубать [-бить]; прокладывать [проложить] (дорогу); высекать [высечь].

hey [hei] эй!

heyday ['heidei] *fig.* зенит, расцвет.

hicc|up, ['hikʌp] *a.* **~ough 1.** икота; **2.** икать [икнуть].

hid [hid], **hidden** ['hidn] *pt* и *p. pt.* от hide.

hide [haid] [*irr.*] [с]прятать(ся); скры(ва)ть(ся); **~-and-seek** игра в прятки.

hidebound ['heidbaund] *fig.* узкий, ограниченный.

hideous ['hidiəs] □ отвратительный, ужасный.

hiding-place потаённое место, убежище.

high [hai] **1.** *adj.* □ *com.* высокий; возвышенный; сильный; высший, верховный; дорогой (о цене); с душком (мясо); with a ~ hand своевольно, властно; ~ spirits *pl.* приподнятое настроение; ~ life высшее общество; ~ light основной момент; ~ words гневные слова *n/pl.*; **2.** *adv.* высоко; сильно; **~-bred** породистый; **~-brow** *Am. sl.* претенциозный интеллигент; **~-class** первоклассный; **~-day** праздник; **~-grade** высокопроцентный; высокосортный; **~-handed** своевольный; повелительный; **~lands** *pl.* горная страна; **~ly** ['haili] очень, весьма; speak ~ of положительно отзываться о (П); **~-minded** возвышенный, благородный; **~ness** ['hainis] возвышенность *f*; *fig.* высочество; **~-power**: ~ station мощная электростанция; **~-road** шоссе *n*, *indecl.*; главная дорога; **~-strung** очень чувствительный; **~way** большая дорога, шоссе; *fig.* прямой путь *m*; **~wayman** разбойник.

hike [haik] F **1.** пешеходная экскурсия; **2.** путешествовать пешком; **~r** ['heikə] пешеходный путешественник; странник (-ица).

hilarious [hi'lɛəriəs] □ (шумно) весёлый.

hill [hil] холм, возвышение; **~billy** *Am.* ['hilbili] человек из глухой стороны; **~ock** ['hilək] холмик; **~y** [-i] холмистый.

hilt [hilt] рукоятка (сабли и т. п.).

him [him] *pron. pers.* (косвенный падеж от he) его, ему; **~self** [him'self] сам; себя, -ся, -сь.

hind [haind] **1.** лань *f*; **2.** ~ leg задняя нога; **~er 1.** ['haində] *adj.* задний; **2.** ['hində] *v/t.* [по]меша́ть, препя́тствовать (Д); **~most** са́мый за́дний.

hindrance ['hindrəns] поме́ха, препя́тствие.

hinge [hindʒ] **1.** пе́тля; крюк; шарни́р; *fig.* сте́ржень *m*, суть *f*; **2.** ~ upon *fig.* зави́сеть от (Р).

hint [hint] **1.** намёк; **2.** намека́ть [-кну́ть] (at на В).

hip [hip] бедро́; ⚘ я́года шипо́вника.

hippopotamus [hipə'pɔtəməs] гиппопота́м.

hire [haiə] **1.** наём, прока́т; **2.** нанима́ть [наня́ть]; ~ out сдава́ть в наём, дава́ть напрока́т.

his [hiz] *pron. poss.* его́, свой.

hiss [his] *v/i.* [про]шипе́ть; *v/t.* осви́стывать [-ста́ть].

histor|ian [his'tɔ:riən] исто́рик; **~ic**(**al** □) [his'tɔrik, -rikəl] истори́ческий; **~y** ['histəri] исто́рия.

hit [hit] **1.** уда́р, толчо́к; попада́ние (в цель); *thea.*, ♪ успе́х, боеви́к; **2.** [*irr.*] ударя́ть [уда́рить]; поража́ть [порази́ть]; попада́ть [попа́сть] в (цель и т. п.); *Am.* F прибы́(ва́)ть в (В); ~ a p. a blow наноси́ть уда́р (Д); F ~ it off with [по-]ла́дить с (Т); ~ (up)on находи́ть [найти́] (В); напада́ть [напа́сть] на (В).

hitch [hitʃ] **1.** толчо́к, рыво́к; ⚓ пе́тля, у́зел; *fig.* препя́тствие; **2.** подта́лкивать [-толкну́ть]; зацепля́ть(ся) [-пи́ть(ся)], прицепля́ть (-ся) [-пи́ть(ся)]; **~-hike** *Am.* F *mot.* путеше́ствовать, по́льзуясь попу́тными автомоби́лями.

hither ['hiðə] *lit.* сюда́; **~to** [-'tu:] *lit.* до сих по́р.

hive [haiv] **1.** у́лей; рой пчёл; *fig.* людско́й мураве́йник; **2.** ~ up запаса́ть [-сти́]; жить вме́сте.

hoard [hɔ:d] **1.** запа́с, склад; **2.** накопля́ть [-пи́ть]; запаса́ть [-сти́] (В); припря́т(ыв)ать.

hoarfrost ['hɔ:'frɔst] и́ней.

hoarse [hɔ:s] □ хри́плый, охри́пший.

hoary ['hɔ:ry] седо́й; покры́тый и́неем.

hoax [houks] **1.** обма́н, мистифика́ция; **2.** подшу́чивать [-ути́ть] над (Т), мистифици́ровать (*im*)*pf*.

hobble ['hɔbl] **1.** прихра́мывающая похо́дка; **2.** *v/i.* прихра́мывать; *v/t.* [с]трено́жить (ло́шадь).

hobby ['hɔbi] *fig.* конёк, люби́мое заня́тие.

hobgoblin ['hɔbgɔblin] домово́й.

hobo ['houbou] *Am.* F бродя́га *m*.

hod [hɔd] лото́к (для подно́са кирпиче́й); коры́то (для и́звести).

hoe [hou] ⚒ **1.** моты́га; **2.** моты́жить; разрыхля́ть [-ли́ть] (моты́гой).

hog [hɔg] **1.** свинья́ (*a. fig.*); бо́ров; **2.** выгиба́ть спи́ну; ко́ротко подстрига́ть (гри́ву); **~gish** ['hɔgiʃ] □ сви́нский; обжо́рливый.

hoist [hɔist] **1.** лебёдка; лифт; **2** поднима́ть [-ня́ть].

hold [hould] **1.** владе́ние; захва́т власть *f*, влия́ние; ⚓ трюм catch (*or* get, lay, take) ~ of схва́тывать [схвати́ть] (В); keep ~ o: уде́рживать [-жа́ть] (В); **2.** [*irr.* *v/t.* держа́ть; выде́рживать [вы́держать]; остана́вливать [-нови́ть]; проводи́ть [-вести́] (собра́ние и т. п.); завладе́(ва́)ть (внима́нием); занима́ть [-ня́ть]; вмеща́ть [вмести́ть]; ~ one's owi отста́ивать свою́ пози́цию; ~ the line! *teleph.* не ве́шайте тру́бку; ~ over откла́дывать [отложи́ть]; ~ up подде́рживать [-жа́ть]; заде́рживать [-жа́ть]; останови́ть с це́лью грабежа́; **3.** *v/i.* остана́вливаться [-нови́ться]; держа́ться (о пого́де); ~ forth рассужда́ть; разглаго́льствовать; ~ good (*or* true име́ть си́лу; ~ off держа́ться поо́даль; ~ on держа́ться за (В); ~ to приде́рживаться (Р); ~ up держа́ться пря́мо; **~er** ['houldə] арендa´тор; владе́лец; **~ing** [-iŋ] уча́сток земли́; владе́ние; **~-over** *Am* пережи́ток; **~-up** *Am.* налёт ограбле́ние.

hole [houl] дыра́, отве́рстие; я́ма нора́; F *fig.* затрудни́тельное положе́ние; pick **~s** in находи́ть недоста́тки в (П).

holiday ['hɔlədi] пра́здник; день о́тдыха; о́тпуск; **~s** *pl.* кани́кулы *f*/*pl*.

hollow ['hɔlou] **1.** □ пусто́й, по́лый; впа́лый, ввали́вшийся; **2** пустота́; дупло́; лощи́на; **3.** выда́лбливать [вы́долбить].

holly ['hɔli] ⚘ остроли́ст, па́дуб.

holster ['houlstə] кобура́.

holy ['houli] свято́й, свяще́нный ~ water свята́я вода́; ♀ Week страстна́я неде́ля.

homage ['hɔmidʒ] почте́ние, уваже́ние; do (*or* pay, render) ~ ока́зывать почте́ние (to Д).

home [houm] **1.** дом, жили́ще; ро́дина; at ~ до́ма; **2.** *adj.* дома́шний вну́тренний; ♀ Office, *Am.* ♀ Departement министе́рство вну́тренних дел; ♀ Secretary мини́стр вну́тренних дел; **3.** *adv.* домо́й hit (*or* strike) ~ попа́сть в цель **~-felt** прочу́вствованный, серде́чный; **~less** ['houmlis] бездо́мный; **~like** ую́тный; **~ly** [-li] *fig* просто́й, обы́денный; дома́шний некраси́вый; **~-made** дома́шнего изготовле́ния; **~sickness** тоска́ по ро́дине; **~stead** дом с уча́стком земли́; уса́дьба; **~ward**(s) [-wəd(s) домо́й.

homicide ['hɔmisaid] уби́йство уби́йца *m*/*f*.

mogeneous [hɔmo'dʒi:niəs] □ ‹нородный.

ne [houn] **1.** оселóк, точи́льный ‹мень *m*; **2.** [на]точи́ть.

nest ['ɔnist] □ чéстный; **~y** [-i] ‹стность *f*.

ney ['hʌni] мёд; my ~! ду́шень‹!; **~comb** ['hʌnikoum] сóты ‹*pl.*; **~ed** ['hʌnid] медóвый; **~‹oon** **1.** медóвый мéсяц; **2.** про‹дить медóвый мéсяц.

norary ['ɔnərəri] почётный.

no(u)r ['ɔnə] **1.** честь *f*; чéст‹ость *f*; почёт; пóчесть *f*; Your ♀ ‹ша честь *f*; **2.** почитáть [-чти́ть]; ‹остáивать [-стóить]; ⚚ плати́ть ‹ срок (по вéкселю); **~able** ['ɔn‹əbl] □ почётный; благорóдный; ‹чтённый.

od [hud] **1.** капюшóн; *mot.* капóт; ‹ покрывáть капюшóном.

odwink ['hudwiŋk] обмáнывать ‹нýть].

of [hu:f] копы́то.

ok [hu:k] **1.** крюк, крючóк; ба‹р; серп; by ~ or by crook прáв‹ами и непрáвдами, так и́ли и́на‹; **2.** зацепля́ть [-пи́ть]; застёги‹ать(ся) [-стегнýть(ся)].

op [hu:p] **1.** óбруч; ⊕ обóйма, ‹гель *m*, кольцó; **2.** набивáть ‹бручи на (В); скрепля́ть óбру‹м.

oping-cough коклю́ш.

ot [hu:t] **1.** крик совы́; ги́канье; ‹ *v/i.* [за]улюлю́кать, [за]ги́кать; ‹*ot.* [за]гудéть; *v/t.* осви́стывать ‹истáть].

p [hop] **1.** ⚘ хмель *m*; прыжóк; ‹ танцевáльный вéчер; **2.** соби‹áть хмель; скакáть, пры́гать на ‹днóй ногé.

pe [houp] **1.** надéжда; **2.** надé‹ться (for на В); ~ in полагáться ‹оложи́ться] на (В); **~ful** ['houp‹l] □ подаю́щий надéжды; на‹éющийся; **~less** [-lis] □ безна‹ёжный.

rde [hɔ:d] ордá; ватáга, шáйка.

rizon [ho'raizn] горизóнт; *fig.* ‹ругозóр.

rn [hɔ:n] рог; *mot.* гудóк; ♪ ‹ожóк; ~ of plenty рог изоби́лия.

rnet ['hɔ:nit] *zo.* шéршень *m*.

rny ['hɔ:ni] □ мозóлистый.

rr|ible ['hɔrəbl] □ стрáшный, ‹жáсный, **~id** ['hɔrid] □ ужáсный; ‹ротивный; **~ify** ['hɔrifai] ужа‹áть [-снýть]; шоки́ровать; **~or** ‹hɔrə] ýжас; отвращéние.

rse [hɔ:s] лóшадь *f*, конь *m*; ‹óзлы *f/pl.*; *sport* конь *m*; take ~ ‹есть на лóшадь; **~back**: on ~ ‹ерхóм; **~hair** кóнский вóлос; **~laugh** F грýбый, грóмкий ‹óхот; **~man** [-mən] всáдник, ‹ерховóй; **~power** лошади́ная ‹и́ла; **~-radish** ⚘ хрен; **~shoe** ‹одкóва.

horticulture ['hɔ:tikʌltʃə] садо-вóдство.

hose [houz] ⚚ *coll.* чулки́ *m/pl.* (как назвáние товáра); шланг.

hosiery ['houʒəri] ⚚ чулóчные издéлия *n/pl.*, трикотáж.

hospitable ['hɔspitəbl] □ госте-приíмный.

hospital ['hɔspitl] больни́ца, гóс-питаль *m*; **~ity** [hɔspi'tæliti] гос-теприи́мство.

host [houst] хозя́ин; содержáтель гости́ницы; *fig.* мнóжество; ~s of heaven *eccl.* áнгелы, си́лы небéс-ные.

hostage ['hɔstidʒ] залóжник (-ица).

hostel ['hɔstəl] общежи́тие; тур-бáза.

hostess ['houstis] хозя́йка (*s.* host).

hostil|e ['hɔstail] враждéбный; **~ity** [hɔs'tiliti] враждéбность *f*; враж-дéбный акт.

hot [hɔt] горя́чий; жáркий; пы́л-кий; ~ dogs горя́чие соси́ски *f/pl.*; **~bed** парни́к; *fig.* очáг.

hotchpotch ['hɔtʃpɔtʃ] овощнóй суп; *fig.* вся́кая вся́чина.

hotel [ho(u)'tel] отéль *m*, гости́ни-ца.

hot|headed опромéтчивый; **~-house** оранжерéя, тепли́ца; **~spur** вспы́льчивый человéк.

hound [haund] **1.** гóнчая собáка; *fig.* негодя́й, подлéц; **2.** трави́ть собáками.

hour [auə] час; врéмя; **~ly** ['auəli] ежечáсный.

house **1.** [haus] *com.* дом; здáние; *parl.* палáта; *univ.* коллéдж; **2.** [hauz] *v/t.* поселя́ть [-ли́ть]; поме-щáть [-ести́ть]; приюти́ть *pf.*; *v/i.* помещáться [-ести́ться]; жить; **~breaker** взлóмщик, громи́ла *m*; **~-check** *Am.* óбыск; **~hold** до-мáшнее хозя́йство; домочáдцы *m/pl.*; **~holder** главá семьи́; **~keeper** эконóмка; **~keeping** до-мáшнее хозя́йство, домоводство; **~warming** новосéлье; **~wife** хо-зя́йка; **~wifery** ['hauswifəri] до-мáшнее хозя́йство; домовóдство.

housing ['hauziŋ] снабжéние жи-ли́щем; жили́щное строи́тельство.

hove [houv] *pt.* и *p. pt.* от heave.

hovel ['hɔvəl] навéс; лачýга, хи-бáрка.

hover ['hɔvə] пари́ть (о пти́це); *fig.* колебáться, не решáться.

how [hau] как?, каки́м óбразом?; ~ about ...? как обстои́т дéло с (Т)?; **~ever** [hau'əvə] **1.** *adv.* как бы ни; **2.** *cj.* однáко, тем не мéнее.

howl [haul] **1.** вой, завывáние; **2.** [за]вы́ть; **~er** ['haulə] *sl.* грýбая оши́бка.

hub [hʌb] ступи́ца (колесá), втýл-ка; *fig.* центр (внимáния).

hubbub ['hʌbʌb] шум, гам.

huckster ['hʌkstə] мелочнóй тор-гóвец; бары́шник.

huddle ['hʌdl] **1.** сва́ливать в ку́чу, укла́дывать кое-ка́к; сверну́ться «кала́чиком»; ~ on надева́ть на́спех; **2.** ку́ча; су́толока, сумато́ха.
hue [hju:] отте́нок; ~ and cry пого́ня с кри́ками.
huff [hʌf] **1.** раздраже́ние; **2.** *v/t.* задира́ть; запу́гивать [-га́ть]; *v/i.* оскорбля́ться [-би́ться], обижа́ться [оби́деться].
hug [hʌg] **1.** объя́тие; **2.** обнима́ть [-ня́ть]; *fig.* быть приве́рженным, скло́нным к (Д).
huge [hju:dʒ] □ огро́мный, гига́нтский; **~ness** ['hju:dʒnis] огро́мность *f.*
hulk [hʌlk] *fig.* большо́й, неуклю́жий челове́к.
hull [hʌl] **1.** ♀ шелуха́, скорлупа́; ко́рпус (корабля́); **2.** [на]шелуши́ть, [об]лущи́ть.
hum [hʌm] [за]жужжа́ть; напева́ть; F make things ~ вноси́ть оживле́ние в рабо́ту.
human ['hju:mən] **1.** □ челове́ческий; **~ly** по-челове́чески; **2.** F челове́к; **~e** [hju:'mein] □ гума́нный, челове́чный; **~itarian** [hjumæni'tεəriən] филантро́п; **2.** гуманита́рный; гума́нный; **~ity** [hju'mæniti] челове́чество; гума́нность *f*; **~kind** ['hju:mən'kaind] людско́й род.
humble ['hʌmbl] **1.** □ скро́мный; поко́рный, смире́нный; **2.** унижа́ть [уни́зить]; смиря́ть [-ри́ть].
humble-bee ['hʌmblbi:] шмель *m.*
humbleness [-nis] скро́мность *f*; поко́рность *f.*
humbug ['hʌmbʌg] чепуха́; хвасту́н.
humdrum ['hʌmdrʌm] бана́льный, ску́чный.
humid ['hju:mid] сыро́й, вла́жный; **~ity** [hju'miditi] сы́рость *f,* вла́га.
humiliat|e [hju'milieit] унижа́ть [уни́зить]; **~ion** [hjumili'eiʃən] униже́ние.
humility [hju'militi] смире́ние; поко́рность *f.*
humming ['hʌmiŋ] F мо́щный; **~bird** *zo.* коли́бри *m/f indecl.*
humorous ['hju:mərəs] □ юмористи́ческий; коми́ческий.
humo(u)r ['hju:mə] **1.** ю́мор; шутли́вость *f*; настрое́ние; out of ~ не в ду́хе; **2.** потака́ть (Д); ублажа́ть [-жи́ть].
hump [hʌmp] **1.** горб; **2.** [с]го́рбить(ся).
hunch [hʌntʃ] **1.** горб; *Am.* подозре́ние; ломо́ть *m*; **2.** [с]го́рбить (-ся) (*a.* ~ out, up); **~back** горбу́н(ья).
hundred ['hʌndrəd] **1.** сто; **2.** со́тня; **~th** [-θ] со́тый; со́тая часть *f*; **~weight** це́нтнер.
hung [hʌŋ] *pt.* и *p.pt.* от hang.

Hungarian [hʌŋ'gεəriən] **1.** венг рец (-рка); **2.** венге́рский.
hunger ['hʌŋgə] **1.** го́лод; *f* жа́жда; **2.** *v/i.* голода́ть; бы голо́дным; *fig.* жа́ждать (for
hungry ['hʌŋgri] □ голо́дный.
hunk [hʌŋk] то́лстый кусо́к.
hunt [hʌnt] **1.** охо́та; по́иски *m,* (for P); **2.** охо́титься на (B) *or* (T); трави́ть; ~ out *or* up оты́ски вать [-ка́ть]; ~ for *fig.* охо́тить за (T), иска́ть (P *or* B); **~er** ['hʌn охо́тник; охо́тничья ло́шадь *f*; **ing-ground** райо́н охо́ты.
hurdle ['hə:dl] препя́тстви барье́р; **~-race** ска́чки с препя ствиями; барье́рный бег.
hurl [hə:l] **1.** си́льный бросо́к; швыря́ть [-рну́ть], мета́ть [ме ну́ть].
hurricane ['hʌrikən] урага́н.
hurried ['hʌrid] □ торопли́вый.
hurry ['hʌri] **1.** торопли́вость поспе́шность *f*; **2.** *v/t.* [по]тор пи́ть; поспе́шно посыла́ть; *v* [по]спеши́ть (*a.* ~ up).
hurt [hə:t] **1.** поврежде́ние; **2.** [*ir* (*a. fig.*) причиня́ть боль; повре да́ть [-еди́ть]; боле́ть (о ча́с те́ла).
husband ['hʌzbənd] **1.** муж, с пру́г; **2.** [с]эконо́мить, эконо́м расхо́довать.
hush [hʌʃ] **1.** тишина́, молча́ни **2.** ти́ше!; **3.** водворя́ть тиши ~ up зама́лчивать [замолча́ть]; *v* успока́иваться [-ко́иться]; ут ха́ть [ути́хнуть].
husk [hʌsk] **1.** ♀ шелуха́; **2.** оч ща́ть от шелухи́, [на]шелуши́т **~y** ['hʌski] □ си́плый, охри́пш (го́лос); *Am.* ро́слый.
hustle ['hʌsl] **1.** *v/t.* толка́ [-кну́ть]; [по]тороп́ить; пону дать [-ну́дить]; *v/i.* толка́ть [-кну́ться]; [по]торопи́ться; *pa Am.* бы́стро де́йствовать; **2.** то котня́; *Am.* F энерги́чная де́ятел ность *f*; ~ and bustle толкотня́ шум.
hut [hʌt] хи́жина, хиба́рка; б ра́к.
hutch [hʌtʃ] кле́тка (для кро́лик и т. п.).
hybrid ['haibrid] 🕮 гибри́д, п месь *f*; **~ize** ['haibridaiz] скре́щ вать [-ести́ть] (расте́ния, живо́ ных).
hydro... ['haidro...] 🕮 водо...; **chloric** [-'klɔrik]: ~ acid соля́н кислота́; **~gen** ['haidridʒən] водоро́д; **~pathy** [hai'drɔpəθi] в долече́ние; **~phobia** ['haid 'foubiə] водобоя́знь *f*; **~pla** ['haidroplein] гидропла́н.
hygiene ['haidʒi:n] гигие́на.
hymn [him] **1.** церко́вный гим **2.** петь ги́мны.
hyphen ['haifən] **1.** дефи́с, сое

нительная чёрточка; 2. писать через чёрточку.
hypnotize ['hipnətaiz] [за]гипнотизировать.
hypo|chondriac [haipo'kɔndriæk] ипохондрик; **~crisy** [hi'pɔkrəsi] лицемерие; **~crite** ['hipokrit] лицемер; **~critical** [hipo'kritikəl] □ лицемерный; **~thesis** [hai'pɔθisis] гипотеза, предположение.
hyster|ical [his'terikəl] □ истеричный; **~ics** [his'teriks] *pl.* истерика.

I

I [ai] *pers. pron.* я.
ice [ais] 1. лёд; мороженое; 2. замораживать [-розить]; покрывать льдом; глазировать *(im)pf.*; **~-age** ледниковый период; **~-bound** затёртый льдами; **~-box**, **~-chest** холодильник, ледник; **~-cream** мороженое.
icicle ['aissikl] (ледяная) сосулька.
icing ['aisiŋ] сахарная глазурь *f*; ✝ обледенение.
icy ['aisi] □ ледяной.
idea [ai'diə] идея; понятие, представление; мысль *f*; **~l** [-l] 1. □ идеальный; воображаемый; 2. идеал.
identi|cal [ai'dentikəl] □ тождественный; одинаковый; **~fication** [aidentifi'keiʃən] отождествление; установление личности; **~fy** [-fai] отождествлять [-вить]; устанавливать личность (тождество) (P); **~ty** [-ti] тождественность *f*; ~ card удостоверение личности.
idiom ['idiəm] идиома; говор.
idiot ['idiət] идиот(ка); **~ic** [idi'ɔtik] (-ally) идиотский.
idle ['aidl] 1. □ незанятый; безработный; ленивый; праздный; тщетный; ⊕ бездействующий, холостой; ~ hours *pl.* часы досуга; 2. *v/t.* проводить (время) без дела (*mst* ~ away); *v/i.* лениться, бездельничать; **~ness** [-nis] праздность *f*, безделье; **~r** [-ə] бездельник (-ица), лентяй(ка).
idol ['aidl] идол; *fig.* кумир; **~atry** [ai'dɔlətri] идолопоклонство; обожание; **~ize** ['aidəlaiz] боготворить.
idyl(l) ['aidil] идиллия.
if [if] *cj.* если; если бы; (= whether) ли: ~ he knows знает ли он.
ignit|e [ig'nait] зажигать [-жечь]; загораться [-реться], воспламеняться [-ниться]; **~ion** [ig'niʃən] *mot.* зажигание; запал; *attr.* запальный.
ignoble [ig'noubl] □ низкий, подлый.
ignor|ance ['ignərəns] невежество; неведение; **~ant** [-rənt] невежественный; несведущий; **~e** [ig'nɔ:] игнорировать *(im)pf.*; ⚖ отвергать [-ергнуть].
ill [il] 1. *adj.* больной, нездоровый; дурной; 2. *adv.* едва ли; плохо, дурно; 3. зло, вред.
ill|-advised неблагоразумный; **~-bred** невоспитанный.
illegal [i'li:gəl] □ незаконный.
illegible [i'ledʒəbl] □ неразборчивый.
illegitimate [ili'dʒitimit] □ незаконный; незаконнорождённый.
ill|-favo(u)red некрасивый; неприятный; **~-humo(u)red** в дурном настроении, не в духе.
illiberal [i'libərəl] □ ограниченный (о взглядах); скупой.
illicit [i'lisit] □ запрещённый (законом).
illiterate [i'litərit] □ 1. неграмотный; 2. необразованный человек; неуч.
ill|-mannered невоспитанный, грубый; **~-natured** □ дурного нрава, злобный.
illness ['ilnis] болезнь *f*.
ill|-timed несвоевременный, неподходящий; **~-treat** плохо обращаться с (T).
illumin|ate [i'lju:mineit] освещать [-етить], озарять [-рить]; просвещать [-етить]; проливать свет на (B); **~ating** [-neitiŋ] освещающий, осветительный; **~ation** [ilju:mi'neiʃən] освещение; иллюминация.
illus|ion [i'lu:ʒən] иллюзия, обман чувств; **~ive** [-siv], □ **~ory** □ обманчивый, иллюзорный.
illustrat|e ['iləstreit] иллюстрировать *(im)pf.*; пояснять [-нить]; **~ion** [iləs'treiʃən] иллюстрация; **~ive** ['iləstreitiv] □ иллюстративный.
illustrious [i'lʌstriəs] □ знаменитый.
ill-will недоброжелательность *f*.
image ['imidʒ] образ; изображение; отражение; подобие.
imagin|able [i'mædʒinəbl] □ вообразимый; **~ary** [-nəri] воображаемый; мнимый; **~ation** [imædʒi'neiʃən] воображение, фантазия; **~ative** [i'mæddʒinətiv] □ одарённый воображением; **~e** [i'mædʒin] воображать [-разить]; представлять [-авить] себе.
imbecile ['imbisail] 1. □ слабоумный; 2. глупец.
imbibe [im'baib] впитывать [впитать], вдыхать [вдохнуть]; *fig.* усваивать [усвоить] (идеи).

imbue [im'bju:] насыща́ть [-ы́тить]; окра́шивать [окра́сить]; *fig.* наполня́ть [-о́лнить].
imita|te ['imiteit] подража́ть (Д); передра́знивать [-ни́ть]; подде́л(ыв)ать; **~tion** [imi'teiʃən] подража́ние; подде́лка, суррога́т; *attr.* подде́льный, иску́сственный.
immaculate [i'mækjulit] □ безукори́зненный; незапя́тнанный (*a. fig.*).
immaterial [imə'tiəriəl] □ несуще́ственный, нева́жный; невеще́ственный.
immature [imə'tjuə] незре́лый; недора́звитый.
immediate [i'mi:djət] □ непосре́дственный; ближа́йший; безотлага́тельный; **~ly** [-li] *adv.* непосре́дственно; неме́дленно.
immense [i'mens] □ огро́мный.
immerse [i'mə:s] погружа́ть [-узи́ть], окуна́ть [-ну́ть]; *fig.* ~ **o. s. in** погружа́ться [-узи́ться] в (В).
immigra|nt ['imigrənt] иммигра́нт(ка); **~te** [greit] иммигри́ровать (*im*)*pf.*; **~tion** [imi'greiʃən] иммигра́ция.
imminent ['iminənt] □ грозя́щий, нави́сший.
immobile [i'moubail] неподви́жный.
immoderate [i'mɔdərit] неуме́ренный, чрезме́рный.
immodest [i'mɔdist] □ нескро́мный.
immoral [i'mɔrəl] □ безнра́вственный.
immortal [i'mɔ:tl] □ бессме́ртный.
immovable [i'mu:vəbl] □ недви́жимый, неподви́жный; непоколеби́мый.
immun|e [i'mju:n] невосприи́мчивый (from к Д); иммýнный; **~ity** [-iti] освобожде́ние (от платежа́); ⚕ иммуните́т, невосприи́мчивость *f* (from к Д); *pol.* иммуните́т.
imp [imp] бесёнок; шалуни́шка *m/f.*
impair [im'pɛə] ослабля́ть [-а́бить]; [ис]по́ртить; поврежда́ть [-еди́ть].
impart [im'pɑ:t] прида(ва́)ть; переда(ва́)ть (но́вости т. п.).
impartial [im'pɑ:ʃəl] □ беспристра́стный, непредвзя́тый; **~ity** ['impɑ:ʃi'æliti] беспристра́стность *f.*
impassable [im'pɑ:səbl] □ непроходи́мый, непрое́зжий.
impassioned [im'pæʃənd] стра́стный, пы́лкий.
impassive [im'pæsiv] □ споко́йный, безмяте́жный.
impatien|ce [im'peiʃəns] нетерпе́ние; **~t** [-t] □ нетерпели́вый.
impeach [im'pi:tʃ] порица́ть; набра́сывать тень на (В).
impeccable [im'pekəbl] □ безупре́чный; непогрсши́мый.

impede [im'pi:d] [вос]препя́тствовать (Д); [по]меша́ть (Д).
impediment [im'pedimənt] поме́ха; заде́ржка.
impel [im'pel] принужда́ть [-у́дить].
impend [im'pend] нависа́ть [-и́снуть]; надвига́ться [-и́нуться].
impenetrable [im'penitrəbl] □ непроходи́мый; непроница́емый *fig.* непостижи́мый.
imperative [im'perətiv] □ повели́тельный, вла́стный; кра́йне необходи́мый.
imperceptible [impə'septəbl] □ незаме́тный.
imperfect [im'pə:fikt] □ непо́лный; несоверше́нный, дефе́ктный.
imperial [im'piəriəl] □ импе́рский импера́торский; госуда́рственный.
imperil [im'peril] подверга́ть опа́сности.
imperious [im'piəriəs] □ вла́стный; настоя́тельный; высокоме́рный.
impermeable [im'pə:miəbl] непроница́емый.
impersonal [im'pə:snl] □ безли́чный.
impersonate [im'pə:səneit] олицетворя́ть [-ри́ть]; исполня́ть роль (Р).
impertinen|ce [im'pə:tinəns] де́рзость *f*; **~t** [-nənt] □ де́рзкий.
impervious [im'pə:viəs] □ непроница́емый, непроходи́мый; глухо́й (to к Д).
impetu|ous [im'petjuəs] □ стреми́тельный; **~s** ['impitəs] дви́жуща я си́ла.
impiety [im'paiəti] неве́рие; неваже́ние.
impinge [im'pindʒ] *v/i.* ударя́ться [уда́риться] (on о В); покуша́ться [-уси́ться] (on на В).
impious ['impiəs] □ нечести́вый
implacable [im'pleikəbl] □ неумли́мый; непримири́мый.
implant [im'plɑ:nt] насажда́ть [насади́ть]; внуша́ть [-ши́ть].
implement ['implimənt] **1.** инструме́нт; ору́дие; принадле́жность **2.** выполня́ть [вы́полнить].
implicat|e ['implikeit] вовлека́ть [-е́чь], впу́т(ыв)ать; заключа́ть в себе́; **~ion** [impli'keiʃən] вовлче́ние; вы́вод.
implicit [im'plisit] □ безогово́рный; подразумева́емый.
implore [im'plɔ:] умоля́ть [-ли́ть]
imply [im'plai] подразумева́ть; намека́ть [-кну́ть] на (В); знчить.
impolite [impo'lait] □ неве́жливый, неучти́вый.
impolitic [im'pɔlitik] □ нецелсообра́зный.

port 1. ['impɔ:t] ввоз, и́мпорт; *pl.* ввози́мые това́ры *m/pl.*; **2.** ı'pɔ:t] ввози́ть [ввезти́], импорровать *(im)pf.*; име́ть значе́ние; **nce** [im'pɔ:təns] значи́тельность ва́жность *f*; **~ant** [-tənt] □ жный, значи́тельный; **~ation** ıpɔ:'teiʃən] ввоз, и́мпорт.

portun|ate [im'pɔ:tjunit] □ найливый; **~e** [im'pɔ:tju:n] докуть (Д), надоеда́ть [-е́сть] (Д).

pos|e [im'pəuz] *v/t.* навя́зывать ıа́ть]; облага́ть [обложи́ть]; *v/i.* upon производи́ть впечатле́ние (В), импони́ровать (Д); **~ition** ıpə'ziʃən] наложе́ние; облое́ние.

possib|ility [im'pɔsə'biliti] незмо́жность *f*; невероя́тность *f*; e [im'pɔsəbl] □ невозмо́жный; вероя́тный.

post|or [im'pɔstə] обма́нщик; мозва́нец; **~ure** [im'pɔstʃə] обıн, плутовство́.

poten|ce ['impotəns] бесси́лие, а́бость *f*; **~t** [-tənt] бесси́льный, а́бый.

poverish [im'pɔvəriʃ] доводи́ть бе́дности; обедня́ть [-ни́ть].

practicable [im'præktikəbl] □ исполни́мый, неосуществи́мый.

pregnate ['impregneit] оплодооря́ть [-ри́ть]; ⚗ насыща́ть ы́тить], пропи́тывать [-пита́ть].

press 1. ['impres] отпеча́ток *fig.*); *typ.* о́ттиск; **2.** [im'pres] печа́т(ыв)ать; запечатле́(ва́)ть; ıуша́ть [-ши́ть] (on Д); произди́ть впечатле́ние на (В); **~ion** n'preʃən] впечатле́ние; *typ.* о́тск; печа́тание; I am under the ~ at у меня́ впечатле́ние, что ...; **ve** [im'presive] □ внуши́тельıй, производя́щий впечатле́ние.

print 1. [im'print] запечатле́а́)ть; отпеча́т(ыв)ать; **2.** ['imint] отпеча́ток; *typ.* выходны́е е́дения *n/pl.*

prison [im'prizn] заключа́ть в рьму́, заточа́ть [-чи́ть]; **~ment** mənt] заточе́ние, заключе́ние тюрьму́).

probable [im'prɔbəbl] □ нероя́тный, неправдоподо́бный.

proper [im'prɔpə] □ неуме́стый; непристо́йный; непра́вильый.

prove [im'pru:v] *v/t.* улучша́ть лу́чшить]; [у]соверше́нствоать; повыша́ть це́нность (Р); *v/i.* лучша́ться [улу́чшиться]; [у]сорше́нствоваться; ~ upon улуча́ть [улу́чшить] (В); **~ment** mənt] усоверше́нствование; лучше́ние.

provise ['improvaiz] импровии́ровать *(im)pf.*

prudent [im'pru:dənt] □ нелагоразу́мный; неосторо́жный.

impuden|ce ['impjudəns] бессты́дство; де́рзость *f*; **~t** [-dənt] □ наха́льный; бессты́дный.

impuls|e ['impʌls], **~ion** [im'pʌlʃən] толчо́к; поры́в; ⚡ возбужде́ние.

impunity [im'pju:niti] безнака́занность *f*; with ~ безнака́занно.

impure [im'pjuə] □ нечи́стый; с при́месью.

imput|ation [impju'teiʃən] обвине́ние; **~e** [im'pju:t] вменя́ть [-ни́ть] (в вину́); припи́сывать [-са́ть] (Д/В).

in [in] **1.** *prp. com.* в, во (П or В); ~ number в коли́честве (Р), число́м в (В); ~ itself само́ по себе́; ~ 1949 в 1949-ом (в ты́сяча девятьсо́т со́рок девя́том) году́; cry out ~ alarm закрича́ть в испу́ге (*or* от стра́ха); ~ the street на у́лице; ~ my opinion по моему́ мне́нию, по-мо́ему; ~ English по-англи́йски; a novel ~ English рома́н на англи́йском языке́; ~ tens по десяти́; ~ the circumstances при да́нных усло́виях; a coat ~ velvet ба́рхатное пальто́ (*or* из ба́рхата); ~ this manner таки́м о́бразом; ~ a word одни́м сло́вом; ~ crossing the road переходя́ че́рез у́лицу; be ~ power быть у вла́сти; be engaged ~ reading занима́ться чте́нием; **2.** *adv.* внутри́; внутрь; be ~ for: a) быть обречённым на (что́-либо неприя́тное); b) I am ~ for an examination мне предстои́т экза́мен; F be ~ with быть в хоро́ших отноше́ниях с (Т).

inability [inə'biliti] неспосо́бность [*f.*]

inaccessible [inæk'sesəbl] □ недосту́пный; недосяга́емый.

inaccurate [in'ækjurit] □ нето́чный; неаккура́тный.

inactiv|e [in'æktiv] □ безде́ятельный; неде́йствующий; **~ity** [inæk'tiviti] безде́ятельность *f*; ине́ртность *f*.

inadequate [in'ædikwit] □ несоразме́рный; недоста́точный.

inadmissible [inəd'misəbl] недопусти́мый, неприе́млемый.

inadvertent [inəd'və:tənt] □ невнима́тельный; ненаме́ренный.

inalienable [in'eiliənəbl] □ неотъе́млемый.

inane [i'nein] □ бессмы́сленный; пусто́й.

inanimate [in'ænimit] □ неодушевлённый; безжи́зненный.

inapproachable [inə'proutʃəbl] недосту́пный, непристу́пный.

inappropriate [-priit] □ неуме́стный, несоотве́тствующий.

inapt [in'æpt] □ неспосо́бный; неподходя́щий.

inarticulate [inɑ:'tikjulit] □ нечленора́здельный, невня́тный.

inasmuch [inəz'mʌtʃ]: ~ as *adv.* так как; ввиду́ того́, что.

inattentive [inə'tentiv] □ невнима́тельный.

inaugura|te [i'nɔ:gjureit] откры́(ва́)ть (вы́ставку и т. п.); вводи́ть в до́лжность; **~tion** [inɔgju'reiʃən] вступле́ние в до́лжность; (торже́ственное) откры́тие.

inborn ['in'bɔ:n] врождённый; приро́дный.

incalculable [in'kælkjuləbl] □ неисчисли́мый, несчётный; ненадёжный (о челове́ке).

incandescent [inkæn'desnt] раскалённый; кали́льный.

incapa|ble [in'keipəbl] □ неспосо́бный (of к Д *or* на В); **~citate** [inkə'pæsiteit] де́лать неспосо́бным, неприго́дным.

incarnate [in'kɑ:nit] воплощённый; олицетворённый.

incautious [in'kɔ:ʃəs] □ неосторо́жный, опроме́тчивый.

incendiary [in'sendjəri] **1.** поджига́тель *m*; *fig.* подстрека́тель *m*; **2.** зажига́тельный (*a.* ⚔); *fig.* подстрека́ющий.

incense[1] ['insens] ла́дан, фимиа́м.

incense[2] [in'sens] [рас]серди́ть, приводи́ть в я́рость.

incentive [in'sentiv] побуди́тельный моти́в, побужде́ние.

incessant [in'sesnt] □ непреры́вный.

incest ['insest] кровосмеше́ние.

inch [intʃ] дюйм (= 2,54 см); *fig.* пядь *f*; by **~es** мало-пома́лу.

inciden|ce ['insidəns] сфе́ра де́йствия; **~t** [-t] **1.** слу́чай, случа́йность *f*; происше́ствие; **2.** случа́йный; прису́щий (to Д); **~tal** [insi'dentl] □ случа́йный; побо́чный; прису́щий (Д); **~ly** случа́йно; ме́жду про́чим.

incinerate [in'sinəreit] сжига́ть [сжечь]; испепеля́ть [-ли́ть].

incis|e [in'saiz] надре́з(ыв)ать; де́лать надре́з на (П); **~ion** [in'siʒən] разре́з, надре́з; насе́чка; **~ive** [in'saisiv] □ ре́жущий; о́стрый.

incite [in'sait] подстрека́ть [-кну́ть]; побужда́ть [-уди́ть]; **~ment** [-mənt] подстрека́тельство; побужде́ние, сти́мул.

inclement [in'klemənt] суро́вый, холо́дный.

inclin|ation [inkli'neiʃən] накло́н, отко́с; отклоне́ние; накло́нность *f*, скло́нность *f*; **~e** [in'klain] **1.** *v/i.* склоня́ться [-ни́ться]; ~ to *fig.* быть скло́нным к (Д); *v/t.* склоня́ть [-ни́ть] (*a fig.*); располага́ть [-ложи́ть]; **2.** накло́н; скло́нность *f.*

inclose [in'klouz] *s.* enclose.

inclu|de [in'klu:d] заключа́ть [-чи́ть], содержа́ть (в себе́); включа́ть [-чи́ть]; **~sive** [-siv] □ включа́ющий в себя́, содержа́щий.

incoheren|ce [inko'hiərəns] несвя́зность *f*, непосле́довательность; **~t** [-t] □ несвя́зный, непоследовательный.

income ['inkəm] дохо́д.

incommode [inkə'moud] [по]беспоко́ить.

incomparable [in'kɔmpərəbl] несравни́мый; несравне́нный.

incompatible [inkəm'pætəbl] несовмести́мый.

incompetent [in'kɔmpitənt] □ све́дущий, неуме́лый; ⚖ непраспосо́бный.

incomplete [inkəm'pli:t] □ непный; незако́нченный.

incomprehensible [in'kɔm''hensəbl] □ непоня́тный, нестижи́мый. [невообрази́мы

inconceivable [inkən'si:vəbl]

incongruous [in'kɔŋgruəs] □ нме́стный, неле́пый; несовмесмый.

inconsequent(ial) [in'kɔnsikw-'kwenʃəl] □ непосле́довательн

inconsidera|ble [inkən'sidərəbl] незначи́тельный, нева́жный; [-rit] □ неосмотри́тельный; обду́манный; невнима́тельный други́м).

inconsisten|cy [inkən'sistənsi] совмести́мость *f*; **~t** [-tənt] несовмести́мый.

inconstant [in'kɔnstənt] □ непося́нный, неусто́йчивый.

incontinent [in'kɔntinənt] □ сде́ржанный; невозде́ржанны

inconvenien|ce [inkən'vi:njəns] неудо́бство; беспоко́йство; **2.** [п беспоко́ить; **~t** [-njənt] □ неуд ный, затрудни́тельный.

incorporat|e **1.** [in'kɔ:pəreit] о единя́ть(ся) [-ни́ть(ся)]; включ [-чи́ть] (into в В); **2.** [-rit] соенённый, объединённый; **~ed** [-r tid] зарегистри́рованный (об щесте; **~ion** [in'kɔ:pə''reiʃ объедине́ние; регистра́ция.

incorrect [inkə'rekt] □ непра́виный; неиспра́вный.

incorrigible [in'kɔridʒəbl] □ исправи́мый.

increase **1.** [in'kri:s] увели́ч (ва)ть(ся); уси́ли(ва)ть(ся); **2.** [' kri:s] рост; увеличе́ние; приро́

incredible [in'kredəbl] □ невер я́тный.

incredul|ity [inkri'dju:liti] неве́рчивость *f*; **~ous** [in'kredjul □ недове́рчивый, скепти́ческ

incriminate [in'krimineit] ⚖ и кримини́ровать (*im*)*pf.*, обвиня́ в преступле́нии.

incrustation [inkrʌs'teiʃən] ко ко́рка; ⊕ на́кипь *f.*

incub|ate ['inkjubeit] выводи́ [вы́вести] (цыпля́т); **~ator** [-bei инкуба́тор.

inculcate ['inkʌlkeit] внедря́ [-ри́ть], вселя́ть [-ли́ть] (upon

cumbent [inˈkʌmbənt] воз-
бженный, (воз)лежа́щий.
cur [inˈkəː] подверга́ться [-е́рг-
уться] (Д); наде́лать *pf.* (дол-
ов).
curable [inˈkjuərəbl] **1.** неизле-
и́мый; **2.** страда́ющий неизле-
и́мой боле́знью.
curious [inˈkjuəriəs] □ нелюбо-
ытный; невнима́тельный.
cursion [inˈkəːʃən] вторже́ние.
lebted [inˈdetid] в долгу́; *fig.*
бя́занный.
lecen|cy [inˈdiːsnsi] непристо́й-
ость *f*, неприли́чие; **~t** [-snt] □
еприли́чный.
lecisi|on [indiˈsiʒən] нереши́-
льность *f*; колеба́ние; **~ve**
saisiv] □ нереши́тельный; не
ша́ющий.
lecorous [inˈdekərəs] □ некор-
е́ктный; неприли́чный.
leed [inˈdiːd] в са́мом де́ле, дей-
зви́тельно; неуже́ли!
lefensible [indiˈfensəbl] □ не-
ригóдный для оборо́ны; *fig.* не-
остоя́тельный.
lefinite [inˈdefinit] □ неопреде-
е́нный; неограни́ченный.
lelible [inˈdelibl] □ неизглади́-
ый; несмыва́емый.
lelicate [inˈdelikit] □ неделика́т-
ый, нескро́мный.
lemni|fy [inˈdemnifai] возме-
а́ть убы́тки (Р); обезопа́сить *pf.*;
омпенси́ровать (*im*)*pf.*; **~ty** [-ti]
ра́нтия от убы́тков; возмеще́-
е, компенса́ция.
lent [inˈdent] **1.** зазу́бривать
ри́ть]; выреза́ть [вы́резать];
едъявля́ть тре́бование; ✝ за-
зывать това́ры; **2.** тре́бование;
заказ на това́ры; о́рдер; **~ation**
ıdenˈteiʃən] зубе́ц; вы́резка;
ıre [inˈdentʃə] **1.** докуме́нт, кон-
а́кт, догово́р; **2.** обя́зывать до-
во́ром.
lependen|ce [indiˈpendəns] не-
ви́симость *f*, самостоя́тельность
~t [-t] □ незави́симый, само-
оя́тельный.
lescribable [indisˈkraibəbl] □
опису́емый.
lestructible [-ˈstrʌktəbl] □ не-
зруши́мый.
leterminate [indiˈtəːminit] □
определённый; нея́сный.
lex [ˈindeks] **1.** и́ндекс, указа́-
ль *m*; показа́тель *m*; указа́тель-
ый па́лец; **2.** заноси́ть в и́ндекс.
lia [ˈindjə] ʼИндия; ~ rubber
учу́к; рези́на; **~n** [-n] **1.** инди́й-
ий; инде́йский; ~ corn маи́с,
куру́за; **2.** инди́ец, индиа́нка;
ed ~) инде́ец, индиа́нка.
licat|e [ˈindikeit] ука́зывать
а́ть]; предпи́сывать [-са́ть];
on [indiˈkeiʃən] указа́ние.
lict [inˈdait] предъявля́ть обви-
не́ние (for в П); **~ment** [-mənt]
обвини́тельный акт.
indifferen|ce [inˈdifrəns] равно-
ду́шие, безразли́чие; **~t** [-t] □
равноду́шный, беспристра́стный;
незначи́тельный.
indigenous [inˈdidʒinəs] ме́стный,
тузе́мный.
indigent [ˈindidʒənt] □ нужда́ю-
щийся.
indigest|ible [indiˈdʒestəbl] □ неу-
добовари́мый; **~ion** [-tʃən] рас-
стро́йство желу́дка.
indign|ant [inˈdignənt] □ негоду́ю-
щий; **~ation** [indigˈneiʃən] негодо-
ва́ние; **~ity** [inˈdigniti] пренебре-
же́ние, оскорбле́ние.
indirect [indiˈrekt] □ непрямо́й;
око́льный; укло́нчивый.
indiscre|et [indisˈkriːt] □ нескро́м-
ный; неблагоразу́мный; болтли́-
вый; **~tion** [-ˈkreʃən] нескро́мность
f; неосмотри́тельность *f*; болтли́-
вость *f*.
indiscriminate [indisˈkriminit] □
неразбо́рчивый.
indispensable [indisˈpensəbl] □
необходи́мый, обяза́тельный.
indispos|ed [indisˈpouzd] нездоро́-
вый; **~ition** [ˈindispəˈˈziʃən] недо-
мога́ние, нездоро́вье; нерасполо-
же́ние (to к Д).
indistinct [indisˈtiŋkt] □ нея́сный,
неотчётливый; невня́тный.
indite [inˈdait] выража́ть в слова́х;
сочиня́ть [-ни́ть].
individual [indiˈvidjuəl] **1.** □ ли́ч-
ный, индивидуа́льный; характе́р-
ный; отде́льный; **2.** индиви́дуум;
ли́чность *f*; **~ity** [-vidjuˈæliti] ин-
дивидуа́льность *f*.
indivisible [indiˈvizəbl] недели́-
мый.
indolen|ce [ˈindoləns] пра́здность *f*;
вя́лость *f*; **~t** [-t] □ пра́здный;
вя́лый.
indomitable [inˈdɔmitəbl] □ упо́р-
ный; неукроти́мый.
indoor [ˈindɔː] вну́тренний; ко́м-
натный; **~s** [ˈinˈdɔːz] в до́ме, вну-
три́ до́ма.
indorse *s.* endorse.
induce [inˈdjuːs] побужда́ть
[-уди́ть]; вызыва́ть [вы́звать];
~ment [-mənt] побужде́ние.
induct [inˈdʌkt] водворя́ть [-ри́ть];
вводи́ть в до́лжность; **~ion** [in-
ˈdʌkʃən] вступле́ние, введе́ние.
indulge [inˈdʌldʒ] *v/t.* доставля́ть
удово́льствие (Д with T); бало-
ва́ть; потво́рствовать (Д); *v/i.* ~ in
a th. увлека́ться [-е́чься] (T);
пред(ав)а́ться (Д); **~nce** [-əns]
снисхожде́ние; потво́рство; **~nt**
[-ənt] □ снисходи́тельный; по-
тво́рствующий.
industri|al [inˈdʌstriəl] □ про-
мы́шленный; производи́тельный;
~alist [-ist] промы́шленник; **~ous**

[in'dʌstriəs] □ трудолюби́вый, приле́жный.
industry ['indəstri] промы́шленность *f*, инду́стрия; прилежа́ние.
inebriate **1.** [in'i:briit] пья́ный; опьяне́вший; **2.** [-ieeit] опьяня́ть [-ни́ть].
ineffable [in'efəbl] □ невырази́мый.
ineffect|ive [ini'fektiv], **~ual** [-tjuəl] □ безрезульта́тный; недействи́тельный.
inefficient [ini'fiʃənt] □ неспосо́бный, неуме́лый; непроизводи́тельный.
inelegant [in'eligənt] □ грубова́тый, безвку́сный.
inept [i'nept] □ неуме́стный, неподходя́щий; глу́пый.
inequality [ini'kwɔliti] нера́венство; неодина́ковость *f*.
inequitable [in'ekwitəbl] пристра́стный.
inert [i'nə:t] □ ине́ртный; вя́лый; ко́сный; **~ia** [i'nə:ʃiə], **~ness** [i'nə:tnis] ине́рция; вя́лость *f*.
inestimable [in'estiməbl] □ неоцени́мый.
inevitable [in'evitəbl] □ неизбе́жный, немину́емый.
inexact [inig'zækt] □ нето́чный.
inexhaustible [inig'zɔ:stəbl] □ неистощи́мый, неисчерпа́емый.
inexorable [in'eksərəbl] □ неумоли́мый, непрекло́нный.
inexpedient [iniks'pi:diənt] □ нецелесообра́зный.
inexpensive [iniks'pensiv] □ недорого́й, дешёвый.
inexperience [iniks'piəriəns] нео́пытность *f*; **~d** [-t] нео́пытный.
inexpert [ineks'pə:t] □ нео́пытный; неиску́сный, неуме́лый.
inexplicable [in'eksplikəbl] □ необъясни́мый, непоня́тный.
inexpressi|ble [iniks'presəbl] □ невырази́мый, неопису́емый; **~ve** [-siv] □ невырази́тельный.
inextinguishable [iniks'tiŋgwiʃəbl] □ неугаси́мый.
inextricable [in'ekstrikəbl] □ запу́танный; безвы́ходный.
infallible [in'fæləbl] □ безоши́бочный, непогреши́мый.
infam|ous ['infəməs] □ посты́дный, позо́рный, бесче́стный; **~y** [-mi] бесче́стье, позо́р; ни́зость *f*, по́длость *f*.
infan|cy ['infənsi] младе́нчество; **~t** [-t] младе́нец.
infanti|le ['infəntail], **~ne** [-tain] младе́нческий; инфанти́льный.
infantry ['infəntri] ⚔ пехо́та, инфанте́рия.
infatuate [in'fætjueit] вскружи́ть го́лову (Д); увлека́ть [-е́чь].
infect [in'fekt] заража́ть [-рази́ть]; **~ion** [in'fekʃən] инфе́кция, зара́за; зарази́тельность *f*; **~ious** [-ʃəs] □, **~ive** [-tiv] инфекцио́нный, зара[зный]; зарази́тельный.
infer [in'fə:] де́лать вы́вод; по[д]разумева́ть; **~ence** ['infərəns] вы[вод], заключе́ние; подразум[е]ва́емое.
inferior [in'fiəriə] **1.** ни́зший (по чи́ну); ху́дший, неполноце́нны[й]; **2.** подчинённый; **~ity** [in'fiəri'ɔri[ti]] бо́лее ни́зкое ка́чество (положе[ние]), досто́инство); неполноце[н]ность *f*.
infernal [in'fə:nl] □ а́дский.
infertile [in'fə:tail] беспло́дны[й], неплодоро́дный.
infest [in'fest] *fig.* наводня[ть] [-ни́ть]; be **~ed** with кише́ть (Т).
infidelity [infi'deliti] неве́рие; [не]ве́рность *f* (to Д).
infiltrate [in'filtreit] *v/t.* пропу[с]ка́ть сквозь фильтр; *v/i.* прон[и]ка́ть [-и́кнуть]; проса́чивать[ся] [-сочи́ться].
infinit|e ['infinit] □ бесконе́чны[й], безграни́чный; **~y** [in'finiti] бес[ко]не́чность *f*, безграни́чность *f*.
infirm [in'fə:m] □ не́мощны[й], дря́хлый; слабохара́ктерны[й]; **~ary** [-əri] больни́ца; **~ity** [-iti] не́мощь *f*; недоста́ток.
inflame [in'fleim] воспламеня[ть] (-ся) [-ни́ть(ся)]; ⚕ воспаля́ть(ся) [-ли́ть(ся)]; **~ed** [-d] воспалё[н]ный.
inflamma|ble [in'flæməbl] □ во[с]пламеня́ющийся; огнеопа́сны[й]; **~tion** [inflə'meiʃən] воспламе[не]ние; ⚕ воспале́ние; **~tory** [in'fl[æ]mətəri] поджига́тельский; в[о]спали́тельный.
inflat|e [in'fleit] наду́(ва́)ть (га́з[ом], во́здухом); ✝ взду(ва́)ть; **~i[on]** [-ʃən] надува́ние; *fig.* напы́щ[ен]ность *f*; инфля́ция.
inflexi|ble [in'fleksəbl] □ неги́бк[ий], негну́щийся; *fig.* непрекло́нн[ый], непоколеби́мый; **~on** [-ʃən] изг[иб]; модуля́ция.
inflict [in'flikt] налага́ть [-ложи́ть]; наноси́ть [-нести́] (ра́ну и т. [д.]); причиня́ть [-ни́ть] (боль); **~i[on]** [infli'kʃən] наложе́ние и т. д.
influen|ce ['influəns] **1.** влия́н[ие], возде́йствие; **2.** возде́йствов[ать] на (В) (*im*)*pf.*, [по]влия́ть на (В); **~tial** [influ'enʃəl] □ влияте[ль]ный.
influx ['inflʌks] впаде́ние (ри[ч]ка); *fig.* наплы́в, прили́в.
inform [in'fɔ:m] *v/t.* информи́р[о]вать (*im*)*pf.*, уведомля́ть [уве́[до]мить] (of о П); *v/i.* доно[си́ть] [-нести́] (against a p. на В); **~al** □ неофициа́льный; неприну[ж]дённый; **~ality** [infɔ:'mæliti] [не]соблюде́ние форма́льностей; [от]су́тствие церемо́ний; **~ation** [in[fə]'meiʃən] информа́ция, све́де[ния] *n*/*pl.*; спра́вка; осведомле́н[ие]

~ative [in'fɔ:mətiv] информацио́нный.
nfrequent [in'fri:kwənt] □ ре́дкий.
nfringe [in'frindʒ] наруша́ть [-ру́шить] (*a.* ~ upon).
nfuriate [in'fjuərieit] [вз]беси́ть.
nfuse [in'fju:z] ⚕ вли(ва́)ть; *fig.* вселя́ть [-ли́ть]; наста́ивать [настоя́ть] (тра́вы и т. п.).
ngen|ious [in'dʒi:njəs] □ изобрета́тельный; ~uity [indʒi'njuiti] изобрета́тельность *f*; ~uous [in'dʒenjuəs] □ чистосерде́чный; просто́й, бесхи́тростный.
ngot ['iŋgət] сли́ток, брусо́к (мета́лла).
ngratitude [in'grætitju:d] неблагода́рность *f*.
ngredient [in'gri:diənt] составна́я часть *f*, ингредие́нт.
nhabit [in'hæbit] обита́ть, жить в (П); ~ant [-itənt] жи́тель(ница *f*) *m*, обита́тель(ница *f*) *m*.
nhal|ation [inhə'leiʃən] вдыха́ние; ⚕ ингаля́ция; ~e [in'heil] вдыха́ть [вдохну́ть].
nherent [in'hiərənt] □ прису́щий; прирождённый.
nherit [in'herit] насле́довать (*im*)*pf.*; унасле́довать *pf.*; ~ance [-itəns] насле́дство; *biol.* насле́дственность *f*.
nhibit [in'hibit] [вос]препя́тствовать (Д); *biol.* [за]тормози́ть; ~ion [inhi'biʃən] сде́рживание; *biol.* торможе́ние.
nhospitable [in'hɔspitəbl] □ негостеприи́мный.
nhuman [in'hju:mən] □ бесчелове́чный, нечелове́ческий.
nimitable [i'nimitəbl] □ неподража́емый; несравне́нный.
niquity [i'nikwiti] несправедли́вость *f*; беззако́ние.
nitia|l [i'niʃəl] 1. □ нача́льный, первонача́льный; 2. нача́льная бу́ква; ~s *pl.* инициа́лы *m*/*pl.*; ~te 1. [-iit] при́нятый (в о́бщество), посвящённый (в та́йну); 2. [-ieit] вводи́ть [ввести́]; посвяща́ть [-вяти́ть]; положи́ть нача́ло (Д); ~tive [i'niʃiətiv] инициати́ва, почи́н; ~tor [-ieitə] инициа́тор.
nject [in'dʒekt] впры́скивать [-снуть].
njunction [in'dʒʌŋkʃən] прика́з; постановле́ние суда́.
njur|e ['indʒə] [по]вреди́ть по-; вреди́ть [-еди́ть]; ра́нить (*im*)*pf.*; ~ious [in'dʒuəriəs] □ вре́дный; оскорби́тельный; ~y ['indʒəri] оскорбле́ние; поврежде́ние, ра́на.
njustice [in'dʒʌstis] несправедли́вость *f*.
nk [iŋk] 1. черни́ла *n*/*pl.*; (*mst* printer's ~) типогра́фская кра́ска; 2. ме́тить черни́лами; сади́ть кля́ксы на (В).

inkling ['iŋkliŋ] намёк (of на В); подозре́ние.
ink|pot черни́льница; ~stand пи́сьменный прибо́р; ~y ['iŋki] черни́льный.
inland ['inlənd] 1. вну́тренняя террито́рия страны́; 2. вну́тренний; 3. [in'lænd] внутрь, внутри́ (страны́).
inlay [in'lei] 1. [*irr.* (lay)] вкла́дывать [вложи́ть]; выстила́ть [вы́стлать]; покрыва́ть моза́икой; 2. ['in'lei] моза́ика, инкруста́ция.
inlet ['inlet] у́зкий зали́в, бу́хта; входно́е (*or* вво́дное) отве́рстие.
inmate ['inmeit] сожи́тель(ница *f*) *m* (по ко́мнате).
inmost ['inmoust] глубоча́йший, сокрове́нный.
inn [in] гости́ница.
innate ['in'neit] □ врождённый. приро́дный.
inner ['inə] вну́тренний; ~most [-moust] *s.* inmost.
innings ['iniŋz] о́чередь пода́чи мяча́.
innkeeper хозя́ин гости́ницы.
innocen|ce ['inosns] ⚖ невино́вность *f*; неви́нность *f*; простота́; ~t [-snt] 1. □ неви́нный; ⚖ невино́вный; 2. проста́к, наи́вный челове́к.
innocuous [i'nɔkjuəs] □ безвре́дный, безоби́дный.
innovation [ino'veiʃən] нововведе́ние, но́вшество; нова́торство.
innuendo [inju'endou] ко́свенный намёк, инсинуа́ция.
innumerable [in'ju:mərəbl] □ бессчётный, бесчи́сленный.
inoculate [i'nɔkjuleit] де́лать приви́вку (Д), приви́(ва́)ть; *fig.* внуша́ть [-ши́ть].
inoffensive [inə'fensiv] безоби́дный, безвре́дный.
inoperative [in'ɔpərətiv] безде́ятельный; неде́йствующий.
inopportune [in'ɔpətju:n] □ несвоевре́менный, неподходя́щий.
inordinate [i'nɔ:dinit] □ неуме́ренный, чрезме́рный.
inquest ['inkwest] ⚖ сле́дствие, дозна́ние; coroner's ~ суде́бный осмо́тр тру́па.
inquir|e [in'kwaiə] узн(ав)а́ть; наводи́ть спра́вки (about, after, for о П; of у Р); ~ into иссле́довать (*im*)*pf*; ~ing [-riŋ] □ пытли́вый; ~y [-ri] спра́вка; рассле́дование, сле́дствие.
inquisit|ion [inkwi'ziʃən] рассле́дование; ~ive [in'kwizitiv] □ любозна́тельный; лыбопы́тный.
inroad ['inroud] набе́г, наше́ствие; *fig.* посяга́тельство.
insan|e [in'sein] □ душевнобольно́й; безу́мный; ~ity [in'sæniti] умопомеша́тельство; безу́мие.

insatia|ble [in'seiʃiəbl] □, **~te** [-ʃiət] ненасы́тный, жа́дный.
inscribe [in'skraib] впи́сывать [-са́ть]; надпи́сывать [-са́ть] (in, on В/Т *or* В на П); посвяща́ть [-яти́ть] (кни́гу).
inscription [in'skripʃən] на́дпись *f*; посвяще́ние (кни́ги).
inscrutable [ins'kru:təbl] □ непостижи́мый, зага́дочный.
insect ['insekt] насеко́мое; **~icide** [in'sektisaid] сре́дство для истребле́ния насеко́мых.
insecure [insi'kjuə] □ ненадёжный; небезопа́сный.
insens|ate [in'senseit] бесчу́вственный; бессмы́сленный; **~ible** [-əbl] □ нечувстви́тельный; потеря́вший созна́ние; незаме́тный; **~itive** [-itiv] нечувстви́тельный.
inseparable [in'sepərəbl] □ неразлу́чный; неотдели́мый.
insert 1. [in'sə:t] вставля́ть [-а́вить]; помеща́ть [-ести́ть] (в газе́те); **2.** ['insə:t] вста́вка, вкла́дыш; **~ion** [in'sə:ʃən] вста́вка; объявле́ние.
inside ['in'said] **1.** вну́тренняя сторона́; вну́тренность *f*; изна́нка (оде́жды); **2.** *adj.* вну́тренний; **3.** *adv.* внутрь, внутри́; **4.** *prp.* внутри́ (Р).
insidious [in'sidiəs] □ хи́трый, кова́рный.
insight ['insait] проница́тельность *f*; интуи́ция.
insignia [in'signiə] *pl.* зна́ки отли́чия; значки́ *m/pl.*
insignificant [insig'nifikənt] незначи́тельный.
insincere [insin'siə] неи́скренний.
insinuat|e [in'sinjueit] инсинуи́ровать *(im)pf.*; намека́ть [-кну́ть] на (В); ~ o. s. *fig.* вкра́дываться [вкра́сться]; **~ion** [in'sinju''eiʃən] инсинуа́ция; вкра́дчивость *f*.
insipid [in'sipid] безвку́сный, пре́сный.
insist [in'sist] ~ (up)on: наста́ивать [-сто́ять] на (П), утвержда́ть (В); **~ence** [-əns] насто́йчивость *f*; **~ent** [-ənt] □ насто́йчивый.
insolent ['insələnt] □ на́глый.
insoluble [in'sɔljubl] нераствори́мый; неразреши́мый.
insolvent [in'sɔlvənt] несостоя́тельный (должни́к).
inspect [in'spekt] осма́тривать [осмотре́ть]; инспекти́ровать; **~ion** [in'spekʃən] осмо́тр; инспе́кция.
inspir|ation [inspə'reiʃən] вдыха́ние; вдохнове́ние; воодушевле́ние; **~e** [in'spaiə] вдыха́ть [вдохну́ть]; *fig.* вдохновля́ть [-ви́ть].
install [in'stɔ:l] устана́вливать [-нови́ть]; вводи́ть в до́лжность; ⊕ [с]монти́ровать; **~ation** [instɔ:'leiʃən] устано́вка; устро́йство.
instalment [in'stɔ:lmənt] очередно́й взнос (при рассро́чке); о[…] де́льный вы́пуск (кни́ги).
instance ['instəns] слу́чай; приме́[р] тре́бование; ⚖ инста́нция; for ~ наприме́р.
instant ['instənt] □ **1.** неме́длен[]ный, безотлага́тельный; on th[e] 10th ~ 10-го теку́щего ме́сяца; [2.] мгнове́ние, моме́нт; **~aneou[s]** [instən'teinjəs] □ мгнове́нны[й]; **~ly** ['instəntli] неме́дленно, то́тча[с].
instead [in'sted] взаме́н, вме́ст[о]; ~ of вме́сто (Р).
instep ['instep] подъём (ноги́).
instigat|e ['instigeit] побужда́[ть] [-уди́ть]; подстрека́ть [-кну́ть]; **~or** [-ə] подстрека́тель(ница *f*) *m*.
instil(l) [in'stil] влива́ть по ка́пл[е]; *fig.* внуша́ть [-ши́ть] (into Д).
instinct ['instiŋkt] инсти́нкт; **~iv[e]** [in'stiŋktiv] □ инстинкти́вный.
institut|e ['institju:t] нау́чн[ое] учрежде́ние, институ́т; **2.** учреж[]да́ть [-еди́ть]; устана́вливать [-но[]ви́ть]; **~ion** [insti'tju:ʃən] устано[в]ле́ние; учрежде́ние, заведе́ние.
instruct [in'strʌkt] [на]учи́т[ь], обуча́ть [-чи́ть]; инструкти́роват[ь] *(im)pf.*; **~ion** [in'strʌkʃən] обуч[е]ние; предписа́ние; инстру́кци[я]; **~ive** [-tiv] □ поучи́тельный; **~o[r]** [-tə] руководи́тель *m*, инстру́кто[р], преподава́тель *m*.
instrument ['instrumənt] инстру[]ме́нт; ору́дие (*a. fig.*); прибо́[р], аппара́т; ⚖ докуме́нт; **~al** [instru]'mentl] □ слу́жащий сре́дство[м]; инструмента́льный; **~ality** [-men]'tæliti] сре́дство, спо́соб.
insubordinate [insə'bɔ:dnit] н[е]подчиня́ющийся дисципли́не.
insufferable [in'sʌfərəbl] □ невы[]носи́мый, нестерпи́мый.
insufficient [insə'fiʃənt] недост[а]то́чный.
insula|r ['insjulə] □ островно́[й]; *fig.* за́мкнутый; **~te** [-leit] ⚡ изо[]ли́ровать *(im)pf.*; **~tion** [insju]'leiʃən] ⚡ изоля́ция.
insult 1. ['insʌlt] оскорбле́ние; [2.] [in'sʌlt] оскорбля́ть [-би́ть].
insur|ance [in'ʃuərəns] страхова[]ние; *attr.* страхово́й; **~e** [in'ʃu[ə]] [за]страхова́ть(ся).
insurgent [in'sə:dʒənt] **1.** мятё[ж]ный; **2.** повста́нец; мятё́жник.
insurmountable [insə'mauntabl] [□] непреодоли́мый.
insurrection [insə'rekʃən] восст[а]ние; мяте́ж.
intact [in'tækt] нетро́нутый; н[е]повреждённый.
intangible [in'tændʒəbl] □ неос[я]за́емый; *fig.* неуловимый.
integ|ral ['intigrəl] □ неотъе́мле[]мый; це́лый; це́лостный; **~rat[e]** [-greit] объединя́ть [-ни́ть]; инте[]гри́ровать *(im)pf.*; **~rity** [in'tegrit[y]] че́стность *f*; це́лостность *f*.

:ellect ['intilekt] ум, рассу́док; **ual** [inti'lektjuəl] **1.** □ интеллек-у́альный, у́мственный; **2.** интел-иге́нт(ка); ~s *pl.* интеллиге́нция.
:elligence [in'telidʒəns] ум, рас-у́док, интелле́кт; Intelligence ervice разве́дывательная слу́жба, азве́дка.
:ellig|ent [in'telidʒənt] □ у́мный; мышлённый; **~ible** [-dʒəbl] □ оня́тный.
:emperance [in'tempərəns] неу-е́ренность *f*; невозде́рж(ан)-ость *f*; пристра́стие к спиртны́м апи́ткам.
:end [in'tend] намерева́ться; ме́ть в виду́; ~ for предназнача́ть зна́чить] для (Р).
:ense [in'tens] □ си́льный; ин-енси́вный, напряжённый.
:ensify [in'tensifai] уси́ли(ва)ть ся); интенсифици́ровать (*im*)*pf*.
:ensity [in'tensiti] интенси́вность си́ла; я́ркость *f* (кра́ски).
:ent [in'tent] **1.** □ стремя́щийся, кло́нный (on к Д); внима́тель-ый, при́стальный; **2.** наме́рение, ель *f*; to all ~s and purposes в у́щности; во всех отноше́ниях; **ion** [in'tenʃən] наме́рение; **~ional** l] □ наме́ренный, умы́шленный.
:er [in'tə:] предава́ть земле́, [по-] орони́ть.
:er... ['intə] *pref.* меж..., между...; ере...; взаимо...
:eract [intər'ækt] де́йствовать руг на дру́га, взаимоде́йствовать.
:ercede [intə'si:d] хода́тайство-ать.
:ercept [-'sept] перехва́тывать хвати́ть]; пре(ы)ва́ть; прегра-а́ть путь (Д); **~ion** [-pʃən] пере-ва́т(ывание); пересече́ние.
:ercess|ion [intə'seʃən] хода́-а́йство, засту́пничество; **~or** [-sə] ода́тай, засту́пник.
:erchange **1.** [intə'tʃeindʒ] *v/t.* ередова́ть; обме́ниваться [-ня́ть-я] (Т); *v/i.* чередова́ться; **2.** intə'tʃeindʒ] обме́н; чередова́ние, ме́на.
:ercourse ['intəkɔ:s] обще́ние, вязь *f*; отноше́ния *n/pl.*; сноше́-ия *n/pl.*
:erdict **1.** [intə'dikt] запреща́ть рети́ть]; лиша́ть пра́ва по́льзо-ания; **2.** ['intədikt], **~ion** [intə-ikʃən] запреще́ние.
:erest ['intrist] **1.** *com.* интере́с; интересо́ванность *f* (in в П); ы́года; проце́нты *m/pl.* (на капи-а́л); **2.** *com.* интересова́ть; заинте-есо́вывать [-сова́ть]; **~ing** [-iŋ]] интере́сный.
:erfere [intə'fiə] вме́шиваться ша́ться]; [по]меша́ть, надоеда́ть е́сть] (with Д); **~nce** [-rəns] меша́тельство; поме́ха.
:erim ['intərim] **1.** промежу́ток вре́мени; **2.** вре́менный, проме-жу́точный.
interior [in'tiəriə] **1.** □ вну́трен-ний; **2.** вну́тренность *f*; вну́трен-ние о́бласти страны́; *pol.* вну́трен-ние дела́ *n/pl.*
interjection [intə'dʒekʃən] воскли-ца́ние; *gr.* междоме́тие.
interlace [intəl'eis] переплета́ть(ся) [-плести́(сь)].
interlock [intə'lɔk] сцепля́ть(ся) [-пи́ть(ся)].
interlocut|ion [intəlo'kju:ʃən] бесе́-да, диало́г; **~or** [intə'lɔkjutə] со-бесе́дник.
interlope [intə'loup] вме́шиваться [-ша́ться]; **~r** [-ə] вме́шивающий-ся в чужи́е дела́.
interlude ['intəlu:d] антра́кт; про-межу́точный эпизо́д.
intermeddle [intə'medl] вме́ши-ваться [-ша́ться] (with, in в В); сова́ться не в своё де́ло.
intermedia|ry [-'mi:diəri] **1.** = intermediate; посре́днический; **2.** посре́дник; **~te** [-'mi:djət] □ про-межу́точный; сре́дний.
interment [in'tə:mənt] погребе́ние.
interminable [in'tə:minəbl] □ бесконе́чный.
intermingle [intə'miŋgl] сме́ши-вать(ся) [-ша́ть(ся)]; обща́ться.
intermission [-'miʃən] переры́в, па́уза, переме́на (в шко́ле).
intermit [intə'mit] пре(ы)ва́ть (-ся); **~tent** [-ənt] □ преры́вистый; перемежа́ющийся.
intermix [intə'miks] переме́ши-вать(ся) [-ша́ть(ся)].
intern [in'tə:n] интерни́ровать (*im*)*pf*.
internal [in'tə:nl] □ вну́тренний.
international [intə'næʃnl] □ меж-дунаро́дный, интернациона́ль-ный; ~ law междунаро́дное пра́во.
interpolate [in'tə:poleit] интерпо-ли́ровать (*im*)*pf*.
interpose [intə'pouz] *v/t.* встав-ля́ть [-а́вить], вводи́ть [ввести́]; *v/i.* станови́ться [стать] (between ме́жду Т); вме́шиваться [-ша́ть-ся] (в В).
interpret [in'tə:prit] объясня́ть [-ни́ть], растолко́вывать [-ко-ва́ть]; переводи́ть [-вести́] (у́стно); **~ation** [-''eiʃən] толкова́ние, ин-терпрета́ция, объясне́ние; **~er** [-ə] перево́дчик (-ица).
interrogat|e [in'terogeit] допра́ши-вать [-роси́ть]; спра́шивать [спро-си́ть]; **~ion** [-''geiʃən] допро́с; вопро́с; **~ive** [intə'rɔgətiv] □ вопроси́тельный.
interrupt [intə'rʌpt] пре(ы)ва́ть; **~ion** [-'rʌpʃən] переры́в.
intersect [intə'sekt] пересека́ть(ся) [-се́чь(ся)]; скре́щивать(ся) [-ес-ти́ть(ся)]; **~ion** [-kʃən] пере-сече́ние.

intersperse [intəˈspəːs] разбра́сывать [-броса́ть], рассыпа́ть [-ы́пать]; усе́ивать [усе́ять].
intertwine [intəˈtwain] сплета́ть (-ся) [-ести́(сь)].
interval [ˈintəvəl] промежу́ток, расстоя́ние, интерва́л; па́уза, переме́на.
interven|e [intəˈviːn] вме́шиваться [-ша́ться]; вступа́ться [-пи́ться]; **~tion** [-ˈvenʃən] интерве́нция; вмеша́тельство.
interview [ˈintəvjuː] **1.** свида́ние, встре́ча; интервью́ *n indecl.*; **2.** интервьюи́ровать *(im)pf.*, име́ть бесе́ду с (Т).
intestine [inˈtestin] **1.** вну́тренний; **2.** кишка́; **~s** *pl.* кишки́ *f/pl.*, кише́чник.
intima|cy [ˈintiməsi] инти́мность *f*, бли́зость *f*; **~te 1.** [-meit] сообща́ть [-щи́ть]; намека́ть [-кну́ть] на (В); **2.** [-mit] a) □ инти́мный, ли́чный; бли́зкий; b) бли́зкий друг; **~tion** [intiˈmeiʃən] сообще́ние; намёк.
intimidate [inˈtimideit] [ис]пуга́ть; запу́гивать [-га́ть].
into [ˈintu, intə] *prp.* в, во (В).
intolera|ble [inˈtɔlərəbl] □ невыноси́мый, нестерпи́мый; **~nt** [-rənt] □ нетерпи́мый.
intonation [intouˈneiʃən] интона́ция.
intoxica|nt [inˈtɔksikənt] опьяня́ющий (напи́ток); **~te** [-keit] опьяня́ть [-ни́ть]; **~tion** [-ˈˈkeiʃən] опьяне́ние.
intractable [inˈtræktəbl] □ непода́тливый.
intrepid [inˈtrepid] неустраши́мый, бесстра́шный, отва́жный.
intricate [ˈintrikit] □ сло́жный, затрудни́тельный.
intrigue [inˈtriːg] **1.** интри́га; любо́вная связь *f*; **2.** интригова́ть; [за]интригова́ть, [за]интересова́ть; **~r** [-ə] интрига́н(ка).
intrinsic(al □) [inˈtrinsik, -sikəl] вну́тренний; сво́йственный; суще́ственный.
introduc|e [intrəˈdjuːs] вводи́ть [ввести́]; представля́ть [-а́вить]; **~tion** [-ˈdʌkʃən] введе́ние; представле́ние; ♪ интроду́кция; **~tory** [-ˈdʌktəri] вступи́тельный, вво́дный.
intru|de [inˈtruːd] вторга́ться [вто́ргнуться]; навя́зываться [-за́ться]; **~der** [-ə] проны́ра *m/f*; незва́ный гость *m*; **~sion** [-ʒən] вторже́ние; появле́ние без приглаше́ния; **~sive** [-siv] □ назо́йливый, навя́зчивый.
intrust [inˈtrʌst] *s.* entrust.
intuition [intjuˈiʃən] интуи́ция.
inundate [ˈinʌndeit] затопля́ть [-пи́ть], наводня́ть [-ни́ть].
inure [iˈnjuə] приуча́ть [-чи́ть] (to к Д).

invade [inˈveid] вторга́ться [вто́р-нуться]; *fig.* овладе́(ва́)ть (Т); [-ə] захва́тчик, интерве́нт.
invalid 1. [inˈvælid] недействите-ный, не име́ющий зако́нной си́л **2.** [ˈinvəliːd] a) нетрудоспосо́бн b) инвали́д; **~ate** [inˈvælid лиша́ть зако́нной си́лы, сде́л недействи́тельным.
invaluable [inˈvæljuəbl] □ нео ни́мый.
invariable [inˈvɛəriəbl] □ не ме́нный; неизменя́емый.
invasion [inˈveiʒən] вторже́н набе́г; ⚖ посяга́тельство; инва́зия.
inveigh [inˈvei]: **~** against поноси́ [об]руга́ть (В).
invent [inˈvent] изобрета́ть [-б сти́]; выду́мывать [вы́думат **~ion** [inˈvenʃən] изобрете́ние; и бретáтельность *f*; **~ive** [-tiv] изобрета́тельный; **~or** [-tə] и брета́тель *m*; **~ory** [ˈinvəntri] о́пись *f*, инвента́рь *m*; *Am.* пер чёт това́ра, инвентариза́ция; составля́ть о́пись (Р); вноси́т инвента́рь.
inverse [ˈinvəːs] □ перевёрнут обра́тный.
invert [inˈvəːt] перевёртыв [переверну́ть], переставл [-а́вить].
invest [inˈvest] вкла́дывать [в жи́ть] (капита́л); *fig.* облек [обле́чь] (with Т); ⚔ обложи́ть (кре́пость).
investigat|e [inˈvestigeit] рассле́ вать *(im)pf.*; разузн(ав)а́ть; исс дова́ть *(im)pf.* **~ion** [investiˈgeiʃ ⚖ сле́дствие; иссле́дование; [inˈvestigeitə] иссле́дователь ⚖ сле́дователь *m*.
invest|ment [inˈvestmənt] влож ние де́нег, инвести́рован вклад; **~or** [-ə] вкла́дчик.
inveterate [inˈvetərit] зако не́лый; F зая́длый; застаре́лы
invidious [inˈvidiəs] □ вызыва щий вражде́бное чу́вство; не ви́стный; зави́дный.
invigorate [inˈvigəreit] дав си́лы (Д); воодушевля́ть [-ви
invincible [inˈvinsəbl] □ непо ди́мый.
inviola|ble [inˈvaiələbl] □ не ши́мый; неприкоснове́нный; [-lit] ненару́шенный.
invisible [inˈvizəbl] неви́дим
invit|ation [inviˈteiʃən] приглаш ние; **~e** [inˈvait] приглаш [-ласи́ть].
invoice [ˈinvɔis] ✝ накладн факту́ра.
invoke [inˈvouk] вызыва́ть [в зва́ть] (ду́ха); взыва́ть [воззва о (П); приз(ы)ва́ть.
involuntary [inˈvɔləntəri] □ во́льный; непроизво́льный.

involve [in'vɔlv] включáть в себя́; вовлекáть [-éчь]; впу́т(ыв)ать.
invulnerable [in'vʌlnərəbl] □ неуязви́мый.
inward ['inwəd] **1.** вну́тренний; умственный; **2.** *adv.* (*mst* ~s [-z]) внутрь; вну́тренне; **3.** ~s *pl.* вну́тренности *f/pl.*
inwrought ['in'rɔ:t] во́тканный в матéрию (об узо́ре); *fig.* тéсно свя́занный (with с Т).
iodine ['aiədi:n] йод.
IOU ['aiou'ju:] (= I owe you) долгова́я распи́ска.
irascible [i'ræsibl] □ раздражи́тельный.
irate [ai'reit] гнéвный.
iridescent [iri'desnt] ра́дужный, перели́вчатый.
iris ['aiəris] *anat.* ра́дужная оболо́чка (глáза); ⚘ и́рис, каса́тик.
Irish ['aiəriʃ] **1.** ирла́ндский; **2.** the ~ ирла́ндцы *m/pl.*
irksome ['ə:ksəm] утоми́тельный, ску́чный.
iron ['aiən] **1.** желéзо; (*mst* flat-~) утю́г; ~s *pl.* око́вы *f/pl.*, кандалы́ *m/pl.*; **2.** желéзный; **3.** [вы́]утю́жить, [вы́]гла́дить; ~**clad** **1.** покры́тый бронёй, бронирóванный; **2.** броненóсец; ~**-hearted** *fig.* жестокосéрдный.
ironic(**al** □) [aiə'rɔnik, -nikəl] ирони́ческий.
iron|ing ['aiəniŋ] **1.** гла́женье; вéщи для гла́женья; **2.** глади́льный; ~**mongery** скобяно́й товáр; ~**mould** ржа́вое пятно́; ~**works** *mst sg.* чугуноплави́льный и́ли железодéлательный заво́д.
irony ['aiərəni] иро́ния.
irradiate [i'reidieit] озаря́ть [-ри́ть]; ⚕ облуча́ть [-чи́ть]; *phys.* испуска́ть лучи́; *fig.* распространя́ть [-ни́ть] (зна́ния и т. п.); проливáть свет на (В).
irrational [i'ræʃnl] неразу́мный; ⅟ иррациона́льный.
irreconcilable [i'rekənsailəbl] □ непримири́мый; несовмести́мый.
irrecoverable [iri'kʌvərəbl] □ непоправи́мый, невозвра́тный.
irredeemable [iri'di:məbl] □ невозвра́тимый; безысхо́дный; не подлежа́щий вы́купу.
irrefutable [i'refjutəbl] □ неопровержи́мый.
irregular [i'regjulə] □ непра́вильный (*a. gr.*); беспоря́дочный; нерегуля́рный.
irrelevant [i'relivənt] □ не относя́щийся к дéлу; неумéстный.
irreligious [iri'lidʒəs] □ нерелигио́зный; невéрующий.
irremediable [iri'mi:diəbl] □ непоправи́мый; неизлечи́мый.
irreparable [i'repərəbl] □ непоправи́мый.
irreproachable [iri'proutʃəbl] □ безукори́зненный, безупрéчный.
irresistible [iri'zistəbl] □ неотрази́мый; непреодоли́мый (о жела́нии и т. п.).
irresolute [i'rezəlu:t] □ нереши́тельный.
irrespective [iris'pektiv] □ безотноси́тельный (of к Д); независи́мый (of от Р).
irresponsible [iris'pɔnsəbl] □ безотвéтственный; невменя́емый.
irreverent [i'revərənt] □ непочти́тельный.
irrevocable [i'revəkəbl] □ безвозвра́тный.
irrigate ['irigeit] ороша́ть [ороси́ть].
irrita|ble ['iritəbl] □ раздражи́тельный; болéзненно чувстви́тельный; ~**nt** [-tənt] раздража́ющее срéдство; ~**te** [-teit] раздража́ть [-жи́ть]; ~**tion** [iri'teiʃən] раздражéние.
irruption [i'rʌpʃən] набéг, нашéствие.
is [iz] 3. *p. sg. pres.* от be.
island ['ailənd] о́стров; ~**er** [-ə] островитя́нин (-тя́нка).
isle [ail] о́стров; ~**t** [ai'lit] острово́к.
isolat|e ['aisəleit] изоли́ровать; (*im*)*pf.*, отделя́ть [-ли́ть]; ~**ion** [aisə'leiʃən] изоли́рование.
issue ['isju:] **1.** вытека́ние, излия́ние; вы́ход; пото́мство; спо́рный вопро́с; вы́пуск, изда́ние; исхо́д, результа́т; ~ in law разногла́сие о пра́вильности применéния зако́на; be at ~ быть в разногла́сии; быть предмéтом спо́ра; point at ~ предмéт обсуждéния; **2.** *v/i.* исходи́ть [изойти́] (from из Р); вытека́ть [вы́течь] (from из Р); происходи́ть [произойти́] (from от Р); *v/t.* выпуска́ть [вы́пустить], изд(ав)а́ть.
isthmus ['isməs] перешéек.
it [it] *pron. pers.* он, она́, оно́; э́то.
Italian [i'tæljən] **1.** италья́нский; **2.** италья́нец (-нка); **3.** италья́нский язы́к.
italics [i'tæliks] *typ.* курси́в.
itch [itʃ] **1.** ⚕ чесо́тка; зуд; **2.** чеса́ться, зудéть; be ~ing to *inf* горéть жела́нием (+ *inf.*).
item ['aitem] **1.** пункт, пара́граф; вопро́с (на повéстке); но́мер (програ́ммы); **2.** *adv.* та́кже, то́же; ~**ize** ['aitəmaiz] *part. Am.* перечисля́ть по пу́нктам.
iterate ['itəreit] повторя́ть [-ри́ть].
itinerary [i'tinərəri, ai't-] маршру́т, путь *m*; путеводи́тель *m*.
its [its] *pron. poss.* от it его́, её, свой.
itself [it'self] (сам *m*, сама́ *f.*) само́ *n*; себя́, -ся, -сь; себé; in ~ само́ по себé; by ~ само́ собо́й; отдéльно.
ivory ['aivəri] слоно́вая кость *f*.
ivy ['aivi] ⚘ плющ.

J

jab [dʒæb] F **1.** толкáть [-кнýть]; тыкать [ткнуть]; пырять [-рнýть]; **2.** толчóк, пинóк, (кóлющий) удáр.
jabber ['dʒæbə] болтáть, таратóрить.
jack [dʒæk] **1.** пáрень *m*; валéт (кáрта); ⊕ домкрáт; ⚓ матрóс; флаг, гюйс; **2.** поднимáть домкрáтом; *Am. sl.* повышáть [-ы́сить] (цéны); **~ass** осёл; дурáк.
jacket ['dʒækit] жакéт; кýртка; ⊕ чехóл, кожýх.
jack|-knife складнóй нож; **~-of--all-trades** на все рýки мáстер.
jade [dʒeid] клячa; *contp.* шлю́ха; неря́ха.
jag [dʒæg] зубéц; зазýбрина; дырá, прорéха; **~ged** ['dʒægid], **~gy** [-i] зубчáтый; зазýбренный.
jail [dʒeil] тюрьмá; тюрéмное заключéние; **~er** ['dʒeilə] тюрéмщик.
jam[1] [dzæm] варéнье.
jam[2] [~] **1.** сжáтие, сжимáние; ⊕ перебóй; traffic ~ затóр в ýличном движéнии; *Am.* be in a ~ быть в затруднúтельном положéнии; **2.** заж(им)áть; защемля́ть [-мúть]; набивáть биткóм; загромождáть [-моздúть]; глушúть (радиопередáчи).
jangle ['dʒæŋgl] издавáть рéзкие звýки; нестрóйно звучáть.
janitor ['dʒænitə] швейцáр; двóрник.
January ['dʒænjuəri] янвáрь *m*.
Japanese [dʒæpə'ni:z] **1.** япóнский; **2.** япóнец (-нка); the ~ *pl.* япóнцы *pl.*
jar [dʒɑ:] **1.** кувшúн; бáнка; ссóра; неприя́тный, рéзкий звук; дребезжáние; **2.** [за]дребезжáть; [по-]корóбить; дисгармонúровать.
jaundice ['dʒɔ:ndis] ⚕ желтýха; жёлчность *f*; *fig.* зáвисть *f*; **~d** [-t] желтýшный; *fig.* завúстливый.
jaunt [dʒɔ:nt] **1.** увеселúтельная поéздка, прогýлка; **2.** предпринимáть увеселúтельную поéздку и т. п.; **~y** ['dʒɔ:nti] □ весёлый, бóйкий.
javelin ['dʒævlin] копьё.
jaw [dʒɔ:] чéлюсть *f*; **~s** *pl.* рот, пасть *f*; ⊕ *mst pl.* губá (клещéй); **~-bone** челюстнáя кость *f*.
jealous ['dʒeləs] □ ревнúвый; завúстливый; **~y** [-i] рéвность *f*; зáвисть *f*.
jeep [dʒi:p] *Am.* ⚔ джип.
jeer [dʒiə] **1.** насмéшка, глумлéние; **2.** насмехáться [-еяться], [по]глумúться (at над Т).
jejune [dʒi'dʒu:n] □ прéсный; пустóй, неинтерéсный.
jelly ['dʒeli] **1.** желé *n indecl.*; студень *m*; **2.** засты́(вá)ть; **~-fish** медýза.
jeopardize ['dʒepədaiz] подвергáть опáсности.
jerk [dʒə:k] **1.** рывóк; толчóк; подёргивание (мýскула); **2.** рéзко толкáть или дёргать; двúгаться толчкáми; **~y** ['dʒə:ki] □ отрывистый; **~ily** *adv.* рывкáми.
jersey ['dʒə:zi] фуфáйка; вя́заный жакéт.
jest [dʒest] **1.** шýтка; насмéшка; **2.** [по]шутúть; насмéшничать; **~er** ['dʒestə] шутнúк (-úца); шут.
jet [dʒet] **1.** струя́ (воды́, гáза и т. п.); ⊕ жиклёр, форсýнка; *attr.* реактúвный; **2.** бить струёй; выпускáть струёй.
jetty ['dʒeti] ⚓ прúстань *f*; мол; дáмба.
Jew [dʒu:] еврéй; *attr.* еврéйский.
jewel ['dʒu:əl] драгоцéнный кáмень *m*; **~(l)er** [-ə] ювелúр; **~(le)ry** [-ri] драгоцéнности *f/pl.*
Jew|ess ['dʒu:is] еврéйка; **~ish** [-iʃ] еврéйский.
jib [dʒib] ⚓ клúвер.
jiffy ['dʒifi] F миг, мгновéние.
jig-saw *Am.* машúнная ножóвка; ~ puzzle составнáя картúнка-загáдка.
jilt [dʒilt] **1.** кокéтка, обмáнщица; **2.** увлéчь и обманýть (о жéнщине).
jingle ['dʒiŋgl] **1.** звон, звя́канье; **2.** [за]звенéть, звя́кать [-кнуть].
job [dʒɔb] **1.** рабóта, труд; дéло; задáние; by the ~ сдéльно, поурóчно; ~ lot вéщи кýпленные гуртóм по дешёвке; ~ work сдéльная рабóта; **2.** *v/t.* брать (давáть) внаём; *v/i.* рабóтать поштýчно, сдéльно; быть мáклером; **~ber** ['dʒɔbə] занимáющийся случáйной рабóтой; сдéльщик; мáклер; спекуля́нт.
jockey ['dʒɔki] **1.** жокéй; **2.** обманывать [-нýть], надý(вá)ть.
jocose [dʒə'kous] шутлúвый, игрúвый.
jocular ['dʒɔkjulə] шутлúвый; юмористúческий.
jocund ['dʒɔkənd] □ весёлый; живóй; приятный.
jog [dʒɔg] **1.** толчóк; тря́ская езда; мéдленная ходьбá; **2.** *v/t.* толкáть [-кнýть]; *v/i.* (*mst* ~ along,) éхать подпры́гивая, трястúсь.
join [dʒɔin] **1.** *v/t.* соединя́ть [-нúть], присоединя́ть [-нúть]; присоединя́ться [-нúться] к (Д); войтú в компáнию (Р); вступúть в члéны (Р); ~ battle вступáть в бой; ~ hands объединя́ться [-нúться]; брáться зá руки; *v/i.*

соединя́ться [-ни́ться]; объединя́ться [-ни́ться]; ~ in with присоединя́ться [-ни́ться] к (Д); ~ up вступа́ть в а́рмию; **2.** соедине́ние; то́чка (ли́ния, пло́скость) соедине́ния.

joiner ['dʒɔinə] столя́р; **~y** [-ri] столя́рничество.

joint [dʒɔint] **1.** ме́сто соедине́ния; *anat.* суста́в; ♀ у́зел; кусо́к мя́са для жа́рения; put out of ~ вы́вихивать [вы́вихнуть]; **2.** □ соединённый; о́бщий; ~ heir сонасле́дник; **3.** соединя́ть [-ни́ть]; расчленя́ть [-ни́ть]; **~-stock** акционе́рый капита́л; ~ company акционе́рное о́бщество.

jok|e [dʒouk] **1.** шу́тка, острота́; **2.** *v/i.* [по]шути́ть; *v/t.* поддра́знивать [-ни́ть], **~er** ['dʒoukə] шутни́к (-и́ца); **~y** [-ki] □ шутли́вый; шу́точный.

jolly ['dʒɔli] весёлый, ра́достный; F преле́стный, сла́вный.

jolt [dʒoult] **1.** трясти́ [тряхну́ть], встря́хивать [-хну́ть]; **2.** толчо́к; тря́ска.

jostle ['dʒɔsl] **1.** толка́ть(ся) [-кну́ть(ся)]; тесни́ть(ся); **2.** толчо́к; толкотня́, да́вка (в толпе́).

jot [dʒɔt] **1.** ничто́жное коли́чество, йо́та; **2.** ~ down бе́гло наброса́ть, кра́тко записа́ть.

journal ['dʒə:nl] дневни́к; журна́л; *parl.* протоко́л заседа́ния; ⊕ ше́йка (ва́ла), ца́пфа; **~ism** ['dʒə:nlizm] журнали́стика.

journey ['dʒə:ni] **1.** пое́здка, путеше́ствие; **2.** путеше́ствовать; **~-man** подмасте́рье; наёмник.

jovial ['dʒouviəl] весёлый, общи́тельный.

joy [dʒɔi] ра́дость *f*, удово́льствие; **~ful** ['dʒɔiful] □ ра́достный, весёлый; **~less** [-lis] □ безра́достный; **~ous** [-əs] □ ра́достный, весёлый.

jubil|ant ['dʒu:bilənt] лику́ющий; **~ate** [-leit] ликова́ть, торжествова́ть; **~ee** ['dʒu:bili:] юбиле́й.

judge [dʒʌdʒ] **1.** судья́ *m*; арби́тр; знато́к, цени́тель; **2.** *v/i.* суди́ть, посуди́ть *pf.*; быть арби́тром; *v/t.* суди́ть о (П); оце́нивать [-ни́ть]; осужда́ть [осуди́ть], порица́ть.

judg(e)ment ['dʒʌdʒmənt] пригово́р, реше́ние суда́; сужде́ние; рассуди́тельность *f*; мне́ние, взгляд.

judicature ['dʒu:dikətʃə] суде́йская корпора́ция; судоустро́йство; отправле́ние правосу́дия.

judicial [dʒu:'diʃəl] □ суде́бный; суде́йский; рассуди́тельный.

judicious [dʒu:'diʃəs] □ здравомы́слящий, рассуди́тельный; **~ness** [-nis] рассуди́тельность *f*.

jug [dʒʌg] кувши́н; F тюрьма́.

juggle ['dʒʌgl] **1.** фо́кус, трюк; **2.** жонгли́ровать; обма́нывать [-ну́ть]; **~r** [-ə] жонглёр; фо́кусник (-ица).

juic|e [dʒu:s] сок; **~y** ['dʒu:si] □ со́чный; F колори́тный; интере́сный.

July [dʒu'lai] ию́ль *m*.

jumble ['dʒʌmbl] **1.** пу́таница, беспоря́док; **2.** толка́ться; сме́шивать(ся) [-ша́ть(ся)]; дви́гаться в беспоря́дке; **~-sale** прода́жа вся́ких сбо́рных веще́й с благотвори́тельной це́лью.

jump [dʒʌmp] **1.** прыжо́к; скачо́к; вздра́гивание (от испу́га); **2.** *v/i.* пры́гать [-гнуть]; скака́ть [-кну́ть]; ~ at охо́тно приня́ть (предложе́ние, пода́рок), ухва́тываться [ухвати́ться] за (В); ~ to conclusions де́лать поспе́шные вы́воды; *v/t.* перепры́гивать [-гнуть]; **~er** ['dʒʌmpə] прыгу́н; скаку́н; дже́мпер; **~y** [-pi] не́рвный, легко́ вздра́гивающий.

junct|ion ['dʒʌŋkʃən] соедине́ние; 🚂 железнодоро́жный у́зел; **~ure** [-ktʃə] соедине́ние; стече́ние обстоя́тельств, положе́ние дел; (крити́ческий) моме́нт; at this ~ of things при подо́бном положе́нии дел.

June [dʒu:n] ию́нь *m*.

jungle ['dʒʌŋgl] джу́нгли *f/pl.*; густы́е за́росли *f/pl.*

junior ['dʒu:njə] **1.** мла́дший; моло́же (to Р *or* чем И); **2.** мла́дший.

junk [dʒʌŋk] □ джо́нка; *Am.* старьё; *sl.* хлам, отбро́сы *m/pl.*

juris|diction [dʒuəris'dikʃən] отправле́ние правосу́дия; юрисди́кция; **~prudence** ['dʒuərispru:dəns] юриспруде́нция, законове́дение.

juror ['dʒuərə] ⚖ прися́жный; член жюри́.

jury [-ri] ⚖ прися́жные *m/pl.*; жюри́ *n indecl.*; **~man** прися́жный; член жюри́.

just [dʒʌst] **1.** □ *adj.* справедли́вый; пра́ведный; ве́рный, то́чный; **2.** *adv.* то́чно, как раз, и́менно; то́лько что; пря́мо; ~ now сейча́с, сию́ мину́ту; то́лько что.

justice ['dʒʌstis] справедли́вость *f*; правосу́дие; судья́ *m*; court of ~ суд.

justification [dʒʌstifi'keiʃən] оправда́ние; реабилита́ция.

justify ['dʒʌstifai] опра́вдывать [-да́ть], извиня́ть [-ни́ть].

justly ['dʒʌstli] справедли́во.

justness [-nis] справедли́вость *f*.

jut [dʒʌt] (*a.* ~ out) выступа́ть; вы́да(ва́)ться.

juvenile ['dʒu:vinail] **1.** ю́ный, ю́ношеский; **2.** ю́ноша *m*, подро́сток.

K

kangaroo [kæŋgə'ru:] кенгуру́ *m/f. indecl.*
keel [ki:l] **1.** киль *m*; **2.** ~ over опроки́дывать(ся) [-и́нуть(ся)].
keen [ki:n] □ о́стрый; ре́зкий; проница́тельный; си́льный; be ~ on о́чень люби́ть (В), стра́стно увлека́ться (Т); **~ness** ['ki:nnis] острота́; проница́тельность *f*.
keep [ki:p] **1.** содержа́ние; пропита́ние; for ~s F *part. Am.* навсегда́; **2.** [*irr.*] *v/t. com.* держа́ть; сохраня́ть [-ни́ть], храни́ть; содержа́ть; вести́ (кни́ги и т. п.); [с]держа́ть (сло́во и т. п.); ~ company with подде́рживать знако́мство с (Т); ~ waiting заставля́ть ждать; ~ away не подпуска́ть (from к Д); ~ a th. from a p. уде́рживать что́-либо от (Р); ~ in не выпуска́ть; оставля́ть (шко́льника) по́сле уро́ков; ~ on не снима́ть (шля́пы и т. п.); ~ up подде́рживать [-жа́ть]; **3.** *v/i.* держа́ться; уде́рживаться [-жа́ться] (from от Р); ост(ав)а́ться; не по́ртиться (о пи́ще); F и́ли *Am.* жить, обрета́ться; ~ doing продолжа́ть де́лать; ~ away держа́ться в отдале́нии; ~ from возде́рживаться [-жа́ться] от (Р); ~ off держа́ться в отдале́нии от (Р); ~ on (talking) продолжа́ть (говори́ть); ~ to приде́рживаться (Р); ~ up держа́ться бо́дро; ~ up with держа́ться наравне́ с (Т), идти́ в но́гу с (Т).
keep|er ['ki:pə] храни́тель *m*; сто́рож; **~ing** ['ki:piŋ] хране́ние; содержа́ние; be in (out of) ~ with ... (не) согласова́ться с (Т); **~sake** ['ki:pseik] пода́рок на па́мять.
keg [keg] бочо́нок.
kennel ['kenl] конура́.
kept [kept] *pt.* и *p. pt.* от keep.
kerb(stone) ['kə:b(stoun)] край тротуа́ра; бордю́рный ка́мень *m*.
kerchief ['kə:tʃif] (головно́й) плато́к; косы́нка.
kernel ['kə:nl] зерно́, зёрнышко; ядро́; *fig.* суть *f*.
kettle ['ketl] ча́йник (для кипяче́ния воды́); котёл; **~drum** ♪ лита́вра; F зва́ный вече́рний чай.
key [ki:] **1.** ключ; код; ⊕ клин; шпо́нка; кла́виш(а); ♪ ключ, тона́льность *f*; *fig.* тон; **2.** запира́ть [запере́ть] (на ключ); ♪ настра́ивать [-ро́ить]; ~ up *fig.* придава́ть реши́мость (Д); be ~ed up *Am.* быть в взви́нченном состоя́нии; **~board** клавиату́ра; **~hole** замо́чная сква́жина; **~-note** тона́льность *f*; *fig.* основна́я мысль *f*; **~stone** △ ключево́й ка́мень *m*.
kick [kik] **1.** уда́р (ного́й, копы́том); пино́к; F си́ла сопротивле́ния; **2.** *v/t.* ударя́ть [уда́рить] (ного́й); брыка́ть [-кну́ть]; ~ out *Am. sl.* вышвы́ривать [вы́швырнуть]; выгоня́ть [вы́гнать]; *v/i.* брыка́ться [-кну́ться], ляга́ться [лягну́ться]; [вос]проти́виться; **~er** ['kikə] брыкли́вая ло́шадь *f*; футболи́ст.
kid [kid] **1.** козлёнок; ла́йка (ко́жа); F ребёнок; **2.** *sl.* поддра́знивать [-ни́ть].
kidnap ['kidnæp] похища́ть [-хи́тить] (люде́й); **~(p)er** [-ə] похити́тель-вымога́тель *m*.
kidney ['kidni] *anat.* по́чка; F тип, хара́ктер.
kill [kil] уби́(ва́)ть; бить (скот); *fig.* [по]губи́ть; *parl.* прова́ливать [-ли́ть] (законопрое́кт и т. п.); ~ off уничтожа́ть [-о́жить]; ~ time убива́ть вре́мя; **~er** ['kilə] уби́йца *m/f*.
kiln [kiln] обжига́тельная печь *f*.
kin [kin] семья́; родня́.
kind [kaind] **1.** □ до́брый, серде́чный, любе́зный; **2.** сорт, разнови́дность *f*; род; pay in ~ плати́ть нату́рой; **~-hearted** мягкосерде́чный, до́брый.
kindle ['kindl] зажига́ть(ся) [заже́чь(ся)]; воспламеня́ть [-ни́ть].
kindling ['kindliŋ] расто́пка.
kind|ly ['kaindli] до́брый; **~ness** [-nis] доброта́; до́брый посту́пок.
kindred ['kindrid] **1.** ро́дственный; **2.** кро́вное родство́.
king [kiŋ] коро́ль *m*; **~dom** ['kiŋdəm] короле́вство; ⚘, *zo.* (расти́тельное, живо́тное) ца́рство; **~like** [-laik], **~ly** [-li] короле́вский; вели́чественный.
kink [kiŋk] изги́б; пе́тля; у́зел; *fig.* стра́нность *f*, причу́да.
kin|ship ['kinʃip] родство́; **~sman** ['kinzmən] ро́дственник.
kiss [kis] **1.** поцелу́й; **2.** [по]целова́ть(ся).
kit [kit] ка́дка; ра́нец; ⚔ ли́чное обмундирова́ние; **~-bag** ⚔ вещево́й мешо́к; ⊕ набо́р инструме́нтов.
kitchen ['kitʃin] ку́хня.
kite [kait] (бума́жный) змей.
kitten ['kitn] котёнок.
knack [næk] уда́чный приём; уме́ние, сноро́вка.
knapsack ['næpsæk] ра́нец, рюкза́к.
knave [neiv] моше́нник; вале́т (ка́рта).
knead [ni:d] [с]меси́ть.
knee [ni:] коле́но; **~-cap** *anat.* коле́нная ча́шечка; **~l** [ni:l] [*irr.*]

становиться на колени; стоять на коленях (to перед Т).
nell [nel] похоронный звон.
nelt [nelt] *pt.* и *p. pt.* от kneel.
new [nju:] *pt.* и *p. pt.* от know.
nickknack ['niknæk] безделушка.
nife [naif] **1.** (*pl.* knives) нож; **2.** резать, колоть ножом.
night [nait] **1.** рыцарь *m*; *chess* конь *m*; **2.** возводить в рыцари; **~-errant** странствующий рыцарь *m*; **~hood** ['naithud] рыцарство; **~ly** [-li] рыцарский.
nit [nit] [*irr.*] [с]вязать; связывать [-зать]; срастаться [срастись]; ~ the brows хмурить брови; **~ting** ['nitiŋ] **1.** вязание; **2.** вязальный.
nives [naivz] *pl.* от knife.
nob [nɔb] шишка; набалдашник; ручка; кнопка; головка.
nock [nɔk] **1.** удар, стук; **2.** ударять(ся) [ударить(ся)]; [по]стучать(ся); F ~ about рыскать по свету; ~ down сбивать с ног; ⊕ разбирать [-зобрать]; be ~ed down попадать под автомобиль и т. п.; ~ off work прекращать работу; ~ off стряхивать [-хнуть], смахивать [-хнуть]; ~ out выби(ва)ть, выколачивать [выколотить]; *sport.* нокаутировать (*im*)*pf.*; **~-kneed** с вывернутыми внутрь коленями; *fig.* слабый; **~-out** нокаут (*a.* ~ blow).
knoll [noul] холм, бугор.
knot [nɔt] **1.** узел; союз, узы *f/pl.*; **2.** завязывать узел (или узлом); спут(ыв)ать; **~ty** ['nɔti] узловатый; сучковатый; *fig.* затруднительный.
know [nou] [*irr.*] знать; быть знакомым с (Т); узн(ав)ать; [с]уметь; ~ French говорить по-французски; come to ~ узн(ав)ать; **~ing** ['nouiŋ] □ ловкий, хитрый; проницательный; **~ledge** ['nɔlidʒ] знание; to my ~ по моим сведениям; **~n** [noun] *p. pt.* от know; come to be ~ сделаться известным; make ~ объявлять [-вить].
knuckle ['nʌkl] **1.** сустав пальца; **2.** ~ down, ~ under уступать [-пить]; подчиняться [-ниться].

L

abel ['leibl] **1.** ярлык, этикетка; **2.** наклеивать ярлык на (В); *fig.* относить к категории (as P).
aboratory [lə'bɔrətəri] лаборатория; ~ assistant лабораторный (-ная) ассистент(ка).
aborious [lə'bɔ:riəs] □ трудный; старательный.
abo(u)r ['leibə] **1.** труд; работа; родовые муки *f/pl.*; hard ~ принудительный труд; ♀ Exchange биржа труда; **2.** рабочий; трудовой; **3.** *v/i.* трудиться, работать; прилагать усилия; *v/t.* вырабатывать [выработать]; **~-creation** предоставление работы; **~ed** вымученный; трудный; **~er** [-rə] рабочий
ace [leis] **1.** кружево; шнурок; **2.** [за]шнуровать; окаймлять [-мить] (кружевом и т. п.); хлестать [-тнуть], [вы]пороть (*a.* ~ into *a p.*).
acerate ['læsəreit] разрывать [разорвать], раздирать [разодрать].
ack [læk] **1.** недостаток, нужда; отсутствие (P); **2.** испытывать недостаток, нужду в (П) he ~s money у него недостаток денег; be ~ing недост(ав)ать: water is ~ing недостаёт воды; **~-lustre** тусклый.
acquer ['lækə] **1.** лак, политура; **2.** [от]лакировать.
ad [læd] парень *m*, юноша *m*.
adder ['lædə] лестница; ⚓ трап.
laden ['leidn] нагружённый; *fig.* обременённый.
lading ['leidiŋ] погрузка; груз, фрахт.
ladle ['leidl] **1.** ковш; черпак; половник; **2.** вычерпывать [вычерпнуть]; разли(ва)ть (суп) (*a.* ~ out).
lady ['leidi] дама; леди *f. indecl.* (титул); **~like** имеющая манеры леди; **~love** возлюбленная; **~ship** [-ʃip]: your ~ ваша милость *f.*
lag [læg] **1.** запаздывать; отст(ав)ать (*a.* ~ behind); **2.** запаздывание; отставание.
laggard ['lægəd] медленный, вялый человек.
lagoon [lə'gu:n] лагуна.
laid [leid] *pt.* и *p. pt.* от lay; **~-up** лежачий (больной).
lain [lein] *p. pt.* от lie².
lair [leə] логовище, берлога.
laity ['leiiti] миряне *pl.*; профаны [*m/pl.*]
lake [leik] озеро.
lamb [læm] **1.** ягнёнок; **2.** [о]ягниться.
lambent ['læmbənt] играющий, колыхающийся (о пламени).
lambkin ['læmkin] ягнёночек.
lame [leim] **1.** □ хромой; *fig.* неубедительный; **2.** [из]увечить, [ис]калечить.
lament [lə'ment] **1.** стенание, жалоба; **2.** стенать; оплак(ив)ать; [по]жаловаться; **~able** ['læməntəbl] жалкий; печальный; **~ation** [læmən'teiʃən] жалоба, плач.

lamp [læmp] ла́мпа; фона́рь *m*; *fig.* све́точ, свети́ло.
lampoon [læmˈpu:n] **1.** памфле́т, па́сквиль *m*; **2.** писа́ть па́сквиль на (В).
lamp-post фона́рный столб.
lampshade абажу́р.
lance [lɑ:ns] **1.** пи́ка; острога́; **2.** пронза́ть пи́кой; вскрыва́ть ланце́том; **~-corporal** *Brit.* ⚔ ефре́йтор.
land [lænd] **1.** земля́, су́ша; страна́; ~s *pl.* поме́стья *n/pl.*; ~ register позе́мельная кни́га; **2.** ⚓ выса́живать(ся) [вы́садить(ся)]; вытаскивать на бе́рег; ⚓ пристава́ть к бе́регу, прича́ли(ва)ть; ✈ приземля́ться [-ли́ться]; **~ed** [ˈlændid] земе́льный; **~holder** владе́лец земе́льного уча́стка.
landing [ˈlændiŋ] вы́садка; ✈ приземле́ние, поса́дка; ~ ground поса́дочная площа́дка; **~-stage** при́стань *f*.
land|lady хозя́йка (меблиро́ванных ко́мнат); поме́щица; **~lord** поме́щик; хозя́ин (кварти́ры, гости́ницы); **~mark** межево́й знак, ве́ха; ориенти́р; **~-owner** землевладе́лец; **~scape** [ˈlænskeip] ландша́фт, пейза́ж; **~slide** о́ползень *m*; *pol.* ре́зкое измене́ние (в распределе́нии голосо́в ме́жду па́ртиями).
lane [lein] тропи́нка; переу́лок.
language [ˈlæŋgwidʒ] язы́к (речь); strong ~ си́льные выраже́ния *n/pl.*, брань *f*.
languid [ˈlæŋgwid] □ то́мный.
languish [ˈlæŋgwiʃ] [за]ча́хнуть; тоскова́ть, томи́ться.
languor [ˈlæŋgə] апати́чность *f*; томле́ние; то́мность *f*.
lank [ˈlæŋk] □ высо́кий и худо́й; прямо́й (о волоса́х); **~y** [ˈlæŋki] □ долговя́зый.
lantern [ˈlæntən] фона́рь *m*; **~-slide** диапозити́в.
lap [læp] **1.** пола́; коле́ни *n/pl.*; *fig.* ло́но; ⊕ накла́дка; перекры́тие; *sport.* круг; **2.** перекры́(ва́)ть; [вы́]лака́ть; жа́дно пить; плеска́ться.
lapel [ləˈpel] отворо́т (пальто́ и т. п.).
lapse [læps] **1.** ход (вре́мени); оши́бка, опи́ска; (мора́льное) паде́ние; **2.** па́дать [упа́сть] (мора́льно); приня́ться за ста́рое; теря́ть си́лу (о пра́ве).
larceny [ˈlɑ:sni] ⚖ воровство́.
lard [lɑ:d] **1.** свино́е са́ло; **2.** [на-]шпигова́ть; **~er** [ˈlɑ:də] кладова́я.
large [lɑ:dʒ] □ большо́й, кру́пный; оби́льный; ще́дрый; at ~ на свобо́де; простра́нно, подро́бно; **~ly** [ˈlɑ:dʒli] в значи́тельной сте́пени; оби́льно, ще́дро; на широ́кую но́гу, в широ́ком масшта́бе; **~ness** [-nis] большо́й разме́р; широт (взгля́дов).
lark [lɑ:k] жа́воронок; *fig.* шу́тк прока́за, заба́ва.
larva [ˈlɑ:və] *zo.* личи́нка.
larynx [ˈlæ:riŋks] горта́нь *f*.
lascivious [ləˈsiviəs] □ похотли́вый.
lash [læʃ] **1.** плеть *f*; бич; реме́нь *m* (часть кнута́); уда́р (плётьы и т. п.); ресни́ца; **2.** хлеста́т [-тну́ть]; привя́зывать [-за́ть]; *fig* бичева́ть.
lass, ~ie [læs, ˈlæsi] де́вушка, де́вочка.
lassitude [ˈlæsitju:d] уста́лость *f*.
last¹ [lɑ:st] **1.** *adj.* после́дний про́шлый; кра́йний; ~ but on предпосле́дний; ~ night вчер ве́чером; **2.** коне́ц; at ~ наконе́ц **3.** *adv.* в после́дний раз; по́сл всех; в конце́.
last² [~] продолжа́ться [-до́лжить ся]; [про]дли́ться; хвата́ть [-ти́ть] сохраня́ться [-ни́ться].
last³ [~] коло́дка.
lasting [ˈlɑ:stiŋ] □ дли́тельный постоя́нный; про́чный.
lastly [ˈlɑ:stli] наконе́ц.
latch [lætʃ] **1.** щеко́лда, задви́жка америка́нский замо́к; **2.** запира́т [запере́ть].
late [leit] по́здний; запозда́лый неда́вний; уме́рший, поко́йный *adv.* по́здно; at (the) ~st не позд не́е; of ~ за после́днее вре́мя; b ~ опа́здывать [опозда́ть]; **~l** [ˈleitli] неда́вно; за после́дне вре́мя. [лате́нтный.
latent [ˈleitənt] □ скры́тый;
lateral [ˈlætərəl] □ боково́й; по бо́чный, втори́чный.
lath [lɑ:θ] **1.** дра́нка; пла́нка; **2** прибива́ть пла́нки к (Д).
lathe [leið] тока́рный стано́к.
lather [ˈlɑ:ðə] **1.** мы́льная пе́на; **2** *v/t.* намы́ли(ва)ть; *v/i.* мы́литься намы́ли(ва)ться; взмы́ли(ва)тьс (о ло́шади).
Latin [ˈlætin] **1.** лати́нский язы́к **2.** лати́нский.
latitude [ˈlætitju:d] *geogr.*, *ast.* широта́; *fig.* свобо́да де́йствий.
latter [ˈlætə] неда́вний; после́дни **~ly** [-li] неда́вно; к концу́.
lattice [ˈlætis] решётка (*a.* **~-work**
laud [lɔ:d] **1.** хвала́; **2.** [по]хвали́ть **~able** [ˈlɔ:dəbl] □ похва́льный.
laugh [lɑ:f] **1.** смех; **2.** смея́ться ~ at a p. высме́ивать [вы́смеять (В), смея́ться над (Т); **~able** [ˈlɑ:fəbl] □ смешно́й; **~ter** [ˈlɑ:ftə] смех
launch [lɔ:ntʃ] **1.** барка́с; мото́рна ло́дка; **2.** запуска́ть [-сти́ть] спуска́ть [-сти́ть] (су́дно на́ воду *fig.* пуска́ть в ход.
laund|ress [ˈlɔ:ndris] пра́чка; **~r** [-ri] пра́чечная; бельё для сти́р-[ки.
laurel [ˈlɔrəl] ♀ лавр.

avatory ['lævətəri] убо́рная.
avender ['lævində] ⚘ лава́нда.
avish ['læviʃ] **1.** □ ще́дрый, расточи́тельный; **2.** расточа́ть [-чи́ть].
aw [lɔ:] зако́н; пра́вило; ⚖ пра́во; ⚖ юриспруде́нция; go to ~ нача́ть суде́бный проце́сс; lay down the ~ задава́ть тон; **~-abiding** ⚖ законопослу́шный, соблюда́ющий зако́н; **~-court** суд; **~ful** ['lɔ:ful] □ зако́нный; **~less** ['lɔ:lis] □ беззако́нный.
awn [lɔ:n] лужа́йка, газо́н; бати́ст [(ткань).
aw|suit ['lɔ:sju:t] суде́бный проце́сс; **~yer** ['lɔ:jə] юри́ст; адвока́т.
ax [læks] □ вя́лый; ры́хлый; небре́жный; неря́шливый; **~ative** ['læksətiv] слаби́тельное.
ay[1] [lei] **1.** *pt.* от lie[2]; **2.** све́тский, мирско́й (не духо́вный).
ay[2] [~] **1.** положе́ние, направле́ние; **2.** [*irr.*] *v/t.* класть [положи́ть]; возлага́ть [-ложи́ть; успока́ивать [-ко́ить]; накры́(ва́)ть (на стол); ~ before a p. предъявля́ть [-ви́ть] (Д); ~ in stocks запаса́ться [запасти́сь] (of T); ~ low опроки́дывать [-и́нуть]; ~ open излага́ть [изложи́ть]; откры́(ва́)ть; ~ out выкла́дывать [вы́ложить]; разби́(ва́)ть (сад, парк и т. п.); ~ up [на]копи́ть; прико́вывать к посте́ли; ~ with обкла́дывать [обложи́ть] (T); *v/i.* [с]нести́сь (о пти́цах); держа́ть пари́ (*a.* ~ a wager).
ayer ['leiə] слой, пласт, наслое́ние.
ayman ['leimən] миря́нин; неспециали́ст, люби́тель *m.*
ay|off приостано́вка произво́дства; **~-out** план; разби́вка.
azy ['leizi] □ лени́вый.
ead[1] [led] свине́ц; ⚓ лот; грузи́ло; *typ.* шпо́ны *m/f pl.*
ead[2] [li:d] **1.** руково́дство; инициати́ва; *sport.* ли́дерство; *thea.* гла́вная роль *f*; ⚡ вво́дный про́вод; **2.** [*irr.*] *v/t.* води́ть, [по-] вести́; приводи́ть [-вести́]; склоня́ть [-ни́ть] (to к Д); руководи́ть (T); ходи́ть [пойти́] с (P *pl.*) (о ка́рточной игре́); ~ on соблазня́ть [-ни́ть]; *v/t.* вести́; быть пе́рвым ~ off нач(ин)а́ть, класть нача́ло.
leaden ['ledn] свинцо́вый (*a. fig.*).
eader ['li:də] руководи́тель(ница *f*) *m*; вождь *m*; передова́я статья́.
leading ['li:diŋ] **1.** руководя́щий; веду́щий; передово́й; выдаю́щийся; **2.** руково́дство; веде́ние.
leaf [li:f] (*pl.*: leaves) лист (⚘ *pl.*: ли́стья); листва́; **~let** ['li:flit] листо́вка; **~y** ['li:fi] покры́тый ли́стьями.
league [li:g] **1.** ли́га, сою́з; **2.** вступа́ть в сою́з; объединя́ть(ся) [-ни́ть(ся)].
leak [li:k] **1.** течь *f*; уте́чка, **2.** дава́ть течь, пропуска́ть во́ду; ~ out проса́чиваться [-сочи́ться]; *fig.* обнару́жи(ва)ться; **~age** ['li:kidʒ] проса́чивание; *fig.* обнару́жение (та́йны и т. п.); **~y** ['li:ki] с те́чью.
lean [li:n] **1.** [*irr.*] прислоня́ть(ся) [-ни́ть(ся)] (against к Д); опира́ться [опере́ться] (on на В) (*a. fig.*); наклоня́ть(ся) [-ни́ть(ся)]; **2.** то́щий, худо́й.
leant [lent] *pt.* и *p. pt.* от lean.
leap [li:p] **1.** прыжо́к, скачо́к; **2.** [*a. irr.*] пры́гать [-гнуть], скака́ть [скакну́ть]; **~t** [lept] *pt.* и *p. pt.* от leap; **~-year** високо́сный год.
learn [lə:n] [*a. irr.*] изуча́ть [-чи́ть], [на]учи́ться (Д); ~ from узн(ав)а́ть от (P); **~ed** [lə:nid] □ учёный; **~ing** ['lə:niŋ] уче́ние; учёность *f*, эруди́ция; **~t** [lə:nt] *pt.* и *p. pt.* от learn.
lease [li:s] **1.** аре́нда; наём; **2.** сдава́ть внаём, в аре́нду; брать внаём, в аре́нду.
least [li:st] *adj.* мале́йший; наиме́ньший; *adv.* ме́нее всего́, в наиме́ньшей сте́пени; at (the) ~ по кра́йней ме́ре.
leather ['leðə] **1.** ко́жа; реме́нь *m*; **2.** (*a.* ~n) ко́жаный.
leave [li:v] **1.** разреше́ние, позволе́ние; о́тпуск; **2.** [*irr.*] *v/t.* оставля́ть [-а́вить]; покида́ть [поки́нуть]; предоставля́ть [-а́вить]; *Am.* позволя́ть [-о́лить]; ~ off броса́ть [бро́сить] (де́лать что́-либо); *v/i.* уезжа́ть [уе́хать]; уходи́ть [уйти́].
leaves [li:vz] *pl.* от leaf.
leavings ['li:viŋz] оста́тки *m/pl.*; отбро́сы *m/pl.*
lecture ['lektʃə] **1.** докла́д; ле́кция; наставле́ние; **2.** *v/i.* чита́ть ле́кции; *v/t.* отчи́тывать [-ита́ть]; **~r** [-rə] докла́дчик (-ица); ле́ктор; *univ.* преподава́тель *m.*
led [led] *pt.* и *p. pt.* от lead.
ledge [ledʒ] вы́ступ, усту́п; риф.
ledger ['ledʒə] ⚚ гроссбу́х, гла́вная кни́га.
leech [li:tʃ] *zo.* пия́вка.
leer [liə] **1.** взгляд и́скоса; **2.** смотре́ть, гляде́ть и́скоса (at на В).
leeway ['li:wei] ⚓ дрейф; *fig.* make up for ~ навёрстывать упу́щенное.
left[1] [left] *pt.* и *p. pt.* от leave; be ~ ост(ав)а́ться.
left[2] [~] **1.** ле́вый; **2.** ле́вая сторона́; **~-hander** левша́ *m/f.*
leg [leg] нога́ (от бедра́ до ступни́); но́жка (стола́ и т. п.); штани́на.
legacy ['legəsi] насле́дство.
legal ['li:gəl] □ зако́нный, лега́льный; правово́й; **~ize** [-aiz] узако́ни(ва)ть, легализова́ть (*im*)*pf.*
legation [li'geiʃən] дипломати́ческая ми́ссия.
legend ['ledʒənd] леге́нда; на́дпись *f*; **~ary** [-əri] легенда́рный.

leggings ['legiŋz] гамаши *f/pl.*, краги *f/pl.*
legible ['ledʒəbl] □ разборчивый.
legionary ['li:dʒənəri] легионер.
legislat|ion [ledʒis'leiʃən] законодательство; **~ive** ['ledʒisleitiv] законодательный; **~or** законодатель *m.*
legitima|cy [li'dʒitiməsi] законность *f*; **~te 1.** [-meit] узакони(ва)ть; **2.** [-mit] законный.
leisure ['leʒə] досуг; at your ~ когда вам удобно; **~ly** не спеша, спокойно.
lemon ['lemən] лимон; **~ade** [lemə'neid] лимонад.
lend [lend] [*irr.*] одалживать [одолжить]; давать взаймы; *fig.* д(ав)ать, прид(ав)ать.
length [leŋθ] длина; расстояние; продолжительность *f*; отрез (материи); at ~ подробно; go all ~s пойти на всё; **~en** ['leŋθən] удлинять(ся) [-нить(ся)]; **~wise** [-waiz] в длину; вдоль; **~y** [-i] растянутый; многословный.
lenient ['li:niənt] □ мягкий; снисходительный.
lens [lenz] линза.
lent[1] [lent] *pt.* и *p. pt.* от lend.
Lent[2] [~] великий пост.
less [les] **1.** (*comp.* от little) меньший; **2.** *adv.* меньше, менее; **3.** *prp.* без (Р).
lessen ['lesn] *v/t.* уменьшать [уменьшить]; недооценивать [-нить]; *v/i.* уменьшаться [уменьшиться].
lesser ['lesə] меньший.
lesson ['lesn] урок; *fig.* give a ~ to a p. проучить (В) *pf.*; предостережение.
lest [lest] чтобы не, как бы не.
let [let] [*irr.*] оставлять [-авить]; сдавать внаём; позволять [-волить] (Д), пускать [пустить]; ~ alone оставить в покое; *adv.* не говоря уже о ... (П); ~ down опускать [-стить]; *fig.* подводить [-вести]; ~ go выпускать из рук; выкинуть из головы (мысль); ~ into посвящать [-ятить] в (тайну и т. п.); ~ off стрелять [выстрелить] из (Р); *fig.* выпаливать [выпалить] (шутку); ~ out выпускать [выпустить]; ~ up *Am.* ослабе(ва)ть.
lethargy ['leθədʒi] летаргия; апатичность *f.*
letter ['letə] **1.** буква; литера; письмо; ~s *pl.* литература; учёность *f*; *attr.* письменный; to the ~ буквально; **2.** помечать буквами; делать надпись на (П); **~-case** бумажник; **~-cover** конверт; **~ed** [-d] начитанный, образованный; **~-file** регистратор (папка); **~ing** [-riŋ] надпись *f*; тиснение; **~press** текст в книге (в отличие от иллюстраций).

lettuce ['letis] салат.
level ['levl] **1.** горизонтальный; ровный; одинаковый, равный; равномерный; my ~ best всё, что в моих силах; **2.** уровень *m*; ватерпас, нивелир; *fig.* масштаб; ~ of the sea уровень моря; on the ~ *Am.* честно, правдиво; **3.** *v/t.* выравнивать [выровнять]; уравнивать [-внять]; сглаживать [сгладить]; сравнивать, [с]ровнять (с землёй); ~ up повышать уравнивая; *v/i.* ~ at прицели(ва)ться в (В); **~-headed** уравновешенный.
lever ['li:və] рычаг, вага; **~age** [-ridʒ] подъёмная сила.
levity ['leviti] легкомыслие, ветренность *f.*
levy ['levi] **1.** сбор, взимание (налогов); ⚔ набор (рекрутов); **2.** взимать (налог); ⚔ наб(и)рать.
lewd [lju:d] □ похотливый.
liability [laiə'biliti] ответственность *f* (*a.* ⚖); обязательство; задолженность *f*; *fig.* подверженность *f*, склонность *f*; liabilities *pl.* обязательства *n/pl.*; ✝ долги *m/pl.*
liable ['laiəbl] □ ответственный (за В); обязанный; подверженный; be ~ to быть предрасположенным к (Д).
liar ['laiə] лгун(ья).
libel ['laibəl] **1.** клевета; **2.** [на-] клеветать на (В).
liberal ['libərəl] **1.** □ щедрый, обильный; *pol.* либеральный; **2.** либерал(ка); **~ity** [libə'ræliti] щедрость *f*; либеральность *f.*
liberat|e ['libəreit] освобождать [-бодить]; **~ion** [libə'reiʃən] освобождение; **~or** ['libəreitə] освободитель *m.*
libertine ['libətain] распутник; вольнодумец.
liberty [-ti] свобода; вольность *f*; бесцеремонность *f*; be at ~ быть свободным.
librar|ian [lai'brɛəriən] библиотекарь *m*; **~y** ['laibrəri] библиотека.
lice [lais] *pl.* от louse.
licen|ce, *Am.* **~se** ['laisəns] **1.** разрешение, ✝ лицензия; вольность *f*; driving ~ водительские права *n/pl.*; **2.** разрешать [-шить]; давать право, патент на (В).
licentious [lai'senʃəs] □ распущенный, безнравственный.
lick [lik] **1.** облизывание; **2.** лизать [лизнуть]; облизывать [-зать]; F [по]бить, [по]колотить; ~ the dust быть поверженным наземь; быть убитым; ~ into shape привести в порядок.
lid [lid] крышка; веко.
lie[1] [lai] **1.** ложь *f*, обман; give the ~ обличать во лжи; **2.** [со]лгать.
lie[2] [~] **1.** положение; направление; **2.** [*irr.*] лежать; быть рас-

положенным, находиться; заключаться; ~ by оставаться без употребления; ~ down ложиться [лечь]; ~ in wait for поджидать (В).

ien ['liən] ⚖ право наложения ареста на имущество должника.

ieu [lju:]: in ~ of вместо (Р).

ieutenant [lef'tenənt, ⚓ and *Am.* lut-] лейтенант; **~-commander** капитан-лейтенант.

ife [laif] жизнь *f*; образ жизни; биография; живость *f*; for ~ пожизненный; на всю жизнь; ~ sentence пожизненное заключение; **~-assurance** страхование жизни; **~-boat** спасательная лодка; **~-guard** лейб-гвардия; **~less** □ бездыханный, безжизненный; **~-like** словно живой; **~-long** пожизненный; **~-preserver** спасательный пояс; трость, налитая свинцом; **~-time** вся жизнь *f*, целая жизнь *f*.

ift [lift] **1.** лифт; подъёмная машина; *phys.*, ✈ подъёмная сила; *fig.* возвышение; give a p. a ~ подвозить [-везти] кого-либо; **2.** *v/t.* поднимать [-нять]; возвышать [-высить]; *sl.* [у]красть; *v/i.* возвышаться [-выситься]; подниматься [-няться].

ight[1] [lait] **1.** свет, освещение; огонь *m*; *fig.* светило; аспект; will you give me a ~ позвольте прикурить; put a ~ to зажигать [зажечь]; **2.** светлый, ясный; **3.** [*a. irr.*] *v/t.* зажигать [зажечь]; освещать [-етить]; *v/i.* (*mst* ~ up) загораться [-реться]; освещаться [-етиться].

ight[2] [~] **1.** *adj.* □ лёгкий, легковесный; незначительный; пустой, легкомысленный; ~ current ⚡ ток слабого напряжения; make ~ of относиться несерьёзно к (Д); **2.** ~ on неожиданно натолкнуться на (В), случайно напасть на (В).

ighten ['laitn] освещать [-етить]; [по]светлеть; сверкать [-кнуть] (о молнии); делать(ся) более лёгким.

ighter ['laitə] зажигалка; запал; ⚓ лихтер.

ight|headed легкомысленный; в бреду; **~-hearted** □ беззаботный; весёлый; **~house** маяк.

ighting ['laitiŋ] освещение.

ight|-minded легкомысленный; **~ness** лёгкость *f*.

ightning [-niŋ] молния; **~-conductor**, **~-rod** громоотвод.

ight-weight *sport* легковес.

ike [laik] **1.** похожий, подобный; равный; such ~ подобный тому, такой; F feel ~ хотеть (+ *inf.*); what is he ~? что он за человек?; **2.** нечто подобное; ~s *pl.* склонности *f/pl.*, влечения *n/pl.*; his ~ ему подобные; **3.** любить; [за-] хотеть; how do you ~ London? как вам нравится Лондон? I should ~ to know я хотел бы знать.

like|lihood ['laiklihud] вероятность *f*; **~ly** ['laikli] вероятный; подходящий; he is ~ to die он вероятно умрёт.

like|n ['laikən] уподоблять [-обить]; сравнивать [-нить]; **~ness** ['laiknis] сходство, подобие; **~wise** [-waiz] тоже, также; подобно.

liking ['laikiŋ] расположение (for к Д).

lilac ['lailək] **1.** сирень *f*; **2.** лиловый.

lily ['lili] лилия; ~ of the valley ландыш.

limb [lim] член, конечность *f*; ветка.

limber ['limbə] гибкий, мягкий.

lime [laim] известь *f*; ♀ лиметта (разновидность лимона); **~light** свет рампы; *fig.* центр общего внимания.

limit ['limit] граница, предел; off ~s вход воспрещён (надпись); be ~ed to ограничи(ва)ться (Т); **~ation** [limi'teiʃən] ограничение; ⚖ предельный срок; **~ed** ['limitid]: ~ (liability) company общество с ограниченной ответственностью; **~less** ['limitlis] □ безграничный.

limp [limp] **1.** [за]хромать; **2.** прихрамывание, хромота; **3.** мягкий, нетвёрдый; слабый.

limpid ['limpid] прозрачный.

line [lain] **1.** линия (*a.* 🚂, *tel.*); строка; черта, штрих; шнурок; леса (удочки); специальность *f*, занятие; ⚔ развёрнутый строй; ⚔ рубеж; ~s *pl.* стихи; ~ of conduct образ действия; hard ~s *pl.* неудача; in ~ with в согласии с (Т); stand in ~ *Am.* стоять в очереди; **2.** *v/t.* разлиновывать [-новать]; класть на подкладку; ~ out набрасывать [-росать]; тянуться вдоль (Р).; *v/i.* ~ up выстраиваться [выстроиться] (в ряд).

linea|ge ['liniidʒ] родословная, происхождение; **~ment** [-mənt] черты (лица); очертание (гор); **~r** ['liniə] линейный.

linen ['linin] **1.** полотно; *coll.* бельё; **2.** полотняный.

liner ['lainə] пассажирский пароход или самолёт.

linger ['liŋgə] [по]медлить, [про-] мешкать; ~ over задерживаться [-жаться] на (П).

lingerie ['læ:nʒəri:] ✝ дамское бельё.

lining ['lainiŋ] подкладка; ⊕ обивка, облицовка, футеровка.

link [liŋk] **1.** звено; связь *f*; соеди-

не́ние; *fig.* у́зы *f/pl.*; **2.** соединя́ть [-ни́ть]; смыка́ть [сомкну́ть]; примыка́ть [-мкну́ть].
linseed ['linsi:d] льняно́е се́мя *n*; ~ oil льняно́е ма́сло.
lion ['laiən] лев; **~ess** [-is] льви́ца.
lip [lip] губа́; край; F де́рзкая болтовня́; **~-stick** губна́я пома́да.
liquefy ['likwifai] превраща́ть(ся) в жи́дкость.
liquid ['likwid] **1.** жи́дкий; прозра́чный; ✝ легко́ реализу́емый; **2.** жи́дкость *f*.
liquidat|e ['likwideit] ликвиди́ровать *im(pf.)*; выпла́чивать [вы́платить] (долг); **~ion** [likwi'deiʃən] ликвида́ция; вы́плата до́лга.
liquor ['likə] жи́дкость *f*; (*a.* strong ~) спиртно́й напи́ток.
lisp [lisp] **1.** шепеля́вость *f*; ле́пет; **2.** шепеля́вить, сюсю́кать.
list [list] **1.** спи́сок, рее́стр, пе́речень *m*; крен (су́дна); **2.** вноси́ть в спи́сок; составля́ть спи́сок (P); [на]крени́ться.
listen ['lisn] [по]слу́шать; прислу́ш(ив)аться; (to к Д); ~ in подслу́ш(ив)ать (to В); слу́шать ра́дио; **~er, ~er-in** [-ə'rin] слу́шатель(ница *f*) *m*.
listless ['listlis] апати́чный.
lit [lit] *pt.*и *p. pt.* от light[1].
literal ['litərəl] □ буква́льный, досло́вный.
litera|ry ['litərəri] □ литерату́рный; **~ture** ['litəritʃə] литерату́ра.
lithe [laið] ги́бкий.
lithography [li'θɔgrəfi] литогра́фия.
litigation [liti'geiʃən] тя́жба; спор.
litter ['litə] **1.** носи́лки *f/pl.*; подсти́лка (для скота́); помёт (припло́д); беспоря́док; **2.** подстила́ть [подостла́ть] (соло́му и т. п.); [о]щени́ться, [о]пороси́ться и т. п.; разбра́сывать в беспоря́дке.
little ['litl] **1.** *adj.* ма́ленький, небольшо́й; коро́ткий (о вре́мени); a ~ one малы́ш; **2.** *adv.* немно́го, ма́ло; **3.** пустя́к, ме́лочь *f*; a ~ немно́го; ~ by ~ ма́ло-пома́лу, постепе́нно; not a ~ нема́ло.
live 1. [liv] *com.* жить; существова́ть; ~ to see дожи́(ва́)ть до (P); ~ down загла́живать [-ла́дить]; ~ out пережи́(ва́)ть; ~ up to a standard жить согла́сно тре́бованиям; **2.** [laiv] живо́й; жи́зненный; горя́щий; ⚔ боево́й, де́йствующий (снаря́д); ⚡ под напряже́нием; **~lihood** ['laivlihud] сре́дства к жи́зни; **~liness** [-nis] жи́вость *f*; оживле́ние; **~ly** ['laivli] живо́й; оживлённый.
liver ['livə] *anat.* пе́чень *f*; *cook.* печёнка.
livery ['livəri] ливре́я.
live|s [laivz] *pl.* от life; **~-stock** ['laivstɔk] живо́й инвента́рь *m*.
livid ['livid] ме́ртвенно бле́дный.
living ['liviŋ] **1.** □ живо́й; живу́щий, существу́ющий; **2.** сре́дства к жи́зни; жизнь *f*, о́браз жи́зни; **~-room** жила́я ко́мната.
lizard ['lizəd] я́щерица.
load [loud] **1.** груз; тя́жесть *f*, бре́мя *n*; заря́д; **2.** [на]грузи́ть; отягоща́ть [-готи́ть]; заряжа́ть [-яди́ть] (об ору́жии); *fig.* обременя́ть [-ни́ть]; **~ing** ['loudiŋ] погру́зка; груз; заря́дка.
loaf [loaf] **1.** (*pl.* loaves) хлеб, карава́й; **2.** безде́льничать; шата́ться, слоня́ться без де́ла.
loafer ['loufə] безде́льник; бродя́га *m*.
loam [loum] жи́рная гли́на; плодоро́дная земля́.
loan [loun] **1.** заём; on ~ взаймы́; **2.** дава́ть взаймы́, ссужа́ть [ссуди́ть].
lo(a)th [louθ] □ несклóнный; **~e** [louð] пита́ть отвраще́ние к (Д); **~some** ['louðsəm] □ отврати́тельный.
loaves [louvz] *pl.* хле́бы *m/pl.*
lobby ['lɔbi] **1.** прихо́жая; *parl.* кулуа́ры *m/pl.*; *thea.* фойе́ *n indecl.*; **2.** *part. Am. parl.* пыта́ться возде́йствовать на чле́нов конгре́сса.
lobe [loub] ⚘ *anat.* до́ля; мо́чка (у́ха).
lobster ['lɔbstə] ома́р.
local ['loukəl] **1.** □ ме́стный; ~ government ме́стное самоуправле́ние; **2.** ме́стное изве́стие; (*a.* ~ train) при́городный по́езд; **~ity** [lou'kæliti] ме́стность *f*, райо́н; окре́стность *f*; **~ize** ['loukəlaiz] локализова́ть (*im*)*pf.*; ограни́чивать распростране́ние (P).
locat|e [lou'keit] *v/t.* определя́ть ме́сто (P); располага́ть в определённом ме́сте; назнача́ть ме́сто для (P); *Am.* отмеча́ть грани́цу (P); be ~d быть располо́женным; *v/i.* поселя́ться [-ли́ться]; **~ion** [-ʃən] размеще́ние; определе́ние ме́ста; *Am.* местонахожде́ние.
lock [lɔk] **1.** замо́к; запо́р; зато́р; шлюз; ло́кон; пучо́к; **2.** *v/t.* запира́ть [запере́ть]; ⊕ [за]тормози́ть; ~ in запира́ть [запере́ть]; ~ up вложи́ть (капита́л) в тру́дно реализу́емые бума́ги; *v/i.* запира́ться [запере́ться]; замыка́ться [замкну́ться].
lock|er ['lɔkə] запира́ющийся шка́фчик; **~et** ['lɔkit] медальо́н; **~-out** лока́ут; **~smith** сле́сарь *m*; **~-up** вре́мя закры́тия (школ, магази́нов и т. п.); арестáнтская ка́мера.
locomotive ['loukəmoutiv] **1.** дви́жущий(ся); **2.** (и́ли ~ engine) локо-

мотив, паровоз, тепловоз, электровоз.
cust ['loukəst] саранча.
destar путеводная звезда.
dg|e [lɔdʒ] **1.** сторожка; (*mst* охотничий) домик; (масонская) ложа; **2.** *v/t.* дать помещение (Д); депонировать (*im*)*pf.* (деньги); по(ав)ать (жалобу); *v/i.* квартировать; застревать [-рять] (о пуле и т. п.); **~er** ['lɔdʒə] жилец, жилица; **~ing** ['lɔdʒiŋ] жилище; ~s *pl.* квартира; комната (снимаемая).
ft [lɔft] чердак; галерея; **~y** ['lɔfti] □ высокомерный; величественный.
g [lɔg] колода; бревно; ⚓ лаг; **~-cabin** бревенчатая хижина; **~gerhead** ['lɔgəhed]: be at ~s быть в ссоре, ссориться (with с Т).
gic ['lɔdʒik] логика; **~al** ['lɔdʒikəl] □ логический.
in [lɔin] филейная часть *f*; ~s *pl.* поясница.
iter ['lɔitə] слоняться без дела; мешкать.
ll [lɔl] сидеть развалясь; стоять облокотясь.
ne|liness ['lounlinis] одиночество; **~ly** [-li] □, **~some** [-səm] □ одинокий.
ng[1] [lɔŋ] **1.** долгий срок, долгое время *n*; before ~ вскоре; for ~ надолго; **2.** *adj.* длинный; долгий; медленный; in the ~ run в конце концов; be ~ медлить; долго длиться; **3.** *adv.* долго; ~ ago давно; so ~! пока (до свидания)!; ~er дольше; больше.
ng[2] [~] страстно желать, жаждать (for P), тосковать (по Д).
ng|-distance *attr.* дальний; *sport* на длинные дистанции; **~evity** [lɔn'dʒeviti] долговечность *f*.
nging ['lɔŋiŋ] **1.** □ тоскующий; **2.** сильное желание, стремление (к Д), тоска (по Д).
ngitude ['lɔndʒitju:d] *geogr.* долгота.
ng|shoreman ['lɔŋʃɔ:mən] портовый грузчик; **~sighted** дальнозоркий; **~-suffering 1.** многострадальный; долготерпеливый; **2.** долготерпение; **~-term** долгосрочный; **~-winded** □ могущий долго бежать, не задыхаясь; многоречивый.
ok [luk] **1.** взгляд; выражение (глаз, лица); вид, наружность *f* (*a.* ~s *pl.*); have a ~ at a th. посмотреть на (В); ознакомиться [-комиться] с (Т); **2.** *v/i.* [по-] смотреть (at на В); выглядеть; ~ for искать (В *or* Р); ~ forward to предвкушать [-усить] (В); с радостью ожидать (Р); ~ into исследовать (*im*)*pf.*; ~ out! берегись!, смотри!; ~ (up)on *fig.* смотреть как на (В), считать за (В); *v/t.* ~ disdain смотреть с презрением; ~ over не замечать [-етить]; просматривать [-мотреть]; ~ up [по]искать (в словаре и т. п.); навещать [-естить].
looker-on ['lukər'ɔn] зритель(ница *f*) *m*; наблюдатель(ница *f*) *m*.
looking-glass зеркало.
look-out ['luk'aut] вид (на море и т. п.); виды *m/pl.*, шансы *m/pl.*; that is my ~ это моё дело.
loom [lu:m] **1.** ткацкий станок; **2.** маячить, неясно вырисовываться.
loop [lu:p] **1.** (✈ мёртвая) петля; **2.** делать (✈ мёртвую) петлю; закреплять петлей; **~hole** лазейка (*a. fig.*); *fig.* увёртка; ⚔ бойница, амбразура.
loose [lu:s] **1.** □ *com.* свободный; неопределённый; просторный; болтающийся, шатающийся; распущенный (о нравах); несвязанный; рыхлый; **2.** освобождать [-бодить]; развязывать [-язать]; **~n** ['lu:sn] ослаблять(ся) [-абить (-ся)]; развязывать [-язать]; разрыхлять [-лить]; расшатывать [-шатать].
loot [lu:t] **1.** [о]грабить; **2.** добыча, награбленное добро.
lop [lɔp] обрубать [-бить] (ветки); **~-sided** кривобокий; накренённый. [вый.]
loquacious [lo'kweiʃəs] болтли-
lord [lɔ:d] господин, барин; лорд; повелитель *m*; the ♀ господь *m*; my ~ [mi'lɔ:d] милорд (обращение); the ♀'s prayer отче наш (молитва); the ♀'s Supper тайная вечеря; **~ly** ['lɔ:dli] высокомерный; **~ship** ['lɔ:dʃip]: your ~ ваша светлость *f*.
lorry ['lɔri] 🚘 грузовик; вагон-платформа; подвода; полок.
lose [lu:z] [*irr.*] *v/t.* [по]терять; упускать [-стить]; проигрывать [-рать]; ~ o. s. заблудиться *pf.*; *v/i.* [по]терять; проигрывать(ся) [-рать(ся)]; отст(ав)ать (о часах).
loss [lɔs] потеря, утрата; урон; убыток; проигрыш; at a ~ в затруднении.
lost [lɔst] *pt.* и *p. pt.* от lose; be ~ пропадать [-пасть]; погибать [-гибнуть]; *fig.* растеряться *pf.*
lot [lɔt] жребий; ✝ вещи продаваемые партией на аукционе; участь *f*, доля; *Am.* участок земли; F масса, уйма; draw ~s бросать жребий; fall to a p.'s ~ выпасть на долю кого-нибудь.
lotion ['louʃən] жидкое косметическое средство, жидкий крем.
lottery ['lɔtəri] лотерея.
loud [laud] □ громкий, звучный; шумный, крикливый; *fig.* кричащий (о красках).
lounge [laundʒ] **1.** сидеть разва-

ля́сь; стоя́ть опира́ясь; **2.** пра́здное времяпрепровожде́ние; дива́н; *thea.* фойе́ *n indecl.*

lour ['lauə] смотре́ть угрю́мо; [на]хму́риться.

lous|e [laus] (*pl.*: lice) вошь *f* (*pl.*: вши); **~y** ['lauzi] вши́вый; *fig.* парши́вый.

lout [laut] неуклю́жий, неотёсанный челове́к.

lovable ['lʌvəbl] □ привлека́тельный, ми́лый.

love [lʌv] **1.** любо́вь *f*; влюблённость *f*; предме́т любви́; give (*or* send) one's ~ to a p. передава́ть, посыла́ть приве́т (Д); in ~ with влюблённый в (В); make ~ to уха́живать за (Т); **2.** люби́ть; ~ to do де́лать с удово́льствием; **~-affair** любо́вная интри́га; **~ly** ['lʌvli] прекра́сный, чу́дный; **~r** ['lʌvə] любо́вник; возлю́бленный; люби́тель(ница *f*) *m.*

loving ['lʌviŋ] □ лю́бящий.

low[1] [lou] ни́зкий, невысо́кий; *fig.* сла́бый; ти́хий (о го́лосе); ни́зкий, непристо́йный; ~est bid са́мая ни́зкая цена́, предло́женная на аукцио́не.

low[2] [~] **1.** мыча́ние; **2.** [за]мыча́ть.

lower[1] ['louə] **1.** *compr.* от low[1]; ни́зший; ни́жний; **2.** *v/t.* спуска́ть [-сти́ть] (ло́дку, па́рус); опуска́ть [-сти́ть] (глаза́); снижа́ть [-и́зить]; *v/i.* снижа́ться [-и́зиться] (о це́нах, звуке и т. п.); уменьша́ться [уме́ньши́ться].

lower[2] ['lauə] *s.* lour.

low|land ни́зменная ме́стность *f*, ни́зменность *f*; **~liness** ['loulinis] скро́мность *f*; **~ly** скро́мный; **~-necked** с ни́зким вы́резом; **~-spirited** пода́вленный, уны́лый.

loyal ['lɔiəl] □ ве́рный, лоя́льный; **~ty** [-ti] ве́рность *f*, лоя́льность *f*.

lozenge ['lɔzindʒ] табле́тка; ромб.

lubber ['lʌbə] у́валень *m.*

lubric|ant ['lu:brikənt] сма́зка; **~ate** [-keit] сма́з(ыв)ать (маши́ну); **~ation** [lu:bri'keiʃən] сма́зка.

lucid ['lu:sid] □ я́сный; прозра́чный.

luck [lʌk] уда́ча, сча́стье; good ~ счастли́вый слу́чай, уда́ча; bad ~, hard ~, ill ~ неуда́ча; **~ily** ['lʌkili] к сча́стью; **~y** ['lʌki] □ счастли́вый, уда́чный; приносящий уда́чу.

lucr|ative ['lu:krətiv] □ при́быльный, вы́годный; **~e** ['lu:kə] бары́ш, при́быль *f*.

ludicrous ['lu:dikrəs] □ неле́пый, смешно́й.

lug [lʌg] [по]тащи́ть, [по]волочи́ть.

luggage ['lʌgidʒ] бага́ж; **~-office** 🚂 ка́мера хране́ния багажа́.

lugubrious [lu:gju:briəs] □ мра́чный.

lukewarm ['lu:kwɔ:m] теплова́тый; *fig.* равноду́шный.

lull [lʌl] **1.** убаю́к(ив)ать; усыпля́ть [-пи́ть]; **2.** вре́менное зати́шье; вре́менное успокое́ние.

lullaby ['lʌləbai] колыбе́льная пе́сня.

lumber ['lʌmbə] нену́жные громо́здкие ве́щи *f/pl.*; *Am.* пиломатериа́лы *m/pl.*; **~man** *Am.* лесопромы́шленник; лесору́б.

lumin|ary ['lu:minəri] свети́ло; **~ous** [-əs] □ светя́щийся, све́тлый; *fig.* пролива́ющий свет.

lump [lʌmp] **1.** глы́ба, ком; *fig.* чурба́н; кусо́к (са́хара и т. п.); in the ~ о́птом, гурто́м; ~ sum о́бщая су́мма; **2.** *v/t.* брать огу́лом; сме́шивать в ку́чу; *v/i.* свёртываться в ко́мья; **~ish** ['lʌmpiʃ] неуклю́жий; тупоу́мный; **~y** ['lʌmpi] □ комкова́тый.

lunatic ['lu:nətik] **1.** сумасше́дший, безу́мный; **2.** психи́чески больно́й; ~ asylum психиатри́ческая больница.

lunch(eon) ['lʌntʃ(ən)] **1.** второ́й за́втрак; **2.** [по]за́втракать.

lung [lʌŋ] лёгкое; (a pair of) ~s *pl* лёгкие *n/pl.*

lunge [lʌndʒ] **1.** вы́пад, уда́р (рапи рой, шпа́гой) **2.** *v/i.* наноси́ть уда (at Д).

lurch [lə:tʃ] **1.** [на]крени́ться; идт шата́ясь; **2.** leave a. p. in the ~ по ки́нуть кого́-нибудь в беде́, в тя жёлом положе́нии.

lure [ljuə] **1.** прима́нка; *fig.* со блазн; **2.** прима́нивать [-ни́ть]; *fig* соблазня́ть [-ни́ть].

lurid ['ljuərid] мра́чный.

lurk [lə:k] скрыва́ться в заса́де тaíться.

luscious ['lʌʃəs] □ со́чный; при́торный.

lustr|e ['lʌstə] гля́нец; лю́стра; **~ous** ['lʌstrəs] □ глянцеви́тый.

lute[1] [lu:t, lju:t] ♪ лю́тня.

lute[2] [~] **1.** зама́зка, масти́ка; **2.** зама́зывать зама́зкой.

Lutheran ['lu:θərən] лютера́нский.

luxur|iant [lʌg'zjuəriənt] □ пы́шный; **~ious** [-riəs] □ роско́шный, пы́шный; **~y** ['lʌkʃəri] ро́скошь *f*, предме́т ро́скоши.

lye [lai] щёлок.

lying ['laiiŋ] **1.** *p. pr.* от lie[1] и lie[2] **2.** *adj.* лжи́вый, ло́жный; лежа́щий; **~-in** [-'in] ро́ды *m/pl.*; ~ hospital роди́льный дом.

lymph [limf] ли́мфа.

lynch [lintʃ] расправля́ться сам су́дом с (Т); **~-law** ['lintʃlɔ:] сам суд; зако́н Ли́нча.

lynx [links] *zo.* рысь *f*.

lyric ['lirik], **~al** [-ikəl] □ лири́ческий; **~s** *pl.* ли́рика.

M

macaroni [mækə'rouni] макаро́ны *f/pl.*

macaroon [mækə'ru:n] минда́льное пече́нье.

machin|ation [mæki'neiʃən] махина́ция, интри́га; ~s *pl.* ко́зни *f/pl.*; **~e** [mə'ʃi:n] **1.** маши́на; механи́зм; *attr.* маши́нный; ~ fitter сле́сарь-монта́жник; **2.** подверга́ть маши́нной обрабо́тке; **~e-made** сде́ланный механи́ческим спо́собом; **~ery** [-əri] маши́нное обору́дование; **~ist** [-ist] меха́ник; машини́ст.

mackerel ['mækrəl] *zo.* макре́ль *f.*

mackintosh ['mækintɔʃ] макинто́ш, плащ.

mad [mæd] □ сумаше́дший, поме́шанный; бе́шеный; *fig.* ди́кий; *Am.* взбешённый; go ~ сходи́ть с ума́; drive ~ своди́ть с ума́.

madam ['mædəm] мада́м *f indecl.*; суда́рыня.

mad|cap **1.** сорвиголова́ *m/f*; **2.** сумасбро́дный; **~den** ['mædn] [вз]беси́ть; своди́ть с ума́.

made [meid] *pt.* и *p. pt.* от make.

made-up прихоро́шенный; гото́вый (об оде́жде); ~ of состоя́щий из (Р).

mad|house дом умалишённых; **~man** сумасше́дший; **~ness** ['mædnis] сумасше́ствие.

magazine [mægə'zi:n] склад боеприпа́сов; журна́л; ⊕, ⚔ магази́н.

maggot ['mægət] личи́нка.

magic ['mædʒik] **1.** (*a.* **~al** ['mædʒikəl] □) волше́бный; **2.** волшебство́; **~ian** [mə'dʒiʃən] волше́бник.

magistra|cy ['mædʒistrəsi] до́лжность судьи́; магистра́т; **~te** [-trit] мирово́й судья́ *m.*

magnanimous [mæg'næniməs] □ великоду́шный.

magnet ['mægnit] магни́т; **~ic** [mæg'netik] (~ally) магни́тный; магнети́ческий.

magni|ficence [mæg'nifisns] великоле́пие; **~ficent** [-snt] великоле́пный; **~fy** ['mægnifai] увели́чи(ва)ть; **~tude** ['mægnitju:d] величина́; разме́ры *m/pl.*; ва́жность *f.*

mahogany [mə'hɔgəni] кра́сное де́рево.

maid [meid] деви́ца, де́вушка; го́рничная, служа́нка; old ~ ста́рая де́ва; ~ of honour фре́йлина; *Am.* подру́жка неве́сты.

maiden ['meidn] **1.** деви́ца, де́вушка; **2.** незаму́жняя; *fig.* де́вственный; *fig.* пе́рвый; ~ name де́вичья фами́лия; **~head, ~hood** деви́чество; де́вственность *f*; **~ly** [-li] деви́чий.

mail[1] [meil] кольчу́га.

mail[2] [~] **1.** по́чта; *attr.* почто́вый; **2.** *Am.* сдава́ть на по́чту; посыла́ть по́чтой; **~-bag** почто́вая су́мка; **~man** *Am.* почтальо́н.

maim [meim] [ис]калéчить, [из-]уве́чить.

main [mein] **1.** гла́вная часть *f*; ~s *pl.* ↯ магистра́ль *f*; ↯ сеть си́льного то́ка; *f*; in the ~ в основно́м; **2.** гла́вный, основно́й; **~land** ['meinlənd] матери́к; **~ly** ['meinli] гла́вным о́бразом; бо́льшей ча́стью; **~spring** *fig.* гла́вная дви́жущая си́ла; **~stay** *fig.* гла́вная подде́ржка, опо́ра.

maintain [men'tein] подде́рживать [-жа́ть]; утвержда́ть [-рди́ть]; сохраня́ть [-ни́ть].

maintenance ['meintinəns] содержа́ние, сре́дства к существова́нию; подде́ржка; сохране́ние.

maize [meiz] ⚘ маис, кукуру́за.

majest|ic [mə'dʒestik] (~ally) вели́чественный; **~y** ['mædʒisti] вели́чество; вели́чественность *f.*

major ['meidʒə] **1.** ста́рший, бо́льший; ♪ мажо́рный; ~ key мажо́р; совершенноле́тний; **2.** майо́р; *Am. univ.* гла́вный предме́т; **~-general** генера́л-майо́р; **~ity** [mə'dʒɔriti] совершенноле́тие; большинство́; чин майо́ра.

make [meik] **1.** [*irr.*] *v/t. com.* [с]де́лать, производи́ть [-вести́]; [при-]гото́вить; составля́ть [-а́вить]; заключа́ть [-чи́ть] (мир и т. п.); заставля́ть [-ста́вить]; ~ good исправля́ть [-а́вить; [с]держа́ть (сло́во); do you ~ one of us? вы с на́ми? ~ a port входи́ть в порт, га́вань; ~ sure of удостоверя́ться [-ве́риться] в (П); ~ way уступа́ть доро́гу (for Д); ~ into превраща́ть [-рати́ть], переде́л(ыв)ать в (В); ~ out разбира́ть [разобра́ть]; выпи́сывать [вы́писать]; ~ over переда(ва́)ть; ~ up составля́ть [-а́вить] ула́живать [ула́дить] (о ссо́ре); [за]гримирова́ть; навёрстывать [наверста́ть] (вре́мя); = ~ up for (*v/i.*); ~ up one's mind реша́ться [-ши́ться]; **2.** *v/i.* направля́ться [-а́виться] (for к Д); ~ away with отде́л(ыв)аться от (Р); ~ off уезжа́ть [уе́хать]; уходи́ть [уйти́]; ~ up for возмеща́ть [-мести́ть]; **3.** тип, моде́ль *f*; изде́лие; ма́рка (фи́рмы); **~-believe** притво́рство; предло́г; **~-shift** заме́на; подру́чное сре́дство; **~-up** соста́в; грим, косме́тика.

maladjustment ['mæləd'dʒʌstmənt] неуда́чное приспособле́ние.

maladministration ['mælədminis'treiʃən] плохо́е управле́ние.

malady [ˈmælədi] болéзнь *f*.
malcontent [ˈmælkəntent] **1.** недовóльный; **2.** недовóльный (человéк).
male [meil] **1.** мужскóй; **2.** мужчи́на; самéц.
malediction [mæliˈdikʃən] прокля́тие.
malefactor [ˈmælifæktə] злодéй.
malevolen|ce [məˈlevələns] злорáдство; недоброжелáтельность *f*; **~t** [-lənt] □ злорáдный; недоброжелáтельный.
malice [ˈmælis] злóба.
malicious [məˈliʃəs] □ злóбный; **~ness** [-nis] злóбность *f*.
malign [məˈlain] **1.** □ пáгубный, врéдный; **2.** [на]клеветáть на (В); злослóвить; **~ant** [məˈlignənt] □ зловрéдный; злóбный, злóстный; ⚕ злокáчественный; **~ity** [-niti] злóбность *f*; пáгубность *f*; ⚕ злокáчественность *f*.
malleable [ˈmæliəbl] кóвкий; *fig.* подáтливый.
mallet [ˈmælit] колотýшка.
malnutrition [ˈmælnju:ˈtriʃən] недостáточное питáние.
malodorous [ˈmæˈloudərəs] □ зловóнный, вонючий.
malt [mɔ:lt] сóлод; F пи́во.
maltreat [mælˈtri:t] дýрно обращáться с (Т).
mammal [ˈmæməl] млекопитáющее (живóтное).
mammoth [ˈmæməθ] **1.** громáдный; **2.** мáмонт.
man [mæn] **1.** (*pl.* men) человéк; мужчи́на *m*; человéчество; слугá *m*; фигýра (игры́); **2.** ⚔ ⚓ укомплектóвывать состáвом; ~ o. s. мужáться.
manage [ˈmænidʒ] *v/t.* управля́ть (Т), завéдовать (Т); стоя́ть во главé (Р); справля́ться [-áвиться] с (Т); обходи́ться [обои́тись] (with (Т, without без Р); ~ to (+ *inf.*) [с]умéть ...; **~able** [-əbl] □ послýшный, сми́рный; сговóрчивый; **~ment** [-mənt] управлéние, завéдование; умéние спрáвиться; **~r** [-ə] завéдующий; дирéктор; **~ress** [-əres] завéдующая.
managing [ˈmænidʒiŋ] руководя́щий; деловóй.
mandat|e [ˈmændeit] мандáт; накáз; **~ory** [ˈmændətəri] мандáтный; повели́тельный.
mane [mein] гри́ва; *fig.* кóсмы *f/pl.*
manful [ˈmænful] □ мýжественный.
mange [meindʒ] *vet.* чесóтка.
manger [ˈmeindʒə] я́сли *m/pl.*, кормýшка.
mangle [ˈmæŋgl] **1.** катóк (для белья́); **2.** [вы́]катáть (бельё); *fig.* искажáть [искази́ть].
mangy [ˈmeindʒi] чесóточный; парши́вый.
manhood [ˈmænhud] возмужáлость *f*; мýжественность *f*.
mania [ˈmeiniə] мáния; **~c** [ˈmeiniæk] **1.** маньяк (-я́чка); **2.** помéшанный.
manicure [ˈmænikjuə] **1.** маникю́р **2.** дéлать маникю́р (Д).
manifest [ˈmænifest] **1.** □ очеви́дный, я́вный; **2.** ⚓ декларáция судовóго грýза; **3.** *v/t.* обнарýживать; обнарóдовать *pf.*; проявля́ть [-ви́ть]; **~ation** [ˈmænifesˈteiʃən] проявлéние; манифестáция; **~o** [-ˈfestou] манифéст.
manifold [ˈmænifould] □ **1.** разнообрáзный, разнорóдный; **2.** размножáть [-óжить] (докумéнты).
manipulat|e [məˈnipjuleit] манипули́ровать; **~ion** [mənipjuˈleiʃən] манипуля́ция; подтасóвка.
man|kind [mænˈkaind] **1.** человéчество; **2.** [ˈmænkaind] мужскóй род; **~ly** [-li] мýжественный.
manner [ˈmænə] спóсоб, мéтод, манéра; óбраз дéйствий; **~s** *pl* умéние держáть себя́; манéры *f/pl.*; обы́чаи *m/pl.*; in a ~ в нéкоторой стéпени; **~ed** [-d] вы́чурный; **~ly** [-li] вéжливый.
manoeuvre [məˈnu:və] **1.** манёвр **2.** проводи́ть манёвры; маневри́ровать.
man-of-war воéнный корáбль *f*
manor [ˈmænə] помéстье.
mansion [ˈmænʃən] большóй помéщичий дом.
manslaughter [ˈmænslɔ:tə] непредумы́шленное уби́йство.
mantel [mæntl] облицóвкаками́на **~piece, ~shelf** пóлкаками́на.
mantle [mæntl] **1.** мáнтия; *fig.* покрóв; **2.** *v/t.* окýт(ыв)ать; покры́(вá)ть; *v/i.* [по]краснéть.
manual [-juəl] **1.** ручнóй; **2.** руковóдство (кни́га), учéбник, спрáвочник.
manufactory [mænjuˈfæktəri] фáбрика.
manufactur|e [mænjuˈfæktʃə] **1** произвóдство; издéлие; **2.** вырабáтывать [вы́делать], [с]фабриковáть; **~er** [-rə] фабрикáнт; заводчик; **~ing** [-riŋ] произвóдство вы́делка; *attr.* фабри́чный, промы́шленный.
manure [mənˈjuə] **1.** удобрéние **2.** удобря́ть [-óбрить].
many [ˈmeni] **1.** мнóгие, многочи́сленные; мнóго; ~ a инóй; **2** мнóжество; a good ~ поря́дочное коли́чество; a great ~ громáдное коли́чество.
map [mæp] **1.** кáрта; **2.** наноси́ть на кáрту; ~ out [с]плани́ровать.
mar [mɑ:] искажáть [искази́ть]; [ис]пóртить.
marble [mɑ:bl] **1.** мрáмор; **2.** распи́сывать под мрáмор.
March[1] [mɑ:tʃ] март.

ıarch[2] [~] **1.** ⚔ марш; похóд; *fig.* ›азвитие (собы́тий); **2.** марши›овáть; *fig.* идти́ вперёд (*a.* ~ on).
archioness ['mɑːʃənis] маркиза ти́тул).
are [mɛə] кобы́ла; ~'s nest ил›ю́зия; газéтная у́тка.
argin ['mɑːdʒin] крáй; поля́ *n/pl.* страни́цы); опу́шка (лéса); **~al** -l] □ находя́щийся на краю́; ~ ıote замéтка на поля́х страни́цы.
arine [mə'riːn] **1.** морскóй; **2.** олдáт морскóй пехóты; *paint.* ıорскóй вид (карти́на); **~r** ['mæ›inə] моря́к, матрóс.
arital [mə'raitl] □ супру́жеский.
aritime ['mæritaim] примóр›кий; морскóй.
ark[1] [mɑːk] мáрка (дéнежная диница).
ark[2] [~] **1.** мéтка, знак; балл, тмéтка (оцéнка знáний); фабри́ч›ая мáрка; мишéнь *f*; нóрма; a ıan of ~ выдаю́щийся человéк; ıp to the ~ *fig.* на дóлжной вы›оте́; **2.** *v/t.* отмечáть [-éтить]; стáвить расцéнку на (товáр); стá›ить отмéтку в (П); ~ off отделя́ть -ли́ть]; ~ out расставля́ть указá›ельные знáки на (П); ~ time ⚔ тбивáть шаг на мéсте; **~ed** ma:kt] □ отмéченный; замéтный.
arket ['mɑːkit] **1.** ры́нок, базáр; ✝ сбыт; in the ~ в продáже; **2.** ›ривози́ть на ры́нок (для про›áжи); покупáть на ры́нке; про›á(вá)ть; go ~ing ходи́ть на ры́нок;
able [-əbl] □ хóдкий.
arksman ['mɑːksmən] мéткий трелóк.
armalade ['mɑːməleid] (апель›и́нное) варéнье; мармелáд.
aroon [mə'ruːn] высáживать на ıеобитáемом óстрове.
arquee [mɑː'kiː] шатёр.
arquis ['mɑːkwis] марки́з.
arriage ['mæridʒ] брак; свáдьба; ivil ~ граждáнский брак; **~able** -əbl] дости́гший (-шая) брáчного ›óзраста; **~-lines** *pl.* свидéтель›тво о брáке.
arried ['mærid] женáтый; за›у́жняя; ~ couple супру́ги *pl.*
arrow ['mærou] кóстный мозг; *ig.* су́щность *f*; **~y** [-i] костно›озговóй; *fig.* крéпкий.
arry ['mæri] *v/t.* жени́ть; вы›авáть зáмуж; *eccl.* сочетáть брá›ом; жени́ться на (П), вы́йти зá›уж за (В); *v/i.* жени́ться; вы́йти áмуж.
arsh [mɑːʃ] болóто.
arshal ['mɑːʃəl] **1.** мáршал; цере›онимéйстер; *Am.* начáльник ›олиции; **2.** выстрáивать [вы́›троить] (войскá и т. п.); торжест›енно вести́.
arshy ['mɑːʃi] болóтистый, бо›óтный.

mart [mɑːt] ры́нок; аукциóнный зал.
marten ['mɑːtin] *zo.* куни́ца.
martial ['mɑːʃl] □ воéнный; вои́нственный; ~ law воéнное положéние.
martyr ['mɑːtə] **1.** му́ченик (-ица); **2.** за]му́чить (дó смерти).
marvel ['mɑːvel] **1.** ди́во, чу́до; **2.** удивля́ться [-ви́ться]; **~lous** ['mɑːvələs] □ изуми́тельный, удиви́тельный.
mascot ['mæskət] талисмáн.
masculine ['mɑːskjulin] мужскóй; му́жественный.
mash [mæʃ] **1.** мешани́на; су́сло; **2.** разминáть [-мя́ть]; раздáвливать [-дави́ть]; ~ed potatoes *pl.* картóфельное пюрé *n indecl.*
mask [mɑːsk] **1.** мáска; **2.** [за]маски́ровáть; скры(вá)ть; **~ed** [-t]: ~ ball маскарáд.
mason ['meisn] кáменщик; масóн; **~ry** [-ri] кáменная (и́ли кирпи́чная) клáдка; масóнство.
masquerade [mæskə'reid] **1.** маскарáд; **2.** *fig.* притворя́ться [-ри́ться].
mass [mæs] **1.** мáсса; *eccl.* мéсса; ~ meeting мáссовое собрáние; **2.** собирáться толпóй, собирáть(ся) в ку́чу; ⚔ масси́ровать *(im)pf.*
massacre ['mæsəkə] **1.** резня́, избиéние; **2.** вырезáть [вы́резать] (людéй).
massage ['mæsɑːʒ] **1.** массáж; **2.** масси́ровать.
massive ['mæsiv] масси́вный; крýпный.
mast [mɑːst] ⚓ мáчта.
master ['mɑːstə] **1.** хозя́ин; господи́н; капитáн (су́дна); учи́тель *m*; мáстер; *univ.* главá коллéджа; ♀ of Arts маги́стр иску́сств; **2.** одолé(вá)ть; справля́ться [-áвиться] с (Т); овладé(вá)ть (Т); владéть (языкóм); **3.** *attr.* мастерскóй; ведýщий; **~-builder** строи́тель *m*; **~ful** ['mɑːstəful] □ влáстный; мастерскóй; **~key** отмы́чка; **~ly** [-li] мастерскóй; **~piece** шедéвр; **~ship** [-ʃip] мастерствó; дóлжность учи́теля; **~y** ['mɑːstəri] госпóдство, власть *f*; мастерствó.
masticate ['mæstikeit] [с]жевáть.
mastiff ['mæstif] англи́йский дог.
mat [mæt] **1.** цинóвка, рогóжа; **2.** *fig.* спу́т(ыв)ать.
match[1] [mætʃ] спи́чка; ⚔ фити́ль [*m.*]
match[2] [~] **1.** рóвня *m/f*; матч, состязáние; вы́годный брак, пáртия; be a ~ for быть рóвней (Д); **2.** *v/t.* [с]равня́ться с (Т); подбирáть под пáру; well ~ed couple хорóшая пáра; *v/i.* соотвéтствовать; сочетáться; to ~ подходя́щий (по цвéту, тóну и т. п.); **~less** ['mætʃlis] □ несравнéнный, бесподóбный.
mate [meit] **1.** товáрищ; сожи́тель

(-ница *f*) *m*; супру́г(а); саме́ц (са́мка); ⚓ помо́щник капита́на; **2.** сочета́ть(ся) бра́ком.

material [məˈtiəriəl] **1.** □ материа́льный; суще́ственный; **2.** материа́л (*a. fig.*); мате́рия; вещество́.

matern|al [məˈtə:nl] □ матери́нский; **~ity** [-niti] матери́нство; (*mst* ~ hospital) роди́льный дом.

mathematic|ian [mæθiməˈtiʃən] матема́тик; **~s** [-mæˈtiks] (*mst sg.*) матема́тика.

matriculate [məˈtrikjuleit] приня́ть и́ли быть при́нятым в университе́т.

matrimon|ial [mætriˈmounjəl] □ бра́чный; супру́жеский; **~y** [ˈmætriməni] супру́жество, брак.

matrix [ˈmeitriks] ма́трица.

matron [ˈmeitrən] заму́жняя же́нщина; эконо́мка; сестра́-хозя́йка (в больни́це).

matter [ˈmætə] **1.** вещество́; материа́л; предме́т; де́ло; по́вод; what's the ~? что случи́лось?, в чём де́ло?; no ~ who ... всё равно́, кто ...; ~ of course само́ собо́й разуме́ющееся де́ло; for that ~ что каса́ется э́того; ~ of fact факт; **2.** име́ть значе́ние; it ˈdoes not ~ ничего́; **~-of-fact** факти́ческий; делово́й.

mattress [ˈmætris] матра́ц, тюфя́к.

matur|e [məˈtjuə] **1.** □ зре́лый; вы́держанный; † подлежа́щий упла́те; **2.** созре́(ва́)ть; вполне́ развива́ться; † наступа́ть [-пи́ть] (о сро́ке); **~ity** [-riti] зре́лость *f*; † срок платежа́ по ве́кселю.

maudlin [ˈmɔ:dlin] □ плакси́вый.

maul [mɔ:l] [рас]терза́ть; *fig.* жесто́ко критикова́ть.

mawkish [ˈmɔ:kiʃ] □ сентимента́льный; неприя́тный на вкус.

maxim [ˈmæksim] афори́зм; при́нцип; **~um** [-siməm] **1.** ма́ксимум; вы́сшая сте́пень *f*; **2.** максима́льный.

May[1] [mei] май.

may[2] [~] [*irr.*] (мода́льный глаго́л без инфинити́ва и прича́стий) [с]мочь; име́ть разреше́ние.

maybe [ˈmeibi:] *Am.* мо́жет быть.

May-day [ˈmeidei] пра́здник пе́рвого ма́я.

mayor [mɛə] мэр.

maz|e [meiz] лабири́нт; *fig.* пу́таница; be ~d и́ли in a ~ быть расте́рянным; **~y** [ˈmeizi] □ запу́танный.

me [mi:, mi] ко́свенный паде́ж от I: мне, меня́; F я.

meadow [ˈmedou] луг.

meagre [ˈmi:gə] худо́й, то́щий; ску́дный.

meal [mi:l] еда́ (за́втрак, обе́д, у́жин); мука́.

mean[1] [mi:n] □ по́длый, ни́зкий; ска́редный.

mean[2] [~] **1.** сре́дний; in the ~ time тем вре́менем; **2.** середи́на; ~s *pl.* состоя́ние, бога́тство; (*a. sg.*) сре́дство; спо́соб; by all ~s любо́й цено́й; коне́чно; by no ~s нисколько; отню́дь не ...; by ~s of посре́дством (Р).

mean[3] [~] [*irr.*] намерева́ться; име́ть в виду́; хоте́ть сказа́ть, подразумева́ть; предназнача́ть [-зна́чить]; зна́чить; ~ well (ill) име́ть до́брые (плохи́е) наме́рения.

meaning [ˈmi:niŋ] **1.** □ зна́чащий; **2.** значе́ние; смысл; **~less** [-lis] бессмы́сленный.

meant [ment] *pt.* и *p. pt.* от mean.

mean|time, ~while тем вре́менем.

measles [ˈmi:zlz] *pl.* ⚕ корь *f*.

measure [ˈmeʒə] **1.** ме́ра; ме́рка; мероприя́тие; масшта́б; ♪ такт; ~ of capacity ме́ра объёма; beyond ~ непоме́рно; in a great ~ в большо́й сте́пени; made to ~ сде́ланный по ме́рке; **2.** измеря́ть [-е́рить]; [с]ме́рить; снима́ть ме́рку с (Р); **~less** [-lis] □ неизмери́мый; **~ment** [-mənt] разме́р; измере́ние.

meat [mi:t] мя́со; *fig.* содержа́ние; **~y** [ˈmi:ti] мяси́стый; *fig.* содержа́тельный.

mechanic [miˈkænik] меха́ник; реме́сленник; **~al** [-nikəl] □ маши́нный; механи́ческий; машина́льный; **~ian** [mekəˈniʃən] меха́ник; **~s** (*mst sg.*) меха́ника.

mechanize [ˈmekənaiz] механизи́ровать (*im*)*pf.*; ⚔ моторизова́ть [(*im*)*pf.*].

medal [medl] меда́ль *f*.

meddle [medl] (with, in) вме́шиваться [-ша́ться] (в В); **~some** [-səm] □ надое́дливый.

media|l [ˈmi:diəl] □, **~n** [-ən] сре́дний; среди́нный.

mediat|e [ˈmi:dieit] посре́дничать; **~ion** [mi:diˈeiʃən] посре́дничество; **~or** [ˈmi:dieitə] посре́дник.

medical [ˈmedikəl] □ медици́нский; враче́бный; ~ certificate больни́чный листо́к; медици́нское свиде́тельство; ~ man врач, меди́к.

medicin|al [meˈdisinl] □ лека́рственный; целе́бный; **~e** [ˈmed(i)sin] медици́на; лека́рство.

medi(a)eval [mediˈi:vəl] □ средневеко́вый.

mediocre [ˈmi:dioukə] посре́дственный.

meditat|e [ˈmediteit] *v/i.* размышля́ть [-ы́слить]; *v/t.* обду́м(ыв)ать (В); **~ion** [mediˈteiʃən] размышле́ние; созерца́ние; **~ive** [ˈmediteitiv] □ созерца́тельный.

Mediterranean [meditəˈreinjən] (и́ли ~ Sea) Средизе́мное мо́ре.

medium [ˈmi:diəm] **1.** середи́на; сре́дство, спо́соб; ме́диум (у спири́тов); аге́нт; **2.** сре́дний; уме́ренный.

medley ['medli] смесь *f*; ♪ попурри́ *n indecl.*
meek [mi:k] □ кро́ткий, мя́гкий; **~ness** ['miknis] кро́тость *f*, мя́гкость *f*.
meet [mi:t] [*irr.*] *v/t.* встреча́ть [-е́тить]; [по]знако́миться с (Т); удовлетворя́ть [-ри́ть] (тре́бования и т. п.); опла́чивать [-лати́ть] (долги́); go to ~ a p. идти́ навстре́чу (Д); *v/i.* [по]знако́миться; сходи́ться [сойти́сь], соб(и)ра́ться; ~ with испы́тывать [-пыта́ть] (В), подверга́ться [-ве́ргнуться] (Д); **~ing** ['mi:tiŋ] заседа́ние; встре́ча; ми́тинг, собра́ние.
melancholy ['melənkəli] **1.** уны́ние; грусть *f*; **2.** пода́вленный; уны́лый.
mellow ['melou] **1.** □ спе́лый; прия́тный на вкус; **2.** смягча́ть (-ся) [-чи́ть(ся)]; созре́(ва́)ть.
melo|dious [mi'loudjəs] □ мелоди́чный; **~dy** ['melədi] мело́дия.
melon ['melən] ♀ ды́ня.
melt [melt] [рас]та́ять; [рас]плави́ть(ся); *fig.* смягча́ть(ся) [-чи́ть (-ся)].
member ['membə] член (*a. parl.*); **~ship** [-ʃip] чле́нство.
membrane ['membrein] плева́, оболо́чка; перепо́нка; ⊕ мембра́на.
memento [me'mentou] напомина́ние.
memoir ['memwɑ:] мемориа́льная статья́; ~s *pl.* мемуа́ры *m/pl.*
memorable ['memərəbl] □ незабве́нный.
memorandum [memə'rændəm] заме́тка; *pol.* меморандум.
memorial [mi'mɔ:riəl] **1.** па́мятник; ~s *pl.* хро́ника; **2.** мемориа́льный.
memorize ['meməraiz] *part. Am.* зау́чивать наизу́сть.
memory ['meməri] па́мять *f*; воспомина́ние.
men [men] (*pl.* от man) лю́ди *m/pl.*; мужчи́ны *m/pl.*
menace ['menəs] **1.** угрожа́ть [-ози́ть], [по]грози́ть (Д; with Т); **2.** угро́за; опа́сность *f*.
mend [mend] **1.** *v/t.* исправля́ть [-а́вить]; [по]чини́ть; ~ one's ways исправля́ться [-а́виться]; *v/i.* улучша́ться [улу́чшиться]; поправля́ться [-а́виться]; **2.** почи́нка; on the ~ на попра́вку (о здоро́вье).
mendacious [men'deiʃəs] □ лжи́вый.
mendicant ['mendikənt] ни́щий; ни́щенствующий мона́х.
menial ['mi:niəl] *contp.* **1.** □ рабо-ле́пный, лаке́йский; **2.** слуга́ *m*, лаке́й.
mental [mentl] □ у́мственный; психи́ческий; ~ arithmetic счёт в уме́; **~ity** [men'tæliti] спосо́бность мышле́ния; склад ума́.
mention ['menʃən] **1.** упомина́ние; **2.** упомина́ть [-мяну́ть] (В *or* о П); don't ~ it! не сто́ит!, не́ за что!
mercantile ['mə:kəntail] торго́вый, комме́рческий.
mercenary ['mə:sinəri] **1.** □ корыстный; наёмный; **2.** наёмник.
mercer ['mə:sə] торго́вец шёлком и ба́рхатом.
merchandise ['mə:tʃəndaiz] това́р (-ы *pl.*).
merchant ['mə:tʃənt] торго́вец, купе́ц; law ~ торго́вое пра́во; **~man** [-mən] торго́вое су́дно.
merci|ful ['mə:siful] □ милосе́рдный; **~less** [-lis] □ немилосе́рдный.
mercury ['mə:kjuri] ртуть *f*.
mercy [-si] милосе́рдие; сострада́ние; проще́ние; be at a p.'s ~ быть во вла́сти кого́-либо.
mere [miə] □ просто́й; сплошно́й; **~ly** то́лько, про́сто.
meretricious [meri'triʃəs] □ показно́й; мишу́рный; распу́тный.
merge [mə:dʒ] сли́(ва́)ть(ся) (in с Т); **~r** ['mə:dʒə] слия́ние, объедине́ние.
meridian [mə'ridiən] **1.** полу́денный; *fig.* вы́сший; **2.** по́лдень *m*; *geogr.* меридиа́н; *fig.* вы́сшая то́чка; расцве́т.
merit ['merit] **1.** заслу́га; досто́инство; make a ~ of a th. ста́вить что́-либо себе́ в заслу́гу; **2.** заслу́живать [-ужи́ть]; **~orious** [meri'tɔ:riəs] □ досто́йный награ́ды; похва́льный.
mermaid ['mə:meid] руса́лка, ная́да.
merriment ['merimənt] весе́лье.
merry ['meri] □ весёлый, ра́достный; make ~ весели́ться; **~-go-round** карусе́ль *f*; **~-making** весе́лье; пра́здество.
mesh [meʃ] **1.** пе́тля; ~(es *pl.*) се́ти *f/pl.*; ⊕ be in ~ сцепля́ться [-пи́ться]; **2.** *fig.* опу́тывать сетя́ми; запу́таться в сетя́х.
mess[1] [mes] **1.** беспоря́док, пу́таница; неприя́тность *f*; кава́рда́к; make a ~ of a th. прова́ливать де́ло; **2.** *v/t.* приводи́ть в беспоря́док; *v/i.* F ~ about рабо́тать ко́е-ка́к.
mess[2] [~] ⚔ о́бщий стол; столо́вая.
message ['mesidʒ] сообще́ние; посла́ние; поруче́ние.
messenger ['mesindʒə] посы́льный; предве́стник.
met [met] *pt.* и *p. pt.* от meet.
metal ['metl] **1.** мета́лл; ще́бень *m*; **2.** мости́ть ще́бнем; **~lic** [mi'tælik] (**~ally**) металли́ческий; **~lurgy** ['metələ:dʒi] металлу́ргия.
meteor ['mi:tjə] метео́р; **~ology** [mi:tjə'rɔlədʒi] метеороло́гия.
meter ['mi:tə] счётчик; измери́тель *m*.

method ['meθəd] мéтод, спóсоб; систéма, порядок; **~ic**, *mst.* **~ical** □ [mi'θɔdik, -dikəl] систематúческий; методúческий, методúчный.
meticulous [mi'tikjuləs] □ дотóшный; щепетúльный.
metre ['mi:tə] метр.
metric ['metrik] (~ally) метрúческий; ~ system метрúческая систéма.
metropoli|s [mi'trɔpəlis] столúца; метропóлия; **~tan** [metrə'pɔlitən] столúчный.
mettle [metl] темперáмент; пыл.
Mexican ['meksikən] **1.** мексикáнский; **2.** мексикáнец (-нка).
miauw [mi'au] [за]мяýкать.
mice [mais] *pl.* мы́ши *f/pl.*
Michaelmas ['miklməs] Михáйлов день *m* (29 сентября́).
micro... ['maikro] микро...
micro|phone ['maikrəfoun] микрофóн; **~scope** микроскóп.
mid [mid] срéдний; сединный; **~air**: in ~ высокó в вóздухе; **~day** **1.** пóлдень *m*; **2.** полýденный.
middle [midl] **1.** серединá; **2.** срéдний; ♀ Ages *pl.* срéдние векá *m/pl.*, средневекóвье; **~-aged** срéдних лет; **~-class** срéдняя буржуазúя; **~man** посрéдник; **~-sized** срéдней величины́; **~-weight** срéдний вéс (о бóксе); (боксёр) срéднего вéса.
middling ['midliŋ] посрéдственный.
middy ['midi] F = midshipman.
midge [midʒ] мóшка; **~t** ['midʒit] кáрлик; *attr.* миниатю́рный.
mid|land ['midlənd] внýтренняя часть страны́; **~most** центрáльный; **~night** пóлночь *f*; **~riff** ['midrif] *anat.* диафрáгма; **~ship** мúдель *m*; **~shipman** корабéльный гардемарúн; **~st** [midst] серединá; средá; in the ~ of средú (Р); in our ~ в нáшей средé; **~summer** серединá лéта; **~way** на полпутú; **~wife** акушéрка; **~wifery** ['midwifəri] акушéрство; **~winter** серединá зимы́.
mien [mi:n] мúна (выражéние лицá).
might [mait] **1.** мощь *f*; могýщество; with ~ and main изо всех сил; **2.** *pt.* и *p.pt.* от may; **~y** ['maiti] могýщественный; громáдный.
migrat|e [mai'greit] мигрúровать; **~ion** [-ʃən] мигрáция; перелёт; **~ory** ['maigrətəri] кочýющий; перелётный.
mild [maild] □ мя́гкий; крóткий; слáбый (о напúтке, табакé и т. п.).
mildew ['mildju:] ⚘ мúлдью *n indecl.*; плéсень *f*.
mildness ['maildnis] мя́гкость *f*; крóткость *f.*; умéренность *f.*
mile [mail] мúля (= 1609,33 м).
mil(e)age ['mailidʒ] расстоя́ние в мúлях.
milit|ary ['militəri] **1.** □ воéнный; вóинский; ♀ Government воéнное правúтельство; **2.** воéнные; воéнные влáсти *f/pl.*; **~ia** [mi'liʃə] милúция; ополчéние.
milk [milk] **1.** молокó; powdered ~ молóчный порошóк; whole ~ цéльное молокó; **2.** [вы́]доить; **~maid** доя́рка; **~man** молóчник; **~sop** бесхарáктерный человéк, «тря́пка»; **~y** ['milki] молóчный; ♀ Way Млéчный путь *m.*
mill¹ [mil] **1.** мéльница; фáбрика, завóд; **2.** [с]молóть; ⊕ [от]фрезеровáть *(im)pf.*
mill² [~] *Am.* (= 1/10 *cent*) милл (ты́сячная часть дóллара).
millepede ['milipi:d] *zo.* многонóжка.
miller ['milə] мéльник; ⊕ фрéзерный станóк; фрезерóвщик.
millet ['milit] ⚘ прóсо.
milliner ['milinə] модúстка; **~y** [-ri] магазúн дáмских шляп.
million ['miljən] миллиóн; **~aire** [miljə'nɛə] миллионéр; **~th** ['miljənθ] **1.** миллиóнный; **2.** миллиóнная часть *f*.
mill-pond мéльничный пруд; **~stone** жёрнов.
milt [milt] молóки *f/pl.*
mimic ['mimik] **1.** подражáтельный; **2.** имитáтор; **3.** пародúровать *(im)pf.*; подражáть (Д); **~ry** [-ri] подражáние; *zo.* мимикрúя.
mince [mins] **1.** *v/t.* [из]рубúть (мя́со); he does not ~ matters он говорúт без обиняков; *v/i.* говорúть жемáнно; **2.** рýбленое мя́со (*mst* ~d meat); **~meat** фарш из изю́ма, я́блок и т. п.; **~-pie** пирóг (*s.* mincemeat).
mincing-machine мясорýбка.
mind [maind] **1.** ум, рáзум; мнéние; намéрение; охóта; пáмять *f*; to my ~ по моемý мнéнию; out of one's ~ без умá; change one's ~ передýм(ыв)ать; bear in ~ пóмнить, не забы́(вá)ть; have a ~ to имéть желáние (+ *inf.*); have a th. on one's ~ беспокóиться о чём-либо; make up one's ~ решáться [-шúться]; **2.** пóмнить; [по]забóтиться о (П); остерегáться [-рéчься] (Р); never ~! ничегó!; I don't ~ (it) я ничегó не имéю прóтив; would you ~ taking off your hat? бýдьте дóбры, снять шля́пу; **~ful** ['maindful] □ (of) внимáтельный (к Д); забóтливый.
mine¹ [main] *pred.* мой *m*, моя́ *f*, моё *n*, мой *pl.*; **2.** мой (родны́е), моя́ семья́.
mine² [~] **1.** рудни́к, копь *f*, шáхта; *fig.* истóчник; ⚔ мúна; **2.** добы́(вá)ть; рыть; производúть гóрные рабóты; ⚔ минúровать

(*im*)*pf*.; подры́(ва́)ть; *fig*. подрыва́ть [подорва́ть]; **~r** ['mainə] горня́к, шахтёр.
mineral ['minərəl] **1.** минера́л; **~s** *pl*. минера́льные во́ды *f/pl*.; **2.** минера́льный.
mingle ['miŋgl] сме́шивать(ся) [-ша́ть(ся)].
miniature ['minjətʃə] **1.** миниатю́ра; **2.** миниатю́рный.
minim|ize ['minimaiz] доводи́ть до ми́нимума; *fig*. преуменьша́ть [-е́ньши́ть]; **~um** [-iməm] **1.** ми́нимум; **2.** минима́льный.
mining ['mainiŋ] го́рная промы́шленность *f*.
minister ['ministə] **1.** мини́стр; посла́нник; свяще́нник; **2.** *v/i*. соверша́ть богослуже́ние; [по-] служи́ть.
ministry ['ministri] министе́рство; служе́ние;
mink [miŋk] *zo*. но́рка.
minor ['mainə] **1.** мла́дший; ме́ньший; второстепе́нный; ♪ мино́рный; A ~ ля мино́р; **2.** несовершенноле́тний; *Am. univ*. второстепе́нный предме́т; **~ity** [mai'nɔriti] несовершенноле́тие; меньшинство́.
minstrel ['minstrəl] менестре́ль *m*; **~s** *pl*. исполни́тели негритя́нских пе́сен.
mint [mint] ♀ мя́та; моне́та; моне́тный двор; *fig*. «золото́е дно»; a ~ of money больша́я су́мма; **2.** [вы́-, от]чека́нить.
minuet [minju'et] ♪ менуэ́т.
minus ['mainəs] **1.** *prp*. без (P), ми́нус; **2.** *adj*. отрица́тельный.
minute 1. [mai'nju:t] □ ме́лкий; незначи́тельный; подро́бный, дета́льный; **2.** ['minit] мину́та; моме́нт; **~s** *pl*. протоко́л; **~ness** [mai'nju:tnis] ма́лость *f*; то́чность *f*.
mirac|le ['mirəkl] чу́до; **~ulous** [mi'rækjuləs] □ чуде́сный.
mirage ['mirɑ:ʒ] мира́ж.
mire ['maiə] **1.** треси́на; грязь *f*; **2.** завя́знуть в треси́не.
mirror ['mirə] **1.** зе́ркало; **2.** отража́ть [отрази́ть].
mirth [mə:θ] весе́лье, ра́дость *f*; **~ful** ['mə:θful] □ весёлый, ра́достный; **~less** [-lis] □ безра́достный.
miry ['maiəri] то́пкий.
mis... [mis] *pref*. означа́ет непра́вильность и́ли недоста́ток, напр.: misadvise дать непра́вильный сове́т.
misadventure ['misəd'ventʃə] несча́стье; несча́стный слу́чай.
misanthrop|e ['mizənθroup], **~ist** [mi'zænθropist] мизантро́п, человеконенави́стник.
misapply ['misə'plai] злоупотребля́ть [-би́ть] (T); непра́вильно испо́льзовать.
misapprehend ['misæpri'hend] понима́ть оши́бочно.
misbehave ['misbi'heiv] ду́рно вести́ себя́.
misbelief ['misbi'li:f] заблужде́ние; е́ресь *f*.
miscalculate ['mis'kælkjuleit] ошиба́ться в расчёте; непра́вильно рассчи́тывать.
miscarr|iage ['mis'kæridʒ] неуда́ча; недоста́вка по а́дресу; вы́кидыш, або́рт; ~ of justice суде́бная оши́бка; **~y** [-ri] терпе́ть неуда́чу; сде́лать вы́кидыш.
miscellaneous [misi'leinjəs] □ сме́шанный; разносторо́нний.
mischief ['mistʃif] озорство́; прока́зы *f/pl*; вред; зло.
mischievous ['mistʃivəs] □ вре́дный; озорно́й, шаловли́вый.
misconceive ['miskən'si:v] непра́вильно понима́ть.
misconduct 1. ['mis'kɔndəkt] дурно́е поведе́ние; плохо́е управле́ние; **2.** [-kən'dʌkt] пло́хо управля́ть (T); ~ o. s. ду́рно вести́ себя́.
misconstrue ['miskən'stru:] непра́вильно истолко́вывать.
miscreant ['miskriənt] негодя́й, злоде́й.
misdeed ['mis'di:d] злодея́ние.
misdemeano(u)r ['misdi'mi:nə] ⚖ суде́бно наказу́емый просту́пок.
misdirect ['misdi'rekt] неве́рно напра́вить; непра́вильно адресова́ть.
miser ['maizə] скупе́ц, скря́га *m/f*.
miserable ['mizərəbl] □ жа́лкий, несча́стный; убо́гий, ску́дный.
miserly ['maizəli] скупо́й.
misery ['mizəri] невзго́да, несча́стье, страда́ние; нищета́.
misfortune [mis'fɔ:tʃən] неуда́ча, несча́стье.
misgiving [mis'giviŋ] опасе́ние, предчу́вствие дурно́го.
misguide [mis'gaid] вводи́ть в заблужде́ние; непра́вильно напра́вить.
mishap ['mishæp] неуда́ча.
misinform ['misin'fɔ:m] непра́вильно информи́ровать.
misinterpret ['misin'tə:prit] неве́рно истолко́вывать.
mislay [mis'lei] [*irr*. (lay)] положи́ть не на ме́сто.
mislead [mis'li:d] [*irr*. (lead)] вводи́ть в заблужде́ние.
mismanage ['mis'mænidʒ] пло́хо управля́ть (T); [ис]по́ртить.
misplace ['mis'pleis] положи́ть не на ме́сто; *p.pt*. **~d** *fig*. неуме́стный.
misprint ['mis'print] **1.** непра́вильно печа́тать; сде́лать опеча́тку; **2.** опеча́тка.
misread ['mis'ri:d] [*irr*. (read)] чита́ть непра́вильно; непра́вильно истолко́вывать.
misrepresent ['misrepri'zent] представля́ть в ло́жном све́те.
miss[1] [mis] мисс, ба́рышня.

miss[2] [~] **1.** про́мах; отсу́тствие; поте́ря; **2.** *v/t.* упуска́ть [-сти́ть]; опа́здывать [-да́ть] на (В); прогляде́ть *pf.*, не заме́тить; не заста́ть до́ма; чу́вствовать отсу́тствие (кого́-либо); *v/i.* прома́хиваться [-хну́ться]; не попада́ть в цель.

missile ['misail] мета́тельный снаря́д; раке́та.

missing ['misiŋ] отсутствующий, недостающий; ⚔ бе́з вести пропа́вший; be ~ отсу́тствовать.

mission ['miʃən] ми́ссия, делега́ция; призва́ние; поруче́ние; *eccl.* миссионе́рская де́ятельность *f*; **~ary** ['miʃnəri] миссионе́р.

mis-spell ['mis'spel] [*a. irr.* (spell)] орфографи́чески непра́вильно писа́ть.

mist [mist] лёгкий тума́н; ды́мка.

mistake [mis'teik] **1.** [*irr.* (take)] ошиба́ться [-би́ться]; непра́вильно понима́ть; принима́ть [-ня́ть] (for за (В); be **~n** ошиба́ться [-би́ться]; **2.** оши́бка; заблужде́ние; **~n** [ən] □ оши́бочный, непра́вильно по́нятый; неуме́стный.

mister ['mistə] ми́стер, господи́н (ста́вится перед фами́лией).

mistletoe ['misltou] ⚘ оме́ла.

mistress ['mistris] хозя́йка до́ма; учи́тельница; мастери́ца; любо́вница; сокращённо: Mrs. ['misiz] ми́ссис, госпожа́ (ста́вится пе́ред фами́лией заму́жней же́нщины).

mistrust ['mis'trʌst] **1.** не доверя́ть (Д): **2.** недове́рие; **~ful** [-ful] □ недове́рчивый.

misty ['misti] □ тума́нный; нея́сный.

misunderstand ['misʌndə'stænd] [*irr.* (stand)] непра́вильно понима́ть; **~ing** [-iŋ] недоразуме́ние; размо́лвка.

misuse **1.** ['mis'ju:z] злоупотребля́ть [-би́ть](Т); ду́рно обраща́ться с (Т); **2.** [-'ju:s] злоупотребле́ние.

mite [mait] *zo.* клещ; ле́пта; малю́тка *m/f.*

mitigate ['mitigeit] смягча́ть [-чи́ть]; уменьша́ть [уме́ньши́ть].

mitre ['maitə] ми́тра.

mitten ['mitn] рукави́ца.

mix [miks] [с]меша́ть(ся); переме́шивать [-ша́ть]; враща́ться (в о́бществе); ~ed переме́шанный, сме́шанный; разноро́дный; ~ up перепу́т(ыв)ать; be ~ed up with быть заме́шанным в (П); **~ture** ['mikstʃə] смесь *f.*

moan [moun] **1.** стон; **2.** [за]стона́ть.

moat [mout] крепостно́й ров.

mob [mɔb] **1.** толпа́; чернь *f.* **2.** [с]толпи́ться; напада́ть толпо́й на (В).

mobil|e ['moubail] подвижно́й; ⚔ моби́льный, подвижно́й; **~ization** [moubilai'zeiʃən] ⚔ мобилиза́ция; **~ize** ['moubilaiz] ⚔ мобилизова́ть (*im*)*pf.*;

moccasin ['mɔkəsin] мокаси́н (о́бувь инде́йцев).

mock [mɔk] **1.** насме́шка; **2.** подде́льный; мни́мый; **3.** *v/t.* осме́ивать [-ея́ть]; *v/i.* ~ at насмеха́ться [-ея́ться] над (Т); **~ery** [-ri] насме́шка.

mode [moud] ме́тод, спо́соб; обы́чай; фо́рма; мо́да.

model [mɔdl] **1.** моде́ль *f*; манеке́н; нату́рщик (-ица); *fig.* приме́р, образе́ц; *attr.* образцо́вый, приме́рный; **2.** модели́ровать (*im*)*pf.*; [вы́]лепи́ть; оформля́ть [офо́рмить].

moderat|e **1.** ['mɔdərit] □ уме́ренный; возде́ржанный; вы́держанный; **2.** ['mɔdəreit] умеря́ть [уме́рить]; смягча́ть(ся) [-чи́ть(ся)]; **~ion** [mɔdə'reiʃən] уме́ренность *f*; воздержа́ние.

modern ['mɔdən] совреме́нный; **ize** [-aiz] модернизи́ровать (*im*)*pf.*

modest ['mɔdist] □ скро́мный; благопристо́йный; **~y** [-i] скро́мность *f.*

modi|fication [mɔdifi'keiʃən] видоизмене́ние; модифика́ция; **~fy** ['mɔdifai] видоизменя́ть [-ни́ть]; смягча́ть [-чи́ть].

modulate ['mɔdjuleit] модули́ровать.

moist [mɔist] вла́жный; **~en** ['mɔisn] увлажня́ть(ся) [-ни́ть(ся)]; **~ure** ['mɔistʃə] вла́жность; вла́га.

molar ['moulə] коренно́й зуб.

molasses [mə'læsiz] чёрная па́тока.

mole [moul] *zo.* крот; ро́динка; мол, да́мба.

molecule ['mɔlikju:l] моле́кула.

molest [mo'lest] приста́(ва́)ть к (Д).

mollify ['mɔlifai] успока́ивать [-ко́ить], смягча́ть [-чи́ть].

mollycoddle ['mɔlikɔdl] **1.** не́женка *m/f.*; **2.** изне́жи(ват)ь.

molten ['moultən] распла́вленный; лито́й.

moment ['moumənt] моме́нт, миг, мгнове́ние; = ~um; **~ary** [-əri] □ момента́льный; кратковре́менный; **~ous** [mou'mentəs] □ ва́жный; **~um** [-təm] дви́жущая си́ла; *phys.* моме́нт.

monarch ['mɔnək] мона́рх; **~y** ['mɔnəki] мона́рхия.

monastery ['mɔnəstri] монасты́рь *m.*

Monday ['mʌndi] понеде́льник.

monetary ['mʌnitəri] моне́тный; валю́тный; де́нежный.

money ['mʌni] де́ньги *f/pl.*; ready ~ нали́чные де́ньги *f/pl* ; **~-box** копи́лка; **~-changer** меня́ла *m*; **~-order** почто́вый де́нежный перево́д.

mongrel ['mʌŋgrəl] **1.** *biol.* мети́с;

помесь *f*; дворняжка; **2.** нечистокровный.
monitor ['mɔnitə] наставник; ⚓ монитор.
monk [mʌŋk] монах.
monkey ['mʌŋki] **1.** обезьяна; ⊕ копровая баба; **2.** F [по]дурачиться; ~ with возиться с (T); ~-wrench ⊕ раздвижной гаечный ключ.
monkish ['mʌŋkiʃ] монашеский.
mono|cle ['mɔnɔkl] монокль *m*; **~gamy** [mɔ'nɔgəmi] единобрачие; **~logue** [-lɔg] монолог; **~polist** [mə'nɔpəlist] монополист; **~polize** [-laiz] монополизировать (*im*)*pf.*; *fig.* присваивать себе (B); **~poly** [-li] монополия (P); **~tonous** [mə'nɔtənəs] □ монотонный; однозвучный; **~tony** [-təni] монотонность *f.*
monsoon [mɔn'su:n] муссон.
monster ['mɔnstə] чудовище; урод; *fig.* изверг; *attr.* исполинский.
monstro|sity [mɔns'trɔsiti] чудовищность *f*; уродство; **~us** ['mɔnstrəs] □ уродливый; чудовищный.
month [mʌnθ] месяц; **~ly** ['mʌnθli] **1.** (еже)месячный; **2.** ежемесячный журнал.
monument ['mɔnjumənt] памятник; **~al** [mɔnju'mentl] □ монументальный.
mood [mu:d] настроение, расположение духа.
moody [mu:di] □ капризный; угрюмый, унылый; не в духе.
moon [mu:n] **1.** луна, месяц; **2.** F проводить время в мечтаниях; **~light** лунный свет; **~lit** залитый лунным светом; **~struck** лунатический.
Moor[1] [muə] марокканец (-нка); мавр(итанка).
moor[2] [~] торфянистая местность, поросшая вереском.
moor[3] [~] ⚓ причали(ва)ть; **~ings** ['muəriŋz] *pl.* ⚓ швартовы *m/pl.*
moot [mu:t] : ~ point спорный вопрос.
mop [mɔp] **1.** швабра; **2.** чистить шваброй.
mope [moup] хандрить.
moral ['mɔrəl] **1.** □ моральный, нравственный; **2.** нравоучение, мораль *f*; ~s *pl.* нравы *m/pl.*; **~e** [mɔ'ra:l] *part.* ⚔ моральное состояние; **~ity** [mə'ræliti] мораль *f*, этика; **~ize** ['mɔrəlaiz] морализировать.
morass [mə'ræs] болото, трясина.
morbid ['mɔ:bid] □ болезненный.
more [mɔ:] больше; более; ещё; once ~ ещё раз; so much the ~ тем более; no ~ больше не ...; **~over** [mɔ:'rouvə] сверх того, кроме того.
moribund ['mɔribʌnd] умирающий.
morning ['mɔ:niŋ] утро; tomorrow ~ завтра утром; ~ **coat** визитка.
morose [mə'rous] □ угрюмый.
morphia ['mɔ:fiə], **morphine** ['mɔ:fi:n] морфий.
morsel ['mɔ:səl] кусочек.
mortal ['mɔ:tl] **1.** □ смертный; смертельный; **2.** смертный, человек; **~ity** [mɔ:'tæliti] смертельность *f*; смертность *f.*
mortar ['mɔ:tə] ступка; известковый раствор; ⚔ мортира; миномёт.
mortgage ['mɔ:gidʒ] **1.** заклад; ипотека, закладная; **2.** закладывать [заложить]; **~e** [mɔ:gə'dʒi:] кредитор по закладной.
mortgag|er, ~or ['mɔ:gədʒə] должник по закладной.
morti|fication [mɔ:tifi'keiʃən] умерщвление (плоти); унижение; **~fy** ['mɔ:tifai] умерщвлять [-ртвить] (плоть); огорчать [-чить], унижать [унизить].
morti|ce, ~se ['mɔ:tis] ⊕ гнездо шипа.
mortuary ['mɔ:tjuəri] мертвецкая.
mosaic [mə'zeiik] мозаика.
moss [mɔs] мох; **~y** мшистый.
most [moust] **1.** *adj.* □ наибольший; **2.** *adv.* больше всего; ~ beautiful самый красивый; **3.** наибольшее количество; большая часть *f*; at (the) ~ самое большее, не больше чем; **~ly** ['moustli] по большей части; главным образом; чаще всего.
moth [mɔθ] моль *f*; мотылёк; **~-eaten** изъеденный молью.
mother ['mʌðə] **1.** мать *f*; **2.** относиться по-матерински к (Д); **~hood** ['mʌðəhud] материнство; **~-in-law** [-rinlɔ:] тёща; свекровь *f*; **~ly** [-li] материнский; **~-of-pearl** [-rev'pə:l] перламутровый; **~-tongue** родной язык.
motif [mou'ti:f] мотив.
motion ['mouʃən] **1.** движение; ход; *parl.* предложение; **2.** *v/t.* показывать жестом; *v/i.* кивать [кивнуть] (to на B); **~less** [-lis] неподвижный; **~-picture** *Am.* кино...; ~s *pl.* фильм; кино *n indecl.*
motive ['moutiv] **1.** движущий; двигательный; **2.** повод, мотив; **3.** побуждать [-удить]; мотивировать (*im*)*pf.*; **~less** беспричинный.
motley ['mɔtli] разноцветный; пёстрый.
motor ['moutə] **1.** двигатель *m*, мотор; = ~-car; **2.** моторный; авто..., автомобильный; ~ mechanic, ~fitter авторемонтный механик; **3.** ехать (или везти) на автомобиле; **~-bicycle** мотоцикл; **~-bus** автобус; **~-car** автомобиль

m, F маши́на; **~-cycle** мотоци́кл; **~ing** ['moutəriŋ] автомоби́льное де́ло; автомоби́льный спорт; **~ist** [-rist] автомобили́ст(ка); **~lorry,** *Am.* **~truck** грузово́й автомоби́ль *m*, грузови́к.
mottled [mɔtld] кра́пчатый.
mould [mould] **1.** садо́вая земля́; по́чва; пле́сень *f*; фо́рма (лите́йная); шабло́н; склад, хара́ктер; **2.** отлива́ть в фо́рму; *fig.* [с]формирова́ть.
moulder ['mouldə] рассыпа́ться [-ы́паться].
moulding ['mouldiŋ] ⚠ карни́з.
mouldy ['mouldi] запле́сневелый.
moult [moult] *zo.* [по]линя́ть.
mound [maund] на́сыпь *f*; холм; курга́н.
mount [maunt] **1.** гора́; ло́шадь под седло́м; **2.** *v/i.* восходи́ть [взойти́]; поднима́ться [-ня́ться]; сади́ться на ло́шадь; *v/t.* устана́вливать [-нови́ть] (ра́дио и т. п.), [с]монти́ровать; вставля́ть в ра́му (в опра́ву).
mountain ['mauntin] **1.** гора́; **2.** го́рный, наго́рный; **~eer** [maunti'niə] альпини́ст(ка); **~ous** ['mauntinəs] гори́стый.
mourn [mɔ:n] горева́ть; опла́к(ив)ать; **~er** ['mɔ:nə] скорбя́щий; **~ful** ['mɔ:nful] □ тра́урный; **~ing** ['mɔ:niŋ] тра́ур; плач; *attr.* тра́урный.
mouse [maus] (*pl.* mice) мышь *f*.
m(o)ustache [məs'tɑ:ʃ] усы́ *m/pl.*
mouth [mauθ], *pl.* **~s** [-z] рот, уста́ *n/pl.*; у́стье (реки́); вход (в га́вань); **~-organ** губна́я гармо́ника; **~piece** мундшту́к; *fig.* ру́пор.
move [mu:v] **1.** *v/t. com.* дви́гать [дви́нуть]; передвига́ть [-и́нуть]; тро́гать [тро́нуть]; вноси́ть [внести́] (предложе́ние); *v/i.* дви́гаться [дви́нуться]; переезжа́ть [перее́хать]; разви́(ва́)ться (о собы́тиях); идти́ [пойти́] (о дела́х); *fig.* враща́ться (в о́бществе и т. п.); ~ for a th. предлага́ть [-ложи́ть] что́-либо; ~ in въезжа́ть [въе́хать]; ~ on дви́гаться вперёд; **2.** движе́ние; перее́зд; ход (в игре́); *fig.* шаг; on the ~ на ходу́; make a ~ встать из-за стола́; предпринима́ть что́-либо; **~ment** ['mu:vmənt] движе́ние; ♪ темп, ритм; ♪ часть *f* (симфо́нии и т. п.); ⊕ ход (маши́ны).
movies ['mu:viz] *s. pl.* кино́ *n indecl.*
moving ['mu:viŋ] □ дви́жущийся; ~ staircase эскала́тор.
mow [mou] [*irr.*] [с]коси́ть; **~n** [-n] *p. pt.* от mow.
Mr ['mistə] *s.* mister.
Mrs ['misiz] *s.* mistress.
much [mʌtʃ] *adj.* мно́го; *adv.* мно́го, о́чень; I thought as ~ я так и ду́мал; make ~ of высоко́ цени́ть (В); I am not ~ of a dancer я нева́жн… танцу́ю.
muck [mʌk] наво́з; *fig.* дрянь *f*.
mucus ['mju:kəs] слизь *f*.
mud [mʌd] грязь *f*; **~dle** [mʌdl] … *v/t.* запу́тывать [-тать]; [с]пу́та… (*a.* ~ up, together); F опьяня́т… [-ни́ть]; *v/i.* халту́рить; де́йство… вать без пла́на; **2.** F пу́таница, не… разбери́ха; **~dy** ['mʌdi] гря́зный… **~-guard** крыло́.
muff [mʌf] му́фта; **~etee** [mʌfi'ti… напу́льсник.
muffin ['mʌfin] сдо́бная бу́лка.
muffle ['mʌfl] глуши́ть, заглуша́т… [-ши́ть] (го́лос и т. п.); заку́т(ы… в)ать; **~r** [-ə] кашне́ *n indecl.*; *mo…* глуши́тель *m*.
mug [mʌg] кру́жка.
muggy ['mʌgi] ду́шный, вла́жный…
mulatto [mju'lætou] мула́т(ка).
mulberry ['mʌlbəri] ту́товое де́… рево, шелкови́ца; ту́товая я́год…
mule [mju:l] мул; упря́мый чело… ве́к; **~teer** [mju:li'tiə] пого́нщик…
mull[1] [mʌl] мусли́н. [му́лов…
mull[2] [~] *Am.*: ~ over обду́м(ы… в)ать; размышля́ть [-мы́слить].
mulled [mʌld]: ~ wine глинтве́йн…
multi|farious [mʌlti'fɛəriəs] □ ра… нообра́зный; **~form** ['mʌltifɔ:m… многообра́зный; **~ple** ['mʌltipl] … ⚠ кра́тный; **2.** ⚠ кра́тное число́… многокра́тный; разнообра́зный… **~plication** [mʌltipli'keiʃən] умно… же́ние; увеличе́ние; ~ table таб… ли́ца умноже́ния; **~plicity** [-'plis… iti] многочи́сленность *f*; разно… обра́зие; **~ply** ['mʌltiplai] увели… чи(ва)ть(-ся); ⚠ умножа́ть [-о́… жить]; **~tude** [-tju:d] мно́жество… ма́сса; толпа́; **~tudinous** [mʌlti… 'tju:dinəs] многочи́сленный.
mum [mʌm] ти́ше!
mumble [mʌmbl] [про]бормота́ть… с трудо́м жева́ть.
mummery ['mʌməri] пантоми́м… маскара́д; *contp.* «представле́ние»
mumm|ify ['mʌmifai] мумифици́… ровать; (*im*)*pf.*; **~y** ['mʌmi] му́мия…
mumps [mʌmps] *sg.* ⚕ сви́нка.
mundane ['mʌndein] □ мирско́й… све́тский.
municipal [mju'nisipəl] □ муници… па́льный; **~ity** [-nisi'pæliti] муни… ципалите́т.
munificen|ce [mju:'nifisns] ще́д… рость *f*; **~t** [-t] ще́дрый.
murder ['mə:də] **1.** уби́йство… **2.** уби́(ва́)ть; *fig.* прова́ливат… [-ли́ть] (пье́су и т. п.); **~er** [-rə… уби́йца; **~ess** [-ris] же́нщина… -уби́йца; **~ous** [-rəs] □ уби́йствен… ный. [ный…
murky ['mə:ki] □ тёмный; па́смур-
murmur ['mə:mə] **1.** журча́ние… шо́рох (ли́стьев); ро́пот; **2.** [за]журча́ть; ропта́ть. [скота́).
murrain ['mʌrin] чума́ (рога́того

musc|le [mʌsl] му́скул, мы́шца; **~ular** ['mʌskjulə] му́скулистый; му́скульный.
Muse[1] [mju:z] му́за.
muse[2] [~] заду́м(ыв)аться (on над [Т).
museum [mju:'ziəm] музе́й.
mushroom ['mʌʃrum] **1.** гриб; **2.** расплю́щи(ва)ть(ся); *Am.* ~ up расти́ как грибы́.
music ['mju:zik] му́зыка; музыка́льное произведе́ние; но́ты *f/pl.*; set to ~ положи́ть на му́зыку; **~al** ['mju:zikəl] □ музыка́льный; мелоди́чный; ~ box шарма́нка; **~-hall** мю́зик-холл, эстра́дный теа́тр; **~ian** [mju:'ziʃən] музыка́нт (-ша); **~stand** пюпи́тр для нот; **~-stool** табуре́т для роя́ля.
musketry ['mʌskitri] руже́йный ого́нь *m*; стрелко́вая подгото́вка.
muslin ['mʌzlin] мусли́н (ткань).
mussel [mʌsl] ми́дия.
must [mʌst]: I ~ я до́лжен (+ *inf.*); I ~ not мне нельзя́; **2.** виногра́дное су́сло; пле́сень *f.*
mustache *Am.* усы́ *m/pl.*
mustard ['mʌstəd] горчи́ца.
muster ['mʌstə] **1.** смотр, осмо́тр; ⚔ сбор; **2.** проверя́ть [-е́рить].
musty ['mʌsti] за́тхлый.
muta|ble ['mju:təbl] □ изме́нчивый, непостоя́нный; **~tion** [mju:'teiʃən] измене́ние, переме́на.
mute [mju:t] **1.** □ немо́й; **2.** немо́й; стати́ст; **3.** надева́ть сурди́нку **на** (В).
mutilat|e ['mju:tileit] [из]уве́чить; **~ion** [-'eiʃən] уве́чье.
mutin|eer [mju:ti'niə] мяте́жник; **~ous** ['mju:tinəs] □ мяте́жный; **~y** [-ni] **1.** мяте́ж; **2.** поднима́ть мяте́ж.
mutter ['mʌtə] **1.** бормота́нье; ворча́ние; **2.** [про]бормота́ть; [за-]ворча́ть.
mutton [mʌtn] бара́нина; leg of ~ бара́нья но́жка; ~ chop бара́нья котле́та.
mutual ['mju:tjuəl] □ обою́дный, взаи́мный; о́бщий.
muzzle ['mʌzl] **1.** мо́рда, ры́ло; ду́ло, жерло́; намо́рдник; **2.** надева́ть намо́рдник (Д); *fig.* заста́вить молча́ть.
my [mai, *a.* mi] *pron. poss.* мой *m*, моя́ *f*, моё *n*; мои́ *pl.*
myrtle [mə:tl] ⚘ мирт.
myself [mai'self, mi-] *pron. refl.* **1.** себя́, меня́ самого́; -ся, -сь; **2.** (для усиле́ния) сам.
myster|ious [mis'tiəriəs] □ таи́нственный; **~y** [-ri] та́йна; таи́нство.
mysti|c ['mistik] (*a.* ~al [-ikəl] □) мисти́ческий; **~fy** [-tifai] мистифици́ровать (*im*)*pf.*; озада́чи(ва)ть.
myth [miθ] миф; мифи́ческое лицо́.

N

nab [næb] *sl.* схвати́ть на ме́сте преступле́ния.
nacre ['neikə] перламу́тр.
nag [næg] F **1.** кля́ча; **2.** прид(и)ра́ться к (Д).
nail [neil] **1.** *anat.* но́готь *m*; гвоздь *m*; **2.** заби́(ва́)ть гвоздя́ми, пригвожда́ть [-озди́ть], прибі́(ва́)ть; *fig.* прико́вывать [-ова́ть].
naïve [nai'i:v, nɑ:'iv] □, **naive** [neiv] □ наи́вный; безыску́сственный.
naked ['neikid] □ наго́й, го́лый; я́вный; **~ness** [-nis] нагота́; обнажённость *f.*
name [neim] **1.** и́мя *n*; фами́лия; назва́ние; of (F by) the ~ of под и́менем (Р), по и́мени (И); in the ~ of во и́мя (Р); от и́мени (Р); call a p. ~s [об]руга́ть (В); **2.** наз(ы)ва́ть; дава́ть и́мя (Д); **~less** ['neimlis] □ безымя́нный; **~ly** [-li] и́менно; **~-plate** доще́чка с фами́лией; **~sake** тёзка *m/f.*
nap [næp] **1.** ворс; лёгкий сон; **2.** дрема́ть [вздремну́ть].
nape [neip] заты́лок.
napkin ['næpkin] салфе́тка; подгу́зник.
narcotic [nɑ:'kɔtik] **1.** (~ally) наркоти́ческий; **2.** нарко́тик.
narrat|e [næ'reit] расска́зывать [-за́ть]; **~ion** [-ʃən] расска́з; **~ive** ['nærətiv] **1.** □ повествова́тельный; **2.** расска́з.
narrow ['nærou] **1.** □ у́зкий; те́сный; ограни́ченный (об интелле́кте); **2.** ~s *pl.* проли́в; **3.** су́живать(ся) [су́зить(ся)]; уменьша́ть(-ся) [уме́ньши́ть(ся)]; ограни́чи(ва)ть; **~-chested** узкогру́дый; **~-minded** □ ограни́ченный, у́зкий; недалёкий; **~ness** [-nis] у́зость *f.*
nasal ['neizəl] □ носово́й; гнуса́вый.
nasty ['nɑ:sti] □ проти́вный; неприя́тный; гря́зный; зло́бный.
natal ['neitl]: ~ day день рожде́ния.
nation ['neiʃən] на́ция.
national ['næʃnl] **1.** □ национа́льный, наро́дный; госуда́рственный; **2.** соотéчественник; по́дданный; **~ity** [næʃə'næliti] национа́льность *f*; по́дданство; **~ize** ['næʃnəlaiz] национализи́ровать (*im*)*pf.*; натурализова́ть (*im*)*pf.*
native ['neitiv] **1.** □ родно́й; ту-

зе́мный; ~ language родно́й язы́к; **2.** уроже́нец (-нка); тузе́мец (-мка).
natural ['nætʃrəl] □ есте́ственный; ~ sciences есте́ственные нау́ки *f/pl.*; **~ist** [-ist] натурали́ст (в иску́сстве); естествоиспыта́тель *m*; **~ize** [-aiz] натурализова́ть (*im*)*pf.*; **~ness** [-nis] есте́ственность *f.*
nature ['neitʃə] приро́да; хара́ктер.
naught [nɔ:t] ничто́; но́ль *m*; set at ~ пренебрега́ть [-бре́чь] (Т); **~y** ['nɔ:ti] □ непослу́шный, капри́зный.
nause|a ['nɔ:siə] тошнота́; отвраще́ние; **~ate** [-eit] *v/t.* тошни́ть; it ~s me меня́ тошни́т от э́того; внуша́ть отвраще́ние (Д); be ~d испы́тывать тошноту́; *v/i.* чу́вствовать тошноту́; **~ous** [-əs] □ тошнотво́рный. [хо́дный.]
nautical ['nɔ:tikəl] морско́й; море-}
naval ['neivəl] (вое́нно-)морско́й.
nave [neiv] ⚠ неф (це́ркви).
navel ['neivəl] пуп, пупо́к.
naviga|ble ['nævigəbl] □ судохо́дный; **~te** [-geit] *v/i.* управля́ть (су́дном, аэропла́ном); пла́вать (на су́дне); лета́ть (на аэропла́не); *v/t.* управля́ть (су́дном и т. д.); пла́вать по (Д); **~tion** [nævi'geiʃən] морехо́дство; навига́ция; **~tor** ['nævigeitə] морепла́ватель *m*; шту́рман.
navy ['neivi] вое́нный флот.
nay [nei] нет; да́же; бо́лее того́.
near [niə] **1.** *adj.* бли́зкий; бли́жний; скупо́й; ~ at hand под руко́й; ~ silk полушёлк; **2.** *adv.* по́дле; бли́зко, недалеко́; почти́; **3.** *prp.* о́коло (Р), у (Р); **4.** приближа́ться [-ли́зиться] к (Д); **~by** ['niə'bai] ря́дом; **~ly** ['niəli] почти́; **~ness** [-nis] бли́зость *f.*
neat [ni:t] □ чи́стый, опря́тный; стро́йный; иску́сный; кра́ткий; **~ness** ['ni:tnis] опря́тность *f* и т. д.
nebulous ['nebjuləs] □ о́блачный; тума́нный.
necess|ary ['nesisəri] **1.** □ необходи́мый, ну́жный; **2.** необходи́мое; **~itate** [ni'sesiteit] де́лать необходи́мым; **~ity** [-ti] необходи́мость *f*, нужда́.
neck [nek] ше́я; го́рлышко (буты́лки и т. п.); вы́рез (в пла́тье); ~ of land переше́ек; ~ and ~ голова́ в го́лову; **~band** во́рот (руба́шки); **~erchief** ['nekətʃif] ше́йный плато́к; **~lace** [-lis] ожере́лье; **~tie**} [га́лстук.]
née [nei] урождённая.
need [ni:d] **1.** на́добность *f*; потре́бность *f*; нужда́; недоста́ток; be in ~ of нужда́ться в (П); **2.** бе́дствовать; нужда́ться в (П); I ~ it мне э́то ну́жно; **~ful** ['ni:dful] □ ну́жный.
needle ['ni:dl] игла́, иго́лка; спи́ца (вяза́льная).
needless ['ni:dlis] □ нену́жный.
needlewoman швея́.
needy ['ni:di] □ нужда́ющийся; бе́дствующий.
nefarious [ni'fɛəriəs] бесче́стный.
negat|ion [ni'geiʃən] отрица́ние; **~ive** ['negətiv] **1.** □ отрица́тельный; негати́вный *f*; **2.** отрица́ние; *phot.* негати́в; **3.** отрица́ть.
neglect [ni'glekt] **1.** пренебреже́ние; небре́жность *f*; **2.** пренебрега́ть [-бре́чь] (Т); **~ful** [-ful] □ небре́жный.
negligen|ce ['neglidʒəns] небре́жность *f*; **~t** [-t] □ небре́жный.
negotia|te [ni'gouʃieit] вести́ перегово́ры; догова́риваться [-вори́ться] о (П); F преодоле́(ва́)ть; **~tion** [nigouʃi'eiʃən] перегово́ры *m/pl.*; преодоле́ние (затрудне́ний); **~tor** [ni'gouʃieitə] лицо́, веду́щее перегово́ры.
negr|ess ['ni:gris] негритя́нка; **~o** ['ni:grou], *pl.* ~es [-z] негр.
neigh [nei] **1.** ржа́ние; **2.** [за]ржа́ть.
neighbo(u)r ['neibə] сосе́д(ка); **~hood** [-hud] сосе́дство; **~ing** [-riŋ] сосе́дний, сме́жный.
neither ['neiðə] **1.** ни тот, ни друго́й; **2.** *adv.* та́кже не; ~ ... nor ... ни ... ни...
nephew ['nevju:] племя́нник.
nerve [nə:v] **1.** нерв; му́жество, хладнокро́вие; на́глость *f*; **2.** придава́ть си́лы (хра́брости) (Д); **~less** ['nə:vlis] □ беcси́льный, вя́лый.
nervous ['nə:vəs] □ не́рвный; нерво́зный; си́льный; **~ness** [-nis] не́рвность *f*, нерво́зность *f*; эне́ргия.
nest [nest] **1.** гнездо́ (*a. fig.*); **2.** вить гнездо́; **~le** [nesl] *v/i.* удо́бно устро́иться; приж(им)а́ться (to, on, against к Д); *v/t.* приж(им)а́ть (го́лову).
net[1] [net] **1.** сеть *f*; **2.** расставля́ть се́ти; пойма́ть и́ли покры́ть се́тью.
net[2] [~] **1.** не́тто *adj. indecl.*, чи́стый (вес, дохо́д); **2.** приноси́ть (и́ли получа́ть) чи́стого дохо́да.
nettle [netl] **1.** ⚘ крапи́ва; **2.** обжига́ть крапи́вой; *fig.* уязвля́ть [-ви́ть].
network ['netwə:k] плетёнка; сеть *f* (желе́зных доро́г, радиоста́нций и т. п.).
neuter ['nju:tə] **1.** *gr.* сре́дний; ⚘ беспо́лый; **2.** сре́дний род; кастри́рованное живо́тное.
neutral ['nju:trəl] **1.** □ нейтра́льный; сре́дний, неопределённый; **2.** нейтра́льное госуда́рство; граждани́н нейтра́льного госуда́рства; **~ity** [nju'træliti] нейтралите́т; **~ize** ['nju:trəlaiz] нейтрализова́ть (*im*)*pf.*
never ['nevə] никогда́; совсе́м не; **~more** никогда́ бо́льше; **~theless** [nevəðə'les] тем не ме́нее; несмотря́ на э́то.

new [nju:] новый; молодой (об овощах); свежий; **~-comer** новоприбывший; **~ly** ['nju:li] заново, вновь; недавно.
news [nju:z] новости *f/pl.*, известия *n/pl.*; **~-agent** газетчик; **~-boy** газетчик-разносчик; **~-monger** сплетник (-ица); **~-paper** газета; **~-print** газетная бумага; **~-reel** киножурнал; **~stall,** *Am.* **~-stand** газетный киоск.
New Year Новый год; **~'s** Eve канун Нового года.
next [nekst] **1.** *adj.* следующий; ближайший; ~ door to *fig.* чуть (ли) не, почти; ~ to возле (P); вслед за (T); **2.** *adv.* потом, после; в следующий раз.
nibble [nibl] *v/t.* обгры́з(а)ть; [о]щипать (*a. v/i.* ~ at); *v/i.* ~ at *fig.* прид(и)раться к (Д).
nice [nais] □ приятный, милый, славный; хорошенький; тонкий; привередливый; **~ty** ['naisiti] точность *f*; разборчивость *f*; *pl.* тонкости *f/pl.*, детали *f/pl.*
niche [nitʃ] ниша.
nick [nik] **1.** зарубка; in the ~ of time как раз во-время; **2.** сделать зарубку в (П); поспеть во-время на (В).
nickel [nikl] **1.** *min.* никель *m*; *Am.* монета в 5 центов; **2.** [от]никелировать.
nickname ['nikneim] **1.** прозвище; **2.** да(ва)ть прозвище (Д).
niece [ni:s] племянница.
niggard ['nigəd] скупец; **~ly** [-li] скупой, скаредный.
night [nait] ночь *f*, вечер; by ~, at ~ ночью, вечером; **~-club** ночной клуб; **~fall** сумерки *f/pl.*; **~-dress, ~gown** (женская) ночная сорочка; **~ingale** ['naitiŋgeil] соловей; **~ly** ['naitli] ночной; *adv.* ночью; еженощно; **~mare** кошмар; **~-shirt** ночная рубашка.
nil [nil] *particul. sport* ноль *m or* нуль *m*; ничего.
nimble [nimbl] □ проворный, ловкий; живой.
nimbus ['nimbəs] сияние, ореол.
nine [nain] девять; **~pins** *pl.* кегли *f/pl.*; **~teen** ['nain'ti:n] девятнадцать; **~ty** ['nainti] девяносто.
ninny ['nini] F простофиля *m/f.*
ninth [nainθ] **1.** девятый; **2.** девятая часть *f*; **~ly** ['nainθli] в-девятых.
nip [nip] **1.** щипок; укус; сильный мороз; **2.** щипать [щипнуть]; прищемлять [-мить]; побить морозом; ~ in the bud пресекать в зародыше.
nipper ['nipə] клешня; (a pair of) **~s** *pl.* щипцы *m/pl.*
nipple [nipl] сосок.
nitre ['naitə] ⚗ селитра.
nitrogen ['naitridʒən] азот.

no [nou) **1.** *adj.* никакой; in ~ time в мгновение ока; ~ one никто; **2.** *adv.* нет; **3.** отрицание.
nobility [nou'biliti] дворянство; благородство.
noble ['noubl] **1.** □ благородный; знатный; **2.** = **~man** титулованное лицо, дворянин; **~ness** ['noublnis] благородство.
nobody ['noubədi] никто.
nocturnal [nɔk'tə:nl] ночной.
nod [nɔd] **1.** кивать головой; дремать, «клевать носом»; **2.** кивок головой.
node [noud] ♀ узел; ⚕ нарост, утолщение.
noise [nɔiz] **1.** шум, гам; грохот; **2.** ~ abroad разглашать [-ласить]; **~less** ['nɔizlis] □ бесшумный.
noisome ['nɔisəm] вредный; нездоровый; зловонный.
noisy ['nɔizi] □ шумный; шумливый; *fig.* кричащий (о красках).
nomin|al ['nɔminl] □ номинальный; именной; ~ value номинальная цена; **~ate** ['nɔmineit] назначать [-значить]; выставлять [выставить] (кандидата); **~ation** [nɔmi'neiʃən] выставление (кандидата); назначение.
non [nɔn] *prf.* не..., бес..., без...
nonage ['nounidʒ] несовершеннолетие.
non-alcoholic безалкогольный.
nonce [nɔns]: for the ~ только для данного случая.
non-commissioned ['nɔnkə'miʃənd]: ~ officer сержант, унтер-офицер.
non-committal уклончивый.
non-conductor ⚡ непроводник.
nonconformist ['nɔnkən'fɔ:mist] человек не подчиняющийся общим правилам.
nondescript ['nɔndiskript] неопределённый; неопределимый.
none [nʌn] **1.** ничто, никто; ни один; никакой; **2.** нисколько, совсем не ...; ~ the less тем не менее.
nonentity [nɔ'nentiti] небытие; ничтожество (о человеке); фикция.
non-existence небытие.
non-party ['nɔn'pɑ:ti] беспартийный.
non-performance неисполнение.
nonplus [-'plʌs] **1.** замешательство; **2.** приводить в замешательство.
non-resident не проживающий в данном месте.
nonsens|e ['nɔnsəns] вздор, бессмыслица; **~ical** [nɔn'sensikəl] □ бессмысленный.
non-skid ['nɔn'skid] приспособление против буксования колёс.
non-stop безостановочный; ✈ беспосадочный.
non-union не состоящий членом профсоюза.
noodle ['nu:dl]: **~s** *pl.* лапша.

nook [nuk] укрóмный уголóк; закоýлок.

noon [nu:n] пóлдень *m* (*a.* ~day, ~tide, ~time).

noose [nu:s] **1.** пéтля; аркáн; **2.** ловúть аркáном; вéшать [повéсить].

nor [nɔ:] и не; тáкже не; ни.

norm [nɔ:m] нóрма; стандáрт, образéц; **~al** ['nɔ:məl] □ нормáльный; **~alize** [-aiz] нормировáть (*im*)*pf*.; нормализовáть (*im*)*pf*.

north [nɔ:θ] **1.** сéвер; **2.** сéверный; **3.** *adv.* ~ of к сéверу от (Р); **~-east 1.** сéверо-востóк; **2.** сéверо-востóчный (*a.* **~-eastern** [-ən]); **~erly** ['nɔ:ðəli], **~ern** ['nɔ:ðən] сéверный; **~ward**(s) ['nɔ:θwəd(z)] *adv.* на сéвер; к сéверу; **~-west 1.** сéверо-зáпад; ⚓ норд-вéст; **2.** сéверо-зáпадный (*a.* **~-western** [-ən]).

nose [nouz] **1.** нос; нóсик (чáйника и т. п.); чутьё; нос (лóдки и т. п.); **2.** *v/t.* [по]нюхать; разнюх(ив)ать; **~-dive** ✈ пикирóвка; **~gay** букéт цветóв.

nostril ['nɔstril] ноздря́.

nosy ['nouzi] F любопы́тный.

not [nɔt] не.

notable ['noutəbl] **1.** □ достопримечáтельный; **2.** выдаю́щийся человéк.

notary ['noutəri] нотáриус (*a.* ~ public).

notation [nou'teiʃən] нотáция; зáпись *f*.

notch [nɔtʃ] **1.** зарýбка; зазýбрина; **2.** зарубáть [-бúть]; зазýбри(ва)ть.

note [nout] **1.** замéтка; зáпись *f*; примечáние; долговáя распúска; (дипломатúческая) нóта; ♪ нóта; репутáция; вниммáние; **2.** замечáть [-éтить]; упоминáть [-мянýть]; (*a* ~ down) дéлать замéтки, записывать [-сáть]; отмечáть [-éтить]; **~book** записнáя кнúжка; **~d** ['noutid] хорошó извéстный; **~-worthy** достопримечáтельный.

nothing ['nʌθiŋ] ничтó, ничегó; for ~ зря, дáром; bring (come) to ~ свестú (сойтú) на нет.

notice ['noutis] **1.** внимáние; извещéние, уведомлéние; предупреждéние; at short ~ без предупреждéния; give ~ предупреждáть об увольнéнии (úли об ухóде); извещáть [-естúть]; **2.** замечáть [-éтить]; обращáть внимáние на (В); **~able** ['noutisəbl] □ достóйный внимáния; замéтный.

noti|fication [noutifi'keiʃən] извещéние, сообщéние; объявлéние; **~fy** ['noutifai] извещáть [-естúть], уведомлять [увéдомить].

notion ['nouʃən] понятие, представлéние; **~s** *pl. Am.* галантерéя.

notorious [nou'tɔ:riəs] □ преслóвутый.

notwithstanding [nɔtwiθ'stændiŋ] несмотря́ на (В), вопрекú (Д).

nought [nɔ:t] ничтó; ⅍ ноль *m* or нуль *m*.

nourish ['nʌriʃ] питáть (*a. fig.*); [на-, по]кормúть; *fig.* [вз]лелéять (надéжду и т. п.); **~ing** [-iŋ] питáтельный; **~ment** [-mənt] питáние; пúща (*a. fig.*).

novel ['nɔvəl] **1.** нóвый; необы́чный; **2.** ромáн; **~ist** [-ist] романúст (áвтор); **~ty** ['nɔvəlti] новúнка; новизнá.

November [no'vembə] ноябрь *m*.

novice ['nɔvis] начинáющий; новичóк; *eccl.* послýшник (-ица).

now [nau] **1.** тепéрь, сейчáс; тóтчас; just ~ тóлько что; ~ and again (úли then) от врéмени до врéмени; **2.** *cj.* когдá, раз.

nowadays ['nauədeiz] в нáше врéмя.

nowhere ['nouwɛə] нигдé, никудá.

noxious ['nɔkʃəs] □ врéдный.

nozzle [nɔzl] нóсик (чáйника и т.п.); ⊕ соплó.

nucle|ar ['nju:kliə] я́дерный; ~ pile я́дерный реáктор; **~us** [-s] ядрó.

nude [nju:d] нагóй; *paint.* обнажённая фигýра.

nudge [nʌdʒ] F **1.** подтáлкивать лóктем; **2.** лёгкий толчóк лóктем.

nuisance [nju:sns] неприя́тность *f*; досáда; *fig.* надоéдливый человéк.

null [nʌl] невыразúтельный; недéйствительный; ~ and void потеря́вший закóнную сúлу (о договóре); **~ify** ['nʌlifai] аннулúровать (*im*)*pf*.; **~ity** [-ti] ничтóжность *f*; ничтóжество (о человéке); ⚖ недéйствительность *f*.

numb [nʌm] **1.** онемéлый, оцепенéлый; окоченéлый; **2.** вызывáть онемéние (úли окоченéние) (Р).

number ['nʌmbə] **1.** числó; нóмер; **2.** [за]нумеровáть; насчúтывать; **~less** [-lis] бесчúсленный.

numera|l ['nju:mərəl] **1.** úмя числúтельное; цúфра; **2.** числовóй; **~tion** [nju:mə'reiʃən] исчислéние; нумерáция.

numerical [nju:'merikəl] □ числовóй; цифровóй.

numerous ['nju:mərəs] □ многочúсленный.

nun [nʌn] монáхиня; *zo.* синúца-лазóревка.

nunnery ['nʌnəri] жéнский монастырь *m*.

nuptial ['nʌpʃəl] **1.** брáчный, свáдебный; **2. ~s** [-z] *pl.* свáдьба.

nurse [nə:s] **1.** кормúлица (*mst* wet-~); ня́ня (*a.* ~-maid); сидéлка (в больнúце); медицúнская сестрá; at ~ на попечéнии ня́ни; **2.** кормúть, вскáрмливать грýдью; ня́нчить; ухáживать за (Т); **~ry** ['nə:sri] дéтская (кóмната); 🌱 питóмник, рассáдник; ~ school дéтский сад.

nurs(e)ling ['nə:sliŋ] питóмец (-мица).

urture ['nə:tʃə] **1.** пита́ние; вос-
пита́ние; **2.** пита́ть; воспи́тывать
-та́ть].
ut [nʌt] оре́х; ⊕ га́йка; ~s *pl.*
ме́лкий у́голь *m*; **~cracker** щипцы́
для оре́хов; щелку́нчик; **~meg**
'nʌtmeg] муска́тный оре́х.
nutri|tion [nju:'triʃən] пита́ние;
пи́ща; **~tious** [-ʃəs], **~tive** ['nju:tri-
tiv] □ пита́тельный.
nut|shell оре́ховая скорлупа́; in a ~
кра́тко, в двух слова́х; **~ty** ['nʌti]
име́ющий вкус оре́ха; щеголь-
ско́й.
nymph [nimf] ни́мфа.

O

af [ouf] дурачо́к; неуклю́жий
челове́к.
ak [ouk] дуб.
ar [ɔ:] **1.** весло́; **2.** *poet.* грести́;
~sman ['ɔ:zmən] гребе́ц.
asis [ou'eisis] оа́зис.
at [out] овёс (*mst* ~s *pl.*).
ath [ouθ] кля́тва; ⚔, ⚖ прися́га;
руга́тельство.
atmeal ['outmi:l] овся́нка (крупа́).
bdurate ['ɔbdjurit] □ закосне́лый.
bedien|ce [o'bi:djəns] послуша́-
ние, повинове́ние; **~t** [-t] □ по-
слу́шный, поко́рный.
beisance [o'beisəns] ни́зкий по-
кло́н, префера́нс; почте́ние; do ~
выража́ть почте́ние.
besity [ou'bi:siti] ту́чность *f*,
полнота́.
bey [o'bei] повинова́ться (*im*)*pf.*
(Д); [по]слу́шаться (Р).
bituary [o'bitjuəri] некроло́г;
спи́сок уме́рших.
bject 1. ['ɔbdʒikt] предме́т, вещь
f; объе́кт; *fig.* цель *f*, наме́рение;
2. [əb'dʒekt] не люби́ть, не одоб-
ря́ть (Р); возража́ть [-рази́ть] (to
про́тив Р).
bjection [əb'dʒekʃən] возраже́-
ние; **~able** [-əbl] □ нежела́тель-
ный; неприя́тный.
bjective [ɔb'dʒektiv] **1.** □ объек-
ти́вный; целево́й; **2.** ⚔ объе́кт,
цель *f*.
bject-lens *opt.* ли́нза объекти́ва.
bligat|ion [ɔbli'geiʃən] обяза́тель-
ство; обя́занность *f*; **~ory** [ɔ'bli-
gətəri] □ обяза́тельный.
blig|e [ə'blaidʒ] обя́зывать [-за́ть];
принужда́ть [-у́дить]; ~ a p. де́лать
одолже́ние кому́-либо; much ~d
о́чень благода́рен (-рна); **~ing**
[-iŋ] □ услу́жливый, любе́зный.
blique [o'bli:k] □ косо́й; око́ль-
ный; *gr.* ко́свенный.
bliterate [o'blitəreit] изгла́жи-
вать(ся) [-ла́дить(ся)]; вычёркивать [вы́черкнуть].
blivi|on [o'bliviən] забве́ние; **~ous**
[-əs] □ забы́вчивый.
bnoxious [əb'nɔkʃəs] □ неприя́т-
ный, проти́вный, несно́сный.
bscene [ɔb'si:n] □ непристо́йный.
bscur|e [əb'skjuə] **1.** □ тёмный;
мра́чный; нея́сный; неизве́стный;
непоня́тный; **2.** затемня́ть [-ни́ть];
~ity [-riti] мрак, темнота́ и т. д.
obsequies ['ɔbsikwiz] *pl.* погребе́-
ние.
obsequious [əb'si:kwiəs] □ рабо-
ле́пный, подобостра́стный.
observ|able [əb'zə:vəbl] □ заме́т-
ный; **~ance** [-vəns] соблюде́ние
(зако́на, обря́да и т. п.); обря́д;
~ant [-vənt] □ наблюда́тельный;
~ation [ɔbzə'veiʃən] наблюде́ние;
наблюда́тельность *f*; замеча́ние;
~atory [əb'zə:vətri] обсервато́рия;
~e [əb'zə:v] *v/t.* наблюда́ть; *fig.* со-
блюда́ть [-юсти́]; замеча́ть [-е́тить]
(В); *v/i.* замеча́ть [-е́тить].
obsess [əb'ses] завладе́(ва́)ть (Т);
~ed by, *a.* with одержи́мый (Т);
пресле́дуемый (Т).
obsolete ['ɔbsoli:t, -səl-] устаре́лый.
obstacle ['ɔbstəkl] препя́тствие.
obstinate ['ɔbstinit] □ упря́мый.
obstruct [əb'strʌkt] [по]меша́ть (Д),
затрудня́ть [-ни́ть]; загражда́ть
[-ради́ть]; **~ion** [əb'strʌkʃən] пре-
пя́тствие, поме́ха; загражде́ние;
обстру́кция; **~ive** [-tiv] меша́ю-
щий; обструкцио́нный.
obtain [əb'tein] *v/t.* добы́(ва́)ть,
доста́(ва́)ть; *v/i.* быть в обы́чае;
~able [-əbl] ☨ получа́емый; до-
стижи́мый.
obtru|de [əb'tru:d] навя́зывать(ся)
[-за́ть(ся)] (on Д); **~sive** [-siv] на-
вя́зчивый.
obtuse [əb'tju:s] □ тупо́й (*a. fig.*).
obviate ['ɔbvieit] избега́ть [-ежа́ть]
(Р).
obvious ['ɔbviəs] □ очеви́дный,
я́сный.
occasion [ə'keiʒən] **1.** слу́чай; воз-
мо́жность *f*; по́вод; причи́на; F
собы́тие; on the ~ of по слу́чаю
(Р); **2.** причиня́ть [-ни́ть]; дава́ть
по́вод к (Д); **~al** [-ʒnl] □ случа́й-
ный; ре́дкий.
Occident ['ɔksidənt] За́пад, стра-
ны́ За́пада; **⁀al** [ɔksi'dentl] □ за́-
падный.
occult [ɔ'kʌlt] □ окку́льтный, та́й-
ный.
occup|ant ['ɔkjupənt] жи́тель(ница
f) *m*; владе́лец (-лица); **~ation**
[ɔkju'peiʃən] завладе́ние; ⚔ окку-
па́ция; заня́тие, профе́ссия; **~y**
['ɔkjupai] занима́ть [заня́ть]; за-
владе́(ва́)ть (Т); оккупи́ровать
(*im*)*pf*.
occur [ə'kə:] случа́ться [-чи́ться];

встреча́ться [-е́титься]; ~ to a p. приходи́ть в го́лову кому́; **~rence** [ə'kʌrəns] происше́ствие, слу́чай.
ocean ['ouʃən] океа́н.
o'clock [ə'klɔk]: five ~ пять часо́в.
ocul|ar ['ɔkjulə] □ глазно́й; **~ist** ['ɔkjulist] окули́ст, глазно́й врач.
odd [ɔd] □ нечётный; непа́рный; ли́шний; разро́зненный; чудно́й, стра́нный; **~ity** ['ɔditi] чудакова́тость *f*; **~s** [ɔdz] *pl.* нера́венство; разногла́сие; ра́зница; преиму́щество; гандика́п; ша́нсы *m/pl.*; be at ~ with не ла́дить с (Т); ~ and ends оста́тки *m/pl.*; то да сё.
odious ['oudiəs] ненави́стный; отврати́тельный.
odo(u)r ['oudə] за́пах; арома́т.
of [ov; *mst* əv, v] *prp.* о, об (П); из (Р); от (Р); ука́зывает на причи́ну, принадле́жность, объе́кт де́йствия, ка́чество, исто́чник; ча́сто соотве́тствует ру́сскому роди́тельному падежу́; think ~ a th. ду́мать о (П); ~ charity из милосе́рдия; die ~ умере́ть от (Р); cheat ~ обсчи́тывать на (В); the battle ~ Quebec би́тва под Кве́беком; proud ~ го́рдый (Т); the roof ~ the house кры́ша до́ма.
off [ɔ:f, ɔf] **1.** *adv.* прочь; far ~ далеко́; ча́ще всего́ перево́дится верба́льными приста́вками: go ~ уходи́ть [уйти́]; switch ~ выключа́ть [вы́ключить]; take ~ снима́ть [снять]; ~ and on от вре́мени до вре́мени; be well (badly) ~ быть зажи́точным (бе́дным), быть в хоро́шем (плохо́м) положе́нии; **2.** *prp.* с (Р), со (Р) (выража́ет удале́ние предме́та с пове́рхности); от (Р) (ука́зывает на расстоя́ние); **3.** *adj.* свобо́дный от слу́жбы (рабо́ты); да́льний, бо́лее удалённый; боково́й; пра́вый (о стороне́).
offal ['ɔfəl] отбро́сы *m/pl.*; па́даль *f*; **~s** *pl.* потроха́ *m/pl.*
offen|ce, *Am.* **~se** [ə'fens] просту́пок; оби́да, оскорбле́ние; наступле́ние.
offend [ə'fend] *v/t.* обижа́ть [оби́деть], оскорбля́ть [-би́ть]; *v/i.* наруша́ть [-у́шить] (against В); **~er** оби́дчик; правонаруши́тель(ница *f*) *m*; first ~ престу́пник, суди́мый впервы́е.
offensive [ə'fensiv] **1.** □ оскорби́тельный, оби́дный; агресси́вный, наступа́тельный; проти́вный; **2.** наступле́ние.
offer ['ɔfə] **1.** предложе́ние; **2.** *v/t.* предлага́ть [-ложи́ть]; приноси́ть в же́ртву; *v/i.* выража́ть гото́вность (+ *inf.*); [по]пыта́ться; явля́ться [яви́ться]; **~ing** [-riŋ] же́ртва; предложе́ние.
off-hand ['ɔ:f'hænd] *adv.* F бесцеремо́нно; без подгото́вки.
office ['ɔfis] слу́жба, до́лжность *f*; конто́ра, канцеля́рия; ec… богослуже́ние; ♀ министе́рств… **~r** ['ɔfisə] должностно́е лицо́, ч… но́вник (-ица); ⚔ офице́р.
official [ə'fiʃəl] **1.** □ официа́льны… служе́бный; ~ channel служе́… ный поря́док; ~ hours *pl.* сл… же́бные часы́ *m/pl.*; **2.** служе́бн… лицо́, слу́жащий; чино́вник.
officiate [ə'fiʃieit] исполня́ть об… занности (as P).
officious [ə'fiʃəs] □ назо́йливы… официо́зный.
off|set возмеща́ть [-ести́ть]; **~sho…** побе́г; о́тпрыск; ответвле́ни… **~spring** о́тпрыск, пото́мок.
often ['ɔ:fn; *a.* 'ɔ:ftən] ча́сто, мно́… раз.
ogle [ougl] **1.** стро́ить гла́зки (Д… **2.** влюблённый взгляд.
ogre ['ougə] людое́д.
oil [ɔil] **1.** ма́сло (расти́тельное, м… нера́льное); нефть *f*; **2.** см… з(ыв)ать; *fig.* подма́з(ыв)а… **~cloth** клеёнка; **~skin** дождеви́… **~y** ['ɔili] □ масляни́стый, ма́сл… ный; *fig.* еле́йный.
ointment ['ɔintmənt] мазь *f*.
O. K., okay ['ou'kei] F **1.** *pred.* в… в поря́дке, хорошо́; **2.** *int.* хор… шо́!, ла́дно!, есть!
old [ould] *com.* ста́рый; (in time… of ~ в старину́; ~ age ста́рость… **~-fashioned** ['ould'fæʃənd] ст… ромо́дный; **~ish** ['ouldiʃ] стар… ва́тый.
olfactory [ɔl'fæktəri] *anat.* об… ня́тельный. [цве…
olive ['ɔliv] ♀ оли́ва; оли́вковы…
ominous ['ɔminəs] □ злове́щи…
omission [o'miʃən] упуще́ние; пр… пуск.
omit [o'mit] пропуска́ть [-сти́т… упуска́ть [-сти́ть].
omnipoten|ce [ɔm'nipotəns] вс… могу́щество; **~t** [-tənt] □ всем… гу́щий.
on [ɔn] **1.** *prp. mst* на (П *or* В); ~ t… wall на стене́; march ~ Lond… марш на Ло́ндон; ~ good authori… из достове́рного исто́чника; ~ t… 1st of April пе́рвого апре́ля; ~ … arrival по его́ прибы́тии; talk ~ … subject говори́ть на те́му; ~ t… model по э́тому образцу́; ~ heari… it услы́шав э́то; **2.** *adv.* да́льш… вперёд; да́лее; keep one's hat … остава́ться в шля́пе; have a coat… быть в пальто́; and so ~ и так д… лее (и т. д.); be ~ быть пу́щенн… в ход, включённым (и т. п.).
once [wʌns] **1.** *adv.* раз; не́когд… когда́-то; at ~ сейча́с же; ~ for … раз навсегда́; ~ in a while и́зредк… this ~ на э́тот раз; **2.** *cj.* как то́льк…
one [wʌn] **1.** оди́н; еди́ный; еди́нс… венный; како́й-то; ~ day одна́ж… ды; ~ never knows никогда́ … зна́ешь; **2.** (число́) оди́н; едини́…

:he little ~s малыши́ *m/pl.*; ~ another друг дру́га; at ~ заодно́, сра́зу; ~ by ~ оди́н за други́м; I for ~ я со своей стороны́.

nerous ['ɔnərəs] □ обремени́тельный.

ne|self [wʌn'self] *pron. refl.* -ся, -сь, (самого́) себя́; **~-sided** □ односторо́нний; **~-way**: ~ street у́лица односторо́ннего движе́ния.

nion ['ʌnjən] лук, лу́ковица.

nlooker ['ɔnlukə] зри́тель(ница *f*) *m*; наблюда́тель(ница *f*) *m*.

nly ['ounli] **1.** *adj.* еди́нственный; **2.** *adv.* еди́нственно; то́лько; исключи́тельно; ~ yesterday то́лько вчера́; **3.** *cj.* но; ~ that ... е́сли бы не то, что ...

nset ['ɔnset], **onslaught** [-slɔ:t] ата́ка, на́тиск, нападе́ние.

nward ['ɔnwəd] **1.** *adj.* продвига́ющийся вперёд; **2.** *adv.* вперёд; впереди́.

oze [u:z] **1.** ил, ти́на; **2.** проса́чиваться [-сочи́ться]; ~ away убы́(ва́)ть.

paque [ou'peik] □ непрозра́чный.

pen ['oupən] **1.** □ *com.* откры́тый; открове́нный; я́вный; ~ to досту́пный (Д); in the ~ air на откры́том во́здухе; **2.** bring into the ~ обнару́жи(ва)ть; **3.** *v/t.* откры́(ва́)ть; нач(ин)а́ть; *v/i.* откры́(ва́)ться; нач(ин)а́ться; ~ into откры́(ва́)ться в (В) (о две́ри); ~ on to выходи́ть на *or* в (В); **~-handed** ще́дрый; **~ing** ['oupniŋ] отве́рстие; нача́ло; откры́тие; **~-minded** *fig.* непредубеждённый.

pera ['ɔpərə] о́пера; **~-glass**(es *pl.*) бино́кль *m*.

perat|e ['ɔpəreit] *v/t.* управля́ть (Т); *part. Am.* приводи́ть в де́йствие; *v/i.* опери́ровать *(im)pf.*; ока́зывать влия́ние; рабо́тать; де́йствовать; **~ion** [ɔpə'reiʃən] де́йствие; ⚕, ⚔, ✝ опера́ция; проце́сс; be in ~ быть в де́йствии; **~ive** **1.** ['ɔpərеitiv] □ де́йствующий; действи́тельный; операти́вный (*a.* ⚕); **2.** ['ɔpərətiv] (фабри́чный) рабо́чий; **~or** ['ɔpəreitə] опера́тор; телеграфи́ст(ка).

pinion [ə'pinjən] мне́ние; взгляд; in my ~ по-мо́ему.

pponent [ə'pounənt] оппоне́нт, [проти́вник.]

pportun|e ['ɔpətju:n] □ благоприя́тный; подходя́щий; своевре́менный; **~ity** [ɔpə'tju:niti] удо́бный слу́чай, возмо́жность *f*.

ppos|e [ə'pouz] противопоставля́ть [-ста́вить]; [вос]проти́виться (Д); **~ed** [-d] противопоста́вленный; be ~ то быть про́тив (Р); **~ite** ['ɔpəzit] **1.** □ противополо́жный; **2.** *prp.*, *adv.* напро́тив, про́тив (Р); **3.** противополо́жность *f*; **~ition** [ɔpə'ziʃən] сопротивле́ние; оппози́ция; контра́ст.

oppress [ə'pres] притесня́ть [-ни́ть], угнета́ть; **~ion** [-ʃən] притесне́ние, угнете́ние; угнетённость *f*; **~ive** [-siv] □ гнету́щий, угнета́ющий; ду́шный.

optic ['ɔptik] глазно́й, зри́тельный; **~al** [-tikəl] □ опти́ческий; **~ian** [ɔp'tiʃən] о́птик.

option ['ɔpʃən] вы́бор, пра́во вы́бора; ~ right пра́во преиму́щественной поку́пки; **~al** ['ɔpʃənl] □ необяза́тельный, факультати́вный.

opulence ['ɔpjuləns] бога́тство.

or [ɔ:] и́ли; ~ else и́наче; и́ли же.

oracular [ɔ'rækjulə] □ проро́ческий.

oral ['ɔ:rəl] □ у́стный; слове́сный.

orange ['ɔrindʒ] **1.** апельси́н; ора́нжевый цвет; **2.** ора́нжевый.

orat|ion [o'reiʃən] речь *f*; **~or** ['ɔrətə] ора́тор; **~ory** [-ri] красноре́чие; часо́вня.

orb [ɔ:b] шар; орби́та; *fig.* небе́сное свети́ло; держа́ва.

orchard ['ɔ:tʃəd] фрукто́вый сад.

orchestra ['ɔ:kistrə] ♪ орке́стр.

ordain [ɔ:'dein] посвяща́ть в духо́вный сан; предпи́сывать [-са́ть].

ordeal [ɔ:'di:l] *fig.* испыта́ние.

order ['ɔ:də] **1.** поря́док; знак отли́чия; прика́з; ✝ зака́з; ранг; ⚔ строй; take (holy) ~s принима́ть духо́вный сан; in ~ to что́бы; in ~ that с тем, что́бы; make to ~ де́лать на зака́з; *parl.* standing ~s *pl.* пра́вила процеду́ры; **2.** прика́зывать [-за́ть]; назнача́ть [-на́чить]; ✝ зака́зывать [-за́ть]; **~ly** [-li] **1.** аккура́тный; споко́йный; регуля́рный; **2.** ⚔ вестово́й, ордина́рец.

ordinance ['ɔ:dinəns] ука́з, декре́т.

ordinary ['ɔ:dnri] □ обыкнове́нный; зауря́дный.

ordnance ['ɔ:dnəns] ⚔, ⚓ артиллери́йские ору́дия *n/pl.*; артиллери́йское и техни́ческое снабже́ние.

ordure ['ɔ:djuə] наво́з; отбро́сы *m/pl*; грязь *f*.

ore ['ɔ:] руда́.

organ ['ɔ:gən] о́рган; го́лос; ♪ орга́н; **~grinder** арма́нщик; **~ic** [ɔ:'gænik] (~ally) органи́ческий; **~ization** [ɔ:gənai'zeiʃən] организа́ция; **~ize** ['ɔ:gənaiz] организова́ть *(im)pf.*; **~izer** [-ə] организа́тор.

orgy ['ɔ:dʒi] о́ргия.

orient ['ɔ:rient] **1.** восто́к; Восто́к, восто́чные стра́ны *f/pl.*; **2.** ориенти́ровать *(im)pf.*; **~al** [ɔ:ri'entl] **1.** □ восто́чный, азиа́тский; **2.** жи́тель Восто́ка; **~ate** ['ɔ:rienteit] ориенти́ровать *(im)pf.*

orifice ['ɔrifis] отве́рстие; у́стье.

origin ['ɔridʒin] исто́чник; происхожде́ние; нача́ло.

original [əˈridʒənl] **1.** □ первонача́льный; оригина́льный; по́длинный; **2.** оригина́л, по́длинник; чуда́к; **~ity** [əridʒiˈnæliti] оригина́льность *f*.
originat|e [əˈridʒineit] *v/t.* дава́ть нача́ло (Д), порожда́ть [породи́ть]; *v/i.* происходи́ть [-изойти́] (from от Р); **~or** [-ə] созда́тель *m*; инициа́тор.
ornament 1. [ˈɔːnəmənt] украше́ние, орна́мент; *fig.* краса́; **2.** [-ment] украша́ть [укра́сить]; **~al** [ɔːnəˈmentl] □ декорати́вный.
ornate [ɔːˈneit] □ разукра́шенный; витиева́тый (стиль).
orphan [ˈɔːfən] **1.** сирота́ *m/f.*; **2.** осироте́лый (*a.* ~ed); **~age** [-idʒ], **~-asylum** прию́т для сиро́т.
orthodox [ˈɔːθədɔks] □ правове́рный; *eccl.* правосла́вный.
oscillate [ˈɔsileit] вибри́ровать; *fig.* колеба́ться.
ossify [ˈɔsifai] [о]костене́ть.
ostensible [ɔsˈtensəbl] □ очеви́дный.
ostentatio|n [ɔstənˈteiʃən] хвастовство́; выставле́ние напока́з; **~us** [-ʃəs] □ показно́й.
ostler [ˈɔslə] ко́нюх.
ostrich [ˈɔstritʃ] *zo.* стра́ус.
other [ˈʌðə] друго́й; ино́й; the ~ day на дня́х; the ~ morning неда́вно у́тром; every ~ day че́рез день; **~wise** [waiz] и́наче; и́ли же.
otter [ˈɔtə] *zo.* вы́дра.
ought [ɔːt]: I ~ to мне сле́довало бы; you ~ to have done it вам сле́довало э́то сде́лать.
ounce [auns] у́нция (= 28,3 г).
our [ˈauə] *pron. poss.* **~s** [ˈauəz] *pron. poss. pred.* наш, на́ша, на́ше; на́ши *pl.*; **~selves** [auəˈselvz] *pron.* **1.** *refl.* себя́, -ся, -сь; **2.** (для усиле́ния) (мы) са́ми.
oust [aust] выгоня́ть [вы́гнать], вытесня́ть [вы́теснить].
out [aut] **1.** *adv.* нару́жу; вон; до конца́; ча́сто перево́дится приста́вкой вы- : take ~ вынима́ть [вы́нуть]; be ~ with быть в ссо́ре с (Т); ~ and ~ соверше́нно; way ~ вы́ход; **2.** *parl.* the ~s *pl.* оппози́ция; **3.** ✝ ~ size разме́р бо́льше норма́льного; **4.** *prp.* ~ of: из (Р); вне (Р); из-за (Р).
out... [~] пере...; вы...; рас...; про...; воз..., вз...; из...; **~balance** [autˈbæləns] переве́шивать [-ве́сить]; **~bid** [-ˈbid] [*irr.* (bid)] перебива́ть це́ну; **~-break** [ˈautbreik] взрыв, вспы́шка (гне́ва); (внеза́пное) нача́ло (войны́, эпиде́мии и т. п.); **~building** [ˈautbildiŋ] надво́рное строе́ние; **~burst** [-ˈbəːst] взрыв, вспы́шка; **~cast** [-kɑːst] **1.** изгна́нник (-ица); па́рия *m/f*; **2.** и́згнанный; **~come** [-ˈkʌm] результа́т; **~cry** [-krai] вы́крик; проте́ст; **~do** [autˈduː] [*irr.* (do)] превосходи́ть [-взойти́]; **~door** [ˈautdɔː] *adj.* (находя́щийся) вне до́ма и́ли на откры́том во́здухе; нару́жный; **~doors** [ˈautˈdɔː... *adv.* на откры́том во́здухе, вне до́ма.
outer [ˈautə] вне́шний, нару́жный; **~most** [ˈautəmoust] кра́йний.
out|fit [-fit] снаряже́ние; обмунди́ровка; обору́дование; **~going** [-gouiŋ] **1.** уходя́щий; исходя́щий (о бума́гах, пи́сьмах и т. п.); **2.** ~s *pl.* расхо́ды *m/pl.*; **~grow** [auˈgrou] [*irr.* (grow)] выраста́ть [вы́расти] из (пла́тья и т. п.); **~house** [-haus] надво́рное строе́ние; фли́гель *m*.
outing [ˈautiŋ] (за́городная) прогу́лка.
out|last [autˈlɑːst] продолжа́ться до́льше, чем ...; пережи́(ва́)ть; **~law** [ˈautlɔː] **1.** челове́к вне зако́на; **2.** объявля́ть вне зако́на; **~lay** [-lei] изде́ржки *f/pl.*; **~let** [-let] выпускно́е отве́рстие; вы́ход; **~line** [-lain] **1.** (*a. pl.*) очерта́ние, ко́нтур; **2.** рисова́ть ко́нтур (Р); де́лать набро́сок (Р); **~live** [autˈliv] пережи́(ва́)ть; **~look** [ˈautluk] вид, перспекти́ва; то́чка зре́ния, взгляд; **~lying** [-laiiŋ] отдалённый; **~number** [autˈnʌmbə] превосходи́ть чи́сленностью; **~-post** [-poust] аванпо́ст; **~pouring** [-pɔːriŋ] *mst pl.* излия́ние (чувств); **~put** [-put] вы́пуск; производи́тельность *f*; проду́кция.
outrage [ˈautreidʒ] **1.** гру́бое наруше́ние (on Р); **2.** гру́бо наруша́ть (зако́н); **~ous** [autˈreidʒəs] □ неи́стовый; возмути́тельный.
out|right [ˈautˈrait] откры́то; сра́зу; вполне́; **~run** [autˈrʌn] [*irr.* (run)] перегоня́ть [-гна́ть], опережа́ть [-реди́ть]; *fig.* преступа́ть преде́лы (Р); **~set** [ˈautset] нача́ло, отправле́ние; **~shine** [autˈʃain] [*irr.* (shine)] затмева́ть [-ми́ть]; **~side** [ˈautˈsaid] нару́жная сторона́; вне́шняя пове́рхность *f*; вне́шность *f*; кра́йность *f*; at the ~ в кра́йнем слу́чае; **2.** нару́жный; вне́шний; кра́йний; **3.** *adv.* нару́жу; снару́жи; на (откры́том) во́здухе; **4.** *prp.* вне (Р); **~sider** [ˈautˈsaidə] посторо́нний (челове́к); **~skirts** [ˈautskəːts] *pl.* окра́ина; **~spoken** [autˈspoukən] □ открове́нный; **~standing** [ˈautstændiŋ] выступа́ющий; *fig.* выдающийся; неупла́ченный (счёт); **~stretch** [autˈstretʃ] протя́гивать [-тяну́ть]; **~strip** [-ˈstrip] опережа́ть [-реди́ть]; превосходи́ть [-взойти́].
outward [ˈautwəd] **1.** вне́шний, пове́рхностный; **2.** *adv.* (*mst* ~s [-z]) нару́жу; за преде́лы.

ıtweigh [aut'wei] превосходи́ть ıéсом; *fig.* переве́шивать [пере-ıе́сить].

ven ['ʌvn] (хле́бная) печь *f*; ду-:о́вка.

ver ['ouvə] **1.** *adv.* ча́ще всего́ ıерево́дится приста́вками глаго́-:ов: пере..., вы..., про...; сно́ва; ıдоба́вок; сли́шком; ~ and above :ро́ме того́; (all) ~ again сно́ва, ещё)аз; ~ against напро́тив; ~ and ~ again) то и де́ло; read ~ перечи́-:ывать [-чита́ть]; **2.** *prp.* над (Т); ıо (Д); за (В); свы́ше (Р); сверх Р); че́рез (В); о(б) (П); all ~ the own по всему́ го́роду.

ver... ['ouvə] *pref.* как приста́вка,)значáет: сверх...; над...; пере...; ıрезме́рно; **~act** ['ouver'ækt] пе-)еигрывать [-гра́ть] (роль); **~all** 'ouvərɔ:l] спецоде́жда; **~awe** [ou-/ər'ɔ:] держа́ть в благогове́йном :тра́хе; **~balance** [ouvə'bæləns] :еря́ть равнове́сие; переве́шивать -ве́сить]; **~bearing** [-'bɛəriŋ] □ ıла́стный; **~board** ['ouvəbɔ:d] ⚓ ıá борт, за бо́ртом; **~cast** ['ouvə-kɑ:st] па́смурный; **~-charge** [ou-/ə'tʃɑ:dʒ] **1.** сли́шком высо́кая цена́; **2.** перегружа́ть [-узи́ть]; за-ıра́шивать сли́шком высо́кую це́-ıу с (Р) (for за В); **~coat** [-kout] ıальто́ *n indecl.*; **~come** [-'kʌm] *irr.* (come)] преодоле́(ва́)ть, по-)ежда́ть [-еди́ть]; **~crowd** [ouvə-kraud] переполня́ть [-о́лнить] (за́л ı т. п.); **~do** [-'du:] [*irr.* (do)] пере-ıка́ри(ва)ть (мя́со и т. п.); де́лать :ли́шком усе́рдно, утри́ровать *im*)*pf.*; **~draw** ['ouvə'drɔ:] [*irr.* draw)] ✝ превыша́ть [-вы́сить] кредит); **~dress** [-'dres] одева́ться :ли́шком пы́шно; **~due** [-'dju:] ıросро́ченный; **~eat** [ouvər'i:t] *irr.* (eat)]: ~ o. s. объеда́ться [объ-е́сться]; **~flow** **1.** [ouvə'flou] [*irr.* flow)] *v/t.* затопля́ть [-пи́ть]; *v/i.* ıерели́(ва́)ться; **2.** ['ouvəflou] на-)однéние; разли́в; **~grow** ['ouvə-grou] [*irr.* (grow)] заглуша́ть -ши́ть] (о расте́ниях); расти́ сли́ш-:ом бы́стро; **~hang** **1.** ['ouvə'hæŋ] *irr.* (hang)] *v/i.* нависа́ть [-и́снуть]; 2. ['ouvəhæŋ] свес; вы́ступ; **~haul** ouvə'hɔ:l] [от]ремонти́ровать; **~-head** **1.** ['ouvə'hed] *adv.* над голо-)о́й, наверху́; **2.** ['ouvəhed] *adj.* ве́рхний; ✝ накладно́й; **3.** ~s *pl.* ✝ ıакладны́е расхо́ды *m/pl.*; **~hear** ouvə'hiə] [*irr.* (hear)] подслу́ш(и-)ать; нечáянно слы́шать; **~lap** ouvə'læp] *v/t.* части́чно покры-)ать; *v/i.* заходи́ть оди́н за дру-го́й; **~lay** [ouvə'lei] [*irr.* (lay)] ⊕ покры́(ва́)ть; **~load** [ouvə'loud] ıерегружа́ть [-узи́ть]; **~look** [ou-/ə'luk] обозре́(ва́)ть; прогля́ды-)ать [-де́ть]; **~master** [ouvə'mɑ:-stə] подчиня́ть себе́; **~much** ['ouvə'mʌtʃ] чрезме́рно; **~pay** [-'pei] [*irr.* (pay)] перепла́чивать [-лати́ть]; **~power** [ouvə'pauə] переси́ли(ва)ть; **~reach** [ouvə'ri:tʃ] перехитри́ть *pf.*; ~ o. s. брать сли́шком мно́го на себя́, сли́шком напряга́ть си́лы; **~ride** [-'raid] [*irr.* (ride)] перее́хать ло́шадью; *fig.* отверга́ть [-е́ргнуть]; **~run** [-'rʌn] [*irr.* (run)] перелива́ться че́рез край; **~sea** ['ouvə'si:] **1.** за-мо́рский; загра́ничный; **2.** (*a.* ~seas) за́ морем, за́ море; **~see** [-'si:] [*irr.* (see)] надзира́ть за (Т); **~seer** ['ouvəsiə] надзира́тель(ница *f*) *m*; **~shadow** [ouvə'ʃædou] броса́ть тень на (В); омрача́ть [-чи́ть]; **~sight** [-sait] недосмо́тр; **~sleep** ['ouvəsli:p] [*irr.* (sleep)] прос(ы)-па́ть; **~spread** [ouvə'spred] [*irr.* (spread)] покры́(ва́)ть; **~state** ['ouvə'steit] преувели́чи(ва)ть; **~-strain** [-'strein] **1.** переутомле́ние; **2.** переутомля́ть [-ми́ть]; **~take** [ouvə'teik] [*irr.* (take)] догоня́ть [догна́ть]; засти́гнуть врасплóх; **~tax** ['ouvə'tæks] обременя́ть чрез-ме́рным нало́гом; *fig.* сли́шком напряга́ть (си́лы и т. п.) **~throw** **1.** [ouvə'θrou] [*irr.* (throw)] сверга́ть [све́ргнуть]; опроки́дывать [-и́-нуть]; **2.** ['ouvəθrou] сверже́ние; ниспроверже́ние; **~time** ['ouvə-taim] **1.** сверхуро́чные часы́ *m/pl.*; **2.** *adv.* сверхуро́чно.

overture ['ouvətjuə] ♪ увертю́ра; нача́ло (перегово́ров и т. п.); фор-ма́льное предложе́ние.

over|turn [ouvə'tə:n] опроки́ды-вать [-и́нуть]; **~weening** [ouvə'wi:-niŋ] высокоме́рный; **~whelm** [ouvə'welm] подавля́ть [-ви́ть]; переси́ли(ва)ть; **~work** [-wə:k] **1.** перегру́зка; переутомле́ние; **2.** [*irr.* (work)] переутомля́ть(ся) [-ми́ть(ся)]; **~wrought** ['ouvə'rɔ:t] переутомлённый; возбуждённый (о не́рвах).

owe [ou] быть до́лжным (Д/В); быть обя́занным (Д/Т).

owing ['ouiŋ] до́лжный; неупла́-ченный; ~ to *prp.* благодаря́ (Д).

owl [aul] сова́.

own [oun] **1.** свой, со́бственный; родно́й; **2.** my ~ моя́ со́бственность *f*; a house of one's ~ со́бственный дом; hold one's ~ сохраня́ть свои́ пози́ции; **3.** владе́ть (Т); при-зна́(ва́)ть (В); призна́(ва́)ться в (П).

owner ['ounə] владе́лец (-лица *f*); **~ship** [-ʃip] со́бственность *f*; пра́-во со́бственности.

ox [ɔks], *pl.* **oxen** вол, бык.

oxid|e ['ɔksaid] ⚗ о́кись *f*; **~ize** ['ɔksidaiz] окисля́ть(ся) [-ли́ть (-ся)].

oxygen ['ɔksidʒən] ⚗ кислоро́д.

oyster ['ɔistə] у́стрица.

P

pace [peis] **1.** шаг; похо́дка, по́ступь *f*; темп; **2.** *v/t.* измеря́ть шага́ми; *v/i.* [за]шага́ть.
pacific [pə'sifik] (~ally) миролюби́вый; ♀ Ocean Ти́хий океа́н; **~-ation** ['pæsifi'keiʃən] умиротворе́ние; усмире́ние.
pacify ['pæsifai] умиротворя́ть [-ри́ть]; усмиря́ть [-ри́ть].
pack [pæk] **1.** па́чка; вьюк; свя́зка; ки́па; коло́да (карт); сво́ра (соба́к); ста́я (волко́в); **2.** *v/t.* (*often* ~ up) упако́вывать [-кова́ть]; заполня́ть [запо́лнить], наби́(ва́)ть; (*a.* ~ off) выпрова́живать [вы́проводить]; ⊕ уплотня́ть [-ни́ть]; *v/i.* упако́вываться [-ова́ться]; (*often* ~ up) укла́дываться [уложи́ться]; **~age** ['pækidʒ] тюк; ки́па; упако́вка; ме́сто (багажа́); **~er** ['pækə] упако́вщик (-ица); **~et** ['pækit] паке́т; почто́вый парохо́д; **~thread** бечёвка, шпага́т.
pact [pækt] пакт, догово́р.
pad [pæd] **1.** мя́гкая прокла́дка; блокно́т; **2.** подби(ва́)ть, наби(ва́)ть (ва́той и т. п.); **~ding** ['pædiŋ] наби́вочный материа́л; *fig.* многосло́вие.
paddle [pædl] **1.** весло́, гребо́к; ⚓ ло́пасть *f* (гребно́го колеса́); **2.** грести́ гребко́м; плыть на байда́рке; **~-wheel** гребно́е колесо́.
paddock ['pædək] вы́гон, заго́н.
padlock ['pædlɔk] вися́чий замо́к.
pagan ['peigən] **1.** язы́чник; **2.** язы́ческий.
page [peidʒ] **1.** паж; страни́ца; **2.** нумерова́ть страни́цы (P).
pageant ['pædʒənt] пы́шное (истори́ческое) зре́лище; карнава́льное ше́ствие.
paid [peid] *pt.* и *p. pt.* от pay.
pail [peil] ведро́, бадья́.
pain [pein] **1.** боль *f*; страда́ние; наказа́ние; ~s *pl.* (*often sg.*) стара́ния *n/pl.*; on ~ of под стра́хом (P); be in ~ испы́тывать боль; take ~s [по]стара́ться; **2.** причиня́ть боль (Д); **~ful** ['peinful] □ боле́зненный; мучи́тельный; **~less** [-lis] □ безболе́зненный; **~staking** ['peinzteikiŋ] усе́рдный, стара́тельный.
paint [peint] **1.** кра́ска; румя́на *n/pl.*; **2.** [по]кра́сить; [на]румя́нить(ся); **~-brush** кисть *f*; **~er** ['peintə] худо́жник; маля́р; **~ing** ['peintiŋ] жи́вопись *f*; карти́на; **~ress** [-tris] худо́жница.
pair [pεə] **1.** па́ра; чета́; a ~ of scissors но́жницы *f/pl.*; **2.** соединя́ть(ся) по́ двое; спа́ривать(ся).
pal [pæl] *sl.* прия́тель(ница *f*) *m.*
palace ['pælis] дворе́ц.
palatable ['pælətəbl] вку́сный.
palate [-it] нёбо; вкус.
pale[1] [peil] **1.** □ бле́дный; ту́склый; ~ ale све́тлое пи́во; **2.** [по]бледне́ть.
pale[2] [~] кол; *fig.* преде́лы *m/pl.*
paleness ['peilnis] бле́дность *f*.
pall [pɔ:l] оку́тывать покро́вом.
pallet ['pælit] соло́менный тюфя́к.
palliat|e ['pælieit] облегча́ть [-чи́ть] (боле́знь); *fig.* покры́(ва́)ть; **~ive** ['pælietiv] паллиати́вный; смягча́ющий.
pall|id ['pælid] □ бле́дный; **~idness** [-nis], **~or** [-lə] бле́дность *f*.
palm [pα:m] **1.** ладо́нь *f*; ⚘ па́льма; **2.** тро́гать, гла́дить ладо́нью; пря́тать в руке́; ~ off on a p. всу́чивать [-чи́ть] (Д); **~tree** па́льмовое де́рево.
palpable ['pælpəbl] □ осяза́емый; *fig.* очеви́дный, я́вный.
palpitat|e ['pælpiteit] трепета́ть; би́ться (о се́рдце); **~ion** [-ʃən] сердцебие́ние.
palsy ['pɔ:lzi] **1.** парали́ч; *fig.* сла́бость *f*; **2.** парализова́ть (*im*)*pf.*
palter ['pɔ:ltə] [с]плутова́ть; криви́ть душо́й.
paltry ['pɔ:ltri] □ пустяко́вый, ничто́жный.
pamper ['pæmpə] [из]балова́ть, изне́жи(ва)ть.
pamphlet ['pæmflit] брошю́ра.
pan [pæn] кастрю́ля; сковорода́
pan... [~] *pref.* пан...; обще...
panacea [pænə'siə] панаце́я, универса́льное сре́дство.
pancake ['pænkeik] блин; ола́дья
pandemonium [pændi'mounjəm] 🕮 *fig.* «ад кроме́шный».
pander ['pændə] **1.** потво́рствовать (to Д); сво́дничать; **2.** сво́дник (-ица).
pane [pein] (око́нное) стекло́.
panegyric [pæni'dʒirik] панеги́рик похвала́.
panel [pænl] **1.** ⚠ пане́ль *f*; филёнка; ⚖ спи́сок прися́жных заседа́телей; **2.** обшива́ть пане́лями (сте́ны).
pang [pæŋ] внеза́пная о́страя боль *f*; ~s *pl. fig.* угрызе́ния (со́вести).
panic ['pænik] **1.** пани́ческий; **2.** па́ника.
pansy ['pænzi] ⚘ аню́тины гла́зки *m/pl.*
pant [pænt] задыха́ться [задохну́ться]; тяжело́ дыша́ть; стра́стно жела́ть (for, after P).
panties ['pæntiz] *Am.* F (a pair of ~) (да́мские) пантало́ны *m/pl.*
pantry ['pæntri] кладова́я; буфе́тная (для посу́ды).
pants [pænts] *pl. Am.* и́ли P (a pair of ~) подшта́нники *m/pl.*; штаны *m/pl.*

ap [pæp] ка́шка (для дете́й).
apal ['peipəl] □ па́пский.
aper ['peipə] 1. бума́га; газе́та; обо́и m/pl.; нау́чный докла́д; документ; 2. о(б)кле́ивать обо́ями; ~-bag кулёк; ~-clip, ~-fastener кре́пка; ~-hanger обо́йщик; ~-weight пресс-папье́ n indecl.
appy ['pæpi] кашицеобра́зный.
ar [pɑ:] ра́венство; † номина́льная сто́имость f; at ~ альпа́ри; be on a ~ with быть наравне́, на одно́м у́ровне с (Т).
arable ['pærəbl] при́тча.
arachut|e ['pærəʃu:t] парашю́т; ~ist [-ist] парашюти́ст.
arade [pə'reid] 1. выставле́ние напока́з; ⚔ пара́д; ⚔ плац (= ~-ground); ме́сто для гуля́нья; make a ~ of выставля́ть напока́з; 2. выставля́ть напока́з; ⚔ выстра́ивать(ся) на пара́д.
aradise ['pærədais] рай.
aragon [-gən] образе́ц (совершенства, доброде́тели).
aragraph ['pærəgrɑ:f] абза́ц; параграф; газе́тная заме́тка.
arallel ['pærəlel] 1. паралле́льный; 2. паралле́ль f (a. fig.); geogr. паралле́ль f; without ~ несравни́мый; 3. быть паралле́льным с (Т), проходи́ть паралле́льно (Д); сра́внивать [-ни́ть].
araly|se ['pærəleiz] парализова́ть (im)pf.; ~sis [pə'rælisis] ⚕ паралич.
aramount ['pærəmaunt] верхо́вный, вы́сший; первостепе́нный.
arapet ['pærəpit] ⚔ бру́ствер; парапе́т, пери́ла n/pl.
araphernalia [pærəfə'nei'ljə] pl. принадле́жности f/pl.
arasite ['pærəsait] паразит (a. fig.); fig. тунея́дец (-дка).
arasol [pærə'sɔl] зо́нтик (от со́лнца).
aratroops ['pærətru:ps] pl. ⚔ парашю́тно-деса́нтные войска́ f/pl.
arboil ['pɑ:bɔil] слегка́ прова́ривать.
arcel [pɑ:sl] 1. паке́т; посы́лка; 2. (mst ~ out) дели́ть на уча́стки; выделя́ть [вы́делить].
arch [pɑ:tʃ] иссуша́ть [-ши́ть]; опаля́ть [-ли́ть] (о со́лнце).
archment [-mənt] перга́мент.
ardon [pɑ:dn] 1. проще́ние; ⚖ поми́лование; 2. проща́ть [простить]; поми́ловать pf.; ~able [-əbl] □ прости́тельный.
are [pɛə] [по]чи́стить (о́вощи и т. п.); обреза́ть [-ре́зать]; fig. уре́з(ыв)ать.
arent ['pɛərənt] роди́тель(ница f) m; fig. исто́чник; ~s pl. роди́тели m/pl.; ~age [-idʒ] происхожде́ние; ~al [pə'rentl] □ роди́тельский.

parenthe|sis [pə'renθisis], pl. ~ses [-si:z] вво́дное сло́во, вво́дное предложе́ние; pl. typ. (кру́глые) ско́бки f/pl.
paring ['pɛəriŋ] кожура́, ко́рка, шелуха́; ~s pl. обре́зки m/pl.; очи́стки f/pl.
parish ['pæriʃ] 1. церко́вный прихо́д; прихожа́не pl.; (a. civil ~) гражда́нский о́круг; 2. прихо́дский.
parity ['pæriti] ра́венство; равноце́нность f.
park [pɑ:k] 1. парк; mot. стоя́нка; 2. mot. ста́вить на стоя́нку; ~ing ['pɑ:kiŋ] mot. стоя́нка; attr. стоя́ночный.
parlance ['pɑ:ləns] спо́соб выраже́ния, язы́к.
parley [pɑ:li] 1. перегово́ры m/pl.; 2. вести́ перегово́ры.
parliament ['pɑ:ləmənt] парла́мент; ~ary [-'mentəri] парламента́рный, парла́ментский.
parlo(u)r ['pɑ:lə] приёмная; жила́я ко́мната; гости́ная; Am. зал, ателье́ n indecl.; ~-maid го́рничная.
parochial [pə'roukjəl] □ прихо́дский; fig. ме́стный; у́зкий, ограни́ченный.
parole [pə'roul] ⚔ паро́ль m; че́стное сло́во.
parquet ['pɑ:kei] парке́т; thea. пере́дние ряды́ парте́ра.
parrot ['pærət] 1. попуга́й; 2. повторя́ть как попуга́й.
parry ['pæri] отража́ть [отрази́ть], [от]пари́ровать (уда́р).
parsimonious [pɑ:si'mounjəs] □ бережли́вый, эконо́мный; скупо́й.
parsley ['pɑ:sli] ♀ петру́шка.
parson [pɑ:sn] прихо́дский свяще́нник, па́стор.
part [pɑ:t] 1. часть f, до́ля; уча́стие; thea. a. fig. роль f; ме́стность f; ♪ па́ртия; a man of ~s спосо́бный челове́к; take in good (bad) ~ хорошо́ (пло́хо) принима́ть (слова́ и т. п.); for my (own) ~ с мое́й стороны́; in ~ части́чно; on the ~ of со стороны́ (Р); 2. adv. ча́стью, отча́сти; 3. v/t. разделя́ть [-ли́ть]; ~ the hair де́лать пробо́р; v/i. разлуча́ться [-чи́ться], расст(ав)а́ться (with, from с Т).
partake [pɑ:'teik] [irr. (takə)] принима́ть уча́стие; разделя́ть [-ли́ть].
partial ['pɑ:ʃəl] □ части́чный; пристра́стный; неравноду́шный (to к Д); ~ity [pɑ:ʃi'æliti] пристра́стие; скло́нность f.
particip|ant [pɑ:'tisipənt] уча́стник (-ица); ~ate [-peit] уча́ствовать (in в П); ~ation [-peiʃən] уча́стие.
particle ['pɑ:tikl] части́ца; крупи́ца.
particular [pə'tikjulə] 1. □ осо́бенный; осо́бый; ча́стный; разбо́рчивый; 2. подро́бность f, де-

та́ль *f*; in ~ в осо́бенности; **~ity** [pətikju'læriti] осо́бенность *f*; тща́тельность *f*; **~ly** [pə'tikjuləli] осо́бенно; чрезвыча́йно.

parting ['pɑ:tiŋ] **1.** разлу́ка; пробо́р; ~ of the ways *part. fig.* перепу́тье; **2.** проща́льный.

partisan [pɑ:ti'zæn] **1.** сторо́нник (-ица); ⚔ партиза́н; **2.** партиза́нский.

partition [pɑ:'tiʃən] **1.** разде́л; перегоро́дка; **2.** ~ off отделя́ть перегоро́дкой.

partly ['pɑ:tli] ча́стью, отча́сти.

partner ['pɑ:tnə] **1.** уча́стник (-ица); ✝ компаньо́н(ка); партнёр(ша); **2.** ста́вить в па́ру; де́лать партнёром; быть партнёром; **~ship** [-ʃip] уча́стие; ✝ това́рищество, компа́ния.

part-owner совладе́лец.

part-time непо́лная за́нятость *f*; *attr.* не по́лностью за́нятый; ~ worker рабо́чий, за́нятый не по́лный рабо́чий день.

party ['pɑ:ti] па́ртия; отря́д; уча́стник (to в П); компа́ния; вечери́нка; ~ line *parl.* парти́йные директи́вы *f/pl.*; ~ ticket *Am.* парти́йная програ́мма.

pass ['pɑ:s] **1.** прохо́д; перева́л; па́спорт; про́пуск; беспла́тный биле́т; *univ.* посре́дственная сда́ча экза́мена; **2.** *v/i.* проходи́ть [пройти́]; прекраща́ться [-крати́ться]; умира́ть [умере́ть]; происходи́ть [-изойти́], случа́ться [-чи́ться]; переходи́ть [перейти́] (from ... to ... из [P] ... в [B] ...); име́ть хожде́ние; *cards* [с]пасова́ть; come to ~ случа́ться [-чи́ться]; ~ as, for счита́ться (T), слыть (T); ~ away исчеза́ть [-е́знуть]; умира́ть [умере́ть]; ~ by проходи́ть ми́мо; ~ into переходи́ть [перейти́] в (B); ~ off проходи́ть [пройти́] (о бо́ли и т. п.); ~ on идти́ да́льше; ~ out выходи́ть [вы́йти]; **3.** *v/t.* проходи́ть [пройти́]; проезжа́ть [-е́хать]; минова́ть (*im*)*pf.*; выде́рживать [вы́держать] (экза́мен); обгоня́ть [обогна́ть], опережа́ть [-реди́ть]; переправля́ть(ся) [-а́вить(ся)] че́рез (B); (*a.* ~ on) переда(ва́)ть; выноси́ть [вы́нести] (пригово́р); проводи́ть [-вести́] (вре́мя); принима́ть [-ня́ть] (зако́н); **~able** ['pɑ:səbl] □ проходи́мый; ходя́чий (о деньга́х); посре́дственный, сно́сный.

passage ['pæsidʒ] прохо́д; тече́ние (вре́мени); перее́зд, перепра́ва; коридо́р; отры́вок (из кни́ги).

passenger ['pæsindʒə] пассажи́р; седо́к; **~-train** пассажи́рский по́езд.

passer-by ['pɑ:sə'bai] прохо́жий.

passion ['pæʃən] страсть *f*; гнев; ♀ *eccl.* кре́стные му́ки *f/pl.*; ♀ Week страстна́я неде́ля; **~ate** [-it] □ стра́стный.

passive ['pæsiv] □ пасси́вный; поко́рный.

passport ['pɑ:spɔ:t] па́спорт.

password [-wə:d] ⚔ паро́ль *m.*

past [pɑ:st] **1.** *adj.* про́шлый; мину́вший; for some time ~ за после́днее вре́мя; **2.** *adv.* ми́мо; **3.** *prp.* за (T); по́сле (P); ми́мо (P); свы́ше (P); half ~ two полови́на тре́тьего; ~ endurance нестерпи́мый; ~ hope безнадёжный; **4.** про́шлое.

paste [peist] **1.** те́сто; па́ста; клей; **2.** кле́ить, прикле́и(ва)ть; **~board** карто́н; *attr.* карто́нный.

pastel ['pæstel] пасте́ль *f.*

pasteurize ['pæstəraiz] пастеризова́ть (*im*)*pf.*

pastime ['pɑ:staim] времяпрепрово́ждение.

pastor ['pɑ:stə] па́стор; па́стырь *m*; **~al** [-rəl] пастора́льный; пасту́шеский.

pastry ['peistri] пиро́жное, пече́нье; **~-cook** конди́тер.

pasture ['pɑ:stʃə] **1.** па́стбище; вы́гон; **2.** пасти́(сь).

pat [pæt] **1.** похло́пывание; кружо́чек (ма́сла); **2.** похло́п(ыв)ать; **3.** кста́ти; во́-время.

patch [pætʃ] **1.** запла́та; клочо́к земли́; обры́вок; лоску́т; **2.** [за-] лата́ть, [по]чини́ть.

pate [peit] F башка́, голова́.

patent ['peitənt] **1.** я́вный; откры́тый; патенто́ванный; ~ fastener кно́пка (застёжка); ~ leather лакиро́ванная ко́жа; **2.** (*a.* letters ~ *pl.*) пате́нт; дипло́м; **3.** [за]патентова́ть; **~ee** [peitən'ti:] владе́лец пате́нта.

patern|al [pə'tə:nl] □ отцо́вский; оте́ческий; **~ity** [-niti] отцо́вство.

path [pɑ:θ], *pl.* **~s** [pɑ:ðz] тропи́нка, доро́жка.

pathetic [pə'θetik] (**~ally**) патети́ческий; тро́гательный.

patien|ce ['peiʃəns] терпе́ние; насто́йчивость *f*; **~t** [-t] **1.** □ терпели́вый; **2.** пацие́нт(ка).

patrimony ['pætriməni] родово́е поме́стье, во́тчина.

patrol [pə'troul] ⚔ **1.** патру́ль *m*; дозо́р; **2.** патрули́ровать.

patron ['peitrən] патро́н; покрови́тель *m*; клие́нт; **~age** ['pætrənidʒ] покрови́тельство; клиенту́ра; **~ize** [-naiz] покрови́тельствовать; снисходи́тельно относи́ться к (Д); постоя́нно покупа́ть у (P).

patter ['pætə] говори́ть скорогово́ркой; [про]бормота́ть; бараба́нить (о дожде́); топота́ть, семени́ть.

pattern ['pætən] **1.** образе́ц; моде́ль *f*; узо́р; **2.** де́лать по образцу́ (с P).

paunch [pɔ:ntʃ] брюшко́, пу́зо.
pauper ['pɔ:pə] ни́щий (-щая); **~ize** [-raiz] доводи́ть до нищеты́.
pause [pɔ:z] **1.** па́уза, переры́в, остано́вка; **2.** де́лать па́узу.
pave [peiv] [на]мости́ть; *fig.* прокла́дывать [проложи́ть] (путь); **~ment** ['peivmənt] тротуа́р, пане́ль *f*; мостова́я.
paw [pɔ:] **1.** ла́па; F рука́; **2.** тро́гать ла́пой; бить копы́том.
pawn [pɔ:n] **1.** зало́г, закла́д; *chess* пе́шка; in, at ~ в закла́де; **2.** закла́дывать [заложи́ть]; **~broker** ростовщи́к; **~shop** ломба́рд, ссу́дная ка́сса.
pay [pei] **1.** пла́та, упла́та; зарпла́та, жа́лованье; **2.** [*irr.*] *v/t.* [за]плати́ть; опла́чивать [оплати́ть]; вознагражда́ть [-ради́ть]; [с]де́лать (визи́т); ~ attention to обраща́ть внима́ние на (В); ~ down плати́ть нали́чными; *v/i.* окупа́ться [-пи́ться] (*a. fig.*); ~ for [у-, за]плати́ть за (В), опла́чивать [оплати́ть] (В); *fig.* [по]плати́ться за (В); **~able** ['peiəbl] подлежа́щий упла́те; **~-day** день вы́платы жа́лованья; **~ing** ['peiiŋ] вы́годный; **~master** казначе́й, касси́р; **~ment** [mənt] упла́та, платёж; **~roll** платёжная ве́домость *f*.
pea [pi:] ♀ горо́х; горо́шина; **~s** *pl.* горох; *attr.* горо́ховый.
peace [pi:s] мир; споко́йствие; **~able** ['pi:səbl] □ миролюби́вый, ми́рный; **~ful** [-ful] □ ми́рный, споко́йный; **~maker** миротво́рец.
peach [pi:tʃ] пе́рсик; пе́рсиковое де́рево.
pea|cock ['pi:kɔk] павли́н; **~hen** [-hen] па́ва.
peak [pi:k] верши́на (горы́); козырёк (ке́пки); *attr.* максима́льный; вы́сший.
peal [pi:l] **1.** звон колоколо́в; раска́т (гро́ма); ~ of laughter взрыв сме́ха; **2.** разда́(ва́)ться; греме́ть; трезво́нить.
peanut ['pi:nʌt] земляно́й оре́х.
pear [pɛə] ♀ гру́ша; гру́шевое де́рево.
pearl [pə:l] *coll.* же́мчуг; жемчу́жина *a. fig.*; *attr.* жемчу́жный; **~y** ['pə:li] как же́мчуг.
peasant ['pezənt] **1.** крестья́нин; **2.** крестья́нский; **~ry** [-ri] крестья́нство.
peat [pi:t] торф.
pebble ['pebl] голы́ш, га́лька.
peck [pek] **1.** пек, ме́ра сыпу́чих тел (= 9,087 ли́тра); *fig.* мно́жество; **2.** клева́ть [клю́нуть].
peculate ['pekjuleit] (незако́нно) растра́чивать [-ра́тить].
peculiar [pi'kju:ljə] □ своеобра́зный; осо́бенный; стра́нный; **~ity** [pikju:li'æriti] осо́бенность *f*; стра́нность *f*.
pecuniary [pi'kju:njəri] де́нежный.
pedagogue ['pedəgɔg] педаго́г, учи́тель(ница *f*) *m*.
pedal [pedl] **1.** педа́ль *f*; **2.** ножно́й; **3.** е́хать на велосипе́де; рабо́тать педа́лями.
peddle [pedl] торгова́ть вразно́с.
pedest|al ['pedistl] пьедеста́л (*a. fig.*); **~rian** [pi'destriən] **1.** пешехо́д; **2.** пешехо́дный.
pedigree ['pedigri:] родосло́вная.
pedlar ['pedlə] разно́счик, коробе́йник.
peek [pi:k] *Am.* **1.** ~ in загля́дывать [-яну́ть]; **2.** бе́глый взгляд.
peel [pi:l] **1.** ко́рка, ко́жица, шелуха́; **2.** (*a.* ~ off) *v/t.* снима́ть ко́жицу, ко́рку, шелуху́ с (Р); [по-] чи́стить (фру́кты, о́вощи); *v/i.* [об]лупи́ться, сходи́ть [сойти́] (о ко́же).
peep [pi:p] **1.** взгляд укра́дкой; **2.** взгля́дывать укра́дкой; *fig.* проявля́ться [-ви́ться]; [про]пища́ть; **~-hole** глазо́к (око́шечко).
peer [piə] **1.** [с]равня́ться с (Т); ~ at вгля́дываться [-де́ться] в (В); **2.** ро́вня́ *m/f.*; пэр; **~less** ['piəlis] □ несравне́нный.
peevish ['pi:viʃ] □ брюзгли́вый.
peg [pəg] **1.** ко́лышек; ве́шалка; ♪ коло́к; зажи́мка для белья́; *fig.* take a p. down a ~ сбива́ть спесь с кого́-либо; **2.** прикрепля́ть ко́лышком; отмеча́ть ко́лышками; ~ away, along F упо́рно рабо́тать; **~-top** юла́ (игру́шка).
pellet ['pelit] ша́рик; пилю́ля; дроби́нка.
pell-mell ['pel'mel] вперемéшку.
pelt [pelt] **1.** ко́жа, шку́ра; **2.** *v/t.* обстре́ливать [-ля́ть]; забра́сывать [-роса́ть]; *v/i.* бараба́нить (о дожде́ и т. п.).
pen [pen] **1.** перо́; заго́н; **2.** [на-] писа́ть; [*irr.*] загоня́ть в заго́н.
penal [pi:nl] □ уголо́вный; кара́тельный; ~ servitude ка́торжные рабо́ты *f/pl.*; **~ize** ['pi:nəlaiz] нака́зывать [-за́ть]; **~ty** ['penlti] наказа́ние; ✝, *sport.* штраф; *attr.* штрафно́й.
penance ['penəns] эпитими́я.
pence [pens] *pl.* от penny.
pencil [pensl] **1.** каранда́ш; кисть *f* (живопи́сца); **2.** [на]рисова́ть; писа́ть карандашо́м; вычéрчивать [вы́чертить].
pendant ['pendənt] кулóн, брело́к.
pending ['pendiŋ] **1.** ⚖ ожида́ющий реше́ния; **2.** *prp.* в продолже́ние (Р); (вплоть) до (Р).
pendulum ['pendjuləm] ма́ятник.
penetra|ble ['penitrəbl] □ проница́емый; **~te** [-treit] проника́ть [-ни́кнуть] в (В); глубоко́ тро́гать; прони́зывать [-за́ть]; *fig.* вника́ть [вни́кнуть] в (В); **~tion** [peni'treiʃən] проника́ние; проница́тель-

ность *f*; **~tive** ['penitreitiv] □ проникáющий; проницáтельный.
penholder рýчка (для перá).
peninsula [pi'ninsjulə] полуóстров.
peniten|ce ['penitəns] раскáяние; покая́ние; **~t 1.** □ раскáивающийся; **2.** кáющийся грéшник; **~tiary** [peni'tenʃəri] исправи́тельный дом; *Am.* кáторжная тюрьмá.
penman ['penmən] писáтель *m*; [писéц.]
pen-name псевдони́м.
pennant ['penənt] ⚓ вы́мпел.
penniless ['penilis] □ без копéйки.
penny ['peni] пéнни *n indecl.*, пенс; *Am.* монéта в 1 цент; **~weight** 24 грáна (= 1,5552 гр).
pension 1. ['penʃən] пéнсия; **2.** увольня́ть на пéнсию; давáть пéнсию (Д); **~ary, ~er** ['penʃənəri, -ʃənə] пенсионéр(ка).
pensive ['pensiv] □ задýмчивый.
pent [pent] заключённый; **~-up** накóпленный (о гнéве и т. п.).
penthouse ['penthaus] навéс.
penu|rious [pi'njuəriəs] скýдный; скупóй; **~ry** ['penjuri] нуждá; недостáток.
people [pi:pl] **1.** нарóд; *coll.* лю́ди *m/pl.*; населéние; **2.** заселя́ть [-ли́ть]; населя́ть [-ли́ть].
pepper ['pepə] **1.** пéрец; **2.** [по-, на-] пéрчить; **~mint** ⚘ мя́та; **~y** [-ri] □ напéрченный; *fig.* вспы́льчивый.
per [pə:] по (Д), чéрез (В), посрéдством (Р); за (В), на (В), в (В); ~ cent процéнт.
perambulat|e [pə'ræmbjuleit] обходи́ть [обойти́], объезжáть [-éхать]; **~or** ['præmbjuleitə] дéтская коля́ска.
perceive [pə'si:v] воспринимáть [-ня́ть]; ощущáть [ощути́ть]; понимáть [-ня́ть].
percentage [pə'sentidʒ] процéнт; процéнтное отношéние и́ли содержáние.
percepti|ble [pə'septəbl] □ ощути́мый; **~on** [-ʃən] ощущéние; восприя́тие.
perch [pə:tʃ] **1.** *zo.* óкунь *m*; перч, мéра длины́ (= 5.029 м); насéст; **2.** сади́ться [сесть]; усáживаться [усéсться]; сажáть на насéст.
percolate ['pə:kəleit] [про]фильтровáть; процéживать [-цеди́ть].
percussion [pə:'kʌʃən] удáр.
perdition [pə:'diʃən] ги́бель *f*.
peregrination [perigri'neiʃən] стрáнствование; путешéствие.
peremptory [pə'remptəri] безапелляциóнный; повели́тельный, влáстный.
perennial [pə'renjəl] □ вéчный, неувядáемый; ⚘ многолéтний.
perfect 1. ['pə:fikt] □ совершéнный; закóнченный; **2.** [pə'fekt] [у]совершéнствовать; завершáть [-ши́ть]; **~ion** [-ʃən] совершéнство; *fig.* вы́сшая стéпень *f*.
perfidious [pə'fidiəs] □ верolóмный.
perfidy ['pə:fidi] верolóмство.
perforate ['pə:fəreit] перфори́ровать (*im*)*pf*.
perform [pə'fɔ:m] исполня́ть [-óлнить] (*a. thea.*); *thea.*, ♪ игрáть [сыгрáть] (роль, пьéсу и т. п.), представля́ть [-áвить]; **~ance** [əns] исполнéние (*a. thea.*); *thea.* представлéние; *sport* достижéние; **~er** [-ə] исполни́тель(ница *f*) *m*.
perfume 1. ['pə:fju:m] духи́ *m/pl.*; благоухáние; **2.** [pə'fju:m] [на-] души́ть; **~ry** [-əri] парфюмéрия.
perfunctory [pə'fʌŋktəri] □ *fig.* механи́ческий; повéрхностный.
perhaps [pə'hæps, præps] мóжет быть.
peril ['peril] **1.** опáсность *f*; **2.** подвергáть опáсности; **~ous** [-əs] □ опáсный.
period ['piəriəd] пери́од; абзáц; **~ic** [piəri'ɔdik] периоди́ческий; **~ical** [-dikəl] **1.** □ периоди́ческий; **2.** периоди́ческое издáние.
perish ['periʃ] погибáть [-и́бнуть]; [по]губи́ть; **~able** ['periʃəbl] □ скоропóртящийся; тлéнный.
periwig ['periwig] пари́к.
perjur|e ['pə:dʒə]: ~ o. s. лжесвидéтельствовать; нарушáть кля́тву; **~y** [-ri] лжесвидéтельство; клятвопреступлéние.
perk [pə:k] F: *mst* ~ up *v/i.* задирáть нос; *v/t.* ~ o. s. прихорáшиваться.
perky ['pə:ki] □ дéрзкий; самоувéренный.
permanen|ce ['pə:mənəns] постоя́нство; **~t** [-t] □ постоя́нный, неизмéнный.
permea|ble ['pə:miəbl] проницáемый; **~te** [-mieit] проникáть [-и́кнуть], пропи́тывать [-итáть].
permissi|ble [pə'misəbl] □ позволи́тельный; **~on** [-ʃən] позволéние, разрешéние.
permit 1. [pə'mit] разрешáть [-ши́ть], позволя́ть [-вóлить]; допускáть [-усти́ть]; **2.** ['pə:mit] разрешéние; прóпуск.
pernicious [pə:'niʃəs] пáгубный.
perpendicular [pə:pən'dikjulə] □ перпендикуля́рный.
perpetrate ['pə:pitreit] совершáть [-ши́ть] (преступлéние и т. п.).
perpetu|al [pə'petjuəl] постоя́нный, вéчный; **~ate** [-jueit] увековéчи(ва)ть.
perplex [pə'pleks] озадáчи(ва)ть, сбивáть с тóлку; **~ity** [-iti] озадáченность *f*; недоумéние; затруднéние.
perquisites ['pə:kwizits] *pl.* случáйные дохóды *m/pl.*
persecut|e ['pə:sikju:t] преслéдовать; **~ion** [pə:si'kju:ʃən] преслéдование.

perseverance [pə:si'viərəns] настóйчивость *f*, упóрство; **~e** [-'viə] *v/i.* выдéрживать [вы́держать]; упóрно продолжáть (in В).
persist [pə'sist] упóрствовать (in в П); **~ence** [-əns] настóйчивость *f*; **~ent** [-ənt] □ настóйчивый.
person ['pə:sn] лицó, ли́чность *f*, осóба, человéк; **~age** [-idʒ] вáжная персóна; персонáж; **~al** [-l] □ ли́чный; **~ality** [pə:sə'næliti] ли́чность *f*; кóлкость *f*; **~ate** ['pə:səneit] игрáть роль (Р); выдавáть себя́ за (В); **~ify** [pə:'sɔnifai] олицетворя́ть [-ри́ть], воплощáть [-лоти́ть]; **~nel** [pə:sə'nel] персонáл, ли́чный состáв.
perspective [pə'spektiv] перспекти́ва; ви́д.
perspicuous [pə'spikjuəs] □ я́сный.
perspiration [pə:spə'reiʃən] потéние; пот; **~e** [pəs'paiə] [вс]потéть.
persuade [pə'sweid] убеждáть [убеди́ть]; склоня́ть [-ни́ть] (into к Д); **~sion** [-ʒən] убеждéние; убеди́тельность *f*; **~sive** [-siv] □ убеди́тельный.
pert [pə:t] □ дéрзкий; развя́зный.
pertain [pə:'tein] (to) принадлежáть (Д); относи́ться [отнести́сь] (к Д).
pertinacious [pə:ti'neiʃəs] □ упря́мый, неусту́пчивый.
pertinent ['pə:tinənt] □ умéстный; относя́щийся к дéлу.
perturb [pə'tə:b] нарушáть [-у́шить] (спокóйствие); [о]беспокóить.
perusal [pə'ru:zəl] внимáтельное прочтéние; **~e** [pə'ru:z] [про]читáть; внимáтельно прочи́тывать.
pervade [pə:'veid] распространя́ться [-ни́ться] по (Д) (о зáпахе и т. п.).
perverse [pə'və:s] □ преврáтный, оши́бочный; ⚕ извращённый; **~ion** [-ʃən] ⚕ извращéние.
pervert 1. [pə'və:t] извращáть [-рати́ть]; совращáть [-рати́ть]; 2. ['pə:və:t] отсту́пник (-ица).
pest [pest] *fig.* я́зва, бич; паразит; **~er** ['pestə] докучáть (Д), надоедáть [-éсть] (Д).
pestiferous [pes'tifərəs] □ зарáзный; **~lence** ['pestiləns] чумá; **~lent** [-t] смертонóсный; **~lential** [pesti'lenʃəl] □ чумнóй; зловóнный.
pet [pet] 1. кóмнатное живóтное; люби́мец, бáловень *m*; 2. люби́мый; ~ dog кóмнатная собáчка, болóнка; ~ name ласкáтельное и́мя; 3. баловáть; ласкáть.
petition [pi'tiʃən] 1. прошéние, пети́ция; прóсьба; 2. [по]проси́ть; подавáть прошéние.
petrify ['petrifai] превращáть(ся) в кáмень; приводи́ть в оцепенéние.
petrol ['petrəl] *Brit. mot.* бензи́н.
petticoat ['petikout] ни́жняя ю́бка.
pettish ['petiʃ] □ оби́дчивый.
petty ['peti] □ мéлкий; мéлочный.
petulant ['petjulənt] раздражи́тельный.
pew [pju:] церкóвная скамья́.
pewter ['pju:tə] оловя́нная посу́да.
phantasm ['fæntæzm] фантóм; иллю́зия.
phantom ['fæntəm] фантóм, при́зрак; иллю́зия.
Pharisee ['færisi:] фарисéй.
pharmacy ['fɑ:məsi] фармаци́я; аптéка.
phase [feiz] фáза; пери́од.
phenomenon [fi'nɔminən], *pl.* **~a** [-nə] явлéние; фенóмен.
phial ['faiəl] скля́нка, пузырёк.
philander ['fi'lændə] флиртовáть.
philanthropist [fi'lænθrəpist] филантрóп.
philologist [fi'lɔlədʒist] филóлог.
philosopher [fi'lɔsəfə] филóсоф; **~ize** [-faiz] филосóфствовать; **~y** [-fi] филосóфия.
phlegm [flem] мокрóта; флегмати́чность *f*.
phone [foun] F *s.* telephone.
phonetics [fo'netiks] *pl.* фонéтика.
phosphorus ['fɔsfərəs] фóсфор.
photograph ['foutəgrɑ:f] 1. фотогрáфия, сни́мок; 2. [с]фотографи́ровать; **~er** [fə'tɔgrəfə] фотóграф; **~y** [-fi] фотогрáфия (дéло).
phrase [freiz] 1. фрáза, выражéние; слог; 2. выражáть [вы́разить].
physical ['fizikəl] □ физи́ческий; телéсный; **~ian** [fi'ziʃən] врач; **~ist** ['fizisist] фи́зик; **~s** ['fiziks] *sg.* фи́зика.
physique [fi'zi:k] телосложéние.
pick [pik] 1. удáр (óстрым); вы́бор; киркá; 2. выбирáть [вы́брать]; ковыря́ть [-рну́ть] в (П); соб(и)рáть (цветы́, плоды́); оглáдывать [оглодáть]; [по]клевáть; срывáть [сорвáть] (цветóк, фрукт); ~ out выбирáть [вы́брать]; ~ up соб(и)рáть; подбирáть [подобрáть]; поднимáть [-ня́ть]; заезжáть [заéхать] за (Т); **~-a-back** ['pikəbæk] (о дéтях) на спинé (отцá и т. п.); **~axe** киркá.
picket ['pikit] 1. кол; ⚔ сторожевáя застáва; стáчечный пикéт; 2. выставля́ть пикéты вокру́г (Р); обноси́ть частокóлом.
picking ['pikiŋ] собирáние, отбóр и т. д. (*s. verb*); **~s** *pl.* остáтки *m/pl.*, объéдки *m/pl.*; *mst* **~s** *pl.* мéлкая пожи́ва.
pickle [pikl] 1. рассóл; *pl.* пи́кули *f/pl.*; F неприя́тности *f/pl.*; 2. [по-] соли́ть; **~d** herring солёная селёдка.

pick|lock ['piklɔk] отмы́чка; **~-pocket** карма́нный вор.
pictorial [pik'tɔ:riəl] **1.** иллюстри́рованный; изобрази́тельный; **2.** иллюстри́рованный журна́л.
picture ['piktʃə] **1.** карти́на; the ~s *pl.* кино́ *indecl.*; ~-gallery карти́нная галере́я; ~ (post)card откры́тка с ви́дом; **2.** изобража́ть [-рази́ть]; опи́сывать [-са́ть]; вообража́ть [-рази́ть]; **~sque** [piktʃə'resk] живопи́сный.
pie [pai] паште́т; пиро́г; торт.
piebald ['paibɔ:ld] пе́гий (о ло́шади).
piece [pi:s] **1.** кусо́к, часть *f*; обры́вок, обло́мок; шту́ка; ~ of advice сове́т; ~ of news но́вость *f*; by the ~ пошту́чно; give a ~ of one's mind выска́зывать своё мне́ние; take to ~s разбира́ть на ча́сти; **2.** [по]чини́ть; соединя́ть в одно́ це́лое, собира́ть из кусо́чков; **~meal** по частя́м, постепе́нно; **~work** сде́льная рабо́та.
pier [piə] усто́й; бык (моста́); мол; волноло́м; при́стань *f*.
pierce [piəs] пронза́ть [-зи́ть]; просве́рливать [-ли́ть]; прони́зывать [-за́ть].
piety ['paiəti] благоче́стие, на́божность *f*.
pig [pig] свинья́.
pigeon ['pidʒin] го́лубь *m*; **~-hole** **1.** отделе́ние (пи́сьменного стола́ и т. п.); **2.** раскла́дывать по я́щикам; откла́дывать в до́лгий я́щик.
pig|headed ['pig'hedid] упря́мый; **~-iron** чугу́н в болва́нках; **~skin** свина́я ко́жа; **~sty** свина́рник; **~tail** коси́чка, коса́.
pike [paik] ⚔ копьё; пи́ка; *zo.* щу́ка.
pile [pail] **1.** ку́ча, гру́да; ⚡ батаре́я; костёр; шта́бель *m*; ~s *pl.* геморро́й; **2.** скла́дывать [сложи́ть]; сва́ливать в ку́чу.
pilfer ['pilfə] [у]ворова́ть.
pilgrim ['pilgrim] пало́мник; **~age** ['pilgrimidʒ] пало́мничество.
pill [pil] пилю́ля.
pillage ['pilidʒ] **1.** грабёж; **2.** [о]гра́бить.
pillar ['pilə] столб, коло́нна; **~-box** почто́вый я́щик.
pillion ['piljən] *mot.* за́днее сиде́нье.
pillory ['piləri] **1.** позо́рный столб; **2.** поста́вить к позо́рному столбу́.
pillow ['pilou] поду́шка; **~-case, ~-slip** на́волочка.
pilot ['pailət] **1.** ✈ пило́т; ⚓ ло́цман; **2.** ⚓ проводи́ть [-вести́]; ✈ пилоти́ровать; **~-balloon** шар-пило́т.
pimp [pimp] **1.** сво́дник (-ица); **2.** сво́дничать.
pimple [pimpl] пры́щик.
pin [pin] **1.** була́вка; шпи́лька; кно́пка; ке́гля; ♪ коло́к; **2.** прика́лывать [-коло́ть]; *fig.* пригвожда́ть [-озди́ть].
pinafore ['pinəfɔ:] пере́дник.
pincers ['pinsəz] *pl.* клещи́ *f/pl.*; щипцы́ *m/pl.*
pinch [pintʃ] **1.** щипо́к; щепо́тка (со́ли и т. п.); стеснённое положе́ние, кра́йность *f*; **2.** *v/t.* щипа́ть [щипну́ть]; прищемля́ть [-ми́ть]; *v/i.* [по]скупи́ться; жать (об о́буви).
pine [pain] **1.** ⚘ сосна́; **2.** [за]ча́хнуть; изны́(ва́)ть; **~-apple** анана́с; **~-cone** сосно́вая ши́шка.
pinion ['pinjən] **1.** оконе́чность пти́чьего крыла́; перо́ (крыла́); ⊕ шестерня́; **2.** подреза́ть кры́лья (Д); *fig.* свя́зывать ру́ки (Д).
pink [piŋk] **1.** ⚘ гвозди́ка; *fig.* вы́сшая сте́пень *f*; **2.** ро́зовый.
pinnacle ['pinəkl] ⚠ остроконе́чная ба́шенка; верши́на (горы́); *fig.* верх.
pint [paint] пи́нта (= 0,47 ли́тра).
pioneer [paiə'niə] **1.** пионе́р; ⚔ сапёр; **2.** прокла́дывать путь (for Д); руководи́ть (ке́м-либо).
pious ['paiəs] □ на́божный.
pip [pip] *vet.* типу́н; ко́сточка, зёрнышко (плода́); очко́ (на ка́ртах); звёздочка (на пого́не).
pipe [paip) **1.** труба́; тру́бка; ♪ свире́ль *f*, ду́дка; бо́чка (для вина́); **2.** игра́ть на свире́ли и т. п.; [за-] пища́ть; **~-layer** прокла́дчик труб; **~-line** трубопрово́д; нефтепрово́д; **~r** ['paipə] ду́дочник; волы́нщик.
piping ['paipiŋ]: **1.** ~ hot о́чень горя́чий; **2.** кант (на пла́тье).
pique [pi:k] **1.** доса́да; **2.** возбужда́ть [-уди́ть] (любопы́тство); коло́ть [кольну́ть], заде́(ва́)ть (самолю́бие); ~ o. s. on чва́ниться (Т).
pira|cy ['paiərəsi] пира́тство; наруше́ние а́вторского пра́ва; **~te** [-rit] **1.** пира́т; наруши́тель а́вторского пра́ва; **2.** самово́льно переиздава́ть.
pistol [pistl] пистоле́т.
piston ['pistən] ⊕ по́ршень *m*; **~-rod** шату́н; **~-stroke** ход по́ршня.
pit [pit] **1.** я́ма; ша́хта; о́спина; *thea.* парте́р; *Am.* отде́л това́рной би́ржи; **2.** скла́дывать в я́му (на́ зиму).
pitch [pitʃ] **1.** смола́; дёготь *m*; бросо́к; сте́пень *f*; ♪ высота́ то́на; ⚓ килева́я ка́чка; ⊕ накло́н; **2.** *v/t.* разби́(ва́)ть (пала́тку); мета́ть [метну́ть], броса́ть [бро́сить]; ♪ дава́ть основно́й тон (Д); *v/i.* ⚔ располага́ться ла́герем; подверга́ться ка́чке; F ~ into наброса́ться [-ро́ситься] на (В).
pitcher ['pitʃə] кувши́н.
pitchfork ['pitʃfɔ:k] ви́лы *f/pl.*; ♪ камерто́н.
pitfall ['pitfɔ:l] *fig.* лову́шка.
pith [piθ] спинно́й мозг; сердцеви́на; *fig.* су́щность *f*, суть *f*; **~y**

['piθi] с сердцеви́ной; энерги́чный.
pitiable ['pitiəbl] □ жа́лкий.
pitiful ['pitiful] □ жа́лостливый; жа́лостный; (*a. contp.*) жа́лкий.
pitiless ['pitilis] □ безжа́лостный
pittance ['pitəns] ску́дное жа́лование.
pity ['piti] **1.** жа́лость *f* (for к Д), it is a ~ жаль; **2.** [по]жале́ть.
pivot ['pivət] **1.** то́чка враще́ния; ⊕ сте́ржень *m* (*a. fig.*); штифт; **2.** враща́ться ([up]on вокру́г Р).
placable ['pleikəbl] □ кро́ткий, незлопа́мятный.
placard ['plækɑ:d] **1.** плака́т; **2.** раскле́и(ва)ть (объявле́ния); реклами́ровать плака́тами.
place [pleis] **1.** ме́сто; месте́чко, селе́ние; пло́щадь *f*; жили́ще; уса́дьба; до́лжность *f*, слу́жба; ~ of delivery ме́сто доста́вки; give ~ to уступа́ть ме́сто (Д); in ~ of вме́сто (Р); out of ~ неуме́стный; **2.** [по]ста́вить, класть [положи́ть]; размеща́ть [-ести́ть], помеща́ть [-ести́ть].
placid ['plæsid] □ споко́йный, безмяте́жный.
plagiar|ism ['pleidʒiərizm] плагиа́т; **~ize** [-raiz] незако́нно заи́мствовать (мы́сли и т. п.).
plague [pleig] **1.** бе́дствие, бич; чума́; **2.** [из]му́чить; F надоеда́ть [-е́сть] (Д).
plaid [plæd] шотла́ндка; плед.
plain [plein] **1.** □ просто́й; поня́тный; я́сный, я́вный; очеви́дный; обыкнове́нный; гла́дкий, ро́вный; **2.** *adv.* я́сно; разбо́рчиво; открове́нно; **3.** равни́на; пло́скость *f*; **~-clothes man** сы́щик; **~dealing** прямота́.
plaint|iff ['pleintif] исте́ц, исти́ца; **~ive** ['pleintiv] □ жа́лобный, зауны́вный.
plait [plæt, *Am.* pleit] **1.** коса́ (воло́с); **2.** заплета́ть [-ести́].
plan [plæn] **1.** план; **2.** составля́ть план; *fig.* намеча́ть [-е́тить]; намерева́ться.
plane [plein] **1.** пло́ский; **2.** пло́скость *f*; прое́кция; ✈ несу́щая пове́рхность *f*; самолёт; *fig.* у́ровень *m*; ⊕ руба́нок; **3.** [вы́]строга́ть; ✈ [с]плани́ровать.
plank [plæŋk] **1.** доска́, пла́нка; *Am. pol.* пункт парти́йной програ́ммы; **2.** настила́ть и́ли обшива́ть до́сками; *sl.* ~ down выкла́дывать [вы́ложить] (де́ньги).
plant [plɑ:nt] **1.** расте́ние; ⊕ заво́д, фа́брика; **2.** сажа́ть [посади́ть] (расте́ние); устана́вливать [-нови́ть]; **~ation** [plæn'teiʃən] планта́ция; насажде́ние; **~er** ['plɑ:ntə] планта́тор.
plaque [plɑ:k] таре́лка (как стенно́е украше́ние); доще́чка.
plash [plæʃ] плеска́ть(ся) [-сну́ть].
plaster ['plɑ:stə] **1.** *pharm.* пла́стырь *m*; ⊕ штукату́рка; (*mst* ~ of Paris) гипс; **2.** [о]штукату́рить; накла́дывать пла́стырь на (В).
plastic ['plæstik] (~ally) пласти́ческий; ~ material пластма́сса.
plat [plæt] план, съёмка; уча́сток.
plate [pleit] **1.** пласти́нка; плита́; полоса́ (мета́лла); доще́чка с на́дписью; столо́вое серебро́; таре́лка; ⊕ листово́е желе́зо; **2.** покрыва́ть мета́ллом.
plat(t)en [plætn] ва́лик (пи́шущей маши́нки).
platform ['plætfɔ:m] перро́н, платфо́рма; трибу́на; площа́дка (ваго́на); полити́ческая програ́мма.
platinum ['plætinəm] *min.* пла́тина.
platitude [-titju:d] бана́льность *f*.
platoon [plə'tu:n] ⚔ взвод.
platter ['plætə] деревя́нная таре́лка.
plaudit ['plɔ:dit] рукоплеска́ния [*n/pl.*]
plausible ['plɔ:zəbl] □ правдоподо́бный.
play [plei] **1.** игра́; пье́са; ⊕ зазо́р; мёртвый ход; **2.** игра́ть [сыгра́ть] (в В, ♪ на П); свобо́дно дви́гаться (о механи́зме); ~ off *fig.* разы́грывать [-ра́ть]; стра́вливать [страви́ть] (against с Т); **~ed out** вы́дохшийся; **~bill** театра́льная афи́ша; **~er** ['pleiə] игро́к; актёр; **~er-piano** пиано́ла; **~fellow, ~-mate** това́рищ игр, друг де́тства; партнёр; **~ful** ['pleiful] □ игри́вый; **~goer** театра́л; **~-ground** площа́дка для игр; **~-house** теа́тр; **~thing** игру́шка; **~wright** драмату́рг.
plea [pli:] оправда́ние, до́вод; мольба́; on the ~ (of и́ли that ...) под предло́гом (Р *or* что ...).
plead [pli:d] *v/i.* обраща́ться к суду́; ~ for вступа́ться [-пи́ться] за (В); говори́ть за (В); ~ guilty признава́ть себя́ вино́вным; *v/t.* защища́ть [-ити́ть] (в суде́); приводи́ть в оправда́ние; **~er** ['pli:də] ⚖ защи́тник; **~ing** ['pli:diŋ] ⚖ защи́та.
pleasant [pleznt] □ прия́тный; **~ry** [-ri] шу́тка.
please [pli:z] [по]нра́виться (Д); угожда́ть [угоди́ть] (Д); if you ~ с ва́шего позволе́ния; изво́льте! ~ come in! войди́те пожа́луйста!; доставля́ть удово́льствие (Д); be ~d to do де́лать с удово́льствием; be ~d with быть дово́льным (Т); ~d [pli:zd] дово́льный.
pleasing ['pli:ziŋ] □ прия́тный.
pleasure ['pleʒə] удово́льствие, наслажде́ние; *attr.* увесели́тельный; at ~ по жела́нию.
pleat [pli:t] **1.** скла́дка; **2.** де́лать скла́дки на (П).

pledge [pledʒ] **1.** зало́г, закла́д; обе́т, обеща́ние; **2.** закла́дывать [заложи́ть]; руча́ться [поручи́ться] (T); he ~d himself он связа́л себя́ обеща́нием.

plenary [pli:nəri] по́лный, плена́рный.

plenipotentiary [plenipə'tenʃəri] полномо́чный представи́тель *m.*

plentiful ['plentiful] □ оби́льный.

plenty [-ti] **1.** изоби́лие; доста́ток; избы́ток; ~ of мно́го (P); **2.** F чрезвыча́йно; вполне́.

pliable ['plaiəbl] □ ги́бкий; *fig.* пода́тливый, мя́гкий.

pliancy ['plaiənsi] ги́бкость *f.*

pliers ['pleiəz] *pl.* плоскогу́бцы *m/pl.*

plight [plait] **1.** свя́зывать обеща́нием; помо́лвить *pf.*; **2.** (плохо́е) положе́ние.

plod [plɔd] (*a.* ~ along, on) таска́ться, [по]тащи́ться; корпе́ть (at над T).

plot [plɔt] **1.** уча́сток земли́. деля́нка; за́говор; план; фа́була, сюже́т; **2.** *v/i.* составля́ть за́говор; [за]интригова́ть; *v/t.* наноси́ть [нанести́] (на ка́рту); *b. s.* замышля́ть [-ы́слить].

plough, *Am. a.* plow [plau] **1.** плуг; **2.** [вс]паха́ть; *fig.* [из]бороздить; **~share** ле́ме́х.

pluck [plʌk] **1.** дёрганье; F сме́лость *f,* му́жество; потроха́ *m/pl.*; **2.** срыва́ть [сорва́ть] (цвето́к); ощи́пывать [-па́ть] (пти́цу); ~ at дёргать [дёрнуть] (B); хвата́ть(ся) [схвати́ть(ся)] за (B); ~ up courage собра́ться с ду́хом; **~y** ['plʌki] сме́лый, отва́жный.

plug [plʌg] **1.** вту́лка; заты́чка; ⚡ ште́псель *m*; ~ socket ште́псельная розе́тка; **2.** *v/t.* затыка́ть [заткну́ть]; [за]пломбирова́ть (зуб).

plum [plʌm] сли́ва.

plumage ['plu:midʒ] опере́ние.

plumb [plʌm] **1.** вертика́льный; отве́сный; **2.** отве́с; лот; **3.** *v/t.* ста́вить по отве́су; измеря́ть ло́том; проника́ть вглубь (P); *v/i.* рабо́тать водопрово́дчиком; **~er** ['plʌmə] водопрово́дчик; **~ing** [-iŋ] водопрово́д(ное де́ло).

plume [plu:m] **1.** перо́; плюма́ж; **2.** украша́ть плюма́жем; ~ o. s. on кичи́ться (T).

plummet ['plʌmit] свинцо́вый отве́с; грузи́ло.

plump [plʌmp] **1.** *adj.* пу́хлый, по́лный; F □ реши́тельный; **2.** [по]толсте́ть; бу́хать(ся) [-хнуть (-ся)]; **3.** тяжёлое паде́ние; **4.** F *adv.* пря́мо, без обиняко́в.

plunder ['plʌndə] **1.** грабёж; награ́бленные ве́щи *f/pl.*; **2.** [о]гра́бить.

plunge [plʌndʒ] **1.** ныря́ть [нырну́ть]; окуна́ть(ся) [-ну́ть(ся)]; **2.** ныря́ние; погруже́ние; take the ~ де́лать реши́тельный шаг.

plurality [pluə'ræliti] мно́жество; большинство́; мно́жественность *f.*

plush [plʌʃ] плюш, плис.

ply [plai] **1.** слой; скла́дка; оборо́т; three-~ трёхсло́йный; **2.** *v/t.* засыпа́ть [засы́пать], забра́сывать [-роса́ть] (вопро́сами); *v/i.* курси́ровать; **~-wood** фане́ра.

pneumatic [nju:'mætik] **1.** (~ally) пневмати́ческий; ~ post пневмати́ческая по́чта; **2.** пневмати́ческая ши́на.

pneumonia [nju:'mounjə] ⚕ воспале́ние лёгких.

poach [poutʃ] браконье́рствовать; ~ed egg яйцо́-пашо́т.

poacher ['poutʃə] браконье́р.

pocket ['pɔkit] **1.** карма́н; ✈ возду́шная я́ма; **2.** класть в карма́н; прикарма́ни(ва)ть; присва́ивать [-сво́ить]; подавля́ть [-ви́ть] (чу́вство); прогла́тывать [-лоти́ть] (оби́ду); **3.** карма́нный.

pod [pɔd] ♀ стручо́к; шелуха́.

poem ['pouim] поэ́ма; стихотворе́ние.

poet ['pouit] поэ́т; **~ess** [-is] поэте́сса; **~ic**(**al** □) [pou'etik, -tikəl] поэти́ческий; поэти́чный; **~ics** [-tiks] *pl.* поэ́тика; **~ry** ['pouitri] поэ́зия.

poignan|cy ['pɔi(g)nənsi] острота́; **~t** [-t] о́стрый; *fig.* мучи́тельный.

point [pɔint] **1.** то́чка; пункт, смысл; суть де́ла; очко́; деле́ние (шкалы́); остриё, о́стрый коне́ц; 🚂 стре́лка; ~ of view то́чка зре́ния; the ~ is that ... де́ло в том, что ...; make a ~ of *ger.* поста́вить себе́ зада́чей (+ *inf.*); in ~ of в отноше́нии (P); off the ~ не (относя́щийся) к де́лу; be on the ~ of *ger.* соб(и)ра́ться (+ *inf.*); win on ~s выи́грывать по пу́нктам; to the ~ к де́лу (относя́щийся); **2.** *v/t.* ~ one's finger пока́зывать па́льцем (at на B); заостря́ть [-ри́ть]; (*often* ~ out) ука́зывать [-за́ть]; ~ at направля́ть [-ра́вить] (ору́жие) на (B); *v/i.* ~ at ука́зывать [-за́ть] на (B); ~ to быть напра́вленным на (B); **~ed** ['pɔintid] □ остроконе́чный; о́стрый; *fig.* ко́лкий; **~er** ['pɔintə] указа́тель *m*; ука́зка; по́йнтер; **~less** [-lis] пло́ский; бессмы́сленный.

poise [pɔiz] **1.** равнове́сие; оса́нка; **2.** *v/t.* уравнове́шивать [-е́сить]; держа́ть (го́лову и т. п.); *v/i.* находи́ться в равнове́сии; пари́ть.

poison ['pɔizn] **1.** яд, отра́ва; **2.** отравля́ть [-ви́ть]; **~ous** [-əs] (*fig. a.*) ядови́тый.

poke [pouk] **1.** толчо́к, тычо́к; **2.** *v/t.* ты́кать [ткнуть]; толка́ть [-кну́ть]; сова́ть [су́нуть]; меша́ть кочерго́й; ~ fun at подшу́чивать [-шути́ть] над (T); *v/i.* сова́ть нос

(into в В); иска́ть о́щупью (for В *or* P).
poker ['poukə] кочерга́.
poky ['pouki] те́сный; убо́гий.
polar ['poulə] поля́рный; ~ bear бе́лый медве́дь *m*.
pole [poul] по́люс; шест; жердь *f*; кол; ♀ поля́к, по́лька; **~cat** *zo.* хорёк.
polemic [po'lemik] (*a.* **~al** [-mikəl] □) полеми́ческий.
pole-star Поля́рная звезда́; *fig.* путево́дная звезда́.
police [pə'li:s] **1.** поли́ция; **2.** подде́рживать поря́док в (П); **~-man** полице́йский; **~-station** полице́йский уча́сток.
policy ['pɔlisi] поли́тика; ли́ния поведе́ния; страхово́й по́лис.
Polish[1] ['pouliʃ] по́льский.
polish[2] ['pɔliʃ] **1.** полиро́вка; *fig.* лоск; **2.** [на]полирова́ть; *fig.* утонча́ть [-чи́ть].
polite [pə'lait] □ ве́жливый, благовоспи́танный; **~ness** [-nis] ве́жливость *f*.
politic ['pɔlitik] □ полити́чный; расчётливый; **~al** [pə'litikəl] □ полити́ческий; госуда́рственный; **~ian** [pɔli'tiʃən] поли́тик; **~s** ['pɔlitiks] *pl.* поли́тика.
poll [poul] **1.** голосова́ние; подсчёт голосо́в; спи́сок избира́телей; **2.** *v/t.* получа́ть [-чи́ть] (голоса́); *v/i.* [про]голосова́ть; **~-book** спи́сок избира́телей.
pollen ['pɔlin] ⚘ пыльца́.
poll-tax ['pɔltæks] поду́шный нало́г.
pollute [pə'lu:t] загрязня́ть [-ни́ть]; оскверня́ть [-ни́ть].
polyp(e) ['pɔlip] *zo.*, **~us** [-lipəs] ⚕ поли́п.
pommel ['pʌml] **1.** голо́вка (эфе́са шпа́ги); лука́ (седла́), **2.** [по]би́ть; [по]колоти́ть.
pomp [pɔmp] по́мпа; великоле́пие.
pompous ['pɔmpəs] □ напы́щенный.
pond [pɔnd] пруд.
ponder ['pɔndə] *v/t.* обду́м(ыв)ать; *v/i.* заду́м(ыв)аться; **~able** [-rəbl] весо́мый; **~ous** [-rəs] □ *fig.* тяжелове́сный.
pontiff ['pɔntif] первосвяще́нник.
pontoon [pɔn'tu:n] ⚔ понто́н; **~-bridge** понто́нный мост.
pony ['pouni] по́ни *m indecl.* (лоша́дка).
poodle [pu:dl] пу́дель *m*.
pool [pu:l] **1.** лу́жа; бассе́йн; о́мут; *cards* пу́лька; † пул; **2.** † объедини́ть в о́бщий фонд; скла́дываться [сложи́ться] (with с Т).
poop [pu:p] ⚓ корма́.
poor [puə] □ бе́дный, неиму́щий; несча́стный; ску́дный; плохо́й; **~-house** богаде́льня; **~-law** зако́н о бе́дных; **~ly** ['puəli] *adj.* нездоро́вый; **~ness** ['puənis] бе́дность *f*.
pop [pɔp] **1.** хло́панье; F шипу́чий напи́ток; **2.** *v/t.* сова́ть [су́нуть]; *v/i.* хло́пать [-пнуть] (о про́бке); [по]тре́скаться (о кашта́нах и т.п.); ~ in внеза́пно появи́ться.
popcorn ['pɔpkɔ:n] *Am.* калёные зёрна кукуру́зы.
pope [poup] (ри́мский) па́па *m*.
poplar ['pɔplə] ⚘ то́поль *m*.
poppy ['pɔpi] ⚘ мак.
popula|ce ['pɔpjuləs] простонаро́дье; **~r** [-lə] □ наро́дный; популя́рный; **~rity** [-'læriti] популя́рность *f*.
populat|e ['pɔpjuleit] населя́ть [-ли́ть]; **~ion** [pɔpju'leiʃən] населе́ние.
populous ['pɔpjuləs] □ многолю́дный.
porcelain ['pɔ:slin] фарфо́р.
porch [pɔ:tʃ] подъе́зд; по́ртик; *Am.* вера́нда.
pore [pɔ:] **1.** по́ра; **2.** погружа́ться [-узи́ться] (over в В).
pork [pɔ:k] свини́на.
porous ['pɔ:rəs] □ по́ристый.
porridge ['pɔridʒ] овся́ная ка́ша.
port [pɔ:t] **1.** га́вань *f*, порт; ⚓ ле́вый борт; портве́йн; **2.** ⚓ брать нале́во.
portable ['pɔ:təbl] портати́вный.
portal [pɔ:tl] порта́л; та́мбур (двере́й).
portend [pɔ:'tend] предвеща́ть.
portent ['pɔ:tent] предве́стник, зна́мение (плохо́го); чу́до; **~ous** [pɔ:'tentəs] □ злове́щий; знамена́тельный.
porter ['pɔ:tə] привра́тник, швейца́р; носи́льщик; по́ртер (пи́во).
portion ['pɔ:ʃən] **1.** часть *f*; по́рция; *fig.* уде́л, у́часть *f*; **2.** дели́ть (на ча́сти); наделя́ть [-ли́ть].
portly ['pɔ:tli] доро́дный; представи́тельный.
portmanteau [pɔ:t'mæntou] чемода́н.
portrait ['pɔ:trit] портре́т.
portray [pɔ:'trei] рисова́ть портре́т с (Р); изобража́ть [-рази́ть]; опи́сывать [-са́ть]; **~al** [-əl] рисова́ние портре́та; изображе́ние; описа́ние.
pose [pouz] **1.** по́за; **2.** пози́ровать; ста́вить в по́зу; [по]ста́вить (вопро́с); ~ as выдава́ть себя́ за (В).
position [pə'ziʃən] ме́сто; положе́ние; пози́ция; состоя́ние; то́чка зре́ния.
positive ['pɔzətiv] **1.** □ положи́тельный; позити́вный; уве́ренный; самоуве́ренный; абсолю́тный; **2.** *gr.* положи́тельная сте́пень *f*; *phot.* позити́в.
possess [pə'zes] облада́ть (Т); владе́ть (Т); *fig.* овладе́(ва́)ть (Т); be **~ed** быть одержи́мым; ~ o. s. of завладе́(ва́)ть (Т); **~ion** [-ʃən] владе́ние; облада́ние; *fig.* одержи́мость *f*; **~or** [-sə] владе́лец.
possib|ility [pɔsə'biliti] возмо́жность *f*; **~le** ['pɔsəbl] □ возмо́ж-

ный; **~ly** [-i] возмо́жно; if I ~ can е́сли у меня́ бу́дет возмо́жность *f*.
post [poust] **1.** по́чта; столб; до́лжность *f*; пост; *Am.* ~ exchange гарнизо́нный магази́н; **2.** *v/t.* отправля́ть по по́чте; раскле́и(ва)ть (афи́ши); расставля́ть [-а́вить]; well ~ed хорошо́ осведомлённый; *v/i.* [по]спеши́ть.
postage [-tidʒ] почто́вая опла́та; **~-stamp** почто́вая ма́рка.
postal ['poustəl] □ почто́вый; ~ order де́нежный почто́вый перево́д.
post-card откры́тка.
poster ['poustə] афи́ша, плака́т.
posterior [pɔs'tiəriə] **1.** □ после́дующий; за́дний; **2.** зад.
posterity [pɔs'teriti] пото́мство.
post-free без почто́вой опла́ты.
post-haste ['poust'heist] поспе́шно.
posthumous ['pɔstjuməs] □ посме́ртный; рождённый по́сле сме́рти отца́.
post|man почтальо́н; **~mark 1.** почто́вый ште́мпель *m*; **2.** [за-] штемпелева́ть; **~master** почтме́йстер.
post-mortem ['poust'mɔ:tem] **1.** посме́ртный; **2.** вскры́тие тру́па.
post|(-)office по́чта, почто́вая конто́ра; ~ box абонеме́нтный почто́вый я́щик; **~-paid** франки́рованный.
postpone [poust'poun] отсро́чи(ва)ть; откла́дывать [отложи́ть]; **~ment** [-mənt] отсро́чка.
postscript ['pous(s)kript] постскри́птум.
postulate 1. ['pɔstjulit] постула́т; **2.** [-leit] ста́вить усло́вием; постули́ровать (*im*)*pf.*; [по]тре́бовать.
posture ['pɔstʃə] **1.** по́за; положе́ние; **2.** пози́ровать; ста́вить в по́зу.
post-war ['poust'wɔ:] послевое́нный.
posy ['pouzi] буке́т цвето́в.
pot [pɔt] **1.** горшо́к; котело́к; **2.** класть и́ли сажа́ть в горшо́к; заготовля́ть впрок.
potation [pou'teiʃən] питьё, напи́ток; (*part.* ~s *pl.*) попо́йка.
potato [pə'teitou] карто́фелина; **~es** *pl.* карто́фель *m*; F карто́шка.
pot-belly пу́зо; пуза́тый челове́к.
poten|cy ['poutənsi] си́ла, могу́щество; **~t** [-tənt] □ могу́щественный; кре́пкий; **~tial** [pə'tenʃəl] **1.** потенциа́льный, возмо́жный; **2.** потенциа́л.
pother ['pɔðə] сумато́ха; шум.
pot|-herb пря́ное расте́ние; **~house** каба́к.
potion ['pouʃən] ⚕ миксту́ра; зе́лье.
potter ['pɔtə] гонча́р; **~y** [-ri] гли́няные изде́лия *n/pl.*; гонча́рня.
pouch [pautʃ] **1.** су́мка (*a. biol.*); мешо́чек; **2.** прикарма́ни(ва)ть; класть в су́мку.
poultry ['poultri] дома́шняя пти́ца.
pounce [pauns] **1.** прыжо́к, наско́к; **2.** набра́сываться [-ро́ситься] ([up]on на В).
pound [paund] **1.** фунт; заго́н; ~ (sterling) фунт сте́рлингов (сокр. £ = 20 ш.); **2.** [ис]толо́чь; колоти́ть(ся); ~ at бомбардирова́ть.
pour [pɔ:] *v/t.* лить; ~ out нали́(ва́)ть; сы́пать, насыпа́ть [насы́пать]; *v/i.* ли́ться; [по]сы́паться.
pout [paut] **1.** наду́тые гу́бы *f/pl.*; **2.** *v/t.* наду́(ва́)ть (гу́бы); *v/i.* [на-] ду́ться.
poverty ['pɔvəti] бе́дность *f*.
powder ['paudə] **1.** порошо́к; пу́дра; по́рох; **2.** [ис]толо́чь; [на-] пу́дрить(ся); посыпа́ть [посы́пать]; **~-box** пу́дреница.
power ['pauə] си́ла; мо́щность *f*; *pol.* держа́ва; власть *f*; ⚖ полномо́чие; ⚗ сте́пень *f*; **~-current** ток высо́кого напряже́ния; **~ful** [-ful] □ мо́щный, могу́щественный; си́льный; **~less** [-lis] бесси́льный; **~ plant** силова́я устано́вка; **~-station** электроста́нция.
pow-wow ['pau'wau] зна́харь (у инде́йцев) *m*; *Am.* шу́мное собра́ние.
practica|ble ['præktikəbl] □ осуществи́мый; проходи́мый (о доро́ге); **~l** [-kəl] □ практи́ческий; практи́чный; факти́ческий; ~ joke (гру́бая) шу́тка, прока́за.
practice ['præktis] пра́ктика; упражне́ние, трениро́вка; привы́чка; обы́чай; **put into** ~ осуществля́ть [-ви́ть].
practise [~] *v/t.* применя́ть [-ни́ть]; занима́ться [-ня́ться] (Т); упражня́ться в (П); практикова́ть; *v/i.* упражня́ться; ~ (up)on злоупотребля́ть [-би́ть] (Т); **~d** [-t] о́пытный.
practitioner [præk'tiʃnə] практику́ющий врач.
praise [preiz] **1.** хвала́; **2.** [по]хвали́ть.
praiseworthy ['preizwə:ði] досто́йный похвалы́.
prance [prɑ:ns] станови́ться на дыбы́; гарцева́ть.
prank [præŋk] вы́ходка, прока́за.
prate [preit] **1.** пустосло́вие; **2.** пустосло́вить, болта́ть.
pray [prei] [по]моли́ться; [по]проси́ть; ~! прошу́ вас!
prayer [prɛə] моли́тва; про́сьба; Lord's ~ о́тче наш; **~-book** моли́твенник; **~ful** [-ful] □ богомо́льный.
pre... [pri:, pri] до...; пред...
preach [pri:tʃ] пропове́довать; **~er** ['pri:tʃə] пропове́дник.
preamble [pri:'æmbl] преа́мбула; вступле́ние.
precarious [pri'kɛəriəs] ненадёжный.
precaution [pri'kɔ:ʃən] предосторо́жность *f*.
precede [pri'si:d] предше́ствовать

(Д); **~nce, ~ncy** [-əns(i)] первенство,; преимущественное значение; **~nt** ['presidənt] прецедент.
recept ['pri:sept] наставление; заповедь *f*; **~or** [pri'septə] наставник.
recinct ['pri:siŋkt] предел; (полицейский) участок; (избирательный округ; **~s** *pl.* окрестности *f/pl.*
recious ['preʃəs] **1.** □ драгоценный; **2.** F *adv.* очень; ~! здорово!
recipi|ce ['presipis] пропасть *f*; **~tate** **1.** [pri'sipiteit] низвергать [-ергнуть]; [по]торопить; ⚗ осаждать [осадить]; **2.** [-tit] a) □ опрометчивый; стремительный; b) ⚗ осадок; **~tation** [prisipi'teiʃən] низвержение; стремительность *f*; осадки *m/pl.*; ⚗ осаждение; **~tous** [pri'sipitəs] □ крутой; обрывистый.
recis|e [pri'sais] □ точный; **~ion** [-'siʒən] точность *f*.
reclude [pri'klu:d] исключать заранее; предотвращать [-ратить] (В); [по]мешать (Д).
recocious [pri'kouʃəs] □ преждевременно развитой.
reconceive ['pri:kən'si:v] представлять себе заранее; **~d** предвзятый. [предвзятое мнение.]
reconception ['pri:kən'sepʃən]
recursor [pri'kə:sə] предтеча *m/f*; предшественник (-ица).
redatory ['predətəri] хищный.
redecessor ['pri:disesə] предшественник (-ица).
redestin|ate [pri:'destineit] предопределять [-лить]; **~ed** [-tind] предопределённый.
redicament [pri'dikəmənt] серьёзное затруднение.
redicate ['predikit] предикат.
redict [pri'dikt] предсказывать [-зать]; **~ion** [-kʃən] предсказание.
redilection [pri:di'lekʃən] склонность *f*, пристрастие (for к Д).
redispos|e ['pri:dis'pouz] предрасполагать [-ложить].
redomina|nce [pri'dɔminəns] господство, преобладание; **~nt** [-nənt] □ преобладающий; доминирующий; **~te** [-neit] господствовать, преобладать (over над Т).
re-eminent [pri:'eminənt] □ выдающийся.
re-emption [pri:'emʃən] (*a.* right of ~) преимущественное право на покупку.
refabricate ['pri:'fæbrikeit] изготовлять заранее (части стандартного дома и т. п.).
reface ['prefis] **1.** предисловие; **2.** предпос(ы)лать (Д with В); снабжать предисловием.
refect ['pri:fekt] префект.
refer [pri'fə:] предпочитать [-почесть]; повышать [-ысить] (в чине); под(ав)ать (прошение); выдвигать [выдвинуть] (требование); **~able** ['prefərəbl] □ предпочтительный; **~ence** [rəns] предпочтение; **~ential** [prefə'renʃəl] □ предпочтительный; льготный.
prefix ['pri:fiks] префикс, приставка.
pregnan|cy ['pregnənsi] беременность *f*; богатство (воображения и т. п.); **~t** [-nənt] □ беременная; *fig.* чреватый; богатый.
prejud|ge ['pri:'dʒʌdʒ] осуждать, не выслушав; **~ice** ['predʒudis] **1.** предрассудок; предубеждение; **2.** предубеждать [-бедить] (против Р); наносить ущерб (Д); **~icial** [predʒu'diʃəl] пагубный.
prelate ['prelit] прелат.
preliminar|y [pri'liminəri] **1.** □ предварительный; вступительный; **2.** подготовительное мероприятие.
prelude ['prelju:d] ♪ прелюдия.
prematur|e [premə'tjuə] преждевременный.
premeditation [primedi'teiʃən] преднамеренность *f*.
premier ['premjə] **1.** первый; **2.** премьер-министр.
premises ['premisiz] *pl.* помещение; дом (с пристройками).
premium ['pri:mjəm] награда, премия; ☤ лаж; страховая премия; at a ~ выше номинальной стоимости; в большом спросе.
premonit|ion [pri:mo'niʃən] предчувствие; предупреждение.
preoccup|ied [pri'ɔkjupaid] озабоченный; **~y** [-pai] поглощать внимание (Р); занимать раньше (чем кто-либо).
preparat|ion [prepə'reiʃən] приготовление; подготовка; **~ory** [pri:pærətəri] □ предварительный; подготовительный, приготовительный.
prepare [pri'pɛə] *v/t.* приготовлять [-товить]; [при]готовить; подготовлять [-товить]; *v/i.* [при]готовиться; подготовляться [-товиться] (for к Д); **~d** [-d] □ подготовленный; готовый.
prepondera|nce [pri'pɔndərəns] преобладание; **~nt** [-rənt] □ преобладающий; **~te** [-reit] иметь перевес; ~ over превосходить [-взойти] (В).
prepossess [pri:pə'zes] располагать к себе; **~ing** [-iŋ] □ располагающий.
preposterous [pri'pɔstərəs] несообразный, нелепый, абсурдный.
prerequisite ['pri:'rekwizit] предпосылка.
presage ['presidʒ] **1.** предзнаменование; предчувствие; **2.** (*a.* [pri'seidʒ]) предзнаменовать, предвещать; предчувствовать.
prescribe [pris'kraib] предписы-

вать [-писа́ть]; ⚕ пропи́сывать [-писа́ть].
prescription [pris'kripʃən] предписа́ние; ⚕ реце́пт.
presence [prezns] прису́тствие; ~ of mind прису́тствие ду́ха.
present[1] [preznt] **1.** □ прису́тствующий; тепе́решний, настоя́щий; да́нный; **2.** настоя́щее вре́мя; пода́рок; at ~ в да́нное вре́мя; for the ~ на э́тот раз.
present[2] [pri'zent] представля́ть [-а́вить]; преподноси́ть [-нести́]; под(ав)а́ть (проше́ние); [по]ста́вить (пье́су); одаря́ть [-ри́ть]; под(ав)а́ть.
presentation [prezen'teiʃən] представле́ние; подноше́ние; пода́ча.
presentiment [pri'zentimənt] предчу́вствие. [ча́с.
presently ['prezntli] вско́ре; сей-
preservati|on [prezə'veiʃən] сохране́ние; сохра́нность *f*; **~ve** [pri'zə:vətiv] **1.** предохрани́тельный; **2.** предохрани́тельное сре́дство.
preserve [pri'zə:v] **1.** сохраня́ть [-ни́ть]; предохраня́ть [-ни́ть]; заготовля́ть впрок (о́вощи и т. п.); **2.** (*mst pl.*) консе́рвы *m/pl.* (*a. opt.*); варе́нье; запове́дник.
preside [pri'zaid] председа́тельствовать (over на П).
presiden|cy ['prezidənsi] президе́нтство; председа́тельство; **~t** [-dənt] президе́нт; председа́тель *m.*
press [pres] **1.** печа́ть *f*, пре́сса; да́вка; ⊕ пресс; **2.** *v/t.* жать; дави́ть; наж(им)а́ть; навя́зывать [-за́ть] (on Д); *Am.* [вы́]гла́дить; be **~ed** for time спеши́ть; *v/i.* дави́ть (on на В); ~ for наста́ивать [настоя́ть] на (П); ~ on [по]спеши́ть; ~ (up)on наседа́ть [-е́сть] на (В); **~ing** ['presiŋ] □ неотло́жный; **~ure** ['preʃə] давле́ние (*a. fig.*); сжа́тие.
presum|able [pri'zju:məbl] □ предположи́тельный; **~e** [pri'zju:m] *v/t.* предполага́ть [-ложи́ть]; *v/i.* полага́ть; осме́ли(ва)ться; ~ (up)on злоупотребля́ть [-би́ть] (Т); кичи́ться (Т).
presumpt|ion [pri'zʌmpʃən] самонаде́янность *f*; предположе́ние; **~ive** [-tiv] □ предполага́емый; **~uous** [-tjuəs] □ самонаде́янный.
presuppos|e [pri:sə'pouz] предполага́ть [-ложи́ть]; **~ition** [pri:sʌpə'ziʃən] предположе́ние.
pretence [pri'tens] претéнзия, тре́бование; притво́рство; предло́г.
pretend [pri'tend] притворя́ться [-ри́ться]; симули́ровать (*im*)*pf.*; претендова́ть (to на В).
pretension [pri'tenʃən] претéнзия, притяза́ние (to на В).
pretentious [-ʃəs] претенцио́зный.
pretext ['pri:tekst] предло́г.
pretty ['priti] **1.** □ хоро́шенький приятный; **2.** *adv.* дово́льно.
prevail [pri'veil] превозмога́ть [-мо́чь] (over В); преоблада́ть (over над Т *or* среди́ Р); ~ (up)on a p. to do убеди́ть кого́-нибудь что́-либо сде́лать; **~ing** [-iŋ] □ преоблада́ющий.
prevalent ['prevələnt] □ преоблада́ющий; широко́ распространённый.
prevaricat|e [pri'værikeit] отклоня́ться от прямо́го отве́та, увили́вать [-льну́ть].
prevent [pri'vent] предотвраща́ть [-ати́ть]; [по]меша́ть (Д); предупрежда́ть [-упреди́ть]; **~ion** [pri'venʃən] предупрежде́ние; предотвраще́ние; **~ive** [-tiv] **1.** □ предупреди́тельный; профилакти́ческий; **2.** ⚕ профилакти́ческое сре́дство.
pre|view ['pri:vju:] предвари́тельный осмо́тр (фи́льма, мод и т. п.)
previous ['pri:vjəs] □ предыду́щий; преждевре́менный; предвари́тельный; ~ to до (Р); **~ly** пре́жде.
pre-war ['pri:wɔ:] довое́нный.
prey [prei] **1.** добы́ча; же́ртва; beast (bird) of ~ хи́щный зверь *m* (хи́щная пти́ца); **2.** ~ (up)on: (о)гра́бить, терза́ть; подта́чивать [-точи́ть].
price [prais] **1.** цена́; **2.** оце́нивать [-ни́ть]; назнача́ть це́ну (Д); **~less** ['praislis] бесце́нный.
prick [prik] **1.** проко́л; уко́л; шип **2.** *v/t.* коло́ть [кольну́ть]; ~ up one's ears навостри́ть у́ши; *v/i.* коло́ться; **~le** [prikl] шип, колю́чка; **~ly** ['prikli] колю́чий.
pride [praid] **1.** го́рдость *f*; take ~ in горди́ться (Т); **2.** ~ o. s. горди́ться ([up]on Т).
priest [pri:st] свяще́нник. [нутый.
prim [prim] □ чо́порный; натя́-
prima|cy ['praiməsi] пе́рвенство **~ry** [-ri] □ первонача́льный; основно́й; нача́льный; перви́чный.
prime [praim] **1.** □ гла́вный; первонача́льный; перви́чный; основно́й; превосхо́дный; ~ cost ✝ себесто́имость *f*; ♀ Minister премье́р-мини́стр; **2.** *fig.* расцве́т; **3.** *v/t* снабжа́ть информа́цией; учи́ть гото́вым отве́там.
primer ['primə] буква́рь *m*; нача́льный уче́бник.
primeval [prai'mi:vəl] первобы́тный.
primitive ['primitiv] □ первобы́тный; примити́вный; основно́й.
primrose ['primrouz] ⚘ при́мула
prince [prins] принц; князь *m*; **~ss** [prin'ses] принце́сса; княги́ня, княжна́.
principal ['prinsəpəl] **1.** □ гла́вный, основно́й; **2.** принципа́л

глава́; ре́ктор университе́та; дире́ктор шко́лы; основно́й капита́л.

principle ['prinsəpl] при́нцип; пра́вило; причи́на, исто́чник; on ~ из при́нципа.

print [print] **1.** *typ.* печа́ть *f*; о́ттиск; шрифт; след; отпеча́ток; штамп; гравю́ра; произведе́ние печа́ти; ✝ набивна́я ткань *f*; out of ~ распро́данный (о печа́тном); **2.** [на]печа́тать; *phot.* отпеча́т(ы-в)ать; *fig.* запечатле́(ва́)ть (on на П); **~er** ['printə] печа́тник.

printing ['printiŋ] печа́тание; печа́тное изда́ние; *attr.* печа́тный; **~-ink** типогра́фская кра́ска; **~-office** типогра́фия.

prior ['praiə] **1.** предше́ствующий (to Д); **2.** *adv.* ~ to до (Р); **3.** *eccl.* настоя́тель *m*; **~ity** [prai'ɔriti] приорите́т; очерёдность *f*.

prism [prizm] при́зма.

prison ['prizn] тюрьма́; **~er** [-ə] заключённый; пле́нный.

privacy ['praivəsi] уедине́ние; сохране́ние в та́йне.

private ['praivit] **1.** □ ча́стный; ли́чный; уединённый; конфиденциа́льный; **2.** ⚔ рядово́й; **in ~** конфиденциа́льно.

privation [prai'veiʃən] лише́ние, нужда́.

privilege ['privilidʒ] **1.** привиле́гия; **2.** дава́ть привиле́гию (Д).

privy ['privi]: ~ to посвящённый в (В); ♀ Council та́йный сове́т; ♀ Councillor член та́йного сове́та; ♀ Seal ма́лая госуда́рственная печа́ть *f*.

prize [praiz] **1.** пре́мия, приз; ⚓ приз; трофе́й; вы́игрыш; **2.** удосто́енный пре́мии; **3.** высоко́ цени́ть; взла́мывать [взлома́ть]; **~-fighter** боксёр-профессиона́л.

probab|ility [prɔbə'biliti] вероя́тность *f*; **~le** ['prɔbəbl] □ вероя́тный.

probation [prə'beiʃən] испыта́ние; испыта́тельный стаж; ⚖ усло́вное освобожде́ние.

probe [proub] ⚕ **1.** зонд; **2.** зонди́ровать.

probity ['proubiti] че́стность *f*.

problem ['prɔbləm] пробле́ма; A зада́ча; **~atic(al** □) [prɔbli'mætik, -tikəl] проблемати́чный.

procedure [prə'si:dʒə] процеду́ра; о́браз де́йствия.

proceed [prə'si:d] отправля́ться да́льше; приступа́ть [-пи́ть] (to к Д); поступа́ть [-пи́ть]; продолжа́ть [-до́лжить] (with В); ~ from исходи́ть (от Р); **~ing** [-iŋ] посту́пок; **~s** *pl.* ⚖ судопроизво́дство; протоко́лы *m/pl.*, труды́ *m/pl.*; **~s** ['prousi:dz] дохо́д; вы́ручка, вы́рученная су́мма.

process 1. ['prouses] проце́сс; движе́ние, тече́ние; ход; спо́соб; in ~ на ходу́; in ~ of construction стро́ящийся; **2.** [prə'ses] привлека́ть к суду́; ⊕ обраба́тывать [-бо́тать]; **~ion** [-ʃən] проце́ссия.

proclaim [prə'kleim] провозглаша́ть [-ласи́ть]; объявля́ть [-ви́ть] (войну́ и т. п.).

proclamation [prɔklə'meiʃən] воззва́ние; объявле́ние; прокламация.

proclivity [prə'kliviti] скло́нность *f*.

procurat|ion [prɔkjuə'reiʃən] полномо́чие, дове́ренность *f*; **~or** ['prɔkjuəreitə] пове́ренный.

procure [prə'kjuə] *v/t.* дост(ав)а́ть; *v/i.* сво́дничать.

prod [prɔd] **1.** тычо́к, толчо́к; **2.** ты́кать [ткнуть]; толка́ть [-кну́ть]; *fig.* подстрека́ть [-кну́ть].

prodigal ['prɔdigəl] **1.** расточи́тельный; ~ son блу́дный сын; **2.** мот(о́вка).

prodig|ious [prə'didʒəs] □ удиви́тельный; грома́дный; **~y** ['prɔdidʒi] чу́до.

produc|e 1. [prə'dju:s] предъявля́ть [-ви́ть]; представля́ть [-а́вить]; производи́ть [-вести́]; [по]ста́вить (фильм и т. п.); изд(ав)а́ть; **2.** ['prɔdju:s] проду́кция; проду́кт; **~er** [prə'dju:sə] производи́тель *m*; режиссёр *m*.

product ['prɔdəkt] проду́кт, изде́лие; **~ion** [prə'dʌkʃən] произво́дство; проду́кция; постано́вка; (худо́жественное) произведе́ние; **~ive** [prə'dʌktiv] □ производи́тельный, продукти́вный; плодоро́дный; **~iveness** [-nis], **~ivity** [prɔdʌk'tiviti] продукти́вность *f*, производи́тельность *f*.

profan|e [prə'fein] **1.** □ мирско́й, све́тский; богоху́льный; **2.** оскверня́ть [-ни́ть]; профани́ровать (*im*)*pf.*; **~ity** [prə'fæniti] богоху́льство.

profess [prə'fes] испове́довать (ве́ру); откры́то признава́ть; заявля́ть [-ви́ть]; претендова́ть на (В); *univ.* преподава́ть; **~ion** [prə'feʃən] профе́ссия; заявле́ние; вероисповеда́ние; **~ional** [-l] **1.** □ профессиона́льный; **2.** специали́ст; профессиона́л (*a. sport*); **~or** [-sə] профе́ссор.

proffer ['prɔfə] **1.** предлага́ть [-ложи́ть]; **2.** предложе́ние.

proficien|cy [prə'fiʃənsi] о́пытность *f*; уме́ние; **~t** [-ʃənt] **1.** □ уме́лый; иску́сный; **2.** ма́стер, знато́к.

profile ['proufi:l] про́филь *m*.

profit ['prɔfit] **1.** при́быль *f*; вы́года, по́льза; **2.** *v/t.* приноси́ть по́льзу (Д); *v/i.* ~ by [вос]по́льзоваться (Т); извлека́ть по́льзу из (Р); **~able** ['prɔfitəbl] □ при́быльный; вы́годный; поле́зный; **~eer** [prɔfi'tiə] **1.** спекуля́нт; **2.** спекулиро́вать; **~-sharing** уча́стие в при́были.

profligate ['prɔfligit] **1.** □ распу́тный; **2.** распу́тник.

profound [prə'faund] □ глубо́кий; основа́тельный; проникнове́нный.

profundity [prə'fʌnditi] глубина́.

profus|e [prə'fju:s] □ изоби́льный; ще́дрый; **~ion** [prə'fju:ʒən] изоби́лие.

progen|itor [prou'dʒenitə] прароди́тель(ница *f*) *m*; **~y** ['prɔdʒini] пото́мство.

program, ~me ['prougræm] програ́мма.

progress 1. ['prougres] прогре́сс; продвиже́ние; успе́хи *m/pl.*; be in ~ развива́ться; вести́сь; **2.** [prə'gres] продвига́ться вперёд; де́лать успе́хи; **~ion** [prə'greʃən] движе́ние вперёд; 𝔄 прогре́ссия; **~ive** [-siv] **1.** □ передово́й, прогресси́вный; прогресси́рующий; **2.** *pol.* член прогресси́вной па́ртии.

prohibit [prə'hibit] запреща́ть [-ети́ть]; препя́тствовать (Д); **~ion** [proui'biʃən] запреще́ние; **~ive** [prə'hibitiv] □ запрети́тельный.

project 1. ['prɔdʒekt] прое́кт; план; **2.** [prə'dʒekt] *v/t.* броса́ть [бро́сить]; [с-, за]проекти́ровать; *v/i.* обду́мывать план; вы́да(ва́)ться; **~ile** [prə'dʒektail] снаря́д; **~ion** [prə'dʒekʃən] мета́ние; проекти́рование; прое́кт; вы́ступ; прое́кция; **~or** [-tə] ⚚ проектиро́вщик; *opt.* проже́ктор; волше́бный фона́рь *m*.

proletarian [proule'tɛəriən] **1.** пролета́рий; **2.** пролета́рский.

prolific [prə'lifik] (~ally) плодоро́дный; плодови́тый.

prolix ['prouliks] □ многосло́вный.

prologue ['proulɔg] проло́г.

prolong [prə'lɔŋ] продлева́ть [-ли́ть]; продолжа́ть [-до́лжить].

promenade [prɔmi'nɑ:d] **1.** прогу́лка; ме́сто для прогу́лки; **2.** прогу́ливаться [-ля́ться].

prominent ['prɔminənt] □ выступа́ющий; релье́фный; *fig.* выдаю́щийся.

promiscuous [prə'miskjuəs] □ разноро́дный; сме́шанный; неразбо́рчивый.

promis|e ['prɔmis] **1.** обеща́ние; **2.** обеща́ть (*im*)*pf.*, *pf. a.* [по-]; **~ing** [-iŋ] □ *fig.* подаю́щий наде́жды; **~sory** [-əri] заключа́ющий в себе́ обеща́ние; ~ note ⚚ долгово́е обяза́тельство.

promontory ['prɔməntri] мыс.

promot|e [prə'mout] спосо́бствовать (*im*)*pf.*, *pf. a.* [по-] (Д); соде́йствовать (*im*)*pf.*, *pf. a.* [по-] (Д); выдвига́ть [вы́двинуть]; продвига́ть [-и́нуть]; повыша́ть по слу́жбе; ⚔ присво́ить зва́ние (Р); **~ion** [prə'mouʃən] повыше́ние (в чи́не и т. п.); продвиже́ние.

prompt [prɔmpt] **1.** □ бы́стрый; прово́рный; **2.** побужда́ть [-уди́ть]; внуша́ть [-ши́ть]; подска́зывать [-за́ть] (Д); суфли́ровать (Д); **~er** ['prɔmptə] суфлёр; **~ness** ['prɔmptnis] быстрота́; прово́рство.

promulgate ['prɔməlgeit] провозглаша́ть [-ласи́ть].

prone [proun] □ (лежа́щий) ничко́м; распростёртый; ~ to скло́нный к (Д).

prong [prɔŋ] зубе́ц (ви́лки); шпенёк.

pronounce [prə'nauns] произноси́ть [-нести́]; объявля́ть [-ви́ть].

pronunciation [-nʌnsi'eiʃən] произноше́ние.

proof [pru:f] **1.** доказа́тельство; про́ба. испыта́ние; *typ.* корректу́ра, про́бный о́ттиск; **2.** непроница́емый; недосту́пный; **~-reader** корре́ктор.

prop [prɔp] подпо́рка; опо́ра.

propaga|te ['prɔpəgeit] размножа́ть(ся) [-о́жить(ся)]; распространя́ть(ся) [-ни́ть(ся)]; **~tion** [prɔpə'geiʃən] размноже́ние; распростране́ние.

propel [prə'pel] продвига́ть вперёд; **~ler** [-ə] пропе́ллер, возду́шный винт; гребно́й винт.

propensity [prə'pensiti] скло́нность *f*.

proper ['prɔpə] □ сво́йственный, прису́щий; подходя́щий; пра́вильный; со́бственный; прили́чный; **~ty** [-ti] иму́щество, со́бственность *f*; сво́йство.

prophe|cy ['prɔfisi] проро́чество; **~sy** [-sai] [на]проро́чить.

prophet ['prɔfit] проро́к.

propi|tiate [prə'piʃieit] умилостивля́ть [уми́лостивить]; **~tious** [prə'piʃəs] □ благоскло́нный; благоприя́тный.

proportion [prə'pɔ:ʃən] **1.** пропо́рция; соразме́рность *f*; часть *f*; ~s *pl.* разме́ры *m/pl.*; **2.** соразмеря́ть [-ме́рить]; **~al** [-l] □ пропорциона́льный.

propos|al [prə'pouzəl] предложе́ние; план; **~e** [prə'pouz] *v/t* предлага́ть [-ложи́ть]; ~ to o. s. ста́вить себе́ це́лью; *v/i.* де́лать предложе́ние (бра́ка); намерева́ться, предполага́ть; **~ition** [prɔpə'ziʃən] предложе́ние.

propound [prə'paund] предлага́ть на обсужде́ние.

propriet|ary [prə'praiətəri] со́бственнический; ча́стный; *pharm.* патенто́ванный; **~or** [-tə] владе́лец (-лица); **~y** [-ti] уме́стность *f*; присто́йность *f*; the proprieties *pl.* прили́чия *n/pl.*

propulsion [prə'pʌlʃən] ⊕ приво́д; движе́ние вперёд.

pro-rate [prou'reit] распределя́ть пропорциона́льно.

prosaic [prou'zeiik] (~ally) *fig.* прозаичный.
proscribe [pros'kraib] объявлять вне закона; запрещать [-етить].
prose [prouz] **1.** проза; **2.** прозаический; *fig.* прозаичный.
prosecut|e ['prɔsikju:t] проводить [-вести], [по]вести; преследовать судебным порядком; **~ion** [prɔsi'kju:ʃən] судебное преследование; **~or** ['prɔsikju:tə] ⚖ обвинитель *m*; public ~ прокурор.
prospect 1. ['prɔspekt] перспектива, вид (*a. fig.*); ✝ предполагаемый покупатель *m* (клиент и т. п.); **2.** [prəs'pekt] ⚒ развед(ыв)ать (for на В); **~ive** [prəs'pektiv] □ будущий, ожидаемый; **~us** [-təs] проспект.
prosper ['prɔspə] *v/t.* благоприятствовать (Д); *v/i.* процветать; преуспевать; **~ity** [prɔs'periti] процветание; благосостояние; *fig.* расцвет; **~ous** ['prɔspərəs] □ благоприятный; состоятельный; процветающий.
prostitute ['prɔstitju:t] **1.** проститутка; **2.** проституировать (*im*) *pf.*; [о]бесчестить.
prostrat|e 1. ['prɔstreit] распростёртый; поверженный; обессиленный; **2.** [prɔs'treit] повергать ниц; унижать [унизить]; истощать [-щить]; ~ o. s. падать ниц; **~ion** [-ʃən] распростёртое положение; изнеможение.
prosy ['prouzi] □ *fig.* прозаичный; банальный.
protect [prə'tekt] защищать [-итить]; (пред)охранять [-нить] (from от Р); **~ion** [prə'tekʃən] защита; **~ive** [-tiv] защитный; предохранительный; ~ duty покровительственная пошлина; **~or** [-tə] защитник; **~orate** [-tərit] протекторат.
protest 1. ['proutest] протест; опротестование (векселя); **2.** [prə'test] [за]протестовать; опротестовывать [-стовать] (вексель).
Protestant ['prɔtistənt] **1.** протестант(ка); **2.** протестантский.
protestation [proutes'teiʃən] торжественное заявление.
protocol ['proutəkɔl] протокол.
prototype [-taip] прототип.
protract [prə'trækt] тянуть (В *or* с Т); продолжать [-должить].
protru|de [prə'tru:d] выдаваться наружу, торчать; **~sion** [-ʒən] выступ.
protuberance [prə'tju:bərəns] выпуклость *f*; опухлость *f*.
proud [praud] □ гордый (of Т).
prove [pru:v] *v/t.* доказывать [-зать]; удостоверять [-верить]; испытывать [-пытать]; *v/i.* оказываться [-заться].
provender ['prɔvində] корм.
proverb ['prɔvəb] пословица.
provide [prə'vaid] *v/t.* заготовлять [-товить]; снабжать [-бдить]; обеспечи(ва)ть; ⚖ ставить условием; *v/i.* запасаться [-стись]; **~d** (that) при условии (что).
providen|ce ['prɔvidəns] провидение; предусмотрительность *f*; **~t** [-dənt] □ предусмотрительный; **~tial** [prɔvi'denʃəl] □ провиденциальный.
provider [prə'vaidə] поставщик [(-ица).
provin|ce ['prɔvins] область *f*; провинция; *fig.* сфера деятельности; **~cial** [prə'vinʃəl] **1.** провинциальный; **2.** провинциал(ка).
provision [prə'viʒən] снабжение; обеспечение; ⚖ положение (договора и т. п.); **~s** *pl.* провизия; **~al** [-l] □ предварительный; временный.
proviso [prə'vaizou] условие.
provocat|ion [prɔvə'keiʃən] вызов; провокация; раздражение; **~ive** [prə'vɔkətiv] вызывающий (о поведении и т. п.); провокационный.
provoke [prə'vouk] [с]провоцировать; возбуждать [-будить]; вызывать [вызвать]; [рас]сердить.
provost 1. ['prɔvest] ректор; декан; **2.** [prə'vou] ⚔ офицер военной полиции.
prow [prau] ⚓ нос (судна).
prowess ['prauis] доблесть *f*.
prowl [praul] красться; бродить.
proximity [prɔk'simiti] близость *f*.
proxy ['prɔksi] заместитель *m*; полномочие; передача голоса; доверенность *f*.
prude [pru:d] щепетильная, стыдливая женщина.
pruden|ce ['pru:dəns] благоразумие; предусмотрительность *f*; осторожность *f*; **~t** [-t] □ благоразумный; осторожный.
prud|ery ['pru:dəri] чрезмерная стыдливость *f*; **~ish** [-diʃ] □ чрезмерно стыдливый.
prune [pru:n] **1.** чернослив; **2.** ✂ подрезать [-резать], обрезать [обрезать]; *fig.* сокращать [-ратить].
prurient ['pruəriənt] □ похотливый.
pry [prai] **1.** подглядывать [-ядеть]; ~ into совать нос в (В); *Am.* ~ open вскры(ва)ть, взламывать [взломать]; ~ up поднимать [-нять]; **2.** рычаг.
psalm [sa:m] псалом.
pseudonym ['(p)sju:dənim] псевдоним.
psychiatrist [sai'kaiətrist] психиатр.
psychic ['saikik], **~al** [-kikəl] □ психический.
psycholog|ical [saikə'lɔdʒikəl] □ психологический; **~ist** [sai'kɔlədʒist] психолог; **~y** [-dʒi] психология.
pub [pʌb] F трактир, кабак.

puberty ['pju:bəti] половáя зрéлость *f*.

public ['pʌblik] **1.** □ публи́чный, общéственный; госудáрственный; коммунáльный; ~ house трактúр; ~ law междунарóдное прáво; ~ spirit дух солидáрности, патриоти́зма; **2.** пýблика; общéственность *f*; **~an** ['pʌblikən] трактúрщик; **~ation** [pʌbli'keiʃən] опубликовáние; издáние; monthly ~ ежемéсячник; **~ity** [pʌ'blisiti] глáсность *f*; реклáма.

publish ['pʌbliʃ] [о]публиковáть, изд(ав)áть; опубликóвывать [-ковáть]; оглашáть [-ласи́ть]; **~ing** house издáтельство; **~er** [-ə] издáтель *m*; **~s** *pl.* издáтельство.

pucker ['pʌkə] **1.** [с]мóрщить(ся); **2.** морщи́на.

pudding ['pudiŋ] пýдинг; black ~ кровянáя колбасá.

puddle ['pʌdl] лýжа.

puerile ['pjuərail] □ ребя́ческий.

puff [pʌf] **1.** дуновéние (вéтра); клуб (ды́ма); пухóвка; **2.** *v/t.* надý(вá)ть; выпя́чивать [вы́пятить]; расхвáливать [-ли́ть], преувели́ченно реклами́ровать; **~ed** eyes распýхшие глазá *m/pl.*; *v/i.* дуть поры́вами; пыхтéть; ~ away at попы́хивать (T); ~ out надý(вá)ться; **~-paste** слоёное тéсто; **~y** ['pʌfi] запыхáвшийся; отёкший; одутловáтый.

pug [pʌg], **~-dog** мопс.

pugnacious [pʌg'neiʃəs] драчли́вый.

pug-nosed ['pʌgnouz] курнóсый.

puke [pju:k] рвóта.

pull [pul] **1.** тя́га; рýчка (звонкá и т. п.); затя́жка (ды́мом); **2.** [по-] тянýть; таскáть, [по]тащи́ть; выдёргивать [вы́дернуть]; дёргать [-рнуть]; ~ down сноси́ть [снести́] (здáние и т. п.); ~ out 🚂 отходи́ть [отойти́] (от стáнции); ⚕ ~ through выхáживать [вы́ходить]; поправля́ться [-áвиться] (от болéзни); ~ o. s. together взять себя́ в рýки; ~ up подтя́гивать [-янýть]; осáживать [осади́ть] (лошадéй); останáвливать(ся) [-нови́ть(ся)].

pulley ['puli] ⊕ блок; вóрот; ремённый шкив.

pulp [pʌlp] мя́коть плодá; пýльпа (зýба); ⊕ бумáжная мáсса.

pulpit ['pulpit] кáфедра (проповéдника).

pulpy ['pʌlpi] □ мя́гкий; мяси́стый.

puls|ate [pʌl'seit] пульси́ровать; би́ться; **~e** [pʌls] пульс.

pulverize ['pʌlvəraiz] *v/t.* распыля́ть [-ли́ть]; размельчáть в порошóк; *v/i.* распыля́ться [-ли́ться].

pumice ['pʌmis] пéмза.

pump [pʌmp] **1.** насóс; лёгкая бáльная тýфля; **2.** качáть [качнýть] (насóсом); ~ up накáчивать [-чáть].

pumpkin ['pʌmpkin] ⚘ ты́ква.

pun [pʌn] **1.** каламбýр; **2.** каламбýрить.

Punch[1] [pʌntʃ] полишинéль *m*.

punch[2] [~] **1.** ⊕ кéрнер, пробóйник; компóстер; удáр кулакóм; **2.** проби́(вá)ть (отвéрстия); [от-] штамповáть; бить кулакóм.

punctilious [pʌŋk'tiliəs] педанти́чный; щепети́льный до мелочéй.

punctual ['pʌŋktjuəl] □ пунктуáльный; **~ity** [pʌŋktju'æliti] пунктуáльность *f*.

punctuat|e ['pʌŋktjueit] стáвить знáки препинáния; *fig.* перемежáть; **~ion** [pʌŋktju'eiʃən] пунктуáция.

puncture ['pʌŋktʃə] **1.** прокóл; ⚡ пробóй; **2.** прокáлывать [-колóть]; получáть прокóл.

pungen|cy ['pʌndʒənsi] остротá, éдкость *f*; **~t** [-t] óстрый, éдкий.

punish ['pʌniʃ] накáзывать [-зáть]; **~able** [-əbl] □ наказýемый; **~ment** [-mənt] наказáние.

puny ['pju:ni] □ крóхотный; тщеду́шный.

pupil [pju:pl] *anat.* зрачóк; учени́к (-и́ца).

puppet ['pʌpit] марионéтка (*a. fig.*); **~show** кýкольный теáтр.

puppy ['pʌpi] щенóк; *fig.* молокосóс; фат.

purchase ['pə:tʃəs] **1.** покýпка, закýпка; приобретéние; ⊕ механи́зм для поднятия грýзов (рычáг; лебёдка и т. п.); *fig.* тóчка опóры; **2.** покупáть [купи́ть]; приобретáть [-рести́]; **~r** [-ə] покупáтель(ница *f*) *m*.

pure [pjuə] □ *com.* чи́стый; беспорóчный; беспри́месный; **~-bred** ['pjuəbred] *Am.* чистокрóвный.

purgat|ive ['pə:gətiv] слаби́тельное; **~ory** [-t(ə)ri] чисти́лище.

purge [pə:dʒ] **1.** ⚕ слаби́тельное; *pol.* чи́стка; **2.** очищáть [очи́стить]; *pol.* проводи́ть чи́стку в (П).

purify ['pjuərifai] очищáть [очи́стить].

purity ['pjuəriti] чистотá; непорóчность *f*.

purl [pə:l] журчáть.

purlieus ['pə:lju:z] *pl.* окрéстности *f/pl.*

purloin [pə:'lɔin] [у]воровáть.

purple [pə:pl] **1.** пурпýрный; багрóвый; **2.** пýрпур; **3.** turn ~ [по-] багровéть.

purport ['pə:pət] смысл, содержáние.

purpose ['pə:pəs] **1.** намéрение, цель *f*; ýмысел; on ~ нарóчно; to the ~ кстáти; к дéлу; to no ~ напрáсно; **2.** имéть цéлью; намеревáться [намéриться]; **~ful** [-ful] □ умы́шленный; целеустремлённый; **~less** [-lis] □ бесцéльный; **~ly** [-li] нарóчно.

purr [pə:] [за]мурлы́кать.

purse [pə:s] **1.** кошелёк; дéнежный приз; public ~ казнá; **2.** подж(им)áть (гýбы); зажмýри(ва)ть (глазá).

pursuan|ce [pəˈsju(:)əns]: in ~ of согла́сно (Д); **~t** [-ənt]: ~ to согла́сно (Д).
pursu|e [pəˈsju:] пресле́довать (В); занима́ться [заня́ться] (Т); продолжа́ть [-до́лжить]; **~er** [-ə] пресле́дователь(ница *f*) *m*; **~it** [pəˈsju:t] пого́ня *f*; *mst* ~s *pl.* заня́тие.
purvey [pə:ˈvei] поставля́ть [-а́вить] (проду́кты); снабжа́ть [-бди́ть] (Т); **~or** [-ə] поставщи́к.
pus [pʌs] 🕮 гной.
push [puʃ] **1.** толчо́к; уда́р; давле́ние; напо́р; уси́лие; **2.** толка́ть [-кну́ть]; нажи(им)а́ть (на В); продвига́ть(ся) [-ви́нуть(ся)] (*a.* ~ on); притесня́ть [-ни́ть]; [по]торопи́ть; ~ one's way прота́лкиваться [протолка́ться]; **~-button** ⚡ кно́пка (звонка́ и т. п.).
pusillanimous [pju:siˈlænimәs] □ малоду́шный.
puss(y) [ˈpus(i)] ко́шечка, ки́ска.
put [put] [*irr.*] **1.** класть [положи́ть]; [по]ста́вить; сажа́ть [посади́ть]; зад(ав)а́ть (вопро́с, зада́чу и т. п.); сова́ть [су́нуть]; ~ across успе́шно проводи́ть (ме́ру); перевози́ть [-везти́]; ~ back ста́вить на ме́сто (обра́тно); ста́вить наза́д; ~ by откла́дывать [отложи́ть] (де́ньги); ~ down подавля́ть [-ви́ть] (восста́ние); запи́сывать [-са́ть]; заставля́ть замолча́ть; припи́сывать [-са́ть] (to Д); ~ forth проявля́ть [-ви́ть]; пуска́ть [пусти́ть] (побе́ги); пуска́ть в обраще́ние; ~ in вставля́ть [-а́вить]; всо́вывать [всу́нуть]; ~ off снима́ть [снять] (оде́жду); отде́л(ы-в)аться от (P with T); отта́лкивать [оттолкну́ть]; откла́дывать [отложи́ть]; ~ on наде́(ва́)ть (пла́тье и т. п.); *fig.* принима́ть [-ня́ть] (вид); прибавля́ть [-а́вить]; ~ out выкла́дывать [вы́ложить]; протя́гивать [-тяну́ть]; выгоня́ть [вы́гнать]; [по]туши́ть (ого́нь); ~ through *teleph.* соединя́ть [-ни́ть] (to с Т); ~ to прибавля́ть [-ба́вить]; ~ to death казни́ть (*im*)*pf.*; ~ to the rack пыта́ть; ~ up [по-] стро́ить, возводи́ть [-вести́] (зда́ние); [по]ста́вить (пье́су); дава́ть прию́т (Д); **2.** *v/i.*: ⚓ ~ off, ~ to sea уходи́ть в мо́ре; ~ in ⚓ заходи́ть в порт; ~ up at остана́вливаться [останови́ться] в (П); ~ up with [по]мири́ться с (Т).
putrefy [ˈpju:trifai] (с)гнить.
putrid [ˈpju:trid] □ гнило́й; воню́чий; **~ity** [pju:ˈtriditi] гниль *f.*
putty [ˈpʌti] **1.** (око́нная) зама́зка; **2.** зама́з(ыв)ать (о́кна).
puzzle [pʌzl] **1.** недоуме́ние; затрудне́ние; зага́дка; головоло́мка; **2.** *v/t.* озада́чи(ва)ть; ста́вить в тупи́к; ~ out распу́т(ыв)ать; *v/i.* би́ться (over над Т); **~-headed** [ˈpʌzlˈhedid] бестолко́вый; сумбу́рный.
pygm|ean [pigˈmi:ən] ка́рликовый; **~y** [ˈpigmi] ка́рлик, пигме́й.
pyjamas [pəˈdʒɑ:məz] *pl.* пижа́ма.
pyramid [ˈpirəmid] пирами́да; **~al** [piˈræmidl] □ пирамида́льный.
pyre [ˈpaiə] погреба́льный костёр.
pyrotechnic [pairoˈteknik] пироте́хни́ческий; ~ display фейерве́рк.
Pythagorean [paiˈθægəˈri:ən] пифаго́ре́йский.
pyx [piks] *eccl.* дарохрани́тельница.

Q

quack [kwæk] **1.** зна́харь *m* (-рка); шарлата́н; кря́канье (у́ток); **2.** шарлата́нский; **3.** кря́кать [-кнуть]; **~ery** [ˈkwækəri] шарлата́нство.
quadrangle [kwɔˈdræŋgl] четырёхуго́льник; шко́льный двор.
quadrennial [kwɔˈdreniəl] □ четырёхле́тний; происходя́щий раз в четы́ре го́да.
quadru|ped [ˈkwɔdruped] четвероно́гое живо́тное; **~ple** [ˈkwɔdrupl] □ учетверённый; четверно́й.
quagmire [ˈkwægmaie] тряси́на, боло́то.
quail [kweil] дро́гнуть *pf.*; [с]тру́сить.
quaint [kweint] □ стра́нный, необы́чный.
quake [kweik] [за]трясти́сь; [за-] дрожа́ть; дро́гнуть *pf.*
Quaker [ˈkweikə] ква́кер.
quali|fication [kwɔlifiˈkeiʃən] квалифика́ция; сво́йство; ограниче́ние; **~fy** [ˈkwɔlifai] *v/t.* квалифици́ровать (*im*)*pf.*; ограни́чи(ва)ть; смягча́ть [-чи́ть]; наз(ы)ва́ть (as Т); *v/i.* подгота́вливаться [-гото́виться] (for к Д); **~ty** [-ti] ка́чество; сво́йство; досто́инство.
qualm [kwɔ:m, kwɑ:m] тошнота́; сомне́ние; при́ступ малоду́шия.
quantity [ˈkwɔntiti] коли́чество; 𝔄 величина́; мно́жество.
quarantine [ˈkwɔrənti:n] **1.** каранти́н; **2.** подверга́ть каранти́ну.
quarrel [ˈkwɔrəl] **1.** ссо́ра, перебра́нка; **2.** [по]ссо́риться; **~some** [-səm] □ вздо́рный; приди́рчивый.
quarry [ˈkwɔri] **1.** каменоло́мня; добы́ча (на охо́те) **2.** добы(ва́)ть (ка́мни); *fig.* [по]ры́ться.
quart [kwɔ:t] ква́рта (=1,14 ли́тра).
quarter [ˈkwɔ:tə] **1.** че́тверть *f*; че́тверть часа́; кварта́л; ме́сто, сторона́; поща́да; ~s *pl.* кварти́ра; ⚔ каза́рмы *f/pl.*; *fig.* исто́чники

m/pl.; from all ~s со всех сторо́н; **2.** дели́ть на четы́ре ча́сти; ⚔ расквартиро́вывать [-ирова́ть]; четвертова́ть (*im*)*pf.*; **~-day** день, начина́ющий кварта́л го́да; **~-deck** шка́нцы *m/pl.*; **~ly** [-li] **1.** кварта́льный; **2.** журна́л, выходя́щий ка́ждый кварта́л го́да; **~master** ⚔ квартирме́йстер.

quartet(**te**) [kwɔ:'tet] ♪ кварте́т.

quash [kwɔʃ] ⚖ аннули́ровать (*im*)*pf.*

quaver ['kweivə] **1.** дрожь *f*; ♪ трель *f*; **2.** вибри́ровать; говори́ть дрожа́щим го́лосом.

quay [ki:] на́бережная.

queasy ['kwi:zi] □ сла́бый (о желу́дке); тошнотво́рный.

queen [kwi:n] короле́ва; *chess* ферзь *m*; **~like, ~ly** ['kwi:nli] подоба́ющий короле́ве; ца́рственный.

queer [kwiə] стра́нный, эксцентри́чный.

quench [kwentʃ] утоля́ть [-ли́ть] (жа́жду); [по]туши́ть; охлажда́ть [охлади́ть].

querulous ['kweruləs] □ ворчли́вый.

query ['kwiəri] **1.** вопро́с; **2.** спра́шивать [спроси́ть]; подверга́ть сомне́нию.

quest [kwest] **1.** по́иски *m/pl.*; **2.** оты́скивать [-ка́ть], разы́скивать [-ка́ть].

question ['kwestʃən] **1.** вопро́с; сомне́ние; пробле́ма; beyond (all) ~ вне вся́кого сомне́ния; in ~ (лицо́, вопро́с,) о кото́ром идёт речь; call in ~ подверга́ть сомне́нию; that is out of the ~ об э́том не мо́жет быть и ре́чи; **2.** расспра́шивать [-роси́ть]; задава́ть вопро́с (Д); допра́шивать [-роси́ть]; подверга́ть сомне́нию; **~able** [-əbl] □ сомни́тельный; **~naire** [kestiə'nɛə, kwestʃə'nɛə] анке́та.

queue [kju:] **1.** о́чередь *f*, «хвост»; коса́ (воло́с); **2.** заплета́ть в ко́су; (*mst* ~ up) стоя́ть в о́череди.

quibble [kwibl] **1.** игра́ слов, каламбу́р; увёртка; **2.** [с]остри́ть; уклоня́ться [-ни́ться].

quick [kwik] **1.** живо́й; бы́стрый, ско́рый; прово́рный; о́стрый (слух и т. п.); **2.** чувстви́тельное ме́сто; to the ~ *fig.* за живо́е; до мо́зга косте́й; cut to the ~ заде́вать за живо́е; **~en** ['kwikən] *v/t.* ускоря́ть [-о́рить]; оживля́ть [-ви́ть]; *v/i.* ускоря́ться [-о́риться]; оживля́ться [-ви́ться]; **~ness** ['kwiknis] быстрота́; оживлённость *f*; сообрази́тельность *f*; **~sand** плыву́н, сыпу́чие пески́ *m/pl.*; **~silver** ртуть *f*; **~-witted** нахо́дчивый.

quiescen|ce [kwai'esns] поко́й; неподви́жность *f*; **~t** [-t] неподви́жный; *fig.* споко́йный.

quiet ['kwaiət] **1.** □ споко́йный, ти́хий; бесшу́мный; сми́рный; **2.** поко́й; тишина́; **3.** успока́ивать(ся), [-ко́ить(ся)]; **~ness** [-nis], **~ude** [-ju:d] тишина́; поко́й; споко́йствие.

quill [kwil] пти́чье перо́; ствол пера́; *fig.* перо́ (для письма́); игла́ (ежа́ и т. п.); **~ing** ['kwiliŋ] рюш (на пла́тье).

quilt [kwilt] **1.** стёганое одея́ло; **2.** [вы́]стега́ть.

quince [kwins] ⚘ айва́.

quinine [kwi'ni:n, *Am.* 'kwainain] *pharm.* хини́н.

quintuple ['kwintjupl] пятикра́тный.

quip [kwip] сарка́зм; острота́; ко́лкость *f*.

quirk [kwə:k] = quibble, quip; причу́да; ро́счерк пера́; завито́к (рису́нка).

quit [kwit] **1.** покида́ть [-и́нуть]; оставля́ть [-а́вить]; give notice to ~ заявля́ть об ухо́де (с рабо́ты); **2.** свобо́дный, отде́лавшийся (of от Р).

quite [kwait] вполне́, соверше́нно, совсе́м; дово́льно; ~ a hero настоя́щий геро́й; ~ (so)!, ~ that! так!, соверше́нно ве́рно!

quittance ['kwitəns] квита́нция.

quiver ['kwivə] [за]дрожа́ть; [за-]трепета́ть.

quiz [kwiz] **1.** шу́тка; мистифика́ция; насме́шка; *part. Am.* опро́с, прове́рка зна́ний; **2.** подшу́чивать [-ути́ть] над (Т); *part. Am.* опра́шивать [опроси́ть].

quorum ['kwɔ:rəm] *parl.* кво́рум.

quota ['kwoutə] до́ля, часть *f*, кво́та.

quotation [kwou'teiʃən] цита́та; цити́рование; ☤ котиро́вка, курс.

quote [kwout] [про]цити́ровать; ☤ коти́ровать (*im*)*pf.*; дава́ть расце́нку на (В).

R

rabbi ['ræbai] равви́н.

rabbit ['ræbit] кро́лик.

rabble [ræbl] сброд; толпа́.

rabid ['ræbid] □ неи́стовый, я́ростный; бе́шеный.

rabies ['reibii:z] бе́шенство.

race [reis] **1.** ра́са; род; поро́да; состяза́ние в ско́рости; бег; го́нки *f/pl.*; (*mst* ~s *pl.*) ска́чки *f/pl.*; бега́ *m/pl.*; **2.** [по]мча́ться; состяза́ться в ско́рости; уча́ствовать в ска́чках и т. п.; **~-course** доро́жка; трек; **~r** ['reisə] уча́стник го́нок и́ли ска́чек (ло́шадь, автомоби́ль и т. п.).

racial ['reiʃəl] ра́совый.

rack [ræk] **1.** вéшалка; подстáвка; пóлка; стóйка; кормýшка; 🚂 luggage ~ сéтка для вещéй; **2.** класть в сéтку *или* на пóлку; пытáть; ~ one's brains ломáть себé гóлову; go to ~ and ruin погибáть [-йбнуть]; разоря́ться [-ри́ться].
racket ['rækit] тéннисная ракéтка; шум, гам; *Am.* шантáж; **~eer** [ræki'tiə] *Am.* вымогáтель *m.*
racy ['reisi] □ характéрный; крéпкий; пикáнтный; колори́тный.
radar ['reidɑ:] радáр; ~ set радиолокáтор.
radian|ce ['reidiəns] сия́ние; **~t** [-t] □ лучи́стый; сия́ющий, лучезáрный.
radiat|e ['reidieit] излучáть [-чи́ть] (свет, теплó); **~ion** [reidi'eiʃən] излучéние; **~or** ['reidieitə] излучáтель *m*; ⚠, *mot.* радиáтор.
radical ['rædikəl] **1.** □ основнóй, коренной; фундаментáльный; радикáльный; **2.** *pol.* радикáл.
radio ['reidiou] **1.** рáдио *n indecl.*; ~ drama, ~ play радиопостанóвка; ~ set радиоприёмник; **2.** передавáть по рáдио; **~graph** [-grɑ:f] **1.** рентгéновский сни́мок; **2.** дéлать рентгéновский сни́мок с (Р); **~scopy** [reidi'ɔskəpi] исслéдование рентгéновскими лучáми; **~-telegram** радио(теле)грáмма.
radish ['rædiʃ] рéдька; (red) ~ редиска.
raffle [ræfl] **1.** *v/t.* разы́грывать в лотерéю; *v/i.* учáствовать в лотерéе; **2.** лотерéя.
raft [rɑ:ft] **1.** плот; парóм **2.** сплавля́ть [-áвить] (лес); **~er** ['rɑ:ftə] ⊕ стропи́ло.
rag [ræg] тря́пка; **~s** *pl.* тряпьё, вéтошь *f*; лохмóтья *m/pl.*
ragamuffin ['rægəmʌfin] оборвáнец; ýличный мáльчик.
rage [reidʒ] **1.** я́рость *f*, гнев; повáльное увлечéние; предмéт увлечéния; it is all the ~ э́то послéдний крик мóды; **2.** [вз]беси́ться; бушевáть.
ragged ['rægid] □ нерóвный; рвáный, понóшенный.
raid [reid] **1.** налёт; набéг; облáва; **2.** дéлать набéг, налёт на (В); вторгáться [втóргнуться] в (В).
rail [reil] **1.** пери́ла *n/pl.*; огрáда; 🚂 рельс; поперéчина; (main) ~ ⚓ пóручень *m*; run off the **~s** сойти́ с рéльсов; **2.** éхать по желéзной дорóге; [вы́]ругáть, [вы́]брани́ть (at, against В).
railing ['reiliŋ] огрáда; пери́ла *n/pl.*
raillery ['reiləri] беззлóбная насмéшка, подшýчивание.
railroad ['reilroud] *part. Am.*, **railway** [-wei] желéзная дорóга.
rain [rein] **1.** дождь *m*; **2.** идти́ (о дождé); *fig.* [по]сы́паться; **~bow** рáдуга; **~coat** *Am.* дождеви́к, непромокáемое пальтó *n indecl.*; **~fall** коли́чество осáдков; **~-proof** непромокáемый; **~y** ['reini] □ дождли́вый.
raise [reiz] (*often* ~ up) поднимáть [-ня́ть]; воздвигáть [-ви́гнуть] (пáмятник и т. п.); возвышáть [-ы́сить]; воспи́тывать [-итáть]; вызывáть [вы́звать] (смех, гнев и т. п.); возбуждáть [-уди́ть] (чýвство); добы́(вá)ть (дéньги).
raisin [reizn] изю́минка; *pl.* изю́м.
rake [reik] **1.** грáбли *f/pl.*; кочергá; повéса *m*; распýтник; **2.** *v/t.* сгребáть [-ести́]; разгребáть [-ести́]; *fig.* ~ for тщáтельно искáть (В *or* Р).
rally ['ræli] **1.** вновь собирáть(ся); овладé(вá)ть собóй; **2.** *Am.* мáссовый ми́тинг; объединéние; съезд.
ram [ræm] **1.** барáн; тарáн; **2.** [про-] тарáнить; заби́(вá)ть.
rambl|e ['ræmbl] **1.** прогýлка (без цéли); **2.** броди́ть без цéли; говори́ть бессвя́зно; **~er** [-ə] праздношатáющийся; ползýчее растéние; **~ing** [-iŋ] бродя́чий; бессвя́зный; разбрóсанный; ползýчий.
ramify ['ræmifai] разветвля́ться [-етви́ться].
ramp [ræmp] скат, уклóн; **~ant** ['ræmpənt] стоя́щий на зáдних лáпах (о геральди́ческом живóтном); *fig.* необýзданный.
rampart ['ræmpɑ:t] вал.
ramshackle ['ræmʃækl] вéтхий.
ran [ræn] *pt.* от run.
ranch [ræntʃ] *Am.* скотовóдная фéрма.
rancid ['rænsid] □ прогóрклый.
ranco(u)r ['ræŋkə] злóба, затаённая враждá.
random ['rændəm] **1.** at ~ наугáд, наобýм; **2.** сдéланный (вы́бранный и т. д.) наугáд; случáйный.
rang [ræŋ] *pt.* от ring.
range [reindʒ] **1.** ряд; ли́ния (домóв); цепь *f* (гор); óбласть распространéния (растéний и т. п.); предéл, амплитýда; диапазóн (гóлоса); ⚔ дáльность дéйствия; стрéльбище; **2.** *v/t.* выстрáивать в ряд; стáвить в порядке; классифици́ровать (*im*)*pf.*; ⚓ плáвать, [по]плы́ть вдоль (Р); *v/i.* выстрáиваться в ряд; простирáться; броди́ть, ры́скать.
rank [ræŋk] **1.** ряд; ⚔ шерéнга; звáние, чин; категóрия; ~ and file рядовóй состáв; *fig.* людскáя мáсса; **2.** *v/t.* стрóить в шерéнгу; выстрáивать в ряд; классифици́ровать (*im*)*pf.*; *v/i.* стрóиться в шерéнгу; равня́ться (with Д); **3.** бýйный (о расти́тельности); прогóрклый (о мáсле); отъя́вленный.
rankle [ræŋkl] *fig.* мýчить, терзáть (об оби́де и т. п.); ~ in терзáть (В).
ransack ['rænsæk] [по]ры́ться в (П); [о]грáбить.
ransom ['rænsəm] **1.** вы́куп; **2.** выкупáть [вы́купить].

rant [rænt] **1.** деклама́ция; высокопа́рная речь *f*; **2.** говори́ть напы́щенно; [про]деклами́ровать; шу́мно весели́ться.
rap [ræp] **1.** лёгкий уда́р; стук (в дверь и т. п.); *fig.* not a ~ ни гроша́; **2.** ударя́ть [уда́рить]; [по-] стуча́ть.
rapaci|ous [rəˈpeiʃəs] □ жа́дный; хи́щный; **~ty** [rəˈpæsiti] жа́дность *f*; хи́щность *f*.
rape [reip] **1.** похище́ние; изнаси́лование; **2.** похища́ть [-и́тить]; [из]наси́ловать.
rapid [ˈræpid] **1.** □ бы́стрый, ско́рый; круто́й; **2.** **~s** *pl.* поро́ги *m/pl.*, стремни́ны *f/pl.*; **~ity** [rəˈpiditi] ско́рость *f*.
rapt [ræpt] восхищённый; увлечённый; **~ure** [ˈræptʃə] восто́рг, экста́з; go into **~s** приходи́ть в восто́рг.
rare [rɛə] □ ре́дкий; *phys.* разреженный.
rarefy [ˈrɛərifai] разрежа́ть(ся) [-еди́ть(ся)].
rarity [-riti] ре́дкость *f*.
rascal [ˈrɑːskəl] моше́нник; **~ity** [rɑːsˈkæliti] моше́нничество; **~ly** [ˈrɑːskəli] моше́ннический.
rash¹ [ræʃ] □ стреми́тельный; опроме́тчивый; необду́манный.
rash² [~] сыпь *f*.
rasp [rɑːsp] **1.** ра́шпиль *m*; скре́жет; **2.** подпи́ливать ра́шпилем; соскреба́ть [-ести́]; раздража́ть [-жи́ть].
raspberry [ˈrɑːzbəri] мали́на.
rat [ræt] кры́са; *sl.* изме́нник; smell a ~ чу́ять недо́брое.
rate [reit] **1.** но́рма; ста́вка; пропо́рция; сте́пень *f*; ме́стный нало́г; разря́д; ско́рость *f*; at any ~ во вся́ком слу́чае; ~ of exchange (валю́тный) курс; **2.** оце́нивать [-ни́ть], расце́нивать [-ни́ть]; [вы́-] брани́ть; ~ among счита́ться среди́ (Р).
rather [rɑːðə] скоре́е; предпочти́тельно; верне́е; дово́льно; I had ~ ... я предпочёл бы ...
ratify [ˈrætifai] ратифици́ровать (*im*)*pf.*; утвержда́ть [-рди́ть].
rating [ˈreitiŋ] оце́нка; су́мма нало́га; ранг; класс.
ratio [ˈreiʃiou] Ⓤ отноше́ние.
ration [ˈræʃən] **1.** рацио́н; паёк; **2.** снабжа́ть продово́льствием; нормирова́ть вы́дачу (Р).
rational [ræʃnl] □ рациона́льный; разу́мный; **~ity** [ræʃˈnæliti] рациона́льность *f*; разу́мность *f*; **~ize** [ˈræʃnəlaiz] рационализи́ровать (*im*)*pf*.
ratten [rætn] саботи́ровать (*im*)*pf*.
rattle [rætl] **1.** треск; дребезжа́ние; трещо́тка (*a. fig.*); погрему́шка; **2.** [про]треща́ть; [за]дребезжа́ть; [за]греме́ть (Т); говори́ть без у́молку; ~ off отбараба́нить *pf.*; **~snake** гремя́чая змея́; **~trap** *fig.* ве́тхий экипа́ж, автомоби́ль и т. п.
rattling [ˈrætliŋ] *fig.* бы́стрый; великоле́пный.
raucous [ˈrɔkəs] □ хри́плый.
ravage [ˈrævidʒ] **1.** опустоше́ние; **2.** опустоша́ть [-ши́ть]; разоря́ть [-ри́ть].
rave [reiv] бре́дить (*a. fig.*), говори́ть бессвя́зно; неистовствовать.
ravel [rævl] *v/t.* запу́т(ыв)ать; распу́т(ыв)ать; *v/i.* запу́т(ыв)аться; (*a.* ~ out) располза́ться по швам.
raven [reivn] во́рон.
raven|ing [ˈrævniŋ], **~ous** [-əs] прожо́рливый; хи́щный.
ravine [rəˈviːn] овра́г, лощи́на.
ravish [ˈræviʃ] приводи́ть в восто́рг; [из]наси́ловать; похища́ть [-и́тить]; **~ment** [-mənt] похище́ние; восхище́ние; изнаси́лование.
raw [rɔː] □ сыро́й; необрабо́танный; нео́пытный; ободра́нный; **~-boned** худо́й, костля́вый.
ray [rei] **1.** луч; *fig.* про́блеск; ⚕ ~ treatment облуче́ние.
raze [reiz] разруша́ть до основа́ния; сноси́ть [снести́] (зда́ние и т. п.); вычёркивать [вы́черкнуть].
razor [ˈreizə] бри́тва; **~-blade** ле́звие безопа́сной бри́твы.
re... [riː] *pref.* (придаёт сло́ву значе́ния:) сно́ва, за́ново, ещё раз, обра́тно.
reach [riːtʃ] **1.** преде́л досяга́емости; круг понима́ния, кругозо́р; о́бласть влия́ния; beyond ~ вне преде́лов досяга́емости; within easy ~ побли́зости; под руко́й; **2.** *v/t.* достига́ть [-и́гнуть] (Р); доезжа́ть [дое́хать], доходи́ть [дойти́] до (Р); простира́ться [-стере́ться] до (Р); протя́гивать [-яну́ть]; дост(ав)а́ть до (Р); *v/i.* протя́гивать ру́ку (for за Т).
react [riˈækt] реаги́ровать; ~ upon each other взаимоде́йствовать; противоде́йствовать (against Д).
reaction [riˈækʃən] реа́кция; **~ary** [-ʃənəri] **1.** реакцио́нный; **2.** реакционе́р(ка).
read **1.** [riːd] [*irr.*] [про]чита́ть; изуча́ть [-чи́ть]; истолко́вывать [-кова́ть]; пока́зывать [-за́ть] (о прибо́ре); гласи́ть; ~ to a p. чита́ть кому́-нибудь вслух; **2.** [red] a) *pt.* и *p. pt.* от read 1.; b) *adj.* начи́танный; **~able** [ˈriːdəbl] □ интере́сный; чёткий; **~er** [ˈriːdə] чита́тель(ница *f*) *m*; чтец; ле́ктор; хрестома́тия.
readi|ly [ˈredili] *adv.* охо́тно; бы́стро; легко́; **~ness** [-nis] гото́вность *f*; подгото́вленность *f*.
reading [ˈriːdiŋ] чте́ние; ле́кция; толкова́ние, понима́ние; *parl.* чте́ние (законопрое́кта).
readjust [ˈriːəˈdʒʌst] сно́ва приводи́ть в поря́док; переде́л(ыв)ать;

~ment [-mənt] приведе́ние в поря́док; переде́лка.
ready [ˈredi] □ гото́вый; скло́нный; ⚕ нали́чный; make (или get) ~ [при]гото́вить(ся); **~-made** гото́вый (о пла́тье).
reagent [riˈeidʒənt] ⚗ реакти́в.
real [riəl] □ действи́тельный; реа́льный; настоя́щий; ~ estate недви́жимость *f*; **~ity** [riˈæliti] действи́тельность *f*; **~ization** [riəlaiˈzeiʃən] понима́ние, осозна́ние; осуществле́ние; ⚕ реализа́ция; **~ize** [ˈriəlaiz] представля́ть себе́; осуществля́ть [-ви́ть]; осозн(ав)а́ть; реализова́ть (*im*)*pf*.
realm [relm] короле́вство; ца́рство; сфе́ра.
realty [ˈriəlti] недви́жимое иму́щество.
reap [ri:p] [с]жать (рожь и т. п.); *fig*. пож(ин)а́ть; **~er** [ˈri:pə] жнец, жни́ца.
reappear [ˈri:əˈpiə] появля́ться сно́ва.
rear [riə] **1.** *v/t*. воспи́тывать [-та́ть]; выра́щивать [вы́растить]; *v/i*. станови́ться на дыбы́; **2.** за́дняя сторона́; ⚔ тыл; at the ~ of, in (the) ~ of позади́ (Р); **3.** за́дний; ты́льный; ⚔ тылово́й; **~-admiral** ⚓ контр-адмира́л; **~-guard** ⚔ арьерга́рд.
re-arm [ˈri:ɑ:m] перевооружа́ть(-ся) [-жи́ть(ся)].
reason [ri:zn] **1.** ра́зум; рассу́док; основа́ние; причи́на; by ~ of по причи́не (Р); for this ~ поэ́тому; it stands to ~ that ... я́сно, что ..., очеви́дно, что ...; **2.** *v/i*. рассужда́ть [-уди́ть]; заключа́ть [-чи́ть]; резюми́ровать (*im*)*pf*.; *v/t*. ~ out проду́мать до конца́; ~ out of разубежда́ть [-еди́ть] в (П); **~able** [ˈri:znəbl] □ (благо)разу́мный; уме́ренный; недорого́й.
reassure [ˈri:əˈʃuə] сно́ва уверя́ть; успока́ивать [-ко́ить].
rebate [ˈri:beit] ⚕ ски́дка; усту́пка.
rebel 1. [rebl] бунтовщи́к (-и́ца); повста́нец; **2.** [~] (*a*. **~lious** [riˈbeljəs]) мяте́жный; **3.** [riˈbel] восст(ав)а́ть; бунтова́ть [вз-ся]; **~lion** [riˈbeljən] мяте́ж, восста́ние; бунт.
rebirth [ˈribə:θ] возрожде́ние.
rebound [riˈbaund] **1.** отска́кивать [-скочи́ть]; **2.** рикоше́т; отско́к.
rebuff [riˈbʌf] **1.** отпо́р; ре́зкий отка́з; **2.** дава́ть отпо́р (Д).
rebuild [ˈri:ˈbild] [*irr*. (build)] восстана́вливать [-нови́ть] (зда́ние и т. п.).
rebuke [riˈbju:k] **1.** упрёк; вы́говор; **2.** упрека́ть [-кну́ть]; де́лать вы́говор (Д).
rebut [riˈbʌt] дава́ть отпо́р (Д).
recall [riˈkɔ:l] **1.** отозва́ние (депута́та, посла́ и т. п.); ⚕ отме́на; **2.** отзыва́ть [отозва́ть]; призыва́ть обра́тно; отменя́ть [-ни́ть]; напомина́ть [-о́мнить]; вспомина́ть [-о́мнить] (В); ⚕ брать (или тре́бовать) обра́тно (капита́л); отменя́ть [-ни́ть].
recapitulate [ri:kəˈpitjuleit] резюми́ровать (*im*)*pf*.
recast [ˈri:ˈkɑ:st] [*irr*. (cast)] придава́ть но́вую фо́рму (Д); ⊕ отлива́ть за́ново.
recede [riˈsi:d] отступа́ть [-пи́ть]; удаля́ться [-ли́ться].
receipt [riˈsi:t] **1.** распи́ска, квита́нция; получе́ние; реце́пт (кулина́рный); **~s** *pl*. прихо́д; **2.** распи́сываться [-са́ться] на (П).
receiv|able [riˈsi:vəbl] ⚕ неопла́ченный (счёт); **~e** [riˈsi:v] получа́ть [-чи́ть]; принима́ть [-ня́ть]; воспринима́ть [-ня́ть]; **~ed** [-d] общепри́знанный; **~er** [-ə] получа́тель(ница *f*) *m*; *teleph*. телефо́нная тру́бка; ⚖ суде́бный исполни́тель *m*.
recent [ri:snt] □ неда́вний; све́жий; но́вый; **~ly** [-li] неда́вно.
receptacle [riˈseptəkl] вмести́лище.
reception [riˈsepʃən] получе́ние; приём; приня́тие.
receptive [riˈseptiv] □ восприи́мчивый (к Д).
recess [riˈses] кани́кулы *f/pl*.; переры́в; ни́ша; уединённое ме́сто; **~es** *pl*. *fig*. тайники́ *m/pl*.; **~ion** [-ʃən] удале́ние; углубле́ние; ⚕ спад.
recipe [ˈresipi] реце́пт.
recipient [riˈsipiənt] получа́тель (-ница *f*) *m*.
reciproc|al [riˈsiprəkəl] взаи́мный; обою́дный; эквивале́нтный; **~ate** [-keit] ⊕ дви́гать(ся) взад и вперёд; обме́ниваться [-ня́ться] (услу́гами и т. п.); **~ity** [resiˈprɔsiti] взаи́мность *f*.
recit|al [riˈsaitl] чте́ние, деклама́ция; повествова́ние; ♪ конце́рт (соли́ста); **~ation** [resiˈteiʃən] деклама́ция; **~e** [riˈsait] [про]деклами́ровать; расска́зывать [-за́ть].
reckless [ˈreklis] □ безрассу́дный; опроме́тчивый; беспе́чный.
reckon [ˈrekən] *v/t*. исчисля́ть [-чи́слить]; причисля́ть [-чи́слить] (among к Д); счита́ть [счесть] за (В); *v/i*. предполага́ть [-ложи́ть]; ~ (up)on *fig*. рассчи́тывать на (В); **~ing** [-iŋ] подсчёт; счёт; распла́та.
reclaim [riˈkleim] исправля́ть [-а́вить]; поднима́ть [-ня́ть] (целину́).
recline [riˈklain] отки́дывать(ся) [-и́нуть(ся)]; полулежа́ть.
recluse [riˈklu:s] отше́льник (-ица).
recogni|tion [rekəgˈniʃən] опозна́ние; узнава́ние; призна́ние (Р); **~ze** [ˈrekəgnaiz] узн(ав)а́ть; призн(ав)а́ть.

recoil [riˈkɔil] **1.** отскóк; ⚔ отдáча, откáт; **2.** отскáкивать [-скочи́ть]; откáтываться [-кати́ться].
recollect [rekəˈlekt] вспоминáть [вспóмнить] (В); **~ion** [rekəˈlekʃən] воспоминáние, пáмять *f* (of о П).
recommend [rekəˈmend] рекомендовáть (*im*)*pf.*, *pf. a.* [по-]; **~ation** [rekəmenˈdeiʃən] рекомендáция.
recompense [ˈrekəmpəns] **1.** вознаграждéние; компенсáция; **2.** вознаграждáть [-ради́ть]; отплáчивать [отплати́ть] (Д).
reconcil|e [ˈrekənsail] примиря́ть [-ри́ть] (to с Т); улáживать [улáдить]; ~e o. s. примиря́ться [-ри́ться]; **~iation** [ˈrekənsiliˈeiʃən] примирéние.
recondition [ˈri:kənˈdiʃən] [от]ремонти́ровать; переоборýдовать.
reconn|aissance [riˈkɔnisəns] ⚔ развéдка; **~oitre** [rekəˈnɔitə] производи́ть развéдку; развéд(ыв)ать.
reconsider [ˈri:kənˈsidə] пересмáтривать [-мотрéть].
reconstitute [ˈri:kɔnstitju:t] восстанáвливать [-нови́ть].
reconstruct [ˈri:kənsˈtrʌkt] восстанáвливать [-нови́ть]; перестрáивать [-стрóить]; **~ion** [-sˈtrʌkʃən] реконстрýкция; восстановлéние.
reconvert [ˈri:kənˈvə:t] перестрáивать на ми́рный лад.
record 1. [ˈrekɔ:d] зáпись *f*; *sport* рекóрд; ⚖ протокóл (заседáния и т. п.); place on ~ запи́сывать [-сáть]; граммофóнная пласти́нка; репутáция; ♀ Office государственный архи́в; off the ~ *Am.* неофициáльно; on ~ зарегистри́рованный; **2.** [riˈkɔ:d] запи́сывать [-сáть]; [за]регистри́ровать; **~er** [riˈkɔ:də] регистрáтор; регистри́рующий прибóр.
recount [riˈkaunt] излагáть [изложи́ть] (подрóбно).
recoup [riˈku:p] компенси́ровать (*im*)*pf.*, возмещáть [-ести́ть] (Д for В).
recourse [riˈkɔ:s] обращéние за пóмощью; прибéжище; have ~ to прибегáть к пóмощи (Р).
recover [riˈkʌvə] *v/t.* получáть обрáтно; вернýть (себé) *pf.*; навёрстывать [-верстáть] (врéмя); *v/i.* оправля́ться [-áвиться] (*a.* ~ o. s.); **~y** [-ri] восстановлéние; выздоровлéние; возмещéние; ⚖ взыскáние.
recreat|e [ˈrekrieit] *v/t.* освежáть [-жи́ть]; развлекáть [-éчь]; *v/i.* освежáться [-жи́ться] (пóсле рабóты и т. п.) (*a.* ~ o. s.); развлекáться [-éчься]; **~ion** [rekriˈeiʃən] óтдых; развлечéние.
recrimination [rikrimiˈneiʃən] взаи́мное (и́ли встрéчное) обвинéние.
recruit [riˈkru:t] **1.** рéкрут новобрáнец; *fig.* новичóк; **2.** [у]комплектовáть; [за]вербовáть (новобрáнцев).
rectangle [ˈrektæŋgl] прямоугóльник.
recti|fy [ˈrektifai] исправля́ть [-áвить]; выверя́ть [вы́верить]; ⚡ выпрямля́ть [вы́прямить]; **~tude** [ˈrektitju:d] прямотá, чéстность *f.*
rector [ˈrektə] рéктор; пáстор, свящéнник; **~y** [-ri] дом свящéнника.
recumbent [riˈkʌmbənt] □ лежáчий.
recuperate [riˈkju:pəreit] восстанáвливать си́лы; оправля́ться [опрáвиться].
recur [riˈkə:] возвращáться [-рати́ться] (to к Д); приходи́ть снóва на ýм; происходи́ть вновь; **~rence** [riˈkʌrəns] повторéние; **~rent** [-rənt] □ повторя́ющийся; периоди́ческий; ⚕ возврáтный.
red [red] **1.** крáсный; ~ heat крáсное калéние; ~ herring *fig.* отвлечéние внимáния; ~ tape канцеля́рщина; **2.** крáсный цвéт; ~s *pl.* (*part. pol.*) крáсные *pl.*
red|breast [ˈredbrest] мали́новка; **~den** [redn] [по]краснéть; **~dish** [ˈrediʃ] красновáтый.
redeem [riˈdi:m] искупáть [-пи́ть]; выкупáть [вы́купить]; спасáть [-сти́]; **~er** [-ə] спаси́тель *m.*
redemption [riˈdempʃən] искуплéние; вы́куп; спасéние.
red-handed [ˈredˈhændid]: take a p. ~ поймáть когó-либо на мéсте преступлéния.
red-hot накалённый дóкраснá; *fig.* взбешённый; горя́чий.
red-letter: ~ day прáздничный день *m.*
redness [ˈrednis] краснотá.
redolent [ˈredolənt] благоухáющий.
redouble [riˈdʌbl] удвáивать(ся) [удвóить(ся)].
redound [riˈdaund]: ~ to спосóбствовать (Д), помогáть [помóчь] (Д).
redress [riˈdres] **1.** исправлéние; ⚖ возмещéние; **2.** исправля́ть [-áвить]; заглáживать [-лáдить] (вину́); возмещáть [-ести́ть].
reduc|e [riˈdju:s] понижáть [-и́зить]; снижáть [-и́зить]; доводи́ть [довести́] (to до Р); уменьшáть [умéньши́ть]; сокращáть [-рати́ть]; урéз(ыв)ать; ~ to writing излагáть пи́сьменно; **~tion** [riˈdʌkʃən] снижéние (цен), ски́дка; уменьшéние; сокращéние; умéньшенная кóпия (карти́ны и т. п.).
redundant [riˈdʌndənt] □ изли́шний; чрезмéрный.
reed [ri:d] тростни́к; свирéль *f.*
reef [ri:f] риф, подвóдная скалá.
reek [ri:k] **1.** вонь *f*, зáтхлый зáпах; дым; пар; **2.** *v/i.* дыми́ться; (неприя́тно) пáхнуть (of Т); испускáть пар.

reel [ri:l] **1.** катушка; бобина; барабан, во́рот; **2.** *v/i.* [за]кружиться, [за]вертеться; шататься [шатнуться]; *v/t.* [на]мотать; ~ off разматывать [-мотать]; *fig.* отбарабанить *pf.*; ~ up наматывать на катушку.
re-elect ['ri:i'lekt] переизб(и)рать.
re-enter ['ri:'entə] входить снова в (В).
re-establish ['ri:is'tæbliʃ] восстанавливать [-новить].
refection [ri'fekʃən] закуска.
refer [ri'fə:]: ~ to *v/t.* приписывать [-сать] (Д); относить [отнести] (к Д); направлять [-равить] (к Д); передавать на рассмотрение (Д); *v/i.* ссылаться [сослаться] на (В); относиться [отнестись] к (Д); **~ee** [refə'ri:] *sport* судья *m*; **~ence** ['refrəns] справка; ссылка; рекомендация; упоминание; отношение; лицо, давшее рекомендацию; in ~ to относительно (Р); ~ book справочник; ~ library справочная библиотека; make ~ to ссылаться [сослаться] на (В).
referendum [refə'rendəm] референдум.
refill ['ri:'fil] наполнять снова; пополнять(ся) [-полнить(ся)].
refine [ri'fain] ⊕ очищать [очистить] рафинировать (*im*)*pf.*; делать(ся) более утончённым; ~ (up)on [у]совершенствовать; **~ment** [-mənt] очищение, рафинирование; отделка; усовершенствование; утончённость *f*; **~ry** [-əri] ⊕ очистительный завод.
reflect [ri'flekt] *v/t.* отражать [отразить]; *v/i.* ~ (up)on: бросать тень на (В); размышлять [-ыслить] о (П); отражаться [-разиться] на (В); **~ion** [ri'flekʃən] отражение; отсвет; размышление, обдумывание; *fig.* тень *f*; рефлексия.
reflex ['ri:fleks] **1.** отражение; отсвет, отблеск; рефлекс; **2.** рефлекторный.
reforest ['ri:fɔrist] снова засаждать лесом.
reform [ri'fɔ:m] **1.** реформа; улучшение; **2.** улучшать(ся) [улучшить(ся)]; реформировать (*im*)*pf.*; исправлять(ся); **~ation** [refə'meiʃən] преобразование; исправление (моральное); *eccl.* ♀ Реформация; **~atory** [ri'fɔ:mətəri] исправительное заведение; **~er** [-mə] реформатор.
refract|ion [ri'frækʃən] рефракция, преломление; **~ory** [-təri] □ упрямый; непокорный; ⊕ огнеупорный.
refrain [ri'frein] **1.** *v/t.* сдерживать [-жать]; *v/i.* воздерживаться [-жаться] (from от Р); **2.** припев, рефрен.
refresh [ri'freʃ] освежать [-жить]; подкреплять(ся) [-пить(ся)]; подновлять [-вить]; **~ment** [-mənt] подкрепление; закуска.
refrigerat|e [ri'fridʒəreit] замораживать [-розить]; охлаждать(ся) [охладить(ся)]; **~ion** [rifridʒə'reiʃən] замораживание; охлаждение.
refuel ['ri:'fjuəl] *mot.* заправляться горючим.
refuge ['refju:dʒ] убежище; **~e** [refju'dʒi:] беженец (-нка).
refulgent [ri'fʌldʒənt] лучезарный.
refund [ri'fʌnd] возмещать расходы (Д); возвращать [-ратить].
refusal [ri'fju:zəl] отказ.
refuse 1. [ri'fju:z] *v/t.* отказываться [-заться] от (Р); отказывать [-зать] в (П); отвергать [отвергнуть]; *v/i.* отказываться [-заться]; [за]артачиться (о лошади); **2.** ['refju:s] брак ⊕; отбросы *m/pl.*; мусор.
refute [ri'fju:t] опровергать [-вергнуть].
regain [ri'gein] получать обратно; снова достигать.
regal [ri:gəl] □ королевский; царственный.
regale [ri'geil] *v/t.* угощать [угостить]; *v/i.* пировать; угощаться [угоститься] (on Т).
regard [ri'gɑ:d] **1.** взгляд, взор; внимание; уважение; with ~ to по отношению к (Д); kind ~s сердечный привет; **2.** [по]смотреть на (В); рассматривать (as как); [по]считаться с (Т); относиться [отнестись] к (Д); as ~s ... что касается (Р); **~ing** [-iŋ] относительно (Р); **~less** [-lis] *adv.* ~ of не обращая внимания на (В); не считаясь с (Т).
regenerate 1. [ri'dʒenəreit] перерождать(ся) [-одить(ся)]; возрождаться [-родиться]; ⊕ регенерировать; **2.** [-rit] возрождённый.
regent ['ri:dʒənt] регент.
regiment ['redʒimənt] **1.** полк; **2.** формировать полк(и) из (Р); организовать (*im*)*pf.*; **~als** [redʒi'mentlz] *pl.* полковая форма.
region ['ri:dʒən] область *f*; район; **~al** [-l] □ областной; местный.
register ['redʒistə] **1.** журнал (записей); реестр; официальный список; ♪ регистр; ⊕ заслонка; **2.** регистрировать(ся) (*im*)*pf.*, *pf. a.* [за-]; заносить в список; ✉ посылать заказным.
registr|ar [redʒis'trɑ:] регистратор; служащий загса; **~ation** [redʒis'treiʃən] регистрация; **~y** ['redʒistri] регистратура; регистрация; регистрационная запись *f*; реестр.
regret [ri'gret] **1.** сожаление; раскаяние; **2.** [по]жалеть (that ... что ...); сожалеть о (П); горевать

о (П); раска́иваться [-ка́яться] в (П); **~ful** [-ful] □ по́лный сожале́ния; **~table** [-əbl] □ приско́рбный.
regular ['regjulə] □ пра́вильный; регуля́рный (*a.* ⚔); форма́льный; **~ity** [regju'læriti] регуля́рность *f.*
regulat|e ['regjuleit] [у]регули́ровать, упоря́дочи(ва)ть; ⊕ [от]регули́ровать; **~ion** [regju'leiʃən] **1.** регули́рование; предписа́ние; ~s *pl.* уста́в; **2.** *attr.* устано́вленный.
rehears|al [ri'hə:səl] *thea.*, ♪ репети́ция; **~e** [ri'hə:s] *thea.* [про]репети́ровать.
reign [rein] **1.** ца́рствование; *fig.* власть *f*; **2.** ца́рствовать; госпо́дствовать (*a. fig.*); *fig.* цари́ть.
reimburse [ri:im'bə:s] возвраща́ть [-рати́ть]; возмеща́ть расхо́ды (Д).
rein [rein] **1.** вожжа́; **2.** пра́вить (лошадьми́); сде́рживать [-жа́ть].
reinforce [ri:in'fɔ:s] подкрепля́ть [-пи́ть]; уси́ли(ва)ть; **~ment** [-mənt] подкрепле́ние.
reinstate ['ri:in'steit] восстана́вливать [-нови́ть] (в права́х и т. п.).
reinsure ['ri:in'ʃuə] перестрахо́вывать [-ова́ть].
reiterate [ri:'itəreit] повторя́ть [-ри́ть] (*mst* многокра́тно).
reject [ri'dʒekt] отверга́ть [отве́ргнуть]; отка́зываться [-за́ться] от (Р); отклоня́ть [-ни́ть]; **~ion** [ri'dʒekʃən] отклоне́ние; отка́з.
rejoic|e [ri'dʒɔis] *v/t.* [об]ра́довать *v/i.* [об]ра́доваться (at, in Д); **~ing** [-iŋ] (ча́сто ~s *pl.*) весе́лье; пра́зднование.
rejoin 1. ['ri:'dʒɔin] сно́ва соединя́ться [-ни́ться] с (Т); сно́ва примыка́ть [-мкну́ть] к (Д); **2.** [ri'dʒɔin] возража́ть [-рази́ть].
rejuvenate [ri'dʒu:vineit] омола́живать(ся) [омолоди́ть(ся)].
relapse [ri'læps] **1.** рециди́в (⚖, ⚕); **2.** сно́ва впада́ть (в е́ресь, заблужде́ние и т. п.); сно́ва заболева́ть.
relate [ri'leit] *v/t.* расска́зывать [-за́ть]; приводи́ть в связь; *v/i.* относи́ться [отнести́сь]; **~d** [-id] ро́дственный (to с Т).
relation [ri'leiʃən] отноше́ние; связь *f*; родство́; ро́дственник (-ица); in ~ to по отноше́нию к (Д); **~ship** [-ʃip] родство́.
relative ['relətiv] **1.** □ относи́тельный; сравни́тельный (to с Т); усло́вный; **2.** ро́дственник (-ица).
relax [ri'læks] уменьша́ть напряже́ние (Р); смягча́ть(ся) [-чи́ть (-ся)]; де́лать(ся) ме́нее стро́гим; **~ation** [ri:læk'seiʃən] ослабле́ние; смягче́ние; о́тдых от рабо́т; развлече́ние.
relay [ri'lei] **1.** сме́на; *sport* эстафе́та; *attr.* эстафе́тный; **2.** *radio* трансли́ровать (*im*)*pf.*
release [ri'li:s] **1.** освобожде́ние; высвобожде́ние; избавле́ние; вы́пуск (фи́льма на прока́т и т. п.); **2.** освобожда́ть [-боди́ть]; высвобожда́ть [вы́свободить]; избавля́ть [-а́вить]; выпуска́ть [вы́пустить]; отпуска́ть [-сти́ть]; проща́ть [прости́ть] (долг).
relegate ['religeit] отсыла́ть [отосла́ть]; направля́ть [-ра́вить] (to к Д); ссыла́ть [сосла́ть].
relent [ri'lent] смягча́ться [-чи́ться]; **~less** [-lis] □ безжа́лостный.
relevant ['relivənt] уме́стный; относя́щийся к де́лу.
reliab|ility [rilaiə'biliti] надёжность *f*; про́чность *f*; **~le** [ri'laiəbl] □ надёжный; достове́рный.
reliance [ri'laiəns] дове́рие; уве́ренность *f.*
relic ['relik] пережи́ток; рели́квия; рели́кт; ~s *pl.* оста́нки *m/pl.*
relief [ri'li:f] облегче́ние; по́мощь *f*; посо́бие; подкрепле́ние; сме́на (*a.* ⚔); ⚔ сня́тие оса́ды; релье́ф; ~ works *pl.* обще́ственные рабо́ты для безрабо́тных.
relieve [ri'li:v] облегча́ть [-чи́ть]; освобожда́ть [-боди́ть]; ока́зывать по́мощь (Д); выруча́ть [вы́ручить]; ⚔ снять оса́ду с (Р); сменя́ть [-ни́ть].
religion [ri'lidʒən] рели́гия.
religious [ri'lidʒəs] □ религио́зный; благогове́йный; добросо́вестный; *eccl.* мона́шеский.
relinquish [ri'liŋkwiʃ] оставля́ть [-а́вить] (наде́жду и т. п.); броса́ть [бро́сить] (привы́чку).
relish ['reliʃ] **1.** вкус; при́вкус; припра́ва; **2.** наслажда́ться [-лади́ться] (Т); получа́ть удово́льствие от (Р); придава́ть вкус (Д).
reluctan|ce [ri'lʌktəns] нежела́ние; нерасположе́ние; **~t** [-t] □ сопротивля́ющийся; неохо́тный.
rely [ri'lai]: ~ (up)on полага́ться [-ложи́ться] на (В), наде́яться на (В).
remain [ri'mein] ост(ав)а́ться; **~der** [-də] оста́ток.
remark [ri'mɑ:k] **1.** замеча́ние; заме́тка; **2.** замеча́ть [-е́тить]; выска́зываться [вы́сказаться] (on о П); **~able** [ri'mɑ:kəbl] □ замеча́тельный.
remedy ['remidi] **1.** сре́дство, лека́рство; ме́ра (for про́тив Р); **2.** исправля́ть [-а́вить]; выле́чивать [вы́лечить].
rememb|er [ri'membə] по́мнить; вспомина́ть [-о́мнить]; ~ me to ... переда́й(те) приве́т (Д); **~rance** [-brəns] воспомина́ние; па́мять *f*; сувени́р; ~s *pl.* приве́т.
remind [ri'maind] напомина́ть [-о́мнить] (Д; of о П *or* В); **~er** [-ə] напомина́ние.
reminiscence [remi'nisns] воспомина́ние.
remiss [ri'mis] □ неради́вый;

невнимáтельный; вя́лый; **~ion** [ri'miʃən] прощéние; отпущение (грехóв); освобождéние от уплáты; уменьшéние.
emit [ri'mit] отпускáть [-сти́ть] (грехи́); перес(ы)лáть (товáры); уменьшáть(ся) [умéньши́ть(ся)]; **~tance** [-əns] дéнежный перевóд.
emnant ['remnənt] остáток; пережи́ток. [[-стрóить].
emodel ['ri:mɔdl] перестрáивать
emonstra|nce [ri'mɔnstrəns] протéст; увещáние; **~te** [-treit] протестовáть; увещевáть, увещáть (with В).
emorse [ri'mɔ:s] угрызéния (*n/pl.*) сóвести; раскáяние; **~less** [-lis] □ безжáлостный.
emote [ri'mout] □ отдалённый; дáльний; уединённый; **~ness** [-nis] отдалённость *f*.
emov|al [ri'mu:vəl] переéзд; устранéние; смещéние; ~ van фургóн для перевóза мéбели; **~e** [ri'mu:v] *v/t.* удаля́ть [-ли́ть]; уноси́ть [унести́]; передвигáть [-и́нуть]; смещáть [смести́ть]; *v/i.* переезжáть [переéхать]; **~er** [-ə] перевóзчик мéбели.
emunerat|e [ri'mju:nəreit] вознаграждáть [-ради́ть]; оплáчивать [оплати́ть]; **~ive** [ri'mju:nərətiv] □ хорошó оплáчиваемый, вы́годный. [ние; возобновлéние.
enascence [ri'næsns] возрождé-
end [rend] [*irr.*] разрывáть(ся) [разорвáть(ся)]; раздирáть(ся) [разодрáть(ся)].
ender ['rendə] возд(ав)áть; окáзывать [оказáть] (услýгу и т. п.); представля́ть [-áвить]; изображáть [-рази́ть]; [за]плати́ть (Т for за В); ♪ исполня́ть [-óлнить]; переводи́ть [-вести́] (на другóй язы́к); растáпливать [-топи́ть] (сáло).
enew [ri'nju:] возобновля́ть [-нови́ть]; **~al** [-əl] возобновлéние.
enounce [ri'nauns] откáзываться [-зáться] от (Р); отрекáться [-рéчься] от (Р).
enovate ['renoveit] восстанáвливать [-нови́ть]; освежáть [-жи́ть].
enown [ri'naun] *rhet.* извéстность *f*; **~ed** [-d] *rhet.* знамени́тый.
ent[1] [rent] **1.** *pt.* и *p. pt.* от rend; **2.** прорéха; дырá.
ent[2] [~] **1.** арéндная плáта; квартúрная плáта; рéнта; **2.** нанимáть [наня́ть] и́ли сда(вá)ть (дом и т. п.); **~al** [rentl] арéндная плáта.
enunciation [rinʌnsi'eiʃən] отречéние; откáз (of от Р).
epair[1] [ri'pɛə] **1.** почи́нка, ремóнт; in (good) ~ в испрáвном состоя́нии; **2.** [по]чини́ть, [от]ремонти́ровать; исправля́ть [-áвить].
epair[2]: ~ to отправля́ться [-áвиться] в (В).
reparation [repə'reiʃən] возмещéние; исправлéние; *pol.* make ~s *pl.* плати́ть репарáции.
repartee [repɑ:'ti:] находчивость *f*; остроýмный отвéт.
repast [ri'pɑ:st] трáпеза.
repay [*irr.* (pay)] [ri'pei] отплáчивать [-лати́ть]; отдавáть дóлг (Д); возвращáть [-рати́ть] (дéньги); возмещáть [-ести́ть]; **~ment** [-mənt] возврáт (дéнег); возмещéние.
repeal [ri'pi:l] **1.** аннули́рование; **2.** аннули́ровать (*im*)*pf.*; отменя́ть [-ни́ть].
repeat [ri'pi:t] **1.** повторя́ть(ся) [-ри́ть(ся)]; говори́ть наизýсть; **2.** ♪ повторéние; знак повторéния; ☤ повтóрный закáз.
repel [ri'pel] оттáлкивать [оттолкнýть]; ⚔ отражáть [-рази́ть]; отвергáть [-éргнуть].
repent [ri'pent] раскáиваться [-кáяться] (of в П); **~ance** [-əns] раскáяние; **~ant** [-ənt] кáющийся.
repetition [repi'tiʃən] повторéние; повторéние наизýсть.
replace [ri:'pleis] стáвить, класть обрáтно; заменя́ть [-ни́ть]; замещáть [-ести́ть] (когó-либо); **~ment** [-mənt] замещéние.
replenish [ri'pleniʃ] пополня́ть [-óлнить]; **~ment** [-mənt] пополнéние (*a.* ⚔). [насы́щенный.
replete [ri'pli:t] напóлненный;
replica ['replikə] тóчная кóпия.
reply [ri'plai] **1.** отвéт (to на В); **2.** отвечáть [-éтить]; возражáть [-рази́ть].
report [ri'pɔ:t] **1.** отчёт; сообщéние; донесéние; доклáд; молвá, слух; свидéтельство; звук (взры́ва и т. п.); **2.** сообщáть [-щи́ть] (В *or* о П); доноси́ть [-нести́] о (П); доклáдывать [доложи́ть]; рапортовáть (*im*)*pf.* о (П); **~er** [-ə] доклáдчик (-ица); репортёр(ша F).
repos|e [ri'pouz] **1.** óтдых; покóй; **2.** *v/t.* давáть óтдых (Д); *v/i.* отдыхáть [отдохнýть] (*a.* ~ o. s.); покóиться; быть оснóванным (на П); **~itory** [ri'pɔzitəri] склад; храни́лище. [говор (Д).
reprehend [repri'hend] дéлать вы́-
represent [repri'zent] представля́ть [-áвить]; изображáть [-рази́ть]; *thea.* исполня́ть роль (Р); **~ation** [-zən'teiʃən] изображéние; представи́тельство; *thea.* представлéние; **~ative** □ [repri'zentətiv] **1.** характéрный; показáтельный; представля́ющий (of В); *parl.* представи́тельный; **2.** представи́тель(ница *f*) *m*; House of ⁓s *pl. Am. parl.* палáта представи́телей.
repress [ri'pres] подавля́ть [-ви́ть]; **~ion** [ri'preʃən] подавлéние.
reprimand ['reprimɑ:nd] **1.** вы́говор; **2.** дéлать вы́говор (Д).

reprisal [ri'praizəl] репрессáлия.
reproach [ri'proutʃ] **1.** упрёк; укóр; **2.** (~ a p. with a th.) упрекáть [-кнýть], укорять [-рить] (когó-либо в чём-либо).
reprobate ['reprobeit] распýтник; подлéц.
reproduc|e [ri:prə'dju:s] воспроизводить [-извести]; размножáться [-óжиться]; **~tion** [-'dʌkʃən] воспроизведéние; размножéние; репродýкция
reproof [ri'pru:f] порицáние; вы́говор.
reprove [ri'pru:v] порицáть; дéлать вы́говор (Д).
reptile ['reptail] пресмыкáющееся (живóтное).
republic [ri'pʌblik] респýблика; **~an** [-likən] **1.** республикáнский; **2.** республикáнец (-нка).
repudiate [ri'pju:dieit] отрекáться [-éчься] от (Р); отвергáть [-вéргнуть].
repugnan|ce [ri'pʌgnəns] отвращéние; нерасположéние; противорéчие; **~t** [-nənt] □ противный, оттáлкивающий.
repuls|e [ri'pʌls] **1.** откáз; отпóр; **2.** ⚔ отражáть [отразить]; оттáлкивать [оттолкнýть]; **~ive** [-iv] □ оттáлкивающий.
reput|able ['repjutəbl] □ почтéнный; **~ation** [repju:'teiʃən] репутáция; **~e** [ri'pju:t] óбщее мнéние; репутáция; **~ed** [ri'pju:tid] извéстный; предполагáемый; be ~ed (to be ...) слыть (за В).
request [ri'kwest] **1.** трéбование; прóсьба; ☤ спрос; in (great) ~ в (большóм) спрóсе; (*a. radio*) заявка; **2.** [по]просить (В or P or о П).
require [ri'kwaiə] нуждáться в (П); [по]трéбовать (Р); **~d** [-d] потрéбный; обязáтельный; трéбуемый; **~ment** [-mənt] трéбование; потрéбность *f*.
requisite ['rekwizit] **1.** необходимый; **2.** ~s *pl.* всё необходимое, нýжное; **~ion** [rekwi'ziʃən] **1.** официáльное предписáние; трéбование; ⚔ реквизиция; **2.** дéлать заявку на (В); ⚔ реквизировать (*im*)*pf*.
requital [ri'kwaitl] вознаграждéние; возмéздие.
requite [ri'kwait] отплáчивать [-латить] (Д for за В); вознаграждáть [-радить]; [ото]мстить за (В).
rescind [ri'sind] аннулировать (*im*)*pf*.
rescission [ri'siʒən] аннулировáние, отмéна.
rescue ['reskju:] **1.** освобождéние; спасéние; ⚖ незакóнное освобождéние; **2.** освобождáть [-бодить]; спасáть [-сти]; ⚖ незакóнно освобождáть.
research [ri'sə:tʃ] изыскáние (*mst pl.*); исслéдование (наýчное).
resembl|ance [ri'zembləns] схóдство (to с Т); **~e** [ri'zembl] походить на (В), имéть схóдство с (Т).
resent [ri'zent] обижáться [обидеться] за (В); **~ful** [-ful] □ обиженный; злопáмятный; **~ment** [-mənt] негодовáние; чýвство обиды.
reservation [rezə'veiʃən] оговóрка; скрывáние; *Am.* резервáция, заповéдник; резервировáние, предварительный закáз.
reserve [ri'zə:v] **1.** запáс; ☤ резéрвный фонд; ⚔ резéрв; сдéржанность *f*; скры́тность *f*; **2.** сберегáть [-рéчь]; приберегáть [-рéчь], отклáдывать [отложить]; резервировать (*im*)*pf*.; оставлять за собóй; **~d** [-d] □ скры́тный; закáзанный зарáнее.
reside [ri'zaid] проживáть; ~ in быть присýщим (Д); **~nce** ['rezidəns] местожительство; резидéнция; **~nt** [-dənt] **1.** проживáющий, живýщий; **2.** постоянный житель *m*; резидéнт.
residu|al [ri'zidjuəl] остáточный; **~e** ['rezidju:] остáток; осáдок.
resign [ri'zain] *v/t.* откáзываться [-зáться] от (дóлжности, прáва), оставлять [-áвить] (надéжду); слагáть [сложить] (обязанности); уступáть [-пить] (правá); ~ o. s. to покоряться [-риться] (Д); *v/i.* уходить в отстáвку; **~ation** [rezig'neiʃən] отстáвка; откáз от дóлжности; **~ed** [ri'zaind] □ покóрный, безрóпотный.
resilien|ce [ri'ziliəns] упрýгость *f*, эластичность *f*; **~t** [-t] упрýгий, эластичный.
resin ['rezin] **1.** смолá; **2.** [вы́]смолить.
resist [ri'zist] сопротивляться (Д); противостоять (Д); **~ance** [-əns] сопротивлéние; **~ant** [-ent] сопротивляющийся.
resolut|e ['rezəlu:t] □ решительный; **~ion** [rezə'lu:ʃən] резолюция; решительность *f*, решимость *f*.
resolve [ri'zɔlv] **1.** *v/t.* растворять [-орить]; *fig.* решáть [решить], разрешáть [-шить]; *v/i.* решáть(ся) [решить(ся)]; ~ (up)on решáться [-шиться] на (В); **2.** решéние; **~d** [-d] □ пóлный решимости.
resonant ['reznənt] □ звýчный, резонирующий.
resort [ri'zɔ:t] **1.** прибéжище; курóрт; summer ~ дáчное мéсто; **2.** ~ to: прибегáть [-éгнуть] к (Д); чáсто посещáть (В).
resound [ri'zaund] [про]звучáть, оглашáть(ся) [огласить(ся)]; отражáть [-разить] (звук).
resource [ri'sɔ:s] ресýрс; срéдство; возмóжность *f*; нахóдчивость *f*; **~ful** [-ful] □ нахóдчивый.

respect [ri'spekt] **1.** уважéние; отношéние; почтéние (of к Д); ~s *pl.* привéт, поклóн; **2.** *v/t.* уважáть, почитáть; **~able** [-əbl] □ почтéнный; представи́тельный; *part.* ✝ соли́дный; **~ful** [-ful] □ почти́тельный; **~ing** [-iŋ] относи́тельно (Р); **~ive** [-iv] □ соответ́ственный; we went to our ~ places мы пошли́ по местáм; **~ively** [-ivli] и́ли; соответ́ственно.

respirat|ion [respə'reiʃən] дыхáние; вдох и вы́дох; **~or** ['respəreitə] респирáтор; противогáз.

respire [ris'paiə] дышáть; переводи́ть дыхáние.

respite ['respait] переды́шка; отсрóчка.

respond [ris'pɔnd] отвечáть [-éтить]; ~ to реаги́ровать на; отзывáться [отозвáться] на (В).

response [ris'pɔns] отвéт; *fig.* óтклик; óтзыв.

responsi|bility [rispɔnsə'biliti] отвéтственность *f*; **~ble** [ris'pɔnsəbl] отвéтственный (to пéред Т).

rest [rest] **1.** óтдых; покóй; лóже; опóра; **2.** *v/i.* отдыхáть [отдохнýть]; [по]лежáть; опирáться [оперéться] (on на В); *fig.* ~ (up)on оснóвываться [-овáться] на (П); *v/t.* давáть óтдых (Д).

restaurant ['restərɔ:ŋ] ресторáн.

restitution [resti'tju:ʃən] возврáт (об имýществе); восстановлéние; возмещéние убы́тков.

restive ['restiv] □ норови́стый (о лóшади); упря́мый.

restless ['restlis] непосéдливый; беспокóйный, неугомóнный; **~ness** [-nis] непосéдливость *f*; неугомóнность *f*.

restorat|ion [resto'reiʃən] реставрáция; восстановлéние; **~ive** [ris'tɔrətiv] укрепля́ющий, тони́ческий.

restore [ris'tɔ:] восстанáвливать [-нови́ть]; возвращáть [-рати́ть]; *paint.* реставри́ровать (*im*)*pf.*; ~ to health вылéчивать [вы́лечить].

restrain [ris'trein] сдéрживать [-жáть]; задéрживать [-жáть]; подавля́ть [-ви́ть] (чýвства); **~t** [-t] сдéржанность *f*; ограничéние; обуздáние.

restrict [ris'trikt] ограни́чи(ва)ть; **~ion** [ris'trikʃən] ограничéние.

result [ri'zʌlt] **1.** результáт; исхóд; **2.** происте кáть [-éчь] (from от, из Р); ~ in приводи́ть [-вести́] к (Д).

resum|e [ri'zju:m] возобновля́ть [-ви́ть]; получáть обрáтно; резюми́ровать (*im*)*pf.*; **~ption** [ri'zʌmpʃən] возобновлéние; продолжéние.

resurrection [rezə'rekʃən] воскресéние; воскрешéние (обы́чая и т. п.).

resuscitate [ri'sʌsiteit] воскрешáть [-еси́ть]; оживля́ть [-ви́ть].

retail 1. ['ri:teil] рóзничная продáжа; by ~ в рóзницу; *attr.* рóзничный; **2.** [ri:'teil] продавáть(ся) в рóзницу; **~er** [-ə] рóзничный торгóвец.

retain [ri'tein] удéрживать [-жáть]; сохраня́ть [-ни́ть].

retaliat|e [ri'tælieit] отплáчивать [-лати́ть] (тем же); **~ion** [ritæli'eiʃən] отплáта, возмéздие.

retard [ri'tɑ:d] задéрживать [-жáть]; замедля́ть [-éдлить]; запáздывать [запоздáть].

retention [ri'tenʃən] удержáние; сохранéние.

reticent ['retisənt] сдéржанный; молчали́вый.

retinue ['retinju:] сви́та.

retir|e [ri'taiə] *v/t.* увольня́ть в отстáвку; изымáть из обращéния; *v/i.* выходи́ть в отстáвку; удаля́ться [-ли́ться]; уединя́ться [-ни́ться]; **~ed** [-d] □ уединённый; отставнóй, в отстáвке; ~ pay пéнсия; **~ement** [-mənt] отстáвка; уединéние; **~ing** [-riŋ] скрóмный, застéнчивый.

retort [ri'tɔ:t] **1.** рéзкий (и́ли нахóдчивый) отвéт; ⚗ retóрта; **2.** отпари́ровать *pf.* (кóлкость); возражáть [-рази́ть].

retouch ['ri:tʌtʃ] дéлать попрáвки в (П); *phot.* ретуши́ровать (*im*)*pf.*

retrace [ri'treis] прослéживать до истóчника; ~ one's steps возвращáться по свои́м следáм (*a. fig.*).

retract [ri'trækt] отрекáться [отрéчься] от (Р); брать назáд (словá и т. п.); втя́гивать [втянýть].

retreat [ri'tri:t] **1.** отступлéние (*part.* ⚔); уединéние; пристáнище; ⚔ отбóй; ⚔ вечéрняя заря́; **2.** уходи́ть [уйти́]; удаля́ться [-ли́ться]; (*part.* ⚔) отступáть [-пи́ть].

retrench [ri'trentʃ] урéз(ыв)ать, сокращáть [-рати́ть] (расхóды).

retrieve [ri'tri:v] (снóва) находи́ть [найти́]; восстанáвливать [-нови́ть].

retro... ['retro(u), 'ri:tro(u)] обрáтно...; **~active** [retrou'æktiv] имéющий обрáтную си́лу; **~grade** ['retrougreid] **1.** ретрогрáдный; реакциóнный; **2.** регресси́ровать; **~gression** [retrou'greʃən] регрéсс, упáдок; **~spect** ['retrouspekt] взгляд на прóшлое; **~spective** [retrou'spektiv] □ ретроспекти́вный; имéющий обрáтную си́лу.

return [ri'tə:n] **1.** возвращéние; возврáт; ✝ оборóт; дохóд, при́быль *f*; отдáча; результáт вы́боров; *attr.* обрáтный (билéт и т. п.); many happy ~s of the day поздравля́ю с днём рождéния; in ~ в обмéн (for на В); в отвéт; by ~ (of post) с обрáтной пóчтой; ~ ticket обрáтный билéт; **2.** *v/i.* возвращáться [-рати́ться]; вернýться *pf.*;

v/t. возвращáть [-ратúть]; вернýть *pf.*; отплáчивать [-латúть]; приносúть [-нестú] (дохóд); присылáть назáд; отвечáть [-éтить]; *parl.* изб(и)рáть. [воссоединéние.]
reunion ['ri:'ju:njən] собрáние;
revalorization [ri:væləraiˈzeiʃən] переоцéнка.
reveal [riˈvi:l] обнарýжи(ва)ть; откры́(вá)ть; **~ing** [-iŋ] обнарýживающий; показáтельный.
revel [revl] **1.** пировáть; упú(вá)ться (in T); **2.** пирýшка.
revelation [reviˈleiʃən] откровéние; обнарýжéние; откры́тие.
revel|(l)er ['revlə] гулякá *m*; **~ry** [-ri] разгýл, кутёж.
revenge [riˈvendʒ] **1.** месть *f*; ревáнш; отмéстка; **2** [ото]мстúть за (В); **~ful** [-ful] □ мстúтельный.
revenue ['revinju:] (годовóй) дохóд; *pl.* дохóдные статьú *f/pl.*; ~ board, ~ office департáмент госудáрственных сбóров.
reverberate [reˈvə:bəreit] отражáть(ся) [отразúть(ся)].
revere [riˈviə] уважáть, почитáть; **~nce** ['revərəns] **1.** почтéние; **2.** уважáть; благоговéть пéред (T); **~nd** [-d] **1.** почтéнный; **2.** *eccl.* преподóбие.
reverent(ial) ['revərənt, revəˈrenʃəl] почтúтельный; пóлный благоговéния.
reverie ['revəri] мечты́ *f/pl.*; мечтáтельность *f.*
revers|al [riˈvə:səl] перемéна; обрáтный ход; отмéна; изменéние; **~e** [riˈvə:s] **1.** обрáтная сторонá; перемéна; противополóжное; **~s** *pl.* преврáтности *f/pl.*; **2.** □ обрáтный; противополóжный; **3.** поворáчивать назáд; ⊕ давáть обрáтный ход; ⚖ отменять [-нúть]; **~ion** [riˈvə:ʃən] возвращéние; *biol.* атавúзм.
revert [riˈvə:t] возвращáться [-ратúться] (в прéжнее состояние úли к вопрóсу).
review [riˈvju:] **1.** обзóр; провéрка; ⚖ пересмóтр; ⚔, ⚓ смотр; обозрéние (журнáл); рецéнзия; **2.** пересмáтривать [-смотрéть]; писáть рецéнзию о (П); обозрé(вá)ть (В); ⚔, ⚓ производúть смотр (P).
revile [riˈvail] оскорблять [-бúть].
revis|e [riˈvaiz] пересмáтривать [-смотрéть]; исправлять [-áвить]; **~ion** [riˈviʒən] пересмóтр; ревúзия; испрáвленное издáние.
reviv|al [riˈvaivəl] возрождéние; оживлéние; **~e** [riˈvaiv] приходúть úли приводúть в чýвство; оживлять [-вúть]; ожú(вá)ть.
revocation [revəˈkeiʃən] отмéна, аннулúрование (закóна и т. п.).
revoke [riˈvouk] *v/t.* отменять [-нúть] (закóн и т. п.); *v/i.* дéлать ренóнс.
revolt [riˈvoult] **1.** восстáние; мятéж; **2.** *v/i.* восст(ав)áть; *fig.* отпадáть [отпáсть] (from от P); *v/t. fig.* оттáлкивать [оттолкнýть].
revolution [revəˈlu:ʃən] круговóе вращéние; ⊕ оборóт; *pol.* революция; **~ary** [-əri] **1.** революциóнный; **2.** революционéр(ка); **~ize** [-aiz] революционизúровать (*im*)*pf.*
revolv|e [riˈvɔlv] *v/i.* вращáться; периодúчески возвращáться; *v/t.* вращáть; обдýм(ыв)ать; **~ing** [-iŋ] вращáющийся; поворóтный.
revulsion [riˈvʌlʃən] внезáпное изменéние (чувств и т. п.).
reward [riˈwɔ:d] **1.** наградá; вознаграждéние; **2.** вознаграждáть [-радúть]; награждáть [-радúть].
rewrite ['ri:ˈrait] [*irr.* (write)] перепúсывать [-сáть].
rhapsody ['ræpsədi] рапсóдия.
rheumatism ['ru:mətizm] ревматúзм.
rhubarb ['ru:bɑ:b] ⚘ ревéнь *m.*
rhyme [raim] **1.** рúфма; (рифмóванный) стих; without ~ or reason без смы́сла; **2.** рифмовáть(ся) (with, to с T).
rhythm [riðm] ритм; **~ic(al)** [-mik, -mikəl] ритмúчный, ритмúческий.
rib [rib] **1.** ребрó; **2.** ⊕ укреплять рёбрами.
ribald ['ribəld] грýбый, непристóйный.
ribbon ['ribən] лéнта; **~s** *pl.* клóчья *m/pl.*
rice [rais] рис.
rich [ritʃ] □ богáтый (in T); роскóшный; плодорóдный (о пóчве); жúрный (о пúще); пóлный (тон); густóй (о крáсках); ~ milk цéльное молокó; **~es** ['ritʃiz] *pl.* богáтство; сокрóвища *n/pl.*
rick [rik] ⚒ стог, скирд(á).
ricket|s ['rikits] рахúт; **~y** [-i] рахитúчный; шáткий.
rid [rid] [*irr.*] избавлять [-áвить] (of от P); get ~ of отдéл(ыв)аться от (P), избавляться [-áвиться] от (P).
ridden [ridn] **1.** *p. pt.* от ride; **2.** (в слóжных словáх) одержúмый (стрáхом, предрассýдками и т. п.), под влáстью (чегó-либо).
riddle [ridl] **1.** загáдка; решетó; **2.** изрешéчивать [-шетúть].
ride [raid] **1.** уздá верхóм; катáние; прогýлка; **2.** [*irr.*] *v/i.* éздить, [по]éхать (на лóшади, автомобúле и т. п.); катáться верхóм; *v/t.* éздить, [по]éхать на (П); катáть (на спинé); **~r** ['raidə] верховóй; наéздник (-ица) (в цúрке); всáдник (-ица).
ridge [ridʒ] гóрный кряж, хребéт; ⌂ конёк (кры́ши); ⚒ грядка.
ridicul|e ['ridikju:l] **1.** осмеяние, насмéшка; **2.** высмéивать [вы-

смеять]; **~ous** [ri'dikjuləs] □ нелепый, смешной.
riding ['raidiŋ] верховая езда; *attr.* верховой.
rife [raif] □: ~ with изобилующий (T).
riff-raff ['rifræf] подонки (общества) *m/pl.*
rifle [raifl] **1.** винтовка; **2.** [о]грабить; **~man** ⚔ стрелок.
rift [rift] трещина, расселина.
rig [rig] **1.** ⚓ оснастка; F наряд; **2.** оснащать [оснастить]; F наряжать [-ядить]; **~ging** ['rigiŋ] ⚓ такелаж, снасти *f/pl.*
right [rait] **1.** □ правильный, верный; правый; be ~ быть правым; put ~ приводить в порядок; **2.** *adv.* прямо; правильно; справедливо; как раз; ~ away сразу; ~ on прямо вперёд; **3.** право; справедливость *f*; the ~s *pl.* (of a story) настоящие факты *m/pl.*; by ~ of на основании (P); on (*or* to) the ~ направо; **4.** приводить в порядок; выпрямлять(ся) [выпрямить(ся)]; **~eous** ['raitʃəs] □ праведный; **~ful** ['raitful] □ справедливый; законный.
rigid ['ridʒid] □ негнущийся, негибкий, жёсткий; *fig.* суровый; непреклонный; **~ity** [ri'dʒiditi] жёсткость *f*; непреклонность *f.*
rigo(u)r ['rigə] суровость *f*; строгость *f.*
rigorous [-rəs] □ суровый; строгий.
rim [rim] ободок; край; обод; оправа (очков).
rime [raim] иней; изморозь *f*; = rhyme.
rind [raind] кора, кожура, корка.
ring [riŋ] **1.** кольцо; круг; звон (колоколов); звонок; ✝, *sport* ринг; **2.** надевать кольцо на (B); (*mst* ~ in, round, about) окружать [-жить]; [*irr.*] [за]звучать; ~ the bell [по]звонить (у двери); звонить в колокол; ~ a p. up позвонить кому-нибудь по телефону; **~-leader** зачинщик (-ица); **~let** ['riŋlit] колечко; локон.
rink [riŋk] каток, скетинг-ринк.
rinse [rins] [вы]полоскать.
riot ['raiət] **1.** бунт; буйство; разгул; run ~ вести себя буйно; разгуливаться [-ляться]; **2.** принимать участие в бунте; предаваться разгулу; **~er** [-ə] бунтарь *m*; **~ous** [-əs] □ буйный, разгульный.
rip [rip] [рас]пороть(ся).
ripe [raip] □ зрелый (*a. fig.*); спелый; готовый; **~n** [raipn] созре(ва)ть, [по]спеть; **~ness** ['raipnis] спелость *f*; зрелость *f.*
ripple [ripl] **1.** рябь *f*, зыбь *f*; журчание; **2.** покрывать(ся) рябью; журчать.
rise [raiz] **1.** повышение; восход; подъём; выход (на поверхность); возвышенность *f*; происхождение; take (one's) ~ происходить [произойти]; **2.** [*irr.*] подниматься [-няться]; всходить [взойти]; вст(ав)ать; восст(ав)ать; нач(ин)аться; ~ to быть в состоянии справиться с (T); **~n** [rizn] *p. pt.* от rise.
rising ['raiziŋ] вставание; возвышение; восстание; восход.
risk [risk] **1.** риск; run a (*or* the) ~ рисковать [-кнуть]; **2.** отваживаться на (B); рисковать [-кнуть] (T); **~y** ['riski] □ рискованный.
rit|e [rait] обряд, церемония; **~ual** ['ritjuəl] **1.** ритуальный; **2.** ритуал.
rival ['raivəl] **1.** соперник (-ица); ✝ конкурент; **2.** соперничающий; **3.** соперничать с (T); **~ry** [-ri] соперничество; соревнование.
rive [raiv] [*irr.*] раскалывать(ся) [расколоть(ся)].
river ['rivə] река; поток (*a. fig.*); **~side** берег реки; *attr.* прибрежный.
rivet ['rivit] **1.** заклёпка; **2.** заклёпывать [-лепать]; *fig.* приковывать [-овать] (B к Д).
rivulet ['rivjulit] ручей; речушка.
road [roud] дорога; путь *m*; *mst* ~s *pl.* ⚓ рейд (*a.* ~stead); **~ster** ['roudstə] дорожный велосипед; родстер (двухместный открытый автомобиль *m*); **~way** мостовая.
roam [roum] *v/t.* бродить по (Д); *v/i.* странствовать; скитаться.
roar [rɔ:] **1.** [за]реветь; [за]грохотать; ~ with laughter хохотать во всё горло; **2.** рёв; грохот; громкий хохот.
roast [roust] **1.** [из]жарить(ся); калить (орехи и т. п.); **2.** жареный; ~ meat жареное, жаркое.
rob [rɔb] [о]грабить; *fig.* лишать [-шить] (of P); **~ber** ['rɔbə] грабитель *m*; **~bery** [-ri] грабёж.
robe [roub] мантия (судьи); ряса; халат.
robust [ro'bʌst] □ крепкий, здоровый.
rock [rɔk] **1.** скала; утёс; горная порода; ~ crystal горный хрусталь *m*; **2.** качать(ся) [качнуть (-ся)]; убаюк(ив)ать.
rocket ['rɔkit] ракета; *attr.* ракетный; **~-powered** с ракетным двигателем.
rocking-chair кресло-качалка.
rocky ['rɔki] каменистый; скалистый.
rod [rɔd] жезл; прут (*a.* ⊕); розга, розги; удочка; ⊕ шток; стержень *m*; род (мера длины, около 5-ти метров).
rode [roud] *pt.* от ride.
rodent ['roudənt] грызун.
rodeo [rou'deiou] *Am.* загон для клеймения скота; состязание ковбоев.

roe [rou] косу́ля; икра́; soft ~ молоки *n/pl.*
rogu|e [roug] жу́лик, моше́нник; **~ish** ['rougiʃ] жуликова́тый, моше́ннический.
roister ['rɔistə] бесчи́нствовать.
rôle [roul] *thea.* роль *f* (*a. fig.*).
roll [roul] **1.** свёрток (мате́рии и т. п.); руло́н; кату́шка; рее́стр, спи́сок; раска́т (гро́ма); бу́лочка; **2.** *v/t.* ката́ть, [по]кати́ть; враща́ть; раска́тывать [-ката́ть] (те́сто); прока́тывать [-ката́ть] (мета́лл); ~ up свёртывать [сверну́ть]; ска́тывать [ската́ть]; *v/i.* ката́ться, [по]кати́ться; валя́ться (in в П); (о гро́ме) грохота́ть; ⚓ име́ть бокову́ю ка́чку; **~-call** ⚔ перекли́чка; **~er** ['roulə] ро́лик; вал; ~ skate конёк на ро́ликах.
rollick ['rɔlik] шу́мно весели́ться.
rolling ['rouliŋ] прока́тный; холми́стый; ~ mill ⊕ прока́тный стан.
Roman ['roumən] **1.** □ ри́мский; **2.** ри́млянин (-янка); *typ.* прямо́й све́тлый шрифт.
romance [rə'mæns] **1.** ♪ рома́нс; рома́н; **2.** *fig.* прикра́шивать действи́тельность; **3.** ♀ рома́нский; **~r** [-ə] романи́ст (а́втор).
romantic [ro'mæntik] (**~ally**) романти́чный; **~ism** [-tisizm] романти́зм, рома́нтика; **~ist** [-tisist] рома́нтик.
romp [rɔmp] **1.** возня́; сорвиголова́ *m/f*; **2.** вози́ться, шу́мно игра́ть.
röntgenogram [rɔnt'genəgræm] рентгеногра́мма.
rood [ru:d] че́тверть а́кра = 0,1 гекта́ра; распя́тие.
roof [ru:f] **1.** кры́ша; ~ of the mouth нёбо; **2.** [по]кры́ть (дом); **~ing** ['ru:fiŋ] **1.** кро́вельный материа́л; **2.** кро́вля; ~ felt кро́вельный толь *m.*
rook [ruk] **1.** грач; *chess* ладья́; *fig.* моше́нник; **2.** обма́нывать [-ну́ть].
room [ru:m] **1.** ко́мната; ме́сто; помеще́ние; простра́нство; ~s *pl.* кварти́ра; ко́мнаты *f/pl.*; **2.** *Am.* жить квартира́нтом (-ткой); **~er** ['rumə] квартира́нт(ка), жиле́ц, жили́ца; **~mate** сожи́тель(ница *f*) *m*; **~y** ['rumi] □ просто́рный.
roost [ru:st] **1.** насе́ст; **2.** уса́живаться на насе́ст; *fig.* устра́иваться на́ ночь; **~er** ['ru:stə] пету́х.
root [ru:t] ко́рень *m*; strike ~ пуска́ть ко́рни; укореня́ться [-ни́ться]; ~ out вырыва́ть с ко́рнем (*a. fig.*); вы́искивать [вы́искать] (*a.* ~ up); **~ed** ['ru:tid] укорени́вшийся.
rope [roup] **1.** кана́т; верёвка; трос; ни́тка (же́мчуга, бус); F come to the end of one's ~ дойти́ до то́чки; know the ~s *pl.* знать все ходы́ и вы́ходы; **2.** свя́зывать верёвкой; привя́зывать кана́том; (*mst* ~ off) оцепля́ть кана́том.
rosary ['rouzəri] *eccl.* чётки *f/pl.*
rose [rouz] **1.** ро́за; се́тка (на ле́йке); ро́зовый цвет; **2.** *pt.* от rise.
rosin ['rɔzin] канифо́ль *f.*
rostrum ['rɔstrəm] ка́федра; трибу́на.
rosy ['rouzi] □ ро́зовый; румя́ный; *fig.* ра́дужный.
rot [rɔt] **1.** гние́ние; гниль *f*; **2.** *v/t.* [с]гнои́ть; *v/i.* сгни(ва́)ть, [с]гнить.
rota|ry ['routəri] враща́тельный; ротацио́нный; **~te** [rou'teit] враща́ть(ся); чередова́ть(ся); **~tion** [rou'teiʃən] враще́ние; чередова́ние; **~tory** [rou'teitəri]: *s.* rotary; ⚡ многофа́зный.
rote [rout]: by ~ *fig.* механи́чески.
rotten [rɔtn] □ гнило́й; испо́рченный; F отврати́тельный.
rouge [ru:ʒ] **1.** румя́на *n/pl.*; **2.** [на-] румя́нить(ся).
rough [rʌf] **1.** □ гру́бый; шерша́вый; шерохова́тый; косма́тый; бу́рный; неделика́тный; ~ and ready сде́ланный кое-ка́к, на́спех; грубова́тый; **2.** буя́н; **3.** ~ it перебива́ться с трудо́м; **~cast 1.** ⊕ штукату́рка намётом; **2.** на́черно разрабо́танный; **3.** ⊕ штукату́рить намётом; **~en** ['rʌfən] де́лать(ся) гру́бым, шерохова́тым; **~ness** ['rʌfnis] шерохова́тость *f*; гру́бость *f*; **~shod**: ride ~ over обходи́ться гру́бо, суро́во с (Т).
round [raund] **1.** □ кру́глый; кругово́й; прямо́й, и́скренний; ~ trip *Am.* пое́здка ту́да и обра́тно; **2.** *adv.* круго́м, вокру́г; обра́тно; (*often* ~ about) вокру́г да о́коло; all the year ~ кру́глый год; **3.** *prp.* вокру́г, круго́м (Р); за (В *or* Т); по (Д); **4.** круг; цикл; тур (в та́нце); *sport* ра́унд; обхо́д; объе́зд; 100 ~s ⚔ сто патро́нов; **5.** *v/t.* закругля́ть [-ли́ть]; огиба́ть [обогну́ть]; ~ up окружа́ть [-жи́ть]; *v/i.* закругля́ться [-ли́ться]; **~about** ['raundəbaut] **1.** око́льный; **2.** око́льный путь *m*; карусе́ль *f*; **~ish** ['raundiʃ] круглова́тый; **~-up** обла́ва.
rous|e [rauz] *v/t.* [раз]буди́ть; возбужда́ть [-уди́ть]; воодушевля́ть [-ви́ть]; ~ o. s. стряхну́ть лень; *v/i.* просыпа́ться [-сну́ться]; **~ing** ['rauziŋ] возбужда́ющий; бу́рный.
rout [raut] **1.** разгро́м; бе́гство; put to ~ разгроми́ть на́голову; обраща́ть в бе́гство; **2.** = put to ~; рыть ры́лом.
route [ru:t, ⚔ raut] путь *m*; ⚔ маршру́т.
routine [ru:'ti:n] **1.** заведённый поря́док; рути́на; **2.** рути́нный.
rove [rouv] скита́ться; броди́ть.
row[1] [rou] **1.** ряд; прогу́лка в ло́дке; **2.** грести́ (весло́м); пра́вить (ло́дкой).

row² [rau] F **1.** галдёж, гвалт; дра́ка; ссо́ра; **2.** задава́ть нагоня́й (Д).
row-boat ['roubout] гребна́я ло́дка.
rower ['rouə] гребе́ц (*wo*)*man*.
royal ['rɔiəl] □ короле́вский; великоле́пный; **~ty** [-ti] член короле́вской семьи́; короле́вская власть *f*; ~s *pl.* а́вторский гонора́р.
rub [rʌb] **1.** тре́ние; растира́ние; *fig.* препя́тствие; **2.** *v/t.* тере́ть; протира́ть [-тере́ть]; натира́ть [натере́ть]; ~ out стира́ть [стере́ть]; ~ up [от]полирова́ть; освежа́ть [-жи́ть] (в па́мяти); *v/i.* тере́ться (against о В); *fig.* ~ along, on проби́(ва́)ться с трудо́м.
rubber ['rʌbə] каучу́к; рези́на; рези́нка; *cards* ро́ббер; ~s *pl. Am.* гало́ши *f/pl.*; *attr.* рези́новый.
rubbish ['rʌbiʃ] му́сор; хлам; *fig.* вздор; глу́пости *f/pl.*
rubble [rʌbl] щебе́нь *m*; ⚠ бут.
ruby ['ru:bi] руби́н; руби́новый цвет.
rudder ['rʌdə] ⚓ руль *m*; ✈ руль поворо́та.
rudd|iness ['rʌdinis] краснота́; румя́нец; **~y** ['rʌdi] я́рко-кра́сный; румя́ный.
rude [ru:d] □ неотёсанный; гру́бый; неве́жливый; *fig.* кре́пкий (о здоро́вье).
rudiment ['ru:diment] *biol.* рудиме́нт, зача́ток; ~s *pl.* нача́тки *m/pl.*
rueful ['ru:ful] □ уны́лый, печа́льный.
ruff [rʌf] бры́жи *f/pl.*; *zo.* ёрш.
ruffian ['rʌfjən] грубия́н; хулига́н.
ruffle [rʌfl] **1.** манже́тка; рюш; сумато́ха; рябь *f*; **2.** [взъ]еро́шить (во́лосы); ряби́ть (во́ду); *fig.* наруша́ть споко́йствие (Р), [вс]трево́жить.
rug [rʌg] плед; ковёр, ко́врик; **~ged** ['rʌgid] □ неро́вный; шерохова́тый; суро́вый; пересечённый; ре́зкий.
ruin ['ruin] **1.** ги́бель *f*; разоре́ние; круше́ние (наде́жд и т. п.); *mst* ~s *pl.* разва́лины *f/pl.*; **2.** [по]губи́ть; разоря́ть [-ри́ть]; разруша́ть [-у́шить]; [о]бесче́стить; **~ous** ['ruinəs] □ разори́тельный; губи́тельный.
rul|e [ru:l] **1.** пра́вило; уста́в; правле́ние; власть *f*; лине́йка; as a ~ обы́чно; **2.** *v/t.* управля́ть (Т); постановля́ть [-ви́ть]; [на]линова́ть; [раз]графи́ть; ~ out исключа́ть [-чи́ть]; *v/i.* госпо́дствовать; **~er** ['ru:lə] прави́тель(ница *f*) *m*; лине́йка.
rum [rʌm] ром; *Am.* спиртно́й напи́ток.
Rumanian [ru(:)'meinjən] **1.** румы́нский; **2.** румы́н(ка).
rumble ['rʌmbl] **1.** громыха́ние; гро́хот; (*Am.* ~-seat) откидно́е сиде́нье; **2.** [за]громыха́ть; [за-]грохота́ть; [за]греме́ть (о гро́ме).
rumina|nt ['ru:minənt] жва́чное живо́тное; **~te** [-neit] жева́ть жва́чку; *fig.* размышля́ть [-мы́слить].
rummage ['rʌmidʒ] **1.** распрода́жа ме́лочей (с благотвори́тельной це́лью); **2.** *v/t.* выта́скивать [вы́тащить]; переры́(ва́)ть; *v/i.* ры́ться.
rumo(u)r ['ru:mə] **1.** слух; молва́; **2.** it is ~ed ... хо́дят слу́хи ...
rump [rʌmp] огу́зок.
rumple [rʌmpl] [с]мять; [взъ]еро́шить (во́лосы, пе́рья и т. п.).
run [rʌn] **1.** [*irr.*] *v/i. com.* бе́гать, [по]бежа́ть; [по]те́чь; расплы́(ва́)ться (о кра́сках и т. п.); враща́ться, рабо́тать (о маши́не); гласи́ть; ~ across a p. натáлкиваться [натолкну́ться] на (В); ~ away убега́ть [убежа́ть]; понести́ *pf.* (о ло́шади); ~ down сбега́ть [сбежа́ть]; остана́вливаться [-нови́ться (о часа́х и т. п.); истоща́ться [-щи́ться]; ~ dry иссяка́ть [-я́кнуть]; ~ for *parl.* выставля́ть свою́ кадидату́ру на (В); ~ into впада́ть [впасть] в (В); доходи́ть [дойти́] до (Р); встреча́ть [-е́тить]; ~ on продолжа́ться [-до́лжиться]; говори́ть без у́молку; ~ out, short конча́ться [ко́нчиться]; ~ through прочита́ть бе́гло; прома́тывать]-мота́ть]; ~ to достига́ть [-и́гнуть] (су́ммы); ~ up to доходи́ть [дойти́] до (Р); **2.** *v/t.* пробега́ть [-бежа́ть] (расстоя́ние); нали́(ва́)ть (во́ду и т. п.); вести́ (дела́); выгоня́ть в по́ле (скот); вонза́ть [-зи́ть]; управля́ть (конто́рой и т. п.); проводи́ть [-вести́] (Т, over по Д); ~ the blockade прорва́ть блока́ду; ~ down задавля́ть [-ви́ть]; *fig.* говори́ть пло́хо о (П); унижа́ть [уни́зить]; переутомля́ть [-ми́ть]; ~ over переезжа́ть [-е́хать], задавля́ть [-ви́ть]; прочита́ть бе́гло; ~ up взду(ва́)ть (це́ны); возводи́ть [-вести́] (зда́ние); ~ up a bill at [за]должа́ть (Д); **3.** бег; пробе́г; ход, рабо́та, де́йствие (маши́ны); тече́ние, ход (вре́мени); ряд; пое́здка, прогу́лка; ☤ спрос; управле́ние; *Am.* руче́й, пото́к; заго́н; па́стбище; разреше́ние по́льзоваться (of T); the common ~ обыкнове́нные лю́ди *m/pl.*; *thea.* have a ~ of 20 nights идти́ два́дцать вечеро́в подря́д (о пье́се); in the long ~ со вре́менем; в конце́ концо́в.
run|about ['rʌnəbaut] лёгкий автомоби́ль *m*; **~away** беглéц; дезерти́р.
rung¹ [rʌŋ] *p. pt.* от ring.
rung² [~] ступе́нька.
run|let ['rʌnlit], **~nel** ['rʌnl] руче́ёк; кана́ва.
runner ['rʌnə] бегу́н; по́лоз (у сане́й); побе́г (расте́ния); **~-up** [-'rʌp] занима́ющий второ́е ме́сто (в состяза́нии).

running ['rʌniŋ] **1.** бегу́щий; беговóй; текýщий; two days ~ два дня подря́д; ~ fire ⚔ бе́глый огóнь *m*; ~ hand бе́глый пóчерк; **2.** бе́ганье; бег; бегá *m/pl.*; де́йствие; **~-board** поднóжка.

runway ['rʌnwei] ✈ взлётно-посáдочная полосá.

rupture ['rʌptʃə] **1.** перелóм; разры́в; ⚕ гры́жа; **2.** разрывáть [разорвáть] (*a. fig.*); прор(ы)вáть.

rural ['ruərəl] □ се́льский, дереве́нский

rush [rʌʃ] **1.** ⚘ тростни́к, камы́ш; нáтиск; † напл́ыв (покупáтелей); ~ hours *pl.* часы́-пик; ⚔ перебе́жка; **2.** *v/i.* мчáться; бросáться [брóситься]; носи́ться, [по]нести́сь; ~ into бросáться необдýманно в (В); ~ into print сли́шком поспе́шно выступáть в печáти; *v/t.* мчать; увлекáть [увле́чь]; [по]торопи́ть; *fig.* ⚔ брать стреми́тельным нáтиском.

russet ['rʌsit] крáсно-кори́чневый.

Russia ['rʌʃə] Росси́я; **~n** [-n] **1.** рýсский; **2.** рýсский, рýсская; рýсский язы́к.

rust [rʌst] **1.** ржáвчина; **2.** [за]ржавéть.

rustic ['rʌstik] **1.** (~ally) дереве́нский; простóй; грýбый; **2.** се́льский жи́тель *m*.

rustle [rʌsl] **1.** [за]шелесте́ть; **2.** ше́лест, шóрох.

rust|less ['rʌstlis] нержаве́ющий; **~y** ['rʌsti] заржáвленный, ржáвый; порыже́вший.

rut [rʌt] колея́ (*a. fig.*); ⊕ фальц, жёлоб; *zo.* те́чка.

ruthless ['ru:θlis] □ безжáлостный.

rutted ['rʌtid], **rutty** ['rʌti] изре́занный колея́ми.

rye [rai] ⚘ рожь *f*.

S

sabotage ['sæbotɑ:ʒ] **1.** саботáж; **2.** саботи́ровать (В) (*a.* ~ on *a th.*) (*im*)*pf*.

sabre ['seibə] сáбля, шáшка.

sack [sæk] **1.** грабёж; мешóк, куль *m*; сак (пальтó); **2.** класть, ссыпáть в мешóк; [о]грáбить; F увольня́ть [увóлить] (В); **~cloth, ~ing** ['sækiŋ] дерю́га, холст.

sacrament ['sækrəmənt] *eccl.* тáинство, причáстие.

sacred ['seikrid] □ святóй; свяще́нный; ♪ духóвный.

sacrifice ['sækrifais] **1.** же́ртва; жертвоприноше́ние; at a ~ † себе́ в убы́ток; **2.** [по]же́ртвовать.

sacrileg|e ['sækrilidʒ] святотáтство, кощýнство; **~ious** [sækri'lidʒəs] □ святотáтственный.

sad [sæd] □ печáльный, грýстный; досáдный; тýсклый.

sadden [sædn] [о]печáлить(ся).

saddle [sædl] **1.** седлó; **2.** [о]седлáть; *fig.* взвáливать [-ли́ть] (upon на В); обременя́ть [-ни́ть]; **~r** шóрник.

sadism ['sɑ:dizm] сади́зм.

sadness ['sædnis] печáль *f*, грусть *f*.

safe [seif] **1.** □ невреди́мый; надёжный; безопáсный; (бýдучи) в безопáсности; **2.** сейф, несгорáемый шкаф; шкаф для прови́зии; **~-conduct** охрáнное свидéтельство; **~guard 1.** охрáна; предосторóжность *f*; защи́та; **2.** охраня́ть [-ни́ть]; защищáть [-ити́ть].

safety ['seifti] **1.** безопáсность *f*; надёжность *f*; **2.** безопáсный; **~-pin** англи́йская булáвка; **~-razor** безопáсная бри́тва.

saffron ['sæfrən] шафрáн.

sag [sæg] оседáть [осе́сть]; прогибáться [-гнýться]; обвисáть [-и́снуть]; ⚓ отклоня́ться от кýрса.

sagacious [sə'geiʃəs] проницáтельный, прозорли́вый; **~ty** [sə'gæsiti] проницáтельность *f*, прозорли́вость *f*.

sage [seidʒ] **1.** □ мýдрый; разýмный; **2.** мудре́ц; ⚘ шалфе́й.

said [sed] *pt.* и *p. pt.* от say.

sail [seil] **1.** пáрус; плáвание под парусáми; пáрусное сýдно; **2.** *v/i.* идти́ под парусáми; плáвать, [по-] плы́ть; отплы́(вá)ть; носи́ться, [по]нести́сь (об облакáх); *v/t.* управля́ть (сýдном); плáвать по (Д); **~-boat** *Am.* пáрусная лóдка; **~or** ['seilə] моря́к, матрóс; be a (good) bad ~ (не) страдáть морскóй болéзнью; **~-plane** планёр.

saint [seint] **1.** святóй; **2.** причисля́ть к ли́ку святы́х; **~ly** ['seintli] *adj.* святóй.

sake [seik]: for the ~ of рáди (Р); for my ~ рáди меня́.

sal(e)able ['seiləbl] хóдкий (товáр).

salad ['sæləd] салáт.

salary ['lsæləri] **1.** жáлованье; **2.** плати́ть жáлованье (Д).

sale [seil] продáжа; распродáжа; аукциóн; be for ~, be on ~ продавáться.

sales|man продаве́ц; *Am.* коммивояжёр; **~woman** продавщи́ца.

salient ['seiljənt] выдаю́щийся, выступáющий; вы́пуклый.

saline ['seilain] солянóй; солёный.

saliva [sə'laivə] 🕮 слюнá.

sallow ['sælou] болéзненный, желтовáтый (о цвéте лицá).

sally ['sæli] **1.** ⚔ вы́лазка; ре́плика,

острота́; 2. ⚔ де́лать вы́лазку; ~ forth, ~ out отправля́ться [-а́виться].
salmon ['sæmən] сёмга; ло́со́сь *m*.
saloon [sə'lu:n] зал; сало́н (на парохо́де); сало́н-ваго́н; *Am.* бар, пивна́я.
salt [sɔ:lt] 1. соль *f*; *fig.* остроу́мие; old ~ быва́лый моря́к; 2. солёный; жгу́чий; е́дкий; 3. [по]соли́ть; заса́ливать [-соли́ть]; **~-cellar** соло́нка; **~petre** ['sɔ:ltpitə] сели́тра; **~y** ['sɔ:lti] солёный.
salubrious [sə'lu:briəs] □, **salutary** ['sæljutəri] □ благотво́рный; поле́зный для здоро́вья.
salut|ation [sælju'teiʃən] приве́тствие; **~e** [sə'lu:t] 1. приве́тствие; ⚔ салю́т; ⚔ отда́ние че́сти; 2. приве́тствовать; ⚔ салютова́ть (*im*)*pf.* (Д); ⚔ отдава́ть честь (Д).
salvage ['sælvidʒ] 1. спасе́ние (иму́щества и́ли су́дна); спасённое иму́щество; подъём (затону́вших судо́в); 2. спаса́ть [спасти́] (иму́щество от огня́, су́дно на мо́ре и т. п.).
salvation [sæl'veiʃən] спасе́ние; ♀ Army 'Армия спасе́ния.
salve[1] [sælv] = salvage.
salve[2] [sɑ:v] 1. сре́дство для успоко́ения; 2. успока́ивать [-ко́ить] (со́весть); сгла́живать [сгла́дить] (тру́дность).
salvo ['sælvou] (оруди́йный) залп; *fig.* взрыв аплодисме́нтов.
same [seim]: the ~ тот же са́мый; та же са́мая; то же са́мое; it is all the ~ to me мне всё равно́.
sample [sɑ:mpl] 1. про́ба; обра́зчик, образе́ц; 2. [по]про́бовать; отбира́ть образцы́ (Р).
sanct|ify ['sæŋktifai] освяща́ть [-яти́ть]; **~imonious** [sæŋkti'mounjəs] □ ха́нжеский; **~ion** ['sæŋkʃən] 1. са́нкция; утвержде́ние; принуди́тельная ме́ра; 2. санкциони́ровать (*im*)*pf.*; утвержда́ть [-рди́ть]; **~ity** [-titi] свя́тость *f*; **~uary** [-tjuəri] святи́лище; убе́жище.
sand [sænd] 1. песо́к; ~s *pl.* песча́ный пляж; о́тмель *f*; пески́ *m/pl.* (пусты́ни); 2. посыпа́ть песко́м.
sandal [sændl] санда́лия.
sandwich ['sænwidʒ, -witʃ] 1. бутербро́д, са́ндвич; 2. просла́ивать [-сло́ить].
sandy ['sændi] песча́ный; песо́чный; песо́чного цве́та.
sane [sein] норма́льный; здра́вый; здравомы́слящий.
sang [sæŋ] *pt.* от sing.
sanguin|ary ['sæŋgwinəri] □ крова́вый; кровожа́дный; **~e** [-gwin] сангвини́ческий; оптимисти́ческий.
sanitary ['sænitəri] □ санита́рный; гигиени́ческий.
sanit|ation [sæni'teiʃən] оздоровле́ние; улучше́ние санита́рных усло́вий; санитари́я; **~y** ['sæniti] здра́вый ум.
sank [sæŋk] *pt.* от sink.
sap [sæp] 1. сок (расте́ний); *fig.* жи́зненные си́лы *f/pl.*; ⚔ са́па; 2. истоща́ть [-щи́ть]; подка́пывать [-копа́ть]; **~less** ['sæplis] худосо́чный; истощённый; **~ling** ['sæpliŋ] молодо́е деревцо́.
sapphire ['sæfaiə] *min.* сапфи́р.
sappy ['sæpi] со́чный; *fig.* си́льный.
sarcasm ['sɑ:kæzm] сарка́зм.
sardine [sɑ:'di:n] сарди́н(к)а.
sardonic [sɑ:'dɔnik] (~ally) сардони́ческий.
sash [sæʃ] куша́к, по́яс.
sash-window подъёмное окно́.
sat [sæt] *pt.* и *p. pt.* от sit.
satchel ['sætʃəl] (шко́льный) ра́нец.
sate [seit] насыща́ть [-ы́тить]; пресыща́ть [-ы́тить].
sateen [sæ'ti:n] сати́н.
satellite ['sætəlait] сателли́т (*a. astr.*); приспе́шник; *astr.* спу́тник.
satiate ['seiʃieit] пресыща́ть [-ы́тить]; насыща́ть [-ы́тить].
satin ['sætin] атла́с.
satir|e ['sætaiə] сати́ра; **~ist** ['sætərist] сати́рик; **~ize** [-raiz] высме́ивать [вы́смеять].
satisfaction [sætis'fækʃən] удовлетворе́ние.
satisfactory [sætis'fæktəri] удовлетвори́тельный.
satisfy ['sætisfai] удовлетворя́ть [-ри́ть]; утоля́ть [-ли́ть] (го́лод, любопы́тство и т. п.); выполня́ть [вы́полнить] (обяза́тельства); убежда́ть [убеди́ть].
saturate ['sætʃəreit] ⚗ насыща́ть [-ы́тить]; пропи́тывать [-ита́ть].
Saturday ['sætədi] суббо́та.
sauce [sɔ:s] 1. со́ус; *fig.* припра́ва; F де́рзость *f*; 2. приправля́ть со́усом; F [на]дерзи́ть (Д); **~pan** кастрю́ля; **~r** ['sɔ:sə] блю́дце.
saucy ['sɔ:si] □ F де́рзкий.
saunter ['sɔ:ntə] 1. прогу́ливаться; флани́ровать; шата́ться; 2. прогу́лка.
sausage ['sɔsidʒ] соси́ска, колбаса́.
savage ['sævidʒ] 1. □ ди́кий; жесто́кий; свире́пый; 2. дика́рь *m* (-а́рка); *fig.* ва́рвар(ка *f*); **~ry** [-ri] ди́кость *f*; жесто́кость *f*.
save [seiv] спаса́ть [спасти́]; избавля́ть [-а́вить] (from от Р); сберега́ть [-ре́чь]; откла́дывать [отложи́ть].
saving ['seiviŋ] 1. □ спаси́тельный; сберега́тельный; 2. спасе́ние; ~s *pl.* сбереже́ния *n/pl.*
savings-bank сберега́тельная ка́сса.
saviour ['seivjə] спаси́тель *m*; ♀ Спаси́тель *m*.
savo(u)r ['seivə] 1. вкус; F смак; *fig.* пика́нтность *f*; при́вкус; 2. F смакова́ть; ~ of: отзыва́ться (Т); па́хнуть (Т); **~y** [-ri] □ вку́сный; пика́нтный; F сма́чный.

saw [sɔ:] **1.** *pt.* от see; **2.** поговóрка; пилá; **3.** [*irr.*] пили́ть; **~dust** опи́лки *f/pl.*; **~-mill** лесопи́льный завóд; **~n** [sɔ:n] *p. pt.* от saw.
Saxon ['sæksn] **1.** саксóнский; **2.** саксóнец (-нка).
say [sei] **1.** [*irr.*] говори́ть [сказáть]; ~ grace читáть моли́тву (пéред едóй); that is to ~ тó есть, т. е.; you don't ~ so! неужéли!; I ~! послу́шай(те)!; he is said to be ... говоря́т, что он ...; **2.** речь *f*; слóво; it is my ~ now óчередь за мной тепéрь говори́ть; **~ing** ['seiiŋ] поговóрка.
scab [skæb] струп (на я́зве); чесóтка; *sl.* штрейкбрéхер.
scabbard ['skæbəd] нóжны *f/pl.*
scabrous ['skeibrəs] скабрёзный.
scaffold ['skæfəld] ⚠ лесá *m/pl.*; подмóстки *pl.*; эшафóт; **~ing** [-iŋ] ⚠ лесá *m/pl.*
scald [skɔ:ld] **1.** ожóг (кипя́щей жи́дкостью); **2.** [о]шпáрить; обвáривать [-ри́ть].
scale[1] [skeil] **1.** чешу́йка (*coll.*: чешуя́); ви́нный кáмень *m* (на зубáх); нáкипь *f*, окáлина (в котлé и т. п.); (a pair of) **~s** *pl.* весы́ *m/pl.*; **2.** соскобля́ть чешую́ с (Р); ⊕ снимáть окáлину с (Р); шелуши́ться; чи́стить от ви́нного кáмня; взвéшивать [-éсить].
scale[2] [~] **1.** лéстница; масштáб; размéр; шкалá; ♪ гáмма; *fig.* размéр; **2.** взбирáться [взобрáться] (по лéстнице и т. п.); ~ up увели́чивать по масштáбу; ~ down уменьшáть по масштáбу.
scallop ['skɔləp] **1.** *zo.* гребешóк (моллю́ск); **~s** *pl.* фестóны *m/pl.*; **2.** украшáть фестóнами.
scalp [skælp] **1.** скальп; **2.** скальпи́ровать (*im*)*pf.*, *pf. a.* [о-].
scaly ['skeili] чешу́йчатый; покры́тый нáкипью.
scamp [skæmp] **1.** бездéльник; **2.** рабóтать кое-кáк; **~er** [-ə] **1.** бежáть стремглáв; уд(и)рáть; **2.** поспéшное бéгство; галóп; *fig.* бéглое чтéние.
scandal ['skændl] скандáл; позóр; сплéтни *f/pl.*; **~ize** ['skændəlaiz] скандализи́ровать (*im*)*pf.*; **~ous** [-ləs] □ скандáльный; клеветни́ческий.
scant, ~y [skænt, 'skænti] ску́дный; [ограни́ченный.
scapegoat ['skeipgout] козёл отпущéния.
scapegrace [-greis] повéса *m*, шалопáй.
scar [skɑ:] **1.** шрам; рубéц; **2.** *v/t.* покрывáть рубцáми; *v/i.* [за]рубцевáться.
scarc|e [skɛəs] недостáточный; ску́дный; рéдкий; **~ely** ['skɛəsli] едвá ли; как тóлько, едвá; **~ity** [-siti] недостáток; дороговизнá.
scare [skɛə] **1.** [на-, ис]пугáть; отпу́гивать [-гну́ть] (*a.* ~ away); **2.** пáника; **~crow** пу́гало, чу́чело (*a. fig.*).
scarf [skɑ:f] шарф; шаль *f*; гáлстук.
scarlet ['skɑ:lit] **1.** áлый цвет; **2.** áлый; ~ fever ⚕ скарлати́на.
scarred [skɑ:d] в рубцáх.
scathing ['skeiðiŋ] éдкий; рéзкий; *fig.* уничтожáющий.
scatter ['skætə] разбрáсывать [-бросáть]; рассыпáть(ся) [-ы́пать (-ся)]; рассéивать(ся) [-éять(ся)].
scavenger ['skævindʒə] му́сорщик.
scenario [si'nɑ:riou] сценáрий.
scene [si:n] сцéна; мéсто дéйствия; декорáция; **~s** *pl.* кули́сы *f/pl.*; **~ry** ['si:nəri] декорáции *f/pl.*; пейзáж.
scent [sent] **1.** аромáт, зáпах; духи́ *m/pl.*; *hunt.* чутьё, нюх; **2.** [по-] чу́ять; [на]души́ть; **~less** ['sentlis] без аромáта, зáпаха.
sceptic ['skeptik] скéптик; **~al** [-tikəl] □ скепти́ческий.
scept|er, ~re ['septə] ски́петр.
schedule ['ʃedju:l, *Am.* 'skedju:l] **1.** табли́ца; грáфик, плáн; *Am.* расписáние поездóв; **2.** составля́ть расписáние (Р); назначáть [назнáчить, намечáть [-éтить].
scheme [ski:m] **1.** схéма; план; проéкт; **2.** *v/t.* [за]проекти́ровать; *v/i.* интриговáть.
schism ['sizm] схи́зма, раскóл.
scholar ['skɔlə] учёный; учени́к (-и́ца); **~ly** [-li] *adj.* учёный; **~ship** [-ʃip] учёность *f*, эруди́ция; *univ.* стипéндия.
scholastic [skə'læstik] (**~ally**) схоласти́ческий; шкóльный.
school [sku:l] **1.** шкóла; класс (помещéние); at ~ в шкóле; primary ~ начáльная шкóла; secondary ~ срéдняя шкóла; **2.** дисциплини́ровать (*im*)*pf.*; [вы́]шкóлить]; **~boy** шкóльник; **~fellow** шкóльный товáрищ; **~girl** шкóльница; **~ing** ['sku:liŋ] обучéние в шкóле; **~master** учи́тель *m*; **~mate** *s.* schoolfellow; **~mistress** учи́тельница; **~room** клáссная кóмната.
science ['saiəns] нау́ка; естéственные нау́ки *f/pl.*
scientific [saiən'tifik] [**~ally**] нау́чный; умéлый.
scientist ['saiəntist] учёный; естествовéд.
scintillate ['sintileit] сверкáть [-кну́ть]; мерцáть.
scion ['saiən] побéг (растéния); óтпрыск, потóмок.
scissors ['sizəz] *pl.* (a pair of ~) нóжницы *f/pl.*
scoff [skɔf] **1.** насмéшка; **2.** [по-] глуми́ться (at над Т).
scold [skould] **1.** сварли́вая жéнщина; **2.** [вы́]брани́ть.
scon(e) [skɔn, skoun] лепёшка.
scoop [sku:p] **1.** совóк; черпáк;

ковш; углубле́ние; сенсацио́нная но́вость (одно́й определённой газе́ты); **2.** зачёрпывать [-пну́ть].
scooter [ˈsku:tə] *mot.* мото-ро́ллер; ⚓ ску́тер; самока́т (игру́шка).
scope [skoup] кругозо́р; разма́х; охва́т; просто́р.
scorch [skɔ:tʃ] *v/t.* обжига́ть [обже́чь]; опаля́ть [-ли́ть]; *v/i.* пали́ть; F бе́шено нести́сь.
score [skɔ:] **1.** зару́бка; ме́тка; счёт (в игре́); два деся́тка; ♪ партиту́ра; ~s *pl.* мно́жество; run up ~s *pl.* де́лать долги́; on the ~ of по причи́не (Р); what's the ~? како́в счёт? (в игре́); **2.** отмеча́ть [-е́тить]; засчи́тывать [-ита́ть]; выи́грывать [вы́играть]; забива́ть гол; оркестрова́ть *(im)pf.*; *Am.* [вы́]брани́ть.
scorn [skɔ:n] **1.** презре́ние; **2.** презира́ть [-зре́ть]; **~ful** [ˈskɔ:nful] □ презри́тельный.
Scotch [skɔtʃ] **1.** шотла́ндский; **2.** шотла́ндский диале́кт; the ~ шотла́ндцы *m/pl.*; **~man** [ˈskɔtʃmən] шотла́ндец.
scot-free [ˈskɔtˈfri:] невреди́мый; ненака́занный.
scoundrel [ˈskaundrəl] негодя́й, подле́ц.
scour [ˈskauə] *v/t.* [по]чи́стить; отчища́ть [отчи́стить]; [вы́]мыть; смы(ва́)ть; ры́скать по (Д); *v/i.* ры́скать (*a.* ~ about).
scourge [skə:dʒ] **1.** бич; бе́дствие; **2.** бичева́ть; [по]кара́ть.
scout [skaut] **1.** разве́дчик (*a.* ✈); Boy ♀s *pl.* бойска́уты *m/pl.*; ~ party ⚔ разве́дочный отря́д; **2.** производи́ть разве́дку; отверга́ть с презре́нием.
scowl [skaul] **1.** хму́рый вид; **2.** [на]хму́риться.
scrabble [ˈskræbl] цара́пать; [вс]кара́бкаться; сгреба́ть [сгрести́].
scramble [ˈskræmbl] **1.** [вс]кара́бкаться; [по]дра́ться (for за В); ~d eggs *pl.* яи́чница-болту́нья; **2.** сва́лка, борьба́; кара́бканье.
scrap [skræp] **1.** клочо́к; кусо́чек; лоскуто́к; вы́резка (из газе́ты); ⊕ лом; утильсырьё; ~s *pl.* оста́тки *m/pl.*; объе́дки *m/pl.*; **2.** отдава́ть на слом; выбра́сывать [вы́бросить]; **~-book** альбо́м для газе́тных вы́резок.
scrap|e [skreip] **1.** скобле́ние; цара́пина; затрудне́ние; **2.** скобли́ть; скрести́(сь); соскреба́ть [-ести́] (*mst* ~ off); отчища́ть [-и́стить]; заде́(ва́)ть; ша́ркать [-кнуть] (Т); скаре́дничать; **~er** [ˈskreipə] скоба́ для чи́стки о́буви.
scrap|-heap сва́лка отбро́сов (и́ли ло́ма); **~-iron** желе́зный лом.
scratch [skrætʃ] **1.** цара́пина; *sport* черта́ ста́рта; **2.** случа́йный; разношёрстный; *sport* без гандика́па; **3.** [о]цара́пать; [по]чеса́ть; ~ out вычёркивать [вы́черкнуть].
scrawl [skrɔ:l] **1.** кара́кули *f/pl.*; **2.** писа́ть кара́кулями.
scream [skri:m] **1.** вопль *m*; крик; **2.** пронзи́тельно крича́ть; **~y** [-i] крикли́вый; крича́щий (о кра́сках).
screech [skri:tʃ] пронзи́тельно крича́ть; взви́згивать [-гнуть].
screen [skri:n] **1.** ши́рма; экра́н; щит; перегоро́дка; плете́нь *m*; ⚠ та́мбур; гро́хот, си́то; ⚔ прикры́тие; the ~ кино́ *n indecl.*; **2.** прикры́(ва́)ть; заслоня́ть [-ни́ть]; *opt.* пока́зывать на экра́не; просе́ивать [-е́ять].
screw [skru:] **1.** га́йка; винт; = screw-propeller; **2.** приви́нчивать [-нти́ть] (*mst* ~ on); скрепля́ть винта́ми; *fig.* притесня́ть [-ни́ть]; ~ up [с]мо́рщить (лицо́); **~driver** отвёртка; **~-propeller** гребно́й винт.
scribble [ˈskribl] **1.** кара́кули *f/pl.*; **2.** [на]цара́пать.
scrimp [skrimp] *v/t.* уре́з(ыв)ать; *v/i.* [по]скупи́ться.
scrip [skrip] ✝ квита́нция о подпи́ске на а́кции.
script [skript] рукопи́сный шрифт; *film* сцена́рий.
Scripture [ˈskriptʃə] свяще́нное писа́ние.
scroll [skroul] сви́ток (перга́мента); спи́сок; ⚠ завито́к (украше́ние).
scrub [skrʌb] **1.** куст; ~s *pl.* куста́рник; по́росль *f*; **2.** скрести́; чи́стить щёткой.
scrubby [ˈskrʌbi] низкоро́слый; захуда́лый.
scrup|le [ˈskru:pl] **1.** сомне́ния *n/pl.*, колеба́ния *n/pl.*; **2.** [по]стесня́ться; **~ulous** [ˈskru:pjuləs] □ щепети́льный; добросо́вестный.
scrutin|ize [ˈskru:tinaiz] рассма́тривать [-мотре́ть]; тща́тельно проверя́ть; **~y** [ˈskru:tini] испыту́ющий взгляд; то́чная прове́рка.
scud [skʌd] **1.** гони́мые ве́тром облака́ *n/pl.*; стреми́тельный бег; **2.** носи́ться, [по]нести́сь; скользи́ть [-зну́ть].
scuff [skʌf] идти́, волоча́ но́ги.
scuffle [ˈskʌfl] **1.** дра́ка; **2.** [по-]дра́ться.
scullery [ˈskʌləri] помеще́ние при ку́хне для мытья́ посу́ды.
sculptor [ˈskʌlptə] ску́льптор, ва́ятель *m*.
sculptur|e [ˈskʌlptʃə] **1.** скульпту́ра; **2.** [из]вая́ть; высека́ть [вы́сечь].
scum [skʌm] пе́на; на́кипь *f*; *fig.* подо́нки *m/pl.*
scurf [skə:f] пе́рхоть *f*.
scurrilous [ˈskʌriləs] гру́бый, непристо́йный.

scurry ['skʌri] бы́стро бе́гать; сновáть (тудá и сюдá).
scurvy ['skə:vi] ⚕ цингá.
scuttle ['skʌtl] 1. ведёрко для ýгля; 2. уд(и)рáть; дезерти́ровать (*im*)*pf*.
scythe [saið] ⚒ косá.
sea [si:] мóре; *attr.* морскóй; be at ~ *fig.* не знать, что дéлать; недоумевáть; **~board** бéрег мóря; **~faring** ['si:fɛəriŋ] мореплáвание; **~-going** дáльнего плáвания (о сýдне).
seal [si:l] 1. *zo.* тюлéнь *m*; печáть *f*; плóмба; клеймó; 2. запечáт(ыв)ать; скрепля́ть печáтью; опечáт(ыв)ать; ~ up ⊕ гермети́чески укýпоривать; замáз(ыв)ать; ~ (with lead) [за]пломби́ровать.
sea-level ['levl] ýровень мóря.
sealing-wax сургýч.
seam [si:m] 1. шов (*a.* ⊕); рубéц; *geol.* прослóйка; 2. сши(вá)ть; [из]борозди́ть.
seaman ['si:mən] моря́к; матрóс.
seamstress ['semstris] швея́.
sea-plane гидроплáн.
sear [siə] иссушáть [-ши́ть]; опаля́ть [-ли́ть]; ⚕ прижигáть [-жéчь]; *fig.* притупля́ть [-пи́ть].
search [sə:tʃ] 1. пóиски *m/pl.*; óбыск; рóзыск; in ~ of в пóисках (Р); 2. *v/t.* обы́скивать [-кáть]; зонди́ровать (рáну); прони́зывать [-зáть]; *v/i.* разы́скивать [-кáть] (for В); ~ into проникáть [-и́кнуть] в (В); **~ing** [-iŋ] тщáтельный; испытýющий; **~-light** прожéктор; **~-warrant** докумéнт на прáво óбыска.
sea|-shore морскóй бéрег; **~sick** страдáющий морскóй болéзнью; **~side** поберéжье; взмóрье; *attr.* примóрский; ~ place, ~ resort морскóй курóрт.
season ['si:zn] 1. врéмя гóда; перИод; сезóн; out of ~ не вóвремя; with the compliments of the ~ с лýчшими пожелáниями к прáзднику; 2. *v/t.* приправля́ть [-áвить] (пи́щу); выдéрживать [вы́держать] (винó, лес и т. п.); закаля́ть [-ли́ть] (to прóтив Р); **~-able** [-əbl] □ своеврéменный; по сезóну; **~al** ['si:zənl] □ сезóнный; **~ing** ['si:zniŋ] припрáва; **~-ticket** сезóнный билéт.
seat [si:t] 1. сидéнье; стул; скамья́; мéсто (в теáтре и т. п.); посáдка (на лóшади); усáдьба; подстáвка; 2. усáживать [усади́ть]; снабжáть стýльями; вмещáть [вмести́ть]; **~ed** сидя́щий; be ~ed сидéть, сади́ться [сесть].
sea|-urchin морскóй ёж; **~ward** ['si:wəd] *adj.* напрáвленный к мóрю; *adv.* (*a.* ~s) к мóрю; **~weed** морскáя вóдоросль *f*; **~worthy** гóдный для мореплáвания.
secede [si'si:d] откáлываться [отколóться], отпадáть [отпáсть] (от союза и т. п.).
secession [si'seʃən] раскóл; отпадéние; *hist.* вы́ход из сою́за (США); **~ist** [-ist] отстýпник (-ица).
seclu|de [si'klu:d] уединя́ть [-ни́ть]; **~sion** [si'klu:ʒən] уединéние.
second ['sekənd] 1. □ вторóй; втори́чный; уступáющий (to Д); on ~ thoughts по зрéлом размышлéнии; 2. секýнда; помóщник; секундáнт; **~s** *pl.* ☨ товáр вторóго сóрта; 3. поддéрживать [-жáть]; подкрепля́ть [-пи́ть]; **~ary** [-əri] □ втори́чный; второстепéнный; побóчный; **~-hand** подéржанный; из вторы́х рук; **~ly** [-li] во-вторы́х; **~-rate** второсóртный; второразря́дный.
secre|cy ['si:krisi] скры́тность *f*; секрéтность *f*; **~t** ['si:krit] 1. □ тáйный, секрéтный; скры́тный; 2. тáйна, секрéт; in ~ секрéтно, тайкóм; be in the ~ быть посвящённым в секрéт.
secretary ['sekrətri] секретáрь *m*, секретáрша; мини́стр.
secret|e [si'kri:t] (с)пря́тать; выделя́ть [вы́делить]; **~ion** [-ʃən] секрéция, выделéние; **~ive** [-iv] скры́тный.
section ['sekʃən] сечéние; разрéз; отрéзок; ⚕ вскры́тие, сéкция; отдéл; раздéл (кни́ги); ⚔ отделéние.
secular ['sekjulə] □ мирскóй, свéтский; вековóй.
secur|e [si'kjuə] 1. □ безопáсный; надёжный; увéренный; 2. закрепля́ть [-пи́ть]; обеспéчи(ва)ть; обезопáсить *pf*; дост(ав)áть; **~ity** [-riti] безопáсность *f*; надёжность *f*; обеспéчение; залóг; **~ities** *pl.* цéнные бумáги *f/pl.*
sedate [si'deit] □ степéнный; уравновéшенный.
sedative ['sedətiv] *mst* ⚕ успокáивающее срéдство.
sedentary ['sedntəri] □ сидя́чий.
sediment ['sedimənt] осáдок.
sedition [si'diʃən] призы́в к бýнту.
seditious [-ʃəs] □ бунтáрский.
seduc|e [si'dju:s] соблазня́ть [-ни́ть]; **~tion** [si'dʌkʃən] соблáзн; **~tive** [-tiv] □ соблазни́тельный.
sedulous ['sedjuləs] □ прилéжный.
see [si:] [*irr.*] *v/i.* [у]ви́деть; I ~ я понимáю; ~ about a th. [по]заботиться о (П); ~ through a p. ви́деть насквóзь когó-либо; ~ to присмáтривать [-смотрéть] за (Т); *v/t.* [у]ви́деть; [по]смотрéть (фильм, и т. п.); замечáть [-éтить]; понимáть [-ня́ть]; посещáть [-ети́ть]; ~ a p. home провожáть когó-нибудь домóй; ~ off провóжать [-води́ть]; ~ a th. through доводи́ть [довести́] что-нибудь до концá; ~ a p. through

помогáть [помóчь] (Д); live to ~ дожи́(вáт)ь до (Р).
seed [si:d] **1.** сéмя *n*; зернó; *coll.* семенá *n/pl.*; засéв; зёрнышко (яблока и т. п.); потóмство; go to ~ пойти́ в семенá; *fig.* опускáться [-сти́ться]; **2.** *v/t.* засевáть [засéять]; [по]сéять; *v/i.* пойти́ в сéмя; **~ling** ['si:dliŋ] ⚘ сéянец; **~s** *pl.* рассáда; **~y** ['si:di] напóлненный семенáми; потрёпанный, обноси́вшийся; F нездорóвый.
seek [si:k] [*irr.*] *mst fig.* [по]искáть (Р); [по]пытáться; [по]старáться; ~ after добивáться (Р).
seem [si:m] [по]казáться; **~ing** ['si:miŋ] □ кáжущийся; мни́мый; **~ly** [-li] подобáющий; пристóйный.
seen [si:n] *p. pt.* от see.
seep [si:p] просáчиваться [-сочи́ться]; протекáть [-éчь].
seer ['si(:)ə] прови́дец.
seesaw ['si:'sɔ:] **1.** качéли *f/pl.*; качáние на доскé; **2.** качáться на доскé.
seethe [si:ð] кипéть, бурли́ть.
segment ['segmənt] сегмéнт, отрéзок; дóля, дóлька.
segregate ['segrigeit] отделя́ть [-ли́ть].
seiz|e [si:z] хватáть [схвати́ть]; захвáтывать [захвати́ть]; ухвати́ться за (В) *pf.* (*a. fig.*); конфисковáть (*im*)*pf.*; *fig.* охвáтывать [-ти́ть] (о чу́встве); **~ure** ['si:ʒə] конфискáция; захвáт; ⚕ апоплекси́ческий удáр.
seldom ['seldəm] *adv.* рéдко, и́зредка.
select [si'lekt] **1.** отбирáть [отобрáть]; подбирáть [подобрáть]; **2.** отбóрный; и́збранный; **~ion** [si'lekʃən] вы́бор; подбóр; отбóр.
self [self] **1.** *pron.* сам; себя́; ✝ и́ли F = myself etc. я сам и т. д.; **2.** *adj.* одноцвéтный; **3.** *su.* (*pl.* **selves**, selvz) ли́чность *f*; **~-centred** эгоцентри́чный; **~-command** самообладáние; **~-conceit** самомнéние; **~-conceited** чванли́вый; **~-conscious** застéнчивый; **~-contained** самостоя́тельный; *fig.* зáмкнутый; **~-control** самооблáдание; **~-defence**: in ~ при самозащи́те; **~-denial** самоотречéние; **~-evident** очеви́дный; **~interest** своекоры́стие; **~ish** ['selfiʃ] □ эгоисти́чный; **~-possession** самооблáдание; **~-reliant** самоувéренный; **~-seeking** своекоры́стный; **~-willed** своевóльный.
sell [sel] [*irr.*] прод(ав)áть; торговáть; ~ off, ~ out ✝ распрод(ав)áть; **~er** ['selə] продавéц (-вщи́ца); good ~ ✝ хóдкий товáр.
semblance ['sembləns] подóбие; нару́жность *f*; вид.
semi... ['semi...] полу...; **~-final** полуфи́нал.
seminary ['seminəri] духóвная семинáрия; рассáдник (*fig.*).
sempstress [-stris] швея́.
senate ['senit] сенáт; *univ.* совéт.
senator ['senətə] сенáтор.
send [send] [*irr.*] пос(ы)лáть; отправля́ть [-áвить]; ~ for пос(ы)лáть за (Т); ~ forth испускáть [-усти́ть]; изд(ав)áть; ~ up вызывáть повышéние (Р); ~ word сообщáть [-щи́ть].
senil|e ['si:nail] стáрческий; **~ity** [si'niliti] стáрость *f*; дря́хлость *f*.
senior ['si:njə] **1.** стáрший; ~ partner ✝ главá фи́рмы; **2.** пожилóй человéк; стáрший; he is my ~ by a year он стáрше меня́ нá год; **~ity** [si:ni'ɔriti] старшинствó.
sensation [sen'seiʃən] ощущéние; чу́вство; сенсáция; **~al** [-ʃnl] □ сенсациóнный; сенсуáльный.
sense [sens] **1.** чу́вство; ощущéние; смысл; значéние; in (out of) one's ~s *pl.* (не) в своём умé; bring one to his ~s *pl.* привести́ когó-либо в себя́; make ~ имéть смысл; быть поня́тным; **2.** ощущáть [ощути́ть], [по]чу́вствовать.
senseless ['senslis] □ бесчу́вственный; бессмы́сленный; бессодержáтельный; **~ness** [-nis] бесчу́вственность *f* и т. д.
sensibility [-i'biliti] чувстви́тельность *f*; тóчность *f* (прибóра).
sensible ['sensəbl] □ (благо)разу́мный; здравомы́слящий; ощути́мый, замéтный; be ~ of сознá(ва)ть (В).
sensitiv|e ['sensitiv] □ чувстви́тельный (to к Д); **~ity** [-'tiviti] чувстви́тельность *f* (to к Д).
sensual ['sensjuəl] □ чу́вственный.
sensuous ['sensjuəs] □ чу́вственный; эстети́чный.
sent [sent] *pt.* и *p. pt.* от send.
sentence ['sentəns] **1.** ⚖ приговóр; *gr.* предложéние; serve one's ~ отбывáть наказáние; **2.** приговáривать [-говори́ть].
sententious [sen'tenʃəs] нравоучи́тели́ный; сентенциóзный.
sentient ['senʃənt] чу́вствующий.
sentiment ['sentimənt] чу́вство; настроéние; мнéние; мысль *f*; *s.* ~ality; **~al** [senti'mentl] сентиментáльный; **~ality** [sentimen'tæliti] сентиментáльность *f*.
sentinel ['sentinl], **sentry** ['sentri] ⚔ часовóй; карау́льный.
separa|ble ['sepərəbl] □ отдели́мый; **~te 1.** ['seprit] □ отдéльный, осóбый; сепарáтный; **2.** ['sepəreit] отделя́ть(ся) [-ли́ть(ся)]; разлучáть(ся) [-чи́ть(ся)]; расходи́ться [разойти́сь]; **~tion** [sepə'reiʃən] отделéние; разлучéние; разобщéние.
September [sep'tembə] сентя́брь *m*.

sepul|chre ['sepəlkə] *rhet.* гробни́ца; **~ture** ['sepəltʃə] погребе́ние.
sequel ['si:kwəl] продолже́ние; после́дствие.
sequen|ce ['si:kwəns] после́довательность *f*; **~t** [-kwənt] сле́дующий.
sequestrate [si'kwestreit] ⚖ секвестрова́ть (*im*)*pf.*; конфискова́ть (*im*)*pf.*
serenade [seri'neid] **1.** ♪ серена́да; **2.** петь серена́ду (Д).
seren|e [si'ri:n] □ безо́блачный (*a. fig.*); я́сный; безмяте́жный; Your ♀ Highness ва́ша све́тлость *f*; **~ity** [si'reniti] **1.** безмяте́жность *f*; безо́блачность *f*; **2.** ♀ све́тлость *f*.
serf [sə:f] крепостно́й; раб.
sergeant ['sɑ:dʒənt] ⚔ сержа́нт.
serial ['siəriəl] **1.** □ сери́йный; после́довательный; **2.** рома́н или фильм в не́скольких частя́х.
series ['siəri:z] *pl.* се́рия; ряд.
serious ['siəriəs] □ серьёзный; be ~ серьёзно говори́ть; **~ness** [-nis] серьёзность *f*.
sermon ['sə:mən] про́поведь *f*.
serpent ['sə:pənt] змея́; **~ine** [-ain] изви́листый; змееви́дный.
servant ['sə:vənt] слуга́ *m/f*; служа́нка; служи́тель *m*; прислу́га.
serve [sə:v] **1.** *v/t.* [по]служи́ть (Д); под(ав)а́ть (обе́д, мяч в те́ннисе и т. п.); обслу́живать [-жи́ть]; вруча́ть [-чи́ть] (on Д); отбы́(ва́)ть (срок и т. п.); удовлетворя́ть [-ри́ть]; (it) ~s him right так ему́ и на́до; ~ out вы́да(ва́)ть, разд(ав)а́ть; *v/i.* [по]служи́ть (*a.* ⚔) (as Т); ~ at table прислу́живать за столо́м; **2.** *tennis*: пода́ча.
service ['sə:vis] **1.** слу́жба; обслу́живание; услу́га; (*a.* divine ~) богослуже́ние; сообще́ние; *tennis*: пода́ча (мяча́); the ~s *pl.* ⚔ а́рмия, флот и вое́нная авиа́ция; be at a p.'s ~ быть к чьи́м-либо услу́гам; **2.** *Am.* ⊕ [от]ремонти́ровать; **~able** ['se:visəbl] □ поле́зный; про́чный.
servil|e ['sə:vail] □ ра́бский; рабо-ле́пный; холо́пский; **~ity** [sə:viliti] ра́бство; рабо́ле́пство.
servitude ['sə:vitju:d] ра́бство; penal ~ ка́торга.
session ['seʃən] се́ссия; заседа́ние.
set [set] **1.** [*irr.*] *v/t.* [по]ста́вить; класть [положи́ть]; помеща́ть [-ести́ть]; размеща́ть [-ести́ть]; сажа́ть [посади́ть] (насе́дку на я́йца); зад(ав)а́ть (уро́ки и т. п.); вставля́ть в ра́му (карти́ну и т. п.); уса́живать [усади́ть] (to за В); ⚕ вправля́ть [-а́вить] (ру́ку, но́гу); ~ a p. laughing [рас]смеши́ть кого́-нибудь; ~ sail пуска́ться в пла́вание; ~ one's teeth сти́снуть зу́бы; ~ aside откла́дывать [отложи́ть]; ~ store by высоко́ цени́ть (В); счита́ть ва́жным (В); ~ forth излага́ть [изложи́ть]; ~ off оттеня́ть [-ни́ть]; ~ up учрежда́ть [-еди́ть]; устра́ивать [-ро́ить]; **2.** *v/i. ast.* заходи́ть [зайти́], сади́ться [сесть]; засты́(ва́)ть; ~ about a th. принима́ться [-ня́ться] за что́-нибудь; ~ forth отправля́ться [-а́виться]; ~ (up)on нач(ин)а́ть (В); ~ out отправляться [-а́виться]; ~ to вступа́ть в бой; бра́ться [взя́ться] за (рабо́ту, еду́); ~ up for выдава́ть себя́ за (В); **3.** неподви́жный; устано́вленный; засты́вший (взгляд); твёрдый; ~ (up)on поглощённый (Т); ~ with опра́вленный (Т); hard ~ нужда́ющийся; ~ speech пригото́вленная ре́чь *f*; **4.** набо́р; компле́кт; прибо́р; се́рия; ряд; систе́ма; гарниту́р; серви́з (обе́денный и т. п.); (ра́дио)приёмник; круг (о́бщества); *tennis*: сет; покро́й (пла́тья); *thea.* обстано́вка.
set|back ['set'bæk] неуда́ча; **~-down** отпо́р; **~-off** контра́ст; украше́ние.
setting ['setiŋ] опра́ва (камне́й); декора́ции и костю́мы; *fig.* окружа́ющая обстано́вка; захо́д (со́лнца); ♪ му́зыка на слова́.
settle ['setl] *v/t.* водворя́ть [-ри́ть]; приводи́ть в поря́док; успока́ивать [-ко́ить]; реша́ть [-и́ть] (вопро́с); ула́живать [-а́дить]; заселя́ть [-ли́ть]; опла́чивать [-ати́ть] (счёт); устра́ивать [-ро́ить] (дела́); *v/i.* (*often* ~ down) поселя́ться [-ли́ться]; водворя́ться [-ри́ться]; устра́иваться [-ро́иться]; уса́живаться [усе́сться]; приходи́ть к реше́нию; отста́иваться [-тоя́ться]; оседа́ть [осе́сть]; устана́вливаться [-нови́ться] (о пого́де); **~d** ['setld] постоя́нный; усто́йчивый; **~ment** ['setlmənt] реше́ние; урегули́рование; поселе́ние; ⚖ да́рственная за́пись *f*; **~r** ['setlə] поселе́нец.
set-to (кула́чный) бой; схва́тка.
seven ['sevn] семь; **~teen(th)** [-ti:n(θ)] семна́дцать(-тый); **~th** ['sevnθ] **1.** □ седьмо́й; **2.** седьма́я часть *f*; **~tieth** ['sevntiiθ] семидеся́тый; **~ty** ['sevnti] се́мьдесят.
sever ['sevə] разъединя́ть [-ни́ть]; разлуча́ть [-чи́ть]; [по]рва́ть(ся).
several ['sevrəl] не́сколько (Р); □ отде́льный; **~ly** в отде́льности.
severance ['sevərəns] разры́в; отделе́ние.
sever|e [si'viə] □ стро́гий, суро́вый; ре́зкий; си́льный; жесто́кий; е́дкий; кру́пный (убы́ток); **~ity** [si'veriti] стро́гость *f*; суро́вость *f*; жесто́кость *f*.
sew [sou] [*irr.*] [с]шить.
sewer ['sjuə] сто́чная труба́; **~age** ['sjuəridʒ] канализа́ция.

sew|ing ['souiŋ] шитьё; *attr.* швейный; **~n** [soun] *p. pt.* от sew.
sex [seks] пол.
sexton ['sekstən] церковный сторож, пономарь *m*; могильщик.
sexual ['seksjuəl] □ половой; сексуальный.
shabby ['ʃæbi] □ потёртый; жалкий; захудалый; подлый.
shack [ʃæk] *Am.* лачуга, хижина.
shackle ['ʃækl] **1.** ~s *pl.* кандалы *m/pl.*; оковы *f/pl.*; **2.** заковывать в кандалы.
shade [ʃeid] **1.** тень *f*; оттенок; абажур (для лампы); нюанс; тени *f/pl.* (в живописи); **2.** затенять [-нить]; омрачать [-чить]; [за-]штриховать; ♪ нюансировать (*im*)*pf.*; ~ off незаметно переходить (into в В).
shadow ['ʃædou] **1.** тень *f*; призрак; **2.** осенять [-нить]; (*mst* ~ forth) излагать туманно; следить тайно за (Т); **~y** [-i] тенистый; призрачный; смутный.
shady ['ʃeidi] тенистый; F тёмный, сомнительный; теневой.
shaft [ʃɑ:ft] древко; рукоятка; оглобля; *fig.* стрела (*a.* ⚘); ⊕ вал.
shaggy ['ʃægi] косматый; волосатый.
shake [ʃeik] **1.** [*irr.*] *v/t.* трясти (В *or* Т); тряхнуть (Т) *pf.*; встряхивать [-хнуть]; потрясать [-сти]; [по-]колебать; ~ hands пожать руку друг другу, обменяться рукопожатием; *v/i.* [за]трястись; [за]дрожать (with, at от Р); ♪ пускать трель; **2.** встряска; дрожь *f*; потрясение; ♪ трель *f*; **~-hands** *pl.* рукопожатие; **~n** ['ʃeikən] **1.** *p. pt.* от shake; **2.** *adj.* потрясённый.
shaky ['ʃeiki] □ нетвёрдый (на ногах); трясущийся; шаткий.
shall [ʃæl] [*irr.*] *v/aux.* вспом. глагол, образующий будущее (1-ое лицо единственного и множественного числа:) I shall do я буду делать, я сделаю.
shallow ['ʃælou] **1.** мелкий; *fig.* поверхностный; **2.** отмель *f*.
sham [ʃæm] **1.** притворный; поддельный; **2.** притворство; подделка; притворщик (-ица); **3.** *v/t.* симулировать (*im*)*pf.*; *v/i.* притворяться [-риться].
shamble ['ʃæmbl] волочить ноги; **~s** [-z] бойня.
shame [ʃeim] **1.** стыд; позор; for ~! стыдно!; put to ~ [при]стыдить; **2.** [при]стыдить; [о]срамить; **~-faced** ['ʃeimfeist] □ застенчивый; **~ful** ['ʃeimful] □ стыдный; позорный; **~less** ['ʃeimlis] □ бесстыдный.
shampoo [ʃæm'pu:] **1.** шампунь *m*; мытьё головы; **2.** мыть шампунем.
shamrock ['ʃæmrɔk] ⚘ трилистник.
shank [ʃæŋk] голень *f*; ствол.
shanty ['ʃænti] хибарка, хижина.
shape [ʃeip] **1.** форма; образ; очертание; **2.** *v/t.* созд(ав)ать; придавать форму, вид (Д); *v/i.* [с]формироваться; **~less** ['ʃeiplis] бесформенный; **~ly** [-li] хорошо сложённый; приятной формы.
share [ʃɛə] **1.** доля, часть *f*; участие; акция; лемех, сошник (плуга); go ~s *pl.* делиться поровну; **2.** *v/t.* [по]делиться (Т); *v/i.* участвовать (in в П); **~holder** ✝ пайщик (-ица).
shark [ʃɑ:k] акула; *fig.* мошенник.
sharp [ʃɑ:p] **1.** □ *com.* острый (*a. fig.*); *fig.* отчётливый; крутой; едкий; кислый; резкий; пронзительный; колкий; F продувной; **2.** *adv.* круто; точно; look ~! живо!; **3.** ♪ диез; **~en** ['ʃɑ:pən] [на-]точить; заострять [-рить]; **~er** ['ʃɑ:pə] шулер; **~ness** ['ʃɑ:pnis] острота; резкость *f* (и т. д.); **~-sighted** зоркий; **~-witted** остроумный.
shatter ['ʃætə] разбивать вдребезги; разрушать [-рушить] (надежды); расстраивать [-роить] (нервы, здоровье).
shave [ʃeiv] **1.** [*irr.*] [по]брить(ся); [вы]строгать (доску и т. п.); едва не задеть (В); **2.** бритьё; have a ~ [по]бриться; have a close ~ едва избежать опасности; **~n** ['ʃeivn] бритый.
shaving ['ʃeiviŋ] **1.** бритьё; ~s *pl.* стружки *f/pl.*
shawl [ʃɔ:l] шаль *f*; большой платок (на плечи).
she [ʃi:] **1.** она; **2.** женщина; **she-...** самка (животного): she-wolf волчица.
sheaf [ʃi:f] сноп; связка; пучок.
shear [ʃiə] **1.** [*irr.*] [о]стричь (овец); *fig.* обдирать как липку; **2.** ~s *pl.* (большие) ножницы *f/pl.*
sheath [ʃi:θ] ножны *f/pl.*; **~e** [ʃi:ð] вкладывать в ножны; ⊕ обши(ва)ть.
sheaves [ʃi:vz] *pl.* от sheaf.
shed[1] [ʃed] [*irr.*] [по]терять (волосы, зубы); проли(ва)ть (слёзы, кровь); сбрасывать [сбросить] (одежду, кожу).
shed[2] [~] навес, сарай; ангар.
sheen [ʃi:n] блеск; отблеск.
sheep [ʃi:p] овца; **~-dog** овчарка; **~-fold** овчарня; **~ish** ['ʃi:piʃ] □ глуповатый; робкий; **~skin** овчина; баранья кожа.
sheer [ʃiə] явный; полнейший; *Am.* прозрачный (о ткани); отвесный.
sheet [ʃi:t] простыня; лист (бумаги, железа); широкая полоса; ✝ таблица; ~ iron листовое железо; ~ lightning зарница.
shelf [ʃelf] полка; уступ; риф; on the ~ *fig.* сданный в архив.

shell [ʃel] **1.** скорлупа́; ра́ковина; щит (черепа́хи); ⚔ снаря́д; ги́льза; **2.** снима́ть скорлупу́ с (Р); [об]лущи́ть; обстре́ливать [-ля́ть]; **~-fish** моллю́ск; **~-proof** непробива́емый снаря́дами.
shelter [ˈʃeltə] **1.** прию́т, *fig.* кров; убе́жище (*a.* ⚔); **2.** *v/t.* дава́ть прию́т (Д), приюти́ть *pf.*; *v/i.* (*a.* take **~**) укры́(ва́)ться; приюти́ться *pf.*
shelve [ʃelv] ста́вить на по́лку; *fig.* откла́дывать в до́лгий я́щик; увольня́ть [уво́лить].
shelves [ʃelvz] *pl.* от shelf.
shepherd [ˈʃepəd] **1.** пасту́х; па́стырь *m*; **2.** пасти́; направля́ть [-а́вить] (люде́й как ста́до).
sherbet [ˈʃə:bət] шербе́т.
shield [ʃi:ld] **1.** щит; защи́та; **2.** заслоня́ть [-ни́ть] (from от Р).
shift [ʃift] **1.** сме́на (на заво́де и т. п.); измене́ние; сдвиг; переме́на; уло́вка; make **~** ухитря́ться [-ри́ться]; [у]дово́льствоваться (with Т); **2.** *v/t.* [по]меня́ть; перемеща́ть [-мести́ть]; *v/i.* извора́чиваться [изверну́ться]; перемеща́ться [-мести́ться]; **~** for o. s. обходи́ться без по́мощи; **~less** [ˈʃiftlis] □ беспо́мощный; **~y** [ˈʃifti] □ *fig.* изворо́тливый, ло́вкий.
shilling [ˈʃiliŋ] ши́ллинг.
shin [ʃin] **1.** (и́ли **~**-bone) го́лень *f*; **2.** **~** up вскара́бк(ив)аться.
shine [ʃain] **1.** сия́ние; свет; блеск, гля́нец, лоск; **2.** [*irr.*] сия́ть; свети́ть; блесте́ть; [от]полирова́ть; [по]чи́стить (о́бувь); *fig.* блиста́ть.
shingle [ˈʃiŋgl] га́лька; кро́вельная дра́нка; *Am.* вы́веска; **~s** *pl.* ⚕ опоя́сывающий лиша́й.
shiny [ˈʃaini] □ со́лнечный; лосня́щийся; блестя́щий.
ship [ʃip] **1.** су́дно, кора́бль *m*; **2.** грузи́ть на су́дно; перевози́ть [-везти́]; производи́ть поса́дку, нагру́зку (Р на су́дно); **~board**: ⚓ on **~** на корабле́; **~ment** [ˈʃipmənt] нагру́зка; погру́зка; **~-owner** владе́лец су́дна; **~ping** [ˈʃipiŋ] погру́зка; торго́вый флот, суда́ *n/pl.*; судохо́дство; *attr.* судохо́дный; **~wreck** **1.** кораблекруше́ние; **2.** потерпе́ть кораблекруше́ние; **~-wrecked** потерпе́вший кораблекруше́ние; **~yard** верфь *f*.
shire [ˈʃaiə, …ʃiə] гра́фство.
shirk [ʃə:k] увиливать [-льну́ть] от (Р); **~er** [ˈʃə:kə] прогу́льщик.
shirt [ʃə:t] мужска́я руба́шка, соро́чка; (*a.* **~**-blouse) блу́за.
shiver [ˈʃivə] **1.** дрожь *f*; **2.** [за]дрожа́ть; вздра́гивать [-ро́гнуть]; **~y** [-ri] дрожа́щий.
shoal [ʃoul] **1.** мелково́дье; мель *f*; ста́я, кося́к (ры́бы); **2.** ме́лкий; **3.** [об]меле́ть.
shock [ʃɔk] **1.** уда́р, толчо́к; потрясе́ние; копна́; ⚕ шок; **2.** *fig.* потряса́ть [-ясти́]; шоки́ровать; **~ing** [ˈʃɔkiŋ] □ потряса́ющий; сканда́льный; ужа́сный.
shod [ʃɔd] *pt.* и *p. pt.* от shoe.
shoddy [ˈʃɔdi] **1.** волокно́ из шерстяны́х тря́пок; *fig.* хлам; **2.** подде́льный; дрянно́й.
shoe [ʃu:] **1.** ту́фля; башма́к; полуботи́нок; подко́ва; **2.** [*irr.*] обу́(ва́)ть; подко́вывать [-кова́ть]; **~black** чи́стильщик сапо́г; **~blacking** ва́кса; **~horn** рожо́к (для о́буви); **~-lace,** *Am.* **~-string** шнуро́к для боти́нок; **~maker** сапо́жник; **~polish** *s.* shoeblacking.
shone [ʃɔn] *pt.* и *p. pt.* от shine.
shook [ʃuk] *pt.* от shake.
shoot [ʃu:t] **1.** стрельба́; ⚘ росто́к, побе́г; **2.** [*irr.*] *v/t.* стреля́ть; застрели́ть *pf.*; расстре́ливать [-ля́ть]; снима́ть [сня́ть], засня́ть *pf.* (фильм); *v/i.* стреля́ть [вы́стрелить]; дёргать (о бо́ли); (*a.* **~** along, past) проноси́ться [-нести́сь]; промелькну́ть *pf.*; промча́ться *pf.*; ⚘ расти́ (бы́стро); **~** ahead ри́нуться вперёд; **~er** [ˈʃu:tə] стрело́к.
shooting [ˈʃu:tiŋ] стрельба́; охо́та; **~** star па́дающая звезда́.
shop [ʃɔp] **1.** ла́вка, магази́н; мастерска́я; talk **~** говори́ть в о́бществе о свое́й профе́ссии; **2.** де́лать поку́пки (*mst* go **~**ping); **~keeper** ла́вочник (-ица); **~man** ла́вочник; продаве́ц; **~-steward** цехово́й ста́роста *m*; **~-window** витри́на.
shore [ʃɔ:] **1.** бе́рег; взмо́рье, побере́жье; on **~** на́ берег, на берегу́; подпо́рка; **2.** **~** up подпира́ть [-пере́ть].
shorn [ʃɔ:n] *p. pt.* от shear.
short [ʃɔ:t] коро́ткий; кра́ткий; невысо́кий (рост); недоста́точный; непо́лный; отры́вистый, сухо́й (отве́т); песо́чный (о пече́нье); in **~** вкра́тце; come (и́ли fall) **~** of име́ть недоста́ток в (П); не достига́ть [-и́чь] *or* [-и́гнуть] (Р); не опра́вдывать [-да́ть] (ожида́ний); cut **~** прер(ы)ва́ть; fall (и́ли run) **~** истоща́ться [-щи́ться], иссяка́ть [-я́кнуть]; stop **~** of не доезжа́ть [дое́хать], не доходи́ть [дойти́] до (Р); **~age** [ˈʃɔ:tidʒ] нехва́тка; **~coming** недоста́ток; изъя́н; **~cut** сокраще́ние доро́ги; **~-dated** † краткосро́чный; **~en** [ˈʃɔ:tn] *v/t.* сокраща́ть [-рати́ть]; укора́чивать [-роти́ть]; *v/i.* сокраща́ться [-рати́ться]; укора́чиваться [-роти́ться];**~ ening** [-iŋ] жир для те́ста; **~hand** стеногра́фия; **~ly** [ˈʃɔ:tli] *adv.* вско́ре; ко́ротко; **~ness** [-nis] коро́ткость *f*; кра́ткость *f*; **~-sighted** близору́кий; **~-term** краткосро́чный; **~-winded** страда́ющий оды́шкой.

shot [ʃɔt] **1.** *pt.* и *p. pt.* от shoot; **2.** вы́стрел; ядро́ (пу́шки); дробь *f*, дроби́нка (*mst* small ~); стрело́к; *sport* ядро́ (для толка́ния); уда́р; *phot.* сни́мок; ⚕ инъе́кция; have a ~ сде́лать попы́тку; F not by a long ~ отню́дь не; **~-gun** дробови́к.
should [ʃud, ʃəd] *pt.* от shall.
shoulder [ˈʃouldə] **1.** плечо́; усту́п, вы́ступ; **2.** взва́ливать на пле́чи; *fig.* брать на себя́; ⚔ брать к плечу́ (ружьё); **~-blade** лопа́тка (*anat.*).
shout [ʃaut] **1.** крик; во́зглас; **2.** [за]крича́ть [кри́кнуть]; [на]крича́ть (at на В).
shove [ʃʌv] **1.** толчо́к; **2.** пиха́ть [пихну́ть]; толка́ть [-кну́ть].
shovel [ˈʃʌvl] **1.** лопа́та, сово́к; **2.** копа́ть [копну́ть]; сгреба́ть лопа́той.
show [ʃou] **1.** [*irr.*] *v/t.* пока́зывать [-за́ть]; выставля́ть [вы́ставить]; проявля́ть [-ви́ть]; дока́зывать [-за́ть]; ~ in вводи́ть [ввести́]; ~ up изоблича́ть [-чи́ть]; *v/i.* пока́зываться [-за́ться]; проявля́ться [-ви́ться]; ~ off пуска́ть пыль в глаза́; **2.** зре́лище; вы́ставка; ви́димость *f*; пока́зывание; **~-case** витри́на.
shower [ˈʃauə] **1.** ли́вень *m*; душ; **2.** ли́ться ли́внем; ороша́ть [ороси́ть]; поли́(ва́)ть; *fig.* осыпа́ть [осы́пать]; **~y** [ˈʃauəri] дождли́вый.
show|n [ʃoun] *p. pt.* от show; **~-room** вы́ставочный зал; **~-window** *Am.* витри́на; **~y** [ˈʃoui] □ роско́шный; эффе́ктный.
shrank [ʃræŋk] *pt.* от shrink.
shred [ʃred] **1.** лоскуто́к, клочо́к; кусо́к; **2.** [*irr.*] ре́зать, рвать на клочки́; F [ис]кромса́ть.
shrew [ʃruː] сварли́вая же́нщина.
shrewd [ʃruːd] проница́тельный; хи́трый.
shriek [ʃriːk] **1.** пронзи́тельный крик, вопль *m*; **2.** [за]вопи́ть.
shrill [ʃril] **1.** □ пронзи́тельный; **2.** пронзи́тельно крича́ть, [за]визжа́ть.
shrimp [ʃrimp] *zo.* креве́тка; *fig.* сморчо́к.
shrine [ʃrain] ра́ка; святы́ня.
shrink [ʃriŋk] [*irr.*] сокраща́ться [-рати́ться]; усыха́ть [усо́хнуть]; сади́ться [сесть] (о мате́рии, ше́рсти); устраша́ться [-ши́ться] (from, at P); **~age** [ˈʃriŋkidʒ] сокраще́ние; уса́дка; усу́шка.
shrivel [ˈʃrivl] смо́рщи(ва)ть(ся); съёжи(ва)ться.
shroud [ʃraud] **1.** са́ван; *fig.* покро́в; **2.** завёртывать в са́ван; оку́т(ыв)ать (*a. fig.*).
shrub [ʃrʌb] куст; **~s** *pl.* куста́рник.
shrug [ʃrʌg] **1.** пож(им)а́ть (плеча́ми); **2.** пожима́ние (плеча́ми).
shrunk [ʃrʌŋk] *pt.* и *p. pt.* от shrink (*a.* ~en).
shudder [ˈʃʌdə] **1.** вздра́гивать [-ро́гнуть]; содрога́ться [-гну́ться]; **2.** дрожь *f*; содрога́ние.
shuffle [ˈʃʌfl] **1.** ша́ркать [-кнуть] (при ходьбе́); волочи́ть (но́ги); [с]тасова́ть (ка́рты); виля́ть (лука́вить); ~ off свали́ть с себя́ (отве́тственность); **2.** ша́рканье; тасова́ние (карт); увёртка.
shun [ʃʌn] избега́ть [-ежа́ть] (P); остерега́ться [-ре́чься] (P).
shunt [ʃʌnt] **1.** 🚂 маневри́ровать; ⚡ шунти́ровать; *fig.* откла́дывать [отложи́ть]; **2.** 🚂 стре́лка; перево́д на запа́сный путь; ⚡ шунт.
shut [ʃʌt] [*irr.*] **1.** закры́(ва́)ть(ся), затворя́ть(ся) [-ри́ть(ся)]; ~ down прекраща́ть рабо́ту; ~ up! замолчи́!; **2.** закры́тый; **~ter** [ˈʃʌtə] ста́вень *m*; *phot.* затво́р.
shuttle [ˈʃʌtl] ⊕ челно́к; ~ train при́городный по́езд.
shy [ʃai] **1.** пугли́вый; засте́нчивый; **2.** [ис]пуга́ться (at P).
shyness [ˈʃainis] засте́нчивость *f*.
Siberian [saiˈbiəriən] **1.** сиби́рский; **2.** сибиря́к (-я́чка).
sick [sik] **1.** больно́й (of T); чу́вствующий тошноту́; уста́вший (of от P); be ~ for тоскова́ть по (Д *or* П); **~en** [ˈsikn] *v/i.* заболе́(ва́)ть; [за]ча́хнуть; ~ at чу́вствовать отвраще́ние к (Д); *v/t.* де́лать больны́м; вызыва́ть тошноту́ у (P); **~fund** больни́чная ка́сса.
sickle [ˈsikl] серп.
sick|-leave о́тпуск по боле́зни; **~ly** [ˈsikli] боле́зненный; тошното́рный; нездоро́вый (кли́мат); **~ness** (-nis) боле́знь *f*; тошнота́.
side [said] **1.** *com.* сторона́; бок; край; ~ by ~ бок о́ бок; take ~ with примыка́ть к стороне́ (P); **2.** *attr.* боково́й; побо́чный; **3.** ~ with стать на сто́рону (P); **~board** буфе́т; **~-car** *mot.* коля́ска мотоци́кла; **~-light** боково́й фона́рь *m*; **~long** *adv.* вкось; *adj.* косо́й; боково́й; **~-path** тротуа́р; **~-stroke** пла́вание на боку́; **~-track** **1.** 🚂 запасно́й путь *m*; **2.** переводи́ть (по́езд) на запа́сный путь; **~walk** *Am.* тротуа́р; **~ward** (-s) [ˈsaidwədz], **~ways** в сто́рону; вкось; бо́ком.
siding [ˈsaidiŋ] 🚂 ве́тка.
sidle [ˈsaidl] подходи́ть (и́ли ходи́ть) бочко́м.
siege [siːdʒ] оса́да; lay ~ to осажда́ть [осади́ть].
sieve [siːv] си́то.
sift [sift] просе́ивать [-е́ять]; *fig.* [про]анализи́ровать.
sigh [sai] **1.** вздох; **2.** вздыха́ть [вздохну́ть].

sight [sait] **1.** зрéние; вид; взгляд; зрéлище; прицéл; ~s *pl.* достопримечáтельности *f/pl.*; catch ~ of увидеть *pf.*, замéтить *pf.*; lose ~ of потерять из виду; **2.** увидеть *pf.*; вы́смотреть *pf.*; прицéли(ва)ться (at в B); **~ly** ['saitli] красивый; приятный на вид; **~-seeing** ['sait-si:iŋ] осмóтр достопримечáтельностей.
sign [sain] **1.** знак; признак; симптóм; вы́веска; in ~ of в знак (P); **2.** *v/i.* подавáть знáк (Д); *v/t.* подпи́сывать [-сáть].
signal ['signl] **1.** сигнáл; **2.** □ выдаю́щийся, замечáтельный; **3.** [про]сигнализи́ровать; **~ize** ['signəlaiz] отмечáть [-éтить].
signat|ory ['signətəri] **1.** подписáвший; **2.** сторонá, подписáвшая (договóр); ~ powers *pl.* держáвы-участницы (договóра); **~ure** ['signitʃə] пóдпись *f.*
sign|board вы́веска; **~er** ['sainə] лицó, подписáвшее какóй-либо докумéнт.
signet ['signit] печáтка.
signific|ance [sig'nifikəns] значéние; **~ant** [-kənt] □ значи́тельный, многозначи́тельный; характéрный (of для P); **~ation** [signifi'keiʃən] значéние; смысл.
signify ['signifai] знáчить, означáть; выкáзывать [вы́казать].
signpost указáтельный столб.
silence ['sailəns] **1,** молчáние; безмóлвие; ~! молчáть!; **2.** застáвить молчáть; заглушáть [-ши́ть]; **~r** [-ə] глуши́тель *m.*
silent ['sailənt] □ безмóлвный; молчали́вый; бесшу́мный.
silk [silk] **1.** шёлк; **2.** шёлковый; **~en** ['silkən] □ шелкови́стый; **~worm** шелкови́чный червь *m*; **~y** ['silki] шелкови́стый.
sill [sil] подокóнник; порóг.
silly ['sili] □ глу́пый, дурáшливый.
silt [silt] **1.** ил; **2.** засоря́ть(ся) и́лом (*mst* ~ up).
silver ['silvə] **1.** серебрó; **2.** серéбряный; **3.** [по]серебри́ть; **~y** [-ri] серебри́стый.
similar ['similə] □ схóдный (с Т), похóжий (на В); подóбный; **~ity** [simi'læriti] схóдство; подóбие.
simile ['simili] сравнéние (как ритори́ческая фигу́ра).
similitude [si'militju:d] подóбие; óбраз; схóдство.
simmer ['simə] мéдленно кипéть (и́ли кипяти́ть).
simper ['simpə] **1.** жемáнная улы́бка; **2.** жемáнно улыбáться.
simple ['simpl] □ простóй; неслóжный; простоду́шный; **~-hearted** наи́вный; **~ton** [-tən] простáк.
simpli|city [sim'plisiti] простотá; простоду́шие; **~fy** [-fai] упрощáть [-ости́ть].
simply ['simpli] прóсто; неслóжно.
simulate ['simjuleit] симули́ровать (*im*)*pf.*, притворя́ться [-ори́ться].
simultaneous [siməl'teinjəs] □ одноврéмéнный.
sin [sin] **1.** грех; **2.** согрешáть [-ши́ть], греши́ть.
since [sins] **1.** *prp.* с (P); **2.** *adv.* с тех пор; ... тому́ назáд; **3.** *cj.* с тех пор, как; так как; поскóльку.
sincer|e [sin'siə] □ и́скренний; **~ity** [sin'seriti] и́скренность *f.*
sinew ['sinju:] сухожи́лие; *fig. mst* ~s *pl.* физи́ческая си́ла; **~y** [-jui] му́скулистый; си́льный.
sinful ['sinful] □ гре́шный.
sing [siŋ] [*irr.*] [с]петь; воспé(вá)ть; ~ing bird пéвчая пти́ца.
singe [sindʒ] опаля́ть [-ли́ть].
singer ['siŋə] певéц, певи́ца.
single ['siŋgl] **1.** □ еди́нственный; одинóчный; одинóкий; холостóй, незаму́жняя; ~ entry простáя бухгалтéрия; in ~ file гуськóм; **2.** одинóчная игрá (в тéннисе); **3.** ~ out отбирáть [отобрáть]; **~-breasted** однобóртный (пиджáк); **~-handed** самостоя́тельно, без посторóнней пóмощи; **~t** ['siŋglit] тéльная фуфáйка; **~-track** одноколéйный.
singular ['siŋgjulə] необычáйный; стрáнный; еди́нственный; **~ity** [siŋgju'læriti] необычáйность *f.*
sinister ['sinistə] зловéщий.
sink [siŋk] **1.** [*irr.*] *v/i.* опускáться [-сти́ться]; [по-, у]тону́ть; погружáться [-узи́ться]; *v/t.* затопля́ть [-пи́ть]; [вы́]рыть (колóдец); проклáдывать [проложи́ть] (тру́бы); помещáть невы́годно (капитáл); замáлчивать [замолчáть] (фáкты); **2.** рáковина (водопровóдная); **~ing** [-iŋ] ⚕ внезáпная слáбость *f*; ~ fund амортизациóнный фонд.
sinless ['sinlis] безгрéшный.
sinner ['sinə] грéшник (-ица).
sinuous ['sinjuəs] □ изви́листый.
sip [sip] **1.** мáленький глотóк; **2.** пить мáленькими глоткáми.
sir [sə:] су́дарь *m* (обращéние); ♀ сэр (ти́тул).
siren ['saiərin] сирéна.
sirloin ['sə:lɔin] филéй.
sister ['sistə] сестрá; **~hood** [-hud] сéстринская общи́на; **~-in-law** [-rinlɔ:] невéстка; золóвка; свояченица; **~ly** [-li] сéстринский.
sit [sit] [*irr.*] *v/i.* сидéть; заседáть; *fig.* быть расположéнным; ~ down сади́ться [сесть]; *v/t.* сажáть [посади́ть] (на я́йца).
site [sait] местоположéние; учáсток (для строи́тельства).
sitting ['sitiŋ] заседáние; **~-room** гости́ная.
situat|ed ['sitjueitid] расположéнный; **~ion** [sitju'eiʃən] положéние; ситуáция; дóлжность *f.*

six [siks] **1.** шесть; **2.** шестёрка; **~teen** ['siks'ti:n] шестна́дцать; **~teenth** [-θ] шестна́дцатый; **~th** [siksθ] **1.** шесто́й; **2.** шеста́я часть *f*; **~tieth** ['sikstiiθ] шестидеся́тый; **~ty** ['siksti] шестьдеся́т.
size [saiz] **1.** разме́р, величина́; форма́т; но́мер (о́буви и т. п.); **2.** сортирова́ть по разме́рам; ~ up определя́ть величину́ (P); ... **~d** [-d] ... разме́ра.
siz(e)able ['saizəbl] поря́дочного разме́ра.
sizzle ['sizl] [за]шипе́ть.
skat|e [skeit] **1.** конёк (*pl.*: коньки́); (= roller-~) конёк на ро́ликах; **2.** ката́ться на конька́х; **~er** ['skeitə] конькобе́жец (-жка).
skein [skein] мото́к пря́жи.
skeleton ['skelitn] скеле́т, о́стов; карка́с; *attr.* ⚔ недоукомплекто́ванный (полк и т. д.); ~ key отмы́чка.
sketch [sketʃ] **1.** эски́з, набро́сок; **2.** де́лать набро́сок (P); рисова́ть эски́зы.
ski [ʃi:, *Am.* ski:] **1.** (*pl.* ~ и́ли ~s) лы́жа; **2.** ходи́ть на лы́жах.
skid [skid] **1.** тормозно́й башма́к; буксова́ние; ✈ хвостово́й косты́ль *m*; **2.** *v/t.* [за]тормози́ть; *v/i.* буксова́ть.
skilful ['skilful] □ искýсный, уме́лый.
skill [skil] мастерство́, уме́ние; **~ed** квалифици́рованный; иску́сный.
skim [skim] **1.** снима́ть [снять] (на́кипь, сли́вки и т. п.); [по-] нести́сь по (Д), скользи́ть [-зну́ть] по (Д); просма́тривать [-смотре́ть]; ~ over бе́гло прочи́тывать; **2.** ~ milk снято́е молоко́.
skimp [skimp] ску́дно снабжа́ть; уре́з(ыв)ать; [по]скупи́ться (in на В); **~y** ['skimpi] □ ску́дный; у́зкий.
skin [skin] **1.** ко́жа; шку́ра; кожура́; оболо́чка; **2.** *v/t.* сдира́ть ко́жу, шку́ру, кору́ с (Р); ~ off F снима́ть [снять] (перча́тки, чулки́ и т. п.); *v/i.* зажи́(ва́)ть (о ра́не) (*a.* ~ over); **~-deep** пове́рхностный; **~flint** скря́га *m*; **~ny** ['skini] то́щий.
skip [skip] **1.** прыжо́к; ⚒ бадья́; **2.** *v/i.* [по]скака́ть; *fig.* переска́кивать [-скочи́ть] (from с [P]), to на [В]); *v/t.* пропуска́ть [-сти́ть] (страни́цу и т. п.).
skipper ['skipə] шки́пер, капита́н.
skirmish ['skə:miʃ] **1.** ⚔ перестре́лка; сты́чка; **2.** перестре́ливаться.
skirt [skə:t] **1.** ю́бка; пола́; край, окра́ина; **2.** окаймля́ть [-ми́ть]; идти́ вдоль кра́я (P); быть располо́женным на окра́ине (P).
skit [skit] сати́ра, паро́дия; **~tish** ['skitiʃ] □ игри́вый, коке́тливый.
skittle ['skitl] ке́гля; play (at) ~s *pl.* игра́ть в ке́гли; **~-alley** кегельба́н.
skulk [skʌlk] скрыва́ться; пря́таться; кра́сться; **~er** ['skʌlkə] скрыва́ющийся; прогу́льщик.
skull [skʌl] че́реп.
sky [skai] не́бо (*eccl.*: небеса́); **~lark** **1.** жа́воронок; **2.** выки́дывать шту́ки; **~light** ве́рхний свет; све́тлый люк; **~line** горизо́нт; очерта́ние (на фо́не не́ба); **~-scraper** небоскрёб; **~ward(s)** ['skaiwəd(z)] к не́бу.
slab [slæb] плита́; пласти́на.
slack [slæk) **1.** нерадивый; расхля́банный; сла́бый; ме́дленный; ненатя́нутый (о пово́дьях и т. п.); (*a.* ✝) вя́лый; **2.** ⚓ слабина́ (кана́та); ✝ засто́й; ~s *pl.* свобо́дные (рабо́чие) брю́ки *f/pl.*; **3.** = ~en; = slake; **~en** ['slækn] ослабля́ть [-а́бить]; [о]сла́бнуть; замедля́ть [-е́длить]; ло́дырничать.
slag [slæg] шлак, ока́лина.
slain [slein] *p. pt.* от slay.
slake [sleik] утоля́ть [-ли́ть] (жа́жду); гаси́ть (и́звесть).
slam [slæm] **1.** хло́панье; (в ка́рточной игре́) шлем; **2.** хло́пать [-пнуть] (Т); захло́пывать(ся) [-пнуть(ся)].
slander ['slɑ:ndə] **1.** клевета́; **2.** [на]клевета́ть; **~ous** [-rəs] □ клеветни́ческий.
slang [slæŋ] слэнг; жарго́н.
slant [slɑ:nt] **1.** склон, укло́н; *Am.* то́чка зре́ния; **2.** *v/t.* класть ко́со; направля́ть вкось; *v/i.* лежа́ть ко́со; **~ing** ['slɑ:ntiŋ] *adj.* □ косо́й; **~wise** [-waiz] *adv.* ко́со.
slap [slæp] **1.** шлепо́к; ~ in the face пощёчина; **2.** шлёпать [-пнуть].
slash [slæʃ] **1.** уда́р сплеча́; разре́з; вы́рубка; **2.** руби́ть [рубану́ть] (са́блей); [по]ра́нить (ножо́м); [ис]полосова́ть [полосну́ть] (кнуто́м и т. п.).
slate [sleit] **1.** сла́нец, ши́фер; гри́фельная доска́; **2.** крыть ши́ферными пли́тами; **~-pencil** гри́фель *m*.
slattern [slætən] неря́ха (же́нщина).
slaughter ['slɔ:tə] **1.** убо́й (скота́); резня́, кровопроли́тие; **2.** [за]ре́зать (дома́шнее живо́тное); **~-house** бо́йня.
Slav [slɑ:v] **1** славяни́н (-я́нка); **2.** славя́нский.
slave [sleiv] **1.** раб(ы́ня); *attr.* ра́бский; **2.** рабо́тать как ка́торжник.
slaver ['slævə] **1.** слю́ни *f/pl.*; **2.** [за]слюня́вить; пуска́ть слю́ни.
slav|ery ['sleivəri] ра́бство; **~ish** [-viʃ] □ ра́бский.
slay [slei] [*irr.*] уби́(ва́)ть.
sled [sled], **~ge**[1] [sledʒ] са́ни *f/pl.*; сала́зки *f/pl.*
sledge[2] [~] кузне́чный мо́лот.
sleek [sli:k] **1.** □ гла́дкий, прили́-

занный; хо́леный; **2.** пригла́живать [-гла́дить]; **~ness** [sli:knis] гла́дкость *f*.
sleep [sli:p] **1.** [*irr.*] *v/i.* спать; ~ (up-) on отложи́ть до за́втра; *v/t.* дава́ть (кому́-нибудь) ночле́г; ~ away прос(ы)па́ть; **2.** сон; **~er** [-ə] спя́щий; 🚂 шпа́ла; F спа́льный ваго́н; **~ing** [-iŋ]: ~ partner компаньо́н, не уча́ствующий акти́вно в дела́х; **~ing-car(riage)** 🚂 спа́льный ваго́н; **~less** [-lis] □ бессо́нный; **~-walker** луна́тик; **~y** [-i] □ со́нный, за́спанный.
sleet [sli:t] **1.** дождь со сне́гом и́ли гра́дом; **2.** it ~s идёт дождь со сне́гом; **~y** ['sli:ti] сля́котный.
sleeve [sli:v] рука́в; ⊕ му́фта; вту́лка.
sleigh [slei] са́ни *f/pl.*; сала́зки *f/pl.*
sleight [slait] (*mst* ~ of hand) ло́вкость *f* (рук); фо́кусничество.
slender ['slendə] □ стро́йный; то́нкий; ску́дный.
slept [slept] *pt.* и *p. pt.* от sleep.
sleuth [slu:θ] соба́ка-ище́йка; *fig.* сы́щик.
slew [slu:] *pt.* от slay.
slice [slais] **1.** ло́мтик; то́нкий слой; часть *f*; **2.** ре́зать ло́мтиками.
slick [slik] F гла́дкий; *Am.* хи́трый; **~er** *Am.* ['slikə] жу́лик.
slid [slid] *pt.* и *p. pt.* от slide.
slide [slaid] **1.** [*irr.*] скользи́ть [-зну́ть]; ката́ться по льду; вдвига́ть [-и́нуть], всо́вывать [всу́нуть] (into в В); let things ~ относи́ться ко всему́ спустя́ рукава́; **2.** скольже́ние; ледяна́я гора́ и́ли доро́жка; о́ползень *m*; накло́нная пло́скость *f*; ⊕ сала́зки *f/pl.*; диапозити́в; **~-rule** логарифми́ческая лине́йка.
slight [slait] **1.** □ то́нкий, хру́пкий; незначи́тельный; сла́бый; **2.** пренебреже́ние; **3.** пренебрега́ть [-бре́чь] (Т); трети́ровать.
slim|e [slaim] слизь *f*; ли́пкий ил; **~y** ['slaimi] сли́зистый; вя́зкий.
sling [sliŋ] **1.** (руже́йный) реме́нь *m*; рога́тка; праща́; ⚕ повя́зка; **2.** [*irr.*] швыря́ть [швырну́ть]; ве́шать через плечо́; подве́шивать [-е́сить].
slink [sliŋk] [*irr.*] кра́сться.
slip [slip] **1.** [*irr.*] *v/i.* скользи́ть [-зну́ть]; поскользну́ться *pf.*; выскольза́ть [вы́скользнуть] (*a.* ~ away); буксова́ть (о колёсах); ошиба́ться [-би́ться]; *v/t.* сова́ть [су́нуть]; спуска́ть [спусти́ть] (соба́ку); выпуска́ть [вы́пустить] (стрелу́); ~ a p.'s memory ускольза́ть из па́мяти (Р); ~ on (off) наде́(ва́)ть (сбра́сывать [сбро́сить]); **2.** скольже́ние; полоса́; про́мах; оши́бка; опи́ска; опеча́тка; комбина́ция (бельё); ⚓ э́ллинг, ста́пель *m*; на́волочка; give a p. the ~ ускольза́ть [-зну́ть] от (Р); **~per** ['slipə] ко́мнатная ту́фля, ~s *pl.* щлёпанцы *m/pl.*; **~pery** ['slipəri] □ ско́льзкий; ненадёжный; **~shod** ['slipʃɔd] неря́шливый; небре́жный; **~t** [slipt] *pt.* и *p. pt.* от slip.
slit [slit] **1.** разре́з; щель *f*; **2.** [*irr.*] разреза́ть в длину́.
sliver ['slivə] ще́пка, лучи́на.
slogan [slougən] ло́зунг, деви́з.
sloop [slu:p] ⚓ шлюп.
slop [slɔp]: **1.** лу́жа; ~s *pl.* жи́дкая пи́ща; ~s *pl.* помо́и *m/pl.*; **2.** проли́(ва́)ть; расплёскивать(ся) [-еска́ть(ся)].
slope [sloup] **1.** накло́н, склон, скат; **2.** клони́ться; име́ть накло́н.
sloppy ['slɔpi] □ мо́крый (о доро́ге); жи́дкий (о пи́ще); неря́шливый.
slot [slɔt] щель *f*; паз.
sloth [slouθ] лень *f*, ле́ность *f*; *zo.* лени́вец.
slot-machine автома́т (для прода́жи папиро́с и т. п.).
slouch [slautʃ] **1.** [с]суту́литься; неуклю́же держа́ться; свиса́ть [сви́снуть]; **2.** суту́лость *f*; ~ hat мя́гкая шля́па.
slough[1] [slau] боло́то; топь *f*.
slough[2] [slʌf] сбро́шенная ко́жа (змеи́).
sloven ['slʌvn] неря́ха *m/f*; **~ly** [-li] неря́шливый.
slow [slou] **1.** □ ме́дленный; медли́тельный; тупо́й; вя́лый; be ~ отст(ав)а́ть (о часа́х); **2.** (*a.* ~ down, up, off) замедля́ть(ся) [заме́длить (-ся)]; **~coach** тугоду́м; отста́лый челове́к; **~-worm** *zo.* медяни́ца.
sludge [slʌdʒ] *f*; отсто́й; ти́на.
slug [slʌg] **1.** слизня́к; *Am.* F жето́н для телефо́нных автома́тов; **2.** *Am.* F [от]тузи́ть.
slugg|ard ['slʌgəd] лежебо́ка *m/f.*; **~ish** ['slʌgiʃ] □ ме́дленный, вя́лый.
sluice [slu:s] **1.** шлюз; **2.** отводи́ть шлю́зом; шлюзова́ть (*im*)*pf.*; обли́(ва́)ть (over В).
slum [slʌm] *mst* ~s *pl.* трущо́ба.
slumber ['slʌmbə] **1.** (*a.* ~s *pl.*) сон; **2.** дрема́ть; спать.
slump [slʌmp] **1.** ре́зкое паде́ние (цен, спро́са); **2.** ре́зко па́дать; тяжело́ опуска́ться (на стул и т. п.).
slung [slʌŋ] *pt.* и *p. pt.* от sling.
slunk [slʌŋk] *pt.* и *p. pt.* от slink.
slur [slə:] **1.** слия́ние (зву́ков); *fig.* пятно́ (на репута́ции); ♪ ли́га; **2.** *v/t.* сли(ва́)ть (слова́); ~ over зама́зы(ва)ть; ♪ игра́ть лега́то.
slush [slʌʃ] сля́коть *f*; та́лый снег.
sly [slai] □ хи́трый; лука́вый; on the ~ тайко́м.
smack [smæk] **1.** (при́)вкус; за́пах; чмо́канье; зво́нкий поцелу́й; *fig.*

оттéнок; **2.** отзывáться [отозвáться] (of T); пáхнуть (of T); имéть прúвкус (of P); чмóкать [-кнуть] (губáми); хлóпать [-пнуть] (T); шлёпать [-пнуть].

small [smɔ:l] *com.* мáленький, небольшóй; мéлкий; незначúтельный; ~ change мéлочь *f*; ~ fry мéлкая рыбёшка; мелюзгá; ~ of the back *anat.* пояснúца; **~-arms** *pl.* ручнóе огнестрéльное орýжие; **~ish** [smɔ:liʃ] довóльно мáленький; **~pox** *pl.* ⚕ óспа; **~-talk** лёгкий, бессодержáтельный разговóр.

smart [smɑ:t] **1.** □ рéзкий, сúльный (удáр); сурóвый (о наказáнии); лóвкий; остроýмный; щеголевáтый; нарядный; **2.** боль *f*; **3.** болéть (о чáсти тéла); страдáть; **~-money** компенсáция за увéчье; отступны́е дéньги *f/pl.*; **~ness** ['smɑ:tnis] нарядность *f*; элегáнтность *f*; лóвкость *f*.

smash [smæʃ] **1.** *v/t.* сокрушáть [-шúть] *a. fig.*; разбивáть вдрéбезги; *v/i.* разбú(вá)ться; стáлкиваться [столкнýться] (into с T); † [о]банкрóтиться; **2.** битьё вдрéбезги; столкновéние (поездóв и т. п.); **~-up** катастрóфа; банкрóтство.

smattering ['smætəriŋ] повéрхностное знáние.

smear [smiə] **1.** пятнó; мазóк; **2.** [на]мáзать, измáз(ыв)ать.

smell [smel] **1.** зáпах; обоняние; **2.** [*irr.*] обонять (B); [по]чýять (B); (*a.* ~ at) [по]нюхать (B); ~ of пáхнуть (T).

smelt[1] [smelt] *pt.* и *p. pt.* от smell.

smelt[2] [~] выплавлять [вы́плавить] (метáлл).

smile [smail] **1.** улы́бка; **2.** улыбáться [-бнýться].

smirch [smə:tʃ] *rhet.* [за]пятнáть.

smirk [smə:k] ухмыляться [-льнýться].

smite [smait] [*irr.*] поражáть [поразúть]; ударять [удáрить]; разбú(вá)ть (неприятеля); разрушáть [-рýшить].

smith [smiθ] кузнéц.

smithereens ['smiðə'ri:nz] *pl.* оскóлки *m/pl.*; черепкú *m/pl.*; (in)to ~ вдрéбезги.

smithy ['smiði] кýзница.

smitten ['smitn] **1.** *p.pt.* от smite; **2.** поражённый (with T); очарóванный (with T).

smock [smɔk] **1.** украшáть обóрками; **2. ~-frock** рабóчий халáт.

smoke [smouk] **1.** дым; have a ~ покурúть *pf.*; **2.** курúть; [на-]дымúть; [за]дымúться; выкýривать [вы́курить] (*a.* ~ out); **~-dried** копчёный; **~r** ['smoukə] курящий; 🚃 F вагóн для курящих; отделéние для курящих; **~-stack** 🚃 ⚓ дымовáя трубá.

smoking ['smoukiŋ] курящий; курúтельный (о кóмнате); **~-compartment** отделéние для курящих.

smoky [-ki] ды́мный; закоптéлый.

smooth [smu:ð] **1.** □ глáдкий; *fig.* плáвный; спокóйный; вкрáдчивый, льстúвый; **2.** приглáживать [-лáдить]; разглáживать [-лáдить]; *fig.* (*a.* ~ over) смягчáть [-чúть], смáз(ыв)ать; **~ness** ['smu:ðnis] глáдкость *f* и т. д.

smote [smout] *pt.* от smite.

smother ['smʌðə] [за]душúть.

smoulder ['smouldə] тлеть.

smudge [smʌdʒ] **1.** [за]пáчкать(ся); **2.** грязное пятнó.

smug [smʌg] самодовóльный.

smuggle ['smʌgl] занимáться контрабáндой; протáскивать контрабáндой; **~r** [-ə] контрабандúст(ка).

smut [smʌt] **1.** сáжа, ýгольная пыль *f* и т. п.; грязное пятнó; непристóйности *f/pl.*; ❦ головня; **2.** [за-]пáчкать.

smutty ['smʌti] □ грязный.

snack [snæk] лёгкая закýска; **~-bar** закýсочная.

snaffle ['snæfl] трéнзель *m.*

snag [snæg] коряга; сучóк; обломанный зуб; *fig.* препятствие.

snail [sneil] *zo.* улúтка.

snake [sneik] *zo.* змея.

snap [snæp] **1.** щёлк, треск; застёжка; хрустящее печéнье; дéтская кáрточная игрá; *fig.* энергúчность *f*; cold ~ внезáпное похолодáние; **2.** *v/i.* [с]ломáться; щёлкать [-кнуть]; ухвáтываться [ухватúться] (at за B); огрызáться [-знýться] (at на B); [по]рвáться; цáпать [цáпнуть] (at B); *v/t.* защёлкивать [защелкнýть]; *phot.* дéлать моментáльный снúмок (P); ~ out отрéзать *pf.*; ~ up подхвáтывать [-хватúть]; **~fastener** кнóпка (застёжка); **~pish** ['snæpiʃ] □ раздражúтельный; **~py** ['snæpi] F энергúчный; живóй; **~shot** *phot.* моментáльный снúмок.

snare [snɛə] **1.** силóк; *fig.* ловýшка; западня; **2.** поймáть в ловýшку.

snarl [snɑ:l] **1.** рычáние; **2.** [про-]рычáть; *fig.* огрызáться [-знýться].

snatch [snætʃ] **1.** рывóк; хватáние; обры́вок; кусóчек; **2.** хватáть [схватúть]; ~ at хватáться [схватúться] за (B); ~ up подхвáтывать [-хватúть].

sneak [sni:k] **1.** *v/i.* крáсться; *v/t.* F стащúть *pf.*, укрáсть *pf.*; **2.** трус; ябедник (-ица); **~ers** ['sni:kəz] *pl.* тéннисные тýфли *f/pl*; тáпочки *f/pl.*

sneer [sniə] **1.** усмéшка; насмéшка; **2.** насмéшливо улыбáться; [по-]глумúться (at над T).

sneeze [sni:z] **1.** чихáнье; **2.** чихáть [чихнýть].

snicker ['snikə] тихо ржать; хихикать [-кнуть].
sniff [snif] фыркать [-кнуть] (в знак презрения); [за]сопеть; [по-]нюхать.
snigger ['snigə] подавленный смешок.
snip [snip] **1.** обрезок; надрез; **2.** резать ножницами.
snipe [snaip] стрелять из укрытия.
snippy ['snipi] F отрывисто-грубый; надменный.
snivel ['snivl] [за]хныкать; F распускать сопли.
snob [snɔb] сноб; **~bery** ['snɔbəri] снобизм.
snoop [snu:p] *Am.* **1.** совать нос в чужие дела; **2.** проныра *m/f.*
snooze [snu:z] F **1.** лёгкий, короткий сон; **2.** дремать, вздремнуть *pf.*
snore [snɔ:] [за]храпеть.
snort [snɔ:t] фыркать [-кнуть]; [за]храпеть (о лошади).
snout [snaut] рыло; морда.
snow [snou] **1.** снег; **2.** it ~s снег идёт; be ~ed under быть занесённым снегом; **~-drift** снежный сугроб; **~y** ['snoui] □ снежный; белоснежный.
snub [snʌb] **1.** *fig.* осаживать [осадить]; **2.** выговор; **~-nosed** курносый.
snuff [snʌf] **1.** нюхательный табак; **2.** снимать нагар (со свечи); (*a.* take ~) нюхать табак; **~le** ['snʌfl] гнусавить, говорить в нос.
snug [snʌg] □ уютный; достаточный; **~gle** ['snʌgl] (ласково) прижимать(ся) (to к Д).
so [sou] так; итак; таким образом; I hope ~ я надеюсь; are you tired? ~ I am вы устали? — да; you are tired, ~ am I вы устали и я тоже; ~ far до сих пор.
soak [souk] *v/t.* [на]мочить; впитывать [впитать]; *v/i.* промокать; пропитываться [-питаться]; просачиваться [-сочиться].
soap [soup] **1.** мыло; soft ~ жидкое мыло; **2.** намыли(ва)ть; **~-box** мыльница; импровизированная трибуна; **~y** ['soupi] □ мыльный.
soar [sɔ:] высоко летать; парить; ✈ [с]планировать.
sob [sɔb] **1.** рыдание; **2.** [за]рыдать, разрыдаться *pf.*
sober ['soubə] **1.** □ трезвый; умеренный; **2.** вытрезвлять [вытрезвить]; **~ness** [-nis], **~sobriety** [sou'braiəti] трезвость *f.*
so-called ['soukɔ:ld] так называемый.
sociable ['souʃəbl] **1.** □ общительный; дружеский; **2.** *Am.* вечеринка.
social ['souʃəl] **1.** □ общественный; социальный; светский; ~ service социальное учреждение; **2.** вечеринка; **~ize** [-aiz] социализировать (*im*)*pf.*
society [sə'saiəti] общество; компания (торговая); общественность *f*; объединение.
sociology [sousi'ɔləʤi] социология.
sock [sɔk] носок; стелька.
socket ['sɔkit] впадина (глазная); углубление; ⚡ патрон (электрической лампочки); ⊕ муфта.
soda ['soudə] сода; содовая вода; **~-fountain** сифон.
sodden ['sɔdn] промокший.
soft [sɔft] □ *com.* мягкий; нежный; тихий; неяркий; кроткий; изнеженный; придурковатый; ~ drink *Am.* F безалкогольный напиток; **~en** ['sɔfn] смягчать(ся) [-чить(ся)].
soggy ['sɔgi] сырой; пропитанный водой.
soil [sɔil] **1.** почва, земля; грязь *f*; пятно; **2.** [за]пачкать(ся).
sojourn ['sɔdʒə:n, 'sʌdʒ-] **1.** пребывание; **2.** (временно) проживать.
solace ['sɔləs] **1.** утешение; **2.** утешать [утешить].
sold [sould] *pt.* и *p. pt.* от sell.
solder ['sɔ(l)də] **1.** спайка; **2.** паять, запаивать [запаять].
soldier ['souldʒə] солдат; **~like, ~ly** [-li] воинский; воинственный; **~y** [-ri] солдаты *m/pl.*
sole[1] [soul] □ единственный; исключительный.
sole[2] [~] **1.** подошва; подмётка; **2.** ставить подмётку к (Д).
solemn ['sɔləm] □ торжественный; важный; **~ity** [sə'lemniti] торжественность *f*; **~ize** ['sɔləmnaiz] [от]праздновать; торжественно отмечать.
solicit [sə'lisit] [по]ходатайствовать; выпрашивать [выпросить]; прист(ав)ать (к мужчине на улице); **~ation** [səlisi'teiʃən] ходатайство; настойчивая просьба; **~or** [sə'lisitə] ⚖ стряпчий; поверенный; *Am.* агент фирмы; **~ous** [-əs] □ заботливый; ~ of стремящийся к (Д); **~ude** [-ju:d] заботливость *f*, забота.
solid ['sɔlid] **1.** □ твёрдый; прочный; сплошной; массивный; ⩓ пространственный, кубический; *fig.* солидный; надёжный; единогласный; сплочённый; a ~ hour целый час; ~ tire массивная шина; **2.** твёрдое тело; **~arity** [sɔli'dæriti] солидарность *f*; **~ify** [sə'lidifai] [за]твердеть; делать твёрдым; **~ity** [-ti] твёрдость *f*; прочность *f.*
soliloquy [sə'liləkwi] монолог; разговор с самим собой.
solit|ary ['sɔlitəri] □ одинокий; уединённый; отдельный; **~ude** [-tju:d] одиночество; уединённое место.

solo ['soulou] со́ло *n indecl.*; ✈ одино́чный полёт; **~ist** ['soulouist] соли́ст(ка).
solu|ble ['sɔljubl] раствори́мый; разреши́мый; **~tion** [sə'lu:ʃən] растворе́ние; реше́ние; ⊕ раство́р; рези́новый клей.
solv|e [sɔlv] реша́ть [реши́ть], разреша́ть [-ши́ть]; **~ent** [-vənt] **1.** растворя́ющий; ✝ платёжеспосо́бный; **2.** раствори́тель *m.*
somb|er, ~re ['sɔmbə] □ мра́чный.
some [sʌm, səm] не́кий; како́й-то; како́й-нибудь; не́сколько; не́которые; о́коло (P); ~ 20 miles миль два́дцать; in ~ degree, to ~ extent до изве́стной сте́пени; **~body** ['sʌmbədi] кто́-то; кто́-нибудь; **~how** [-hau] ка́к-то; ка́к-нибудь; ~ or other так и́ли ина́че; **~one** [~wʌn] *s.* somebody.
somer|sault ['sʌməsɔ:lt], **~set** [-set] кувырка́ние; turn ~s *pl.* кувырка́ться, turn a ~ кувыркну́ться *pf.*
some|thing ['sʌmθiŋ] что́-то; что́-нибудь; кое-что́; ~ like приблизи́тельно; что-то вро́де (P): **~time** [-taim] **1.** когда́-то; не́когда; **2.** бы́вший, пре́жний; **~times** иногда́; **~what** [-wɔt] слегка́, немно́го; до не́которой сте́пени; **~where** [-wεə] где́-то, куда́-то; где́-нибудь, куда́-нибудь.
son [sʌn] сын (*pl.*: сыновья́; *fig. pl.*: сыны́).
song [sɔŋ] пе́сня; рома́нс; F for a mere ~ за бесце́нок; **~-bird** пе́вчая пти́ца; **~ster** ['sɔŋstə] певе́ц; пе́вчая пти́ца.
son-in-law зять *m.*
sonorous [sə'nɔ:rəs] □ зву́чный.
soon [su:n] ско́ро, вско́ре; ра́но; охо́тно; as (*or* so) ~ as как то́лько; **~er** ['su:nə] скоре́е; no ~ ... than едва́ ..., как; no ~ said than done ска́зано — сде́лано.
soot [su:t] **1.** са́жа; ко́поть *f*; **2.** покрыва́ть са́жей.
sooth|e [su:ð] успока́ивать [-ко́ить]; утеша́ть [уте́шить]; **~sayer** ['su:θseiə] предсказа́тель(ница *f*) *m.*
sooty ['su:ti] □ закопчённый; чёрный как са́жа.
sop [sɔp] **1.** обмакну́тый (в подли́вку и т. п.) кусо́к хле́ба и т. п.; *fig.* взя́тка; **2.** обма́кивать [-макну́ть]; нама́чивать [-мочи́ть].
sophist|icate [so'fistikeit] извраща́ть [-рати́ть]; подде́л(ыв)ать; лиша́ть наи́вности; **~icated** [-id] извращённый, искажённый; лишённый наи́вности; искушённый; **~ry** ['sɔfistri] софи́стика.
soporific [soupə'rifik] усыпля́ющее, снотво́рное сре́дство.
sorcer|er ['sɔ:sərə] волше́бник; **~ess** [-ris] волше́бница; ве́дьма; **~y** [-ri] волшебство́.
sordid ['sɔ:did] □ гря́зный; убо́гий.
sore [sɔ:] **1.** □ чувстви́тельный; боле́зненный; больно́й, воспалённый; оби́женный; ~ throat боль в го́рле; **2.** боля́чка; я́зва (*a. fig.*).
sorrel ['sɔ:rəl] **1.** гнедо́й (о ло́шади); **2.** гнеда́я ло́шадь *f.*
sorrow ['sɔrou] **1.** го́ре, печа́ль *f*; **2.** горева́ть, печа́литься; **~ful** ['sɔrouful] □ печа́льный, ско́рбный.
sorry ['sɔri] □ по́лный сожале́ния; (I am) (so) ~! мне о́чень жаль!; винова́т!; I am ~ for you мне вас жаль.
sort [sɔ:t] **1.** род, сорт; people of all ~s *pl.* всевозмо́жные лю́ди *m/pl.*; ~ of F как бу́дто; be out of ~s *pl.* быть не в ду́хе; пло́хо чу́вствовать себя́; **2.** сортирова́ть; ~ out рассортиро́вывать [-ирова́ть].
sot [sɔt] го́рький пья́ница *m.*
sough [sau] **1.** ше́лест; **2.** [за-] шелесте́ть.
sought [sɔ:t] *pt.* и *p. pt.* от seek
soul [soul] душа́.
sound [saund] **1.** □ здоро́вый, кре́пкий, про́чный; здра́вый; норма́льный; ✝ платёжеспосо́бный; ⚖ зако́нный; **2.** звук, шум; звон; зонд; проли́в; пла́вательный пузы́рь *m* (у ры́бы); **3.** звуча́ть (*a. fig.*); разд(ав)а́ться; зонди́ровать (*a. fig.*); измеря́ть глубину́ (P); выслу́шивать [вы́слушать] (больно́го); **~ing** ['saundiŋ] ⚓ проме́р глубины́ ло́том; зонди́рование; **~less** [-lis] □ беззву́чный; **~ness** [-nis] здоро́вье и т. д.; **~-proof** звуконепроница́емый.
soup [su:p] суп.
sour ['sauə] **1.** □ ки́слый; *fig.* угрю́мый; раздражи́тельный; **2.** *v/t.* [за]ква́сить; *fig.* озлобля́ть [озло́бить]; *v/i.* закиса́ть [-и́снуть]; прокиса́ть [-и́снуть].
source [sɔ:s] исто́к; исто́чник (*mst fig.*), ключ, родни́к.
sour|ish ['sauəriʃ] □ кислова́тый; **~ness** [-nis] кислота́; *fig.* го́речь *f*; раздражи́тельность *f.*
souse [saus] [за]соли́ть; [за]маринова́ть; ока́чивать [окати́ть].
south [sauθ] **1.** юг; **2.** ю́жный; **~-east** **1.** юго-восто́к; **2.** юго-восто́чный (*a.* ~-eastern).
souther|ly ['sʌðəli], **~n** ['sʌðən] ю́жный; **~ner** [-ə] южа́нин, южа́нка; *Am.* жи́тель(ница) ю́жных шта́тов.
southernmost [-moust] са́мый ю́жный.
southward, ~ly ['sauθwəd, -li], **~s** [-dz] *adv.* к ю́гу, на юг.
south|-west **1.** юго-за́пад; **2.** юго-за́падный (*a.* ~-westerly, ~-western); **~-wester** юго-за́падный ве́тер; ⚓ зюйдве́стка.

souvenir ['su:vəniə] сувени́р.
sovereign ['sɔvrin] **1.** □ верхо́вный; сувере́нный; превосхо́дный; **2.** мона́рх; соверéн (моне́та в оди́н фунт сте́рлингов); **~ty** [-ti] верхо́вная власть *f*; суверените́т.
soviet ['souviet] **1.** сове́т; **2.** сове́тский.
sow[1] [sau] *zo.* свинья́, свинома́тка; ⊕ чу́шка.
sow[2] [sou] [*irr.*] [по]се́ять; засева́ть [засе́ять]; **~n** [soun] *p. pt.* от sow[2].
spa [spɑ:] куро́рт (с минера́льными во́дами); целе́бные во́ды *f/pl.*
space [speis] **1.** простра́нство; ме́сто; промежу́ток; срок; *attr.* косми́ческий; **2.** *typ.* набира́ть в разря́дку.
spacious ['speiʃəs] □ просто́рный; обши́рный; вмести́тельный.
spade [speid] лопа́та; **~s** пи́ки *f/pl.* (ка́рточная масть).
span [spæn] **1.** пролёт (мо́ста́); коро́ткое расстоя́ние и́ли вре́мя; *Am.* па́ра лошаде́й (воло́в и т. п.); **2.** стро́ить мост че́рез (В); измеря́ть [-е́рить].
spangle ['spæŋgl] **1.** блёстка; **2.** украша́ть блёстками; *fig.* усе́ивать [усе́ять].
Spaniard ['spænjəd] испа́нец (-нка).
Spanish ['spæniʃ] испа́нский.
spank [spæŋk] F **1.** шлёпать [-пнуть]; отшлёп(ыв)ать; **2.** шлепо́к; **~ing** ['spæŋkiŋ] све́жий (ве́тер).
spar [spɑ:] **1.** ⚓ рангоу́тное де́рево; ✈ лонжеро́н; **2.** бокси́ровать (в трениро́вке); *fig.* [по]спо́рить, препира́ться.
spare [spɛə] **1.** □ запасно́й; ли́шний, свобо́дный; ску́дный; худоща́вый; скро́мный; ~ time свобо́дное вре́мя *n*; **2.** ⊕ запасна́я часть *f*; **3.** [по]щади́ть; [по]жале́ть; [с]бере́чь; уделя́ть [-ли́ть] (вре́мя); избавля́ть [-а́вить] от (Р).
sparing ['spɛəriŋ] □ уме́ренный; бережли́вый; ску́дный.
spark [spɑ:k] **1.** и́скра; щёголь *m*; **2.** [за]и́скриться; **~(ing)-plug** *mot.* запа́льная свеча́.
sparkle ['spɑ:kl] **1.** и́скра; сверка́ние; **2.** [за]и́скриться, [за]сверка́ть; sparkling wine шипу́чее вино́.
sparrow ['spærou] воробе́й.
sparse [spɑ:s] □ ре́дкий; разбро́санный.
spasm [spæzm] спа́зма, су́дорога; **~odic(al** □) [spæz'mɔdik, -dikəl] су́дорожный.
spat [spæt] **1.** ге́тра; **2.** *pt.* и *p.pt.* от spit.
spatter ['spætə] бры́згать [-знуть]; расплёскивать [-плеска́ть].
spawn [spɔ:n] **1.** икра́; *fig. contp.* отро́дье; **2.** мета́ть икру́; *contp.* [рас]плоди́ться.
speak [spi:k] [*irr.*] *v/i.* говори́ть; [по]говори́ть (with, to с Т); разгова́ривать; ~ out, ~ up выска́зываться [вы́сказаться]; говори́ть гро́мко; *v/t.* выска́зывать [вы́сказать]; говори́ть [сказа́ть] (пра́вду и т. п.); **~er** ['spi:kə] ора́тор; *parl.* спи́кер (председа́тель пала́ты); **~ing-trumpet** ру́пор.
spear [spiə] **1.** копьё; дро́тик; острога́; **2.** пронза́ть копьём; бить острого́й (ры́бу).
special ['speʃəl] **1.** □ специа́льный; осо́бенный; осо́бый; э́кстренный; **2.** специа́льный корреспонде́нт; э́кстренный по́езд; **~ist** [-ist] специали́ст; **~ity** [speʃi'æliti] осо́бенность *f*; специа́льность *f*; **~ize** ['speʃəlaiz] специализи́ровать(ся) (*im*)*pf.* (в П *or* по Д); **~ty**['speʃəlti] *s.* speciality.
specie ['spi:ʃi:] зво́нкая моне́та; **~s** ['spi:ʃi:z] вид; разнови́дность *f.*
speci|fic [spi'sifik] (~ally) характе́рный; осо́бенный; определённый; **~fy** [-fai] специфици́ровать (*im*)*pf.*; то́чно определя́ть; **~men** [-min] образе́ц; обра́зчик; экземпля́р.
specious ['spi:ʃəs] □ благови́дный; показно́й.
speck [spek] **1.** пя́тнышко; кра́пинка; **2** [за]пятна́ть; **~le** ['spekl] **1.** пя́тнышко; **2.** испещря́ть [-ри́ть]; [за]пятна́ть.
spectacle ['spektəkl] зре́лище; ~s *pl.* очки́ *n/pl.*
spectacular [spek'tækjulə] □ эффе́ктный, импоза́нтный.
spectator [spek'teitə] зри́тель(ница *f*) *m.*
spect|er ['spektə] при́зрак; **~ral** ['spektrəl] □ при́зрачный; **~re** *s.* ~er.
speculat|e ['spekjuleit] размышля́ть [-ы́слить]; ☨ спекули́ровать (in Т); **~ion** [spekju'leiʃən] размышле́ние; предположе́ние; ☨ спекуля́ция; **~ive** ['spekjulətiv] □ умозри́тельный; спекуляти́вный; **~or** [-leitə] ☨ спекуля́нт.
sped [sped] *pt.* и *p. pt.* от speed.
speech [spi:tʃ] речь *f*; го́вор; **~less** ['spi:tʃlis] □ безмо́лвный.
speed [spi:d] **1.** ско́рость *f*, быстрота́; *mot.* ход, ско́рость *f*; good ~! всего́ хоро́шего!; **2.** [*irr.*] *v/i.* [по]спеши́ть; идти́ поспе́шно; успева́ть (в заня́тиях); *v/t.* ~ up ускоря́ть [-о́рить]; **~-limit** допуска́емая ско́рость *f* (езды́); **~ometer** [spi:'dɔmitə] *mot.* спидо́метр; **~y** ['spi:di] □ бы́стрый.
spell [spel] **1.** (коро́ткий) пери́од; промежу́ток вре́мени; рабо́чее вре́мя *n*; ча́ры *f/pl.*; обая́ние; **2.** [*a. irr.*] писа́ть, чита́ть по бу́квам; писа́ть пра́вильно; означа́ть [означи́ть]; **~bound** *fig.* очаро́ванный;

~er ['spelə] *part. Am.* буква́рь *m*; **~ing** [-iŋ] правописа́ние; **~ing-book** буква́рь *m*.
spelt [spelt] *pt.* и *p. pt.* от spell.
spend [spend] [*irr.*] [по]тра́тить, [из]расхо́довать (де́ньги); проводи́ть [-вести́] (вре́мя); истоща́ть [-щи́ть]; **~thrift** ['spendθrift] мот (-о́вка), расточи́тель(ница *f*) *m*.
spent [spent] **1.** *pt.* и *p. pt.* от spend. **2.** *adj.* истощённый.
sperm [spə:m] спе́рма; кашало́т.
spher|e [sfiə] шар; земно́й шар; небе́сная сфе́ра; гло́бус; *fig.* сфе́ра; круг, по́ле де́ятельности; среда́; **~ical** ['sferikəl] □ сфери́ческий.
spice [spais] **1.** спе́ция, пря́ность *f*; *fig.* соль *f*; при́вкус; **2.** приправля́ть [-а́вить].
spick and span ['spikən'spæn] щегольско́й, с иго́лочки.
spicy ['spaisi] □ пря́ный; пика́нтный.
spider ['spaidə] *zo.* пау́к.
spigot ['spigət] *Am.* кран (бо́чки).
spike [spaik] **1.** остриё; шип, гвоздь *m* (на подо́шве); ⚘ ко́лос; **2.** прибива́ть гвоздя́ми; снабжа́ть шипа́ми; пронза́ть [-зи́ть].
spill [spil] **1.** [*irr.*] *v/t.* проли́(ва́)ть; рассыпа́ть [-ы́пать]; F вывáливать [вы́валить] (седока́); *v/i.* проли́(ва́)ться; **2.** F паде́ние.
spilt [spilt] *pt.* и *p. pt.* от spill.
spin [spin] **1.** [*irr.*] [с]прясть; [с]сучи́ть (кана́т и т. п.); крути́ться; [за]кружи́ть(ся); ~ a yarn расска́зывать небыли́цы; ~ along ката́ться, [по]кати́ться; **2.** круже́ние; бы́страя езда́.
spinach ['spinidʒ] ⚘ шпина́т.
spinal ['spainl] спинно́й; ~ column спинно́й хребе́т; ~ cord, ~ marrow спинно́й мозг.
spindle ['spindl] веретено́.
spine [spain] *anat.* спинно́й хребе́т, позвоно́чный столб; колю́чка.
spinning|-mill пряди́льная фа́брика; **~-wheel** пря́лка.
spinster ['spinstə] ста́рая де́ва; ⚖ незаму́жняя (же́нщина).
spiny ['spaini] колю́чий.
spiral ['spaiərəl] **1.** □ спира́льный; ~ staircase винтова́я ле́стница; **2.** спира́ль *f*.
spire ['spaiə] шпиль *m*; шпиц; остроконе́чная верши́на.
spirit ['spirit] **1.** *com.* дух; привиде́ние; смысл; воодушевле́ние; спирт; ~s *pl.* (high припо́днятое, low пода́вленное) настрое́ние; спиртны́е напи́тки *m/pl.*; **2.** ~ away, off таи́нственно похища́ть; **~ed** [-id] □ живо́й; сме́лый; энерги́чный; **~less** [-lis] □ вя́лый; ро́бкий; безжи́зненный.
spiritual ['spiritjuəl] □ духо́вный; одухотворённый; религио́зный; **~ism** [-izm] спирит(уал)и́зм.
spirituous ['spiritjuəs] спиртно́й, алкого́льный.
spirt [spə:t] *s* spurt.
spit [spit] **1.** ве́ртел; слюна́; плево́к; *fig.* подо́бие; **2.** [*irr.*] плева́ть [плю́нуть]; треща́ть (об огне́); шипе́ть (о ко́шке); мороси́ть.
spite [spait] **1.** зло́ба, злость *f*; in ~ of не смотря́ на (В); **2.** досажда́ть [досади́ть]; **~ful** ['spaitful] зло́бный.
spitfire ['spitfaiə] вспы́льчивый челове́к.
spittle ['spitl] слюна́; плево́к.
spittoon [spi'tu:n] плева́тельница.
splash [splæʃ] **1.** бры́зги *f/pl.* (*mst* ~es *pl.*); плеск; **2.** бры́згать [-знуть]; плеска́ть(ся) [-сну́ть].
splayfoot ['spleifut] косола́пый.
spleen [spli:n] *anat.* селезёнка; хандра́.
splend|id ['splendid] □ блестя́щий; великоле́пный, роско́шный; **~o(u)r** [-də] блеск; великоле́пие, ро́скошь *f*; пы́шность *f*.
splice [splais] ⚓ сплета́ть [-ести́] (кана́ты), сплёсни(ва)ть.
splint [splint] **1.** ⚕ лубо́к; **2.** накла́дывать лубо́к на (В); **~er** ['splintə] **1.** оско́лок; лучи́на; зано́за; **2.** расщепля́ть(ся) [-пи́ть(ся)].
split [split] **1.** тре́щина; щель *f*; *fig.* раско́л; **2.** расщеплённый; раско́лотый; **3.** [*irr.*] *v/t.* раска́лывать [-коло́ть]; расщепля́ть [-пи́ть]; ~ hairs вдава́ться в то́нкости; ~ one's sides with laughing надрыва́ться от сме́ха; *v/i.* раска́лываться [-коло́ться]; ло́паться [ло́пнуть]; **~ting** ['splitiŋ] ужа́сный (о головно́й бо́ли); оглуши́тельный.
splutter ['splʌtə] *s.* sputter.
spoil [spɔil] **1.** (*a.* ~s *pl.*) награ́бленное добро́, добы́ча; *pol. part. Am.* ~s system распределе́ние госуда́рственных должносте́й за услу́ги; **2.** [*irr.*] [ис]по́ртить; [по]губи́ть; [ис]по́ртиться (о пи́ще); [из]балова́ть (ребёнка).
spoke [spouk] **1.** *pt.* от speak; **2.** спи́ца (колеса́); ступе́нька, перекла́дина; **~n** ['spoukən] *p. pt.* от speak; **~sman** ['spouksmən] представи́тель *m*.
sponge [spʌndʒ] **1.** гу́бка; **2.** *v/t.* вытира́ть или мыть гу́бкой; ~ up впи́тывать гу́бкой; *v/i.* жить на чужо́й счёт; **~-cake** бискви́т; **~r** ['spʌndʒə] прижива́льщик (-лка).
spongy ['spʌndʒi] гу́бчатый.
sponsor ['spɔnsə] **1.** покрови́тель (-ница *f*) *m*; поручи́тель(ница *f*) *m*; крёстный оте́ц, крёстная мать *f*; *Am.* абоне́нт радиорекла́мы; **2.** руча́ться [поручи́ться] за (В); быть крёстным отцо́м (крёстной ма́терью) у (Р).
spontane|ity [spɔntə'ni:iti] непо-

сре́дственность *f*; самопроизво́льность *f*; **~ous** [spɔn'teinjəs] □ непосре́дственный; непринуждённый; самопроизво́льный.
spook [spu:k] привиде́ние.
spool [spu:l] **1.** шпу́лька; **2.** нама́тывать на шпу́льку.
spoon [spu:n] **1.** ло́жка; **2.** че́рпать ло́жкой; **~ful** ['spu:nful] ло́жка (ме́ра).
sport [spɔ:t] **1.** спорт; **~s** *pl.* спорти́вные и́гры *f/pl.*; *attr.* спорти́вный; *fig.* игру́шка; развлече́ние, заба́ва; *sl.* молоде́ц; **2.** *v/i.* игра́ть, весели́ться, резви́ться; *v/t.* F щеголя́ть [-льну́ть] (T); **~ive** ['spɔ:tiv] □ игри́вый; весёлый; **~sman** ['spɔ:tsmən] спортсме́н.
spot [spɔt] **1.** *com.* пятно́; кра́пинка; ме́сто; on the ~ на ме́сте; сра́зу, неме́дленно; **2.** нали́чный; подлежа́щий неме́дленной упла́те; **3.** [за]пятна́ть; ⚔ обнару́жи(ва)ть; F опозн(ав)а́ть; **~less** ['spɔtlis] □ безупре́чный; незапя́тнанный; **~-light** проже́ктор; *fig.* центр внима́ния; **~ty** ['spɔti] пятни́стый; кра́пчатый; прыщева́тый.
spouse [spauz] супру́г(а).
spout [spaut] **1.** струя́; но́сик (ча́йника и т. п.); водосто́чная труба́; **2.** выпуска́ть струёй (B); би́ть струёй; F ора́торствовать.
sprain [sprein] **1.** растяже́ние (свя́зок); **2.** растя́гивать [-тяну́ть]; вы́вихнуть *pf.*
sprang [spræŋ] *pt.* от spring.
sprawl [sprɔ:l] растя́гивать(ся) [-яну́ть(ся)]; разва́ливаться [-ли́ться] (в кре́сле); ⚘ бу́йно разраста́ться.
spray [sprei] **1.** водяна́я пыль *f*; бры́зги *f/pl.*; пульвериза́тор, распыли́тель *m* (*a.* ~er); **2.** распыля́ть [-ли́ть]; обры́зг(ив)ать.
spread [spred] **1.** [*irr.*] *v/t.* (*a.* ~ out) расстила́ть [разостла́ть]; распространя́ть [-ни́ть]; нама́з(ыв)ать (T); ~ the table накры́(ва́)ть на стол; *v/i.* простира́ться [простере́ться]; распространя́ться [-ни́ться]; **2.** *pt.* и *p pt.* от spread 1.; **3.** распростране́ние; протяже́ние.
spree [spri:] весе́лье; ша́лость *f*; кутёж.
sprig [sprig] ве́точка, побе́г; *fig.* о́тпрыск; ⊕ шти́фтик; гво́здик.
sprightly ['spraitli] оживлённый, весёлый.
spring [spriŋ] **1.** прыжо́к, скачо́к; родни́к, ключ; (*a.* ~*time*) весна́; ⊕ пружи́на, рессо́ра; *fig.* моти́в; **2.** [*irr.*] *v/t.* взрыва́ть [взорва́ть]; вспу́гивать [-гну́ть] (дичь); ~ a leak ⚓ дава́ть течь (о корабле́); ~ a th. (up)on a p. неожи́данно сообщи́ть (В/Д); *v/i.* пры́гать [-гнуть]; вска́кивать [вскочи́ть]; ⚘ появля́ться [-ви́ться] (о по́чках); ~ up возника́ть [-и́кнуть]; **~-board** трампли́н; **~tide** весна́; ~ tide сизиги́йный прили́в; **~y** ['spriŋi] □ упру́гий.
sprinkl|e ['spriŋkl) бры́згать [-знуть]; [о]кропи́ть; **~ing** [-iŋ] лёгкий дождь *m*; a ~ немно́го.
sprint [sprint] *sport* **1.** спринт (бег на коро́ткую диста́нцию); **2.** бе́гать на ско́рость.
sprite [sprait] эльф.
sprout [spraut] **1.** пуска́ть ростки́; всходи́ть [взойти́] (о семена́х); отра́щивать [отрасти́ть]; **2.** ⚘ росто́к, побе́г.
spruce[1] [spru:s] □ щеголева́тый; наря́дный.
spruce[2] [~] ⚘ ель *f*.
sprung [sprʌŋ] *pt.* и *p. pt.* от spring.
spry [sprai] *part. Am.* живо́й; сообрази́тельный; прово́рный.
spun [spʌn] *pt.* и *p. pt.* от spin.
spur [spə:] **1.** шпо́ра; *fig.* побужде́ние; act on the ~ of the moment де́йствовать под влия́нием мину́ты; **2.** пришпо́ри(ва)ть; побужда́ть [-уди́ть].
spurious ['spuəriəs] □ подде́льный, подло́жный.
spurn [spə:n] отверга́ть с презре́нием; отта́лкивать [оттолкну́ть] (ного́й).
spurt [spə:t] **1.** наддава́ть хо́ду; бить струёй; выбра́сывать [вы́бросить] (пла́мя); **2.** струя́; поры́в ве́тра; рыво́к; *sport* спурт.
sputter ['spʌtə] **1.** бры́зги *f/pl.*; шипе́ние; **2.** [за]шипе́ть (об огне́); бры́згать слюно́й; говори́ть бессвя́зно.
spy [spai] **1.** шпио́н(ка); та́йный аге́нт; **2.** шпио́нить, следи́ть (on за T); **~-glass** подзо́рная труба́.
squabble ['skwɔbl] **1.** перебра́нка, ссо́ра; **2.** [по]вздо́рить.
squad [skwɔd] брига́да; отря́д; ⚔ отделе́ние; гру́ппа, кома́нда; **~ron** ['skwɔdrən] ⚔ эскадро́н; ✈ эскадри́лья; ⚓ эска́дра.
squalid ['skwɔlid] □ убо́гий.
squall [skwɔ:l] **1.** шквал; вопль *m*; крик; **2.** [за]вопи́ть.
squander ['skwɔndə] прома́тывать [-мота́ть]; расточа́ть [-чи́ть].
square [skwɛə] **1.** □ квадра́тный; прямоуго́льный; пра́вильный; ро́вный; то́чный; прямо́й, че́стный; недвусмы́сленный; ~ measure квадра́тная ме́ра; 2 feet ~ 2 фу́та в квадра́те; **2.** квадра́т; прямоуго́льник; пло́щадь *f*; **3.** *v/t.* де́лать прямоуго́льным; опла́чивать [оплати́ть] (счёт); согласо́вывать [-сова́ть]; *v/i.* согласо́вываться [-сова́ться]; сходи́ться [сойти́сь]; **~-toes** F педа́нт.
squash [skwɔʃ] **1.** фрукто́вый напи́ток; разда́вленная ма́сса; F толчея́; **2.** разда́вливать [-дави́ть].
squat [skwɔt] **1.** призе́мистый;

2. сидеть на корточках; ~ter ['skwɔ:tə] *Am.* поселившийся самовольно в незанятом доме, на незанятой земле.
squawk [skwɔ:k] **1.** пронзительный крик (птицы); **2.** пронзительно кричать.
squeak [skwi:k] [про]пищать; *sl.* доносить [донести].
squeal [skwi:l] [за]визжать; *s.* squeak.
squeamish ['skwi:miʃ] □ щепетильный; обидчивый; привередливый; брезгливый.
squeeze [skwi:z] **1.** сж(им)ать; стискивать [-снуть]; выжимать [выжать]; *fig.* вымогать (from у Р); **2.** сжатие; пожатие; давление; давка; ~r ['skwi:zə] выжималка.
squelch [skweltʃ] F хлюпать; раздавливать ногой; *fig.* подавлять [-вить].
squint [skwint] косить (глазами); [со]щуриться.
squire ['skwaiə] **1.** сквайр (титул); **2.** сопровождать (даму).
squirm [skwə:m] F изви(ва)ться, [с]корчиться.
squirrel [skwirəl, *Am.* 'skwə:rəl] белка.
squirt [skwə:t] **1.** струя; шприц; F выскочка *m/f*; **2.** пускать струю (Р); бить струёй.
stab [stæb] **1.** удар (чем-либо острым); **2.** *v/t.* закалывать [заколоть]; *v/i.* наносить удар (at Д).
stabili|ty [stə'biliti] устойчивость *f*; прочность *f*; ~ze ['stæbilaiz] стабилизировать (*im*)*pf.*
stable[1] ['steibl] □ стойкий; устойчивый.
stable[2] [~] **1.** конюшня; хлев; **2.** ставить в конюшню (или в хлев).
stack [stæk] **1.** стог (сена и т. п.); штабель *m*; труба (парохода); куча; **2.** складывать в стог и т. д.; нагромождать [-моздить].
stadium ['steidiəm] *sport* стадион; ⚕ стадия.
staff [stɑ:f] **1.** посох; жезл; древко; ⚔ штаб; *attr.* штабной; ♪ нотная линейка; служебный персонал; **2.** снабжать персоналом.
stag [stæg] *zo.* олень-самец.
stage [steidʒ] **1.** подмостки *m/pl.*; сцена; эстрада; стадия; перегон; этап; **2.** [по]ставить (пьесу), инсценировать (*im*)*pf.*; ~**-coach** дилижанс; ~**-manager** режиссёр.
stagger ['stægə] **1.** *v/i.* шататься [(по)шатнуться]; *v/t.* потрясать [-ясти]; поражать [поразить]; **2.** шатание.
stagna|nt ['stægnənt] □ стоячий (о воде); *fig.* косный; ~te [-neit] застаиваться [застояться]; *fig.* [за-]коснеть.
staid [steid] □ солидный, уравновешенный.
stain [stein] **1.** пятно; ⊕ протрава; **2.** [за]пачкать; [за]пятнать; ⊕ протравливать [-равить] (дерево); [по]красить; ~ed glass цветное стекло; ~less ['steinlis] незапятнанный; нержавеющий (о стали); *fig.* безупречный.
stair [stɛə] ступенька; ~s *pl.* лестница; ~**case**, *Am.* ~**way** лестница; лестничная клетка.
stake [steik] **1.** кол; ставка, заклад (в пари); ~s *pl.* приз; be at ~ быть поставленным на карту (*a. fig.*); **2.** подпирать (или огораживать) кольями; ставить на карту; ~ out, off отмечать вехами.
stale [steil] □ несвежий; выдохшийся; спёртый (воздух); избитый.
stalk [stɔ:k] **1.** стебель *m*, черенок; *hunt.* подкрадывание; **2.** *v/i.* важно шествовать, гордо выступать; *v/t.* подкрадываться [-расться] к (Д).
stall [stɔ:l] **1.** стойло; прилавок; киоск, ларёк; *thea.* место в партере; **2.** ставить в стойло; застревать [-рять] (в снегу и т. п.); ✈ терять скорость.
stallion ['stæljən] жеребец.
stalwart ['stɔ:lwət] рослый, дюжий; стойкий.
stamina ['stæminə] выносливость *f.*
stammer ['stæmə] **1.** заикаться [-кнуться]; запинаться [запнуться]; **2.** заикание.
stamp [stæmp] **1.** штамп, штемпель *m*; печать *f* (*a. fig.*); клеймо; (почтовая, гербовая) марка; топанье; **2.** [от]штамповать; [за]штемпелевать; [за]клеймить; топать ногой.
stampede [stæm'pi:d] **1.** паническое бегство; **2.** обращать(ся) в паническое бегство.
stanch [stɑ:ntʃ] **1.** останавливать кровотечение из (Р); **2.** верный, лояльный.
stand [stænd] **1.** [*irr.*] *v/i. com.* стоять; постоять *pf.*; простаивать [-стоять]; останавливаться [-новиться]; держаться; устоять *pf.*; ~ against [вос]противиться, сопротивляться (Д); ~ aside [по]сторониться; ~ back отступать [-пить]; ~ by присутствовать; *fig.* быть наготове; поддерживать [-жать] (В); ~ for быть кандидатом (Р); стоять за (В); значить; ~ off отодвигаться [-инуться] от (Р); ~ out выделяться [выделиться] (against на П); ~ over оставаться нерешённым; ~ to держаться (Р); ~ up вст(ав)ать, подниматься [-няться]; ~ up for защищать [-итить]; **2.** *v/t.* [по]ставить; выдерживать [выдержать], выносить [вынести]; F угощать [угостить] (Т); **3.** остановка; сопротивление; точка зрения; ки-

óск; позиция; мéсто; подстáвка; трибýна; make a ~ against сопротивля́ться (Д).
standard ['stændəd] **1.** знáмя *n*, флаг, штандáрт; нóрма, стандáрт; образéц; ýровень *m*; **2.** стандáртный; образцóвый; **~ize** [-aiz] нормировáть (*im*)*pf.*
stand-by ['stænd'bai] опóра.
standing ['stændiŋ] **1.** □ стоя́щий; стоя́чий; постоя́нный; ~ orders *pl.* устáв; *parl.* прáвила процедýры; **2.** стоя́ние; положéние; продолжи́тельность *f*; **~-room** мéсто для стоя́щих (пассажи́ров, зри́телей).
stand|-offish сдéржанный; **~point** тóчка зрéния; **~still** бездéйствие; мёртвая тóчка; **~-up**: ~ collar стоя́чий воротничóк.
stank [stæŋk] *pt.* от stink.
stanza ['stænzə] строфá, станс.
staple ['steipl] **1.** глáвный прóдукт; глáвная тéма; **2.** основнóй.
star [stɑ:] **1.** звездá (*a. fig.*); *fig.* судьбá; ~s and stripes *pl. Am.* национáльный флаг США; **2.** украшáть звёздами; игрáть глáвную роль; предоставля́ть глáвную роль (Д).
starboard ['stɑ:bəd] ⚓ **1.** прáвый бóрт; **2.** класть руль напрáво.
starch [stɑ:tʃ] **1.** крахмáл; *fig.* чóпорность *f*; **2.** [на]крахмáлить.
stare [stɛə] **1.** при́стальный взгляд; **2.** смотрéть при́стально; тарáщить глазá (at на В).
stark [stɑ:k] окоченéлый; совершéнный; *adv.* совершéнно.
star|ry ['stɑ:ri] звёздный; как звёзды; **~-spangled** [-'spæŋgld] усéянный звёздами; ~ banner *Am.* национáльный флаг США.
start [stɑ:t] **1.** вздрáгивание; отправлéние; ✈ взлёт; *sport* старт; начáло; *fig.* преимýщество; get the ~ of a p. получи́ть преимýщество пéред кéм-либо; **2.** *v/i.* вздрáгивать [-рóгнуть]; вскáкивать [вскочи́ть]; отправля́ться в путь; *sport* стартовáть (*im*)*pf.*; нач(ин)áться; ✈ взлетáть [-етéть]; *v/t.* пускáть [пусти́ть] (в ход); *sport* давáть старт (Д); *fig.* нач(ин)áть; учреждáть [-еди́ть]; вспýгивать [-гнýть]; побуждáть [-уди́ть] (a p. doing когó-либо дéлать); **~er** ['stɑ:tə] *mot.* стáртер; *sport* стáртер, F стартёр; *fig.* инициáтор.
startl|e [stɑ:tl] поражáть [поразúть]; вздрáгивать [-рóгнуть]; **~ing** ['stɑ:tliŋ] поразúтельный.
starv|ation [stɑ:'veiʃən] гóлод; голодáние; **~e** [stɑ:v] голодáть; умирáть с гóлоду; мори́ть гóлодом; ~ for *fig.* жáждать (Р).
state [steit] **1.** состоя́ние; положéние; госудáрство (*pol. a.* ♀); штат; *attr.* госудáрственный; in ~ с пóмпой; **2.** заявля́ть [-ви́ть]; констати́ровать (*im*)*pf.*; [с]формули́ровать; излагáть [изложи́ть]; **~ly** величáвый, вели́чественный; **~ment** утверждéние; заявлéние; официáльный отчёт; ✝ ~ of account извлечéние (и́ли вы́писка) из счёта; **~room** парáдный зал; ⚓ отдéльная каю́та (на парохóде); **~sman** ['steitsmən] госудáрственный (*Am. a.* полити́ческий) дéятель *m.*
static ['stætik] стати́ческий; стационáрный.
station ['steiʃən] **1.** мéсто, пост; стáнция; вокзáл; остановка; ⚓ воéнно-морскáя бáза; **2.** [по]стáвить, помещáть [-ести́ть]; ⚔ размещáть [-ести́ть]; **~ary** ['steiʃnəri] □ неподви́жный; стационáрный; **~ery** [~] канцеля́рские принадлéжности *f/pl.*; **~-master** 🚂 начáльник стáнции.
statistics [stə'tistiks] статúстика.
statu|ary ['stætjuəri] скульптýрный; **~e** [-ju:] стáтуя, изваяние.
stature ['stætʃə] рост, стан, фигýра.
status ['steitəs] положéние, состоя́ние; стáтус.
statute ['stætju:t] статýт; закóн; законодáтельный акт; устáв.
staunch [stɔ:ntʃ] *s.* stanch.
stave [steiv] **1.** клёпка (бочáрная); переклáдина; строфá; **2.** [*irr.*] (*mst* ~ in) пролáмывать [-ломи́ть], разби́(вá)ть (бóчку и т. п.); ~ off предотвращáть [-врати́ть].
stay [stei] **1.** ⚓ штаг; опóра, поддéржка; останóвка; пребывáние; ~s *pl.* корсéт; **2.** *v/t.* поддéрживать [-жáть]; задéрживать [-жáть]; *v/i.* ост(ав)áться; остáнавливаться [-нови́ться], жить (at в П); *sport* проявля́ть вынóсливость; **~er** ['steiə] вынóсливый человéк; *sport* стáйер; ~ race велосипéдная гóнка за ли́дером.
stead [sted]: in ~ of вмéсто (Р); **~fast** ['stedfəst] стóйкий, непоколеби́мый.
steady ['stedi] **1.** □ устóйчивый; установи́вшийся; твёрдый; равномéрный; степéнный; **2.** дéлать (-ся) устóйчивым; приходи́ть в равновéсие.
steal [sti:l] [*irr.*] *v/t.* [у]воровáть, [у]крáсть; *v/i.* крáсться, прокрáдываться [-рáсться].
stealth [stelθ]: by ~ укрáдкой, таикóм; **~y** ['stelθi] □ тáйный; бесшýмный.
steam [sti:m] **1.** пар; испарéние; **2.** *attr.* паровóй; **3.** *v/i.* выпускáть пар; плáвать [по]плы́ть, (о парохóде); *v/t.* вари́ть на парý; пáрить; выпáривать [вы́парить]; **~er** ['sti:mə] ⚓ парохóд; **~y** ['sti:mi] □ парообрáзный; насы́щенный парáми.
steel [sti:l] **1.** сталь *f*; **2.** стальнóй

(*a.* ~у); *fig.* жесто́кий; **3.** покрыва́ть ста́лью, *fig.* закаля́ть [-ли́ть].
steep [sti:p] **1.** крутой; F невероятный; **2.** погружа́ть [-узи́ть] (в жи́дкость); пропи́тывать [-ита́ть]; *fig.* погружа́ться [-узи́ться] (in в В).
steeple ['sti:pl] шпиль *m*; колоко́льня; **~-chase** ска́чки с препя́тствиями.
steer¹ [stiə] кастри́рованный бычо́к.
steer² [~] пра́вить рулём; управля́ть (Т); води́ть, [по]вести́ ((су́дно); **~age** ['stiəridʒ] ⚓ управле́ние рулём; сре́дняя па́луба; **~sman** ['stiəzmən] рулево́й.
stem [stem] **1.** ствол; сте́бель *m*; *gr.* осно́ва; ⚓ нос; **2.** заде́рживать [-жа́ть]; сопротивля́ться (Д).
stench [stentʃ] зловоние.
stencil ['stensl] трафаре́т.
stenographer [ste'nɔgrəfə] стенографи́ст(ка).
step¹ [step] **1.** шаг; похо́дка; ступе́нька; подно́жка; *fig.* ме́ра; посту́пок; tread in the ~s of *fig.* идти́ по стопа́м (Р); ~s *pl.* стремя́нка; **2.** *v/i.* шага́ть [шагну́ть]; ступа́ть [-пну́ть]; ходи́ть, идти́ [пойти́]; ~ out бо́дро шага́ть; *v/t.* измеря́ть шага́ми (*a.* ~ out); ~ up продвига́ть [-и́нуть].
step² [~]: **~daughter** па́дчерица; **~-father** ['stepfɑ:ðə] о́тчим; **~-mother** ма́чеха; **~son** па́сынок.
steppe [step] степь *f*.
stepping-stone *fig.* трампли́н.
steril|e ['sterail] беспло́дный; стери́льный; **~ity** [ste'riliti] беспло́дие; стери́льность *f*; **~ize** ['sterilaiz] стерилизова́ть (*im*)*pf*.
sterling ['stə:liŋ] полнове́сный; полноце́нный; † сте́рлинговый.
stern [stə:n] **1.** □ стро́гий, суро́вый; неумоли́мый; **2.** ⚓ корма́; **~ness** ['stə:nnis] стро́гость *f*, суро́вость *f*; **~-post** ⚓ ахтерште́вень *m*.
stevedore ['sti:vidɔ:] ⚓ гру́зчик.
stew [stju:] **1.** [с]туши́ть(ся); **2.** тушёное мя́со; F беспоко́йство.
steward [stjuəd] эконо́м; управля́ющий; ⚓, ✈ стю́ард, бортпроводни́к; распоряди́тель *m*; **~ess** ['stjuədis] ⚓, ✈ стюарде́сса, бортпроводни́ца.
stick [stik] **1.** па́лка; трость *f*; прут; по́сох; **2.** [*irr.*] *v/i.* прикле́и(ва)ться, прилипа́ть [-ли́пнуть]; застрева́ть [-ря́ть]; завяза́ть [-я́знуть]; торча́ть (до́ма и т. п.); ~ to приде́рживаться [-жа́ться] (Р); ~ at nothing не остана́вливаться ни пе́ред че́м; ~ out, ~ up торча́ть; стоя́ть торчко́м; *v/t.* вка́лывать [вколо́ть]; втыка́ть [воткну́ть]; прикле́и(ва)ть; раскле́и(ва)ть; F терпе́ть, вы́терпеть *pf*.
sticky ['stiki] □ ли́пкий, кле́йкий.
stiff [stif] □ жёсткий, неги́бкий; туго́й; тру́дный; окостене́лый; натя́нутый; **~en** ['stifn] де́лать (-ся) жёстким и т. д.; окостене́(ва́)ть; **~necked** ['stif'nekt] упря́мый.
stifle ['staifl] [за]души́ть; задыха́ться [задохну́ться].
stigma ['stigmə] *eccl.* стигма́т; *fig.* пятно́, клеймо́; **~tize** [-taiz] [за-] клейми́ть.
still [stil] **1.** *adj.* ти́хий; неподви́жный; **2.** *adv.* ещё, всё ещё; **3.** *cj.* всё же, одна́ко; **4.** успока́ивать [-ко́ить]; **5.** дистилля́тор; **~-born** мертворождённый; **~-life** натюрмо́рт; **~ness** ['stilnis] тишина́.
stilt [stilt] ходу́ля; **~ed** ['stiltid] ходу́льный, высокопа́рный.
stimul|ant ['stimjulənt] **1.** ⚕ возбужда́ющее сре́дство; **2.** ⚕ стимули́рующий, возбужда́ющий; **~ate** [-leit] возбужда́ть [-уди́ть]; поощря́ть [-ри́ть]; **~ation** [stimju'leiʃən] возбужде́ние; поощре́ние; **~us** ['stimjuləs] сти́мул.
sting [stiŋ] **1.** жа́ло; уку́с (насеко́мого); о́страя боль *f*; *fig.* ко́лкость *f*; **2.** [*irr.*] [у]жа́лить; жечь (-ся)(о крапи́ве); уязвля́ть [-ви́ть]; **~iness** ['stindʒinis] ска́редность *f*; **~y** ['stindʒi] ска́редный, скупо́й.
stink [stiŋk] **1.** вонь *f*; **2.** [*irr.*] воня́ть.
stint [stint] **1.** ограниче́ние; преде́л; **2.** уре́з(ыв)ать; ограни́чи(ва)ть; [по]скупи́ться на (В).
stipend ['staipend] жа́лованье, окла́д (*mst* свяще́нника).
stipulat|e ['stipjuleit] ста́вить усло́вием; обусло́вливать [-вить]; **~ion** [stipju'leiʃən] усло́вие; кла́узула, огово́рка.
stir [stə:] **1.** шевеле́ние; суета́, сумато́ха; движе́ние; *fig.* оживле́ние; **2.** шевели́ть(ся) [-льну́ть (-ся)]; [по]меша́ть (чай и т. п.); [вз]волнова́ть; ~ up возбужда́ть [-уди́ть]; разме́шивать [-ша́ть].
stirrup ['stirəp] стре́мя *n* (*pl.*: стремена́).
stitch [stitʃ] **1.** стежо́к (о шитье́); пе́тля (о вяза́нии); ⚕ шов; **2.** [с]шить, проши́(ва́)ть.
stock [stɔk] **1.** ствол; опо́ра; ру́чка; ло́жа (винто́вки); инвента́рь *m*; запа́с; † сырьё; live ~ живо́й инвента́рь *m*; скот; † основно́й капита́л; фо́нды *m/pl.*; *Am.* а́кция, а́кции; ~s *pl.* госуда́рственный долг; ~s *pl.* ⚓ ста́пель *m*; † take ~ of де́лать переучёт (Р); *fig.* крити́чески оце́нивать; **2.** име́ющийся в запа́се (и́ли нагото́ве); изби́тый, шабло́нный; **3.** обору́довать (хозя́йство); снабжа́ть [-бди́ть]; † име́ть на скла́де.
stockade [stɔ'keid] частоко́л.
stock|-breeder животново́д; **~-**

broker биржевóй мáклер; ~ exchange фóндовая бúржа; **~holder** *Am.* акционéр.
stockinet ['stɔkinet] трикотáж.
stocking ['stɔkiŋ] чулóк.
stock|-jobber биржевóй спекулянт, мáклер; **~-taking** переучёт товáра; провéрка инвентаря́; *fig.* обзóр результáтов; **~y** ['stɔki] коренáстый.
stoic ['stouik] **1.** стóик; **2.** стóический.
stoker ['stoukə] кочегáр; истопнúк.
stole [stoul] *pt.* от steal; **~n** ['stoulən] *p. pt.* от steal.
stolid ['stɔlid] □ флегматúчный; бесстрáстный; тупóй.
stomach ['stʌmək] **1.** желýдок; живóт; *fig.* охóта (for к Д); **2.** перевáривать [-варúть] (*a. fig.*); *fig.* сносúть [снестú].
stone [stoun] **1.** кáмень *m*; кóсточка (плодá); **2.** кáменный; **3.** облицóвывать камня́ми; забрáсывать камня́ми; вынимáть кóсточки из (Р); **~-blind** совсéм слепóй; **~ware** гончáрные издéлия *n/pl.*
stony ['stouni] кáменный; каменúстый; *fig.* кáменный.
stood [stud] *pt.* и *p. pt.* от stand.
stool [stu:l] табурéтка; ⚕ стул; **~-pigeon** *Am.* провокáтор.
stoop [stu:p] **1.** *v/i.* наклоня́ться [-нúться], нагибáться [нагнýться]; [с]сутýлиться; унижáться [унúзиться] (to до Р); снисходúть [снизойтú]; *v/t.* [с]сутýлить; **2.** сутýлость *f*; *Am.* верáнда.
stop [stɔp] **1.** *v/t.* затыкáть [заткнýть] (*a.* ~ up); задéл(ыв)ать; [за]пломбировáть (зуб); преграждáть [-градúть]; удéрживать [-жáть]; прекращáть [-кратúть]; останáвливать [-новúть]; ~ it! брось!; *v/i.* перест(ав)áть; останáвливаться [-новúться]; прекращáться [-кратúться]; кончáться [кóнчиться]; **2.** остановка; пáуза; задéржка; ⊕ стóпор; упóр; ♪ клáпан; ♪ лад (стрýнного инструмéнта); ♪ педáль *f* (оргáна); *gr.* (*a.* full ~) тóчка; **~-gap** затычка; подрýчное срéдство; **~page** ['stɔpidʒ] задéржка, останóвка; прекращéние рабóты; ⊕ засорéние; **~per** ['stɔpə] прóбка; **~ping** ['stɔpiŋ] (зубнáя) плóмба.
storage ['stɔ:ridʒ] хранéние; склад.
store [stɔ:] **1.** запáс; склад; амбáр; *fig.* изобúлие; *Am.* лáвка; ~s *pl.* припáсы *m/pl.*; универмáг; in ~ наготóве; про запáс; **2.** снабжáть [снабдúть]; запасáть [-стú]; хранúть на склáде; **~house** склад; *fig.* сокрóвищница; **~-keeper** кладовщúк; *Am.* лáвочник.
stor(e)y ['stɔ:ri] этáж.
stork [stɔ:k] áист.
storm [stɔ:m] **1.** бýря; ⚓ *a.* шторм; ⚔ штурм; **2.** бушевáть, свирéпствовать (*a. fig.*); it ~s бýря бушýет; ⚔ штурмовáть; **~y** □ бýрный; штормовóй; я́ростный.
story ['stɔ:ri] расскáз; пóвесть *f*; *thea.* фáбула; F ложь *f*.
stout [staut] **1.** □ крéпкий, прóчный, плóтный; тýчный; отвáжный; **2.** крéпкое пúво.
stove [stouv] печь *f*, пéчка; (кýхонная) плитá.
stow [stou] уклáдывать [уложúть] (о грýзе и т. п.); **~away** ⚓ безбилéтный пассажúр, «зáяц».
straddle ['strædl] расставля́ть [-áвить] (нóги); ходúть, расставля́я нóги; стоя́ть, расстáвив нóги; сидéть верхóм на (П).
straggl|e ['strægl] отст(ав)áть; идтú вразбрóд; быть разбрóсанным; **~ing** [-iŋ] разбрóсанный (о домáх и т. п.); беспоря́дочный.
straight [streit] **1.** *adj.* прямóй; прáвильный; чéстный; *Am.* неразбáвленный; put ~ приводúть в поря́док; **2.** *adv.* пря́мо; срáзу; **~en** ['streitn] выпрямля́ть(ся) [вы́прямить(ся)]; ~ out приводúть в поря́док; **~forward** ['fɔ:wəd] □ чéстный, прямóй, откровéнный.
strain [strein] **1** порóда; плéмя *n*; ⊕ деформáция; напряжéние; растяжéние (*a.* ⚕); ♪ *mst* ~s *pl.* напéв, мелóдия; влечéние (of к Д); **2.** *v/t.* натя́гивать [натянýть]; (*a.* ⊕) напрягáть [-я́чь]; процéживать [-едúть]; переутомля́ть [-мúть]; ⊕ деформúровать (*im*)*pf.*, сгибáть [согнýть]; ⚕ растя́гивать [-янýть]; *v/i.* напрягáться [-я́чься]; тянýться (after за Т); тянýть изо всех сил (at В); [по]старáться; **~er** ['streinə] дуршлáг; сúто; фильтр.
strait [streit] пролúв; ~s *pl.* затруднúтельное положéние; ~ waistcoat смирúтельная рубáшка; **~ened** ['streitnd] стеснённый.
strand [strænd] **1.** бéрег (морскóй); прядь *f*; **2.** сесть на мель; be ~ed *fig.* быть без средств.
strange [streindʒ] □ чужóй; чýждый; стрáнный; **~r** ['streindʒə] чужезéмец (-мка); чужóй (человéк); посторóнний (человéк).
strangle ['stræŋgl] [у]давúть.
strap [stræp] **1.** ремéнь *m*; ля́мка; штрúпка; ⊕ крепúтельная плáнка; **2.** стя́гивать ремнём; порóть ремнём.
stratagem ['strætidʒəm] стратагéма, (воéнная) хúтрость *f*.
strateg|ic [strə'ti:dʒik] (~ally) стратегúческий; **~y** ['strætidʒi] стратéгия.
strat|um ['streitəm], *pl.* **~a** [-tə] *geol.* пласт; слой (óбщества).
straw [strɔ:] **1.** солóма; солóминка; **2.** солóменный; ~ vote *Am.*

неофициа́льное про́бное голосова́ние; **~berry** клубни́ка; (*a.* wild ~) земляни́ка.

stray [strei] **1.** сбива́ться с пути́; заблуди́ться *pf.*; отби́(ва́)ться (from от Р); блужда́ть; **2.** (*a.* ~ed) заблуди́вшийся; бездо́мный; случа́йный; **3.** отби́вшееся живо́тное; беспризо́рник (-ница)

streak [stri:k] **1.** просло́йка; поло́ска; *fig.* черта́; **2.** проводи́ть по́лосы на (П).

stream [stri:m] **1.** пото́к; руче́й; струя́; **2.** *v/i.* [по]те́чь; струи́ться; развева́ться; **~er** ['stri:mə] вы́мпел; дли́нная ле́нта; транспара́нт; столб (се́верного сия́ния); *typ.* кру́пный газе́тный заголо́вок.

street [stri:t] у́лица; *attr.* у́личный; **~-car** *Am.* трамва́й.

strength [streŋθ] си́ла; кре́пость *f* (материа́ла); on the ~ of в си́лу (Р); на основа́нии (Р); **~en** ['streŋθən] *v/t.* уси́ли(ва)ть; укрепля́ть [-пи́ть]; *v/i.* уси́ли(ва)ться.

strenuous ['strenjuəs] □ си́льный; энерги́чный; напряжённый.

stress [stres] **1.** давле́ние; напряже́ние; ударе́ние; **2.** подчёркивать [-черкну́ть]; ста́вить ударе́ние на (П).

stretch [stretʃ] **1.** *v/t.* натя́гивать [-яну́ть]; растя́гивать [-яну́ть]; вытя́гивать [вы́тянуть]; раски́дывать [-ки́нуть]; протя́гивать [-яну́ть] (*mst* ~ out); *fig.* преувели́чи(ва)ть; *v/i.* тяну́ться; растя́гиваться [-яну́ться]; натя́гиваться [-яну́ться]; **2.** растя́гивание; напряже́ние; протяже́ние; натя́жка; преувеличе́ние; простра́нство; промежу́ток вре́мени; **~er** ['stretʃə] носи́лки *f/pl.*

strew [stru:] [*irr.*] посыпа́ть [посы́пать]; разбра́сывать [-роса́ть].

stricken ['strikən] *p. pt.* от strike.

strict [strikt] то́чный; стро́гий; **~ness** ['striktnis] то́чность *f*; стро́гость *f*.

stridden ['stridn] *p. pt.* от stride.

stride [straid] **1.** [*irr.*] шага́ть [шагну́ть]; ~ over переша́гивать [-гну́ть]; **2.** большо́й шаг.

strident ['straidnt] □ скрипу́чий.

strike [straik] **1.** ста́чка; забасто́вка; be on ~ бастова́ть; **2.** [*irr.*] *v/t.* ударя́ть [уда́рить]; высека́ть [вы́сечь] (ого́нь); [от]чека́нить; спуска́ть [-сти́ть] (флаг); поража́ть [порази́ть]; находи́ть [найти́]; подводи́ть [-вести́] (бала́нс); заключа́ть [-чи́ть] (сде́лку); принима́ть [-ня́ть] (по́зу); наноси́ть [нанести́] (уда́р); ~ up завя́зывать [-за́ть] (знако́мство); *v/i.* [про]би́ть (о часа́х); [за]бастова́ть; ⚓ сесть на мель; ~ home *fig.* попада́ть в са́мую то́чку; **~r** ['straikə] забасто́вщик (-ица).

striking ['straikiŋ] □ порази́тельный; замеча́тельный; уда́рный.

string [striŋ] **1.** верёвка; бечёвка; тетива́ (лу́ка); ♪ струна́; ни́тка (бус); ~s *pl.* ♪ стру́нные инструме́нты *m/pl.*; pull the ~s быть закули́сным руководи́телем; **2.** [*irr.*] натя́гивать стру́ны на (В); напряга́ть [-ря́чь]; *Am.* завя́зывать [завяза́ть]; нани́зывать [-за́ть]; *Am. sl.* води́ть за́ нос; **~-band** стру́нный орке́стр.

stringent ['strindʒənt] стро́гий; то́чный; обяза́тельный; стеснённый (в деньга́х).

strip [strip] **1.** сдира́ть [содра́ть] (*a.* ~ off); обдира́ть [ободра́ть]; разде́(ва́)ть(ся); *fig.* лиша́ть [-ши́ть] (of Р); [о]гра́бить; ⊕ разбира́ть [разобра́ть] (на ча́сти); ⚓ разоружа́ть [-жи́ть] (су́дно); **2.** полоса́; ле́нта.

stripe [straip] полоса́; ⚔ наши́вка.

strive [straiv] [*irr.*] [по]стара́ться; стреми́ться (for к Д); **~n** [-n] *p. pt.* от strive.

strode [stroud] *pt.* от stride.

stroke [strouk] **1.** уда́р (*a.* ⚕); взмах; штрих, черта́; ⊕ ход (по́ршня); ~ of luck уда́ча; **2.** [по]гла́дить; приласка́ть *pf.*

stroll [stroul] **1.** прогу́ливаться [-ля́ться]; **2.** прогу́лка.

strong [strɔŋ] □ *com.* си́льный; про́чный; кре́пкий; о́стрый; твёрдый; **~hold** кре́пость *f*; *fig.* опло́т; **~-willed** реши́тельный; упря́мый.

strop [strɔp] **1.** реме́нь для пра́вки бритв; **2.** пра́вить (бри́тву).

strove [strouv] *pt.* от strive.

struck [strʌk] *pt.* и *p. pt.* от strike.

structure ['strʌktʃə] структу́ра, строй; устро́йство; ⚠ строе́ние, сооруже́ние.

struggle ['strʌgl] **1.** боро́ться; вся́чески стара́ться; би́ться (with над Т); ~ through с трудо́м пробива́ться; **2.** борьба́.

strung [strʌŋ] *pt.* и *p. pt.* от string.

strut [strʌt] **1.** *v/i.* ходи́ть го́голем; *v/t.* ⊕ подпира́ть [-пере́ть]; **2.** ва́жная похо́дка; ⊕ подпо́рка.

stub [stʌb] **1.** пень *m*; оку́рок; огры́зок; **2.** выкорчёвывать [вы́корчевать]; ударя́ться [уда́риться] (ного́й) (against о В).

stubble ['stʌbl] жнивьё.

stubborn ['stʌbən] □ упря́мый; неподатливый; упо́рный.

stuck [stʌk] *pt.* и *p. pt.* от stick; **~-up** F высокоме́рный.

stud [stʌd] **1.** гвоздь *m* (для украше́ния); за́понка; ко́нный заво́д; **2.** оби́(ва́)ть (гвоздя́ми); усе́ивать [усе́ять] (with Т); **~-horse** племенно́й жеребе́ц.

student ['stju:dənt] студе́нт(ка).

studied ['stʌdid] обду́манный;

преднаме́ренный; изы́сканный; де́ланный.
studio ['stju:diou] сту́дия; ателье́ *n indecl.*; мастерска́я.
studious ['stju:djəs] □ приле́жный, стара́тельный, усе́рдный.
study ['stʌdi] **1.** изуче́ние; нау́чное заня́тие; нау́ка; заду́мчивость *f*; кабине́т; *paint.* этю́д, эски́з; **2.** учи́ться (Д); изуча́ть [-чи́ть]; иссле́довать (*im*)*pf*.
stuff [stʌf] **1.** материа́л; вещество́; мате́рия; F дря́нь *f*; чепуха́; **2.** *v/t.* наби́(ва́)ть; заби́(ва́)ть; начиня́ть [-ни́ть]; засо́вывать [засу́нуть]; *v/i.* объеда́ться [объе́сться]; **~ing** ['stʌfiŋ] наби́вка (поду́шки и т. п.); начи́нка; **~y** ['stʌfi] □ спёртый, ду́шный.
stultify ['stʌltifai] выставля́ть в смешно́м ви́де; своди́ть на не́т.
stumble ['stʌmbl] **1.** спотыка́ние; запи́нка; **2.** спотыка́ться [-ткну́ться]; запина́ться [запну́ться]; **~ upon** натыка́ться [наткну́ться] на (В).
stump [stʌmp] **1.** пень *m*; обру́бок; оку́рок; **2.** *v/t.* F ста́вить в тупи́к; **~ the country** агити́ровать по стране́; *v/i.* тяжело́ ступа́ть; **~y** ['stʌmpi] □ призе́мистый.
stun [stʌn] оглуша́ть [-ши́ть] (*a. fig.*); *fig.* ошеломля́ть [-ми́ть].
stung [stʌŋ] *pt.* и *p. pt.* от sting.
stunk [stʌŋk] *pt.* и *p. pt.* от stink.
stunning ['stʌniŋ] F сногсшиба́тельный.
stunt[1] [stʌnt] *Am.* F трюк; ✈ фигу́ра вы́сшего пилота́жа.
stunt[2] [~] заде́рживать рост (Р); **~ed** ['stʌntid] ча́хлый.
stup|efy ['stju:pifai] изумля́ть [-ми́ть]; поража́ть [порази́ть]; **~endous** [stju:'pendəs] □ изуми́тельный; **~id** ['stju:pid] □ глу́пый, тупо́й; **~idity** [stju'piditi] глу́пость *f*; **~or** ['stju:pə] оцепене́ние.
sturdy ['stə:di] си́льный, кре́пкий; здоро́вый.
stutter ['stʌtə] заика́ться [-кну́ться]; запина́ться [запну́ться].
sty [stai] свина́рник; ячме́нь *m* (на глазу́).
style [stail] **1.** стиль *m*; слог; мо́да; фасо́н; ти́тул; **2.** титулова́ть (*im*)*pf*.
stylish ['stailiʃ] □ мо́дный; элега́нтный; **~ness** [-nis] элега́нтность *f*.
suave [sweiv] учти́вый; мя́гкий.
sub... [sʌb] *mst* под...; суб...
subdivision ['sʌbdi'viʒən] подразделе́ние.
subdue [səb'dju:] подчиня́ть [-ни́ть]; покоря́ть [-ри́ть]; подавля́ть [-ви́ть].
subject ['sʌbdʒikt] **1.** подчинённый; подвла́стный; *fig.* **~ to** подлежа́щий (Д); **2.** *adv.* **~ to** при усло́вии (Р); **3.** по́дданный; предме́т; сюже́т; (*a.* **~ matter**) те́ма; **4.** [səb'dʒekt] подчиня́ть [-ни́ть]; *fig.* подверга́ть [-е́ргнуть]; **~ion** [səb'dʒekʃən] покоре́ние; подчине́ние.
subjugate ['sʌbdʒugeit] поработи́ть [-боти́ть].
sublease ['sʌb'li:s], **sublet** ['sʌb'let] [*irr.* (let)] сдать на права́х суба-ре́нды
sublime [[sə'blaim] □ возвы́шенный.
submachine ['sʌbmə'ʃi:n]: **~ gun** автома́т.
submarine ['sʌbməri:n] **1.** подво́дный; **2.** ⚓ подво́дная ло́дка.
submerge [sʌb'mə:dʒ] погружа́ть (-ся) [-узи́ть(ся)]; затопля́ть [-пи́ть].
submiss|ion [səb'miʃən] подчине́ние; поко́рность *f*; представле́ние (докуме́нта и т. п.); **~ive** [səb'misiv] □ поко́рный.
submit [səb'mit] подчиня́ть(ся) [-ни́ть(ся)] (Д); представля́ть [-а́вить] (на рассмотре́ние).
subordinate 1. [sə'bɔ:dnit] подчинённый; *gr.* прида́точный; **2.** [~] подчинённый (-ённая); **3.** [sə'bɔ:dineit] подчиня́ть [-ни́ть].
suborn [sʌ'bɔ:n] подкупа́ть [-пи́ть].
subscribe [səb'skraib] *v/t.* подпи́сывать [-са́ть]; [по]же́ртвовать; *v/i.* присоединя́ться [-ни́ться] (to к Д); подпи́сываться [-са́ться] (to на В; ✝ for на В); абони́роваться (to на В); **~r** [-ə] подпи́счик (-чица); абоне́нт(ка).
subscription [səb'skripʃən] подпи́ска (на журна́л и́ли на заём); абонеме́нт.
subsequent ['sʌbsikwənt] □ после́дующий; **~ly** впосле́дствии.
subservient [səb'sə:vient] раболе́пный; соде́йствующий (to Д).
subsid|e [səb'said] спада́ть [спа́сть] (о температу́ре); убы́(ва́)ть (о воде́); утиха́ть [ути́хнуть], уле́чься *pf.*; **~iary** [səb'sidjəri] **1.** □ вспомога́тельный; **2.** филиа́л; **~ize** ['sʌbsidaiz] субсиди́ровать (*im*)*pf.*; **~y** [-di] субси́дия.
subsist [səb'sist] существова́ть; жить (on, by Т); **~ence** [-əns] существова́ние; сре́дства к существова́нию.
substance ['sʌbstəns] су́щность *f*, суть *f*; содержа́ние; вещество́; иму́щество.
substantial [səb'stænʃəl] □ суще́ственный, ва́жный; про́чный; веще́ственный; состоя́тельный; пита́тельный.
substantiate [səb'stænʃieit] дока́зывать справедли́вость (Р); подтвержда́ть [-рди́ть].
substitut|e ['sʌbstitju:t] **1.** заменя́ть [-ни́ть]; замеща́ть [-ести́ть] (for В); **2.** замести́тель(ница *f*) *m*; за-

ме́на; суррога́т; ~ion [sʌbsti'tju:ʃən] заме́на; замеще́ние.
subterfuge ['sʌbtəfju:dʒ] увёртка, отгово́рка.
subterranean [sʌbtə'reinjən] □ подзе́мный.
subtle ['sʌtl] □ то́нкий; неулови́мый; утончённый; **~ty** [-ti] то́нкость *f*; неулови́мость *f*.
subtract [səb'trækt] ⅄ вычита́ть [вы́честь].
suburb ['sʌbə:b] при́город; предме́стье; **~an** [sə'bə:bən] при́городный.
subver|sion [sʌb'və:ʃən] ниспроверже́ние; **~sive** [-siv] *fig.* подрывно́й; разруши́тельный; **~t** [sʌb'və:t] ниспроверга́ть [-е́ргнуть]; разруша́ть [-у́шить].
subway ['sʌbwei] тонне́ль *m* (*a.* тунне́ль); *Am.* метро́(полите́н) *n indecl.*
succeed [sək'si:d] [по]сле́довать за (Т); быть прее́мником (Р); достига́ть це́ли; преуспе́(ва́)ть.
success [sək'ses] успе́х; уда́ча; **~ful** [sək'sesful] □ успе́шный; уда́чный; уда́чливый; **~ion** [-'seʃən] после́довательность *f*; непреры́вный ряд; прее́мственность *f*; in ~ оди́н за други́м; подря́д; **~ive** [-'sesiv] □ после́дующий; после́довательный; **~or** [-'sesə] прее́мник (-ица); насле́дник (-ица).
succo(u)r ['sʌkə] **1.** по́мощь *f*; **2.** приходи́ть на по́мощь (Д).
succulent ['sʌkjulənt] со́чный.
succumb [sə'kʌm] уступа́ть [-пи́ть] (to Д); не выде́рживать [вы́держать] (to Р); быть побеждённым.
such [sʌtʃ] тако́й; *pred.* тако́в, -а́ и т. д.; ~ a man тако́й челове́к; ~ as тако́й, как ...; как наприме́р.
suck [sʌk] **1.** соса́ть; выса́сывать [вы́сосать] (*a.* ~ out); вса́сывать [всоса́ть] (*a.* ~ in); **2.** соса́ние; **~er** ['sʌkə] сосуно́к; ⚘, *zo.* присо́ска, присо́сок; *Am.* проста́к; **~le** ['sʌkl] корми́ть гру́дью; **~ling** ['sʌkliŋ] грудно́й ребёнок; сосу́н(о́к).
suction ['sʌkʃən] **1.** вса́сывание; **2.** *attr.* вса́сывающий.
sudden ['sʌdn] □ внеза́пный; all of a ~ внеза́пно, вдруг.
suds [sʌdz] *pl.* мы́льная вода́.
sue [sju:] *v/t.* пресле́довать суде́бным поря́дком; ~ out выхлопа́тывать [вы́хлопота́ть]; *v/i.* возбужда́ть иск (for о П).
suéde [sweid] за́мша.
suet [sjuit] по́чечное са́ло.
suffer ['sʌfə] *v/i.* [по]страда́ть (from от Р *or* Т); *v/t.* [по]терпе́ть; сноси́ть [снести́]; **~ance** [-rəns] попусти́тельство; **~er** [-rə] страда́лец (-лица); **~ing** [-riŋ] страда́ние.
suffice [sə'fais] хвата́ть [-ти́ть], быть доста́точным.
sufficien|cy [sə'fiʃənsi] доста́точность *f*; доста́ток; **~t** [-ənt] □ доста́точный.
suffocate ['sʌfəkeit] души́ть, удуша́ть [-ши́ть]; задыха́ться [задохну́ться].
suffrage ['sʌfridʒ] избира́тельное пра́во.
suffuse [sə'fju:z] зали́(ва́)ть) слеза́ми); покры́(ва́)ть (кра́ской).
sugar ['ʃugə] **1.** са́хар; **2.** са́харный; **~y** [-ri] са́харный (*a. fig.*); *fig.* при́торный, слаща́вый.
suggest [sə'dʒest] внуша́ть [-ши́ть]; подска́зывать [-за́ть]; наводи́ть на мысль о (П); [по]сове́товать; предлага́ть [-ложи́ть]; **~ion** [-ʃən] внуше́ние; сове́т, предложе́ние; намёк; **~ive** [-iv] □ наводя́щий на размышле́ние; соблазни́тельный; двусмы́сленный.
suicide ['sjuisaid] самоуби́йца *m/f*; самоуби́йство.
suit [sju:t] **1.** проше́ние; набо́р; (*a.* ~ of clothes) костю́м; (ка́рточная) масть *f*; ⚖ тя́жба; иск; **2.** *v/t.* приспоса́бливать [-осо́бить] (to, with к Д); соотве́тствовать (Д); удовлетворя́ть [-ри́ть]; быть (кому́-либо) к лицу́ (*a.* with a p.); устра́ивать [-ро́ить]; подходи́ть [подойти́] (Д); ~ed подходя́щий; *v/i.* годи́ться; **~able** ['sju:təbl] □ подходя́щий; соотве́тствующий; **~-case** чемода́н; **~e** [swi:t] сви́та; набо́р; ♪ сю́ита; (и́ли ~ of rooms) анфила́да ко́мнат; гарниту́р (ме́бели); **~or** ['sju:tə] уха́живатель *m*; ⚖ исте́ц; проси́тель(ница *f*) *m*.
sulk [sʌlk] **1.** [на]ду́ться; быть не в ду́хе; **2.** ~s [-s] *pl.* плохо́е настрое́ние; **~y** ['sʌlki] □ наду́тый, угрю́мый.
sullen ['sʌlən] угрю́мый, мра́чный; серди́тый.
sully ['sʌli] *mst fig.* [за]пятна́ть.
sulphur ['sʌlfə] ⚗ се́ра; **~ic** [sʌl'fjuərik] се́рный.
sultriness ['sʌltrinis] духота́, зной.
sultry ['sʌltri] □ ду́шный, зно́йный.
sum [sʌm] **1.** су́мма; ито́г; *fig.* содержа́ние; су́щность; ~s *pl.* арифме́тика; **2.** (*a.* ~ up) ⅄ скла́дывать [сложи́ть]; *fig.* подводи́ть ито́г.
summar|ize ['sʌməraiz] сумми́ровать (*im*)*pf.*; резюми́ровать (*im*-)*pf.*; **~y** [-ri] **1.** □ кра́ткий; сокращённый; ⚖ дисциплина́рный; **2.** (кра́ткое) изложе́ние, резюме́ *n indecl.*
summer ['sʌmə] ле́то; **~(l)y** [-ri, -li] ле́тний.
summit ['sʌmit] верши́на (*a. fig.*); преде́л; верх.
summon ['sʌmən] соз(ы)ва́ть (собра́ние и т. п.); ⚖ вызыва́ть [вы́звать] (в суд); приз(ы)ва́ть; **~s** [-z] вы́зов (в суд); суде́бная пове́стка; ⚔ предложе́ние сда́ться.

sumptuous ['sʌmptjuəs] роскóшный; пы́шный.
sun [sʌn] **1.** сóлнце; **2.** сóлнечный; **3.** грéть(ся) на сóлнце; **~burn** ['sʌnbə:n] загáр.
Sunday ['sʌndi] воскресéнье.
sun|-dial сóлнечные часы́ *m/pl.*; **~-down** *Am.* закáт, захóд сóлнца.
sundries ['sʌndriz] *pl.* вся́кая вся́чина; ⚕ разные расхóды *m/pl.*
sung [sʌŋ] *p. pt.* от sing.
sun-glasses *pl.* тёмные очки́ *n/pl.*
sunk [sʌŋk] *p. pt.* от sink.
sunken [sʌŋkən] *fig.* впáлый.
sun|ny ['sʌni] □ сóлнечный; **~rise** восхóд сóлнца; **~set** захóд сóлнца, закáт; **~shade** зóнт(ик) от сóлнца; **~shine** сóлнечный свет; in the ~ на сóлнце; **~stroke** ⚕ сóлнечный удáр; **~up** ['sʌnʌp] *Am.* восхóд сóлнца.
sup [sʌp] [по]у́жинать.
super... ['sju:pə] *pref.*: пере..., пре...; сверх...; над...; супер...; **~abundant** [sju:pərə'bʌndənt] □ изоби́льный· **~annuate** [sju:pə'rænjueit] переводи́ть на пéнсию; *fig.* сдавáть в архи́в; **~d** престарéлый; устарéлый. [прекрáсный.]
superb [sju'pə:b] роскóшный,
super|charger ['sju:pətʃɑ:dʒə] ⊕ нагнетáтель *m*; **~cilious** [sju:pə'siliəs] □ высокомéрный; **~ficial** [sju:pə'fiʃəl] □ повéрхностный; **~fine** ['sju:pə'fain] чрезмéрно утончённый; вы́сшего сóрта; **~fluity** [sju:pə'fluiti] изоби́лие, изли́шек; изли́шество; **~fluous** [sju'pə:fluəs] □ изли́шний; **~heat** [sju:pə'hi:t] ⊕ перегрé(вá)ть; **~intend** [sju:prin'tend] надзирáть за (Т); заведовать (Т); **~intendent** [-ənt] надзирáтель *m*; завéдующий; управдóм.
superior [sju'piəriə] **1.** □ вы́сший; стáрший (по чи́ну); лу́чший; превосхóдный; превосходя́щий (to В); **2.** стáрший, начáльник; *eccl.* настоя́тель *m*, (*mst* lady ~) настоя́тельница; **~ity** [sjupiəri'ɔriti] превосхóдство.
super|lative [sju'pə:lətiv] **1.** □ высочáйший; величáйший; **2.** превосхóдная стéпень *f*; **~numerary** [sju:pə'nju:mərəri] **1.** сверхштáтный; **2.** сверхштáтный рабóтник; *thea.* стати́ст; **~scription** [sju:pə'skripʃən] нáдпись *f*; **~sede** [-si:d] заменя́ть [-ни́ть]; вытесня́ть [вы́теснить]; *fig.* обгоня́ть [обогнáть]; **~stition** [-'stiʃən] суевéрие; **~stitious** [-'stiʃəs] суевéрный; **~vene** [sju:pə'vi:n] добавля́ться [-áвиться]; неожи́данно возникáть; **~vise** ['sju:pəvaiz] надзирáть за (Т); **~vision** [sju:pə'viʒən] надзóр; **~visor** ['sju:pəvaizə] надзирáтель *m*. [♀ тáйная вéчеря.]
supper ['sʌpə] у́жин; the (Lord's)

supplant [sə'plɑ:nt] вытесня́ть [вы́теснить] (В).
supple ['sʌpl] ги́бкий; подáтливый.
supplement **1.** ['sʌplimənt] добавлéние, дополнéние; приложéние; **2.** [-'ment] дополня́ть [допóлнить]; **~al** [sʌpli'mentl] □, **~ary** [-təri] дополни́тельный, добáвочный.
suppliant ['sʌpliənt] проси́тель (-ница *f*) *m*.
supplicat|e ['sʌplikeit] умоля́ть (for о П); **~ion** [sʌpli'keiʃən] мольбá; прóсьба.
supplier [sə'plaiə] поставщи́к (-и́ца).
supply [sə'plai] **1.** снабжáть [-бди́ть] (with Т); поставля́ть [-áвить]; доставля́ть [-áвить]; возмещáть [-ести́ть]; замещáть [-ести́ть]; **2.** снабжéние; постáвка; запáс; врéменный заместáтель *m*; *pl.* продовóльствие; припáсы *m/pl.*; ⚕ предложéние; *mst pl. parl.* ассигновáния *n/pl.* (утверждённые парлáментом).
support [sə'pɔ:t] **1.** поддéржка; опóра; **2.** подпирáть [-перéть]; поддéрживать [-жáть]; содержáть (семью́ и т. п.).
suppose [sə'pouz] предполагáть [-ложи́ть]; полагáть; F ~ we do so? а éсли мы э́то сдéлаем?
supposed [sə'pouzd] □ предполагáемый; **~ly** [-zidli] предположи́тельно; я́кобы.
supposition [sʌpə'ziʃən] предположéние.
suppress [sə'pres] подавля́ть [-ви́ть]; запрещáть [-ети́ть] (газéту); сдéрживать [-жáть] (смéх, гнев и т. п.); **~ion** [sə'preʃən] подавлéние и т. д.
suppurate ['sʌpjuəreit] гнои́ться.
suprem|acy [sju'preməsi] превосхóдство; верхóвная власть *f*; **~e** [sju'pri:m] □ верхóвный; вы́сший; крáйний.
surcharge [sə:'tʃɑ:dʒ] **1.** перегружáть [-узи́ть]; **2.** ['sə:tʃa:dʒ] перегру́зка; приплáта, доплáта (за письмó и т. п.); надпечáтка.
sure [ʃuə] □ *com.* вéрный; увéренный; безопáсный; надёжный; to be ~! *Am.* ~! безуслóвно, конéчно; **~ly** ['ʃuəli] несомнéнно; навéрно; **~ty** [-ti] пору́ка; поручи́тель *m*.
surf [sə:f] прибóй.
surface ['sə:fis] **1.** повéрхность *f*; **2.** повéрхностный.
surfeit ['sə:fit] **1.** изли́шество; пресыщéние; **2.** пресыщáть(ся) [-ы́тить(ся)] (on Т); переедáть [переéсть] (on P).
surge [sə:dʒ] **1.** волнá; **2.** вздымáться (о вóлнах); *fig.* [вз]волновáться.

surg|eon ['sə:dʒen] хиру́рг; **~ery** ['sə:dʒəri] хирурги́я; хирурги́ческий кабине́т.
surgical ['sə:dʒikəl] □ хирурги́ческий.
surly [sə:li] □ угрю́мый; гру́бый.
surmise ['sə:maiz] **1.** предположе́ние, дога́дка; **2.** [sə:'maiz] предполага́ть [-ложи́ть].
surmount [sə:'maunt] преодоле́(ва́)ть, превозмога́ть [-мо́чь].
surname ['sə:neim] фами́лия; про́звище.
surpass [sə:'pɑ:s] перегоня́ть [-гна́ть]; превосходи́ть [-взойти́]; **~ing** [-iŋ] превосхо́дный.
surplus ['sə:pləs] **1.** изли́шек; оста́ток; **2.** изли́шний; доба́вочный, приба́вочный.
surprise [sə'praiz] **1.** удивле́ние; неожи́данность *f*, сюрпри́з; *attr.* неожи́данный; ⚔ внеза́пный; **2.** удивля́ть [-ви́ть]; застава́ть врасплóх.
surrender [sə'rendə] **1.** сда́ча; капитуля́ция; **2.** *v/t.* сда(ва́)ть; отка́зываться [-за́ться] от (Р); *v/i.* сд(ав)а́ться (*a.* ~ o. s.).
surround [sə'raund] окружа́ть [-жи́ть]; **~ing** [-iŋ] окружа́ющий; **~ings** [-iŋz] *pl.* окре́стности *f/pl.*
surtax ['sə:tæks] доба́вочный нало́г.
survey 1. [sə:'vei] обозре́(ва́)ть; осма́тривать [осмотре́ть]; *surv.* межева́ть; **2.** ['sə:vei] осмо́тр; обзо́р; *fig.* обсле́дование; *surv.* межева́ние; *attr.* обзо́рный; **~or** [sə:'veiə] землеме́р; *Am.* инспе́ктор.
surviv|al [sə'vaivəl] выжива́ние; пережи́ток; **~e** [sə'vaiv] *v/t.* пережи́(ва́)ть; вы́живать по́сле (Р); *v/i.* остава́ться в живы́х, вы́жи(ва́)ть; **~or** [-ə] оста́вшийся в живы́х.
susceptible [sə'septəbl] □ восприи́мчивый (to к Д); оби́дчивый; be ~ of допуска́ть [-сти́ть] (В).
suspect [səs'pekt] **1.** подозрева́ть, заподáзривать [-до́зрить] (of в П); сомнева́ться [усомни́ться] в (по́длинности и т. п.); полага́ть; **2.** подозри́тельный; подозрева́емый.
suspend [səs'pend] ве́шать [пове́сить]; приостана́вливать [-нови́ть]; откла́дывать [отложи́ть]; вре́менно прекраща́ть; **~ed** подвесно́й; **~ers** [-əz] *pl. Am.* подтя́жки *f/pl.*; подвя́зки *f/pl.*
suspens|e [səs'pens] напряжённое внима́ние; состоя́ние неизве́стности; be in ~ быть нерешённым; **~ion** [səs'penʃən] подве́шивание; прекраще́ние; вре́менная отста́вка; ~ bridge вися́чий мост.
suspici|on [səs'piʃən] подозре́ние; *fig.* чу́точка; **~ous** [-əs] □ подозри́тельный.
sustain [səs'tein] подпира́ть [-пере́ть]; подде́рживать [-жа́ть]; подтвержда́ть [-рди́ть]; выде́рживать [вы́держать]; выноси́ть [вы́нести], испы́тывать [испыта́ть].
sustenance ['sʌstinəns] пи́ща; сре́дства к существова́нию.
svelte [svelt] стро́йный.
swab [swɔb] **1.** шва́бра; ⚕ мазо́к; **2.** (*a.* ~ down) мыть шва́брой.
swaddle ['swɔdl] [с-, за]пелена́ть; swaddling clothes *pl.* пелёнки *f/pl.*
swagger ['swægə] ва́жничать; чва́ниться; [по]хва́стать (*a.* -ся).
swallow ['swɔlou] **1.** *zo.* ла́сточка; глото́к; **2.** глота́ть; прогла́тывать [-лоти́ть].
swam [swæm] *pt.* от swim.
swamp [swɔmp] **1.** боло́то, топь *f*; **2.** затопля́ть [-пи́ть], зали́(ва́)ть; **~y** ['swɔmpi] боло́тистый.
swan [swɔn] ле́бедь *m.* (*poet. a. f.*).
swap [swɔp] F **1.** обме́нивать(ся) [-ня́ть(ся)]; [по]меня́ть; **2.** обме́н.
sward [swɔ:d] газо́н; дёрн.
swarm [swɔ:m] **1.** рой (пчёл); стая (птиц); толпа́; **2.** рои́ться (о пчёлах); кише́ть (with T).
swarthy ['swɔ:ði] сму́глый.
swash [swɔʃ] плеска́ть [-сну́ть]; плеска́ться.
swath [swɔ:θ] 🌾 проко́с.
swathe [sweið] [за]бинтова́ть; заку́т(ыв)ать.
sway [swei] **1.** колеба́ние; кача́ние; влия́ние; **2.** кача́ть(ся) [качну́ть(-ся)]; [по]колеба́ться; име́ть влия́ние на (В); вла́ствовать над (Т).
swear [swɛə] [*irr.*] [по]кля́сться (by T); заставля́ть покля́сться (to в П); *b. s.* [вы́]руга́ться.
sweat [swet] **1.** пот; поте́ние; **2.** [*irr.*] *v/i.* [вс]поте́ть; исполня́ть тяжёлую рабо́ту; *v/t.* заставля́ть поте́ть; эксплуати́ровать; выделя́ть [вы́делить] (вла́гу); **~y** ['sweti] по́тный.
Swede [swi:d] шве́д(ка).
Swedish ['swi:diʃ] шве́дский.
sweep [swi:p] **1.** [*irr.*] мести́, подмета́ть [-ести́]; [по]чи́стить; проноси́ться [-нести́сь] (*a.* ~ past, along); *fig.* увлека́ть [-е́чь] (*a.* ~ along); ⚔ обстре́ливать [-ля́ть]; **2.** подмета́ние; разма́х; взмах; трубочи́ст; make a clean ~ (of) отде́л(ыв)аться (от Р); **~er** ['swi:pə] мете́льщик; **~ing** ['swi:piŋ] □ стреми́тельный; широ́кий, разма́шистый; огу́льный; **~ings** [-z] *pl.* му́сор.
sweet [swi:t] **1.** □ сла́дкий; све́жий; души́стый; ми́лый; have a ~ tooth быть сластёной; **2.** конфе́та; **~s** *pl.* сла́дости *f/pl.*, сла́сти *f/pl.*; **~en** ['swi:tn] подсла́щивать [-ласти́ть]; **~heart** возлю́бленный (-енная); **~ish** ['swi:tiʃ] сладкова́тый; **~meat** конфе́та; **~ness** ['swi:tnis] сла́дость *f*.
swell [swel] **1.** [*irr.*] *v/i.* [о]пу́хнуть; разду́(ва́)ться; набуха́ть [-у́хнуть];

нараста́ть [-сти́] (о зву́ке); *v/t.* разду́(ва́)ть; увели́чи(ва)ть; **2.** F щегольско́й; шика́рный; великоле́пный; **3.** вы́пуклость *f*; о́пухоль *f*; ⚓ мёртвая зыбь *f*; F щёголь *m*; све́тский челове́к; **~ing** ['sweliŋ] о́пухоль *f*.
swelter ['sweltə] томи́ться от жары́.
swept [swept] *pt.* и *p. pt.* от sweep.
swerve [swə:v] **1.** отклоня́ться от прямо́го пути́; (вдруг) свора́чивать в сто́рону; **2.** отклоне́ние.
swift [swift] □ бы́стрый, ско́рый; **~ness** ['swiftnis] быстрота́.
swill [swil] **1.** помо́и *m/pl.*; по́йло; **2.** [про]полоска́ть; [вы́]лака́ть.
swim [swim] **1.** [*irr.*] пла́вать, [по-] плы́ть; переплы́(ва́)ть; my head ~s у меня́ голова́ кру́жится; **2.** пла́вание; be in the ~ быть в ку́рсе де́ла.
swindle ['swindl] **1.** обма́нывать [-ну́ть], наду́(ва́)ть; **2.** обма́н, надува́тельство.
swine [swain] (*sg. mst fig.*) свинья́; сви́ньи *f/pl.*
swing [swiŋ] **1.** [*irr.*] кача́ть(ся) [качну́ть(ся)]; [по]колеба́ть(ся); разма́хивать (рука́ми); болта́ть (нога́ми); висе́ть; Г быть пове́шенным; **2.** кача́ние, колеба́ние; разма́х; взмах; ритм; каче́ли *f/pl.*; in full ~ в по́лном разга́ре; **~-door** дверь, открыва́ющаяся в любу́ю сто́рону.
swinish ['swainiʃ] □ сви́нский.
swipe [swaip] **1.** ударя́ть сплеча́; **2.** уда́р сплеча́.
swirl [swə:l] **1.** кружи́ть(ся) в водоворо́те; клуби́ться; **2.** водоворо́т; круже́ние; ви́хрь *m*.
Swiss [swis] **1.** швейца́рский; **2.** швейца́рец (-рка); the ~ *pl.* швейца́рцы *m/pl.*
switch [switʃ] **1.** прут; 🚂 стре́лка; ⚡ выключа́тель *m*; фальши́вая коса́; **2.** хлеста́ть [-стну́ть]; 🚂 маневри́ровать; ⚡ переключа́ть [-чи́ть] (*often* ~ over) (*a. fig.*); *fig.* переменя́ть направле́ние (Р); ~ on ⚡ включа́ть [-чи́ть]; ~ off выключа́ть [вы́ключить]; **~-board** ⚡ коммута́тор.
swollen ['swoulən] *p. pt.* от swell.
swoon [swu:n] **1.** о́бморок; **2.** па́дать в о́бморок.
swoop [swu:p] **1.** (*a.* ~ down), устремля́ться вниз (на добы́чу и т. п.); налета́ть [-ете́ть] (on на В); **2.** налёт, внеза́пное нападе́ние.
sword [sɔ:d] шпа́га; меч.
swordsman ['sɔdzmən] фехтова́льщик.
swore [swɔ:] *pt.* от swear.
sworn [swɔ:n] *p. pt.* от swear.
swum [swʌm] *p. pt.* от swim.
swung [swʌŋ] *pt.* и *p. pt.* от swing.
sycophant ['sikofənt] льстец.
syllable ['siləbl] слог.
symbol ['simbəl] си́мвол, эмбле́ма; знак; **~ic(al** □) [sim'bɔlik, -əl] символи́ческий; **~ism** ['simbəlizm] символи́зм.
symmetr|ical [si'metrikəl] □ симметри́чный; **~y** ['simitri] симметри́я.
sympath|etic [simpə'θetik] (~ally) сочу́вственный; симпати́чный; ~ strike забасто́вка солида́рности; **~ize** ['simpəθaiz] [по]сочу́вствовать (with Д); симпатизи́ровать (with Д); **~y** [-θi] сочу́вствие (with к Д); симпа́тия (for к Д).
symphony ['simfəni] симфо́ния.
symptom ['simptəm] симпто́м.
synchron|ize ['siŋkrənaiz] *v/i.* совпада́ть по вре́мени; *v/t.* синхронизи́ровать (*im*)*pf.*; устана́вливать одновре́ме́нность (собы́тий); сверя́ть [све́рить] (часы́); **~ous** [-nəs] □ синхро́нный.
syndicate **1.** ['sindikit] синдика́т; **2.** [-keit] синдици́ровать (*im*)*pf.*
synonym ['sinənim] сино́ним; **~ous** [si'nɔniməs] синоними́ческий.
synopsis [si'nɔpsis] конспе́кт; сино́псис.
synthe|sis ['sinθisis] си́нтез; **~tic(al** □) [sin'θetik, -tikəl] синтети́ческий.
syringe ['sirindʒ] **1.** шприц; **2.** спринцева́ть.
syrup ['sirəp] сиро́п; па́тока.
system ['sistim] систе́ма; **~atic** [sistə'mætik] (~ally) системати́ческий.

T

tab [tæb] ве́шалка; пе́телька; ⚔ петли́ца (на воротнике́).
table ['teibl] **1.** стол; о́бщество за столо́м; плита́; доще́чка; табли́ца; та́бель *m*; ~ of contents оглавле́ние; **2.** класть на стол; представля́ть [-а́вить] (предложе́ние и т. п.); **~-cloth** ска́терть *f*; **~-spoon** столо́вая ло́жка.
tablet ['tæblit] доще́чка; блокно́т; табле́тка; кусо́к (мы́ла и т. п.).
taboo [tə'bu:] **1.** табу́ *n ndecl.*; запреще́ние, запре́т; **2.** подверга́ть табу́; запреща́ть [-ети́ть]; **3.** запрещённый.
tabulate ['tæbjuleit] располага́ть в ви́де табли́ц.
tacit ['tæsit] □ молчали́вый (о согла́сии и т. п.); подразумева́емый; **~urn** ['tæsitə:n] □ молчали́вый, неразгово́рчивый.
tack [tæk] **1.** гво́здик с широ́кой

шля́пкой; кно́пка (канцеля́рская); стежо́к; ⚓ галс; *fig.* полити́ческая ли́ния; **2.** *v/t.* прикрепля́ть гво́здиками или кно́пками; смётывать [смета́ть]; присоединя́ть [-ни́ть], добавля́ть [-а́вить] (to, on к Д); *v/i.* ⚓ повора́чивать на друго́й галс; *fig.* меня́ть полити́ческий курс.

tackle ['tækl] **1.** принадле́жности *f/pl.*; снасть *f*; ⊕, ⚓ та́ли *f/pl.*; **2.** энерги́чно бра́ться за (В); би́ться над (Т).

tact [tækt] такт, такти́чность *f*; **~ful** ['tæktful] □ такти́чный.

tactics ['tæktiks] та́ктика.

tactless ['tæktlis] □ беста́ктный.

taffeta ['tæfitə] тафта́.

tag [tæg] **1.** ярлычо́к, этике́тка; ушко́ (сапога́); *fig.* изби́тая фра́за; **2.** прикрепля́ть ярлы́к, ушко́ к (Д).

tail [teil] **1.** хвост; коса́ (воло́с); пола́, фа́лда; обра́тная сторона́ (моне́ты); **2.** *v/t.* снабжа́ть хвосто́м; отруба́ть хвост (щеня́т); высле́живать [вы́следить]; *v/i.* тяну́ться дли́нной верени́цей; ~ off отст(ав)а́ть; **~-coat** фрак; **~-light** *mot.*, 🚃 за́дний фона́рь *m*; ✈ хвостово́й ого́нь *m*.

tailor ['teilə] **1.** портно́й; **2.** портня́жничать; [с]шить; **~-made** сши́тый на зака́з.

taint [teint] **1.** поро́к; пятно́ позо́ра; зара́за; испо́рченность *f*; **2.** [за]пятна́ть; [ис]по́ртить(ся); ⚕ заража́ть(ся) [зарази́ть(ся)].

take [teik] **1.** [*irr.*] *v/t.* брать [взять]; принима́ть [-ня́ть]; [съ]есть, [вы́-]пить; занима́ть [заня́ть] (ме́сто); *phot.* снима́ть [снять]; отнима́ть [-ня́ть] (вре́мя); I ~ it that я полага́ю, что ...; ~ the air выходи́ть на во́здух; ✈ отлета́ть [-ете́ть]; ~ fire загора́ться [-ре́ться]; ~ in hand бра́ться [взя́ться] за (В), предпринима́ть [-ня́ть]; ~ pity on сжа́литься *pf.* над (Т); ~ place случа́ться [-чи́ться], происходи́ть [произойти́]; ~ rest отдыха́ть [отдохну́ть]; ~ a seat сади́ться [сесть]; ~ a view выска́зывать свою́ то́чку зре́ния; ~ a walk [по]гуля́ть, прогу́ливаться [-ля́ться]; ~ down снима́ть [снять]; запи́сывать [-са́ть]; ~ for принима́ть [-ня́ть] за (В); ~ from брать [взять] у (Р); отнима́ть [отня́ть] у (Р) *or* от (Р); ~ in обма́нывать [-ну́ть]; принима́ть [-ня́ть] (го́стя); получа́ть (газе́ту и т. п.); ~ off снима́ть [снять] (оде́жду); ~ out вынима́ть [вы́нуть]; ~ to pieces разбира́ть [разобра́ть] (на ча́сти); ~ up бра́ться [взя́ться] за (В); занима́ть [заня́ть], отнима́ть [отня́ть] (ме́сто, вре́мя); **2.** *v/i.* [по]де́йствовать; име́ть успе́х; ~ after походи́ть на (В); ~ off уменьша́ться [уме́ньши́ться]; ✈ взлета́ть [-ете́ть]; оторва́ться от земли́; ~ over принима́ть до́лжность (from от Р); ~ to пристрасти́ться к (Д) *pf.*; привяза́ться к (Д) *pf.*; that won't ~ with me э́тим меня́ не возьмёшь; **3.** уло́в (ры́бы); (театра́льный) сбор; **~s** *pl.* бары́ши́ *m/pl.*; **~n** ['teikən] *p. pt.* от take; be ~ ill заболе́(ва́)ть; **~-off** ['tei'kɔf] карикату́ра; подража́ние; ✈ взлёт.

taking ['teikiŋ] **1.** □ привлека́тельный; зара́зный; **2. ~s** [-z] *pl.* † бары́ши́ *m/pl.*

tale [teil] расска́з, по́весть *f*; вы́думка; спле́тня.

talent ['tælənt] тала́нт; **~ed** [-id] тала́нтливый.

talk [tɔ:k] **1.** разгово́р; бесе́да; слух; **2.** [по]говори́ть; разгова́ривать; [по]бесе́довать; [на]спле́тничать; **~ative** ['tɔ:kətiv] болтли́вый; **~er** ['tɔ:kə] **1.** говору́н(ья), болту́н(ья); собесе́дник (-ница).

tall [tɔ:l] высо́кий; F невероя́тный; ~ order чрезме́рное тре́бование; ~ story *Am.* F неправдоподо́бный расска́з, небыли́ца.

tallow ['tælou] топлёное са́ло (для свече́й).

tally ['tæli] **1.** би́рка; ко́пия, дублика́т; опознава́тельный ярлы́к; **2.** отмеча́ть [-е́тить]; подсчи́тывать [-ита́ть]; соотве́тствовать (with Д).

tame [teim] **1.** □ ручно́й, приручённый; поко́рный; пасси́вный; ску́чный; **2.** прируча́ть [-чи́ть]; смиря́ть [-ри́ть].

tamper ['tæmpə]: ~ with вме́шиваться [-ша́ться] в (В); неуме́ло вози́ться с (Т); подде́л(ыв)ать (В); стара́ться подкупи́ть (В).

tan [tæn] **1.** зага́р; корьё, толчёная дубо́вая кора́; **2.** рыжева́то-кори́чневый; **3.** [вы́]дуби́ть (ко́жу); загора́ть.

tang [tæŋ] ре́зкий при́вкус; налёт.

tangent ['tændʒənt] ⅍ та́нгенс; go (*a.* fly) off at a ~ внеза́пно отклоня́ться (от те́мы и т. п.).

tangible ['tændʒəbl] □ осяза́емый, ощути́мый.

tangle ['tæŋgl] **1.** пу́таница, неразбери́ха; **2.** запу́т(ыв)ать(ся).

tank [tæŋk] **1.** цисте́рна; бак; ⚔ танк, *attr.* та́нковый; **2.** налива́ть в бак.

tankard ['tæŋkəd] высо́кая кру́жка.

tannery ['tænəri] коже́венный заво́д.

tantalize ['tæntəlaiz] [за-, из]му́чить.

tantrum ['tæntrəm] F вспы́шка гне́ва или раздраже́ния.

tap[1] [tæp] **1.** вту́лка; кран; F сорт, ма́рка (напи́тка); **2.** вставля́ть кран в (бо́чку); де́лать проко́л (для выпуска́ния жи́дкости) у

(больно́го); дела́ть надре́з на (де́реве для получе́ния со́ка); выпра́шивать де́ньги у (Р).
tap[2] [~] **1.** [по]стуча́ть; хло́пать [-пнуть]; **2.** лёгкий стук; шлепо́к; **~-dance** чечётка.
tape [teip] тесьма́; *sport* фи́нишная ле́нточка; телегра́фная ле́нта; red ~ бюрократи́зм, канцеля́рщина; **~-measure** [ˈteipmeʒə] руле́тка.
taper [ˈteipə] **1.** то́нкая восковая свеча́; **2.** *adj.* су́живающийся к концу́; кони́ческий; **3.** *v/i.* су́живаться к концу́; *v/t.* заостря́ть [-ри́ть].
tape-recorder магнитофо́н.
tapestry [ˈtæpistri] гобеле́н.
tape-worm ⚕ солитёр.
tap-room [ˈtæprum] пивна́я.
tar [tɑ:] **1.** дёготь *m*; смола́; **2.** обма́зывать дёгтем; [вы́]смоли́ть.
tardy [ˈtɑ:di] □ медли́тельный; запозда́лый, по́здний.
tare[1] [tɛə] та́ра; ски́дка на та́ру.
tare[2] [~] ⚘ посевна́я ви́ка.
target [ˈtɑ:git] цель *f*; мише́нь (*a. fig.*); ~ practice стрельба́ по мише́ням.
tariff [ˈtærif] тари́ф.
tarnish [ˈtɑ:niʃ] **1.** *v/t.* лиша́ть бле́ска (мета́лл); *fig.* [о]поро́чить; *v/i.* [по]тускне́ть (о мета́лле); **2.** ту́склость *f*; *fig.* пятно́.
tarry[1] [ˈtæri] ме́длить, ме́шкать; ~ for ждать (В *or* Р), дожида́ться (Р).
tarry[2] [ˈtɑ:ri] вы́мазанный дёгтем.
tart [tɑ:t] **1.** сла́дкая ватру́шка; **2.** ки́слый, те́рпкий; е́дкий; *fig.* ко́лкий.
task [tɑ:sk] **1.** зада́ча; уро́к; take to ~ призыва́ть к отве́ту; отчи́тывать [-ита́ть]; **2.** дава́ть зада́ние (Д); обременя́ть [-ни́ть], перегружа́ть [-узи́ть].
tassel [ˈtæsl] ки́сточка (украше́ние).
taste [teist] **1.** вкус; скло́нность *f* (for к Д); про́ба; **2.** [по]про́бовать (на вкус), отве́д(ыв)ать; *fig.* испы́тывать [-пыта́ть]; ~ sweet быть сла́дким на вкус; **~ful** [ˈteistful] □ (сде́ланный) со вку́сом; **~less** [-lis] □ безвку́сный.
tasty [ˈteisti] □ F вку́сный; прия́тный.
tatter [ˈtætə] **1.** изна́шивать(ся) в лохмо́тья; рва́ть(ся) в кло́чья; **2.** **~s** *pl.* лохмо́тья *n/pl.*; кло́чья *m/pl.* (*sg.* клок).
tattle [ˈtætl] **1.** болтовня́; **2.** [по-] болта́ть; [по]суда́чить.
tattoo [təˈtu:] **1.** ⚔ сигна́л вече́рней зари́; татуиро́вка; **2.** татуи́ровать (*im*)*pf*.
taught [tɔ:t] *pt.* и *p. pt.* от teach.
taunt [tɔ:nt] **1.** насме́шка, «шпи́лька»; **2.** говори́ть ко́лкости (Д); [съ]язви́ть.
taut [tɔ:t] ⚓ ту́го натя́нутый; вполне́ испра́вный (о корабле́).
tavern [ˈtævən] таве́рна.
tawdry [ˈtɔ:dri] □ мишу́рный, безвку́сный.
tawny [ˈtɔ:ni] рыжева́то-кори́чневый.
tax [tæks] **1.** нало́г (on на В); *fig.* напряже́ние; бре́мя *n*; испыта́ние; **2.** облага́ть нало́гом; ⚖ таксиро́вать (*im*)*pf.*; определя́ть разме́р (изде́ржек, штра́фа и т. п.); чрезме́рно напряга́ть (си́лы); подверга́ть испыта́нию; ~ a p. with a th. обвиня́ть [-ни́ть] кого́-либо в чём-либо; **~ation** [tækˈseiʃən] обложе́ние нало́гом; взима́ние нало́га; ⚖ такса́ция.
taxi [ˈtæksi] **1.** = **~-cab** такси́ *n indecl.*; **2.** е́хать в такси́; ✈ рули́ть.
taxpayer [ˈtækspeiə] налогопла́тельщик.
tea [ti:] чай.
teach [ti:tʃ] [*irr.*] [на]учи́ть, обуча́ть [-чи́ть]; преподава́ть; **~able** [ˈti:tʃəbl] □ спосо́бный к уче́нию; подлежа́щий обуче́нию; **~er** [ˈti:tʃə] учи́тель(ница *f*) *m*, преподава́тель (-ница *f*) *m*.
team [ti:m] упря́жка (лошаде́й и т. п.); *sport* кома́нда; брига́да, арте́ль *f* (рабо́чих); **~ster** [ˈti:mstə] возни́ца *m*; **~-work** совме́стная рабо́та; согласо́ванная рабо́та.
teapot [ˈti:pɔt] ча́йник (для зава́рки).
tear[1] [tɛə] **1.** [*irr.*] дыра́, проре́ха; **2.** [по]рва́ть(ся); разрыва́ть(ся) [разорва́ть(ся)]; *fig.* раздира́ть (-ся); [по]мча́ться.
tear[2] [tiə] слеза́ (*pl.* слёзы).
tearful [ˈtiəful] □ слезли́вый; по́лный слёз (о глаза́х).
tease [ti:z] **1.** задира *m/f*; челове́к, лю́бящий дразни́ть; **2.** F дразни́ть; задира́ть (В); прист(ав)а́ть к (Д).
teat [ti:t] сосо́к.
technic|al [ˈteknikəl] □ техни́ческий; **~ality** [tekniˈkæliti] техни́ческая сторона́ де́ла; техни́ческая дета́ль *f*; **~ian** [tekˈniʃən] те́хник.
technique [tekˈni:k] те́хника.
technology [tekˈnɔlədʒi] техноло́гия; техни́ческие нау́ки *f/pl.*
tedious [ˈti:diəs] □ ску́чный, утоми́тельный.
tedium [ˈti:diəm] ску́ка.
tee [ti:] мише́нь *f* (в и́грах); ме́тка для мяча́ (в го́льфе).
teem [ti:m] изоби́ловать, кише́ть (with T).
teens [ti:nz] *pl.* во́зраст от трина́дцати до девятна́дцати лет.
teeth [ti:θ] *pl.* от tooth; **~e** [ti:ð]: the child is teething у ребёнка проре́заются зу́бы.
teetotal(l)er [ti:ˈtoutlə] тре́звенник.
telegram [ˈteligræm] телегра́мма.
telegraph [ˈteligrɑ:f] **1.** телегра́ф; **2.** телеграфи́ровать (*im*)*pf.*; **3.** *attr.*

телегра́фный; ~ic [teli'græfik] (~ally) телегра́фный; ~y [ti'legrəfi] телеграфи́я.

telephon|e ['telifoun] 1. телефо́н; 2. телефони́ровать (*im*)*pf*.; ~ic [teli'fɔnik] (~ally) телефо́нный; ~y [ti'lefəni] телефони́я; телефони́рование.

telephoto ['teli'foutou] *phot.* телефотогра́фия.

telescope ['teliskoup] 1. телеско́п; 2. скла́дывать(ся) [сложи́ть(ся)] (подо́бно телеско́пу); вреза́ться друг в дру́га (о ваго́нах при круше́нии).

televis|ion ['teli'viʒən] телеви́дение; ~or [-vaizə] телеви́зор.

tell [tel] [*irr.*] *v/t.* говори́ть [сказа́ть]; расска́зывать [-за́ть]; уверя́ть [уве́рить]; отлича́ть [-чи́ть]; ~ a p. to do a th. веле́ть кому́-либо что́-либо де́лать; ~ off F [вы́]брани́ть, «отде́л(ыв)ать»; *v/i.* ска́зываться [сказа́ться]; выделя́ться [вы́делиться]; расска́зывать [-за́ть] (about о П); ~er ['telə] расска́зчик; касси́р (в ба́нке); ~ing ['teliŋ] □ многоговоря́щий, многозначи́тельный; ~tale ['telteil] спле́тник (-ица); болту́н(ья); доно́счик (-ица); ⊕ предупреди́тельное сигна́льное приспособле́ние.

temper ['tempə] 1. умеря́ть [уме́рить]; смягча́ть [-чи́ть]; ⊕ отпуска́ть [-сти́ть]; закаля́ть [-ли́ть] (*a fig.*); 2. хара́ктер; настрое́ние; раздраже́ние, гнев; ⊕ о́тпуск (мета́лла); ~ament [-rəmənt] темпера́мент; ~amental [tempərə'mentl] □ темпера́ментный; ~ance ['tempərəns] уме́ренность *f*; ~ate [-rit] □ уме́ренный, возде́ржанный; ~ature ['tempritʃə] температу́ра.

tempest ['tempist] бу́ря; ~uous [tem'pestjuəs] □ бу́рный, бу́йный.

temple ['templ] храм; *anat.* висо́к.

tempor|al ['tempərəl] □ вре́менный; мирско́й, све́тский; ~ary [-rəri] □ вре́менный; ~ize [-raiz] стара́ться вы́играть вре́мя; приспособля́ться к обстоя́тельствам.

tempt [tempt] искуша́ть [-уси́ть], соблазня́ть [-ни́ть]; привлека́ть [-е́чь]; ~ation [temp'teiʃən] искуше́ние, собла́зн; ~ing [-tiŋ] □ зама́нчивый, соблазни́тельный.

ten [ten] 1. де́сять; 2. деся́ток.

tenable ['tenəbl] про́чный; ⚔ обороноспосо́бный.

tenaci|ous [ti'neiʃəs] □ упо́рный; це́пкий; вя́зкий; ~ty [ti'næsiti] це́пкость *f*; сто́йкость *f*, упо́рство.

tenant ['tenənt] нанима́тель(ница *f*) *m*; аренда́тор; жи́тель(ница *f*) *m*.

tend [tend] *v/i.* име́ть скло́нность (to к Д); клони́ться; направля́ться [-ра́виться]; *v/t.* [по]забо́титься о (П); уха́живать, [по]смотре́ть за (Т); ⊕ обслу́живать [-и́ть]; ~ance ['tendəns] уха́живание (of за Т); присмо́тр (of за Т); ~ency [-si] тенде́нция; накло́нность *f*.

tender ['tendə] 1. □ *com.* не́жный; мя́гкий; сла́бый (о здоро́вье); чувстви́тельный; ла́сковый; чу́ткий; 2. (официа́льное) предложе́ние; зая́вка (*part.* ✝); 🚂 те́ндер; ⚓ посы́льное су́дно; плаву́чая ба́за; legal ~ зако́нное платёжное сре́дство; 3. предлага́ть [-ложи́ть]; представля́ть [-а́вить] (докуме́нты); приноси́ть [-нести́] (извине́ние, благода́рность); ~foot F новичо́к; ~ness [-nis] не́жность *f*.

tendon ['tendən] *anat.* сухожи́лие.

tendril ['tendril] ⚘ у́сик.

tenement ['tenimənt] снима́емая кварти́ра; ~ house многокварти́рный дом.

tenor ['tenə] ♪ те́нор; тече́ние, направле́ние; укла́д (жи́зни); о́бщий смысл (ре́чи и т. п.).

tens|e [tens] 1. *gr.* вре́мя *n*; 2. □ натя́нутый; возбуждённый; напряжённый; ~ion ['tenʃən] напряже́ние (*a.* ⚡); натяже́ние; *pol.* напряжённость *f*; натя́нутость *f*.

tent[1] [tent] 1. пала́тка, тент; 2. размеща́ть в пала́тках; жить в пала́тках.

tent[2] [~] 1. тампо́н; 2. вставля́ть [тампо́н в (В).]

tentacle ['tentəkl] *zo.* щу́пальце.

tentative ['tentətiv] □ про́бный; эксперимента́льный; ~ly в ви́де о́пыта.

tenth [tenθ] 1. деся́тый; 2. деся́тая часть *f*.

tenure ['tenjuə] владе́ние; пребыва́ние (в до́лжности); срок владе́ния.

tepid ['tepid] □ теплова́тый.

term [tə:m] 1. преде́л; срок; семе́стр; те́рмин; ⅌ член; ⚖ се́ссия; день упла́ты аре́нды и т. п.; ~s *pl.* усло́вия; be on good (bad) ~s быть в хоро́ших (плохи́х) отноше́ниях; come to ~s прийти́ к соглаше́нию; 2. выража́ть [вы́разить]; наз(ы)ва́ть; [на]именова́ть.

termina|l ['tə:minl] 1. □ заключи́тельный; коне́чный; семестро́вый; 2. коне́чный пункт; коне́чный слог; экза́мен в конце́ семе́стра; ⚡ зажи́м; *Am.* 🚂 коне́чная ста́нция; ~te [-neit] конча́ть(ся) [ко́нчить(ся)]; ~tion [tə:mi'neiʃən] оконча́ние; коне́ц.

terminus ['tə:minəs] 🚂 коне́чная ста́нция.

terrace ['terəs] терра́са; на́сыпь *f*; ряд домо́в; ~d [-t] располо́женный терра́сами.

terrestrial [ti'restriəl] □ земно́й; *zo.* сухопу́тный.

terrible ['terəbl] □ ужа́сный, стра́шный.

terri|fic [tə'rifik] (~ally) ужаса́ющий; F великоле́пный; **~fy** ['terifai] *v/t.* ужаса́ть [-сну́ть].
territor|ial [teri'tɔ:riəl] 1. □ территориа́льный; земе́льный; ♀ Army, Force территориа́льная а́рмия; 2. ⚔ солда́т территориа́льной а́рмии; **~y** ['teritəri] террито́рия; о́бласть *f*; сфе́ра.
terror ['terə] у́жас; терро́р; **~ize** [-raiz] терроризова́ть (*im*)*pf*.
terse [tə:s] □ сжа́тый, вырази́тельный (стиль).
test [test] 1. испыта́ние; крите́рий; про́ба; ана́лиз; ⚗ реакти́в; *attr.* испыта́тельный; про́бный; 2. подверга́ть испыта́нию, прове́рке, (⚗) де́йствию реакти́ва.
testify ['testifai] дава́ть показа́ние, свиде́тельствовать (to в по́льзу Р, against про́тив Р, on о П).
testimon|ial [testi'mounjəl] аттеста́т; рекоменда́тельное письмо́; **~y** ['testimeni] у́стное показа́ние; пи́сьменное свиде́тельство.
test-tube ⚗ проби́рка.
testy ['testi] □ вспы́льчивый, раздражи́тельный.
tether ['teðə] 1. при́вязь *f* (живо́тного); come to the end of one's ~ дойти́ до то́чки; 2. привя́зывать [-за́ть] (живо́тное).
text [tekst] текст; те́ма (про́поведи); **~book** уче́бник, руково́дство.
textile ['tekstail] 1. тексти́льный; 2. ~s *pl.* тексти́льные изде́лия *n/pl.*; тка́ни *f/pl.*
texture ['tekstʃə] ткань *f*; ка́чество тка́ни; строе́ние, структу́ра (ко́жи и т. п.).
than [ðæn,ðən] чем, не́жели.
thank [θæŋk] 1. [по]благода́ри́ть (В); ~ you благодарю́ вас; 2. ~s *pl.* спаси́бо!; ~s to благодаря́ (Д); **~ful** ['θæŋkful] □ благода́рный; **~less** [-lis] □ неблагода́рный; **~sgiving** [θæŋksgiviŋ] благода́рственный моле́бен.
that [ðæt, ðət] 1. *pron.* тот, та, то; те *pl.*; (*a.* э́тот и т. д.); кото́рый и т. д.; 2. *cj.* что; что́бы.
thatch (θætʃ] 1. соло́менная и́ли тростнико́вая кры́ша; 2. крыть соло́мой и́ли тростнико́м.
thaw [θɔ:] 1. о́ттепель *f*; та́яние; 2. *v/i.* [рас]та́ять; отта́ивать [отта́ять]; *v/t.* раста́пливать [растопи́ть] (снег и т. п.).
the [ði:; пе́ред гла́сными ði; пе́ред согла́сными ðə] 1. определённый член, арти́кль; 2. *adv.* ~ ... ~ ... чем ..., тем ...
theatr|e ['θiətə] теа́тр; *fig.* аре́на; ~ of war теа́тр вое́нных де́йствий; **~ic(al** □) [θi'ætrik, -trikəl] театра́льный (*a. fig.*); сцени́ческий.
theft [θeft] воровство́ кра́жа.
their [ðɛə] *pron. poss.* (от they) их; свой, своя́, своё, свои́ *pl.*; **~s** [ðɛəz] *pron. poss. pred.* их, свой и т. д.
them [ðem, ðəm] *pron. pers.* (ко́свенный паде́ж от they) их, им.
theme [θi:m] те́ма, предме́т (разгово́ра и т. п.); шко́льное сочине́ние.
themselves [ðem'selvz] *pron. refl.* себя́, -ся; *emphasis* са́ми.
then [ðen] 1. *adv.* тогда́; пото́м, зате́м; 2. *cj.* тогда́, в тако́м слу́чае; зна́чит; 3. *adj.* тогда́шний.
thence *lit.* [ðens] отту́да; с того́ вре́мени; *fig.* отсю́да, из э́того.
theolog|ian [θiə'loudʒiən] богосло́в; **~y** [θi'ɔlədʒi] богосло́вие.
theor|etic(al □) [θiə'retik, -tikəl] теорети́ческий; **~ist** ['θiərist] теоре́тик; **~y** ['θiəri] тео́рия.
there [ðɛə] там, туда́; ~! вот!, ну!; ~ is, ~ are [ðə'riz, ðə'rɑ:] есть, име́ется, име́ются; **~about(s)** ['ðɛərəbaut(s)] побли́зости; о́коло э́того, приблизи́тельно; **~after** [ðɛər'ɑ:ftə] с э́того вре́мени; **~by** ['ðɛə'bai] посре́дством э́того; таки́м о́бразом; **~fore** ['ðɛəfɔ:] поэ́тому; сле́довательно; **~upon** ['ðɛərə'pɔn] по́сле того́, вслед за те́м; всле́дствие того́.
thermo|meter [θə'mɔmitə] термо́метр, гра́дусник; **~s** ['θə:mɔs] (*or* ~ flask, ~ bottle) те́рмос.
these [ði:z] *pl.* от this.
thes|is ['θi:sis], *pl.* **~es** [-si:z] те́зис; диссерта́ция.
they [ðei] *pron. pers.* они́.
thick [θik] 1. □ *com.* то́лстый; густо́й; пло́тный; хри́плый (го́лос); F глу́пый; ~ with гу́сто покры́тый (Т); 2. ча́ща; *fig.* гу́ща; in the ~ of в са́мой гу́ще (Р); в разга́ре (Р); **~en** ['θikən] [по]толсте́ть; сгуща́ть(ся) [сгусти́ть(ся)]; учаща́ться [участи́ться]; **~et** ['θikit] ча́ща; за́росли *f/pl.*; **~-headed** тупоголо́вый, тупоу́мный; **~ness** ['θiknis] толщина́; пло́тность *f*; сгущённость *f*; **~-set** ['θik'set] гу́сто наса́женный; корена́стый; **~-skinned** (*a. fig.*) толстоко́жий.
thie|f [θi:f], *pl.* **~ves** [θi:vz] вор; **~ve** [θi:v] *v/t.* [у]кра́сть; *v/i.* ворова́ть.
thigh [θai] бедро́.
thimble ['θimbl] напёрсток.
thin [θin] 1. □ *com.* то́нкий; худо́й, худоща́вый; ре́дкий; жи́дкий; in a ~ house в полупусто́м за́ле (теа́тра); 2. де́лать(ся) то́нким, утонча́ть(ся) [-чи́ть(ся)]; [по]реде́ть; [по]худе́ть.
thing [θiŋ] вещь *f*; предме́т; де́ло; ~s *pl.* ли́чные ве́щи *f/pl.*; бага́ж; оде́жда; принадле́жности *f/pl.*; the ~ (не́что) са́мое ва́жное, ну́жное; ~s are going better положе́ние улучша́ется.

think [θiŋk] [*irr.*] *v/i.* [по]ду́мать (of, about о П); мы́слить; полага́ть; вспомина́ть [вспо́мнить] (of о П); намерева́ться (+ *inf.*); приду́м(ыв)ать (of В); *v/t.* счита́ть [счесть]; ~ much of быть высо́кого мне́ния о (П).
third [θə:d] **1.** тре́тий; **2.** треть *f.*
thirst [θə:st] **1.** жа́жда; **2.** жа́ждать (for, after Р) (*part. fig.*); **~y** ['θə:sti] □ томи́мый жа́ждой; I am ~ я хочу́ пить.
thirt|een ['θə:ti:n] трина́дцать; **~eenth** ['θə:'ti:nθ] трина́дцатый; **~ieth** ['θə:tiiθ] тридца́тый; **~y** ['θə:ti] три́дцать.
this [ðis] *pron. demonstr.* (*pl.* these) э́тот, э́та, э́то; э́ти *pl.*; ~ morning сего́дня у́тром.
thistle ['θisl] ♀ чертополо́х.
thong [θɔŋ] реме́нь *m*; плеть *f.*
thorn [θɔ:n] ♀ шип; колю́чка; *fig.* ~ s *pl.* те́рния *n/pl.*; **~y** ['θɔ:ni] колю́чий; *fig.* тяжёлый, терни́стый.
thorough ['θʌrə] □ основа́тельный; совершённый; **~ly** *adv.* основа́тельно, доскона́льно; совершённо; **~bred 1.** чистокро́вный; **2.** чистокро́вное живо́тное; **~fare** прохо́д; прое́зд; гла́вная арте́рия (го́рода); **~going** радика́льный.
those [ðouz] *pl.* от that.
though [ðou] *conj.* хотя́; да́же е́сли бы, хотя́ бы; *adv.* тем не ме́нее; одна́ко; всё-таки; as ~ как бу́дто, сло́вно.
thought [θɔ:t] **1.** *pt.* и *p. pt.* от think; **2.** мысль *f*; мышле́ние; размышле́ние; забо́та; внима́тельность *f*; **~ful** ['θɔ:tful] □ заду́мчивый; глубокомы́сленный; забо́тливый; внима́тельный (of к Д); **~less** ['θɔ:tlis] □ беспе́чный; необду́манный; невнима́тельный (of к Д).
thousand ['θauzənd] ты́сяча; **~th** ['θauzən(t)θ] **1.** ты́сячный; **2.** ты́сячная часть *f.*
thrash [θræʃ] [с]молоти́ть; [по]би́ть; F побежда́ть [-еди́ть] (в состяза́нии); ~ out тща́тельно обсужда́ть (вопро́с и т. п.); *s.* thresh; **~ing** ['θræʃiŋ] молотьба́; побо́и *m/pl.*, F взбу́чка.
thread [θred] **1.** ни́тка, нить *f*; *fig.* нить *f*; ⊕ (винтова́я) резьба́, наре́зка; **2.** продева́ть ни́тку в (иго́лку); нани́зывать [-за́ть] (бу́сы); ⊕ нареза́ть [-е́зать]; **~bare** ['θredbɛə] потёртый, изно́шенный; *fig.* изби́тый.
threat [θret] угро́за; **~en** ['θretn] *v/t.* [при]грози́ть, угрожа́ть (Д with Т); *v/i.* грози́ть.
three [θri:] **1.** три; **2.** тро́йка; **~fold** ['θri:fould] тройно́й; *adv.* втройне́; **~pence** ['θrepəns] три пе́нса (моне́та); **~-score** ['θri:'skɔ:] шестьдеся́т.
thresh [θreʃ] ✓ [с]молоти́ть; *s.* thrash; ~ out *fig.* = thrash out.
threshold ['θreʃ(h)ould] поро́г.
threw [θru:] *pt.* от throw.
thrice [θrais] три́жды.
thrift [θrift] бережли́вость *f*, эконо́мность *f*; **~less** ['θriftlis] □ расточи́тельный; **~y** ['θrifti] □ эконо́мный, бережли́вый.
thrill [θril] **1.** *v/t.* [вз]волнова́ть; приводи́ть в тре́пет, [вз]будора́жить; *v/i.* [за]трепета́ть (with от Р); [вз]волнова́ться; **2.** тре́пет; глубо́кое волне́ние; не́рвная дрожь *f*; **~er** ['θrilə] сенсацио́нный рома́н (*mst* детекти́вный).
thrive [θraiv] [*irr.*] процвета́ть; преуспева́ть; разраста́ться; **~n** ['θrivn] *p. pt.* от thrive.
throat [θrout] го́рло, гло́тка; clear one's ~ отка́шливаться [-ляться].
throb [θrɔb] **1.** пульси́ровать; си́льно би́ться; **2.** пульса́ция; бие́ние; *fig.* тре́пет.
throes [θrouz] *pl.* му́ки *f/pl.*; аго́ния; родовы́е му́ки *f/pl.*
throne [θroun] трон, престо́л.
throng [θrɔŋ] **1.** толпа́, толчея́; **2.** [с]толпи́ться; заполня́ть [-о́лнить] (о толпе́).
throttle ['θrɔtl] **1.** [за]души́ть (за го́рло); ⊕ дроссели́ровать; **2.** ⊕ дро́ссель *m.*
through [θru:] **1.** че́рез (В); сквозь (В); по (Д); *adv.* насквозь; от нача́ла до конца́; **2.** прямо́й, беспереса́дочный (по́езд и т. п.); сквозно́й (биле́т); **~out** [θru:'aut] **1.** *prp.* че́рез (В); по всему́, всей ...; **2.** повсю́ду; во всех отноше́ниях.
throve [θrouv] *pt.* от thrive.
throw [θrou] **1.** [*irr.*] броса́ть [бро́сить], кида́ть [ки́нуть], мета́ть [метну́ть]; ~ over перебра́сывать [-бро́сить]; покида́ть [-и́нуть] (друзе́й); ~ up изверга́ть [-е́ргнуть]; вски́дывать [вски́нуть]; **2.** бросо́к; броса́ние; **~n** [-n] *p. pt.* от throw.
thru *Am.* = through.
thrum [θrʌm] бренча́ть, тре́ньkать.
thrush [θrʌʃ] дрозд.
thrust [θrʌst] **1.** толчо́к; уда́р; ⊕ распо́р; end ~ осево́е давле́ние; **2.** [*irr.*] толка́ть [-кну́ть]; ты́кать [ткнуть]; ~ o. s. into *fig.* втира́ться [втере́ться] в (В); ~ upon a p. навя́зывать [-за́ть] (Д).
thud [θʌd] **1.** глухо́й звук; **2.** па́дать с глухи́м зву́ком.
thug *Am.* [θʌg] уби́йца *m*, головоре́з.
thumb [θʌm] **1.** большо́й па́лец (руки́); **2.** захва́тывать [захвата́ть], загрязня́ть [-ни́ть] (па́льцами); **~tack** *Am.* чертёжная кно́пка.
thump [θʌmp] **1.** глухо́й стук; тяжёлый уда́р; **2.** наноси́ть тяжёлый уда́р (Д).

thunder ['θʌndə] **1.** гром; **2.** [за-] греме́ть; it ~s гром греми́т; *fig.* мета́ть гро́мы и мо́лнии; **~bolt** уда́р мо́лнии; **~clap** уда́р гро́ма; **~ous** ['θʌndərəs] □ грозово́й; громово́й, оглуша́ющий; **~-storm** гроза́; **~-struck** сражённый уда́ром мо́лнии; *fig.* как гро́мом поражённый.
Thursday ['θə:zdi] четве́рг.
thus [ðʌs] так, таки́м о́бразом.
thwart [θwɔ:t] **1.** ба́нка (скамья́ для гребца́); **2.** меша́ть исполне́нию (жела́ний и т. п.), расстра́ивать [-ро́ить].
tick [tik] **1.** *zo.* клещ; креди́т, счёт; ти́канье; тик (мате́рия); **2.** *v/i.* ти́кать; *v/t.* брать и́ли отпуска́ть в креди́т; ~ off отмеча́ть «пти́чкой»; F проб(и)ра́ть, отде́л(ыв)ать.
ticket ['tikit] **1.** биле́т; ярлы́к; удостовере́ние; квита́нция; *Am.* спи́сок кандида́тов па́ртии; **2.** прикрепля́ть ярлы́к к (Д); **~office,** *Am.* **~-window** биле́тная ка́сса.
tickl|e ['tikl] [по]щекота́ть; **~ish** [-iʃ] □ щекотли́вый.
tidal ['taidl]: ~ wave прили́вная волна́.
tide [taid] **1.** low ~ отли́в; high ~ прили́в; *fig.* тече́ние; **2.** *fig.* ~ over преодоле́(ва́)ть.
tidings ['taidiŋz] *pl.* но́вости *f/pl.*, изве́стия *n/pl.*
tidy ['taidi] **1.** опря́тный, аккура́тный; значи́тельный; **2.** приб(и)ра́ть; приводи́ть в поря́док.
tie [tai] **1.** связь *f*; га́лстук; ра́вный счёт (голосо́в и́ли очко́в); ничья́; ⊕ скре́па; *pl.* у́зы *f/pl.*; **2.** *v/t.* завя́зывать [-за́ть]; свя́зывать [-за́ть]; *v/i.* игра́ть вничью́; сравня́ть счёт.
tier [tiə] ряд; я́рус.
tie-up связь *f*; сою́з; *Am.* прекраще́ние рабо́ты и́ли у́личного движе́ния.
tiger ['taigə] тигр.
tight [tait] □ пло́тный, компа́ктный; непроница́емый; туго́й; ту́го натя́нутый; те́сный; F подвы́пивший; F ~ place *fig.* затрудни́тельное положе́ние; **~en** ['taitn] стя́гивать(ся) [стяну́ть(ся)] (*a.* ~ up); затя́гивать [-яну́ть]; подтя́гивать [-яну́ть]; **~-fisted** скупо́й; **~ness** ['taitnis] пло́тность *f* и т. д.; **~s** [taits] *pl.* трико́ *n indecl.*
tigress ['taigris] тигри́ца.
tile [tail] **1.** черепи́ца; ка́фель *m*, изразе́ц; **2.** крыть черепи́цей и т. д.
till [til] **1.** де́нежный я́щик, ка́сса (в прила́вке); **2.** *prp.* до (Р); **3.** *cj.* пока́; **4.** ⚒ возде́л(ыв)ать (В); [вс]паха́ть; **~age** ['tilidʒ] па́шня; обрабо́тка земли́.

tilt [tilt] **1.** накло́нное положе́ние, накло́н; уда́р копьём; **2.** наклоня́ть(ся) [-ни́ть(ся)]; опроки́дывать(ся) [-и́нуть(ся)]; би́ться на ко́пьях; ~ against боро́ться с (Т).
timber ['timbə] **1.** лесоматериа́л, строево́й лес; ба́лка; **2.** пло́тничать; столя́рничать; стро́ить из де́рева.
time [taim] **1.** вре́мя *n*; пери́од; пора́; раз; такт; темп; at the same ~ в то же вре́мя; for the ~ being пока́, на вре́мя; in (*or* on) ~ во́время; **2.** (уда́чно) выбира́ть вре́мя для (Р); назнача́ть вре́мя для (Р); хронометри́ровать (*im*)*pf.*; **~ly** ['taimli] своевре́менный; **~-piece** часы́ *m/pl.*; **~-table** 🚂 расписа́ние.
timid ['timid] □, **timorous** ['timərəs] □ ро́бкий.
tin [tin] **1.** о́лово; (*a.* ~-plate) жесть *f*; жестя́нка; **2.** [по]луди́ть; [за-] консерви́ровать (в жестя́нках).
tincture ['tiŋktʃə] **1.** ⚕ тинкту́ра; *fig.* отте́нок; **2.** окра́шивать [окра́сить].
tinfoil ['tin'fɔil] фо́льга.
tinge [tindʒ] **1.** слегка́ окра́шивать; *fig.* придава́ть отте́нок (Д); **2.** лёгкая окра́ска; *fig.* отте́нок.
tingle ['tiŋgl] испы́тывать и́ли вызыва́ть пока́лывание (в онеме́вших чле́нах), пощи́пывание (на моро́зе), зуд, звон в уша́х и т. п.
tinker ['tiŋkə] **1.** луди́льщик; **2.** неуме́ло чини́ть (at В); вози́ться (at с Т).
tinkle ['tiŋkl] звя́кать [-кнуть].
tin-plate ['tin'pleit] (бе́лая) жесть *f.*
tinsel ['tinsəl] блёстки *f/pl.*; мишура́.
tinsmith ['tinsmiθ] жестя́н(щ)ик.
tint [tint] **1.** кра́ска; отте́нок, тон; **2.** слегка́ окра́шивать.
tiny ['taini] □ о́чень ма́ленький, кро́шечный.
tip [tip] **1.** (то́нкий) коне́ц; наконе́чник; ко́нчик; чаевы́е *pl.*; ча́стная информа́ция; намёк; лёгкий толчо́к; **2.** снабжа́ть наконе́чником; опроки́дывать [-и́нуть]; дава́ть на чай (Д); дава́ть ча́стную информа́цию (Д).
tipple ['tipl] пья́нствовать; вы́пи(ва́)ть, пить.
tipsy ['tipsi] подвы́пивший.
tiptoe ['tip(')tou]: on ~ на цы́почках.
tire [taiə] **1.** обод колеса́; *mot.* ши́на; **2.** утомля́ть [-ми́ть]; уст(ав)а́ть; **~d** [-d] уста́лый; **~less** ['taiəlis] неутоми́мый; **~some** [-səm] утоми́тельный; надое́дливый; ску́чный.
tiro ['taiərou] нович́ок.
tissue ['tisju:] ткань *f* (*a. biol.*); *fig.* сплете́ние (лжи и т. п.); **~-paper** [-'peipə] шёлковая бума́га; папиро́сная бума́га.

titbit ['titbit] ла́комый кусо́чек; *fig.* пика́нтная но́вость *f.*
titillate ['titileit] [по]щекота́ть.
title ['taitl] загла́вие; ти́тул; зва́ние; ⚖ пра́во со́бственности (to на В); ~d титуло́ванный.
titter ['titə] **1.** хихи́канье; **2.** хихи́кать [-кнуть].
tittle ['titl] мале́йшая части́ца; to a ~ тю́телька в тю́тельку; **~-tattle** [-tætl] спле́тни *f/pl.*, болтовня́.
to [tu:, tu, tə] *prp.* (ука́зывает на направле́ние движе́ния, цель): к (Д); в (В); на (В); (ука́зывает на лицо́, по отноше́нию к кото́рому что́-либо происхо́дит, и соотве́тствует ру́сскому да́тельному падежу́): ~ me *etc.* мне и т. д.; ~ and fro *adv.* взад и вперёд; (части́ца, слу́жащая показа́телем инфинити́ва): ~ work рабо́тать; I weep ~ think of it я пла́чу, ду́мая об э́том.
toad [toud] жа́ба; **~stool** пога́нка (гриб); **~y** ['toudi] **1.** подхали́м; **2.** подхали́мничать пе́ред (Т).
toast [toust] **1.** грено́к; тост; **2.** приготовля́ть гренки́; поджа́ри(ва)ть; *fig.* гре́ть(ся) (у огня́); пить за чьё-либо здоро́вье, пить за (В).
tobacco [tə'bækou] таба́к; **~nist** [tə'bækənist] торго́вец таба́чными изде́лиями.
toboggan [tə'bɔgən] **1.** сала́зки *f/pl.*; **2.** ката́ться на сала́зках (с горы́).
today [tə'dei] сего́дня; в на́ше вре́мя.
toe [tou] **1.** па́лец (на ноге́); носо́к (чулка́, башмака́); **2.** каса́ться ноcко́м (Р).
together [tə'geðə] вме́сте; друг с дру́гом; подря́д, непреры́вно.
toil [tɔil] **1.** тяжёлый труд; **2.** уси́ленно труди́ться; идти́ с трудо́м.
toilet ['tɔilit] туале́т (одева́ние и костю́м); убо́рная; **~-table** туале́тный сто́лик.
toilsome ['tɔilsəm] □ тру́дный, утоми́тельный.
token ['toukən] знак; приме́та; пода́рок на па́мять; ~ money билло́нные де́ньги *f/pl.*
told [tould] *pt.* и *p. pt.* от tell.
tolera|ble ['tɔlərəbl] □ терпи́мый; сно́сный; **~nce** [-rəns] терпи́мость *f*; **~nt** [-rənt] □ терпи́мый; **~te** [-reit] [по]терпе́ть, допуска́ть [-сти́ть]; **~tion** [tɔlə'reiʃən] терпи́мость *f*; допуще́ние.
toll [toul] по́шлина; *fig.* дань *f*; **~-bar, ~-gate** заста́ва (где взима́ется по́шлина).
tom [tɔm]: ~ cat кот.
tomato [tə'mɑ:tou, *Am.* tə'meitou], *pl.* **~es** [-z] помидо́р, тома́т.
tomb [tu:m] моги́ла; надгро́бный па́мятник.
tomboy ['tɔmbɔi] сорване́ц (о де́вочке).
tomfool ['tɔm'fu:l] шут; дура́к.
tomorrow [tə'mɔrou] за́втра.
ton [tʌn] (metric) то́нна (= 1000 кг).
tone [toun] **1.** тон (♪, *paint.*, *fig.*); интона́ция; **2.** придава́ть жела́тельный тон (зву́ку, кра́ске); настра́ивать [-ро́ить] (инструме́нт).
tongs [tɔŋz] *pl.* щипцы́ *m/pl.*, клещи́ *f/pl.*
tongue [tʌŋ] язы́к; hold one's ~ держа́ть язы́к за зуба́ми; **~-tied** ['tʌŋtaid] косноязы́чный; молчали́вый.
tonic ['tɔnik] **1.** (~ally) тони́ческий (*a.* ♪); укрепля́ющий; **2.** ♪ основно́й тон; ⚕ укрепля́ющее сре́дство.
tonight [tə'nait] сего́дня ве́чером.
tonnage ['tʌnidʒ] ⚓ тонна́ж; грузоподъёмность *f*; грузова́я по́шлина.
tonsil ['tɔnsl] *anat.* гла́нда, минда́лина.
too [tu:] та́кже, то́же; сли́шком; о́чень.
took [tuk] *pt.* от take.
tool [tu:l] (рабо́чий) инструме́нт; ору́дие (*a. fig.*)
toot [tu:t] **1.** звук рожка́, гудо́к; **2.** труби́ть в рожо́к.
tooth [tu:θ] (*pl.* teeth) зуб; **~ache** зубна́я боль *f*; **~-brush** зубна́я щётка; **~less** ['tu:θlis] □ беззу́бый; **~pick** зубочи́стка; **~some** ['tu:θsəm] вку́сный.
top [tɔp] **1.** ве́рхняя часть *f*; верху́шка вершина (горы́); маку́шка (головы́, де́рева); верх (автомоби́ля, ле́стницы, страни́цы); волчо́к; at the ~ of one's voice во весь го́лос; on ~ наверху́; **2.** вы́сший, пе́рвый; максима́льный (о ско́рости и т. п.); **3.** покры́(ва́)ть (све́рху); *fig.* превыша́ть [-ы́сить]; быть во главе́ (Р).
toper ['toupə] пья́ница *m/f.*
top-hat F цили́ндр (шля́па).
topic ['tɔpik] те́ма, предме́т; **~al** ['tɔpikəl] ме́стный; злободне́вный.
topmost ['tɔpmoust] са́мый ве́рхний; са́мый ва́жный.
topple ['tɔpl] опроки́дывать(ся) [-и́нуть(ся)] (*a.* ~ over).
topsyturvy ['tɔpsi'tə:vi] □ вверх дном; ши́ворот-навы́ворот.
torch [tɔtʃ] фа́кел; electric ~ карма́нный электри́ческий фона́рь *m*; **~-light** свет фа́кела; ~ procession фа́кельное ше́ствие.
tore [tɔ:] *pt.* от tear.
torment **1.** ['tɔ:ment] муче́ние, му́ка; **2.** [tɔ:'ment] [из-, за]му́чить; изводи́ть [извести́].
torn [tɔ:n] *p. pt.* от tear.
tornado [tɔ:'neidou] торна́до *m indecl.*, смерч; урага́н *a. fig.*
torpedo [tɔ:'pi:dou] **1.** торпе́да; **2.**

торпеди́ровать (*im*)*pf.*; *fig.* взрыва́ть [взорва́ть].

torpid ['tɔ:pid] □ онеме́лый, оцепене́лый; вя́лый, апати́чный; **~ity** [tɔ:'piditi], **torpor** ['tɔ:pə] оцепене́ние; апа́тия.

torrent ['tɔrənt] пото́к (*a. fig.*).

torrid ['tɔrid] жа́ркий, зно́йный.

tortoise ['tɔ:təs] *zo.* черепа́ха.

tortuous ['tɔ:tjuəs] □ изви́листый; *fig.* укло́нчивый, нейскренний.

torture ['tɔ:tʃə] **1.** пы́тка; **2.** пыта́ть, [из-, за]му́чить.

toss [tɔs] **1.** мета́ние, броса́ние; толчо́к, сотрясе́ние; (*a.* ~-up) броса́ние моне́ты (в орля́нке); **2.** броса́ть [бро́сить]; беспоко́йно мета́ться (о больно́м); вски́дывать [-и́нуть] (го́лову); подбра́сывать [-ро́сить] (*mst* ~ up); ~ (up) игра́ть в орля́нку; *sport* разы́грывать воро́та.

tot [tɔt] F ма́ленький ребёнок, малы́ш.

total ['toutl] **1.** □ по́лный, абсолю́тный; тота́льный; о́бщий; **2.** це́лое, су́мма; ито́г; **3.** подводи́ть ито́г, подсчи́тывать [-ита́ть]; составля́ть в ито́ге; равня́ться (Д); **~itarian** [toutæli'tɛəriən] тоталита́рный; **~ity** [tou'tæliti] вся су́мма, всё коли́чество.

totter ['tɔtə] идти́ неве́рной похо́дкой; шата́ться [(по)шатну́ться].

touch [tʌtʃ] **1.** осяза́ние; прикоснове́ние; *fig.* соприкоснове́ние, обще́ние; чу́точка; при́месь *f*; лёгкий при́ступ (боле́зни); ♪ туше́ *n indecl.*; штрих; **2.** тро́гать [тро́нуть] (В) (*a. fig.*); прикаса́ться [-косну́ться], притра́гиваться [-тро́нуться] к (Д); *fig.* каса́ться [косну́ться] (Р), затра́гивать [-ро́нуть] (В) (те́му и т. п.); be ~ed *fig.* быть тро́нутым; быть слегка́ поме́шанным; ~ up отде́л(ыв)ать, поправля́ть [-а́вить] (не́сколькими штриха́ми); ~ at ⚓ заходи́ть [зайти́] в (порт); **~ing** ['tʌtʃiŋ] тро́гательный; **~stone** проби́рный ка́мень *m*, осело́к; *fig.* про́бный ка́мень *m*; **~y** ['tʌtʃi] □ оби́дчивый; сли́шком чувстви́тельный.

tough [tʌf] **1.** жёсткий; вя́зкий; упру́гий; выно́сливый; тру́дный; **2.** *Am.* хулига́н; **~en** ['tʌfn] де́лать(ся) жёстким, пло́тным и т. д.; **~ness** ['tʌfnis] жёсткость *f* и т. д.

tour [tuə] **1.** кругово́е путеше́ствие; турне́ *n indecl.*; тур, объе́зд; **2.** соверша́ть путеше́ствие или турне́ по (Д); путеше́ствовать (through по Д); **~ist** ['tuərist] тури́ст(ка); ~ agency бюро́ путеше́ствий.

tournament [-nəmənt] турни́р.

tousle ['tauzl] взъеро́ши(ва)ть, растрёпывать [-репа́ть].

tow [tou] ⚓ **1.** букси́рный кана́т, трос; букси́ровка; take in ~ брать на букси́р; **2.** букси́ровать; тяну́ть (ба́ржу) на бечеве́.

towards [tə'wɔ:dz, tɔ:dʒ] *prp.* (ука́зывает на направле́ние к предме́ту, отноше́ние к чему́-либо) по направле́нию к (Д); к (Д), по отноше́нию к (Д); для (Р).

towel ['tauəl] полоте́нце.

tower ['tauə] **1.** ба́шня; вы́шка; *fig.* опо́ра; **2.** возвыша́ться [-ы́ситься] (above, over над Т) (*a. fig.*).

town [taun] **1.** го́род; **2.** *attr.* городско́й; ~ council городско́й сове́т; ~ hall ра́туша; **~sfolk** ['taunzfouk], **~speople** [-pi:pl] горожа́не *m/pl.*; **~sman** ['taunzmən] горожа́нин; согражда́нин.

toxi|c(al □) ['tɔksik, -sikəl] ядови́тый; **~n** ['tɔksin] токси́н.

toy [tɔi] **1.** игру́шка; заба́ва; безделу́шка; **2.** *attr.* игру́шечный; **3.** игра́ть; забавля́ться; флиртова́ть; **~book** де́тская кни́га с карти́нками.

trace [treis] **1.** след; черта́; постро́мка; **2.** [на]черти́ть; высле́живать [вы́следить] (В); просле́живать [-еди́ть] (В); *a. fig.* [с]кальки́ровать.

tracing [treisiŋ] чертёж на ка́льке.

track [træk] **1.** след; просёлочная доро́га; тропи́нка; беговая доро́жка; 🚂 колея́, ре́льсовый путь *m*; **2.** следи́ть за (Т); просле́живать [-еди́ть] (В); ~ down, ~ out высле́живать [вы́следить] (В).

tract [trækt] тракта́т; брошю́ра; простра́нство, полоса́ (земли́, воды́).

tractable ['træktəbl] сгово́рчивый; поддаю́щийся обрабо́тке.

tract|ion ['trækʃən] тя́га; волоче́ние; ~ engine тяга́ч; **~or** [træ'ktə] ⊕ тра́ктор.

trade [treid] **1.** профе́ссия; ремесло́; торго́вля; **2.** торгова́ть (in Т; with с Т); обме́нивать [-ня́ть] (for на В); ~ on испо́льзовать (*im*)*pf.*; **~-mark** фабри́чная ма́рка; **~-price** опто́вая цена́; **~r** ['treidə] торго́вец; торго́вое су́дно; **~sman** ['treidzmən] торго́вец, ла́вочник; реме́сленник; **~(s)-union** ['treid(z)'ju:njən] профсою́з; **~wind** ⚓ пасса́тный ве́тер.

tradition [trə'diʃən] тради́ция; преда́ние; ста́рый обы́чай; **~al** □ традицио́нный.

traffic [træfik] **1.** движе́ние (у́личное, железнодоро́жное и т. п.); торго́вля; ~ jam зато́р у́личного движе́ния; **2.** торгова́ть.

traged|ian (trə'dʒi:diən] а́втор траге́дии; тра́гик; **~y** ['trædʒidi] траге́дия.

tragic(al □) ['trædʒik, -dʒikəl] траги́ческий, траги́чный.

trail [treil] **1.** след; тропа́; **2.** *v/t.* таска́ть, [по]тащи́ть, [по]волочи́ть; идти́ по сле́ду (P); *v/i.* таска́ться, [по]тащи́ться; ♀ свиса́ть [свисну́ть]; **~er** ['treilə] *mot.* прице́п.

train [trein] **1.** по́езд; шлейф (пла́тья); цепь *f*, верени́ца; хвост (коме́ты, павли́на); сви́та, толпа́ (покло́нников); by ~ по́ездом; **2.** воспи́тывать [-та́ть]; приуча́ть [-чи́ть]; [на]тренирова́ть(ся); ⚔ обуча́ть [-чи́ть]; [вы́]дрессирова́ть.

trait [treit] черта́ (лица́, хара́ктера).

traitor ['treitə] преда́тель *m*, изме́нник.

tram [træm] *s.* ~-car, ~way; **~-car** ['træmkɑ:] ваго́н трамва́я.

tramp [træmp] **1.** бродя́га *m*; (до́лгое) путеше́ствие пешко́м; звук тяжёлых шаго́в; **2.** тяжело́ ступа́ть; тащи́ться с трудо́м; F то́пать; бродя́жничать; **~le** ['træmpl] топта́ть; тяжело́ ступа́ть; поп(и)ра́ть (B); ~ down зата́птывать [-топта́ть].

tramway ['træmwei] трамва́й.

trance [trɑ:ns] ⚕ транс; экста́з.

tranquil ['træŋkwil] □ споко́йный; **~lity** [træŋ'kwiliti] споко́йствие; **~lize** ['træŋkwilaiz] успока́ивать (-ся) [-ко́ить(ся)].

transact [træn'zækt] проводи́ть [-вести́] (де́ло), соверша́ть [-ши́ть]; **~ion** [-'zækʃən] де́ло, сде́лка; веде́ние, отправле́ние (де́ла); ~s *pl.* труды́ *m/pl.*, протоко́лы *m/pl.* (нау́чного о́бщества).

transatlantic ['trænzət'læntik] трансатланти́ческий.

transcend [træn'send] переступа́ть преде́лы (P); превосходи́ть [-взойти́], превыша́ть [-вы́сить].

transcribe [træns'kraib] перепи́сывать [-са́ть]; *gr.*, ♪ транскриби́ровать (*im*)*pf.*

transcript ['trænskript] ко́пия; **~ion** [træn'skripʃən] перепи́сывание; ко́пия; *gr.*, ♪ транскри́пция.

transfer 1. [træns'fə:] *v/t.* переноси́ть [-нести́], перемеща́ть [-мести́ть]; перед(ав)а́ть; переводи́ть [-вести́] (в друго́й го́род, на другу́ю рабо́ту); *v/i. Am.* переса́живаться [-се́сть]; **2.** ['trænsfə:] перено́с; переда́ча; трансфе́рт; перево́д; *Am.* переса́дка; **~able** [træns'fə:rəbl] предоста́вленный с пра́вом переда́чи; допуска́ющий переда́чу.

transfigure [træns'figə] видоизменя́ть [-ни́ть]; преобража́ть [-рази́ть].

transfix [-'fiks] пронза́ть [-зи́ть]; прока́лывать [-коло́ть]; **~ed** *fig.* прико́ванный к ме́сту (with от P).

transform (-'fɔ:m] превраща́ть [-врати́ть]; преобразо́вывать [-зова́ть]; **~ation** [-fə'meiʃən] преобразова́ние; превраще́ние; ⚡ трансформа́ция.

transfuse [-'fu:z] перели́(ва́)ть; ⚕ де́лать перелива́ние (кро́ви); *fig.* перед(ав)а́ть (свой энтузиа́зм и т. п.).

transgress (-'gres] *v/t.* преступа́ть [-пи́ть], наруша́ть [-у́шить] (зако́н и т. п.); *v/i.* [со]греши́ть; **~ion** [-'greʃən] просту́пок; наруше́ние (зако́на и т. п.); **~or** [-'gresə] (право)наруши́тель(ница *f*) *m*; гре́шник (-ица).

transient ['trænʃənt] **1.** *s.* transitory; **2.** *Am.* прое́зжий (-жая).

transition [træn'siʒən] перехо́д; перехо́дный пери́од.

transitory ['trænsitəri] □ мимолётный, скороте́чный, скоропреходя́щий.

translat|e [trɑ:ns'leit] переводи́ть [-вести́] (from с P, into на B); *fig.* перемеща́ть [-мести́ть]; **~ion** [trɑ:ns'leiʃən] перево́д.

translucent [trænz'lu:snt] просве́чивающий; полупрозра́чный.

transmigration [trænzmai'greiʃən] переселе́ние.

transmission [trænz'miʃən] переда́ча (*a.* ⊕); пересы́лка; ⊕ трансми́ссия; *radio* переда́ча; трансля́ция; *opt.* пропуска́ние.

transmit [trænz'mit] отправля́ть [-а́вить]; пос(ы)ла́ть; перед(ав)а́ть (*a. radio*); *opt.* пропуска́ть [-сти́ть]; **~ter** [-ə] переда́тчик (*a. radio*); *tel.* микрофо́н.

transmute [trænz'mju:t] превраща́ть [-рати́ть].

transparent [træns'pεərənt] □ прозра́чный.

transpire [-'paiə] испаря́ться [-ри́ться]; проса́чиваться [-сочи́ться]; *fig.* обнару́жи(ва)ться.

transplant [-'plɑ:nt] переса́живать [-сади́ть]; *fig.* переселя́ть [-ли́ть].

transport 1. [træns'pɔ:t] перевози́ть [-везти́]; перемеща́ть [-мести́ть]; *fig.* увлека́ть [-е́чь], восхища́ть [-ити́ть]; **2.** ['trænspɔ:t] тра́нспорт; перево́зка; тра́нспортное (-ные) сре́дство (-ства *n/pl.*); be in ~s быть вне себя́ (of от P); **~ation** [trænspɔ:'teiʃən] перево́зка.

transpose [træns'pouz] перемеща́ть [-мести́ть]; переставля́ть [-а́вить] (слова́ и т. п.); ♪ транспони́ровать (*im*)*pf.*

transverse ['trænzvə:s] □ попере́чный.

trap [træp] **1.** лову́шка, западня́; капка́н; **2.** расставля́ть лову́шки; лови́ть в лову́шку; *fig.* замани́ть в лову́шку; **~-door** ['træpdɔ:] люк; опускна́я дверь *f.*

trapeze [trə'pi:z] трапе́ция.

trapper ['træpə] охо́тник, ста́вящий капка́ны.

trappings [ˈtræpiŋz] *pl.* ко́нская (пара́дная) сбру́я; пара́дный мунди́р.

traps [træps] *pl.* F ли́чные ве́щи *f/pl.*; бага́ж.

trash [træʃ] хлам; отбро́сы *m/pl.*; *fig.* дрянь *f*; макулату́ра (о кни́ге); вздор, ерунда́; **~y** [ˈtræʃi] □ дрянно́й.

travel [ˈtrævl] **1.** *v/i.* путеше́ствовать; е́здить, [по]е́хать; передвига́ться [-и́нуться]; распространя́ться [-ни́ться] (о све́те, зву́ке); *v/t.* объезжа́ть [-е́здить, -е́хать]; проезжа́ть [-е́хать] (... км в час и т. п.); **2.** путеше́ствие; ⊕ ход; (пере)движе́ние; **~(l)er** [-ə] путеше́ственник (-ица).

traverse [ˈtrævə:s] **1.** пересека́ть [-се́чь]; проходи́ть [пройти́] (В); **2.** попере́чина; ⚓, ⚔ тра́верс.

travesty [ˈtrævisti] **1.** паро́дия; искаже́ние; **2.** пароди́ровать; искажа́ть [искази́ть].

trawler [ˈtrɔ:lə] тра́льщик.

tray [trei] подно́с; лото́к.

treacher|ous [ˈtretʃərəs] □ преда́тельский, вероло́мный; ненадёжный; **~y** [-ri] преда́тельство, вероло́мство.

treacle [ˈtri:kl] па́тока.

tread [tred] **1.** [*irr.*] ступа́ть [-пи́ть]; ~ down зата́птывать [затопта́ть]; **2.** по́ступь *f*, похо́дка; ступе́нька; *mot.* проте́ктор; **~le** [ˈtredl] педа́ль *f* (велосипе́да); подно́жка (шве́йной маши́ны).

treason (ˈtri:zn] изме́на; **~able** [-əbl] □ изме́ннический.

treasure [ˈtreʒə] **1.** сокро́вище; **2.** храни́ть; высо́ко́ цени́ть; **~r** [-rə] казначе́й.

treasury [ˈtreʒəri] казначе́йство; сокро́вищница.

treat [tri:t] **1.** *v/t.* обраба́тывать [-бо́тать]; ⚕ лечи́ть; угоща́ть [угости́ть] (to Т); обраща́ться [обрати́ться] с (Т), обходи́ться [обойти́сь] с (Т); *v/i.* ~ of име́ть предме́том, обсужда́ть [-уди́ть] (В); ~ with вести́ перегово́ры с (Т); **2.** удово́льствие, наслажде́ние; угоще́ние; **~ise** [ˈtri:tiz] тракта́т; **~-ment** [ˈtri:tmənt]; обрабо́тка (Т); лече́ние; обраще́ние (of с Т); **~y** [ˈtri:ti] догово́р.

treble [ˈtrebl] **1.** □ тройно́й, утро́енный; **2.** тройно́е коли́чество; ♪ ди́скант; **3.** утра́ивать(ся) [утро́ить(ся)].

tree [tri:] де́рево; родосло́вное де́рево; (сапо́жная) коло́дка.

trefoil [ˈtrefɔil] трили́стник.

trellis [ˈtrelis] **1.** решётка; ⚘ шпале́ра; **2.** обноси́ть решёткой; сажа́ть (расте́ния) шпале́рой.

tremble [ˈtrembl] [за]дрожа́ть, [за-]трясти́сь (with от Р).

tremendous [triˈmendəs] □ стра́шный, ужа́сный; F грома́дный.

tremor [ˈtremə] дрожа́ние.

tremulous [ˈtremjuləs] □ дрожа́щий; тре́петный, ро́бкий.

trench [trentʃ] **1.** кана́ва; ⚔ транше́я, око́п; **2.** рыть рвы, транше́и и т. п.; вска́пывать [вскопа́ть]; ~ (up)on посяга́ть [-гну́ть] на (В); **~ant** [ˈtren(t)ʃənt] □ ре́зкий, ко́лкий.

trend [trend] **1.** направле́ние (*a. fig.*); *fig.* тече́ние; напра́вленность *f*; **2.** отклоня́ться [-ни́ться] (to к Д) (о грани́це и т. п.); име́ть тенде́нцию (towards к Д).

trespass [ˈtrespəs] **1.** наруша́ть грани́цы (on P); соверша́ть просту́пок; злоупотребля́ть [-би́ть] (on Т); **2.** наруше́ние грани́ц; злоупотребле́ние ([up]on Т); **~er** [-ə] наруши́тель грани́ц; правонаруши́тель *m.*

tress [tres] ло́кон; коса́.

trestle [ˈtresl] ко́злы *f/pl.*; подста́вка.

trial [ˈtraiəl] испыта́ние; о́пыт, про́ба; ⚖ суде́бное разбира́тельство; суд; on ~ на испыта́нии, на испыта́ние; под судо́м; give *a. p.* a ~ нанима́ть кого́-либо на испыта́тельный срок; ~ ... *attr.* про́бный, испыта́тельный.

triang|le [ˈtraiæŋgl] треуго́льник; **~ular** [traiˈæŋgjulə] □ треуго́льный.

tribe [traib] пле́мя *n*; *contp.* компа́ния.

tribun|al [traiˈbju:nl] суд; трибуна́л; **~e** [ˈtribju:n] трибу́на; трибу́н.

tribut|ary [ˈtribjutəri] **1.** □ платя́щий дань; *fig.* подчинённый; спосо́бствующий; **2.** да́нник (-ица); *geogr.* прито́к; **~e** [ˈtribju:t] дань *f*; подноше́ние.

trice [trais]: in a ~ мгнове́нно.

trick [trik] **1.** шту́ка, ша́лость *f*; фо́кус, трюк; уло́вка; сноро́вка; **2.** обма́нывать [-ну́ть]; наду́(ва́)ть; иску́сно украша́ть; **~ery** [ˈtrikəri] надува́тельство; проде́лка.

trickle [ˈtrikl] те́чь стру́йкой; сочи́ться.

trick|ster [ˈtrikstə] обма́нщик; **~y** [ˈtriki] □ хи́трий; мудрёный, сло́жный, тру́дный.

tricycle [ˈtraisikl] трёхколёсный велосипе́д.

trifl|e [ˈtraifl] **1.** пустя́к; ме́лочь *f*; a ~ *fig.* немно́жко; **2.** *v/i.* [по]шути́ть; занима́ться пустяка́ми; *v/t.* ~ away зря тра́тить; **~ing** [ˈtraifliŋ] пустя́чный, пустяко́вый.

trig [trig] **1.** опря́тный; наря́дный; **2.** наряжа́ть [-яди́ть]; [за]тормози́ть.

trigger [ˈtrigə] ⚔ спусково́й крючо́к; ⊕ соба́чка, защёлка.

trill [tril] **1.** трель *f*; **2.** выводи́ть трель.

trim [trim] **1.** □ наря́дный; приведённый в поря́док; **2.** наря́д;

поря́док; состоя́ние гото́вности; ⚓ (пра́вильное) размеще́ние гру́за; **3.** приводи́ть в поря́док; (~ up) подреза́ть [-е́зать], подстрига́ть [-и́чь]; отде́л(ыв)ать (пла́тье); ⚓ уравнове́шивать [-е́сить] (су́дно); **~ming** ['trimiŋ] *mst* ~s *pl.* отде́лка (на пла́тье); припра́ва, гарни́р.
trinket ['triŋkit] безделу́шка; брело́к; ~s *pl. contp.* финтифлю́шки *f/pl.*
trip [trip] **1.** путеше́ствие; пое́здка; экску́рсия; спотыка́ние; *fig.* обмо́лвка, оши́бка; **2.** *v/i.* идти́ легко́ и бы́стро; спотыка́ться [споткну́ться]; обмо́лвиться *pf.*; *v/t.* подставля́ть но́жку (Д).
tripartite ['trai'pɑ:tait] тро́йственный; состоя́щий из трёх часте́й.
tripe [traip] *cook.* рубе́ц.
triple ['tripl] тройно́й; утро́енный; **~ts** ['triplits] *pl.* тро́йня *sg.*
tripper [tripə] F экскурса́нт(ка).
trite [trait] □ бана́льный, изби́тый.
triturate ['tritjəreit] растира́ть в порошо́к.
triumph ['traiəmf] **1.** триу́мф; торжество́; **2.** пра́здновать побе́ду, триу́мф; торжествова́ть, восторжествова́ть *pf.* (over над Т); **~al** [trai'ʌmfəl] триумфа́льный; **~ant** [-fənt] □ победоно́сный; торжеству́ющий.
trivial ['triviəl] □ обы́денный; ме́лкий, пусто́й; тривиа́льный.
trod [trɔd] *pt.* от tread; **~den** ['trɔdn] *p. pt.* от tread.
troll [troul] напева́ть.
troll(**e**)**y** ['trɔli] ваго́нетка; 🚂 дрези́на; *Am.* трамва́й.
trollop ['trɔləp] *contp.* неря́ха *m/f*; проститу́тка.
trombone [trɔm'boun] ♪ тромбо́н.
troop [tru:p] **1.** толпа́; отря́д; ⚔ кавалери́йский и́ли та́нковый взвод; *Am.* эскадро́н; **2.** дви́гаться и́ли собира́ться толпо́й; ~ away, ~ off удаля́ться [-ли́ться]; **~er** ['tru:pə] (рядово́й) кавалери́ст; рядово́й-танки́ст; **~s** *pl.* войска́ *n/pl.*
trophy ['troufi] трофе́й, добы́ча.
tropic ['trɔpik] тро́пик; ~s *pl.* тро́пики *m/pl.* (зо́на); **~**(**al** □) [~, -pikəl] тропи́ческий.
trot [trɔt] **1.** рысь (ло́шади); бы́стрый ход (челове́ка); **2.** бе́гать ры́сью; пуска́ть ры́сью; [по]спеши́ть.
trouble ['trʌbl] **1.** беспоко́йство; волне́ние; забо́ты *f/pl.*, хло́поты *f/pl.*; затрудне́ния *n/pl.*; го́ре, беда́; take ~ утружда́ться; **2.** [по-] беспоко́ить(ся); [по]проси́ть; утружда́ть [-уди́ть]; don't ~! не труди́тесь!; **~some** [-səm] тру́дный; причиня́ющий беспоко́йство.
trough [trɔf] коры́то, корму́шка; квашня́; жёлоб.
trounce [trauns] F [по]би́ть, [вы́-] поро́ть.
troupe [tru:p] *thea.* тру́ппа.
trousers ['trauzəz] *pl.* брю́ки *f/pl.*
trout [traut] форе́ль *f.*
trowel ['trauəl] лопа́тка (штукату́ра).
truant ['tru:ənt] **1.** лентя́й; прогу́льщик; учени́к, прогуля́вший уро́ки; **2.** лени́вый; пра́здный.
truce [tru:s] переми́рие.
truck [trʌk] **1.** ваго́нетка; теле́жка; *Am.* грузови́к; 🚂 (откры́тая) това́рная платфо́рма; ме́на; товарообме́н; **2.** перевози́ть на грузовика́х; вести́ менову́ю торго́влю; обме́нивать [-ня́ть]; **~-farmer** *Am.* огоро́дник.
truckle ['trʌkl] раболе́пствовать.
truculent ['trʌkjulənt] свире́пый; гру́бый.
trudge [trʌdʒ] идти́ с трудо́м; таска́ться, [по]тащи́ться.
true [tru:] ве́рный; пра́вильный; настоя́щий; it is ~ пра́вда; come ~ сбы́(ва́)ться; ~ to nature то́чно тако́й, как в нату́ре.
truism ['tru:izm] трюи́зм.
truly ['tru:li] правди́во; лоя́льно; пои́стине; то́чно; yours ~ пре́данный (-ная) вам.
trump [trʌmp] **1.** ко́зырь *m*; **2.** козыря́ть [-рну́ть]; бить ко́зырем; ~ up выду́мывать [вы́думать]; **~ery** ['trʌmpəri] мишура́; дрянь *f.*
trumpet ['trʌmpit] **1.** труба́; **2.** [за-, про]труби́ть; *fig.* возвеща́ть [-ести́ть].
truncheon ['trʌntʃən] ⚒ (ма́ршальский) жезл; дуби́нка (полице́йского).
trundle ['trʌndl] ката́ть(ся), [по-] кати́ть(ся).
trunk [trʌŋk] ствол (де́рева); ту́ловище; хо́бот (слона́); доро́жный сунду́к; **~-call** *teleph.* вы́зов по междугоро́дному телефо́ну; **~-line** 🚂 магистра́ль *f*; *teleph.* междугоро́дная ли́ния.
truss [trʌs] **1.** связка; большо́й пук; ⚕ банда́ж; ⚠ стропи́льная фе́рма; **2.** увя́зывать в пуки́; скру́чивать ру́ки (Д); ⚠ связывать [-за́ть]; укрепля́ть [-пи́ть].
trust [trʌst] **1.** дове́рие; ве́ра; отве́тственное положе́ние; ✝ креди́т; трест; on ~ в креди́т; на ве́ру; **2.** *v/t.* доверя́ть, [по]ве́рить (Д); вверя́ть [вве́рить], доверя́ть [-е́рить] (Д with В); *v/i.* полага́ться [положи́ться] (in. to на В); наде́яться (in, to на В); **~ee** [trʌs'ti:] ⚖ опеку́н; попечи́тель *m*; **~ful** ['trʌstful] □, **~ing** ['trʌstiŋ] □ дове́рчивый; **~worthy** [-wə:ði] заслу́живающий дове́рия.
truth [tru:θ] пра́вда; и́стина; **~ful** ['tru:θful] □ правди́вый; ве́рный.
try [trai] **1.** испы́тывать [испы-

та́ть]; [по]про́бовать; [по]пыта́ться; [по]стара́ться; утомля́ть [-ми́ть]; ⚖ суди́ть; ~ on примеря́ть [-е́рить] (на себя́); **2.** попы́тка; **~ing** ['traiiŋ] □ тру́дный; тяжёлый; раздража́ющий.
tub [tʌb] ка́дка; лоха́нь *f*; бадья́; F ва́нна.
tube [tju:b] труба́, тру́бка; F метро́ *n indecl.* (в Ло́ндоне).
tuber ['tju:bə] ⚘ клу́бень *m*; **~culous** [tju:'bə:kjuləs] ⚕ туберкулёзный.
tubular ['tju:bjulə] □ тру́бчатый, цилиндри́ческий.
tuck [tʌk] **1.** скла́дка, сбо́рка (на пла́тье); **2.** де́лать скла́дки; подбира́ть под себя́; запря́т(ыв)ать; ~ up подвёртывать [-верну́ть] (подо́л); засу́чивать [-чи́ть] (рукава́).
Tuesday ['tju:zdi] вто́рник.
tuft [tʌft] пучо́к (травы́); хохоло́к; боро́дка кли́нышком.
tug [tʌg] **1.** рыво́к; гуж; ⚓ букси́р; **2.** тащи́ть с уси́лием; дёргать [дёрнуть] (изо всех сил); ⚓ букси́ровать.
tuition [tju'iʃən] обуче́ние.
tulip ['tju:lip] тюльпа́н.
tumble ['tʌmbl] **1.** *v/i.* па́дать [упа́сть] (споткну́вшись); кувырка́ться [-кну́ться]; опроки́дываться [-и́нуться]; мета́ться (в посте́ли); *v/t.* приводи́ть в беспоря́док, [по]мя́ть; **2.** паде́ние; беспоря́док; **~-down** [-daun] полуразру́шенный; **~r** [-ə] акроба́т; бока́л, (высо́кий) стака́н.
tumid ['tju:mid] □ распу́хший; *fig.* напы́щенный.
tumo(u)r ['tju:mə] о́пухоль *f*.
tumult ['tju:mʌlt] шум и кри́ки; бу́йство; душе́вное возбужде́ние; **~uous** [tju'mʌltjuəs] шу́мный, бу́йный; возбуждённый.
tun [tʌn] больша́я бо́чка.
tuna ['tju:nə] туне́ц.
tune [tju:n] **1.** мело́дия, моти́в; тон; строй; звук; in ~ настро́енный (роя́ль); в тон; out of ~ расстро́енный (роя́ль); не в тон; **2.** настра́ивать [-ро́ить] (инструме́нт); ~ in *radio* настра́ивать приёмник (to на В); **~ful** ['tju:nful] □ мелоди́чный, гармони́чный; **~less** ['tju:nlis] □ немелоди́чный.
tunnel ['tʌnl] **1.** тунне́ль *m* (*a.* тонне́ль *m*); ⚒ што́льня; **2.** проводи́ть тунне́ль че́рез (В).
turbid ['tə:bid] му́тный; тума́нный.
turbulent ['tə:bjulənt] бу́рный; бу́йный, непоко́рный.
tureen [tə'ri:n, tju'r-] супова́я ми́ска.
turf [tə:f] **1.** дёрн; торф; ко́нный спорт, ска́чки *f/pl.*; **2.** обдерня́ть [-ни́ть]; **~y** ['tə:fi] покры́тый дёрном, дерни́стый; торфяно́й.
turgid ['tə:dʒid] □ опу́хший; *fig.* напы́щенный.
Turk [tə:k] ту́рок, турча́нка.
turkey ['tə:ki] индю́к, инде́йка.
Turkish ['tə:kiʃ] **1.** туре́цкий; **2.** туре́цкий язы́к.
turmoil ['tə:mɔil] шум, сумато́ха; беспоря́док.
turn [tə:n] **1.** *v/t.* враща́ть, верте́ть; повора́чивать [поверну́ть]; обора́чивать [оберну́ть]; точи́ть (на тока́рном станке́); превраща́ть [-рати́ть]; направля́ть [-ра́вить]; ~ a corner заверну́ть за́ угол; ~ down отверга́ть [-е́ргнуть] (предложе́ние); загиба́ть [загну́ть]; ~ off закры́(ва́)ть (кран); выключа́ть [вы́ключить]; ~ on откры́(ва́)ть (кран); включа́ть [-чи́ть]; ~ out выгоня́ть [вы́гнать]; увольня́ть [уво́лить]; выпуска́ть [вы́пустить] (изде́лия); ~ over перевёртывать [-верну́ть]; *fig.* перед(ав)а́ть (дове́ренность и т. п.); ~ up поднима́ть вверх; **2.** *v/i.* враща́ться, верте́ться; повора́чиваться [поверну́ться]; [с]де́латься, станови́ться [стать]; превраща́ться [-врати́ться]; ~ about обёртываться [оберну́ться]; ⚔ повора́чиваться круго́м; ~ in заходи́ть мимохо́дом; F ложи́ться спать; ~ out ока́зываться [-за́ться]; ~ to принима́ться [-ня́ться] за (В); обраща́ться [обрати́ться] к (Д); ~ up появля́ться [-ви́ться]; случа́ться [-чи́ться]; ~ upon обраща́ться [обрати́ться] про́тив (Р); **3.** *su.* оборо́т; поворо́т; изги́б; переме́на; о́чередь *f*; услу́га; оборо́т (ре́чи); F испу́г; at every ~ на ка́ждом шагу́, постоя́нно; by или in ~s по о́череди; it is my ~ моя́ о́чередь *f*; take ~s де́лать поочерёдно; does it serve your ~? э́то вам подхо́дит?, э́то вам годи́тся?; **~coat** перебе́жчик, хамелео́н *fig.*; **~er** ['tə:nə] то́карь *m*; **~ery** [-ri] тока́рное ремесло́; тока́рные изде́лия *n/pl.*
turning ['tə:niŋ] поворо́т (у́лицы и т. п.); враще́ние; тока́рное ремесло́; **~-point** *fig.* поворо́тный пункт; перело́м.
turnip ['tə:nip] ⚘ ре́па.
turn|key ['tə:nki:] тюре́мщик; **~-out** ['tə:n'aut] ⚚ вы́пуск проду́кции; **~over** ['tə:nouvə] ⚚ оборо́т; **~pike** шлагба́ум; **~stile** турнике́т.
turpentine ['tə:pəntain] скипида́р.
turpitude ['tə:pitju:d] позо́р; ни́зость *f*.
turret ['tʌrit] ба́шенка; ✈ туре́ль *f*; ⚔, ⚓ оруди́йная ба́шня.
turtle ['tə:tl] *zo.* черепа́ха.
tusk [tʌsk] клык (слона́, моржа́).
tussle ['tʌsl] **1.** борьба́, дра́ка; **2.** (упо́рно) боро́ться, [по]дра́ться.
tussock ['tʌsək] ко́чка.
tutelage ['tju:tilidʒ] опеку́нство; опе́ка.

tutor ['tjuːtə] **1.** домашний учитель *m*; репетитор; ⚖ опекун; **2.** обучать [-чить]; наставлять [наставить].
tuxedo [tʌk'siːdou] *Am.* смокинг.
twaddle ['twɔdl] **1.** пустая болтовня; **2.** пустословить.
twang [twæŋ] **1.** звук натянутой струны; (*mst* nasal ~) гнусавый выговор; **2.** звенеть (о струне); гнусавить.
tweak [twiːk] щипать [щипнуть].
tweezers ['twiːzəz] *pl.* пинцет.
twelfth [twelfθ] двенадцатый.
twelve [twelv] двенадцать.
twent|ieth ['twentiiθ] двадцатый; **~y** ['twenti] двадцать.
twice [twais] дважды; вдвое.
twiddle ['twidl] вертеть (в руках); играть (T); *fig.* бездельничать.
twig [twig] веточка, прут.
twilight ['twailait] сумерки *f/pl.*
twin [twin] **1.** близнец; двойник; парная вещь *f*; **2.** двойной; парный.
twine [twain] **1.** бечёвка, шпагат, шнурок; **2.** [с]вить; [с]плести; обви(ва)ть(ся).
twinge [twindʒ] приступ боли.
twinkle ['twiŋkl] **1.** мерцание; мигание; мелькание; **2.** [за]мерцать; [за]сверкать; мигать [мигнуть].
twirl [twəːl] **1.** кручение; вращение; **2.** вертеть; закручивать [-утить].
twist [twist] **1.** кручение; скручивание; сучение; изгиб; поворот; вывих; **2.** [с]крутить; [с]сучить; [с]вить(ся); сплетать(ся) [-ести(сь)].
twit [twit]: ~ a p. with a th. попрекать [-кнуть] кого-либо (T).
twitch [twitʃ] **1.** подёргивание, судорога; **2.** дёргать(ся) [дёрнуть (-ся)].
twitter ['twitə] **1.** щебет; **2.** [за-] щебетать; чирикать [-кнуть]; be in a ~ дрожать.
two [tuː] **1.** два, две; двое; пара; in ~ надвое, пополам; **2.** двойка; in ~s попарно; **~fold** ['tuːfould] **1.** двойной; **2.** *adv.* вдвое; **~pence** ['tʌpəns] два пенса; **~-storey** двухэтажный; **~-way** двусторонний; ~ plug двойной штепсель *m.*
tyke [taik] дворняжка; шустрый ребёнок.
type [taip] тип; типичный представитель *m*; *typ.* литера; шрифт; true to ~ типичный; set in ~ *typ.* наб(и)рать; **~write** [*irr.* (write)] писать на машинке; **~writer** пишущая машинка.
typhoid ['taifɔid] ⚕ (*a.* ~ fever) брюшной тиф.
typhoon [tai'fuːn] тайфун.
typhus ['taifəs] ⚕ сыпной тиф.
typi|cal ['tipikəl] □ типичный; **~fy** [-fai] служить типичным примером для (P); **~st** ['taipist] переписчик (-чица) (на машинке), машинистка; shorthand ~ стенографист(ка).
tyrann|ic(al □) [ti'rænik, -ikəl] тиранический; **~ize** ['tirənaiz] тиранить; **~y** [-ni] тирания, деспотизм.
tyrant ['taiərənt] тиран, деспот.
tyre ['taiə] шина (колеса).
tyro ['taiərou] новичок.

U

ubiquitous [juː'bikwitəs] □ вездесущий.
udder ['ʌdə] вымя *n.*
ugly ['ʌgli] □ безобразный; дурной; противный.
ulcer ['ʌlsə] 🕮 язва; **~ate** [-reit] изъязвлять(ся) [-вить(ся)]; **~ous** [-rəs] изъязвлённый; язвенный.
ulterior [ʌl'tiəriə] □ более отдалённый; *fig.* дальнейший; скрытый (мотив и т. п.).
ultimate ['ʌltimit] □ последний; конечный; максимальный; **~ly** [-li] в конце концов.
ultimo ['ʌltimou] *adv.* истекшего месяца
ultra¹ ['ʌltrə] крайний.
ultra²... [~...] *pref.* сверх..., ультра-...
umbel ['ʌmbəl] ⚘ зонтик.
umbrage ['ʌmbridʒ] обида; *poet.* тень *f*, сень *f.*
umbrella [ʌm'brelə] зонтик.
umpire ['ʌmpaiə] **1.** посредник; третейский судья *m*; *sport* судья *m*; **2.** быть (третейским) судьёй; быть посредником.
un... [ʌn...] *pref.* (придаёт отрицательное или противоположное значение) не..., без...
unable ['ʌn'eibl] неспособный; be ~ не быть в состоянии, не [с]мочь.
unaccountable ['ʌnə'kauntəbl] □ необъяснимый; безответственный.
unaccustomed ['ʌnə'kʌstəmd] не привыкший; непривычный.
unacquainted [-'kweintid]: ~ with незнакомый с (T); не знающий (P).
unadvised ['ʌnəd'vaizd] □ неблагоразумный; необдуманный.
unaffected ['ʌnə'fektid] □ непритворный, искренний; не(за)тронутый (by T).
unaided ['ʌn'eidid] лишённый помощи; без посторонней помощи.
unalterable [ʌn'ɔːltərəbl] □ неизменный.

unanim|ity [ju:nə'nimiti] единоду́шие; **~ous** [ju:'næniməs] □ единоду́шный, единогла́сный.
unanswerable [ʌn'ɑ:nsərəbl] □ неопровержи́мый.
unapproachable [ʌnə'proutʃəbl] □ непристу́пный; недосту́пный.
unapt [ʌ'næpt] □ неподходя́щий; неспосо́бный, неуме́лый.
unasked ['ʌn'ɑ:skt] непро́шенный.
unassisted ['ʌnə'sistid] без по́мощи.
unassuming ['ʌnə'sju:miŋ] скро́мный, непритяза́тельный.
unattractive ['ʌnə'træktiv] □ непривлека́тельный.
unauthorized ['ʌn'ɔ:θəraizd] неразрешённый; неправомо́чный.
unavail|able ['ʌnə'veiləbl] не име́ющийся в распоряже́нии; **~ing** [-liŋ] бесполе́зный.
unavoidable [ʌnə'vɔidebl] □ неизбе́жный.
unaware ['ʌnə'wɛə] не зна́ющий, не подозрева́ющий (of P); be ~ of ничего́ не знать о (П); не замеча́ть [-е́тить] (P); **~s** [-z] неожи́данно, врасплóх; нечáянно.
unbacked [ʌn'bækt] *fig.* не име́ющий подде́ржки.
unbalanced ['ʌn'bælənst] неуравнове́шенный.
unbearable [ʌn'bɛərəbl] □ невыноси́мый.
unbecoming ['ʌnbi'kʌmiŋ] □ неподходя́щий; не иду́щий к лицу́; неприли́чный.
unbelie|f ['ʌnbi'li:f] неве́рие; **~vable** ['ʌnbi'li:vəbl] □ невероя́тный; **~ving** [-iŋ] □ неве́рующий.
unbend ['ʌn'bend] [*irr.* (bend)] выпрямля́ть(ся) [вы́прямить(ся)]; станови́ться непринуждённым; **~ing** [-iŋ] □ негну́щийся; *fig.* непреклóнный.
unbias(s)ed ['ʌn'baiəst] □ беспристра́стный.
unbind ['ʌn'baind] [*irr.* (bind)] развя́зывать [-за́ть]; *fig.* освобожда́ть [-боди́ть].
unblushing [ʌn'blʌʃiŋ] бессты́дный.
unbosom [ʌn'buzəm] поверя́ть [-е́рить] (та́йну); ~ o. s. излива́ть ду́шу.
unbounded [ʌn'baundid] □ неограни́ченный; беспреде́льный.
unbroken ['ʌn'broukn] неразби́тый; не поби́тый (реко́рд); непреры́вный.
unbutton ['ʌn'bʌtn] расстёгивать [расстегну́ть].
uncalled [ʌn'kɔ:ld]: ~-for непро́шенный; неуме́стный.
uncanny [ʌn'kæni] □ жу́ткий, сверхъесте́ственный.
uncared ['ʌn'kɛəd]: ~-for забро́шенный.
unceasing [ʌn'si:siŋ] □ непрекраща́ющийся, безостано́вочный.
unceremonious ['ʌnseri'mounjəs] □ бесцеремо́нный.
uncertain [ʌn'sə:tn] □ неуве́ренный; неопределённый; неизве́стный; **~ty** [-ti] неуве́ренность *f*; неизве́стность *f*; неопределённость *f*.
unchang|eable [ʌn'tʃeindʒəbl] □, **~ing** [-iŋ] неизме́нный; неизменя́емый.
uncharitable [ʌn'tʃæritəbl] □ немилосе́рдный.
unchecked ['ʌn'tʃekt] беспрепя́тственный; непрове́ренный.
uncivil ['ʌn'sivl] □ неве́жливый; **~ized** ['ʌn'sivilaizd] нецивилизо́ванный.
uncle ['ʌŋkl] дя́дя *m*.
unclean ['ʌn'kli:n] □ нечи́стый.
unclose ['ʌn'klouz] откры́(ва́)ть (-ся).
uncomfortable [ʌn'kʌmfətəbl] □ неудо́бный; нело́вкий.
uncommon [ʌn'kɔmən] □ необыкнове́нный; замеча́тельный.
uncommunicative ['ʌnkə'mju:nikeitiv] необщи́тельный, неразгово́рчивый.
uncomplaining ['ʌnkəm'pleiniŋ] □ безро́потный.
uncompromising [ʌn'kɔmprəmaiziŋ] □ бескомпроми́ссный.
unconcern ['ʌnkən'sə:n] беззабо́тность *f*; беспе́чность *f*; **~ed** [-d] □ беззабо́тный; беспе́чный.
unconditional ['ʌnkən'diʃnl] □ безогово́рочный, безусло́вный.
unconquerable [ʌn'kɔŋkərəbl] □ непобеди́мый.
unconscionable [ʌn'kɔnʃnəbl] □ бессо́вестный.
unconscious [ʌn'kɔnʃəs] □ бессозна́тельный; потеря́вший созна́ние; be ~ of не созн(ав)а́ть (P); **~ness** [-nis] бессозна́тельность *f*.
unconstitutional ['ʌnkɔnsti'tju:ʃnl] □ противоре́чащий конститу́ции.
uncontrollable [ʌnkən'trouləbl] □ неудержи́мый; не поддаю́щийся контро́лю.
unconventional ['ʌnkən'venʃənl] □ чу́ждый усло́вности; необы́чный; нешабло́нный.
uncork ['ʌn'kɔ:k] отку́пори(ва)ть.
uncount|able ['ʌn'kauntəbl] бесчи́сленный; **~ed** [-tid] несчётный.
uncouple ['ʌn'kʌpl] расцепля́ть [-пи́ть].
uncouth [ʌn'ku:θ] неуклю́жий.
uncover [ʌn'kʌvə] откры́(ва́)ть (лицо́ и т. п.); снима́ть кры́шку с (P); обнажа́ть [-жи́ть] (го́лову).
unct|ion ['ʌŋkʃən] пома́зание; мазь *f*; **~uous** ['ʌŋktjuəs] □ масляни́стый; *fig.* еле́йный.
uncult|ivated ['ʌn'kʌltiveitid] невозде́ланный; некульту́рный.
undamaged ['ʌn'dæmidʒd] неповреждённый.

undaunted [ʌn'dɔ:ntid] □ неустраши́мый.
undeceive ['ʌndi'si:v] выводи́ть из заблужде́ния.
undecided ['ʌndi'saidid] □ нерешённый; нереши́тельный.
undefined ['ʌndi'faind] □ неопределённый.
undeniable [ʌndi'naiəbl] □ неоспори́мый; несомне́нный.
under ['ʌndə] **1.** *adv.* ни́же; внизу́, вниз; **2.** *prp.* под (В, Т); ни́же (Р); ме́ньше (Р); при (П); **3.** *pref.* ниже..., под..., недо...; **4.** ни́жний; ни́зший; **~bid** ['ʌndə'bid] [*irr.* (bid)] предлага́ть бо́лее ни́зкую це́ну чем (И); **~brush** [-brʌʃ] подле́сок; **~carriage** [-'kæridʒ] шасси́ *n indecl.*; **~clothing** [-klouðiŋ] ни́жнее бельё; **~cut** [-kʌt] сбива́ть це́ны; подреза́ть [-е́зать]; **~done** [-dʌn] недожа́ренный; **~estimate** [-r'estimeit] недооце́нивать [-и́ть]; **~fed** [-fed] истощённый от недоеда́ния; **~go** [-'gou] [*irr.* (go)] испы́тывать [испыта́ть]; подверга́ться [-е́ргнуться] (Д); **~graduate** [-'grædjuit] студе́нт(ка) после́днего ку́рса; **~ground** ['ʌndəgraund] **1.** подзе́мный; подпо́льный; **2.** метро́(полите́н) *n indecl.*; подпо́лье; **~hand** [-hænd] **1.** та́йный, закули́сный; **2.** *adv.* та́йно, «за спино́й»; **~lie** [ʌndə'lai] [*irr.* (lie)] лежа́ть в основа́нии (Р); **~line** [-'lain] подчёркивать [-черкну́ть]; **~ling** [-liŋ] подчинённый; **~mine** [ʌndə'main] [за]мини́ровать (*im*)*pf.*; подка́пывать [-копа́ть] (*a. fig.*); *fig.* подрыва́ть [подорва́ть]; **~most** ['ʌndəmoust] са́мый ни́жний; ни́зший; **~neath** [ʌndə'ni:θ] **1.** *prp.* под (Т/В); **2.** *adv.* вниз, внизу́; **~privileged** [-'privilidʒd] лишённый привиле́гий; **~rate** [ʌndə'reit] недооце́нивать [-и́ть]; **~-secretary** ['ʌndə'sekrətəri] замести́тель мини́стра (в Англии и США); **~sell** [-'sel] [*irr.* (sell)] † продава́ть деше́вле други́х; **~signed** [-'saind] нижеподписа́вшийся; **~stand** [ʌndə'stænd] [*irr.* (stand)] *com.* понима́ть [поня́ть]; подразумева́ть (by под Т); make o. s. understood уме́ть объясни́ться; an understood thing решённое де́ло; **~standable** [-əbl] поня́тный; **~standing** [-iŋ] понима́ние; соглаше́ние; взаимопонима́ние; **~state** ['ʌndə'steit] преуменьша́ть [-ме́ньши́ть]; **~stood** [ʌndə'stud] *pt.* и *p. pt.* от understand; **~take** [ʌndə'teik] [*irr.* (take)] предпринима́ть [-ня́ть]; бра́ть на себя́; обя́зываться [-за́ться]; **~taker** **1.** [ʌndə'teikə] предпринима́тель *m*; **2.** ['ʌndəteikə] содержа́тель похоро́нного бюро́; **~taking** **1.** [ʌndə'teikiŋ] предприя́тие; обяза́тельство; **2.** ['ʌndəteikiŋ] похоро́нное бюро́; **~tone** [-toun]: in an ~ вполго́лоса; **~value** [-'vælju:] недооце́нивать [-и́ть]; **~wear** [-wεə] ни́жнее бельё; **~wood** [-wud] подле́сок; **~write** [-rait] [*irr.* (write)] подпи́сывать поли́с морско́го страхова́ния; принима́ть в страхо́вку; **~writer** [-raitə] морско́й страхо́вщик.
undeserved ['ʌndi'zə:vd] □ незаслу́женный.
undesirable [-'zaiərəbl] □ нежела́тельный; неудо́бный, неподходя́щий.
undisciplined [ʌn'disiplind] недисциплини́рованный.
undisguised ['ʌndis'gaizd] □ незамаскиро́ванный; я́вный.
undo ['ʌn'du:, ʌn'du:] [*irr.* (do)] уничтожа́ть [-о́жить] (сде́ланное); развя́зывать [-за́ть]; расстёгивать [расстегну́ть]; расторга́ть [-о́ргнуть] (догово́р и т. п.); **~ing** [-iŋ] уничтоже́ние; ги́бель *f*; развя́зывание; расстёгивание и т. д.
undoubted [ʌn'dautid] □ несомне́нный, бесспо́рный.
undreamt [ʌn'dremt]: ~-of невообрази́мый, неожи́данный.
undress ['ʌn'dres] **1.** дома́шний костю́м; **2.** разде́(ва́)ть(ся); **~ed** ['ʌn'drest] неоде́тый; невы́деланный (о ко́же).
undue ['ʌn'dju:] □ неподходя́щий; чрезме́рный; ненадлежа́щий; ещё не подлежа́щий опла́те.
undulat|e ['ʌndjuleit] быть волни́стым, волнообра́зным; **~ion** [ʌndju'leiʃən] волнообра́зное движе́ние; неро́вность пове́рхности.
unearth ['ʌn'ə:θ] вырыва́ть из земли́; *fig.* раска́пывать [-копа́ть]; **~ly** [ʌn'ə:θli] неземно́й; стра́нный, ди́кий.
uneas|iness [ʌn'i:zinis] беспоко́йство; трево́жность *f*; стесне́ние; **~y** [ʌn'i:zi] □ беспоко́йный, трево́жный; стеснённый (о движе́ниях и т. п.).
uneducated ['ʌn'edjukeitid] необразо́ванный; невоспи́танный.
unemotional ['ʌni'mouʃnl] □ пасси́вный; бесстра́стный; сухо́й *fig.*
unemploy|ed ['ʌnim'plɔid] безрабо́тный; neза́нятый; **~ment** [-'plɔimənt] безрабо́тица.
unending [ʌn'endiŋ] □ несконча́емый, бесконе́чный.
unendurable ['ʌnin'djuərəbl] нестерпи́мый.
unengaged ['ʌnin'geidʒd] neза́нятый; свобо́дный.
unequal ['ʌn'i:kwəl] □ нера́вный; неро́вный; **~led** [-d] непревзойдённый.
unerring ['ʌn'ə:riŋ] □ непогреши́мый; безоши́бочный.

unessential [ˈʌniˈsenʃəl] □ несущéственный (to для P).
uneven [ˈʌnˈi:vn] □ неро́вный; шерохова́тый (*a. fig.*).
uneventful [ˈʌniˈventful] □ без осо́бых собы́тий.
unexampled [ʌnigˈzɑ:mpld] беспримéрный.
unexpected [ˈʌniksˈpektid] □ неожи́данный.
unfailing [ʌnˈfeiliŋ] □ неизмéнный; неисчерпа́емый.
unfair [ˈʌnˈfɛə] □ несправедли́вый; нечéстный (о спортсмéне, игрé и т. п.).
unfaithful [ˈʌnˈfeiθful] □ невéрный, вероло́мный; нето́чный.
unfamiliar [ˈʌnfəˈmiljə] незнако́мый; непривы́чный.
unfasten [ˈʌnˈfɑ:sn] открепля́ть [-пи́ть]; расстёгивать [расстегну́ть]; **~ed** [-d] расстёгнутый; неприкреплённый.
unfavo(u)rable [ˈʌnˈfeivərəbl] □ неблагоприя́тный; невы́годный.
unfeeling [ʌnˈfi:liŋ] □ бесчу́вственный.
unfinished [ˈʌnˈfiniʃt] незако́нченный.
unfit 1. [ˈʌnˈfit] □ него́дный, неподходя́щий; **2.** [ʌnˈfit] дéлать неприго́дным.
unfix [ˈʌnˈfiks] открепля́ть [-пи́ть]; дéлать неусто́йчивым.
unfledged [ˈʌnˈfledʒd] неопери́вшийся (*a. fig.*).
unflinching [ʌnˈflintʃiŋ] □ неукло́нный.
unfold [ʌnˈfould] развёртывать(ся) [-верну́ть(ся)]; откры́(ва́)ть (та́йну и т. п.).
unforced [ˈʌnˈfɔ:st] □ непринуждённый.
unforgettable [ˈʌnfəˈgetəbl] □ незабвéнный.
unfortunate [ʌnˈfɔ:tʃnit] **1.** несча́стный; неуда́чный; неуда́чливый; **2.** неуда́чник (-ица); **~ly** [-li] к несча́стью; к сожалéнию.
unfounded [ˈʌnˈfaundid] □ необосно́ванный; неосновáтельный.
unfriendly [ˈʌnˈfrendli] недружелю́бный; непривéтливый.
unfurl [ʌnˈfə:l] развёртывать [разверну́ть].
unfurnished [ˈʌnˈfə:niʃt] немебли́рованный.
ungainly [ʌnˈgeinli] нескла́дный.
ungenerous [ˈʌnˈdʒenərəs] □ не великоду́шный, не щéдрый.
ungentle [ˈʌnˈdʒentl] □ неделика́тный, неучти́вый.
ungodly [ʌnˈgɔdli] □ безбо́жный.
ungovern|able [ʌnˈgʌvənəbl] □ неукроти́мый; распу́щенный.
ungraceful [ˈʌnˈgreisful] □ неизя́щный, неграцио́зный.
ungracious [ˈʌnˈgreiʃəs] □ неми́лостивый.
ungrateful [ʌnˈgreitful] □ неблагода́рный.
unguarded [ˈʌnˈgɑ:did] □ неохраня́емый; неосторо́жный; незащищённый.
unguent [ˈʌŋgwənt] мазь *f*.
unhampered [ˈʌnˈhæmpəd] беспрепя́тственный.
unhandsome [ʌnˈhænsəm] □ некраси́вый.
unhandy [ʌnˈhændi] □ неудо́бный; нело́вкий.
unhappy [ʌnˈhæpi] □ несча́стный.
unharmed [ˈʌnˈhɑ:md] благополу́чный; невреди́мый.
unhealthy [ʌnˈhelθi] □ нездоро́вый, болéзненный; врéдный.
unheard-of [ʌnˈhə:dɔv] неслы́ханный.
unhesitating [ʌnˈheziteitiŋ] □ неколéблющийся, реши́тельный.
unholy [ʌnˈhouli] безбо́жный; дья́вольский.
unhonoured [ˈʌnˈɔnəd] не уважа́емый; неопла́ченный.
unhope|d-for [ʌnˈhouptˈfɔ:] неожи́данный; **~ful** [-ful] не подаю́щий надéжды, безнадёжный.
unhurt [ˈʌnˈhə:t] невреди́мый, цéлый.
uniform [ˈju:nifɔ:m] **1.** □ однообра́зный; одноро́дный; **2.** фо́рма, мунди́р; **3.** дéлать однообра́зным; обмундиро́вывать [-рова́ть]; **~ity** [ju:niˈfɔ:miti] единообра́зие, однообра́зие.
unify [ˈju:nifai] объединя́ть [-ни́ть]; унифици́ровать (*im*)*pf*.
unilateral [ˈju:niˈlætərəl] односторо́нний.
unimaginable [ʌniˈmædʒinəbl] □ невообрази́мый.
unimportant [ˈʌnimˈpɔ:tənt] □ нева́жный.
uninformed [ˈʌninˈfɔ:md] несвéдущий; неосведомлённый.
uninhabit|able [ˈʌninˈhæbitəbl] него́дный для жилья́; **~ed** [-tid] нежило́й; необита́емый.
uninjured [ˈʌnˈindʒəd] неповреждённый, невреди́мый.
unintelligible [ˈʌninˈtelidʒəbl] □ непоня́тный.
unintentional [ˈʌninˈtenʃnl] □ непреднамéренный, неумы́шленный.
uninteresting [ˈʌnˈintristiŋ] □ неинтерéсный, безынтерéсный.
uninterrupted [ˈʌnintəˈrʌptid] □ непреры́вный, беспреры́вный.
union [ˈju:njən] объединéние; соединéние (*a.* ⊕); сою́з, федера́ция; профсою́з; ♀ Jack брита́нский национа́льный флаг; **~ist** [-ist] член профсою́за.
unique [ju:ˈni:k] еди́нственный в своём ро́де; бесподо́бный.
unison [ˈju:nizn] ♪ унисо́н; *fig.* согла́сие.

unit ['ju:nit] ⚔ часть *f*, подразделе́ние; ⚓ едини́ца; ⊕ агрега́т; **~e** [ju:'nait] соединя́ть(ся) [-ни́ть (-ся)]; объединя́ть(ся) [-ни́ть(ся)]; **~y** ['ju:niti] едине́ние; еди́нство.
univers|al [juni'və:sl] □ всео́бщий; всеми́рный; универса́льный; **~ality** [ju:nivə:'sæliti] универса́льность *f*; **~e** ['ju:nivə:s] мир, вселе́нная; **~ity** [juni'və:siti] университе́т.
unjust ['ʌn'dʒʌst] □ несправедли́вый; **~ified** [ʌn'dʒʌstifaid] неопра́вданный.
unkempt ['ʌn'kempt] нечёсаный; неопря́тный.
unkind [ʌn'kaind] □ недо́брый.
unknown ['ʌn'noun] **1.** неизве́стный; ~ to me *adv.* та́йно от меня́; **2.** незнако́мец (-мка).
unlace ['ʌn'leis] расшнуро́вывать [-ова́ть].
unlawful ['ʌn'lɔ:ful] □ незако́нный.
unlearn ['ʌn'lə:n] разу́чиваться [[-и́ться].
unless [ən'les, ʌn'les] *cj.* е́сли ... не.
unlike ['ʌn'laik] **1.** непохо́жий на (В); **2.** *prp.* в отли́чие от (Р); **~ly** [ʌn'laikli] неправдопсдо́бный; невероя́тный.
unlimited [ʌn'limitid] безграни́чный, неограни́ченный.
unload ['ʌn'loud] выгружа́ть [вы́грузить], разгружа́ть [-узи́ть]; ⚔ разряжа́ть [-яди́ть].
unlock ['ʌn'lɔk] отпира́ть [отпере́ть]; **~ed** [-t] неза́пертый.
unlooked-for [ʌn'lukt'fɔ:] неожи́данный, непредви́денный.
unlovely ['ʌn'lʌvli] некраси́вый, непривлека́тельный.
unlucky [ʌn'lʌki] □ неуда́чный, несчастли́вый.
unman ['ʌn'mæn] лиша́ть му́жественности.
unmanageable [ʌn'mænidʒəbl] □ тру́дно поддаю́щийся контро́лю; непоко́рный.
unmarried ['ʌn'mærid] нежена́тый, холосто́й; незаму́жняя.
unmask ['ʌn'mɑ:sk] снима́ть ма́ску с (Р); *fig.* разоблача́ть [-чи́ть].
unmatched ['ʌn'mætʃt] бесподо́бный.
unmeaning [ʌn'mi:niŋ] □ бессмы́сленный.
unmeasured [ʌn'meʒəd] неизме́ренный; неизмери́мый.
unmeet ['ʌn'mi:t] неподходя́щий.
unmentionable [ʌn'menʃnəbl] невырази́мый; нецензу́рный.
unmerited ['ʌn'meritid] незаслу́женный.
unmindful [ʌn'maindful] □ забы́вчивый; невнима́тельный (of к Д).
unmistakable ['ʌnmis'teikəbl] □ несомне́нный; легко́ узнава́емый.
unmitigated [ʌn'mitigeitid] несмягчённый; *fig.* абсолю́тный.
unmounted ['ʌn'mauntid] пе́ший; неопра́вленный (драгоце́нный ка́мень); не смонти́рованный.
unmoved ['ʌn'mu:ved] нетро́нутый.
unnamed ['ʌn'neimd] безымя́нный; неупомя́нутый.
unnatural [ʌn'nætʃrəl] □ неесте́ственный; противоесте́ственный.
unnecessary [ʌn'nesisəri] □ нену́жный, изли́шний.
unnerve ['ʌn'nə:v] лиша́ть прису́тствия ду́ха
unnoticed ['ʌn'noutist] незаме́ченный.
unobjectionable ['ʌnəb'dʒekʃnəbl] □ безукори́зненный.
unobserved ['ʌnəb'zə:vd] □ незаме́ченный.
unobtainable ['ʌnəb'teinəbl]: ~ thing вещь, кото́рой нельзя́ доста́ть и́ли получи́ть.
unoccupied ['ʌn'ɔkjupaid] неза́нятый.
unoffending ['ʌnə'fendiŋ] безоби́дный.
unofficial ['ʌnə'fiʃəl] □ неофициа́льный.
unopposed ['ʌnə'pouzd] не встреча́ющий сопротивле́ния.
unostentatious ['ʌnɔstən'teiʃəs] □ скро́мный; не показно́й.
unpack ['ʌn'pæk] распако́вывать [-ова́ть].
unpaid ['ʌn'peid] неупла́ченный, неопла́ченный.
unparalleled [ʌn'pærəleld] несравне́нный, бесприме́рный.
unpeople ['ʌn'pi:pl] обезлю́дить *pf*.
unpleasant [ʌn'pleznt] □ неприя́тный; **~ness** [-nis] неприя́тность *f*.
unpolished ['ʌn'pɔliʃt] неотполиро́ванный; *fig.* неотёсанный.
unpolluted ['ʌnpə'lu:tid] незапя́тнанный, непоро́чный.
unpopular ['ʌn'pɔpjulə] □ непопуля́рный, нелюби́мый.
unpracti|cal ['ʌn'præktikəl] □ непракти́чный; **~sed** [-tist] нео́пытный; неприменённый.
unprecedented [ʌn'presidəntid] □ беспрецеде́нтный; бесприме́рный.
unprejudiced [ʌn'predʒudist] □ непредубеждённый, беспристра́стный.
unprepared ['ʌnpri'pɛəd] □ неподгото́вленный; без подгото́вки.
unpreten|ding ['ʌnpri'tendiŋ] □, **~tious** [-ʃəs] □ скро́мный, без претéнзий.
unprincipled ['ʌn'prinsəpld] беспринци́пный; безнра́вственный.
unprofitable [ʌn'prɔfitəbl] невы́годный; нерента́бельный.
unproved ['ʌn'pru:vd] недока́занный.

unprovided [ˈʌnprəˈvaidid] не обеспе́ченный, не снабжённый (with T); **~-for** непредви́денный.
unprovoked [ˈʌnprəˈvoukt] □ ниче́м не вы́званный.
unqualified [ˈʌnˈkwɔlifaid] □ неквалифици́рованный; безогово́рочный.
unquestionable [ʌnˈkwestʃənəbl] □ несомне́нный, неоспори́мый.
unravel [ʌnˈrævəl] распу́т(ыв)ать; разга́дывать [-да́ть].
unready [ˈʌnˈredi] □ негото́вый.
unreal [ˈʌnˈriəl] □ ненастоя́щий; нереа́льный.
unreasonable [ʌnˈri:znəbl] □ не(благо)разу́мный; безрассу́дный; непоме́рный.
unrecognizable [ˈʌnˈrekəgnaizəbl] □ неузнава́емый.
unredeemed [ˈʌnriˈdi:md] □ неиспо́лненный (об обеща́нии); невы́купленный (закла́д); неопла́ченный (долг).
unrefined [ˈʌnriˈfaind] неочи́щенный.
unreflecting [ˈʌnriˈflektiŋ] □ легкомы́сленный, не размышля́ющий.
unregarded [ˈʌnriˈgɑ:did] не при́нятый в расчёт.
unrelenting [ʌnriˈlentiŋ] □ безжа́лостный.
unreliable [ˈʌnriˈlaiəbl] ненадёжный.
unrelieved [ˈʌnriˈli:vd] □ необлегчённый; не получа́ющий по́мощи.
unremitting [ʌnriˈmitiŋ] □ беспреры́вный; неосла́бный.
unreserved [ˈʌnriˈzə:vd] □ открове́нный; невозде́ржанный; безогово́рочный.
unresisting [ˈʌnriˈzistiŋ] □ не сопротивля́ющийся.
unrest [ˈʌnˈrest] беспоко́йство, волне́ние.
unrestrained [ˈʌnrisˈtreind] □ несде́ржанный; необу́зданный.
unrestricted [ˈʌnrisˈtriktid] □ неограни́ченный.
unriddle [ʌnˈridl] разга́дывать [-да́ть].
unrighteous [ʌnˈraitʃəs] □ непра́ведный; несправедли́вый.
unripe [ˈʌnˈraip] незре́лый, неспе́лый.
unrival(l)ed [ʌnˈraivəld] непревзойдённый; без сопе́рника.
unroll [ˈʌnˈroul] развёртывать [-верну́ть].
unruffled [ˈʌnˈrʌfld] гла́дкий (о мо́ре и т. п.); невозмути́мый.
unruly [ʌnˈruli] непоко́рный.
unsafe [ˈʌnˈseif] □ ненадёжный, опа́сный.
unsal(e)able [ˈʌnˈseiləbl] неходово́й (това́р); непрода́жный.
unsanitary [ˈʌnˈsænitəri] негигиени́чный; антисанита́рный.
unsatisfactory [ˈʌnsætisˈfæktəri] □ неудовлетвори́тельный.
unsavo(u)ry [ˈʌnˈseivəri] □ невку́сный; непривлека́тельный.
unsay [ˈʌnˈsei] [*irr.* (say)] брать наза́д (ска́занное).
unscathed [ˈʌnˈskeiðd] невреди́мый.
unschooled [ˈʌnˈsku:ld] необу́ченный; недисциплини́рованный.
unscrew [ˈʌnˈskru:] отви́нчивать (-ся) [-нти́ть(ся)].
unscrupulous [ʌnˈskru:pjuləs] □ беспринци́пный; бессо́вестный; неразбо́рчивый (в сре́дствах).
unsearchable [ʌnˈsə:tʃəbl] □ непостижи́мый, необъясни́мый.
unseasonable [ʌnˈsi:znəbl] □ несвоевре́менный.
unseemly [ʌnˈsi:mli] неподоба́ющий; непристо́йный.
unseen [ˈʌnˈsi:n] неви́димый; неви́данный.
unselfish [ˈʌnˈseilfiʃ] □ бескоры́стный.
unsettle [ˈʌnˈsetl] приводи́ть в беспоря́док; расстра́ивать [-ро́ить]; **~d** [-d] неустро́енный; неустанови́вшийся; не решённый; неопла́ченный (счёт).
unshaken [ˈʌnˈʃeikən] непоколе́бленный.
unshaven [ˈʌnˈʃeivn] небри́тый.
unship [ˈʌnˈʃip] сгружа́ть с корабля́.
unshrink|able [ˈʌnˈʃriŋkəbl] не садя́щийся при сти́рке (о мате́рии); **~ing** [-iŋ] □ непоколеби́мый, бесстра́шный.
unsightly [ʌnˈsaitli] непригля́дный.
unskil|ful [ˈʌnˈskilful] □ неуме́лый, неиску́сный; **~led** [ˈʌnˈskild] неквалифици́рованный.
unsoci|able [ʌnˈsouʃəbl] необщи́тельный.
unsolder [ˈʌnˈsɔldə] распа́ивать [-пая́ть].
unsolicited [ˈʌnsəˈlisitid] непро́шенный, невостре́бованный.
unsophisticated [ˈʌnsəˈfistikeitid] безыску́ственный; бесхи́тростный.
unsound [ˈʌnˈsaund] □ нездоро́вый; испо́рченный; необосно́ванный.
unsparing [ʌnˈspɛəriŋ] □ беспоща́дный; ще́дрый.
unspeakable [ʌnˈspi:kəbl] □ невырази́мый.
unspent [ˈʌnˈspent] неистра́ченный; неутомлённый.
unstable [ˈʌnˈsteibl] □ нетвёрдый, неусто́йчивый; *phys.*, ⚗ нестойкий.
unsteady [ˈʌnˈstedi] □ *s.* **unstable**; ша́ткий; непостоя́нный.
unstring [ˈʌnˈstriŋ] [*irr.* (string)] снима́ть стру́ны с (P); распуска́ть

[-усти́ть] (бу́сы и т. п.); расша́тывать [-шата́ть] (не́рвы).
unstudied ['ʌn'stʌdid] есте́ственный непринуждённый.
unsubstantial ['ʌnsəb'stænʃəl] □ нереа́льный; несуще́ственный.
unsuccessful ['ʌnsək'sesful] □ неуда́чный, безуспе́шный; неуда́чливый.
unsuitable ['ʌn'sju:təbl] □ неподходя́щий.
unsurpassable ['ʌnsə'pɑ:səbl] □ не могу́щий быть превзойдённым.
unsuspect|ed ['ʌnsəs'pektid] неподозрева́емый; неожи́данный; **~ing** [-iŋ] неподозрева́ющий (of о П).
unsuspicious ['ʌnsəs'piʃəs] □ неподозрева́ющий; не вызыва́ющий подозре́ний.
unswerving [ʌn'swə:viŋ] □ неукло́нный.
untangle ['ʌn'tæŋgl] распу́т(ыв)ать.
untarnished ['ʌn'tɑ:niʃt] неопоро́ченный.
unthink|able ['ʌn'θiŋkəbl] невообрази́мый, немы́слимый; **~ing** [-iŋ] □ опроме́тчивый.
unthought ['ʌn'θɔ:t] (и́ли ~-of) неожи́данный.
untidy [ʌn'taidi] □ неопря́тный, неаккура́тный; неу́бранный.
untie ['ʌn'tai] развя́зывать [-за́ть].
until [ən'til, ʌn'til] **1.** *prp.* до (Р); **2.** *cj.* (до тех пор) пока́ ... (не) ...
untimely [ʌn'taimli] несвоевре́менный.
untiring [ʌn'taiəriŋ] □ неутоми́мый.
untold ['ʌn'tould] нерасска́занный; несчётный.
untouched ['ʌn'tʌtʃt] нетро́нутый (*a. fig.*); *phot.* неретуши́рованный.
untried ['ʌn'traid] неиспы́танный; ⚖ недопро́шенный.
untroubled ['ʌn'trʌbld] беспрепя́тственный; ненару́шенный.
untrue ['ʌn'tru:] □ непра́вильный; неве́рный.
untrustworthy ['ʌn'trʌstwə:ði] □ не заслу́живающий дове́рия.
unus|ed **1.** ['ʌn'ju:zd] неупотреби́тельный; не бы́вший в употребле́нии; неиспо́льзованный; **2.** ['ʌn'ju:st] непривы́кший (to к Д); **~ual** [ʌn'ju:ʒuəl] □ необыкнове́нный, необы́чный.
unutterable [ʌn'ʌtərəbl] □ невырази́мый.
unvarnished ['ʌn'va:niʃt] *fig.* неприкра́шенный.
unvarying [ʌn'vɛəriiŋ] □ неизменя́ющийся, неизме́нный.
unveil [ʌn'veil] снима́ть покрыва́ло с (Р); откры́(ва́)ть (па́мятник, та́йну).
unwanted ['ʌn'wɔntid] нежела́нный; нену́жный.
unwarrant|able [ʌn'wɔrəntəbl] □ недопусти́мый; **~ed** [-tid] ниче́м не опра́вданный; негаранти́рованный.
unwary [ʌn'wɛəri] □ необду́манный, неосторо́жный.
unwholesome ['ʌn'houlsəm] нездоро́вый, неблаготво́рный.
unwieldy [ʌn'wi:ldi] □ неуклю́жий; громо́здкий.
unwilling ['ʌn'wiliŋ] □ несклóнный, нерасполо́женный.
unwise ['ʌn'waiz] □ неразу́мный.
unwitting [ʌn'witiŋ] □ нево́льный, непреднаме́ренный.
unworkable [ʌn'wə:kəbl] непримени́мый, него́дный для рабо́ты.
unworthy [ʌn'wə:ði] □ недосто́йный.
unwrap ['ʌn'ræp] развёртывать (-ся) [-верну́ть(ся)].
unyielding [ʌn'ji:ldiŋ] □ непода́тливый, неусту́пчивый.
up [ʌp] **1.** *adv.* вверх, наве́рх; вверху́, наверху́; вы́ше; *fig.* be ~ to the mark быть на до́лжной высоте́ (нау́ки и т. п.); be ~ against a task стоя́ть пе́ред зада́чей; ~ to вплоть до (Р); it is ~ to me (to do) мне прихо́дится (де́лать); what's ~? *sl.* что случи́лось?, в чём де́ло?; **2.** *prp.* вверх по (Д); по направле́нию к (Д); вдоль по (Д); ~ the river вверх по реке́; **3.** *adj.* ~ train по́езд, иду́щий в го́род; **4.** *su.* the ~s and downs *fig.* превра́тности судьбы́; **5.** *vb.* F поднима́ть [-ня́ть]; повыша́ть [-ы́сить]; вст(ав)а́ть.
up|braid [ʌp'breid] [вы́]брани́ть; **~bringing** ['ʌpbriŋiŋ] воспита́ние; **~heaval** [ʌp'hi:vl] переворо́т; **~hill** ['ʌp'hil] (иду́щий) в го́ру; *fig.* тяжёлый; **~hold** [ʌp'hould] [*irr.* (hold)] подде́рживать [-жа́ть]; приде́рживаться (взгля́да) **~holster** [ʌp'houlstə] оби́(ва́)ть (ме́бель); [за]драпирова́ть (ко́мнату); **~holsterer** [-rə] обо́йщик; драпиро́вщик; **~holstery** [-ri] ремесло́ драпиро́вщика и́ли обо́йщика.
up|keep ['ʌpki:p] содержа́ние; сто́имость содержа́ния; **~land** ['ʌplənd] наго́рная страна́; **~lift** **1.** ['ʌplift] (духо́вный) подъём; **2.** [ʌp'lift] поднима́ть [-ня́ть]; возвыша́ть [-ы́сить].
upon [ə'pɔn] *s.* **on.**
upper ['ʌpə] ве́рхний; вы́сший; **~most** [-moust] са́мый ве́рхний; наивы́сший.
up|raise [ʌp'reiz] возвыша́ть [-ы́сить]; **~right** ['ʌp'rait] **1.** □ прямо́й, вертика́льный; *adv. a.* стоймя́; **2.** сто́йка; (*a.* ~ piano) пиани́но *n indecl.*; **~rising** [ʌp'raiziŋ] восста́ние.
uproar ['ʌprɔ:] шум, гам, волне́-

ние; **~ious** [ʌp'rɔːriəs] □ шу́мный, бу́йный.
up|root [ʌp'ruːt] искореня́ть [-ни́ть]; вырыва́ть с ко́рнем; **~set** [ʌp'set] [*irr.* (set)] опроки́дывать(ся) [-и́нуть(ся)]; расстра́ивать [-ро́ить]; выводи́ть из (душе́вного) равнове́сия; **~shot** ['ʌpʃɔt] развя́зка; заключе́ние; **~side** ['ʌpsaid] *adv.*: ~ down вверх дном; **~stairs** ['ʌp'stɛəz] вверх (по ле́стнице), наве́рх(у́); **~start** ['ʌpstɑːt] вы́скочка *m/f*; **~stream** ['ʌp'striːm] вве́рх по тече́нию; **~turn** [ʌp'təːn] переве́ртывать [перевернуть]; **~ward(s)** ['ʌpwəd(z)] вверх, наве́рх.
urban ['əːbən] городско́й; **~e** [əː'bein] □ ве́жливый; изы́сканный.
urchin ['əːtʃin] постре́л, мальчи́шка *m*.
urge [əːdʒ] **1.** понужда́ть [-у́дить]; подгоня́ть [подогна́ть] (*often* ~ on); **2.** стремле́ние, толчо́к *fig.*; **~ncy** ['əːdʒənsi] насто́ятельность *f*; сро́чность *f*; насто́йчивость *f*; **~nt** ['əːdʒənt] □ сро́чный; настоя́тельный, насто́йчивый.
urin|al ['juərinl] писсуа́р; **~ate** [-rineit] [по]мочи́ться; **~e** [-rin] моча́.
urn [əːn] у́рна.
us [ʌs; əs] *pron. pers.* (ко́свенный паде́ж от we) нас, нам, на́ми.
usage ['juːzidʒ] употребле́ние; обы́чай.
usance ['juːzəns] ⚕: bill at ~ ве́ксель на срок, устано́вленный торго́вым обы́чаем.
use 1. [juːs] употребле́ние; примене́ние; по́льзование; по́льза; привы́чка; (of) no ~ бесполе́зный; **2.** [juːz] употребля́ть [-би́ть]; по́льзоваться (T); воспо́льзоваться (T) *pf.*; испо́льзовать (*im*)*pf.*; обраща́ться [обрати́ться] с (T), обходи́ться [обойти́сь] с (T); I **~d** [juːs(t)] to do я, быва́ло, ча́сто де́лал; **~d** [juːst]: ~ to привы́кший к (Д); **~ful** ['juːsful] □ поле́зный; приго́дный; **~less** ['juːslis] □ бесполе́зный; неприго́дный, него́дный.
usher ['ʌʃə] **1.** капельди́нер; швейца́р; при́став (в суде́); **2.** проводи́ть [-вести́] (на ме́сто); вводи́ть [ввести́].
usual ['juːʒuəl] □ обыкнове́нный, обы́чный.
usurer ['juːʒərə] ростовщи́к.
usurp [juː'zəːp] узурпи́ровать (*im*)*pf.*; **~er** [juː'zəːpə] узурпа́тор.
usury ['juːʒuri] ростовщи́чество.
utensil [juː'tensl] (*mst pl.* ~s) посу́да, у́тварь *f*; принадле́жность *f*.
utility [juː'tiliti] поле́зность *f*; вы́годность *f*; public ~ коммуна́льное предприя́тие; *pl.* предприя́тия обще́ственного по́льзования; коммуна́льные услу́ги *f/pl.*
utiliz|ation [juːtilai'zeiʃən] испо́льзование, утилиза́ция; **~e** ['juːtilaiz] испо́льзовать (*im*)*pf.*, утилизи́ровать (*im*)*pf.*
utmost ['ʌtmoust] кра́йний, преде́льный.
utter ['ʌtə] **1.** □ *fig.* по́лный; кра́йний; абсолю́тный; **2.** изд(ав)а́ть (зву́ки); выража́ть слова́ми; **~ance** [-rəns] выраже́ние; произнесе́ние; выска́зывание; **~most** [-moust] кра́йний; преде́льный.

V

vacan|cy ['veikənsi] пустота́; вака́нсия, свобо́дное ме́сто; пробе́л; рассе́янность *f*; **~t** ['veikənt] □ неза́нятый, вака́нтный; пусто́й; рассе́янный (взгляд и т. п.).
vacat|e [və'keit, *Am.* 'veikeit] освобожда́ть [-боди́ть] (дом и т. п.); покида́ть [-и́нуть], оставля́ть [-а́вить] (до́лжность); упраздня́ть [-ни́ть]; **~ion** [və'keiʃən, *Am.* vei'keiʃən] оставле́ние; кани́кулы *f/pl.*; о́тпуск.
vaccin|ate ['væksineit] ⚕ привива́(ва́)ть; **~ation** [væksi'neiʃən] ⚕ приви́вка; **~e** ['væksiːn] ⚕ вакци́на.
vacillate ['væsileit] колеба́ться.
vacuum ['vækjuəm] *phys.* ва́куум; пустота́; ~ cleaner пылесо́с; ~ flask, ~ bottle те́рмос.
vagabond ['vægəbənd] **1.** бродя́га *m*; **2.** бродя́жничать.
vagrant ['veigrənt] **1.** бродя́га *m*; праздношата́ющийся; **2.** стра́нствующий; бродя́чий.
vague [veig] неопределённый, нея́сный, сму́тный.
vain [vein] □ тще́тный, напра́сный; пусто́й, су́етный; тщесла́вный; in ~ напра́сно, тще́тно; **~glorious** [vein'glɔːriəs] тщесла́вный; хвастли́вый.
valediction [væli'dikʃən] проща́ние; проща́льная речь *f*.
valet ['vælit] **1.** камерди́нер; **2.** служи́ть камерди́нером.
valiant ['væljənt] □ *rhet.* хра́брый, до́блестный.
valid ['vælid] ⚖ действи́тельный, име́ющий си́лу; ве́ский, обосно́ванный; **~ity** [və'liditi] действи́тельность *f* и т. д.
valley ['væli] доли́на.
valo(u)r ['vælə] *rhet.* до́блесть *f*.

valuable ['væljuəbl] **1.** □ це́нный; **2.** ~s *pl.* це́нности *f/pl.*
valuation [vælju'eiʃən] оце́нка (иму́щества).
value ['vælju:] **1.** це́нность *f*; цена́; ✝ сто́имость *f*; ✝ валю́та; значе́ние; **2.** оце́нивать [-и́ть] (В); [о-] цени́ть (В); дорожи́ть (Т); **~less** ['vælju:lis] ничего́ не сто́ящий.
valve ['vælv] ⊕ кла́пан, ве́нтиль *m*; *radio* электро́нная ла́мпа.
van [væn] фурго́н; 🚂 бага́жный и́ли това́рный ваго́н; ⚔ аванга́рд.
vane [vein] флю́гер; крыло́ (ветряно́й ме́льницы); ло́пасть *f* (винта́); лопа́тка (турби́ны).
vanguard ['vængɑ:d] ⚔ аванга́рд.
vanish ['væniʃ] исчеза́ть [-е́знуть].
vanity ['væniti] су́етность *f*; тщесла́вие; ~ bag да́мская су́мочка.
vanquish ['væŋkwiʃ] побежда́ть [-еди́ть].
vantage ['vɑ:ntidʒ] преиму́щество.
vapid ['væpid] □ безвку́сный, пре́сный; *fig.* ску́чный.
vapor|ize ['veipəraiz] испаря́ть(ся) [-ри́ть(ся)]; **~ous** [-rəs] парообра́зный; (*mst fig.*) тума́нный.
vapo(u)r ['veipə] **1.** пар; пары́; тума́н; *fig.* химе́ра, фанта́зия; **2.** бахва́литься.
varia|ble ['vɛəriəbl] □ непостоя́нный, изме́нчивый; переме́нный; **~nce** [-riəns] разногла́сие; ссо́ра; be at ~ расходи́ться во мне́ниях; находи́ться в противоре́чии; **~nt** [-riənt] **1.** ино́й; разли́чный; **2.** вариа́нт; **~tion** [vɛəri'eiʃən] измене́ние; отклоне́ние; ♪ вариа́ция.
varie|d ['vɛərid] □ *s.* various; **~gate** ['vɛərigeit] де́лать пёстрым; разнообра́зить; **~ty** [və'raiəti] разнообра́зие; многосторо́нность *f*; разнови́дность *f*; ряд, мно́жество; ~ show варьете́ *n indecl.*
various ['vɛəriəs] ра́зный; разли́чный; разнообра́зный.
varnish ['vɑ:niʃ] **1.** лак; оли́фа; лакиро́вка (*a. fig.*); *fig.* прикра́са; **2.** [от]лакирова́ть; придава́ть лоск (Д); *fig.* прикра́шивать [-ра́сить] (недоста́тки).
vary ['vɛəri] изменя́ть(ся) [-ни́ть (-ся)]; ра́зниться; расходи́ться [разойти́сь] (о мне́ниях); разнообра́зить.
vase [vɑ:z] ва́за.
vast [vɑ:st] □ обши́рный, грома́дный.
vat [væt] чан; бо́чка, ка́дка.
vault [vɔ:lt] **1.** свод; склеп; подва́л, по́греб; *sport* прыжо́к (с упо́ром); **2.** выводи́ть свод над (Т); перепры́гивать [-гнуть].
vaunt [vɔ:nt] [по]хва́статься (of Т).
veal [vi:l] теля́тина; *attr.* теля́чий.
veer [viə] меня́ть направле́ние (о ве́тре); *fig.* изменя́ть взгля́ды и т. п.
vegeta|ble ['vedʒitəbl] **1.** о́вощ; ~s *pl.* зе́лень *f*, о́вощи *m/pl.*; **2.** расти́тельный; овощно́й; **~rian** [vedʒi'tɛəriən] **1.** вегетариа́нец (-нка); **2.** вегетариа́нский; **~te** ['vedʒiteit] *fig.* прозяба́ть.
vehemen|ce ['vi:iməns] си́ла; стреми́тельность *f*; стра́стность *f*; **~t** [-t] стреми́тельный; стра́стный.
vehicle ['vi:ikl] экипа́ж, пово́зка (и любо́е друго́е сре́дство тра́нспорта и́ли передвиже́ния); *fig.* сре́дство выраже́ния (мы́слей); проводни́к (зара́зы и т. п.).
veil [veil] **1.** покрыва́ло; вуа́ль *f*; *fig.* заве́са; **2.** закрыва́ть покрыва́лом, вуа́лью; *fig.* [за]маскирова́ть.
vein [vein] ве́на; жи́ла (*a.* ⚒); *fig.* жи́лка; настрое́ние.
velocity [vi'lɔsiti] ско́рость *f*.
velvet ['velvit] ба́рхат; *attr.* ба́рхатный; **~y** [-i] ба́рхатный (*fig.*); бархати́стый.
venal ['vi:nl] прода́жный, подкупно́й (*a.* подку́пный).
vend [vend] прод(ав)а́ть; **~er, ~or** ['vendə] продаве́ц.
veneer [və'niə] **1.** фане́ра; **2.** обкле́ивать фане́рой; *fig.* придава́ть (Д) вне́шний лоск.
venera|ble ['venərəbl] □ почте́нный; **~te** [-reit] благогове́ть пе́ред (Т); **~tion** [venə'reiʃən] благогове́ние, почита́ние.
venereal [vi'niəriəl] венери́ческий.
Venetian [vi'ni:ʃən] венециа́нский; ~ blind жалюзи́ *n indecl.*
vengeance ['vendʒəns] месть *f*, мще́ние.
venison ['venzn] оле́нина.
venom ['venəm] (*part.* змеи́ный) яд (*a. fig.*); **~ous** [-əs] □ ядови́тый (*a. fig.*).
vent [vent] **1.** отве́рстие; отду́шина; give ~ to изли́(ва́)ть (В); **2.** *fig.* изли́(ва́)ть (В), дава́ть вы́ход (Д).
ventilat|e ['ventileit] прове́три(ва)ть; [про]вентили́ровать; *fig.* обсужда́ть [-уди́ть], выясня́ть [вы́яснить] (вопро́с); **~ion** [venti'leiʃən] прове́тривание; вентиля́ция; *fig.* выясне́ние, обсужде́ние (вопро́са).
venture ['ventʃə] **1.** риско́ванное предприя́тие; спекуля́ция; at a ~ наугад, науда́чу; **2.** рискова́ть [-кну́ть] (Т); отва́жи(ва)ться на (В) (*a.* ~ upon); **~some** [-səm] □, **venturous** [-rəs] □ сме́лый; риско́ванный.
veracious [və'reiʃəs] правди́вый.
verb|al ['və:bəl] □ слове́сный; у́стный; *gr.* глаго́льный; **~iage** ['və:biidʒ] многосло́вие; **~ose** [və:'bous] □ многосло́вный.
verdant ['və:dənt] □ зелене́ющий, зелёный.

verdict ['və:dikt] ⚖ верди́кт; пригово́р (прися́жных) (*a. fig.*).
verdigris ['və:digris] ярь-медя́нка.
verdure ['və:dʒə] зе́лень *f*.
verge [və:dʒ] **1.** край; кайма́ (вокру́г клу́мбы); *fig.* грань *f*; on the ~ of на гра́ни (P); **2.** клони́ться (to к Д); приближа́ться [-ли́зиться] (to к Д); ~ (up)on грани́чить с (T).
veri|fy ['verifai] проверя́ть [-е́рить]; подтвержда́ть [-рди́ть]; **~table** ['veritəbl] □ настоя́щий, и́стинный.
vermin ['və:min] *coll.* вреди́тели *m/pl.*, парази́ты *m/pl.*; **~ous** ['və:minəs] киша́щий парази́тами.
vernacular [və'nækjulə] **1.** □ наро́дный (о выраже́нии); родно́й (о языке́); ме́стный (о диале́кте); **2.** наро́дный язы́к; ме́стный диале́кт; жарго́н.
versatile ['və:sətail] □ многосторо́нний; подвижно́й.
verse [və:s] стих; стихи́ *m/pl.*; поэ́зия; строфа́; **~d** [və:st] о́пытный, све́дущий.
versify ['və:sifai] *v/t.* перелага́ть на стихи́; *v/i.* писа́ть стихи́.
version ['və:ʃən] вариа́нт; ве́рсия; перево́д.
vertebral ['və:tibrəl] позвоно́чный.
vertical ['və:tikəl] □ вертика́льный; отве́сный.
vertig|inous [və:'tidʒinəs] □ головокружи́тельный.
verve [vɛəv] жи́вость *f* (изображе́ния); разма́х.
very ['veri] **1.** *adv.* о́чень; the ~ best са́мое лу́чшее; **2.** *adj.* настоя́щий, су́щий; са́мый (как усиле́ние); the ~ same тот са́мый; the ~ thing и́менно то, что ну́жно; the ~ thought уже́ одна́ мысль *f*, сама́ мысль *f*; the ~ stones да́же ка́мни *m/pl.*; the veriest rascal после́дний негодя́й.
vesicle ['vesikl] пузырёк.
vessel ['vesl] сосу́д; су́дно, кора́бль *m.*
vest [vest] **1.** жиле́т; нате́льная фуфа́йка; вста́вка (в пла́тье); **2.** *v/t.* облека́ть [-е́чь] (with T); *v/i.* переходи́ть во владе́ние (in P).
vestibule ['vestibju:l] вестибю́ль *m.*
vestige ['vestidʒ] след.
vestment ['vestment] одея́ние; *eccl.* облаче́ние, ри́за.
vestry ['vestri] *eccl.* ри́зница; **~man** [-mən] член прихо́дского управле́ния.
veteran ['vetərən] **1.** ветера́н; быва́лый солда́т; **2.** *attr.* ста́рый, о́пытный.
veterinary ['vetnri] **1.** ветерина́р (*mst* ~ surgeon); **2.** ветерина́рный.
veto ['vi:tou] **1.** ве́то *n indecl.*; **2.** налага́ть ве́то на (B).
vex [veks] досажда́ть [досади́ть], раздража́ть [-жи́ть]; **~ation** [vek'seiʃən] доса́да, неприя́тность *f*; **~atious** [-ʃəs] доса́дный.
via ['vaiə] че́рез (B) (на пи́сьмах и т. п.).
vial ['vaiəl] пузырёк, буты́лочка.
viands ['vaiəndz] *pl.* я́ства *n/pl.*
vibrat|e [vai'breit] [по]колеба́ться, вибри́ровать; **~ion** [-ʃən] вибра́ция.
vice [vais] **1.** поро́к; недоста́ток; ⊕ тиски́ *m/pl.*; **2.** *pref.* ви́це...; **~roy** ['vaisroi] ви́це-коро́ль *m.*
vice versa ['vaisi'və:sə] наоборо́т.
vicinity [vi'siniti] окре́стность *f*; бли́зость *f*.
vicious ['viʃəs] □ поро́чный; зло́й.
vicissitude [vi'sisitju:d] : *mst* ~s *pl.* превра́тности *f/pl.*
victim ['viktim] же́ртва; **~ize** [-timaiz] де́лать свое́й же́ртвой; [за]му́чить.
victor ['viktə] победи́тель *m*; **~ious** [vik'tɔ:riəs] □ победоно́сный; **~y** ['viktəri] побе́да.
victual ['vitl] **1.** *v/i.* запаса́ться прови́зией; *v/t.* снабжа́ть прови́зией; **2.** *mst* ~s *pl.* продово́льствие, прови́зия; **~ler** ['vitlə] поставщи́к продово́льствия.
video ['vidiou] *adj.* телевизио́нный.
vie [vai] сопе́рничать.
view [vju:] **1.** вид (of на B); по́ле зре́ния, кругозо́р; взгляд; наме́рение; осмо́тр; in ~ of ввиду́ (P); on ~ (вы́ставленный) для обозре́ния; with a ~ to *or* of + *ger.* с наме́рением (+ *inf.*); have in ~ име́ть в виду́; **2.** осма́тривать [осмотре́ть]; рассма́тривать [-мотре́ть]; [по]смотре́ть на (B); **~point** то́чка зре́ния.
vigil|ance ['vidʒiləns] бди́тельность *f*; **~ant** [-lənt] □ бди́тельный.
vigo|rous ['vigərəs] □ си́льный, энерги́чный; **~(u)r** ['vigə] си́ла, эне́ргия.
vile [vail] □ ме́рзкий, ни́зкий.
vilify ['vilifai] поно́сить, [о]черни́ть.
village ['vilidʒ] село́, дере́вня; *attr.* се́льский, дереве́нский; **~r** [-ə] се́льский (-кая) жи́тель(ница *f*) *m.*
villain ['vilən] злоде́й, негодя́й; **~ous** [-əs] злоде́йский; по́длый; **~y** [-i] злоде́йство; по́длость *f*.
vim [vim] F эне́ргия, си́ла.
vindic|ate ['vindikeit] отста́ивать [отстоя́ть] (пра́во и т. п.); реабилити́ровать (*im*)*pf.*; опра́вдывать [-да́ть]; **~tive** [vin'diktiv] □ мсти́тельный.
vine [vain] виногра́дная лоза́; **~gar** ['vinigə] у́ксус; **~-growing** виногра́дарство; **~yard** ['vinjəd] виногра́дник.

vintage ['vintidʒ] сбор виногра́да; вино́ (из сбо́ра определённого го́да).
violat|e ['vaiəleit] наруша́ть [-у́шить], преступа́ть [-пи́ть] (кля́тву, зако́н и т. п.); [из]наси́ловать; **~ion** [vaiə'leiʃən] наруше́ние; изнаси́лование.
violen|ce ['vaiələns] нейстовство; наси́лие; **~t** [-t] □ нейстовый; я́ростный; наси́льственный.
violet ['vaiəlit] фиа́лка; фиоле́товый цвет.
violin [vaiə'lin] ♪ скри́пка.
viper ['vaipə] гадю́ка.
virago [vi'reigou] сварли́вая же́нщина.
virgin ['və:dʒin] **1.** де́вственница; *poet. a. eccl.* де́ва; **2.** □ де́вственный (*a.* ~al); **~ity** [və:'dʒiniti] де́вственность *f*.
viril|e ['virail] возмужа́лый; му́жественный; **~ity** [vi'riliti] му́жество; возмужа́лость *f*.
virtu ['və:tu:] понима́ние то́нкостей иску́сства; article of ~ худо́жественная ре́дкость *f*; **~al** ['və:tjuəl] □ факти́ческий; **~e** ['və:tju:] доброде́тель *f*; досто́инство; in ~ of посре́дством (P); в си́лу (P); **~ous** ['və:tjuəs] □ доброде́тельный; целому́дренный.
virulent ['virulənt] вируле́нтный (яд); опа́сный (о боле́зни); *fig.* зло́бный.
visa ['vi:zə] *s.* visé.
viscount ['vaikaunt] вико́нт.
viscous ['viskəs] □ вя́зкий; тягу́чий (о жи́дкости).
visé ['vi:zei] **1.** ви́за; **2.** визи́ровать (*im*)*pf.*, *pf. a.* [за-].
visible ['vizəbl] □ ви́димый; ви́дный; *fig.* я́вный, очеви́дный; *pred.* is he ~? принима́ет ли он?
vision ['viʒən] зре́ние; вид; виде́ние; *fig.* проница́тельность *f*; **~ary** ['viʒənəri] **1.** при́зрачный; фантасти́ческий; мечта́тельный; **2.** прови́дец (-дица); мечта́тель(ница *f*) *m*.
visit ['vizit] **1.** *v/t.* навеща́ть [-ести́ть]; посеща́ть [-ети́ть]; осма́тривать [-мотре́ть]; *fig.* постига́ть [-и́гнуть] *or* [-и́чь]; *v/i.* де́лать визи́ты; гости́ть; **2.** посеще́ние, визи́т; **~ation** [vizi'teiʃən] официа́льное посеще́ние; *fig.* испыта́ние, ка́ра; **~or** ['vizitə] посети́тель (-ница *f*) *m*, го́сть(я *f*) *m*; инспе́ктор.
vista ['vistə] перспекти́ва; вид.
visual ['vizjuəl] □ зри́тельный; нагля́дный; опти́ческий; **~ize** [-aiz] нагля́дно представля́ть себе́, мы́сленно ви́деть.
vital ['vaitl] □ жи́зненный; насу́щный, суще́ственный; живо́й (стиль); ~s, ~ parts *pl.* жи́зненно ва́жные о́рганы *m/pl.*; **~ity** [vai'tæliti] жизнеспосо́бность *f*, жи́зненность *f*, живу́честь *f*; **~ize** ['vaitəlaiz] оживля́ть [-ви́ть].
vitamin(e) ['vaitəmin] витами́н.
vitiate ['viʃieit] [ис]по́ртить; де́лать недействи́тельным.
vivaci|ous [vi'veiʃəs] □ живо́й, оживлённый; **~ty** [-'væsiti] жи́вость *f*, оживлённость *f*.
vivid ['vivid] □ *fig.* живо́й, я́ркий.
vivify ['vivifai] оживля́ть [-ви́ть].
vixen ['viksn] лиси́ца-са́мка.
vocabulary [və'kæbjuləri] слова́рь *m*, спи́сок слов; запа́с слов.
vocal ['voukəl] □ голосово́й; звуча́щий; ♪ вока́льный.
vocation [vou'keiʃən] призва́ние; профе́ссия; **~al** [-l] □ профессиона́льный.
vociferate [vou'sifəreit] гро́мко крича́ть, горла́нить.
vogue [voug] мо́да; популя́рность *f*.
voice [vɔis] **1.** го́лос; give ~ to выража́ть [вы́разить] (B); **2.** выража́ть [вы́разить] (слова́ми).
void [vɔid] **1.** пусто́й; лишённый (of P); недействи́тельный; **2.** пустота́; ва́куум; **3.** ⚕ опорожня́ть [-ро́жнить]; де́лать недействи́тельным.
volatile ['vɔlətail] ⚗ лету́чий (*a. fig.*); *fig.* изме́нчивый.
volcano [vɔl'keinou] (*pl.*: volcanoes) вулка́н.
volition [vou'liʃən] волево́й акт, хоте́ние; во́ля.
volley ['vɔli] **1.** залп; *fig.* град (упрёков и т. п.); **2.** стреля́ть за́лпами; сы́паться гра́дом; *fig.* испуска́ть [-усти́ть] (кри́ки, жа́лобы).
voltage ['voultidʒ] ⚡ напряже́ние.
voluble ['vɔljubl] речи́стый, многоречи́вый.
volum|e ['vɔljum] том; объём; ёмкость *f*, вмести́тельность *f*; *fig.* си́ла, полнота́ (зву́ка и т. п.); **~inous** [və'lju:minəs] □ объёмистый; многото́мный; обши́рный.
volunt|ary ['vɔləntəri] □ доброво́льный; доброво́льческий; **~eer** [vɔlən'tiə] **1.** доброво́лец; **2.** *v/i.* вызыва́ться [вы́зваться] (for на B); идти́ доброво́льцем; *v/t.* предлага́ть [-ложи́ть] (свою́ по́мощь и т. п.).
voluptu|ary [və'lʌptjuəri] сладостра́стник, сластолю́бец; **~ous** [-s] сладостра́стный; (*of people*) сластолюби́вый.
vomit ['vɔmit] **1.** рво́та; **2.** [вы́-]рвать: he ~s его́ рвёт; *fig.* изверга́ть [-е́ргнуть].
voraci|ous [vo'reiʃəs] □ прожо́рливый, жа́дный; **~ty** [vo'ræsiti] прожо́рливость *f*.
vortex ['vɔ:teks] *mst fig.* водоворо́т; *mst fig.* вихрь

vote [vout] **1.** голосова́ние; баллотиро́вка; (избира́тельный) го́лос; пра́во го́лоса; во́тум; реше́ние; cast a ~ отдава́ть го́лос (for за В; against про́тив Р); **2.** *v/i.* голосова́ть (*im*)*pf*., *pf. a.* [про-] (for за В; against про́тив Р); *v/t.* голосова́ть (*im*)*pf*., *pf. a.* [про-]; **~r** [ˈvoutə] избира́тель(ница *f*) *m*.

voting... [ˈvoutiŋ] избира́тельный.

vouch [vautʃ]: ~ for руча́ться [поручи́ться] за (В); **~er** [ˈvautʃə] распи́ска; оправда́тельный докуме́нт; поручи́тель *m*; **~safe** [vautʃˈseif] удоста́ивать [-сто́ить] (В/Т).

vow [vau] **1.** обе́т, кля́тва; **2.** *v/t.* [по]кля́сться в (П).

vowel [ˈvauəl] гла́сный (звук).

voyage [vɔidʒ] **1.** путеше́ствие (мо́рем); **2.** путеше́ствовать (по́ морю).

vulgar [ˈvʌlgə] □ гру́бый, вульга́рный; по́шлый; широко́ распространённый; ~ tongue наро́дный язы́к; **~ize** [-raiz] опошля́ть [опо́шлить]; вульгаризи́ровать (*im*)*pf*.

vulnerable [ˈvʌlnərəbl] □ *fig.* уязви́мый.

vulture [ˈvʌltʃə] *zo.* стервя́тник; *fig.* хи́щник.

W

wad [wɔd] **1.** клочо́к ва́ты, ше́рсти и т. п.; пыж; **2.** набива́ть и́ли подбива́ть ва́той; забива́ть пыжо́м; **~ding** [ˈwɔdiŋ] наби́вка, подби́вка.

waddle [ˈwɔdl] ходи́ть вперева́лку.

wade [weid] *v/t.* переходи́ть вброд; *v/i.* проб(и)ра́ться (through по Д *or* че́рез В).

wafer [ˈweifə] обла́тка; ва́фля.

waffle [ˈwɔfl] *part. Am.* ва́фля.

waft [wɑːft] **1.** дунове́ние (ве́тра); струя́ (за́паха); **2.** носи́ть(ся), [понести́(сь) (по во́здуху).

wag [wæg] **1.** шутни́к; **2.** маха́ть [махну́ть] (Т), виля́ть [вильну́ть] (Т); ~ one's finger грози́ть па́льцем.

wage [weidʒ] **1.** вести́ (войну́); **2.** *mst* ~s [ˈweidʒiz] *pl.* за́работная пла́та.

waggish [ˈwægiʃ] □ шаловли́вый; заба́вный, коми́чный.

waggle [ˈwægl] F пома́хивать (Т); пока́чивать(ся).

wag(g)on [ˈwægən] пово́зка, теле́га; F де́тская коля́ска; 🚂 *Brit.* ваго́н-платфо́рма; **~er** [-ə] во́зчик.

waif [weif] беспризо́рник; бездо́мный челове́к; бро́шенная вещь *f*.

wail [weil] **1.** вопль *m*; вой (ве́тра); причита́ние; **2.** [за]вопи́ть; выть, завы́(ва́)ть; причита́ть.

waist [weist] та́лия; ⚓ шкафу́т; **~coat** [ˈweiskout, ˈweskət] жиле́т.

wait [weit] *v/i.* ждать (for В *or* Р), ожида́ть (for Р), подожда́ть *pf*. (for В *or* Р); (ча́сто: ~ at table) прислу́живать [-жи́ть] (за столо́м); ~ (up)on прислу́живать (Д); ~ and see занима́ть выжида́тельную пози́цию; *v/t.* выжида́ть [вы́ждать] (В); ~ dinner подожда́ть с обе́дом (for В); **~er** [ˈweitə] официа́нт.

waiting [ˈweitiŋ] ожида́ние; **~-room** приёмная; 🚂 зал ожида́ния.

waitress [ˈweitris] официа́нтка.

waive [weiv] отка́зываться [-за́ться] от (пра́ва и т. п.); **~r** [ˈweivə] ⚖ отка́з (от пра́ва, тре́бования).

wake [weik] **1.** ⚓ кильва́тер; **2.** [*irr.*] *v/i.* бо́дрствовать; (*mst* ~ up) просыпа́ться [просну́ться], пробужда́ться [-уди́ться]; *v/t.* [раз]буди́ть, пробужда́ть [-уди́ть]; возбужда́ть [-уди́ть] (жела́ния и т. п.); **~ful** [ˈweikful] □ бессо́нный; бди́тельный; **~n** [ˈweikən] *s.* wake 2.

wale [weil] полоса́, рубе́ц.

walk [wɔːk] **1.** *v/i.* ходи́ть, идти́ [пойти́] (пешко́м); [по]гуля́ть; появля́ться [-ви́ться] (о привиде́нии); *v/t.* прогу́ливать (ло́шадь и т. п.); обходи́ть [обойти́]; **2.** ходьба́; похо́дка; прогу́лка пешко́м; тропа́, алле́я; ~ of life обще́ственное положе́ние; профе́ссия.

walking [ˈwɔːkiŋ] **1.** ходьба́; **2.** гуля́ющий; ходя́чий; ~ tour экску́рсия пешко́м; **~-stick** трость *f*.

walk|-out [ˈwɔːkˈaut] *Am.* забасто́вка; **~-over** лёгкая побе́да.

wall [wɔːl] **1.** стена́; сте́нка (сосу́да); **2.** обноси́ть стено́й; ~ up заде́л(ыв)ать (дверь и т. п.).

wallet [ˈwɔlit] бума́жник.

wallflower ⚘ желтофио́ль *f*; *fig.* де́вушка, оста́вшаяся без кавале́ра (на балу́).

wallop [ˈwɔləp] F [по]би́ть, [поот]колоти́ть.

wallow [ˈwɔlou] валя́ться, бара́хтаться.

wall|-paper [ˈwɔːlpeipə] обо́и *m/pl.*; **~-socket** ⚡ ште́псельная розе́тка.

walnut [-nət] ⚘ гре́цкий оре́х.

walrus [ˈwɔːlrəs] *zo.* морж.

waltz [wɔːls] **1.** вальс; **2.** вальси́ровать.

wan [wɔn] □ бле́дный; изнурённый; ту́склый.

wand [wɔnd] (волшебная) палочка.
wander [ˈwɔːndə] бродить; странствовать; блуждать (также о взгляде, мыслях и т. п.).
wane [wein] 1. убывание (луны); 2. уменьшаться [уменьшиться]; убы(ва)ть, быть на ущербе (о луне); подходить к концу.
wangle [ˈwæŋgl] *sl.* ухитряться получить.
want [wɔnt] 1. недостаток (of P *or* в П); нужда; потребность *f*; бедность *f*; 2. *v/i.* be ~ing: he is ~ing in patience ему недостаёт терпения; ~ for нуждаться в (П); *v/t.* [за]хотеть (P *a.* B); [по]желать (P *a.* B); нуждаться в (Д); he ~s energy ему недостаёт энергии; what do you ~? что вам нужно?; ~ed (в объявлениях) требуется, ⚖ разыскивается.
wanton [ˈwɔntən] 1. □ резвый; произвольный; буйный (о росте); похотливый; распутный; 2. резвиться.
war [wɔː] 1. война; *fig.* борьба; make ~ вести войну ([up]on с T); 2. *attr.* военный; 3. воевать.
warble [ˈwɔːbl] издавать трели; [с]петь (о птицах).
ward [wɔːd] 1. опекаемый; район (города); (больничная) палата; (тюремная) камера; ~s *pl.* бородка (ключа); 2. ~ (off) отражать [отразить], отвращать [-ратить] (удар); ~er [ˈwɔːdə] тюремщик; ~robe [ˈwɔːdroub] гардероб; ~ trunk чемодан-шкаф.
ware [wɛə] (в сложный словах) посуда; ~s *pl.* товар(ы *pl.*).
warehouse 1. [ˈwɛəhaus] товарный склад; пакгауз; 2. [-hauz] помещать в склад; хранить на складе.
warfare [ˈwɔːfɛə] война, ведение войны.
wariness [ˈwɛərinis] осторожность *f*.
warlike [ˈwɔːlaik] воинственный.
warm [wɔːm] 1. □ тёплый (*a. fig.*); *fig.* горячий; 2. согревание; 3. [на-, со]греть, нагре(ва)ть(ся), согре(ва)ть(ся) (*a.* ~ up); ~th [-θ] тепло; теплота (*a. fig.*).
warn [wɔːn] предупреждать [-редить] (of, against о П); предостерегать [-стеречь] (of, against от P); ~ing [ˈwɔːniŋ] предупреждение; предостережение.
warp [wɔːp] [по]коробить(ся) (о дереве); *fig.* извращать [-ратить], искажать [исказить] (взгляды и т. п.).
warrant [ˈwɔrənt] 1. правомочие; ручательство; ⚖ доверенность *f*; ~ of arrest приказ об аресте; 2. оправдывать [-дать]; ручаться [поручиться] за (B); ✝ гарантировать (*im*)*pf.*; ~y [-i] гарантия; ручательство.
warrior [ˈwɔriə] *poet.* боец, воин.
wart [wɔːt] бородавка; нарост (на стволе дерева).
wary [ˈwɛəri] □ осторожный.
was [wɔz, wəz] *pt.* от be.
wash [wɔʃ] 1. *v/t.* [вы]мыть; обмы(ва)ть; промы(ва)ть; [вы]стирать; *v/i.* [вы]мыться; стираться (о материи); плескаться; 2. мытьё; стирка; бельё (для стирки); прибой; помои *m/pl.*; *pharm.* примочка; ~able [ˈwɔʃəbl] (хорошо) стирающийся; ~-basin [ˈwɔʃbeisn] таз; умывальная раковина; ~-cloth тряпочка для мытья, ~er [ˈwɔʃə] мойщик (-ица); промыватель *m*; стиральная машина; ⊕ шайба, прокладка; ~(er)woman прачка; ~ing [ˈwɔʃiŋ] 1. мытьё; стирка; бельё (для стирки); 2. стиральный; стирающийся; ~y [ˈwɔʃi] жидкий, водянистый.
wasp [wɔsp] оса.
wastage [ˈweistidʒ] изнашивание; потери утечкой, усушкой и т. п.
waste [weist] 1. пустыня; потеря; излишняя трата; отбросы *m/pl.*; ⊕ отходы *m/pl.*; угар; lay ~ опустошать [-шить]; 2. пустынный; невозделанный; опустошённый; 3. *v/t.* расточать [-чить] (деньги и т. п.); [по]терять (время); опустошать [-шить]; изнурять [-рить] (организм); *v/i.* истощаться [-щиться]; ~ful [ˈweistful] □ расточительный; ~-paper: ~ basket корзина для бумаги.
watch [wɔtʃ] 1. стража; сторож; ⚓ вахта; (карманные или наручные) часы *m/pl.*; 2. *v/i.* [по]караулить (over B); стоять на страже; бодрствовать; ~ for выжидать [выждать] (B); *v/t.* [по]сторожить; наблюдать, следить за (T); выжидать [выждать]; ~-dog сторожевой пёс; ~ful [ˈwɔtʃful] □ бдительный; ~maker часовщик; ~man [-mən] (ночной) сторож; ~word пароль *m*; лозунг.
water [ˈwɔːtə] 1. вода; ~s *pl.* воды *f/pl.*; drink the ~s пить целебные воды; *attr.* водяной; водный; водо...; 2. *v/t.* орошать [оросить]; [на]поить (животных); поли(ва)ть; (*a.* ~ down) разбавлять водой; *fig.* чересчур смягчать; *v/i.* слезиться; ходить на водопой; набирать воду (о корабле); ~fall водопад; ~-gauge водомер.
watering [ˈwɔːtəriŋ]: ~-can, ~-pot лейка; ~-place водопой; воды *f/pl.*, курорт с минеральными водами; морской курорт.
water|-level уровень воды; ⊕ ватерпас; ~man [ˈwɔːtəmən] лодочник, перевозчик; ~proof 1. непромокаемый; 2. непромокаемый плащ *m*; 3. придавать водонепроницаемость (Д); ~shed

водораздéл; бассéйн рекú; ~-side бéрег; *attr.* располóженный на берегý; ~tight водонепроницáемый; *fig.* выдéрживающий крúтику; ~-way вóдный путь *m*; фарвáтер; ~works *pl.*, *a. sg.* водопровóдная стáнция; ~y ['wɔːtəri] водянúстый (*a. fig.*).

wattle ['wɔtl] **1.** плетéнь *m*; **2.** [с]плестú; стрóить из плетня.

wave (weiv) **1.** волнá; знак (рукóй); завúвка (причёски); **2.** *v/t.* [по-]махáть, дéлать знак (Т); завú(вá)ть (вóлосы); ~ a p. away дéлать знак комý-либо, чтóбы он удалúлся; ~ aside *fig.* отмáхиваться [-хнýться] от (Р); *v/i.* развевáться (о знамёнах); волновáться (о нúве); качáться (о вéтке); вúться (о волосáх); **~-length** длинá волны́.

waver ['weivə] [по]колебáться; колыхáться [-хнýться] (о плáмени); дрóгнуть (о войскáх) *pf.*

wavy ['weivi] волнúстый.

wax[1] [wæks] **1.** воск; сургýч; ушнáя сéра; *attr.* восковóй; **2.** [на-]вощúть.

wax[2] [~] [*irr.*] прибы́(вá)ть (о лунé).

wax|en ['wæksən] (*mst fig.*) восковóй; *fig.* мя́гкий как воск; **~y** ['wæksi] □ восковóй; похóжий на воск.

way [wei] *mst* дорóга, путь *m*; сторонá, направлéние; мéтод; срéдство; обы́чай, привы́чка; óбласть *f*, сфéра; состоя́ние; отношéние; (*a.* ~s *pl.*) óбраз (жúзни, мы́слей); ~ in, out вход, вы́ход; this ~ сюдá; by the ~ кстáти, мéжду прóчим; по дорóге; by ~ of рáди (Р); в кáчестве (Р); on the ~ в путú; по дорóге; out of the ~ находя́щийся в сторонé; необы́чный; необыкновéнный; under ~ ⚓ на ходý (*a. fig.*); give ~ уступáть [-пúть] (Д); have one's ~ добивáться своегó; настáивать на своём; lead the ~ идтú во главé; покáзывать примéр; **~-bill** накладнáя; спúсок пассажúров; **~farer** пýтник; **~lay** [wei'lei] [*irr.* (lay)] подстерегáть [-рéчь]; **~side 1.** обóчина; **2.** придорóжный; **~ward** ['weiwəd] □ своенрáвный; капрúзный.

we [wiː, wi] *pron. pers.* мы.

weak [wiːk] □ слáбый; **~en** ['wiːkən] *v/t.* ослабля́ть [-áбить]; *v/i.* [о]слабéть; **~ly** [-li] хúлый; *adv.* слáбо; **~-minded** ['wiːk'maindid] слабоýмный; **~ness** [-nis] слáбость *f.*

weal[1] [wiːl] блáго.

weal[2] [~] *s.* wale.

wealth [welθ] богáтство; изобúлие; **~y** ['welθi] □ богáтый.

wean [wiːn] отнимáть от грудú; отучáть [-чúть] (from, of от Р).

weapon ['wepən] орýжие; *fig.* срéдство (самозащúты).

wear [wɛə] **1.** [*irr.*] *v/t.* носúть (одéжду); (*a.* ~ away, down, off) стирáть [стерéть], изнáшивать [износúть]; *fig.* изнуря́ть [-рúть], истощáть [-щúть] (*mst* ~ out); *v/i.* носúться (о плáтье); ~ on мéдленно тянýться (о врéмени); **2.** ношéние, нóска (одéжды); одéжда, плáтье; (*a.* ~ and tear, *part.* ⊕) изнóс, изнáшивание; be the ~ быть в мóде.

wear|iness ['wiərinis] устáлость *f*; утомлённость *f*; **~isome** [-səm] □ утомúтельный; **~y** ['wiəri] **1.** □ утомлённый; утомúтельный; **2.** утомля́ть(ся) [-мúть(ся)].

weasel ['wiːzl] *zo.* лáска.

weather ['weðə] **1.** погóда; **2.** *v/t.* вывéтривать [вы́ветрить]; выдéрживать [вы́держать] (бýрю) (*a. fig.*); подвергáть атмосфéрному влия́нию; *v/i.* вывéтриваться [вы́ветриться]; подвергáться атмосфéрному влия́нию; **~-beaten, ~-worn** обвéтренный; закалённый (о человéке); повреждённый бýрями.

weav|e [wiːv] [*irr.*] [со]ткáть; [с]плестú; *fig.* сочиня́ть [-нúть]; **~er** ['wiːvə] ткач, ткачúха.

web [web] ткань *f*; паутúна; (плáвательная) перепóнка; **~bing** ['webiŋ] ткáная тесьмá.

wed [wed] выдавáть зáмуж; женúть (*im*)*pf.*; сочетáть брáком; **~ding** ['wediŋ] **1.** свáдьба; **2.** свáдебный.

wedge [wedʒ] **1.** клин; **2.** закрепля́ть клúном; раскáлывать при пóмощи клúна; (*a.* ~ in) вклúнивать(ся) [-нúть(ся)]; ~ o. s. in втúскиваться [втúснуться].

wedlock ['wedlɔk] брак.

Wednesday ['wenzdi] средá (день).

wee [wiː] крóшечный, мáленький.

weed [wiːd] **1.** сóрная травá, сорня́к; **2.** [вы́]полóть; **~s** [-z] *pl.* вдóвий трáур; **~y** ['wiːdi] заросший сóрной травóй; F *fig.* долговя́зый, тóщий.

week [wiːk] недéля; by the ~ понедéльно; this day ~ недéлю томý назáд; чéрез недéлю; **~-day** бýдний день *m*; **~-end** нерабóчее врéмя от суббóты до понедéльника; **~ly** ['wiːkli] **1.** еженедéльный; недéльный; **2.** еженедéльник.

weep [wiːp] [*irr.*] [за]плáкать; покрывáться кáплями; **~ing** ['wiːpiŋ] плакýчий (об úве, берёзе).

weigh [wei] *v/t.* взвéшивать [-éсить] (*a. fig.*); ~ anchor поднимáть я́корь; ~ed down отягощённый; *v/i.* вéсить; взвéшиваться [-éситься]; *fig.* имéть вес, значéние; ~ (up)on тяготéть над (Т).

weight [weit] **1.** вес; тя́жесть *f*; гúря; *sport* штáнга; брéмя *n*; вли-

я́ние; **2.** отягоща́ть [-готи́ть]; *fig.* обременя́ть [-ни́ть]; **~y** ['weiti] □ тяжёлый; *fig.* ва́жный, ве́ский.
weird [wiəd] таи́нственный; роково́й; F стра́нный, непоня́тный.
welcome ['welkəm] **1.** приве́тствие; you are ~ to *inf.* я охо́тно позволя́ю вам (+ *inf.*); (you are) ~ не́ за что!; ~! добро́ пожа́ловать!; **2.** жела́нный; прия́тный; **3.** приве́тствовать (*a. fig.*); раду́шно принима́ть.
weld [weld] ⊕ сва́ривать(ся) [-и́ть (-ся)].
welfare ['welfɛə] благосостоя́ние; ~ work рабо́та по улучше́нию бытовы́х усло́вий населе́ния.
well[1] [wel] **1.** коло́дец; родни́к; *fig.* исто́чник; пролёт (ле́стницы); ⊕ бурова́я сква́жина; **2.** хлы́нуть *pf.*; бить ключо́м.
well[2] [~] **1.** хорошо́; ~ off состоя́тельный; I am not ~ мне нездоро́вится; **2.** *int.* ну! *or* ну,...; **~-being** благополу́чие; **~-bred** благовоспи́танный; **~-favo(u)red** привлека́тельный; **~-mannered** с хоро́шими мане́рами; **~-timed** своевре́менный; **~-to-do** [-tə'du:] состоя́тельный, зажи́точный; **~-worn** поно́шенный; *fig.* изби́тый.
Welsh [welʃ] **1.** уэ́льский, валли́йский; **2.** валли́йский язы́к; the ~ валли́йцы *m/pl.*
welt [welt] рант (на о́буви); полоса́ (от уда́ра кнуто́м и т. п.).
welter ['weltə] **1.** сумато́ха, сумбу́р; **2.** валя́ться, бара́хтаться.
wench [wentʃ] де́вка, (крестья́нская) де́вушка.
went [went] *pt.* от go.
wept [wept] *pt.* и *p. pt.* от weap.
were [wə:, wə] *pt. pl.* от be.
west [west] **1.** за́пад; **2.** за́падный; **3.** *adv.* к за́паду, на за́пад; ~ of к за́паду от (P); **~erly** ['westəli], **~ern** ['westən] за́падный; **~ward**(s) ['westwəd(z)] на за́пад.
wet [wet] **1.** дождли́вая пого́да; мокрота́; **2.** мо́крый; вла́жный, сыро́й; дождли́вый; **3.** [*irr.*] [на-] мочи́ть, нама́чивать [-мочи́ть]; увлажня́ть [-ни́ть].
wether ['weðə] кастри́рованный бара́н.
wet-nurse ['wetnə:s] корми́лица.
whale [weil] кит; **~bone** ['weilboun] кито́вый ус; **~r** ['weilə] китобо́йное су́дно; китоло́в.
whaling ['weiliŋ] охо́та на кито́в.
wharf [wɔ:f] (това́рная) при́стань *f*; на́бережная.
what [wɔt] **1.** что?; ско́лько ...?; **2.** то, что; что; ~ about ...? что но́вого о ...?; ну, как ...?; ~ for? заче́м?; ~ a blessing! кака́я благода́ть!; **3.** ~ with ... ~ with отча́сти от (P) ... отча́сти от (P); **~(so)ever** [wɔt(sou)'evə] како́й бы ни; что бы ни; there is no doubt whatever нет никако́го сомне́ния.
wheat [wi:t] пшени́ца.
wheel [wi:l] **1.** колесо́; гонча́рный круг; *mot.* руль *m*; **2.** ката́ть, [по-] кати́ть (katя́ску и т. п.); е́хать на велосипе́де; опи́сывать круги́; повора́чивать(ся) [поверну́ть(ся)]; ⚔ заходи́ть фла́нгом; ⚔ right ~! ле́вое плечо́ вперёд — марш!; **~-barrow** та́чка; **~-chair** кре́сло на колёсах (для инвали́да); **~ed** [wi:ld] колёсный, на колёсах.
wheeze [wi:z] дыша́ть с при́свистом.
when [wen] **1.** когда́?; **2.** *conj.* когда́, в то вре́мя как, как то́лько; тогда́ как.
whence [wens] отку́да.
when(so)ever [wen(sou)'evə] вся́кий раз когда́; когда́ бы ни.
where [wɛə] где, куда́; from ~ отку́да; **~about(s)** **1.** ['wɛərə'baut(s)] где?, о́коло како́го ме́ста?; **2.** ['wɛərəbaut(s)] местонахожде́ние; **~as** [wɛər'æz] тогда́ как; поско́льку; **~by** [wɛə'bai] посре́дством чего́; **~fore** ['wɛəfɔ:] почему́?; **~in** [wɛər'in] в чём; **~of** [wɛər'ɔv] из кото́рого; о кото́ром; о чём; **~upon** [wɛərə'pɔn] по́сле чего́; **~ver** [wɛər'evə] где бы ни, куда́ бы ни; **~withal** [-wi'ðɔ:l] необходи́мые сре́дства *n/pl.*
whet [wet] [на]точи́ть (на оселке́).
whether ['weðə] ... ли; ~ or no так и́ли и́наче; во вся́ком слу́чае.
whetstone ['wetstoun] точи́льный ка́мень *m.*
whey [wei] сы́воротка.
which [witʃ] **1.** кото́рый?; како́й?; **2.** кото́рый; что; **~ever** [-'evə] како́й уго́дно, како́й бы ни ...
whiff [wif] **1.** дунове́ние, струя́ (во́здуха); дымо́к; затя́жка (при куре́нии); **2.** пуска́ть клубы́ (ды́ма); попы́хивать (T).
while [wail] **1.** вре́мя *n*, промежу́ток вре́мени; for a ~ на вре́мя; F worth ~ сто́ящий затра́ченного труда́; **2.** ~ away проводи́ть [-вести́] (вре́мя); **3.** (*a.* whilst [wailst]) пока́, в то вре́мя как; тогда́ как.
whim [wim] при́хоть *f*, капри́з.
whimper ['wimpə] [за]хны́кать.
whim|sical ['wimzikəl] □ прихотли́вый, причу́дливый; **~sy** ['wimzi] при́хоть *f*; причу́да.
whine [wain] [за]скули́ть; [за]хны́кать.
whip [wip] **1.** *v/t.* хлеста́ть [-стну́ть]; [вы́]сечь; сби(ва́)ть (сли́вки, я́йца и т. п.); *pol.* ~ in со-з(ы)ва́ть]; ~ up расшеве́ливать [-ли́ть]; подстёгивать [-стегну́ть]; *v/i.* ю́ркать [юркну́ть]; трепа́ться (о па́русе); **2.** кнут (*a.* riding-~) хлыст; ку́чер; *parl.* организа́тор па́ртии.

whippet *zo.* ['wipit] гончая собака.
whipping ['wipiŋ] подстёгивание (кнутом); взбучка; **~-top** волчок.
whirl [wə:l] **1.** вихревое движение; вихрь *m*; кружение; **2.** кружить(ся); **~-pool** водоворот; **~-wind** вихрь *m*.
whisk [wisk] **1.** веничек, метёлочка; мутовка; **2.** *v/t.* сби(ва)ть (сливки и т. п.); смахивать [-хнуть]; помахивать (хвостом); *v/i.* юркать [юркнуть]; **~ers** ['wiskəz] *pl. zo.* усы (кошки и т. п.) *m/pl.*; бакенбарды *f/pl.*
whisper ['wispə] **1.** шёпот; **2.** шептать [шепнуть].
whistle ['wisl] **1.** свист; свисток; **2.** свистать, свистеть [свистнуть].
white [wait] **1.** *com.* белый; бледный; F честный; невинный, чистый: ~ heat белое каление; ~ lie невинная (*or* святая) ложь *f*; **2.** белый цвет; белизна; белок (глаза, яйца); белила *n/pl.*; **~n** ['waitn] [по]белить; [по]белеть; **~ness** ['waitnis] белизна; **~wash 1.** побелка; **2.** [по]белить; *fig.* обелять [лить].
whither *lit.* ['wiðə] куда.
whitish ['waitiʃ] бел(ес)оватый.
Whitsun ['witsn] *eccl.* троица.
whittle ['witl] строгать или оттачивать ножом; *fig.* ~ away свести на нет.
whiz(z) [wiz] свистеть (о пулях и т. п.).
who [hu:] *pron.* **1.** кто?; **2.** который; кто; тот, кто ...; *pl.*: те, кто.
whoever [hu:'evə] *pron.* кто бы ни ...; который бы ни ...
whole [houl] **1.** □ целый, весь; невредимый; ~ milk цельное молоко; **2.** целое; всё *n*; итог; (up)on the ~ в целом; в общем; **~-hearted** □ искренний, от всего сердца; **~sale 1.** (*mst* ~ trade) оптовая торговля; **2.** оптовый; *fig.* в больших размерах; ~ dealer оптовый торговец; **3.** оптом; **~some** [houlsəm'] □ полезный, здоровый.
wholly ['houli] *adv.* целиком, всецело.
whom [hu:m] *pron.* (винительный падеж от who) кого и т. д.; которого и т. д.
whoop [hu:p] **1.** гиканье; **2.** гикать [гикнуть]; **~ing-cough** ['hu:piŋkɔf] ⚕ коклюш.
whose [hu:z] (родительный падеж от who) чей *m*, чья *f*, чьё *n*, чьи *pl.*; *rel. pron. mst*: которого, которой: ~ father отец которого ...
why [wai] **1** почему?, отчего?, зачем?; **2.** да ведь ...; что же...
wick [wik] фитиль *m*.
wicked ['wikid] □ злой, злобный; безнравственный; **~ness** [-nis] злобность *f*; безнравственность *f*.
wicker ['wikə] прутья для плетения; ~ basket плетёная корзинка; ~ chair плетёный стул.
wicket ['wikit] калитка; воротца *n/pl.* (в крикете).
wide [waid] *a.* □ *and adv.* широкий; просторный; далёкий; широко; далеко, далёко (of от P); ~ awake бдительный; осмотрительный; 3 feet ~ три фута в ширину, шириной в три фута; **~n** ['waidn] расширять(ся) [-ирить (-ся)] **~-spread** широко распространённый.
widow ['widou] вдова; *attr.* вдовий; **~er** [-ə] вдовец.
width [widθ] ширина; широта.
wield [wi:ld] *lit.* владеть (T); иметь в руках.
wife [waif] жена; **~ly** ['waifli] свойственный жене.
wig [wig] парик.
wild [waild] **1.** □ дикий; бурный; буйный; run ~ расти без присмотра; talk ~ говорить не думая; **2.** ~, ~s [-z] дикая местность *f*; дебри *f/pl.*; **~cat** *zo.* дикая кошка; *fig.* недобросовестное рискованное предприятие; *attr.* рискованный; нелегальный; **~erness** ['wildənis] пустыня, дикая местность *f*; **~-fire**: like ~ с быстротой молнии.
wile [wail] *mst* ~s *pl.* хитрость *f*; уловка.
wil(l)ful ['wilful] □ упрямый, своевольный; преднамеренный.
will [wil] **1.** воля; сила воли; желание; завещание; with a ~ энергично; **2.** [*irr.*] *v/aux.*: he ~ come он придёт; he ~ do it он это сделает; он хочет это сделать; он обычно это делает; **3.** завещать (*im*)*pf.*; [по]желать, [за]хотеть; ~ o. s. заставлять [-ставить] себя.
willing ['wiliŋ] □ охотно готовый (to на B *or* + *inf.*); **~ness** [nis] готовность *f*.
will-o-the-wisp ['wiləðəwisp] блуждающий огонёк.
willow ['wilou] ⚘ ива.
wily ['waili] □ хитрый, коварный.
win [win] [*irr.*] *v/t.* выигрывать [выиграть]; одерживать [-жать] (победу); получать [-чить]; снискать *pf.*; (to do) склонять [-нить] (сделать); ~ a p. over склонить кого-либо на свою сторону; *v/i.* выигрывать [выиграть]; одерживать победу.
wince [wins] вздрагивать [вздрогнуть].
winch [wintʃ] лебёдка; ворот.
wind[1] [wind, *poet.* waind] **1.** ветер; дыхание; ⚕ газы *m/pl.*; ♪ духовые инструменты *m/pl.*; **2.** заставлять запыхаться; давать перевести дух; [по]чуять.
wind[2] [waind] [*irr.*] *v/t.* наматывать [намотать]; обматывать [об-

мота́ть]; обви́(ва́)ть; ~ up заводи́ть [завести́] (часы́); ✝ ликвиди́ровать (im)pf.; зака́нчивать [зако́нчить] (де́ло, пре́ния и т. п.); v/i. нама́тываться [намота́ться]; обви́(ва́)ться.
wind|bag ['windbæg] sl. болту́н, пустозво́н; **~fall** па́данец; бурело́м; fig. неожи́данное сча́стье.
winding ['waindiŋ] 1. изги́б, изви́лина; нама́тывание; ⚡ обмо́тка; 2. изви́листый; спира́льный; ~ stairs pl. винтова́я ле́стница; **~-sheet** са́ван.
wind-instrument ['windinstrumənt] ♪ духово́й инструме́нт
windlass ['windləs] ⚓ бра́шпиль m; ⊕ во́рот.
windmill [-mil] ветряна́я ме́льница.
window ['windou] окно́; витри́на; **~-dressing** декори́рование витри́ны; fig. пока́з в лу́чшем ви́де.
wind|pipe ['windpaip] anat. трахе́я; **~-screen** mot. ветрово́е стекло́.
windy ['windi] □ ве́треный; fig. несерьёзный; многосло́вный.
wine [wain] вино́; **~press** виноде́льный пресс.
wing [wiŋ] 1. крыло́; co. рука́; ✈, ⚔ авиапо́лк, Am. авиабрига́да; ⚔ фланг; ⌂ фли́гель m; thea. ~s pl. кули́сы f/pl.; take ~ полете́ть pf.; on the ~ на лету́; 2. fig. окрыля́ть [-ли́ть]; ускоря́ть [-о́рить]; [по]лете́ть.
wink [wiŋk] 1. морга́ние; миг; F not get a ~ of sleep не смыка́ть глаз; 2. морга́ть [-гну́ть] мига́ть [мигну́ть]; ~ at подми́гивать [-гну́ть] (Д); смотре́ть сквозь па́льцы на (В).
win|ner ['winə] победи́тель(ница f) m; призёр; **~ning** ['winiŋ] 1. выи́грывающий; побежда́ющий; fig. привлека́тельный (a. ~some [-səm]); 2. ~s pl. вы́игрыш.
wint|er ['wintə] 1. зима́; attr. зи́мний; 2. проводи́ть зи́му, [пере-, про]зимова́ть; **~ry** ['wintri] зи́мний; холо́дный; fig. неприве́тливый.
wipe [waip] вытира́ть [вы́тереть]; утира́ть [утере́ть]; ~ out fig. смы(ва́)ть (позо́р); уничтожа́ть [-о́жить].
wire ['waiə] 1. про́волока; про́вод; F телегра́мма; 2. монти́ровать провода́ на (П); телеграфи́ровать (im)pf.; скрепля́ть и́ли свя́зывать про́волокой; **~drawn** ['waiə'drɔ:n] то́нкий, казуисти́ческий; **~less** ['waiəlis] 1. □ беспро́волочный; attr. ра́дио...; 2. ра́дио n indecl.; on the ~ по ра́дио; ~ (message) радиогра́мма; ~ (telegraphy) беспро́волочный телегра́ф, радиотелеграфи́я; ~ operator ради́ст; ~ pirate радиоза́яц; ~ (set) радиоприёмник; 2. передава́ть по ра́дио; **~-netting** про́волочная се́тка.
wiry ['waiəri] про́волочный; fig. жи́листый; выно́сливый.
wisdom ['wizdəm] му́дрость f; ~ tooth зуб му́дрости.
wise [waiz] 1. му́дрый; благоразу́мный; ~crack Am. уда́чное и́ли саркасти́ческое замеча́ние; 2. о́браз, спо́соб.
wish [wiʃ] 1. жела́ние; пожела́ние; 2. [по]жела́ть (Р) (a. ~ for); ~ well (ill) (не) благоволи́ть (к Д); **~ful** ['wiʃful] □ жела́ющий, жа́ждущий; тоскли́вый.
wisp [wisp] пучо́к (соло́мы, се́на и т. п.).
wistful ['wistful] □ заду́мчивый, тоскли́вый.
wit [wit] 1. остроу́мие; ра́зум (a. ~s pl.); остря́к; be at one's ~'s end быть в тупике́; 2. to ~ то́ есть, а и́менно.
witch [witʃ] колду́нья, ве́дьма; fig. чароде́йка; **~craft** ['witʃkrɑ:ft] колдовство́.
with [wið] с (Т), со (Т); от (Р); у (Р); при (П); ~ a knife ножо́м, ~ a pen перо́м и т. д.
withdraw [wið'drɔ:] [irr. (draw)] v/t. отдёргивать [-рнуть]; брать наза́д; изыма́ть [изъя́ть] (кни́гу из прода́жи, де́ньги из обраще́ния); v/i. удаля́ться [-ли́ться]; ретирова́ться (im)pf.; ⚔ отходи́ть [отойти́]; **~al** [-əl] отдёргивание; изъя́тие; удале́ние; ⚔ отхо́д.
wither ['wiðə] v/i. [за]вя́нуть; [по-]блёкнуть; v/t. иссуша́ть [-ши́ть].
with|hold [wið'hould] [irr. (hold)] уде́рживать(ся) [-жа́ть(ся)]; отка́зывать [-за́ть] в (П); скры(ва́)ть (from от Р); **~in** [-'in] 1. lit. adv. внутри́; 2. prp. в (П), в преде́лах (Р); внутри́ (Р); ~ doors в до́ме; ~ call в преде́лах слы́шимости; **~out** [-'aut] 1. lit. adv. вне, снару́жи; 2. prp. без (Р); вне (Р); **~stand** [-'stænd] [irr. (stand)] противостоя́ть (Д).
witness ['witnis] 1. свиде́тель(ница f) m; очеви́дец (-дица); bear ~ свиде́тельствовать (to, of о П); in ~ of в доказа́тельство (Р); 2. свиде́тельствовать о (П); засвиде́тельствовать (В) pf.; быть свиде́телем (Р); заверя́ть [-е́рить] (по́дпись и т. п.).
wit|ticism ['witisizm] остро́та, шу́тка; **~ty** ['witi] □ остроу́мный.
wives [waivz] pl. от wife.
wizard ['wizəd] волше́бник, маг.
wizen(ed) ['wizn(d)] вы́сохший; смо́рщенный.
wobble ['wɔbl] кача́ться [качну́ться]; ковыля́ть [-льну́ть].
woe [wou] го́ре, скорбь f; ~ is me! го́ре мне!; **~begone** ['woubigɔn] удручённый го́рем; мра́чный;

~ful ['wouful] □ скóрбный, гóрестный; жáлкий.
woke [wouk] *pt.* от wake; **~n** ['woukən] *p. pt.* от wake.
wolf [wulf] **1.** волк; **2.** пожирáть с жáдностью; **~ish** ['wulfiʃ] вóлчий; хи́щный.
wolves [wulvz] *pl.* от wolf 1.
woman ['wumən] **1.** жéнщина; **2.** жéнский; ~ doctor жéнщина-врач; ~ student студéнтка; **~hood** [-hud] жéнский пол; жéнственность *f*; **~ish** [-iʃ] □ женоподóбный, бáбий; **~kind** [-'kaind] *coll.* жéнщины *f/pl.*; **~like** [-laik] женоподóбный; **~ly** [-li] жéнственный.
womb [wu:m] *anat.* мáтка; чрéво (мáтери); *fig.* лóно.
women ['wimin] *pl.* от woman; **~folk** [-fouk] жéнщины *f/pl.*
won [wʌn] *pt.* и *p. pt.* от win.
wonder ['wʌndə] **1.** удивлéние, изумлéние; чу́до; дикóвина; **2.** удивля́ться [-ви́ться] (at Д); I ~ (мне) интерéсно знать; **~ful** [-ful] □ удиви́тельный, замечáтельный.
won't [wount] не бу́ду и т. д.; не хочу́ и т. д.
wont [~] **1.** be ~ имéть обыкновéние; **2.** обыкновéние, привы́чка; **~ed** привы́чный.
woo [wu:] ухáживать за (Т); [по-] свáтаться за (В).
wood [wud] лес; дéрево, лесоматериáл; дровá *n/pl.*; *attr.* леснóй; деревя́нный; дровянóй; ♪ деревя́нные духовы́е инструменты *m/pl.*; **~cut** гравю́ра на дéреве; **~-cutter** дровосéк; гравёр по дéреву; **~ed** ['wudid] леси́стый; **~en** ['wudn] деревя́нный; *fig.* безжи́зненный; **~man** [-mən] лесни́к; лесору́б; **~pecker** ['pekə] дя́тел; **~-winds** [-windz] деревя́нные духовы́е инструмéнты *m/pl.*; **~work** деревя́нные издéлия *n/pl.*; деревя́нные чáсти *f/pl.* (строéния); **~y** ['wudi] леси́стый; *fig.* деревяни́стый.
wool [wul] шерсть *f*; *attr.* шерстянóй; **~-gathering** ['wulgæðəriŋ] витáние в облакáх; **~(l)en** ['wulin] **1.** шерстянóй; **2.** шерстянáя матéрия; **~ly** ['wuli] **1.** покры́тый шéрстью; шерсти́стый; си́плый; **2.** wollies *pl.* шерстяны́е вéщи *f/pl.*
word [wə:d] **1.** *mst* слóво; разговóр; вéсть *f*; сообщéние; ⚔ парóль *m*; ~s *pl.* ♪ словá (пéсни) *n/pl.*; *fig.* кру́пный разговóр; **2.** выражáть словáми; формули́ровать *(im)pf.*, *pf. a.* [c-]; **~ing** ['wə:diŋ] формулирóвка; **~-splitting** софи́стика; буквоéдство.
wordy ['wə:di] □ многослóвный; словéсный.
wore [wɔ:] *pt.* от wear 1.
work [wə:k] **1.** рабóта; труд; дéло; заня́тие; произведéние, сочинéние; *attr.* рабóто...; рабóчий; **~s** *pl.* механи́зм; строи́тельные рабóты *f/pl.*; завóд; мастерски́е *f/pl.*; be in (out of) ~ имéть рабóту (быть безрабóтным); set to ~ брáться за рабóту; ~s council произвóдственный совéт; **2.** *v/i.* рабóтать; занимáться [-ня́ться]; дéйствовать; *v/t.* [*irr.*] обрабáтывать [-бóтать]; отдéл(ыв)ать; [*regular vb.*] разрабáтывать [-бóтать] (рудни́к и т. п.); приводи́ть в дéйствие; ~ one's way проби́(вá)ться; ~ off отрабáтывать [-бóтать]; отдéл(ыв)аться от (Р); ✝ распрод(ав)áть; ~ out решáть [реши́ть] (задáчу); разрабáтывать [-бóтать] (план) [*a. irr.*]; ~ up отдéл(ыв)ать; взбудорáжи(ва)ть; подстрекáть [-кну́ть] на (В).
work|able ['wə:kəbl] □ примени́мый; выполни́мый; пригóдный для рабóты; **~aday** ['wə:kədai] бу́дничный; **~day** бу́дний (*or* рабóчий) день *m*; **~er** ['wə:kə] рабóчий; рабóтник (-ица); **~-house** рабóтный дом; *Am.* исправи́тельный дом; **~ing** ['wə:kiŋ] **1.** рабóта, дéйствие; разрабóтка; обрабóтка; **2.** рабóтающий; рабóчий; дéйствующий.
workman ['wə:kmən] рабóчий; рабóтник; **~like** [-laik] иску́сный; **~ship** мастерствó (ремéсленника); отдéлка (рабóты).
work|shop ['wə:kʃɔp] мастерскáя; цех; **~woman** рабóтница.
world [wə:ld] *com.* мир, свет; *attr.* мировóй; всеми́рный; *fig.* a ~ of мнóжество, ку́ча (Р); bring (come) into the ~ рождáть [роди́ть] (рождáться [роди́ться]); champion of the ~ чемпиóн ми́ра.
wordly ['wə:ldli] мирскóй; свéтский; **~-wise** ['wə:ldli'waiz] óпытный бывáлый.
world-power мировáя держáва.
worm [wə:m] **1.** червя́к, червь *m*; ⚕ глист; **2.** вывéдывать [вы́ведать], выпы́тывать [вы́пытать] (out of у Р); ~ o. s. *fig.* вкрáдываться [вкрáсться] (into в В); **~eaten** истóченный червя́ми; *fig.* устарéлый.
worn [wɔ:n] *p. pt.* от wear 1; **~-out** [wɔ:n'aut] изнóшенный; *fig.* изму́ченный.
worry ['wʌri] **1.** беспокóйство; тревóга; забóта; **2.** беспокóить(ся); надоедáть [-éсть] (Д); прист(ав)áть к (Д); [за]му́чить
worse [wə:s] ху́дший; *adv.* ху́же; сильнéе; from bad to ~ всё ху́же и ху́же; **~n** ['wə:sn] ухудшáть(ся) [уху́дшить(ся)].
worship ['wə:ʃip] **1.** культ; почитáние; поклонéние; богослужéние; **2.** поклоня́ться (Д); почитáть; обожáть; **~per** [-ə] поклóнник (-ица); почитáтель(ница *f*) *m*.

worst [wəːst] **1.** (са́мый) ху́дший, наиху́дший; *adv.* ху́же всего́; **2.** оде́рживать верх над (Т), побежда́ть [-еди́ть].
worsted ['wustid] **1.** *attr.* камво́льный; **2.** га́рус; камво́льная пря́жа.
worth [wəːθ] **1.** сто́ящий; заслу́живающий; be ~ заслу́живать, сто́ить; **2.** цена́, сто́имость *f*; це́нность *f*; досто́инство; **~less** ['wəːθlis] □ ничего́ не сто́ящий; **~-while** ['wəːθ'wail] F сто́ящий; be ~ име́ть смысл; be not ~ не сто́ить труда́; **~y** ['wəːði] □ досто́йный (of P); заслу́живающий (of B).
would [wud] (*pt.* от will) *v/aux.*: he ~ do it он сде́лал бы э́то; он обы́чно э́то де́лал; **~-be** ['wudbi] мни́мый; так называ́емый; самозва́нный.
wound[1] [wuːnd] **1.** ра́на, ране́ние; **2.** ра́нить (*im*)*pf.*; *fig.* заде́(ва́)ть.
wound[2] [waund] *pt.* и *p. pt.* от wind.
wove ['wouv] *pt.* от weave; **~n** ['wouvn] *p. pt.* от weave.
wrangle ['ræŋgl] **1.** препира́ния *n/pl.*, **2.** препира́ться.
wrap [ræp] **1.** *v/t.* (ча́сто ~ up) завёртывать [заверну́ть]; обёртывать [оберну́ть] (бума́гой); заку́т(ыв)ать; оку́т(ыв)ать (*a. fig.*); be ~ped up in быть погружённым в (B); *v/i.* ~ up заку́т(ыв)аться; **2.** обёртка; шаль *f*; плед; **~per** ['ræpə] обёртка; хала́т, капо́т; бандеро́ль *f*; суперобло́жка (кни́ги); **~ping** ['ræpiŋ] упако́вка; обёртка.
wrath [rɔːθ] гнев.
wreath [riːθ], *pl.* **~s** [riːðz] вено́к; гирля́нда; *fig.* кольцо́, коле́чко (ды́ма); **~e** [riːð] [*irr.*] *v/t.* сви(ва́)ть; сплета́ть [сплести́]; *v/i.* обви́(ва́)ться; клуби́ться.
wreck [rek] **1.** ⚓ обло́мки су́дна; круше́ние, ава́рия; разва́лина (о челове́ке); **2.** разруша́ть [-у́шить]; [по]топи́ть (су́дно); be ~ed потерпе́ть ава́рию, круше́ние; *fig.* разруша́ться [-у́шиться] (о пла́нах); **~age** ['rekidʒ] обло́мки (су́дна и т. п. по́сле круше́ния); круше́ние; крах; **~er** ['rekə] граби́тель разби́тых судо́в; рабо́чий авари́йной кома́нды и́ли ремо́нтной брига́ды.
wrench [rentʃ] **1.** дёрганье; скру́чивание; вы́вих; *fig.* тоска́, боль *f*; искаже́ние; ⊕ га́ечный ключ; **2.** вывёртывать [вы́вернуть]; выви́хивать [вы́вихнуть]; *fig.* искажа́ть [искази́ть] (факт, и́стину); ~ open взла́мывать [взлома́ть].
wrest [rest] вырыва́ть [вы́рвать] (from у P) (*a. fig.*); истолко́вывать в свою́ по́льзу; **~le** ['resl] *mst sport* боро́ться; **~ling** [-liŋ] борьба́.
wretch [retʃ] негодя́й; несча́стный.
wretched ['retʃid] □ несча́стный; жа́лкий.
wriggle ['rigl] изви́(ва́)ться (о червяке́ и т. п.); ~ out of уклоня́ться [-ни́ться] от (P).
wright [rait]: ship~ кораблестрои́тель *m*; cart~ каре́тник; play~ драмату́рг.
wring [riŋ] [*irr.*] скру́чивать [-у-ти́ть]; лома́ть (ру́ки); (*a.* ~ out) выжима́ть [вы́жать] (бельё и т. п.); вымога́ть (from у P).
wrinkle ['riŋkl] **1.** морщи́на; скла́дка; **2.** [с]мо́рщить(ся).
wrist [rist] запя́стье; ~ watch ручны́е (*or* нару́чные) часы́ *m/pl.*
writ [rit] ⚖ предписа́ние, пове́стка; Holy ♀ Свяще́нное писа́ние.
write [rait] [*irr.*] [на]писа́ть; ~ up подро́бно опи́сывать; дописывать [-са́ть]; восхваля́ть в печа́ти; **~r** ['raitə] писа́тель(ница *f*) *m*; письмоводи́тель *m*.
writhe [raið] [с]ко́рчиться (от бо́ли).
writing ['raitiŋ] **1.** писа́ние; (литерату́рное) произведе́ние, сочине́ние; (*a* hand~) по́черк; докуме́нт; in ~ пи́сьменно; **2.** пи́сьменный; пи́счий; **~-case** несессе́р для пи́сьменных принадле́жностей; **~-paper** почто́вая (*or* пи́счая) бума́га.
written ['ritn] **1.** *p. pt.* от write; **2.** пи́сьменный.
wrong [rɔŋ] **1.** □ непра́вильный, оши́бочный; не тот (,кото́рый ну́жен); be ~ быть непра́вым; go ~ уклоня́ться от пра́вильного пути́; не получа́ться [-чи́ться], срыва́ться [сорва́ться] (о де́ле); *adv.* непра́вильно, не так; **2.** неправота́; непра́вильность *f*; оби́да; несправедли́вость *f*; зло; **3.** поступа́ть несправедли́во с (T); причиня́ть зло (Д); обижа́ть [оби́деть]; **~doer** злоде́й(ка); **~ful** ['rɔŋful] □ незако́нный (посту́пок); несправедли́вый.
wrote [rout] *pt.* от write.
wrought [rɔːt] *pt.* и *p. pt.* от work 2 [irr.]: ~ goods гото́вые изде́лия *n/pl.*; ~ iron ⊕ сва́рочное желе́зо.
wrung [rʌŋ] *pt.* и *p. pt.* от wring.
wry [rai] □ криво́й, перекошенный; искажённый.

X

X-ray ['eks'rei] **1.** ~s *pl.* рентге́новские лучи́ *m/pl.*; **2.** просве́чивать рентге́новскими луча́ми; **3.** рентге́новский.
xylophone ['zailəfoun] ♪ ксилофо́н.

Y

yacht [jɔt] ⚓ **1.** я́хта; **2.** плы́ть на я́хте; **~ing** ['jɔtiŋ] я́хтенный спорт.
yankee ['jæŋki] F америка́нец, я́нки *m indecl.*
yap [jæp] **1.** тя́вкать [-кнуть]; *Am. sl.* болта́ть.
yard [jɑ:d] ярд (о́коло 91 см); двор; лесно́й склад; **~stick** измери́тельная лине́йка длино́й в 1 ярд; *fig.* ме́рка, «арши́н».
yarn [jɑ:n] **1.** пря́жа; F *fig.* расска́з; (фантасти́ческая) исто́рия; **2.** F расска́зывать ска́зки, небыли́цы.
yawn [jɔ:n] **1.** зево́та; **2.** зева́ть [зевну́ть]; *fig.* зия́ть.
year [jə:, jiə] год (*pl.* года́, го́ды, лета́ *n/pl.*); **~ly** ежего́дный.
yearn [jə:n] томи́ться, тоскова́ть (for, after по Д).
yeast [ji:st] дро́жжи *f/pl.*
yell [jel] **1.** пронзи́тельный крик; **2.** пронзи́тельно крича́ть, [за]вопи́ть.
yellow ['jelou] **1.** жёлтый; F трусли́вый; ~ press жёлтая пре́сса, бульва́рная пре́сса; **2.** [по]желте́ть; [за]желти́ть; ~ed пожелте́вший; **~ish** ['jelouiʃ] желтова́тый.
yelp [jelp] **1.** лай, визг; **2.** [за]визжа́ть, [за]ла́ять.
yes [jes] **1.** да; **2.** согла́сие.
yesterday ['jestədi] вчера́.
yet [jet] **1.** *adv.* ещё, всё ещё; уже́; до сих пор; да́же; тем не ме́нее; as ~ пока́, до сих пор; not ~ ещё не(т); **2.** *cj.* одна́ко, всё же, несмотря́ на э́то.
yield [ji:ld] **1.** *v/t.* приноси́ть [-нести́] (плоды́, урожа́й, дохо́д и т. п.); сда(ва́)ть; *v/i.* уступа́ть [-пи́ть] (to Д); подд(ав)а́ться; сд(ав)а́ться; **2.** урожа́й, (урожа́йный) сбор; ⚒ вы́ход; дохо́д; **~ing** ['ji:ldiŋ] □ *fig.* усту́пчивый.
yoke [jouk] **1.** ярмо́ (*a. fig.*); па́ра запряжённых воло́в; коромы́сло; *fig.* и́го; **2.** впряга́ть в ярмо́; *fig.* спа́ри(ва)ть; подходи́ть друг к дру́гу.
yolk [jouk] желто́к.
yonder ['jɔndə] *lit.* **1.** вон тот, вон та и т. д.; **2.** *adv.* вон там.
you [ju:, ju] *pron. pers.* ты, вы; тебя́, вас; тебе́, ва́м (ча́сто to ~) и т. д.
young [jʌŋ] **1.** □ молодо́й; ю́ный; **2.** the ~ молодёжь *f*; *zo.* детёныши *m/pl.*; with ~ супоро́с(н)ая, сте́льная и т. п.; **~ster** ['jʌŋstə] F подро́сток, ю́ноша *m.*
your [jɔ:, juə] *pron. poss.* твой *m*, твоя́ *f*, твоё *n*, твои́ *pl.*; ваш *m*, ва́ша *f*, ва́ше *n*, ва́ши *pl.*; **~s** [jɔ:z, juəz] *pron. poss. absolute form* твой *m*, твоя́ *f* и т. д.; **~self** [jɔ:'self], *pl.* **~selves** [-'selvz] сам *m*, сама́ *f*, само́ *n*, са́ми *pl.*; себя́, -ся.
youth [ju:θ] *coll.* молодёжь *f*; ю́ноша *m*; мо́лодость *f*; **~ful** ['ju:θful] □ ю́ношеский; моложа́вый.
yule [ju:l] *lit.* свя́тки *f/pl.*

Z

zeal [zi:l] рве́ние, усе́рдие; **~ot** ['zelət] ревни́тель *m*; **~ous** ['zeləs] □ рья́ный, усе́рдный, ре́вностный.
zenith ['zeniθ] зени́т (*a. fig.*).
zero ['ziərou] нуль *m* (*a.* ноль *m*); нулева́я то́чка.
zest [zest] **1.** пика́нтность *f*, «изю́минка»; F наслажде́ние, жар; **2.** придава́ть пика́нтность (Д), де́лать пика́нтным.
zigzag ['zigzæg] зигза́г.
zinc [ziŋk] **1.** цинк; **2.** оцинко́вывать [-ова́ть].
zip [zip] свист (пу́ли); F эне́ргия; ~ fastener = **~per** ['zipə] (застёжка-)мо́лния.
zone [zoun] зо́на (*a. pol.*); по́яс; райо́н.
zoolog|ical [zouə'lɔdʒikəl] □ зоологи́ческий; **~y** [zou'ɔlədʒi] зооло́гия.

APPENDIX

Grammatical Tables

Грамматические таблицы

Conjugation and Declension

The following two rules relative to the spelling of endings in Russian inflected words must be observed:

1. Stems terminating in г, к, х, ж, ш, ч, щ are never followed by ы, ю, я, but by **и, у, а.**

2. Stems terminating in ц are never followed by и, ю, я, but by **ы, у, а.**

Besides these, a third spelling rule, dependent on phonetic conditions, viz. position of stress, is likewise important:

3. Stems terminating in ж, ш, ч, щ, ц can be followed by an о in the ending only if the syllable in question bears the stress; otherwise, i. e. in unstressed position, **е** is used instead.

A. Conjugation

Prefixed forms of the perfective aspect are represented by adding the prefix in square brackets, e. g.: [про]чита́ть = чита́ть *impf.*, прочита́ть *pf.*

Personal endings of the present (and perfective future) tense:

1st conjugation:	-ю (-у)	-ешь	-ет	-ем	-ете	-ют (-ут)
(stressed)		(-ёшь)	(-ёт)	(-ём)	(-ёте)	
2nd conjugation:	-ю (-у)	-ишь	-ит	-им	-ите	-ят (-ат)

Reflexive:

1st conjugation:	-юсь (-усь)	-ешься	-ется	-емся	-етесь	-ются (-утся)
2nd conjugation:	-юсь (-усь)	-ишься	-ится	-имся	-итесь	-ятся (-атся)

Suffixes and endings of the other verbal forms:

imp.	-й(те)	-и(те)	-ь(те)	
reflexive	-йся (-йтесь)	-ись (-итесь)	-ься (-ьтесь)	
	m	*f*	*n*	*pl.*
p.pr.a.	-щий(ся)	-щая(ся)	-щее(ся)	-щие(ся)
p.pr.p.	-мый	-мая	-мое	-мые
short form	-м	-ма	-мо	-мы
g.pr.	-я(сь), after ж, ш, ч, щ: -а(сь)			
pt.	-л	-ла	-ло	-ли
refl.	-лся	-лась	-лось	-лись
p.pt.a.	-вший(ся)	-вшая(ся)	-вшее(ся)	-вшие(ся)

p.pt.p.	-нный	-нная	-нное	-нные
	-тый	-тая	-тое	-тые
short form	-н	-на	-но	-ны
	-т	-та	-то	-ты
g.pt.	-в, -вши(сь)			

Stress:

a) There is *no change of stress unless the final syllable of the infinitive is stressed,* i. e. in all forms of the respective verb stress remains invariably on the root syllable accentuated in the infinitive, e. g.: пла́кать. The forms of пла́кать correspond to paradigm [3], except for the stress, which is always on пла́-. The imperative of such verbs also differs from the paradigms concerned: it is in **-ь(те)** provided their stem ends in **one consonant** only, e. g.: пла́кать — пла́чь(те), ве́рить — ве́рь(те); and in **-и(те)** (unstressed!) in cases of **two and more consonants** preceding the imperative ending, e. g.: по́мнить — по́мни(те). Verbs with a vowel stem termination, however, generally form their imperative in **-й(те)**: успоко́ить — успоко́й(те).

b) The prefix вы- in perfective verbs always bears the stress: вы́полнить (but *impf.*: выполня́ть). Imperfective (iterative) verbs with the suffix -ыв-/-ив- are always stressed on the syllable preceding the suffix: пока́зывать (but *pf.* показа́ть), спра́шивать (but *pf.* спроси́ть).

c) In the past participle passive of verbs in **-а́ть (-я́ть)**, there is usually a shift of stress back onto the root syllable as compared with the infinitive (see paradigms [1]—[4], [6], [7], [28]). With verbs in **-е́ть** and **-и́ть** such a shift may occur as well, very often in agreement with a parallel accent shift in the 2nd p. sg. present tense, e. g.: [про]смотре́ть: [про]смотрю́, смо́тришь — просмо́тренный; see also paradigms [14] — [16] as against [13]: [по]мири́ть: [по]мирю́, -и́шь — помирённый. In this latter case the short forms of the participles are stressed on the last syllable throughout: -ённый: -ён, -ена́, -ено́, -ены́. In the former examples, however, stress remains on the same root syllable as in the long form: -ˈенный: -ˈен, -ˈена, -ˈено, -ˈены.

Any details differing from the following paradigms and not explained in the foregoing notes are either mentioned in special remarks attached to the individual paradigms or, if not, pointed out after the entry word itself.

Verbs in -ать

1 [про]**чита́ть**

pr. [*ft.*]	[про]чита́ю, -а́ешь, -а́ют
imp.	[про]чита́й(те)
p.pr.a.	чита́ющий
p.pr.p.	чита́емый
g.pr.	чита́я
pt.	[про]чита́л, -а, -о, -и
p.pt.a.	[про]чита́вший
p.pt.p.	прочи́танный
g.pt.	прочита́в(ши)

2 [по]**трепа́ть** (with л after б, в, м, п, ф)

pr. [*ft.*]	[по]треплю́, -е́плешь, -е́плют
imp.	[по]трепли́(те)
p.pr.a.	тре́плющий
p.pr.p.	—
g.pr.	трепля́
pt.	[по]трепа́л, -а, -о, -и
p.pt.a.	[по]трепа́вший
p.pt.p.	потрёпанный
g.pt.	потрепа́в(ши)

3 [об]**глода́ть** (with changing consonant:
г, д, з > ж
к, т > ч
х, с > ш
ск, ст > щ)

pr. [*ft.*] [об]гложу́, -о́жешь, -о́жут
imp. [об]гложи́(те)
p.pr.a. гло́жущий
p.pr.p. —
g.pr. гложа́
pt. [об]глода́л, -а, -о, -и
p.pt.a. [об]глода́вший
p.pt.p. обгло́данный
g.pt. обглода́в(ши)

---

4 [по]**держа́ть**
(with preceding ж, ш, ч, щ)

pr. [*ft.*] [по]держу́, -е́ржишь, -е́ржат
imp. [по]держи́(те)
p.pr.a. держа́щий
p.pr.p. —
g.pr. держа́
pt. [по]держа́л, -а, -о, -и
p.pt.a. [по]держа́вший
p.pt.p. поде́ржанный
g.pt. подержа́в(ши)

Verbs in -авать

5 **дава́ть**
(*st.* = -ешь, -ет, *etc.*)

pr. [*ft.*] даю́, даёшь, даю́т
imp. дава́й(те)
p.pr.a. даю́щий
p.pr.p. дава́емый
g.pr. дава́я
pt. дава́л, -а, -о, -и
p.pt.a. дава́вший
p.pt.p. —
g.pt. —

Verbs in -евать

6 [на]**малева́ть**
(*e.* = -ю́, -ёшь, *etc.*)

pr. [*ft.*] [на]малю́ю, -ю́ешь, -ю́ют
imp. [на]малю́й(те)
p.pr.a. малю́ющий
p.pr.p. малю́емый
g.pr. малю́я
pt. [на]малева́л, -а, -о, -и
p.pt.a. [на]малева́вший
p.pt.p. намалёванный
g.pt. намалева́в(ши)

Verbs in -овать (and in -евать with preceding ж, ш, ч, щ, ц)

7 [на]**рисова́ть**
(*e.* = -ю́, -ёшь, *etc.*)

pr. [*ft.*] [на]рису́ю, -у́ешь, -у́ют
imp. [на]рису́й(те)
p.pr.a. рису́ющий
p.pr.p. рису́емый
g.pr. рису́я
pt. [на]рисова́л, -а, -о, -и
p.pt.a. [на]рисова́вший
p.pt.p. нарисо́ванный
g.pt. нарисова́в(ши)

Verbs in -еть

8 [по]**жале́ть**

pr. [*ft.*] [по]жале́ю, -е́ешь, -е́ют
imp. [по]жале́й(те)
p.pr.a. жале́ющий
p.pr.p. жале́емый
g.pr. жале́я
pt. [по]жале́л, -а, -о, -и
p.pt.a. [по]жале́вший
p.pt.p. ...ённый (*e. g.* одолённый)
g.pt. пожале́в(ши)

---

9 [с]**горе́ть**

pr. [*ft.*] [с]горю́, -и́шь, -я́т
imp. [с]гори́(те)
p.pr.a. горя́щий
p.pr.p. —
g.pr. горя́
pt. [с]горе́л, -а, -о, -и
p.pt.a. [с]горе́вший
p.pt.p. ...е́нный (*e.g.* презре́нный)
g.pt. сгоре́в(ши)

---

10 [по]**терпе́ть**

pr. [*ft.*] [по]терплю́, -е́рпишь, -е́рпят
imp. [по]терпи́(те)
p.pr.a. терпя́щий
p.pr.p. терпи́мый
g.pr. терпя́
pt. [по]терпе́л, -а, -о, -и
p.pt.a. [по]терпе́вший
p.pt.a. ...енный (*e. g.* претерпенный)
g.pt. потерпе́в(ши)

---

11 [по]**лете́ть**
(with changing consonant:
д, з > ж
к, т > ч
х, с > ш
ск, ст > щ)

pr. [*ft.*] [по]лечу́, -ети́шь, -етя́т
imp. [по]лети́(те)
p.pr.a. летя́щий
p.pr.p. —
g.pr. летя́
pt. [по]лете́л, -а, -о, -и

p.pt.a.	[по]летéвший
p.pt.p.	...енный (*e. g.* вéрченный)
g.pt.	полетéв(ши)

Verbs in **-ерéть**

12	[по]**терéть** (*st.* = -ешь, -ет, *etc.*)
pr. [*ft.*]	[по]трý, -трёшь, -трýт
imp.	[по]трй(те)
p.pr.a.	трýщий
p.pr.p.	—
g.pr.	—
pt.	[по]тёр, -рла, -о, -и
p.pt.a.	[по]тёрший
p.pt.p.	[по]тёртый
g.pt.	потерéв *or* потёрши

Verbs in **-ить**

13	[по]**мирúть**
pr. [*ft.*]	[по]мирю́, -рúшь, -ря́т
imp.	[по]мирú(те)
p.pr.a.	миря́щий
p.pr.p.	мирúмый
g.pr.	миря́
pt.	[по]мирúл, -а, -о, -и
p.pt.a.	[по]мирúвший
p.pt.p.	помирённый
g.pt.	помирúв(ши)

14	[на]**кормúть** (with л after б, в, м, п, ф)
pr. [*ft.*]	[на]кормлю́, -óрмишь, -óрмят
imp.	[на]кормú(те)
p.pr.a.	кóрмящий
p.pr.p.	кормúмый
g.pr.	кормя́
pt.	[на]кормúл, -а, -о, -и
p.pt.a.	[на]кормúвший
p.pt.p.	накóрмленный
g.pt.	накормúв(ши)

15	[по]**просúть** (with changing consonant: д, з > ж; к, т > ч; х, с > ш; ск, ст > щ)
pr. [*ft.*]	[по]прошý, -óсишь, -óсят
imp.	[по]просú(те)
p.pr.a.	прося́щий
p.pr.p.	просúмый
g.pr.	прося́
pt.	[по]просúл, -а, -о, -и
p.pt.a.	[по]просúвший
p.pt.p.	попрóшенный
g.pt.	попросúв(ши)

16	[на]**точúть** (with preceding ж, ш, ч, щ)
pr. [*ft.*]	[на]точý, -óчишь, -óчат
imp.	[на]точú(те)
p.pr.a.	точáщий
p.pr.p.	точúмый
g.pr.	точá
pt.	[на]точúл, -а, -о, -и
p.pt.a.	[на]точúвший
p.pt.p.	натóченный
g.pt.	наточúв(ши)

Verbs in **-оть**

17	[рас]**колóть**
pr. [*ft.*]	[рас]колю́, -óлешь, -óлют
imp.	[рас]колú(те)
p.pr.a.	кóлющий
p.pr.p.	—
g.pr.	кóля
pt.	[рас]колóл, -а, -о, -и
p.pt.a.	[рас]колóвший
p.pt.p.	раскóлотый
g.pt.	расколóв(ши)

Verbs in **-уть**

18	[по]**дýть**
pr. [*ft.*]	[по]дýю, -ýешь, -ýют
imp.	[по]дýй(те)
p.pr.a.	дýющий
p.pr.p.	—
g.pr.	дýя
pt.	[по]дýл, -а, -о, -и
p.pt.a.	[по]дýвший
p.pt.p.	дýтый
g.pt.	подýв(ши)

19	[по]**тянýть**
pr. [*ft.*]	[по]тянý, -я́нешь, -я́нут
imp.	[по]тянú(те)
p.pr.a.	тя́нущий
p.pr.p.	—
g.pr.	—
pt.	[по]тянýл, -а, -о, -и
p.pt.a.	[по]тянýвший
p.pt.p.	[по]тя́нутый
g.pt.	потянýв(ши)

20	[со]**гнýть** (*st.* = -ешь, -ет, *etc.*)
pr. [*ft.*]	[со]гнý, -нёшь, -нýт
imp.	[со]гнú(те)
p.pr.a.	гнýщий
p.pr.p.	—
g.pr.	—

pt. [со]гну́л, -а, -о, -и
p.pt.a. [со]гну́вший
p.pt.p. [со́]гну́тый
g.pt. согну́в(ши)

---

21 [по]**ту́хнуть**
(-г- = -г- instead of -х- throughout)
pr. [*ft.*] [по]ту́хну, -нешь, -нут
imp. [по]ту́хни(те)
p.pr.a. ту́хнущий
p.pr.p. —
g.pr. —
pt. [по]ту́х, -хла, -о, -и
p.pt.a. [по]ту́хший
p.pt.p. ...нутый (*e. g.* дости́гнутый)
g.pt. поту́хши

Verbs in **-ыть**

22 [по]**кры́ть**
pr. [*ft.*] [по]кро́ю, -о́ешь, -о́ют
imp. [по]кро́й(те)
p.pr.a. кро́ющий
p.pr.p. —
g.pr. кро́я
pt. [по]кры́л, -а, -о, -и
p.pt.a. [по]кры́вший
p.pt.p. [по]кры́тый
g.pt. покры́в(ши)

---

23 [по]**плы́ть**
(*st.* = -ешь, -ет, *etc.*)
pr. [*ft.*] [по]плыву́, -вёшь, -ву́т
imp. [по]плыви́(те)
p.pr.a. плыву́щий
p.pr.p. —
g.pr. плывя́
pt. [по]плы́л, -а́, -о, -и
p.pt.a. [по]плы́вший
p.pt.p. ...ы́тый (*e.g.* проплы́тый)
g.pt. поплы́вши

Verbs in **-зти, -зть, (-сти)**

24 [по]**везти́**
(-с[т]- = -с[т]- instead of -з- throughout)
(*st.* = -ешь, -ет, *etc.*)
pr. [*ft.*] [по]везу́, -зёшь, -зу́т
imp. [по]вези́(те)
p.pr.a. везу́щий
p.pr.p. везо́мый
g.pr. везя́
pt. [по]вёз, -везла́, -о́, -и́
p.pt.a. [по]вёзший
p.pt.p. повезённый
g.pt. повёзши

Verbs in **-сти, -сть**

25 [по]**вести́**
(-т- = -т- instead of -д- throughout)
(*st.* = -ешь, -ет, *etc.*)
pr. [*ft.*] [по]веду́, -дёшь, -ду́т
imp. [по]веди́(те)
p.pr.a. веду́щий
p.pr.p. ведо́мый
pt. [по]вёл, -вела́, -о́, -и́
p.pt.a. [по]ве́дший
p.pt.p. поведённый
g.pt. поведя́

Verbs in **-чь**

26 [по]**вле́чь**
(г/ж = г instead of к, and ж instead of ч) (-б- = -б- instead of к/ч)
(*st.* = -ешь, -ет, *etc.*)
pr. [*ft.*] [по]влеку́, -ечёшь, -еку́т
imp. [по]влеки́(те)
p.pr.a. влеку́щий
p.pr.p. влеко́мый
g.pr. —
pt. [по]влёк, -екла́, -о́, -и́
p.pt.a. [по]влёкший
p.pt.p. повлечённый
g.pt. повлёкши

Verbs in **-ять**

27 [рас]**та́ять**
(*e.* = -ю́, -ёшь, -ёт, *etc.*)
pr. [*ft.*] [рас]та́ю, -а́ешь, -а́ют
imp. [рас]та́й(те)
p.pr.a. та́ющий
p.pr.p. —
g.pr. та́я
pt. [рас]та́ял, -а, -о, -и
p.pt.a. [рас]та́явший
p.pt.p. ...янный (*e. g.* обла́янный)
g.pt. раста́яв(ши)

---

28 [по]**теря́ть**
pr. [*ft.*] [по]теря́ю, -я́ешь, -я́ют
imp. [по]теря́й(те)
p.pr.a. теря́ющий
p.pr.p. теря́емый
g.pr. теря́я
pt. [по]теря́л, -а, -о, -и
p.pt.a. [по]теря́вший
p.pt.p. поте́рянный
g.pt. потеря́в(ши)

B. Declension

Noun

a) Succession of the six cases (horizontally): nominative, genitive, dative, accusative, instrumental and prepositional in the singular and (thereunder) the plural. *With nouns denoting animate beings (persons and animals) there is a coincidence of endings in the accusative and genitive both singular and plural of the masculine, but only in the plural of the feminine and neuter genders.* This rule also applies, of course, to adjectives as well as various pronouns and numerals that must in syntactical connections agree with their respective nouns.

b) Variants of the following paradigms are pointed out in notes added to the individual declension types or, if not, mentioned after the entry word itself.

Masculine nouns:

1	ви́д	—	-а	-у	—	-ом	о -е
		-ы	-ов	-ам	-ы	-ами	о -ах

Note: Nouns in -ж, -ш, -ч, -щ have in the *g/pl.* the ending -ей.

2	реб	**-ёнок**	-ёнка	-ёнку	-ёнка	-ёнком	о -ёнке
		-я́та	-я́т	-я́там	-я́т	-я́тами	о -я́тах

3	слу́ча	**-й**	-я	-ю	-й	-ем	о -е
		-и	-ев	-ям	-и	-ями	о -ях

Notes: Nouns in -ий have in the *prpos/sg.* the ending -ии.
When *e.*, the ending of the *instr/sg.* is -ём, and of the *g/pl.* -ёв.

4	про́фил	**-ь**	-я	-ю	-ь	-ем	о -е
		-и	-ей	-ям	-и	-ями	о -ях

Note: When *e.*, the ending of the *instr/sg.* is -ём.

Feminine nouns:

5	рабо́т	**-а**	-ы	-е	-у	-ой (-ою)	о -е
		-ы	—	-ам	-ы	-ами	о -ах

Note: In the *g/pl.* with many nouns having two final stem consonants -о- or -е- is inserted between these (cf. p. 15 and entry words concerned).

6	неде́л	**-я**	-и	-е	-ю	-ей (-ею)	о -е
		-и	-ь	-ям	-и	-ями	о -ях

Notes: Nouns in -ья have in the *g/pl.* the ending -ий (unstressed) or -е́й (stressed), the latter being also the termination of nouns in -е́я. Nouns in -я with preceding vowel terminate in the *g/pl.* in -й (for -ий see also No. 7).
When *e.*, the ending of the *instr/sg.* is -ёй (-ёю).
For the insertion of -е-, -о- in the *g/pl.* cf. note with No. 5.

7	а́рм**и**	**-я** -и	-и -й	-и -ям	-ю -и	-ей (-ею) -ями	об -и об -ях
8	тетра́д	**-ь** -и	-и -ей	-и -ям	-ь -и	-ью -ями	о -и о -ях

Neuter nouns:

9	блю́д	**-о** -а	-а —	-у -ам	-о -а	-ом -ами	о -е о -ах

Note: For the insertion of -о-, -е- in the *g/pl.* cf. note with No. **5**.

10	по́л	**-е** -я́	-я -е́й	-ю -я́м	-е -я́	-ем -я́ми	о -е о -я́х

Note: Nouns in **-ье** have in the *g/pl.* the ending **-ий**. Besides, they do not shift their stress.

11	жили́**щ**	**-е** -а	-а —	-у -ам	-е -а	-ем -ами	о -е о -ах
12	жела́н**и**	**-е** -я	-я -й	-ю -ям	-е -я	-ем -ями	о -и о -ях
13	вре́м	**-я** -ена́	-ени -ён	-ени -ена́м	-я -ена́	-енем -ена́ми	о -ени о -ена́х

Adjective

(also ordinal numbers, etc.)

Notes

a) Adjectives in **-ский** have no predicative (short) forms.

b) Variants of the following paradigms have been recorded with the individual entry words. See also p. 15.

		m	*f*	*n*	*pl.*	
14	бе́л	**-ый (-о́й)** -ого -ому -ый (-ого) -ым о -ом	**-ая** -ой -ой -ую -ой (-ою) о -ой	**-ое** -ого -ому -ое -ым о -ом	**-ые** -ых -ым -ые (-ых) -ыми о -ых	long form
		—*	-а́	-о (*a.*: -о́)	-ы (*a.*: -ы́)	short form
15	си́н	**-ий** -его -ему -ий (-его) -им о -ем	**-яя** -ей -ей -юю -ей (-ею) о -ей	**-ее** -его -ему -ее -им о -ем	**-ие** -их -им -ие (-их) -ими о -их	long form
		-(ь)*	-я́	-е	-и	short form
16	стро́**г**	**-ий** -ого -ому -ий (-ого) -им о -ом	**-ая** -ой -ой -ую -ой (-ою) о -ой	**-ое** -ого -ому -ое -им о -ом	**-ие** -их -им -ие (-их) -ими о -их	long form
		—*	-а́	-о	-и	short form

17	то́щ	**-ий**	**-ая**	**-ее**	**-ие**	long form
		-его	-ей	-его	-их	
		-ему	-ей	-ему	-им	
		-ий (-его)	-ую	-ее	-ие (-их)	
		-им	-ей (-ею)	-им	-ими	
		о -ем	о -ей	о -ем	о -их	
		—	-а́	-е(о́)	-и	short form
18	оле́н	**-ий**	**-ья**	**-ье**	**-ьи**	
		-ьего	-ьей	-ьего	-ьих	
		-ьему	-ьей	-ьему	-ьим	
		-ий(-ьего)	-ью	-ье	-ьи (-ьих)	
		-ьим	-ьей (-ьею)	-ьим	-ьими	
		об -ьем	об -ьей	об -ьем	об -ьих	
19	дя́дин	**—**	**-а**	**-о**	**-ы**	
		-а	-ой	-а	-ых	
		-у	-ой	-у	-ым	
		— (-а)	-у	-о	-ы (-ых)	
		-ым	-ой (-ою)	-ым	-ыми	
		о -ом**	о -ой	о -ом	о -ых	

* In the masculine short form of many adjectives having two final stem consonants -о- or -е- is inserted between these (cf. p. 15 and entry words concerned).

** Masculine surnames in -ов, -ев, -ин, -ын have the ending -е.

Pronoun

20	**я**	меня́	мне	меня́	мной (мно́ю)	обо мне
	мы	нас	нам	нас	на́ми	о нас
21	**ты**	тебя́	тебе́	тебя́	тобо́й (тобо́ю)	о тебе́
	вы	вас	вам	вас	ва́ми	о вас
22	**он**	его́	ему́	его́	им	о нём
	она́	её	ей	её	е́ю (ей)	о ней
	оно́	его́	ему́	его́	им	о нём
	они́	их	им	их	и́ми	о них

Note: After prepositions the oblique forms receive an н-prothesis, e.g.: для него́, с не́ю (ней).

23	**кто**	кого́	кому́	кого́	кем	о ком
	что	чего́	чему́	что	чем	о чём

Note: In combinations with ни-, не- a preposition separates such compounds, e.g. ничто́: ни от чего́, ни к чему́.

24	**мой**	моего́	моему́	мой (моего́)	мои́м	о моём
	моя́	мое́й	мое́й	мою́	мое́й (мое́ю)	о мое́й
	моё	моего́	моему́	моё	мои́м	о моём
	мои́	мои́х	мои́м	мои́ (мои́х)	мои́ми	о мои́х
25	**наш**	на́шего	на́шему	наш (на́шего)	на́шим	о на́шем
	на́ша	на́шей	на́шей	на́шу	на́шей (на́шею)	о на́шей
	на́ше	на́шего	на́шему	на́ше	на́шим	о на́шем
	на́ши	на́ших	на́шим	на́ши (на́ших)	на́шими	о на́ших

26	**чей**	чьего́	чьему́	чей (чьего́)	чьим	о чьём
	чья	чьей	чьей	чью	чьей (чье́ю)	о чьей
	чьё	чьего́	чьему́	чьё	чьим	о чьём
	чьи	чьих	чьим	чьи (чьих)	чьи́ми	о чьих
27	**э́тот**	э́того	э́тому	э́тот (э́того)	э́тим	об э́том
	э́та	э́той	э́той	э́ту	э́той (э́тою)	об э́той
	э́то	э́того	э́тому	э́то	э́тим	об э́том
	э́ти	э́тих	э́тим	э́ти (э́тих)	э́тими	об э́тих
28	**тот**	того́	тому́	тот (того́)	тем	о том
	та	той	той	ту	той (то́ю)	о той
	то	того́	тому́	то	тем	о том
	те	тех	тем	те (тех)	те́ми	о тех
29	**сей**	сего́	сему́	сей (сего́)	сим	о сём
	сия́	сей	сей	сию́	сей (се́ю)	о сей
	сие́	сего́	сему́	сие́	сим	о сём
	сии́	сих	сим	сии́ (сих)	си́ми	о сих
30	**сам**	самого́	самому́	самого́	сами́м	о само́м
	сама́	само́й	само́й	самоё	само́й (само́ю)	о само́й
	само́	самого́	самому́	само́	сами́м	о само́м
	са́ми	сами́х	сами́м	сами́х	сами́ми	о сами́х
31	**весь**	всего́	всему́	весь (всего́)	всем	обо всём
	вся	всей	всей	всю	всей (все́ю)	обо всей
	всё	всего́	всему́	всё	всем	обо всём
	все	всех	всем	все (всех)	все́ми	обо всех
32	**не́сколько**	не́скольких	не́скольким	не́сколько (не́скольких)	не́сколькими	о не́скольких

Numeral

33	**оди́н**	одного́	одному́	оди́н (одного́)	одни́м	об одно́м
	одна́	одно́й	одно́й	одну́	одно́й (одно́ю)	об одно́й
	одно́	одного́	одному́	одно́	одни́м	об одно́м
	одни́	одни́х	одни́м	одни́ (одни́х)	одни́ми	об одни́х

34	**два**	**две**	**три**	**четы́ре**
	двух	двух	трёх	четырёх
	двум	двум	трём	четырём
	два (двух)	две (двух)	три (трёх)	четы́ре (четырёх)
	двумя́	двумя́	тремя́	четырьмя́
	о двух	о двух	о трёх	о четырёх

35	**пять**	**пятна́дцать**	**пятьдеся́т**	**сто**	**со́рок**
	пяти́	пятна́дцати	пяти́десяти	ста	сорока́
	пяти́	пятна́дцати	пяти́десяти	ста	сорока́
	пять	пятна́дцать	пятьдеся́т	сто	со́рок
	пятью́	пятна́дцатью	пятью́десятью	ста	сорока́
	о пяти́	о пятна́дцати	о пяти́десяти	о ста	о сорока́

36	**двéсти**	**трúста**	**четы́реста**	**пятьсóт**
	двухсóт	трёхсóт	четырёхсóт	пятисóт
	двумстáм	трёмстáм	четырёмстáм	пятистáм
	двéсти	трúста	четы́реста	пятьсóт
	двумястáми	тремястáми	четырьмястáми	пятьюстáми
	о двухстáх	о трёхстáх	о четырёхстáх	о пятистáх
37	**óба**	**óбе**	**двóе**	**чéтверо**
	обóих	обéих	двоúх	четверы́х
	обóим	обéим	двоúм	четверы́м
	óба (обóих)	óбе (обéих)	двóе (двоúх)	чéтверо (четверы́х)
	обóими	обéими	двоúми	четверы́ми
	об обóих	об обéих	о двоúх	о четверы́х

American and British Geographical Names

Американские и британские географические названия

A

Aberdeen (æbə'di:n) г. Абердúн.
Adelaide ('ædəleid) г. Аделайда.
Aden ('eidn) г. 'Аден.
Africa ('æfrikə) 'Африка.
Alabama (ælə'bɑ:mə) Алабáма.
Alaska (ə'læskə) Аля́ска.
Albany ('ɔ:lbəni) 'Олбани.
Alleghany ('æligeini) **1.** Аллегáны *pl.* (горы); **2.** Аллегéйни (река).
America (ə'merikə) Амéрика.
Antilles (æn'tili:z) Антúльские островá.
Antwerp ('æntwə:p) Антвéрпен.
Arabia (ə'reibjə) Арáвия.
Argentina (ɑ:dʒən'ti:nə) Аргентúна.
Arizona (æri'zounə) Аризóна.
Arkansas ('ɑ:kənsɔ: штат в США, ɑ:'kænsəs река в США) Аркáнзáс.
Ascot ('æskət) г. 'Эскот.
Asia ('eiʃə) 'Азия; ~ *Minor* Мáлая 'Азия.
Auckland ('ɔ:klənd) г. 'Окленд (порт в Новой Зеландии).
Australia (ɔ:s'treiljə) Австрáлия.
Austria ('ɔ:striə) 'Австрия.
Azores (ə'zɔ:z) Азóрские островá.

B

Bahamas (bə'hɑ:məz) Багáмские островá.
Balkans ('bɔ:lkənz): *the* ~ Балкáны.
Baltic Sea ('bɔ:ltik'si:) Балтúйское мóре.
Baltimore ('bɔ:ltimɔ:) г. Бáлтимор.
Barents Sea ('bɑ:rənts'si:) Бáренцово мóре.
Bavaria (bə'vɛəriə) Бавáрия.
Belfast ('belfɑ:st) г. Бéлфаст (столица Северной Ирландии).
Belgium ('beldʒəm) Бéльгия.
Bengal (beŋ'gɔ:l) Бенгáлия.
Berlin ('bə:'lin, bə:'lin) г. Берлúн.
Bermudas (bə[:]'mju:dəz) Бермýдские островá.
Birmingham ('bə:miŋəm) г. Бúрмингем.
Biscay ('biskei): *Bay of* ~ Бискáйский залúв.
Black Sea ('blæk'si:) Чёрное мóре.
Boston ('bɔstən) г. Бостóн.
Brazil (brə'zil) Брази́лия.
Brighton ('braitn) г. Брáйтон.
Bristol ('bristl) г. Брúстóль (порт и торговый город на юге Англии).
Britain ('britən) (*Great* Велико-) Британия; *Greater* ~ Великобритáния с колóниями, Британская импéрия.
Brooklyn ('bruklin) Брýклин.
Brussels ('brʌslz) г. Брюссéль.
Burma ('bə:mə) Бúрма.
Bulgaria (bʌl'gɛəriə) Болгáрия.
Byelorussia (bjelou'rʌʃə) Белорýссия.

C

Calcutta (kæl'kʌtə) г. Калькýтта.
California (kæli'fɔ:njə) Калифóрния.
Cambridge ('keimbridʒ) г. Кéмбридж.
Canada ('kænədə) Канáда.
Canary (kə'nɛəri): ~ *Islands* Канáрские островá.
Canterbury ('kæntəbəri) г. Кéнтербери.
Capetown ('keiptaun) г. Кéйптаун.
Cardiff ('kɑ:dif) г. Кáрдифф.
Caribbean Sea (kæ'ribi:ən'si:) Карúбское мóре.
Carolina (kærə'lainə) Каролúна (*North* Сéверная, *South* 'Южная).
Ceylon (si'lɔn) о-в Цейлóн.
Chesterfield ('tʃestəfi:ld) г. Чéстерфильд.
Cheviot ('tʃeviət): ~ *Hills* Чевиóтские гóры.
Chicago (ʃi'kɑ:gou, *a.* ʃi'kɔ:gou) г. Чикáго.
Chile ('tʃili) Чúли.
China ('tʃainə) Китáй.
Cincinnati (sinsi'næti) г. Цинциннáти.
Cleveland ('kli:vlənd) г. Клúвленд.
Clyde (klaid) р. Клайд.
Colorado (kɔlə'rɑ:dou) Колорáдо.
Columbia (kə'lʌmbiə) Колýмбия (река, город, адм. округ).
Connecticut (kə'nektikət) Коннéктикут (река и штат в США).
Cordilleras (kɔ:di'ljɛərəz) Кордильéры (горы).
Coventry ('kɔvəntri) г. Кóвентри.
Cyprus ('saiprəs) о-в Кипр.

D

Dakota (də'koutə) Дакóта (*North* Сéверная, *South* 'Южная).
Denmark ('denmɑ:rk) Дáния.
Danube ('dænju:b) р. Дунáй.
Delhi ('deli) г. Дéли.
Detroit (də'trɔit) г. Детрóйт.
Dover ('douvə) г. Дувр.
Dublin ('dʌblin) г. Дýблин.
Dunkirk (dʌn'kə:k) г. Дюнкéрк.

E

Edinburgh ('edinbərə) г. 'Эдинбург.
Egypt ('i:dʒipt) Еги́пет.
Eire ('ɛərə) 'Эйре.
England ('iŋglənd) 'Англия.
Erie ('iəri): *Lake* ~ óзеро 'Эри.
Eton ('i:tn) г. 'Итон.
Europe ('juərəp) Еврóпа.

F

Falkland ('fɔ:klənd): ~ *Islands* Фолклéндские островá.
Florida ('flɔridə) Флори́да.
Folkestone ('foukstən) г. Фóлкстон.
France (frɑ:ns) Фрáнция.

G

Galveston(e) ('gælvistən) г. Гáлвестон.
Geneva (dʒi'ni:və) г. Женéва.
Georgia ('dʒɔ:dʒiə) Джóрджия (штат в США).
Germany ('dʒə:məni) Гермáния.
Gettysburg ('getizbə:g) г. Гéттисберг.
Ghana (gɑ:nə) Гáна.
Glasgow ('glɑ:sgou) г. Глáзго.
Gloucester ('glɔstə) г. Глóстер.
Greenwich ('grinidʒ) г. Гри́н(в)ич.
Guernsey ('gə:nzi) о-в Гéрнси.
Guiana (gi'ɑ:nə) Гвиáна.
Guinea ('gini) Гвинéя.

H

Haiti ('he:iti) Гаи́ти.
Halifax ('hælifæks) г. Гáлифакс.
Harwich ('hæridʒ) г. Хáридж.
Hawaii (hɑ:'waii) о-в Гавáйи.
Hebrides ('hebridi:z) Гебри́дские островá.
Heligoland ('heligoulænd) о-в Гéльголанд.
Hindustan (hindu'stæn, -'stɑ:n) Индостáн.
Hollywood ('hɔliwud) г. Гóлливуд.
Hudson ('hʌdsn) р. Гýдзóн.
Hull (hʌl) г. Гулль.
Hungary ('hʌŋgəri) Вéнгрия.
Huron ('hjuərən): *Lake* ~ óзеро Гýрóн.

I

Iceland ('aislənd) Ислáндия.
Idaho ('aidəhou) Айдáхо.
Illinois (ili'nɔi) 'Иллинóйс.
India ('indjə) 'Индия.
Indiana (indi'ænə) Индиáна.
Iowa ('aiouə) 'Айова.
Irak, Iraq (i'rɑ:k) Ирáк.
Iran (iə'rɑ:n) Ирáн.
Ireland ('aiələnd) Ирлáндия.
Italy ('itəli) Итáлия.

J

Jersey ('dʒə:zi) **1.** о-в Джéрси; **2.** ~ *City* г. Джéрси-Си́ти.

K

Kansas ('kænzəs) Кáнзáс.
Karachi (kə'rɑ:tʃi) г. Карáчи.
Kashmir (kæʃ'miə) Кашми́р.
Kentucky (ken'tʌki) Кентýкки.
Kenya ('ki:njə, 'kenjə) Кéния.
Klondike ('klɔndaik) Клóндайк.
Korea (ko'riə) Корéя.

L

Labrador ('læbrədɔ:) п-в Лабрадóр.
Lancaster ('læŋkəstə) г. Лáнкáстер.
Leeds (li:dz) г. Лидс.
Leicester ('lestə) Лéстер.
Lincoln ('liŋkən) г. Линкольн.
Liverpool ('livəpu:l) г. Ли́верпýл(ь).
London ('lʌndən) г. Лóндон.
Los Angeles (lɔs'ændʒili:z) г. Лос-'Анжелос.
Louisiana (lu[:]i:zi'ænə) Луизиáна.

M

Mackenzie (mə'kenzi) р. Макéнзи.
Madras (mə'dræs) г. Мадрáс.
Maine (mein) Мэн (штат в США).
Malta ('mɔ:ltə) о-в Мáльта.
Manchester ('mæntʃistə) г. Мáнчестер.
Manhattan (mæn'hætən) Манхáттан.
Manitoba (mæni'toubə) Манитóба.
Maryland ('merilənd, *Brt.* mɛəri-) Мэ́риленд.
Massachusetts (mæsə'tʃu:sets) Массачýсетс.
Melbourne ('melbən) г. Мéльбурн.
Miami (mai'æmi) г. Майáми.
Michigan ('miʃigən) Ми́чиган (штат в США); *Lake* ~ óзеро Ми́чиган.
Milwaukee (mil'wɔ:ki[:]) г. Милуóки.
Minneapolis (mini'æpəlis) г. Миннеáполис.
Minnesota (mini'soutə) Миннесóта.

Mississippi (misi'sipi) Миссиси́пи (река и штат).
Missouri (mi'zuəri, *Brt.* mi'suəri) Миссу́ри (река и штат).
Montana (mɔn'tɑ:nə) Монта́на (штат в США).
Montreal (mɔntri'ɔ:l) г. Монреа́ль.
Moscow ('mɔskou) г. Москва́.
Munich ('mju:nik) г. Мю́нхен.
Murray ('mʌri) р. Му́ррей (Ма́рри).

N

Natal (nə'tæl) Ната́ль.
Nebraska (ni'bræskə) Небра́ска (штат в США).
Nevada (ne'vɑ:də) Нева́да (штат в США).
Newcastle ('nju:kɑ:sl) г. Ньюка́сл.
Newfoundland (nju:'faundlənd, ⚓ nju:fənd'lænd) о-в Ньюфаундле́нд.
New Hampshire (nju:'hæmpʃiə) Нью-Хэ́мпшир (штат в США).
New Jersey (nju:'dʒə:zi) Нью-Дже́рси (штат в США).
New Mexico (nju:'meksikou) Нью-Ме́ксико (штат в США).
New Orleans (nju:'ɔ:liənz) г. Но́вый Орлеа́н.
New York ('nju:'jɔ:k) Нью-Йо́рк (город и штат).
New Zealand (nju:'zi:lənd) Но́вая Зела́ндия.
Niagara (nai'ægərə) р. Ниага́ра, ~ *Falls* Ниага́рские водопа́ды.
Nigeria (nai'dʒiəriə) Ниге́рия.
Northampton (nɔ:'θæmptən) Нортге́мптон.
Norway ('nɔ:wei) Норве́гия.
Nottingham ('nɔtiŋəm) Но́ттингем.

O

Oceania (ouʃi'einiə) Океа́ния.
Ohio (ou'haiou) Ога́йо (река и штат).
Oklahoma (ouklə'houmə) Оклахо́ма (штат в США).
Ontario (ɔn'tɛəriou) Онта́рио; *Lake* ~ о́зеро Онта́рио.
Oregon ('ɔrigən) Орего́н (штат в США).
Orkney ('ɔ:kni): ~ *Islands* Оркне́йские острова́.
Ottawa ('ɔtəwə) г. Отта́ва.
Oxford ('ɔksfəd) г. 'Оксфорд.

P

Pakistan ('pɑ:kis'tɑ:n) Пакиста́н.
Paris ('pæris) г. Пари́ж.
Pennsylvania (pensil'veinjə) Пенсильва́ния (штат в США).
Philadelphia (filə'delfjə) г. Филаде́льфия.
Philippines ('filipi:nz) Филиппи́ны.
Pittsburg(h) ('pitsbə:g) г. Пи́тсбург.
Plymouth ('pliməθ) г. Пли́мут.
Poland ('poulənd) По́льша.
Portsmouth ('pɔ:tsmeθ) г. По́ртсмут.
Portugal ('pɔ:tjugəl) Португа́лия.
Punjab (pʌn'dʒɑ:b) Пенджа́б.

Q

Quebec (kwi'bek) Квебе́к.

R

Rhine (rain) р. Рейн.
Richmond ('ritʃmənd) г. Ри́чмонд.
Rhode Island (roud'ailənd) Род-'Айленд (штат в США).
Rhodes (roudz) о-в Ро́дос.
Rhodesia (rou'di:ziə) Роде́зия.
Rome (roum) г. Рим.
Russia ('rʌʃə) Росси́я.

S

Scandinavia (skændi'neivjə) Скандина́вия.
Scotland ('skɔtlənd) Шотла́ндия.
Seattle (si'ætl) г. Сиэ́тл.
Seoul (soul) г. Сеу́л.
Sheffield ('ʃefi:ld) г. Ше́ффилд.
Shetland ('ʃetlənd): *the ~ Islands* Шетла́ндские острова́.
Siberia (sai'biəriə) Сиби́рь.
Singapore (siŋgə'pɔ:) г. Сингапу́р.
Soudan (su[:]'dæn) Суда́н.
Southampton (sauθ'æmptən) г. Саутге́мптон.
Spain (spein) Испа́ния.
St. Louis (snt'luis) г. Сент-Лу́ис.
Stratford ('strætfəd): ~ **on Avon** г. Стра́тфорд-на-'Эйвоне.
Sweden ('swi:dn) Шве́ция.
Switzerland ('switsələnd) Швейца́рия.
Sydney ('sidni) г. Си́дней.

T

Tennessee (tene'si:) Теннесси́ (река и штат в США).
Texas ('teksəs) Теха́с (штат в США).
Thames (temz) р. Те́мза.
Toronto (tə'rɔntou) г. Торо́нто.
Trafalgar (trə'fælgə) Трафальга́р.
Transvaal ('trænzvɑ:l) Трансваа́ль.
Turkey ('tə:ki) Ту́рция.

U

Utah ('ju:tɑ:) 'Юта (штат в США).

V

Vancouver (væn'ku:və) г. Ванку́вер.
Vermont (və:'mɔnt) Вермо́нт (штат в США).

Vienna (vi'enə) г. Ве́на.
Virginia (və'dʒinjə) Вирги́ния (штат в США).

W

Wales (weilz) Уэ́льс.
Washington ('wɔʃiŋtən) Ва́шингто́н (город и штат в США).
Wellington ('weliŋtən) г. Ве́ллингтон (столица Новой Зеландии).
West Virginia ('westvə'dʒinjə) За́падная Вирги́ния (штат в США).
Winnipeg ('winipeg) Ви́ннипег (город и озеро в Канаде).
Wisconsin (wis'kɔnsin) Виско́нсин (река и штат в США).
Worcester ('wustə) г. Ву́стер.
Wyoming (wai'oumiŋ) Вайо́минг (штат в США).

Y

York (jɔ:k) Йорк.
Yugoslavia ('ju:gou'slɑ:viə) Югосла́вия.

Наиболее употребительные сокращения, принятые в СССР

Current Russian Abbreviations

авт. (авто́бус) (motor) bus
Азербайджа́нская ССР (Сове́тская Социалисти́ческая Респу́блика) Azerbaijan S.S.R. (Soviet Socialist Republic)
акад. (акаде́мик) academician
АН СССР (Акаде́мия нау́к Сою́за Сове́тских Социалисти́ческих Респу́блик) Academy of Sciences of the U.S.S.R. (Union of Soviet Socialist Republics)
Армя́нская ССР (Сове́тская Социалисти́ческая Респу́блика) Armenian S.S.R. (Soviet Socialist Republic)
арх. (архите́ктор) architect
АССР (Автоно́мная Сове́тская Социалисти́ческая Респу́блика) Autonomous Soviet Socialist Republic
АТС (автомати́ческая телефо́нная ста́нция) telephone exchange

б-ка (библиоте́ка) library
БССР (Белору́сская Сове́тская Социалисти́ческая Респу́блика) Byelorussian S.S.R. (Soviet Socialist Republic)
БСЭ (Больша́я Сове́тская Энциклопе́дия) Big Soviet Encyclopedia

в. (век) century
вв. (века́) centuries
ВВА (Вое́нно-возду́шная акаде́мия) Air Force College
ВВС (Вое́нно-возду́шные си́лы) Air Forces
ВЛКСМ (Всесою́зный Ле́нинский Коммунисти́ческий Сою́з Молодёжи) Leninist Young Communist League of the Soviet Union
вм. (вме́сто) instead of
ВС (Верхо́вный Сове́т) Supreme Soviet
ВСХВ (Всесою́зная сельскохозя́йственная вы́ставка) Agricultural Fair of the U.S.S.R.
втуз (вы́сшее техни́ческое уче́бное заведе́ние) technical college, institute of technology
вуз (вы́сшее уче́бное заведе́ние) university, college
ВЦИК (Всеросси́йский Центра́льный Исполни́тельный Комите́т) All-Russian Central Executive Committee
ВЦСПС (Всесою́зный Центра́льный Сове́т Профессиона́льный Сою́зов) the All-Union Central Council of Trade Unions
ВЧК (Всеросси́йская Чрезвыча́йная Коми́ссия по борьбе́ с контрреволю́цией, сабота́жем и спекуля́цией) All-Russian Special Committee for the Suppression of Counter-Revolution, Sabotage, and Black Marketeering (*historical*)

г (грамм) gram(me)
г. **1.** (год) year; **2.** (го́род) city
га (гекта́р) hectare
гг. (го́ды) years
ГДР (Герма́нская Демократи́ческая Респу́блика) German Democratic Republic
г-жа (госпожа́) Mrs.
глав... in compounds (гла́вный)
главвра́ч (гла́вный врач) head physician
г-н (господи́н) Mr.
гос... in compounds (госуда́рственный)
Госба́нк (госуда́рственный банк) State Bank
Гослитизда́т (Госуда́рственное изда́тельство худо́жественной литерату́ры) State Publishing House for Literature
Госполитизда́т (Госуда́рственное изда́тельство полити́ческой литерату́ры) State Publishing House for Political Literature

ГПУ (Госуда́рственное полити́ческое управле́ние) G.P.U. Political State Administration (*historical*)
гр. (гражда́нин) citizen
Грузи́нская ССР (Сове́тская Социалисти́ческая Респу́блика) Georgian S.S.R. (Soviet Socialist Republic)
ГСО (Гото́в к санита́рной оборо́не) Ready to do medical service
ГТО (Гото́в к труду́ и оборо́не) Ready to work and defend
ГУМ (Госуда́рственный универса́льный магази́н) department store
ГУС (Госуда́рственный учёный сове́т) State Advisory Board of Scholars

Детги́з (Госуда́рственное изда́тельство де́тской литерату́ры) State Publishing House for Children's Books
дир. (дире́ктор) director
ДКА (Дом Кра́сной 'Армии) House of the Red Army
доб. (доба́вочный) additional
Донба́сс (Доне́цкий бассе́йн) Donets Basin
доц. (доце́нт) lecturer, instructor
д-р (до́ктор) doctor

ж. д. (желе́зная доро́га) railroad, railway
ж.-д. (железнодоро́жный) relating to railroads *or* railways

завко́м (заводско́й комите́т) works council
загс (отде́л за́писей а́ктов гражда́нского состоя́ния) registrar's (registry) office

и др. (и други́е) etc.
им. (и́мени) called
и мн. др. (и мно́гие други́е) and many (much) more
и пр., и проч. (и про́чее) etc.
и т. д. (и так да́лее) and so on
и т. п. (и тому́ подо́бное) etc.

к. (копе́йка) kopeck
Каза́хская ССР (Сове́тская Социалисти́ческая Респу́блика) Kazak S.S.R. (Soviet Socialist Republic)
кв. **1.** (квадра́тный) square; **2.** (кварти́ра) apartment, flat
кг (килогра́мм) kg (kilogram[me])
КИМ (Коммунисти́ческий интернациона́л молодёжи) Communist Youth International
Кирги́зская ССР (Сове́тская Социалисти́ческая Респу́блика) Kirghiz S.S.R. (Soviet Socialist Republic)
км/час (киломе́тров в час) km/h (kilometers per hour)
колхо́з (коллекти́вное хозя́йство) collective farm, kolkhoz
комсомо́л (Коммунисти́ческий Сою́з Молодёжи) Young Communist League
коп. (копе́йка) kopeck
КПСС (Коммунисти́ческая па́ртия Сове́тского Сою́за) C.P.S.U. (Communist Party of the Soviet Union)
куб. (куби́ческий) cubic

Латви́йская ССР (Сове́тская Социалисти́ческая Респу́блика) Latvian S.S.R. (Soviet Socialist Republic)
Лито́вская ССР (Сове́тская Социалисти́ческая Респу́блика) Lithuanian S.S.R. (Soviet Socialist Republic)
л. с. (лошади́ная си́ла) h.p. (horse power)

МВД (Министе́рство вну́тренних дел) Ministry of Internal Affairs
МГУ (Моско́вский госуда́рственный университе́т) Moscow State University
МГФ (Моско́вская городска́я филармо́ния) Moscow Municipal Philharmonic Hall
Молда́вская ССР (Сове́тская Социалисти́ческая Респу́блика) Moldavian S.S.R. (Soviet Socialist Republic)
м. пр. (ме́жду про́чим) by the way, incidentally; among other things
МТС (маши́нно-тра́кторная ста́нция) machine and tractor station (*hist.*)
Музги́з (Музыка́льное госуда́рственное изда́тельство) State Publishing House for Music
МХАТ (Моско́вский худо́жественный академи́ческий теа́тр) Academic Artists' Theater, Moscow

напр. (наприме́р) for instance

НКВД (Наро́дный комиссариа́т вну́тренних дел) People's Commissariat of Internal Affairs (*1935 to 1946; since 1946* МВД, *cf.*)
№ (но́мер) number
н. ст. (но́вый стиль) new style (*Gregorian calendar*)
н. э. (на́шей э́ры) A. D.
нэп (но́вая экономи́ческая поли́тика) New Economic Policy

о. (о́стров) island
обл. (о́бласть) region; province, sphere, field (*fig.*)
о-во (о́бщество) society
ОГИЗ (Объедине́ние госуда́рственных изда́тельств) Union of the State Publishing Houses
оз. (о́зеро) lake
ОНО (отде́л наро́дного образова́ния) Department of Popular Education
ООН (Организа́ция Объединённых На́ций) United Nations Organization
отд. (отде́л) section, (отделе́ние) department

п. (пункт) point, paragraph
п. г. (про́шлого го́да) of last year
пер. (переу́лок) lane, alleyway, side street
пл. (пло́щадь *f*) square; area (*a.* ⚕); (*living*) space
п. м. (про́шлого ме́сяца) of last month
проф. (профе́ссор) professor

р. **1.** (река́) river; **2.** (ру́бль *m*) r(o)uble
райко́м (райо́нный комите́т) district committee (*Sov.*)
РСФСР (Росси́йская Сове́тская Федерати́вная Социалисти́ческая Респу́блика) Russian Soviet Federative Socialist Republic

с. г. (сего́ го́да) (of) this year
след. (сле́дующий) following
см (сантиме́тр) cm. (centimeter)
с. м. (сего́ ме́сяца) (of) this month
см. (смотри́) see
совхо́з (сове́тское хозя́йство) state farm
ср. (сравни́) cf. (compare)
СССР (Сою́з Сове́тских Социалисти́ческих Респу́блик) U.S.S.R. (Union of Soviet Socialist Republics)
ст. **1.** (ста́нция) station; **2.** (стани́ца) Cossack village
стенгазе́та (стенна́я газе́та) wall newspaper
стр. (страни́ца) page
ст. ст. (ста́рый стиль) old style (*Julian calendar*)
с. х. (се́льское хозя́йство) agriculture
с.-х. (сельскохозя́йственный) agricultural
с. ч. (сего́ числа́) this day's
США (Соединённые Шта́ты Аме́рики) U.S.A. (United States of America)

т (то́нна) ton
т. **1.** (това́рищ) comrade; **2.** (том) volume
Таджи́кская ССР (Сове́тская Социалисти́ческая Респу́блика) Tadzhik S.S.R. (Soviet Socialist Republic)
ТАСС (Телегра́фное Аге́нтство Сове́тского Сою́за) TASS (Telegraph Agency of the Soviet Union)
т-во (това́рищество) company, association
т. г. (теку́щего го́да) of the current year
т. е. (то́ есть) i. e. (that is)
тел. (телефо́н) telephone
тел. комм. (телефо́нный коммута́тор) telephone switchboard
т. к. (та́к как) *cf.* так
т. м. (теку́щего ме́сяца) instant
т. наз. (так называ́емый) so-called
тов. *s.* т. 1.
торгпре́дство (торго́вое представи́тельство) trade agency of the U.S.S.R.
тролл. (тролле́йбус) trolley bus
тт. (тома́) volumes
Туркме́нская ССР (Сове́тская Социалисти́ческая Респу́блика) Turkmen S.S.R. (Soviet Socialist Republic)
тыс. (ты́сяча) thousand

Узбéкская ССР (Совéтская Социалисти́ческая Респу́блика) Uzbek S.S.R. (Soviet Socialist Republic)
ул. (у́лица) street
УССР (Украи́нская Совéтская Социалисти́ческая Респу́блика) Ukrainian S.S.R. (Soviet Socialist Republic)
Учпедги́з (Госуда́рственное изда́тельство учéбно-педагоги́ческой литерату́ры) State Publishing House for Educational Books

ФРГ (Федерати́вная Респу́блика Герма́нии) Federal Republic of Germany

ЦИК (Центра́льный Исполни́тельный Комитéт) Central Executive Committee (*Sov.*); *cf.* ЦК
ЦК (Центра́льный Комитéт) Central Committee
ЦПКиО (Центра́льный парк культу́ры и óтдыха) Central Park for Culture and Recreation

ч. (час) hour, (часть) part
ЧК (Чрезвыча́йная коми́ссия ...) Cheka (*predecessor, 1917—22,* of the ГПУ, *cf.*)

Эстóнская ССР (Совéтская Социалисти́ческая Респу́блика) Estonian S.S.R (Soviet Socialist Republic)

Current British and American Abbreviations

Наиболее употребительные сокращения, принятые в Великобритании и США

A

A.B.C. *American Broadcasting Company* Америка́нская радиовеща́тельная корпора́ция.

A-bomb *atomic bomb* а́томная бо́мба.

A.C. *alternating current* переме́нный ток.

A/C *account (current)* контокорре́нт, теку́щий счёт.

acc(t). *account* отчёт; счёт.

A.E.C. *Atomic Energy Commission* Коми́ссия по а́томной эне́ргии.

AFL-CIO *American Federation of Labor & Congress of Industrial Organizations* Америка́нская федера́ция труда́ и Конгре́сс произво́дственных профсою́зов, АФТ/КПП.

A.F.N. *American Forces Network* радиосе́ть америка́нских войск (в Европе).

Ala. *Alabama* Алаба́ма (штат в США).

Alas. *Alaska* Аля́ска (территория в США).

a.m. *ante meridiem* (лат. = *before noon*) до полу́дня.

A.P. *Associated Press* Ассо́шиэйтед пресс.

A.R.C. *American Red Cross* Америка́нский Кра́сный Крест.

Ariz. *Arizona* Аризо́на (штат в США).

Ark. *Arkansas* Арка́нза́с (штат в США).

A.R.P. *Air-Raid Precautions* гражда́нская ПВО (противовозду́шная оборо́на).

B

B.A. *Bachelor of Arts* бакала́вр филосо́фии.

B.B.C. *British Broadcasting Corporation* Брита́нская радиовеща́тельная корпора́ция.

B/E *Bill of Exchange* ве́ксель *m*, тра́тта.

B.E.A.C. *British European Airways Corporation* Брита́нская корпора́ция европе́йских возду́шных сообще́ний.

Benelux *Belgium, Netherlands, Luxemburg* экономи́ческий и тамо́женный сою́з, БЕНИЛЮКС.

B.F.B.S. *British Forces Broadcasting Service* радиовеща́тельная организа́ция брита́нских вооружённых сил.

B.L. *Bachelor of Law* бакала́вр пра́ва.

B/L *bill of lading* коносаме́нт; тра́нспортная накладна́я.

B.M. *Bachelor of Medicine* бакала́вр медици́ны.

B.O.A.C. *British Overseas Airways Corporation* Брита́нская корпора́ция трансокеа́нских возду́шных сообще́ний.

B.O.T. *Board of Trade* министе́рство торго́вли (в Англии).

B.R. *British Railways* Брита́нская желе́зная доро́га.

Br(it). *Britain* Великобрита́ния; *British* брита́нский, англи́йский.

Bros. *brothers* бра́тья *pl.* (в названиях фирм).

B.S.A. *British South Africa* Брита́нская 'Южная 'Африка.

B.T.U. *British Thermal Unit(s)* брита́нская теплова́я едини́ца.

B.U.P. *British United Press* информацио́нное аге́нтство „Бри́тиш Юна́йтед Пресс".

C

c. 1. *cent(s)* цент (американская монета); **2.** *circa* приблизи́тельно, о́коло; **3.** *cubic* куби́ческий.

C/A *current account* теку́щий счёт.

Cal(if). *California* Калифо́рния (штат в США).

Can. *Canada* Кана́да; *Canadian* кана́дский.

C.C. *continuous current* постоя́нный ток.

C.I.C. *Counter Intelligence Corps* слу́жба контрразве́дки США.

C.I.D. *Criminal Investigation Division* кримина́льная поли́ция.

c.i.f. *cost, insurance, freight* цена́, включа́ющая сто́имость, расхо́ды по страхова́нию и фрахт.

c/o *care of* че́рез, по а́дресу (надпись на конвертах).

Co. 1. *company* о́бщество, компа́ния; **2.** (в США и Ирландии также) *County* о́круг.

C.O.D. *cash* (ам. *collect.*) *on delivery* нало́женный платёж, упла́та при доста́вке.
Col. *Colorado* Колора́до (штат в США).
Conn. *Connecticut* Конне́ктикут (штат в США).
c.w.o. *cash with order* нали́чный расчёт при вы́даче зака́за.
cwt. *hundredweight* це́нтнер.

D

d. *penny* (*pence pl.*) (условное обозначение английской монеты) пе́нни (пе́нс[ы] *pl.*).
D.C. 1. *direct current* постоя́нный ток; **2.** *District of Columbia* федера́льный о́круг Колу́мбия (с американской столицей).
Del. *Delaware* Де́лавэр (штат в США).
Dept. *Department* отде́л; управле́ние; министе́рство; ве́домство.
disc(t). *discount* ски́дка; диско́нт, учёт векселе́й.
div(d). *dividend* дивиде́нд.
dol. *dollar* до́ллар.
doz. *dozen* дю́жина.
D.P. *Displaced Person* перемещённое лицо́.
d/p *documents against payment* докуме́нты за нали́чный расчёт.
Dpt. *Department* отде́л; управле́ние; министе́рство; ве́домство.

E

E. 1. *East* восто́к; *Eastern* восто́чный; **2.** *English* англи́йский.
E. & O.E. *errors and omissions excepted* исключа́я оши́бки и про́пуски.
E.C.E. *Economic Commission for Europe* Экономи́ческая коми́ссия ООН для Евро́пы.
ECOSOC *Economic and Social Council* Экономи́ческий и социа́льный сове́т ООН.
EE., E./E. *errors excepted* исключа́я оши́бки.
e.g. *exempli gratia* (лат. = *for instance*) напр. (наприме́р).
Enc. *enclosure(s)* приложе́ние (-ния).
E.R.P. *European Recovery Program(me)* програ́мма „восстановле́ния Евро́пы", т. наз. „план Ма́ршалла".
Esq. *Esquire* эсква́йр (титул дворянина, должностного лица; обычно ставится в письме после фамилии).

F

. 1. *farthing* (брит. монета) че́тверть пе́нса, фа́ртинг; **2.** *fathom* морска́я саже́нь f; **3.** *feminine* же́нский; *gram.* же́нский род; **4.** *foot* фут, *feet* фу́ты; **5.** *following* сле́дующий.
FBI *Federal Bureau of Investigation* федера́льное бюро́ рассле́дований (в США).
FIFA *Fédération Internationale de Football Association* Междунаро́дная федера́ция футбо́льных о́бществ, ФИФА.
Fla. *Florida* Флори́да (штат в США).
F.O. *Foreign Office* министе́рство иностра́нных дел.
fo(l). *folio* фо́лио *indecl. n* (формат в пол-листа); лист (бухгалтерской книги).
f.o.b. *free on board* фра́нко-борт, ФОБ.
f.o.q. *free on quay* фра́нко-на́бережная.
f.o.r. *free on rail* фра́нко-ре́льсы, фра́нко желе́зная доро́га.
f.o.t. *free on truck* фра́нко ж.-д. платфо́рма; фра́нко-грузови́к.
f.o.w. *free on waggon* фра́нко-ваго́н.
fr. *franc(s)* фра́нк(и).
ft. *foot* фут, *feet* фу́ты.

G

g. 1. *gram(me)* грамм; **2.** *guinea* гине́я (денежная единица = 21 шиллингу).
Ga. *Georgia* Гео́ргия (штат в США).
G.A.T.T. *General Agreement on Tariffs and Trade* 'Общее соглаше́ние по тамо́женным тари́фам и торго́вле.
G.I. *government issue* казённый; госуда́рственная со́бственность f; *fig.* америка́нский солда́т.
G.M.T. *Greenwich Mean Time* сре́днее вре́мя по гри́нвичскому меридиа́ну.
gns. *guineas* гине́и.
gr. *gross* бру́тто.
gr.wt. *gross weight* вес бру́тто.
Gt.Br. *Great Britain* Великобрита́ния.

H

h. *hour(s)* час(ы́).
H.B.M. *His (Her) Britannic Majesty* Его́ (Её) Брита́нское Вели́чество.
H-bomb *hydrogen bomb* водоро́дная бо́мба.
H.C. *House of Commons* пала́та о́бщин (в Англии).
hf. *half* полови́на.
H.L. *House of Lords* пала́та ло́рдов (в Англии).
H.M. *His (Her) Majesty* Его́ (Её) Вели́чество.
H.M.S. 1. *His (Her) Majesty's Service* на слу́жбе Его́ (Её) Вели́чества; ✆ служе́бное де́ло; **2.** *His (Her)*

Majesty's Ship корáбль англи́йского воéнно-морскóго флóта.
H.O. *Home Office* министéрство внýтренних дел (в Англии).
H.P., h.p. *horse-power* лошади́ная си́ла (единица мощности).
H.Q., Hq. *Headquarters* штаб.
H.R. *House of Representatives* палáта представи́телей (в США).
H.R.H. *His (Her) Royal Highness* Егó (Её) Королéвское Высóчество.
hrs. *hours* часы́.

I

Ia. *Iowa* 'Айова (штат в США).
Id. *Idaho* Айдáхо (штат в США).
I.D. *Intelligence Department* развéдывательное управлéние.
i.e. *id est* (лат. = *that is to say*) т. е. (тó есть).
Ill. *Illinois* 'Иллинóйс (штат в США).
I.M.F. *International Monetary Fund* Междунарóдный валю́тный фонд ООН.
in. *inch(es)* дюйм(ы).
Inc. 1. *Incorporated* объединённый; зарегистри́рованный как корпорáция; **2.** *Including* включи́тельно; **3.** *Inclosure* приложéние.
Ind. *Indiana* Индиáна (штат в США).
I.N.S. *International News Service* Междунарóдное телегрáфное агéнтство.
inst. (лат. = *instant*) с. м. (сегó мéсяца).
Ir. *Ireland* Ирлáндия; *Irish* ирлáндский.

J

J.P. *Justice of the Peace* мировóй судья́ *m.*
Jr. *junior* млáдший.

K

Kan(s). *Kansas* Кáнзáс (штат в США).
k.o. *knock(ed) out* спорт.: нокáут; *fig.* (окончательно) раздéлаться с кéм-либо.
Ky. *Kentucky* Кентýкки (штат в США).

L

l. *litre* литр.
£ *pound sterling* фунт стéрлингов.
La. *Louisiana* Луизиáна (штат в США).
£A *Australian pound* австрали́йский фунт (денежная единица).
lb. *pound* фунт (мера веса).
L/C *letter of credit* аккредити́в.
£E *Egyptian pound* еги́петский фунт (денежная единица).
L.P. *Labour Party* лейбори́стская пáртия.
LP *long-playing* долгоигрáющий; ~ *record* долгоигрáющая пласти́нка.
Ltd. *limited* с ограни́ченной отвéтственностью.

M

m. 1. *male* мужскóй; **2.** *metre* метр; **3.** *mile* ми́ля; **4.** *minute* минýта.
M.A. *Master of Arts* маги́стр филосóфии.
Man. *Manitoba* Манитóба (провинция Канады).
Mass. *Massachusetts* Массачýсетс (штат в США).
M.D. *medicinae doctor* (лат. = *Doctor of Medicine*) дóктор медици́ны.
Md. *Maryland* Мэ́риленд (штат в США).
Me. *Maine* Мэн (штат в США).
mg. *milligramme* миллигрáмм.
Mich. *Michigan* Ми́чигáн (штат в США).
Minn. *Minnesota* Миннесóта (штат в США).
Miss. *Mississippi* Миссиси́пи (штат в США).
mm. *millimetre* миллимéтр.
Mo. *Missouri* Миссýри (штат в США).
M.O. *money order* дéнежный перевóд по пóчте.
Mont. *Montana* Монтáна (штат в США).
MP, M.P. 1. *Member of Parliament* член парлáмента; **2.** *Military Police* воéнная поли́ция.
m.p.h. *miles per hour* (столько-то) миль в час.
Mr. *Mister* ми́стер, господи́н.
Mrs. *Mistress* ми́ссис, госпожá.
MS. *manuscript* рýкопись f.
M.S. *motorship* теплохóд.

N

N. *North* сéвер; *Northern* сéверный.
N.A.A.F.I. *Navy, Army, and Air Force Institutes* воéнно-торгóвая слýжба ВМС (воéнно-морски́х сил), ВВС (воéнно-воздýшных сил) и сухопýтных войск.
NATO *North Atlantic Treaty Organization* Североатланти́ческий союз, НАТО.
N.C. *North Carolina* Сéверная Кароли́на (штат в США).
N.Dak. *North Dakota* Сéверная Дакóта (штат в США).
N.E. *Northeast* северо-востóк.
Neb. *Nebraska* Небрáска (штат в США).
Nev. *Nevada* Невáда (штат в США).
N.H. *New Hampshire* Нью-Хэ́мпшир (штат в США).
N.J. *New Jersey* Нью-Джéрси (штат в США).

N.Mex. *New Mexico* Нью-Мéксико (штат в США).
nt.wt. *net weight* вес нéтто, чи́стый вес.
N.W. *Northwestern* северо-зáпадный.
N.Y. *New York* Нью-Йóрк (штат в США).
N.Y.C. *New York City* Нью-Йóрк (город).

O

O. 1. *Ohio* Огáйо (штат в США); **2.** *order* поручéние, закáз.
o/a *on account of* за (чей-либо) счёт.
O.E.E.C. *Organization of European Economic Co-operation* Организáция европéйского экономи́ческого сотрýдничества.
O.H.M.S. *On His (Her) Majesty's Service* состоя́щий на королéвской (государственной или военной) слýжбе; ✉ служéбное дéло.
O.K. *all correct* всё в поря́дке, всё прáвильно; утверждено́, согласо́вано.
Okla. *Oklahoma* Оклахо́ма (штат в США).
Ore(g). *Oregon* Орего́н (штат в США).

P

p.a. *per annum* (лат.) в год; ежего́дно.
Pa. *Pennsylvania* Пенсильвáния (штат в США).
P. A. A. *Pan American Airways* Панамерикáнская авиакомпáния.
P.C. 1. *post-card* почто́вая кáрточка, откры́тка; **2.** *police constable* полицéйский.
p.c. *per cent* процéнт, процéнты.
pd. *paid* уплáчено; оплáченный.
Penn(a). *Pennsylvania* Пенсильвáния (штат в США).
per pro(c). *per procurationem* (лат. = *by proxy*) по довéренности.
p.m. *post meridiem* (лат. = *after noon*) ... часо́в (часá) дня.
P.O. 1. *Post Office* почто́вое отделéние; **2.** *postal order* дéнежный перево́д по по́чте.
P.O.B. *Post Office Box* почто́вый абонемéнтный я́щик.
p.o.d. *pay on delivery* нало́женный платёж.
P.O.S.B. *Post Office Savings Bank* сберегáтельная кáсса при почто́вом отдéлении.
P.S. *Postscript* постскри́птум, припи́ска.
P.T.O., p.t.o. *please turn over* см. н/об. (смотри́ на оборо́те).
PX *Post Exchange* воéнно-торго́вый магази́н.

Q

quot. *quotation* котиро́вка.

R

R.A.F. *Royal Air Force* воéнно-воздýшные си́лы Великобритáнии.
ref(c). *reference* ссы́лка, указáние.
regd. *registered* зарегистри́рованный; ✉ заказно́й.
reg. ton *register ton* реги́стровая тóнна.
ret. *retired* изъя́тый из обращéния; вы́купленный, оплáченный.
Rev. *Reverend* преподо́бный.
R.I. *Rhode Island* Род-'Айленд (штат в США).
R.N. *Royal Navy* англи́йский воéнно-морско́й флот Великобритáнии.
R.P. *reply paid* отвéт оплáчен.
R.R. *Railroad Am.* желéзная доро́га.

S

S. *South* юг; *Southern* ю́жный.
s. 1. *second* секýнда; **2.** *shilling* ши́ллинг.
S.A. 1. *South Africa* 'Южная 'Африка; **2.** *South America* 'Южная Амéрика; **3.** *Salvation Army* 'Армия спасéния.
S.C. 1. *South Carolina* 'Южная Кароли́на (штат в США); **2.** *Security Council* Совéт Безопáсности ООН.
S.Dak. *South Dakota* 'Южная Дако́та (штат в США).
S.E. 1. *Southeast* юго-восто́к; *Southeastern* юго-восто́чный; **2.** *Stock Exchange* фо́ндовая би́ржа (в Лондоне).
sh. *shilling* ши́ллинг.
Soc. *society* о́бщество.
sov. *sovereign* соверéн (золотая монета в один фунт стерлингов).
Sq. *Square* плóщадь f.
sq. *square...* квадрáтный.
S.S. *steamship* парохо́д.
St. *Station* стáнция; вокзáл.
St. Ex. Stock Exchange фо́ндовая би́ржа.
stg. *sterling* фунт стéрлингов.
suppl. *supplement* дополнéние, приложéние.
S.W. *Southwest* юго-восто́к; *Southwestern* юго-восто́чный.

T

t. *ton* то́нна.
T.D. *Treasury Department* министéрство финáнсов (в США).
Tenn. *Tennessee* Теннесси́ (штат в США).
Tex. *Texas* Техáс (штат в США).
T.M.O. *telegraphic money order* дéнежный перево́д по телегрáфу.
T.O. *Telegraph (Telephone) Office* телегрáфное (телефо́нное) отделéние.
T.U. *Trade Union* тред-юнио́н профессионáльный сою́з.

T.U.C. *Trade Unions Congress* конгре́сс (брита́нских) тред-юнио́нов.

U

U.K. *United Kingdom* Соединённое Короле́вство (Англия, Шотландия, Уэльс и Северная Ирландия).
U.N. *United Nations* Объединённые На́ции.
UNESCO *United Nations Educational, Scientific, and Cultural Organization* Организа́ция Объединённых На́ций по вопро́сам просвеще́ния, нау́ки и культу́ры, ЮНЕСКО.
U.N.S.C. *United Nations Security Council* Сове́т Безопа́сности ООН.
U.P. *United Press* телегра́фное аге́нтство „Юна́йтед Пресс".
U.S.(A.) *United States (of America)* Соединённые Шта́ты (Аме́рики).
Ut. *Utah* 'Юта (штат в США).

V

Va. *Virginia* Вирги́ния (штат в США).
VE-day *Victory in Europe-day* День побе́ды в Евро́пе (над Германией в 1945).
viz. *videlicet* (лат.) а и́менно.
vol. *volume* том.
vols. *volumes* тома́ *pl.*
Vt. *Vermont* Вермо́нт (штат в США).

W

W. *West* за́пад; *Western* за́падный.
Wash. *Washington* Ва́шингто́н (штат в США).
W.D. *War Department* вое́нное министе́рство США.
W.F.T.U. *World Federation of Trade Unions* Всеми́рная федера́ция профессиона́льных сою́зов, ВФП.
W.H.O. *World Health Organization* Всеми́рная организа́ция здравоохране́ния, ВОЗ.
W.I. *West Indies* Вест-'Индия.
Wis. *Wisconsin* Виско́нсин (штат в США).
W.O. *War Office* (британское) вое́нное министе́рство.
wt. *weight* вес.
W.Va. *West Virginia* За́падная Вирги́ния (штат в США).
Wyo. *Wyoming* Вайо́минг (штат в США).

X

Xmas *Christmas* рождество́.

Y

yd(s). *yard(s)* я́рд(ы).
Y.M.C.A. *Young Men's Christian Association* Христиа́нская ассоциа́ция молоды́х людей́.
Y.W.C.A. *Young Women's Christian Association* Христиа́нская ассоциа́ция (молоды́х) де́вушек.

Числительные — Numerals

Количественные

Cardinals

0	ноль *&* нуль *m* naught, zero, cipher
1	оди́н *m*, одна́ *f*, одно́ *n* one
2	два *m/n*, две *f* two
3	три three
4	четы́ре four
5	пять five
6	шесть six
7	семь seven
8	во́семь eight
9	де́вять nine
10	де́сять ten
11	оди́ннадцать eleven
12	двена́дцать twelve
13	трина́дцать thirteen
14	четы́рнадцать fourteen
15	пятна́дцать fifteen
16	шестна́дцать sixteen
17	семна́дцать seventeen
18	восемна́дцать eighteen
19	девятна́дцать nineteen
20	два́дцать twenty
21	два́дцать оди́н *m* (одна́ *f*, одно́ *n*) twenty-one
22	два́дцать два *m/n* (две *f*) twenty-two
23	два́дцать три twenty-three
30	три́дцать thirty
40	со́рок forty
50	пятьдеся́т fifty
60	шестьдеся́т sixty
70	се́мьдесят seventy
80	во́семьдесят eighty
90	девяно́сто ninety
100	сто (а *и́ли* one) hundred
200	две́сти two hundred
300	три́ста three hundred
400	четы́реста four hundred
500	пятьсо́т five hundred
600	шестьсо́т six hundred
700	семьсо́т seven hundred
800	восемьсо́т eight hundred
900	девятьсо́т nine hundred
1000	(одна́) ты́сяча *f* (а *и́ли* one) thousand
60 140	шестьдеся́т ты́сяч сто со́рок sixty thousand one hundred and forty
1 000 000	(оди́н) миллио́н *m* (а *и́ли* one) million
1 000 000 000	(оди́н) миллиа́рд *or* биллио́н *m* milliard, *Am.* billion

Порядковые

Ordinals

1st	пе́рвый first
2nd	второ́й second
3rd	тре́тий third
4th	четвёртый fourth
5th	пя́тый fifth
6th	шесто́й sixth
7th	седьмо́й seventh
8th	восьмо́й eighth
9th	девя́тый ninth
10th	деся́тый tenth
11th	оди́ннадцатый eleventh
12th	двена́дцатый twelfth
13th	трина́дцатый thirteenth
14th	четы́рнадцатый fourteenth
15th	пятна́дцатый fifteenth
16th	шестна́дцатый sixteenth
17th	семна́дцатый seventeenth
18th	восемна́дцатый eighteenth
19th	девятна́дцатый nineteenth
20th	двадца́тый twentieth
21st	два́дцать пе́рвый twenty-first
22nd	два́дцать второ́й twenty-second
23rd	два́дцать тре́тий twenty-third
30th	тридца́тый thirtieth
40th	сороково́й fortieth
50th	пятидеся́тый fiftieth
60th	шестидеся́тый sixtieth
70th	семидеся́тый seventieth
80th	восьмидеся́тый eightieth
90th	девяно́стый ninetieth
100th	со́тый (one) hundredth
200th	двухсо́тый two hundredth
300th	трёхсо́тый three hundredth
400th	четырёхсо́тый four hundredth
500th	пятисо́тый five hundredth
600th	шестисо́тый six hundredth
700th	семисо́тый seven hundredth
800th	восьмисо́тый eight hundredth
900th	девятисо́тый nine hundredth
1000th	ты́сячный (one) thousandth
60 140th	шестьдеся́т ты́сяч сто сороково́й sixty thousand one hundred and fortieth
1 000 000th	миллио́нный millionth

Русские меры длины и веса

Russian Measures and Weights

In the U.S.S.R. the metric system is in force since January 1st, 1927. Hence measures and weights are in accordance with the international metric system.

Moreover the following old Russian measures and weights are occasionally still used within the Soviet Union:

1. Ме́ры длины́. Long measures

1 верста́ (verst) = 500 саже́ням (саже́нь, fathom) = 1500 арши́нам (arshin) = 1066.78 m.

1 арши́н (arshin) = 2.333 фу́та (фут, foot) = 16 вершка́м (вершо́к, vershock) = 28 дю́ймам (дюйм, inch) = 0.71 m.

2. Квадра́тные ме́ры. Square measures

1 квадра́тная верста́ (square verst) = 104.167 десяти́ны (dessiatine) = 250 000 квадра́тным саже́ням (square sagene)

1 десяти́на (dessiatine) = 2400 кв. саже́ням (square sagene) = 109.254 acres

3. Ме́ры объёма. Cubic measures

куби́ческий фут (cubic foot); куби́ческая саже́нь (cubic sagene); куби́ческий арши́н (cubic arshin)

4. Хле́бные ме́ры. Dry measures

1 че́тверть (chetvert) = 2 осьми́нам (осьми́на, osmina, eighth) = 4 полуосьми́нам (poluosmina) = 8 четверика́м (четвери́к, chetverik) = 64 га́рнцам (га́рнец, garnetz) = 209.9 l.

5. Ме́ры жи́дкостей. Liquid measures

1 ведро́ (bucket) = 10 кру́жкам (кру́жка, mug) = 100 ча́ркам (ча́рка, cup, gin-glas) = 12.30 l.

6. Ме́ры ма́ссы (ве́са). Weights

1 пуд (pood) = 40 фу́нтам (фунт, pound) = 1280 ло́там (small weight) = 16.38 kg.

1 лот (small weight) = 3 золотника́м (золотни́к, zolotnick) = 288 до́лям (до́ля, dolya)

Валю́та. Currency

1 рубль (rouble) = 100 копе́йкам (копе́йка, copeck)

British and American Measures and Weights

Британские и американские меры длины и веса

1. Ме́ры длины́

1 line (l.) ли́ния = 2,12 мм
1 inch (in.) дюйм = 2,54 см
1 foot (ft.) фут = 30,48 см
1 yard (yd.) ярд = 91,44 см

2. Морски́е ме́ры

1 fathom (f., fm.) морска́я саже́нь = 1,83 м
1 cable('s) length ка́бельтов = 183 м, в США = 120 морски́м саже́ням = 219 м
1 nautical mile (n. m.) *or* **1 knot** морска́я ми́ля = 1852 м

3. Квадра́тные ме́ры

1 square inch (sq. in.) квадра́тный дюйм = 6,45 кв. см
1 square foot (sq. ft.) квадра́тный фут = 929,03 кв. см
1 square yard (sq. yd.) квадра́тный ярд = 8 361,26 кв. см
1 square rod (sq. rd.) квадра́тный род = 25,29 кв. м
1 rood (ro.) руд = 0,25 а́кра
1 acre (a.) акр = 0,4 га
1 square mile (sq. mi.) квадра́тная ми́ля = 259 га

4. Ме́ры объёма

1 cubic inch (cu. in.) куби́ческий дюйм = 16,387 куб. см
1 cubic foot (cu. ft.) куби́ческий фут = 28 316,75 куб. см
1 cubic yard (cu. yd.) куби́ческий ярд = 0,765 куб. м
1 register ton (reg. ton) реги́стровая то́нна = 2,832 куб. м

5. Ме́ры ёмкости

Ме́ры жи́дких и сыпу́чих тел

1 British *or* **Imperial gill (gl., gi.)** станда́ртный и́ли англи́йский джилл = 0,142 л
1 British *or* **Imperial pint (pt.)** станда́ртная и́ли англи́йская пи́нта = 0,568 л
1 British *or* **Imperial quart (qt.)** станда́ртная и́ли англи́йская ква́рта = 1,136 л
1 British *or* **Imp. gallon (Imp. gal.)** станда́ртный и́ли англи́йский галло́н = 4,546 л

6. Ме́ры сыпу́чих тел

1 British *or* **Imperial peck (pk.)** станда́ртный и́ли англи́йский пек = 9,086 л
1 Brit. *or* **Imp. bushel (bu., bus.)** станда́ртный и́ли англи́йский бу́шель = 36,35 л
1 Brit. *or* **Imperial quarter (qr.)** станда́ртная и́ли англи́йская че́тверть = 290,8 л

7. Ме́ры жи́дких тел

1 Brit. *or* **Imperial barrel (bbl., bl.)** станда́ртный и́ли англи́йский ба́ррель = 1,636 гл

Америка́нские ме́ры жи́дких и сыпу́чих тел

Ме́ры сыпу́чих тел

1 U.S. dry pint америка́нская суха́я пи́нта = 0,551 л
1 U.S. dry quart америка́нская суха́я ква́рта = 1,1 л
1 U.S. dry gallon америка́нский сухо́й галло́н = 4,4 л
1 U.S. peck америка́нский пек = 8,81 л
1 U.S. bushel америка́нский бу́шель = 35,24 л

Ме́ры жи́дких тел

1 U.S. liquid gill америка́нский джилл (жи́дкости) = 0,118 л
1 U.S. liquid pint америка́нская пи́нта (жи́дкости) = 0,473 л
1 U.S. liquid quart америка́нская ква́рта (жи́дкости) = 0,946 л
1 U.S. liquid gallon америка́нский галло́н (жи́дкости) = 3,785 л
1 U.S. barrel америка́нский ба́ррель = 119 л
1 U.S. barrel petroleum америка́нский ба́ррель не́фти = 158,97 л

8. Торго́вые ме́ры ве́са

1 grain (gr.) гран = 0,0648 г
1 dram (dr.) дра́хма = 1,77 г
1 ounce (oz.) у́нция = 28,35 г
1 pound (lb.) фунт = 453,59 г
1 quarter (qr.) че́тверть = 12,7 кг, в США = 11,34 кг
1 hundredweight (cwt.) це́нтнер = 50,8 кг, в США = 45,36 кг
1 stone (st.) стон = 6,35 кг
1 ton (tn., t.) = 1016 кг (тж long ton: tn. l.), в США = 907,18 кг (тж short ton: tn. sh.)